cheat

Want to check out the real-time, on-line marketing of hundreds of today's hottest companies? Don't go surfing without a net! Use the Zikmund & d'Amico CHEAT SHEET for quick access to all the sites featured in MARKETING! Tear this CHEAT SHEET out, fold it up, take it to class, keep it by your computer, add your own favorite sites, set your coffee on it—it's yours! And for hot links to these and other great sites—including study aids, career resources, and more—head to the official MARKETING Web site at zikmund.swcollege.com

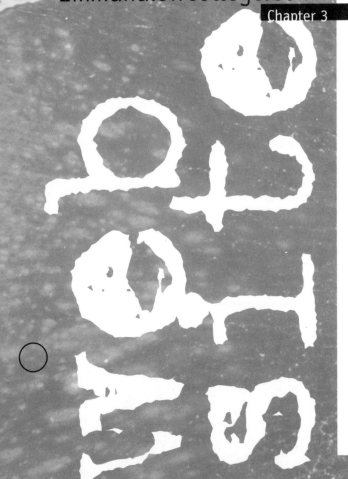

Chapter 1

Atlanta Braves	www.atlantabraves.com
Bandai	www.bandai.com
American Heart Association	www.amhrt.org
Crayola	www.crayola.com
Energizer	www.energizer.com
Kellogg's	www.kelloggs.com
Wearever	www.mirro.com/bakeware.htm
Ford Motor Company	www.ford.com
The Body Shop	www.bodyshop.com
American Marketing Association	www.ama.org

Chapter 2

Enterprise	www.erac.com
Parmalat	www.parmalat.com.br
McDonald's	www.mcdonalds.com
The Limited	www.limited.com
General Electric	www.ge.com
Dow Chemical	www.dow.com
Union Carbide	www.unioncarbide.com
Xerox Corporation	www.xerox.com
Chicago Bulls	www.nba.com/bulls
Kodak	www.kodak.com
Reveries	www.reveries.com
Gallup Organization	www.gallup.com
Johnson & Johnson Company	www.jnj.com
Better World 'Zine	www.betterworld.com

Chapter 3

Motorola	www.mot.com
Telstra	www.telstra.com.au
U.S. Bureau of the Census	www.census.gov
National Restaurant Association	www.restaurant.org
U.S. Census Bureau World Population Clock	www.census.gov/cgi-bin/ipc/popclockw
PCWEBOPEDIA	www.pcwebopedia.com
Microsoft	www.microsoft.com
Netscape	www.netscape.com
Yahoo!	www.yahoo.com
Excite	www.excite.com
Hotbot	www.hotbot.com
Lycos	www.lycos.com
Chicago Tribune	www.chicago.tribune.com
Excite (powered by Jango)	www.jango.excite.com
CD Universe	www.cduniverse.com
PowerAgent	www.poweragent.com
MatchLogic	www.matchlogic.com
U.S. Department of Justice	www.usdoj.gov
U.S. Food and Drug Administration	www.fda.gov
Federal Trade Commission	www.ftc.gov
Bonny Doon Vineyard	www.bonnydoonvineyard.com
USA TODAY Interactive	www.usatoday.com
Australian National University	http://coombs.anu.edu.au/ResFacilities/DemographyPage.html
American Demographics Magazine	www.marketingtools.com/publications/AD/index.htm
National Museum of Natural History, Paris, France	www.popexpo.net/home.htm
Popular Science	www.popsci.com
Home of Mister Economy	http://amos.bus.okstate.edu

sheet

Chapter 4

Whirlpool	www.whirlpool.com
Kodak	www.kodak.com
Nike	www.nike.com
Burger King	www.burgerking.com
Honda	www.honda.com
European Union	www.eurunion.org
NAFTA	www.nafta.org
Yahoo!	www.yahoo.com
Indonesia	www.indonesiatoday.com
CIA FACTBOOK	www.odci.gov/cia/publications/factbook/index.html
Online Atlas	www.magellangeo.com
Current Exchange Rates	www.travelfinder.com/currency.html

Chapter 5

Frito-Lay	www.fritolay.com
United Parcel Service	www.ups.com
Pizza Hut	www.pizzahut.com
Library of Congress	www.loc.gov
Hotbot	www.hotbot.com
Wall Street Journal Interactive	www.wsj.com
U.S. Census Bureau	www.census.gov
Fedworld	www.stat.fedworld.gov
Advertising Age	www.adage.com
Inc. ONLINE	www.inc.com
BusinessWeek ONLINE	www.businessweek.com
WhoWhere?	www.whowhere.com
A. C. Nielsen	www.acnielsen.com
Chicago Museum of Science and Industry	www.msichicago.org
Sales & Marketing Management	www.salesandmarketing.com
Spider's Apprentice	www.monash.com/spidap.html
Gallup Organization	www.gallup.com
NPD Group Inc.	www.npd.com
ASI Market Research Center	www.asiresearch.com
IBM (data mining)	www.software.ibm.com
Advertising Research Foundation	www.arfsite.org
New York Public Library	www.nypl.org
Penn Library Business Reference Desk	www.library.upenn.edu/resources/business/business.html
National Restaurant Association	www.restaurant.org

Chapter 6

Creative Memories	www.creative-memories.com
Infiniti Motors	www.infinitimotors.com
Allstate Insurance	www.allstate.com
Principal Financial Group	www.principal.com
Nike	www.nike.com
Kodak	www.kodak.com
Harley-Davidson	www.harley-davidson.com
Association for Consumer Research	www.acr.webpage.com:8080/acr/
Society for Consumer Psychology	www.cob.ohio-state.edu/scp/
Yankelovich Partners Monitor	www.yankelovich.com/products/MONITOR

Chapter 7

New Pig	www.newpig.com
Data Fellows	www.datafellows.com
Silicon Valley Online	www.silvalonline.com
Lucent Technologies	www.lucent.com
GE Trading Process Network	www.tpn.geis.com
General Electric	www.ge.com
American Express Corporate Services	www.americanexpress.com
North American Industry Classification System	www.census.gov/epcd/www/naics.html
International Standards Organization	www.iso.ch/
Dun & Bradstreet	www.dnb.com
Manufacturing Extension Partnership	www.mep.nist.gov/

marketing

EDITION 6

William G. Zikmund
OKLAHOMA STATE UNIVERSITY

Michael d'Amico
UNIVERSITY OF AKRON

South-Western College Publishing
an International Thomson Publishing company I(T)P®

Cincinnati • Albany • Boston • Detroit • Johannesburg • London • Madrid • Melbourne • Mexico City
New York • Pacific Grove • San Francisco • Scottsdale • Singapore • Tokyo • Toronto

to Tobin and Noah Zikmund
Kathy and Alyse d'Amico

Publishing Team Director: John Szilagyi
Sponsoring Editors: Dreis Van Landuyt, Steve Scoble
Developmental Editor: Atietie O. Tonwe
Production Editor: Barbara Fuller Jacobsen
Production House: Lifland et al., Bookmakers
Photo Manager: Cary Benbow
Typesetter: Parkwood Composition
Internal Design: Michael H. Stratton
Cover Design: Michael H. Stratton
Cover Image: Russ Willms
Marketing Manager: Sarah Woelfel

Copyright © 1999
by South-Western College Publishing
Cincinnati, Ohio

Library of Congress Cataloging-in-Publication Data

Zikmund, William G.
    Marketing/William G. Zikmund, Michael d'Amico.—6th ed.
        p.   cm.
    Includes bibliographical references and index.
    ISBN 0-538-88215-8
    1. Marketing.   I. d'Amico, Michael.   II. Title.
    HF5415.Z54   1998
    658.8—dc21   98-18863
                                                                 CIP

I(T)P®

International Thomson Publishing

South-Western College Publishing is an ITP Company.
The ITP trademark is used under license.

ISBN 0-538-88215-8

  2 3 4 5 6 7 8 C1 5 4 3 2 1 0 9

Printed in the United States of America

bookataglance

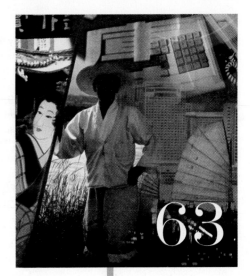

115

part 2
Analysis of Market and Buyer Behavior 125

97

part 3
**Product Strategy for Global
Competition** 259

350

336

part 4
Distribution Strategy 363

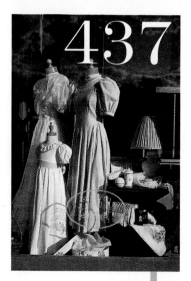

part 5
Integrated Marketing Communications 459

16 ADVERTISING 495

part 6
Pricing Strategy 589

514

preface

With the 21st century on the horizon and the emergence of the digital age, marketing has seen, over the past few years, the most dramatic changes ever to occur in the discipline.

Marketing has always been about adapting to change. However, during the last decade of the 20th century, the astonishing developments in information technology have changed virtually every aspect of marketing. Today, effective marketers can gain competitive advantage through information technology and time-based competition. Consider Cisco Systems, Inc., the leading supplier of networking hardware including routers, local- and wide-area-network switches, and dial-up access servers, which has been marketing its products through its World Wide Web site for a little more than a year. It expects its annual sales of networking products on the Internet to approach $1 billion, or nearly one-fourth of its business. Cisco is an effective marketer which has successfully adapted to recent technological change. Adapting to change and using information technology to gain competitive advantage are two major themes of this sixth edition of our book.

Although many changes have taken place, some things remain the same. Marketing is still an academic discipline about a dynamic, competitive, and creative activity that is part of our everyday lives. *Marketing,* Sixth Edition, presents a lively picture of the field. This book discusses academic theory, yet it is contemporary and practical. It is also very readable. In a straightforward and conversational prose style, it offers balanced coverage of marketing concepts and the practical examples that make marketing easy to understand. To enhance readers' understanding of marketing concepts and strategies, it employs current illustrations from domestic and global markets in the real world.

Marketing, Sixth Edition, stresses that marketing is essential to gaining a competitive advantage in a global marketplace. Readers will not find a separate chapter on international marketing, but the fact that conceptual issues about international marketing are not isolated in a single chapter does not mean that they are ignored. The global dimensions of the marketplace have become so pervasive that they affect virtually every aspect of marketing. These dimensions are discussed whenever a global perspective can help explain how marketing principles are applied in the global economy. Our book is structured to make it easy for instructors to discuss global markets when explaining market segmentation, international advertising when explaining advertising, international pricing when explaining pricing, and so on. Thus, the discussion of marketing strategies used by international marketers does not come too early, before students know the basics of market segmentation, advertising, pricing, or any other marketing topic. Nor does it come too late, when the semester's time pressures are greatest. We hope this structure will help students understand that 21st-century marketing managers cannot think of the international aspects of marketing as independent from the overall marketing strategy.

Marketing, Sixth Edition, provides many examples so that students can understand the role marketing plays in business and not-for-profit organizations. For example, Chapter 1 discusses how nine innings of baseball is only one aspect of the product offered in the technologically sophisticated home of the Atlanta Braves. A discussion about Yahoo, Hotbot, and other search engines for the World Wide Web adds a new "wired" dimension to Chapter 5, Information Technology and Marketing Research. Examples of push technology can be found throughout the book. Chapter 6 begins with a vignette about changing social values; the vignette illustrates why women are no longer waiting for "Mr. Right" to buy expensive jewelry for them. References to the Spice Girls, Garth Brooks, Chumbawamba, the Volkswagen Beetle, the *Star Wars* prequel, and the Chicago Cubs are among the many student-oriented examples that can be found in this new edition.

Marketing, Sixth Edition, stresses the logic of marketing management, relating strategy and tactics to the environmental opportunities and constraints that managers must deal with daily. Effective marketing principles related to competitive strategy, total quality management, relationship marketing, and team building are emphasized throughout the book so that readers can see that there is a difference between intuitive decision making and sound marketing management.

The theories and strategies that marketing managers use to create competitive advantages have central importance in *Marketing*, Sixth Edition. Theoretical concepts, such as those found in the study of buyer behavior, are presented so that students will understand their practical value for marketing managers. Competitive market strategies, such as those used for segmenting, targeting, and positioning, appear early in the book. They provide a foundation to build on when marketing mix strategies are discussed later in the book.

Relationship marketing is a recurring theme in *Marketing*, Sixth Edition. Our book stresses the fact that the marketing process does not end with the sale; it discusses how marketers establish and build relationships with customers. Many examples illustrate that both large and small businesses can apply these concepts. For instance, Chapter 1 portrays Fletcher Music Centers in Clearwater, Florida, as a retailer that understands that the key to winning and keeping customers is determining what they need, sometimes before they figure it out themselves. Our discussion of relationship marketing recognizes that the way companies like American Express and Harley-Davidson conduct business has changed dramatically in recent years. Many companies, especially those engaged in multinational marketing, are coming to rely on collaborating organizations. Chapter 4 introduces the role of collaborators, and the remainder of the book provides insights into managing relationships with suppliers, intermediaries, and customers.

Commenting on A. Bartlett Giamatti (former president of Yale University and former commissioner of major league baseball), Whitey Herzog said, "For being book smart, he had an awful lot of street smarts." We wrote the sixth edition of *Marketing* with the goal of helping students become both book smart and street smart about marketing.

Marketing, Sixth Edition, serves the needs of professors as well as those of students. Our book was written to be teachable. We made considerable effort to ensure that the pedagogy would meet the needs of modern marketing professors. Learning objectives and chapter summaries are coordinated to help students organize their thoughts. Experts in color graphics and graphic design assisted us and the editors in designing a book that highlights key concepts and ideas to the benefit of both the reader and the instructor. As further aids to students and professors, various exhibits and features offer practical examples of advertising, brand management, pricing, and every other facet of marketing.

"The essence of knowledge is having it to apply it." This adage expresses our belief that students must experience a situation to truly learn. Our end-of-chapter materials and end-of-part materials have been developed with experiential learning in mind.

End-of-chapter materials include Questions for Review & Critical Thinking, video cases and regular cases, Internet Insights, Marketing Plan—Right or Wrong? and Ethically Right or Wrong? The feature Marketing Plan—Right or Wrong? is unique to our book. This innovative feature profiles aspects of real business plans. Students are asked to evaluate the potential of these ideas, some of which were hits and others flops. Internet Insights are composed of Internet exercises and an address book of useful URLs that will take students to a wide variety of Web sites. Some exercises require students to collect specific information; others are meant to hone Internet search skills. Both add interactivity to the student's education.

The end-of-part materials consist of Cross-Functional Insights and Enhance Your Marketing Skills with CD-ROM. Both features provide materials that go beyond the traditional marketing class. Cross-Functional Insights will help professors explain how marketing fits into the broader picture of business and society. Our CD-ROM gives students the opportunity to experience marketing through exciting full-motion video clips, photo montages, and animated slide shows. The CD-ROM covers a broad range of topics.

ORGANIZATION OF THE BOOK

The organization of the sixth edition of *Marketing* differs from that of previous editions. The book is organized into six parts. The first discusses the nature of marketing, the fundamentals of marketing strategy, and the marketing environment.

Chapter 1, The Nature of Marketing, places increased emphasis on the importance of creating superior customer value and using a marketing orientation to build relationships. It introduces the marketing concept, total quality management, and global competition, themes that run throughout the book.

Chapter 2, Marketing Management: Strategy and Ethical Behavior, includes broad coverage of ethical principles and moral behavior, to serve as a framework and a springboard for further delineation of ethical concerns in the remaining chapters. We chose this organization because students need some background in marketing principles before they can truly understand how an organization's ethical principles influence its marketing decision making. To support an emphasis on ethics, *Marketing*, Sixth Edition, features a section entitled Ethically Right or Wrong? at the ends of the chapters. This section encourages students to think about ethical principles and how they affect decision making in specific situations.

Coverage of environmental factors has undergone major revision. Chapter 3 now deals with the macroenvironment, and Chapter 4 discusses the microenvironment. Chapter 3, Environmental Forces in a Digital World: The Macroenvironment, lays the foundation for the text's extensive technological focus and introduces ways in which information technology can create true competitive advantage. Many aspects of the Internet are introduced here.

Chapter 4, The Microenvironment in an Era of Global Competition, introduces the value chain and builds a four Cs framework—Company, Customer, Competition, and Collaboration—to provide insight into managing both domestic and global relationships with suppliers, intermediaries, and customers. The chapter explains many strategic global issues within the four Cs framework. This chapter helps set the stage for a continuing discussion of the nature of competition based on quality, time, location, and price. The unique needs of global marketers—especially the need for collaborators in international marketing activity—are introduced.

Part 2, Analysis of Market and Buyer Behavior, discusses information management, buyer behavior, market segmentation, targeting, and positioning.

Chapter 5, Information Technology and Marketing Research, examines information technology as an ingredient vital to successful marketing research. The revised chapter describes how data mining, collecting data on the Internet, and database management make marketing research faster, more accurate, and more efficient. Additional coverage is given to the Internet, which clearly will be an indispensable research tool in the 21st century.

Chapter 6, Consumer Behavior, provides a model and an overview of consumer behavior. It concentrates on both the psychological dimensions of the decision-making process and the sociological and cultural factors influencing the consumer.

Chapter 7, Business Markets and Organizational Buying, has been revised to reflect how the advent of e-commerce and global business has remarkably changed organizational buying. The growing importance of the Internet in business-to-business marketing is explained in engaging examples such as the one about Cisco Systems, Inc.

Chapter 8, Market Segmentation, Targeting, and Positioning Strategies, applies the behavioral theories discussed in other chapters to the concept of market segmentation. It explains how market and positioning strategies apply to both domestic and international markets. For instance, one example explains why the National Basketball Association is targeting women. The chapter shows how both large multinational firms and small domestic marketers can use market segmentation, targeting, and positioning strategies. The discussion of data-based marketing has been greatly expanded. The chapter includes a discussion of mass customization and flexible manufacturing.

Part 3, Product Strategy for Global Competition, deals with both the marketing of goods and services by commercial organizations and the marketing of ideas by not-for-profit organizations.

Chapter 9, Basic Concepts about Goods and Services, discusses the elements of products and explains branding and packaging strategies. For example, it explains the basic idea for Lunchables, which was to provide convenient meal solutions for parents and kids, and why the product had to be modified when its sales began to flatten.

Chapter 10, Strategies for New Products and the Product Life Cycle, opens with a discussion of the Piccolo Point-of-Care Whole Blood Analyzer, an innovative product that provides blood test results in about 12 minutes. It then addresses the nature of new products and the characteristics associated with new product successes. It goes on to depict the new product development process and to address the fact that most new products fail. The discussion of various strategies used over the course of product life cycles and the ethical issues associated with the marketing of products provides students with a practical understanding of how these issues can be addressed in both domestic and foreign markets.

Chapter 11, Strategies for Services and Relationship Marketing, begins with a discussion of the special concerns of the marketers of services. For example, it explains how Progressive Corporation, an insurance company that specializes in high-risk drivers, provides fast, innovative, and customized service as it strives for competitive advantage. The chapter also focuses attention on relationship marketing. It explores three prominent methods of creating and maintaining customer relationships: frequency marketing, social marketing, and structural marketing.

The major purpose of marketing is to satisfy human needs by delivering products of various types to buyers when and where they want them and at a reasonable cost. Part 4, Distribution Strategy, consists of three chapters discussing how products are placed in the hands of those who need them. This part of the book focuses on the nature of distribution, retailing and wholesaling strategies, and the physical distribution process. As the economy becomes increasingly global, international channels of distribution and worldwide physical distribution are becoming key factors in determining competitive advantage. The sixth edition of *Marketing* reflects the new importance of logistical systems in the success of the firm.

Chapter 12, The Nature of Distribution, sets the stage for the discussion of the place element of the marketing mix. It now incorporates a new section about electronic information brokers as emerging intermediaries that are reshaping the concept of channels of distribution.

Chapter 13, Retailing, Direct Marketing, and Wholesaling, has greatly expanded coverage of direct marketing, a topic of growing importance in any course on marketing principles. As in many other chapters, technology is stressed throughout and numerous examples, such as Excite Shopping and Bloomingdale's on the Internet, are provided.

Chapter 14, Logistics and Physical Distribution Management, offers insights into the importance of these two aspects of business and their influence on marketing strategy.

Part 5, Integrated Marketing Communications, includes chapters introducing promotional concepts, advertising, publicity, public relations, personal selling, and sales promotion. All the chapters have been revised to place a greater emphasis on integrated marketing communications and direct marketing. However, the emphasis on creative promotional strategy remains.

Chapter 15, Integrated Marketing Communications, focuses on the need for all elements of the promotional mix to work together. Special attention is paid to the emergence of new media. The chapter concludes with a discussion of the ethics of persuasion.

Chapter 16, Advertising, has been updated to reflect the reclassification in media caused by recent technological changes. The categories of personal and mass media no longer accurately describe the tools of marketing. We now must separate interactive (non-human) technologies such as the Internet from media that involve interaction with a person. Among the new topics included is push technology—custom delivery of personalized marketing messages.

Chapter 17, Personal Selling and Sales Management, explains the changing role of the salesperson in today's digital world. The chapter includes extensive coverage of sales force automation and explains how the Internet has made personal selling more efficient and effective. It also highlights the importance of relationship management in personal selling.

Chapter 18, Sales Promotion, Publicity, and Public Relations, begins with a story about the vice president of Cakebread Cellars of Rutherford, California, whose idea of public relations is rounding up 20 customers and going salmon fishing. This chapter's inclusion in the book reflects the growing importance of sales promotion, publicity, and public relations in marketing strategies.

Part 6, Pricing Strategy, consists of two chapters: Chapter 19, Introduction to Pricing Concepts, and Chapter 20, Pricing Strategies and Tactics. These chapters address the function of price in the allocation of goods within economies and the practical role price plays in the marketing mix. Much of the material deals with pricing objectives and discusses how pricing strategy is developed to satisfy these objectives. The book retains a very pragmatic approach to this key element of the marketing mix.

Our end-of-the-book appendixes are now supplemented with a series of Internet appendixes. Thus, the appendixes that end the book are different from those that appeared in previous editions. Material on career opportunities now appears in both an in-book appendix and an Internet appendix. The book's Appendix A, Internet Insights into Marketing Careers, provides information to help students learn how to identify career options using the Internet. Appendix B, The Marketing Audit, has a sample outline for conducting a marketing audit. Appendix C, Organizing the Marketing Function, discusses ways of assigning tasks, grouping tasks into organizational units, and allocating resources to those units.

Several additional appendixes appear on the Internet at zikmund.swcollege.com. Additional material about marketing job descriptions and how to prepare for employment in these fields is in Planning a Marketing Career. This on-line appendix provides insightful comments on a wide range of careers, from sales management to marketing research to advertising. The appendix entitled Financial and Economic Analysis for Marketers explains financial concepts and many analytical ratios that marketing managers use in their decision making. Evaluating and Controlling Marketing Performance discusses how sales analysis and other means of control are utilized to assess marketing productivity. Because these are Internet appendixes, professors can introduce this material at any point in the academic term.

SOME DISTINCTIVE FEATURES STUDENTS WILL LIKE

Marketing, Sixth Edition, offers a number of distinctive and interesting features. Each chapter opens with a vignette, which describes an actual situation relevant to the material in the chapter and focuses students' attention on the pragmatic aspects of the chapter. For example, Chapter 3 begins by showing how Motorola has benefited from the fact that resourceful Chinese who cannot afford telephones use pagers as primitive substitutes for telephones. And Chapter 15 opens with a discussion of how Trivial Pursuit went on the Web to recapture some of its past glory by getting consumers involved.

Each chapter begins with a clear statement of learning objectives so that students will know what to expect. The chapter summaries are designed around these learning objectives.

Graphics and exhibits are designed to encourage student involvement and learning. Most photos are accompanied by a clear, understandable caption that reinforces a theory or principle explained in the text.

Interesting and relevant end-of-chapter materials such as video cases and Questions for Review & Critical Thinking address practical marketing problems. Many questions are designed to stimulate the student to search for additional information about marketing. Every chapter now includes a team-building question/exercise designed to enhance students' ability to work with others.

Because information technologies are changing the way business is conducted around the world, we have added an innovative feature to the end of each chapter in the book: Internet Insights—a section containing Internet exercises and an address book of useful URLs. A related feature is our Web page (zikmund.swcollege.com), which allows both professors and students to access supplemental information about the text and its teaching materials. The "In Case You Missed It" Web page has received particularly high praise.

To help students learn the vocabulary of marketing, key terms are listed at the end of each chapter. These terms are defined in a marginal glossary that runs through the text. In addition, a complete glossary appears at the end of the book as a reference source.

Throughout the text, numerous easy-to-understand real-world examples are designed to help students gain insight and perspective. Many examples reflect the changing global markets and increased competition from foreign firms faced by today's marketers. For example, one story notes that one of the latest food rages in Japan is to eat fish live. This example is part of the discussion of the macromarketing environment, in which we point out how cultural values are not the same in different countries.

Cross-Functional Insights and Enhancing Your Marketing Skills with CD-ROM exercises are important features of this textbook. They appear at the end of each part of the book. The Cross-Functional Insights section recognizes that many theories and principles from other business disciplines can provide additional insights into the role of marketing within an organization. The questions in the Cross-Functional Insights sections are designed to help students think about integrating what they have learned about management, finance, production, and other functional areas taught in business school courses with the marketing principles explained in *Marketing*, Sixth Edition.

What Went Right? What Went Wrong? Unique features called What Went Right? and What Went Wrong? illustrate successes and failures in specific marketing situations. They focus on decisions made by particular organizations and the outcomes of those decisions. For example, one What Went Right? feature tells how three notes and three words from a minor hit record by Bob Seger transformed the image of Chevy trucks. Another example explains how the House of Blues restaurant generates so much publicity that it does not need to purchase any mass media advertising. A What Went Wrong? box describes how Porsche's targeting of the wrong psychographic segment caused a dramatic decline in sales. Another explains why many disgruntled customers canceled subscriptions to *Reader's Digest*.

Adapting to Change   The Adapting to Change features examine technological, social, demographic, and other developments that require companies to change their product offerings and marketing approaches. The ability to recognize and adapt to market needs quickly is presented as a key source of competitive advantage. For example, one Adapting to Change feature describes why one Kroger supermarket in a suburb north of Atlanta has a fitness area with treadmills, stair-climbing machines, and even a trainer with a degree in exercise physiology.

Focus Sections   *Marketing*, Sixth Edition, includes special sections that focus on two important aspects of marketing: global competition and relationship marketing. Each Focus on Global Competition and Focus on Relationships section features a particular company's application of the theoretical concepts that have just been discussed in the text.

Focus on Global Competition   At home, contemporary marketers face competition from global organizations that operate in the United States. Abroad, marketers must adapt their strategies to the countries where their products are marketed. The challenge of global competition is addressed in the Focus on Global Competition features, which describe increased competition from foreign competitors at home and abroad. For example, one feature tells what happened when British Airways looked beyond its core service, air transportation: It redefined its view of what an airline does to emphasize what happens on the ground as much as what happens in the air. Another explains that when per-capita income starts going up, the first thing people do with their extra money is eat out. That's why American fast-food restaurants are spreading rapidly in Asia.

Focus on Relationships   Effective marketers focus on creating and keeping customers. Often they work with collaborators to provide greater value to customers. One Focus on Relationship section shows how Caterpillar builds lifetime relationships with its dealers.

Ethically Right or Wrong?   Ethical issues are first introduced in Chapter 2. Ethically Right or Wrong? sections at the ends of the remaining chapters require students to take a stand on ethical issues. These sections give students the chance to think about ethical principles and how they apply in specific situations. For example, one exercise asks students to think critically about the ethical implications of marketing realistic toy guns.

Student Learning Guide   The *Student Learning Guide* for *Marketing*, Sixth Edition, was written by Ron E. LaFreniere of Shoreline Community College. For each chapter, this comprehensive guide includes a summary outline, chapter summary, vocabulary-building matching exercises, vocabulary-building fill-in-the-blank exercises, true/false questions, multiple-choice questions, and experiential activities. In addition to the quizzes that reinforce each chapter objective, students will benefit from up-to-date materials in a section entitled Marketing on the Web, which deals with such topics as product marketing strategies on the Web, distance distribution opportunities on the Web, and measuring Web effectiveness. The *Student Learning Guide* can be purchased chapter by chapter or in full.

PowerNotes   A unique bound supplement, *PowerNotes*, includes copies of the PowerPoint slides provided to instructors, printed at fifty percent of their normal size on full sheets, with space for students to take notes during lectures. Detailed outlines are also provided for each chapter of the book. The complete version of *PowerNotes* is available for purchase.

SPECIAL FEATURES PROFESSORS WILL LIKE

A professor's job is demanding. Thus, we expect professors to demand a lot from the publisher and the authors of *Marketing*, Sixth Edition. Both the textbook and the accompanying instructor's materials have been developed to help instructors excel when performing their vital teaching function.

The extensive learning support package that accompanies *Marketing*, Sixth Edition, includes an *Instructor's Resource Manual* with materials about cases, Questions for Review & Critical Thinking, Marketing Plan—Right or Wrong? sections, and Ethically Right or Wrong? sections. The *Test Bank* is also available in a computerized version. Three hundred full-color transparency acetates and six hundred PowerPoint software presentation slides are designed to help the professor prepare lecture and discussion materials. Furthermore, there is a comprehensive multimedia program. Videotapes and CD-ROM ancillary materials enable professors to bring the contemporary world of marketing into the classroom. A *Student Learning Guide* and *MarketingBuilder Express*, a manual and software for developing a marketing plan, are also available. Highlights of some of the instructor's materials appear below.

The Web @ Its Best   For a closer look at the technological focus of *Marketing*, Sixth Edition, visit the on-line complement to the text at zikmund.swcollege.com. There you will find the following features:

- *In Case You Missed It:* Interesting marketing examples and useful tidbits from Michael d'Amico; updated monthly during the academic year to add spice to your lectures
- *Confessions of a Marketer:* A monthly special-interest column for the world of marketing
- *Online Supplements:* A preview of the *Student Learning Guide* and a preview of *PowerNotes*, for students, ready for downloading.
- *Marketing Trivia:* A great source for unusual marketing facts
- *Unique Online Appendixes:* In-depth treatment of three important subjects in marketing. Financial and Economic Analysis for Marketers covers profit and loss statements, financial ratios, elasticity, break-even point, economic order quantity, and other important business and marketing calculations. Planning a Marketing Career offers insightful comments on a wide range of careers, from sales management to market research to advertising. Evaluating and Controlling Marketing Performance addresses key indicators for judging effectiveness and controlling marketing strategies and programs.

Test Bank   The *Test Bank* for *Marketing*, Sixth Edition, is new. Joe Ballenger of Stephen F. Austin State University prepared this *Test Bank* with special attention to matching the questions closely with the text. There are well over 5,000 questions, drawn from every aspect of the text material, to enhance the instructor's ability to test students' understanding of the concepts. For example, the *Test Bank* includes both multiple-choice and true/false questions on many of the boxed features and all of the opening vignettes. All of the end-of-chapter cases are also covered by multiple-choice and true/false questions. The questions are organized by the heads and subheads within the textbook chapters, and the page number of each subhead and question is given for easy reference. To further facilitate use, the questions have been categorized according to Bloom's taxonomy for cognitive complexity—recall, comprehension, calculation, and application. Also, difficulty rankings allow the instructor to know in advance whether students will find a question easy, medium, or hard.

Thomson World Class Testing Tools™, the computerized version of the *Test Bank*, gives instructors a convenient means of generating tests. The menu-driven testing package provides many user-oriented features, including the ability to edit and add exam questions, scramble questions within sections of the exam, and merge questions. Call-in testing is also available.

Multimedia Program   Video materials bring excitement to physical distribution, advertising, personal selling, market segmentation, and other topics. Both videotapes and a CD-ROM have been prepared to accompany *Marketing,* Sixth Edition. This comprehensive multimedia program has three major parts: the end-of-chapter video cases, a group of additional videos, and a CD-ROM.

End-of-Chapter Video Cases   The video cases are much like regular end-of-chapter cases but with an accompanying video segment that portrays some elements of the case. For example, video cases feature marketers such as World's Gym, Red Roof Inn, V8 vegetable juice, and the Minnesota Twins baseball team. Many video cases, such as the one on Weather Or Not, Inc., focus on small businesses.

Additional Video Series   Two different additional video series are available separately to qualified adopters: the Supplemental Video Lecture Support Series and the INC. Video Lecture Support Series.

The Supplemental Video Lecture Support Series, includes 14 separate video segments on international topics, total quality management, advertising, small businesses, and entrepreneurship. These exciting videos reinforce the fact that marketing is not an isolated business activity. Each video segment shows marketing decisions and explores how these decisions must be integrated with other functional areas of the corporation, such as finance, human resources, and operations.

The INC. Video Lecture Support Series is made up of videotapes from the *INC. Magazine* Video Library. These videos deal with some of the most important and timely issues in marketing. Qualified adopters may select from videos on personal selling, customer service, starting a new business, and other important topics.

Principles of Marketing CD-ROM   South-Western's Principles of Marketing CD-ROM provides a unique multimedia-based approach to learning introductory marketing concepts. Instead of simply reading text on a CD-ROM, students can experience marketing through exciting full-motion video clips, photo montages, and animated slide shows. Students can also learn and explore topics via interactive exhibits, process models, and diagrams. This CD-ROM supplement contains 32 interactive modules covering a broad range of concepts. Many of the Enhancing Your Marketing Skills with CD-ROM exercises can be used in class to enliven lectures.

Instructor's Resource Manual   The *Instructor's Resource Manual for Marketing,* Sixth Edition, was prepared by the authors and Craig Hollingshead of Marshall University. It provides an average of 50 pages of important information for each chapter. The manual is also available on disk for instructors who prefer to work on disk. Each chapter contains the following information:

- *Chapter Scan:* A brief overview of the chapter
- *Suggested Learning Objectives:* Expanded versions of the objectives presented in the textbook
- *Chapter Outline:* A detailed, three-level outline of chapter material
- *The Chapter Summarized:* An extended outline, with narratives under each major point to flesh out the discussion and suggest alternative examples and issues to bring forward
- *Answer Guidelines for End-of-Chapter Materials:* Extensive and detailed responses to the Questions for Review & Critical Thinking, Marketing Plan—Right or Wrong? sections, Ethically Right or Wrong? sections, and case discussion questions.

PowerPoint Presentation Software   PowerPoint is a state-of-the-art presentation graphics program for IBM-compatible computers. Prepared by Jack Gifford of Miami University (Ohio), this integrated program allows instructors to retrieve any of the preloaded slides that accompany the book. Images can easily be edited, added, or deleted. The instructor can present the slides electronically in the classroom; make four-color prints of slides (a four-color printer is required); prepare notes pages from the slides; and animate a slide show with transition effects.

Transparency Acetates   Three hundred full-color transparency acetates are provided with *Marketing,* Sixth Edition. The transparencies were selected from the text features and also from materials that do not appear in the text.

INC. Reader   A readings book is available for professors who wish to supplement text assignments with articles from *INC. Magazine.* This softcover book contains selections that discuss contemporary issues and trends in marketing.

JIAN MarketingBuilder Express   The JIAN *MarketingBuilder Express* was written by Erika Matulich of Texas Christian University. The book and software provide hands-on assistance to instructors who assign a marketing plan to students. *MarketingBuilder Express* covers topics such as selecting a client, presenting information, creating a marketing plan outline, preparing a situation analysis, writing strategies, and evaluating performance.

OUR REVIEWERS ARE APPRECIATED

The following colleagues reviewed various drafts of the manuscript to evaluate scholarly accuracy, writing style, and pedagogy. The many changes in this edition are based on their suggestions. We gratefully acknowledge their contributions in helping us point *Marketing* toward the 21st century.

Bruce L. Alford
University of Evansville

Joe Ballenger
Stephen F. Austin State University

Fred M. Beasley
Northern Kentucky University

Thomas G. Delaughter
University of Florida

A. Cemal Ekin
Providence College

Steven Engel
University of Colorado–Boulder

Jack Gifford
Miami University (Ohio)

Donald R. Glover
Metropolitan State College of Denver

Donald H. Granbois
Indiana University

Blaine S. Greenfield
Bucks County Community College

David A. Griffith
University of Oklahoma

Bob Heiser
Metropolitan State College of Denver

Craig A. Hollingshead
Marshall University

Ron E. LaFreniere
Shoreline Community College

Kenneth Lawrence
New Jersey Institute of Technology

David Loudon
Northeast Louisiana University

Shekhar Misra
California State University–Chico

Kim A. Nelson
University of Arizona

Hale A. Newcomer
University of North Texas

Pallab Paul
University of Denver

Stuart C. Rogers
University of Denver

David Shani
Kean University

Elizabeth A. Sinclair-Colando
Kent State University

Dilip Soman
University of Colorado–Boulder

Frederick J. Stephenson
University of Georgia

Jerry W. Wilson
Georgia Southern University

Linda Wright
Mississippi State University

Our thanks also go to the individuals listed on the next page for their earlier contributions.

Joe Alexander
University of Northern Colorado

David Andrus
Kansas State University

Ramon Avila
Ball State University

Gul Bataney
Bentley College

Sharon E. Beatty
University of Alabama

Bradley Becu
Xavier University

Robert G. Benson
St. Cloud State University

Jackie Brown
University of Nevada–Las Vegas

Gordon Bruner
Southern Illinois University

Wendy Bryce
Western Washington University

Laura Bulas
Central Community College

David Burns
Youngstown State University

Joseph Cangelosi
University of Central Arkansas

Fred Capossela
California State Polytechnic University–Pomona

Ted Clark
SUNY–New Paltz

Barbara Coe
University of North Texas

Richard Colombo
New York University

Jerry Conover
Northern Arizona University

Kenneth E. Crocker
Bowling Green State University

J. Joseph Cronin, Jr.
Florida State University

Roger Davis
Baylor University

Casey Donoho
Northern Arizona University

Patrick Dunne
Texas Tech University

Vicky Evans
Procter & Gamble

Raymond P. Fisk
University of Central Florida

Douglas Fugate
Western Kentucky University

S. J. Garner
Eastern Kentucky University

Charles Goeldner
University of Colorado–Boulder

Debbie Goodman
Salisbury State University

Vicki Griffis
University of South Florida

Dean Headley
Wichita State University

Ronn Herr
Southeast Missouri State University

Nathan Himelstein
Essex Community College

Frederick B. Hoyt
Illinois Wesleyan University

Ray Javalgi
Cleveland State University

Russel Jones
Central State University

Madhav Kacker
Suffolk University

Peter Kaminski
Northern Illinois University

Bill Kawashima
University of North Carolina–Greensboro

Terry Kearney
Marquette University

Craig Kelley
California State University–Sacramento

Steven Kelly
DePaul University

Maryon King
Southern Illinois University

Brad Kleindl
Missouri Southern State College

Kathleen A. Krentler
San Diego State University

Russell Laczniak
Iowa State University

Geoffrey Lantos
Stonehill College

Jay Laughlin
Kansas State University

Richard Leventhal
Metropolitan State University

Marilyn Liebrenz-Himes
George Washington University

Sandra Loeb
University of South Dakota

Tim Longfellow
Illinois State University

Lynn Loudenback
New Mexico State University

Jim McAlexander
Oregon State University

Barbara McCuen
University of Nebraska–Omaha

Martha McEnally
University of North Carolina–Greensboro

Lee Meadow
Northern Illinois University

Susan Mikutis
University of North Florida

Shirley Miller
Bryant College

Fred Morgan
University of Kentucky

Al Moseley
Miami-Dade Community College

Bill Motz
Lansing Community College

Keith Murray
Northeastern University

George Prough
University of Akron

Daniel Rajaratnam
Baylor University

James Rakowski
University of Memphis

Linda Riley
New Mexico State University

Saeed Samiee
University of South Carolina

Donald Scglimpaglia
San Diego State University

Matthew Shank
Northern Kentucky University

Surendra Singh
University of Kansas

Roger Singley
Illinois State University

Dick Skinner
Kent State University

Bob Smiley
Indiana State University

J. B. Spalding
Bellarmine College

Thaddeus Spratlen
University of Washington

Marion Stamps
University of South Florida

Fred Stephenson
University of Georgia

Glenn T. Stoops
Bowling Green State University

Robert A. Swerdlow
Lamar University

Edwin Tang
North Carolina State University

Janice Taylor
Miami University

Raymond Taylor
Louisiana State University–Shreveport

Ron Taylor
Mississippi State University

Donald L. Thompson
Georgia Southern University

Howard Thompson
Eastern Kentucky University

Ken Thompson
University of North Texas

Tom Trittipo
University of Central Oklahoma

Richard Utecht
University of Texas–San Antonio

Charles Vitaska
Metropolitan State University

Blaise Waguespack
Embry-Riddle Aeronautical University

Terrell Williams
California State University–Northridge

Phillip H. Wilson
University of North Texas

Tim Wright
Lakeland Community College

Geoffrey G. Zoeckler
St. Norbert College

ACKNOWLEDGMENTS

The first five editions of *Marketing* were well received by professors and, more importantly, by students of marketing. We appreciate the compliments and praise we have received from our fellow professors in universities and colleges around the country.

The sixth edition of *Marketing* was the result of the hard work of many people at South-Western College Publishing. John Szilagyi, publishing team director, was very supportive. Our sponsoring editor, Steve Scoble, helped to slay many dragons and demons that plagued us. His thorough understanding of the needs of both instructors and students and the depth of his experience in many areas of publishing showed on this project. It is an understatement to say that we greatly appreciate his help. Dreis Van Landuyt made several important decisions that gave the new focus to this revision. His time on the watch kept our ship afloat. For deftly navigating this project and managing its myriad daily details and for ensuring that the supplements meet our high standards, we thank our developmental editor, Atietie O. Tonwe. His sincere and always optimistic efforts encouraged us on many occasions. Production editor Barb Fuller Jacobsen was always available and acted as a necessary sounding board about production issues as well as the plight of the 1908 World Championship team's more recent efforts. We appreciate the rapport we shared with her. Moreover, her meticulous attention to detail and her concern for the quality of our book made a big difference. We are in her debt.

The efforts of copy editor Quica Ostrander, designer Mike Stratton, photo manager Cary Benbow, and production coordinator Sally Lifland resulted in a book that is lucid in exposition and a paragon of the state of the art in publishing. Sarah Woelfel and Julia Batsch did a great job. Their creative talent and special skills provide evidence that marketing is both an art and a science.

Preparing the instructional materials to enhance classroom efforts required an army of people. Joe Ballenger of Stephen F. Austin State University prepared the *Test Bank* for this edition. Craig A. Hollingshead of Marshall University contributed a significant portion of the *Instructor's Resource Manual.* Ron E. LaFreniere of Shoreline Community College prepared the *Student Learning Guide.* The PowerPoint Presentation package and the transparency acetates were prepared by Jack Gifford of Miami University (Ohio). Geoff Lantos of Stonehill College helped prepare the instructor's materials for the Ethically Right or Wrong? sections. Media technology editor Kevin von Gillern and media production editor Robin Browning, both at South-Western, deserve appreciation for creating a cool Web site and for providing indispensable help with the video and other multimedia materials.

We owe many long-term debts as well to our parents, professors, families, and friends. George Zikmund, who spent his entire life in sales and sales management, was responsible for leaving to his son an indelible sense of the practical side of marketing. Philip Cateora, as an assistant professor of Principles of Marketing at the University of Colorado, inspired a directionless young man to major in marketing. Phil Campagna later served as a wise marketing mentor at Remington Arms company. Learning to understand marketing—and to be both book smart and street smart—takes many years, and these long-term debts are impossible to repay. We hope this book will pass on our parents', teachers', and mentors' insights to others.

William G. Zikmund
Michael F. d'Amico

ZIKMUND
authors
D'AMICO
&

William G. Zikmund above,
Michael d'Amico below

william g. zikmund

A native of the Chicago area, William G. Zikmund now lives in Tulsa, Oklahoma. He is a professor of marketing at Oklahoma State University. He received his bachelor's degree in marketing from the University of Colorado, a master's degree from Southern Illinois University, and a Ph.D. in business administration from the University of Colorado.

Zikmund worked in marketing research for Conway Millikin Company and Remington Arms Company before beginning his academic career. In addition, he has extensive consulting experience with many business and not-for-profit organizations.

During his academic career, Zikmund has published dozens of articles and papers in diverse scholarly journals. In addition to *Marketing*, Zikmund has written *Effective Marketing, Exploring Marketing Research, Essentials of Marketing Research, Business Research Methods*, and a work of fiction, *A Corporate Bestiary*.

A member of many professional organizations, Zikmund has served on the editorial review boards of the *Journal of Marketing Education, Marketing Education Review*, the *Journal of the Academy of Marketing Science*, and the *Journal of Business Research*.

He is an active teacher who strives to be creative and innovative in the classroom.

michael d'amico

Michael d'Amico was born and bred in Hoboken, New Jersey. He now lives in Akron, Ohio and is a professor of marketing at the University of Akron. D'Amico graduated from the Georgetown University School of Foreign Service, received his master's degree from Rutgers University, and earned his Ph.D. in business administration at Texas Tech University. Before attending Rutgers, he worked in sales and marketing positions in Washington, D.C. and New York City, and he now serves frequently as a consultant to not-for-profit, political, and commercial organizations and as a board member for such organizations as Goodwill Industries.

D'Amico has published over one hundred proceedings, journal, and business press articles and has co-edited several proceedings and texts. Currently co-editor of the *Journal of Marketing Management*, he is also a past president of the Marketing Management Association and past National Vice-President of Pi Sigma Epsilon, the national marketing fraternity.

D'Amico has won a number of teaching awards and was selected by the Professional Fraternities Association as its 1997–1998 Outstanding Collegiate Chapter Advisor for his work with Pi Sigma Epsilon. He is currently national president of Mu Kappa Tau, the Marketing Honorary Society.

once tech-nology is out of the jar you can't put it back in

–WHO SAID THIS?

nce tech-
ology is out
f the jar

THAT'S WHO SAID IT!

ou can't put
back in —ANONYMOUS

The unidentified person who said this clearly understood how a
new technology can dramatically change an industry. Today's
digital technology, which allows instantaneous and interactive
access to information around the globe, will transform the nature
of marketing in the 21st century. Like birds set free from a cage,
we confront unlimited opportunity.

chapter
1

The Nature of Marketing

LEARNING OBJECTIVES

After you have studied this chapter, you will be able to:

Understand how marketing affects people's daily lives.  **1**

Define marketing and discuss marketing in its broadened sense. **2**

Identify the elements of the marketing mix. **3**

Understand that marketers must contend with external environmental forces. **4**

(continued on next page)

a visit to Turner Field, the Atlanta Braves' $242.5 million, state-of-the-art ballpark, feels like a trip back to the future.

BellSouth, one of the team's corporate sponsors, describes the stadium as "20th century tradition meets 21st century technology."

The Braves' marketing campaign reflects the charm and nostalgia of baseball's past, but it has a futuristic slogan, "Turner Field: Not just baseball. A baseball theme park."

Sure, baseball purists will love the fact that they're closer to the action at Turner Field than at any other major league ballpark. It's only 45 feet from first and third base to the dugouts. On top of that, there's a Braves Museum and Hall of Fame with more than two hundred artifacts. Cybernauts will find Turner Field awesome because it's a ballpark that makes them a part of the action. At the stadium, built for the 1996 summer Olympics and converted for baseball use since the Games, there are

- Interactive games to test fans' hitting and pitching skills, as well as knowledge of baseball trivia; electronic kiosks with touch screens and data banks filled with scouting reports on three hundred past and present Braves, along with the Braves' Internet home page; a dozen 27-inch television monitors mounted above the Braves' Clubhouse Store, broadcasting all the other major league games in progress, and a video ticker-tape screen underneath, spitting out up-to-the-minute scores and stats.
- A sophisticated BellSouth communications system, with four miles of fiber-optic cable underneath the playing field that will allow for World Series games to be simulcast around the globe, as well as special black boxes placed throughout the stadium to allow for as many as 5,500 cellular phone calls an hour.

Welcome to the future of baseball. The idea behind the marketing of Turner Field is that for many fans, it is not enough to just provide nine innings of baseball.

Turner Field's theme-park concept was the brainchild of Braves President Stan Kasten. In the early 1990s, as the Braves grew into one of the best teams in baseball, Kasten increasingly became frustrated while watching fans flock to Atlanta–Fulton County Stadium a few hours before games, with little to do but eat overcooked hot dogs and watch batting practice.

As Kasten saw it, they spent too much time milling on the club-level concourse and too little time spending money.

What if he could find a way for families to make an outing of it, bring the amenities of the city to Hank Aaron Drive, and create a neighborhood feel in a main plaza at the ballpark?

"I wanted to broaden fans' experience at the ballpark and broaden our fan base," Kasten says. "People have no problem spending money when they're getting value. We have one of the highest payrolls in baseball, and I needed to find new ways to sustain our revenues."

Turner Field's main entry plaza opens three hours before games—compared to two hours for the rest of the ballpark—and will stay open about two hours after games. On weekends, there'll be live music.

Everyone's invited—$1 "skyline seats" are available for each game—and that buck gets you anywhere, from the open-air porch at the Chop House restaurant, which specializes in barbecue, bison

dogs, Moon Pies, and Tomahawk lager, to the grassy roof at Coke's Sky Field, where fans can keep cool under a mist machine.

Interactive games in Scouts Alley range from $1 to $4, and the chroma-key studios in the East and West Pavilions, where fans can have their picture inserted into a baseball card or into a photograph of a great moment in Braves history, cost $10–$20. The Museum is $2.

And, it should come as no surprise that there are seven ATMs located throughout the ballpark.

One of the Braves' key marketing objectives is to help build a new generation of baseball fans. The new stadium was planned so that fans will find something to be loved and learned at every turn.

The minute a fan's ticket is torn, that person becomes part of the happening Turner Field. Turner Field is the result of creative marketing.[1]

> **THE IDEA BEHIND THE MARKETING OF TURNER FIELD IS THAT FOR MANY FANS, IT IS NOT ENOUGH TO JUST PROVIDE NINE INNINGS OF BASEBALL.**

Why do people go to baseball games? What role does a winning team play in increasing the number of fans who visit the stadium? How important is the price of a ticket? What do baseball marketers and stadium managers do that motivates consumers to buy a ticket? Are all baseball teams and ballparks thought of as the same? Is being socially responsible an important concern for a marketing organization? The answers to questions like these lie in the field of marketing, the subject of this book.

Atlanta Braves
www.atlantabraves.com

Marketing Affects Our Daily Lives

Perhaps you have thought of some answers to the questions asked in the introduction. After all, you have visited shopping centers, examined retail displays, compared prices, dealt with salespeople, and evaluated and purchased a wide range of products. If you think about it, as customers, we all play a part in the marketing system, so we all know something about marketing. We all recognize brand names such as Nike and Nintendo 64 and their corporate and product symbols, the Nike "Swoosh" and Super Mario. Television advertising has been both an irritant and a source of pleasure to us all.

Some aspects of marketing are, of course, more widely known than others. The brand names shown in Exhibit 1-1 are probably quite familiar to you. The brand names in Exhibit 1-2 probably are not—they identify corporations most consumers seldom encounter directly. These companies buy goods and services that are used to produce other goods and services, thus performing important marketing activities *behind the scenes*. Although most of us deal regularly with retailers and sales clerks, we encounter wholesalers, industrial sales representatives, and advertising agents less frequently. Indeed, there are many aspects of marketing that many people have never considered systematically. Most people do not fully understand marketing's place in society or how marketing activities should be managed. To fully understand marketing, you must first know what it is and what it includes.

You Already Know Something About Marketing

Marketing—What Is It?

As you will see, there are several ways to consider the subject of marketing, so there are a number of ways to define the term itself. Because for most people marketing has a business connotation, it is best to begin by discussing marketing from a business perspective. Marketing, as the term implies, is focused on the marketplace. (In fact, for shoppers of past generations, the word *marketing* meant going to a store or market to buy groceries.) A businessperson who is asked the question "What is marketing?" might answer that marketing is selling, or advertis-

Many Companies Engaged in Marketing Operate "Behind the Scenes"

ing, or retailing. But notice that these are marketing activities, not definitions of marketing as a whole.

At the broadest level, the function of marketing activities is to bring buyers and sellers together. At the beach, the thirsty sunbather seeks the Coke stand owner. The owner is, in turn, interested in selling soft drinks to satisfy the customer's thirst. The owner's marketing activities, such as locating the stand at the beach and advertising the price on a sign, help bring buyer and seller together. The owner's goal is to consummate a sale to satisfy a customer. This, of course, is a simple example. A more sophisticated situation requires more complex marketing activities.

Suppose you were the vice-president of marketing for Bandai America, a company in Cerritos, California, that markets the Mighty Morphin Power Ranger toys. The company's headquarters is in Japan, and most of Bandai's toys are produced in Asia and Mexico. Thus, manufacturing—which is an important business activity, but not a marketing activity—would not be directly under your control. Instead, your marketing activities might be identified as developing and planning products, determining prices, advertising, selling, distributing products to consumers, and servicing the products after sales have been made. And even this extensive list is not complete.

A full understanding of marketing requires recognition of the fact that product development activities and product modifications are planned in response to the public's changing needs and wants. A major marketing activity, then, is paying continuous attention to customers' needs— identifying and interpreting those needs before undertaking other activities, including production.

AT THE BROADEST LEVEL, THE FUNCTION OF MARKETING ACTIVITIES IS TO BRING BUYERS AND SELLERS TOGETHER.

Although most marketing activities are intended to direct the flow of goods and services from producer to consumer, the marketing process begins with customer analysis even before the product is manufactured.

Consider again Bandai's Mighty Morphin Power Ranger toys. These action figures are toy replicas of the multi-ethnic characters on television's popular Mighty Morphin Power Rangers show. The program features six teenage characters who, armed with power derived from prehistoric animals, do battle against evil forces and robot vehicles to save the earth.[2]

Before it began marketing the Power Rangers, Bandai's main business— creating toys based on popular Japanese movie and television characters—had been very successful in Japan but had failed abroad. Popular Japanese toys such as Ultraman, a metallic superhero with laser-beam eyes, were "too foreign" for the U.S. market.[3] In essence, Bandai had failed to mount the marketing efforts needed to adapt its toys to U.S. markets.

However, with the support of Japanese moviemaker Toei Company, California producer Saban Entertainment, and Fox Children's Network, Bandai was able to make the long-running Japanese Jyu Rangah (Power Ranger) television series and toys work for U.S. consumers.

Bandai
www.bandai.com

A major marketing activity is paying continuous attention to customers' needs. Bandai marketers developed an understanding of the differing needs of Japanese and American children when the company developed its Mighty Morphin Power Ranger toys. Bandai's U.S. operation does not merely manufacture toys; it interprets the U.S. market's needs.

Based on American needs, Bandai made some changes in the Japanese models. The violence of the television program was toned down for the U.S. audience; the off-duty Rangers were portrayed as normal kids who shoot baskets, mall-hop, and do aerobics when they aren't battling evil space aliens. And Bandai added a moral at the end of each show. It also "Americanized" the toys, making the unmasked characters look American and giving more focus to the female part of the team. It did, however, retain the toys' original technical intricacy—ensuring, for example, that the index finger moves to hold a laser gun—because both Japanese and American children like such features.

By discussing the new product idea with Americans before beginning to manufacture the toys, Bandai marketers developed a better understanding of the differing needs of Japanese and American children. Thus, Bandai's U.S. operation does not merely manufacture toys; it interprets the U.S. market's needs. Today, Power Rangers can be found adorning all sorts of products. The distinctive images of Billy the Blue Ranger, Jason the Red Ranger, Trini the Yellow Ranger, Zak the Black Ranger, Kimberly the Pink Ranger, and Tommy the Green Ranger have popped up on underwear, T-shirts, bottles of bubble bath, jigsaw puzzles, stickers, coloring books, paper plates, and wastebaskets.

Not-for-Profit Organizations Are Marketers Too!

"Perform a death-defying act—eat less saturated fat." The American Heart Association offered this admonition in an advertisement, yet the American Heart Association does not seek to make a profit, nor does it charge a price for most services. Is the American Heart Association engaging in marketing? Are your university, church, and local police department marketers? If we take a broadened perspective of marketing, the answer is unquestionably "Yes."

American Heart Association
www.amhrt.org

Exchange process
The interchange of something of value between two or more parties.

If the concept of marketing is broadened to include not-for-profit organizations, then the primary characteristic of marketing is that it involves an **exchange process** requiring that two or more parties exchange, or trade, something of value.[4] An economic transfer of goods or services in exchange for a price expressed in monetary terms is the most frequently analyzed marketing exchange. However, exchanges also occur in a politician's campaign, a zoo's fund-raising drive, or an antismoking group's program. When a donation is made to a political campaign, to a zoo, or to an antismoking effort, something is given and something is received—even though what is received may be intangible, such as a feeling of goodwill or a sense of satisfaction. In each situation, there has been a transaction, either between an individual and a group or between two individuals. The common characteristic in these situations is the set of activities necessary to bring about exchange relationships. Additional examples of exchanges include offering to vote or volunteer for a candidate who pledges to work hard for his or her constituents, donating blood to help the sick and injured, and spending time working for a United Way campaign—the reward for all of which is a sense of satisfaction. Because all these activities involve an exchange, they may be viewed from a marketing perspective.[5]

A Definition of Marketing

The Atlanta Braves and Bandai examples illustrate what marketing is like in well-managed businesses. The American Heart Association example illustrates that not-for-profit organizations engage in marketing. Thinking about these examples should help you understand that the three organizations share a common marketing goal—to facilitate the exchange or transfer of goods, services, or ideas so that both the marketer and the "customer" profit in some way. This principle of exchange comprises the key aspect of the American Marketing Association's definition of marketing: **Marketing** is the process of planning and executing the conception, pricing, promotion, and distribution of ideas, goods, and services to create exchanges that will satisfy individual and organizational objectives.[6]

Effective marketing requires the conception and development of goods, services, or ideas so that they can be brought to market and purchased by buyers. Pricing, promotion, and distribution of these goods, services, or ideas facilitate the basic function of bringing marketers (suppliers) together with consumers (buyers). Each party must gain something; revenues satisfy the marketer's objectives, and products satisfy the consumer's needs. Each party contributes something of value because each expects to be satisfied by the exchange. Effective marketing involves using the resources of an *entire* organization to create exchanges between the marketer and the customer so that both parties are satisfied.

Keeping Customers and Building Relationships

So far, our discussion of marketing has focused on the idea of creating exchanges. To put it another way, we have talked about getting customers; but keeping customers is equally important. Marketers want customers for life. Effective marketers work to build long-term relationships with their customers. The term **relationship marketing** (or relationship management) communicates the idea that a major goal of marketing is to build long-term relationships with the parties who contribute to a company's success.

Once an exchange is made, effective marketing stresses managing relationships that will bring about additional exchanges. Effective marketers view making a sale not as the end of a process but as the start of the organization's relationship with a customer. Satisfied customers who want to purchase the same product in the future will return to a company that has treated them well. If they need a related

This is San Xavier del Bac, just outside of Tucson. They call it the "White Dove of the Desert." I don't know what's more beautiful—the mission itself or the captivating smiles of the little children I met.

For a free travel packet, call 1-800-944-9668.

From a broad perspective, marketing includes the activities of not-for-profit organizations. The Arizona Visitors and Convention Bureau recognizes that it markets Arizona's natural beauty and unique history to tourists, who make a contribution to the state's economy.

Marketing
The process of planning and executing the conception, pricing, promotion, and distribution of ideas, goods, and services to create exchanges that will satisfy individual and organizational objectives.

Relationship marketing
Marketing activities aimed at building long-term relationships with the people (especially customers) and organizations that contribute to the company's success.

| ORGANIZATION | EXCHANGE | | CUSTOMER SATISFACTION/ RELATIONSHIP BUILDING |
	ORGANIZATION	CONSUMER	
Atlanta Braves' Turner Field	Offers nine innings of baseball, interactive entertainment, food and beverages, and television broadcasts of games, all of which have value for the fan	Pays for tickets, interactive games, food, beverages, souvenirs, etc., providing revenue for the Braves	Enjoyment of game and ballpark visit Sense of involvement with team Sense of loyalty
American Heart Association	Dispenses useful public service information, provides health care, and conducts medical research Expresses gratitude for donations	Donates money or volunteer time that helps the American Heart Association provide services	Sense of doing good Knowledge that time or money is well spent to benefit others Knowledge that "someone might do the same for me or one of my loved ones" in a time of need

item, satisfied customers know the first place to look. The key aspects of our definition of marketing are illustrated in Exhibit 1-3.

In summary, marketers strive to initiate exchanges and build relationships. More simply, you can think of marketing as an activity aimed at getting and keeping customers. It is the marketer's job to use the resources of the entire organization to create, interpret, and maintain the relationship between the company and the customer.[7]

What Is a Market?

Market
A group of potential customers who may want the product offered and who have the resources, the willingness, and the ability to purchase it.

The root word in the term *marketing* is *market*.[8] A **market** is a group of potential customers for a particular product who are willing and able to spend money or exchange other resources to obtain the product. The term can be somewhat confusing, because it has been used to designate buildings or places (the Fulton Fish Market, the European Market), institutions (the stock market), and stores (the supermarket), as well as many other things. But each usage—even the name of a building in which trading is carried out—suggests people or groups with purchasing power who are willing to exchange their resources for something else. It will become clear as you read this book that the nature of the market is a primary concern of marketing decision makers.

The Marketing Mix

Marketing mix
The specific combination of interrelated and interdependent marketing activities in which an organization engages to meet its objectives.

Our definition of marketing indicates that marketing includes many interrelated and interdependent activities meant to encourage exchange and build relationships. The term **marketing mix** describes the result of management's creative efforts to combine these activities.[9] Faced with a wide choice of product features, messages, prices, distribution methods, and other marketing variables, the marketing manager must select and combine ingredients to create a marketing mix that will achieve organizational objectives.

Four Ps of marketing
The basic elements of the marketing mix: product, place (distribution), price, and promotion; also called the controllable variables of marketing, because they can be controlled and manipulated by the marketer.

The marketing mix may have many facets, but its elements can be placed in four basic categories: product, place (distribution), promotion, and price. These are commonly referred to as the **four Ps of marketing,** or—because they can be influenced by managers—as the *controllable variables* of marketing.[10] Because virtually every possible marketing activity can be placed in one of these categories, the four Ps constitute a framework that can be used to develop plans for marketing efforts. Preparing a marketing strategy requires considering each major category of the marketing mix and making decisions about the development of substrategies within the category.

A product is what is offered to customers. A rock concert by the Spice Girls is not a tangible good, but it is a product nonetheless. Developing a product, even a concert, requires making certain that it has the characteristics and features the customer wants. Every product, whether it is a good, a service, or an idea, requires marketing. Some organizations are effective marketers that create value for their customers, and others are not.

THE FIRST ELEMENT—PRODUCT

The term **product** refers to what the business or nonprofit organization offers to its prospective customers or clients. The offering may be a tangible good, such as a car; a service, such as an airline trip; or an intangible idea, such as the importance of parents' reading to their children.

Because customers often expect more from an organization than a simple, tangible product, the task of marketing management is to provide a complete offering—a "total product"—that includes not only the basic good or service but also the "extras" that go with it. The core product of a city bus line may be rides or transportation, for example, but its total product offering should include courteous service, buses that run on time, and assistance in finding appropriate bus routes. The chairman of Binney and Smith, marketers of Crayola Crayons, once said, "We are no longer just a crayon company. We are in the business of providing assorted products that are fun to use and inspire creative self-expression."[11] This effective marketer realizes what a product is. One of Xerox Corporation's products is a copying machine plus repair service, supplies, advice, and other customer services that extend beyond the initial sale. Xerox's product definition shows that the company understands that the sale is not the end of the marketing process.

The product the customer receives in the exchange process is the result of a number of product strategy decisions. Developing and planning a product involves making sure that it has the characteristics and features customers want. Selecting a brand name, designing a package, developing appropriate warranties and service plans, and other product decisions are also part of developing the "right" product. Product strategies are addressed in Chapters 9–11.

As you will see, product strategies must take into consideration the other three elements of the marketing mix. Price, distribution, and promotion enhance the attractiveness of the product offering.

Product
A good, service, or idea that offers a bundle of tangible and intangible attributes to satisfy consumers.

Crayola
www.crayola.com

Place (distribution)
The element of the marketing mix that encompasses all aspects of getting products to the consumer in the right location at the right time.

THE SECOND ELEMENT—PLACE

Determining how goods get to the customer, how quickly, and in what condition involves formulating a strategy regarding **place,** or distribution. Transportation, storage, materials handling, and the like are

w h a t w e n t wrong?

McDonald's McDonald's in the United Kingdom chose a tartan design for new "host" and "hostess" uniforms in all of its 764 U.K. restaurants. By most accounts, the ties, scarves, and waistcoats in the tartan fabric were considered to be attractive. However, soon after the uniforms began to appear in the restaurants, it became clear that McDonald's had breached British etiquette. What went wrong?

Different Scottish tartans historically belong to individual clans, or families, whose members in days gone by were typically fiercely competitive with each other, sometimes to the point of bloodshed. Where McDonald's tripped up was in choosing the tartan belonging to Clan Lindsay, rivals of the Donalds. An enraged Godfrey Lord Macdonald, chief of Clan Donald (who allegedly commands the allegiance of every Donald, Macdonald, and McDonald worldwide), complained of a "complete lack of understanding of the name." He says there are nineteen Macdonald tartans the company could have chosen from.[12]

Channel of distribution
The sequence of marketing organizations involved in bringing a product from the producer to the consumer.

Manufacturer
An organization that recognizes a consumer need and produces a product from raw materials, component parts, or labor to satisfy that need.

Wholesaler
An organization that serves as an intermediary between manufacturer and retailer to facilitate the transfer of products or the exchange of title to those products, or an organization that sells to manufacturers or institutions that resell the product (perhaps in another form). Wholesalers neither produce nor consume the finished product.

physical distribution activities. Selecting wholesalers, retailers, and other types of distributors is also a place activity.

The examples so far have shown that every organization engages in marketing. Not every organization, however, has the resources or ability to manage all the activities required in the distribution process. Thus, organizations may concentrate on activities in which they have a unique advantage and rely on wholesalers, retailers, and various other specialists to make the distribution process more efficient. For example, the Pepsi-Cola Corporation, which specializes in the production and promotion of soft drinks, finds it efficient to utilize independent bottlers and retailers to distribute its products to the ultimate consumer.

A **channel of distribution** is the complete sequence of marketing organizations involved in bringing a product from the producer to the consumer. Its purpose is to make possible transfer of ownership and/or possession of the product. Exhibit 1-4 illustrates a basic channel of distribution consisting of the manufacturer, the wholesaler, the retailer, and the ultimate consumer. Each of these four engages in a transaction that involves movement of the physical good and/or a transfer of title (ownership) of that product. As you look at Exhibit 1-4, consider the following definitions:

A **manufacturer** is an organization that recognizes a consumer need and produces a product from raw materials, component parts, or labor to satisfy that need.

A **wholesaler** is an organization that serves as an intermediary between manufacturer and retailer to facilitate the transfer of products or the exchange of title to those products, or an organization that sells products to manufacturers or

e x h i b i t 1-4

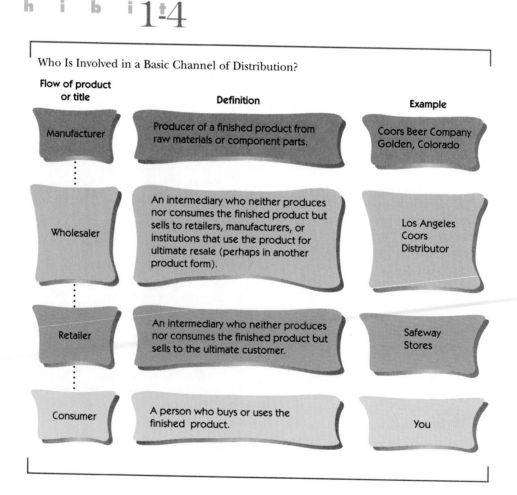

Who Is Involved in a Basic Channel of Distribution?

Flow of product or title	Definition	Example
Manufacturer	Producer of a finished product from raw materials or component parts.	Coors Beer Company Golden, Colorado
Wholesaler	An intermediary who neither produces nor consumes the finished product but sells to retailers, manufacturers, or institutions that use the product for ultimate resale (perhaps in another product form).	Los Angeles Coors Distributor
Retailer	An intermediary who neither produces nor consumes the finished product but sells to the ultimate customer.	Safeway Stores
Consumer	A person who buys or uses the finished product.	You

institutions that resell the products (sometimes in another form). Exhibit 1-4 shows the type of wholesaler that sells to retailers. Wholesalers neither produce nor consume the finished product.

A **retailer** is an organization that sells products it has obtained from a manufacturer or wholesaler to the ultimate consumer. Retailers neither produce nor consume the product.

The **ultimate consumer** is the individual who buys or uses the product for personal consumption.

The actual distribution path that a product or title takes may be simpler or much more complex than the one illustrated in Exhibit 1-4. For example, a computer manufacturer such as Gateway 2000 or Dell may provide information about its products on the Internet and ship directly to a buyer. Various distribution systems are explained in Chapters 12–14.

Excluded from the channel of distribution are numerous specialists that perform specific facilitating activities for manufacturers, wholesalers, or retailers—for example, the airline or the railway that transports a product from Boston to Philadelphia or the advertising agency on Madison Avenue that creates the advertising message and selects the appropriate media. These specialists, or *collaborators,* are hired because they can perform a certain marketing activity in a basic marketing channel more efficiently or more effectively than a producer can. However, they are not among the organizations included in our definition of channel of distribution.[13]

It is important to realize that distribution mixes vary widely even among companies selling directly competitive products. For example, Avon and Amway use sales representatives selling directly to consumers as their primary source of distribution; Gillette and Colgate-Palmolive, selling similar goods, deal with many wholesalers and retailers in their distribution systems. Further, a single organization may use different methods of distribution in different parts of the world.

THE THIRD ELEMENT—PROMOTION

Marketers need to communicate with consumers. **Promotion** is the means by which marketers "talk to" existing customers and potential buyers. Promotion may convey a message about the organization, a product, or some other element of the marketing mix, such as the new low price being offered during a sale period. Simply put, promotion is marketing communication.

As an illustration of the value of promotional efforts in a marketing mix, think about Energizer batteries. You probably have seen one of the television commercials featuring a pink mechanical Energizer bunny in some hilarious situation. Perhaps you recall the tireless drum-playing bunny crossing a desert, Darth Vader's light saber failing because he did not have Energizer batteries, or, in a spoof of the movie *Twister,* a team of bunny spotters attempting to follow the pink bunny's path. However, from the marketer's point of view, the most important thing you probably remember is that the Energizer "keeps going, and going, and going." Energizer's promotion accomplishes its task: It communicates the message about the long-lasting battery to consumers.

Retailer
An organization that sells products it has obtained from a manufacturer or wholesaler to the ultimate consumer. Retailers neither produce nor consume the product.

Ultimate consumer
An individual who buys or uses a product for personal consumption.

Promotion
The element of the marketing mix that includes all forms of marketing communication.

Energizer
www.energizer.com

Marketers need to communicate how their products satisfy consumers' needs. This Kellogg's advertisement says "Cereal. Eat it for life." It promotes the healthful benefits of eating cereal. It conveys Kellogg's message that kids who eat cereal for breakfast perform better in school.

Kellogg's
www.kelloggs.com

Advertising, personal selling, publicity, and sales promotion are all forms of promotion. Each offers unique benefits, but all are forms of communication that inform, remind, or persuade. For example, advertising that tells us "Always Coca-Cola" or "Always the Real Thing—Coca-Cola" reminds us of our experiences with a familiar cola.

An IBM sales representative delivers a personal message that explains how a computer network will help provide business solutions for an organization and then attempts to persuade the company to purchase the product. The essence of all promotion is communication aimed at informing, reminding, or persuading potential buyers.

Different firms emphasize different forms of promotional communication. Some firms advertise heavily, for example, whereas others advertise hardly at all. A firm's particular combination of communication tools is its promotional mix. The topic of promotion is addressed in greater detail in Chapters 15–18.

THE FOURTH ELEMENT—PRICE

The amount of money, or sometimes goods or services, given in exchange for something is its price. In other words, **price** is what is exchanged for a product. Just as the customer buys a product with cash, so a company "buys" the customer's cash with the product. In not-for-profit situations, price may be expressed in terms of volunteered time or effort, votes, or donations.

Price
The amount of money or other consideration—that is, something of value— given in exchange for a product.

Marketers must determine the best price for their products. To do so, they must ascertain a product's value, or what it is worth to consumers. Once the value of a product is established, the marketer knows what price to charge. However, because consumers' evaluations of a product's worth change over time, prices are subject to rapid change.

According to economists, prices are always "on trial." Pricing strategies and decisions require establishing appropriate prices and carefully monitoring the competitive marketplace. Price is discussed in Chapters 19 and 20.

THE ART OF BLENDING THE ELEMENTS

A manager selecting a marketing mix may be likened to a chef preparing a meal. Each realizes that there is no one best way to mix ingredients. Different combinations may be used, and the result will still be satisfactory. In marketing, as in cooking, there is no standard formula for a successful combination of ingredients. Marketing mixes vary from company to company and from situation to situation.

Exhibit 1-5 provides examples of many marketing mix elements. The vast majority of marketers agree that the blending of these elements is a creative activity. For example, though both firms are successful at selling motorcycles, the marketing mix strategies of Honda and Harley-Davidson differ greatly. Far greater differences can be seen in marketing mixes for different products, such as Penn tennis balls and Steinway pianos. The field of marketing encompasses such differ-e x h i b i 1-5

MARKETING MIX ELEMENT	COMPANY OR ORGANIZATION	EXAMPLE
PRODUCT		
Product development	Procter & Gamble	Olestra fat substitute
	Coca-Cola	Citra, a new citrus soft drink
Product modification	Pizza Hut	Higher-quality, better-tasting pepperoni pizza
	Charles Schwab	Schwab's broker service can now be accessed via the Internet
	Disney	DisneyWorld's Tomorrowland has been remodeled and modernized
Branding	3M Company	Scotch brand cellophane tape
	National Multiple Sclerosis Society	"Help fight MS."
Trademark	Michelin	Tire Man
Warranty	Sears	"If any Craftsman hand tool ever fails to give complete satisfaction, Sears will replace it free."
PLACE (DISTRIBUTION)		
Channel of distribution	Hoover Vacuum	Ships directly to Wal-Mart
	U.S. Postal Service	Sells stamps by mail order, in vending machines, and at post offices
Physical distribution	South-Western College Publishing	Uses FedEx to transport rush orders
PROMOTION		
Advertising	Australia Office of Tourism	"Australia—come and say g'day."
	The Advertising Council	"Remember, only you can prevent forest fires."
Personal selling	Girl Scouts	Door-to-door cookie sales
	Hitachi	Sales representatives sell fiber-optic communication systems to business organizations
Sales promotion	Metropolitan Life Insurance	Gives away "Let's Go Mets" T-shirts at New York Mets baseball games
	The American Red Cross	Emphasizes the importance of donating blood by giving Nabisco Lifesaver candies and a T-shirt with the "life saver" theme
Publicity	Garth Brooks (singer)	Gives free concert in Central Park
PRICE		
Price strategy	Absolut Country of Sweden Vodka	Expensive
	AT&T	"True Savings"
	Southwestern Bell	"The Works"—twelve best-selling services offered together at a price 45 percent lower than what a customer would pay if the services were ordered separately

ing approaches because the design, implementation, and revision of a marketing mix is a creative activity.

Some experts claim that marketing is, or could be, a science. Certain aspects of marketing, such as the gathering and analyzing of information by marketing researchers, are indeed scientific in nature. The fact remains, however, that there are no pat solutions in marketing. Even frequently encountered problems have unique aspects requiring creative solutions. This absence of certainty may annoy those who are accustomed to solving math or accounting problems and arriving at one "right" answer. But marketing is different. Its relationship to the ever-changing environment requires that it be dynamic, constantly altering its approaches to suit the marketplace.[14] Each product's marketing mix must be critically analyzed and altered as the environment changes and new problems develop.

The Marketing Environment— Coping with the Uncontrollable

All organizations operate within environments. That is, all organizations, whether for profit or not for profit, are surrounded by, and must contend with, external forces. Except in rare instances, managers cannot govern these external, or environmental, forces; therefore, the forces are called **uncontrollable variables.** Uncontrollable variables affect both consumers' behavior and organizations' development of effective marketing mixes, as shown in Exhibit 1-6.

Inflation provides an example. Organizations' reactions to high inflation rates are easy to spot in their pricing policies. Consumers' reactions to economic forces such as shortages of materials and high land prices are similarly predictable; they are likely to build fewer homes. Such a decline will in turn reduce the demand for bulldozers, concrete mixers, nails, and even work clothes.

The influence of some environmental forces—for example, changes in social values and lifestyles—may be more subtle. Consider that most people in your grandparents' day—and certainly your great-grandparents' day—thought it a vice for children to eat between meals.[15] Today, most parents allow children to eat a series of small meals and snacks throughout the day. Parents today differ from those of past generations in their beliefs about such issues as whether a 5 p.m. cookie can "spoil" their children's dinner. Many view snacks not just as a form of sustenance but as a means to buy peace. Mothers tuck lollipops in their purses to appease restless children in church. They prepare goody bags for car trips of more than 30 minutes.

Marketing managers must be able to recognize and analyze subtle uncontrollable variables of this kind so that they can plan marketing mixes compatible with the environment. For example, marketers have responded to the snacking trend with convenient, disposable, single-serving packages containing sweet and

Uncontrollable variable
A force or influence external to the organization and beyond its control.

e x h i b i t 1-6

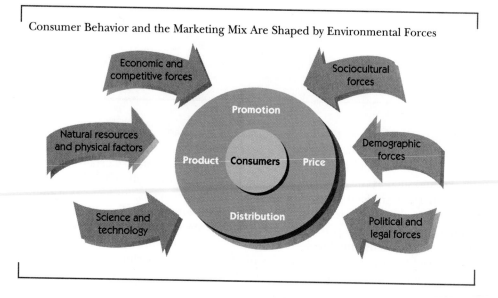

Consumer Behavior and the Marketing Mix Are Shaped by Environmental Forces

Economic and competitive forces

Sociocultural forces

Natural resources and physical factors

Demographic forces

Promotion

Product Consumers Price

Distribution

Science and technology

Political and legal forces

colorful snacks that appeal to children. To win parents, they communicate health claims that stress the real fruit juice or added nutrients in candy and cereals.

Reacting and adapting to competition, economic forces, social trends, government regulations, and the many other environmental influences surrounding an organization is a major part of a marketing manager's job. On one hand, the manager may try to change or influence the environment in some way. Although environmental forces are, for the most part, beyond the control of any individual organization, a group of organizations may be able to influence some aspect of its environment through political lobbying or some other such activity. On the other hand, the marketing mix is controlled by the organization. The marketing manager can adjust the marketing mix to reflect changes in the environment. The proper timing of a marketing decision is often the factor that determines success. Determining the correct time to enter and exit a market, for example, may rest on an analysis of the external environment.

Environmental factors affect all organizations, even the largest and wealthiest companies. Because of their important influence on marketing decisions, environmental forces are discussed in depth in Chapters 3 and 4.

Modern Marketers Use the Marketing Concept

An organization's level of marketing sophistication is often reflected in its goals and in the general principles underlying the way it conducts its activities. Marketing sophistication can be judged in terms of whether an organization is oriented toward production, sales, or marketing. These orientations also describe the prevailing philosophies of certain historical eras.[16] Exhibit 1-7 illustrates the differences among the orientations.

Orientations toward Marketing

e x h i b i t 1-7

	FOCUS	MEANS	GOAL	ILLUSTRATIVE COMMENTS
PRODUCTION ORIENTATION	Manufacturing	Making high-quality products	Produce as much product as possible	"You can have any color you want as long as it's black." "Make the best product you can and people will buy it." "I know people want my kind of product."
SALES ORIENTATION	Selling existing products	Aggressive sales and advertising efforts	Maximize sales volume	"You don't like black? I'll throw in a set of glassware!" "Sell this inventory no matter what it takes." "Who cares what they want? Sell what we've got."
MARKETING ORIENTATION	Fulfilling actual and potential customer needs and wants	Consumer orientation, profit orientation, and integrated marketing	Make profits by ensuring customer satisfaction	"Find out what consumers want before you make the product." "Maybe people don't want the 'best' product. Find out what they do want." "I'm going to find out what the people want."

PRODUCTION ORIENTATION—"AS LONG AS IT'S BLACK"

Marketing managers with a **production orientation** and philosophy focus their efforts on physical production and stress developments in technology. Henry Ford's famous description of the Model T—"You can have any color you want as long as it's black"—sums up the prevailing attitude of the production orientation.

Organizations with a production orientation typically do best in a seller's market, in which demand exceeds supply. Manufacturers simply produce a high-quality product and expect to sell it easily. Before the turn of the century, production-oriented organizations were more common than they are today. Today, few organizations in the United States can survive for long if they maintain a philosophy that gives little thought to marketing.

SALES ORIENTATION—FOCUS ON TRANSACTIONS

The philosophy of an organization with a **sales orientation** is to change consumers' minds to fit the product. This philosophy is epitomized by the slogan "Push! Push! Sell! Sell!"

Organizations with a sales orientation stress aggressive promotional campaigns to "push" their existing products. These organizations concentrate on selling what they make rather than on learning what will best satisfy consumers and then marketing those products. Sales-oriented organizations focus their efforts on the **transaction**, which is the completion of a single exchange agreement or, more simply put, an immediate sale. This focus on transactions (sometimes called *transaction marketing*) encourages organizations to emphasize short-run increases in sales of existing products rather than long-run profits. Short-term sales maximization is a paramount goal of these organizations.

> SALES-ORIENTED ORGANIZATIONS FOCUS THEIR EFFORTS ON THE TRANSACTION, WHICH IS THE COMPLETION OF A SINGLE EXCHANGE AGREEMENT OR, MORE SIMPLY PUT, AN IMMEDIATE SALE.

The sales orientation is perhaps most common during economic periods when supply exceeds demand, such as the Great Depression (1929–1933). Companies that maintain a sales orientation while competitors move on to a marketing-oriented philosophy may find themselves in difficulty.

MARKETING ORIENTATION—ESTABLISHING AND MAINTAINING RELATIONSHIPS

Companies that have superior skill in understanding and satisfying customers are said to have a **marketing orientation** or to be market-driven.[17] Marketing-oriented organizations embrace the idea of an organization-wide focus on learning customers' needs so that they can offer **superior customer value**—that is, so that they can satisfy customer needs better than their competitors do. These organizations realize that the organization must see itself not as producing goods and services but as developing long-term relationships with customers—as doing the things that will make people want to continue to do business with it rather than with its competitors.[18]

THE MARKETING CONCEPT—THE FOUNDATION OF A MARKETING ORIENTATION

Being marketing-oriented means adopting the philosophy known as the marketing concept. The **marketing concept,** which is central to all effective marketing thinking, planning, and action, relates marketing to the organization's overall purpose—to survive and prosper by satisfying a clientele—and calls on management and employees to do three things.[19]

Production orientation
Organizational philosophy that emphasizes physical production and technology rather than sales or marketing.

Sales orientation
Organizational philosophy that emphasizes selling existing products, whether or not they meet consumer needs, often through aggressive sales techniques and advertising.

Transaction
A single exchange agreement; the completion of a one-time sale.

Marketing orientation
Organizational philosophy that emphasizes developing exceptional skill in understanding and satisfying customers so that the organization can offer superior customer value.

Superior customer value
The consumer's attribution of greater worth or better ability to fulfill a need to a certain product compared to its competitors.

Marketing concept
Organizational philosophy that stresses consumer orientation, long-range profitability, and the integration of marketing and other organizational functions. The marketing concept, which focuses on satisfying consumers' wants and needs, is the foundation of a marketing orientation.

1. To be consumer-oriented in all matters, from product development to honoring warranties and service contracts
2. To stress long-run profitability rather than short-term profits or sales volume
3. To adopt a cross-functional perspective to achieve a consumer orientation and long-run profitability

Companies that subscribe to this philosophy have a marketing orientation.

Consumer Orientation

Consumer orientation is the first aspect of the marketing concept. The consumer, or customer, should be seen as "the fulcrum, the pivot point about which the business moves in operating for the balanced interests of all concerned."[20] Organizations that have accepted the marketing concept try to create goods and services with the customer's needs in mind. Effective marketers recognize that they must offer products that consumers perceive to have greater value than those offered by competitors.

It follows that a marketing manager's first determination must be what the customer wants. The marketing concept rightly suggests that it is better to find out

In marketing-oriented organizations, products are designed to solve customer problems. Marketing managers for Wearever recognized that bakers want to avoid burned cookies at all costs. When they created insulated cookie sheets to solve this consumer problem, sales soared.

www.mirro.com/bakeware.htm

Fletcher Music Centers   Fletcher Music Centers in Clearwater, Florida, understands that the key to winning and keeping customers is to figure out what they need, sometimes before they figure it out themselves. A few years ago Fletcher was struggling along with other retailers in the ailing business of selling organs. "There is no natural market for organs," says Fletcher president John Riley, 42. "No one goes to a mall to shop for one." But after conducting [research] with its main clientele, senior citizens who retire to Florida, Fletcher realized that what these people wanted wasn't so much a musical instrument as companionship.

Today Fletcher drums up business by positioning a "meet 'em and greet 'em" salesman at the keyboard within earshot of elderly mall patrons. "What's your favorite song?" he'll ask. And to the peals of "Chattanooga Choo Choo," he'll begin his line of patter: "Where ya from? You must have just moved here? Do you play the organ at all? Ever seen one like this? It's specially designed for someone just like you with no musical background. Come on inside and try it out."

Once inside, the prospect is treated to a sales pitch heavy with subtext: Buy from us because we can help enliven your retirement years. Whether the customer springs for the $500 used model or the $47,000 top of the line, free weekly group lessons—good for a lifetime—come with the package. Says Riley: "We've seen a fair share of romances develop at these lessons."

Then there are the small details that show elderly customers how much Fletcher cares about their needs: large type on the keys and oversized knobs that arthritic fingers can easily manipulate. Says Sherman Wantz, 75, who just bought his fourth Fletcher organ: "They know how to treat elderly people without making them feel like children. They appeal to a desire in older people to continue accomplishing things in their lives." Such satisfaction is music to Fletcher's ears.[21]

Sauder Woodworking Sauder Woodworking, a manufacturer of church pews in northwest Ohio, became a leader in the red-hot ready-to-assemble furniture business by adopting a marketing orientation. It promotes its ready-to-assemble furniture not as a cheap alternative to factory-ready furniture but as good furniture that just happens to come in a box. The company is highly skilled at anticipating changing lifestyle and retail trends, but it also recognizes that it must offer furniture that consumers perceive to have greater value than products offered by competitors. Attention to the small detail is an important part of Sauder's marketing effort. For instance, Sauder's products—from computer workstations to entertainment centers to stand-alone wardrobes—are famous for their easy-to-follow assembly instructions. The company believes the instructions are as much a part of the product as the wood that goes into it. All instructions are tested in sixth-grade classrooms to ensure that customers will be able to assemble a product that has superior customer value.[22]

what the customer wants and offer that product than to make a product and then try to sell it to somebody. A company that subscribes to the marketing concept, then, must figure out what customers need—sometimes before they figure it out themselves (which is what Fletcher Music Centers did, as described in the Adapting to Change feature). In many instances, the technological innovations of visionaries are the roads to customer need satisfaction. However, most effective marketers must gather and analyze information to understand factors, such as competitive alternatives, that influence consumer needs.

According to most marketing thinkers, consumer orientation—the satisfaction of customer wants—is the justification for an organization's existence. Consider the following examples:

- While visiting one of McDonald's outlets, the chairman of the board of McDonald's restaurants encountered a sign ordering customers to "MOVE TO THE NEXT POSITION." He made sure that such signs were removed from all McDonald's outlets, stating, "It's up to us to move to the customer."
- Crisco Savory Seasonings, a new line of flavored vegetable oils patterned after more expensive gourmet cooking oils, come in four all-natural flavors: Roasted Garlic, Hot & Spicy, Classic Herb, and Lemon Butter.[23] The flavored oils fill a consumer need for quick and easy meal preparation. They can be used in a number of ways—for stir-frying, sauteing, pan-frying, marinades, or dressings. Savory Seasonings can be thought of as a "speed-scratch product" that helps consumers cut down on meal preparation time, yet satisfies their desire to give meals a homemade touch.

Many organizations that have adopted the marketing concept realize that the organization must see itself not as producing goods and services but as "buying customers, as doing the things that will make people want to do business with it."[24] Progressive companies wisely spend a great deal of time and effort learning about consumers.

Unfortunately, not all firms have adopted a consumer orientation as their philosophy. To some extent, the consumerism movement and consumer activists like Ralph Nader represent a protest against firms that have failed to adopt a consumer orientation, instead holding onto a sales or production orientation.

Long-Term Profitability Even though the marketing concept stresses consumer orientation, an organization need not meet every fleeting whim of every customer. Implicit in the marketing concept are two assumptions: that the organization has competition and that it wishes to continue to exist. Therefore, long-term profits, not simply current profitability, are accented in this philosophy. Consumers would prefer that the price of a new Mercedes-Benz be under $15,000. But because the manufacturing and marketing costs associated with such a car far exceed that figure, Daimler-Benz, manufacturer of the Mercedes, and its distributors would soon be out of business if they attempted to satisfy that particular consumer desire. Not only consumer wants but also costs and profits must be taken into consideration in determining a competitive market offering.

The marketing concept's focus on long-term profitability leads to the idea that organizations should not seek sales volume for the sake of volume alone. Sales volume can be profitless, and a firm can actually increase its sales volume while decreasing its profits—for example, when big discounts attract more customers but result in less income. It may be possible to "buy volume" by advertising heavily, cutting prices to levels below cost, or using other methods. Few marketing analysts see this as a profitable strategy, however. As most aggressive price cutters ultimately find out, the profit requirements of an operation regulate marketing activities over all but the shortest time periods.

Marketing Is a Cross-Functional Activity

Marketing personnel do not work in a vacuum, isolated from other company activities. The actions of people in such areas as production, credit, and research and development may affect an organization's marketing efforts. Similarly, the work of marketers affects these other departments. Managers must integrate and coordinate marketing functions with other corporate functions so that they are all directed toward achieving the same objectives.

Problems are almost certain to develop unless an integrated, company-wide effort is maintained. Difficulties may arise when a focus on consumer needs is viewed as the responsibility solely of the enterprise's marketing department. Other functional areas may have goals that conflict with customer satisfaction or long-term profitability. For instance, the engineering department will want long lead times for product design, with simplicity and economy as major design goals. Marketing, however, will want short lead times and more complex designs, including optional features and custom components. Similarly, the finance department may want fixed budgets, strict spending justifications, and short-term prices that always cover costs, whereas the marketing department may seek flexible budgets, looser spending rationales, and short-term prices that may be less than costs but that allow markets to be developed quickly. Similar differences in outlook occur between marketing and other functional areas of the organization, and these too may be sources of serious conflicts.

In the 1990s, many organizations recognized that to achieve many consumer-oriented goals, such as new product development, marketing had to be carried out as a cross-functional activity, not a distinct and separate business function. To say that marketing is a **cross-functional activity** is to say that people with many different job titles and functions within the organization (and even outside the organization) have an impact on the goals set by marketing executives. In today's business organization, traditional functional distinctions have become blurred. This book takes a cross-functional perspective on marketing. Much more

MARKETING PERSONNEL DO NOT WORK IN A VACUUM, ISOLATED FROM OTHER COMPANY ACTIVITIES.

Cross-functional activity
An activity carried out by individuals from various departments within an organization and from outside the organization, all of whom have a common purpose.

It's been said that "Marketing is an attitude, not a department." This phrase expresses the perspective of marketing-oriented organizations, which expect other business functions, such as operations, to perform certain marketing activities. In marketing-oriented hotels, for example, doormen, reservations clerks, maids, and other service personnel strongly influence guests' satisfaction with the hotel. An aspect of their jobs is to understand the important role their services play in the hotel's marketing activities.

will be said about the cross-functional nature of marketing in future chapters. For the moment, we will consider total quality management, which is one area where a cross-functional perspective is essential.

Total Quality Management (TQM)

The management principle known as total quality management (TQM) derives from a business philosophy that has much in common with the marketing concept's focus on customer satisfaction, long-run profitability, and integrated activities. **Total quality management** involves instilling the idea of customer-driven quality throughout an organization and managing all employees so that there will be continuous quality improvement. Quality is no longer viewed narrowly as something the manufacturing department achieves by inspecting products for compliance with specifications and eliminating defective ones. Total quality management means that everyone in all parts of the organization places top priority on *continuous improvement* of customer-driven quality and organizational efficiency. As you can see, the marketing concept and total quality management are closely intertwined.

Total quality management (TQM)
A management principle calling for managers to seek to instill the idea of customer-driven quality throughout an organization and to manage all employees so that there will be continuous improvement in the quality of goods and/or services.

In a company that practices total quality management, manufacturing's orientation toward achieving lowest-cost productivity must be balanced with marketing's commitment to offering high-quality products at an acceptable price. For example, if Ford Motor Company advertises that "Quality is Job 1," the production department must offer the assurance that every automobile that comes off the assembly line will meet the quality specifications that consumers expect. The notion that quality improvement is every employee's job must be integrated throughout the organization so that marketing and production will be in harmony. But this focus may conflict with manufacturing's desire to increase weekly production by allowing variations from quality standards. To avoid such conflicts, the firm must combine its systems for statistical quality controls with improvements in the manufacturing operation so that productivity will increase along with quality.

Total quality management and continuous improvement will be discussed in greater detail throughout this book. In particular, Chapter 2 considers total quality management as a corporate philosophy, Chapter 9 investigates continuous quality improvement as a product strategy, and Chapter 11 examines the nature of service quality.

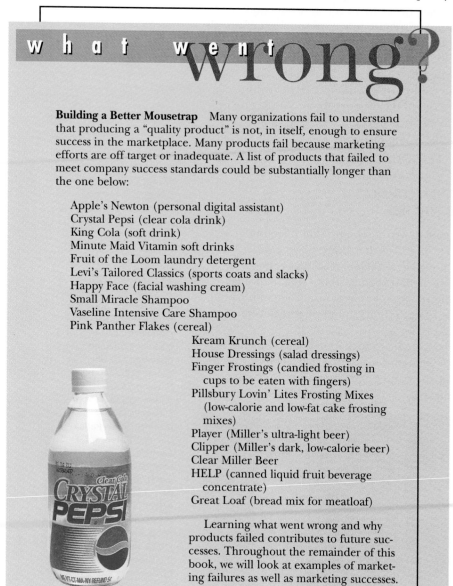

what went wrong?

Building a Better Mousetrap Many organizations fail to understand that producing a "quality product" is not, in itself, enough to ensure success in the marketplace. Many products fail because marketing efforts are off target or inadequate. A list of products that failed to meet company success standards could be substantially longer than the one below:

Apple's Newton (personal digital assistant)
Crystal Pepsi (clear cola drink)
King Cola (soft drink)
Minute Maid Vitamin soft drinks
Fruit of the Loom laundry detergent
Levi's Tailored Classics (sports coats and slacks)
Happy Face (facial washing cream)
Small Miracle Shampoo
Vaseline Intensive Care Shampoo
Pink Panther Flakes (cereal)
Kream Krunch (cereal)
House Dressings (salad dressings)
Finger Frostings (candied frosting in cups to be eaten with fingers)
Pillsbury Lovin' Lites Frosting Mixes (low-calorie and low-fat cake frosting mixes)
Player (Miller's ultra-light beer)
Clipper (Miller's dark, low-calorie beer)
Clear Miller Beer
HELP (canned liquid fruit beverage concentrate)
Great Loaf (bread mix for meatloaf)

Learning what went wrong and why products failed contributes to future successes. Throughout the remainder of this book, we will look at examples of marketing failures as well as marketing successes.

Marketing and Society

Marketing must be examined not only in terms of its role in individual organizations but also in terms of the important role it plays in society. Before we explain, a note on terminology is in order. When referring to marketing as the aggregate of marketing activities within an economy or as the marketing system within a society, some prefer to use the term **macromarketing.** Thus, marketing may be split in the same way economics is split into microeconomics and macroeconomics. Our preference is simply to use the term *marketing*, making its meaning clear by the context in which it is discussed. Marketing's role in society can be illustrated by the description of marketing (or macromarketing) as "the delivery of a standard of living to society." It may seem a bit grandiose to describe marketing in this way, but some reflection will bear out the truth of that statement.

When you think of the aggregate of all organizations' marketing activities (especially if you include transportation and distribution activities), you can see that the efficiency of the system for moving goods from producers to consumers may substantially affect a society's well-being. Consider undeveloped countries. Transportation, storage, and other facets of distribution are vital undertakings; but in many undeveloped nations, marketing intermediaries such as wholesalers are inefficient or even nonexistent. In at least some cases, less developed countries may be poor because their marketing systems are too primitive or inefficient to deliver an improved quality of life. To reach a higher level of economic well-being, such a country must improve its macromarketing.

The recognition that marketing activity plays an important role in society has led a number of marketing thinkers to refine the marketing concept philosophy. The marketing concept stresses satisfying consumer needs at a profit. The **societal marketing concept,** which can be in perfect harmony with the marketing concept, requires that marketers consider the collective needs of society as well as individual consumers' desires and the organization's need for profits.[25]

An example of a company that emphasizes the societal marketing concept is the Body Shop, which sells products bearing names like Rhassoul Mud Shampoo, Raspberry Ripple Bathing Bubbles, and Peppermint Foot Lotion. The colorful shampoos, lotions, soaps, and cosmetics all carry the label "Against animal testing." The Body Shop develops most of its products from natural ingredients such as fruit and vegetable oils. The plastic bottles are returnable for a discount, and customers are supplied with biodegradable plastic bags. And part of the profits from the sale of the Body Shop's products goes to fund environmental campaigns such as saving Amazon rain forests. These actions reflect a marketing philosophy that recognizes that every customer, as a member of society, has a long-term stake in conserving the earth's resources as well as a short-term need for cosmetics. The Body Shop, then, has adopted a societal marketing philosophy that integrates the fulfillment of consumers' short-term preferences with what is best for consumers and society in the long run.

What consumers want and what benefits society often are in harmony. That appears to be the case with the Body Shop. Consumers, society, and the organization may all benefit from the business's societal concerns. Sometimes, however, there can be conflicts between consumers' expressed preferences and an organization's interpretation of what is good for society. Many McDonald's customers, especially teenagers, loved McDonald's french fries when they were cooked in beef tallow. However, McDonald's believed that the fat content of some of its menu items, like french fries, was too high. It stopped frying french fries in beef tallow because it felt a responsibility to offer as healthy a menu as possible. Marketers adhering to the societal marketing concept believe that the organization must reconcile any differences between customers' expressed preferences for goods and services and the organization's interpretation of what is good for society.

Macromarketing
The aggregate of marketing activities in an economy or the marketing system of a society, rather than the marketing activities in a single firm (micromarketing).

Societal marketing concept
Organizational philosophy that stresses the importance of considering the collective needs of society as well as individual consumers' desires and organizational profits.

The Body Shop
www.bodyshop.com

This advertisement for NEC proclaims: "If we live in peace with the environment, we won't have to put the pieces back together." The socially responsive advertising communicates that NEC markets products that are compatible with nature. The company's management believes its environmentally conscious marketing efforts are an important part of its success.

Why Study Marketing?

Why study marketing? One practical reason is that marketing offers many career opportunities, including opportunities in advertising, sales, product management, retail store management, and other fields. Appendix A at the end of this book and the Zikmund/d'Amico Web page (zikmund.swcollege.com) provide additional information to help you learn what career options are available and what preparation is required for employment in these fields.

You may not be planning a career in marketing. This does not mean that the study of marketing holds nothing for you. You may end up working for a business organization in some capacity, in which case you will work with employees who are actively engaged in marketing activity. The study of marketing principles can help you become a more productive, valuable co-worker. In addition, many of the skills and tools of marketing can be applied in other functional areas of business.

If you are planning to own your own business, marketing is the name of the game, and you must understand it to be successful. After you finish this course, you will know why this is so.

We have already mentioned that marketing is used by organizations and people outside the business world. Indeed, when you look for a job, you will be engaged in marketing yourself. The marketing principles and skills you learn in this course will help you achieve the goals you have set for your career. Marketing skills can also help you become a more knowledgeable consumer, as you will better understand the marketing practices that influence your purchases.

There is yet another reason for studying marketing. Learning how people in a society view marketing and how it functions in an increasingly global environment is part of being an educated person. Marketing is a pervasive aspect of our culture that has a dramatic impact on world affairs. It is a fascinating subject, and we hope you will enjoy studying it.

summary

The function of marketing is to bring buyers and sellers together, and the primary emphasis of marketing is an exchange process requiring that two or more parties trade things of value.

1 *Understand how marketing affects people's daily lives.*

Virtually everyone sees or hears advertisements, goes to stores, and uses products manufactured thousands of miles away. Marketing makes these activities possible and allows people to consume products that have become essential to their way of life. Marketing brings buyers and sellers together by directing the flow of goods and services from producer to consumer. Marketing activities are basic to the operation of all organizations as they attempt to satisfy consumer needs.

2 *Define marketing and discuss marketing in its broadened sense.*

Marketing is the process of planning and executing the conception, pricing, promotion, and distribution of ideas, goods, and services to create exchanges that will satisfy individual and organizational objectives. Effective marketing consists of a consumer-oriented mix of business activities planned and implemented by a marketer to facilitate an exchange so that both parties profit in some way. Consumers may exchange money, votes, blood, or something else to obtain the marketer's offering.

3 *Identify the elements of the marketing mix.*

The marketing mix consists of four major elements: product, place (distribution), promotion, and price. These are basic to any organization and are adjusted and combined by the marketing manager to achieve the organization's goals.

4 *Understand that marketers must contend with external environmental forces.*

The marketing environment consists of uncontrollable forces that influence consumer behavior and represent both opportunities for and constraints on an organization. The marketing manager's task is to adjust an organization's marketing mix to cope with the external environment. This involves anticipating environmental changes that will affect the organization. Correct environmental assessment makes marketing decisions more successful.

5 *Explain the marketing concept.*

The marketing concept is a philosophy of business and a set of objectives enabling organizations to offer superior customer value. According to this concept, marketing-oriented organizations can succeed by focusing on consumers' wants and needs, long-term profitability, and an integrated marketing effort. Marketing-oriented organizations embrace the idea that they can satisfy customer needs better than their competitors. Production orientation and sales orientation are less effective alternative philosophies.

6 *Explain total quality management.*

Total quality management is a management philosophy that focuses on integrating the idea of customer-driven quality throughout an organization. Under total quality management, all employees strive for continuous quality improvement.

7 *Recognize the contribution of marketing to a country's economy and way of life.*

Marketing delivers a standard of living to society. The aggregate of all organizations' marketing activities, especially their transportation and distribution activities, affects a society's economic well-being. The efficiency of the system for moving goods from producers to consumers is an important factor determining a country's quality of life.

8 *Define the societal marketing concept.*

The societal marketing concept, which can be in perfect harmony with the marketing concept, stresses the need for marketers to consider the collective needs of society as well as individual consumer desires and the organization's need for profits. It recognizes that every consumer, as a member of society, has both long-term and short-term needs.

key terms

exchange process (p. 8)
marketing (p. 9)
relationship marketing (p. 9)
market (p. 10)

marketing mix (p. 10)
four Ps of marketing (p. 10)
product (p. 11)
place (distribution) (p. 11)

channel of distribution (p. 12)
manufacturer (p. 12)
wholesaler (p. 12)
retailer (p. 13)

ultimate consumer (p. 13)
promotion (p. 13)
price (p. 14)
uncontrollable variable (p. 16)
production orientation (p. 18)
sales orientation (p. 18)

transaction (p. 18)
marketing orientation (p. 18)
superior customer value (p. 18)
marketing concept (p. 18)
cross-functional activity (p. 21)

total quality management
 (TQM) (p. 22)
macromarketing (p. 23)
societal marketing concept (p. 23)

questions for review & critical thinking

1. Think about what you did this morning. In what ways did marketing affect your activities?
2. Define marketing in your own words.
3. If marketing activities involve exchange, what isn't a marketing activity?
4. Do lawyers, accountants, doctors, and dentists need marketing?
5. Why is relationship marketing important?
6. Identify some goods, services, or ideas that are marketed by not-for-profit organizations.
7. What are the elements of the marketing mix?
8. Describe the marketing mixes used by these organizations:
   a. McDonald's
   b. Your local zoo
   c. A group attempting to reduce air pollution
   d. The Xerox Corporation
9. The marketing concept is profit-oriented. What kinds of profit does it stress? How does this orientation apply to nonprofit organizations?
10. Identify an organization in your college town that, in your opinion, has not yet adopted the marketing concept. What evidence can you offer?
11. How might a firm such as Pillsbury conduct its business if it were (a) a product-oriented

company, (b) a sales-oriented company, and (c) a marketing-oriented company?
12. Given the existence of the marketing concept, why do so many products fail? Why are consumer groups still displeased with many products and companies?
13. How can an organization's management prove that it has adopted the marketing concept?
14. A zoo designer says she begins work by asking "In what sort of landscape would I want to observe this animal?" Discuss this approach to design in terms of the marketing concept.
15. Can a small business embrace the marketing concept philosophy as discussed in this chapter?
16. What role does marketing play in society?
17. What is the societal marketing concept?
18. Form small groups as directed by your instructor. Select an international company such as Nike, a local bank, or another familiar company, and identify the key aspects of the company's marketing mix. Discuss as a class the decisions each group makes.

marketing plan—right or wrong?
what's ahead

An old adage says "The essence of knowledge is having to apply it." Beginning with Chapter 2, a feature called **Marketing Plan—Right or Wrong?** at the end of each chapter will ask you to apply the knowledge gained from reading the chapter. Each one will present a particular aspect of a marketing plan or action. You will have a chance to evaluate whether, in your opinion, the plan will go right or wrong.

internet insights

The Internet is first discussed in Chapter 2. As a new communication medium, the Internet is having a dramatic impact, and it is discussed in many other chapters of this textbook. Because of the importance of the Internet to marketing, all of the remaining chapters contain an Internet exercise feature called **Internet Insights.** The exercises in this feature will give you the chance to enhance your understanding of marketing by using the Internet.

Another aspect of Internet Insights is Address Book (useful URLs)—a Web directory of interesting and educational Web addresses. The first of these appears below.

address book (useful urls)

American Marketing Association	www.ama.org
South-Western College Publishing	zikmund.swcollege.com

ethically right or wrong?

Ethical issues are discussed in Chapter 2. A feature entitled **Ethically Right or Wrong?** ends each of the remaining chapters. This feature gives you the chance to take a stand on ethical issues and think about your ethical principles and how they would apply in specific situations.

1-1 video case

Lawn Care of Wisconsin
Focus on Small Business

It's hard to imagine anything worse befalling a business that promises customers lush, green grass than what happened to Terry Kurth's Lawn Care of Wisconsin, Inc., a few years ago. To Kurth's horror, grass of customers who had signed up for a top-of-the-line lawn-care program was mysteriously turning brown.

Kurth had begun the business, which operates Barefoot Grass Lawn Service franchises in Madison and Little Chute, Wis., nine years earlier, and it grew healthily, thanks to a reputation for quality lawn maintenance. When customers began calling to report brown areas, and competitors got wind of an epidemic of "burned" Barefoot Grass lawns, its reputation and health were in grave danger.

Sleuthing solved the brown grass mystery. The company keeps extensive records—date, employee name, products applied, etc.—on each property worked on. The affected lawns had a common denominator: All had been treated with a granular fertilizer that contained a fungicide. Kurth, who has an agronomy degree, asked a University of Wisconsin plant pathologist to inspect some of the lawns, and he said they looked like they had been damaged by atrazine.

Atrazine? It is designed to eliminate grass in cornfields, corn being one of the few plants it doesn't affect. Kurth called the fertilizer supplier, asking that someone fly in to meet with him. A representative of the supplier arrived the next day; he reported his company had already performed lab tests and had found random atrazine contamination. The supplier stopped making atrazine at the plant where the fertilizer came from, but what of the problem at hand?

The supplier agreed to pay for damage repair, but it was up to Kurth and his managers to do the repairing. They gave affected customers an information sheet—most of them before their grass started turning brown. Then, calling in outside landscaping firms to help get the job done faster, they applied activated charcoal to affected lawns. There were 325 in all, and the process was messy, staining clothing and equipment. However, the atrazine was neutralized, and lawns were renovated. Sometimes reseeding was adequate; sometimes an entire lawn was removed and replaced with sod.

"Though our customers were overwhelmingly impressed," Kurth says, "we felt they deserved an additional thank-you for their understanding." Each received a gift box containing an assortment of meats that could, over a long period, be grilled while they were out on their lawns, reminding them of how Barefoot Grass Lawn Service had taken care of them.[26]

QUESTIONS

1. What is the product being marketed by Lawn Care of Wisconsin? What customer needs does this product satisfy?
2. Which of the philosophies/orientations toward marketing discussed in the text has Lawn Care of Wisconsin embraced?
3. Why did the company provide its customers with a gift assortment of meats?

chapter 2

Marketing Management: Strategy and Ethical Behavior

After you have studied this chapter, you will be able to:

Differentiate between marketing strategy and marketing tactics.
1

Discuss the role of marketing planning at the corporate level, at the strategic business unit level, and at the operational level of management.
2

Understand the concept of the organizational mission.
3

Understand the nature of a competitive advantage.
4

Understand the importance of total quality management strategies in product differentiation.
5

(continued on next page)

what if you were asked to name

the biggest rent-a-car company. And what if you were told that the answer is not Hertz or Avis, but Enterprise Rent-a-Car. Would you say you've barely heard of them? It's okay; most frequent fliers have never come near an Enterprise office. And that's just fine with Enterprise. While Hertz, Avis, and lots of little companies were cutting one another's throats to win a point or two of the "suits and shorts" market from business and vacation travelers at airports, Enterprise invaded the hinterlands with a completely different strategy—one that relies heavily on doughnuts, ex–college frat house jocks, and your problems with your family car.

In the 39 years since it was founded in St. Louis, Enterprise has blown past everybody in the industry. It now owns more cars (310,000) and operates in more locations (2,800) than Hertz.

Enterprise's approach is astoundingly simple: It aims to provide a spare family car. Say your car has been hit, or has broken down, or is in for routine maintenance. Once upon a time you could have asked your wife to come get you and borrowed her car, but she's commuting to her own job now and testy about having to hitchhike. Lo and behold, even before you have time to kick the repair shop's Coke machine, a well-dressed, intelligent young Enterprise agent materializes with some paperwork and a car for you. Typically, you pay 30 percent less for an Enterprise car than for one from an airport.

And your insurance or warranty usually picks up part of the tab. You sign and drive off.

Wow! How simple! So why haven't Hertz and Avis made road kill out of Enterprise? And how come Hertz's CEO concedes he "missed a big opportunity" by letting Enterprise run away with this business? Because the replacement business is harder than it looks, and because years ago Enterprise developed a bunch of quirky but simple hiring and promotion practices that have produced a culture perfectly suited to its part of the industry.

Instead of massing 10,000 cars at a few dozen airports, Enterprise sets up inexpensive rental offices just about everywhere. As soon as one branch grows to about 150 cars, the company opens another a few miles away. Once a new office opens, employees fan out to develop chummy relationships with the service managers of every good-size auto dealership and body shop in the area. When your car is being towed, you're in no mood to figure out which local rent-a-car company to use. Enterprise knows that the recommendations of the garage service managers will carry enormous weight, so it has turned courting them into an art form. On most Wednesdays all across the country, Enterprise employees bring pizza and doughnuts to workers at the garages.

Enterprise is also betting that when you're stuck, you won't be in the mood to quibble about prices. Yes, it has cars for $16 a day—the amount many insurance policies pay for replacement rentals. But those are often tiny Geo Metros; about 90 percent of people pay more for a bigger car. Enterprise buys cars from a wide variety of American, Japanese, and European automakers. To reduce costs, it keeps its cars on the road up to 6 months longer than Hertz and Avis do. If your insurance covers a replacement rental, you can get a Chrysler Neon in New Jersey for $21 a day from Enterprise, and a BMW 325 for $49.

Enterprise doesn't just wait for your car to break down to capture you as a customer. A huge chunk of its recent growth has come as auto dealers increasingly offer customers a free or cheap replacement while their cars are in the shop for routine maintenance. Enterprise has agreements with many dealers to provide a replacement for every car brought in for service. At major accounts, the company sets up an office on the premises, staffs it for several hours a day, and keeps cars parked outside so customers don't have to travel back to the Enterprise office to fill out paperwork.

ENTERPRISE'S APPROACH IS ASTOUNDINGLY SIMPLE: IT AIMS TO PROVIDE A SPARE FAMILY CAR.

Unusual hiring and promotion practices drive much of the company's hustle and rapid growth. Virtually every Enterprise employee is a college graduate; in a unionized, labor-intensive industry that seeks to keep wages low, that's unusual enough. But there's more. Hang around Enterprise people long enough, and you'll notice that despite their informal exteriors, most seem to have the competitive, aggressive air of ex-athlete. It's no accident. Brainy introverts need not apply, says the company's chief operating officer. "We hire from the half of the college class that makes the upper half possible," he adds wryly. "We want athletes, fraternity types—especially fraternity presidents and social directors. People people."

The social directors make good salespeople, able to chat up service managers and calm down someone who has just been in a car wreck.[1]

Enterprise built itself around a marketing strategy that differentiated the company from its competitors. As this example illustrates, developing a marketing strategy is crucial to an organization's success. Marketing strategy is the subject of this chapter.

The chapter begins by discussing the activities of marketing managers and defining marketing strategy. Next, it discusses planning at various levels in the organization, giving special attention to the organizational mission and to planning for marketing at the strategic business unit level. It then addresses each stage in the strategic marketing process. A discussion of execution and control follows the material on marketing planning. Finally, the chapter introduces the topic of ethics and social responsibility in marketing, an important and pervasive topic that will be discussed further throughout the text.

Enterprise
www.erac.com

Marketing Management

Organizations, whether charities, universities, or giant global businesses like the Microsoft Corporation, must have managers. Managers develop rules, principles, and ways of thinking and acting that allow the organization to attain its goals and objectives.

Corporate managers, or top managers, are the executives responsible for the entire organization. Every aspect of the organization's operations—production, finance, personnel, marketing—depends on their plans for the organization's long-term future. Top managers, with titles such as chief executive officer (CEO) and executive vice president, provide strategic direction for the organization. They realize that advertising, pricing, distribution, and personal selling are marketing *activities*—not marketing. Top managers recognize that at the corporate level, marketing is a business philosophy rather than a series of activities. Top managers see marketing at all other levels as a process that may require the resources of the entire organization. An important part of their job is to ensure that all business functions work together to achieve marketing success. It is the marketing managers at the middle levels of the organization who are responsible for the management of marketing efforts in the organization's business units and major departments.

Marketing management is the process of planning, executing, and controlling marketing activities to attain marketing goals and objectives effectively and efficiently. Of course, the time, effort, and resources associated with Johnson & Johnson's introduction of a new flavor of dental floss differ from the time, effort, and resources associated with Microsoft's development of computer software that understands normal spoken language, a project that Microsoft has been working on for years. Yet in both cases, success depends on planning, execution, and control. These are the basic functions of management at every level.

Managers in today's dynamic and rapidly changing business world confront extraordinary challenges that were rarely encountered a decade ago. Today's marketing manager must be flexible and versatile to deal with changes that come more quickly and are more dramatic, complex, and unpredictable than ever before.[2] Because marketing managers must deal with change, the marketing management process is a continuous one: Planning, execution, and control are ongoing and repetitive activities.[3] A major aspect of dealing with change is the development of appropriate strategies.

What Is a Marketing Strategy?

Marketers, like admirals and generals, must develop strategies calculated to help them attain the objectives they seek. The military planner's endeavors can end more disastrously than those of business people, but the loss of the means to make a living, the closing of a factory, and the "defeat" of a product in the marketplace are serious matters indeed to the workers, investors, and executives involved. Many executives have noticed similarities between military strategy and marketing strategy. Therefore, a number of military terms—strategy, tactics, campaigns, maneuvers, and so on—have been adopted by business people, just as they have been by football coaches, to relate their organizational activities to those of competitors. Because of its widespread usage, the term *strategy* has been defined in many different ways.[4] For our purposes, a specific definition is appropriate: A **marketing strategy** consists of a plan identifying what basic goals and objectives will be pursued and how they will be achieved in the time available. A strategy entails commitment to certain courses of action and allocation of the resources necessary to achieve the identified goals.

Members of the armed forces describe *strategy* as what generals do and *tactics* as what lower officers, such as captains and lieutenants, do. This description rightly suggests that tactics are less comprehensive in scope than strategies. **Tactics** are specific actions intended to implement strategy. Therefore, tactics are most closely associated with the execution of plans.

The basic strategy at McDonald's, for example, is to have clean, family-type restaurants that offer friendly service, high-quality food, and good value. Offering Happy Meals for children at reasonable prices is a tactic used to implement this strategy. It encourages consumers to bring their families to McDonald's because high-quality children's meals are a good value there. Providing pamphlets explaining that "your fork" is the only thing that is not nutritious in a Chunky Chicken Salad is another specific action that helps convey the idea that McDonald's offers an assortment of high-quality food for the entire family. McDonald's uses many tactics like these to implement its "quality, service, cleanliness, and value" strategy.

Planning—Designing a Framework for the Future

Recall that the basic functions of management are planning, execution, and control. In this part of the chapter, we focus on planning.

Planning is the process of envisioning the future, establishing goals and objectives, and designing organizational and marketing strategies and tactics to be implemented in the future in order to achieve these goals. The planning process consists of analyzing perceived opportunities and selecting courses of action that will help achieve the organization's objectives most efficiently. Marketing managers plan what future activities will be implemented, when they will be performed, and who will be responsible for them.

The purpose of planning is to go beyond analysis of the present and to attempt to predict the future and devise a means to adjust to an ever-changing environment before problems develop. Planning helps an organization shape its own destiny by anticipating changes in the marketplace rather than merely reacting to those changes. For example, an organization that anticipates changes in the public's and legislators' attitudes toward the need for recyclable packaging may plan to convert to "environmentally friendly" packaging before laws require it to do so. Planning allows a manager to follow the maxim "Act! Don't react." In short, planning involves deciding in advance.

Planning goes on at various organizational levels. For simplicity's sake, we will say that there are three such levels: top management, middle management, and operational, or first-line, management. These levels are shown in Exhibit 2-1.

Strategic planning, or long-term planning dealing with an organization's primary goals and objectives, occurs at the top management levels. As we move down the levels in Exhibit 2-2 from top management to middle management, determining long-term goals and planning strategies for the entire organization becomes a less time-consuming part of the job, whereas planning strategy and tactics for business units (such as divisions) and specific products becomes a more important job dimension. In the realm of marketing, middle managers are responsible for planning the marketing mix strategy, allocating resources, and coordinating the activities of operational managers. At the level of operational management, **operational planning,** which concerns day-to-day functional activities, becomes dominant. Thus, whereas a vice president of marketing (a top-level manager) spends most of his or her time planning new products and strategy modifications for entire product lines, a sales manager (an operational manager) concentrates on supervising and motivating the sales force. Exhibit 2-2 shows how the focus of planning and basic strategic and tactical questions vary at the three major levels of the organization.

Tactics
Specific actions intended to implement strategies.

McDonald's
www.mcdonalds.com

Planning
The process of envisioning the future, establishing goals and objectives, and designing organizational and marketing strategies and tactics to be implemented in the future in order to achieve the goals.

Strategic planning
Long-term planning dealing with an organization's primary goals and objectives, carried out primarily by top management; also called corporate strategic planning.

Operational planning
Planning that focuses on day-to-day functional activities, such as supervision of the sales force.

Three Levels of Administration

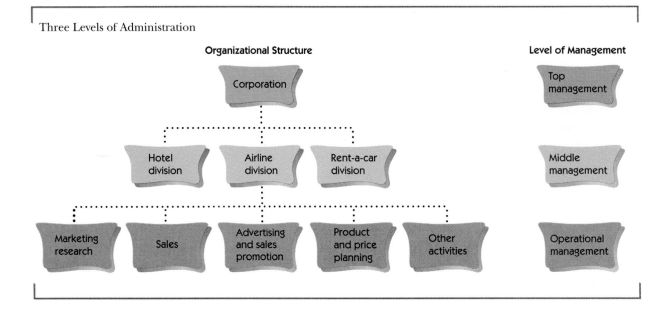

Organizational Structure

Level of Management

Corporation — Top management

Hotel division | Airline division | Rent-a-car division — Middle management

Marketing research | Sales | Advertising and sales promotion | Product and price planning | Other activities — Operational management

A Manager's Level in the Organization Dictates the Focus of Planning

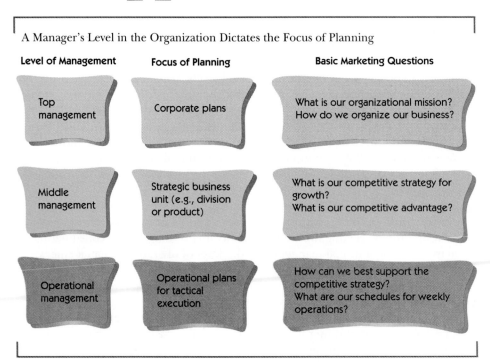

Level of Management	Focus of Planning	Basic Marketing Questions
Top management	Corporate plans	What is our organizational mission? How do we organize our business?
Middle management	Strategic business unit (e.g., division or product)	What is our competitive strategy for growth? What is our competitive advantage?
Operational management	Operational plans for tactical execution	How can we best support the competitive strategy? What are our schedules for weekly operations?

Top Management Makes Corporate Strategic Plans

As noted, strategic planning is the responsibility of top management and is long-term planning for the organization as a whole. It is the process of determining the organization's primary goals and developing a comprehensive organizational framework for accomplishing them. Answers to questions such as "What business are we in?" and "How do we organize our business?" determine the organization's strategies for long-term growth. All organizations, not just major corporations, should engage in strategic planning to determine their direction. **Strategic corporate goals** are broad statements about what the organization wants to accomplish in its long-term future. The organization's mission statement identifies its primary strategic corporate goal.

DEFINING THE ORGANIZATIONAL MISSION

Top managers decide the organizational or corporate mission. It is a strategic decision that influences all other marketing strategies. An **organizational mission statement** is a statement of company purpose. It explains why the organization exists and what it hopes to accomplish. It provides direction for the entire organization. For example, when the Ford Motor Company was founded in 1903, Henry Ford had a clear understanding that cars should not be only for the rich—that the average American family needed economical transportation in the form of a low-priced car. Ford also had the insight to know that he could use product standardization and assembly-line technology to accomplish this mission. Modern marketers should strive to have an equally clear sense of each aspect of the business domain in which they operate.

The mission statement of The Limited, Inc., is a particularly comprehensive one:

> Our commitment is to offer the absolute best customer shopping experience anywhere—the best store, the best merchandise, the best merchandise presentation, the best customer service—the best of everything that a customer sees and experiences. To achieve this goal:
>
> We must maintain a restless, bold and daring business spirit noted for innovation and cutting-edge style;
>
> We must maintain a management culture which is action-oriented, always flexible and never bureaucratic;
>
> We must be tough-minded, disciplined, demanding, self-critical and yet supportive of each other, our team, and our suppliers;
>
> We must seek and retain Associates with an unquestioned reputation for integrity and respect for all people: customers, suppliers, shareholders and fellow Associates;
>
> We must continue to make risk acceptable by rewarding the risk-taker who succeeds—that goes without saying—and not penalizing the one who fails;
>
> And we must utilize our capacity to set qualitative and quantitative standards for our industry.
>
> We are determined to surpass all standards for excellence in retailing by thinking—and thinking small. By staying close to our customer and remaining agile, we will continue as a major force in retailing.[5]

Product success, industry leadership, and even an organization's survival depend on satisfying the consumer. In defining the broad nature of its business, a company must take a consumer-oriented perspective. It must avoid short-sighted, narrow-minded thinking that will lead it to define its purpose from a product/production orientation rather than a consumer orientation. Thus, Motorola defines itself as being in the wireless communication business, not just

Strategic corporate goals
Broad organizational goals related to the long-term future. An organization's primary strategic corporate goal is identified in its organizational mission statement.

Organizational mission statement
A statement of company purpose. It explains why the organization exists and what it hopes to accomplish.

The Limited
www.limited.com

Marketing myopia
The failure of a company to define its organizational purpose from a broad consumer orientation.

as a maker of cellular phones or pagers. Companies, like Disney, that make movies should see themselves as being in the entertainment business rather than the movie business. A firm's failure to define its purpose from a broad consumer orientation is referred to as **marketing myopia.**[6]

Many organizational mission statements include ethical credos. Marketing ethics is discussed later in this chapter.

ESTABLISHING STRATEGIC BUSINESS UNITS

General Electric
www.ge.com

The organizational mission and other strategic corporate goals, once established, provide a framework for determining what organizational structure is most appropriate to the organization's marketing efforts. The organizational structure of a company that markets only a single product or service will be relatively simple. However, many organizations—for example, General Electric—operate a diverse set of businesses. General Electric's businesses range from the marketing of light bulbs to the marketing of aircraft engines. For the medium-sized and large organizations that engage in diverse businesses, establishing strategic business units is another aspect of corporate-level planning.

Strategic business unit (SBU)
A distinct unit—such as a company, division, department, or product line—of an overall parent organization, with a specific marketing focus and a manager who has the authority and responsibility for managing all unit functions.

A **strategic business unit (SBU)** is a distinct unit of the overall parent organization, such as a company, division, department, or product line, with a specific market focus and a manager who has the authority and responsibility for managing all unit functions. For example, a bank may have a real estate division, a commercial division, and a trust division, as well as a retail division that offers traditional banking services for the general public. The logic that underlies the concept of the strategic business unit is best illustrated with an example. Consider these statements: Procter & Gamble does not compete against Kimberly-Clark, and Dow Chemical does not compete against Union Carbide. Competition isn't carried on at the corporate level but at the individual business-unit level. Thus, Procter & Gamble's Pampers compete against Luvs disposable diapers, a Kimberly-Clark product. Dow might compete with Union Carbide for certain types of chemical customers but not others. Acknowledgment of this simple reality has led top managers to identify separate manageable units or autonomous profit centers within their organizations so that performance can be

Dow Chemical
www.dow.com

Union Carbide
www.unioncarbide.com

e x h i b i 2-3

Corporate Strategy Filters Down to Other Levels

Strategic corporate planning
• Define organizational mission
• Establish strategic business units
• Anticipate change

Marketing planning for SBUs
• Set marketing objectives
• Develop marketing strategy
• Formalize marketing plan

Operational marketing plans

monitored at the level of individual business activities rather than at the overall corporate level only.

The idea is that each SBU operates as a "company within a company." The SBU is organized around a cluster of offerings that share some common element, such as being part of the same industry, meeting particular customer needs, being aimed at a particular target market, or being produced with certain technology. An SBU has control over its own marketing strategy, and its sales revenues may be distinguished from those of other SBUs in the organization. It can thus be evaluated individually and its performance measured against that of specific external competitors. This evaluation provides the basis for allocating resources.

STRATEGIES FOR SBUS

Top corporate executives are responsible for an entire organization. They assign the responsibility for planning business-unit strategy and marketing strategy for individual products to middle managers. From a corporation perspective, the managers in charge of SBUs are at a level below the organization's top managers. However, within the SBU they are key executives.

Corporate-level strategies outline broad principles that are expected to cascade down through the organization. Exhibit 2-3 depicts how corporate strategies influence marketing strategies at the business-unit level and at the operational level. Although corporate-level planning strongly influences the marketing planning activities within strategic business units, SBU managers tend to be closer to their customers, and their customer knowledge shapes their planning.

BUSINESS-UNIT STRATEGIES FOR COMPETITIVE ADVANTAGE

One of the most common business-unit goals is to establish and maintain a **competitive advantage**—to be superior to or favorably different from competitors in a way that is important to the market. Illustrations of two basic marketing strategies (there are many others) should help you understand what a business-unit strategy is and how it can allow a company to establish a competitive advantage.

A **price leadership strategy,** or low-cost/low-price strategy, emphasizes producing a standardized product at a very low per-unit cost and underpricing all competitors.[7] For example, Papermate and Parker ballpoint pens were market leaders for many years. Then Bic pens, capitalizing on cheaper resources in foreign countries, produced a standardized product comparable in quality to its competitors and marketed it at a rock-bottom price.

This strategy can work equally well with services. Southwest Airlines, unlike most other domestic airlines, does not have long-distance flights. It links cities with frequent flights, almost like a shuttle airline. It does not offer preflight seat selection, hot meals, or baggage transfer to other airlines. Its low-cost/low-price strategy has been so successful that United Airlines has developed a similar service, Shuttle by United, to compete in this area.

A **differentiation strategy** emphasizes offering a product that is unique in the industry, provides a distinct advantage, or is otherwise set apart from competitors' brands in some way other than by price. The product's styling, a distinctive product feature, likeable advertising, faster delivery, or some other aspect of the marketing mix is designed to produce the perception that the product is unique. The heart of a differentiation strategy is to create, for the consumer, value that is different from or better than what competitors offer. Consider, for example, 3M's strategy to enter the scouring pad business. Steel wool soap pads had been on the market for almost 80 years when 3M introduced Scotch-Brite Never Rust Soap Pads, made from 100 percent recycled plastic beverage bottles with biodegradable and phosphorus-free soap. Scotch-Brite's tremendous success was a result of 3M's differentiation strategy to market soap pads that look and feel like competing brands but do not rust or splinter.

Competitive advantage
Superiority to or favorable difference from competitors along some dimension important to the market.

Price leadership strategy
A strategy whereby a marketer emphasizes underpricing all competitors.

Differentiation strategy
A strategy whereby a marketer offers a product that is unique in the industry, provides a distinct advantage, or is otherwise set apart from competitors' brands in some way other than price.

Xerox Corporation
www.xerox.com

TOTAL QUALITY MANAGEMENT TO ACHIEVE DIFFERENTIATION

In working to differentiate their products, many organizations implement total quality management strategies. These strategies, as noted in Chapter 1, make market-driven quality a top priority.

In the 1980s, U.S. corporations did not keep pace with the product quality strategies of a number of overseas competitors. For example, Xerox Corporation lost a substantial portion of its market share to Ricoh, Canon, and other Japanese copier makers because the Japanese products offered not only lower prices but higher quality as well. Xerox scrutinized its products and its production strategies and discovered it was destroying itself with sloppiness and inefficiency. The conclusion of its internal audit was that Xerox (like many other U.S. businesses) had lost sight of "an axiom as old as business itself . . . focusing on quality that meets the customer's requirements."[8]

Today, Xerox and many other organizations have implemented total quality management programs. These programs are not the exclusive domain of marketing managers, because production quality control and other business activities are integral aspects of their implementation. However, they are in tune with the marketing concept, since the definition of quality comes from the consumer.

The philosophy underlying the implementation of a total quality management strategy is epitomized in the following statement by a Burger King executive: "The customer is the vital key to our success. We are now looking at our business through the customers' eyes and measuring our performance against their expectations, not ours."[9] A company that employs a total quality management strategy must evaluate quality and value through the eyes of the customer. Every aspect of the business must focus on quality. For example, management may institute a performance appraisal system to evaluate employees in terms of the service they provide to customers. Further, the organization may establish cross-functional teams that strive for continuous improvement.

Cross-functional team
A team made up of individuals from various organizational departments who share a common purpose.

Cross-functional teams are composed of individuals from various organizational departments, such as engineering, production, finance, and marketing, who share a common purpose. Current management thinking suggests that cross-functional teams help organizations focus on core business processes, such as customer service or new product development. Working in teams reduces the tendency of employees to focus single-mindedly on an isolated functional activity. The use of cross-functional teams to improve product quality and increase customer value is a major trend in business today.

Demarketing
A strategy (or strategies) intentionally designed to discourage all or some consumers from buying a product.

In some situations, total quality managers determine that a marketing strategy must be aimed at reducing consumption or discouraging buying. **Demarketing** is the name of a strategy (or group of strategies) intentionally designed to discourage all or some customers from buying or consuming a product either temporarily or permanently. Suppose, for example, that a manufacturing firm finds that it has a temporary shortage of finished goods because of a scarcity of raw materials. To reduce customer demand, the firm might use demarketing strategies, such as reducing advertising, increasing prices, instituting a rationing system, or some other, more original activity.

Is demarketing different from the first-come, first-served, take-it-or-leave-it attitude a marketer of goods in short supply might take? Yes. Demarketing stresses a key aspect of marketing, consumer satisfaction. Demarketing attempts to change consumers' attitudes so that they will understand the temporary situation and be satisfied with less. It emphasizes maintaining high quality and trying to keep customers over the long run rather than antagonizing them with a take-it-or-leave-it attitude. This is why demarketing fits into an overall total quality management strategy.

Businesses often encounter situations that warrant demarketing strategies. McDonald's offering of one of ten different Teenie Beanie Baby figures with the purchase of a Happy Meal sold nearly 100 million Happy Meals in only 10 days. But the Beanie Baby promotion was flawed by a great underestimation of demand. The program was supposed to last 35 days, but many retail outlets quickly ran out of stocks of Beanie Babies. In Chicago (at the time home of the NBA world-champion Bulls), newspaper advertisements proclaimed "Harder to get than Bulls tickets" and indicated that McDonald's was sorry if the shortage caused any inconvenience. The demarketing effort's purpose was to maintain customers' trust in their relationship with McDonald's.

When the marketers of new products underestimate demand, advertisements often stress that the shortages will be temporary, with messages such as "We're sorry if you can't find our new [name of brand]. But we're sure you'll find it worth the wait."

In some situations, excess demand or overcrowding is unalterable, and demarketing is a long-term strategy. In Washington, D.C., the Metro subway system engages in selective demarketing by raising rates during morning and evening rush hours. The fare increase discourages tourists, shoppers, and others who could use the subway in non-rush hours from traveling during peak periods.

Chapter 10, which examines product strategies in detail, answers the question "What is quality?" and discusses how to plan total quality management programs.

w h a t   w e n t   right?

Trouble-Shooter Barbie Going into the 1995 holiday shopping season there was no must-have toy. Bad news for some, perhaps, but not for Mattel's Barbie. She was poised for another year of steady sales—until Thanksgiving weekend. That's when Mattel realized its Happy Holidays Barbie, a $30 collector's special bedecked in sequins and white lace, was selling out, with no way to boost production in time for Christmas.

Mattel needed lightning-quick thinking to keep pace with unprecedented consumer demand and maximize sell-through for the rest of the season. In just 10 short days, a marketing team devised and executed Mattel's first-ever certificate redemption program. Consumers who purchased the certificates and mailed them back to Mattel by a certain date were guaranteed receipt of a doll within 4 months.

Among the program components: a "suitable for framing" portrait of Happy Holidays Barbie signed by the doll's designer and Mattel CEO Jill Barad and a certificate for gift-givers with a cover letter from Barad. When retailers depleted their supply of dolls, they restocked shelves with certificates. Sales of redemption certificates exceeded expectations by a whopping 237 percent.[10]

Chicago Bulls
www.nba.com/bulls

PLANNING BUSINESS-UNIT GROWTH STRATEGIES

Managers responsible for strategic business units also focus planning activities on the identification of opportunities for business growth. The **market/product matrix,** which broadly categorizes alternative SBU opportunities in terms of basic strategies for growth, serves as a planning tool. Exhibit 2-4 shows how the matrix cross-classifies market opportunities and product opportunities.

Market-Related Strategies for Existing Products An organization seeking to expand sales of existing products has two major strategy paths available to it.

Market/product matrix
A matrix that includes the four possible combinations of old and new products and old and new markets. The purpose of the matrix is to broadly categorize alternative opportunities in terms of basic strategies for growth.

The Market/Product Matrix

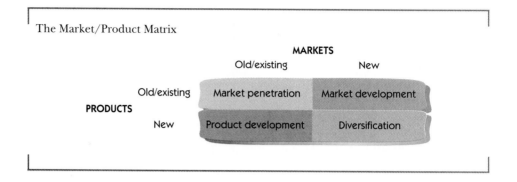

Market penetration
A strategy that seeks to increase sales of an established product by generating increased use of the product in existing markets.

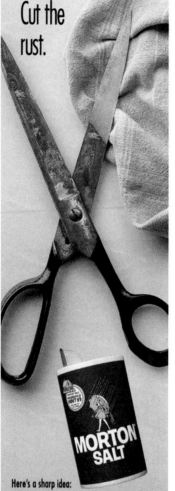

Here's a sharp idea: remove rust from household tools by using Morton® Salt. Just make a paste using 2 tablespoons Morton® Salt and 1 tablespoon lemon juice. Apply the paste to rusted area with a dry cloth and rub. For more ways to use economical, effective and safe Morton® Salt around the house, write: Morton Salt Tips, Dept. B, Chicago, IL 60606-1597.

Market development
A strategy by which an organization attempts to draw new customers to an existing product, most commonly by introducing the product in a new geographical area.

Increased product usage may be an objective for a market penetration strategy. Morton Salt uses a market penetration strategy to encourage existing users to increase usage of its product.

One is **market penetration.** This strategy seeks to augment sales of an established product by increasing use of the product by existing customers in existing markets. Arm & Hammer has, with considerable success, convinced existing customers to purchase more baking soda by showing them new and creative ways to use the product. One suggestion, offered in advertisements and on packages, is to put an open box of baking soda in the refrigerator to reduce food odors. Lest consumers feel that a box of baking soda must be thrown away once it has been in the refrigerator for a time, the company suggests that the product be poured down the kitchen drain to freshen the drain. This strategy gave baking soda two new uses and gave buyers a way to dispose of the product in a manner that performed yet another odor-killing task. A similar technique is used by cereal companies, which frequently demonstrate how a cereal such as Cheerios or Rice Krispies can be used to make cookies, snack foods, and other non-breakfast items. Consumers are encouraged to try, for example, "cooking with Kellogg's."

A somewhat different strategy is **market development,** whereby the organization attempts to draw new customers to an existing product. The most common market development strategy is to enter a new geographical area. The recent changes in Eastern Europe present a market development opportunity for many multinational organizations. The markets that are now growing in the Czech Republic, Slovakia, Lithuania, and other countries previously without market economies expand the sales potential of existing products.

The desire to expand the demand for an existing product need not come from the belief that an existing market is shrinking. It might derive from the fact that an organization has the capacity to produce more products or believes that in some other way its assets are not being utilized to the fullest.

Market-Related Strategies for New Products Nothing is more important to a company's long-term survival and growth than the successful introduction of new products. Consider, for example, that one-third of Rubbermaid's annual sales volume comes from products that are less than 5 years old. Every year, the company introduces more than 400 new products to the market.[11] Rubbermaid understands the critical importance of **product development,** which is the process of marketing innovative products or "new and improved" products in existing markets.

> NOTHING IS MORE IMPORTANT TO A COMPANY'S LONG-TERM SURVIVAL AND GROWTH THAN THE SUCCESSFUL INTRODUCTION OF NEW PRODUCTS.

Product development
A strategy of marketing innovative or "new and improved" products to existing markets.

Another example of a new product is Kodak's Snapshot Photo Scanner, a small, inexpensive device that works with a personal computer to convert 35mm and Polaroid prints into digitized images. Kodak is in the process of developing other new products to adapt its traditional photographic film business to the rapidly evolving world of electronic imaging. Hershey Chocolate USA expanded its product offerings by adding Hugs, Hershey's Kisses "hugged" by white chocolate. This was part of a strategy to offer greater variety in existing markets. Many candy customers increased their purchases of Hershey's products when Hugs became available to go along with Kisses. Using a similar strategy, Clorox developed Clorox Clean-Up, an all-purpose cleaner, and several special-purpose cleaners, such as Clorox Clean-Up Toilet-Bowl Cleaner. Many Clorox customers increased their purchases of Clorox's products as these options became available.

Marketing new products to a new set of customers is called **diversification.** When Sega Corporation felt a need to diversify outside its video-game operations, it created two high-tech, virtual-reality theme parks in Japan. Its expansion into North America with simulator rides that are part video game and part 3D movie is a major diversification effort for Sega.

Diversification
A strategy of marketing new products to a new market.

3M When relationship marketing is successful, marketers and customers reach a level of mutual trust that can lead to the development of new products. 3M's medical and surgical products division in Brookings, South Dakota, has a low-tech program to help build the supplier-customer relationship.

All 750 employees, from production-line workers to senior executives, meet face to face with customers, mostly doctors and nurses, at three area hospitals. Employees don scrubs and go into the operating rooms to watch their surgical tapes, drapes, and prep solutions in action. Says a 3M executive, "We get to feel the pulse of our customers. We see their problems and frustrations up close."

The work teams observed that some products' packaging was difficult to open, and the packaging of other products, designed for reuse, could not be easily closed. They suggested to 3M's product development people that a Ziploc-type seal would make their customers' jobs easier. The suggestion became reality within a few months. Says Valerie Smidt, staff education coordinator for the operating room of Sioux Valley Hospital in Sioux Falls, South Dakota: "The 3M people give us pointers on how to better utilize some items, and we in turn suggest how to make some of their products more user-friendly." The hospital staffs have also been giving the company an unsolicited wish list of future products, which 3M has been evaluating.[12]

A company that diversifies expands into an entirely new business. Often the company's marketing research staff and its engineering research and development staff are instrumental in identifying market opportunities and product ideas for diversification.

An alternative approach to developing new products internally is to acquire new products by merging with another company or purchasing products from other companies. Upon finding that busy Americans were substituting bagels, muffins, and pastries for a bowl of breakfast cereal, Kellogg, the cereal maker, used this strategy when it purchased Lender's, a bagel maker.

The Strategic Marketing Process

Strategic marketing process
The entire sequence of managerial and operational activities required to create and sustain effective and efficient marketing strategies.

Marketing managers engage in many diverse activities, ranging from formulating strategy to evaluating whether existing strategies are effective and efficient. The term **strategic marketing process** refers to the entire sequence of managerial and operational activities required to create and sustain effective and efficient marketing strategies. There are six major stages in the strategic marketing process:

1. Identifying and evaluating opportunities
2. Analyzing market segments and selecting target markets
3. Planning a market position and developing a marketing mix strategy
4. Preparing a formal marketing plan
5. Executing the plan
6. Controlling efforts and evaluating the results

As Exhibit 2-5 shows, the first four stages involve planning activities to develop a marketing strategy that will satisfy customers' needs and meet the goals and objectives of the organization. The latter two stages involve execution and control to make the plan work.

The various activities involved in developing a marketing strategy may be carried out by a number of people over varying time periods, and the actual sequence of decisions may differ among organizations. Nevertheless, each stage is crucial to effective strategy development.

STAGE 1: IDENTIFYING AND EVALUATING OPPORTUNITIES

The powerful and ever-changing impact of environmental factors presents opportunities and threats to every organization. Opportunities occur when environmental

exhibit 2-5

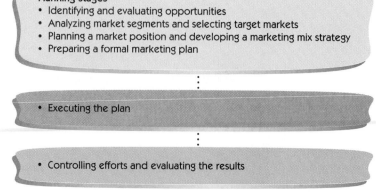

The Six Stages of the Strategic Marketing Process

Planning stages
• Identifying and evaluating opportunities
• Analyzing market segments and selecting target markets
• Planning a market position and developing a marketing mix strategy
• Preparing a formal marketing plan

• Executing the plan

• Controlling efforts and evaluating the results

conditions favor an organization's attaining or improving a competitive advantage. Threats occur when environmental conditions signal potential problems that may jeopardize an organization's competitive position. The marketer must be able to "read" the environment and any changes in it accurately and to translate the analysis of trends into marketing opportunities.

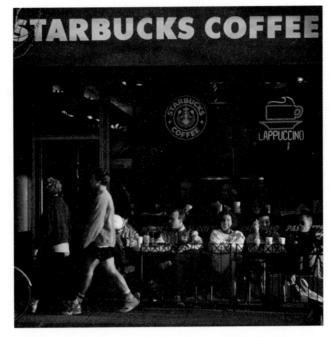

An environmental change may be interpreted as a threat or an opportunity, depending on the nature of an organization's or a strategic business unit's competitive position. Declining at-home per-capita coffee consumption is clearly an unfavorable trend and an environmental threat to coffee marketers. The marketers of soft drinks, however, will see this trend as an opportunity to sell more of their products by convincing consumers to drink cola in the morning. Effective managers analyze threatening situations and foresee problems that may result. Then they adapt their strategies in the hope of turning threats into opportunities. For example, noticing declining coffee consumption at home, Mr. Coffee created an opportunity by developing an appliance for brewing tea. Starbucks created an opportunity from the same trend by developing a chain of gourmet coffee shops.

Situation analysis is the diagnostic activity of interpreting environmental conditions and changes in light of an organization's ability to capitalize on potential opportunities and ward off problems. Kodak is a company that recognizes that such analysis can be crucial to marketing success.

In the late 1980s, Kodak marketed a disposable 35mm camera called Fling.[13] Fling sold poorly, and its name enraged environmentalists. A few years later, the company devised two new versions—a double lens camera that can take wide-angle shots and an underwater version—and renamed the camera the FunSaver 35. The new disposable model sold well—but it still did not please environmentalists because hundreds of thousands of returned cameras ended up in landfills.

After analyzing the situation, Kodak modified the product. The new disposable cameras were designed to be disassembled and recycled. All a customer had to do was take the camera to a photofinisher, which would return it to Kodak for disassembly and recycling of its parts. Some camera parts are tested and reused up to ten times. Kodak sold about 30 million disposable cameras worldwide in 1993, and environmentalists were appeased because 87 percent of each camera was reused or recycled. When situation analysis ascertained that the environmental threats and opportunities facing the company had changed dramatically, Kodak altered its strategy to fit the changing times.

Understanding Change in the Environment Situation analysis requires both environmental scanning and environmental monitoring so that the organization can understand change. **Environmental scanning** is information gathering designed to detect indications of changes that may be beginning to develop. For example, by scanning the environment, Vanity Software Publishing determined that increased

Situation analysis
The interpretation of environmental attributes and changes in light of an organization's ability to capitalize on potential opportunities.

Kodak
www.kodak.com

Environmental scanning
Information gathering designed to detect changes that may be in their initial stages of development.

attention was being paid to repetitive stress injuries suffered by office workers who were spending long periods of time at their computers. In response, the company developed ErgoBreak for Office. ErgoBreak is a software package designed to interrupt, at regular intervals, whatever other program a worker is using. Periodically one of five cartoon characters appears on a worker's computer screen and leads a short exercise to stretch out a body part that may have gone numb from manipulating a mouse or doing some other repetitive action.[14]

Environmental monitoring

Tracking certain phenomena to detect the emergence of meaningful trends.

Environmental monitoring involves tracking certain phenomena, such as sales data and population statistics, to observe whether any meaningful trends are emerging. For example, many women managers, frustrated by the so-called *glass ceiling* that bars women from high executive positions in some corporations, have started their own businesses. The number of women entrepreneurs grew from 1.2 million in 1969 to 2.4 million in 1982; and today, it exceeds 3 million.[15] This is an important trend for organizations that sell to other businesses.

Scanning and monitoring provide information that allows marketers to interpret environmental conditions and to determine the timing and significance of any changes. When these processes accomplish their purpose, situation analysis serves as both a warning system that alerts managers to environmental threats and an appraisal system that makes managers aware of the benefits associated with certain opportunities.

SWOT Analysis   Situation analysis also requires an inward look at the organization. An organization should evaluate its internal strengths and weaknesses in relation to the external environment. You may find the acronym **SWOT**—which stands for internal strengths and weaknesses and external opportunities and threats—helpful in remembering that the purpose of situation analysis is to evaluate both the external environment and the internal environment.

SWOT

Acronym for internal strengths and weaknesses and external opportunities and threats. In analyzing marketing opportunities, the decision maker evaluates all these factors.

Exhibit 2-6 illustrates how situation analysis involves both identifying environmental threats and opportunities and evaluating organizational strengths and weaknesses. Marketing managers consider environmental trends in light of organizational goals to determine the organization's desired position—where it wants to be. Such an analysis allows the organization to assess its present situation. Chances are good that the desired position differs somewhat from the actual position. The difference between the two can be called the **strategic gap.** Planning is aimed at closing the gap so that the organization can move from a situation it doesn't want to one that it does want.

Strategic gap

The difference between where an organization wants to be and where it is.

Matching Opportunities to the Organization   Of course, the world offers thousands of opportunities, but at least some of them may not be realistic for a particular organization, given its resources or interests. Procter & Gamble (P&G) may

exhibit 2-6

Situation Analysis Helps Match Opportunities to the Organization

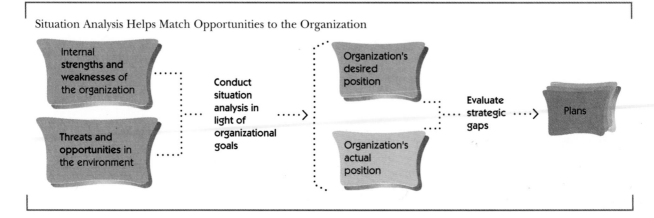

General Electric Lighting   Effective managers analyze threatening situations and foresee problems that may result. Then they adapt their strategies in the hope of turning threats into opportunities. An example comes from General Electric Lighting.

General Electric Lighting is an ancient business, begun in 1878. It is headquartered in Cleveland on a leafy campus of brick Georgian buildings separated by placid lawns. Shockwaves went through the company in 1983, when traditional rival Westinghouse sold its lamp operations to Phillips Electronics of Holland. To John Opie, GE Lighting's chief, the memory is so vivid that he describes it in the present tense: "Suddenly we have bigger, stronger competition. They're coming to our market, but we're not in theirs. So we're on the defensive."

But it was not long until GE turned this threat into an opportunity. GE's 1990 acquisition of Hungarian lighting company Tungsram was the first big move by a Western company in Eastern Europe. After buying Thorn EMI in Britain in 1991, GE had 18 percent of Europe's lighting market and was moving into Asia via a joint venture with Hitachi. Whereas in 1988 GE Lighting got less than 20 percent of its sales from outside the United States, today more than 40 percent of its sales come from abroad. In a few short years, General Electric Lighting's world changed utterly.[16]

identify an opportunity to increase its sales among California's Korean community and may commit resources to development of an advertising campaign to reach that market. It is arguable that P&G is so large a company that it should also take the "opportunity" to go into the nuclear power business, but P&G is unlikely to make that move. Why? Because its managers know that not every environmental opportunity is in fact an **organizational opportunity.** An organization can act profitably only by seizing those opportunities that fit its capabilities. P&G's strength lies in its experience in promoting and distributing consumer products, not in marketing energy to communities.

Consider another example. Vlasic Pickles to Go are refrigerated prepackaged kosher dill pickles.[17] The marketing strategy for the product capitalized on Vlasic's competence in food-processing technology. By developing a new technology that minimizes the amount of brine in the package and creating innovative packaging, the company was able to produce a no-mess pouched pickle that stays crisp. The new packaging allows consumers to pack Pickles to Go in brown-bag lunches.

Vlasic's distribution strategy prescribed having the pickle pouches holepunched so that they could hang in supermarkets' refrigerated display cases next to packaged lunch meats. In addition, having only two pickle spears in each package gave the product entry into convenience stores. Management saw the trend among U.S. consumers toward eating on the go rather than at home as an opportunity to develop Vlasic Pickles to Go as a perfect fit with Vlasic's resources and capabilities.

Identification of opportunities, then, involves not only assessment of the environment but also consideration of an organization's goals, performance capabilities, and limitations. In addition, it involves evaluating opportunities in light of competitors' strengths and weaknesses. An assessment of marketing opportunities typically identifies competitors, reviews their

Organizational opportunity
An environmental opportunity that fits a particular organization's capabilities and resources.

IDENTIFICATION OF OPPORTUNITIES INVOLVES NOT ONLY ASSESSMENT OF THE ENVIRONMENT BUT ALSO CONSIDERATION OF AN ORGANIZATION'S GOALS, PERFORMANCE CAPABILITIES, AND LIMITATIONS.

Try this at home.

Imagine. A crisp, refreshing, mountain waterfall. In your kitchen. That's the beauty of the Brita® Water Filtration Pitcher. It turns tap water into wonderful water. The remarkable filter virtually eliminates lead and chlorine. Copper, water hardness and sediment are dramatically reduced. There's nothing like the great taste of Brita water. And you never have to leave your home sweet home.

BRITA
Tap into great taste.

Brita offers a money-back guarantee (details in box). Brita is available at many fine retailers. For the one nearest you, call 1-800-44-BRITA. *Substances removed may not be in all users' water. ©1997 The Brita Products Company. **Visit our website at www.brita.com.**

Clorox bought U.S. rights to Brita water filtration products after an assessment of marketing opportunities. The company believed that Clorox's distribution channels for bleach and household cleaners would be well-suited to market Brita.

Strategic window of opportunity
The limited time during which an organization has an advantage over its competition because of its capabilities and resources.

marketing programs, assesses their relative capabilities and resources, and evaluates how well they are serving their customers. Although it is important to carefully examine what competitors have done in the past, it is equally important to anticipate what strategies and tactics they might implement in the future. Furthermore, marketing managers should consider the possible emergence of new competitors—including foreign competitors—and their potential impact on the company's marketing opportunities.

An analysis of opportunities relative to an organization's competition may reveal that a window of opportunity is opening.

A **strategic window of opportunity** is a limited time during which an organization's capabilities, resources, or competitive position provides it with certain advantages over the competition. The requirements of the market and the organization's strengths may be in harmony at this moment in time, but the organization must make its move before the window closes. In the mid-1990s, Kodak recognized that very high clarity, or resolution, would be the key to transmitting text and images by computer. Once computer images could exhibit the clarity of photographs, on-line newspapers and magazines and other information businesses would develop. Kodak had the technology and financial resources to conduct research on high-resolution computer images, whereas many of its competitors were not able to exploit this opportunity. Later, however, Kodak's window may begin to close as other companies acquire the technology and resources to compete in this area.

Managers Need Information to Evaluate Opportunities   Marketing managers need information about the marketing environment. Chapters 3 and 4 discuss trends in the external environment. More specific information directly relevant to individual companies may be obtained from feedback from sales personnel, internal records, published information, marketing research surveys, sales forecasts, and other sources. An extensive discussion of how marketing managers obtain and manage information appears in Chapter 5.

STAGE 2: ANALYZING MARKET SEGMENTS AND SELECTING TARGET MARKETS

As stated in Chapter 1, a market is a group of individuals or organizations that are potential customers for the product being offered. There are many types of markets. The most fundamental way of distinguishing among them is on the basis of the buyer's use of the good or service being purchased. When the buyer is an individual consumer who will use the product to satisfy personal or household needs, the good or service is a consumer product sold in the **consumer market.**

Consumer market
The market consisting of buyers who use a product to satisfy personal or household needs.

When the buyer is an organization that will use the product to help operate its business (as when a furniture manufacturer purchases wood) or will resell the product (as when a wholesaler purchases a fax machine), the good or service is an organizational, or business, product sold in the **organizational market,** or the **business market.**

A **market segment** is a portion of a larger market. Thus, African Americans constitute a segment of the total U.S. market. African Americans between the ages of 30 and 40 years are a smaller, more narrowly defined segment. Female African Americans between the ages of 30 and 40 who use electric rather than gas stoves are a still smaller market segment. Market segments can be defined in terms of any number of variables from race or sex to air travel behavior. **Market segmentation** is the dividing of a heterogeneous mass market into a number of segments. The segments considered by analysts to be good potential customers for an organization's product are likely to become the organization's **target markets**—that is, the specific groups toward which the organization aims its marketing plan. Virtually all marketers agree that market segmentation is extremely useful and valuable. Identifying and choosing targets, rather than trying to reach everybody, allows a marketer to tailor marketing mixes to a group's specific needs. As the old adage states, "You can't be all things to all people." A firm selects a target market because it believes it will have a competitive advantage in that particular segment.

Market segmentation is such an important topic that it will be treated more fully in Chapter 8. Suffice it to say here that identifying and evaluating marketing opportunities (the first stage in the six-stage strategic marketing process) must be followed by a decision about where marketing efforts will be directed—that is, by market segmentation and targeting—before the next step, planning a market position and developing a marketing mix, can be undertaken.

STAGE 3: PLANNING A MARKET POSITION AND DEVELOPING A MARKETING MIX

Planning a market position and constructing a marketing mix is the third step in the development of a marketing strategy. After a target market has been selected, marketing managers position the brand in that market and then develop a marketing mix to accomplish the positioning objective. Positioning relates to the way consumers think about all the competitors in a market. A **market position,** or **competitive position,** represents how consumers perceive a brand relative to its competition. Each brand appealing to a given

JASON FORD photo: Curtes

SALOMON BONFIRE
DEDICATED TO QUALITY

Organizational market, or business market
The market consisting of buyers who use a product to help operate a business or for resale.

Market segment
A portion of a larger market, identified according to some shared characteristic or characteristics.

Market segmentation
Dividing a heterogeneous market into segments that share certain characteristics.

Target market
A specific market segment toward which an organization aims its marketing plan.

Market position, or competitive position
The way consumers perceive a product relative to its competition.

Many snowboard manufacturers position their snowboards as high-quality products for risk-taking consumers who want to take the sport to its extreme.

market segment has a position in relation to competitors in the buyer's mind. HBO positions itself as being different from conventional television—"It's not TV. It's HBO." Grasshoppers by Keds are positioned as inexpensive shoes for practical consumers—"If you feel the need to spend more on shoes, you could always buy two pairs." The object of **positioning** is to determine what distinct position is appropriate for the product. Positioning will be discussed more fully in Chapter 8. At this point, however, you should recognize that the marketing mix an organization selects depends on the organization's strategy for positioning its product relative to the competition.

Planning a marketing mix, as mentioned in Chapter 1, requires considering the four Ps: product, price, promotion, and place (distribution). Much of the remainder of this book, especially Chapters 9 through 20, discusses what marketing mix elements are appropriate under varying circumstances. The blend of ingredients, as well as the relative importance of each element in the mix, may differ for different types of products and different positioning strategies. We believe that the way managers fashion marketing mixes is a fascinating subject. Interesting material lies ahead.

STAGE 4: PREPARING A FORMAL MARKETING PLAN

The preparation of the formal marketing plan is the final planning stage of the strategic marketing process. A formal **marketing plan** is a written statement of the marketing objectives and strategies to be followed and the specific courses of action to be taken when (or if) certain future events occur. It outlines the marketing mix, explains who is responsible for managing the specific activities in the plan, and provides a timetable indicating when those activities must be performed. Certain aspects of the plan may ultimately be scrapped or modified because of changes in society or in other portions of the market environment. Establishing action-oriented objectives is a key element of the marketing plan. A **marketing objective** is a statement about the level of performance the organization, SBU, or operating unit intends to achieve. Objectives are more focused than goals because they define results in measurable terms. For example, "to increase our dollar-volume share of the Japanese market from 9 percent to 15 percent by December 31 of this year" describes the nature and amount of change (a 6 percent increase), the performance criterion (market share as measured by percentage of dollar volume), and the target date for achieving the objective.

Marketing plans may be categorized by their duration: long-term (5 or more years), medium-term (2 to 5 years), or short-term (1 year or less). Long-term marketing plans usually outline basic strategies for the strategic business unit's growth. Most organizations prepare an annual marketing plan because marketing activity must be coordinated with annual financial plans and other budgetary plans that follow the fiscal year.

STAGE 5: EXECUTING THE PLAN

Once marketing plans have been developed and approved, they must be executed, or carried out. In fact, the words *executive* and *execute* both come from the Latin word meaning to "follow out" or "carry out." Making a sales presentation, inspecting proofs of advertising copy, setting prices and discounts, and choosing transportation methods are all aspects of executing a marketing plan.

Execution, or implementation, of a plan requires organizing and coordinating people, resources, and activities. Staffing, directing, developing, and leading subordinates are major activities used to implement plans. Clearly, the best marketing plans can fail if they are not properly executed. Speakers at sales meetings are fond of describing the salesperson who read every book on planning for success, spent every waking hour developing approaches to customers and getting all

Positioning
Planning the market position the company wishes to occupy. Positioning strategy is the basis for marketing mix decisions.

Marketing plan
A written statement of the marketing objectives and strategies to be followed and the specific courses of action to be taken when (or if) certain events occur.

Marketing objective
A statement of the level of performance that an organization, SBU, or operating unit intends to achieve. Objectives define results in measurable terms.

Execution
The carrying out of plans; also called *implementation.*

aspects of his sales career in perfect order, but who never sold a thing and was fired. Why? He never got out of the house to sell anything! Planning is extremely important, but it means little without execution.

An important aspect of the middle-level marketing manager's job is to supervise the execution of the marketing plan. Translating the plan into action is a task delegated to operational managers and their staffs. Operational managers, such as a district sales manager or a manager of the jewelry department in a Nordstrom department store, plan activities that will support the business-level marketing strategy. They make specific plans that clearly set out the marketing tactics to be executed. For example, if the organization's marketing plan targets a 25 percent increase in sales volume as an objective, the regional sales manager may plan to employ two additional sales representatives during the next month. Then the manager may implement the necessary marketing activities, such as hiring and training the new employees and directing their selling efforts, so that the objectives can be met.

Mistakes may be made in the completion of any task. These mistakes—some minor, some perhaps unavoidable, but all damaging to some degree—are errors of execution. For example:

- Instructions on the front of Lite Way brand salad dressing packages read, "Just mix with water and cider vinegar." On the reverse side of the package, the instructions read, "Mix with low-fat milk and cider vinegar."
- Jell-O Pudding Pops packages carried a coupon offering a $1 refund. A statement on the front of the coupon directed readers to "details on the back." Unfortunately, the back of the coupon was blank.
- A television commercial for a Cadillac Catera showed the car illegally crossing a double yellow line to pass.[18]

We do not mean to be negative. Most plans are properly

Play 'n Learn   A wrong number in a computer manual has caused headaches and a huge phone bill for a small educational toy distributor.

Compaq Computer Corp., the world's biggest personal computer maker, printed the toll-free number for Play 'n Learn Sales Inc. in manuals as the help line for a WordPerfect program that is installed on its Presario 7100 machines.

As a result, dozens of calls a day come into the family-run Play 'n Learn, sometimes through the night, from people who have a question about the program WordPerfect Works. Some callers turn angry when they realize the tiny firm can't help.

"On top of the nuisance of it, we're losing business because our lines get tied up and our customers can't get through," said owner Kathleen Henn.

She filed suit against Compaq, seeking payment for the more than $6,000 in erroneous calls to her company's toll-free line.

The problem first began in January 1995 when operators for Novell Inc., which then owned WordPerfect, occasionally gave people the wrong number. It snowballed [that] fall when the Compaq manuals were distributed with the wrong number.

The help line for the software is not a toll-free number. It has the area code 801, which is the area code for Utah where Novell and WordPerfect are based.

Play 'n Learn's 1-800 number is the same as the software help line's 1-801 number. Novell runs the help line even though it sold WordPerfect to Corel Inc. [early in 1996].

Henn said her attempts to get any of the companies to fix the problem have produced no concrete response. "It's impossible to get hold of anybody at Compaq, WordPerfect or Novell," she said.

The lawsuit she filed in state court against Compaq alleges negligence, invasion of privacy and emotional harm. Yvonne Donaldson, a spokeswoman for Compaq, declined comment on the lawsuit, saying she was unfamiliar with the mix-up.

Play 'n Learn represents about 30 manufacturers and sells wholesale to about 1,400 stores, specializing in science and nature toys. Three rooms in Henn's home have been converted to offices and three friends and her daughter work at the company.

Henn has ordered a new toll-free number, but she doesn't want to drop her old one because some customers still use it and it's listed in lots of flyers and trade catalogs.

"The worst thing you can do is change your 800 number," she said. "I'm going to be answering WordPerfect's calls forever."

Her attorney, Lee Atkinson, said he suggested that Compaq put out a message on its Internet home page, or send out new manuals.

"They have not been very responsive," Atkinson said. "Their basic response was 'Change your 800 number,' as if her business wasn't as important to her as their business is to them."[19]

executed. We do, however, want to emphasize that "the best-laid plans of mice and men" may go astray. As the What Went Wrong? feature illustrates, proper execution should never be taken for granted.

STAGE 6: CONTROLLING EFFORTS AND EVALUATING THE RESULTS

Control

The process by which managers ensure that planned activities are completely and properly executed.

The purpose of managerial **control** is to ensure that planned activities are executed completely and properly. The first aspect of control is to establish acceptable performance standards. Control also requires investigation and evaluation. Investigation involves "checking up" to determine whether the activities necessary to the execution of the marketing plan are in fact being performed. Actual performance must then be assessed to determine whether organizational objectives have been met. Performance may be evaluated, for example, in terms of the number of sales calls made or new accounts developed. Sales and financial figures may also be judged to appraise individual or organizational successes.

Control activities provide feedback to alert managers, indicating whether to continue with plans and activities or to change them and take corrective action. Marketing executives may discover, by means of a control activity, that actions that were part of the marketing plan are not being carried out "in the field." When this happens, either the marketing plan must be corrected to reflect environmental realities or the persons responsible for carrying out the plan must be more strongly motivated to achieve organizational goals.

Marketing audit

A comprehensive review and appraisal of the total marketing operation, often performed by outside consultants or other unbiased personnel.

A **marketing audit** is a comprehensive review and appraisal of the total marketing operation. It requires a systematic and impartial review of an organization's recent and current operations and its marketing environment. The audit examines the company's strengths and weaknesses in light of the problems and opportunities it faces. Because the marketing audit evaluates the effectiveness of marketing activities, it is often best performed by outside consultants or other unbiased personnel. The topic of managerial control, including a more extensive discussion of the marketing audit, is explored in Appendix B.

INTERRELATIONSHIPS AMONG PLANNING, EXECUTION, AND CONTROL

Planning, execution, and control are closely interrelated. A consideration of the marketing environment leads to the formulation of marketing plans. These in turn must be executed. The execution of the plans must then be controlled through investigation and evaluation. The results or findings generated during the control phase provide a basis for judging both the marketing plans and their execution and serve as new inputs for further planning and execution. Thus, a series of logical steps is maintained, as shown in Exhibit 2-7.

Planning, execution, and control of marketing strategy and tactics are also interrelated because each has ethical dimensions. Understanding the nature of marketing ethics is essential for anyone who plans to be a manager. The remainder of this chapter addresses this issue.

Managerial Ethics and Socially Responsible Behavior

In recent years, many highly publicized stories about organizations—and individuals in organizations—that did not act according to high ethical standards have appeared on television and in newspapers and magazines. For example, there was a barrage of criticism about the Exxon Valdez oil spill and the company's efforts to reduce the damage to the Alaskan environment. And marketers of batteries received so much criticism about the mercury, cadmium, and other toxic metals in batteries that Energizer virtually eliminated mercury from its Green Power batteries, while other battery marketers began to package toxic batteries in such a way that they could be returned to the manufacturer for recycling.

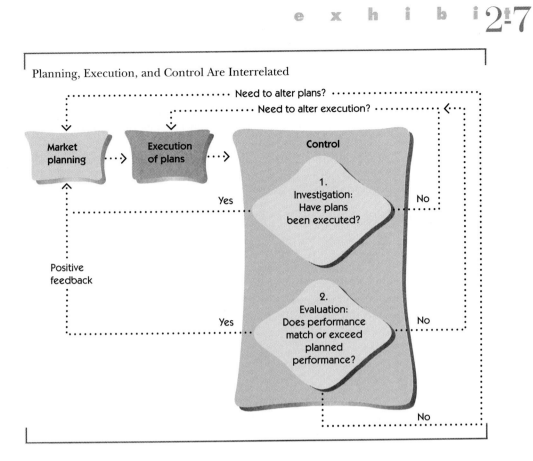

Planning, Execution, and Control Are Interrelated

Society clearly expects marketers to obey the law, but in order to be socially responsible, an organization must acknowledge a responsibility broader than its legal responsibility. **Social responsibility** refers to the ethical principle that a person or an organization must become accountable

> SOCIETY **CLEARLY EXPECTS MARKETERS TO OBEY THE LAW, BUT IN ORDER TO BE SOCIALLY RESPONSIBLE, AN ORGANIZATION MUST ACKNOWLEDGE A RESPONSIBILITY BROADER THAN ITS LEGAL RESPONSIBILITY.**

for how its acts might affect the interests of others.[20] Every marketing manager makes decisions that have ethical implications.

THE NATURE OF ETHICS
Ethics involves values about right and wrong conduct. **Marketing ethics** are the principles that guide an organization's conduct and the values it expects to express in certain situations.[21] In the marketing context, **moral behavior** is individual or organizational activity that exhibits ethical values.

Ethical principles reflect the cultural values and norms of a society. **Norms** suggest what ought to be done under given circumstances. They indicate approval or disapproval, what is good or bad. Many norms in Western society are based on the Judeo-Christian ethic. Being truthful is good. Being fair—doing unto others as you would have them do unto you—meets with approval. Other norms have a utilitarian base.[22] Norms may arise from a concern about the consequences of one's

Social responsibility
The ethical principle that a person or an organization must become accountable for how its acts might affect the interests of others.

Marketing ethics
The principles that guide an organization's conduct and the values it expects to express in certain situations.

Moral behavior
Individual or organizational marketing activity that embodies the ethical values to which the individual or organization subscribes.

Norm
A social principle identifying what action is right or wrong in a given situation.

actions: "You ought to obey product safety laws, or you may go to jail." They may also arise from expectations about how society should function: "It is good that a company's shareholders receive its profits, because profits are the shareholders' reward for investment and risk taking."

Some ethical principles of personal conduct dictated by broad norms have direct counterparts in marketing actions. Being truthful, a societal norm, and avoiding deceptive, untruthful advertising are closely linked. Where such clear-cut links exist, the expected moral behavior is relatively clear. Some actions, such as murdering a competitor, are so noticeably contrary to societal norms that they would be morally indefensible in all circumstances. Although morally acceptable behavior may be clear-cut in many circumstances, in others, determining what is ethical is a complicated matter open to debate.

RESOLVING ETHICAL DILEMMAS

Ethical dilemma

A predicament in which a marketer must resolve whether an action that benefits the organization, the individual decision maker, or both may be considered unethical.

An **ethical dilemma,** for a marketer, is a predicament in which the marketer must resolve whether an action that benefits the organization, the individual decision maker, or both may be considered unethical.[23] An ethical dilemma may arise when two principles or values are in conflict. It may be that a corporation president values both high profits and—like most people in society in general—a pollution-free environment. When one of these values or preferences in any way inhibits the achievement of the other, the business person is faced with an ethical dilemma.

Problems also arise when others do not share the principles or values that guide a marketer's actions. Consider these questions: Is it wrong to pay a bribe in a foreign country where bribery is a standard business practice? Should MTV avoid airing a Madonna video if its sexual overtones offend certain viewers but not others? How a marketer answers these questions involves resolving ethical dilemmas.

In many situations, individuals agree on principles or values but have no fixed measure by which to judge actions. An engineer can calculate exactly how strong a steel girder is and a chemist can usually offer the right formulation of chemicals necessary to perform a task, but the business executive often cannot be so precise. Even in instances where specific laws would seem to guide action, the laws and their application may be subject to debate. Although marketers and other business people often pride themselves on their rational problem-solving abilities, the lack of permanent, objective ethical standards for all situations continues to trouble the person seeking the ethical course of action in business.

Thus, there rarely is an absolute consensus on what constitutes ethical behavior. Different people, and even a single person, can evaluate a question from several different perspectives. For example, the belief that smoking is injurious to health has led to regulations that restrict smoking in airplanes and other public places and bar cigarette commercials from radio and television. Yet to some, this is a controversial matter. Of course, good health is important, but what about the smoker's freedom of choice?

In general, when marketing decision makers encounter ethical dilemmas, they consider the impact of the organization's actions and operate in a way that balances the organization's short-term profit needs with society's long-term needs. For example, a cookie marketer, such as Keebler, knows that people buy cookies because they taste good. It also knows certain inexpensive cooking oils that enhance taste are not as low in saturated fat as other, more expensive ingredients. The company may conduct extensive research to find a way to reformulate the cookies by changing to more healthful ingredients while maintaining the cookies' good taste. More specifically, marketers must ask what is ethical in a particular situation. They must establish the facts of the situation and determine if their plans are compatible with the organization's ethical values. They must

Members of the American Marketing Association (AMA) are committed to ethical professional conduct. They have joined together in subscribing to this Code of Ethics embracing the following topics:

RESPONSIBILITIES OF THE MARKETER

Marketers must accept responsibility for the consequences of their activities and make every effort to ensure that their decisions, recommendations, and actions function to identify, serve, and satisfy all relevant publics: consumers, organizations and society. Marketers' professional conduct must be guided by:

1. The basic rule of professional ethics: not knowingly to do harm;
2. The adherence to all applicable laws and regulations;
3. The accurate representation of their education, training and experience; and
4. The active support, practice and promotion of this Code of Ethics.

HONESTY AND FAIRNESS

Marketers shall uphold and advance the integrity, honor, and dignity of the marketing profession by:

1. Being honest in serving consumers, clients, employees, suppliers, distributors and the public;
2. Not knowingly participating in conflict of interest without prior notice to all parties involved; and
3. Establishing equitable fee schedules including the payment or receipt of usual, customary and/or legal compensation for marketing exchanges.

RIGHTS AND DUTIES OF PARTIES

Participants in the marketing exchange process should be able to expect that:

1. Products and services offered are safe and fit for their intended uses;
2. Communications about offered products and services are not deceptive;

3. All parties intend to discharge their obligations, financial and otherwise, in good faith; and
4. Appropriate internal methods exist for equitable adjustment and/or redress of grievances concerning purchases.

It is understood that the above would include, *but is not limited to,* the following responsibilities of the marketer:

In the area of product development and management:

• Disclosure of all substantial risks associated with product or service usage
• Identification of any product component substitution that might materially change the product or impact on the buyer's purchase decision
• Identification of extra-cost added features

In the area of promotions:

• Avoidance of false and misleading advertising
• Rejection of high pressure manipulations, or misleading sales tactics
• Avoidance of sales promotions that use deception or manipulation

In the area of distribution:

• Not manipulating the availability of a product for purpose of exploitation
• Not using coercion in the marketing channel
• Not exerting undue influence over the resellers' choice to handle a product

In the area of pricing:

• Not engaging in price fixing
• Not practicing predatory pricing
• Disclosing the full price associated with any purchase

In the area of marketing research:

• Prohibiting selling or fund raising under the guise of conducting research
• Maintaining research integrity by avoiding misrepresentation and omission of pertinent research data
• Treating outside clients and suppliers fairly

ORGANIZATIONAL RELATIONSHIPS

Marketers should be aware of how their behavior may influence or impact on the behavior of others in organizational relationships. They should not encourage or apply coercion to obtain unethical behavior in their relationships with others, such as employees, suppliers or customers.

1. Apply confidentiality and anonymity in professional relationships with regard to privileged information.
2. Meet their obligations and responsibilities in contracts and mutual agreements in a timely manner.
3. Avoid taking the work of others, in whole, or in part, and representing this work as their own or directly benefiting from it without compensation or consent of the originator or owner.
4. Avoid manipulation to take advantage of situations to maximize personal welfare in a way that unfairly deprives or damages the organization or others.

Any AMA member found to be in violation of any provision of this Code of Ethics may have his or her Association membership suspended or revoked.

determine at what point certain marketing practices become ethically questionable. Is it ethical for a sales representative to pay for a purchasing agent's lunch? To give the purchasing agent a gift on his or her birthday? To arrange for an all-expenses-paid vacation for the agent if the sales representative's company gets a big contract?[24]

To help marketers act in a socially responsible manner, President John F. Kennedy outlined the consumer's basic rights: the right to be informed, the right to safety, the right to choose, and the right to be heard. Since Kennedy's pronouncement, others have argued that consumers have other rights, such as the right to privacy and the right to a clean and healthy environment. Arguments have been made that children have special rights because they have not developed mature reasoning powers.

Code of conduct

A statement establishing a company's or a professional organization's guidelines with regard to ethical principles and acceptable behavior.

Rights like these are embodied in organizations' and associations' codes of conduct. A **code of conduct** establishes a company's or a professional organization's guidelines with regard to its ethical principles and what behavior it considers proper. The American Marketing Association's Code of Ethics appears in Exhibit 2-8.

Following a code of conduct helps resolve some ethical dilemmas but not others. Many ethical dilemmas involve issues that are not black and white, and individuals often have to resolve such dilemmas by using their own judgment, based on their own ethical values. The checklist that follows offers some good general advice about considering ethical dilemmas.[25]

1. Recognize and clarify the dilemma.
2. Get all possible facts.
3. List the options—all of them.
4. Test each option by asking "Is it legal? Is it right? Is it beneficial?"
5. Make your decision.
6. Double-check your decision by asking "How would I feel if my family found out about this? How would I feel if my decision were printed in the local newspaper?" Do you still feel you made the correct decision?
7. Take the action if warranted.

ETHICAL DIMENSIONS OF MARKETING STRATEGY

It should be clear by now that ethical values influence many aspects of marketing strategy.[26] The cultural values and norms that establish lying and stealing as wrong are reflected in laws dealing with deceptive advertising. The belief that

e x h i b i **2-9** Selected Ethical Questions Related to the Marketing Mix

PRODUCT	PROMOTION	PRICE	DISTRIBUTION
• Who must accept responsibility for an injury caused by a product that was used improperly?	• Can advertising persuade consumers to purchase products that they don't really want?	• Should pricing laws protect consumers or protect small business?	• Should modern shopping malls be built in low-income areas?
• Is the package a source of unnecessary environmental pollution?	• What effect does advertising have on children?	• Do the poor really pay more?	• If a retailer wishes to carry only one of a manufacturer's products, should the manufacturer be able to force the retailer to carry all of its products?

children need extra protection because they are more susceptible than adults to persuasion may ultimately lead to stringent laws governing advertising on children's television programs.

The values and behavior of the public is another marketing issue. Consider that in September 1997 computer hackers vandalized the ValuJet Web site. The hackers who broke in put up pictures of airplane crashes and offensive messages mocking company executives. Such behavior is clearly unethical.

Throughout this book, you will see that laws and ethical considerations can affect every aspect of an organization's marketing mix, which, in turn, can influence the level of its profits. Similarly, ethical considerations can play a part in the development and implementation of that mix. Exhibit 2-9 presents some ethical questions that may be raised concerning all four major portions of the marketing mix. In considering them, remember that ethical issues are philosophical in nature and that not everyone may agree on solutions to ethical dilemmas.[27] However, there has been an undeniable trend toward broadening the social responsibility of marketing organizations beyond their traditional role as economic forces.

summary

This chapter discusses marketing strategy and tactics and how marketing managers must plan, execute, and control the organization's marketing activities.

 1 *Differentiate between marketing strategy and marketing tactics.*
A strategy is a long-range plan to determine what basic goals and objectives will be pursued and how they will be achieved in the time available. A strategy entails a commitment to certain courses of action and allocation of the resources necessary to achieve the identified goals. Tactics are specific actions intended to implement strategy.

2 *Discuss the role of marketing planning at the corporate level, at the strategic business unit level, and at the operational level of management.*
Top management engages in strategic planning to determine long-term goals for the entire organization. Managers at the strategic business unit level plan strategies for the business unit and for individual products. Operational managers are concerned with planning and executing the day-to-day activities of the organization.

3 *Understand the concept of the organizational mission.*
An organizational mission is a statement of a company's purpose. It explains why an organization exists and what it hopes to accomplish.

4 *Understand the nature of a competitive advantage.*
A business or product that is superior to or different from its competitors in a way that is important to the market has a competitive advantage. It may offer the same quality at lower cost or some unique feature, for example.

5 *Understand the importance of total quality management strategies in product differentiation.*
Adopting a total quality management strategy is one of the most common ways marketers differentiate their products. They do this by adjusting marketing strategy to assure that their products offer customers better quality and thus greater satisfaction than competitors' products.

6 *Discuss demarketing.*
In general, marketers engage in demarketing when a product is in short supply. It is a marketing strategy intended to diminish demand while maintaining consumer satisfaction during the shortage period.

7 *Explain the market/product matrix.*
The market/product matrix broadly categorizes the opportunities of a strategic business unit in terms of strategies for growth. The four strategies are market penetration, market development, product development, and product diversification.

8 *Describe marketing objectives and marketing plans.*
Marketing objectives are statements about the level of performance the organization, strategic business unit, or operating unit intends to achieve. Marketing plans are written statements of the marketing objectives and strategies to be followed and

the specific courses of action to be taken when (or if) certain events occur.

9 *Identify the stages in the strategic marketing process.*

The strategic marketing process includes the following six stages:

1. Identifying and evaluating opportunities
2. Analyzing market segments and selecting target markets
3. Planning a market position and developing a marketing mix
4. Preparing a formal marketing plan
5. Executing the plan
6. Controlling efforts and evaluating results

10 *Discuss the concept of positioning.*

Each product occupies a position in the consumer's mind relative to competing products. A key marketing objective is to determine what position the company wishes to occupy. Positioning is accomplished through the development and implementation of a marketing mix.

11 *Understand the nature of marketing ethics and socially responsible behavior.*

Social responsibility refers to the ethical principle that a person or an organization must become accountable for how its acts might affect the interests of others. Ethics involves values about right and wrong conduct. Marketing ethics are the principles that guide an organization's conduct and the values it expects to express in certain situations. Moral behavior on the part of marketers is activity that exhibits ethical values. Ethical principles reflect the cultural values and norms of a society. Marketing decisions often have ethical dimensions and may involve ethical dilemmas.

key terms

marketing management (p. 32)
marketing strategy (p. 32)
tactics (p. 33)
planning (p. 33)
strategic planning (p. 33)
operational planning (p. 33)
strategic corporate goals (p. 35)
organizational mission statement (p. 35)
marketing myopia (p. 36)
strategic business unit (SBU) (p. 36)
competitive advantage (p. 37)
price leadership strategy (p. 37)
differentiation strategy (p. 37)
cross-functional team (p. 38)
demarketing (p. 38)
market/product matrix (p. 39)

market penetration (p. 40)
market development (p. 40)
product development (p. 41)
diversification (p. 41)
strategic marketing process (p. 42)
situation analysis (p. 43)
environmental scanning (p. 43)
environmental monitoring (p. 44)
SWOT (p. 44)
strategic gap (p. 44)
organizational opportunity (p. 45)
strategic window of opportunity (p. 46)
consumer market (p. 46)
organizational market, or business market (p. 47)
market segment (p. 47)

market segmentation (p. 47)
target market (p. 47)
market position, or competitive position (p. 47)
positioning (p. 48)
marketing plan (p. 48)
marketing objective (p. 48)
execution (p. 48)
control (p. 50)
marketing audit (p. 50)
social responsibility (p. 51)
marketing ethics (p. 51)
moral behavior (p. 51)
norm (p. 51)
ethical dilemma (p. 52)
code of conduct (p. 54)

questions for review & critical thinking

1. What are the three major tasks of marketing management?
2. Distinguish between a strategy and a tactic.
3. Based on some of Pepsi's print and television ads, what do you think the company's marketing strategy is?
4. Why are marketing planning activities important?
5. Describe your interpretation of the organizational missions of several corporations or not-for-profit organizations (perhaps Toshiba, Digital Equipment Corporation, Walt

Disney Productions, Eastman Kodak, and Ford Motor Company).
6. Several corporate slogans are listed below. Discuss how each reflects a corporate mission.
   a. FedEx: "When it absolutely, positively has to be there overnight."
   b. Panasonic: "Just slightly ahead of our time."
   c. Smith Corona: "Tomorrow's technology at your touch."
   d. The Equitable Financial Companies: "We have great plans for you."

e. Raytheon: "Where quality starts with fundamentals."

f. Disney: "Using our imagination to bring happiness to millions."

g. Merck: "To preserve and improve life."

7. What is a strategic business unit? What are the basic growth strategies for SBUs?

8. What is the role of total quality management in marketing strategy?

9. What is competitive advantage? Suppose you were the marketing manager for Saturn automobiles. What marketing strategies would you develop to compete with imports?

10. Is it possible for two competing companies to have the same goal but to use different marketing strategies to reach the goal?

11. Describe the stages in the strategic marketing process.

12. What is positioning? How is Dr Pepper positioned relative to Coke and Pepsi?

13. Choose a retail store or a manufacturing company in your local area. Study the company and identify its marketing plan. In your opinion, is the plan a sound one? Is it being executed well or poorly? Give evidence to support your answers.

14. Identify some typical execution errors.

15. What are marketing ethics?

16. What are some examples of socially responsible behavior and socially irresponsible behavior?

17. How do codes of conduct help marketers make strategic decisions?

18. Discuss how marketing managers might work in teams with managers of other functional areas, such as production, in planning a marketing strategy.

marketing plan—right or wrong?

1. A North Dakota aquaculture researcher is raising a freshwater variety of red claw lobsters in the hope of creating a market for the product. The red claw lobster is not as large as the saltwater Maine lobster—in fact, it is actually a large Australian crayfish. If the North Dakota lobsters weigh at least 6 ounces, the law allows them to be marketed as lobsters. That's the product development plan.

2. McDonald's developed a plan to bring out an adult hamburger called the Arch Delux with a premium price. An Arch Delux is a 4-ounce beef patty on a potato-sesame roll with cheese, sliced lettuce (instead of shredded lettuce), tomato, slivered onions (instead of chopped onions), ketchup, and a secret sauce of Dijon mustard, stone-ground mustard, and mayonnaise. Adding a slice of bacon is an option.

3. A black and white (mostly black) photograph of a huge tire dump serves as the background for a Filippo Berio magazine advertisement. An insert in the center of the page shows a bottle of the company's olive oil with the words "Nature Unlimited."

internet insights

zikmund.swcollege.com

exercises

1. Satisfying customer wants is a key aspect of the marketing concept. In order to satisfy customers, marketers must listen to what the market has to say. Some marketers use simple techniques, like suggestion boxes, to listen to the market.

Your marketing professor wants to listen to you, the customer, so that he or she can better satisfy future customers. Send an e-mail message to your marketing professor. Include at least two things in your message: First, tell the professor what you like about this class so far. Then tell the professor what you don't like about this class so far.

chapter 3

Environmental Forces in a Digital World: The Macroenvironment

After you have studied this chapter, you will be able to:

Describe the domestic and foreign environments in which marketers operate and their effects on organizations.

1

Understand that social values and beliefs are important cultural forces.

2

Explain how demographic trends, such as changes that have occurred in the American family, influence marketers.

3

Explain the various ways in which economic conditions influence marketers.

4

Understand that technology, especially digital technology and the Internet, are having a significant impact on marketing and society.

5

(continued on next page)

6   Appreciate how the three levels of U.S. law and the laws of other nations can influence marketing activity.

7   Explain how the various elements of the marketing environment interact.

with so few telephones to be beckoned to, who could have guessed that the Chinese would go bonkers over that familiar summoning device—the pager. The passion spread so quickly in China in the early Nineties that Motorola was astonished. The answer to this mystery: Resourceful Chinese use the pager not as an accessory to the phone, but as a sort of primitive substitute for it. The conventional phone system has a penetration rate of some three to four lines for every 100 Chinese, meaning that even if you find a phone, the other party might not be in a position to receive your call. Only the well-heeled business person can surmount this annoyance with a costly cellular phone.

> RESOURCEFUL **CHINESE USE THE PAGER NOT AS AN ACCESSORY TO THE PHONE, BUT AS A SORT OF PRIMITIVE SUBSTITUTE FOR IT.**

So native genius stepped into the breach. Chinese paging subscribers spontaneously devised a method of carrying code books, allowing them to interpret numeric messages flashed on their pagers: 75416, for example, might mean sell gravel at 6,500 yuan a ton or bring home a cabbage for dinner. Today's pagers have alphanumeric displays that read out short bursts of Chinese characters, eliminating the need for number codes. They also come in stylish packages, priced so a moderately successful worker can afford one: from about $120 for a basic model to $220 for one with a Chinese character readout. . . . There are some 14 million paging subscribers in China, probably half or more of them Motorola customers.[1]

Motorola
www.mot.com

Information technology and culture are two powerful environmental forces that have dramatically interacted to shape the nature of Motorola's marketing. This chapter discusses marketing's environment. It begins with a brief introduction to international aspects of that environment. Then it describes the various components of the macroenvironment: the physical environment, sociocultural forces, demographic forces, economic forces, science and technology, and politics and laws.

A World Perspective for the 21st Century

You may drive a Toyota, a Mazda, or a Mercedes. You may fill your tank at a Shell service station with gasoline refined from crude oil from Nigeria or Venezuela.

You may sign the charge slip with a Bic pen. Each of these products comes from a foreign company and is made available in the United States as a result of international marketing. Today, we live in a global village. It is difficult to think of many business matters that do not influence or are not themselves influenced by events or activities in other areas of the world. Jet age transportation, satellite television networks, computer modems, e-mail, and other electronic technologies are reshaping and restructuring the patterns of business. The world is getting smaller, and the external environment is taking on a more global character.

Some organizations that market products only in their home countries are influenced solely by environmental forces operating in the **domestic environment.** However, in today's global economy, most corporations must anticipate and respond to opportunities and threats in **foreign environments** as well. (See Exhibit 3-1.) It may be easier to envision a large multinational corporation like Xerox or Honda being influenced by forces from both the domestic and foreign environments than to understand how uncontrollable foreign forces affect the marketing activities of, say, a small local electronics retailer. Yet both large and small organizations—indeed, the entire economy—can be influenced by forces thousands of miles away from their home countries.[2] And tomorrow's marketing managers will face even more global competition than managers of the 1990s.

In thinking about marketing in the global economy, it is important to remember two key economic terms. **Imports** are foreign products purchased domestically. **Exports** are domestically produced products sold in foreign markets. In 1996 U.S. exports amounted to $835 billion. The United States' top export products are (1) agricultural products, (2) electrical machinery, such as circuit breakers, (3) data processing and office equipment, (4) aircraft, and (5) general industrial machinery, such as escalators. America's top export customers are (1) Canada, (2) Japan, (3) Mexico, (4) Britain, and (5) Germany. In 1996 imports were approximately $950 billion. The goods accounting for much of this trade were crude oil and refined petroleum products, automobiles, industrial raw materials, and consumer goods.

The Macroenvironment

Whether it is the domestic environment, a foreign environment, or the world environment that is under consideration, the environment can be divided into two categories: the macroenvironment and the microenvironment. The broad societal forces that influence every business and nonprofit marketer comprise the **macroenvironment.** Every company, however, is more directly influenced by a **microenvironment** consisting of its customers and the economic institutions that shape its marketing practices.

The discussion in this chapter describes the macroenvironment. Chapter 4 deals with the more direct influences that comprise the microenvironment. The

Domestic environment
The environment in an organization's home country.

Foreign environment
The environment outside an organization's home country.

Import
A foreign product purchased domestically.

Export
A domestically produced product sold in a foreign market.

Macroenvironment
Broad societal forces that shape the activities of every business and nonprofit marketer. The physical environment, sociocultural forces, demographic factors, economic factors, scientific and technical knowledge, and political and legal factors are components of the macroenvironment.

Microenvironment
Environmental forces, such as customers, that directly and regularly influence a marketer's activity.

e x h i b i 3-1

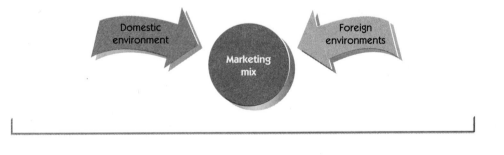

Forces in Both the Domestic and the Foreign Environment Influence the Marketing Mix

Domestic environment → Marketing mix ← Foreign environments

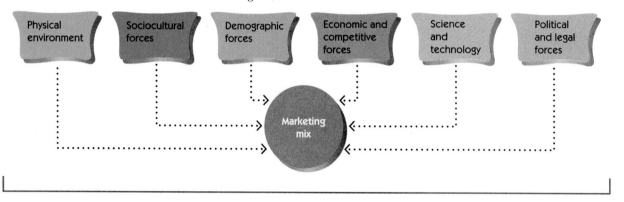

e x h i b i 3-2

Macroenvironment Influences on the Marketing Mix

Physical environment | Sociocultural forces | Demographic forces | Economic and competitive forces | Science and technology | Political and legal forces

Marketing mix

macroenvironment consists of the physical environment, sociocultural forces, demographic forces, economic forces, scientific and technical knowledge, and political and legal forces. (See Exhibit 3-2.)

The Physical Environment

Physical environment
Natural resources and other aspects of the natural world that influence marketing activities.

The **physical environment** consists of natural resources, such as minerals and animal populations, and other aspects of the natural world, such as changes in ecological systems. The availability of natural resources may have a direct and far-reaching impact on marketing activities in a geographic region. Areas rich in petroleum, for example, may concentrate on the production and marketing of fuel oil, kerosene, benzene, naphtha, paraffin, and other products derived from this natural resource.

Marketing is influenced by many other aspects of the natural environment as well. Climate is one example.[3] It is not difficult to understand why umbrella sales are greater in rainy Seattle than in desert-like Tucson or why more winter clothing is sold in Minneapolis than in Miami.

Climate also greatly influences the timing of marketing activities. In India, more than 65 percent of all soft drinks are sold during the blazing hot months of June through September, for instance. Marketers adapt their strategies to such environmental differences. Kmart, for example, identifies every item stocked in its stores by climate. It knows that climate influences not only what is purchased but when. Grass seed, insect sprays, snow shovels, and many other goods must be in the right stores at the correct time of year.

Finally, consideration of the physical environment of marketing must include an awareness of activities or substances harmful to the earth's ecology. Smog, acid rain, and pollution of the ocean are among the many issues in this category. Such issues are highly interrelated with aspects of the sociocultural environment.

Patagonia, a very successful marketer of outdoor apparel, offers an example of how an ecological consideration can influence marketing strategy. Patagonia was the first clothing company in the United States to introduce post-consumer recycled Synchilla fleece, a synthetic fleece made of recycled plastic bottles. The company worked with a leading fiber manufacturer to develop a recycled fiber suitable for clothing. Environmental impact studies showed that the recycled fiber was significantly less burdensome to the environment in virtually every category when compared to virgin polyester. Today, almost all of Patagonia's fleece garments have at least 90 percent post-consumer recycled plastic bottle content. Every PCR garment snatches 25 (2-liter) bottles from the jaws of the dumpster. The company estimates that its own use of PCR since its inception has conserved about 20,000 barrels of oil and kept about 10,000 tons of toxic emissions out of the atmosphere.[4] Marketing ecologically sage products and making efforts, as Patagonia is, to help preserve or revitalize the physical environment is often called **green marketing.**

Green marketing
Marketing ecologically safe products and promoting activities beneficial to the physical environment.

Sociocultural Forces

Every society has a culture that guides everyday life. In the environment of marketing, the word **culture** refers not to classical music, art, and literature but to social institutions, values, beliefs, and behaviors. Culture includes everything people learn as members of a society, but does not include the basic drives with which people are born.

Culture
The institutions, values, beliefs, and behaviors of a society; everything people learn, as opposed to the basic drives with which people are born.

Culture is shaped by humankind. It is learned rather than innate. For example, people are born with a need to eat—but what, when, and where they eat, and whether they season their food with ketchup or curdled goat's milk, is learned from a particular culture. (Japanese eating habits are the subject of the What Went Right? feature.) Similarly, the fact that many U.S. women are free from traditional restraints, whereas few Saudi women are, is a cultural phenomenon. Material artifacts and the symbolic meanings associated with them also vary by culture.

VALUES AND BELIEFS

A **social value** embodies the goals a society views as important and expresses a culture's shared ideas of preferred ways of acting. Social values reflect abstract ideas about what is good, right, and desirable (and bad, wrong, and undesirable). For example, we learn from those around us that it is wrong to lie or steal. The following social values reflect the beliefs of most people in the United States:

Freedom. The freedom of the individual to act as he or she pleases is a fundamental aspect of U.S. culture.

Achievement and success. The achievement of wealth and prestige through honest efforts is highly valued. Such achievement leads to a higher standard of living and improves the quality of life.

Work ethic. The importance of working on a regular basis is strongly emphasized. Those who are idle are considered lazy.

Japanese Like Seafood Really Fresh The latest in food rages in Japan is to eat fish live—flounder that flap around on the plate, finger-length eel swallowed raw. "The food moves around a lot—that's the whole idea," said Sunao Uehara, a chef at Chunagon, a well-known seafood restaurant in Ginza, one of Tokyo's most expensive entertainment districts.

Shrimp, flounder, and lobster are by no means the only energetic entrees on the trendy diners' menu. Other attractions include firefly squid, loaches, sea bream, and young yellowtail. Waiters bring the fish in wiggling, their eyes and mouths moving, then quickly slice open the midsection and gut it, so the fish is ready to eat. Like sushi or sashimi, the slices are dipped in a soy sauce and horseradish.

Lobster is served belly up, with an incision made along the length of the tail so diners can get at the meat. Small squid and eels are eaten whole. Shrimp are featured in a dish called "dance," and are expected to do just that.

Though some Japanese express misgivings about eating live food, it is a concept that fits in easily with the emphasis on freshness and au naturel presentation upon which Japanese gastronomy is based.

Toshio Fujii, an X-ray technician from a stretch of Japan's western coast where discerning seafood eaters are the rule, said he prefers to eat his fish live because "they don't come any fresher. My 7-year-old daughter likes them, too," he said. "But eels are kind of gross. I had them in my beer one time. Too many little bones."

The resurgence in the popularity of eating live food in Japan—practiced for centuries by hungry Japanese fishermen—is part of a larger "gourmet boom" fueled by Japan's ever-growing economy.

Japanese consumers, who have extra money to spend on meals outside the home, are looking for better-tasting, more unusual dishes. Live fish tend to be expensive. Lobster courses at Chunagon range from a basic $44 meal to the top-of-the-line $120 dinner. "The expense just makes it all the more appealing," said Fujii. "The more it costs, the better we expect it to taste."

A spokesman for the Japan Society for the Prevention of Cruelty to Animals said the group doesn't consider the practice to be cruel. In fact, many believe eating live fish is a unique aspect of Japan's culinary culture.[5]

Equality. Most Americans profess a high regard for human equality, especially equal opportunity, and generally relate to one another as equals.

Patriotism/nationalism. Americans take pride in living in the "best country in the world." They are proud of their country's democratic heritage and its achievements.

Individual responsibility and self-fulfillment. Americans are oriented toward developing themselves as individuals. They value being responsible for their achievements. The U.S. Army's slogan "Be all that you can be" captures the essence of the desirability of personal growth.[6]

A **belief** is a conviction concerning the existence or the characteristics of physical and social phenomena. A person may believe, for example, that a high-fat diet causes cancer or that chocolate causes acne. Whether a belief is correct is not particularly important in terms of a person's actions. Even a totally foolish belief may affect how people behave and what they buy.

It is the marketer's job to "read" the social environment and reflect the surrounding culture's values and beliefs in a marketing strategy. For example, a marketer might consider indications that American women's values about the importance of careers may be chang-

> IT IS THE MARKETER'S JOB TO "READ" THE SOCIAL ENVIRONMENT AND REFLECT THE SURROUNDING CULTURE'S VALUES AND BELIEFS IN A MARKETING STRATEGY.

ing. Research has shown that many women believe that the stress caused by their multiple roles—wife, mother, career woman, nurse, chauffeur—is too intense. Social values are changing to play down work and to focus on family and on emotional enhancement of personal life. (An associated trend toward casual living and relaxed dress codes has caused the sales of sheer pantyhose to decline.) In the 21st century, American women will continue to work, but they will be more interested in leisure and in spending more time with family. Such changing social values could result in more spending on products that offer fantasy, romance, humor, and fun.

Telstra
Your Telecommunications Partner in the Asia-Pacific

Not too familiar with all the customs in Asia? Talk to the Australian telecommunications company that knows its way around.

For newcomers, Asia can be a confusing place. Customs, rituals and ways of doing business completely different to what you're used to. That's why you should talk to Australia's Telstra. We've had people in Asia for over 40 years, working in telecommunications with local partners and multinationals from Hong Kong to the Middle East. As you'd imagine, that sort of experience means we know our way around pretty well. Everything from telecommunications solutions to the correct etiquette for cable-car spas. If your corporation needs a telecommunications partner in the Asia-Pacific region, call us at our American regional headquarters today.

1800 799 6283
http://www.Telstra.com.au

CIRCLE ACTION #19

Values and beliefs vary from culture to culture. Understanding why people in foreign countries behave and react as they do requires knowing how their values and beliefs affect the success of marketing efforts.[7] What seems like a normal idea, or even a great idea, to marketers in one country may be seen as unacceptable or even laughable by citizens of other lands. For example, when Campbell's offered its familiar (to Americans) red and white–labeled cans of soup in Brazil, it found cultural values there too strong for this product to overcome. Brazilian housewives apparently felt guilty using the prepared soups that Americans take for granted. They believed that they would not be fulfilling their roles as homemakers if they served their families a soup they could not call their own. Faced with this difficulty, Campbell's withdrew the product. However, the company discovered that Brazilian women felt comfortable using a dehydrated "soup starter" to which they could add their own special ingredients and flair. To market soup in Japan, the marketer must realize that soup is regarded there as a breakfast drink rather than a dish served for lunch or dinner.

Industrial buyers and government workers may also behave differently in different cultures. In some countries, business dealings are carried on so slowly that U.S. business people are frustrated by what they perceive as delays. Yet this customary slowness may be seen by their hosts as contributing to a friendly atmosphere. Government officials in some countries openly demand "gifts" or "tips," without which nothing gets done. Of course, this practice is illegal in the United States because it conflicts with American social values.

LANGUAGE

Language is an important part of culture, and the international marketer must be aware of its subtleties. For example, although the French words *tu* and *vous* both mean "you," the former is used to address a social equal or an inferior and the latter to signify formality and social respect. In Japan, "yes" may mean "yes, I understand what you said," not necessarily "yes, I agree." Numerous marketing mistakes have resulted from misinterpretations of language by unwary translators. The Chevrolet brand name Nova translates into Spanish as "no go." Tomato paste becomes "tomato glue" in Arabic. Translated into Spanish, Herculon carpet is "the carpeting with the big derriere."[8] The straightforward slogan "Come alive with Pepsi!" has been translated as "Come out of the grave with Pepsi!" and "Pepsi brings your ancestors back from the grave." Gestures, too, can be misinterpreted, as illustrated in the What Went Wrong? feature.

CULTURAL SYMBOLS

Another aspect of culture involves cultural symbols. A cultural symbol stands for something else and expresses a particular meaning shared by members of a society. Symbols may be verbal or nonverbal. The color white may represent purity, for example. A bull may represent strength. Such symbols may act as powerful unconscious forces,

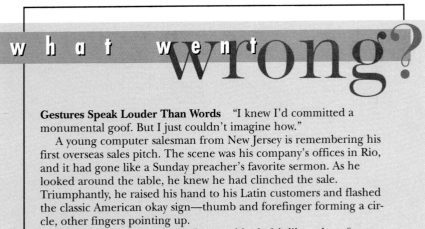

what went wrong?

Gestures Speak Louder Than Words "I knew I'd committed a monumental goof. But I just couldn't imagine how."

A young computer salesman from New Jersey is remembering his first overseas sales pitch. The scene was his company's offices in Rio, and it had gone like a Sunday preacher's favorite sermon. As he looked around the table, he knew he had clinched the sale. Triumphantly, he raised his hand to his Latin customers and flashed the classic American okay sign—thumb and forefinger forming a circle, other fingers pointing up.

The sunny Brazilian atmosphere suddenly felt like a deep freeze. Stony silence. Icy stares. Plus embarrassed smirks from his colleagues.

Calling for a break, they took him outside the conference room and explained. Our hero had just treated everyone to a gesture with roughly the same meaning there as the notorious third-finger sign conveys so vividly here. Apologies saved the sale, but he still turns as pink as a Brazilian sunset when retelling the tale.

It is only natural when you find yourself at sea in the local language to use gestures to bail yourself out. . . . Gestures pack the power to punctuate, to dramatize, to speak a more colorful language than mere words. Yet, like the computer salesman, you may discover that those innocent winks and well-meaning nods are anything but universal.[9]

H.J. Heinz markets its ketchup around the world. In the Czech Republic its television advertising shows three consumer uses for ketchup: one with french fries, one with potato croquettes, and one with spaghetti, a traditional Czech eating habit. Heinz, as a global marketer, has learned not to be ethnocentric. Its advertising also promotes its three varieties of ketchup: Mexican, Hot Tomato, and Original which sell well in the Czech market.

ORDINARY THINGS, EXTRAORDINARY TASTE!

silently working to shape consumer attitudes and behavior. The use of cultural symbols can thus be of great importance in a marketing effort.

As with language, failure to fully understand cultural symbols can produce unpredictable results. According to myth, the site of the Aztec city of Tenochtitlan, now Mexico City, was revealed to its founders by an eagle bearing a snake in its talons. This image, now the official seal of Mexico, appears on the country's flag. To commemorate Mexico's Flag Day, two local McDonald's restaurants managed by U.S. citizens papered their serving trays with placemats embossed with a representation of the national emblem. Mexican government agents were infuriated when they discovered their beloved eagle splattered with ketchup. Authorities swooped down and confiscated the disrespectful placemats.[10]

ETHNOCENTRISM

More often than not, as in the McDonald's placemats example, failure to understand the market leads to unpleasant results. One reason that many managers fail to fully understand foreign cultures and marketing is that people tend to be ethnocentric. **Ethnocentrism** is the tendency to consider one's own culture and way of life as the natural and normal ones.[11] We may mistakenly expect others to share these feelings. This unconscious use of our own cultural values as a reference point has been called the "self-reference criterion."[12] People doing business in a foreign country may be using the self-reference criterion, or being ethnocentric, when they think their domestic strategy or reputation is better than that of any competitor in that country. But exporting one's own biases into foreign markets results in mistakes—such as when large U.S.-built cars with steering wheels on the left side were offered for use in overcrowded Japanese streets where cars are driven on the left side of the road.

Many Americans expect foreign business people to conduct business the same way people do in the United States. However, often this is not the case. For example, assuming that it is appropriate to send a woman sales representative to Saudi Arabia, Yemen, or some other country in the Middle East shows a lack of understanding of cultural values. The women's movement has not had much impact in many Middle Eastern countries. Marketers must avoid such cultural nearsightedness by consciously recognizing its potentially biasing impact.

Ethnocentrism
The tendency to consider one's own culture and way of life as the natural and normal one.

Demographics

The terms *demography* and *demographics* come from the Greek word *demos*, meaning "people" (as does the word *democracy*). **Demography** may be defined as the study of the size, composition (for example, by age or racial group), and distribution of the human population in relation to social factors such as geographic boundaries. The size, composition, and distribution of the population in any geographic market will

Demography
The study of the size, composition, and distribution of the human population in relation to social factors such as geographic boundaries.

clearly influence marketing. Because demographic factors are of great concern to marketing managers, we discuss some basic demographic information and trends in this section. A wealth of demographic statistics for the United States can be found in the *Statistical Abstract of the United States* or on the Internet.[13]

THE U.S. POPULATION

The population of the United States is constantly changing. If marketers are to satisfy the wants and needs of that population, they must be aware of the changes that are occurring and the directions in which these changes are moving the population.

In 1998, the Bureau of the Census estimated that there were 268 million people living in the United States. It has predicted that the population will reach 270 million in the year 2000. The birth rate is 14.8 per thousand, and the death rate is 8.8 per thousand. The birth rate is expected to decline to 14.2 per thousand by the year 2000. About 51.2 percent of the population is female, and about 48.8 percent is male.

U.S. Bureau of the Census
www.census.gov

Migration Migration has always been an overwhelmingly important demographic factor in the United States. Much attention is paid to the effect of the Cuban and Haitian migrations into southern Florida and the general migration into the Sunbelt states. However, migration into and around the country has been going on for hundreds of years.

The center of population is represented by the intersection of two lines, one dividing the population equally into a northern and a southern half and the other, into an eastern and a western half. The 1790 U.S. census showed the center of population to be 23 miles east of Baltimore, Maryland. The 1790 population center was actually under the waters of the Atlantic Ocean because virtually the entire population of the country was concentrated along the East coast because of the curve of the coastline. The 1990 census moved the population center to Crawford County, Missouri, near Cherryville. Each census since 1790 has moved the point farther south and west.

Urbanization The United States—and in fact, the entire world—has become increasingly urbanized since the nineteenth century. In the United States, the expansion of some metropolitan areas has brought neighboring cities and their suburbs so close together that they have, for all practical purposes, merged. Two examples of this phenomenon are the Northeast Corridor, which extends from Boston to Washington, D.C., and the string of communities stretching from north of Los Angeles to Tijuana, Mexico.

In fact, the 1990 census showed that more than half of the people in the United States live in the 39 metropolitan areas (that is, central cities and suburbs) with populations of more than 1 million. Approximately 76 percent live in the nation's 336 metropolitan areas—up from 56 percent in 1950.

Growth in U.S. metropolitan areas has not meant growth in the central cities. Crowded conditions, high crime rates, and other discomforts associated with city life, coupled with the great numbers of private cars owned by Americans, have encouraged the much-discussed "fleeing to the suburbs" of people seeking to enjoy a blend of country and city living. It is growth in suburban areas that has caused the populations of metropolitan areas to remain stable and even to rise. Indeed, the most dramatic growth of the past decade was in the suburbs.[14] Many of these suburbs, such as Palo Alto, California, have become so large that they are in essence cities in themselves. Many citizens of these suburban cities work near their homes and do not commute into the older metropolitan area to work or shop.

Growth in the Sunbelt The states of the southern and western United States, sometimes called the Sunbelt, grew most rapidly during the past two decades. Between 1980 and 1990, almost all (87 percent) of the net gain in the U.S.

State Populations: Projected Percent Change, 2000–2025, and Other Demographic Facts

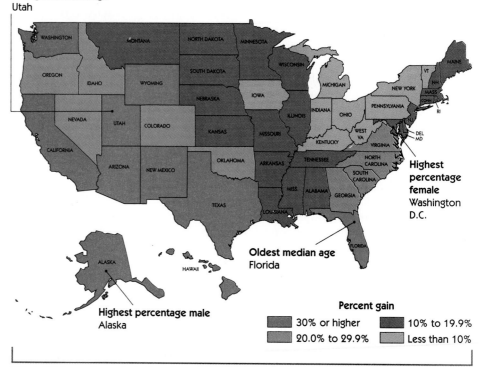

Youngest median age
Utah

Highest percentage female
Washington D.C.

Oldest median age
Florida

Highest percentage male
Alaska

Percent gain

30% or higher	10% to 19.9%
20.0% to 29.9%	Less than 10%

Source: U.S. Census Bureau. Projections: Percentage change of the total population of state: 2000 to 2025 Series A.

population was in the South and West. Between 1990 and 1995, more than 4 million people immigrated to the United States from other countries, and more than half of these people (54 percent) went to California, Texas, and Florida. As a result, 37 percent of the nation's population growth in this period occurred in these three states.[15] California, the most populous state, held the rank of fifth-fastest-growing state in 1990, but dropped to nineteenth during the 1990–1994 period, when it grew by just 8.4 percent. This growth occurred despite California's heavy out-migration—that is, despite the fact that many Californians moved to other states. In fact, California lost more from out-migration than it gained from migration of people from other states into California.[16] Texas grew by 9 percent, and New York grew by 1 percent. As a result, Texas overtook New York as the second most populous state. Nevada and Alaska showed the highest rates of population growth. (However, the rate of population growth can be somewhat misleading; Nevada and Alaska in particular have always been, and continue to be, small in terms of population in spite of high growth rates.)

It is important to remember that long-term trends reflect the past and not necessarily the future. For example, as suggested earlier, it appears that the vast migration of people from other states to California is over. For the year ending July 1, 1993, California grew more slowly than the nation as a whole for the first time in two decades; as noted, California recently has been losing more population to other states than it has been gaining from them. Exhibit 3-3 shows projected state population change between the years 2000 and 2025.

Age When the very first U.S. census was taken in 1790, the median age of the population was only 16 years. Today, the median age is 32.6 years. That means that half the population is older and half younger than 32.6.

GENERATION	AGE	PERCENT OF POPULATION	SIZE (IN MILLIONS)
Kids and teens	Under 18	26%	68
Generation X	18 to 29	17	45
Baby boomers	30 to 49	31	81
Mature market	50 and older	26	68

Source: Adapted from Peter Francese, "America at Mid-Decade," *American Demographics,* February 1995, p. 27. © 1995 *American Demographics* Magazine. Adapted with permission. For subscription information, please call 800/828-1133. Data from Census Bureau surveys.

A consumer's age category—or, as demographers say, *age cohort*—has a major impact on his or her spending behavior. Teenagers spend a great deal of money on soft drinks and fast foods, for example. Many senior citizens spend a lot on travel and prescription drugs. Understanding the age distribution of the population helps marketers anticipate future trends. Exhibit 3-4 shows the distribution of U.S. generations by age for 1995.

The U.S. population has been growing older in recent decades, and this trend is expected to continue. The trend has occurred for two reasons. One is a lowering of the death rate, and the other is aging of the "baby boomers."

The lowering of the death rate means that more people are living longer today. The average life expectancy in the United States has increased to 76 years, and people over 65 years of age constitute a growing segment of the population. Many of these senior citizens do not fit the stereotype of an oldster sitting on a rocking chair waiting for a Social Security check. They are healthy and active, with sufficient finances to enjoy sports, entertainment, international travel, and other products they may have denied themselves while raising families. Some estimates indicate that nearly half of all savings account interest is earned by people over 65. This

fact has particular significance to bank marketers but should be considered by all other marketers as well. The "graying of America" has been as potent an influence on U.S. marketing as was the baby boom of years past.[17]

The baby boom is the tremendous increase in births that occurred between 1946 and 1965, in the 20 years following World War II. Four out of every ten adults are baby boomers. The impact of the baby boom age cohort on U.S. society has been far-reaching, and as these consumers age, they should continue to exert a major influence on marketing strategies for decades. For example, by 2000 all baby boomers will be over 35 years old, and many will be in their mid-50s. These are the peak earning and spending years. The entry of baby boomers into middle age will have a major impact on marketers of investment plans for retirement, health care services, and products such as Centrum Silver vitamins.

Seniors and baby boomers have received a great deal of attention, but other groups should not be overlooked. The generation of Americans born between 1965 and 1976 is often called Generation X. Generation X is smaller than the baby boom generation. Nevertheless, the 45 million adults born between 1965 and 1976 make

adapting to change

up the second-largest group of young adults in U.S. history. It is estimated that a large percentage of those in Generation X are unmarried and still living with their parents. However, as Generation X consumers move into their 30s during the late 1990s, they will get better-paying jobs, buy homes, and start families.[18] Generation X represents $125 billion in annual purchasing power. By the year 2000, this generation is expected to overtake baby boomers as a primary market for most product categories.

Generation X has been stereotyped as an angry, resentful, cynical generation. Like most stereotypes, this one doesn't present a very complete picture. We will have more to say about Generation X throughout the book.

Another group of consumers came into being in the 1980s, when adult baby boomers who had postponed starting families began having children, creating an "echo" of the baby boom known as a "baby boomlet." There were about a half million more births annually in the 1980s than in the late 1970s. By 1990, there were 19 million children under 5 years of age nationwide, compared with 16 million in 1980. And approximately 20.4 million babies were born between January 1990 and December 1994. This was more than in any 5-year period since the last 5 years of the baby boom (1960–1964).[19]

Already the effects of the boomlet are being felt. After years of decline, America's elementary school enrollment began rising in 1985 and continues to do so today. Think of the implications for the marketers of scissors, construction paper, and school glue!

The growth in the pre-teen and teenage groups also has tremendous implications for the economy. These age groups represent a sizable pool of people who will, in 10 or 15 years, be forming households and having and raising children. They will constitute prime markets for homes, furniture, appliances, and other durable products.

Profile of the "Average American Consumer"   What is the "average American consumer" like? Because of the many variables involved, there is no true average American. But it is interesting to try to paint a picture of one. First, there are more women than men in the United States, so the average American is female. And as we mentioned earlier, the median age of Americans is 32.6. The median number of years of schooling in the United States is 12.7. Thus, the "average American" is a woman about 32 years old with a high school education and perhaps a year of college.

Demographers find that more babies are born in August and September than in any other months. This does not occur because parents plan it that way but apparently just the opposite. Married women who wish their babies to be born in the spring stop taking birth control pills nine or ten months before they would like the baby to arrive. Many find that becoming pregnant takes several months longer than anticipated, however. So the marketers of cribs, baby bottles, and other baby products plan to sell more products as larger numbers of babies arrive in late summer.

The Changing American Household

What is the typical U.S. household like? Father, mother, and two children? Wrong! Fewer than 10 percent of all households include husband, wife, and exactly two children. Married couples with any number of children account for only one-fourth of all households. Single-parent households and households composed of unmarried individuals have proliferated in the past 20 years. In 1998, there were almost 100 million U.S. households—up from 81 million in 1980. The number of people in the average household declined from 3.14 in 1970 to 2.76 persons in 1980 and 2.63 persons in 1990.

Single-Person and Single-Parent Households   *Single-person households*—that is, people living alone—account for one of every four households, yet they constitute only 9 percent of the population. The fact that there are single-person households demonstrates that, although many people think a household is the same as a family, it need not be. A household is a dwelling unit occupied by a group of related people, a single person, or several unrelated people who share living quarters. Today, according to the Census Bureau, nonfamily households account for 30 percent of all households.

There are several reasons for the increase in single-person households. More people than ever before have never been married, and young singles are remaining single longer. A high percentage of marriages end in divorce. The longer life expectancy of women means that widows constitute a sizable population segment; an aging mother (or father) may live alone or may live in a "retirement apartment" that provides meal services and other assistance. The number of households maintained by women with no husband present doubled between 1980 and 1990 (from 5.5 million to 10.7 million).

There are 9.7 million *single-parent households*. Many of these are headed by women who are divorced or who have never married. (Approximately 28 percent of all U.S. births are to unmarried women.) But the number of single-parent households headed by men is growing 2.5 times as fast as the number headed by women. Buying behavior in a single-parent household may be different from that in the two-parent household. For example, a teenager may play the shopper role and have the primary responsibility for preparing meals.

Working Women   The advent of the modern career-oriented woman is, in itself, a major change in the American family. With increasing career orientation have come changes in the age at which women have children and the number of women who choose not to have children at all.

The number of people in the work force has grown rapidly in the past decade and will continue to do so. The labor force will grow from 128 million workers in 1993 to at least 137 million (if growth is slow) or as many as 144 million (if growth is rapid) by the year 2000, according to projections by the Bureau of Labor Statistics. Women will account for almost two-thirds of the growth and will represent 47 percent of the labor force by 2000. In more than 60 percent of married-couple households, both husbands and wives work, up from about 40 percent in 1960. Forecasters predict that in 2000, fewer than 20 percent of all households will be "traditional" husband-wife households with only one partner employed outside the home.

Obvious changes in the marketplace reflect these developments: Many stores are open on weekends to permit working people to shop, and it is the rare store that is not open late at least one or two nights per week. Easily prepared microwave dinners are now commonplace. Take-out food, whether from a restaurant or from the prepared-foods section of a supermarket, has gained great popularity.

Family and Household Income   The United States Census Bureau defines a family as a group of two or more persons related by birth, marriage, or adoption and residing together. The annual median family income in the United States was $36,959 in 1993, up from $21,023 in 1980 and $9,867 in 1970.[21]

In 1993, approximately 30 percent of U.S. households had incomes above $50,000, and 24 percent had incomes below $15,000. Only 6 percent had incomes above $100,000. More than two-thirds of all households earning more than $100,000 were headed by college graduates. The average annual income of college graduates was about double that of high school graduates who did not graduate from college.

In the early 1990s, the wealthiest 20 percent of households earned more than the 60 percent of households in the middle classes.[22] Trends in household income (including the income of single-person households) show that there has been a decline in the percentage of middle-income households.

The upper-income group has expanded, in part because of an increase in the number of affluent two-income married couples. Working wives contribute about 40 percent of family income. There are approximately 10 million two-income families earning over $50,000. This affluent group has considerable discretionary income, and it has an impact on the market for luxury goods.

A Multicultural Population   The United States has a *multicultural population*—that is, a population made up of many different ethnic and racial groups. One out of every five U.S. residents is African American, Hispanic, Asian, Native American Indian, Eskimo, or a member of another minority group.[23] In 1995, African Americans represented about 12 percent of the U.S. population, Hispanic Americans about 10 percent, and Asian Americans about 3.4 percent. These three minorities account for approximately 31 million, 26 million, and 9 million people, respectively. (See Exhibit 3-5.) Native Americans account for less than 1 percent of the population.

The trend is clearly toward increased diversity. In the 1960s, nine out of ten Americans were white. Today, about three out of four Americans are non-Hispanic whites. Only a small percentage of immigrants are of European origin. Immigrants, along with Hispanic Americans and African Americans, tend to have

e   x   h   i   b   i   **3-5**   Minority Markets in the United States, 1995

RACE	POPULATION IN MILLIONS	PERCENT OF TOTAL	MEDIAN AGE	PERCENT CHANGE 1990–95	PERCENT OF GROWTH 1990–95
All persons	262	100.0%	34	5.6%	100%
White, non-Hispanic	193	73.8	36	2.8	38
Black, non-Hispanic	31	12.0	29	7.8	16
Asian, non-Hispanic	9	3.4	30	24.8	15
Hispanic	26	10.0	27	18.8	30
American Indian, Eskimo, and Aleut, non-Hispanic	2	0.7	27	7.0	1

Note: Hispanics may be of any race. Numbers may not add to total because of rounding.
Source: Adapted from Peter Francese, "America at Mid-Decade," *American Demographics*, February 1995, p. 28. © 1995 *American Demographics* Magazine. Adapted with permission. For subscription information, please call 800/828-1133. Data from Census Bureau surveys.

more children than the non-Hispanic white population. If these immigration and birth-rate trends continue, the United States will continue to become increasingly diverse.

In recent years, many demographers have predicted that Hispanic Americans will replace African Americans (and other blacks) as the largest U.S. minority group by the year 2010. Data from the 1990 census and other censuses show that although the populace of Hispanic origin increased rapidly in the 1980s (53 percent versus 13 percent for blacks) and between 1990 and 1995 (18.8 percent versus 7.8 percent), there is still a gap of about 5 million people between the two groups. Projections generally assume that present trends will continue. In recent years, however, although the Hispanic population's size has continued to increase, its growth rate has been on the decline. It may be that by the year 2010 African Americans will still outnumber Hispanics.

The Census Bureau revealed other trends in the United States' multicultural population. Perhaps the most significant trend for the entire country was that the number of Asians and Pacific Islanders living in the United States doubled between 1980 and 1990 and increased by almost one-quarter between 1990 and 1995.

The trend toward diversity and a multicultural society has had its greatest impact on certain regions of the country. For example, most of the growth in the Asian American population has been in California, and most of the growth in the Hispanic population has been in Florida, Texas, and California. In certain cities in these states, such as San Diego, non-Hispanic whites account for less than 50 percent of the population.

WORLD POPULATION

The world population exceeds 6 billion people. (See Exhibit 3-6.) Because markets consist of people willing and able to exchange something of value for goods and services, this total is of great marketing significance. However, the exponential growth of population, particularly in less developed countries, puts a heavy burden on marketing. The distribution of food, for instance, is a marketing problem whose solution may prove crucial to the survival of this planet. The world

U.S. Census Bureau
World Population Clock
www.census.gov/
cgi-bin/ipc/popclockw

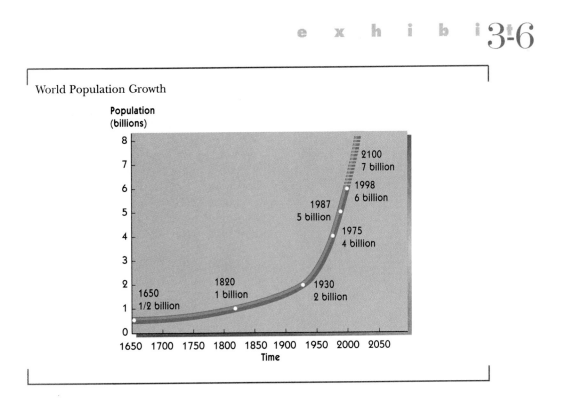

e x h i b i 3-6

World Population Growth

population is expected to grow by at least 140 million per year during the first decade of the 21st century. That's about 16,000 new people per hour.

Although the bulk of this section has dealt with the demography of the U.S. market, it is important to remember that the future of both developed and developing economies is well served by vigorous international trade. Such trade cannot be effectively implemented and maintained unless marketers concern themselves deeply with what is going on in "the rest of the world."

VIGOROUS INTERNATIONAL TRADE CANNOT BE EFFECTIVELY IMPLEMENTED AND MAINTAINED UNLESS MARKETERS CONCERN THEMSELVES DEEPLY WITH WHAT IS GOING ON IN "THE REST OF THE WORLD."

Three areas of the world—North America, Europe, and the Pacific Rim countries surrounding Japan—are economically important areas where global competition can be intense. They will receive special attention in our discussions throughout this book.

Economic and Competitive Forces

Economic and competitive forces strongly influence marketing activity at all levels. In this section, we discuss macromarketing concerns—economic systems and general economic conditions. In Chapter 4, when we discuss the microenvironment, we will consider how competitive forces influence an individual firm's activities.

ECONOMIC SYSTEMS

Economic system
The system whereby a society allocates its scarce resources.

A society's **economic system** determines how it will allocate its scarce resources. Traditionally, capitalism, socialism, and communism have been considered the world's major economic systems. In general, the western world's economies can be classified as modified capitalist systems. Under such systems, competition, both foreign and domestic, influences the interaction of supply and demand. Competition is often discussed in this context in terms of competitive market structures.

The competitive structure of a market is defined by the number of competing firms in some segment of an economy and the proportion of the market held by each competitor. Market structure influences pricing strategies and creates barriers to competitors wishing to enter a market. The four basic types of competitive market structure are pure competition, monopolistic competition, oligopoly, and monopoly.

Pure competition
A market structure characterized by free entry, a homogeneous product, and many sellers and buyers, none of whom can control price.

Pure competition exists when there are no barriers to competition. The market consists of many small, competing firms and many buyers. This means that there is a steady supply of the product and a steady demand for it. Therefore, the price cannot be controlled by either the buyers or the sellers. The product itself is homogeneous—that is, one seller's offering is identical to all the others' offerings. The markets for basic food commodities, such as rice and mushrooms, approximate pure competition.

Monopolistic competition
A market structure characterized by a large number of sellers offering slightly differentiated products and exerting some control over their own prices.

The principal characteristic of **monopolistic competition** is product differentiation—a large number of sellers offering similar products differentiated only by minor differences in, for example, product design, style, or technology. Firms engaged in monopolistic competition have enough influence on the marketplace to exert some control over their own prices. The fast-food industry provides a good example of monopolistic competition.

Oligopoly
A market structure characterized by a small number of sellers who control the market.

Oligopoly, the third type of market structure, exists where a small number of sellers dominate the market. Oligopoly is exemplified by the commercial aircraft industry, which is controlled by two large firms: Boeing and Airbus Industries. Getting established in an oligopoly like the commercial aircraft industry often requires a huge capital investment, which presents a barrier to new firms wishing to enter the industry. The distinguishing characteristic of an oligopoly, however, is not the size of the company measured by assets or sales volume but its control over the marketplace measured by market share. Each of the companies in an oligopoly has a strong influence on product offering, price, and market structure within the industry. The companies do not, however, generally compete on price.

Finally, markets with only one seller, such as a local telephone company or electric utility, are called monopolies. A **monopoly** exists in a market in which there are no suitable substitute products. Antitrust legislation strictly controls monopolies in the United States.

Monopoly
A market structure characterized by a single seller in a market in which there are no suitable substitute products.

ECONOMIC CONDITIONS

Economic conditions around the world are obviously of interest to marketers. The most significant long-term trend in the U.S. economy has been the transition to a service economy. There has been a continuing shift of workers away from manufacturing and into services, where almost 80 percent of U.S. jobs are to be found. This shift has greatly affected economic conditions as well as marketing activity.[24] The marketing of services is an important topic that is discussed throughout this book.

The Business Cycle   The **business cycle** reflects recurrent fluctuations in general economic activity. The various booms and busts in the health of an economy influence unemployment, inflation, and consumer spending and saving patterns, which, in turn, influence marketing activity. The business cycle has four phases:

Business cycle
Recurrent fluctuations in general economic activity. The four phases of the business cycle are prosperity, recession, depression, and recovery.

Prosperity: The phase in which the economy is operating at or near full employment and both consumer spending and business output are high

Recession: The downward phase, in which consumer spending, business output, and employment are decreasing

Depression: The low phase, in which unemployment is highest, consumer spending is low, and business output has declined drastically

Recovery: The upward phase, when employment, consumer spending, and business output are rising

Because marketing activity, such as the successful introduction of new products, is strongly influenced by the business cycle, marketing managers watch the economic environment closely. Unfortunately, the business cycle is not always easy to forecast. The phases of the cycle need not be equal in intensity or duration, and the contractions and expansions of the economy do not always follow a predictable pattern. Furthermore, not all economies of the world are in the same

adapting to change

Wu's Economic Barometer   Gordon Wu is a Hong Kong billionaire who created an index that describes poor countries moving toward wealth. According to Wu's Economic Barometer, when per capita income starts coming up, the first thing people do is eat out. That's why American fast-food restaurants are rapidly growing in Asia. After that period, people in developing countries buy new clothes. The third thing they do is start accumulating new appliances. After that, they buy motorcycles, cars, and apartments. The fifth step—as the country moves toward greater affluence—is to travel overseas.[25]

COUNTRY	1995 PER CAPITA GROSS DOMESTIC PRODUCT (U.S. DOLLARS)	1995 ANNUAL CONSUMER PRICE INFLATION (PERCENT)
Argentina	$ 8,100	1.7%
Belgium	19,500	1.6
Brazil	6,100	23.0
China	2,900	10.1
Czech-Republic	10,200	9.1
Egypt	2,760	9.4
France	20,200	1.7
Greece	9,500	8.1
India	1,500	9.0
Israel	15,500	10.1
Italy	18,700	5.4
Mexico	7,700	52.0
Nigeria	1,300	57.0
Poland	5,800	21.6
Portugal	11,000	4.6
Taiwan	13,500	4.0
Zimbabwe	1,600	25.8

Source: *The World Fact Book: 1996* (Central Intelligence Agency Web page: www.odci.gov/cia).

Gross domestic product (GDP)
The total value of all the goods and services produced by capital and workers in a country.

Gross national product (GNP)
The total value of all the goods and services produced by a nation's residents or corporations, regardless of their location.

Science
The accumulation of knowledge about humans and the environment.

Technology
The application of science for practical purposes.

stage of the business cycle. So a single global forecast may not accurately predict activity in certain countries.

Marketing strategies in a period of prosperity differ substantially from strategies in a period of depression. For example, products with "frills" and "extras" sell better during periods of prosperity than in periods when the economy is stagnant or declining. During periods of depression or recession, when consumers have less spending power, lower prices become more prominent considerations in spending decisions.

GDP and GNP Two common measures of the health of a country's economy are **gross domestic product (GDP)** and **gross national product (GNP).** The GDP measures the value of all the goods and services produced by workers and capital in a country. The GNP measures the value of all the goods and services produced by a country's residents or corporations, regardless of their location. Thus, profits made by U.S. companies on overseas operations are included in GNP, but not in GDP. Profits that foreign companies make on operations in the United States are included in the U.S. GDP, but not in U.S. GNP. Both GDP and GNP provide economic yardsticks of business output. Which of these two measures you use has to do with whether you wish to know what is produced inside our borders or what is produced by Americans around the world.[26]

In the United States, per capita GDP was $27,500 and the inflation rate was 2.5 percent in 1995. Exhibit 3-7 shows per capita GDP (in U.S. dollars) and inflation rates for several countries in 1995. Notice how different economic conditions are around the world.

Science and Technology

Although the two terms are sometimes used interchangeably, **science** is the accumulation of knowledge about human beings and the environment, and **technology** is the application of such knowledge for practical purposes. Thus, the discovery that certain diseases can be prevented by immunization is a scientific discovery, but how and when immunization is administered is a technological issue.

Like other changes in the environment of marketing, scientific and technological advances can revolutionize an industry or destroy one.[27] Think of how advances in the development of virtual reality could change the electronics industry, for instance. The case of oat bran offers an example of how quickly such changes can occur. When the *New England Journal of Medicine* published a study downplaying oat bran's cholesterol-reducing potential, the market share of oat bran cereals fell by almost half within 3 months.[28] However, when the FDA later announced that soluble fiber from oatmeal, as part of a diet low in saturated fat and cholesterol, may reduce heart disease, oatmeal sales rose back to former levels.

The discovery that prolonged exposure to the sun can cause skin cancer certainly affected suntan lotion marketers. Similarly, the knowledge that fish oil and aspirin may help reduce the risk of heart attack has led to the introduction of new diet supplements and changes in the advertising messages of existing products.

Technology from the U.S. space program provided numerous advances that have been seized on by marketers. Besides Tang, freeze-dried ice cream, and some other food products, the space program has yielded solar calculators, liquid crystal wristwatches, and the microchips that are found in personal computer games and personal digital assistants. In addition, space technology has found industrial applications: A firefighter in a lightweight fire-fighting suit can now communicate with others through a built-in communication system. The nonfogging face protector the firefighter wears to improve visibility is also a product of space technology.

Examples of organizations that suffered because they did not adapt to changing technology are easy to find. Western Union's telegrams were sent by an electromechanical device, made obsolete by computers and fax machines. More recently, Atari and several other marketers of video games fell victim to competitors, such as Sony Playstation and Nintendo, that had switched to more technologically advanced, higher-performance microprocessors.

Clearly, then, scientific and technological forces have a pervasive influence on the marketing of most goods and services. Because changes related to science and technology can have a major impact, organizations of all types must monitor these changes and adjust their marketing mixes to meet them.

DIGITAL TECHNOLOGY AND THE INTERNET

Historians and anthropologists have pointed out that technological innovations can change more than the way business is done in an industry. Indeed, major technological innovations can change entire cultures. The mechanical clock made regular working hours possible.[29] The invention of the steam engine and railroads and the mass production of automobiles changed the way people thought about distance—the words *near* and *far* took on new meaning.[30] Television changed the way people think about news and entertainment.[31]

"Today's computer technology can be characterized by the phrase *digital convergence.* Almost all industries, professions, and trades are being pulled closer together by a common technological bond: the digitizing of the work product into the ones and zeros of computer language."[32]

It has been said that "Computing is not about computers anymore. It is about living."[33] Seemingly overnight, thousands of goods and services have become digital. Digital technology is creating unique ways of communicating and performing work. Disposable plastic cards with a computer chip embedded in them that can replace cash for small transactions were used at the Olympics. These smart cards, or stored-value cards, look like credit cards and are sold in $10 to $100 denominations from machines. Some smart cards let customers reload value onto the card at ATMs. A smart card's computer chip can store 80 times more information than the magnetic strip on a credit card. Future smart cards will contain the card holder's name, a credit card, ATM card, account balances, cash card, and other data such as frequent-flier information or critical medical records.[34]

Digital technology (also called information technology) is having such a profound impact on marketing and society that it deserves special attention. Because the Internet is the most important communication medium to come

THE INTERNET IS THE MOST IMPORTANT COMMUNICATION MEDIUM TO COME ALONG SINCE THE INTRODUCTION OF TELEVISION.

along since the introduction of television, we introduce it in this section. (The impact of other digital technologies will be discussed throughout the book.)

The Internet Recent innovations in information technology have been reshaping the way business is conducted around the world. The Internet has been of particular significance because it has influenced so many organizations.[35] The **Internet** is a worldwide network of computers that gives users access to information and documents from distant sources.[36] People using the Internet may be viewing information stored on a host computer halfway around the world. The **World Wide Web (WWW)** refers to the portion of the Internet servers that support a retrieval system that organizes information into documents called Web pages. These World Wide Web documents are formatted in a special programing language (called HTML—

PCWEBOPEDIA is a useful Internet encyclopedia. If you want to learn more about any Internet term go to www.pcwebopedia.com and ask the system to search for a definition. The Web page shown here provides a definition of *search engine.*

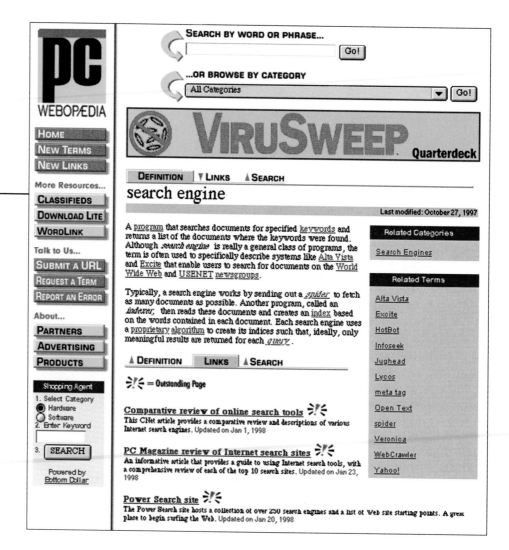

Hypertext Markup Language) that allows for the linking and sharing of information.[37] Hypertext refers to a system that allows related resources to be linked together.[38] HTTP (Hypertext Transfer Protocol) is the traditional method for transferring and displaying HTML information on the Internet.

Over the past few years, academic associations, government agencies, universities, newspapers, TV networks, libraries, and corporations have set up hypertext documents, consisting of various pages, on servers connected to the WWW. An organization's introductory page, or opening screen, is called the *home page* of its Web site. The home page provides basic information about the purpose of the document along with a "menu" of selections, or *links,* that lead to other screens with more specific information. Thus, each page can have connections, or *hyperlinks,* to other pages, which may be on the organization's own computer or on any computer connected to the Internet. The World Wide Web allows users to point and click to innumerable Web sites and then to call up text, graphics, video, and sound bytes from different Web sites.

Navigating the Internet   Using the Internet has become routine for millions of individuals and organizations. Anyone with a computer and a modem can access the Internet by subscribing to a gateway company known as an internet service provider (ISP). In addition, many college and university campus networks offer Internet access, either in computer labs or through off-campus dial-up services.

To access the World Wide Web, the typical home user needs a Web *browser* (a software program with a graphical user interface that can run on that person's particular computer). Popular Web browsers such as Netscape Navigator, Netscape Communicator, and Microsoft Explorer make it easy to move from server to server on the Internet (often called "navigating the 'net," "navigation," or "surfing").

A Web site is a location that can be accessed with browser software. Web browsers require the user to enter a *uniform resource locator,* or URL, into the program. The URL is really just a Web site address that Web browsers recognize.

Microsoft
www.microsoft.com

Netscape
www.netscape.com

In many instances, the user of a Web browser many be unaware that the computer is using a URL. With a Web browser, even a novice can search for information on the Internet simply by pointing and clicking on graphics that resemble the familiar Windows or Macintosh interface. The links to other documents are usually highlighted by color, underlining, or some type of unique icon.

For example, with Netscape, the user may be linked to a series of expanded options containing descriptions of the contents of various files and documents around the Internet. Using a mouse, the user points to highlighted words or colorful icons and then clicks the mouse button to go immediately to the file, regardless of what server it may be stored on. At this point the user can either read or download the material. By clicking on "U.S. Government Information Servers" in one electronic document, for example, a Netscape user might connect to a computer with more information in Washington, D.C. A few more clicks, and the user could be perusing files from the United States Census or the Small Business Administration.

Many Web sites can be accessed by any user or visitor without previous approval. However, some commercial sites require that the user have a valid account and password before access is granted.

A researcher who wants to find a particular site or document on the Internet or is just looking for a resource list on a particular subject can use one of the many Internet search engines.[39] A *search engine* is a computerized "search and retrieval" system that allows anyone to search the World Wide Web for information in a particular way. Some search titles or headers of documents, others search words in the documents themselves, and still others search other indexes or directories. Yahoo is one of the most popular search engines. A person using Yahoo will find lists of broad topics, such as Arts and Humanities, Business and Economy, Entertainment, and Government. Clicking on one of these topics leads

Yahoo!
www.yahoo.com

to other subdirectories or home pages. An alternative way to use a search engine is to type key words and phrases associated with the search; a list of Web sites relevant to the request will be displayed. Excite, Hotbot, and Lycos are also comprehensive and accurate WWW search engines.

Push Technology: A One-on-One Medium   The Internet can be thought of as the world's largest public library. This means that the Internet user can be faced with a retrieval and filtering burden—it takes time to search various Web sites and determine if the information you want is there. This also means that when a content provider, such as the *Chicago Tribune,* publishes on the Web, it faces three challenges: how to get viewers to its Web site, how to get viewers to stay long enough to view the contents, and how to get viewers to return to the Web site.[40]

Push publishing is a form of home or office delivery created to solve these problems. First, it eliminates a user's information overload problem. Second, it gives content providers a way to distribute (push) their information to users. A definition is in order: *Push technology* delivers content to the viewer's desktop, using computer software known as "smart agents" or "intelligent agents" to find information without the user's having to do the searching, or stores entire Web sites, complete with images and links, on a user's computer for later viewing.[41] *Smart agent software* is capable of learning an Internet user's preferences and automatically searching out information in selected Web sites and then distributing the information.

The PointCast Network is a pioneer in the development of personalized Web pages using push technology. PointCast's software can "surf" the Web and automatically send personalized information to an individual user's computer. Users get stock quotes, news, sports, weather, and other information. Users can customize the sections of the service they want delivered. Push technology continuously updates the information and displays it at the user's request. PointCast displays advertising messages for products that reflect the computer user's interests in the upper right-hand corner of each screen.

The PointCast Network is a pioneer in the development of personalized Web pages. PointCast's software "surfs the Web" and automatically sends personalized information to an individual's computer. Users get stock quotes, news, sports, weather, and other information. Advertising messages for products that coincide with the computer user's interests appear in the upper right-hand corner of each screen.

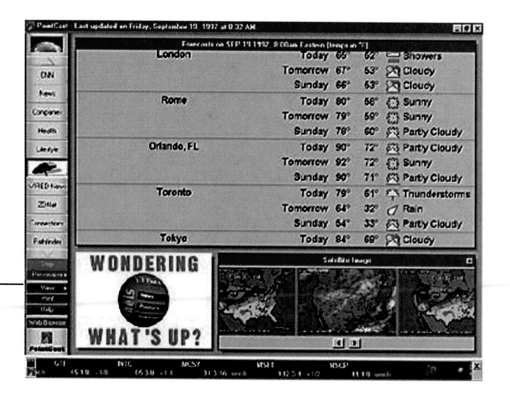

Excite Shopping offers personalized online shopping technology; simultaneous searches can be performed for products available for sale online based on various criteria, among them price and stock levels at different online stores. CD Universe is a similar shopping service for entertainment. PowerAgent is a Web and e-mail alert service that announces timely product bargains to users, who can specify the product categories they are interested in receiving announcements about. MatchLogic works on behalf of advertisers to deliver ads to Web sites automatically when prospective customers access these Web sites.

Push technology may use surveys of customer preferences, or it may use "cookies." *Cookies,* or "magic cookies," are small computer files that a content provider can download onto the computer of someone who visits the provider's Web site. The cookies allow the Web site's computer to record a user's visit, then track other Web sites that person visits, and store these in a file that uses the cookie in place of the person's name (which in most cases the company never knows). For example, if you look up a weather report at Time Warner's Pathfinder Web site by keying in a zip code, the computer notes where you live (or maybe where you wish you lived!). The computer then marks down whether you look up stock quotes (though Time Warner does not capture the symbols of specific stocks). If you visit the Netly News, Pathfinder will record your interest in technology. Then, the next time you visit this Web site, Pathfinder might serve up an ad for a modem or an online brokerage firm or a restaurant in Mountain View, California, depending on what the computer's managed to learn.[42]

WORLDWIDE INFORMATION SYSTEMS

The Internet, along with satellite communications systems, modems, fax machines, and other advances in information technology, has made communication with suppliers, distributors, and customers in other countries much more efficient and in many cases instantaneous.[43] Worldwide information systems, which are discussed in Chapter 5, have been instrumental in the growth of global business. Indeed, many business analysts believe the key to success in the global economy lies in effective use of information technology.

Because of worldwide information systems, the location of a business enterprise has become less important than its ability to keep in touch with other company divisions or other companies via computers and telecommunications. A company in, say, Boise, Idaho, can keep in touch with world financial markets and global customers as easily as a company in Los Angeles or New York. In the future, integration of computers, television, and telephones will further change the way business is conducted. In the not-too-distant future, for example, television viewers will be able to watch an automobile commercial and, with the press of a button, instantly summon up additional information to be delivered on screen or to a printer near the TV set.[44] With another press of a button, the viewer will be able to request a test drive, and within an hour, a local dealer will telephone and schedule a convenient time to stop by with a car. Interactive television with programs on request, home shopping, and travel reservations is now being tested in selected areas.

Politics and Laws

The **political environment**—the practices and policies of governments—and the **legal environment**—laws and regulations and their interpretation—affect marketing activity in several ways. First, they can limit the actions marketers are allowed to take—for example, by barring certain goods from leaving a country, as when Congress passed the Export Administration Act, which prohibited the export of strategic high-technology products to nations such as Iran and Libya. Second, they may require marketers to take certain actions. For instance, cookies called "chocolate chip cookies" are required to contain chips made of real chocolate, and the

Excite Shopping
www.excite.com

CD Universe
www.cduniverse.com

PowerAgent
www.poweragent.com

MatchLogic
www.matchlogic.com

Political environment
The practices and policies of governments.

Legal environment
Laws and regulations and their interpretation.

In 1997, the British colony of Hong Kong was transferred from Britain to Communist China. Though China claims it will maintain Hong Kong's free economy by becoming "one country with two systems," what actually will occur remains uncertain. The results of the transfer could prove to be dramatic.

surgeon general's warning must appear on all cigarette packages. Last, they may absolutely prohibit certain actions by marketers—for example, the sale of products such as narcotic drugs and nuclear weapons—except under the strictest of controls.

Political processes in other countries may have a dramatic impact on international marketers. For example, the dissolution of the former Soviet Union was a historic political action that totally changed the business climate and opened new markets in newly independent states such as Russia, Lithuania, and Ukraine. When the British ended their 156-year colonial control of Hong Kong in 1997, it embarked on an uncertain new era under the sovereignty of Communist China. It remains to be seen how this major political change will affect marketers who do business in Hong Kong.

Developments in Rwanda illustrate how uncertain political situations are and how swiftly they can change. The movie *Gorillas in the Mist* inspired thousands of international tourists to travel to Rwanda to pay $170 per hour to observe mountain gorillas in the Varunga volcanoes. However, soon after the 1994 civil war in Rwanda began, virtually all international tourism stopped—and Rwanda lost the huge revenues that tourism had provided.

Of course, not all political and legal influences involve dramatic changes like those in Rwanda. Laws, in particular, tend to have a stable, long-term influence on marketing strategy. For example, almost all countries with commercial airlines have long-standing bans on foreign ownership of these businesses.

THREE LEVELS OF U.S. LAW

Legislation intended to maintain a competitive business environment, to protect consumers from dangerous products or unethical practices, and to preserve the natural environment can be found at the federal, state, and local levels. Because each of these levels has various departments, subdepartments, regulatory boards, and political subdivisions, such as counties and townships, it is possible that a single marketing organization could confront some 82,688 sets of laws and regulations.[45] When Disney explored the possibility of building a theme park in Virginia to celebrate America's heritage, the company learned that its plans would be reviewed by more than 30 state, local, and federal agencies and it would have to obtain at least 72 permits.[46]

Pepsi in India   Political forces were clearly at play when Pepsi-Cola International was preparing for its introduction of Pepsi products into India. Just when Pepsi's cola, orange, and lemon soft drinks were a few weeks away from introduction to the Indian market, the new nationalist administration in India came up with a costly requisite in the name of patriotism. Pepsi had to change the name of its soft drinks from "Pepsi Era" to "Lehar Pepsi" (Lehar means "wave" in Hindi)—a move that cost the company a maharajah's ransom in design and packaging changes.

After years of political pressure, the name changing was just one final, expensive concession Pepsi was willing to make in order to boost its international market share. It was a struggle to enter this huge market, but Pepsi-Cola International kept fighting to get into the country, which had for many years locked out its chief rival, the Coca-Cola Company.

Pepsi's marketing efforts had been plagued by bad press and government inquiries, but the administration was not its only opponent. Parle Exports Ltd. of Bombay, which dominates India's soft-drink market with an estimated 80 percent share, threw up hurdles of another kind. Parle played up patriotism in an aggressive campaign of propaganda, bad press, and image advertising. After elections in which a nationalistic government defeated the reform-minded Rajiv Gandhi, Parle managing director Ramesh Chauhan decided to launch a marketing war against Pepsi.

"The government should help Indian companies along," Chauhan said. "We are the ones in the fortress. Pepsi is the one trying to break in." Parle used every means at its disposal to keep Pepsi out of the market—including scheming with nationalist government forces and issuing threats.

Chauhan is well connected politically and is part of a large and influential segment of Indian business that harbors a deep-seated fear of multinationals. Chauhan's bare-knuckle style works well in India, where knowing people in high places is key to business success.

When Pepsi began negotiations to set up operations in India several years earlier, no one anticipated it would become the center of one of the most publicized marketing struggles in India's history. However, after working for years to market soda and snacks in India, it now seems that Lehar Pepsi has overcome all the obstacles resulting from the political environment.[47]

The Federal Level   At the federal level of government, the U.S. Department of Justice, the Food and Drug Administration, the Federal Trade Commission, and many other agencies enforce a multitude of laws affecting business. The degree of specialization of some laws and agencies is suggested by the examples in Exhibit 3-8.

Much federal control involves **antitrust legislation,** which prohibits restraint of trade, monopolies, price fixing, price discrimination, deceptive practices, misrepresentations in the labeling of products, and other behavior that tends to lessen competition. The Sherman Antitrust Act (1890), the Clayton Act (1914), and the Federal Trade Commission Act (1914) are the major antitrust laws.

One major federal agency—the **Federal Trade Commission (FTC),** established in 1914—affects virtually all marketers on a regular basis. The FTC was given broad powers of investigation and jurisdiction over "unfair methods of competition." Initially, the FTC was to draft a fixed list of "unfair practices." It soon became clear that no list could be developed to cover all situations. Thus, though the FTC publishes guidelines and uses past decisions as precedents for solving current problems, each situation investigated by the FTC is judged individually. Marketing managers, therefore, face considerable uncertainty in trying to develop programs that can withstand FTC scrutiny. Examples of political and legal constraints on marketing are easy to find. For example, the Food and Drug Administration has ordered cosmetic companies, such as Avon, Revlon, and Estee Lauder, to stop claiming that their so-called anti-aging skin creams can "reverse aging or make basic underlying changes in the skin." According to the FDA, wording such as "rejuvenate, repair or renew skin" and "retard or counteract

U.S. Department of Justice
www.usdoj.gov

U.S. Food and Drug Administration
www.fda.gov

Federal Trade Commission
www.ftc.gov

Antitrust legislation
Federal laws meant to prohibit behavior that tends to lessen competition in U.S. markets. The major antitrust laws are the Sherman Antitrust Act (1890), the Clayton Act (1914), and the Federal Trade Commission Act (1914).

Federal Trade Commission (FTC)
Federal agency established in 1914 by the Federal Trade Commission Act to investigate and put an end to unfair methods of competition.

LEGISLATION	MAJOR PROVISIONS
Federal Hazardous Substances Act (1960)	Requires warning labels on hazardous household chemicals
Kefauver-Harris Drug Amendment (1962)	Requires that manufacturers conduct tests to prove drug effectiveness and safety
Child Protection and Toy Safety Act (1969)	Prevents marketing of products so dangerous that adequate safety warnings cannot be given
Consumer Credit Protection Act (1968)	Requires that lenders fully disclose true interest rates and all other charges to credit customers for loans and installment purchases
Public Health Smoking Act (1970)	Prohibits cigarette advertising on TV and radio and revises the health hazard warning on cigarette packages
Poison Prevention Labeling Act (1970)	Requires safety packaging for products that may be harmful to children
Child Protection Act (1990)	Regulates the number of minutes of advertising on children's television
Telecommunications Act (1996)	Deregulation allows local and long-distance phone companies and other telecommunications companies to compete with each other

aging" could subject anti-aging creams to the same regulations as drugs because it suggests that "a function or structure of the body will be affected by the product."[48]

It would be impossible to discuss all U.S. legislation dealing with marketing in this introductory treatment of the subject. Exhibit 3-9 summarizes selected federal legislation that affects most marketers. Additional milestone legislation affecting major portions of the marketing mix is discussed throughout the book.[49]

The State Level Most states have created laws and agencies that parallel those at the federal level. Most states have departments of agriculture, commerce, labor, and so on, and state-level consumer protection laws dealing with foods, manufactured goods, lending, real estate, banking, and insurance are commonplace.

All states have laws that can affect organizations' marketing mixes. For example, in Oklahoma, distillers must sell their liquor brands to Oklahoma wholesalers at the lowest price in the country. Pennsylvania controls the sale of all hard liquors through a system of "state stores"; Ohio operates state stores and licenses independent stores as well. Ohio does not tax take-out food but does tax food consumed in restaurants. Some farm states do not apply sales taxes if the seller is the actual producer of the goods sold. Michigan prohibits bars from serving free peanuts or potato chips, believing free food might encourage drinking, whereas New York requires that food be available where alcohol is served. California and Arizona prohibit the "importing" from other states of certain fruits, plants, and vegetables. In addition, many states have laws mandating the use of returnable beverage cans and bottles.

ACT	PURPOSE
Sherman Antitrust Act (1890)	Prohibits combinations, contracts, or conspiracies to restrain trade or monopolize
Clayton Act (1914)	Prohibits price discrimination, exclusive dealer arrangements, and interlocking directorates that lessen competition
Federal Trade Commission Act (1914)	Created the FTC and gave it investigatory powers
Robinson-Patman Act (1936)	Expanded Clayton Act to prohibit sellers from offering different deals to different customers
Wheeler-Lea Act (1938)	Expanded powers of FTC to prevent injuries to competition before they occur
Celler-Kefauver Act (1950)	Expanded Clayton Act to prohibit acquisition of physical assets as well as capital stock in another corporation when the effect is to injure competition
Magnuson-Moss Act (1975)	Grants the FTC the power to determine rules concerning warranties and provides the means for class action suits and other forms of redress
Consumer Goods Pricing Act (1975)	Repealed "fair-trade" laws and prohibited price maintenance agreements among producers and resellers
Fair Debt Collection Act (1980)	Requires creditors to act responsibly in debt collection (e.g., bans false statements) and makes harassment of debtors illegal
FTC Improvement Act (1980)	Provides Congress with the power to veto the FTC industrywide Trade Regulation Rules (TRR) and limits the power of the FTC
Federal Antitampering Act (1983)	Prohibits tampering with a product and threats to tamper with a product
Americans with Disabilities Act (1990)	Prohibits discrimination against consumers with disabilities (e.g., stores and hotels must be accessible to shoppers or guests who use wheelchairs)
North American Free Trade Agreement (1993)	Allows for free trade between U.S., Mexico, and Canada without tariffs and trade restrictions
Nutritional Labeling and Education Act (1990)	Requires that certain nutritional facts be printed on food product labels

The Local Level Cities, townships, villages, and counties are all empowered to pass laws and ordinances and to create regulatory agencies. In most areas, health department inspectors check restaurants and motels, weights and measures inspectors check to ensure that scales are honest, and city and county prosecutors investigate misleading and unfair business practices. Local zoning laws affect where businesses such as meat processors, wholesalers, and retailers may be located. Local government units may tax some products but not others, require that certain stores be closed on Sunday, or, as in New York City, legislate that all bars must be closed for at least one hour a day and all customers

Jet Skis, WaveRunners, and other personal watercraft propelled by powerful jets of water can travel at speeds up to 60 miles per hour. With personal watercraft-related injuries and fatalities on the rise, states and localities are beginning to regulate their use. San Juan County in Washington was the first locale to ban the vehicles altogether. The state of Oregon has imposed new water-bike speed limits as strict as 5 mph in certain circumstances. And other states are drafting laws controlling reckless riders. Laws are a powerful environmental force influencing marketing and consumer behavior.

removed from the premises. A common local control on marketing is the issuing of vendors' or similar licenses. In most cases, the licenses are not sold to make money for local governments, although this can be a factor, especially in the case of liquor licenses. The major reason for licensing is so that licenses can be denied to organizations that violate laws or local custom.

One common local law, which affects only door-to-door sellers, is the so-called Green River ordinance, named for the town in Wyoming that pioneered its use. Such ordinances vary widely from place to place, but their purpose is always the same. They require peddlers to obtain licenses but make such licenses very hard to get or restrict door-to-door selling to certain neighborhoods or to specific hours of the day.

Marketing is not only constrained by the legal environment; it can be helped by it as well. For example, retailers use laws to help protect themselves against shoplifting.[50]

Multinational marketing group
A group of countries aligned to form a unified market with minimal trade and tariff barriers among participating member countries.

INTERNATIONAL LAWS

Companies operating their businesses in global markets must pay attention to international laws and the laws of foreign lands. Laws and legal systems that govern the marketing of products in foreign countries vary tremendously. For example, in Brazil, advertisers found guilty of harming or misleading consumers may be fined up to $500,000 or given a prison sentence of up to 5 years. This is a harsh punishment by U.S. standards. The rules of competition, trademark rights, price controls, product quality laws, and a number of other legal issues in individual countries may be of immense importance to a global marketer, such as Coca-Cola.

In France a law prohibits flying saucers from landing in the vineyards in the southern Rhone region. California's Bonny Doon Vineyard capitalized on this law when it introduced a wine called Le Cigare Volant, which translates as "flying saucer" or literally, "flying cigar."

Bonny Doon Vineyard
www.bonnydoonvineyard.com

1995

LE CIGARE VOLANT

RED WINE

CALIFORNIA

ALCOHOL 13.5% BY VOLUME
PRODUCED AND BOTTLED BY BONNY DOON VINEYARD
SANTA CRUZ, CA • U.S.A. • EARTH

Furthermore, not only individual countries, but also multinational bodies, have legal systems to deal with international commerce. **Multinational marketing groups** are groups of countries aligned to form a unified market with minimal trade and tariff barriers among participating member countries. An example is the European Union (formerly called the Common Market). The European Parliament and the Court of Justice deal with legal issues for the European Union.

Environmental Interactions

Before ending this discussion of the macroenvironment, we should emphasize that the parts of the macroenvironment interact with each other. Therefore, effective marketers must consider the whole of marketing's macroenvironment, not just its parts. For example, natural phenomena such as the eruption of volcanoes can affect tourism, agriculture, weather patterns, and radio and television transmission; can heighten public interest in "disaster" movies and books; and can even inspire race-track customers to bet on horses whose names suggest volcanic explosions.

There are many examples of interactions between changes in the economic, technological, and social environments. When the U.S. economy is in a period of decline, the divorce rate also declines, because fewer couples can afford the expense of divorce. When medical science reduces the infant mortality rate in a country, that country's birth rate eventually declines, because parents realize that their children can be expected to survive to adulthood. These kinds of interactions make the job of environmental analysis a complex one. Nonetheless, marketing success cannot be achieved without a careful consideration of environmental constraints and opportunities.

summary

All organizations are influenced by the environments in which they operate.

1 *Describe the domestic and foreign environments in which marketers operate and their effects on organizations.*
Marketing managers must adjust an organization's marketing mix to cope with the domestic environment and often foreign environments as well. In both cases, the marketing environment consists of uncontrollable forces that provide both opportunities and constraints. The environment can be divided into two categories: the macroenvironment and the microenvironment. The macroenvironment includes the physical environment, sociocultural forces, demographic forces, economic forces, science and technology, and politics and laws. The microenvironment consists of forces directly influencing the marketer,

such as customers. Correct environmental assessment makes marketing decisions more successful.

2 *Understand that social values and beliefs are important cultural forces.*
A social value embodies the goals a society views as important and expresses a culture's shared ideas of preferred ways of acting. A belief is a conviction concerning something's existence or characteristics. It is the marketer's job to "read" the social environment and reflect the surrounding culture's values and beliefs in a marketing strategy.

3 *Explain how demographic trends, such as changes that have occurred in the American family, influence marketers.*
Important demographic trends include the aging of the population, a general trend toward having

fewer children, an increase in the number of households, and greater cultural diversity. These and other demographic factors not only affect the demand for goods and services but also lead to variations in pricing, distribution, and promotion.

4 *Explain the various ways in which economic conditions influence marketers.*

The competitive market structure is defined by the number of competing firms in some segment of an economy and the proportion of the market held by each competitor. Pure competition, monopolistic competition, oligopoly, and monopoly are the four basic market structures, and they have different influences on pricing strategies and barriers to competition. Two common measures of economic conditions are gross domestic product (GDP) and gross national product (GNP). The business cycle—prosperity, recession, depression, and recovery—reflects recurrent fluctuations in general economic activity. The various booms and busts in the economy influence unemployment, inflation, and consumer spending and savings patterns, which, in turn, influence marketing activity.

5 *Understand that technology, especially digital technology and the Internet, are having a significant impact on marketing and society.*

Scientific and technological advances can revolutionize an industry or destroy one. Information technology has reshaped the way business is conducted around the world. The Internet has been of particular significance because it has influenced so many organizations. The Internet is a worldwide network of computers that gives users access to information and documents from distant sources.

6 *Appreciate how the three levels of U.S. law and the laws of other nations can influence marketing activity.*

Federal laws control many business activities, such as pricing and advertising by manufacturers, wholesalers, and retailers. The FTC, in particular, affects almost all marketers. State laws also deal with many areas of business, including foods, manufactured goods, lending, real estate, banking, and insurance. Local laws affect zoning and licensing, among other things. Laws that govern the marketing of products in foreign countries and in multinational marketing groups vary tremendously and will affect any organization that engages in international marketing.

7 *Explain how the various elements of the marketing environment interact.*

Changes in any aspect of the environment usually bring about changes elsewhere in the environment. Several environmental forces may combine to encourage changes in consumer behavior or marketing mixes.

key terms

domestic environment (p. 65)
foreign environment (p. 65)
import (p. 65)
export (p. 65)
macroenvironment (p. 65)
microenvironment (p. 65)
physical environment (p. 66)
green marketing (p. 67)
culture (p. 67)
social value (p. 68)
belief (p. 68)

ethnocentrism (p. 70)
demography (p. 70)
economic system (p. 78)
pure competition (p. 78)
monopolistic competition (p. 78)
oligopoly (p. 78)
monopoly (p. 79)
business cycle (p. 79)
gross domestic product (GDP) (p. 80)
gross national product (GNP) (p. 80)

science (p. 80)
technology (p. 80)
Internet (p. 82)
World Wide Web (p. 82)
political environment (p. 85)
legal environment (p. 85)
antitrust legislation (p. 87)
Federal Trade Commission (FTC) (p. 87)
multinational marketing group (p. 90)

questions for review & critical thinking

1. What domestic and foreign environmental factors might have the greatest influence on each of the following firms?
   a. General Motors
   b. McDonald's
   c. Starbucks (coffee)
   d. Humana Hospitals

2. What impact would the development of efficient solar energy have on each of the following industries?
   a. The housing industry
   b. The automobile industry
   c. Another industry of interest to you

3. Evaluate society's continuing concern for physical fitness from the point of view of each of the following:
   a. A manufacturer of packaged foods
   b. A leasing agent for an office building
   c. A maker of athletic shoes and clothing

4. World population is rising much more quickly than the U.S. population. What opportunities does this present to U.S. marketers? What constraints?

5. What is a household? What do you predict will be the nature of households in the year 2010?

6. Ethnic or racial groups are often served by small companies, such as makers of specialty foods. Why might a large firm such as Procter & Gamble, Toyota, or Stroh's Brewing Company avoid marketing to such groups?

7. What businesses would be influenced if a fire destroyed a telephone switching station and it took two weeks to get local service working?

8. What U.S. states seem to be bellwether states— that is, states that predict future environmental trends in the rest of the country?

9. Are economic forces the most important environmental influences on marketing activities?

10. The text mentioned that over the course of history, the development of new technologies, such as the steam engine and the automobile, has profoundly changed the marketplace. What technologies are the driving forces changing today's marketplace?

11. What laws are unique to your state?

12. How much can marketers control political and legal influences on the marketing mix?

13. Form small groups as directed by your instructor. As a group, come to a consensus on the five environmental factors that will most strongly influence an industry designated by your instructor. Discuss as a class the groups' conclusions and how each group came to a consensus.

marketing plan—right or wrong?

1. *Seinfeld* is one of the most successful television shows in the United States. The plan is to show *Seinfeld* on German cable television with German language dubbed in.

2. An automobile manufacturer is setting up a Web page to highlight the unique features of its cars. It plans to include an interactive feature so that visitors to the Web site can easily e-mail the company.

internet insights

zikmund.swcollege.com

exercises

1. Go to www.census.gov and open the link to the POP CLOCK to find the Census Bureau's estimate of the U.S. population on today's date.

2. *USATODAY Interactive* is a good place to keep track of environmental changes. Go to www.usatoday.com and write a short report on trends affecting marketing activity.

3. The Australian National University maintains a Web page that keeps track of leading demographic information facilities worldwide. Go to http://coombs.anu.edu.au/ResFacilities/ DemographyPage.html to find a list of more than 150 interesting Web pages.

address book (useful urls)

American Demographics Magazine	www.marketingtools.com/ publications/AD/index.htm
National Museum of Natural History, Paris, France	www.popexpo.net/home.htm
Popular Science Magazine	www.popsci.com
Home of Mister Economy	amos.bus.okstate.edu

ethically right or wrong?

The United States has had a series of confrontations with China over trade. Early in 1995, a number of politicians believed that the federal government should impose tariffs on Chinese exports to the United States unless Beijing cracked down immediately on pirating of American music, movies, and computer software.

The Chinese government had refused to close down 29 factories in southern China that churned out 70 million compact discs and other illegally copied products every year. The cost to American industry was estimated at $1 billion in lost sales. American businesses were especially concerned by Chinese exports of these illegal products to other countries in Asia.

"We have to send an unambiguous message to Beijing," said Mickey Kantor, the U.S. trade representative, who has demanded that the Chinese government create "strike forces" to close down the factories. "By the year 2010, China could be the second-largest economy in the world, and now is not the time to let them continue to act as they have in the past. They have too much impact on the world economy."

In February 1995, President Clinton imposed a 100 percent tariff on all goods exported from China to the United States. These sanctions could harm a variety of Chinese industries, including some state-run factories closely linked to government leaders and their families. They could also cost American consumers if, because of the sanctions, prices go up on Chinese-made items ranging from consumer electronics to toys and clothing.

QUESTIONS

1. How might China's culture influence its values about intellectual property rights, such as rights to music, movies, and software?
2. If China continues to pirate American music, movies, and software, should even stronger sanctions be imposed?
3. Since businesses operate in a global economy, should business ethical standards be the same throughout the world?

TAKE A STAND

1. Should products with high sodium levels, such as fast-food hamburgers and breakfast sausage, be advertised on children's television?
2. Should English be made the national language of the United States? Should all products have labels in English only?
3. Tokyo-based Ito-Yokado owns a 70 percent share of the 7-Eleven convenience store chain. Should this fact be stated on a decal posted in store windows?
4. Dr. Dre and Snoop Doggy Dogg, gangsta rappers, have been accused of making rap recordings that promote black-on-black crime, advocate violence, and use derogatory, profane, and misogynist lyrics. Is gangsta rap a product that should be marketed? Marketed aggressively on daytime radio?
5. A lawsuit was filed by men who were denied employment by the Hooters restaurant chain, known for its scantily clad female bartenders and servers. Should the restaurant chain be required to hire men as bartenders and servers?

video case

LION Coffee   *Focus on Small Business*

James Delano, president of a Hawaiian firm that roasts coffee and sells it at wholesale and retail, unexpectedly was faced with regulatory action [in 1991] that could cripple the business.

The Woolson Spice Co.'s annual permit to import green coffee beans was expiring in two weeks. The state's Department of Agriculture notified Woolson, which does business as LION Coffee, of impending catastrophe: The permit might not be renewed because of a provision in an old state law that had not been applied to LION before.

Under the law, coffee beans may not be imported by roasters on Hawaiian islands where coffee is grown. Once, that affected only the state's biggest island, Hawaii, where coffee is grown on the Kona coast. But today, coffee is also grown on other islands, including Oahu, where Woolson is located.

LION produces blends almost exclusively. Without imported beans, its coffee-roasting facility would have to shut down. It was the biggest challenge since Delano had bought a dormant Woolson Spice in 1979 and, with two employees, started roasting and packaging coffee in downtown Honolulu.

Action was required, and fast.[52]

QUESTIONS

1. How uncontrollable is the legal environment in the Hawaiian Islands? What actions might LION take to get the annual permit reissued?
2. What environmental forces, other than legal action, might shape LION's marketing mix?

Thirty Years of Freshmen

Once upon a time boys and girls went to college to learn the meaning of life. They ruminated on Kierkegaard and Kant, dealt with existential dilemmas, argued over war, the Bomb and whether to protest or not to protest. "Thirty years ago," recalls Alexander Astin, a professor of education at the University of California, Los Angeles, "students were preoccupied with questions such as 'What is life all about?' and 'Who is God?'"

Once upon a time is over. A study released [in 1997] by UCLA and the American Council on Education compares the attitudes of 9 million freshmen who have answered questionnaires on 1,500 campuses over the past three decades. In 1967, 82% of entering students said it was "essential" or "very important" to "develop a meaningful philosophy of life"—making that the top goal of college freshmen. Today that objective ranks sixth, endorsed by only 42% of students. Conversely, in 1967 less than half of freshmen said that to be "very well off financially" was "essential" or "very important." Today it is their top goal, endorsed by 74%. Idealism and materialism, says Astin, who has directed the surveys since their creation, "have basically traded places."

Today there is a convergence in the goals of men and women. Three decades ago, less than half of female freshmen planned to get a graduate degree. Now nearly 68% of women plan to get higher degrees, vs. 65% of males. Thirty years ago, men were nine times more likely to want to be lawyers. Today there is less than half a percent difference. Among freshmen who want to be doctors and dentists, females outnumber males.

Feminist values are now entrenched. "It is hard to believe that in 1967 fully two-thirds of men agreed with the statement 'The activities of married women are best confined to the home and family,'" Astin remarks. Today that has dropped to 31%. But a gender gap persists: only 19% of female freshmen agree. University of South Carolina professor John Gardner, head of the National Resource Center for the Freshman Year Experience, laments that the survey also confirms how "women have taken on some of our worst habits. They smoke and drink more—binge drinking has become their problem too." Thirty years ago, male freshmen were nearly 50% more likely to be frequent smokers. Today more females than males smoke frequently—about 16%, vs. 13%. A point of divergence: only 31.9% of women, vs. 53.8% of men, agree that "if two people really like each other, it's all right for them to have sex, even if they've known each other only a very short time."

Freshmen who reported feeling "overwhelmed" nearly doubled, from 16% in 1985 to nearly 30% in 1996. As a result of such anxieties, says Gardner, "students today are practical and grade grubbing." Many scholars blame economic insecurity for the change. Says James Spring, associate admissions director at the State University of New York at Binghamton: "As a student in the '60s, I could think about my philosophy of life because I didn't worry about getting a job." Indeed, those who report a "major concern" that they will lack funds to complete college jumped from less than 9% three decades ago to 18% now. Still, there are positives. Today's freshmen, says Gardner, "hold down jobs after school and volunteer in community service as much as ever. We don't recognize their fine qualities enough."[53]

QUESTIONS

1. Analyze the findings presented in the case. What are the most significant environmental changes that occurred between 1966 and 1996?
2. How should your college or university adapt its marketing strategy based on these environmental trends?

chapter
4

The Microenvironment in an Era of Global Competition

After you have studied this chapter, you will be able to:

Understand how the microenvironment affects a company's marketing activity.

1

Identify the four Cs of marketing.

2

Recognize how marketing creates economic utility for customers.

3

Identify the various types of competitors and understand how marketers anticipate and react to competitors' strategies.

4

(continued on next page)

5   Describe the value chain and explain why it must be managed.

6   Understand the importance of global competition in today's economy.

7   Apply the four Cs in a global business context.

in less than a decade, Whirlpool has gone from being essentially a U.S. company to a major global player.

In addition to having an approximate 35 percent share of market in the U.S., Whirlpool manufactures and markets products under 12 major brand names in about 140 countries. With its affiliates, Whirlpool also claims the No. 1 market share in Latin America, while in Europe it holds the No. 3 slot.

In Latin America, Whirlpool expects its share of market to grow through the next decade at a faster clip than that region's overall economy, which is expected to grow 5 to 8 percent annually. Whirlpool's cause for optimism is linked directly to its equity interests in the Brasmotor Group, which includes Multibras S.A., Brazil's largest appliance producer and marketer under the Brastemp, Consul, and Semer brand names.

In Asia, the establishment of six majority-owned, joint-venture partnerships—five in China, one in India—has gained Whirlpool the distinction of being the largest Western appliance company in Asia. In Japan, Daiichi Corp., Japan's major retailer of electric home appliances,

entered into an agreement with Whirlpool to market and sell Whirlpool products in Japan as well as throughout Asia.

In Europe, Whirlpool for the first time is selling Whirlpool-designed and -produced appliances in every major-appliance category, the result of a four-year effort to renew its product line. Whirlpool's three principal European brands, Bauknecht, Whirlpool and Ignis, are represented by new product introductions.

And in the U.S., Whirlpool began producing freestanding gas and electric ranges at its newly completed manufacturing plant near Tulsa, Oklahoma. The cooking products are being produced under the Whirlpool, Roper and Estate brand names.

As a major global player, Whirlpool is organized into four geographical regions: North America, Asia, Latin America and Europe. Each region maintains an independent organizational structure, with senior management in each region reporting to Whirlpool's corporate headquarters in Benton Harbor, Michigan. The vast majority of products sold in a particular region are made in that region.

Expansion plans include growing sales in Asia,

AS A MAJOR GLOBAL PLAYER, WHIRLPOOL IS ORGANIZED INTO FOUR GEOGRAPHICAL REGIONS: NORTH AMERICA, ASIA, LATIN AMERICA AND EUROPE. EACH REGION MAINTAINS AN INDEPENDENT ORGANIZATIONAL STRUCTURE.

Whirlpool expects its ongoing efforts to leverage technology and reduce product complexity on a global basis to result in more opportunities to respond to national and regional appliance preferences. One example is the company's "World Washer," a product designed as a global platform that can be modified to accommodate the manufacturing and marketing realities in Asia, Latin America and North America.[1]

Whirlpool is typical of companies striving to be competitive in this age of global competition. It is customer-driven. It sees the world as its market. And it works with collaborators to gain competitive advantage.

Whirlpool
www.whirlpool.com

The macroenvironment, that collection of broad societal forces that affect every business and nonprofit marketer, was discussed in Chapter 3. Marketers, however, are more directly influenced by their individual microenvironments. A microenvironment consists of a company, its customers, and the other economic institutions that regularly influence its marketing practices. This chapter discusses the nature of the microenvironment and the ways in which the microenvironmental forces shape marketing strategy.

The Microenvironment—The Four Cs

To explain the dramatic impact of the microenvironment, it is useful to organize all microenvironmental forces into four basic categories—company, customers, competitors, and collaborators—each representing a participant that performs essential business activities. We will call these the **four Cs**.[2]

Four Cs
A name for the microenvironmental participants that perform essential business activities: company, customers, competitors, and collaborators.

COMPANY

The **company** is the business or organization itself. Marketing, although exceedingly important, is only one functional activity of an organization. Every marketer must work with people in the organization who perform nonmarketing tasks. For example, in a large manufacturing company, manufacturing, engineering, purchasing, accounting, finance, and personnel are all part of the internal company environment. These functional activities, the level of technology, and the people who perform them have an impact on marketing. Marketers, for example, work within the framework of the corporate mission set by top managers, who are responsible for the company's operations. Companies like 3M, Sony, and Disney have several divisions and market many different products. The way one of a company's products is marketed often affects the marketing of other company products.

Company
A business or organization that offers products and services to consumers.

Owners and managers in today's companies must strive to be flexible to keep up with dynamically changing business environments. In doing so, they often take an entrepreneurial approach to running the business. An **entrepreneur** is someone willing to undertake a venture to create something new. In the traditional view, an entrepreneur is a single individual who sees an opportunity and is willing to work long and hard to turn an idea into a business. Entrepreneurs are typically creative, optimistic, and hard-working individuals who risk their own money to start small companies to make something happen.[3] The story of the entrepreneurial development of the personal computer is well known. Starting out in a garage, two risk-taking individuals with a vision built the first personal computers and then developed Apple Computer into a multinational corporation. Entrepreneurs throughout the world who assume all the risks associated with their innovative ideas have always been in the forefront of new product development.

Entrepreneur
A risk-taking individual who sees an opportunity and is willing to undertake a venture to create a new product or service.

The top managers of many large organizations try to instill an entrepreneurial spirit in their employees. To avoid confusion with the traditional definition of entrepreneur, we define an **intrapreneurial organization** as a large organization that encourages individuals to take risks and gives them the autonomy to develop new products as they see fit.

Intrapreneurial organization
An organization that encourages individuals to take risks and gives them the autonomy to develop new products as they see fit.

Collaboration in the value chain involves creating new value together. Companies link themselves together to achieve a common purpose. Each company values the skills that its partner brings to the collaboration. Kodak and China Lucky Film plan a collaborative effort to establish Kodak in China. Kodak's capabilities include a well-known brand and established operational skill. Collaboration with China Lucky film and its distribution system will allow Kodak to avoid China's 60 percent duty on imported film.[11]

www.kodak.com

operations, such as production, accounting, and pricing, it engages in upstream activities, such as purchasing equipment and materials from suppliers. Downstream activities, performed after the product has been produced, require dealing with other collaborators, such as transportation companies and retailers. These upstream and downstream activities are called *supportive activities*. They provide the support necessary for carrying out primary activities or for concluding the sale of goods or services to the final buyer.

Collaborators in the value chain create new value together.[10] These companies link themselves together to achieve a common purpose. Each company values the skills that its partners bring to the collaboration. By linking their companies' capabilities, the collaborators can increase the value that the ultimate customer obtains.

> BY LINKING THEIR COMPANIES' CAPABILITIES, COLLABORATORS CAN INCREASE THE VALUE THAT THE ULTIMATE CUSTOMER OBTAINS.

exhibit 4-1

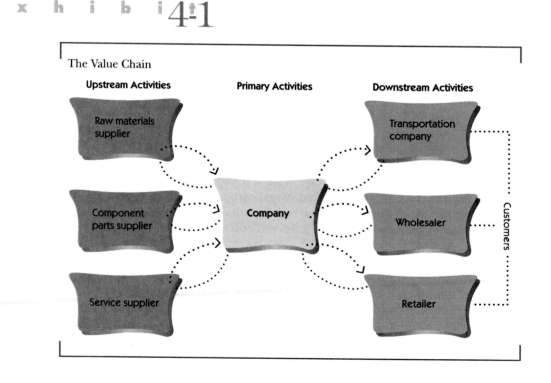

The Value Chain

Core Competencies

Before an organization decides how much it will work with collaborators, its managers should ascertain the company's core competencies.[12] A **core competency** is a proficiency in a critical functional activity—such as technical know-how or a particular business specialization—that helps provide a company's unique competitive advantage. The company may be able to do something that its competitors cannot do at all or that they find difficult to do even poorly.[13] Simply put, core competencies are what the organization does best.

A company enhances its effectiveness by concentrating its resources on a set of core competencies that will allow it to achieve competitive superiority and provide unique or differentiated value for customers. For example, research and development for product design and marketing are Nike's core competencies, not production. Nike manufactures only key technical components of its Nike Air system. All of its shoe production is performed by Asian collaborators.

An understanding of core competencies helps managers determine what value-creating activities can be outsourced. **Outsourcing** means having certain activities performed by collaborators—outside sources. Outsourced activities, such as the production of major parts or subassemblies by suppliers, may be integral to a company's operations. Consider that in Chrysler's Eagle Vision and its other LH series cars, there are ten distinct sections. Chrysler makes the engine, transmission, and metal exterior.[14] The remaining seven sections are made by contract manufacturers such as Textron, which produces and delivers a fully assembled instrument panel containing a speedometer, radio, glove-box door, and air-conditioner louvers. For the 1998 models, Textron became responsible for detailed design and engineering tasks.

> A COMPANY ENHANCES ITS EFFECTIVENESS BY CONCENTRATING ITS RESOURCES ON A SET OF CORE COMPETENCIES THAT WILL ALLOW IT TO ACHIEVE COMPETITIVE SUPERIORITY AND PROVIDE UNIQUE OR DIFFERENTIATED VALUE FOR CUSTOMERS.

The major reason for outsourcing is that, simply put, few companies possess adequate resources and capabilities to perform all primary activities, upstream activities, and downstream activities themselves. In today's era of intense global competition, it would be almost impossible for any organization to have all the necessary competencies that would allow it to excel at every activity in its value chain. Companies that recognize this fact carefully plan their collaborations with other companies so that they can combine complementary strengths to increase customer value.

Companies often have problems when they stray too far from their core competencies. Burger King, for example, expanded its menu with Snickers ice cream bars, chef salads, and Breakfast Buddy and bagel sandwiches. It offered a special dinner service, which included fried shrimp and trays brought to tables by staff.[15] After several years of broadening its offerings, the company realized it had veered too far from its core competencies. Burger King retrenched. It decided to concentrate on the business it knew best—the burger, fries, and drink business. The company now stresses flame broiling, taste, and value.

Relationship Management

Effective executives stress managing the relationships that make the value chain productive. These managers work to build long-term relationships with suppliers,

Core competency
A proficiency in a critical functional area, such as technical know-how or a specialization in a particular aspect of a business, that helps provide a company's unique competitive advantage.

Nike
www.nike.com

Outsourcing
Buying or hiring from outside suppliers.

Burger King
www.burgerking.com

resellers, and ultimately customers who buy their products for consumption. The term **relationship management** is used to communicate the idea that a major goal of business is to build long-term relationships with the parties that contribute to a company's success.

Companies strive to initiate collaborations and build loyalties. It is the manager's job to create, interpret, and maintain the relationships between the company and its collaborators.

Microenvironments and the Four Cs in a Global Economy

"On a political map, the boundaries between countries are as clear as ever. But on a competitive map, a map showing the real flows of financial and industrial activity, those boundaries have largely disappeared."[16]

The world has become a global economy in which corporations market their products in many areas outside their home countries. In consumer electronics, for instance, Japanese marketers like Sony and Panasonic have high market shares in the United States and compete effectively throughout the world. Not only marketing but also manufacturing has taken on an international character

focus on relationships

AMP and Silicon Graphics   Take a look at a dramatic example of successful new-style business relationships. On a recent Saturday afternoon, Rudy Gassner, vice president for capital goods at AMP, a manufacturer of electrical and electronic connectors, was savoring a day off at home in Lemoyne, Pennsylvania, catching up on his reading, when the phone rang. It was Silicon Graphics executive Greg Podshadley. Gassner's eyebrows shot up. Sure, Silicon Graphics was a big, valued customer in a close partnership with AMP, but Podshadley had never butted into his weekend at home before. What Podshadley had to say was equally unexpected. He was in trouble. An electrical connector going into a new workstation was proving so undependable that it threatened major quality problems for the product. No, it wasn't one of AMP's connectors; it was made by a competitor. But could Gassner supply a substitute—and at once? The snafu had brought the whole project to its knees, shutting down the line.

Gassner called his sales manager and sent him and his colleagues to the distribution center to hunt down the needed parts. Combing the cavernous, deserted facility, they hit pay dirt: the right connectors, and enough of them to put Podshadley's line back in business. Trouble was, they needed to use a dauntingly complicated forklift to get the parts, and none of the managers could work it. So, lucky that no underling was around to watch the comedy, they taught themselves by trial and error, picked up the connectors, and drove them to the airport. Silicon Graphics assemblers were soldering them onto circuit boards in California the next day.

Gassner did all this with zero paperwork—and without hinting that that's what happens when you buy from an AMP competitor. Nor did he charge Silicon Graphics a premium for the service. "This is an IOU to collect sometime," says he. Not surprisingly, Podshadley says he owes Gassner a big one. A lot was at stake. "This business is so fast," Podshadley says, "and the technology is so cutting-edge, that there are going to be problems. You can point fingers, and relationships can deteriorate very quickly. You have to work as a team and do what has to be done, or you lose the market."

Companies that succeed at collaborative relationships like this usually set them up routinely, not as exceptions, and with customers and suppliers alike. Effective marketers make clear what it takes to achieve successful collaborations. They spend time determining how to manage them well. They realize what hefty payoffs these relationships can yield—and not just for customer firms taking reduced costs out of suppliers' hides, but for suppliers as well.[17]

for some organizations. Honda lawn mowers, for example, are manufactured in Swepsonville, North Carolina. Is this an American product or a Japanese product?

An organization that sells its products beyond the boundaries of its home nation engages in international marketing. **International marketing** involves the adoption of a marketing strategy that views the world market rather than a domestic market as the forum for marketing operations.

Gillette is one of the many American companies that earn more than half of their profits in foreign markets. This photo shows a retail display in Shanghai, China, where a middle class is emerging.

International marketing
Marketing across international boundaries; also called *multinational marketing*.

Honda
www.honda.com

Many U.S. companies are thoroughly involved in multinational marketing. Gillette, Coca-Cola, and Johnson & Johnson earn well over 50 percent of their profits overseas. The U.S. government encourages U.S. companies to expand their international marketing efforts. The United States is, in fact, a major exporting country in terms of absolute dollar volume.

The United States has passed through a transition period from a domestic orientation to a global orientation. At one time, an American marketer could be content to ignore world trade and compete with other domestic marketers for business in the growing U.S. economy. Today, however, with multinational organizations employing global marketing strategies, a domestic marketer must be aware of foreign competitors' influences not only in international markets but in its own domestic market. Competition is global, and the future of marketing is global. Companies must therefore analyze microenvironments in various parts of the world.[18] For that reason, it is useful to consider global marketing within the framework of the four Cs. We begin by looking at the global consumer.

CUSTOMERS—THE ERA OF THE GLOBAL CONSUMER

International marketers, like marketers in their home countries, focus on satisfying customer needs. These needs often vary by country and culture. For example, Campbell's Soup Company has found that most Americans cringe at the thought of a bowl of pumpkin soup; but in Australia, cream of pumpkin soup is a national favorite—very much what tomato soup is to Americans. Such differences often result from differences in countries' cultural environments.

Sometimes differences are the result of laws shaped by cultural values. For example, foreign marketers are not allowed to advertise their products on Iran's two television channels because of the perceived detrimental Western influence of such products.[20]

Although consumers will no doubt continue

A McDonald's restaurant located in New Delhi, India, is the only one in the world with no beef on the menu.

Some 80 percent of Indians are Hindu, a religion whose adherents don't eat beef and believe cows are a sacred symbol. Instead of the Big Mac, the Indian menu features the Maharaja Mac—"two all-mutton patties, special sauce, lettuce, cheese, pickles, onions on a sesame-seed bun." For the strictest Hindus, who eat no meat at all, there are rice-based patties flavored with peas, carrots, red pepper, beans, coriander, and other spices. McDonald's, which has restaurants in more than 100 countries, adapts its menu to local tastes around the world.[19]

to differ from country to country, they are developing some similar tastes and preferences as the business world becomes more global. Global marketers should recognize both similarities and differences among customers in different areas of the world and incorporate this knowledge into their marketing strategies.[21] The What Went Right? feature describes some similarities among consumers in other countries that may be surprising.

Marketers often view global customers from a regional perspective, reflecting a trend toward formation of multinational economic communities. A **multinational economic community** is a collaboration among countries to increase international trade by reducing trade restrictions. The formation of economic communities not only makes it easier for member nations to trade with each other but also makes it easier for outsiders to trade with member nations.

Perhaps the best-known economic community is the European Union, also known as the European Community or the Common Market. As shown in Exhibit 4-2, it consists of Portugal, France, Ireland, the United Kingdom, Spain, Denmark, Germany, the Netherlands, Belgium, Luxembourg, Italy, Greece, Austria, Finland, and Sweden. Although Europeans have been working on a "borderless" economy for more than 30 years, 1992 finally marked the elimination of

Multinational economic community
A collaboration among countries to increase international trade by reducing trade restrictions. Typically, a group of countries forms a unified market within which there are minimal trade and tariff barriers; the European Union is an example.

European Union
www.eurunion.org

 e x h i b i 4-2

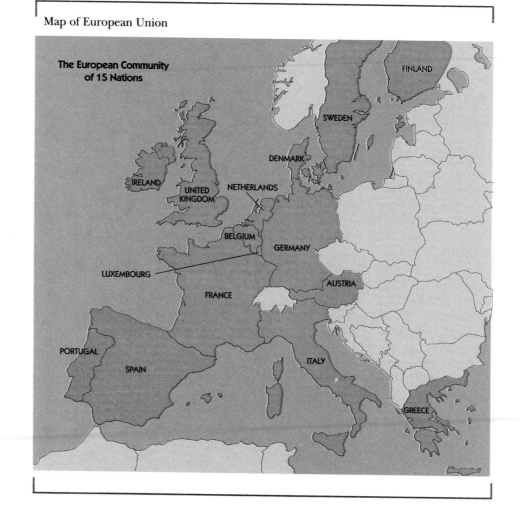

Map of European Union

national trade barriers, differences in tax laws, conflicting product standards, and other restrictions that had kept the member nations from being a single market. Trade within this union almost parallels trade among U.S. states—borders are of minimal significance, and there are no customs controls.

The European Union presents a single market with more than 323 million consumers—an enormous marketing opportunity. It has been estimated that since 1992, the European Union has been the largest single market in the world. Today, market spending within the European Union exceeds $50 trillion. Each year, U.S. companies sell more than $500 billion of goods and services in the European Union.

Furthermore, by the year 2000, this group of economic partners may encompass most of the continent. Iceland, Norway, and Switzerland approved a pact that over time will integrate these countries with the European Union. Three former Eastern bloc countries—the Czech Republic, Hungary, and Poland—are seeking associate status with the European Union, and they may become full members by the turn of the century. Some marketing analysts estimate that in the year 2000, the European Union's trading area will include 450 million people.

In North America, the stage has been set for the development of a single trading market of more than 350 million people. NAFTA, the North American Free Trade Agreement, was passed by the United States Congress in 1993. This agreement, which allows for increased trade among Mexico, Canada, and the United States, has already had a major impact on production location, imports, exports, and unemployment in selected industries.

Tariffs are taxes imposed by a nation on selected imported goods brought into that nation to make those goods more costly in the marketplace. In 1994, as a direct consequence of NAFTA, the United States canceled tariffs on 60 percent of Mexican goods that had been subjected to taxes. Other tariffs are being phased out over a 15-year period. Exports from the United States grew by more than 20 percent in the first 9 months NAFTA was in effect.[23] Mexican

what went right?

American Icons in Europe A television commercial for Dutch radios is set at a railroad crossing in the Arizona desert. A French TV advertisement for cookies features nubile, giggly American girls on a beach somewhere in the United States. Razor blades are being hawked on French television by European actors wearing American football helmets. Meanwhile, a line of French cars is being promoted in a highly stylized TV commercial filmed on a lonely highway in southern California. The accompanying music for the car commercial is the classic American pop tune "On the Road Again" by Canned Heat. A visitor to Europe these days might be astonished to see how American themes and images dominate television and movie commercial advertising. From cookies to razor blades, boom boxes to beer, America increasingly is employed by Europeans to sell European products to fellow Europeans.

American advertising icons such as the Marlboro man and the clean-cut Coca-Cola youth have been familiar faces on European screens for decades. But the widespread use of American settings for European products is something new.

The main reason for the "American sells" trend is simple: In the critical youth and young adult market (ages 15 to 25), American popular culture is more dominant than ever. "The movies they like best are American," said Claire Hakmi, television product director for a French ad agency. "All the sportswear they want is American or modeled on American styles. The sneakers they wear are American. The sweat shirts they wear are American."

Popular fashions are dictated by the powerful American communications industry, but they also represent a casual, open attitude that offers a break from the straitlaced dress and behavior strictures of traditional Europe. "It's the *côté nonchalant*—the relaxed attitude—of the Americans that attracts them," said French advertising executive Jean-Jacques Sibille.

But there is also a more subtle factor behind the Americanization of television and movie trailer advertising on the Old Continent. As Western Europe increasingly becomes a single unified market, advertisers are struggling to find universal, pan-European themes that work in all 15 European Union countries. Experience has shown them that Italian motifs do not necessarily sell soap in Britain; with some exceptions, French themes do not work in Germany. "The German doesn't really want to hear what the French guy has to say about razor blades," said Barrington Hill, an American advertising executive based in London. "But he will listen to an American." Using American themes lets European advertisers bypass historical nationalism and enmities.[22]

consumers bought U.S. products whose production requires technology that Mexico does not yet possess. Consumers in the United States increased purchases of Mexican agricultural products and other goods produced by operations that are labor-intensive. We will continue to discuss global customers and their unique needs throughout this book.

COMPETITORS IN A WORLDWIDE ARENA

We have already mentioned that marketers in the United States and throughout the world are confronted with global competition. Intensified global competition can stimulate and improve domestic competition in an industry. For example, consumers complained for years that American automobile manufacturers were unconcerned about quality and inattentive to market needs. When Japanese and European cars gained a large share of the U.S. auto market, American producers began to remedy these deficiencies. Such improvements in domestic competition spur improvements in living standards as well as general economic well-being.

International marketers hope they can compete on a "level playing field"—an arena in which no one has an "unfair" advantage. However, this is not the case for all products or all markets. Sometimes competitors headquartered in foreign countries enjoy government subsidies or benefit from legislation that grants them other economic advantages in their home markets.

Japanese *keiretsu* provides a good example of a fundamental difference in the way U.S. and Japanese companies conduct business in Japan. A *keiretsu* is a group of companies that form a "corporate family." Bound together by mutual shareholdings or other financial ties, members of the *keiretsu* engage in cooperative business strategies. For example, because Toyota's *keiretsu* includes Koito Manufacturing, an automobile parts company, Koito has special privileges when supplying parts to Toyota. Outside companies find it difficult to market competing products to Toyota in the same way as competitors who are members of Toyota's *keiretsu*.[24]

As mentioned earlier, governments often protect certain domestic industries by imposing **tariffs** on imports, to restrict the activity of foreign companies. Tariffs can have a dramatic impact on foreign competitors. Because the imported products are more expensive (as a result of the tariff), domestic production may be encouraged or consumption of the imported products may be discouraged. For example, at one time the United States imposed a high tariff (50 percent) on imported motorcycles with engines larger than 700cc. Harley-Davidson, the only American-owned motorcycle manufacturer, made no motorcycles with engines smaller than 1000cc and did not care about small-engine motorcycles. As a consequence of the tariff on large-engine imported motorcycles, Harley-Davidson dominated the U.S. market for such machines. Clearly, the existence of high restrictive tariffs in a country can discourage competitors from another nation from marketing in that country.

Import quotas, or government-imposed limits on a type of imported good, are another restrictive factor. Countries trying to promote domestic production or discourage domestic consumption may impose quotas on certain imported products. Some quotas set absolute limits, and goods can be imported only until the set level is reached. After that, no further imports are allowed. Other quotas are linked with tariffs so that an extremely high tariff is levied on goods imported beyond the quota limit. The ultimate forms of restriction are the **embargo**—a government prohibition against trade, often focused on a particular product—and the **boycott**—the refusal of some group or a government to buy a certain product. Either tactic may completely shut down trade with a particular country.

The automotive industry in the United States has been advocating the use of quotas. Faced with increased competition from imported cars and increased pressure from automotive labor unions in the United States, the auto industry and the

Tariff
A tax imposed by a government on an imported product. A tariff is often intended to raise the price of imported goods and thereby give a price advantage to domestic goods.

Import quota
A limit set by a government on how much of a certain type of product can be imported into a country.

Embargo
A government prohibition against trade, especially trade in a particular product.

Boycott
The refusal of some group to buy certain products. A government may enforce a boycott of the products of some other country.

U.S. government have been trying to get Japan to agree to place a limit on the number of cars Japanese companies can export to the United States. Such a restriction would clearly be a form of import quota. Honda and Toyota, as well as Volkswagen and other foreign automobile makers, have established production facilities in the United States partly in response to these pressures.

Governments may impose a variety of other restrictive controls to discourage foreign companies from doing business in their markets. Sometimes countries require that all trade with other nations be approved by some form of central ministry. This allows for the establishment of various types of controls over goods brought into the country. Still other nations set up restrictive criteria to eliminate the importing of certain products. A local government may, for instance, establish buying criteria for food products that effectively prevent food products from being shipped in from certain countries.

Even when there is a level playing field without government restrictions, an exporter may face disadvantages relative to domestic competitors. Procter & Gamble's Pampers, for example, could not beat stiff competition in the Australian and New Zealand markets. Pampers were imported, rather than manufactured locally, and high transportation costs and currency fluctuations meant they had to be priced higher than the competition.[25]

THE COMPANY AS AN INTERNATIONAL MARKETER

Not all U.S.–based companies choose to market their products outside the United States. A bagel bakery may limit its marketing to New York City, for instance. The organization's resources or market demand may justify this strategy. Large corporations, of course, are more likely to find it advantageous to spend considerable time and effort marketing beyond their national boundaries—but not even all large corporations engage in international marketing. Southwest Airlines, for example, chooses to market its services only inside the United States.

focus on global competition

John Deere   Town council members in Greece, New York, a suburb of Rochester, were considering the purchase of a dirt-moving excavator to use for clearing creek beds. The choice was between equipment made by John Deere and equipment made by its only competitor, Komatsu.

During the deliberations, news media reported that a member of Japan's legislature had called American workers lazy. Council members, after receiving many phone calls from constituents urging them to "buy American," voted to buy the John Deere excavator even though the Komatsu machine was $15,000 cheaper.

However, shortly after the decision had been made, local residents and the council learned that the Komatsu brand is made by Komatsu Dresser, an American-Japanese joint venture with headquarters in Lincolnshire, Illinois. Ninety-five percent of the company's dirt movers are made in the United States. The John Deere excavators are produced under a joint venture agreement between Deere and Hitachi. The engines for the John Deere machines are made in the United States, but the machines themselves are made in Japan.

This complicated buying situation reflects how business is conducted in the new global environment. "Who is us?" asks a Harvard professor, illustrating the point that, in today's world—where corporations owned and headquartered in the United States have foreign manufacturing facilities and foreign-owned corporations have assembly plants in the United States—the multinational corporation is truly a world enterprise rather than an organization rooted only in one country. Today's global manager competes in an environment in which the location of the headquarters is not a matter of great significance. "Us" is not necessarily a company, like John Deere, that is headquartered in the United States.[26]

The company that *does* opt to expand into international marketing must consider the same fundamental marketing concepts that apply in domestic marketing. That is, uncontrollable environmental factors must be analyzed, and target markets must be determined. Competitive market positions must be considered, and marketing mix strategies must be planned and executed to appeal to these target markets.

Political stability, tariffs, and exchange rates are some of the factors that a company must take into account when it is making the decision to market in another country. The factors that affect a company's decision to enter a certain market are discussed in Chapter 8, Market Segmentation, Targeting, and Positioning Strategies.

If a company decides to do business in a certain market, it must make decisions about what degree of ownership and management involvement it will pursue. Market potential, the organization's experience in international marketing, the organization's willingness to subject itself to risks, and host country policies often influence these decisions. These factors may cause a multinational marketer to be involved at different levels in different countries.

The basic types of involvement in international markets are direct investment, exporting, and joint venturing. We examine direct investment and exporting next. With joint venturing, we move into the area of collaborations, discussed in the next section. Exhibit 4-3 outlines these strategies.

If foreign market demand is great, a company may invest directly in manufacturing and marketing operations in a host foreign country. This strategy is called

e x h i b i **4-3** Summary of International Involvement

STRATEGY	LOCATION OF PRODUCTION FACILITY	FOREIGN COMPANY'S PRIMARY INVOLVEMENT	OWNER OF FOREIGN OPERATION	CAPITAL OUTLAY REQUIRED BY DOMESTIC COMPANY
DIRECT FOREIGN INVESTMENT	In foreign country	Provides native work force, sales force, and/or intermediaries	Domestic company	High
EXPORTING				
Direct	In domestic country	None	None	Low
Indirect	In domestic country	Acts as intermediary to ensure distribution and sales in foreign country	Company acting as intermediary is foreign owned	Low
JOINT VENTURING				
Licensing/Franchising	In foreign country	Has right to manufacture and service the product and use product name; conducts local marketing efforts	Foreign owned, according to contract	Low
Contract Manufacturing	In foreign country	Manufactures product according to specifications	Production facility is foreign owned	Low
Joint Ownership	In foreign country	Participates as partner	Facilities are owned jointly by domestic and foreign companies, in proportions determined by contract	Moderate to high

direct foreign investment. Coca-Cola owns a bottling plant in Guangzhow (Canton) China, for example. Several Japanese automobile manufacturers have built automobile plants in the United States. This approach enables the automakers to minimize the shipping expenses and political pressures associated with selling foreign-made cars in the U.S. market. In other instances, an organization may invest directly in plant operations in developing countries

WHATEVER THE REASON, DIRECT INVESTMENT IN MANUFACTURING FACILITIES AND MARKETING OPERATIONS REFLECTS A LONG-TERM, HIGH-LEVEL COMMITMENT TO INTERNATIONAL MARKETING.

to take advantage of low-cost labor. Whatever the reason, direct investment in manufacturing facilities and marketing operations reflects a long-term, high-level commitment to international marketing.

Many risks are associated with a long-term direct investment strategy. For example, Iraq's invasion of Kuwait had a major impact on Exxon, Aramco, and other oil companies whose oil-exploration facilities were destroyed or damaged during the Gulf War. In some countries, a change in governments may lead to nationalization of foreign companies' assets—that is, a transfer of the assets to the new government. If the risk of nationalization of a multinational's operations is high, direct investment becomes less attractive.

In contrast to direct investment, **exporting** is a relatively low-level commitment to international marketing. Exporters, manufacturing or harvesting in their home countries, sell some or all of their products in foreign markets. Such distribution may be accomplished either directly, through the company's sales force, or indirectly, through intermediaries. (Thus, exporting may or may not involve collaborators.) There is no investment in overseas plant or equipment in either case.

With indirect exporting, a domestic company does not deal directly with overseas customers. Instead, it sells a portion of its inventory to some intermediary that conducts business in the company's home country; the intermediary then distributes the product in foreign markets. The major strength of the intermediary is its access to and relationship with foreign customers. Some companies that export indirectly do not do so routinely; rather, they view the international marketplace simply as a place to get rid of surplus inventory or unwanted products. Others use indirect exporting continuously and systematically. Whatever the degree of indirect exporting, the company uses its domestic sales force to sell its products to the intermediaries.

A firm may use direct exporting when it wants greater control over the foreign sales of its product. Direct exporting can take several forms. Some companies use their own traveling salespeople, who make occasional visits to overseas markets to try to sell the product there. These salespeople may meet with limited success unless they can cultivate the right prospects and understand what is required to conduct business in another culture. Other companies establish a

German auto maker Mercedes-Benz built a manufacturing plant near Tuscaloosa, Alabama. This action is an example of direct investment.

Export management company
A company that specializes in buying from sellers in one country and marketing the products in other countries. Such companies typically take title to the products.

Joint venturing
In international marketing, an arrangement between a domestic company and a foreign host company to set up production and marketing facilities in a foreign market.

Licensing
In international marketing, an agreement by which a company (the licensor) permits a foreign company (the licensee) to set up a business in the foreign market using the licensor's manufacturing processes, patents, trademarks, trade secrets, and so on, in exchange for payment of a fee or royalty.

domestic-based export department or division. The scope of this unit is determined in part by the degree of commitment the company has to international marketing. Many companies market their products via the World Wide Web to buyers in other countries. When it receives an Internet order the company ships the export order directly to the customer.

In many cases, marketers using direct exporting still maintain a domestic perspective. Organizations with domestic outlooks do not always meet with success in the exporting arena. Therefore, some effective marketers choose to establish overseas sales offices, branches, or distributors to maintain a continuing presence in the host country or overseas market. Such an organization can develop a better understanding of the differences in foreign markets than salespeople making occasional visits.

GLOBAL COLLABORATIONS

Collaborations on a global scale have increased as a result of the globalization of the marketplace. Using export management companies, engaging in joint ventures, and outsourcing to companies operating outside the United States have allowed U.S. companies to marshal more resources for international marketing.

In our discussion of exporting, we mentioned that indirect exporting requires the use of intermediaries. Companies often develop collaborative relationships with **export management companies,** intermediaries that specialize in buying from sellers in one country and marketing the products in other countries. Export management companies, which assume ownership of the goods, reduce the risk of multinational marketing for companies without a great deal of exporting experience. Like other wholesalers, export management companies perform many distribution functions for sellers. However, in most cases, their primary functions are selling and taking responsibility for foreign credit.

Other intermediaries that represent companies in overseas selling activities include various types of export agents, who do not take title to the goods.

In **joint venturing,** domestic and host companies join to set up production and marketing facilities in an overseas market. Unlike exporting, joint venturing involves some agreement for production of the product on foreign soil. The Whirlpool example at the beginning of this chapter discussed joint-venture agreements for operations in the Far East.

There are several forms of joint venturing. (Refer to Exhibit 4-3.) One simple method is **licensing,** in which a domestic company (the licensor) that wishes to do business in a particular overseas market enters into a licensing agreement with an overseas company (the licensee); the agreement permits the licensee to use the licensor's manufacturing processes, patents, trademarks, trade secrets, and so on in exchange for payment of a fee or royalty.

Pepsi Egypt Coca-Cola, which in 1967 left all Arabic countries in the Middle East except Morocco and Tunisia, returned to Egypt in 1978. During Coca-Cola's absence, Pepsi-Cola had become popular with Egyptian consumers.

But ask for a "Peps" in Egypt today and expect to be handed a Coke—a shocking phenomenon in a market where "Peps" has been a generic term for soft drink and the brand of choice for 50 years.

All that changed when the Egyptian government privatized its portion of the soft-drink bottling business. The government's decision to let private enterprise have its portion of the business led to the complete reversal of the two major soft-drink brands' bottling organizations.

Two bottlers previously associated with Pepsi and former partners with the government, Shaher Abdel Hak and his brother Abdel Galil Abdel Hak, turned the Egyptian soft-drink market upside down after they lost a bid for the government's portion of the Pepsi business to another company. When their bid was not accepted, they entered into a joint venture with Atlantic Industries (Coca-Cola Egypt).

Now Coke and Pepsi are battling it out for leadership in Egypt's $400 million market. Before the switch of bottlers, Pepsi brands held 47 percent of the market, compared to Coca-Cola's 38 percent. Today, Coca-Cola has 22 bottling plants and Pepsi has 9. This has boosted Coca-Cola's market share above 60 percent.[27]

Licensing provides a means to conduct business in a country whose laws discourage foreign ownership. One disadvantage of licensing is loss of managerial control. The foreign company makes key decisions without input from the licensor. On the positive side, a licensee may have a greater understanding of the local culture, experience with the local distribution system, and the marketing skill required to succeed in the foreign market.

International franchising is a form of licensing in which a company establishes overseas franchises in much the same way it establishes franchises in its own country. Because many franchisors desire consistency, franchising agreements are most common in markets where conditions are similar to those in the domestic market. A potential disadvantage of international franchising is the possibility that this type of operation will foster future competitors. Sometimes, after gaining enough training and experience, franchisees start their own rival companies.

Some companies believe that the risks of licensing are too great and prefer to maintain greater marketing control. These companies use **contract manufacturing,** under which a company agrees to permit an overseas manufacturer to produce its product. The domestic company supplies the product specifications and the brand name, and the foreign company produces the product under that label for the domestic company. Overseas sales of the product are typically handled and controlled by the domestic company. In Mexico and Spain, for instance, Sears may establish its own stores; but rather than filling these stores with imported products, it often uses local manufacturers to produce Sears-label products to specifications. In many foreign markets, contract manufacturing also offers the opportunity to use labor that is less expensive, thus yielding lower product prices or greater savings to the company.

A final form of joint venturing is the **joint ownership venture.** Under this arrangement, the domestic and foreign partners invest capital and share ownership and control of the partnership in some agreed-on proportion. Ownership is not always equal. AT&T has a joint-venture agreement with PTT Telecom of the Netherlands and Ukraine's State Committee of Communications to modernize phone service in Ukraine, which previously routed long-distance calls through Moscow on poor-quality lines. The venture, which allows Ukrainians to dial foreign countries directly, is owned 39 percent by AT&T, 10 percent by PTT Telecom, and 51 percent by the government of Ukraine.

International franchising
A form of licensing in which a company establishes foreign franchises. Franchising involves a contractual agreement between a franchisor, often a manufacturer or wholesaler, and a franchisee, typically an independent retailer, by which the franchisee distributes the franchisor's product.

Contract manufacturing
In international marketing, an agreement by which a company allows a foreign producer to manufacture its product according to its specifications. Typically, the company then handles foreign sales of the product.

Joint ownership venture
In international marketing, a joint venture in which domestic and foreign partners invest capital and share ownership and control.

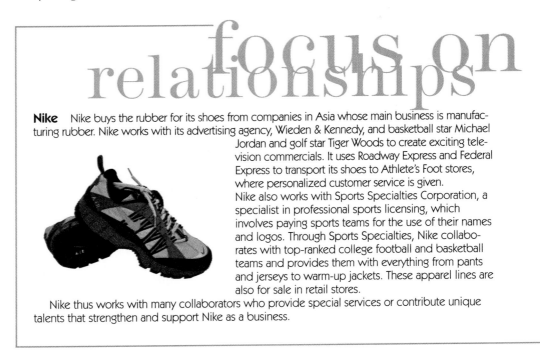

focus on relationships

Nike Nike buys the rubber for its shoes from companies in Asia whose main business is manufacturing rubber. Nike works with its advertising agency, Wieden & Kennedy, and basketball star Michael Jordan and golf star Tiger Woods to create exciting television commercials. It uses Roadway Express and Federal Express to transport its shoes to Athlete's Foot stores, where personalized customer service is given.

Nike also works with Sports Specialties Corporation, a specialist in professional sports licensing, which involves paying sports teams for the use of their names and logos. Through Sports Specialties, Nike collaborates with top-ranked college football and basketball teams and provides them with everything from pants and jerseys to warm-up jackets. These apparel lines are also for sale in retail stores.

Nike thus works with many collaborators who provide special services or contribute unique talents that strengthen and support Nike as a business.

A common reason for entering into a joint ownership venture is that some countries that restrict foreign ownership of investments require such an arrangement. Mexico bars total foreign ownership of Mexican advertising agencies, for example. International agencies such as J. Walter Thompson, Inc., must therefore be involved in joint ownership ventures if they wish to operate in Mexico. In some other countries, the government requires that the local company maintain a majority interest in the venture, keeping foreign control in the company under 50 percent.

Another reason for joint ownership ventures is financial. A U.S. company may wish to set up European operations but may find it economically difficult. A joint ownership venture with a European firm may be the solution.

A key to the success of a joint ownership venture, as with any type of partnership, is finding and keeping the right mix of companies. Foreign and U.S. firms do not always have the same views. Europeans tend to be engineering-oriented, for instance. The term *marketing* may simply mean "sales" to them. In contrast, American companies often put marketing first. Management becomes difficult when the

> A KEY TO THE SUCCESS OF A JOINT OWNERSHIP VENTURE, AS WITH ANY TYPE OF PARTNERSHIP, IS FINDING AND KEEPING THE RIGHT MIX OF COMPANIES.

partners disagree on fundamental components of the business. Whatever the level of collaboration, finding the right partner reduces differences and is vital to success—as illustrated in the accompanying Focus on Relationships feature.

In all global collaborations, technology plays a central role. Satellite communications systems, modems, fax machines, and other advances in information technology have made collaboration with companies in other countries much more efficient. In many cases, instantaneous communication is possible. Global information systems, which are discussed in Chapter 5, have been instrumental in the growth of global business and global collaborations. Many business analysts believe the key to success in the global economy lies in effective use of information technology.

summary

It is useful to organize all microenvironmental forces into four basic categories: company, customers, competitors, and collaborators. These are called the four Cs.

1   *Understand how the microenvironment affects a company's marketing activity.*

The microenvironment consists of the company, its customers, and other economic institutions that shape its marketing practices. Thus, the effect of the microenvironment is regular and direct.

2   *Identify the four Cs of marketing.*

Each C represents a participant that performs essential business activities. The term *company* refers to the business or organization itself. *Customers* are the lifeblood of every company; a company that does not satisfy customers' needs will not stay in business in the long run. *Competitors* are rival companies engaged in the same business. *Collaborators* are persons or companies that work with a marketing company.

3   *Recognize how marketing creates economic utility for customers.*

Marketing includes designing, distributing, and storing products; scheduling their sale; and informing buyers about them. It thus helps to create form utility and creates place, time, and possession utility. Together, these constitute economic utility. By creating economic utility, marketing delivers a standard of living to society.

4 *Identify the various types of competitors and understand how marketers anticipate and react to competitors' strategies.*

Competitors are rival companies interested in selling their products and services to the same group of customers and potential customers. Companies compete on the basis of price, quality, time, and/or location. In general, a price that is lower than competitors' prices will attract customers. Many businesses choose to compete on the basis of quality rather than on the basis of price. Quality-based competition is more complex than price competition because consumers define quality in many different ways. Time-based competition focuses on the fact that buyers prefer to take possession of their goods exactly when they need them, which is often as soon as possible. Location-based competition is based on providing more place utility than competitors do. To establish and maintain a competitive advantage means to be superior to or different from competitors in terms of price, quality, time, or location. This superiority may be accomplished by operating a more efficient factory, by selling at a lower price, by designing better-quality products, or by satisfying customers in other ways.

5 *Describe the value chain and explain why it must be managed.*

The value chain portrays the system of collaborative activities and relationships involved in operating a business. Each link in the chain adds value to the product customers ultimately buy. By managing these collaborations, companies free up their resources so that they can concentrate on what they do best. Having every organization in the value chain focus on core competencies results in lower-cost, better-designed products.

6 *Understand the importance of global competition in today's economy.*

The United States—as well as the rest of the world—has passed through a transition period from a domestic orientation to a global orientation. Today, with multinational organizations employing global marketing strategies, a domestic marketer must be aware of foreign competitors' influence not only in international markets but also in its own domestic market. Markets have been internationalized, competition is global, and the future of marketing is global.

7 *Apply the four Cs in a global business context.*

Because competition is global, companies must analyze microenvironments in various parts of the world. International companies must focus on satisfying customer needs by working with collaborators to gain competitive advantage. The four Cs often vary by country and culture.

key terms

four Cs (p. 99)
company (p. 99)
entrepreneur (p. 99)
intrapreneurial organization (p. 99)
customer (p. 100)
economic utility (p. 100)
form utility (p. 100)
place utility (p. 100)
time utility (p. 100)
possession utility (p. 100)
competitor (p. 100)
product category (p. 101)
product class (p. 101)
brand (p. 101)

price competition (p. 101)
quality-based competition (p. 102)
time-based competition (p. 102)
location-based competition (p. 102)
collaborator (p. 103)
supplier (p. 103)
value chain (p. 103)
core competency (p. 105)
outsourcing (p. 105)
relationship management (p. 106)
international marketing (p. 107)
multinational economic
   community (p. 108)

tariff (p. 110)
import quota (p. 110)
embargo (p. 110)
boycott (p. 110)
direct foreign investment (p. 113)
exporting (p. 113)
export management company (p. 114)
joint venturing (p. 114)
licensing (p. 114)
international franchising (p. 115)
contract manufacturing (p. 115)
joint ownership venture (p. 115)

questions for review & critical thinking

1. State what each of the four Cs stands for, and give an example of each.
2. Who are a professional soccer team's competitors?

3. What are the core competencies of the following organizations?
   a. Levi Strauss
   b. Southwest Airlines

c. Chicago Bulls
d. AT&T

4. Identify the participants in a value chain that brings automobiles to the ultimate consumer.
5. Identify the competitive advantages of the following products:
   a. Lennox air conditioners
   b. Scribner's bookstores
   c. DeBeers diamonds
   d. VISA credit cards
   e. TCI Cablevision
6. Why is global collaboration growing in importance?
7. Explain how global competition affects a small business in your college town.
8. What factors affect a company's ability to compete in international markets?

9. Japan has manufactured automobiles in the United States for more than a decade. What impact has this development had on the world automobile market?
10. Compare and contrast direct foreign investments and joint ownership ventures.
11. Suppose you are the marketing manager of a company that outsources key components of the product it manufactures. What are the job titles of the people in the supplier company with whom you work? As a customer, should your company maintain total control, or should you try to think of the supplier as your collaborator in a joint effort?

marketing plan—right or wrong?

1. Hoover Ltd. sells a variety of floor-care products and other appliances in Europe. The plan was that consumers in Britain and Ireland who bought Hoover appliances would be eligible for a pair of round-trip tickets to destinations in either Europe or the United States. The programs were arranged in collaboration with two travel agencies. The agencies were to obtain low-cost "space-available" tickets and to help Hoover support the expense by sharing commissions on "land packages" such as car rental and hotels at the destination.
2. Pepsi left South Africa in 1985 during the apartheid era. In 1986, Coca-Cola closed its South African concentrate plant but continued to operate out of Swaziland and to market Coca-Cola in the South African market. Pepsi returned after the end of apartheid with a joint venture with a South African bottler. In 1997 Pepsi had less than 5 percent of the market, whereas Coke had a commanding 80 percent of the market. Pepsi's plan was to pull out of South Africa's soft-drink market.

internet insights

zikmund.swcollege.com

exercises

1. Go to the Yahoo search engine (www.yahoo.com) and enter "European Union" as a search phrase. What type of information is available?
2. Use the Internet to learn what you can about Indonesia.
   a. Use your Web browser to go to www.indonesiatoday.com. What type of information is available at this site?
   b. Visit the CIA FACTBOOK (www.odci.gov/cia/publications/factbook/index.html). Then navigate to "Indonesia." What type of information is available?
   c. Use Infoseek and type in "Indonesia" as a search word. How much information is available?

3. If your college or university has an account (identification number and password) with Stat-USA, use the Internet to learn what types of reports are available from the NTDB (National Trade Data Base).

address book (useful urls)

Online Atlas	www.magellangeo.com
Current Exchange Rates	www.travelfinder.com/currency.html

ethically right or wrong?

Not long ago, Disney wanted to build a new theme park that explored American history. The company planned to locate the park in northern Virginia, 35 miles from Washington, D.C., and near many Civil War battlefields and other historical sites that are now part of the national park system. Most Virginians supported the Disney plan—including the governor, who envisioned the creation of 19,000 jobs. However, critics argued that history should not be presented in an amusement park setting and that Disney's "competitive" effort would result in fewer visits to real historical sites. In addition to asserting that Disney would trivialize U.S. history, critics argued that the park would cause air pollution and traffic gridlock. Although some residents of the area welcomed the prospect of a theme park, others believed it would disrupt the community's tranquil lifestyle. In September 1994, Disney abandoned its plans.

QUESTIONS
1. In abandoning its plans, did Disney make a socially responsible decision, or was it forced to abandon the plans because of unfair forces in the microenvironment?
2. Make a judgment as to whether the park should be built at a different location in Virginia or in Maryland.

TAKE A STAND
1. Is it ethical for a company to engage in international trade and work with collaborators in the People's Republic of China, a communist country that has been accused of human rights violations?
2. Often, when a company enters into a collaborative relationship with a single supplier, other suppliers are locked out of doing business with that company for several years. Is this practice consistent with the free enterprise system?
3. A multinational food company markets powdered milk around the world. Critics say that many mothers in underdeveloped countries do not understand that mixing the powder with impure water is unsafe. These critics believe that because many mothers are incapable of using the product properly, the product should be distributed only through physicians and hospitals. Do you agree that this collaboration is necessary?

Gaston's White River Resort *Focus on Small Business*

Gaston's White River Resort, a ten-cottage trout-fishing camp at the end of a country road near Lakeview in northern Arkansas, was having trouble staying afloat in 1965. Revenues were insufficient, and the bank was moving toward foreclosure. Jim Gaston, the resort's young owner, had some ideas about saving it, though, and the bank listened to him. Instead of foreclosing, it granted him a new $15,000 loan.

Gaston was thinking big. In 1965 at an Arkansas fishing resort you rented a room with carpetless, linoleum floors for $7.50 a day. If you wanted TV it was $1 extra, and the same for air conditioning. Gaston began charging $10 a night for a room with carpeting, air conditioning, and TV. The local competition thought he had lost his mind, but a growing clientele supplied evidence that he hadn't.

Actually, Gaston felt the challenge was to compete with much more than the fishing camp down the road. He was after a world market, competing with the fishing experience in New York, or Canada, or Wisconsin, or Alaska.

To help make his resort world-class, he hired his own fishing guides, whom he describes as the best on the White River. He says other fishing camps rely on a pool of guides, and their best customers may not get the best service. His customers do, he says.

He required all his employees (today there are 75 year-round and 47 more in the summer) to pay precise attention to customer satisfaction. You will never find resort employees more helpful than those at Gaston's, he boasts. The resort has a high rate of repeat guests.

Gaston learned to maintain contact with members of the outdoors press, writers for such publications as *Field and Stream* or *Fly Fisherman*, and to promote his resort as a place where corporate types could get away from it all. He installed a landing strip.

He also learned to market to a clientele that changes with the seasons: Arkansans in late winter, Texans and other out-of-staters in the summer; couples in the off season, families with kids in the peak season. Gaston keeps track of customer patterns by computer, to the point where he says he almost knows too much. Operation modes, he says, must change about four times a year to match the crowd.

In that crowd, which is bringing Gaston's White River Resort $5 million in annual sales and has required an increase in the number of its cottages to 73, are faces familiar to many Americans. TV's Phil Donahue, for example, settles in once a year with a group of friends from his college days at Notre Dame. Jim Gaston says he considers it a high compliment that a man who could charter a cruise ship comes back again and again to stay in one of his cottages, eat in his restaurant, and fish for trout in one of his 20-foot john boats.[28]

QUESTIONS

1. Use the four Cs concept to describe Gaston's marketing microenvironment.
2. How has Gaston's established a competitive advantage?
3. How important is relationship management to Gaston's success? Identify several ways Gaston's has built strong relationships with its customers and collaborators.

Sonic Drive-Ins   *Focus on Small Business*

Sonic Corp., of Oklahoma City, Oklahoma, has a history of more than 40 years as a fast-food drive-in franchise chain.

The company has seen growth, decline, and then stronger growth since its start in 1953 in Shawnee, Oklahoma, where founder Troy Smith put covered stalls in his hamburger-stand parking lot, each with a speaker system. Customers ordered a hamburger and a drink from their cars, and a carhop would bring the orders.

By 1958 Smith and a partner had four drive-in hamburger stands. Their slogan was "Service with the speed of sound."

Sonic drive-ins spread across Oklahoma and into neighboring Kansas and Texas. Each drive-in operator was also a part owner. These owner-managers did not contribute to advertising, enjoyed no territorial rights, and paid a one-cent royalty per sandwich bag.

In the late 1960s and early '70s, as the number of drive-ins grew to more than 150, the company was reorganized several times. A group of franchisees bought Sonic's name, slogan, trademark, logos, and supply division. They offered other operators the option to buy stock, and Sonic Industries became a publicly traded company.

By 1978 there were 800 drive-ins in more than a dozen states. But field support was lagging, and some locations did not follow established operating standards. Sonic's sales began to decline. By 1981, 300 drive-ins had closed.

In 1983 C. Stephen Lynn, an experienced franchising and fast-food executive, was brought in as president to turn the company around. He worked to build unity within the owner-operated chain.

To begin, he focused on 17 key markets. He persuaded operators of 200 drive-ins there to commit to purchase and advertise together for one year, promising the arrangement would increase same-store sales 15 percent and cut food costs 3 percent.

Performance was as good as Lynn said it would be. Today 95 percent of the chain, linked in advertising co-ops, spends more than $20 million a year on advertising, and 99 percent of the chain buys food and other supplies together.

Working capital to set up and administer the co-operative programs, and to provide field support, was produced when Lynn orchestrated a $10 million leveraged buyout of the company in 1986. In 1991 a public offering raised $52 million with which Sonic bought out venture capital investors, paid off debt, and added to working capital.

Today there are more than 1,400 Sonic drive-ins in 25 sun-belt states, and sales have been increasing at a 14.4 percent annual compounded rate. The decline under way in the early 1980s has been replaced by something of a Sonic boom.[29]

QUESTIONS

1. Describe Sonic's microenvironment using the four Cs perspective.
2. What were the key elements of Sonic's competitive strategy?
3. What aspects of the macroenvironment are most likely to affect the company's competitive strategy?
4. Why do you think the new president was able to turn the company around?

enhance your
marketing skills

You will find each exercise on the CD-ROM developed for use with this textbook. Each exercise has a name and is located within a module. For example, exercise 2 can be found in the Strategy Module by clicking on The Organizational Context of Marketing.

MACROMARKETING MODULE
Ethics

1. How do other functional activities within an organization, such as production and finance, influence marketing activities?

STRATEGY MODULE
The Organizational Context of Marketing

2. If you were to give an award to companies that have excellent total quality management programs, what criteria would you use to evaluate quality?

STRATEGY MODULE
Managing for Quality as a Strategy

3. What are the factors that influence ethical decision making in marketing?

cross-functional
insights

Many theories and principles from other business disciplines can provide insights about the role marketing plays in an organization. The questions in this section are designed to help you think about integrating what you have learned about management, finance, production, and other functional areas taught in business courses with the marketing principles explained in this textbook.

Marketing Concept/Market-Driven Organizations
The marketing concept stresses consumer orientation, long-run profitability, and integrating marketing functions with other corporate functions. Companies that have superior skill in understanding and satisfying customers are said to be market-driven.

What are the key revenue and expense items that influence an organization's long-run profitability?

Are entrepreneurs consumer-oriented? What characteristics of entrepreneurs would help them become successful marketers?

What traits should a person have to be a leader in a market-driven organization?

Does management contingency theory apply to marketing leadership positions?

Customer Satisfaction Market-oriented organizations embrace an organization-wide focus to learn their customers'

needs so they can offer superior customer value—that is, so they can satisfy customer needs better than their competitors. Marketers should strive to increase customer satisfaction.

How important is a company's corporate culture in such efforts? What type of corporate culture would contribute most to the achievement of the goal of satisfying customers?

What type of performance appraisal system could be used to evaluate employees in terms of customer satisfaction?

Organizational Mission Top managers identify the organizational, or corporate, mission. This strategic decision influences all other marketing strategies. An organizational mission is a statement of company purpose. It explains why the organization exists and what it hopes to accomplish. It provides direction for the entire organization. When we discussed corporate mission statements, we looked at the mission from a marketing perspective.

What aspects of a mission statement would be important to a manager of human resources? A manager of engineering? A financial manager?

Total Quality Management A company that employs a total quality management strategy must evaluate quality through the eyes of the customer. Every aspect of the business must focus on quality—for example, management may institute a performance appraisal system to evaluate employees in terms of the service they provide to customers. Further, all participants must strive for continuous improvement.

Total quality management requires the cooperation of marketing, production, and many other functional areas of the business. How should this coordination be managed?

How important is knowledge of statistical analysis and statistical process control in analyzing a total quality management system?

What type of performance appraisal system could be used to evaluate employees in terms of the quality of goods and services produced?

Do companies need to solicit the opinions of as many employees as possible to be successful in a total quality effort?

Differentiation Strategy A differentiation strategy emphasizes offering a product that is unique in the industry, provides a distinct advantage, or is otherwise set apart from competitors' brands in some way other than price.

How do the laws of supply and demand apply to a marketer of branded goods or services that seeks to differentiate them from those of competitors? Would economists and marketers give the same answer to this question?

SWOT Situation analysis is the diagnostic activity of interpreting environmental conditions and changes in light of the organization's ability to capitalize on potential opportunities and to ward off problems. SWOT stands for external strengths and weaknesses and internal opportunities and threats.

How would a company's financial analysts look at internal opportunities and threats?

How would a top executive's chief concerns about internal opportunities and threats differ from marketers' concerns, if at all?

What is opportunity cost, and how does it relate to the strategic marketing process and SWOT analysis?

Competitive Advantage One of the most common goals of a business unit is to establish and maintain a competitive advantage—to be superior to or favorably different from competitors in a way that is important to the market.

Marketers think increasing customer satisfaction through product development is the key to competitive advantage. In what other ways might a top executive have the organization strive for competitive advantage?

Discuss marketing strategies for competitive advantage in the context of antitrust laws such as the Sherman Antitrust Act and the Federal Trade Commission Act.

Diversification Marketing new products to a new set of customers is called diversification.

What economic factors might bar a company from entering a market?

What organizational changes are necessary when a company diversifies?

Control To marketers, the purpose of managerial control is to ensure that planned activities are completely and properly executed.

What role does accounting play in the marketing control process?

Do organizational conflicts arise between marketers and accountants because of different perspectives on control activities?

Four Cs Working with collaborators is becoming increasingly important.

What organizational adjustments must be made when a company decides to form a strategic alliance or other collaboration with another company?

Core Competencies A core competency is a proficiency in a critical functional activity, such as technical knowhow or a particular business specialization, that helps provide a company's unique competitive advantage.

At what level in the organization are core competencies determined? By what process?

International Marketing International marketing involves the adoption of a marketing strategy that views the world market rather than a domestic market as the basis for marketing operations.

What adjustments must a company make in its organizational structure when it becomes an international organization?

there is one thing stronger than all the armies in the world, and that is an idea whose time has come

Analysis of Market and Buyer Behavior

—WHO SAID THIS?

part 2

ere is one thing ronger than all e armies in e world, and that an idea whose me has me

—VICTOR HUGO

Victor Hugo (1802-1885) was one of the greatest writers of all time. He wrote *Les Miserables* and *The Hunchback of Notre Dame* more than one hundred years ago, yet they remain popular today. The above quote is from his "Histoire d'un Crime" (1852), and concludes, "An invasion of armies can be resisted; but not an idea whose time has come."

chapter 5

Information Technology and Marketing Research

LEARNING OBJECTIVES

After you have studied this chapter, you will be able to:

Explain why information is essential to effective marketing decision making.

1

Explain the importance of worldwide information systems.

2

Describe a decision support system.

3

Explain the contribution of marketing research to effective decision making.

4

Describe the stages in the marketing research process.

5

(continued on next page)

chee-tos,

the cheesy corn puffs, were introduced in the United States almost 50 years ago. Recently, Frito-Lay's Chee-tos became the first major brand of snack food to be made and marketed in China. Frito-Lay's research established that annual per-capita expenditure on snack food in China—nearly zero—was small compared to the $35 per-capita expenditure in the Netherlands and the $52 per person in the United States. Yet the large number of people in China indicated a vast market potential if the company could successfully introduce its brand into the market.

Marketing research also showed that cheese and other dairy products are not regular items in the Chinese diet. In addition, product taste tests revealed that traditional cheese-flavored Chee-tos did not appeal to Chinese consumers.

Rather than be discouraged by these findings, Chee-tos' marketing managers decided that additional marketing research was needed to investigate how the company could creatively adapt its product for the Chinese market. The company conducted consumer research with 600 different flavors to learn what flavors would be most appealing. Among the flavors that Chinese consumers

CHEE-TOS' MARKETING MANAGERS DECIDED THAT MARKETING RESEARCH WAS NEEDED TO INVESTIGATE HOW THE COMPANY COULD CREATIVELY ADAPT ITS PRODUCT FOR THE CHINESE MARKET.

tested and disliked were: ranch dressing, nacho, Italian pizza, Hawaiian barbecue, peanut satay, North Sea crab, chili prawn, coconut milk curry, smoked octopus, caramel, and cuttlefish. Research did show some flavors consumers liked. So, when Chee-tos were introduced to China, they came in two flavors: Savory American Cream and Zesty Japanese Steak.

Although cheese-less Chee-tos may seem like a contradiction in terms, it mattered little in the Chinese market. After 6 months Chee-tos were a such a big hit that processing plants had trouble keeping Chinese retailers' shelves stocked.

The brand name Chee-tos corresponds to the Chinese characters *qi duo,* translated as "new surprise." The name is fortunate for the marketers at Frito-Lay. However, Frito-Lay did not count on good fortune to achieve success in the Chinese market. The company spent considerable effort researching flavors and learning how the Chinese would react to Chester Cheetah as a spokestoon in advertising, because the company did not want a surprise like the one it got in the United Kingdom.

In 1990 Chee-tos were introduced to the United Kingdom with little, if any, consumer research. The

London managers boldly stormed ahead using the American flavors and positioning strategy. The product bombed. The company had not worked diligently to understand the United Kingdom's snacking behaviors and adapt the product characteristics to local tastes.[1]

Although many factors contributed to Chee-tos' success in China, marketing research was a major influence. Frito-Lay understands the importance of information to modern marketing managers in the United States and around the globe. This chapter focuses on how marketing managers use marketing information, especially marketing research.

The chapter begins with a discussion of the role information plays in the marketing decision-making process and goes on to discuss worldwide information systems, decision support systems, data-based marketing, and data mining. The stages in the marketing research process are then described in detail. The chapter ends with an explanation of the importance of accurate sales forecasting.

Frito-Lay
www.fritolay.com

Information: The Basis of Effective Marketing

Marketing managers spend much of their time making decisions. An integral aspect of decision making is the analysis and evaluation of information about the organization's customers, environment, and marketing activities. To be effective, the marketer needs to gather enough information to understand past events, to identify what is occurring now, and to predict what might occur in the future. Good, timely marketing information is an extremely valuable management tool because it reduces uncertainty and the risks associated with decision making. Marketing information can lead the marketing manager to develop new products, to improve existing products, and to make changes in price, promotion, and distribution strategies and tactics. Information can also help define problems or identify opportunities. Once a marketing problem or opportunity is identified, further pertinent information can be systematically gathered to help the marketing manager deal objectively with the situation.

Worldwide Information Systems in the 21st Century

The well-being of business organizations that hope to prosper in the 21st century depends on information about the world economy and global competition. Contemporary marketers require timely and accurate information from around the globe to maintain competitive advantages. In today's world, managers find that much information is available instantaneously. This fact has changed the nature of marketing decision making.

As a result of increased global competition and technological advances, worldwide information systems have developed. A **worldwide information system** is an organized collection—of telecommunications equipment, computer hardware and software, data, and personnel—designed to capture, store, update, manipulate, analyze, and immediately display information about worldwide business activity.[2] Worldwide information systems are made possible by satellite communication, high-speed microcomputers, electronic data interchanges, fiber optics, CD-ROM data storage, fax machines, the Internet, and other technological advances involving interactive media. When executives at Motorola must make pricing decisions about cellular phones for their European markets, they can get information about international currency and exchange rates immediately,

Worldwide information system
An organized collection—of telecommunications equipment, computer hardware and software, data, and personnel—designed to capture, store, update, manipulate, analyze, and immediately display information about worldwide business activity.

without leaving their desks. A salesperson who needs information about a corporation's executives can access a full report on the corporation from a remote location using a personal communication device and the Internet. A marketing manager who requires a bibliography on a particular subject can generate hundreds of abstracts with a few simple keystrokes.

Consider these examples of the dramatic influence of worldwide information systems on the way two companies do business.

United Parcel Service
www.ups.com

- Every evening, Wal-Mart transmits millions of characters of data about the day's sales to its apparel suppliers. Wrangler, a supplier of blue jeans, shares some of the data and a model that interprets the data. It also shares software applications that act to replenish stocks in Wal-Mart stores. This decision support sys-

tem determines when to send specific quantities of specific sizes and colors of jeans to specific stores from specific warehouses. The result is a learning loop that lowers inventory costs and leads to fewer stockouts.

- At any moment, on any day, United Parcel Service (UPS) can track the status of its shipments around the world. UPS drivers use hand-held electronic clipboards, called delivery information acquisition devices (DIAD), to record data about each pickup or delivery. The data are then entered into the company's main computer for record keeping and analysis. Then, using a satellite telecommunications system, UPS can track any shipment for its customers.

The age of global information has begun, and worldwide information systems have already changed the nature of business. Yet, as amazing as today's technology is, it will seem primitive in the 21st century.

Data and Information

We have been discussing information in a general sense. Before we go on, we must define the difference between information and data. **Data** are simply facts—recorded measures of certain phenomena—whereas **information** is a body of facts in a format suitable for use in decision making. The proper collection of data is the cornerstone of any information system. The data collected should be pertinent, timely, and accurate. There are two types of data: primary data and secondary data. **Primary data** are data gathered and assembled specifically for the project at hand. For example, a company that designs an original questionnaire and conducts a survey to learn about its customers' characteristics is collecting primary data. **Secondary data** are data previously collected and assembled for some purpose other than the project at hand. Secondary data come from both internal sources, such as accounting records, and sources external to the organization, such as U.S. Bureau of the Census data on the Internet. Generating information may require collecting secondary data, primary data, or both.

Decision Support Systems

To store data and to transform data into accessible information, companies use computer systems called **decision support systems**.[3] Such systems serve specific business units within a company. A business unit's decision support system is not independent of the corporation's worldwide information system. Indeed, a large organization may have several decision support systems linked into its worldwide information system.

Data
Facts and recorded measures of phenomena.

Information
Data in a format useful to decision makers.

Primary data
Data gathered and assembled specifically for the project at hand.

Secondary data
Data previously collected and assembled for some purpose other than the one at hand.

Decision support system
A computer system that stores data and transforms it into accessible information. It includes databases and software.

The Decision Support System

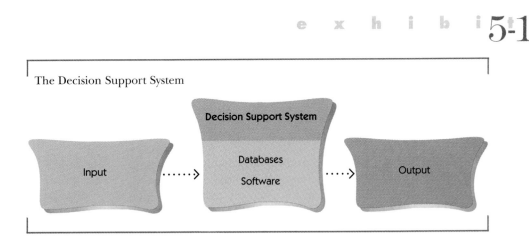

The purpose of a decision support system is to allow decision makers to answer questions through direct interaction with databases. As Exhibit 5-1 shows, the system consists of databases and software.

A **database** is a collection of data, arranged in a logical manner and organized in a form that can be stored and processed by a computer. For example, customer names, addresses, zip codes, and previous purchases may be contained in a company's internal database. Another database may record population and income data by geographical area, based on zip codes.

Many commercial organizations assemble and market computerized databases. For example, Information Resources, Inc. is an innovative organization that is leading the trend toward use of new technologies in marketing research. The organization specializes in providing data about brand and product sales, known as scanner data. Optical scanners in supermarkets read and record the *universal product code (UPC)* of each product sold. The UPC contains product identification information, such as package size, flavor, price, and so on. Information Resources organizes the scanner data into an appropriate format for competitive analysis. Marketers who use the company's reports can analyze them to determine which package sizes sell best, what price is most effective, and how their brands are doing in relation to the competition.

Many commercial databases may be accessed through telecommunication links or via the Internet. Dialog Information Service, ABI/Inform, Dow Jones News/Retrieval, and many other database services make economics statistics, industry news, journal articles, and other data instantaneously accessible to an organization's computers.

Internal records and company reports provide a wealth of information related to costs, shipments, sales, and so on. For example, the database collected by accounting and other personnel can be used to generate a number of reports that managers use to improve performance. A product manager can ask for weekly (or daily) computer-generated reports of sales by

Database
A collection of data, arranged in a logical manner and organized in a form that can be stored and processed by a computer.

Pizza Hut maintains a database on what types of pizza people have previously ordered.

www.pizzahut.com

product line, inventory levels, back orders, and other performance measures. The information about sales of a company's products can be displayed as numerical data or in easy-to-follow, brightly colored graphs.

The **software** portion of a decision support system consists of various types of programs that tell computers, printers, and other hardware what to do. Advances in spreadsheet and statistical software have revolutionized the analysis of marketing data. A decision support system's software allows managers to combine and restructure databases, assess relationships, estimate variables, and otherwise analyze the relevant databases.

Most of today's software is so user-friendly that it is easy for nonexperts to maintain direct control over the computer's tasks and outcomes. A manager can sit at a computer terminal and instantaneously retrieve data files and request special, creative analyses to refine, modify, or generate information in a tailor-made format. At Kmart, a computerized point-of-sale checkout system and a satellite communications system linked to a marketing decision support system allow managers at headquarters to retrieve and analyze up-to-the-minute sales data on all merchandise for the company's 2,400 stores.

Intranets

If a company's decision support system is a private data network that uses Internet standards and technology, it is called an **intranet.**[4] The information on an intranet (data, graphics, even video and voice) is available only inside the organization. Thus, a key difference between the Internet and an intranet is that "firewalls," or security software programs, are installed to limit access to only those employees authorized to enter the system.[5]

A company's intranet uses Internet features, such as electronic mail, Web pages, and browsers, to build a communications and data resource at a specific company.[6] Company information is accessible using the same point and click technology people are accustomed to using to access the Internet. Managers and employees use links to get complete, up-to-date information. An intranet lets authorized personnel—some of whom may previously have been isolated on departmental local area networks—look at product drawings, employee newsletters, sales reports, and other kinds of company information. Whether the information comes from a spreadsheet or a word processing document is not an issue to the user of an intranet. Managers and employees do not have to worry about the format of the information. In short, setting up an intranet involves adding the functionality of the World Wide Web to an organization's existing worldwide information system.

Data-Based Marketing

Many organizations create databases containing huge amounts of data about individual customers and potential customers. Marketers use this information to generate computerized mailing lists and individualized promotional messages. The practice of maintaining customer databases with customers' names, addresses, phone numbers, past purchases, responses to previous offers, and demographic characteristics is referred to as **data-based marketing.** Databases may be compiled by the organization and/or purchased from organizations that specialize in compiling "mailing lists" or other forms of databases. *Relational database software* is an important part of data-based marketing because it allows marketers to relate records in one database, such as sales representatives' customer orders, to records in another database, such as products ready to ship.[7]

In recent years, organizations have begun using the Internet to compile databases. For example, the first time Internet users visit certain Web sites they must fill out a registration form before they get access to the site. The marketer can collect address information and ask visitors about such matters as their interests

Software
Various types of programs that tell computers, printers, and other hardware what to do.

Intranet
A company's private decision support system that uses Internet standards and technology.

Data-based marketing
The practice of using databases of customers' names, addresses, phone numbers, past purchases, responses to previous offers, and demographic characteristics in making marketing decisions.

and demographic background. Then, through use of relational database software, this information can be combined with other databases.

Data-based marketing has implications for many aspects of marketing strategy, especially market segmentation and relationship marketing. This topic will be discussed throughout the book.

DATA-BASED MARKETING HAS IMPLICATIONS FOR MANY ASPECTS OF MARKETING STRATEGY, ESPECIALLY MARKET SEGMENTATION AND RELATIONSHIP MARKETING.

Data Mining

Large corporations' decision support systems often contain millions or even hundreds of millions of records of data.[8] These data volumes are too large and complex for an individual manager to interpret. Consider, for example, a credit card company collecting data on customer purchases. Each customer might make an average of 10 transactions in a month, or 120 per year. With 3 million customers and 5 years of data, it's easy to see how record counts quickly grow beyond the comfort zone for most humans.[9]

Data mining may use powerful computers to dig through exceedingly large volumes of data to discover patterns about an organization's customers. This ad for IBM data mining software showing two very different people says "To our data mining system, they're twins. Both are opera-loving frequent flyers; equally likely prospects for a travel package to La Scala, although unlikely seatmates."

When the number of distinct pieces of information contained in each data record and data volume grows too big, end users don't have the capacity to make sense of it all. Data mining helps managers understand the underlying meaning of the data. The term **data mining** refers to the use of powerful computers to dig through huge volumes of data to discover patterns in an organization's customers and products. One data mining application analyzes a store's point-of-sale transaction records to identify purchases made at the same time or associations between products purchased and other retail shopping information.[10] Consider this example: Grocery chains that have mined the databases provided by their checkout scanners have found that when men go to a supermarket to buy diapers in the evening between 6:00 p.m. and 8:00 p.m., they sometimes walk out with a six-pack of beer as well. Knowing this behavioral pattern, a supermarket chain might lay out its stores so that diapers and beer are closer together.[11]

Data mining
The use of powerful computers to dig through large volumes of data to discover puchasing patterns among an organization's customers.

What Is Marketing Research?

Any discussion of the importance of information to the marketer must include a discussion of marketing research. Marketing research allows managers to make decisions based on objective data, gathered systematically, rather than on intuition.

What is the distinction between marketing research and other forms of marketing information? Even without a formal research program, a manager will have some information about what is going on in the world. Simply by reading the newspaper or watching TV, he or she may discover that a competitor has announced a new product, that the inflation rate is stabilizing, or that a new highway will be built and a shopping mall erected north of town. All of these things may affect the marketer's business, and this information is certainly handy to have, but is it the result of marketing research?

Marketing research
The systematic and objective process of generating information for use in marketing decision making.

The answer to this question is no. **Marketing research** is the systematic and objective process of generating information for use in making marketing decisions. This process includes defining the problem and identifying what information is required to make a decision about the problem, designing a method for collecting information, managing and implementing the collection of data, analyzing the results, and communicating the findings and their implications.[12]

This definition suggests that marketing research is a special effort rather than a haphazard attempt at gathering information. Thus, glancing at a news magazine on an airplane or overhearing a rumor is not conducting marketing research. Even if a rumor or a fact casually overheard becomes the foundation of a marketing strategy, that strategy is not a product of marketing research because it was not based on information that was systematically and objectively gathered and recorded. The term *marketing research* suggests a specific, serious effort to generate new information. The term *research* suggests a patient, objective, and accurate search.

Although marketing managers may perform the research task themselves, they often seek the help of specialists known as marketing researchers. The researchers' role requires detachment from the question under study. If researchers cannot remain impartial, they may try to prove something rather than to generate objective data. If bias of any type enters into the investigative process, the value of the findings must be questioned. Yet this sort of thing can happen relatively easily. For example, a developer who owned a large parcel of land on which she wanted to build a high-price, high-prestige shopping center conducted a study to demonstrate to prospective mall occupants that there was an attractive market for such a center. By conducting the survey only in elite neighborhoods, she generated "proof" that area residents wanted a high-prestige shopping center.

Misleading "research" of this kind must be avoided. Unfortunately, business people with no knowledge of proper marketing research methods may inadvertently conduct poorly designed, biased studies or may be sold such work by marketing research firms. All business people should understand marketing research well enough to avoid these mistakes.

The Stages in the Research Process

Marketing is not an exact science like physics, but that does not mean that marketers and marketing researchers should not try to approach their jobs in a scientific manner. Marketing research is a systematic inquiry into the characteristics of the marketplace, just as astronomy is a systematic investigation of the stars and planets. Both use step-by-step approaches to gain knowledge.

The steps in the research process are highly interrelated, and one step leads to the next. Moreover, the stages in the research process often overlap. Disappointments encountered at one stage may necessitate returning to previous stages or even starting over. Thus, it is something of an oversimplification to present marketing research as a neatly ordered sequence of activities. Still, marketing research often follows a generalized pattern of seven stages. These stages are (1) defining the problem, (2) planning the research design, (3) selecting a sample, (4) collecting data, (5) analyzing data, (6) drawing conclusions and preparing a report, and (7) following up.

Again, these stages overlap and affect one another. For example, the research objectives outlined as part of the problem definition stage will have an impact on sample selection and data collection. In some cases, the "later" stages may be completed before the "early" ones. A decision to sample people of low educational levels (stage 3) will affect the wording of the questions posed to these people (stage 2). The research process, in fact, often becomes cyclical and ongoing, with the conclusions of one study generating new ideas and suggesting problems requiring further investigation. Within each stage of the research process, the researcher faces a number of alternative methods, or paths, from which to choose. In this regard, the research process can be compared to a journey.[13] On any map, some paths are more clearly charted than others. Some roads are direct; others are roundabout. Some paths are free and clear; others require a toll. The point to remember is that there is no "right" or "best" path. The road taken depends on where the traveler wants to go and how much time, money, ability, and other resources are available for the trip.

Although there is no "right" path, the researcher must choose an appropriate one—that is, one that addresses the problem at hand. In some situations, where time is short, the quickest path is best. In other circumstances, where money, time, and personnel are plentiful, the chosen path may be long and demanding.

Exploring the various paths marketing researchers encounter is the main purpose of this section, which describes the seven stages of the research process. Exhibit 5-2 illustrates some choices researchers face at each stage.

STAGE 1: DEFINING THE PROBLEM

The idea that **problem definition** is central to the marketing research process is so obvious that its importance is easily overlooked. Albert Einstein noted that "the formulation of a problem is often more essential than its solution."[14] This is valuable advice for marketing managers and researchers who, in their haste to find the right answer, may fail to ask the right question. Too often, data are collected before the nature of the problem has been carefully established. Except in cases of coincidence or good luck, such data will not help resolve the marketer's difficulties. Researchers are well advised to remember the adage "a problem well defined is a problem half solved."

Problems Can Be Opportunities   On many occasions, the research process is focused not on a problem but on an opportunity. For example, a toy maker who

Problem definition
The crucial first stage in the marketing research process—determining the problem to be solved and the objectives of the research.

The Marketing Research Process

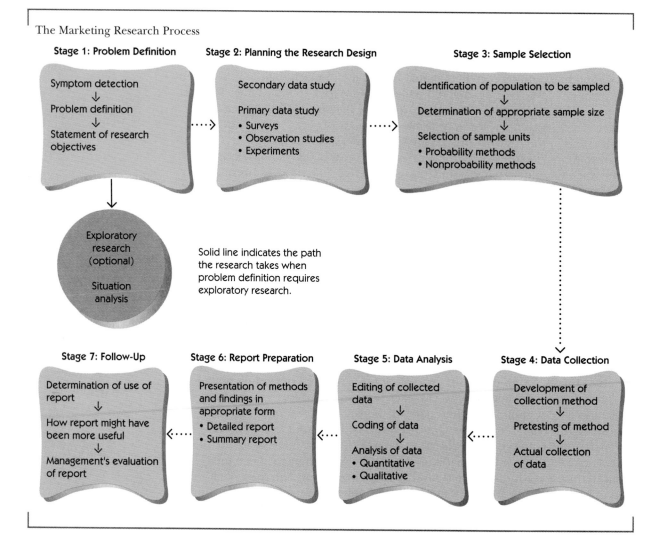

Stage 1: Problem Definition

Symptom detection
↓
Problem definition
↓
Statement of research objectives

Stage 2: Planning the Research Design

Secondary data study

Primary data study
• Surveys
• Observation studies
• Experiments

Stage 3: Sample Selection

Identification of population to be sampled
↓
Determination of appropriate sample size
↓
Selection of sample units
• Probability methods
• Nonprobability methods

Exploratory research (optional)

Situation analysis

Solid line indicates the path the research takes when problem definition requires exploratory research.

Stage 7: Follow-Up

Determination of use of report
↓
How report might have been more useful
↓
Management's evaluation of report

Stage 6: Report Preparation

Presentation of methods and findings in appropriate form
• Detailed report
• Summary report

Stage 5: Data Analysis

Editing of collected data
↓
Coding of data
↓
Analysis of data
• Quantitative
• Qualitative

Stage 4: Data Collection

Development of collection method
↓
Pretesting of method
↓
Actual collection of data

has developed a fabulous new item might face the "problem" of determining what age groups will most likely want the toy or which advertising media are the best to use. In this happy circumstance, the problem definition stage of the research might well be called the "opportunity definition" stage. The

THE PROBLEMS ADDRESSED BY MARKETING RESEARCH ARE FREQUENTLY "GOOD" PROBLEMS AND NOT DISASTERS.

point is that the problems addressed by marketing research are frequently "good" problems and not disasters.

Don't Confuse Symptoms with the Real Problem   There is a difference between a problem and the symptoms of that problem. Pain, for example, is the symptom of a problem. The cause of the pain, perhaps a broken leg, is the problem. In marketing, falling sales are a symptom that some aspect of the marketing mix is not working properly. Sales may be falling because price competition has intensified or because buyer preferences have changed. Defining the general nature of the problem provides a direction for the research.

Consider the case of Ha-Psu-Shu-Tse brand fried Indian bread mix. The owner of the company thought that his product, one of the few Native American food products sold in the United States, was selling poorly because it was not advertised heavily. This feeling led him to hire a management consulting group to research new advertising themes. The consultants suggested, instead, that the product's brand name, Ha-Psu-Shu-Tse (the Pawnee word for "red corn"), might be the main problem. They proposed that consumer attitudes toward the name and product be the starting point of research. In effect, the consultants were reluctant to choose advertising, one component of the marketing mix, as the area of concern without checking for more basic causes of the product's difficulties. The researchers did not confuse symptoms with the real problem. As Exhibit 5-3 shows, the problem definition stage is likely to begin with the detection of symptoms. If managers are uncertain about the exact nature of the problem, they may spend time analyzing and learning about the situation. For example, they may discuss the situation with others, such as sales representatives, who are close to the customers. A small-scale exploratory investigation may be conducted to ensure that Stage 2, planning the research design, does not begin until researchers have an adequate understanding of exactly what information needs to be collected. Exploratory research is optional and is not used in all research projects.

Finally, as Exhibit 5-3 shows, the problem is defined, and a series of research objectives related to the problem are stated. No decisions about the remaining stages of the marketing research process should be made until managers and researchers clearly understand the objectives of the research about to be undertaken.

Exploratory Research   As noted earlier, **exploratory research** is sometimes needed to clarify the nature of a marketing problem. Management may know, from noting a symptom such as declining sales, that some kind of problem is "out there" and may undertake exploratory research to try to identify the problem. Or, management may know what the problem is but not how big or how far-reaching it is. Here too, managers may need research to help them analyze the situation.

Providing conclusions is not the purpose of exploratory research. Its purpose is simply to investigate and explore. Usually, exploratory research is undertaken with the expectation that other types of research will follow and that the subsequent research will be directed at finding possible solutions.

Exploratory research
Research to clarify the nature of a marketing problem.

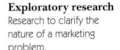

e   x   h   i   b   i   5-3

Stage 1, Defining the Problem, Results in Clear-Cut Research Objectives

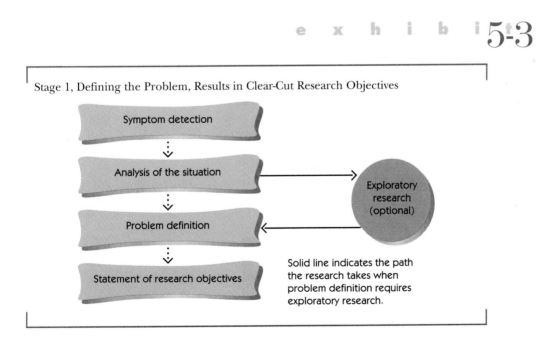

In any research situation, it is generally best to check available secondary data before beginning extensive data collection. Some work at a library, on the Internet, or with an internal database may save time and money.

However, there isn't any set formula prescribing exactly how to analyze a situation. Sometimes checking secondary sources may not be the appropriate first step. Instead, a short series of interviews with a few customers may be in order. For example, suppose a fast-food restaurant is considering adding a low-fat menu or a line of tacos to its standard hamburger fare. Marketing managers might begin their research by conducting some unstructured interviews with customers. Customers might surprise management with negative comments on the proposed additions. Exploratory research in this case could serve to identify problem areas or point to a need for additional information.

Although there are many techniques for exploratory research, our discussion will highlight one popular method—the focus group interview—to illustrate the nature of exploratory techniques. (Another type of exploratory research is described in the What Went Right? feature about Fisher-Price's Play Laboratory.)

Focus group interviews are loosely structured interviews with groups of 6 to 10 people who "focus" on a product or some aspect of buying behavior. During a group session, individuals give their comments and reactions to new product ideas or explain why they buy (or do not buy) certain products. Researchers later analyze those comments for useful ideas, such as that a product is "too high-priced" or "looks like it would break easily." Focus group research is extremely flexible and may be used for many purposes—for example, to learn what problems consumers have with products. During one of Rubbermaid Inc.'s focus groups on housewares, a woman accused the industry of sexism.[15] "Why do companies continue to treat brooms and mops like they were 'women's tools'?" she complained. "They're poorly designed and second-class to hammers and saws, which are balanced and molded to fit men's hands.

<div class="sidebar">

Focus group interview
A loosely structured interview in which a group of 6 to 10 people discuss a product or focus on some aspect of buying behavior.

</div>

<div class="caption">
Focus group interviews are a popular form of exploratory research. Groups of 6 to 10 people give their comments and reactions to new product ideas or explain why they buy certain products.
</div>

Brooms and mops make housework more miserable, not easier." At the time, Rubbermaid did not make cleaning products, but the woman's remarks eventually convinced the company that an opportunity awaited. After 5 years of research and development, Rubbermaid introduced a line of about 50 cleaning products and brushes designed to make cleaning easier, with handles that fit comfortably in consumers' hands and bristles angled to reach tight spaces.

What Is a "Good" Research Objective? Marketers contemplating a research project must decide exactly what they are looking for. The culmination of Stage 1 of the research process must be a formal statement of the problem(s) and the research objective(s). These provide the framework for the study.

The best way to express a research objective is as a well-constructed, testable hypothesis. A **hypothesis** is an unproven proposition or a possible solution to a problem, a statement that can be supported or refuted by empirical data. In its simplest form, it is a guess. In times of inflation or economic recession, an auto manufacturer might hypothesize that lower-income families are cutting back on

<div class="sidebar">

Hypothesis
An unproven proposition that can be supported or refuted by market research. Research objectives are often stated as hypotheses.

</div>

car purchases more than wealthy families. This is a hypothesis that can be tested. A maker of premium beer, in the same situation, may hypothesize that high-income families are reducing consumption of that product while low-income families, seeking some of life's "smaller pleasures," are not cutting down. This, too, is a hypothesis that can be tested.

STAGE 2: PLANNING THE RESEARCH DESIGN

After researchers have clearly identified the research problem and formulated a hypothesis, the next step is to develop a formal research design. The **research design** is a master plan that identifies the specific techniques and procedures that will be used to collect and analyze data relevant to the research problem. The

Research design
A master plan that specifically identifies what techniques and procedures will be used to collect and analyze data relevant to the research problem.

research design must be carefully compared against the objectives developed in Stage 1 to assure that the sources of data, the data collected, the scheduling and costs involved, and so on are consistent with the researchers' main goals.

At the outset, the researchers should determine if the data they need have already been generated by others or if primary research is required. In other words, as Exhibit 5-2 suggests, researchers planning a research design must first choose between using secondary data and using primary data.

Research Designs Using Secondary Data As we have mentioned, data already in the researcher's decision support system or in the library may provide an adequate basis for a formal research effort. For example, a marketer of mobile homes might know that sales of this product rise as building permits for traditional homes decline. Using government figures showing the numbers of building permits issued and trends in home building, the mobile home seller can develop a quantitative model to predict market behavior. In this case, the research design involves the analysis of secondary data only.

Meaningful secondary data may come from internal sources, such as company databases, or external sources, such as government agencies, trade associations, and companies that specialize in supplying specific types of data. Exhibit 5-4 shows some examples of the types of secondary data that are available.

w h a t   w e n t   right?

Fisher-Price's Play Laboratory Seated in a darkened room behind a row of one-way mirrors, designers and marketing researchers observe children who are trying out new toys in Fisher-Price's Play Laboratory. "Somehow there's some magic in a successful toy that catches children's interest, and we have to figure out what that is," Kathleen Alfano tells me. She is the company's manager of the child research department, which includes not only the Play Laboratory but also extensive in-home testing around the country.

On the other side of the mirrors from us, a group of toddlers is hard at work, toy testing. The lab is a large nursery overflowing with toys. The tip-off that this is more than an exceptionally well-stocked day-care center is the pair of professional-looking microphones dangling from the ceiling between a set of fish mobiles.

"It's easy to say what doesn't work," Alfano comments, "but finding out what makes a toy work is harder because children put a little of themselves into it." That all-important feature—play value—isn't some ingredient contained in a toy, she explains; play value arises from the way a child decides to interact with a toy, for whatever reason. Just beyond the mirrors, a 2-year-old girl has stepped up to a two-burner kitchen stove with a plastic telephone mounted on the side. The child moves a pot from one burner to the other, then picks up the phone. She punches a few push buttons without looking at the numbers. Cocking her head to one side and throwing out a hip, she smiles and says, "Hi ya, Mom!" into the receiver. This is play value. If only it could be bottled.

Obviously, the more expensive a toy is, the more guaranteed fun a parent expects it to deliver. During my visit to the Play Laboratory, the company's research and development staff is watching closely to see how its little guinea pigs take to an advance fleet of Fisher-Price's battery-powered, rechargeable, sit-down, two-seater sport cart.

In a small parking lot, five 4-year-olds are motoring about in fast curves and figure eights, fast being about 5 miles per hour. "They all have them set on high," says the project engineer. "Kids don't want to go slow." This propensity does not, however, mean that a dashboard switch offering a slower speed will be dropped from the final version. "The competition provides two speeds," says Schaub. "We have to be equal or better." In other words, some of the features on a toy are not really aimed at the child at all, but at the parents who will pay for it. Fisher-Price's marketing research efforts in the Play Laboratory help take the guesswork out of the design and marketing of fun.[16]

Secondary data show that outdoor cooking has been transformed in recent years. According to the Barbecue Industry Association, sales of gas grills increased 82 percent since 1985, while sales of charcoal grills fell 32 percent.[17] Secondary data also indicate that more people are cooking outdoors more often because gas grilling is faster and cleaner than using charcoal briquettes and lighter fluid. Also, more women are barbecuing, which has resulted in an abundance of new barbecue cookbooks.

Library of Congress
www.loc.gov

The primary advantages of secondary data are that (1) they almost always are less expensive to collect than primary data and (2) they can be obtained rapidly. Secondary sources must be used with care, however, as they have certain disadvantages:

- Secondary data are "old" and possibly outdated.
- Some data are collected only periodically. For example, the population census is taken only once a decade. Comparatively up-to-date estimates are often available in such cases, however.
- Data may not have been collected in the form preferred. Sales figures may be available for a county but not for a particular town within that county, for example.
- Users of secondary data may not be able to assess its accuracy. For example, previous researchers may have "bent" the data to "prove" some point or theory.

In general, an inherent disadvantage of secondary data is that they were not designed specifically to meet the researcher's needs. The manager's task is to determine if the secondary data are pertinent and accurate.

The Internet As described in Chapter 3, the Internet is a worldwide network of computers that gives users access to information and documents from distant sources. Many managers see the Internet as the world's largest public library because both noncommercial and commercial organizations "publish" secondary data there. A wealth of data from reliable sources is available. For example, the United States Library of Congress provides the full text of all versions of House and Senate legislation and the full text of the *Congressional Record*.

e   x   h   i   b   i   5-4

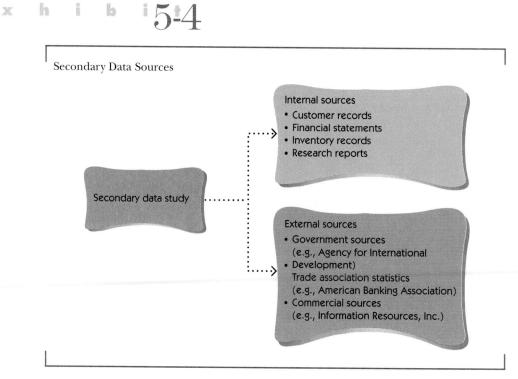

Secondary Data Sources

Secondary data study

Internal sources
• Customer records
• Financial statements
• Inventory records
• Research reports

External sources
• Government sources
  (e.g., Agency for International
• Development)
  Trade association statistics
  (e.g., American Banking Association)
• Commercial sources
  (e.g., Information Resources, Inc.)

The Internet is very user-friendly; information can be called up with point and click techniques and menu-based software systems called *Web browsers.* Netscape and Microsoft Explorer are Web browsers that allow the user to enter a uniform resource locator, or URL. For example, www.sbaonline.sba.gov is the URL for the U.S. Small Business Administration. The URL opens the SBA's Web site, where there are many statistics about small business organizations in the U.S. economy.

Seemingly overnight, secondary data have become digital. For those who are "wired," the Internet is currently the research medium of choice. Every marketing researcher working in the 21st century will have to understand how to access and use the Internet.

A *search engine* is a computerized directory that allows users to search the Internet for information indexed in a particular way. Some search engines search the titles or headers of documents, and others search the documents themselves. Yahoo, Hotbot, Excite, AltaVista, InfoSeek (mentioned in Chapter 3), and Open Text Index are among the most comprehensive and accurate Internet search engines. All a researcher has to do is type the search term in plain English or point and click on key words and phrases.

A user or visitor can access most Web sites without previous approval. However, many commercial sites require that the user have a valid account and password before access is granted. For example, the *Wall Street Journal Interactive* is a valuable resource; however, only subscribers who pay a fee can read it via the Internet.

Exhibit 5-5 is a listing of some popular Internet sites that provide valuable secondary data.

Hotbot
www.hotbot.com

Wall Street Journal Interactive
www.wsj.com

Useful Internet Addresses   exhibi 5-5

ORGANIZATION	DESCRIPTION OF INFORMATION	WEB ADDRESS
U.S. Census Bureau	Demographic information from U.S. census	www.census.gov
Fedworld	A comprehensive source of U.S. government information	www.stat.fedworld.gov
Advertising Age	Magazine providing marketing, media, advertising, and public relations content	www.adage.com
Inc. ONLINE	This online magazine features articles on small business and entrepreneurship	www.inc.com
BusinessWeek ONLINE	A general-interest business magazine with a cross-functional focus	www.businessweek.com
WhoWhere?	A comprehensive easy-to-use White Pages service for locating e-mail addresses of people and organizations on the Internet	www.whowhere.com
Zikmund and d'Amico Home Page at South-Western College Publishing	A valuable resource for professors and students of marketing	zikmund.swcollege.com

Research Designs Using Primary Data Researchers who find that no appropriate secondary data are available can choose from three basic techniques for collecting primary data: surveys, observation studies, and experiments.

Surveys Primary data are commonly generated by survey research. Survey results on one topic or another are reported almost daily by the news media. Most adult Americans have been stopped by interviewers at shopping centers or voting places or have received mailings or phone calls from survey takers. In general, a **survey** is any research effort in which data are gathered systematically from a sample of people by means of a questionnaire. Researchers using surveys may collect data by means of telephone interviews, mailed questionnaires, personal interviews (either door to door or in shopping malls or some other public place), or some other communication method such as fax or the Internet.

Survey research has several advantages. For one thing, surveys involve direct communication. How better to provide buyers with what they want than to first ask them what they want? For example, U.S. automobile makers operate style research clinics to appraise consumer reactions to car designs. First, mock-ups of proposed designs are constructed; then consumers, or respondents, are recruited through short telephone interviews. These respondents are brought in secret to a showroom and shown a car mock-up along with competing autos from around the world. As the "buyers" look over the cars, professional interviewers ask for their reactions to virtually every detail. The survey results are then fed back to designers in Detroit.

When surveys are properly planned and executed, they can prove to be quick, efficient, and accurate means of gathering data. Survey research can involve problems, however. Careless researchers may design or conduct surveys improperly and thus produce incorrect and worthless results—that is, results marked by **systematic bias.** The survey questions might be poorly worded, respondents might be reluctant to provide truthful answers, the sample may not be representative, or mistakes might be made entering data into the computer.

The specific advantages and disadvantages of surveys are best discussed in reference to the form of data collection used. These are outlined in Exhibit 5-6. You can see from this exhibit that choosing one method over another involves trade-

Survey
Any research effort in which data are gathered systematically from a sample of people by means of a questionnaire. Surveys are conducted through face-to-face interviews, telephone interviews, and mailed questionnaires.

Systematic bias
A research shortcoming caused by flaws in the design or execution of a research study.

e x h i b i **5-6** Characteristics of Four Survey Methods

	PERSONAL INTERVIEW DOOR-TO-DOOR	SHOPPING MALL	MAIL-IN QUESTIONNAIRE	TELEPHONE INTERVIEW
Speed of data collection	Moderate to fast	Fast	Researcher has no control over return of questionnaire	Very fast
Respondent cooperation	Good	Moderate	Moderate—poorly designed questionnaire will have low response rate	Good
Flexibility of questioning	Very flexible	Very flexible	Highly standardized format is very inflexible	Moderately flexible
Questionnaire length	Long	Moderate to long	Varies depending on purpose	Moderate
Possibility for respondent misunderstanding	Low	Low	Highest—no interviewer to clarify questions	Moderate
Influence of interviewer on answers	High	High	None	Moderate
Cost	Highest	Moderate to high	Lowest	Low to moderate

offs. For instance, a low-cost mail survey takes more time and is less versatile than a higher-cost personal interview at the consumer's doorstep.

How does the researcher choose the appropriate survey technique? The marketing problem itself generally suggests which technique is most appropriate. An advertiser whose message appears in a broadcast seen by many viewers, like the Super Bowl or the World Series, might contact viewers in their homes via telephone to gather reactions to its commercials. A manufacturer of industrial equipment might choose a mail survey because the executives it wishes to question are hard to reach by phone. A political party might prefer to employ a door-to-door personal survey so that voters can, after some guidance by interviewers, formulate and voice their opinions on current issues. In these examples, the cost, time, and perhaps accuracy involved vary. It is the researcher's job to weigh the advantages and disadvantages of each method and find the most appropriate way to collect the needed data.[18]

Wording survey questions appropriately is a skill that must be learned. The questionnaire writer's goals are to avoid complexity and use simple, accurate, conversational language that does not confuse or bias the respondent. The wording of questions should be simple and unambiguous so that the questions are readily understandable to all respondents.

Consider, for example, the following question:

> The Limited should continue its excellent gift-wrapping program.
> (a) Yes
> (b) No

The gift-wrapping program may not be excellent at all. By answering "yes," a respondent is implying that things are just fine as they are. But by answering "no," she implies that The Limited should discontinue the gift wrapping. Questions should be worded so that the respondent is not put in this sort of bind.[19]

Many respondents are susceptible to leading questions, such as "You do agree that U.S. automobiles are a better value than Japanese automobiles, don't you?" Leading questions should be avoided.

Sometimes rating scales are used to measure consumers' attitudes. Two of the most common attitude scales are the Likert scale and the semantic differential. A

adapting to change

ResearchWeb   ResearchWeb is a banner-based data-gathering system that allows marketers to conduct surveys on the Internet. It is a joint venture between Warwick Baker O'Neill, search engine company Infoseek Corp., and research firm Macro International. In one pilot study, Warwick designed a questionnaire and worked on the nature of the banner's design, Macro processed the data, and Infoseek randomly posted the banners, which lured users with a $1,000 prize given away to one survey respondent. The survey was conducted over a 4-day period in over 100 countries. The results: 1.8 million exposures, 10,000 visits to the survey site, 5,000 completed questionnaires, and 4,129 people who said they would be willing to be contacted again. ResearchWeb says its new method is cheaper, faster, and more actionable (because it is available 24 hours a day) than telephone and mail surveys. Another major benefit of ResearchWeb is that a large percentage of survey respondents are willing to be contacted again in the future. On the downside, respondents are not selected using probability methods. Nonetheless, surveys on the Internet undoubtedly will increase during the 21st century.[20]

Likert scale asks respondents to indicate the degree of agreement with a statement, as in the following example:

Timberland boots are expensive.
Strongly agree   Agree   Undecided   Disagree   Strongly disagree

A semantic differential identifies a company, store, brand, or the like and asks the respondent to place a check mark on a bipolar rating scale, as in the following example:

Timberland boots
Expensive __:__:__:__:__:__:__ Inexpensive

Observation   If the purpose of a research effort is to note actions that are mechanically or visually recordable, observation techniques can form the basis of that effort. **Observation research** involves the systematic recording of behavior, objects, or events as they are witnessed. Companies that sell space on outdoor billboards are interested in traffic patterns—specifically, the numbers of cars and people passing the billboard installations each day. Mass transit organizations may want to know how many people ride each bus and where most of them get on or off. In both cases, the information could be recorded either by human observers or by mechanized counters.

Observation can be more complicated than these simple nose-counting examples might suggest. "Mystery shoppers" can be used to check on the courtesy or product knowledge of retail salespeople. Researchers disguised as customers, store employees, or product demonstrators might subtly observe consumer reactions to prices, products, package designs, or display cases, leaving the consumers unaware that their behavior was observed.

The greatest strength of observation is that it permits the recording of what actually occurs in a particular situation. Its biggest weakness is that the observer cannot be sure *why* the observed behavior occurred. Still, in some cases, it is enough to know that something happened. The A. C. Nielsen Company, for example, uses mechanical observation to rate television shows. Its "peoplemeter," a recording device attached to a family's television, uses a microprocessor to identify which family members are watching the television, when they are watching, and what station is being watched. The questions of why a show is popular and why the ratings of old movies beat those of the president's State of the Union address are often left to the critics.

Experiments   Experiments have long been used by scientists attempting to discover cause-and-effect relationships. Almost every day, you can read news stories about an experimental group of white mice that were exposed to some substance and then developed more cancers than mice in a group not so exposed. The assumption, of course, is that the substance involved increased the chance of developing cancer. A properly run **experiment** allows an investigator to change one variable, such as price, and then observe the effects of the change on another variable, such as sales. Ideally, the experimenter holds all factors steady except the one being manipulated, thus showing that changes are caused by the factor being studied.

Marketing researchers use experimental techniques both in the marketplace ("in the field") and in controlled, or laboratory, situations. For example, McDonald's conducted experiments in the marketplace to determine if it should add a single-slice McPizza to its menu. The company sold the product in *test markets*—cities where a test product is sold just as it would be if it were marketed nationwide. Test markets provide a trial run to determine consumers' reactions and actual sales volume. For McDonald's, sales of the pizza slices were disappointing, and the company discontinued its plans to market pizza.

In contrast, advertisers often use laboratory settings to test advertising copy. One group of subjects is shown a television program that includes one version of

Observation research
The systematic recording of behavior, objects, or events as they are witnessed.

A. C. Nielsen
www.acnielsen.com

Experiment
A research method in which the researcher changes one variable and observes the effects of that change on another variable.

an advertisement. A second group views the same program with a different version. Researchers compare the groups' responses. Research like this is conducted in a controlled setting, rather than a natural setting, to increase researchers' control of environmental variables. Such an experiment is known as a **laboratory experiment.**

Selecting the Research Design   After considering research alternatives, a marketing researcher must pick one. Because there are many ways to tackle a problem, there is no one "best" research design. Certain techniques are simply more appropriate than others.

For example, what technique should the Chicago Museum of Science and Industry use to determine which of its exhibits is the most popular? A survey? (Could you really expect visitors to remember and rate all the museum's exhibits?) Experimentation? (Would you close off the exhibits one at a time and count the complaints associated with each closing?) Secondary data? (That might tell you what exhibits are most popular at other museums.) The Chicago Museum's researcher actually suggested the simple and inexpensive observation technique of keeping track of how frequently the floor tiles had to be replaced in front of each exhibit—indicating which exhibit drew the heaviest traffic. Of course, had the museum been in a hurry for information, another method would have been more appropriate, but the floor tile approach gave museum operators a good measurement over time at a low cost. (Incidentally, the chick-hatching exhibit was the most popular.)

STAGE 3: SELECTING A SAMPLE
Once a researcher has determined which research design to use, the next step is to select a sample of people, organizations, or whatever is of interest. The methods for selecting the sample are important for the accuracy of the study.

Though sampling is a highly developed statistical science, we all apply its basic concepts in daily life. For example, the first taste (or sample) of a bowl of soup may indicate that the soup needs salt, is too salty, or is "just right." **Sampling,** then, is any procedure in which a small part of the whole is used as the basis for conclusions regarding the whole.

A **sample** is simply a portion, or subset, of a larger **population.** It makes sense that a sample can provide a good representation of the whole. A well-chosen sample of lawyers in California should be representative of all California lawyers. Such a sample can be surveyed, and conclusions can be drawn about California lawyers, making surveying all of them unnecessary. A survey of all the members of a group is called a **census.** For a small group—say, a group comprising the presidents of all colleges and universities in Nebraska—sampling is not needed. All the presidents can be easily identified and contacted.

Sampling essentially requires answering these three questions.

1. *Who is to be sampled?* Specifying the **target population,** or the total group of interest, is the first aspect of sampling. The manager must make sure the population to be sampled accurately reflects the population of interest. Suppose a department store manager who wants to analyze the store's image in the community at large uses current credit-card records to develop a survey mailing list. Who will be surveyed? Only current credit-card customers, not noncredit customers, and certainly not noncustomers, though these groups may be important parts of "the community at large."

    Lists of customers, telephone directories, membership lists, and lists of automobile registrations are a few of the many population lists from which a sample may be taken. Selecting a list from which to draw a sample is a crucial aspect of sampling. If the list is inaccurate, the sample may not be representative of the larger population of interest.

Laboratory experiment
An experiment in a highly controlled environment.

Chicago Museum of Science and Industry
www.msichicago.org

Sampling
Any procedure in which a small part of the whole is used as the basis for conclusions regarding the whole.

Sample
A portion or subset of a larger population.

Population
In marketing research, any complete group of entities sharing some common set of characteristics; the group from which a sample is taken.

Census
A survey of all the members of a group (an entire population).

Target population
The population of interest in a marketing research study; the population from which samples are to be drawn.

2. *How big should the sample be?* The traditional tongue-in-cheek response to this question—"big enough"—suggests the true answer. The sample must be big enough to properly portray the characteristics of the target population. In general, bigger samples are better than smaller samples. Nevertheless, if appropriate sampling techniques are used, a small proportion of the total population will give a reliable measure of the whole. For instance, the Nielsen TV ratings survey, which appears to be highly accurate, involves only a few thousand of the 96 million U.S. households. The keys here are that most families' TV viewing habits are similar and that the "Nielsen families" are selected with meticulous care to assure the representativeness of the sample.

3. *How should the sample be selected?* The way sampling units are selected is a major determinant of the accuracy of marketing research. There are two major sampling methods: probability sampling and nonprobability sampling.

When the sampling procedures are such that the laws of probability influence the selection of the sample, the result is a **probability sample.** A *simple random sample* consists of individual names drawn according to chance selection procedures from a complete list of all people in a population. All these people have the same chance of being selected. The procedure is called *simple* because there is only one stage in the sampling process.

When sample units are selected on the basis of convenience or personal judgment (for example, if Portland is selected as a sample city because it appears to be typical), the result is a **nonprobability sample.** In one type of nonprobability sample, a *convenience sample,* data are collected from the people who are most conveniently available. A professor or graduate student who administers a questionnaire to a class is using a convenience sample. It is easy and economical to collect sample data this way; but unfortunately, this type of sampling often produces unrepresentative samples. Another nonprobability sample, the *quota sample,* is often utilized by interviewers who intercept consumers at shopping malls. With this type of sampling, people are chosen because they appear to the interviewers to be of the appropriate age, sex, race, or the like. The What Went Wrong? feature describes a nonprobability sample that was far from representative.

Probability sample
A sample selected by statistical means in such a way that all members of the sampled population had a known, nonzero chance of being selected.

Nonprobability sample
A sample chosen on the basis of convenience or personal judgment.

STAGE 4: COLLECTING DATA

The problem has been defined, the research techniques have been chosen, and the sample to be analyzed has been selected. Now the researcher must actually collect the needed data. Whatever collection method is chosen, it is the researcher's task to minimize errors in the process—and errors are easy to make. For example, interviewers who have not been carefully selected and trained may not phrase their questions properly or may fail to record respondents' comments accurately.

Generally, before the desired data are collected, the collection method is pretested. A proposed questionnaire or interview script might be tried out on a small sample of respondents in an effort to assure that the instructions and questions are clear and comprehensible. The researcher may discover that the survey instrument is too long, causing respondents to

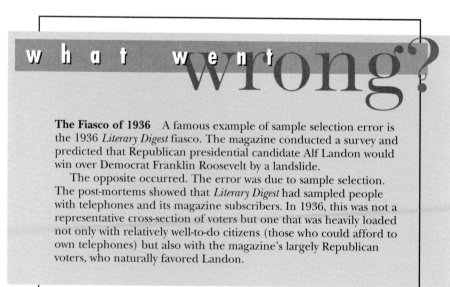

The Fiasco of 1936 A famous example of sample selection error is the 1936 *Literary Digest* fiasco. The magazine conducted a survey and predicted that Republican presidential candidate Alf Landon would win over Democrat Franklin Roosevelt by a landslide.

The opposite occurred. The error was due to sample selection. The post-mortems showed that *Literary Digest* had sampled people with telephones and its magazine subscribers. In 1936, this was not a representative cross-section of voters but one that was heavily loaded not only with relatively well-to-do citizens (those who could afford to own telephones) but also with the magazine's largely Republican voters, who naturally favored Landon.

lose interest, or too short, yielding inadequate information. The **pretesting** provides the researcher with a limited amount of data that will give an idea of what can be expected from the upcoming full-scale study. In some cases, these data will show that the study is not answering the researcher's questions. The study may then have to be redesigned. After pretesting shows the data collection method and questionnaire to be sound, the data can be collected.

STAGE 5: ANALYZING THE DATA

Once a researcher has completed what is called the *fieldwork* by gathering the data germane to solving the research problem, those data must be manipulated, or processed. The purpose is to place the data in a form that will answer the marketing manager's questions.

Processing requires entering the data into a computer. Data processing ordinarily begins with a job called **editing,** in which surveys or other data collection instruments are checked for omissions, incomplete or otherwise unusable responses, illegibility, and obvious inconsistencies. As a result of the editing process, certain collection instruments may be discarded. In research reports, it is common to encounter phrases like this: "One thousand people were interviewed, yielding 856 usable responses." The process may also uncover correctable errors, such as the recording of a usable response on the wrong line of a questionnaire.

Once the data collection forms have been edited, the data undergo **coding.** That is, meaningful categories are established so that responses can be grouped into classifications usable for computer analysis. For example, for a survey focusing on response differences between men and women, a gender code, such as 1 = male and 2 = female, might be used.

After editing and coding, the researcher is ready to undertake the process of analysis. **Data analysis** may involve statistical analysis, qualitative analysis, or both. The type of analysis used should depend on management's information requirements, the research hypothesis, the design of the research itself, and the nature of the data collected.

A review of the many statistical tools that can be used in marketing research is beyond the scope of this book. They range from simple comparisons of numbers and percentages ("100 people, or 25 percent of the sample, agreed") to complex mathematical computations requiring a computer. Statistical tools such as the t-test of two means, the Chi-square test, and correlation analysis are commonly used to analyze data. It may be surprising, in light of the availability of these and many other techniques, that a great number of studies use statistics no more sophisticated than averages and percentages.

STAGE 6: DRAWING CONCLUSIONS AND PREPARING THE REPORT

Remember that the purpose of marketing research is to aid managers in making effective marketing decisions. The researcher's role is to answer the question "What does this mean to marketing managers?" Therefore, the culmination of the research process must be a report that usefully communicates research findings to management. Typically, management is not interested in how the findings were arrived at. Except in special cases, management is likely to want only a summary of the findings. Presenting these clearly, using graphs, charts, and other forms of artwork, is a creative challenge to the researcher and any others involved in the preparation of the final report. If the researcher's findings are not properly communicated to and understood by marketing managers, the research process has been, in effect, a total waste.

STAGE 7: FOLLOWING UP

After the researcher submits a report to management, he or she should follow up to determine if and how management responded to the report. The researcher should ask how the report could have been improved and made more useful. This

Pretesting
Conducting limited trials of a questionnaire or some other aspect of a study to determine its suitability for the planned research project.

Editing
Checking questionnaires or other data collection forms for omissions, incomplete or otherwise unusable responses, illegibility, and obvious inconsistencies.

Coding
Establishing meaningful categories for responses collected by means of surveys or other data collection forms so that the responses can be grouped into usable classifications.

Data analysis
Statistical and/or qualitative consideration of data gathered by research.

is not to say that researchers should expect that managers will always agree with the report's conclusions or pursue its suggested courses of action. Deciding such things is, after all, the role of managers, not of researchers. Marketing management, for its part, should let researchers know how reports could be improved or how future reports might be made more useful.

Marketing Research Is a Global Activity

Marketing research, like all business activity, has become increasingly global. Many companies have far-reaching international marketing research operations. Upjohn, for example, conducts marketing research in 160 different countries.

Companies conducting business in foreign lands must understand the nature of customers in these markets. Although the 15 nations of the European Union now share a single market, research shows that consumers in the EU do not share identical tastes for many consumer products. Marketing researchers have learned that there is no such thing as a typical European consumer—the nations of the European Union are divided by language, religion, climate, and centuries of tradition. Scantel Research, a British firm that advises companies on consumer color preferences, found inexplicable differences in the way Europeans take their medicine. The French pop purple pills; the English and Dutch prefer white ones. Consumers in all three countries dislike bright red capsules, which are big sellers in the United States.[21] This example illustrates that companies doing business in Europe must learn whether and how to adapt to local customs and buying habits.

Decisions about international strategies and tactics should be based on sound market information. But in many foreign nations, U.S. marketing researchers encounter circumstances far different from those to which they are accustomed. To begin with, there is rarely a wealth of secondary data available.

focus on global competition

Domino's   Domino's uses marketing research both at home and abroad to help its managers make decisions about its pizza and its delivery service.

When Domino's investigated marketing pizza in Japan, the marketing research findings suggested that home delivery of pizza wouldn't work there. Japanese diets emphasize such foods as raw fish, rice, and seaweed, and consumers are known to dislike both tomatoes and cheese (which they think looks and tastes like soap). Pizza is considered a snack food rather than a meal, which makes it difficult to justify the high prices necessary to make the home-delivery business profitable. The consumers who like pizza the most are teenage girls, the market segment with the least disposable income. Further, the research showed that because Japanese families typically live in tiny apartments, those who are more likely to pay a premium price for a meal prefer to go out to a more spacious restaurant. Finally, Domino's guarantee of speedy delivery was perceived to be impossible in traffic-congested Tokyo.

Rather than being discouraged by what they learned, the Japanese entrepreneurs made three creative changes in the product strategy. The pizzas were made smaller: the sizes of 12 and 16 inches, common in the United States, were reduced to 10 and 14 inches. Two optional toppings, corn and tuna (toppings that Americans might consider stomach-curdling), were added to make pizza more harmonious with the Japanese diet. And to overcome drivers' problems with Tokyo's narrow streets and heavy traffic, Domino's used souped-up, streamlined motor scooters rather than cars to deliver the pizzas. A few months after the first Domino's opened, the number of scooters doubled, then tripled. Shortly thereafter, additional outlets were opened, and it was clear Domino's had scored a big success.

Although many factors determined Domino's success, its use of marketing research to understand the Japanese perspective, and its willingness to adapt based on what it learned, exerted a major influence.[22]

American researchers are lucky; there are volumes of data about the people and markets in the United States. But in some countries, no census has ever been taken. People in some developing nations seem to take the view that anyone wanting to pry into another person's life must have less than honorable motives. Often, too, lack of data and unfamiliar social patterns make it difficult for a researcher to use all the tools available. It may be impossible to develop carefully planned samples. Telephone directories may not include the entire population and may be woefully out of date. Street maps are unavailable in many cities in South America, Central America, and Asia. In fact, in some large metropolitan areas of the Near East and Asia, streets are unnamed and the houses on them are unnumbered.

In spite of these hardships, marketing research does take place around the globe. A. C. Nielsen, the television ratings company, is the world's largest marketing research company. More than 60 percent of its business comes from outside the United States. Although the nature of marketing research varies around the globe, the need for marketing research and accurate information is universal.

Sales Forecasting: Research About the Future

Marketing managers need information about the future to make decisions today. They need to ask "What will be the size of the market next year?" "How large a share of the market will we have in 5 years?" "What changes in the market can we anticipate?" Sales forecasting involves applying research techniques to answering questions like these.

Sales forecasting is the process of predicting sales totals over some specific future period of time. An accurate sales forecast is one of the most useful pieces of information a marketing manager can have, because the forecast influences so many plans and activities. A good forecast helps in the planning and control of production, distribution, and promotion activity. Forecasting may suggest that price structures need to be adjusted or that inventory holdings should be changed, for example. Because operational planning greatly depends on the sales forecast, ensuring the accuracy of the forecast is important. Mistakes in forecasting can lead to serious errors in other areas of the organization's management. For example, an overestimate of sales can lead to an overstocking of raw materials; an underestimate can mean losing sales because of material shortages.

> AN **ACCURATE SALES FORECAST IS ONE OF THE MOST USEFUL PIECES OF INFORMATION A MARKETING MANAGER CAN HAVE, BECAUSE THE FORECAST INFLUENCES SO MANY PLANS AND ACTIVITIES.**

Sales forecasting
The process of estimating sales volume for a product, an organizational unit, or an entire organization over a specific future time period.

The sales forecast provides information for the control function by establishing an evaluation standard. Management uses it to gauge the organization's marketing successes and failures. Without a standard, there is no way to measure the success or failure of any endeavor.

BREAK-DOWN AND BUILD-UP FORECASTING

Sales forecasts are focused on company sales, but they may also make use of forecasts of general economic conditions, industry sales, and market size. A bank, for example, may use the Wharton forecast of the U.S. economy to develop its own forecast for the banking industry. Based on that forecast, bank management will try to estimate the demand for loans at its various branch locations. This approach—that is, starting with something big, like the U.S. gross domestic product, and working down to an industry forecast, and then a company forecast, and even a product forecast—is called the **break-down method** of forecasting.

The **build-up method** starts with the individual purchaser and then aggregates estimates of sales potential into progressively larger groups. For example, a tool manufacturer might estimate that 10 percent of all electrical contractors in Georgia will buy a drill during a specified period, 15 percent of all carpenters in Georgia will buy a drill, and so on. Adding subtotals for each state leads to a build-up forecast.

Break-down method
A sales forecasting method that starts with large-scale estimates (for example, an estimate of GDP) and works down to industry-wide, company, and product estimates. See also *build-up method.*

Build-up method
A sales forecasting method that starts with small-scale estimates (for example, product estimates) and works up to larger-scale ones. See also *break-down method.*

Market potential
The upper limit of industry demand; the expected sales volume for all brands of a particular product during a given period.

Sales potential
The maximum share of the market an individual organization can expect during a given period.

Sales forecast
The actual sales volume an organization expects during a given period.

THE THREE LEVELS OF FORECASTING

There are three levels of forecasting, which are reflected in the forecast of market potential, the forecast of sales potential, and the sales forecast.

- **Market potential** refers to the upper limit of industry demand, or the expected sales volume for all brands of a particular product type during a given period. Market potential is usually defined for a given geographical area or market segment under certain assumed business conditions. It reflects the market's ability to absorb a type of product.
- **Sales potential** is an estimate of an individual company's maximum share of the market, or the company's maximum sales volume for a particular product during a given period. Sales potential reflects what demand would be if the company undertook the maximum sales-generating activities possible in a given period under certain business conditions.
- The **sales forecast,** or expected actual sales volume, is usually lower than sales potential because the organization is constrained by resources or because management emphasizes the highest profits rather than the largest sales volume.

CONDITIONAL FORECASTING—"WHAT IF?"

Forecasters often assume the upcoming time period will be like the past. However, marketing is carried on in a dynamic environment. An effective forecaster is one who recognizes that the forecast will be accurate only if the assumptions behind it are accurate. Therefore, organizations often create three variants of each forecast: one based on optimistic assumptions, one based on pessimistic assumptions, and one based on conditions thought to be "most likely." The most likely forecast is not always halfway between the other two. In bad times, "most likely" might be awfully close to disaster. The advantage of this threefold forecasting approach is that the forecaster clearly distinguishes between what is predicted and what is possible.

FORECASTING BY TIME PERIODS

A good forecast specifies the time frame during which the forecasted goal is to be

Computers are often used to prepare a long-term forecast.

met. Managers frequently use expressions like "short term," "long term," and "intermediate term" to describe these time periods. Such expressions can mean almost anything, depending on the marketing problem under discussion. For novelty items such as snap bracelets, the difference between the short and the long term may be very short, indeed. Such products may have a life of only a month and then disappear from the market. Established products like Honda motorcycles and Lawn Boy lawn mowers may survive for years or even decades.

Though situations vary, there is general agreement that a short-term forecast covers a period of a year or less and that long-term forecasts cover periods of 5 to 10 years. The intermediate term is anywhere in between.

Generally, forecasting time frames do not go beyond 10 years. For some products, such as automobile tires, it should be safe to assume that a market will exist 10, 20, or even 50 years into the future. But it is not safe to assume that any product will be around "forever." Some forecasters do make such long-range forecasts. The problem is that the longer the time period, the greater the uncertainty and risk involved. The level of uncertainty, as shown in Exhibit 5-7, increases immensely for each year of the forecast.

As time frames become longer, what starts as a forecast can become a fantasy. The history of business is littered with stories of managers who encountered disastrous failure because they assumed that an existing market situation would remain unchanged indefinitely. Marketing's dynamic environment does not offer the safety long-term planners would like to have. Thus, many forecasters revise sales forecasts quarterly, monthly, or weekly, as the situation warrants.

FORECASTING OPTIONS

There is no best way to forecast sales. This does not mean that the marketing manager faces total chaos and confusion. It does mean that there are many different methods, ranging from simple to complex, for forecasting. Some methods that have been used to forecast sales are surveys of executive opinion, analysis of sales force composites, surveys of customer expectations, projection of trends, and analysis of market factors.

Surveys of Executive Opinion   Top-level executives with years of experience in an industry are generally well informed. Surveying executives to obtain estimates of market potential, sales potential, or the direction of demand may be a convenient and inexpensive way to forecast. It is not a scientific technique, however, because

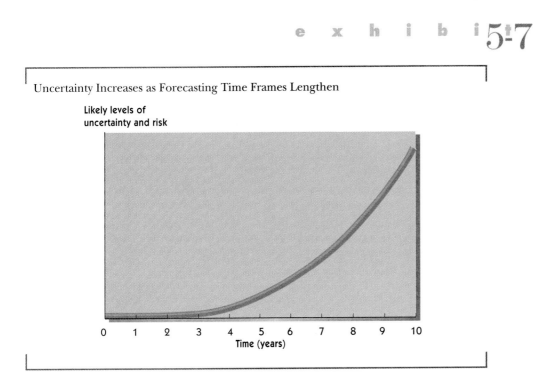

Uncertainty Increases as Forecasting Time Frames Lengthen

executives may be biased, either consciously or unconsciously, and thus overly pessimistic or overly optimistic. Used in isolation, executive opinion has many pitfalls. But the opinions of seasoned industry executives may be a useful supplement to one or more of the other forecasting methods.

Analysis of Sales Force Composites   Asking sales representatives to project their own sales for the upcoming period and then combining all these projections is the sales force composite method of forecasting. The logic underlying this technique is that the sales representative is the person most familiar with the local market area, especially the activity of competitors, and therefore is in the best position to predict local behavior. However, this method may yield subjective predictions and forecasts based on a perspective that is too limited.

Surveys of Customer Expectations

Surveying customer expectations simply involves asking customers if they intend to purchase a service or how many units of a product they intend to buy. This method is best for established products. For a new product concept, customers' expectations may not indicate their actual behavior.

Projection of Trends   Identifying trends and extrapolating past performance into the future is a relatively uncomplicated quantitative forecasting technique. Time series data are identified and even plotted on a graph, and the historical pattern is projected onto the upcoming period. Thus, if sales have increased by 10 percent every year for the last 5 years, the trend suggests that next year's sales should also increase by 10 percent. An advantage of projecting past sales trends is that the company's accounting records can provide the needed data. This common method of forecasting can work well in mature markets that do not experience dynamic changes, since the underlying assumption is that the future will be somewhat like the past. However, if environmental change is radical or if new competitors are entering the market, blindly projecting trends may not be useful and may even be detrimental.

Analysis of Market Factors   The market factor method of forecasting is used when there is an association between sales and another variable, called a **market factor.** For example, population is a general market factor that will help determine whether sales potential for Coca-Cola is higher in Albany, New York, or Salt Lake City, Utah. Similarly, new housing starts may predict lumber sales. When a number of factors are combined into an *index,* the result is referred to as a multiple **market factor index** or market index. Correlation methods and regression methods are mathematical techniques that may be used to identify the degree of association between sales and a market factor.

Sales & Marketing Management magazine's survey of buying power is one of the most widely used market factor indices. The magazine's Buying Power Index is a weighted index of three factors: income (weighted 5), retail sales (weighted 3), and population (weighted 2). The Buying Power Index is calculated for geographical areas. Thus, it can be used as a tool for forecasting at the state, county, or city level. A similar index for industrial purchasing power, which is of great use to industrial marketers, is also published by *Sales & Marketing Management.*

Market factor
A variable, associated with sales, that is analyzed in forecasting sales.

Market factor index
An index derived by combining a number of variables that are associated with sales.

Sales & Marketing Management
www.salesandmarketing.com

SOME PRACTICAL CONSIDERATIONS

Most organizations use several methods to forecast sales; this approach helps them achieve the most accurate forecast possible. Of course, it is reassuring when projections of trends, analyses of market factors, and customer surveys all predict sales at a similar level. However, when this is not the case, executives must use their judgment to determine what the company forecast will be. In making their determination, they may use the methods resulting in the lowest and the highest forecasts to set the pessimistic and optimistic limits. Nevertheless, these methods are an aid to management—not a substitute for managerial decision making. Furthermore, as we have already emphasized, the marketing environment is not stable. Factors such as the length of time a product has been on the market, the arrival of new competitors, and environmental changes may influence the accuracy of forecasting methods. Thus, marketing managers must be willing to update or alter a forecast as additional information becomes available.

summary

Effective marketing management relies on accurate, pertinent, and timely information, supplied in appropriate form by a well-designed decision support system.

1 *Explain why information is essential to effective marketing decision making.*

The marketing manager needs timely, systematically gathered information about the organization's customers, environment, and marketing activities. Without it, the marketing manager has no accurate basis on which to make decisions. Information reduces uncertainty and helps to define problems and identify opportunities.

2 *Explain the importance of worldwide information systems.*

A worldwide information system is an organized collection—of telecommunications equipment, computer hardware and software, data, and personnel—designed to capture, store, update, manipulate, analyze, and immediately display information about worldwide business activity. The well-being of business organizations that hope to prosper in the 21st century depends on such information. The Internet is among the various communication media that are changing the way organizations obtain information from around the globe.

3 *Describe a decision support system.*

A decision support system includes (1) databases that provide logically organized data and (2) a set of software systems for managing data. Decision support systems allow organizations to engage in data-based marketing and data mining.

4 *Explain the contribution of marketing research to effective decision making.*

Marketing research is intended to provide objective information about marketing phenomena to reduce uncertainty and lead to more rational and effective decisions.

5 *Describe the stages in the marketing research process.*

Marketing research studies generally follow seven major steps: (1) defining the problem, (2) planning the research design, (3) selecting a sample, (4) collecting data, (5) analyzing data, (6) drawing conclusions and preparing a report, and (7) following up.

6 *Explain how exploratory research relates to specific marketing management problems.*

Exploratory research clarifies the nature of problems that are not clearly understood so that further research can be conducted.

7 *Understand why secondary data are valuable sources of information.*

Secondary data have already been collected and assembled. They may be obtained quickly and inexpensively.

8 *Understand the uses of surveys, observation, and experiments.*

Primary data are collected through surveys, observation, and experiments. Surveys are used to gather information about large groups of subjects by mail, Internet, telephone, personal interview, or other communication media. Observation is used to record actual behavior. Experiments are tightly controlled research designs that manipulate an experimental variable and measure its effect under controlled conditions.

 9 *Demonstrate your knowledge of the purposes of sales forecasting.*
Sales forecasting is the prediction of an organization's anticipated sales over a specific time period. The forecast is used to plan such activities as production scheduling, distribution, and promotion and to measure the success of these activities. Good forecasting improves planning and control.

 10 *Evaluate the advantages and disadvantages of the various forecasting methods.*
Surveys of executive opinion, sales force composites, and surveys of customers are forecasting methods based on the opinions of experienced individuals or consumers. Personal biases or lack of knowledge may, however, affect the results. Trend analysis is appropriate in some situations but assumes that the future will be like the past. Market factor analysis and published indices are useful when sales are affected by certain external variables.

key terms

worldwide information
   system (p. 129)
data (p. 130)
information (p. 130)
primary data (p. 130)
secondary data (p. 130)
decision support system (p. 130)
database (p. 131)
software (p. 132)
intranet (p. 132)
data-based marketing (p. 132)
data mining (p. 134)
marketing research (p. 134)
problem definition (p. 135)

exploratory research (p. 137)
focus group interview (p. 138)
hypothesis (p. 138)
research design (p. 139)
survey (p. 142)
systematic bias (p. 142)
observation research (p. 144)
experiment (p. 144)
laboratory experiment (p. 145)
sampling (p. 145)
sample (p. 145)
population (p. 145)
census (p. 145)
target population (p. 145)

probability sample (p. 146)
nonprobability sample (p. 146)
pretesting (p. 147)
editing (p. 147)
coding (p. 147)
data analysis (p. 147)
sales forecasting (p. 149)
break-down method (p. 150)
build-up method (p. 150)
market potential (p. 150)
sales potential (p. 150)
sales forecast (p. 150)
market factor (p. 152)
market factor index (p. 152)

questions for review & critical thinking

1. What role does marketing research play in the development of marketing strategies and the implementation of the marketing concept?
2. Some marketing managers seem unable to manage information as well as they perform their other duties. Why might that be?
3. Define or describe, in your own words, each of the following.
   a. Worldwide information system
   b. Internet
   c. Database
   d. Decision support system
   e. Data-based marketing
   f. Data mining
   g. Marketing research
4. What does marketing research do for the manager? What doesn't it do?
5. What is exploratory research? Give an example of its proper application.
6. What are the stages in a formal research project? Which is the most important?

7. Why might a marketing manager choose to investigate secondary rather than primary data?
8. What are the strengths and weaknesses of the following marketing research methods?
   a. Mail surveys
   b. Telephone surveys
   c. Observation studies
   d. Experiments
9. What are the primary considerations in the selection of a sample?
10. Give some examples of population lists from which samples may be drawn.
11. What is the difference between a forecast of market potential, a forecast of sales potential, and a sales forecast?
12. What market factors might help predict market potential for the following products?
   a. Forklift trucks
   b. Chain saws
   c. Soft drinks
   d. Playground equipment

13. What forecasting method would be best for each of the following products?
    a. Cigars
    b. The Newton portable personal digital assistant
    c. Tickets to baseball games at your university
14. What do the executive opinion survey and the sales force composite methods have in common?

15. Form small groups as directed by your instructor. Select a local retailer or a campus organization. Define a marketing problem or a marketing opportunity facing that organization, and design a questionnaire that will yield information to help the organization solve the problem or take advantage of the opportunity.

marketing plan—right or wrong?

1. A retailer plans to have sales clerks ask customers who make purchases for their phone numbers and enter them (via the cash register system) into a computer file. The phone number will be used to learn the customer's name and address so that a database can be developed. Sales clerks are told to ask for the information, but details about the purpose of the phone number are not part of the training.
2. Sales at a sporting goods store have been declining. The store manager plans to survey credit-card customers to learn why people are not shopping at the store.

internet insights

zikmund.swcollege.com

exercises

1. The Spider's Apprentice is a Web site that provides many useful tips about using search engines. Go to www.monash.com/spidap.html to learn the ins and outs of search engines.
2. Marketers scan the environment for changes in social values and beliefs. Go to the Gallup Organization's home page at www.gallup.com. Select the Gallup Poll Archive. Read the results of a recent survey. What are the implications for marketers of the societal attitudes the survey reports? Make a list of five businesses that would be affected by the results of the survey you accessed.

address book (useful urls)

NPD Group Inc.	www.npd.com
ASI Market Research Center	www.asiresearch.com
IBM (data mining)	www.software.ibm.com
Advertising Research Foundation	www.arfsite.org
New York Public Library	www.nypl.org
Penn Library Business Reference Desk	www.library.upenn.edu/resources/business/business.html
National Restaurant Association	www.restaurant.org

Space Wheyfers

Space Wheyfers are new crispy snacks in the shapes of missiles, flying saucers, and rocket ships. They are made from whey. Whey is what is left over from cheese manufacturing. In the past, small cheese producers often dumped this waste from cheese making into streams, where it polluted the water by inducing algae growth.

Space Wheyfers were developed as a snack food to compete with potato chips, pretzels, and other empty-calorie foods. Space Wheyfers have fewer calories and less fat than the snack foods currently being marketed. Because they are made from protein-potent whey, Space Wheyfers contain about 15 percent protein, substantially more than most potato chips.

The Blue Lake Cheese Corporation developed this product because it was a natural for the company. Blue Lake believed that its dairy scientists' development—a yeast process to convert whey into solid protein for the Space Wheyfers—was a major breakthrough for the company.

Because teenagers often eat too much junk food, management believes that teenagers should be the prime market for Space Wheyfers. The space and galactic themes have been very popular since the movie *Star Wars* launched the space-cowboy era.

One of the best things about Space Wheyfers is that they can be given any appealing color or taste. The flavor of the food and the texture of the Wheyfers, however, need to be investigated in a taste test.

QUESTIONS

1. What is the marketing problem facing management at Blue Lake Cheese Corporation?
2. Do you agree that the taste test should be the very first marketing research project?
3. What additional information would be useful in the marketing of this product?
4. How can the company forecast sales?

chapter 6

Consumer Behavior

After you have studied this chapter, you will be able to:

Understand the basic model of consumer behavior.

1

Describe the consumer decision-making process and understand factors, such as consumer involvement, that influence it.

2

Appreciate the importance of perceived risk, choice criteria, purchase satisfaction, and cognitive dissonance.

3

Recognize the influence of individual factors, such as motives, perception, learning, attitude, and personality, on consumer behavior.

4

Explain the nature of culture and subculture in terms of social values, norms, and roles.

5

(continued on next page)

6   Characterize social class in the United States.

7   Explain the influence of reference groups on individual buyers.

8   Examine the roles in the joint decision-making process.

when

Lisa Spence and Tege Millikin of Longview, Texas, first started making scrapbooks in 1996, they merely wanted to preserve memories of their young children. Since then, the two friends have spent thousands of dollars on supplies for their hobby, including dozens of scissors with special blades, acid-free paper so photos won't yellow, and die-cut shapes and stickers to decorate the pages. But they won't specify exactly how much they've spent. "We don't want our husbands to know," confides Mrs. Spence during a recent scrapbook convention in Arlington, Texas, that attracted about 1,000 participants.

Forget quilting. The craft industry's hottest trend is the scrapbook, the fancier the better. The Hobby Industry Association estimates that sales of scrapbooks and supplies topped $200 million in 1996, up from virtually nothing in 1995.

What lifted scrapbooks out of the scrap heap, and why now? Hobbyists say it's a homespun backlash against technology (and something to do when a spouse is on-line), a balm for workaholic guilt and a simple yearning for family tradition. "Families are really disjointed today," says Susan Brandt, assistant executive director of the Hobby Industry

SCRAPBOOKS . . . HARKEN BACK TO A TIME WHEN THINGS WERE SIMPLER AND PEOPLE WERE TOGETHER. . . . ASSEMBLING MEMORY BOOKS HAS BECOME A SOCIAL OUTLET.

Association. Scrapbooks, she adds, harken back to a time "when things were simpler and people were together." Demographics are another factor: "Boomers having babies didn't hurt," she says.

Assembling memory books has become a social outlet for women in their 20s, 30s and 40s. Some devote entire rooms in their homes to the hobby, and host "cropping parties," where neighbors gather to compile pages for their books.

But these aren't your grandmother's scrapbooks. Today's keepsakes are organized by themes, and feature photographs cut with special scissors ($10), pages decorated with mock fabric borders ($10), labels written with fade-resistant pens (about $3), color-coordinated background paper (one pack: $5) and metallic stickers ($5).

Preservation has become another gold mine. Photos in old scrapbooks faded because they were mounted on highly acidic paper and under plastic sheets. Today's scrapbookers demand special buffered paper that costs several dollars per page.

Scrapbook enthusiasts are so gadget-happy that old products are being refashioned to cash in on demand. With a deft bit of labeling, Leeco

Industries, an Olive Branch, Mississippi, manufacturer of office filing systems, has transformed its standard-issue filing box into the "Cropper Hopper," a caddy for scrapbook tools and supplies.

MJDesigns Inc., a Texas-based chain of 57 craft stores, now devotes 100 feet of shelf space in each store to scrapbooks. And it has plans for expansion because its scrapbook departments are jammed with scrapbook customers who spend an average of $60 to $80 per visit.[1]

Creative Memories, a company in St. Cloud, Minnesota, uses a Tupperware-like "party plan" format to promote scrapbooking. Its sales force visits customers in their homes to sell scrapbook products and hosts parties where the scrapbook products can be demonstrated. It's a far cry from the old-fashioned home party. But some of the same business fundamentals apply. There's a captive audience, low marketing costs, and an aura of social pressure that can be lucrative for purveyors. A 1990 University of Chicago study showed that while there's no requirement to buy, 97 percent of party attendees do, in part because they feel an obligation to their host.[2]

Spending extravagantly on scrapbooks and accessories and preserving photos in memory books as a social outlet are examples of consumer behaviors that influence marketing mixes. They also show how fascinating, yet baffling, consumer behavior can be. This chapter begins our explanation of why people buy. The chapter opens by developing a model that gives an overview of consumer behavior. It then explains the consumer decision-making process and the psychological factors that influence this process. Finally, it describes sociocultural factors in consumer behavior.

Creative Memories
www.creative-memories.com

What Is Consumer Behavior?

Effective marketing must begin with careful evaluation of the problems faced by potential customers. This evaluation is essential because, according to the marketing concept, marketing efforts must focus on consumers' needs and provide answers to buyers' problems. A key to understanding consumers' needs and problems lies in the study of consumer behavior. A knowledge of consumer behavior gives the marketing manager information he or she can use to increase the chance of success in the marketplace.

Consumer behavior consists of the activities people engage in when selecting, purchasing, and using products so as to satisfy needs and desires. Such activities involve mental and emotional processes, in addition to physical actions.[3] Consumer behavior includes both the behavior of ultimate consumers and the business behavior of organizational purchasers. However, many marketers prefer to use the term *buyer behavior* when discussing organizational purchasers.

Consumer behavior
The activities people engage in when selecting, purchasing, and using products so as to satisfy needs and desires.

A Simple Start—Some Behavioral Fundamentals

Our discussion of consumer behavior starts with a basic building block: Human behavior of any kind (B) is a function (f) of the interaction between the person (P) and the environment (E)—that is, $B = f(P, E)$. Simple though it is, this formula says it all.[4] Human behavior results when a person interacts with the environment. Whether behaviors are simple or complex, they flow from the person's interaction with environmental variables.

Exhibit 6-1 expands the basic formula for behavior, $B = f(P, E)$, into a more elaborate model of consumer decision making.[5] The model presents a decision-making process influenced by numerous interdependent forces rather than any single factor. Activities of marketers, such as advertising on television, are environmental forces, as are social forces such as culture and family. The characteristics

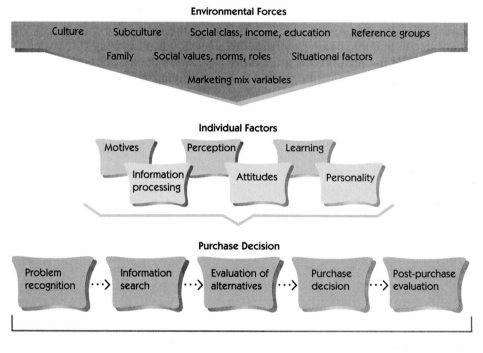

A Consumer Behavior Model of the Decision-Making Process: How It Works and What Influences It

Environmental Forces

Culture   Subculture   Social class, income, education   Reference groups

Family   Social values, norms, roles   Situational factors

Marketing mix variables

Individual Factors

Motives   Perception   Learning

Information processing   Attitudes   Personality

Purchase Decision

Problem recognition · · ·> Information search · · ·> Evaluation of alternatives · · ·> Purchase decision · · ·> Post-purchase evaluation

of the individual, such as the person's attitudes and personality, may also influence the decision-making process at a particular moment.

The Decision-Making Process

Marketers who study consumer behavior are ultimately interested in one central question: How are consumer choices made? One important determinant is the situation in which a decision is made. With regard to situation, there are three categories of consumer decision-making behavior: routinized response behavior, limited problem solving, and extensive problem solving.

Routinized response behavior is the least complex type of decision making. Here, the consumer has considerable experience in dealing with the situation at hand and thus needs no additional information to make a choice. To a cola drinker, deciding on a particular brand is a routine matter accomplished in a matter of seconds. The purchase of a new house by a consumer or a fleet of trucks by an organization, however, usually requires **extensive problem solving.** The process may take months to complete, with a series of identifiable decisions made at different points. **Limited problem solving** is an intermediate level of decision making in which the consumer has some previous purchasing experience but is unfamiliar with stores, brands, or price options.

The "snap judgment" and the more extensive processes are more closely related than they may seem. The routine decision to purchase a particular brand of cola is likely to have been preceded by a series of trials and errors in which the consumer tested different brands of cola before becoming able to make a routine choice. Both the routine choice and the more extensive problem-solving procedures may involve the same series of steps completed at different speeds.

Routinized response behavior
The least complex type of decision making, in which the consumer bases choices on his or her own past behavior and needs no other information.

Extensive problem solving
In-depth search for and evaluation of alternative solutions to a problem.

Limited problem solving
An intermediate level of decision making between routinized response behavior and extensive problem solving, in which the consumer has some purchasing experience but is unfamiliar with stores, brands, or price options.

INFINITI.   OWN ONE AND YOU'LL UNDERSTAND.

Related to these problem-solving situations is the consumer's involvement in the purchase. The level of **consumer involvement** has to do with the importance an individual attaches to a product and the energy he or she directs toward making a decision. High involvement occurs when the decision to be made relates to a product that is of high interest and personally relevant to the individual. The buying situation (buying a birthday gift, for example) and the product's price may also be factors contributing to high involvement. A person who is highly involved with a product will exert more energy in decision making than a person whose involvement is low. Involvement may include both thoughts and feelings, so high involvement can mean thinking more strongly, feeling more strongly, or both.[6] A new mother is likely to be highly involved in the selection of a pediatrician but far less involved in the purchase of safety pins.

Exhibit 6-2 illustrates the decision-making steps in a high-involvement situation in which there is extensive problem solving. It also shows a low-involvement situation, which usually requires only a limited information search and no evaluation.

Let us look more closely at these steps, focusing primarily on situations in which extensive problem solving takes place. Remember, however, that (1) different consumers pass through these steps at different speeds and (2) the five-step process is not necessarily completed once it has begun. Many buyers take a long time to reach the purchase stage, if only because of a shortage of money. Others do not reach the purchase stage at all because they evaluate alternatives and determine that no available alternatives are satisfactory.

STEP 1: PROBLEM RECOGNITION

When a tire blows out on your car as you are driving on an interstate highway, problem recognition is instantaneous. Alternatively, problem recognition can be a more complex, long-term process. A person whose car occasionally "dies" and isn't very shiny or attractive anymore may start to recognize a problem in the making. Perhaps when the new automobile models become available, she

The decision-making process is often shaped by the level of consumer involvement. This advertisement says "Own one and you'll understand." It humorously points out that owners of Infiniti vehicles are highly involved with their cars.

www.infinitimotors.com

Consumer involvement
The extent to which an individual is interested in and attaches importance to a product and is willing to expend energy in making a decision about purchasing the product.

Consumer Decision-Making Processes

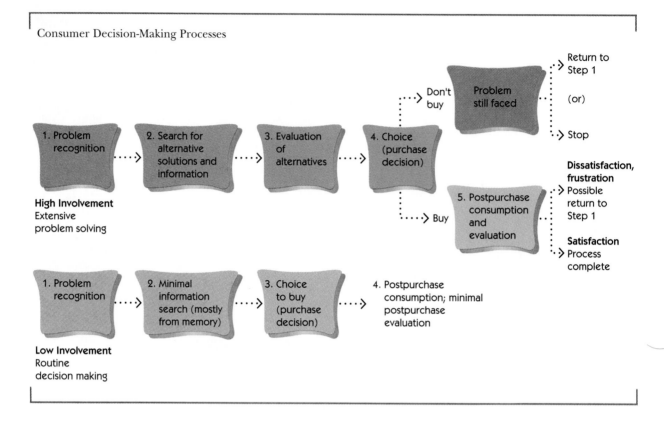

STEP 2: SEARCH FOR ALTERNATIVE SOLUTIONS AND INFORMATION

Problem recognition
The awareness that there is a discrepancy between an actual and a desired condition.

becomes aware that her needs are not completely satisfied. **Problem recognition** is the awareness that there is a discrepancy between an actual and a desired condition. The person who has become aware that a new car is in order may take a bit of time getting one. However, a smoker who realizes that he is lighting the last cigarette in the pack is likely to make a purchase decision very rapidly, passing through steps 2 and 3 of the decision-making process so quickly as to appear to have skipped them. For all practical purposes, he has skipped these stages, because the necessary information is stored in the consumer's memory. Marketers know that routinized buyer behavior is difficult to alter. A buyer who devotes some time and consideration to decision making opens up more opportunities for effective marketers to appeal to him and to offer a product that may satisfy his need. Of course, marketers of the most popular brands of cigarettes, gum, and candy are happy that their regular customers have developed a routinized approach to solving problems.

STEP 2: SEARCH FOR ALTERNATIVE SOLUTIONS AND INFORMATION
Even the habitual buyer of Snickers candy bars is very likely to consider, however briefly, some other choices before selecting Snickers as usual. However, the search for alternatives and information about those alternatives is most easily observed among highly involved buyers who are purchasing a product for the first time or making a purchase that could have major financial, social, or other consequences.[7]

Perceived risk
Consumers' uncertainty about the consequences of their purchase decisions; the perception on the part of a consumer that a product may not do what it is expected to do.

That buyers in such positions behave as they do is explained by the theory of **perceived risk**—the consumer's perception that there is a chance the product may not do what it is expected to do. These consumers perceive that their actions may produce unpleasant consequences that cannot be anticipated with anything approaching certainty.

Consumers encounter several types of risk when they purchase expensive clothing; for example: Is the clothing too expensive? Will it be durable? What will my friends say? Will I look good? Exhibit 6-3 identifies several types of risk that may concern potential buyers. The What Went Right? feature describes how one marketer solved a problem of perceived risk.

Buyers seek to reduce feelings of uncertainty by acquiring information. They may read advertisements. They may take family members or friends shopping with them. They may want the salesperson or some expert to tell them that the product is well made and a very popular item. In other

BUYERS SEEK TO REDUCE FEELINGS OF UNCERTAINTY BY ACQUIRING INFORMATION.

words, consumers engage in an **information search** to acquire information that will reduce uncertainty and provide the basis for evaluation of alternatives. The information search may be internal or external.

Internal search is the mental activity associated with retrieval of information from memory. After an individual has recognized a problem, the first step in solving it is to scan memory for pertinent information. Information stored in memory may have come from prior purchase behavior, advertising, conversations with friends, or other experiences. When the buying situation facing the consumer differs from past situations, however, an internal search may not provide enough information.

External search—the gathering of information from sources other than memory—may require time, effort, and money. External search is most likely to occur in high-involvement situations; it tends to be quite limited in low-involvement situations. Consumers gather external information from experience (such as shopping), personal sources (such as friends), public media (such as newspaper articles and the Internet), and marketer-dominated sources (such as magazine advertisements).

Marketers provide numerous sources of information to satisfy the consumer's need to reduce risk. Guarantees, a liberal return policy, store displays or advertisements showing that a product actually delivers what is promised, and a pledge that "We service what we sell" may reduce the consumer's concern about perceived risk. These efforts are not "tricks." To reduce uncertainty, most consumers prefer to deal with companies that give such assurances.

Information search
An internal or external search for information carried out by a consumer to reduce uncertainty and provide a basis for evaluating alternatives.

Types of Risk That Concern Potential Buyers e x h i b i t **6-3**

TYPE OF RISK	TYPICAL CONCERN
Performance risk	The brand may not perform its function well; it may not work; it may break down.
Financial risk	The buyer may lose money, pay too much, or miss buying something else.
Physical risk	The product may be harmful or unhealthy; it may cause injury.
Social risk	Friends, relatives, or significant others may not approve of the purchase.
Time-loss risk	Maintenance time or time required to return the product to the place of purchase may be excessive.

You'll Be Brilliant Armstrong World Industries, a company that markets sheet-vinyl floor coverings to do-it-yourselfers, learned that women are the catalysts in the residential floor-covering purchase decision but that men do the actual installation. Through its marketing research, Armstrong discovered that a high perceived risk—a fear of the first cut—was associated with the purchase. When interviewers asked people who examined but walked away from an in-store display why they did not buy the product, nearly 60 percent said they feared botching the job.

Armstrong developed a marketing strategy to combat this fear. The company introduced a "Trim and Fit" kit and promoted it with the message "Go on, cut. You'll be brilliant." When retailers were slow to push the kit because of its small retail markup, Armstrong added a sure-fire risk reducer—a "fail safe" guarantee. If the do-it-yourselfer made a mistake, the company would replace the floor covering at no cost. The biggest barrier to the purchase had been substantially reduced. The strategy was a giant success.

In low-involvement situations, in which the customer conducts almost no external search (and even internal search is minimal), it is extremely important for the company's brand name to be prominent in the customer's memory. Thus, assuming consumers spend little time making decisions about soft drink choices, an effective marketing strategy is to make the name Coca-Cola, for example, prominent in consumers' minds. Often, in such situations, the objective of advertising is to create awareness and familiarity through repetition. Messages should remain simple, because the consumer is not highly involved. However, in high-involvement situations, consumers may be more receptive to more complex messages, and the advertising may emphasize information about comparative features of competing brands, stressing the unique benefits of the advertiser's brand.

STEP 3: EVALUATION OF ALTERNATIVES

Evaluation of alternatives begins when an information search has clarified or identified a number of potential solutions to the consumer's problem. Often the alternative solutions are directly competing products. An alternative to a Vermont skiing

Choice criteria
The critical attributes a consumer uses to evaluate product alternatives.

Many consumers desire life simplification. They do not want to evaluate numerous factors when choosing among alternatives. Simplified decision-making increases their purchase satisfaction.

vacation may be a skiing vacation in Aspen or St. Moritz, for example. Other times, however, the alternative to a skiing vacation in Vermont is a new station wagon. The outcome of the evaluation process is usually the ranking of alternatives, the selection of a preferred alternative, or the decision that there is no acceptable alternative and that the search should continue.

In analyzing possible purchases, the prospective buyer considers the appropriate choice criteria. **Choice criteria** are the critical attributes the consumer uses to evaluate alternatives. For an automobile tire, product features such as expected average mileage, warranty, brand name, and price might be typical choice criteria. Which choice criteria are used depends on the consumer and the situation. For example, some people who need automobile tires may buy them at the neighborhood service station even if prices there are higher than at other places. They may feel that the time saved is worth the extra dollars spent. They may know the local station owner and want to give him some business. They may be trying to keep on the station owner's good side just in case they ever need emergency help. Or they may want to deal with a local seller so that they can complain if something goes wrong.

Many buyers appear not to want to evaluate too many factors when choosing among alternatives. The average person looking for a new car does not want (or cannot understand) the kinds of facts and figures mechanical engineers could provide. The typical car buyer wants very simple facts: The car looks good; the car dealer is a good guy. The buyer does not want an analysis of the car's aerodynamics or an art expert's opinion of its looks. In fact, Honda's "We make it simple" promotions were based on the finding that many consumers are confused about optional accessories and mechanical details. Offering only cars with "standard options" simplifies the choice criteria and the buying situation.

STEP 4: CHOICE—PURCHASE DECISIONS AND THE ACT OF BUYING

Sooner or later the prospective buyer must make a purchase decision or choose not to buy any of the alternatives available. Assuming the decision maker has decided which brand to purchase and where it will be purchased, the mechanics of the purchase must be worked out. The actual purchase behavior may be simple, especially if the buyer has either a credit card or a checkbook with a sufficient balance. However, the decision to buy can bring with it a few other related decisions. For example, should the tire buyer get new valve stems too? How about a lifetime wheel-balancing agreement with the seller?

adapting to change

Packard Bell The decision to purchase a multimedia personal computer is a high-involvement decision for most first-time buyers. And before consumption can follow the purchase, the consumer must install and connect the component parts. Packard Bell uses a KISS—"Keep It Simple, Stupid"—philosophy and a color-coding system to avoid frustrating consumers. The computer buyer connects the keyboard to the computer by inserting a purple plug into a purple socket. Next, he or she connects the teal mouse cord into the teal socket and the orange cord for the monitor into the orange slot on the computer. After that, the beige cord is plugged into the electrical outlet. When the computer is turned on, the computer user finds more than 25 software programs preloaded on the computer.[8]

STEP 5: POSTPURCHASE CONSUMPTION AND EVALUATION

Consumption, naturally, follows purchase. If the decision maker is also the user, the matter of **purchase satisfaction** (or dissatisfaction) remains. In some cases, satisfaction is immediate, as when the buyer chews the just-bought gum or feels pleased that the decision-making process is over. Frequently, after making a purchase, we think to ourselves or tell others, "Well, I bought a great set of tires today." Patting ourselves on the back in this way is an attempt to assure satisfaction. We are telling ourselves that we are pleased with the purchase because our expectations have been confirmed. In this case, marketing has achieved its goal of consumer satisfaction.[9]

Orthodontists may increase their patients' satisfaction by giving cards like this one after removing braces. This gesture also decreases the cognitive dissonance of the parents, who have been paying for the dental service for several years, and increases the likelihood that they will choose the same orthodontist for their other children.

Congratulations!
Your Wish Came True!

However, the opposite can occur—a consumer can feel uneasy about a purchase. Will the tires be good on snow? Will someone be surprised that I bought this brand instead of that one? Second thoughts can create an uneasy feeling, a sensation that the decision-making process may have yielded the wrong decision. These feelings of uncertainty can be analyzed in terms of the theory of cognitive dissonance.

In the context of consumer behavior, **cognitive dissonance** is a psychologically uncomfortable postpurchase feeling. More specifically, it refers to the negative feelings, or "buyer's remorse," that can follow a commitment to purchase. Cognitive dissonance results from the fact that people do not like to hold two or more conflicting beliefs or ideas at the same time. Suppose the car owner has bought the tires and has left the shop; there's no turning back now. She wonders, "Should she have bought Michelin tires instead, even though the price was a bit higher?" Dissonance theory describes such feelings as a sense of psychic tension, which the individual will seek to relieve. Each alternative has some advantages and some disadvantages. Buyers reduce cognitive dissonance by focusing on the advantages of the purchase—by carrying out postpurchase evaluation in a way that supports the choice made. Buyers may seek reinforcement from friends or from the seller. They may mentally downgrade the unselected alternatives and play up the advantages of the selected brand to convince themselves that they made the right choice.

Effective marketers don't want dissatisfied customers. When marketers understand that any choice can create cognitive dissonance, they can seek to support their customers' choices. Promising good service, telling the buyer to come right back if there's any trouble and "we'll fix it up," and giving a toll-free hot line number

Cognitive dissonance
The tension that results from holding two conflicting ideas or beliefs at the same time; in terms of consumer behavior, the negative feelings that a consumer may experience after making a commitment to purchase.

WHEN **MARKETERS UNDERSTAND THAT ANY CHOICE CAN CREATE COGNITIVE DISSONANCE, THEY CAN SEEK TO SUPPORT THEIR CUSTOMERS' CHOICES.**

are good business. Fulfilling customer expectations, which leads to satisfaction, is the purpose of many marketing activities.

Individual Factors That Shape the Decision-Making Process

Taking a decision-making perspective reveals a great deal about consumers' problem-solving behavior. But consumer behavior is complex, and there is much more to learn. Now that we have presented an overview of decision-making processes, we can explore the psychological variables that activate and influence them.

MOTIVATION

Marketers wish to know the underlying causes of buying behavior. They wish to know how consumer behavior gets started, is directed toward certain products, and is stopped. Psychologists explain such behavior in terms of motivation.

Motivation and Needs Defined **Motivation** is an activated state within a consumer that causes the consumer to initiate goal-directed behavior. Accordingly, a **motive** is an aroused need that serves to energize behavior and direct it toward a goal. A **need** reflects the lack of something that would benefit the person—a gap between the consumer's actual and desired state. The larger the gap between the consumer's actual and desired state, the more motivated the consumer is to solve the problem. Notice that this definition is consistent with our description of the problem-recognition step of the decision-making process. Problem recognition is, in effect, the creation of a consumer need state. Needs are always within people, but they may not be strong enough to cause the people to act. When, by whatever means, a need is activated, it becomes a motive. Thus, jogging may stimulate the basic human need to quench thirst, which is always present. The motive to find and drink a beverage to satisfy a thirst is an aroused need. An **incentive** (in this case, water or Gatorade) can be any object, person, or situation that an individual believes will satisfy a particular motive.

What is it that arouses motives? What gets people going? In general, it is either an internal force or an external stimulus. For example, when a person is hungry, internal biological mechanisms (grumbling stomach, empty feeling) arouse behaviors aimed at satisfying that hunger. The hungry person satisfies the motive of alleviating hunger by following the steps in Exhibit 6-4, a simple model of motivated behavior. The unfulfilled motive pushes the person toward an incentive that will satisfy the motive. The hungry person may respond by reaching for a candy bar on the desk, strolling to the refrigerator, or going out to a store or restaurant.

Classifying Needs and Motives Many psychologists have attempted to classify needs and motives. There is little agreement among these classifications. In fact, the only area of commonality is the general agreement that two basic groups of needs exist. The first group is made up of **physiological needs**, or needs stemming from biological mechanisms. The second group consists of **social and psychological needs**, or needs resulting from a person's interaction with the social environment. An example of marketers who deal with both sorts of needs is food marketers. Humans need food to live (a physiological need), but the social environment creates other needs. For example, some people patronize elegant restaurants to show that they are more successful than the Joneses next door (a social need).

Motivation
An activated state that causes a person to initiate goal-directed behavior.

Motive
An aroused need that energizes behavior and directs it toward a goal.

Need
The gap between an actual and a desired state.

Incentive
Something believed capable of satisfying a particular motive.

Physiological need
A need based on biological functioning, like the needs for food, water, and air.

Social and psychological need
A need stemming from a person's interactions with the social environment.

Simple Model of Motivated Behavior

satisfy a need for safety may also be seeking social acceptance and self-esteem by exercising, eating healthy foods, and dressing well to gain the respect of others.

Motivation and Emotion   **Emotions** are states involving subjectively experienced feelings of attraction or repulsion. There is a complex interrelationship between motivation and emotion. Romantic love, joy, fear, and anger are some of the emotions that may be associated with a motivated state.

Have you ever gone shopping because you were bored or made an impulsive purchase because you needed a little variety in your life? Most people answer "yes" to this question. The experiential perspective on consumer behavior suggests that consumers shop or buy certain products to have fun, to enjoy the process of shopping, and to achieve increased levels of arousal. These are motivations influenced by emotion.

In the past, marketers classified motives based on the role emotions played in the motivation. Therefore, motives were incorrectly grouped in two distinct categories: "emotional" versus "rational." Although this distinction is inappropriate, dichotomies of this sort are still in use. They persist because they serve to remind marketers that consumers, and even organizational buyers, are not strictly rational.

PERCEPTION

Although the idea of "reality" may at first seem straightforward, individuals differ in how they perceive reality. For example, no two people perceive a product, store, or advertisement in exactly the same way. Perception takes place through the senses. To perceive is to see, hear, taste, feel, or smell some object, person, or event and to assign meaning to it in the process.

Products offered by marketers provide many examples of how perceptions differ. A three-year-old car may appear to be just a used automobile to some, but a teenager may be thrilled to have it as a first car. The teenager's parents may see the car in a different light. The used-car dealer may view it in still another. Their images of the automobile—their perceptions—are very different.

Perception, then, is the process of interpreting sensations and giving meaning to stimuli. This process occurs because people constantly strive to make sense of the world and, when faced with new sensations or data, seek patterns or concepts that relate new bits of information to each other and to past experience. Perception is the interpretation of reality, and each of us views reality from a different perspective.

What Is Selective Perception?   Individuals receive information, or stimuli, by hearing, seeing, touching, tasting, and smelling. How they organize and interpret these stimuli in the decision-making process—that is, how they gain information from them—depends on their involvement in the decision-making process, their abilities to experience sensations, the context in which they encounter the stimuli, their intelligence and thought processes, and even their moods. These factors combine to create a mental phenomenon known as **selective perception**—that is, the tendency of each individual to screen out certain stimuli and to color or interpret other stimuli with meanings drawn from personal background.

The Principal Financial Group magazine advertisement in Exhibit 6-6 shows one way in which people add meaning to and interpret stimuli. The picture contains a star-filled nighttime sky. Yet most people see the stars as the Principal's logo, which is in the shape of a right-angle triangle, because of the human tendency to mentally "fill things in" or "finish things off." This aspect of perception is called **closure**. Many advertisements make use of this concept by not showing the product, showing only part of it, or showing only its shadow. The viewer supposedly becomes more involved with the advertisement through the process of

Emotion
A state involving subjectively experienced feelings of attraction or repulsion.

Perception
The process of interpreting sensations and giving meaning to stimuli.

Selective perception
The screening out of certain stimuli and the interpretation of selected other stimuli according to personal experience, attitudes, or the like.

Closure
An element of perception whereby an observer mentally completes an incomplete stimulus.

Principal Financial Group
www.principal.com

exhibit 6-6

An Example of Closure in the Selective Perception Process

Some of the best-known names in mutual funds look up to us.

The Principal® family of retirement accounts has a truly brilliant track record.

An independent rating company, Lipper Analytical Services, recently analyzed mutual fund families and ranked their performance.

Applying Lipper's criteria, our accounts out-performed fund families like Vanguard, Fidelity, T. Rowe Price, Franklin/Templeton, Merrill Lynch... and on down the line.*

One reason we out-perform them is that generally our expenses are only a fraction of theirs.

At The Principal, our focus is solely on long-term returns for retirement and 401(k) plans. As a result, we manage nearly $40 billion in retirement assets for 33,000 companies and millions of employees.

In fact, we provide administrative services for more 401(k) plans than any bank, mutual fund or insurance company.**

For over 100 years, The Principal has been helping people get the most out of their money.

That's The Principal Edge.®

To learn more about us, visit us at http://www.principal.com on the Internet. And if you'd like to compare the results of the study for yourself, please call 1-800-255-6613.

the Principal

Financial Group

**401(k) • HMO/PPO • Mutual Funds • Securities • Annuities • Home Mortgages
Life, Health, Dental and Disability Insurance**

© 1996 Principal Mutual Life Insurance Company, Des Moines, IA 50392.
*Ranking for mutual fund families stated is based on five-year performance and measurement information provided by Lipper Analytical Services. We applied like criteria to our accounts for comparison. The Principal separate accounts referenced are used with our group annuity contracts and sold to qualified retirement plans. **CFO magazine, April/May 1996, Senior Financial Executive Ranking. Products and services offered through Principal Mutual Life Insurance Company (The Principal) and its subsidiaries. Mutual funds distributed through Princor Financial Services Corporation (member SIPC). Securities through Principal Financial Securities, Inc. Securities and health care products not available in all states.

closure. A person who does not experience closure will be annoyed by the advertisement, so the closure idea is used only when the product is very well known and the advertiser is sure that the viewer can complete the picture.

Selective perception may involve selective exposure, selective attention, or selective interpretation. Selective exposure exists because no individual is exposed to all stimuli; in marketing terms, no one sees every advertisement. For example, many cable TV subscribers choose to block out the reception of certain channels.

Selective exposure
The principle describing the fact that individuals selectively determine whether they will be exposed to certain stimuli.

Selective attention
A perceptual screening device whereby a person does not attend to a particular stimulus.

Selective interpretation
A perceptual screening device whereby a person forms a distorted interpretation of a stimulus whose message is incompatible with his or her values or attitudes.

Stimulus factor
A characteristic of a stimulus—for example, the size, colors, or novelty of a print advertisement—that affects perception.

Individual factor
With reference to perception, a characteristic of a person that affects how the person perceives a stimulus.

Thus, one way consumers avoid stimuli is simply to avoid exposure to them. This is **selective exposure**.

Even if individuals are exposed to information, they may not want to receive certain messages, so they screen these stimuli out of their experience. They pay no attention—at least, no conscious attention—to the stimuli. This is **selective attention**. For example, a person who has just purchased a new Sony TV does not want to hear an advertisement announcing that Sony's prices have just been cut in half, so the person may not pay attention to such advertisements.

Finally, even a person who pays attention may distort a newly encountered message that is incompatible with his or her established values or attitudes. This is **selective interpretation**. The owner of a Ford pickup truck is likely to distort information detailing why Dodge Rams are better trucks than Fords, for example. Looking carefully at perception teaches the truth of the adage, "It's not what you (the marketer) say, it's what they (consumers) hear."

There is not much the marketer can do to overcome selective exposure other than to carefully plan the placement of advertisements so that they reach target customers. Selective attention may be overcome with attention-getting messages. The size of an advertisement, the colors used, the novelty of the pictures included, and many other **stimulus factors** have been shown to have considerable effect on the amount of attention a viewer will give an advertisement.

More subtly, an advertisement may gain increased attention by featuring aspects that speak to the viewer's needs, background, or hopes, because perception is also influenced by **individual factors**. Generally a full-page color advertisement will attract more attention than a quarter-page advertisement in black and white. However, a black-and-white advertisement offering the hope of "a better appearance" to balding men is likely to attract a lot of attention among its target group, balding men, because they are highly involved. Similarly, advertisements promising help in losing weight will be noticed by people who need this help, even if the advertisements don't grab the attention of other people. Many rules of advertising (use color, don't be wordy) are profitably broken when the target consumers are willing to devote attention to a problem that means something to them. This illustrates a basic fact about the perception of advertising: Consumers pay attention to advertisements when the products featured interest them.

This advertisement shows how stimulus factors—colorful products on a black and white background—can be used to attract attention. Runners are likely to pay even more attention because individual factors are also at play. The advertisement speaks to the needs of individuals who are concerned about a healthy lifestyle.

www.nike.com

Perception and Brand Image Marketing Product distinctions often exist in the minds of consumers and not in the products themselves. The symbolic meaning associated with brand distinctions, developed as a result of selective perception, is known as brand image. A **brand image** is a complex of symbols and meanings associated with a brand. Over the years, for example, General Mills has established a strong image for its Betty Crocker brand. The image is one of dependability and honesty—valuable images for a food product. There never was a real Betty Crocker, but the General Mills products are good and reliable, just like Betty's image. Research has shown that brand image can be the key factor in a buying decision.

It has been shown in formal research that with a number of products—among them cola and beer—consumers cannot distinguish between brands once the labels have been removed.[12] That perception of reality is extremely important in brand image marketing is demonstrated in various "taste test" ads on television. Diet 7Up, for example, humorously portrays a blindfolded man nervously awaiting a firing squad. After taking a "taste test" in which he, of course, cannot read the label, the blindfolded man indicates he prefers Diet 7Up to Diet Coke.

Davidoff Cool Water *eau de toilette* is purchased not only for its fragrance but also because of the brand's sexy image.

Brand image
The complex of symbols and meanings associated with a brand.

Copying in Korea A package of gum sold in South Korea has a bright yellow wrapper, bold black lettering, and a small red design at one end. It may look like Juicy Fruit gum, but it isn't. Most likely it's Juicy & Fresh gum from Lotte Confectionery Company. Or it could be Tong Yang, which has a very similar package. Then again, it could be Hearty Juicy, which mimics all three in the hope that consumers will perceive it to be similar to the other brands.

In South Korea, goods copying American brands are everywhere. Even some of the biggest companies imitate the world's best products in the hope that consumers will perceive the copycat brands as similar to the originals. In supermarkets, Tie laundry detergent is packaged in orange boxes with a whirlpool design that differs little from Tide's. This brand is produced by Lucky Goldstar Group, one of South Korea's largest companies. Because of widespread copying like this, protecting intellectual property worldwide is a major problem for global marketers.[13]

Subliminal Perception Can advertisers send messages of which people are not consciously aware? In the 1950s, there was considerable controversy about the possibility of this so-called subliminal advertising. In an alleged movie theater "experiment," the phrases "Eat popcorn" and "Drink Coca-Cola" were supposedly flashed on the screen so rapidly that people were unaware of them. Sales in the movie theater were reported to have increased 58 percent for popcorn and 18

This Pepsi advertisement appeared in the souvenir program of a minor league baseball team. Can you see a batter, a ball, and a fielder? Is this a subliminal advertisement? No, it isn't, because you can see the ball players. Subliminal perception is perception of stimuli at a subconscious level. The Pepsi advertisement is an effective advertisement targeted at a baseball-oriented audience.

percent for Coca-Cola. Psychologists, alarmed at this result, seriously studied the "experiment" and concluded that it had lacked scientific rigor. Subsequent investigations of *subliminal perception* (perception of stimuli at a subconscious level) suggested that advertisers trying to achieve "perception without awareness" would face technical problems so great that the public need not be apprehensive about the possibility. Subliminal stimuli are simply too weak to be effective. For example, only very short messages can be communicated subliminally, and the influence of selective perception tends to be stronger than the weak stimulus factors.[14]

It is interesting to note that the public frequently misuses the word *subliminal*. Symbolism is not subliminal, nor are embedded messages "hidden" in pictures. Neither symbolism nor embedded messages are perceived at a subconscious level—that is, without the individual's knowing of their existence. The picture shown in Exhibit 6-7 allegedly hides an embedded "subliminal" message. Can you see it? If you can, of course, you have not perceived it subliminally.

SYMBOLISM **IS NOT SUBLIMINAL, NOR ARE EMBEDDED IMAGES "HIDDEN" IN PICTURES.**

LEARNING

If you were asked to identify a brand of light bulbs, what brand would you name? Would you say General Electric? If so, you'd be agreeing with 86 percent of consumers asked this question. Furthermore, 55 percent of consumers said they would pick GE the next time they bought a light bulb. Most consumers have learned to be loyal to GE brand light bulbs. How does such learning take place?

How Learning Occurs   Learning occurs as a result of experience or of mental activity associated with experience. Thus, the expression "older and wiser" is not far from the mark, because older people have had the opportunity to learn from many experiences. Experiences related to product usage, shopping, and exposure to advertisements and other aspects of marketing add to consumers' banks of knowledge and influence their habits.

Learning
Any change in behavior or cognition that results from experience or an interpretation of experience.

Learning is defined as any change in behavior or cognition resulting from experience or interpretation of experience. Suppose a package or display—say, for a crayon whose marks can be cleaned away with soap and water—attracts the attention of a shopper, and the shopper gives the product a try. If the crayon works to the customer's satisfaction, she learns through experience that the new product is acceptable. If it does not, she learns that fact instead. This knowledge

Is There a "Subliminal" Message Embedded in This Ad?

becomes information in the consumer's memory. **Memory** is the information-processing function that allows people to store and retrieve information.

A type of learning called *social learning* can occur through observation of the consequences of others' behavior. For example, a younger child observes an older sibling's punishment and learns to avoid that punishment by avoiding the situation that brought it about. Similarly, buyers often purchase products recommended by other people who have used these products. Much television advertising is based on the idea that social learning occurs when people watch others on television. Viewers observe the satisfaction that others, such as Michael Jordan, apparently derive from a product, and they learn by interpreting these experiences.

Many theories attempt to explain exactly how learning occurs. All of the widely accepted theories acknowledge the great importance of experience. One important viewpoint focuses on **operant conditioning**, a form of learning believed to occur when a response, such as a purchase, is followed by a reinforcement, or reward. Exhibit 6-8 illustrates the consumer learning process according to this theory. Here, some aspect of the product (or something or someone associated with the product) provides the stimulus, and the purchase is the consumer's response to the stimulus. If the product proves to be satisfactory, the consumer

Memory
The information-processing function involving the storage and retrieval of information.

Operant conditioning
The process by which reinforcement of a behavior results in repetition of that behavior.

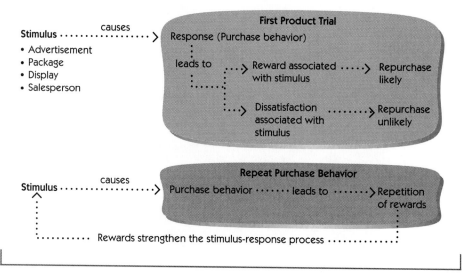

Effects of Reinforcement on Consumer Behavior: First Trial and Repeat Purchase Situations

---

receives a reward—a **reinforcement**. The fact is that the purchase is made in the hope that satisfaction will follow. When it does, the effect is to strengthen (reinforce) the stimulus-response relationship. Learning takes place as this phenomenon occurs over and over.

Some theories of learning stress the importance of repetition in the development of habits. For example, the more you are exposed to a television message such as Levi Strauss & Company's claim "Levi's. They go on," the more likely it is that you will learn the content of the sales message. Similarly, repeatedly rewarding a behavior strengthens the stimulus-response relationship. More simply, repeated satisfaction creates buying habits and loyal customers.

Learning Theories and Marketing   Most learning theories are compatible with marketing activities and marketing's key philosophy, the marketing concept. The theories assert that positive rewards or experiences lead to repeated behaviors. The marketing concept stresses consumer satisfaction, which leads to repeat purchases and long-term profitability for the organization.

ATTITUDES

An **attitude** comprises an individual's general affective, cognitive, and behavioral responses to a given object, issue, or person.[15] People learn attitudes. In terms of marketing, they learn to respond in a consistently favorable or unfavorable manner to products, stores, advertising, and people. Notice that because attitudes are learned, it is possible to change them. This is a goal of much promotional activity.

The ABC Model: A Three-Part Theory of Attitudes   The ABC model is the traditional way to view attitudes. In this view, an attitude has three parts. The A component is the *affective,* or emotional, component. It reflects a person's feelings toward an object. Is the brand good or bad? Is it desirable? Likable? The B component is the *behavioral* component, which reflects intended and actual behaviors toward the object. This component is a predisposition to action. The C component is the *cognitive* component. It involves all the consumer's beliefs, knowledge, and thoughts about the object—the consumer's perception of the product's

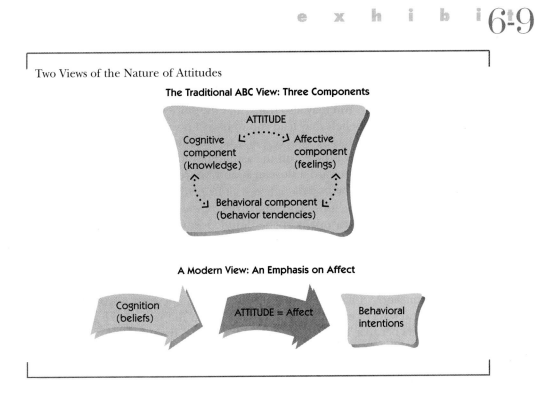

Two Views of the Nature of Attitudes

The Traditional ABC View: Three Components

ATTITUDE

Cognitive component (knowledge) · · · · · · · · Affective component (feelings)

Behavioral component (behavior tendencies)

A Modern View: An Emphasis on Affect

Cognition (beliefs) → ATTITUDE = Affect → Behavioral intentions

attributes or characteristics. Is it durable? Expensive? Suitable as a gift for Aunt Mary? The ABC model is graphically portrayed at the top of Exhibit 6-9.

Modern Attitude Theory Stresses Affect In recent years, attitude theory has changed. The current practice is to define attitude as affect. Attitude is thus seen as comprising feelings about products or brands. The shift in view does not discount the importance of cognitive or behavioral components but simply does not define them as components of attitude. Indeed, as Exhibit 6-9 shows, in this view attitudes are based on cognitive beliefs. Behavioral intentions are in turn influenced by both cognitions and attitude (affect).[16]

How Do Attitudes Influence Buying Behavior? Let's examine a consumer's attitude toward the Kodak Advantix camera. The consumer may hold several cognitive beliefs about the product. One of her beliefs might be that it takes clear pictures. Another might be that its features make it easy to switch back and forth from a regular shot to a wide-angle shot. She may have certain feelings about the camera as well—for example, she may feel that Kodak is a good brand or that the Kodak is desirable because it is the "official camera" of the Olympics. In the current view, these feelings, and her cognitive beliefs, make up her attitude—which may create a predisposition to buy the product.

Kodak
www.kodak.com

Note that the consumer's attitude serves as a general indicator of her possible behavior toward the attitudinal object. That is, the consumer will *consider* buying the product—she will not necessarily buy it. A favorable attitude toward a particular brand may not result in purchase of that brand. After all, consumers have attitudes toward competing brands as well. Furthermore, attitudes are not the sole determinant of behavior. Situational, financial, and motivational forces, as well as attitudes, influence behavior. Because attitudes are situational, their effects are controlled by circumstances. Most Americans have very favorable attitudes toward Rolls Royce and Mercedes automobiles, yet not many own one of these cars. Many people admire—that is, have attitudes that favor—mansions surrounded by well-tended formal gardens. Few people live in such places, however. Attitudes may

Whirlpool   It seemed like a no-brainer. In the late 1980s the U.S. market for refrigerators and other major appliances was mature. But in Western Europe barely 20 percent of households have clothes dryers, versus some 70 percent in the U.S. Here, four producers control 90 percent of the market, whereas Europe can count dozens of appliance makers, nearly all ripe for consolidation.

In 1989 archrivals Whirlpool Corp. and Maytag Corp. leaped across the Atlantic. Maytag bought Britain's Hoover; . . . Whirlpool purchased the appliance unit of Dutch electronics giant Philips and spent another $500 million to retool its plants.

But the invasion has fizzled. [In 1995] Maytag sold its European operations to an Italian appliance maker, booking a $135 million loss.

Whirlpool Chief Executive Donald Whitwam has chosen to fight on, but it looks like a long fight. Whirlpool's European revenues . . . have been flat . . . since 1990. . . .

What went wrong? Why was a Europe that was eager to accept American music and American blue jeans unwilling to accept another American icon, the leading brand name in household appliances?

In part the Americans misjudged the European consumer. [American] consumers have a throwaway philosophy. They want to get the lowest possible price, and when the thing wears out, they'll throw it away. Many Europeans still think of appliances as long-term investments. They will pay more and expect to get more in finish, durability, and appearance.

Whirlpool approached the European market with what it calls a "value gap" strategy. This means that the typical European must work twice as many hours as the average American consumer to buy a refrigerator or other major appliance. Whirlpool figured it could close the value gap and win market share by selling appliances at well below established prices.

To achieve this, Whirlpool centralized purchasing, product design and manufacturing. It redesigned its European appliances to use more parts in common and consolidated warehouses to carry less inventory. . . .

Today Whirlpool sells a midlevel Whirlpool dishwasher in Britain at £330 (about $508); a comparable dishwasher by Britain's Hotpoint goes for £400 (about $616).

What Whirlpool overlooked was this: An American household will often put its washer/dryer in the garage or basement or tuck it away in a closet, where noise and appearance don't matter, but Europeans live in smaller houses and often put their laundry equipment in their kitchens, where noise and looks matter greatly. In 1994 Whirlpool continued to cut costs by reorganizing sales from national teams to trade channel groups. . . . That decision damaged local contacts and Whirlpool turned off more potential customers than it won. Whirlpool admits the sales force reorganization has cost it market share.

Whirlpool did take a big chunk of the market, but the least profitable chunk. Whitwam says European unit sales are up. . . . But much of this increase was in Whirlpool's low-end, thin-margin Ignis line. Whirlpool's average selling price has dropped nearly 15 percent since 1992, to barely $300 per unit in [1995]. Hence, flat dollar sales, even while unit-volume was increasing.

In early 1995 Whirlpool tried to raise prices in Europe, but the increases didn't stick. Europeans apparently considered American products inferior and at higher prices preferred to move to local brands. . . .

Late [in 1995] Whirlpool began rolling out a new range of European products, including clothes dryers that dry more quickly and boast wider doors for easier access.

It now sells three pan-European brands: Bauknecht, for the affluent; Whirlpool, for the middle market; and Ignis, on the low end. Many of the products now use common parts, both within each brand and among the three brands.

Whitwam says over 60 percent of Whirlpool Europe's 1996 sales will come from these new goods, which, he says, provide more value without a proportional price increase. He believes that will help him boost Whirlpool Europe's operating margins—now less than 5 percent— up to the North American level of about 8 percent before the end of the decade. Maybe.[17]

Roles obviously carry over into purchasing situations. There are consumer roles and seller roles. The shopper expects to have certain rights and expects the store employee to fulfill certain obligations.[18] Furthermore, an employee in an expensive fur salon is expected to behave differently from a check-out clerk at Kmart.

CULTURE

Many values, norms, and roles come from a person's overall culture. The term *culture,* though frequently used, is difficult to define clearly because it encompasses so much about the way a society operates. Recall that a culture consists of values, beliefs, and customary behaviors learned and shared by the members of a particular society. Essential to the concept of culture is the notion that culture is learned rather than innate. Thus, that children are born is natural, but how the mating process is conducted and how the children that result from it are treated are "cultural."

It is important for marketers to understand the many aspects of culture. Culture obviously varies from place to place around the globe and affects the success of marketing worldwide. For

In our diverse society, there are many subcultures based on color, language, religion, and geography. Preferences for foods and music and forms of socializing can be strongly influenced by values, norms, and roles prescribed by the subculture.

example, as the What Went Wrong? feature illustrates, Whirlpool's successful global marketing strategy (first described in Chapter 4) was not realized without a few short-term setbacks, particularly in the fiercely competitive Western European market.

SUBCULTURES: CULTURES WITHIN CULTURES

Within any society there is a dominant culture. However, there are also cultural differences. Language differences are an example. Some countries (Canada and Belgium, for example) have two or more official languages (Switzerland has four). In China, five major and many minor languages are spoken. In the United States, several language groups can be identified. Nowadays, almost 20 percent of the U.S. population speaks Spanish.

A **subculture** is a group within a dominant culture that is distinct because it differs from the dominant culture in one or more important ways—language, demographic variables such as ethnic or racial background, or geographical region, for example. The subculture will also differ from the overall culture in some values, norms, and beliefs.

Within the U.S. culture, there are many subcultures. Subcultures made up of particular racial or ethnic groups, such as the African American, Hispanic, and Jewish subcultures, are easiest to identify, but the marketer must recognize the many other subcultural differences. These may be as simple as regional differences in food preferences.[19] In the northeastern states, people often eat lamb chops, for example, but in west Texas, beef is the staple and lamb chops are hard to find. Subcultural differences provide marketers with challenges and with segmentation possibilities that are rich in potential.

SOCIAL CLASSES

Within every culture there are social classes. A **social class** is a group of people with similar levels of prestige, power, and wealth whose thinking and behavior reflect a set of shared beliefs, attitudes, and values. Exhibit 6-10, which summarizes one view of U.S. social classes, shows five discrete groups. Class structure is actually more like an escalator, however, because it runs from bottom to top without any major plateaus.

Social class explains many differences in behavior patterns and lifestyles. Social class may have a major impact on shopping patterns or products purchased. An advertisement for Lucchese boots, which are exquisitely tooled and made from the finest leathers, states that the boots are "available only at finer stores." This simple phrase may stop some readers from further consideration of these boots. Why? One of the classic studies in consumer behavior explains that the lower-status woman believes that if she goes into a high-status department store, the clerks will snub or insult her in various subtle ways, making it clear that she does not "belong." Members of different social classes know which stores and products are for people of their class.

The impact of social class on consumer behavior is often indirect. For example, most people live in neighborhoods made up of people from their own class. If the

Subculture
A group within a dominant culture that is distinct from the culture. Members of a subculture typically display some values or norms that differ from those of the overall culture.

Social class
A group of people with similar levels of prestige, power, and wealth whose thinking and behavior reflect a set of related beliefs, attitudes, and values.

purchases these people make are directly affected by small membership groups within their neighborhoods, they are indirectly touched by the influence of social class.

Among the upper middle class, the *nouveaux riches* are most likely to purchase furs or yachts, because these products signify achievement. The expensive car, the big house, private college for the kids, a summer home, a boat, and frequent vacations are all symbolic expressions of success. This kind of buying behavior was well described by the turn-of-the-century American economist Thorstein Veblen, who coined the term **conspicuous consumption**. Veblen, in criticizing people who buy products simply to be seen consuming them or to display them, hit on a fact of human nature. Consumption of certain items is a means to express one's social class status. Although you may snicker along with Veblen at this behavior, the desire to show off may be real and quite important to an individual who aspires to or has achieved membership in a higher social class, and thus a marketer should not ignore it.

REFERENCE GROUPS

Each individual belongs to many groups. From a marketing perspective, the most important are reference groups. A **reference group** is a group that influences an individual because that individual is a member of the group or aspires to be a member of it. The reference group is used as a point of comparison for self-evaluation.

A **membership group** is a group an individual is actually part of. Examples include clubs, the freshman class, and UCLA alumni. Such groups strongly influence members' behavior—including consumer behavior—by exerting pressure to conform, or peer pressure. The individual is free to join or withdraw from a *voluntary* membership group, such as a group of college peers or a political party. Sometimes, however, the individual has little or no choice about group membership. For example, people approaching middle age may not like that fact, but they nevertheless make changes in their lives as a result of the influence of their middle-aged peers.

Conspicuous consumption
Consumption for the sake of enhancing social prestige.

Reference group
A group that influences an individual because that individual is a member of the group or aspires to be a member.

Membership group
A group to which an individual belongs. If the individual has chosen to belong to the group, it is a voluntary membership group.

e x h i b i 6-10 The American Class System in the 20th Century—an Estimate

CLASS (PERCENTAGE OF POPULATION)	ANNUAL INCOME (1994 DOLLARS)	PROPERTY	OCCUPATIONS	EDUCATION
Upper class (1–3%)	Very high (over $675,000)	Great wealth, old wealth	Investors, heirs, capitalists, corporate executives, highly placed civil and military leaders	Liberal arts education at elite schools
Upper middle class (10–15%)	High ($65,000 or more)	Accumulation of property through savings	Upper managers, professionals, successful small business owners	College, often with graduate training
Middle class (30–34%)	Moderate (average almost $40,000)	Some savings	Small business owners, lower managers, farmers, semiprofessionals, nonretail sales and clerical workers	Some college, high school
Working class (40–45%)	Low (about $25,000)	Some savings	Skilled labor, unskilled labor, retail sales operatives	Some high school, grade school
Lower class (20–25%)	Poverty income (below $18,750)	No savings	Working poor, unemployed, welfare recipients	Grade school or illiterate

Source: Adapted from Dennis Gilbert and Joseph Kahl, *The American Class Structure* (Homewood, IL: Dorsey Press, 1982); and from Daniel W. Rossides, *Social Stratification: The American Class System in Comparative Perspective*, © 1990, Englewood Cliffs, NJ: Prentice Hall, Inc., pp. 406–408.

A second major type of reference group is the **aspirational group**. Individuals may try to behave or look like the people whose group they hope to join. Thus, a little brother may try to act like a big brother and his buddies, or a little sister may try to act like a big sister's teenage friends. Similarly, the young business manager may choose to "dress for success." This usually means dressing like the women or men the manager hopes to join one day in the organization's higher ranks.

Aspirational group
A group to which an individual would like to belong.

Reference Groups Influence Some Products More Than Others   The use of some products is highly subject to group influence. Examples include clothing, cars, and beer consumed publicly. The use of other products is subject to almost no group pressure. These products are so mundane or so lacking in visibility that no one uses them to express self-concept. The risks of using the "wrong" brand in private are small. One rarely hears comments about someone's eating Libby's canned peaches instead of Del Monte's. Note that some product categories can be subject to reference group influences without regard to brand name or design: "Why don't you break down and get an air conditioner, Harry?" "You mean you use instant coffee? No, thank you!" Reference groups, then, may influence the type of product consumed, the brand purchased, or both.

focus on relationships

Harley-Davidson   Owners of Harley-Davidson motorcycles strongly identify with the membership group of Harley owners. They often fancy Harley riders as cowboys, desperadoes, or knights in shining armor. Marketers at Harley-Davidson exert considerable effort to make Harley owners feel special and part of the Harley-Davidson tradition. The company endorses a club (the Harley Owners Group, or HOG), a newsletter (Hog Tales), and many special events. For example, ZZ Top has played at HOG-members-only shows sponsored by Harley-Davidson.

www.harley-davidson.com

Opinion Leaders   Groups frequently include individuals known as opinion leaders. **Opinion leaders** might be friends who are looked up to because of their intelligence, athletic abilities, appearance, or special abilities, such as skill in cooking, mechanics, or languages.[20] In any group, the role of opinion leader with respect to buying behavior moves from member to member, depending on the product involved. If someone is planning to buy a car, that person may seek the opinion or guidance of a friend or family member who is thought to know about cars. The same person might seek a different "expert" when he or she is buying stereo equipment, or good wine, or investment plans.

Opinion leader
A group member who, because of some quality or characteristic, is likely to lead other group members in particular matters.

In certain situations, the most powerful determinant of buying behavior is the attitude of those people the individual respects. Thus, word-of-mouth recommendations may be important buying influences. One reason that marketers try to satisfy their customers is their hope that the customers will recommend the product or organization to members of their social groups. The best thing a homeowner can hear when hiring a house painter, for example, is that the painter did a good job on a neighbor's or friend's house.

THE FAMILY

The United States Census Bureau defines a **family** as a group of two or more persons related by birth, marriage, or adoption and residing together. An individual's family is an important reference group. The family is characterized by frequent face-to-face interaction among family members, who respond to each other on the

Family
A group of two or more persons related by birth, marriage, or adoption and residing together.

basis of their total personalities rather than on the basis of particular roles. It is not surprising that the values people hold, their self-concepts, and the products they buy are influenced by their families. That influence may continue to be strong throughout a person's life. The family is the group primarily responsible for the **socialization process**—that is, the passing down of social values, norms, and roles. Socialization includes the learning of buying behavior. Children observe how their parents evaluate and select products in stores. They see how the exchange process takes place at the cash register and quickly learn that money or a credit card changes hands there. That is how children learn the buying role. When children receive money as a gift or allowance and are permitted to spend it, they act out the buying role, thus learning an activity they will perform throughout their lives.

Socialization process
The process by which a society transmits its values, norms, and roles to its members.

SOCIAL SITUATIONS

Another environmental influence on the decision-making process is the social situation. Consider the gasoline-buying consumer who is late for an appointment and notices the tank is nearly empty. The situational pressure may increase the importance of convenient location as a choice criterion and decrease the importance of other attributes. It would be impossible to list all the social situational influences on buying behavior. However, it is important to appreciate that a consumer may purchase one brand in one social situation and another in a different social situation.

Joint Decision Making

Joint decision making
Decision making shared by all or some members of a group. Often, one decision maker dominates the process.

Some consumer choices are made not by individuals but by groups of two or more people. This is referred to as **joint decision making** (or household decision making). Family members may, for example, choose a car or a house together. Or spouses or partners may sit down together to talk over insurance purchases, furniture purchases, or retirement plans. Despite this image of togetherness, most purchase decisions are dominated by one group member. In the case of the family group, the parents dominate rather than the grade-school children. Older children may have greater influence—as when the teenage son, who "knows all about cars," advises his parents on the selection of a new auto. Typically, different group members take the dominant role

Mothers are often the decision makers and buyers of the food and drinks their children consume.

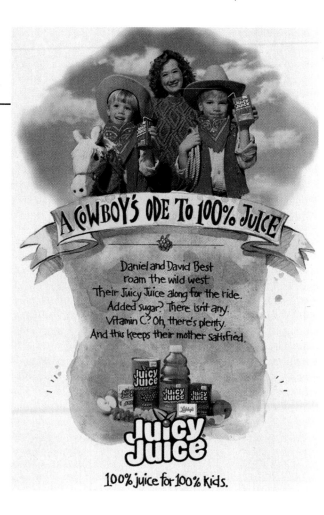

A COWBOY'S ODE TO 100% JUICE

Daniel and David Best
roam the wild west.
Their Juicy Juice along for the ride.
Added sugar? There isn't any.
Vitamin C? Oh, there's plenty.
And this keeps their mother satisfied.

Juicy Juice

100% juice for 100% kids.

in group decision making for different purchases. Even though changing sex roles are influencing traditional roles in family decision making, in most households the husband usually dominates decisions relating to purchases of insurance, while decisions regarding clothing for the children, food, and household furnishings are most often dominated by the wife. This pattern reflects society's norms and traditional role expectations. Decisions made by husband and wife together are common when entertainment, housing, and vacation choices are being made. It should be noted that changes taking place in our society are making the process of identifying the major decision influencer more difficult.

To simplify the discussion, we have not mentioned the distinctions among consumers' roles during the buying effort. However, there are several roles to be played in any buying decision. These roles are (1) the buyer, who, narrowly defined, is the person who goes to a store and actually purchases a product; (2) the user, who, narrowly viewed, is the person who actually consumes or uses the product; and (3) the decision maker, who decides which product or brand to buy. Think about it for a while. Each role could be played by a different person, or all could be played by the same person, or the roles could be played by any combination of people.

The purchase of baby food is the classic example of a situation in which different people play different roles. The baby eats the food but is denied any comment on it. The buyer could be an older child sent to the store by Mom. Mom is the decision maker who, based on her own experience, the influence of advertisements, or her mother's suggestions, has determined which brand of baby food to buy. The purchase of gum or a haircut, however, may involve only one person performing all three roles.

In more complex buying decisions, such as the purchase of a new home or a family automobile, a family member may also play the role of influencer or gatekeeper. The **influencer** expresses an opinion about the product or service to persuade the decision maker ("Dad, we need to sell the station wagon and buy a car that won't embarrass me"). The **gatekeeper** controls the flow of information ("I won't tell Bob about the house on Rockwood Drive because I liked the one on Hazel Boulevard better").

The focus of marketing changes with the role structure of the buying decision. When only one person is involved, marketing can be more concentrated than when several people in different roles are involved. In the baby food example, whom should the marketer attempt to reach? The decision maker—the person with the real say in the matter—should be the target. Thus, baby food advertisements appear in publications read by mothers as well as on TV and radio programs that reach mothers. These advertisements stress the concerns of mothers, such as nutrition. These are matters that neither the baby nor the older sibling sent to the store really cares about.

Influencer
A group member who attempts to persuade the decision maker.

Gatekeeper
A group member who controls the flow of information to the decision maker.

summary

Understanding consumer behavior helps the marketer bring about satisfying exchanges in the marketplace. Consumer behavior is affected by a variety of individual and interpersonal (sociocultural) factors, which influence the decision-making process. Marketers must take these factors into account.

1   *Understand the basic model of consumer behavior.*

Consumer behavior results from the interaction of person and environment, $B = f(P, E)$. Consumer

behavior theorists have expanded and explained this basic model with many theories.

2   *Describe the consumer decision-making process and understand factors, such as consumer involvement, that influence it.*

The decision-making process varies depending on how routine the consumer perceives the situation to be. For decisions involving extensive problem solving, consumers follow a multistep process: (1) recognizing the problem, (2) searching for alternative solutions, (3) evaluating those alternatives, (4) deciding whether to buy, and (5) if a purchase is made, evaluating the product purchased. Many internal and environmental factors affect this process, including consumer involvement as well as situational influences such as physical settings, social circumstances, and economic conditions.

3 *Appreciate the importance of perceived risk, choice criteria, purchase satisfaction, and cognitive dissonance.*

Perceived risk is the consumer's uncertainty about whether a product will do what it is intended to do. Choice criteria are those critical attributes the consumer uses to evaluate a product alternative. Purchase satisfaction on the consumer's part means that marketing has achieved its goal. However, the consumer may instead experience cognitive dissonance—a sense of tension and uncertainty—after deciding to make a purchase. Marketers must address all these issues if satisfactory exchanges are to take place.

4 *Recognize the influence of individual factors, such as motives, perception, learning, attitude, and personality, on consumer behavior.*

Motivation theory attempts to explain the causes of goal-directed behavior in terms of needs, motives, incentives, and drives. Needs can be classified in many ways. Maslow's needs hierarchy ranks human needs from the most basic (physiological) to the highest (self-actualization). As the lower needs are satisfied, the higher needs become more important. Perception is the process of interpreting sensations and stimuli. Each person's perceptions differ at least slightly from everyone else's. Selective perception is the process of screening out or interpreting stimuli—including marketing stimuli. Learning is important to marketing because consumers learn to favor certain products and brands and to dislike others. Consumers also learn to have certain attitudes. Personality reflects the individual's consistent ways of responding to his or her environment. It is gener-

ally agreed that the influence of personality on consumer behavior should be studied only along with other factors, such as attitudes and demographic characteristics, to predict specific behaviors.

5 *Explain the nature of culture and subculture in terms of social values, norms, and roles.*

Marketers look at culture as the values, beliefs, and customary behaviors that the members of a society learn and share. Insofar as consumers in a society share a culture, they think and act in similar ways. A subculture is a group within a dominant culture that has values and distinctive characteristics not shared with the larger culture. Cultures and subcultures prescribe certain values, norms, and roles for the members.

6 *Characterize social class in the United States.*

A social class is a group of people with similar levels of prestige, power, and wealth. According to one view, U.S. society may be roughly divided into five social classes determined by wealth, education, occupation, and other measures of prestige. People in different social classes differ in lifestyle, purchase preferences, and shopping and consumption patterns.

7 *Explain the influence of reference groups on individual buyers.*

Groups strongly influence individuals' behavior. Reference groups, including membership and aspirational groups, provide points of comparison by which an individual evaluates himself or herself. These groups have many direct and indirect influences on purchasing behaviors.

8 *Examine the roles in the joint decision-making process.*

Roles in the joint decision-making process include buyer, user, and decision maker, as well as influencer and gatekeeper for more complex decisions. In general, the decision maker should be the focus of marketing efforts.

key terms

consumer behavior (p. 161)	purchase satisfaction (p. 167)	perception (p. 172)
routinized response behavior (p. 162)	cognitive dissonance (p. 168)	selective perception (p. 172)
extensive problem solving (p. 162)	motivation (p. 169)	closure (p. 172)
limited problem solving (p. 162)	motive (p. 169)	selective exposure (p. 174)
consumer involvement (p. 163)	need (p. 169)	selective attention (p. 174)
problem recognition (p. 164)	incentive (p. 169)	selective interpretation (p. 174)
perceived risk (p. 164)	physiological need (p. 169)	stimulus factor (p. 174)
information search (p. 165)	social and psychological need (p. 169)	individual factor (p. 174)
choice criteria (p. 166)	emotion (p. 172)	brand image (p. 175)

learning (p. 176)
memory (p. 177)
operant conditioning (p. 177)
reinforcement (p. 178)
attitude (p. 178)
personality (p. 180)
self-concept (p. 180)

role (p. 181)
subculture (p. 183)
social class (p. 183)
conspicuous consumption (p. 184)
reference group (p. 184)
membership group (p. 184)
aspirational group (p. 185)

opinion leader (p. 185)
family (p. 185)
socialization process (p. 186)
joint decision making (p. 186)
influencer (p. 187)
gatekeeper (p. 187)

questions for review & critical thinking

1. Use the consumer behavior model shown in Exhibit 6-2 to explain how an individual might arrive at each of the following decisions:
   a. To buy a package of Doublemint chewing gum
   b. Not to buy a BMW convertible
   c. To buy a new house
   d. Not to take a group of three children to the Ice Capades
2. Using examples from your own experience, explain how the following have affected your purchasing behavior:
   a. Extensive problem solving
   b. Perceived risk
   c. Choice criteria
   d. Cognitive dissonance
3. What might a marketer do to reduce cognitive dissonance in the following situations?
   a. A consumer purchases an automobile.
   b. A wholesaler agrees to carry an industrial product line.
   c. A parent purchases an expensive video game for her children.
   d. A man purchases a magazine subscription and wants to be billed later.
4. Tell how the last major purchase you made involved a perceived risk and information search behavior.
5. Name the five levels in Maslow's needs hierarchy. Which group of needs is the most powerful?
6. What is selective perception? How does it influence behavior?
7. Use learning theory to explain why consumers repurchase the same products repeatedly.
8. How do unfavorable consumer attitudes lead to behaviors that are undesirable?
9. What kinds of purchases might be particularly influenced by a buyer's personality and self-image? Name some products and explain your choices.
10. Distinguish between norms and values.

11. How might the marketers at McDonald's be influenced by cultural forces in U.S. marketing? In international marketing?
12. How likely is it that the following people would purchase a ticket to the ballet, to a professional baseball game, and to Disneyland?
    a. A 34-year-old steelworker who graduated from high school
    b. A 44-year-old college professor
    c. A 21-year-old executive secretary
    d. A 21-year-old counter helper at Burger King
13. Is knowledge of consumers' social class useful in marketing planning? Name three products whose purchase might be influenced by the buyer's social class.
14. Is a reference group likely to influence the purchase of the following products or brands?
    a. Laundry detergent
    b. Shampoo
    c. Polo sports shirt
    d. Wristwatch
    e. Athletic club membership
    f. Milk
15. How much joint decision making by a husband and wife would you expect for the following purchases?
    a. Life insurance
    b. Steam iron
    c. Private school education
    d. Box of candy
16. In a family consisting of a father, a mother, and an 11-year-old daughter, what roles might be played, and by whom, in the purchase of a new home?
17. Think of a recent purchase you've made, and identify all the social forces that may have influenced your purchase.
18. Form small groups as directed by your instructor. Outline the consumer decision-making process for choosing a college or university. Discuss as a class each group's outline of the process.

marketing plan—right or wrong?

1. After a customer signs a contract for a new Ford Explorer at a car dealership, the customer must wait a day for the dealership to clean the car and make other final preparations. Overnight the dealer puts a tag on the mirror that reads "Sold to a nice person."

2. Dole Fresh Fruit Company has a plan to create a sticker-collecting trend among kids. Stickers of mascot Bobby Banana or one of his fruit and veggie pals (Anthony Apple, Gus Grape, Pamela Pineapple, Barney Broccoli, Amber Orange, and Sammy Salad Bag) will appear on bananas, oranges, grapefruit, and other fruit or vegetable products.

3. A married couple planned to have their kitchen remodeled. They set their budget at $30,000 and talked extensively to a local builder whom a friend had used before. The remodeler wrote the contract and brought it to the couple's house. They read and signed the builder's version of the contract.

internet insights

zikmund.swcollege.com

exercise

Go to SRI Consulting's Business Intelligence Center home page at future.sri.com. Select the Values and Lifestyles (VALS) Program link and read some of the background information on the VALS system. Select iVALS—Internet VALS—to complete a VALS survey on-line. When you have completed your questionnaire, select the Submit button to submit your completed questionnaire. Wait for the analysis (your answers will be analyzed in less than a minute). What is your primary VALS type? What is your secondary VALS type?

address book (useful urls)

Association for Consumer Research	www.acr.webpage.com:8080/acr/
Society for Consumer Psychology	www.cob.ohio-state.edu/scp/
Yankelovich Partners Monitor	www.yankelovich.com/products/ MONITOR

ethically right or wrong?

Theodore Levitt and Sterling Hayden have both written about human consumption needs. These two views appear below.[21]

Theodore Levitt

The "purpose" of the product is not what the engineer explicitly says it is, but what the consumer implicitly demands that it shall be. Thus the consumer consumes not things, but expected benefits—not cosmetics, but the satisfactions of the allurements they promise; not quarter-inch drills, but quarter-inch holes. . . .

The significance of these distinctions is anything but trivial. Nobody knows this better, for example, than the creators of automobile ads. It is not the generic virtues that they tout, but more likely the car's capacity to enhance its user's status and [sexuality]. . . .

Whether we are aware of it or not, we in effect expect and demand that advertising create these symbols for us to show us what life might be, to bring the possibilities that we cannot see before our eyes and screen out the stark reality in which we must live.

Sterling Hayden

What does a man need—really need? A few pounds of food each day, heat, and shelter, six feet to lie down in—and some form of working activity that will yield a sense of accomplishment. That's all—in a material sense. And we know it. But we are brainwashed by our economic system until we end up in a tomb beneath a pyramid of time payments, mortgages, preposterous gadgetry, playthings that divert our attention from the sheer idiocy of the charade.

QUESTIONS

1. What might each author say about the other's viewpoint?
2. Does advertising create needs?
3. Which of these two views is ethically correct?

TAKE A STAND

1. After a winter storm, your car is covered with ice. There is an old spray can of de-icer in the basement. You read the ingredients and discover it contains chlorofluorocarbons. Do you use the spray?
2. You purchase a new copy of Lotus 1-2-3 at a computer store. Several weeks later a friend says he would like to have a copy of Lotus 1-2-3 and asks you to make a copy for him. Do you make the copy?
3. Is using embedded stimuli in advertisements immoral?
4. You pick up a friend, and she is wearing a fur coat. Do you tell her she shouldn't wear the coat because the fur industry harms animals?
5. After 76 years in the Southwest Athletic Conference, the University of Arkansas switched to the Southeast Conference to obtain higher television revenues. Did the university violate any norms?
6. Some pawnshops are now marketing themselves as "lending institutions for the working poor." Does this service raise any ethical concerns?

6-1 video case

Minnesota Twins:
Take Me Out to the Ball Game

Clay Tucker and his wife Carol are in their late 30s. They have two children, a son age 9 and a daughter age 7. The Tuckers own their own home in Edina, Minnesota, a suburb of Minneapolis. Both Clay and Carol are college graduates. Clay attended college on a track scholarship. Today, he works for a bank in a middle-management position. He drives a four-wheel-drive Ford Explorer. Carol was an art major in college, and she teaches art in high school. She drives a Mazda sedan.

One Monday morning in June, Clay read in the newspaper that the New York Yankees were coming to town for a four-day series beginning on Thursday. His thoughts went back to his high school days in Chicago. He remembered when he and a group of his teenage pals would go to Comiskey Park to root for the White Sox against the arch-rival Yankees. It was always great fun.

The Twins play in the Metrodome, so Clay knew there was no chance for a rain-out. He said to himself, "Why not take the family out to the ball park on Saturday?" The price of a general admission ticket would be about $6, he thought. Grandstand reserved seats might be about $10, and a box seat would probably be less than $15. They could drive to the stadium around 6 p.m., find parking nearby, and buy some hot dogs for dinner.

QUESTIONS
1. Outline the decision-making process for the Tucker family's purchase of tickets to a Twins game.
2. What choice criteria was Clay using to make this decision about family entertainment?
3. Suppose the Tuckers do go to the game. What other purchase decisions are they likely to make while at the game? Identify whether these are routine or problem-solving decisions.
4. What factors will contribute to consumer satisfaction for each member of the Tucker family?
5. What role does learning play in becoming a loyal Twins fan?
6. Describe the sociocultural forces that make a baseball game at the Metrodome a likeable product.

Ore-Best Farms

Ore-Best Farms, a USDA-approved rabbit-processing plant in Oregon City, Oregon, markets vacuum-packed rabbit fryers to Oregon supermarkets. The company, which markets the fresh bunnies in Cryovac packaging similar to bacon packs, is betting that rabbit meat will prove as popular as fish or lamb in the next few years. Company statistics show that rabbit is highest in protein of all meats and lowest in cholesterol, fat, and calories. Ore-Best is marketing it as a nutritious alternative to red meat and fowl for health-conscious consumers.

Rabbit accounts for about ½ cent of the U.S. meat dollar, compared with about 15 cents in Europe, where it is a dietary staple, noted Ore-Best director of operations Leonard Parsons. Ore-Best, aiming to reeducate American tastes, is presenting "tender country-raised rabbit" in transparent packages adorned with colorful labels and illustrated recipes. Where competitors market rabbit domestically, it is sold frozen in cardboard boxes.

"Nutritious rabbit is delicious" is the tag line on the labels, point-of-purchase displays, and newspaper ads. Promotion prepared by Ore-Best's Portland agency, Petzold & Associates, avoids pictures of anything resembling a cute family pet.

The company also has plans to market rabbit legs, cutlets, fillets, ground rabbit, even sausages, patties, and other processed products, in much the same manner as the chicken and turkey industries have marketed their products recently.

The price and texture make rabbit more comparable to beef or pork than to fowl, however. The meat—all white—tastes similar to veal, partisans say.

Ore-Best also intends to sell nonedible portions of its rabbits, including high-fashion rabbit fur garments created in Korea and Hong Kong and rabbit fertilizer. Rabbit blood will be used in medical experiments, rabbit feet sold as lucky charms, and the tail as a zipper pull.

Rabbits may be an accountant's dream. They are inexpensive to raise, take very little care, and reproduce like crazy. For that reason, some Third World countries have expressed keen interest in borrowing some of Ore-Best's rabbit economics. Hospitals, impressed by the nutritional credentials of rabbit meat, are another potential major market.[22]

QUESTIONS
1. Outline the decision-making process a consumer might go through before purchasing Ore-Best's rabbit meat.
2. What choice criteria might be involved in this decision?
3. What cultural factors will help in the marketing of Ore-Best Farms' rabbit meat? Which will be a hindrance?
4. Will social class be a marketing consideration? Will the product be most appealing to one particular class?
5. Will reference groups be influential in a consumer's decision to purchase rabbit meat?

The McGees Buy Three Bicycles

The McGees lived in Riverside, California, west of Los Angeles. Terry was a physics professor at the University of California, Riverside. His wife, Cheryl, worked as a volunteer 10 hours a week at a Crisis Center. They had two children, Judy and Mark.

In February, Cheryl's parents sent her $50 to buy a bicycle for Judy's 11th birthday. They had bought Judy her first bike when she was 5. Now they wanted to buy her a full-size bike. Though Cheryl's parents felt every child should have a bike, Cheryl did not think Judy really wanted one. Judy and most of her friends did not ride their bikes often, and she was afraid to ride to school because of the traffic. So Cheryl decided to buy Judy the cheapest full-size bicycle she could find. Since most of Judy's friends did not have full-size bikes, Cheryl did not know much about them. To learn more about the types available and their prices, Cheryl and Judy checked the JC Penney and Sears catalogs. After looking through the catalogs, Judy said the only thing she cared about was the color. She wanted blue—her favorite color.

Using the Yellow Pages, Cheryl called several retail outlets selling bikes in Riverside. To her surprise, she found that a local department store actually had the best price for a 26-inch bicycle, even lower than Toys ' Я ' Us and Wal-Mart. Cheryl went to the department store, went straight to the toy department, and selected a blue bicycle before a salesperson approached her. She took the bike to the cash register and paid for it. After making the purchase, the McGees found out that the bike was cheap in all senses. The chrome plating on the wheels rusted away in 6 months. Both tires split and had to be replaced.

Later, Cheryl's parents sent another $50 for a bike for Mark's 9th birthday. Based on their experience with Judy's bike, the McGees now realized that the lowest-priced bike might not be the least expensive option in the long run. The McGees wanted to buy Mark a sturdy bike. Mark said he wanted a red, ten-speed, lightweight, imported bike with a lot of accessories—headlights, special pedals, and so forth. The McGees were concerned that Mark would not maintain an expensive bike. When they saw an advertisement for a bicycle sale at Montgomery Ward, Cheryl and Terry went to the store with Mark. A salesperson approached them at an outdoor display of bikes and directed them to the sporting goods department, where they found row after row of red three-speed bikes with minimal accessories—the type of bike Cheryl and Terry felt was ideal for Mark. A salesperson approached them and attempted to interest them in a more expensive bike. Terry interrupted the salesperson in midsentence, saying he wanted to look at the bikes on his own. With a little suggestion, Mark decided he wanted one of these bikes. His need for accessories was satisfied when Terry and Cheryl bought a wire basket for the bike.

After buying a bike for Mark, Terry decided he would like a bike himself, to ride on the weekends. Terry had ridden bikes since he was 5. In graduate school, he had owned a ten-speed bike and had frequently taken 50-mile rides with friends. However, he had not owned a bike since moving to Riverside 15 years ago. Terry really didn't know much about the types of touring bicycles available. He bought a copy of *Touring* and went to the library to read the evaluation of touring bicycles in *Consumer Reports*. Based on this information, he decided he wanted a Serrato. It had all the features he wanted—light weight, durable construction, and flexible setup. When Terry called the discount stores and bicycle shops, he found out that they did not carry Serrato. Since he couldn't find a Serrato, he decided he might not really need a bike—after all, he had done without one for 15 years.

One day after lunch, Terry was walking back to his office and saw a small bicycle shop. The shop was really run-down, with bicycle parts scattered across the floor. The owner, a young man wearing shorts covered in grease, was fixing a bike. As Terry was looking around, the owner approached him and asked him if he liked to bicycle. Terry said he used to but had given it up when he moved to Riverside. The owner said that was a shame because there were a lot of nice places to tour around Riverside. Terry mentioned his interest in a Serrato and his disappointment in not finding a store in Riverside that sold them. The owner said he could order a Serrato for Terry but that they were not very reliable. He suggested a Ross and showed Terry one he had in stock. Terry thought the $400 price was too expensive, but the owner convinced him to try the bike the following weekend. They would ride together in the country. Terry took a 60-mile tour with the bike shop owner and some of his friends. He really enjoyed the experience, recalling his college days. After the tour, Terry bought the Ross.[23]

QUESTIONS

1. Outline the decision-making process the McGees followed for each of their bicycle purchases.
2. Compare the different purchase processes for the three bicycles. What stimulated each of the purchases? What were the factors considered in making the store choice and the purchase decisions?
3. How do the choice criteria vary for the different decisions?

chapter
7

Business Markets and Organizational Buying

After you have studied this chapter, you will be able to:

Identify the types of organizations that make up the business, or organizational, market.

1

Know the steps involved in an organizational buying decision.

2

Characterize the three basic organizational buying situations: the straight rebuy, the modified rebuy, and the new task purchase.

3

Understand that the Internet is changing the way business-to-business marketing occurs.

4

Explain why the buying center concept is important in business-to-business marketing.

5

(continued on next page)

forming strategic alliances with other companies is fast becoming a necessity for small businesses trying to stay competitive.

From biotechnology to retailing, small firms are forming partnerships to achieve goals that would be too costly, time-consuming, or difficult to accomplish on their own. They're also pursuing alliances to encourage product innovation, bring stability to cyclical businesses, expand product portfolios, and forge new kinds of supplier relationships.

New Pig Corporation wanted to make itself a world-class competitor, but having merely good supplier relationships wasn't enough to bring about the dramatic changes necessary to achieve that goal.

The 300-employee company has grown rapidly as a leader in the manufacture of contained absorbents—sock-like bundles of absorbent materials used to soak up industrial spills. New Pig set down a whole host of goals it deemed necessary to propel the company forward.

Because New Pig sells 3,000 products through its catalog and depends on its suppliers for some element of every item, the firm's management decided to focus on improving the firm's purchasing operation.

MANAGEMENT DECIDED THE FIRM HAD TO GO BEYOND TRADITIONAL RELATIONSHIPS WITH ITS KEY SUPPLIERS AND DEVELOP STRATEGIC ALLIANCES WITH THEM.

The company's goals included reducing the time it takes to introduce products, improving product quality, bringing about joint problem solving with suppliers and joint adjustments to market conditions, and involving suppliers early in product development.

To meet those goals, management decided, the firm had to go beyond traditional relationships with its key suppliers and develop strategic alliances with them. New Pig wanted to establish a level of communication with suppliers that fostered continuous improvement and problem solving.

As a starting point, the company began measuring suppliers' performance and, in turn, asked its 30 largest-volume suppliers to evaluate New Pig as a customer.

For these evaluations, absolute candor was the company's guiding principle. "It was quite shocking," says Doug Evans, New Pig's director of strategic purchasing. "We didn't have as close a relationship with suppliers as we thought we did."

His team discovered, for example, why a long-time vendor consistently failed to come up with the innovative approaches that New Pig sought. "We found out that [our people] always faulted them for making mistakes, so they never offered us anything that wasn't time-tested and perfect," says Evans. "Without even knowing it, we were discouraging them from bringing us new ideas."

As such problems began to be addressed, relationships began to improve. In the 18 months since the program has been in place, several joint projects with suppliers have led to improved processes and reduced costs; one change in a shipping method, for instance, produced savings of hundreds of thousands of dollars.

"What's different about this approach is the depth of the relationship," says Evans. "With the usual customer-supplier relationship, you're talking about a phone call as your only contact. With our strategic partners, we have tons of communications, we sit down with product-development teams, and we go out and look at [their] tooling."

The effort that goes into these relationships explains why only 20 to 50 of New Pig's 800 suppliers will be strategic partners. "Like peeling back an onion, you learn things about each other's operation," says Evans. "We've developed a synergy and are moving forward together to cut costs, be more efficient, and increase profits. There's a ton of opportunity out there if you talk."[1]

New Pig markets to business organizations, not to ultimate consumers. But, as the opening vignette illustrates, understanding the buyer-seller relationship is as important in the business market as in the consumer market. This chapter investigates how organizational buying behavior differs from the buying behavior of ultimate consumers.

The chapter begins by defining business-to-business marketing and organizational buying behavior. Then it explains the different types of organizational buying decisions and the role of the buying center. Finally, it discusses the nature of industrial demand and the characteristics of business markets.

Organizational Buying Behavior

A business marketing transaction takes place whenever a good or service is sold for any use other than personal consumption. In other words, any sale to an industrial user, wholesaler, retailer, or organization other than the ultimate consumer is sold in the business market. Such sales involve **business-to-business marketing**.

All products other than consumer products are organizational products, as they are used to help operate an organization's business. The term *organizational* is broader than the term *business* or *industrial,* but both of the latter terms remain in common use. In fact, the term *business market,* which, narrowly defined, would refer only to manufacturers, service marketers, wholesalers, and retailers, is broadly used by marketing writers to include organizational buyers such as governments, churches, and other nonprofit entities.

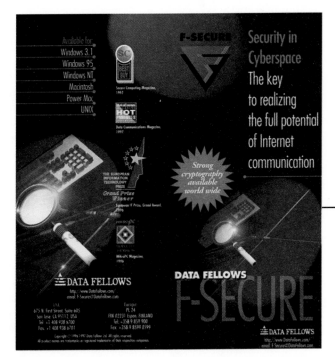

If you are unsure whether a product is a consumer product or an organizational product, ask these two questions:

1. Who bought it?
2. Why did they buy it?

Notice that it is not necessary to ask the question "What did they buy?" For example, airline travel may be a consumer or an organizational product, depending on who bought it and why it was purchased. The fact that it is an airline ticket is not relevant to its classification.

What, then, do organizations buy? Manufacturers require raw materials, equipment, component parts, supplies, and services. Producers of nonmanufactured goods require many of these same products. Wholesalers and retailers purchase products for resale, as well as equipment such as trucks, shelving, and computers. Hospitals, zoos, and other nonprofit organizations use many goods and services to facilitate the performance of their business functions, as do federal, state, and local governments. In fact, the federal government is the largest single buyer of organizational products. In participating in business-to-business exchanges, all these organizations display **organizational buying behavior**. Exhibit 7-1 illustrates some of these behaviors.

Buying is a necessary activity for all business and not-for-profit organizations. In organizational buying situations, the purchase of goods and services, such as semiconductors and accounting services, may involve a complex process. Purchasing agents and other organizational members determine the need to purchase goods and services, engage in information-seeking activities, evaluate alternative purchasing actions, and negotiate the necessary arrangements with suppliers.[2]

Placing an order with a supplier is generally not a simple act. Organizational buying takes place over time, involves communications among several organizational members, and entails financial relationships with suppliers.

Organizational buying behavior
The decision-making activities of organizational buyers that lead to purchases of products.

e x h i b i 7-1 Some Examples of Organizational Buying Behavior

SEGMENT OF ORGANIZATIONAL MARKET	TYPICAL BUYING SITUATION
Agriculture	A farmer purchases a tractor from a farm equipment dealer.
Mining, forestry, fishing	Reading and Bates purchases offshore drilling equipment from the manufacturer.
Construction	A home construction company hires a CPA firm.
Manufacturers of consumer goods	The Smucker Co. supplies fruit filling for Kellogg's Pop Tarts.
Manufacturers of industrial goods	Boeing purchases steel as a raw material from United States Steel.
Wholesalers and retailers (resale market)	Bloomingdale's purchases towels from a wholesaler.
Information	TCI Cablevision makes a decision as to whether to offer WGN as part of its programming.
Service industries	Walker Marketing Research Company purchases software from a distributor of office supplies.
Nonprofit organizations	The San Diego Zoo hires an advertising agency to produce TV commercials.
Government	The federal government asks for competitive bids on solar panels for a space telescope.

Characteristics of the Business Market

The agricultural, financial, and manufacturing industries are quite different from one another, yet they share some basic characteristics that are typical of business markets. First, particular business markets often contain relatively few customers. Second, these customers are often geographically concentrated. For example, Silicon Valley, in the area surrounding San Jose, California, is the headquarters for hundreds of companies that make semiconductors, computer specialty products, and computer software. Of course, foreign competition exists, but business markets abroad also tend to be geographically concentrated.

A third characteristic of organizational buyers is their preference for buying directly from the manufacturer or producer. This preference may come from the desire to buy in large quantities or to avoid intermediaries in an effort to obtain a better price. It may also be a function of the technical complexity of many of the products these buyers use and the fact that many such products are made to order. (Consider how the U.S. government purchases weapon systems, for example.) For all of these reasons, the desire to deal directly with producers is understandable.

A fourth characteristic of organizational purchasers is their comparative expertise in buying. They buy, almost always, in a scientific way, basing decisions on close analyses of the product being offered and careful comparisons with competing products. Moreover, terms of sale, service, guarantees, and other such factors are likely to be carefully weighed. If a product is a highly technical one, the buyer may assign properly trained engineers or scientists to participate in the purchase decision. For a major purchase decision, a committee will likely be formed to evaluate certain factors such as the business-to-business marketer's product, technical abilities, and position vis-à-vis competitors. Here again, strategic alliances may be formed to work out technological problems. For example, Fujitsu's engineers shared technologies and worked closely with product developers at Sun Microsystems to jointly develop a new microchip for Sun's workstations.

A fifth characteristic of the business market is the importance of repeated market transactions. The focus of much business-to-business marketing has shifted from the single transaction to the overall buyer-seller relationship—a focus known as *relationship marketing*. By establishing strong working relationships, suppliers and customers can improve distribution processes and other joint activities. In fact, many business-to-business marketers form **strategic alliances**, or informal partnerships, with their customers. For example, Sherwin-Williams, the paint producer, let Sears executives help select the people who would service the Sears account. Its logic was that the two companies had joint sales goals, so it made sense to jointly select the people responsible for achieving these goals.[3]

We have already discussed the sixth characteristic of the

Silicon Valley Online
www.silvalonline.com

Strategic alliance
An informal partnership or collaboration between a marketer and an organizational buyer.

Lucent Technologies, the former system and technology divisions of AT&T plus Bell Labs, sees its business as making the things that make communications work. Lucent (the word means "luminous, marked by clarity or translucence") created innovative organizational products such as voice mail, the laser, fiber-optic cable, and 56 kbps modem chips. Business-to-business marketers who provide components, such as modem chips, that are used in the production of other products consider relationship marketing to be essential to their businesses. Many form strategic alliances that will benefit both parties.

www.lucent.com

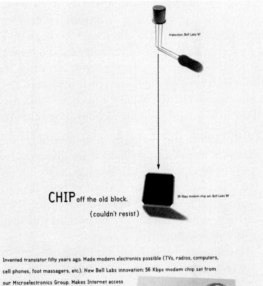

CHIP off the old block.
(couldn't resist)

Invented transistor fifty years ago. Made modern electronics possible (TVs, radios, computers, cell phones, foot massagers, etc.). New Bell Labs innovation: 56 Kbps modem chip set from our Microelectronics Group. Makes Internet access faster over regular phone lines. (Think jet-powered surfing on Net.) Seven of top ten modem makers already use our chips. (Expect other three to call any moment.) To learn more, check our Web site.

Lucent Technologies
Bell Labs Innovations
600 Mountain Avenue
Murray Hill, NJ 07974-0636
http://www.lucent.com
1-888-4-Lucent

We make the things that make communications work."

business market, but it is worth repeating. Business-to-business marketing has become a global activity. Global competition can be intense, and taking a world perspective is essential. In many instances, a business-to-business marketer's main competition does not come from its home country. Indeed, it may have no domestic competitors. Taking a global perspective is important for marketers selling in consumer markets, of course, but in business markets it is so crucial that it may determine whether a marketer's business survives. Managers in business-to-business marketing organizations often find that their decisions about international strategy are the most vital decisions they make.

The characteristics of organizational customers mentioned here do not apply to every organizational buyer. Furthermore, they by no means constitute an exhaustive list of such factors. But they do give some indications of how marketers deal with these special buyers. The fact that there are often relatively few buyers, who may be geographically concentrated and who prefer to deal directly with suppliers, encourages—indeed, often mandates—the extensive use of personal selling. The technical nature of many of the products and the expertise of the people making the purchase decisions demand a well-trained sales force with exten-

THE FOCUS OF MUCH BUSINESS-TO-BUSINESS MARKETING HAS SHIFTED FROM THE SINGLE TRANSACTION TO THE OVERALL BUYER-SELLER RELATIONSHIP—A FOCUS KNOWN AS RELATIONSHIP MARKETING.

sive knowledge of the products they sell. Representing a maker of nuclear power plants is quite different from selling Legos or Loc Blocs to Christmas-shopping grandparents. The various characteristics of business markets often combine to permit the marketer to identify almost all potential customers. This capability can make personal selling, which is usually expensive, a cost-efficient marketing tool.

Three Kinds of Buying

The buyer of organizational goods and services, whether chemicals, machinery, or maintenance services, may go through a decision-making process similar to, but more complex than, the consumer decision-making process discussed in Chapter 6. As shown in Exhibit 7-2, organizational buying behavior may be viewed as a multistage decision-making process. However, the amount of time and effort devoted to each of the stages, or **buy phases**, depends on a number of factors such as the nature of the product, the costs involved, and the experience of the organization in buying the needed goods or services. Consider these three situations:[4]

- An organization regularly buys goods and services from the same suppliers. Careful attention may have been given to selection of the suppliers at some earlier time, but the organization is well satisfied with them and with the products they offer. The organization buys from these suppliers virtually automatically. This is the **straight rebuy** situation. Everything from pencils to legal advice to equipment may be bought this way if the buyer is satisfied with the supplier's past performance.

- An organization is discontent with current suppliers or suspects that "shopping around" may be in its best interest. It knows what products are needed and who the likely suppliers are. This is the **modified rebuy** situation. Here, too, any type of good or service may be involved.

- An organization is facing a new problem or need and is not certain what products or what suppliers will fill the need. If the purchase is expected to be a very expensive one, the sense of concern and uncertainty is heightened. This is **new task buying**.

Buy phase
One of the stages of the multistage process by which organizations make purchase decisions.

Straight rebuy
A type of organizational buying characterized by automatic and regular purchases of familiar products from regular suppliers.

Modified rebuy
An organizational buying situation in which a buyer is not completely satisfied with current suppliers or products and is shopping around rather than rebuying automatically.

New task buying
An organizational buying situation in which a buyer is seeking to fill a need never before addressed. Uncertainty and lack of information about products and suppliers characterize this situation.

Buy Phases: Steps in an Organizational
Buying Decision
e   x   h   i   b   i 7-2

1. Anticipation or recognition of a problem (need)
2. Determination of the characteristics of the product and the quantity needed
3. Description of precise product specifications and critical service needs
4. Search for and qualification of potential sources
5. Acquisition and analysis of proposals
6. Evaluation of proposals and selection of suppliers
7. Selection of an order routine
8. Performance feedback and evaluation

Source: Based on Michael D. Hutt and Thomas W. Speh, *Business Marketing Management* (Hinsdale, IL: Dryden Press, 1995), p. 71.

In each situation, the length of the decision-making process may vary, depending on what is being purchased, as may the time spent on each individual buying phase. These three separate kinds of buying have been associated both with specific types of organizational buyer behaviors and with specific business-to-business marketing activities. Exhibit 7-3 summarizes the characteristics of these three categories of buying decisions. It is important to note that the key element that sets the categories apart from one another is the buyer behavior pattern, not the complexity of the product involved or monetary concerns.

CATEGORY	CHARACTERISTICS
STRAIGHT REBUY	• Arises from a continuing or recurring requirement, handled routinely
	• Usually the decision on each separate transaction is made in the purchasing department.
	• A formal or informal list of acceptable suppliers exists.
	• No supplier not on the list is considered.
	• Buyers have much relevant buying experience, and hence little new information is necessary.
	• Appears to represent the bulk of the individual purchases within companies
	• Items purchased, price paid, delivery time, and the like may vary from transaction to transaction, as long as these variations do not force the company to consider a new source of supply.
MODIFIED REBUY	• May develop from either a new task or a straight rebuy situation
	• The purchase requirement is continuing or recurring but may have expanded to a significantly larger level of operations.
	• The buying alternatives are known, but something about them has changed.
	• Some additional information is needed before the purchase decision can be made.
	• May arise because of outside events, such as an emergency or the actions of a marketer
	• May arise internally because of new buying influences or for potential cost reductions, potential quality improvements, or potential service benefits
	• Marketers who are not active suppliers try to convert the customer's straight rebuys into modified rebuys.
NEW TASK BUYING	• Is undertaken in response to a requirement or problem that has not arisen before
	• Buyers have little or no relevant past buying experience to draw on.
	• A great deal of information is needed.
	• Buyers must seek out alternative ways of solving the problem and alternative suppliers.
	• Occurs infrequently—but is very important to marketers because it sets the pattern for the more routine purchases that will follow
	• May be anticipated and developed by creative marketing

Source: Adapted from P. J. Robinson, C. W. Faris, and Y. Wind, *Industrial Buying and Creative Marketing* (Boston: Allyn & Bacon, 1967), p. 28.

Understanding the types of buying situations and behavior found in organizations is extremely important for organizational marketers, just as understanding consumer behavior patterns is important for marketers of consumer products. Each buying situation suggests a different marketing mix—an adjustment of the four major elements to fit particular circumstances.

A marketing manager facing a new task buying situation, for example, should understand that the target customer is uncertain what steps should be taken to satisfy his or her organization's needs. Such a buyer probably will require a good deal of information about the supplier, its products, and its abilities to deliver and service the products. This suggests a marketing mix that stresses promotion, especially communication of information that will help the customer evaluate alternatives and understand why the company doing the marketing is the one to choose.

A buyer in a modified rebuy mode might require information of another type. This buyer knows something of what is needed and who likely suppliers are. In such a case, communications built around very specific problem areas might be appropriate. If the target buyer is searching for new suppliers, the marketer must find out why. Have deliveries been spotty? Have there been product failures? Are prices perceived as too high? The marketer must come up with responses to these problems that show the target buyer why dealing with this supplier can solve those problems.[5]

In the case of the straight rebuy, the marketer—who is in the strong position of being the supplier benefiting from the rebuy situation—seeks to assure that the target customer does not become discontent and continues to make regular purchases. Maintaining the relationship is the key marketing objective.

In many organizational buying situations, the buyer has either a mental or a formal list of likely suppliers. This list includes those suppliers known to be able to supply the product or service according to specification and to meet time, quality, or other requirements. Suppliers who are on the list obviously have a far greater chance of landing an order than those who are not. Those not on the list will have to exert some extra effort to get an order. Thus, the activities of vendors will reflect their status—either "in" or "out." At a minimum, a firm has to know about a job to bid on it. Firms not on the list might never receive an invitation to bid. Exhibit 7-4 shows how marketing efforts might vary for "in" and "out" suppliers.

e x h i b i 7-4 Strategies Used by "In" Suppliers and "Out" Suppliers in Three Types of Buying Situations

BUYING SITUATION	SUPPLIER STATUS	
	IN SUPPLIER	OUT SUPPLIER
New task buying	Monitor changing or emerging purchasing needs in organization	Actively search for leads
	Isolate specific needs	Isolate specific needs
	If possible, participate actively in early phases of buying process by supplying information and technical advice	If possible, participate actively in early phases of buying process by supplying information and technical advice
Modified rebuy	Act immediately to remedy problems with customer	Define and respond to the organization's problem with existing supplier
	Reexamine and respond to customer needs	Encourage organization to sample alternative offerings
Straight rebuy	Reinforce buyer-seller relationship by meeting or exceeding organization's expectations	Convince organization that the potential benefits or reexamining requirements and suppliers exceed the costs of analysis
	Be alert and responsive to changing needs of customer	Attempt to gain a position on the organization's preferred list of suppliers even as a second or third choice

Source: Adapted from P. J. Robinson, C. W. Faris, and Y. Wind, *Industrial Buying and Creative Marketing* (Boston: Allyn & Bacon, 1967), p. 28.

The Internet and e-Commerce

The Internet is dramatically changing business-to-business marketing and the way organizational buying occurs. Buying over the Internet has been called *electronic commerce*. Consider General Electric, a major corporation that markets power systems, aircraft engines, plastics, medical systems, and hundreds of other products in the business market. GE does $1 billion of business on its Trading Process Network Web site. A salesperson no longer needs to make a call in the case of straight rebuys. Buyers just go to the company's Web site, find information about goods and services, select the products they need, and e-mail their orders. Many business-to-business marketers have found that providing extra customer value on the Internet both increases sales and reduces the cost of making a sales transaction.

GE Trading Process Network
www.tpn.geis.com

An Internet Web site provides a number of advantages to organizational buyers. They appreciate having product and pricing information readily available through a company's Web site. Technical documents and marketing information no longer need to be mailed or faxed to organizational buyers, because they can be sent to customers and collaborators in the value chain over the marketing company's intranet, which is connected to the Web site. Sophisticated Web sites (such as Cisco's, discussed in the What Went Right? feature) allow customers to select a particular product configuration and learn its exact cost.

Customer service representatives may not have to spend as much time on the telephone answering questions about the status of orders in progress. Many Internet sites, such as the Federal Express site, use a tracking number system that permits customers to learn the status of a shipment. Customers also like the idea of being able to get a price quote or other information at their own pace, rather than using e-mail or voice mail to contact a sales representative or customer service worker and then waiting for the company representative to get back to them later on.[6] Simply by eliminating some telephone tag (going back and forth leaving messages for the other party before contact is made), the Internet can save great amounts of time. FAQ (Frequently Asked Questions) pages on Web sites also provide added value to prospective customers.

In competitive bidding situations, the Internet can increase the number of bidders and include suppliers from around the world. General Electric has cut the length of the bidding process in its lighting division from 21 days to 10. Because requesting bids is so easy, purchasing managers contact more suppliers; the increased competition has

The Internet and electronic commerce are dramatically changing business-to-business marketing. General Electric markets power systems, aircraft engines, plastics, medical systems, and hundreds of other products in the business market. GE does $1 billion of business on its Trading Process Network Web site.

www.ge.com

what went right?

Cisco Systems Cisco Systems Inc., the leading supplier of networking hardware including routers, local- and wide-area-network switches, and dial-up access servers, has been selling its products through its World Wide Web site for less than a year. Through its immensely popular Cisco Connection Online (CCO), Cisco expects to sell more than $2 billion worth of networking products annually, making it by far the biggest World Wide Web–based marketer in the world. . . . That figure represents 40% of its business.

Cisco is in the networking business, so it's hardly surprising that a company whose products help connect . . . businesses on the Internet would be selling its wares online. But the company is setting the pace . . . in the way it's employing some fancy new technology to support the cyber-selling process.

. . . The company initially used its Web address (www.cisco.com) to offer customers product information as well as service. But in March 1996, Cisco Marketplace went online, offering customers the ability to configure their own products without having to depend on a salesperson. . . . Cisco Marketplace includes an Internetworking Product Center containing information on 12,800 parts. . . . Customers who have been granted access to do business with the company online can use the e-store 24 hours a day from anywhere in the world.

The secret to the company's e-commerce success is the system's built-in intelligence that filters out erroneous orders before they can even get into the process. This is done through a sophisticated sales-configuration software package from San Jose–based Calico. By shifting much of its business to the Web, Cisco is easing the burden on its order-entry staff, who typically must correct 10 to 15 percent of all orders that come in by fax, about 350,000 during the last fiscal year. "Something about those orders required rework," explains Cisco Connection's senior marketing manager. "With the configurator built in, 100 percent of the orders we receive over the Web site are correct the first time." The placement of a correct order . . . reduces the lead time Cisco needs to deliver the product by 2 to 3 days.

. . . The accuracy of orders is ensured because the system guides the customer through a series of questions to design the product's capabilities. Instead of being turned away, customers who pick combinations that won't work are guided to make alternative choices based on which aspects of the product have greater priority for their needs.

. . . Cisco's Web site has made it better able to meet its customers' demands because its salespeople are not just order takers. The sales force can build relationships with customers and focus on more important issues as a result of not having to handle the transaction carried out on the Internet.

Cisco is enjoying the fruits of being one of the early adopters of Web-based selling technology. . . . Its business-to-business marketing strategy has created a massive advantage for Cisco.[7]

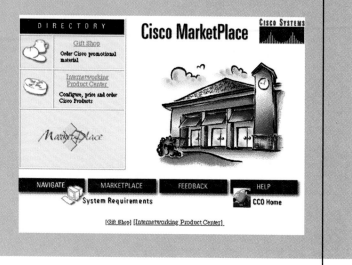

lowered the cost of goods by 5–20 percent. Advanced software lets GE purchasing managers specify to whom they want their request for bids to go and describe the type of information, such as drawings, bidders should provide. The software then manages the bids as they come back, eliminating unacceptable bids and handling further rounds, finally notifying the bidders of the outcome.[8]

The Cross-Functional Buying Center

As mentioned earlier, many people may be involved in an organizational buying decision. How do marketers manage to consider all these persons, their motives, and their special needs? It is a complicated and difficult task. However, the concept of the buying center helps marketing managers to visualize the buying process and to organize their thinking as they develop the marketing mix.[9] The **buying center** in any organization is an informal, cross-departmental decision unit whose primary objective is the acquisition, dissemination, and processing of relevant purchasing-related information. In somewhat simpler terms, the buying center includes all the people and groups that have roles in the decision-making processes of purchasing. Because all these people and groups take part, they are seen as having common goals and as sharing in the risks associated with the ultimate decision. Membership in the buying center and the size of the center vary from organization to organization and from case to case. In smaller organizations, almost everyone may have some input; in larger organizations, a more restricted group may be identifiable. The buying center may range in size from a few people to perhaps 20.

Buying center
An informal, cross-departmental decision unit, the primary objective of which is the acquisition, dissemination, and processing of relevant purchasing-related information.

When thinking in terms of a buying center, keep in mind that the center is not identified on any organization chart. A committee officially created to decide on a purchase is likely to be but one part of the buying center. Other members have unofficial but important roles to play. Indeed, membership in the buying center may actually change as the decision-making process progresses. As the purchasing task moves from step to step, individuals with expertise in certain areas are likely

focus on global competition

Doing Business in France   Effective marketers understand that culture and ingrained traditions for organizational behavior often dictate how companies conduct business meetings. For example, consider doing business in France.

Mainly because of rigid labor laws and a costly system of social benefits and protections, French companies do things strictly by the book. "Old-boy" networking and tradition also exert a heavy influence. Prestige, seniority, and pedigree rule. Widespread lack of flexibility stems from management teams whose members are drawn from identical backgrounds and educational institutions. The man at the head of the table often reflects generations at work. The bottom line: It's difficult to inspire employees to go beyond the narrow limits of their job descriptions.

The French are very attentive to hierarchy and ceremony. The *vous* form of address, for example, is mandatory in business circles. If you use *tu*, you'd best be talking to a toddler. When first meeting a French-speaking business person, stick with *monsieur, madame, or mademoiselle* as a salutation. The use of first names is disrespectful to the French. It's also advisable to apologize if you don't speak French fluently. Such apology shows general respect for the language and dismisses any stigma of American arrogance.

Unfortunately, English is not spoken as widely in France, nor as fluently, as in neighboring countries. When discussing business, the French tend to be very be diplomatic, low key, sober, and discreet. That also applies to their dress, which is strictly conservative (i.e., dark suits and ties). A casual, gregarious American businessman in a blazer and pastel slacks triggers only slightly less scorn than a tourist in a Budweiser cap and polo shirt.

Grabbing a "quick bite" is out. The 2- or 3-hour lunch is alive and well in France. French restaurants are places where business can be conducted at a relaxed pace and the participants can feel at ease with each other while developing open communication. The host should always be the first to bring up the subject of business, which he or she won't do until dessert. The main course is reserved for getting acquainted. Conversation will automatically turn to food, which means some knowledge of French cuisine and wines could ultimately prove to be the first step to landing an order.[10]

RELIABLE DELIVERY AND INVENTORY MANAGEMENT: OPPORTUNITIES FOR ORGANIZATIONAL COLLABORATION

For many organizations, the assurance of reliable delivery of purchases is essential. A related concern, inventory management, may also be an important buying criterion. As business becomes more global and as information technology advances, organizational buyers are increasingly concerned with collaborative efforts and with building strategic alliances with other organizations. Strategic alliances related to inventory management may take the form of single-sourcing.

Single-sourcing
Purchasing a product on a regular basis from a single vendor.

Single-sourcing occurs when an organization buys from a single vendor. Usually in such situations the organizational marketer works closely with the buyer to coordinate delivery of inventory items just as the buyer's inventory is being depleted. The seller may, for example, ship tires to an auto manufacturer so that they arrive exactly when needed in the production process and in the quantity needed. The degree of cooperation may be so great that buyer and seller share information technologies and a common database reflecting the customer's current inventory. Such single-sourcing is likely to involve electronic data interchanges between companies.

THE BOTTOM LINE

The relative importance of each of the major organizational buying criteria—product quality, service, price, and delivery—may vary with the buyer, the situation, or the product. For example, research showed that customers of Copperweld Robotics, a producer of industrial robots, wanted answers to three questions, in the following order: (1) Will it do the job? (2) What service is available? (3) What is the price? Copperweld knows that for the industrial robot industry, service is absolutely the number one priority for creating and maintaining customer relationships. If one component of the robot doesn't work, the customer's whole production line shuts down.

In general, in any organizational buying decision, the criteria interact. Each contributes to the final decision, and each affects the importance of the others. Yet they often boil down to one overriding factor: the need to operate an organization. General Motors' truck and coach division emphasizes features like corrosion resistance and low fuel consumption in its advertising. The strategy is based on the belief that GM customers don't buy trucks because they like them, but because they need them to earn a profit.

American Express Corporate Services provides a business service that helps organizations manage their bottom lines. The advertisement claims that business travelers can do their expense report with their eyes closed. Each night, the company's Expense Manager service gathers and sorts new American Express Credit Card charges. It allows business travelers to use e-mail to retrieve them, add any cash expenses, and then forward the complete report to headquarters for approval.

www.americanexpress.com

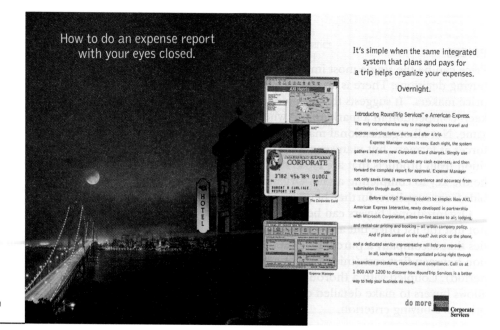

The Nature of Organizational Demand

The nature of the demand for goods and services in the multifaceted organizational marketplace differs greatly from the nature of demand for most consumer goods. Some generalizations may be made about organizational demand and, in particular, about demand in the business segment of the organizational market. This demand is (1) derived, (2) price inelastic, and (3) fluctuating.

DERIVED DEMAND

A reduction in consumer demand for housing has a tremendous and obvious impact on the building supply products industry. The demand for aluminum depends on the demand for products such as airplanes and trucks as well as products packaged in aluminum. Downturns in the economy cause people to cut back on their use of airlines, which in turn reduces the need for airplane fuel and the parts and tools used in airplane maintenance. Ultimately, even the demand for such mundane items as the brooms used to sweep out airline hangars will decline as airline usage declines. All of these examples demonstrate a basic truth: All organizational demand depends ultimately on consumer demand. Organizational demand is **derived demand**—that is, it is derived from consumer demand.

Derived demand
Demand for a product that depends on demand for another product.

Exhibit 7-5 illustrates the power of derived demand in the business marketplace. Notice that derived demand ultimately depends on consumer demand even in purchasing situations quite removed from consumers.

No retailer would buy so much as a can of soup for resale unless management thought that the soup could be sold to a customer. It may be less obvious that no manufacturer of cardboard-box-making machines would buy even a pencil for use at the factory unless management believed that box makers would buy box-making machines, that packers would buy boxes, that wholesalers and retailers would buy boxed items, and that retailers would be able to sell those items to ultimate consumers.

Economists have coined the phrase *acceleration principle* to describe the dramatic effects of derived demand. According to this principle, demand for product B, which derives its demand from the demand for product A, may greatly accelerate if there is a small increase in the demand for product A. For example, consider the demand for VGA graphics cards, which derives from the demand for

e x h i b i **7-5**

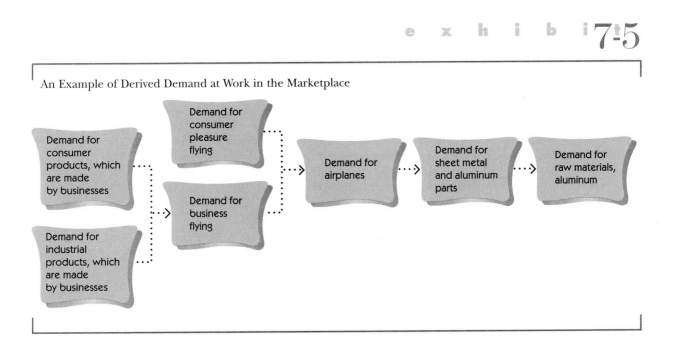

An Example of Derived Demand at Work in the Marketplace

Motorola markets numerous semiconductors that are among the standard equipment that helps make automobiles safe, comfortable, and environmentally friendly. The demand for Motorola semiconductors is derived from the demand for automobiles, trucks, and other vehicles.

www.mot.com

color monitors. Makers of color monitors may increase their purchases of VGA graphics cards by a percentage higher than the percentage increase in sales of color monitors, to protect against the possibility of running out as demand grows. Similarly, when demand for a consumer product declines, the demand for its component parts may decline at an accelerated rate relative to the demand for the consumer product.

Understanding the effects of derived demand on marketing efforts is important for organizational marketers, and not just because those effects are potentially devastating. Derived demand also presents certain opportunities. Under some circumstances, the organizational marketer can stimulate demand for the consumer product on which demand for the organizational product depends. This approach involves drawing demand through the distribution channel until it reaches the seller. For example, advertisements suggesting that milk is better in unbreakable plastic jugs may be sponsored by the producers of plastic jugs or the manufacturers of machines that make plastic jugs. Recognizing a trend of declining per-capita beef consumption, the Beef Industry Council targeted advertisements to consumers in an attempt to reverse the trend. Pork producers and lamb producers have done much the same thing, even though all these organizations represent farmers and ranchers who are several steps removed from the consumer in the channels of distribution.

> UNDERSTANDING THE EFFECTS OF DERIVED DEMAND ON MARKETING EFFORTS IS IMPORTANT FOR ORGANIZATIONAL MARKETERS, AND NOT JUST BECAUSE THOSE EFFECTS ARE POTENTIALLY DEVASTATING. DERIVED DEMAND ALSO PRESENTS CERTAIN OPPORTUNITIES.

The Beef Industry Council's experience suggests another advantage of understanding derived demand. By keeping an eye on the ultimate demand on which they depend, alert marketers can foresee developments that may soon affect their businesses. In some cases, such marketers can take steps to influence these developments or to make adjustments that offset their effects. Responding to trends in the marketplace is an important part of the job of all marketers, of course, but organizational marketers must pay special attention. Unfortunately, their distance from the consumers on whom they ultimately depend may make it more difficult for them to focus attention on developments that may affect their sales.

PRICE INELASTICITY

Compared with the demand for consumer goods, price has only a modest effect on industry demand for an organizational good. Industry demand is relatively price inelastic in the short run—demand for organizational goods and services is not likely to change significantly as a result of price fluctuations. There are two very good reasons for this price inelasticity. First, organizational buyers are in a position to pass along price increases to their customers. If the price of the sheet metal used to make Jeep fenders goes up, Chrysler, maker of Jeep, can raise the price of these products to cover the increased cost of the metal, because the demand for Jeeps is strong. The second, and less obvious, reason for price inelasticity is the tendency for the price of any one product to be an almost insignificant part of the total price of the final product of which it is a part. When the price of sheet metal goes up, raising the cost of a fender by a few dollars, it has little effect on the total price of a finished Jeep. Note, however, that although organizational prices tend to be inelastic in general, buyers are not insensitive to price differences among offerings of several competing sellers. Therefore, marketers must consider price in terms of each customer's special situation.

FLUCTUATING DEMAND

Most organizations prefer steady operating schedules. Thus, you might expect organizational demand to be more or less constant. Actually, compared with the demand for consumer goods, the industry demand for organizational goods is characterized by wide fluctuations. There are three logical reasons for this.

First, organizational purchases can usually be closely linked to the state of the economy. As the economy moves through its up-and-down cycles, demand for many organizational products goes through cycles as well. During prosperous times, firms tend to maintain large inventories. When the economy slows or enters a downturn, retailers, wholesalers, manufacturers, and most other business customers tend to sell off or use up their existing inventories. They also tend to postpone purchases of new supplies, equipment, and other products. If the direction of the economy is uncertain, purchases are again postponed. This is especially true for machine tools, pumps, materials handling equipment, and other products that can be repaired and made to last until better economic times seem imminent. Hence, demand in this part of the organizational market, influenced by environmental dynamics, can fluctuate widely.

Second, many organizational purchasers have a tendency to stock up on the products they buy. They then do not need to make further purchases until their stock is somewhat depleted. Third, many organizational products have long lives, as in the case of buildings and major equipment.

NAICS: Classifying Business Markets

A wide variety of profit and not-for-profit institutions make up the business market. Knowing how many of each kind of organization are in operation, where they are located, their size, and so on can help marketers implement research activities and plan marketing strategies. Fortunately, a great deal of information is available on business markets. Although much of this information is gathered by private companies, governmental agencies are also important sources.

A new tool for use in researching the organizational marketplace is the **North American Industry Classification System (NAICS)**. NAICS, a numerical coding scheme developed by the governments of the partners in the North American Free Trade Agreement, is used to classify a broad range of organizations in terms of the type of economic activity in which they are engaged.

As of 1997, the North American Industry Classification System replaced the United States', Canada's, and Mexico's separate classification systems with one uniform system for classifying industries.[16] In the United States, NAICS replaces the **Standard Industrial Classification (SIC) system** in use since the 1930s. The North American Industry Classification System will allow marketers to better

North American Industry Classification System (NAICS)
A numerical coding scheme developed by the governments of the partners in the North American Free Trade Agreement and used to classify a broad range of organizations in terms of the type of economic activity in which they are engaged.

Standard Industrial Classification (SIC) system
A numerical coding system developed by the U.S. government and (until the advent of NAICS) widely employed by organizational marketers to classify organizations in terms of the economic activities in which they are engaged.

compare economic and financial statistics and ensure that such statistics keep pace with the changing global economy.

In a marked change from the old SIC system, NAICS reflects the enormous changes that have occurred recently in technology and in the growth and diversification of services. New NAICS industry sectors include the following:

1. The Information Sector, which covers industries that create, distribute, or provide access to information, including satellite, cellular, and pager communications; on-line services; software and database publishing; motion picture, video, and sound recording; and radio, television, and cable broadcasting.
2. The Health Care and Social Assistance Sector, which organizes those industries by intensity of care and recognizes new industries, such as HMO medical centers, outpatient mental health care, and elderly continuing care.
3. The Professional, Scientific, and Technical Services Sector, which recognizes industries that rely primarily on human capital, including legal, architectural, engineering, interior design, and advertising services.

The major divisions used in the system are shown in Exhibit 7-6. The two-digit codes in the exhibit can be extended to three digits, four digits, or more to identify finer and finer gradations of differences within any particular area. Consider Information. The two-digit code is 51. Publishing Industries (511), Motion Picture and Video Industries (512), and Broadcasting and Telecommunications (513) are examples of groups with three-digit codes within the Information sector. The four-digit code within the Broadcasting and Telecommunications group for Telecommunications is 5133, and the five-digit code for Wireless Telecommunications Carriers (except Satellite) is 51332.

The new North American Industry Classification System (like the old Standard Industrial Classification System it replaced) is important to marketers because it is a guide to vast amounts of information published by the federal government. The

e   x   h   i   b   i 7-6 Primary NAICS Divisions

SECTOR	TWO-DIGIT CODE
Agriculture, Forestry, Fishing, and Hunting	11
Mining	21
Utilities	22
Construction	23
Manufacturing	31–33
Wholesale Trade	42
Retail Trade	44–45
Transportation and Warehousing	48–49
Information	51
Financial and Insurance	52
Real Estate and Rental Leasing	53
Professional, Scientific, and Technical Services	54
Management of Companies and Enterprises	55
Administrative and Support, Waste Management, and Remediation Services	56
Educational Services	61
Health Care and Social Assistance	62
Arts, Entertainment, and Recreation	71
Accommodation and Food Services	72
Other Services (except Public Administration)	81
Public Administration	92

Census of Retail Trade, the Census of Manufacturing, County Business Patterns, and many other useful government publications are based on the this system. Furthermore, because government agencies use the system so heavily in generating government statistics, most private companies that generate marketing research data also use it.

summary

The behavior of organizational buyers often differs significantly from that of ultimate consumers. Marketing managers must understand the special characteristics of this market.

1 *Identify the types of organizations that make up the business, or organizational, market.*
The business, or organizational, market is composed of businesses, nonprofit groups, charitable and religious organizations, governmental units, and other nonconsumer markets.

2 *Know the steps involved in an organizational buying decision.*
Organizational buying takes place over time, involves communications among several organizational members, and requires financial relationships between an organization and its suppliers. An organizational buying decision is the result of a multistage process that includes (1) anticipating or recognizing a problem, (2) determining the characteristics and quantity of the product needed, (3) describing product specifications and critical service needs, (4) searching for and qualifying potential sources, (5) acquiring and analyzing proposals, (6) evaluating proposals and selecting suppliers, (7) selecting an order routine, and (8) using feedback to evaluate performance.

3 *Characterize the three basic organizational buying situations: the straight rebuy, the modified rebuy, and the new task purchase.*
The straight rebuy requires no review of products or suppliers; materials are reordered automatically when the need arises. The modified rebuy occurs when buyers are discontent with current products or supplier performance and investigate alternative sources. The new task purchase involves evaluating product specifications and reviewing possible vendors in a purchase situation new to the organization.

4 *Understand that the Internet is changing the way business-to-business marketing occurs.*
The Internet has dramatically changed business-to-business marketing and the way organizational buying occurs. In buying over the Internet, or elec-

tronic commerce, organizational buyers go to a supplier's Web site, find information about goods and services, select the products they need, and e-mail their orders. Many business-to-business marketers have found that providing extra customer value on the Internet both increases sales and reduces the cost of making a sales transaction.

5 *Explain why the buying center concept is important in organizational marketing.*
The buying center is an informal network of people who have various roles in the purchasing decision process. The people and their roles vary over time. Roles include users, buyers, gatekeepers, deciders, and influencers. Marketers must identify members of the buying center and evaluate their importance at various stages of the process in order to target marketing efforts most effectively.

6 *Appreciate the needs of organizational buyers and explain how marketers can react to those needs.*
Needs of organizational buyers include product quality, related services, low price, and reliable delivery (perhaps including enhanced inventory management). The relative importance of these factors may vary with the buyer, the situation, or the product. The marketer must first determine what these needs are and then react to them through appropriate adjustments in the marketing mix.

7 *Describe the nature of organizational demand.*
Consumer buying decisions affect many organizations because demand for products in the organizational marketplace is derived demand. That is, organizational demand ultimately depends on consumer demand, even when organizational purchasing decisions are far removed from consumers. Organizational demand is price inelastic in that the amounts of products demanded by organizational buyers do not change significantly as the prices for the products rise and fall. Finally, for a number of reasons, the demand for industrial goods fluctuates widely.

8 *Describe NAICS and analyze its usefulness to marketers.*
NAICS, a coding method used to classify many organizations, can be used to identify products,

individual manufacturers, purchasers of various products, and other useful facts. Governments, trade associations, and other sources use these codes to categorize information. Marketers who understand the system have access to vast amounts of published data and can use the codes to determine market potentials and gain other insights into the structure of markets.

key terms

business-to-business marketing (p. 197)
organizational buying
  behavior (p. 198)
strategic alliance (p. 199)
buy phase (p. 200)
straight rebuy (p. 200)
modified rebuy (p. 200)

new task buying (p. 200)
buying center (p. 205)
user (p. 206)
buyer (p. 206)
gatekeeper (p. 206)
decider (p. 206)
influencer (p. 206)

single-sourcing (p. 210)
derived demand (p. 211)
North American Industry
  Classification System (NAICS)
  (p. 213)
Standard Industrial Classification
  (SIC) system (p. 213)

questions for review & critical thinking

1. In what ways does business-to-business marketing differ from consumer marketing?
2. Compare and contrast the consumer's decision-making process and the organization's decision-making process.
3. For the following products, indicate whether the organization's buying task will be a straight rebuy, a modified rebuy, or new task buying. Briefly explain your answers.
   a. Lawn maintenance for the Mercedes-Benz regional headquarters building in suburban New Jersey
   b. Roller bearings to be a component part for Snapper lawn mowers
   c. An industrial robot to perform a function currently done manually
   d. Personal computers for top-level managers
4. What difficulties for sellers are suggested by the buying center concept?

5. What variables might be used to estimate demand for the following products?
   a. Paper clips
   b. Staplers
   c. Lubricants for industrial-quality drill presses
   d. Forklift trucks
6. Define derived demand, and give an example of its effect on the sale of packaging materials.
7. Is a business-to-business marketer more likely to stress personal selling or advertising in promoting a product? Why?
8. Form small groups as directed by your instructor. Pick a local business organization and identify at least four job titles held by managers and employees. Discuss who might influence the company's buying decisions for straight rebuys, modified rebuys, and new task buying.

marketing plan—right or wrong?

1. A manufacturer of plumbing supplies has traditionally prepared a 50-page catalog listing thousands of parts that it distributes to plumbing wholesalers. The company plans to drop its catalog in favor of an Internet Web site that lists all its supplies.
2. When a retailer runs a credit card through one of those little boxes, the communication device dials a phone number and connects with other computers to verify the customer's credit. The product is actually a highly sophisticated communications terminal. The service provider plans to offer small retailers the option of using the little communication devices to keep track of their employees' working hours and then transmit the information electronically to a company that produces payroll checks.

internet insights

zikmund.swcollege.com

ethically right or wrong?

1. A purchasing agent likes to work with Company A, whose prices are rarely the lowest. The purchasing agent solicits competitive bids from Company A and two other companies that are known for very high quality but also extremely high prices. Two other companies whose products meet the organization's quality specifications and whose prices are generally the lowest in the industry are not invited to submit bids. Company A, whose product meets minimum quality specifications, wins the contract. Is this ethical?

2. A purchasing agent attends a lewd party, sponsored by a company that wants to do business with the agent's company. Should the purchasing agent have attended?

3. A company gives preferential treatment to minority-owned raw materials suppliers. Is this a good policy?

Weather Or Not, Inc.   *Focus on Small Business*

Sara Croke was known for her accuracy as a TV weather forecaster, she says, but that didn't cut any ice when a contract with a Kansas City station ran out and she set up shop as a private forecaster under the name Weather Or Not, Inc. Potential clients kept saying no.

Construction companies and other outdoor businesses insisted they could get what weather information they needed from TV or radio, even though she frequently heard lamentations like: "They said it was going to rain yesterday, so I sent my guys home. Then the sun came out, and now the general contractor's all over me for losing a day."

It wasn't until she went to a small business development center that the cloud over Croke's sales efforts began to lift. The center helped her find her initial market—those already spending money on forecasts.

Walked through her first government bid, Croke got a 6-month contract with KCI Airport. It paid $230 a month which, she says, "I supplemented with unemployment checks."

A business writer, sent her way by the center, wrote about accurate rainout forecasts Croke had given the groundskeeper at Royals Stadium (the writer didn't know the forecasts were gratis) and that led to her first construction-firm contract. Unlike similar firms Croke had approached, this one already had a private forecaster but was dissatisfied.

Next Croke added marketing training to the meteorological training she already had. A sales consultant provided a play-by-play of how to make cold calls, design proposals and marketing packets, and—most important—close sales.

"The No. 1 factor became relating bad weather to bad profits," Croke says. "Instead of 'I know all about weather,' it became 'I know you guys got caught last week with that surprise rain. Weather Or Not's clients had several hours' warning before the rain started. They prepared and didn't lose a dime.'"

Also, Croke would point out that weather broadcasts gave information for an area up to 100 miles wide, while she would find out each morning where clients' projects would be, pinpoint information, and call clients if weather changes were likely. Construction supervisors or tournament-running golf pros had other things to do besides sit and watch the weather all day, she would note. Now they could have "someone baby-sitting the weather for them."

Today Weather Or Not, which started out in 1986 in Croke's one-bedroom apartment, is in two sites in Westwood, Kansas. It is staffed by an office manager;

four forecasters, including a chief meteorologist; and Croke, who pulls a 4–9 a.m. forecasting shift and then concentrates on sales.

Clients have increased along with personnel. They include company CEOs who, for example, change travel plans when warned that ice will glaze over a corporate jet's destination. Thanks in part to satellite technology, Weather Or Not can retrieve the time and place of lightning strikes anywhere in the U.S.—a one-phone-call time-saver of value to insurance companies and lawyers. The same technology makes it possible to warn people running a golf tournament hundreds of miles away that lightning is approaching their area.

Croke sees much growth ahead in these areas, and in mail-order sales of radios that sound an alarm at any hour when severe weather threatens. Dollars that a business spends with her firm in a year can be made back, she says, in minutes.[17]

QUESTIONS

1. What is the broad industry classification for a company like Weather Or Not?
2. The text identifies three characteristics of demand in the business market. How well does demand for Weather Or Not's services match those characteristics?
3. Identify the type of organizational buying situation faced by most of Weather Or Not's customers.

chapter 8

Market Segmentation, Targeting, and Positioning Strategies

After you have studied this chapter, you will be able to:

Define the term *market*.

1

Explain the concept of market segmentation.

2

Relate the identification of meaningful target markets to the development of effective marketing mixes.

3

Distinguish among undifferentiated, concentrated, differentiated, and custom marketing strategies.

4

Demonstrate the effect of the 80/20 rule and the majority fallacy on marketing strategy.

5

(continued on next page)

6 List the market segmentation variables most commonly used by marketing managers and explain how marketers identify which ones are appropriate.

7 Explain the purpose of a positioning strategy.

dana shanler

hated borrowing her mother's jewelry for special occasions. So she did what was once considered unthinkable. She bought an expensive diamond necklace for herself.

"I knew I could afford it, and I decided that I could buy it for myself if I really wanted it," said the 34-year-old attorney. "Now, every time I wear it, I get a real charge out of it."

Jewelry isn't just the gift of love anymore. As women become financially secure and marry later in life, they aren't waiting for someone else to buy them beautiful jewelry. They're treating themselves to gold bracelets, diamond earrings, and those precious gifts they've always wanted.

Realizing women's buying potential, marketers are increasing efforts to target that segment of women who buy jewelry for themselves. Some even encourage women to buy for themselves around Mother's Day, one of the biggest holidays for jewelry gift-giving.

A Sears Mother's Day promotion targeted at women entitled shoppers who spent $50 through Mother's Day anywhere in the store to buy a gold heart pendant on a chain for $29.99, well below the regular retail price of $119.99. "We feel that the woman is the primary purchaser in our stores of all

[WOMEN] WORK, THEY HAVE CAREERS, AND THEY WANT TO REWARD THEMSELVES IN MEANINGFUL WAYS.

merchandise, including jewelry," said Leslie Mann, vice president of fine jewelry and accessories at Sears, the nation's second-largest retailer. "This offers them an extra gift for themselves," she said, "a feel-good purchase."

Marketing to women isn't new in jewelry retailing. The World Gold Council was one of the first to target women in the late 1980s with its "No, you don't have to wrap it" campaign, which told women that buying jewelry can be incorporated into their everyday lives and jewelry doesn't have to be a gift. More retailers and trade groups have since launched their own pitches to women. The Platinum Guild International ran "Platinum: A Reflection of You," which relayed to women that platinum "is for any woman who has come into her own." With sales of gold up about 15 percent and platinum up over 300 percent in the last three years, industry observers attribute some of those gains to new sales to women. The World Gold Council, a New York–based trade group, now estimates that women account for 70 percent of all gold purchases, either for themselves or as gifts for others. "Women are not waiting for a certain person to give them a gift anymore," said Lynn Ramsey, president of the Jewelry Information Center, a New York–based trade group. "They work, they have careers, and they want to reward themselves in meaningful ways."

At Diana Vincent Jewelry Designs, women started buying for themselves about four years ago and now account for a sizable part of the business. Their purchases include diamond pins and platinum rings, with the size of sale usually tied to their income level.

Owner Diana Vincent now sees female patrons at her store who formerly shopped only with their husbands and boyfriends. "They're not just getting allowances from their husbands anymore," Vincent said. "When they buy jewelry, it's a [new] form of independence from everyone else."

According to retailers, women generally stick to small, moderately priced items like simple earrings and pins when making their first purchase for themselves. But once they're accustomed to the routine, they're more inclined to indulge themselves with pricier items.

Executives at QVC heard from their female customers that they wanted more expensive jewelry. In response, the television shopping network launched Arte d'Oro, an 18-karat-gold jewelry line ranging in price from $600 to $3,000. "For women, jewelry today is less about status and more about accessorizing with a quality product that makes them feel good," said John Calnon, vice president of jewelry merchandising at QVC. That's the way Shanler feels when she puts on her diamond necklace and heads out to a business dinner or special family occasion. "Not only is it nice to know I could afford it, but it's mine, I picked it out and I bought it," she said.[1]

Understanding the nature of various market segments is an important aspect of marketing strategy. This chapter considers in greater depth the definitions of the terms *market* and *market segmentation*. It discusses how marketers determine which target marketing strategy will best serve their objectives. Then it examines the many variables used to segment consumer and organizational markets. Finally, it considers how marketers develop positioning strategies.

What Is Market Segmentation?

We have already defined what a market is, but let us look again at that definition. A *market* is a group of actual or potential customers for a particular product. More precisely, a market is a group of individuals or organizations that may want the good or service being offered for sale and that meet these three additional criteria:

1. They have the ability or purchasing power to buy the product being offered.
2. They have the willingness to spend money or exchange other resources to obtain the product.
3. They have the authority to make such expenditures.

Economics textbooks often give the impression that all consumers are alike. Economists frequently draw no distinctions among different types of buyers, as long as they have a willingness and an ability to buy. Young and old buyers, men and women, people who drink 12 beers a day and those who drink one beer on New Year's Eve are all lumped together. Experience tells marketers, however, that in many cases buyers differ from one another even though they may be buying the same products. Marketers try to identify groups and subgroups within total markets—that is, they try to segment markets.

Recall that market segmentation consists of dividing a heterogeneous market into a number of smaller, more homogeneous submarkets. Almost any variable— age, sex, product usage, lifestyle, expected benefit—may be used as a segmenting variable, but the logic behind the strategy is always the same.

- Not all buyers are alike.
- Subgroups of people with similar behavior, values, and/or backgrounds may be identified.

Quaker State 4×4 is a motor oil targeted toward the segment of the market composed of owners of sports utility vehicles, light trucks, and minivans. Historically, motor oil marketers expected drivers to understand the grades of motor oils. However, the distinction between, for example, 10W40 oil and 5W30 oil was not meaningful to most consumers. Quaker State 4×4's segmentation strategy provides a meaningful difference to a distinguishable—and sizable—segment of the market.

www.quakerstate.com

- The subgroups will be smaller and more homogeneous than the market as a whole.
- It should be easier to satisfy smaller groups of similar customers than a large group of dissimilar customers.

Usually, marketers are able to cluster similar customers into specific market segments with different, and sometimes unique, demands. For example, the computer software market can be divided into two segments: the domestic market and the foreign market. The domestic market can be segmented further into business users and home users. And the home user segment can be further subdivided into sophisticated personal computer users, people who hate personal computers but have one so their children can use it for schoolwork, people who use computers only for e-mail, and so on. The number of market segments within the total market depends largely on the strategist's ingenuity and creativity in identifying those segments.

Needless to say, a single company is unlikely to pursue all possible market segments. In fact, the idea behind market segmentation is for an organization to choose one or a few meaningful segments and concentrate its efforts on satisfying those selected parts of the market. Focusing its efforts on these targeted market segments—that is, *targeting*—enables the organization to allocate its marketing resources effectively. Concentrating efforts on a given market segment should result in a more precise marketing program satisfying specific market needs.

As mentioned in Chapter 2, the market segment, or group of buyers, toward which an organization decides to direct its marketing plan is called the *target market*. The target market for Shower Shaver, for example, is that subgroup of women who shave their legs in the shower.

Because it is possible to segment markets in so many ways, target marketing opportunities abound. For example, there are "left-hander" shops specializing in products for left-handed people, tobacco shops catering to wealthy pipe smokers, and dress shops like the 5-7-9 Shops that target women who wear certain clothing sizes. In addition, numerous products bear the names or symbols of sports teams, such as the San Francisco 49ers or the Chicago Bulls, and are marketed to team fans. Some companies even sell items to people who hate particular teams—a once-popular sports-related item was the "I Hate the Yankees Hanky." As you can see, the process of segmentation provides hints on how to market to the targeted segments identified.

Selection of a target market (or markets—in some cases, more than one may be selected for a product) is a three-step process, as shown in Exhibit 8-1. First, the total market, consisting of many different customers, is studied and broken down (or *disaggregated*) into its component parts—that is, individual customers, families, organizations, or other units. The customers are then regrouped by the marketing strategist into market segments on the basis of one or several characteristics that segment members have in common. Then the strategist must target segments to which the organization will appeal. When that is done, the strategist has answered the question "What are our target markets?"

The Major Steps in Market Segmentation and Selection of Target Markets

STEP 1
The market is broken down

STEP 2
and grouped into meaningful market segments

STEP 3
so that a target market can be chosen

c_1 c_3 c_4 c_2 c_6 c_7 c_8 c_5

Heterogeneous group of consumers

c_3 c_4 c_2 c_8 c_5 c_1 c_7 c_6

Individual consumers

#1 c_1 c_2 c_3 #2 c_4 c_5 #3 c_6 c_7 c_8

Fairly homogeneous market segments

#1 #2

• Product
• Price
• Distribution
• Promotion

#3

Target market

CHOOSING MEANINGFUL MARKET SEGMENTS

Target marketing rests on the assumption that differences among buyers are related to meaningful differences in market behavior. The identification of market segments that are not meaningful has little value. The following five criteria make a segment meaningful:

1. The market segment has a characteristic or characteristics that distinguish it from the overall market. This characteristic should be stable over time.
2. The market segment has a market potential of significant size—that is, large enough to be profitable.
3. The market segment is accessible through distribution efforts or reachable through promotional efforts.
4. The market segment is responsive. The market segment has a unique market need, and the likelihood is high that the segment will respond favorably to a marketing mix tailored to this need.
5. The segment's market potential should be measurable. Ease of measurement facilitates effective target marketing by helping to identify and quantify group purchasing power and to indicate the differences among market segments. Although ease of measurement is desirable, it is not mandatory.

Walt Disney World appeals to many diverse groups. Its Internet page allows prospective visitors to click on an icon that best describes their market segment. Those who click on "Attractions for ages 6–13" are connected to a Web page that features different attractions than the Web page for those who click on "Attractions for ages 25–60."

www.disney.com

Determining Whether a Market Segment Is Meaningful

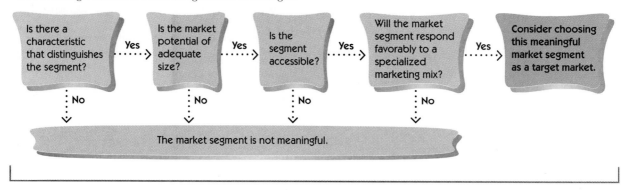

Exhibit 8-2 outlines these criteria. A company's general goal of profitability can depend on how well marketers use the criteria to identify target markets. Selecting a group that is not easily distinguishable or accessible, or appealing to a segment that is too small to generate adequate sales volume, or selecting a group that the company is unable to attract is not effective market segmentation.

Consider an example. Cuban citizens form a possible market segment. This is a large group. But even assuming it has unique market demands, this segment is not meaningful. The U.S. government has placed an embargo on exports to Cuba, and these restrictions have completely shut down trade with the island. Thus, the market segment consisting of Cubans living in Cuba does not meet the criterion of accessibility.

One product that successfully appealed to a meaningful market segment was the First Alert Traveling Smoke and Fire Detector. The product was designed for the sizable number of frequent travelers who worry about hotel fires. Marketers can reach frequent travelers through specific promotional efforts (for example, advertising in in-flight magazines). Offering a high-quality portable smoke alarm

adapting to change

The National Basketball Association   Watch sports on television, and the commercials you see are for beer, razor blades, and trucks—men's stuff.

Those commercials are missing the most important emerging sector of the sports consumer market—girls and women—according to a group of sports marketing executives.

"The total growth of all major (spectator) sports for the remainder of this decade will come from women," Nye Lavalle, chairman of the Sports Marketing Group, said.

Some companies are already targeting women. The National Basketball Association created a women's marketing department last year. Research showed that girls and women account for 44 percent of total NBA merchandise sales, said Michele Brown, director of women's marketing for the league. One out of every five teenage girls in the United States owns or has bought a piece of NBA clothing, Brown said, and those are clothes designed for men.

To broaden its appeal to women, the league plans to begin producing a line of women's wear. "The NBA views women as an untapped market," Brown said.[2]

at a fair price by mail is a marketing mix that may appeal to the specialized needs of this market segment. Thus, First Alert met the criterion of meaningfulness.

THE MARKET SEGMENT CROSS-CLASSIFICATION MATRIX

Effective marketers segment the markets they address and then select attractive target markets.[3] Some do this almost unintentionally, even unwittingly, as did the owner of a small grocery store located in the Seattle area. The store serves only a small portion of the Seattle market, perhaps an area of a few blocks. In a sense, by choosing the store's location, the store's owner has "segmented" and "targeted" the market geographically. However, proper market segmentation and target marketing generally involve serious consideration of a total market, the variables that can be used to identify meaningful segments in that market, and the creation of marketing mixes aimed at satisfying the needs of chosen target segments.

One way marketers can identify target markets is to use a **cross-classification matrix**, a grid that helps isolate variables of interest in the market. Exhibit 8-3 shows the cross-classifications the owners of a new tennis shop in New York City might use to segment the retail tennis equipment market. First, the total group of people interested in tennis is cross-classified using a geographic variable and the variable of sex. Then the chosen segment is cross-classified with income and level of tennis skill. It appears from Exhibit 8-3 that our tennis shop's selected target market is the group of females interested in tennis who shop in Manhattan, are intermediate or advanced players, and have annual incomes over $75,000. The variables used to segment the tennis market can be portrayed on a single, three-dimensional figure, as in Exhibit 8-4. However, if more than three variables are employed, graphical portrayal becomes increasingly difficult.

Cross-classification matrix
A grid that helps isolate variables of interest in the market. For example, a geographic variable might be cross-classified with some other variable of interest, such as income.

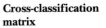

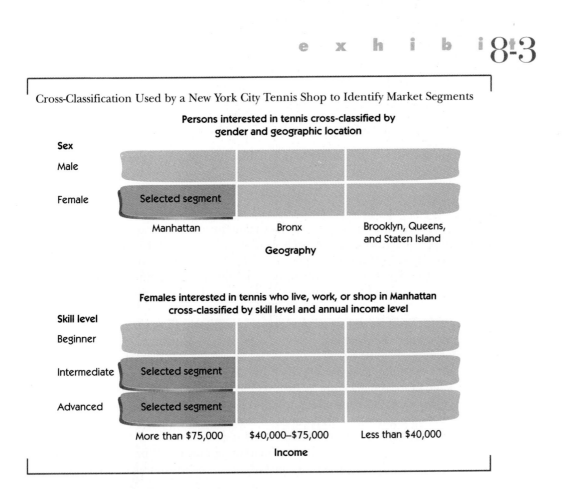

Cross-Classification Used by a New York City Tennis Shop to Identify Market Segments

Persons interested in tennis cross-classified by gender and geographic location

Sex
Male

Female — Selected segment

Manhattan | Bronx | Brooklyn, Queens, and Staten Island

Geography

Females interested in tennis who live, work, or shop in Manhattan cross-classified by skill level and annual income level

Skill level
Beginner

Intermediate — Selected segment

Advanced — Selected segment

More than $75,000 | $40,000–$75,000 | Less than $40,000

Income

A Three-Dimensional Portrayal of the Cross-Classification Matrices Shown in Exhibit 8-3

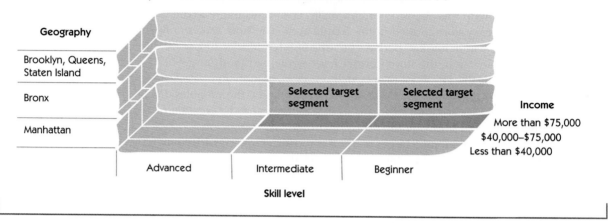

MATCHING THE MIX TO THE TARGET MARKET

Having determined that its target segment will be women with incomes over $75,000 who are intermediate and advanced tennis players, the tennis shop owners must develop a marketing mix aimed at satisfying that group of consumers. This process can be very difficult, even risky. Yet the segmentation effort itself simplifies some of the choices to be made.

1. What brands should be stocked? Those that appeal to female players who are not beginners. Names such as Prince, K-Swiss, and Ellesse appeal to this segment.
2. Should credit cards be accepted? Probably so, because the shop is dealing with women who have high incomes and, therefore, good credit.
3. What newspapers should be used to advertise the store? The best choice is most likely the *New York Times,* which appeals to well-off readers, rather than the *Daily News* or *New York Post,* which appeal to downscale readers.

This example shows how market segmentation and target marketing can help not only in identifying whom to target but also in suggesting how to make the appeal.

Four Strategies for Target Marketing

The idea of zeroing in on a given market segment suggests analogies with rifles and shotguns. The shotgun approach spreads marketing efforts widely, while the rifle approach allows for greater precision by focusing on one target market. We can develop the logic of this analogy by examining four target marketing strategies based on the uniqueness of consumer segments and organizational objectives.

UNDIFFERENTIATED MARKETING: WHEN EVERYONE IS A CUSTOMER

Undifferentiated marketing

A marketing effort not targeted at a specific market segment but designed to appeal to a broad range of customers. The approach is appropriate in a market that lacks diversity of interest.

Sometimes, when a marketing manager asks, "What is our market?" the answer turns out to be "Almost everyone who has any use for our type of product." When marketers determine that there is little diversity among market segments, they may engage in mass marketing. A firm selling hacksaw blades, brass or silver polish, or garbage cans to consumers may find it more efficient not to distinguish among market segments. This absence of segmentation, which is illustrated in Exhibit 8-5, is called **undifferentiated marketing**.

In some situations, undifferentiated marketing may result in savings in production and marketing costs, which can be passed on to consumers in the form of

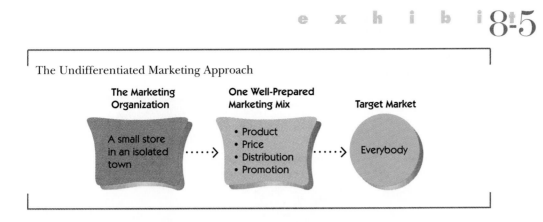

The Undifferentiated Marketing Approach

lower prices. After all, it should be cheaper to make and sell only one car model in one color, as Henry Ford did with the Model T, than to produce and sell tens of models in many colors and with various options, as General Motors does today. However, the attempt to appeal to everyone may make an organization extremely vulnerable to competition.

Even producers of common, unexciting products like salt have found this out. No-Salt, Lite Salt, sea salt, popcorn salt, flavored salts, noniodized salt, and other such products chip away at the customer base of a marketer of common table salt. Similarly, all facial tissues may be pretty much alike, but a product marketed in a package illustrated with Hercules characters from the Disney movie may appeal to buyers with small children. Although "everyone" buys salt and tissues, buyers' secondary desires (for example, to please a child with a Hercules package) may provide the basis for segmentation. The undifferentiated brand cannot offer such specialized benefits.

Undifferentiated marketing can succeed. A small grocery store in a small, isolated town seeks all the people in that town as its customers. The store operator can construct one well-prepared marketing mix to please all, or at least most, customers.

CONCENTRATED MARKETING: ZEROING IN ON A SINGLE TARGET

Suppose a chain saw manufacturer identifies three major market segments: the casual or occasional user (such as the suburban homeowner), the farm segment, and the professional lumberjack segment. Each of these user groups has special needs; each uses chain saws in different ways; each reads different magazines and watches different television programs. If the chain saw marketer selects just one of these segments (say, the farm user), develops an appropriate marketing mix, and directs its marketing efforts and resources toward that segment exclusively, it is engaged in **concentrated marketing**. Exhibit 8-6 illustrates this strategy.

A firm might concentrate on a single market niche because management believes its company has a competitive advantage in dealing with the selected segment. Chain saws sold to the farm and professional segments are generally gasoline-powered. However, the casual-user segment, with less demanding performance standards and far fewer acres to cover, may be content with less powerful electric saws. Thus, a manufacturer of gasoline-powered lawn mowers may decide to produce gas-powered chain saws, while a maker of electric tools might find that its existing production facilities are compatible with the production of electric chain saws. Each can select market segments that provide a match between company goals and abilities and customer needs. Concentrated marketing strategies can be employed by both firms.

Examples of firms that concentrate their marketing efforts are easy to find. There are jewelers and clothing manufacturers that produce goods with price tags

Concentrated marketing
Development of a marketing mix and direction of marketing efforts and resources to appeal to a single market segment.

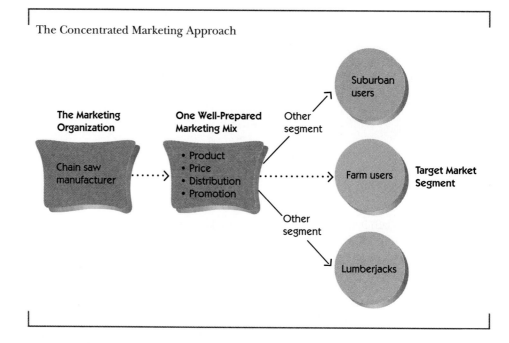

The Concentrated Marketing Approach

The Marketing Organization — Chain saw manufacturer

One Well-Prepared Marketing Mix
• Product
• Price
• Distribution
• Promotion

Other segment → Suburban users

Farm users — Target Market Segment

Other segment → Lumberjacks

that seem ridiculous to most people. Such products are sold to a small but wealthy market segment. Radio stations use concentrated marketing when they target their programming to a market segment that prefers a particular type of music. That is why you don't often hear rock, classical, and country music on the same station.

Can a business-to-business marketer practice concentrated marketing? The answer is yes. An example: Leo Burnett is one of the ten largest advertising agencies in the United States, yet it has fewer than thirty clients. Burnett focuses its efforts on servicing a small number of well-heeled clients with huge advertising budgets. Specializing seems to work, for in this volatile business, more than half of Burnett's clients have been with the agency for more than 10 years.

Concentrated marketing is not without its risks. If an organization specializes its efforts, it lacks diversity and has the problem of "putting all its eggs in one basket." If the market segment is too narrow or if growth in the market segment slows, major financial problems arise.

DeLorean Motor Company
www.usadmc.com

The DeLorean Motor Company, with resources far more limited than those of General Motors, Nissan, or Honda, concentrated its efforts on selling luxury cars to upper-income customers. More specifically, the target market was affluent people with several cars who had never before owned a sports car. A sluggish economy and management's unwillingness to accept the fact that the number of consumers in the targeted segment was very small led to DeLorean's failure. Today, most people barely remember the car, except for its role as a time machine in the *Back to the Future* movies.

An organization that is extremely successful in targeting a single segment may have great difficulty targeting other segments later. Cadillac spent years concentrating on older, affluent consumers who wanted big cars. When it tried to reach younger, upwardly mobile consumers with smaller cars, it was too well entrenched in one market segment to diversify into others.

The 80/20 Principle   Concentrating on one market segment is often more attractive when the marketer knows that a small percentage of all users of a product accounts for a great portion of that product's sales. The **80/20 principle** is the name given to this phenomenon whereby 20 percent of the customers buy 80 percent of the product sold. This 20 percent (which may really be 25 percent or some similar percentage) may be called "heavy users" or

"major customers." For example, marketers of beer know from marketing research that blue-collar workers are the "heavy users" in the beer market. The 80/20 principle operates in both consumer and organizational markets.

The Majority Fallacy Concentrating on the largest segment or the segment of heaviest users may not be the best course of action. Some organizations mistakenly aim at such a segment just because it is so obviously attractive. These organizations have fallen hook, line, and sinker for the majority fallacy. The **majority fallacy** is the name given to the blind pursuit of the largest, or most easily identified, or most accessible market segment. Why is it a fallacy? Simply because the segment they are pursuing is the one that everybody knows is the biggest or "best" segment, it probably attracts the most intense competition and may actually prove less profitable to firms competing for its attention. For example, Procter and Gamble's Prell and Pert are aimed at broader markets than its dandruff-fighting Head and Shoulders, but Head and Shoulders sells more than the other two brands combined.

Clearly, the majority fallacy points out that it may be better for a marketer to go after a small, seemingly less attractive market segment than to pursue the same customers that everyone else is after. Thus, although most brewers market to the heavy user, some brewers succeed by offering smaller bottles of beer to people who don't drink much beer or very expensive

> **CLEARLY, IT MAY BE BETTER FOR A MARKETER TO GO AFTER A SMALL, SEEMINGLY LESS ATTRACTIVE MARKET SEGMENT THAN TO PURSUE THE SAME CUSTOMERS THAT EVERYONE ELSE IS AFTER.**

beer to beer drinkers celebrating a special occasion. Many microbreweries target the gourmet beer drinker segment rather than the blue-collar segment.

DIFFERENTIATED MARKETING: DIFFERENT BUYERS, DIFFERENT STRATEGIES

Of course, it is possible for an organization to target its efforts toward more than one market segment. Once the various segments in a total market have been identified, specific marketing mixes can be developed to appeal to all or some of the submarkets. When an organization chooses more than one target market segment and prepares a marketing mix for each one, it is practicing **differentiated marketing**, or **multiple market segmentation**. For example, Marriott Corporation markets its hotel/motel service in many different price ranges. Residence Inns, Marriott Courtyards, Fairfield Inns, Marriott Hotels, and Marriott Resort Hotels appeal to different buyers attempting to satisfy different needs. Marriott thus practices differentiated marketing.

Using a differentiated marketing strategy exploits the differences between market segments by tailoring a specific marketing mix to each segment. For instance, the chain saw manufacturer that decided to concentrate on only one of three

Business travelers represent about 40 percent of United Airlines passengers but account for more than 70 percent of its revenues.[4] Those business travelers who fly most often, known as "road warriors," represent only 65 percent of all business travelers but 37 percent of United's revenues. Although the percentages are not exactly 80 and 20, this is a good example of the 80/20 principle.

www.ual.com

80/20 principle
In marketing, a principle describing the fact that usually a relatively small percentage of customers accounts for a disproportionately large share of the sales of a product.

Majority fallacy
The blind pursuit of the largest, or most easily identified, or most accessible market segment. The error lies in ignoring the fact that other marketers will be pursuing this same segment.

Differentiated marketing
A marketing effort in which a marketer selects more than one target market and then develops a separate marketing mix for each; also called multiple market segmentation.

market segments could have, given appropriate resources, attempted to appeal to each segment of the chain saw market. This would have meant a greater investment of money and effort, because each segment would have required its own specially tailored product, price, distribution, and promotion.

Of course, some markets are much more diverse than the chain saw illustration suggests. A good example of an industry facing a wide diversity of customers is the hair-coloring industry. Some customers want to change hair color, some want to cover traces of gray, and some want to highlight or brighten hair. Within these large customer groups, additional segments can be found. Exhibit 8-7 illustrates how Clairol segments the hair-coloring market. In this case, identifying the segments is not particularly difficult. The real work and expense come in creating the marketing mixes that satisfy all the segments.

Differentiated marketing is applicable to many situations, and in many cases, it is easy to implement. For example, a popular way for a manufacturer to attract a differentiated market—and one that requires relatively little effort—is by producing different-sized packages of the same product.

Although differentiated marketing is appropriate in many situations, it must be used with care. As this approach becomes more elaborate, costs increase. This fact must be taken into account as the marketing manager considers the value of focusing on different segments' needs. Competitive conditions, corporate objectives, available resources, and alternative marketing opportunities for other prod-

e x h i b i 8-7

The Differentiated Marketing Approach

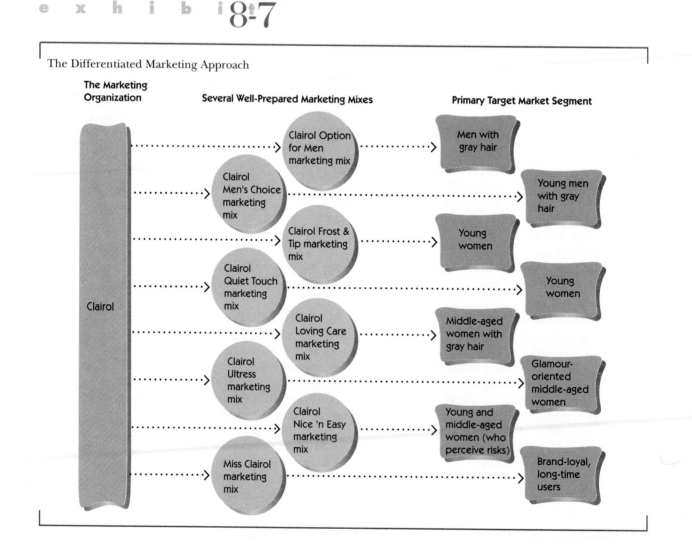

uct lines all influence the decision to utilize a differentiated market segmentation strategy.

CUSTOM MARKETING: TO EACH HIS OR HER OWN

Sometimes the market facing a given marketing manager is so diverse, and its members so dif-

Manufacturers of industrial robots create unique products and marketing mixes to satisfy each customer's unique set of needs. They engage in custom marketing.

ferent from one another, that no meaningful groups of customers can be identified. When this kind of diversity exists, a special kind of marketing effort is necessary. This situation requires **custom marketing**, the attempt to satisfy each customer's unique set of needs. In this case, the marketer must develop a marketing mix suitable to each customer.

A manufacturer of industrial robots faces such a prospect. Industrial robots are usually custom-designed to fit the buyer's special manufacturing problems. Each buyer demands a unique product, with special size and strength characteristics, depending on the job to be done. Each will probably require delivery and installation at a given location, thus somewhat altering the marketer's distribution system. In addition, individual customers may have difficult technical questions, requiring salespeople with broad technical knowledge. The salesperson, who is the key element in promotional efforts, may be required to alter the company's pricing structure to fit the custom-designed product's cost. In all, for our robot maker, each prospect may be considered a market segment, as illustrated in Exhibit 8-8.

Marketers of services, such as architects, tailors, and lawyers, often employ custom marketing strategies. The nature of these services requires that each customer be treated in a unique way. Effective marketers of custom services recognize this need for unique treatment as an opportunity to promote the notion that each customer gets exactly what he or she wants. Customers can have it their way.

Custom marketing
A marketing effort in which a marketer seeks to satisfy each customer's unique set of needs. In effect, each customer is an individual market segment.

Going One-on-One Using Information Technology
Chapter 5 introduced the topic of data-based marketing. The new information technologies available today allow a data-based marketer to track customers individually and then customize its marketing efforts. This form of customized marketing is sometimes called

Mattel For years the prevailing marketing wisdom was "You can't sell software to girls." However, by researching and understanding the needs of a particular market segment, Mattel made this statement a myth.

Mattel made selling software for girls look easy when its "Barbie Fashion Designer" CD-ROM became a runaway success in its first year on the market. The toy marketer spent more than 2 years researching girls' play patterns before going where several software developers have failed: trying to get girls as interested as boys in playing on the computer.

The toy company's research found that dressing up Barbie, perennially the world's best-selling toy, is girls' favorite play activity. With this information in hand, Mattel created a software program allowing girls to design clothes on the PC and print them out for Barbie to wear. The $39.99 product comes with paper "fabric" customizable to different fashions, complete with two-sided sticky paper for creating real seams. A TV commercial took the unprecedented kids' software marketing approach of targeting girls—not just parents—with the theme "Computers are cool for girls."

In less than a year, Barbie Fashion Designer became the best-selling national software product for kids, even though it was targeted at young girls. It was a hit with girls because Mattel built on something girls already love to do, and the company made it even more fun on the computer.

Mattel also expanded the market for Barbie, whose core customer is 8 years old. Girls as old as 14 were clamoring for the Fashion Designer product as soon as it hit retail shelves.[5]

The Custom Marketing Approach

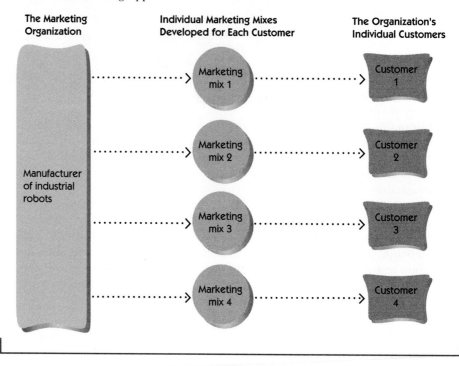

| The Marketing Organization | Individual Marketing Mixes Developed for Each Customer | The Organization's Individual Customers |

one-on-one marketing, but we prefer the term data-based marketing. (Later in the book we will show how data-based marketing is intertwined with relationship marketing and direct marketing strategies.) Going one-on-one with customers is made possible by digital information technologies: customer databases and systems that support mass customization.

GOING ONE-ON-ONE WITH CUSTOMERS IS MADE POSSIBLE BY DIGITAL INFORMATION TECHNOLOGIES: CUSTOMER DATABASES AND SYSTEMS THAT SUPPORT MASS CUSTOMIZATION.

With today's information technology, the role of personalized service can be greatly expanded if a company maintains a customer database. Manhattan East Suite Hotels, for instance, maintains a detailed database on the guests at its nine luxurious New York City properties, which include the Surrey Hotel, the Beekman Tower Hotel, and the Shelburne-Murray Hill. Doormen greet arriving guests by name, and reservation agents know without asking whether a guest prefers a non-smoking room. Manhattan East has been logging occupancy rates much higher than those of the average New York hotel. The hotel relationship marketing goal is to have a circle of friends, with the customer at the center.[6]

Many marketers use information in customer databases to create computer-generated mailing lists and individualized promotional messages. In other words, computer technology has made it possible for a marketer to learn more about customers' habits and preferences and then adopt a custom marketing strategy with individualized promotional messages or personalized product offerings. Data-based marketing helps the company form relationships with customers. The

What Went Right? feature about Lexus provides an excellent example of how an organization can create databases containing large amounts of information about existing customers and potential customers. Chapter 11, Strategies for Services and Relationship Marketing, discusses how to apply this market segmentation strategy.

Exhibit 8-9 (page 236) summarizes the characteristics of the four basic market segmentation strategies.

Mass Customization In addition to making data-based marketing possible, new technologies are changing the face of traditional custom marketing in many ways. Today, for example, marketers offer tennis shoes, basketball shoes, walking shoes, running shoes, aerobics shoes, and many other shoes for specific activities. Marketers of bicycling shoes offer specialized models for off-road use, for specific road and track conditions, and for both racing and recreational riding, with each pair matched to one or more pedal-and-shoe locking systems.[7] This wide variety of shoes is possible because of mass customization rather than traditional mass production.

A mass production process results in low-cost, standard goods and services. **Mass customization** is a strategy that mobilizes the combined power of mass production technologies and computers to make varied, customized products for small market segments. In fact, in many situations, such as in personalized greeting card kiosks, products are customized for one or a very few customers.

Marketers can offer mass customization to very small and specialized market segments because of technological advances in manufacturing that allow for the coordination of relatively autonomous process or task modules. **Flexible manufacturing systems** are replacing mass production with mass customization because more flexible, computerized production technologies are making it possible to make products like bicycle shoes both in large volume and in great variety. These manufacturing systems also allow changes in design or style to be made rapidly. For example, Panasonic consumer electronic products are replaced with modified models approximately every 90 days.

Mass customization calls for flexibility and quick responsiveness to give customers exactly what they want. USAA uses a mass customization strategy to target its financial services to events in a customer's life, such as buying a house or car, getting married, or having a baby. First, a sales representative inputs customer

what went right?

Lexus Lexus would like consumers to feel that ownership of an exclusive car entitles them to membership in an exclusive club: The Lexus Club. Lexus believes that people who have already purchased a Lexus are an important target market. Lexus keeps in steady contact with current owners and prospective buyers through data-based marketing. For example, before ads for its new GS 300 model appeared, all Lexus owners received a letter alerting them to "the new Lexus," the same positioning line used later in traditional media ads. The letter even included an offer for a free videotape on the new car.

Lexus also mailed the letters and videotapes to key prospects, primarily owners of competing models such as the Infiniti J30, the BMW 535i, and the Mercedes-Benz 300E.

At the same time, Lexus has built a dossier on its buyers. The division has logged every new Lexus owner into a database totaling more than 3,000,000 names. The company uses the database to analyze the characteristics of the existing Lexus owners, in hopes of extending those characteristics to a broader market.

Lexus faces a problem common to all luxury car marketers: The buyer group is small. Only about 9 percent of all cars sold are luxury vehicles, with near-luxury cars representing an additional 3.8 percent, according to *Automotive News*.

This makes advertising in the mass media, such as network TV or general magazines, inherently wasteful. So in addition to direct mailings to its customers, Lexus engages in the promotion of special events and sports sponsorships.

But because Lexus owners report higher satisfaction than owners of any other company's cars, they are the best promoters of the brand through a proven tool: word-of-mouth. That's why Lexus strives to keep its customer base excited about what the automaker is doing.

Lexus marketing executives see data-based marketing and special promotions as a means to build relationships. The company's relationship marketing can keep a customer in the fold while identifying common denominators among customers. Because Lexus sees its owner base as a significant source of word-of-mouth endorsements, it attempts to keep this target market excited about the Lexus brand.[8]

Mass customization
A strategy that combines mass production with computers to produce customized products for small market segments.

Flexible manufacturing system
A group of machines integrated through a central computer and able to produce a variety of similar but not identical products.

STRATEGY	MARKET SEGMENT	MARKET CHARACTERISTICS	COMPANY OBJECTIVES	MAJOR DISADVANTAGES	EXAMPLE
Undifferentiated Marketing	Everyone	Little diversity	Production savings	Competitors may identify segments	Chicago Museum of Science and Industry
Concentrated Marketing	One select segment	Targeted segment has special needs	Gain competitive advantage by specialization; match one well-prepared marketing mix with special segment needs	Lack of diversity; market segment may be too narrow; intense competition for majority segment	Rolls Royce
Differentiated Marketing	Multiple segments	Wide diversity of customers	Exploit differences among market segments; maximize market share	Extensive resources required	Starbucks Coffee
Custom Marketing	Complete segmentation	Each customer is unique	Satisfy each customer's unique needs	High marketing costs	Hitachi industrial robots

information into the customer database. Then special software programs analyze the customer's needs and instantly provide customized suggestions for personalized marketing action. Data-based marketing and mass customization help an organization to better meet customers' needs. This ability often allows marketers to charge a higher price for their mass-customized products.

Identifying Market Differences

Marketing is a creative activity, and many marketing success stories are the result of the creative identification of market segments with unsatisfied needs. No More Tangles creme rinse was developed to fill two needs: children's need for "tangle-free hair without tears" and parents' need to get

MARKETING IS A CREATIVE ACTIVITY, AND MANY MARKETING SUCCESS STORIES ARE THE RESULT OF THE CREATIVE IDENTIFICATION OF MARKET SEGMENTS WITH UNSATISFIED NEEDS.

through bathtime without having to endure a lot of crying and fussing. The product

Not every woman has been satisfied with standard-sized blue jeans. Levi Strauss & Co. is solving this problem by using mass customization and flexible manufacturing. At selected Original Levi's Stores, a trained sales associate takes a woman's measurements, inputs the measurements into a computer, and sends the information via modem to a Levi's factory in Tennessee. In approximately 3 weeks, the customer can either pick up her Personal Pair jeans or, for a small extra fee, have them sent directly to her.

was developed and successfully marketed before competitors had even identified the special needs addressed by the product.

The essence of market segmentation strategy is looking for differences within total markets on which to base the development of successful marketing mixes. What are the meaningful differences?

Typical Bases for Segmentation of Consumer Markets

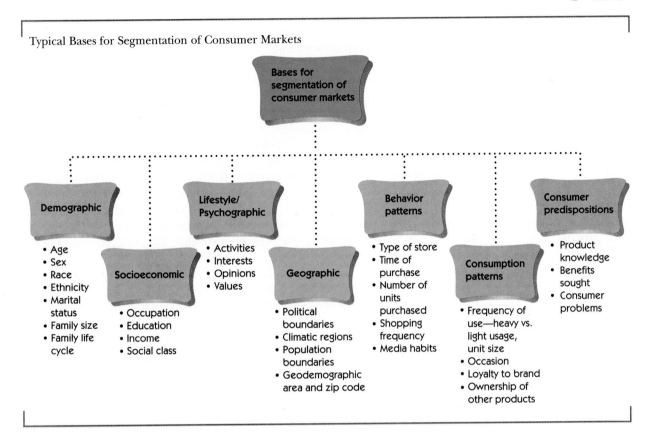

Unfortunately, seldom are there easy answers to this question, because the bases for differentiating market segments are virtually unlimited. Pepsi is aimed at the youth market. Mercedes automobiles are sold to the prestige auto segment. Purina Puppy Chow is marketed to puppy owners, and Purina Dog Chow is marketed to owners of grown dogs. Purina Fit and Trim is aimed at owners of dogs with a tendency to be fat. Winchester brand dog food is marketed to owners of hunting dogs.

Ralston Purina
www.ralston.com

Two things make the task of dealing with the almost limitless bases for market segmentation easier to handle. One is that variables used to segment markets can be categorized into major groups, making them somewhat simpler to use and to remember. Exhibit 8-10 shows just such an arrangement for segmenting consumer markets. The other simplifying factor is that, although the possible segmenting variables are numerous, a far smaller number of variables are, in fact, commonly used. We look next at variables commonly used in segmenting consumer markets. Then we discuss segmentation in organizational markets.

DEMOGRAPHIC SEGMENTATION

Demographic characteristics, such as age, sex, marital status, and family size, are easily understood segmentation variables. Their relationship to various product needs has been well established. Measurement of demographic characteristics and of their relationships to purchasing behavior is not difficult. Further, information about the demographic composition of markets is widely available from a variety of sources. For these reasons, demographic characteristics are among the most commonly used segmentation variables.

Chapters 3 and 6 discussed several demographic trends and how two demographic characteristics may influence decision-making processes. In this section, we illustrate how demographic variables have been used as a basis for segmentation.

Age Infants and toddlers, young children, teenagers, adults, and senior citizens are typical age-based market segments. Classifying consumers into age groups like these is useful when people of different ages have different purchasing behaviors.

Changing age distributions may dramatically affect a company targeting an age-based market. The heaviest consumption of soft drinks, for example, occurs among teenagers. An increase of four million 13- to 24-year-olds would represent an annual consumption gain of three billion cans of soft drinks.

Many marketers target their efforts toward the 45 million Americans born between 1965 and 1976, known as Generation X. Consumers in this first "latchkey" generation are in their 20s and early 30s today. They are heavy consumers of flannel shirts, baggy jeans, Teva sandals, Timberland boots, and baseball caps (which many of them wear backwards). Xers can be reached through magazines such as *Spin* and *Entertainment Weekly* and on MTV. Mountain Dew advertising appeals to this group with commercials that show wild, daredevil activities known as extreme sports.

At the beginning of this century, only one person in 25 was over 65. When the next century dawns, one person in 5 will be over 65. With the growth in the number of older consumers, more firms will be targeting this market segment with products—such as appliances with large letters and big control knobs—that reflect the needs of older people.

Family Life Cycle A marketer of trash compactors, refrigerators, or credit cards might concentrate efforts on households or families rather than on individual consumers. For such marketers, knowing the composition of households is important.

When they hear the word *family,* most people think first of parents and their children. However, families are diverse, in part because they change over time. The **family life cycle,** a series of traditional stages through which most families pass, helps describe how diverse families may be. Exhibit 8-11 shows that, in general, single people marry, raise children, and then live together after the children go out on their own. Different individuals pass through these stages at different rates of speed. Some people skip certain stages, or the process may be disrupted by divorce or the death of a spouse. It is difficult to say exactly what a "normal" family is.

Marketing managers may use the family life cycle as a basis of segmentation for entertainment, household furniture, appliances, and many other product categories. After all, family responsibilities and the presence of children may have a much stronger influence on spending behavior than age, income, or other demographic variables. Consider several people in their 20s: One is single, one is married without children, and one is married with two children, ages 1 and 3. In regard to spending behavior, these consumers are likely to have little in common; so stage in the family life cycle makes a better segmentation variable than age. Exhibit 8-12 lists some products likely to be used during certain life-cycle stages.

Entertainment Weekly
http://cgi.pathfinder.com/ew/

MTV
www.mtv.com

Family life cycle
A series of stages through which most families pass.

This advertisement for Toyota Sienna shows a cute baby and the headline "your life will never be the same." Stage in the family life cycle strongly influences willingness to purchase a van.

your life

is a whole new life. And here to make things a little easier is the affordable new Sienna. A roomy, versatile minivan with front-wheel drive and hefty V6 power. You'll soon find out that it's the best ally

will never

be the same.

a parent can have. So prepare yourself. Ready or not, life will never be the same.

SIENNA

A Modernized Family Life Cycle

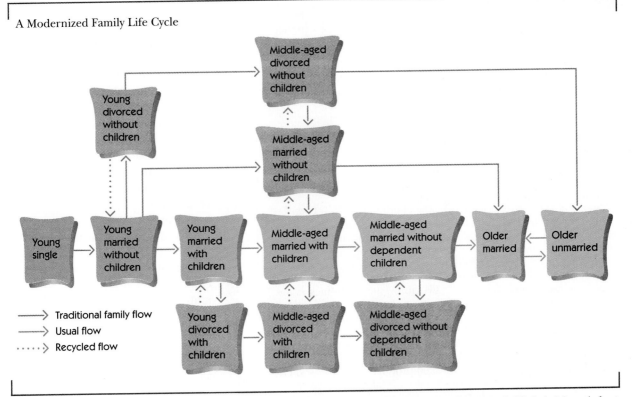

Reprinted by permission of the University of Chicago Press from Patrick E. Murphy and William A. Staples, "A Modernized Family Life Cycle," *Journal of Consumer Research*, January 1979, p. 17.

Consumption Patterns of Families in Several Life-Cycle Stages

STAGE	CONSUMPTION PATTERNS
Young single	Outdoor sporting goods, sports cars, fashion clothing, entertainment and recreation services
Young married without children	Recreation and relaxation products, home furnishings, travel, home appliances High purchase rate of durables
Young married with children	Baby food, clothing, and furniture; starter housing; insurance; washers and dryers; medical services and supplies for children; toys for children
Young single parent	Money-saving products, frozen foods, rental housing, child care, time-saving appliances and foods
Middle-aged married with children at home	Children's lessons (piano, dance, etc.); large food purchases (respond to bulk-buying deals); dental care; higher-priced furniture, autos, and housing; fast food restaurant meals
Middle-aged married without children at home	Luxury products, travel, restaurants, condominiums, recreation Make gifts and contributions; have high discretionary incomes and solid financial position
Older (married or single)	Health care, home security, specialized housing, specialized food products, recreation geared to the retired

Source: CONSUMER BEHAVIOR 3/e by Mowen, John C., © 1993. Reprinted by permission of Prentice-Hall, Inc., Upper Saddle River, NJ.

SOCIOECONOMIC SEGMENTATION

Socioeconomic variables are special demographic characteristics that reflect an individual's social position or economic standing in society. A professor may have a low economic position but a respectable social standing. A surgeon usually rates high in both areas. An unskilled laborer may rate low in both. Socioeconomic factors such as occupation, income, and social class are often combined with other demographic variables to describe consumers.

For example, a socioeconomic and demographic profile comparing heavy users of shotgun ammunition with individuals who purchase little or no shotgun ammunition showed that heavy users are younger than nonusers and are more likely to be blue-collar craftsmen, to live in the rural South, and to have lower incomes. The same type of socioeconomic and demographic profile can be constructed for other products.

As mentioned, social class is one socioeconomic variable that can be used to distinguish groups of customers. Although Americans, perhaps disliking the term *class,* tend to speak of rich and poor people rather than high- and low-class people, class distinctions do exist. There is a considerable difference between a married couple with high-school educations making a combined annual income of $50,000 as toll collectors on the

Lego Lego Systems Inc., the U.S. unit of Denmark's Lego Group, for the past two decades has studied the way girls play to better reach them, but the construction-toy maker has had little success to show for it. About 90% of the company's toys are bought for boys, says Dick Garvey, vice president, marketing, for Lego Systems. "If we could find a way to sell as many Lego sets to girls as we do to boys, we would probably increase our sales volume 75% overnight," he adds.

About 15 years ago, the company introduced a line it thought would appeal to girls: Scala, a specially designed set of Lego parts with which girls could make jewelry. It bombed.

Later, company officials were watching children play with Lego bricks in focus groups and noticed that "if you put identical pieces in front of a group of boys and girls, boys build cars and girls build walls and structures to live in," Mr. Garvey says. That, along with other findings, led in 1992 to the introduction of Paradisa, another girl's line. It highlighted colors such as lavender and pink and was designed to build "socially oriented" structures, such as homes, swimming pools, and stables. Lego's sales to girls increased; but because of continued increases in boys' sales, the company's sales to males remain nine times larger than to females.

Other Lego studies have concluded that girls are less patient than boys with the building process. Mr. Garvey says boys enjoy building, while girls prefer to play with the finished product. So Lego is experimenting with new easy-to-assemble kits and this fall will introduce one called Belville, which it hopes will entice girls to try more complicated construction sets later.

But Meccano Inc., maker of Erector sets, disagrees with this approach. Girls are as capable and keen as builders as boys are, contends its president, Stephane Treppoz. Meccano focus-group research indicates girls generally are more meticulous and have longer attention spans than boys, he says. Indeed, a team of 11-year-old girls from Brooklyn, N.Y., won a $1,500 grand prize last year in a national Erector contest. Their entry was an intricately constructed 6-foot-long suspension bridge.

Meccano will try to put its Erector sets in the hands of more school-age girls, along with boys, by sponsoring a nationwide building contest this fall. The challenge will be to build the perfect baseball stadium. . . .[9]

New Jersey Turnpike and a couple who are both graduates of Harvard Medical School earning a combined income of $400,000 a year practicing in Beverly Hills, California. And the difference is not just the money they make. The doctors may have attended prep schools and prestigious private colleges, inherited wealth, and come from families that have known the good life for generations. They may listen to classical music instead of the "country" music favored by the toll collectors. The doctors may dine frequently at posh restaurants and travel out of the country for their vacations. The other couple probably does not. Consider one final comparison: If each couple were suddenly to earn an extra $20,000, how would each be likely to spend it?

LIFESTYLE AND PSYCHOGRAPHIC SEGMENTATION

A **lifestyle** is a pattern in an individual's pursuit of life goals—in how the person spends his or her time and money. An individual's activities, interests, opinions,

Lifestyle
An individual's activities, interests, opinions, and values as they affect his or her mode of living.

and values represent his or her lifestyle. You probably know someone who has a "workaholic" lifestyle or an "outdoor" lifestyle, for example. Quantitative measures of lifestyles are known as **psychographics**. Such measures are an attempt to "get inside the customer's head" and find out what people actually think about how they live their lives.

Psychographic market segmentation provides a richer portrait of consumer groups than simple demographic information can yield. Psychographic measurement does not replace demographic measures but enhances them. For example, one father of young children may continue the activities that occupied him before the children arrived—perhaps golf, tennis, and partying. Another father in the same stage of the family life cycle may drop his sports and social activities to devote more time to the children. The two demographically similar men differ in terms of lifestyle, or psychographic variables.

As you can imagine, there are many different lifestyles, and there is no agreement among marketers on a standard set of lifestyle categories or psychographic measures. The What Went Wrong? feature illustrates how Porsche used psychographics to supplement its data about its demographic market segments.

Whatever the classification scheme, lifestyles and psychographics are often used to segment markets. *Outdoor Life, Flying, Travel and Leisure,* and many other magazines define their target markets by lifestyle, for example. By reaching certain lifestyle segments, the magazines provide advertising media for other marketers who wish to appeal to those segments.

Psychographic variables are more difficult to deal with than demographic and socioeconomic variables. Library research can tell the marketer approximately how many male Hispanic Americans there are in California, for instance, but there are no statistics on the number of carefree people or good family men. This is one reason marketers typically use psychographic variables in combination with other variables. For example, marketers might decide that the psychographic lifestyle of a Porsche sports car buyer can be tied to more concrete demographic and economic descriptions.[11]

GEOGRAPHIC SEGMENTATION
Simple geography can be an important basis for market segmentation.

Wrangler Jeans knows its core customers live west of the Mississippi River, associate Western wear and jeans with horses, and either live or aspire to live a Western lifestyle.[10] However, the company sees a meaningful market segment beyond rodeo riders and ranchers. It is trying to reach the "emulator consumer" who is not a rodeo fan but who associates with the Western lifestyle through country music.

www.wrangler.com

Psychographics
Quantitative measures of lifestyle.

The market for olestra fat substitute products in foods has been analyzed using psychographic segmentation. Research found that "determined dieters" and "heavy snackers" were most predisposed to embrace olestra. Groups labeled "naturalists" and "taste purists" were least likely to be attracted to olestra products.[12]

www.olean.com

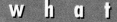

what went wrong?

Porsche After having sold a record 30,000 automobiles in the United States in 1986, Porsche sold only 4,000 or so in 1993. Price was partly responsible. During the 1980s, the price of a Porsche 911 Carrera coupe was less than the average U.S. household's annual income. In 1993, the price was about 25 percent higher because of the strength of the Deutschemark and a luxury tax passed by Congress. However, after conducting marketing research to learn what market segments were prime customers, Porsche Cars North America found out increased price wasn't the only thing that had gone wrong.

The research showed that the demographics of Porsche owners were utterly predictable. The typical owner is a 40-something male college graduate earning over $200,000 per year. The psychographics, however, were of more interest. Porsche owners fell into the rather unusual—and not necessarily flattering—lifestyle categories shown below.

TYPE	PERCENT OF ALL OWNERS	DESCRIPTION
Top Guns	27	Driven, ambitious types. Power and control matter. They expect to be noticed.
Elitists	24	Old-money blue bloods. A car is just a car, no matter how expensive. It is not an extension of personality.
Proud Patrons	23	Ownership is an end in itself. The car is a trophy earned for hard work, and who cares if anyone sees them in it?
Bon Vivants	17	Worldly jet setters and thrill seekers. The car heightens the excitement in their already passionate lives.
Fantasists	9	Walter Mitty types. The car is an escape. Not only are they uninterested in impressing others with it, they also feel a little guilty about owning one.

Porsche's vice president of sales and marketing found the results astonishing. He said, "We were selling to people whose profiles were diametrically opposed. You wouldn't want to tell an elitist how good he looks in the car or how fast he could go."

As a result of its new insights about its target markets, Porsche has cut its prices, launched a new advertising campaign, and introduced a redesign of its classic rear-engine car, the 911.[13]

The demand for suntan lotion is far greater in Florida, for example, than in Saskatchewan. In some cases, a geographic variable might indicate to a marketer that there is absolutely no demand for a certain product in a certain area, such as snow shovels in Puerto Rico.

Most marketers use geography as a basis for segmenting markets. Virtually all marketers decide if they will engage in international business or market only in their home country. International marketers recognize that people in Mexico, Egypt, and Malaysia have different needs and customs. In Argentina, for instance, most Coca-Cola is consumed with food, but in many Asian countries, it is consumed primarily as a refreshment and is rarely served with meals.

Not all U.S.-based firms choose to market their products outside the United States, of course. However, geographical differences are also important in the United States. Domestic marketers should recognize that for many products, such as mass transportation, the needs of people in New York City are different from those of people in Wyoming.

Some Geographic Bases of Segmentation Geographic segmentation includes distinctions based on continents, cultural regions, and climate. Another basis for segmentation is political boundaries, such as state and city lines and the like. However, populations are not always adequately described by political boundaries. Marketers are most often concerned with the population map—where the people are—rather than with such matters as the imaginary line that separates Billings Heights, Montana, from Billings, Montana. Various expressions are used to reflect this fact: "Greater New York," "the Dallas–Fort Worth Metro-Plex," "the Bay Area," "the Twin Cities." These phrases and others like them indicate that for certain market segments there is no distinct political boundary line.

Geodemographic and Zip Code Segmentation   Direct marketers, especially those that sell through catalogs sent by mail, often use zip codes as a basis for market segmentation. The phrase "birds of a feather flock together" is quite appropriate here. People and households in the same zip code area are often similar in demographic characteristics.

Geodemographic segmentation refers to use of a geographic variable, such as zip codes, to characterize clusters of demographically similar individuals. Claritas Corporation's PRIZM system has analyzed each of the 36,000 zip codes in the United States and, based on demographic similarities, classified them into forty market segments. Each has a colorful name like Shotguns and Pickups (large rural families with modest means) and Gray Power (active retirement communities).

Geographical Considerations for Global Marketers   Global marketers who segment markets based on geography must recognize that certain factors may discourage international marketing in certain countries. As explained in Chapter 4, sometimes countries require that all trade with other nations be approved by some form of central ministry. Governments may also impose tariffs, import quotas, or other restrictive controls to discourage foreign companies from doing business in their markets. For example, because of widespread and blatant production and sale of pirated compact discs, laser discs, CD-ROM discs, and other American intellectual property, the United States has threatened to impose trade sanctions against an array of Chinese products, ranging from toys to athletic shoes. China, in turn, has threatened to retaliate with its own sanctions against the United States.

Such restrictive factors may strongly influence decisions to target certain market segments. At the same time, the changing political climate, in which more countries are moving toward market economies, provides many opportunities.

> **Geodemographic segmentation**
> A type of market segmentation by which consumers are grouped according to demographic variables, such as income and age, as identified by a geographic variable, such as zip code.

global focus on competition

Children in China   Xiang Yinchao, a 10-year-old boy, waits quietly in a crowded Shanghai department store while his mother asks a saleswoman a barrage of questions about the VTech alphabet desk, a $70 computer keyboard that helps teach Mandarin-speaking children English. Yinchao's mother knows it's expensive, but she says, "Chinese parents want their kids to speak English. It's the international language." Limited to one child by government regulations and determined to see their kids get ahead, Chinese parents—along with grandparents, great-grandparents, aunts, and uncles—are spoiling, fussing over, and doting on their children as never before.

Known in China as Little Emperors, Chinese kids are being showered with everything from candy to computer games. With at least 300 million people in China under the age of 15, according to government statistics, a huge market is emerging that caters to China's kiddie dynasty. Business is driven by the "six-pocket syndrome," a phrase referring to the fact that as many as six adults may be indulging the whims of each child. The president of Walt Disney's Asian-Pacific consumer products division says, "When you look at the combined spending power of those grown-ups, the Chinese child probably has more spent on him than a child in the West."[14]

BEHAVIOR PATTERN SEGMENTATION

Individual consumers exhibit different behavior patterns and habits worthy of marketers' attention. Some individuals purchase apparel only at specialty men's or women's shops, for example; others buy their clothing at department stores, in discount shops, or from catalogs. Shopping habits and other behavioral differences may be used as bases for segmentation. Why did 7-Up increase efforts to have its products sold in fast-food outlets and in vending machines? Because marketing analysts found that these two types of outlets, which are aimed at people who behave in certain ways, accounted for 40 percent of industry sales but only 20 percent of 7-Up's sales volume.

CONSUMPTION PATTERN SEGMENTATION

Buyers can vary their consumption from heavy to none at all. Therefore, in many cases, consumption patterns provide a good basis for market segmentation. Both the New York Mets and the New York Metropolitan Opera offer season tickets to heavy users of their products. Banks are aware that many of their customers are long-term clients who loyally deal with only one institution—thus banks invent slogans like "a full-service bank" and "the only bank you'll ever need." Light users or nonusers of the same bank's services require a different marketing mix, perhaps one stressing convenient locations or free merchandise for new depositors. Banks and many other marketers of services target some existing customers by using a technique known as cross-selling. **Cross-selling** refers to marketing activities designed to sell new, "extra" services to customers who already buy an existing service. Thus, a bank may make it easy for a customer with a home mortgage loan to obtain a low-cost safety deposit box and a checking account with a credit line.

Consumption patterns may also differ with circumstances. The purchase occasion may prove to be the underlying force creating consumption patterns and thus may be useful in distinguishing among buyer groups. A holiday drinking glass decorated with a Christmas tree or Santa Claus is obviously geared to buyers planning seasonal entertaining rather than to people looking for everyday glassware. Lava soap and other hand cleaners are sold for use in really dirty, messy, or greasy situations.

Of course, some buying patterns are strongly linked to other buying patterns. Ownership of one product may encourage the purchase of additional products. For example, owners of computers that use Windows-based operating systems are likely to buy additional Windows-based software. In contrast, marketers of custom sheepskin van seat covers can expect to sell very few products to people who don't own vans, and people who don't own houses seldom buy storm windows. In many instances, consumption patterns can be the major clue in identifying meaningful marketing segments.

Cross-selling
Marketing activities used to sell new services to customers of an existing service.

focus on relationships

USAA A customer who is brand-loyal—who repeatedly purchases from the same company—is an especially important segment of any market. Effective marketers of services put special efforts into establishing enduring relationships with these customers. USAA, an insurance and financial service company, loses customers at a rate far below the industry rate. USAA retains 98 percent of its auto insurance customers yearly, versus about 85 percent for the industry as a whole, even though the military officers it specializes in covering are constantly on the move. USAA maintains a database in San Antonio that is designed to service its military customers' needs. It includes obvious life events—for example, "new baby," "marriage," and "divorce"— but also "promoted to Colonel," "transferred to Bosnia," and other life events that have insurance and financial impacts on members of the military. It allows clients to relocate anywhere in the world without switching agents. A phone call to any company location will reach a company representative who has access to the caller's file in the database. This gives the sales agent or customer service representative the immediate ability to understand the caller's needs and preference. Having designed its service around agents' access to the information system, USAA conducts virtually all of its business over the telephone and by mail.[15]

CONSUMER PREDISPOSITION SEGMENTATION

Consumers vary widely with respect to product knowledge, beliefs about products and brands, and reasons for purchase. The sophisticated, knowledgeable buyer of stereo equipment is, for marketing purposes, almost totally

This holiday season, give someone you love a little piece of Americana.

For 65 years, Zippo has been a part of America's celebrations. This holiday season, make Zippo a part of yours.

different from the novice buyer. The veteran buyer knows what to look for, what questions to ask, where to buy, where to get service, and even what the price should be. The novice knows almost nothing of these things and so looks to salespeople for guidance. The novice seeks a store with a good reputation and trustworthy salespeople. The veteran buyer trusts his or her own knowledge and judgment.

The major benefits sought by consumers are also likely to vary considerably. Seeking to identify groups of customers by the benefits they seek is called **benefit segmentation**. Even when two or more buyers are purchasing exactly the same product, the expected benefits may vary. Just as in the commercial, some people buy Miller Lite because it tastes great, others because it's less filling. One consumer might buy a mouthwash because it freshens the breath, another because it tastes "mediciney" and therefore must really kill germs.

Segmenting Business Markets

To a great extent, business markets may be segmented by use of variables similar to the ones just discussed. The difference, of course, is that, instead of using characteristics and behavior of the individual consumer, the segmenter uses characteristics and behavior of the organization. For example, when marketers of electrical resistors decided to investigate their market on the basis of benefit segmentation, a study of the benefits sought from electrical resistors uncovered two major benefit segments. Military engineers purchasing for the government and engineers purchasing for consumer electronic companies both sought performance stability and reliability. But military buyers were concerned with failure rate and promptness in review of specifications, while low price was the major benefit sought by the consumer products engineers.

Exhibit 8-13 shows that business markets may be segmented on the basis of geography, organizational characteristics, purchase behavior and usage patterns, and organizational predispositions.

Finding the "Best" Segmentation Variable

As has already been suggested, the "best" segmentation variable is the one that leads the marketer to the identification of a meaningful target market segment. Some experts have argued that the benefits customers seek from products are the basis for all market segments. This may be so. After all, that idea supports the view that consumer orientation is the foundation of the marketing concept.

But contributing to differences in benefits sought are geographical differences and buyers' characteristics. Thus, many segmentation variables may be found to be working together, complementing one another. The heavy user of Coors Light, for example, is somewhere between the ages of 21 and 34, is in the middle or upper income group, lives in an urban or suburban area, belongs to a health club, buys rock music, travels by plane, gives parties and

The marketers of Zippo lighters conducted a survey and realized that 30 percent of the company's customers were collectors. After learning that a large market segment had different reasons for purchasing a Zippo, the company started working more closely with retailers, built a database, established a "collectible of the year" promotion, and increased the lighter line to include more than 500 different models.

Benefit segmentation
A type of market segmentation by which consumers are grouped according to the specific benefits they seek from a product.

Selected Bases for Segmentation of Business Markets

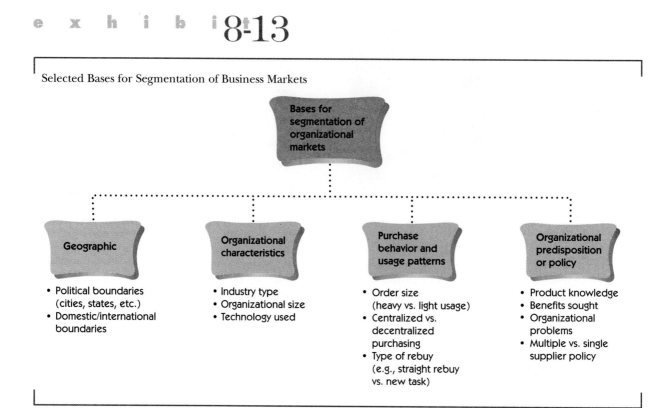

cookouts, rents videos, and is a heavy viewer of television sports.[16] Because variables often complement each other, it is in the marketer's interest to target the best bundle of segmenting variables—two to five or more—so that the most advantageous match of market and marketing mix can be achieved. The marketer's goal is to segment the market in a way that helps the organization select market opportunities compatible with its ability to provide the right marketing mix.

Positioning: The Basic Focus for the Marketing Mix

After a target market has been selected, marketing managers choose the position they hope the brand will occupy in that market. Recall that *market position,* or competitive position, represents the way consumers perceive a brand relative to its competition. The thrust of a typical positioning strategy is to identify a product's or brand's competitive advantage and to stress salient product characteristics or consumer benefits that differentiate the product or brand from those of competitors.

Pepperidge Farm Goldfish
www.pfgoldfish.com

For example, Pepperidge Farm's Goldfish was for years positioned as a premium snack product. However, consumer research indicated that the product had the highest appeal in households with children under 12, especially among mothers who loved Goldfish because they were baked, not fried. And kids liked them because they tasted good. As a result, the Goldfish brand was positioned less as a premium product and more as a fun, kid-oriented snack that moms and kids could agree on. ("It's one snack that it's OK to get hooked on.") Of course, as mentioned in the discussion of market segmentation, a brand cannot be all things to all people. Thus, positioning a brand—perhaps even altering product formulation to emphasize certain product attributes—may cause long-term problems. Further, a competitor may enter the market and position its product directly against the established product. This is known as **head-to-head competition** (or "me, too" competition). The objective here is to occupy the same position as a competitor, rather than to position away from competitors. For example, Burger King recently introduced a Big King burger to compete head-to-head with the Big Mac.

Positioning decisions are easier when marketing research has clearly identified how consumers perceive various

"Think different" is the message in this Apple Computer ad. The company's strategy is to position itself away from IBM and other PC marketers and promote its uniqueness.

www.apple.com

competing offerings. Often, marketers draw positioning maps, sometimes based on sophisticated computer models, to illustrate how consumers see each competitor's product. Exhibit 8-14 shows positioning maps for tea based on two product characteristics: flavor (traditional versus unique) and serving temperature (iced versus hot). A map such as this reflects benefit segmentation.

Head-to-head competition
Positioning a product to occupy the same market position as a competitor.

e   x   h   i   b   i   **8-14**

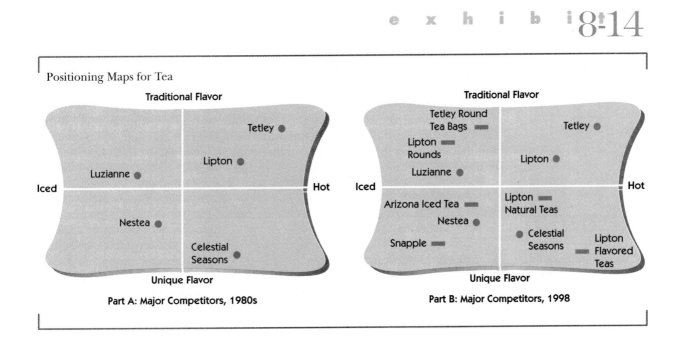

Positioning Maps for Tea

Part A: Major Competitors, 1980s

Part B: Major Competitors, 1998

DiGiorno Rising Crust Pizza, which rises in the oven during pre-heating, positions itself not against other frozen pizzas but as an alternative to delivered pizzeria pizza. DiGiorno Rising Crust Pizza stresses the quality of restaurant pizza and the convenience of frozen pizza.

www.digiorno.com

The map in Part A illustrates that when Luzianne entered the tea market, it was positioned as being exclusively for iced tea, and it was alone in this position. Lipton and Tetley were perceived to be quite similar to each other (served hot and offering a traditional flavor). Positioning maps can help pinpoint opportunities and problems. Part B reflects how competitors, after recognizing Luzianne's success, offered brands that were more clearly differentiated in consumers' minds from the traditional hot teas.

Positioning maps may indicate a void in the market. In other words, if a map shows no brands in a particular quadrant or area, there may be room for a new product. Sometimes research is conducted to determine what characteristics an "ideal brand" would have. If there is no competing product in the "product space" that the ideal brand would occupy on the map, a market opportunity may exist.

In the tea example, positioning was based on certain product characteristics. Consumers view competing offerings from many other perspectives as well. For example, consumers may evaluate a brand or product relative to offerings in another product class—low-saturated-fat olive oil relative to high-saturated-fat butter, for example—or according to purchase situation or usage occasion—an ordinary table wine versus a wine for a celebration. A marketer planning positioning strategy must take these perspectives into account.

When marketing managers are confident that they understand how consumers see their brand's position in relation to the competition, they must decide if they wish to maintain that position or reposition the brand. Ethan Allen introduced a new Country Colors collection, a reasonably priced natural-color furniture line, and advertised it on "Friends" because it wanted to reposition itself as a furniture maker with something for everyone rather than a company that makes expensive furniture for older consumers.[17] **Repositioning** may require rethinking the benefits offered to consumers through the marketing mix. Jello, which for years was positioned to appeal to children as a dessert, was repositioned as a snack food. Its Jiggler recipes and Jiggler forms allow kids to eat Jello with their hands.

Repositioning
Changing the market position of a product.

The target market strategy and the positioning strategy provide the framework for the development of the marketing mix. Thus, target marketing, positioning, and the marketing mix are highly interdependent. More will be said about each of these topics in future chapters.

summary

Market segmentation is one of marketing's most powerful tools. Whatever variables they use, effective marketers try to identify meaningful target segments so that they can develop customer-satisfying marketing mixes.

 Define the term market.

A market is composed of individuals or organizations with the ability, willingness, and authority to exchange their purchasing power for the product offered.

2 *Explain the concept of market segmentation.*

In order to identify homogeneous segments (subgroups) of heterogeneous markets, marketing managers research an entire market, disaggregate it into its parts, and regroup the parts into market segments according to one or more characteristics, such as geography, buying patterns, demography, and psychographic variables.

3 *Relate the identification of meaningful target markets to the development of effective marketing mixes.*

Marketing mixes are effective only if they satisfy the needs of meaningful target markets. A meaningful target market has a significant (and, ideally, measurable) market potential, is distinguishable from the overall market, is responsive, and is accessible through distribution or promotional efforts.

4 *Distinguish among undifferentiated, concentrated, differentiated, and custom marketing strategies.*

An undifferentiated marketing strategy is used if no meaningful segment can be identified. If one meaningful segment is the target of an organization's marketing mix, the concentrated marketing strategy is used. If several market segments are targeted, the differentiated marketing strategy is employed. When markets are so disaggregated that each customer requires a special marketing mix, the custom marketing strategy is appropriate. Data-based marketing and mass customization are changing the nature of traditional custom marketing.

5 *Demonstrate the effect of the 80/20 rule and the majority fallacy on marketing strategy.*

According to the 80/20 principle, the majority of a product's sales are accounted for by a small percentage of the buyers. These users constitute an attractive target market; however, competitors often target this market as well. Failure to take the strength of the competition into account is the majority fallacy. One purpose of market segmentation is to identify segments that may have gone undetected by competitors.

6 *List the market segmentation variables most commonly used by marketing managers and explain how marketers identify which ones are appropriate.*

In consumer markets, segmentation variables include demographic, socioeconomic, psychographic, and geographic factors, as well as behavior and consumption patterns and consumer predispositions. In business markets, geographical areas, organizational characteristics, purchase behavior and usage patterns, and organizational predispositions and policies are used as segmentation variables. The appropriateness of any one variable or combination of variables varies considerably from case to case. The marketing manager must determine which variables will isolate a meaningful target market.

7 *Explain the purpose of a positioning strategy.*

Each brand appealing to a given market segment has a position in the consumer's mind. The purpose of a positioning strategy is to identify a product's or brand's competitive advantage and to stress salient product characteristics or consumer benefits that differentiate the product or brand from those of competitors.

---

key terms

cross-classification matrix (p. 227)
undifferentiated marketing (p. 228)
concentrated marketing (p. 229)
80/20 principle (p. 231)
majority fallacy (p. 231)
differentiated marketing (multiple market segmentation) (p. 231)

custom marketing (p. 233)
mass customization (p. 235)
flexible manufacturing system (p. 235)
family life cycle (p. 238)
lifestyle (p. 240)
psychographics (p. 241)

geodemographic segmentation (p. 243)
cross-selling (p. 244)
benefit segmentation (p. 245)
head-to-head competition (p. 247)
repositioning (p. 248)

---

questions for review & critical thinking

1. Why do organizations practice market segmentation?
2. Think of some creative ways the following organizations might segment the market.

   a. A rental car company
   b. A zoo
   c. A personal computer manufacturer
   d. A science magazine

3. What are some unusual ways markets have been segmented?
4. Identify and evaluate the target market for the following products.
   a. *Wall Street Journal*
   b. The Chicago Cubs
   c. Timberland boots
   d. Perrier bottled water
   e. *Wired* magazine
5. What questions should a marketer ask to determine if a market segment is meaningful?
6. Think of examples of companies that use undifferentiated marketing, concentrated marketing, differentiated marketing, and custom marketing. Why is the strategy appropriate in each instance?
7. Should firms always aim at the largest market segment?
8. What is the relationship between data-based marketing and mass customization?
9. How might Levi's segment the men's clothing market? How might Anheuser-Busch segment the market for beer?
10. What variable do you think is best for segmenting a market?
11. What variables might a business-to-business marketer use to segment a market?
12. What is positioning? Provide some examples.
13. Identify the positioning strategy for the following brands.
    a. 7-Up
    b. American Airlines
    c. AT&T long-distance service
    d. Gateway 2000 computers
14. Form small groups of four or five students. Assume you have been hired by a rental car company as a consultant. Research and identify a market segmentation strategy and a positioning strategy for the company.

marketing plan—right or wrong?

1. The plan at Colgate-Palmolive was to combine laundry detergent and fabric softener in individual laundry packets, which would be used in both washer and dryer. The premium-priced packets, targeted to families with children, would clean and soften in the wash and control static in the dryer.
2. Attitudes toward working women in Japan are changing. Today, more than half of Japan's married women hold full- or part-time jobs, and Japanese women are increasingly looking for products that are convenient and that save time. The plan: market a long-lasting, no-smear lipstick targeted at Japanese business women. The lipsticks would be priced at $30 (American) for a 3.6-gram tube. A cleansing agent to remove the lipstick would cost $10.
3. A physician plans to specialize in the treatment of baldness and will advertise her clinic using the name "The Hair Doctor."

internet i n s i g h t s

z i k m u n d . s w c o l l e g e . c o m

exercises

1. Abbott Wool's Market Segment Resource Locator provides numerous links to information and Web sites related to market segmentation. Go to www.awool.com and answer the following questions.
   a. What type of information can be obtained about the African-American market, the Asian-American market, and the Hispanic-American market?
   b. Select the teen segment. What type of information can be obtained about this market segment?

2. Go to the Census Bureau's home page at www.census.gov. What three states are forecasted to increase the most in population between 1995 and 2020? What is the expected growth of the Asian-American market? The Hispanic market?

address book (useful urls)

Statistics Canada	www.statcan.ca/start.html
Pampers Parenting Institute	www.totalbabycare.com
iGolf	www.igolf.com
Big Yellow: NYNEX Interactive Yellow Pages	www.niyp.com
PRIZM System	www.claritas.com

ethically right or wrong?

After careful research, the Uptown cigarette was targeted to a group that had a higher-than-average number of heavy smokers. Research showed that the target market liked the product, its name, and its attractive black and gold package. However, there were intense protests when the product was introduced to the public, because Uptown was the first cigarette targeted to African Americans. According to some critics, this minority group, which has a higher percentage of smoking-related illnesses than other groups, was a target market chosen on the basis of racism.

QUESTION
1. Is segmentation based on race ethical?

TAKE A STAND
1. Is the marketing of sugar-coated cereals on Saturday morning television programs good for society?
2. There are many people who watch TV evangelists and consider themselves "born again." Is it ethical for a consumer products marketer to sell products to consumers on the basis of religion?
3. Dakota cigarettes were designed to be marketed to active working-class women. Is this ethical?

VALS™ 2

The VALS (Values And Lifestyles) system is a popular psychographic classification scheme. The VALS 2 typology, developed by SRI International, segments U.S. adults based on psychological attributes that drive consumer buying behavior. VALS 2 classifies consumers based on their answers to 35 attitudinal statements and 4 demographic questions.

Using the VALS national database of products, media, and services, manufacturers and advertisers identify the consumer groups who are most naturally attracted to their products and services. This enables them to select an appropriate consumer target. Marketers design their advertising messages for the target using words and images intended to appeal to the target. They then put the advertising in media that the target actually uses. (VALS tracks the television, magazine, and radio preferences of each of the eight consumer groups annually.)

Consumer data by VALS type are provided by linkages with Simmons' annual *Survey of the American Household,* SRI's retail financial services survey, MacroMonitor, and other databases.

case 8-1

Marketers also apply VALS to direct marketing using GeoVALS™ to identify zip codes and block groups that contain large concentrations of their target consumers. Other products include iVALS, which measures and represents consumer preferences in on-line environments, and Japan VALS™, which segments Japanese consumers based on their psychographic profiles.

VALS is built on two key concepts: self-orientation and resources. Self-orientation determines what in particular about the self or the world is the meaningful core that governs a person's activities in life. According to VALS, consumers are motivated by principle, status, or action. Principle-oriented consumers are guided in their choices by abstract, idealized criteria rather than by feelings, events, or desire for approval and opinions of others. Status-oriented consumers look for products and services that demonstrate their success to their peers. Action-oriented consumers are guided by a desire for social or physical activity, variety, and risk taking.

Resources include the full range of psychological, physical, demographic, and material means and capacities consumers have to draw on. Resources encompass education, income, self-confidence, health, eagerness to buy, and energy level. Resources run on a continuum from minimal to abundant.

Based on these dimensions, VALS 2 defines eight segments of adult consumers, as illustrated in the accompanying art and table. Actualizers and Strugglers represent the upper and lower ends of the resource dimension. The other six groups—Fulfilleds, Believers, Achievers, Strivers, Experiencers, and Makers—represent combinations of self-orientation and resource availability.

VALS™ 2 Segmentation System

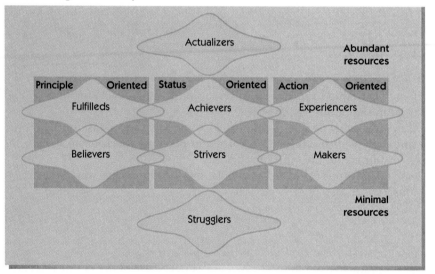

For example, both Achievers and Strivers are status-oriented consumers, but Achievers have more resources. Achievers are successful career and work-oriented people who value structure, predictability, and stability over risk, intimacy, and self-discovery. They are deeply committed to their work and families, and their social lives are structured around family, church, and business. As consumers, they favor established products and services that demonstrate their success to their peers. Strivers seek motivation, self-definition, and approval from the world around them. They are striving to find a secure place in life. Unsure of themselves and with limited economic, social, and psychological resources, they are deeply concerned about the opinions and approval of others. They may try to emulate people who own more impressive possessions, but what they wish to obtain is often beyond their reach.[18]

Characteristics of VALS™ 2 Market Segments

CONSUMER TYPE	PERCENT OF POPULATION	MEDIAN AGE	DISTINCTIVE PURCHASE BEHAVIORS
Actualizers	10%	42	Possessions reflect a cultivated taste for finer things in life
Fulfilleds	10	55	Desire product functionability, value, and durability
Believers	17	58	Favor American products and established brands
Achievers	14	39	Prefer products that demonstrate success to peers
Strivers	14	36	Emulate those with impressive possessions
Experiencers	13	24	Avid consumers of clothing, fast food, music, movies, and videos
Makers	11	35	Unimpressed by material possessions (except those with a practical purpose)
Strugglers	10	67	Modest resources limit purchases to urgent needs

Source: Updated by SRI in April 1995 from VALS2/Simmons Study of Media and Markets database. Used with permission from SRI Consulting, Menlo Park, CA.

QUESTIONS

1. Evaluate VALS 2 as the basis for a market segmentation strategy.
2. What types of products are most likely to benefit from segmentation based on VALS 2?

The Point: 105.7

With his Pauly Shore laugh and a penchant for broadcasting naughty words, Tim Virgin, a weeknight disc jockey for 105.7, The Point, likes to play bands that sound as angry as their names: Rage Against the Machine, Bad Religion, Social Distortion, Rancid. He occasionally taunts callers on the air.

But Virgin's main mission is to give listeners exactly what they want. Before he can have his pudding of punk, he must chew his broccoli—a computer-generated playlist of adolescent confessions from Alanis Morissette and cheery frat anthems from the Dave Matthews Band; self-loathing from Smashing Pumpkins and jingle-jangle from the Gin Blossoms.

"Hey, could you play [Dishwalla's] 'Counting Blue Cars'?" requests one caller.
Virgin rolls his eyes and offers a lame, "I'll see what I can do."
"Yeah, just what you wanted to hear again—Dishwalla," he mutters.

That ability to dance between alternative rage/angst and mainstream Midwestern sensibilities has taken The Point a long way—from its first broadcast 3½ years ago to one of the top-rated alternative rock stations in the nation.

The Point's 300,000 weekly listeners are more loyal and tune in more often than any modern rock audience in the nation, according to Arbitron, the company that compiles radio ratings. KPNT-FM recently tied venerable rock station KSHE for fifth in the overall ratings, which track the 12-and-up age group from 6 a.m. to midnight over a full week. (The Point ranks lower in some important, more narrowly defined categories.)

"They had a mission to make alternative work and they have succeeded in doing so against the odds," said Sky Daniels, who reports on alternative radio for *Radio and Records*, an industry magazine. "The station is being recognized as very successful. Record labels know they need to get The Point on a record."

case 8-2

You will find each exercise on the CD-ROM developed for use with this textbook. Each exercise has a name and is located within a module. For example, the first exercise can be found in the Buyer Behavior Module by clicking on Buying Roles and Decisions.

BUYER BEHAVIOR MODULE
Buying Roles and Decisions

1. The decision-making process is different during routine response behavior, limited problem solving, and extensive problem solving. How do the buying roles of user, influencer, buyer, and decider influence the decision-making process under different decision-making situations?

MICROMARKETING MODULE
Fundamentals of the Marketing Process

2. What criteria might you use to segment the toothpaste market?

cross-functional
insights

Many theories and principles from other business disciplines can provide insights about the role marketing plays in an organization. The questions in this section are designed to help you think about integrating what you have learned in other business courses with the marketing principles explained in this book.

Decision Support Systems for Marketing Decision support systems serve specific business units in a company. A decision support system is a computer system designed to store data and transform the data into accessible information. Its purpose is to allow decision makers to answer questions through direct interaction with databases.

What database software might be used by marketing research managers?

What spreadsheet software might be used by marketing research managers?

What statistical software might be used by marketing research managers?

In what ways must a marketer's decision support system be coordinated with the organization's information system?

Research Is Systematic and Objective Marketing research allows managers to make decisions based on objective, systematically gathered data rather than intuition.

How can a knowledge of statistical hypothesis testing help a marketing researcher?

What steps might a marketing researcher take in testing a statistical hypothesis about a mean?

Simple Random Sampling A sample is simply a portion, or subset, of a larger population. It makes sense that a sample can provide a good representation of the whole. A simple random sample consists of individuals' names drawn according to chance selection procedures from a complete list of all people in a population.

Discuss what type of statistical errors are associated with simple random sampling.

How much control does a statistician have over the probability that an error will occur?

How likely is the occurrence of random sampling error?

A mail questionnaire includes a question that can be answered either *excellent, good, fair,* or *poor.* If simple random sampling is utilized, what statistical test will determine if the observed distribution is different from the expected uniform distribution?

Sales Forecasting Sales forecasting is the process of predicting sales totals over some specific future period. An accurate sales forecast is one of the most useful pieces of information a marketing manager can have because the forecast influences so many plans and activities. Identifying trends and extrapolating past performance into the future is a relatively uncomplicated quantitative forecasting technique. Time series data are identified and even plotted on a graph, and the historical pattern is projected for the upcoming period. The market factor method of forecasting may be used when there is an association between sales and another variable, or factor.

How could correlation analysis be used to identify market factors?

How could regression analysis be used to forecast sales?

How might the moving averages method be used in the projection of sales trends?

Consumer Behavior   Consumer behavior consists of the activities people engage in when selecting, purchasing, and using products so as to satisfy needs and desires. Such activities involve mental and emotional processes in addition to physical actions.

Explain economists' theories about consumer behavior and how they differ from marketers' theories.

The concept *caveat emptor* ("let the buyer beware") was introduced in the 16th century. What is the history of this concept in the 20th century? Is it an important aspect of consumer behavior?

Buying Center   The buying center in any organization is an informal, cross-departmental decision unit whose primary objective is the acquisition, dissemination, and processing of relevant purchasing-related information.

What impact do the management concepts of job description, authority, and responsibility have on the activities of a buying center?

How important is a company's corporate culture in the establishment of buying centers? What type of corporate culture would contribute most to the establishment of effective buying centers?

Suppose an organizational structure identifies profit centers. What impact might they have on organizational buying?

How might purchasing agents with different levels of need for achievement, need for power, and need for affiliation (as explained by McClelland's need theory) differ in their organizational buying behavior?

Gatekeeper Role   The role of collecting and passing on information—or withholding it—is known as the gatekeeper function.

What theories of communication within organizations help explain this function?

necessity is the mother of invention

—WHO SAID THIS?

Product Strategy for Global Competition

necessity is the mother of invention THAT'S WHO SAID IT!

–PLATO

Plato (427 BC–347 BC) was one of the greatest philosophers of all time. Born in Greece, he founded an academy, devoted to philosophy, law, and scientific research, that was the predecessor of today's colleges and universities. Plato was the most renowned teacher of his time. The influence of his thinking has been pervasive and longlived.

chapter 9

Basic Concepts about Goods and Services

LEARNING OBJECTIVES

After you have studied this chapter, you will be able to:

Define *product* and explain why the concept of the total product is important for effective marketing.

1

Differentiate among convenience products, shopping products, and specialty products.

2

Categorize organizational products.

3

Explain the difference between product lines and product mixes.

4

Understand brand-related terminology, including *brand, brand name, brand mark, trademark, manufacturer brand, distributor brand,* and *family brand.*

5

(continued on next page)

for pre-adolescent kids, carrying the wrong lunchbox to school can be as traumatic as wearing no-name sneakers or having a home haircut. Some kids might go so far as to feign illness if Mom and Dad didn't spring for the latest, hippest Hercules or Barbie box.

Though sneakers carry the most status in school-yards today, kids still attach a certain amount of importance to the ol' lunchbox. And Oscar Mayer has discovered a way to tap into those lunchbox dollars with Lunchables.

When Lunchables was first introduced in 1989, Oscar Mayer was simply extending the company's lead in luncheon meats by adding bread and condiments necessary to complete the meal. The basic idea for Lunchables was to provide convenient meal solutions for mothers and kids. This product concept was successful for several years. However, when sales began to flatten out, Oscar Mayer went to its target market, 6- to 12-year-olds, and asked for input. The result was product modification and the introduction of Lunchables Fun Packs, which added juice, candy, and games.[1]

THE BASIC IDEA FOR LUNCHABLES WAS TO PROVIDE CONVENIENT MEAL SOLUTIONS FOR MOTHERS AND KIDS.

Of course, to reach the market, many marketing functions other than product development must be performed. But let's stick with the product itself. Its brand name, Lunchables, is easy to say and remember. It is descriptive. The tag below the name—"lunch combinations"—tells consumers that this is more than just lunch meat.

The package's hip graphics tell that this is a fun pack. Fun is built into the food. Other brand names, such as Kraft cheddar cheese, CapriSun juice drink, and Skittles candy, also appear on the package. Brain teasers and games often appear on the back of the package. Contests such as "Jam with the Pros" offer the chance to have NBA stars visit the winner's school.

Aside from the tangible things, the buyer of a Lunchables Fun Pack purchases intangible things, such as the Oscar Mayer name and reputation. The name Oscar Mayer is associated with the best lunch meats in the world. Consumers associate Oscar Mayer with quality.

A Lunchables is more than a food item; it is a bundle of satisfactions—the particular bundle of benefits that constitutes this Oscar Mayer product.

This is the first of three chapters dealing with product issues. It begins by explaining how marketers view products and product strategy. It then categorizes products using several different classification schemes and goes on to discuss the nature of product lines and product mixes. Next, it discusses the nature of branding, packaging, warranties, and customer service.

Oscar Mayer
www.oscar-mayer.com

What Is a Product?

The product an organization offers to its market is not simply a bar of soap, a rental car, or a charitable cause. As with so many other marketing elements, there is more to the product than meets the eye. A product may be a thing, in the nuts-and-bolts sense, but it does not have to be something tangible. It can be a reward offered to those willing to pay for it: A mowed lawn is the payoff for someone who buys a lawn mower. To an organization, a product is a bundle of benefits. This customer-oriented definition stresses what the buyer gets, not what the seller is selling. For example, a Disney World resort hotel provides more than a place to stay. It offers sun and fun, relaxation and entertainment, and a sense of pride about being a good parent.

Defining the product in terms of benefits allows anything from tangible items to services to ideas to be identified as a product. Whether an organization's offering is largely tangible (a ship), largely intangible (financial counseling), or even more intangible (the idea of world peace), its offering is a product.

Total product
The wide range of tangible and intangible benefits that a buyer might gain from a product after purchasing it.

THE TOTAL PRODUCT

Because a product can have so many aspects and benefits, marketers think in terms of the **total product**—the broad spectrum of tangible and intangible benefits that a buyer might gain from a product once it has been purchased. Marketers view total products as having characteristics and benefits at two levels. **Primary characteristics** are basic features and aspects of the core product. These characteristics provide the essential benefits common to most competing products. Here, consumers expect a basic level of performance.[2] A quarter-inch drill bit, for example, is expected to provide quarter-inch holes. **Auxiliary dimensions** of a product provide supplementary benefits and include special features, aesthetics, package, warranty, instructions for use, repair service contract, reputation, brand name, and so on. Each auxiliary dimension is part of the *augmented product*. Together, these two groups of features fulfill the buyer's needs. Any one of many benefits may be important to a particular buyer. Effective marketers build strategies emphasizing those benefits that are most meaningful to the target markets.

Exhibit 9-1 uses Close-Up toothpaste to illustrate the nature of a core product and the associated auxiliary dimensions. The essential benefits of any toothpaste are cleaning teeth and preventing tooth decay. Close-Up's package (a tube with a flip-cap) also benefits the consumer by making the product convenient to store and easy to use. The brand name Close-Up suggests social confidence and romance. The printing of the manufacturer's name, the country of origin, and a telephone hotline number on the

Primary characteristic
A basic feature or essential aspect of a product.

Auxiliary dimension
An aspect of a product that provides supplementary benefits, such as special features, aesthetics, package, warranty, repair service contract, reputation, brand name, or instructions.

The core product for a hotel is a room to sleep in. However, there are many auxiliary dimensions to this service product. Hotel personnel who provide speedy, friendly personal service and who go out of their way for hotel guests are product characteristics that provide competitive advantage.

The Core Product and the Augmented Product

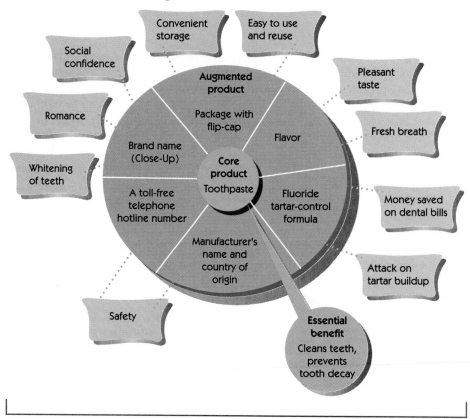

package provides a safety benefit. Each auxiliary dimension adds a benefit that may be important to a buyer.

PRODUCT STRATEGY AND THE PRODUCT CONCEPT

Product strategy
The planning and development of a mix of the primary and auxiliary dimensions of a product.

Product concept
The end result of the marketing strategist's selection and blending of a product's primary and auxiliary dimensions into a basic idea emphasizing a particular set of consumer benefits; also called the product positioning concept.

Product strategy involves planning the product concept and developing a unified mix of product attributes. Successful product strategy requires that all aspects of the product be analyzed and managed in light of competitive offerings. Deciding which product features and which consumer benefits to stress is the creative dimension of product strategy.

The **product concept** (also called the product positioning concept) defines the essence, or core idea, underlying the product features and benefits that appeal to the target market. The product concept reflects the marketing strategist's selection and blending of a product's primary characteristics and auxiliary dimensions into a basic idea or unifying concept. In short, it provides a reason for buying the product. The product concept often is described in the same terms used to characterize the competitive market position that the product is expected to occupy in consumers' minds.

THE **PRODUCT CONCEPT REFLECTS THE MARKETING STRATEGIST'S SELECTION AND BLENDING OF A PRODUCT'S PRIMARY CHARACTERISTICS AND AUXILIARY DIMENSIONS INTO A BASIC IDEA OR UNIFYING CONCEPT.**

For example, the product concept for Ritz Air Crisps stresses that Air Crisps are a new generation of cracker—lighter, air-filled crackers to be eaten by the handful rather that with a slice of cheese. Some widely used product concepts are "Our product has the most advanced technology"; "We build the highest-quality product"; "Our product is made in the USA"; and "Ours is a basic, no-frills product; it's the best value."

PRODUCT DIFFERENTIATION

Calling buyers' attention to aspects of a product that set it apart from its competitors is called

Obsolete, dead, ugly: words that describe the lowly status of hood ornaments today. Hood ornaments are an auxiliary dimension of automobiles. In the 1920s and '30s, hood ornaments, such as sculptures of women, animals, and airplanes, were popular because they were used to dress up radiator caps. Today, most car designers prefer no decorative embellishment. Automakers are dumping hood ornaments in favor of a cleaner, smoother look.[3]

product differentiation. To differentiate their product, marketers may make some adjustment in the product to vary it from the norm or may promote one or more of the product's tangible or intangible attributes. For example, an automobile battery with a selector dial that switches on a supplemental booster battery when the primary battery fails to hold a charge will be more competitive than an ordinary battery. This product feature is a tangible difference that provides a functional benefit.

What differentiates one product from others need not be a scientifically demonstrable improvement. Stylistic and aesthetic differences accomplished through changes in color, design, and shape, as well as technological differences, can play a role in product differentiation. Party Animals, for instance, are "adult crackers" baked in animal shapes to set the brand apart visually from competitors, such as Ritz. If consumers see such variations as important, then the variations differentiate the product from its competitors.

Product differentiation
A strategy that calls buyers' attention to aspects of a product that set it apart from its competitors.

Classifying Products by the Nature of the Market

Many factors influence a buyer's decision-making process. One of the strongest is the product itself because the product includes so many physical, psychological, and purchase-behavior dimensions. For this reason, marketing managers have developed some widely accepted product classifications that describe both products and, more importantly, buyers' perception of them. We begin by discussing consumer products and then consider organizational products.

CLASSIFYING CONSUMER PRODUCTS

Furniture, appliances, groceries, hardware—a seemingly infinite number of categories of consumer products can be identified. The great number and diverse nature of products offered for sale make consumer product classification a complex task. Products may be classified on the basis of many criteria. We will discuss two widely accepted systems: classification by tangibility and durability and classification by consumers' buying behavior. (See Exhibit 9-2.)

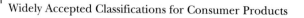

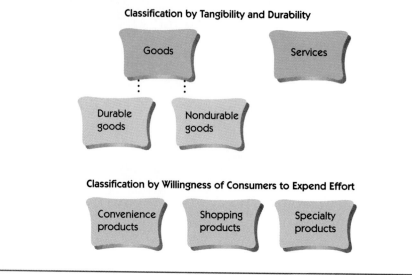

Widely Accepted Classifications for Consumer Products

Classification by Tangibility and Durability

Goods

Services

Durable goods

Nondurable goods

Classification by Willingness of Consumers to Expend Effort

Convenience products

Shopping products

Specialty products

Service
A task or activity performed for a buyer or an intangible that cannot be handled or examined before purchase.

Durable good
A physical, tangible item that can be used over an extended period.

Nondurable good
A physical, tangible item that is quickly consumed, worn out, or outdated.

Tangibility and Durability   Products may be classified according to tangibility and durability—whether they are goods or services and, if goods, whether they are durable or nondurable. Goods have a tangible, physical form, whereas **services** are tasks, activities, or other intangibles. **Durable goods** function over an extended period. Consumers use durable goods, such as automobiles and refrigerators, many times. **Nondurable goods**—which are quickly consumed, worn out, or outdated—are consumed in a single use or a few uses. Chewing gum, paper towels, and hand soap are examples of nondurable goods.

The distinction between goods and services is meaningful, but remember that services, like the physical, tangible items we call goods, should be referred to as *products.* This is especially important now because the service industry accounts for more than half of personal consumption expenditures.[4] If government is included as a service, the proportion of personal consumption accounted for by services is even greater. Because services are so important, a special discussion of strategies for the marketing of services appears in Chapter 11.

For now, however, if you think about a restaurant's product, you will realize that it is difficult to separate goods from services entirely. This reality has led some marketing experts to array products along a continuum from pure good to pure service. A barbecue grill is obviously a tangible good; an employment agency clearly provides a service. But a restaurant provides both a good (the food it prepares) and a service (the cooking and serving of the food, as well as convenience, atmosphere, and other aspects of its total product offering). Thus, you will find a restaurant in the middle of the goods–services scale in Exhibit 9-3.

CONSUMER BEHAVIOR

One of the first product classification systems to be developed is the most widely recognized and the most useful for answering questions regarding marketing mix decisions. This is the consumer product classification scheme developed by Melvin T. Copeland in 1924. Copeland suggested three general classifications of consumer products: convenience, shopping, and specialty.

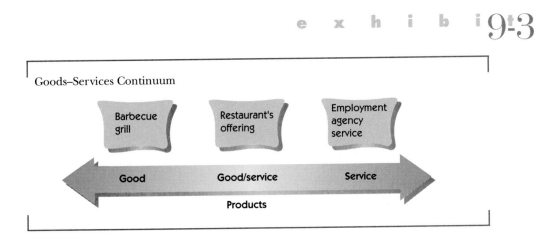

Goods–Services Continuum

Three important points should be made about Copeland's scheme. First, the plan applies to consumer products, not organizational products. Second, and most significant, the classes are primarily based not on the products themselves but on consumers' reasons for buying, their need for information, and their shopping and purchase behaviors. The reason Copeland's plan has remained popular for so long is that it is consumer-oriented. Third, the classifications are somewhat generalized; they are based on a "typical" consumer's reasons for buying. The categories are less useful when applied to specific shoppers, especially very poor or very rich ones.

Convenience Products The first of Copeland's categories is **convenience products**. Bic disposable ball-point pens are convenience goods; so are shoelaces.

Convenience product
A relatively inexpensive, regularly purchased consumer product bought without much thought and with a minimum of shopping effort.

Twizzlers and other candy bars are convenience products. They are purchased on a regular and recurring basis, and they are bought almost reflexively, without a great deal of thought. Silverware and dinnerware, such as Oneida brand, are shopping products. Consumers feel the need to reassure themselves about such products' quality, style, or value before making a purchase.

In most cases, so is gasoline. What do these items have in common? They are relatively inexpensive; they are purchased on a regular and recurring basis; and they are bought almost reflexively, without a great deal of thought. In fact, they are bought with a minimum of consumer shopping effort. Buyers of a particular gasoline brand may be loyal, but their loyalty is not very deep. If they are running low on gas, most drivers will settle for a brand similar to their regular brand rather than drive a few extra miles to get their preferred brand. In short, consumers want to buy products such as these at the most convenient locations. How far out of your way would you go to buy, say, a quart of a particular brand of milk? The answer to such a question provides a guide to determining whether any given product is a convenience product.

Because shoppers rarely expend much shopping effort to obtain convenience products, distribution is a key element in the marketing mix. The object is to make the product available in almost every possible location. For example, thousands of retailers in every large city sell soft drinks and candy bars. These convenience goods are also common vending machine items. Convenience items that are purchased largely on impulse, such as candy bars, are sold in drugstores, discount stores, convenience outlets, and college bookstores. In individual stores, impulse items that are purchased on the spur of the moment are usually placed at the most convenient spots, such as near the checkout counter.

In the convenience goods classification, one brand is fairly easily substituted for another of its type, and personal selling efforts by retailers are almost nonexistent. Therefore, extensive advertising by the manufacturer or service provider may be appropriate. The heavy advertising expenditures of Coca-Cola and Pepsi-Cola attest to the importance of extensive advertising.

Shopping Products **Shopping products**, the second of Copeland's classifications, include products for which consumers feel the need to make product comparisons, seek out additional information, examine merchandise, or otherwise reassure themselves about quality, style, or value before making a purchase. In other words, prospective buyers of these products expect to benefit by shopping around. Decisions about shopping products are not made on the spur of the moment, in part because shopping goods are generally priced higher than convenience goods, and consumers are more involved with the purchases.

There are two types of shopping products. If consumers evaluate product alternatives as similar in quality and features but different in price, these products are *homogeneous shopping products*. For homogeneous shopping products, such as washing machines and undershirts, obtaining the lowest price is the primary reason for making comparisons. *Heterogeneous shopping products* have identifiable product differences. These products tend to be subject to the whims of fashion and are more likely to be noticed by the shopper's family and friends. Thus, the risks, both monetary and social, associated with heterogeneous shopping products are fairly high. Clothing, shoes, furniture, and everyday tableware are examples of heterogeneous shopping products.

Buyers of heterogeneous shopping products are willing to search for the styles, brand names, or quality they want. Furthermore, they may wish to purchase the products in a particular store. You may have heard a friend say, "I got this suit at the Ivy League Shop." But people seldom boast, "I got this Doublemint gum at the 7-Eleven." Thus, the distribution problem differs from that associated with convenience goods. Because people are willing to shop around, the idea is not to place the product everywhere but to place the product in the proper spots. The distribution strategy becomes one of selective distribution. Within a store, shopping products probably will not be placed up front. Furniture can be placed in a distant area of a department store because customers are willing to seek it out.

Marketing mix elements shift somewhat in relative importance when we move from convenience products to shopping products. Product characteristics, includ-

Shopping product
A product for which consumers feel the need to make comparisons, seek out more information, examine merchandise, or otherwise reassure themselves about quality, style, or value before making a purchase.

ing quality, become more important. Price will be a consideration for consumers, but with heterogeneous products it need not be as uniform among competing brands as in the case of easily substituted convenience products. Retail marketers, however, may stress the price of heterogeneous products because they are competing with other retailers of the same brands or similar brands.

Specialty Products In some cases, consumers know exactly what they want. They have selected the brand in advance and will not accept substitutes. For example, they may insist on having Woody at A Cut Above the Others style their hair because they see his service as unique. At the moment of purchase, they no longer need to make shopping comparisons among alternatives. They have thought about their purchase. They regard the brand as having a particular attraction other than price. Products that are the object of this type of consumer preference fall into Copeland's third category, **specialty products**.

Many specialty products are seldom-purchased items, such as stereo equipment, pianos, wedding receptions, and expensive cars. Potential buyers may gather a great amount of information before making the purchase decision. They may go so far as to buy and read books or magazines dealing with the product class. At the time of purchase, they may spend considerable time and effort to get to the appropriate store, but they no longer need to make shopping comparisons; their minds are made up.

Brand insistence can be strong. A shopper may have decided, after considerable thought, that only Wedgwood china and Waterford crystal will do for the dining room. Sales personnel or additional advertising will not sway such a shopper. This brand preference is important to retailers.

The marketer of a specialty product may develop a marketing mix that includes exclusive distribution of the brand. Dealers stocking Jaguar XK8s are few and far between, in part because a potential buyer will travel a considerable distance to purchase the car. Advertising the brand's uniqueness and pricing at a level suitable to, and supportive of, the brand's image are appropriate tactics for the marketer.

As mentioned earlier, Copeland's scheme is a generalized portrayal of consumer goods for the majority of consumers. Unsought purchases, such as the purchase of ambulance services in an emergency, may not fit neatly into this scheme. Furthermore, a particular individual may view some products very differently from most other consumers. Nevertheless, marketers who identify which description best fits their products may use these generalizations to choose appropriate retail outlets and plan other elements of the marketing mix.

Classifying Organizational Products

Organizational products can be categorized in much the same way as consumer products. As Exhibit 9-4 shows, the most commonly used classification system breaks **organizational products** into capital products, production products, and operating products.

CAPITAL PRODUCTS

Capital products consist of installations and accessory equipment. Installations are major capital items necessary to the manufacture of a final product. Buildings and facilities, assembly

> **Specialty product**
> A consumer product that is not bought frequently, is likely to be expensive, and is generally purchased with great care.

> **Organizational product**
> A product or service that is used to produce other products and/or to operate an organization.

> In Germany, Stover Pommes Frites is McDonald's supplier of french fries. The company purchases capital products to perform its production operations.

Classification of Organizational Products

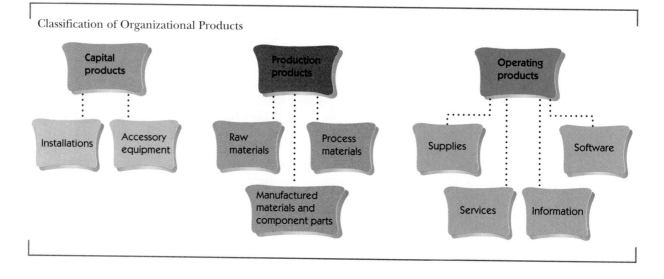

lines, heating plants, and other such major purchases are included in this category. Many of these products are made to order, such as an air-conditioning system for a factory. Accessory equipment facilitates an organization's operations. Generally included in this category are such things as pickup trucks, forklifts, word processors, and copying machines. These items, as a rule, do not involve as large a capital outlay as installations. They are not generally thought of as being specially built to do only one job, although a product such as a pickup truck can be modified to handle specialized tasks.

PRODUCTION PRODUCTS

Production products can be subdivided into raw materials, manufactured materials and component parts, and process materials. Raw materials are organizational products that are still very close to their natural states—that is, they have undergone almost no processing. Bars of aluminum, chunks of granite that will be made into statuary, and trees to be made into lumber or paper are good examples. Manufactured materials and component parts are a step above raw materials in the processing chain. Manufactured materials, such as cloth fabrics, thread, and yarn, have undergone a transformation from raw materials. They are materials that are used as basic ingredients for producing a company's products. Component parts have been processed even more. They include screws, computer chips, and parts of all sorts that end up in a finished product. To a lawn-mower manufacturer, spark plugs, wires, and bushings are all component parts. Notice that unlike raw materials, manufactured materials and component parts have undergone considerable processing. Process materials are used in making finished products but do not become part of these products. An example is an acid used to soak dirt and grime off machine parts.

OPERATING PRODUCTS

Operating products are the closest thing to a convenience good in the organizational products classification scheme. Operating supplies include paper, pencils, brooms, envelopes, light bulbs, and other short-lived stock items that an organization routinely buys and uses up as it operates. Conventional software refers to standard computer packages that can be used by any organization. Lotus 1-2-3, Microsoft PowerPoint, and WordPerfect are examples. Services may be broadly defined as work provided by others. Thus, operating services include everything from janitorial services and machinery maintenance to the services of lawyers,

Collaborating to Turn Jeans to Paper Many ecologically conscious organizations consider recycling and using operating supplies made from recycled materials important aspects of their mission to be socially responsible. Often, they are willing to pay a premium for these products or enter into collaborative relationships to improve the environment. This has created opportunities for marketers.

When Albuquerque paper maker Stefan Watson learned about the nearly 200,000,000 pounds of denim scraps landfilled in the United States each year, he saw it as an answer to a prayer. The only problem was that it was blue, says Watson. Using old-fashioned techniques, Watson developed a system, requiring no caustic or bleach, for converting denim scraps into paper and corrugated board.

Watson looked toward three industry leaders as collaborators in bringing denim paper products to the mainstream. Levi Strauss and Company provided the denim and a ready outlet for paper products, while Crane offered the necessary manufacturing expertise. Cottrell Paper helped develop the corrugated board. It was tricky in the beginning, says Watson. The blue denim created a lot of contamination problems in the mill, which was used to making white paper. But Crane did a fantastic job. Levi Strauss and Company put the products to a variety of uses, from employee pay envelopes and interoffice mailers to clothing labels and hangtags.

If you can get beyond the blues (the color, that is), says Watson, you'll find this paper is much stronger than any other, and there is major potential for reuse and recycling. Watson Paper Company's new denim corrugated board is a case in point. It's a rugged, chambray-colored corrugated stock, ten times as strong as kraft corrugated stock.[5]

accountants, and medical providers. Information consists of news, data, and knowledge pertinent to the operation of the business.

At first glance, this system may appear to be more product-oriented and less buyer-oriented than Copeland's plan. However, the categories do reflect buyer concerns, as major business purchases, such as the acquisition of a new factory building or a computerized assembly system, involve different problems and buyer concerns than do purchases of brooms and sweeping compounds. In this sense, the categories of organizational products are buyer-oriented.

The Product Line and the Product Mix

In discussing consumer and organizational products, we have treated each product type separately, as if a given organization offered just one **product item**—that is, one particular version of a particular good or service. In reality, most organizations market more than one product. Even an industrial cleaning company, whose product would appear to be simply "cleaning," offers an array of services. Does the client want a daily cleanup or a weekly one? Did the client hire the company to do a once-a-year major cleaning or to clean up after some remodeling work? Does the customer want the windows washed? What the cleaning firm has to offer is, in fact, a product line.

From a marketing perspective, then, a firm's **product line** is a group of products that are fairly closely related. The phrase *depth of product line* refers to the number of different product items offered in a product line. For example, Louis Rich's food product line has grown to include several variations: turkey franks, turkey bologna, turkey pastrami, and several other lunch meats made of turkey. All these items are closely related, because they are all in the same product category. A line such as this has considerable depth.

The products that constitute a product line may be related to one another in several ways. They may be similar only in a broad sense, such as **product class**.

Product item
A specific version of a particular good or service.

Product line
A group of products that are fairly closely related. The number of different items in a product line determines the depth of the product line.

Product class
A broad group of products that differ somewhat but perform similar functions or provide similar benefits—for example, all automobiles made for personal use.

Quidel Corporation   Walk into an Osco [Payless] drugstore, and on a shelf near the ovulation testing kits you'll find Conceive brand pregnancy tests. A cherubic infant smiles at you from the pink box. Price: $9.99.

A little farther down the aisle, and near the condoms, you'll find another pregnancy test, called RapidVue. The package features no smiling baby, just brick-red lettering against a mauve background. Price: $6.99.

Both tests are products of San Diego–based Quidel Corp.—and they are identical except for the brand name and the packaging. What's different is the market. "The market definitely divides between the women who want babies and those who don't," explains Quidel Chief Executive Steven Frankel. He explains why the smiling baby sells for more than the plain-wrapper product: "It's like what Charles Revson said about cosmetics: People buy hope. In our case, they pay more for hope than for possible relief."[6]

Procter & Gamble, for example, has a food products line, a paper products line, a cleaning products line, and a cosmetic products line. Products in a line may perform some particular function. Clairol's hair-coloring product line is somewhat different from its shampoo and conditioner line and certainly different from its line of hair dryers, curlers, and other appliances. A product line may also be identified as a group of products that are sold to the same customer groups. For example, Black & Decker, a company that dominates the mass market for power tools sold in stores like Kmart, was losing ground at residential construction sites, where crew members use more profitable, high-end, durable tools. So Black & Decker introduced its DeWalt professional and industrial power-tool line, which consists of 30 drills, saws, and sanders to appeal to this market.[7]

A product line may be identified by price or quality. A&P divides its private label products into lines based on price. Its cheaper brand products are distinct from its more expensive Ann Page brands. Sears, from time to time, has identified its products as Sears, Sears' Better, and Sears' Best.

A marketing organization may offer several product classes and define its various product lines in many ways. A **product mix** encompasses all offerings of the organization, no matter how unrelated they may be. General Motors Corporation manufactures and sells large, medium, and small cars, as well as buses, Army tanks, locomotive engines, and a wide range of parts and other products. Other organizations are similarly diversified. The phrase *width of product mix* is used to identify the extent of the product lines associated with one firm, no matter how diverse or narrow they may be. You might be surprised to discover just how varied the product mix of a firm like Chesebrough-Ponds, Beatrice Foods, or Procter & Gamble really is.

The Marketer's Product Portfolio

Just as the investor or financial advisor seeks to assemble a group of stocks or other investments that form a sound total package, so the marketing manager can view the product mix as a collection of items to be balanced as a group—a **product portfolio**. A balanced product mix might contain some good old standby products, some new products that have already shown promise, and some products in R&D that may be a bit risky but have

THE MARKETING MANAGER CONSIDERS THE INTERRELATIONSHIPS AND CASH FLOWS FOR THE COMPLETE MIX OF PRODUCTS RATHER THAN CONCENTRATING ON THE ISOLATED PROBLEMS OF THE INDIVIDUAL MEMBERS OF THAT MIX.

Product mix
All the product offerings of an organization, no matter how unrelated. The number of product lines within a product mix determines the width of the product mix. A wide mix has a high diversity of product types; a narrow mix has little diversity.

Product portfolio
A collection of products to be balanced as a group. Product portfolio analysis focuses on the interrelationships of products within a product mix. The performance of the mix is emphasized rather than the performance of individual products.

a high payoff potential. The marketing manager considers the interrelationships and cash flows for the complete mix of products rather than concentrating on the isolated problems of the individual members of that mix. Evaluation of a company's or strategic business unit's product mix is called product portfolio analysis.

Product portfolio analysis as envisioned by the Boston Consulting Group is illustrated in Exhibit 9-5. The horizontal scale depicts the market share as high or low. On the vertical scale, the same words refer to the market growth rate. The combinations of these variables yield four quadrants:

High-market-share product in a high-growth market
High-market-share product in a low-growth market
Low-market-share product in a high-growth market
Low-market-share product in a low-growth market

To put this in perspective, let's assign some picturesque names and familiar products to each of the matrix cells. The market for smoking-cessation products is high growth, and Nicorette gum has a high market share. It is a **star**. The canned-meat market is low growth, and Spam has a high market share. It is a **cash cow**. The market for compact disc players is growing rapidly, and Sanyo has a low market share. A product in a high-growth market that seems to be having trouble picking up market share is, for its marketers, a **problem child**, or a question mark. The facial-soap market is low growth, and Palmolive has a low market share. It is a **dog**.

Clearly, every company would like to market a star. But cash cows also have their value. Although Spam may not be part of an exciting and growing market, for example, it does make a lot of money for Hormel. This product and other cash cows are likely to have long-standing records of popularity and to generate cash flow. Excess monies generated by the cows can be used to finance the growth of products the organization hopes will become stars or to correct problems causing a product to be a problem child.

Some marketing experts believe organizations should get rid of dogs to free themselves to concentrate on more profitable projects, but such an approach cannot work for every organization. Not every product can be a star, and dogs can have their uses. They might be profitable in the sense that they contribute to meeting overhead and administrative expenses. Furthermore, products with low shares of low-growth markets may continue to appeal to customers who have special needs or who buy primarily on the basis of price. Many brewers, for example,

Star
A high-market-share product in a high-growth market.

Cash cow
A high-market-share product in a low-growth market.

Problem child
A low-market-share product in a high-growth market.

Dog
A low-market-share product in a low-growth market.

e x h i b i 9-5

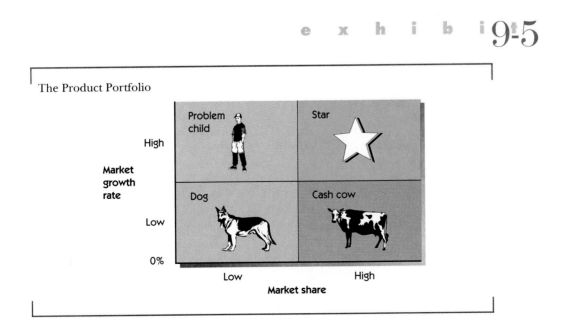

The Product Portfolio

continue to market low-priced beers that appeal to bargain hunters. The investment made in marketing these products is small. If there are no advertising costs and no expenses incurred in improving the product, the brand that is simply placed on the shelf for sale may be profitable. A dog may occupy a safe and secure market niche in which there are few challenges from competitors.

The product portfolio concept does have limitations. The first is that it may give the inexperienced student of marketing an unjustified feeling of security. Simply placing the names of products in the appropriate boxes is not appropriate application of the portfolio concept; that merely helps to describe the portfolio. When the matrix has been formed, the marketing manager's difficult decisions are only beginning. If you have a star, is competition desperately trying to knock it down? Probably. So what steps come next? If you have a cash cow, how vulnerable is it to competition? Wouldn't the competitors like to have a cow of their own? They certainly would. How about the dogs? Should you sell them off? Who would buy them? Should you keep them? How can that be done so as to maximize the cash flow? Should you hold on to them for a longer period, because no competitor seems to be addressing their limited target markets? How much are you willing to spend trying to make the problem child into a star?

A second overriding problem that the portfolio concept only begins to address is the reality of the marketplace and of human nature. On the surface, the portfolio suggests that the marketing manager should work hard either to turn problem children into stars or to develop stars in some other way. However, keeping up a steady flow of stars is difficult, to say the least. The Etch-A-Sketch has been the staple of Ohio Art's toy line for more than 40 years. Although Ohio Art has a cash cow, the company has not been very successful in developing additional items in the star category, and its profits have been declining in recent years. Many organizations and their marketing managers are tempted to build up the cows to make sure they retain a high market share. Often, however, competition or other environmental forces may block the development of stars with money produced by cash cows.

Ohio Art
www.world-of-toys.com

Manitoba Moose   The Manitoba Moose may play minor league professional hockey, but when it comes to creating a brand mark to identify and symbolically represent the team, they are major league. In the first year of the club's first season, the hockey organization sold more than $1 million worth of team paraphernalia, from shirts, hats, and jackets to foam antlers. Its purple, green, and brown logo portrays a goofy moose wearing a hockey helmet and holding a hockey stick.

This success didn't occur by accident. The organization sponsored a write-in contest when it was planning a team name and mascot that would create excitement and not yawns. After the moose was selected by the fans, the club's marketers named it Mick E. Moose. The initial design was that of a natural, tough-looking moose, but the design evolved into a cartoonish moose with a Mona Lisa smile that seems to appeal to women and children as well as men.[9]

Branding—What's in a Name?

According to legend, the practice of branding products originated when an ancient ruler decided that products should bear some sort of symbol so that, if something should go wrong, buyers and the authorities would know who was to blame. Forced to identify their products with themselves, the story goes, producers began to take greater pride in their products and to make them better than those of their competitors, thus reversing the negative intent of the king's order. Whether the story is true or not, it makes the point that branding serves many purposes, both for the buyer and for the seller.

Branding helps buyers to determine which manufacturers' products are to be avoided and which are to be sought. Without branding, a buyer would have difficulty recognizing products that have proved satisfactory in the past. Many consumers are not able to analyze competing items strictly on the basis of physical characteristics. They rely, therefore, on a brand's or firm's reputation as an assurance that the product being purchased meets certain standards. For example, the computer chip marketer's "Intel Inside" stickers on personal computers offer consumers reassurance when they feel confusion and anxiety about making a computer purchase.

Innovation

Mercedes' star symbol is a brand mark that is strongly associated with the company's products. Because the symbol is so powerful, this advertisement features only the brand mark and a single word tied to the Mercedes brand. Use of the word *Mercedes* is not necessary.

www.mercedes-benz.com

Branding helps sellers to develop loyal customers and to show that the firm stands behind what it offers. A brand that has earned a reputation for high quality may pave the way for the introduction of new products. Part of the attraction of Kellogg's Honey Crunch Corn Flakes, for example, is its connection with the original Kellogg's Corn Flakes, a branded product with a long record of public acceptance.

A BRAND THAT HAS EARNED A REPUTATION FOR HIGH QUALITY MAY PAVE THE WAY FOR THE INTRODUCTION OF NEW PRODUCTS.

In large measure, the free enterprise system, with its accent on letting the market decide which firms will succeed and which will fail, depends on branding. Even societies that have tried to do away with branding, such as China, have found that citizens somehow determine which products are good and which are bad, even if they have to use product serial numbers or other bits of information to differentiate among products.

BRANDS AND TRADEMARKS

Despite the common practice of speaking of brands, brand names, and trademarks as if all these terms meant the same thing, there are

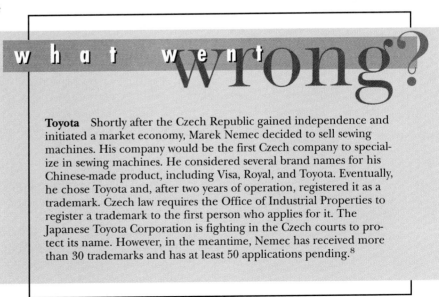

what went wrong?

Toyota Shortly after the Czech Republic gained independence and initiated a market economy, Marek Nemec decided to sell sewing machines. His company would be the first Czech company to specialize in sewing machines. He considered several brand names for his Chinese-made product, including Visa, Royal, and Toyota. Eventually, he chose Toyota and, after two years of operation, registered it as a trademark. Czech law requires the Office of Industrial Properties to register a trademark to the first person who applies for it. The Japanese Toyota Corporation is fighting in the Czech courts to protect its name. However, in the meantime, Nemec has received more than 30 trademarks and has at least 50 applications pending.[8]

Changing technologies have had a major impact on the use of copyrighted material. This advertisement for IBM points out that it is easy for someone to download images and use them commercially without permission. So IBM used its technology to develop a digital watermark. The digital watermark protects images without obscuring them—much like the watermarks on rare manuscripts, such as the one pictured in its advertisement.

Brand
An identifying feature that distinguishes one product from another; more specifically, any name, term, symbol, sign, or design or a unifying combination of these.

Brand name
The verbal part of the brand—the part that can be spoken or written.

Brand mark
A unique symbol that is part of a brand.

Logo
A brand name or company name written in a distinctive way; short for logotype.

Trademark
A legally protected brand name or brand mark. Its owner has exclusive rights to its use. Trademarks are registered with the U.S. Patent and Trademark Office.

Service mark
A symbol that identifies a service. It distinguishes a service in the way a trademark identifies a good.

Generic name
A name so commonly used that it is part of everyday language and is used to describe a product class rather than a particular manufacturer's product.

some technical differences among them.

Brands A **brand** is any name, term, symbol, sign, design, or unifying combination of these. A **brand name** is the verbal part of the brand. For example, Sega, Cover Girl, and WordPerfect are brands. When these words are spoken or written, they are brand names. Many branded goods and services rely heavily on some symbol for identification. Merrill Lynch, a stockbroker, makes considerable use of an image of a bull, and Microsoft Windows is represented by a window that materializes out of an expanding pattern of rectangles floating to its left. Such unique symbols are referred to as **brand marks**. A brand name or company name written in a distinctive way—for example, Coca-Cola written in white script letters on a red background—is called a **logo**, short for *logotype*.

Trademarks A brand or brand name can be almost anything a marketer wants it to be, but it does not have any legal status. A **trademark**, on the other hand, is a legally protected brand name or brand mark. The owners of trademarks have exclusive rights to their use. Thus, the word *trademark* is a legally defined term. Either a brand name is a registered trademark or it is not.

The registered trademark gives a marketer proprietary rights to a symbol or name. The NBC peacock is a registered trademark. So is the name Coca-Cola, the script style in which it is written, and the product's distinctive bottle design. Since the holder of a trademark has exclusive rights to use the trademarked name or symbol, a certain amount of protection is provided to the trademark holder. The name Ball Park Frankfurters is a registered trademark, so no other franks with that name are likely to appear on the market. There is even some protection against similar names, if a legal authority can be induced to agree that the similarity is great enough to constitute an infringement of the original trademark. That's why a small grocery store with a coffee cart called Federal Expresso heard from lawyers representing Federal Express.

Service Marks **Service marks** provide the same identifying function for services that trademarks provide for goods. Like brands, they can be legally protected by registration. The NBC chimes and GM's Mr. Goodwrench are thus legally protected. Service marks may also include slogans like "Fly the Friendly Skies of United."

GENERIC NAMES
Some words are so obviously part of everyday language that no one should be permitted to use them exclusively. These **generic names** describe products or items in terms that are part of our standard vocabulary—for example, *flower* and *cat food*. Other words and terms, such as *nylon, kerosene, escalator, cellophane,* and *formica,* were originally invented to name particular products but have become legally generic through common usage. Therefore, the 3M Company can call its tape Scotch Brand cellophane tape but can no longer claim that it is the one and only cellophane tape. In many instances, a brand name becomes a generic term when a judge determines

that a word, such as *formica,* is in such common usage that the original formulator of the word can no longer hold the right to it.

It is because valuable brand names can and do become legally generic that Muzak advertisements stress that there is only one Muzak, with a capital M. Rollerblade advertisements call attention to the fact that Rollerblade is a brand name and it is technically incorrect to use "rollerblading" as a verb. Coca-Cola exerts every effort to make certain that you do not get a Pepsi when you ask a waiter for a Coke. Vaseline, Kleenex, Frisbee, and other commonly used names—names that are in fact employed to mean a generic product class—may one day be legally declared generic.

You can't Xerox a Xerox on a Xerox.

But we don't mind at all if you copy a copy on a Xerox copier. In fact, we prefer it. Because the Xerox trademark should only identify products made by us. Like Xerox copiers, printers, fax machines, software and multi-function machines.

As a trademark, the Xerox should always be used as an adjective, followed by a noun. And it is never used as a verb. Of course, helping us protect our trademark also helps you.

Because you'll continue to get what you're actually asking for. And not an inferior copy.

THE DOCUMENT COMPANY
XEROX

XEROX® The Document Company® and the stylized X are trademarks of XEROX CORPORATION. 50 USC. 580.

Do you call a copy machine a Xerox machine? Because the Xerox name is worth protecting, the company regularly advertises that Xerox is a registered trademark.

www.xerox.com

One clever marketer of waterproof, all-purpose sealing tape turned the generic issue around. An executive at Manco recognized that most customers pronounced the generic *duct* tape as "duck" tape. So the company registered the trademark Duck brand tape and used a friendly yellow duck as its brand symbol. Today, it is the market leader for this product.

WHAT MAKES A "GOOD" BRAND NAME?

What constitutes a good brand name? Instant Ocean, a synthetic sea salt for use in aquariums, has a good brand name. It is easy to remember. It is easy to say. It is pronounceable, at least in English, in only one way. It has a positive connotation. And it suggests what the product is supposed to do. Irish Spring deodorant soap, Orange Crush soda, and QuickSnap cameras from Fuji are also excellent names in that they associate the product with an image that is meaningful to consumers. Brand names also are often useful in reinforcing an overall product concept. Brands like Land O' Lakes butter, L'Eggs, Duracell, Moist and Easy, and Nature Made may communicate product attributes far better than any other variable in the marketing mix.

Notice that brand names and symbols say something about the product. Jiffy cake mix is quick. Ocean Freeze fish are fresh-frozen. Toast 'Em Pop-Ups tells both what they are and how to cook them. Spic and Span, Dustbuster, and Beautyrest tell what to expect from these products. But brand names also say something about the buyers for whom the products are intended. Narragansett is a beer for New Englanders. Lone Star is a beer for Texans. Eve and Virginia Slims are cigarette brand names that appeal to certain types of women.

A good brand name has a mnemonic quality, something that makes it distinctive and easy to remember. It has something that sticks in buyers' minds.[10] To achieve this quality, most brand names are short, easy to pronounce, and unique. Exxon and Citgo, words coined by petroleum companies, are good brand names. In contrast, Exxon's failed office systems division offered products called Qwip, Qyz, and Vydec—names that were unique but also something of a problem to pronounce. Toys "Я" Us employs backward Rs to conjure an image of children, as well as to make the name unique. When the sign appeared on the first store, which opened in 1954, many customers informed the manager that the R on the sign was backward. That told the founder of the firm he had hit on a name that people noticed and remembered. In fact, the Я had been used instead of the word *Are* simply to shorten the store's name so that bigger letters could be used on the first outlet's sign, since local ordinances prohibited enlarging the sign itself.

Inventors of brand names must be aware of linguistic traps. A vitamin product was introduced into the South American market under the name Fundavit, an English modification of terms suggesting that the product satisfied all the fundamental vitamin requirements. The name had to be changed because it was too close to a Spanish term used to refer to a part of the female anatomy. Exhibit 9-6 summarizes some of the characteristics of good brand names.

Manufacturer brand, or national brand
A brand owned by the maker of the product.

World brand
A product that is widely distributed around the world with a single brand name that is common to all countries and is recognized in all its markets.

MANUFACTURER BRANDS VERSUS DISTRIBUTOR BRANDS

Many of the most familiar brand names are owned and advertised by the firms that actually manufacture the products. Black & Decker tools, for example, are made by the company of the same name. These brands are called **manufacturer brands** or **national brands**, though in an era of global competition the latter name is less accurate.

A product that is widely distributed throughout the world with a single individual brand name that is common to all countries and recognized in all of its markets is known as a **world brand**. Levi's, Marlboro, and Coca-Cola are some of the most widely known world brands. Adopting a single brand name around the

e x h i b i 9-6 t

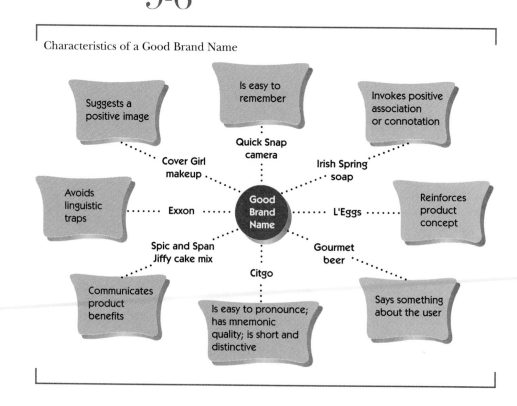

Characteristics of a Good Brand Name

globe, without translation to other languages, can facilitate the marketing of a standardized product and the management of a worldwide image.

Some frequently encountered products have names that are owned by retailers or other intermediaries. The Sears line of Craftsman tools is a good example. Brands owned by Sears, Safeway, Kmart, and other retailers are called **distributor brands** or **private brands**. (Here, the name distributor brand is more descriptive.) Brands owned by wholesalers, such as IGA, are also called distributor brands.

Why are there sometimes two types of brands of the same product, such as Whirlpool and Kenmore, especially when Whirlpool is likely to be the actual manufacturer of the Sears Kenmore line of appliances? Each brand serves a different purpose. The manufacturer brand is intended to create customer loyalty toward the products of a particular manufacturer. Beyond this, it gives the manufacturer a means to control its own products. The products bear its name and are promoted in ways it deems appropriate; furthermore, the flow of profit is directed toward the firm. In contrast, the distributor brand is intended to build loyalty toward a retailer or wholesaler. The retailer, having control over the brand, can advertise it, change its price, label it, and so forth, in any way necessary to please its own customers. Traditionally, distributor brands provide the retailer with a higher margin than do manufacturer brands. To retailers and other distributors supplying retailers, this is an attractive feature.

Why should Whirlpool or any other manufacturer supply a retailer with products to be sold under the distributor's brand rather than the manufacturer's? One reason is that the goods may be produced and sold with minimal effort. The specifications are met, the dealer takes possession of the goods, and the manufacturer's job is finished. There is a certain appeal in letting the distributor handle the pricing, advertising, selling, and guaranteeing of these products that are often sold to noncompeting market segments. The manufacturer may also be able to smooth out production runs or make better use of assets by producing both distributor brands and its own manufacturer brand.

Manufacturers that provide retailers and wholesalers with goods of this type refer to the products as *contract merchandise,* because the products are made to order according to contract. Because a contract is involved, the manufacturer gets the benefit of a guaranteed sale. There is yet another reason for a manufacturer to provide a distributor-labeled product that will be sold, more cheaply, right next to its own nationally branded one: to get the jump on the competition. If, say, Libby's doesn't want to provide the product, Del Monte probably does—and Libby's will lose out.

In today's global economy, many distributor brands do not originate from manufacturers that also market their own brand. For example, there are many Asian and Central American companies that function strictly as contract manufacturers for retailers such as JCPenney. Penney conducts consumer research, designs its private label Arizona Jeans brand, and sets production specification before it contracts with a Mexican company to assemble the jeans.

GENERIC BRANDS

It is possible for a product to carry neither a manufacturer nor a distributor brand. These products, known as **generic products** or **generic brands**, feature a plain package (usually white) with stark, typically black lettering that simply lists the contents. These "no-name" brands offer no guarantees of high quality and are produced and distributed inexpensively. Some portion of the cost savings is passed on to consumers.

The concept of generic brands is not new. Many years ago, shoppers bought most food products from bins and barrels. These were truly generic goods. During periods when increasing cost-of-living pressure is put on household budgets, many no-frills products make gains in supermarket sales, particularly in such product categories as fabric softeners, canned green beans, and facial tissues.

Distributor brand, or private brand
A brand owned by a retailer, wholesaler, or other distributor rather than by the manufacturer of the product.

Generic product, or generic brand
A product that carries neither a manufacturer nor a distributor brand. The goods are plainly packaged with stark lettering that simply lists the contents.

Even among some products for which brand identity is a major factor influencing purchases, such as cosmetics and beer, generics have had a modest success. Many of the same factors that encourage manufacturers to supply distributors with private brands encourage them to produce generic goods.

FAMILY BRANDS AND INDIVIDUAL BRANDS

Family branding involves using a single brand name, like Hunt's, Del Monte, or Campbell's, over a whole line of fairly closely related items. The idea of family branding is to take advantage of a brand's reputation and the goodwill associated with the name. Introduction of a new product, such as Milky Way Lite, is easier because of Milky Way's strong brand recognition. Family branding is used by Levi Strauss, General Electric, MCI, and a host of other corporations.

Use of a family branding strategy does not guarantee success in the marketplace. In what was a relatively rare occurrence, a Campbell's product failed despite the Campbell's name. The product was Campbell's Very Own Special Sauce, a prepared spaghetti sauce. Although many reasons can be offered to account for its failure, the fact that Campbell's name is strongly associated with prepared "American" foods, such as franks and beans, probably was a factor. Most prepared spaghetti sauces on the market bear names like Mama Rosa's and Prego.

Although the failure of its "special" sauce did no serious damage to Campbell's reputation, a product that proves to be dangerous or of poor quality can hurt an organization's overall image. A company's other brands may suffer greatly because of problems with a product of the same name. This is one reason why some firms use individual brand names rather than family brand names. An **individual brand** is not shared by other products in that line.

Besides the motive just mentioned, marketers adopt the individual branding strategy for several other reasons. For one, the products produced by a company might differ substantially from one another. Kraft Foods markets Maxwell House regular and instant coffees, as well as Sanka decaffeinated coffee. An organization may believe that its products are different enough that not much can be gained by identifying the products with one another.

Some organizations practice the individual branding approach because they wish to market several products that appeal to different market segments. There are, for example, many individual brands of detergents within the detergent lines of Procter & Gamble, Lever Brothers, and Colgate-Palmolive. Some contain bleaching crystals; some have fabric softeners; some have extra whitening power; some have extra strength; some have low suds; and so on.

Often, the reason a firm markets many individual brands in a product category is the belief that it is better to lose business to another of its own brands than to lose business to another company's brand. The Mars Company, for example, offers Snickers, Milky Way, Three Musketeers, M&Ms, and many other candies. The matter of shelf space comes into play here. A retailer may have room to dis-

Family branding
The practice of using a single brand name to identify different items in a product line.

Individual brand
A brand that is assigned to a product within a product line and is not shared by other products in that line.

Mars, Inc.
www.mars.com

focus on
global competition

Sony   When Akio Morita began to expand his company, Tokyo Tsushin Kogyo Kabushiki Kaisha, he wisely chose to give it the brand name of his popular transistor radio, Sony. He considered its friendly sounding name (from the Latin *sonus*, for "sound") to be more appealing to world markets than the firm's original name. Today, the four letters, rendered since 1957 in simple, easy-to-read block type, communicate the company's standards with boldness and simplicity to consumers around the world. As Morita had anticipated, it's a name that is musical—and pronounceable—in any language.[11]

play only 25 individual brands of candy bars. If 15 of them are Mars brands, the chances that a customer will select a Mars product are obviously much improved.

Marketers sometimes use a combination of family branding and individual branding strategies. The Kellogg's name is featured on Apple Jacks, Frosted Mini Wheats, Rice Krispies, and many other cereals whose brand names differ. The Willy Wonka name and brand mark appear on packages of candies with more exotic names, including Everlasting Gobstopper, Oompas, Dinasour Eggs, Mix-Ups, and Volcano Rocks. Some marketers refer to these as *sub-brands*.

Co-branding is the use of two individual brands on a single product. Pillsbury's Moist Supreme cake with Jell-o Pudding in the mix is an example of co-branding.

www.pillsbury.com

CO-BRANDING

Co-branding is the use of two individual brands on a single product. For example, Kraft Foods combines its Oscar Mayer Lunchables brand with the Taco Bell brand for tacos and nachos. General Mills' Count Chocula cereal package features the Hershey's brand name because the cereal is made with real Hershey's cocoa. In credit card marketing, MasterCard does almost 30 percent of its business with co-branded cards, many of which are affinity programs. An *affinity program* targets individuals who are inclined to behave in similar ways because they share an interest or a common background, such as alumni of Southern Illinois University. Co-branding partners should be carefully evaluated to make sure their effect will be synergistic and not negative.

Co-branding
The use of two individual brands on a single product.

LICENSING

A product's greatest strength may be an intangible quality or the symbols associated with it. Binney and Smith, for example, has learned that its brand name Crayola and the Crayola logo are valuable assets that other companies may want to use. When a brand name like Crayola, Harley-Davidson, or Disney adds value to a product, it is said to have brand equity. **Brand equity** means that market share or profit margins are greater because of the goodwill associated with the brand.

Brand equity may be a company's strongest asset. High brand equity often indicates that the brand can be effectively used on other products. Thus, the company may enter into a **licensing agreement** with another firm so that the second firm can use the company's trademark. The proliferation of Coca-Cola, Garfield, and other trademarks from movies and television programs is the result of licensing.

Brand equity
The value associated with a brand. Where a brand has brand equity, market share or profit margins are greater because of the goodwill associated with the brand.

Licensing agreement
A legal agreement allowing an organization to use the trademark (or other proprietary rights) of another organization.

Packaging

A package is basically an extension of the product offered for sale. In fact, the package is often more important than the product it contains. The Glue Stic and

the hanging dispenser for Shower Mate are more than simple containers. They offer considerable consumer benefits.

Packages perform many functions. They contain a product and protect it until the consumer is ready to use it. Beyond this, packages facilitate the storage and use of products. (Think again about the Glue Stic container.) Thus, packages should be designed for ease of handling.

Consumers often identify products by their packages. Because distinctive packages on a shelf can attract attention, they can play a major part in promotional strategy. For example, the Good Stuff company markets oval pieces of cedar that help keep moths away from woolen clothing in closets and drawers. The wood chunks are called Sweater Eggs and are packaged in egg cartons. The packaging lends charm to the product and reinforces the brand name. A package on the retailer's shelf may be surrounded by ten or more other packages competing for consumers' attention. In these days of self-service, every package design must attract attention and convey an easily identifiable image. The package must have *shelf impact*. It must tell consumers what the product is and why they should buy it.

Today, environmental considerations may also strongly influence packaging decisions. Packaging waste is piling up, and many industries, such as the fast-food industry, try to make all packaging biodegradable or easy to recycle.

In summary, **packaging** provides a containment function, a protection-in-transit function, a storage function, a usage facilitation function, a promotion function, and an ecological function. Designing packaging thus involves making many decisions, including decisions about labels, inserts, instructions for use, graphic design, and shipping cartons, as well as decisions about the sizes and types of physical containers for individual product items within the outer package.

LABELING—TELLING ABOUT THE PRODUCT

The paper or plastic sticker attached to a can of peas or a mustard jar is technically called a **label**. But as packaging technology improves and cans and bottles become less prominent, labels become incorporated into the protective aspects of the package. In the case of a box of frozen broccoli, for example, a good portion of the vegetable's protection comes from the label, which is more properly called, in this case, the *wrapper*.

Whether the label is a separate entity affixed to a package or is, in effect, the package itself, it must perform certain tasks. It carries the brand name and information concerning the contents of the package, such as cooking instructions and information relating to safe and proper use of the product. A label may also carry instructions for the proper disposal of the product and its package, or at least a plea to consumers to avoid littering. The label must contain any specific nutri-

High-Tech Packaging   Rarely since the advent of cellophane in 1923 has the packaging industry come up with so many new materials and designs. Today's high-tech packages can look better than traditional bottles, boxes, and cans. And when the packaging's work is done and the stuff goes the way of all wrappers, it takes up less space in the local landfill. Some high-tech packages even act on the products they contain.

Printpack of Atlanta used film coated with metal strips, called susceptors, to line the pouch it created for Rudolph's Bacon Snaps pork rind nuggets. When the package is placed in a microwave oven, some of the susceptors heat up to make the nuggets brown and crispy, while others deflect energy from the nuggets to promote more even cooking. Other packaging manufacturers such as Cryovac . . . and Ever-Fresh . . . make films that keep fruits and vegetables fresh by reducing the concentration of gases like oxygen and ethylene that aid ripening.

The packages of the future will be even more versatile. Temperature-sensitive labels will indicate whether products have gotten too hot or too cold during shipping. Microwave films for TV dinners will deep-fry some parts of the meal, like chicken, while keeping others, such as applesauce, cool. Some day, when peaches are covered with protein film and peas come in a bag that dissolves as they cook, we may even be able to eat the packages themselves.[12]

tional information, warnings, or legal restrictions required by law. Some labels, such as those of Procter & Gamble, also give an 800 telephone number that customers with ideas or complaints can use. Consumers' calls are a major source of Procter & Gamble's product improvement ideas.

Most consumer packaged goods are labeled with an appropriate **Universal Product Code (UPC)**, an array of black bars readable by optical scanners. The advantages of the UPC—which allow computerized checkout and computer-generated sales volume information—have become clear to distributors, retailers, and consumers in recent years.

GLOBAL IMPLICATIONS AND LEGAL GUIDELINES FOR PACKAGING

Package designers are relatively free to develop package designs. However, when the package will be used in several countries, marketers must determine whether to use a single package with one language, a single package with two or more languages, or multiple packages tailored to the separate countries. Decisions about use of colors and symbols, protection in transit over long distances, and other aspects of package design should be made only after local culture and usage patterns have been considered.

In particular, a company must follow the legal guidelines and requirements of each country where its product will be marketed. For example, the European Union, shortly after the turn of the century, will require that 90 percent of packaging waste by weight be recoverable through recycling or other uses. In the United States, package designers must follow state and local laws, such as those requiring that soft drink bottles be clearly labeled as returnable. In Germany, recyclable packages display a green dot. These packages can then be disposed of in special yellow garbage cans issued by the government.

Many countries have laws about deceptive packaging. Packages intentionally designed to mislead consumers, labels that bear false or misleading information, or packages that do not provide required warnings soon draw the attention of the Federal Trade Commission, some other official body, or consumer groups.

Universal Product Code (UPC)
The array of black bars, readable by optical scanners, found on many products. The UPC permits computerization of tasks such as checkout and compilation of sales volume information.

Product Warranties

A **product warranty** communicates a written guarantee of a product's integrity and outlines the manufacturer's responsibility for repairing or replacing defective parts. It may substantially reduce the risks the buyer perceives to be associated with the purchase.

As a result of the increase in lawsuits, some labels carry warnings that seem silly. The purchaser of a Batman or Superman costume may read the following warning: "Cape does not enable user to fly."

Product warranty
A written guarantee of a product's integrity and the manufacturer's responsibility for repairing or replacing defective parts.

Magnuson-Moss Warranty Act
Federal law requiring that guarantees provided by sellers be made available to buyers before they purchase and that the guarantees specify who the warrantor is, what products or parts of products are covered, what the warrantor must do if the product is defective, how long the warranty applies, and the obligations of the buyer.

Unfortunately, consumers often find that warranties are difficult-to-understand documents written in legal jargon. Several manufacturers have made use of this fact by offering warranties advertised as simple, short, plain-English documents. Marketers who have not taken this approach may not realize that terms like *fully guaranteed, unconditionally guaranteed,* and *lifetime guarantee* don't mean much to many buyers, especially buyers who have been disappointed with the service received on other guaranteed products.

Some of the difficulties associated with warranties have been mitigated by the **Magnuson-Moss Warranty Act** of 1975. This law requires that any guarantees provided by sellers be made available to buyers prior to purchase of the product. It also grants power to the Federal Trade Commission to specify the manner and form in which guarantees may be used in promotional material. Further, the act stipulates that a warranty must use simple language and disclose precisely who the warrantor is. The warranty must indicate clearly what products or parts of products are covered by the terms of the warranty and which are excluded. The act also specifies what the warrantor is obliged to do in the event of a product defect, how long the warranty applies, and what obligations the buyer has.

A warranty is part of the total product; the seller should not view it as a nuisance. Effective marketers, such as Curtis Mathes television, use the warranty as an opportunity to create satisfied customers and to offer an intangible product attribute that many buyers desire.

Customer Service

Butterball
www.butterball.com

Our earlier discussion identified customer service as one element of the product mix. Effective marketers, knowing that marketing does not end with the sale of products, may create a competitive advantage by emphasizing the amount and quality of customer services they offer. For example, every Thanksgiving the staff of the Butterball Turkey Talk Line provides cooking advice to thousands of callers, helping them prepare—and often salvage—their turkey dinners. Delivery services, gift wrapping, repair, and other customer services all help marketers compete. These services, as auxiliary dimensions of the product, create and maintain goodwill. They provide an opportunity to enhance consumer satisfaction with the total product. Chapter 11 provides a complete discussion of the product strategies for pure services and for tangible goods with a high service component.

summary

The term *product* refers to both goods and services in the consumer and organizational marketplaces. Products should be broadly defined to include their intangible, as well as their tangible, aspects.

1 *Define product and explain why the concept of the total product is important to effective marketing.*
Products can be goods, services, ideas, or any other market offering. The total product concept recognizes the many benefits, both tangible and intangible, that each product incorporates. This total product view permits marketers to identify market segments according to benefits received and to adjust products to appeal to those segments.

2 *Differentiate among convenience products, shopping products, and specialty products.*
Consumer products can be categorized as convenience, shopping, or specialty products. Convenience products are typically inexpensive and are purchased at a convenient location with little shopping effort. Shopping products are purchased after buyers have compared price, quality, and other product attributes. Specialty goods are products for which buyers will accept virtually no substitutes and which they will go to great lengths to obtain.

3 *Categorize organizational products.*
The three classes of organizational products are capital products, production products, and operating products. Capital products include installations and accessory equipment. Production products include raw materials, manufactured materials and component parts, and process materials. Operating supplies, conventional software, services, and information comprise the operating products category.

4 *Explain the difference between product lines and product mixes.*
A firm's product line is a group of products that are fairly closely related. The phrase *depth of product line* describes the number of different product items offered in a product line. A firm's product mix encompasses all offerings of the organization, no matter how unrelated they may be. The marketing manager can view the product mix as a product portfolio to be balanced as a group. The product portfolio concept uses relative market share and market growth to identify whether a product is a star, a cash cow, a problem child, or a dog.

5 *Understand brand-related terminology, including brand, brand name, brand mark, trademark, manufacturer brand, distributor brand, and family brand.*
A brand is a name, term, symbol, sign, or design that distinguishes one product from competing products. A brand name is the verbal part of the brand. A brand mark is a unique symbol used by an organization to identify its product. A trademark is a legally protected brand name or brand mark. Manufacturer, or national, brands are the property of manufacturers; distributor, or private, brands are the property of wholesalers or retailers. A family brand is carried by a group of products with the same brand name.

6 *Discuss the characteristics of effective brand names.*
Most effective brand names are easy to remember and pronounce, short, and distinctive. They suggest positive associations and images, reinforce the product concept, and communicate product benefits. They may also say something about the user. Finally, they avoid linguistic traps. Proposed new brand names must be researched for market acceptability and possible trademark infringement.

7 *Analyze the importance of packaging in the development of an effective product strategy.*
Packaging provides a containment function, a protection-in-transit function, a storage function, a usage facilitation function, a promotion function, and an ecological function. In some instances, packages may be as important as the products they contain.

8 *Discuss the role of customer service in product strategy.*
Marketers can create a competitive advantage by emphasizing the amount and quality of customer services. Delivery, gift wrapping, repair, and other customer services all can be important aspects of a product strategy to create competitive advantage.

key terms

total product (p. 263)
primary characteristic (p. 263)
auxiliary dimension (p. 263)

product strategy (p. 264)
product concept (p. 264)
product differentiation (p. 265)

service (p. 266)
durable good (p. 266)
nondurable good (p. 266)

Dirty Potato Chips

The product is made by Chickasaw Foods. The foil package is bright red with yellow lettering. On the front, at the top, the package says BARBEQUE FLAVOR. Then, in lettering reminiscent of the opening of Star Wars, it goes on:

We don't wash
off the natural
potato juices,
so these are
crisper, potatoier
potato chips
called "Dirty"
Potato Chips.

After that, a yellow background features red lettering that says "Cooked in 100% Peanut Oil" and "Read all about the legend of the Dirty Potato Chip on the back." Here is the Legend of 'Dirty' Potato Chips:

Once upon a time, all potato chips tasted good. Very good. They were very crisp. And they tasted like real potatoes. Then, good ol' American mass production ingenuity took over. Bags of potato chips had to be produced by the millions. Every day. And that was a very sticky problem.

Because when you slice a potato, you know, the juice makes the slices stick together. Well, that was a real bugaboo for potato chip makers who had to cook 'em by the millions. If the slices stuck together, you couldn't send them down a lickety-split production line. So, the potato chip making geniuses solved the problem. "We'll wash off those juices," one said, "and then they won't stick together."

Problem is, when you wash off the juices two things happen. Both bad. You lose a whole lot of the crispness. And you wash off that natural potato flavor.

So, now you know our secret. We don't wash off the natural potato juices. It means we have to hand-cook our chips one batch at a time. Stirring them so they don't stick together.

Are they really "dirty"? No. We just said that because we don't wash off the juices. And it makes it easy to remember the name of the good one. We promise we don't drop any of them on the floor.

And if you show the wisdom of a true potato chip lover you'll tuck this bag on the top of your shopping cart. And you'll never again endure one of those other, squeaky clean chips that taste like . . . well, they don't taste like much of anything.[15]

QUESTIONS

1. In your opinion, what is the product concept behind Dirty Potato Chips?
2. Should this name be registered as a trademark? Is it a good brand name?
3. What makes Dirty Potato Chips different from competitors? Is this difference enough to make the product a success?

chapter 10

Strategies for New Products and the Product Life Cycle

LEARNING OBJECTIVES

After you have studied this chapter, you will be able to:

Define product newness and explain the chances of success and failure for new products. **1**

Identify general characteristics of successful new products. **2**

Characterize the stages of new product development. **3**

Identify some of the most common reasons for new product failures. **4**

Describe the product life cycle and characterize its stages. **5**

(continued on next page)

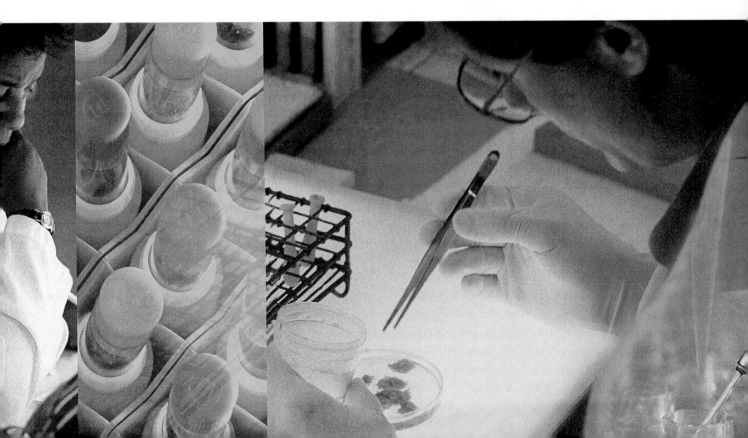

6	Describe the new product diffusion process and list the groups of adopters to which marketers must direct their appeals.
7	Identify strategies for modifying existing products.
8	Explain the total quality management process for goods and services.
9	Understand how marketers manage product lines.
10	Identify some ethical questions associated with product strategy.

anyone who has had a routine physical knows getting a blood test is a pain—and not just because of the needle. First you pray that the technician finds your vein quickly. You watch (or look away squeamishly) as he fills two or three entire test tubes with your precious bodily fluid. Next you wait at least a day for results from the lab. All that may change with the advent of the Piccolo Point-of-Care Whole Blood Analyzer, a desktop machine that provides blood test results in about 12 minutes. This innovative new product from Abaxis Corporation requires only a finger prick's worth of blood. The Piccolo uses standard test chemicals that Abaxis freeze-dries in tiny beads. It seals these in chambers along the rim of a molded plastic disk, or rotor. The technician deposits the blood sample in a well at the rotor's center and pops the disk into the Piccolo, which spins it at about 4,000 rpm. Centrifugal force separates plasma from blood cells and forces precise quantities of it through thin tubes to the chambers. As the plasma and chemicals react, a spectropho-

ALL THAT MAY CHANGE WITH THE ADVENT OF THE PICCOLO POINT-OF-CARE WHOLE BLOOD ANALYZER, A DESKTOP MACHINE THAT PROVIDES BLOOD TEST RESULTS IN ABOUT 12 MINUTES.

tometer reads changes in color and the machine prints out results. Getting data right away lets the doctor prescribe medicine with no need for a follow-up visit or call to discuss the test.

The Federal Food and Drug Administration has approved the Piccolo and a version of the rotor containing five tests. Abaxis plans to offer combinations of about 50 tests; it will charge $8,000 for the analyzer and $8 to $20 for each disposable rotor, making Piccolo testing about as expensive as that done by a large lab. Piccolo is based on U.S. space program efforts to design a blood analyzer for astronauts to use in space. Funding ran out after the Challenger disaster in 1986, and Abaxis founders Gary Stroy and Vladimir Ostoich snapped up exclusive rights in 1988. The Piccolo weighs just 15 pounds, takes up as much room as an oversize toaster, and can operate on a 12-volt battery, making blood tests possible in ambulances, field hospitals, and underdeveloped countries. Nor has Abaxis forgotten space: France's space agency hopes to test the analyzer on a NASA shuttle flight.[1]

This chapter begins by addressing the nature of new products and the characteristics associated with new product successes. It goes on to depict the new product development process and to discuss the fact that most new products fail. Then the focus shifts to the product life cycle, an extremely influential concept in the planning and marketing of products from their births to their deaths. The adoption and diffusion processes, discussed next, help explain a product's acceptance over the course of its life cycle. The chapter then addresses issues related to the marketing of products that have been on the market for some time and discusses strategies for expanding product lines and withdrawing or eliminating goods or services that no longer enjoy adequate market demand. Finally, it considers ethical issues associated with product strategy.

What Is a New Product?

The Piccolo Point-of-Care Whole Blood Analyzer discussed at the beginning of the chapter certainly appears to be a new product. Before reading further, however, pause for a second to decide in your own mind what a **new product** is. Think of an example or two, and try to identify what makes them new. Is Phillips Cool Skin, an electric shaver for men that automatically dispenses Nivea shaving lotion, really a new product? Is a computer workstation that can be linked to other computers with invisible infrared light signals truly different from the first microcomputers? Does the ingenious, and highly practical, voice-activated word-processing software qualify as really new?

To some marketers, a new product may be a major technological innovation. The first computers were introduced in the 1940s. Though primitive by today's standards, at that time they were altogether new to the market. At one time or other, so were microwave ovens, radial tires, adjustable rate mortgages, and automatic teller machines. To other marketers, new products might be simple additions to an otherwise unchanged product line, such as new shades of lipstick or hair coloring introduced by Revlon or Clairol. Even a "me, too" item, developed in imitation of a competitor's successful product, is a new product to the imitating company. Furthermore, a product may be new because it offers some benefit that similar product offerings do not. For example, Velcro tabs on paper diapers, which allow parents to check for wetness and reseal the diaper securely, make these diapers different from those that reseal with ordinary adhesive tape. The marketing concept, after all, tells marketers to consider a product as a bundle of tangible and intangible benefits. If the bundle of benefits offered by a product differs from the bundle already available, then the product can be said to be new.

From the buyer's point of view, a product may be new if it is something never before purchased, even if it has been on the market for years. In international marketing, old products may become "new" again, especially when a manufacturer's established product is being offered to people in a less-developed country. There are, for example, places in the world where VCRs, and even color televisions, are new to most people.

It is clear, then, that the term *new* and the related term *novel* are used in a relative sense. They are influenced by perceptions, whether you are a marketing manager or a consumer. Let's begin by taking the manager's perspective.

New product
A product new to a company. The meaning of this relative term is influenced by the perceptions of marketers and consumers; in general, it refers to any recently introduced product that offers some benefit that other products do not.

Management's Perspective on New Products

Managers may consider a product to be new if it is new to the market or simply new to the company. Products can be either new-to-the-world products, product category extensions, product line extensions, or product modifications. Companies have considerable experience marketing product modifications but far less experience with products in the first three categories.

- **New-to-the-world products** are inventions that create an entirely new market. These are the highest-risk products, because they are new both to the company and to the market. The technology for producing these innovative products, which is itself new to the company, is often the result of a large investment in research and development.
- **Product category extensions** are new products that, for the first time, allow a company to diversify and enter an established market for an existing product category. These products are not entirely new to the market, but the company has had no previous technological or marketing experience with them. If these products imitate competitive products with identical features, they can be described as "me, too" products.
- **Product line extensions** are additions to an existing product line that supplement the basic items in the established line. Line extensions include enhanced models, low-price economy models, and variations in color, flavor, design, and so on. These new products may be family branded or marketed under a new brand name, perhaps a private label that appeals to a different market segment.

- **Product modifications** include product improvements, cost reductions, and repositionings. "New and improved" versions replace existing products and are intended to provide improved performance, enhanced features, or greater perceived value. Cost reductions replace existing products by providing similar performance at a lower cost. Repositionings may modify existing products by targeting new market segments, offering a new benefit, or assuming a different competitive position. The marketing task for these products often is to communicate the benefits of product modifications to consumers who do not see the products as unique or strikingly different from past offerings.

The Consumer's Perspective on Newness

From a consumer perspective, new products vary in degree of newness. There are three types of innovations: discontinuous, dynamically continuous, and continuous, as shown in Exhibit 10-1.

DISCONTINUOUS INNOVATION

Discontinuous innovations are pioneering products so new that no previous product performed an equivalent function. As a result of this near-complete newness, new consumption or usage patterns are required. The lithium battery pacemaker

Discontinuous innovation
A product so new that no previous product performed an equivalent function. Such a product requires the development of new consumption or usage patterns.

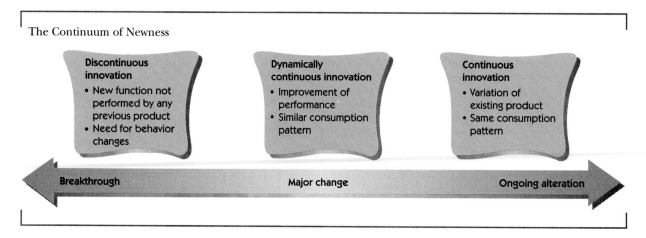

The Continuum of Newness

Discontinuous innovation
- New function not performed by any previous product
- Need for behavior changes

Dynamically continuous innovation
- Improvement of performance
- Similar consumption pattern

Continuous innovation
- Variation of existing product
- Same consumption pattern

Breakthrough   Major change   Ongoing alteration

implanted in heart patients was a discontinuous innovation. The fax machine is another. These products, once new to the world, did things no products before them had done, and using them properly necessitated extensive behavior changes. Artificial hearts and a drug to cure AIDS are still in their developmental stages, but once perfected and made available, they, too, will be discontinuous innovations.

DYNAMICALLY CONTINUOUS INNOVATION

In the newness continuum, somewhere between the breakthrough achieved with the perfected artificial heart and

DON'T LOOK NOW. BUT YOUR MONITOR HAS A BIG BUTT.

The flat-panel computer monitor represents a continuous innovation. This new product is an improvement over the common monitor because it takes up less space. Although the product has a new form, it is used in the traditional manner, so consumers do not have to change their consumption behavior. This is a key characteristic of a continuous innovation.

www.ctxintl.com

the commonplace newness of the *new and improved* consumer product, is the **dynamically continuous innovation.** New products in this middle range represent changes and improvements that do not strikingly change buying and usage patterns.

The electric car is an example of a dynamically continuous innovation. The buying habits of those purchasing cars and fuel may be altered by successful and appealing electric automobiles, but virtually all driving behavior will remain as it is. Compare this situation with the way the Model T Ford affected society. Similarly, word-processing software for personal computers was genuinely new, but its effect on buyers and users was nothing like the effect of the first typewriter. Arista Technologies' Commercial Brake is in the dynamically continuous category. Commercial Brake is a device that works with a VCR to block commercials by automatically fast-forwarding past commercials on TV shows that consumers have taped.

Dynamically continuous innovation
A product that is different from previously available products but that does not strikingly change buying or usage patterns.

CONTINUOUS INNOVATION

A **continuous innovation** is a commonplace change that is part of an ongoing product modification effort, such as a minor alteration of a product or the introduction of an imitative product. The Microsoft Natural Keyboard is an example of a continuous innovation. It has a palm rest and curves upward, slightly parting and angling the left-hand and right-hand keys so that the hands are turned slightly toward each other, allowing the user to maintain a natural position of the wrist and shoulder while typing. It is an improvement on the conventional keyboard. Marketers constantly strive to improve products, because even minor improvements, such as fewer calories or less salt, can provide a competitive advantage. Although this approach may be viewed as fine-tuning the product, these new products are innovations of a sort.

Continuous innovation
A new product that is characterized by minor alterations or improvements to existing products and that produces little change in consumption patterns.

The Slim Chances of Success

Product success is both difficult to define and difficult to achieve. It is problematic to determine the number of new product successes and failures because, like newness, success is so hard to define. How much of a success must a new product be before it is truly "a success"? It is a widely accepted belief that relatively few new product ideas become commercial successes. But because most organizations would rather not talk about their failures, much of this belief must be based on estimates. Moreover, some product ideas wither in their developmental stages, and complete documentation of ideas that were suggested but never made it to market is not likely to be found. For our purpose, failure occurs when a product does not meet the organization's expectations.

Several estimates of new product failure rates are available. Some of these suggest that 80 percent of new product ideas do not become commercial successes.[2] One consulting organization, after considerable study, has suggested that only one successful product is generated from 40 new product ideas. Once a new product has actually appeared on the market, the success rate is much higher because of the research, planning, and effort that have gone into its introduction. It is estimated that there is a one-in-three failure rate among new product introductions.

Clearly, failure and success rates vary from organization to organization. In general, the failure rate is higher for consumer products than for organizational goods. In the consumer package-goods market, for instance, the failure rate is likely to be far higher than in the organizational electrical components field. This difference is due to the dynamic nature of the consumer marketplace and the fact that consumers often cannot tell marketers exactly what new products will satisfy them. In contrast, the organizational buyers of electrical components are able to give detailed information to component manufacturers. No wonder, then, that new product failure and success rates vary greatly.

Relative advantage
The ability of a product to offer clear-cut advantages over competing offerings.

what went wrong?

Not-So-Hot Coffee   Years ago, Kraft's Maxwell House introduced Max-Pax, pre-measured, ground coffee filter rings packed in tins. All the consumer had to do was put the coffee-filled filter in the coffee pot, pour in the necessary water, and brew. No messy paper filters, no spilling loose coffee, and no question about how many scoops per pot. The latter proved to be the product's undoing, as tastes for coffee vary from person to person, locale to locale. Inconsistency was also a problem because a finished pot of coffee was different depending on everything from the amount of water added, to the temperature at which you made the coffee. Water boils at different temperatures depending on the altitude, so the results of brewing a pot using exactly the same amount of coffee (not something you can adjust with a sealed filter) are different in Denver than at the New Jersey shore.

Of course, giving consumers more control isn't always the answer, either. Maxwell House Liquid Concentrated Coffee in a plastic bottle, or ready-to-drink Maxwell House in a gable-top carton with a screw cap were clever enough, but they didn't fly. Americans proved too lazy to add water to the concentrate. But [consumers] weren't lazy enough to see the advantages of a refrigerated, ready-to-drink coffee that could be heated in the microwave. Oddly, there were no directions for iced coffee for the ready-to-drink Maxwell House—perhaps the one idea that consumers could have related to.[3]

The Characteristics of Success

Five characteristics influence a new product's chances for success in the marketplace: relative advantage, compatibility with existing consumption patterns, trialability, observability, and simplicity of usage.[4] When a product lacks one or more of these characteristics, the others might be used effectively to make up for the deficiency. Furthermore, nonproduct elements of the marketing mix—price, promotion, and distribution—must be developed and adjusted with these same characteristics in mind.

RELATIVE ADVANTAGE

Products that offer buyers clear-cut advantages over competing offerings are said to have **relative advantage**. In organizational markets, relative advantage often arises when new products perform exactly the same functions less expensively or faster than existing products. Experience and improved technology, for example, have made possible the replacement of metal parts in many

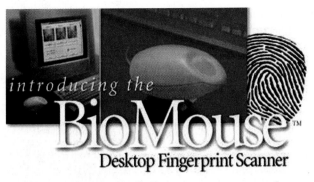

introducing the
BioMouse™
Desktop Fingerprint Scanner

products with cheaper and lighter plastic ones. Similarly, computer systems that use spoken words as input have obvious advantages over earlier generations that require typed input. And when the Miller Brewing Company test-marketed its Clear Miller Beer, the company quickly learned that its colorless beer didn't look or taste like beer. This new product had no relative advantage.

COMPATIBILITY WITH EXISTING CONSUMPTION PATTERNS

Everything else being equal, a new product that is compatible with existing patterns of consumption stands a better chance of market acceptance than one that is incompatible. This is true even when the newer item has some relative advantage.

Consider, for example, the B.A.D. Pack U-Lock, a bicycle antitheft device that features two steel strips to further reinforce the conventional U-lock design and make it impossible to insert a jack or hacksaw. It is completely compatible with cyclists' existing behavior; and because it has a relative advantage, it should achieve rapid market acceptance. On the other hand, it will take time for the market to accept the Handwriter for Windows, a digital pad on which a computer user writes or draws with a pen. The pad converts handwritten characters into computerized text and gives the pen mouselike pointing capabilities with Windows programs. However, the thin pad is quite different from a keyboard or mouse and requires a departure from existing usage patterns.

TRIALABILITY—THE OPPORTUNITY FOR BUYER TESTING

A new product—such as Dior Mascara Flash, an instant "makeup" for hair highlighting—has **trialability** when possible future users can test it with little risk or effort. Electrosol Tabs, a new automatic dishwasher detergent in tablet form, has trialability; it is not expensive, and the buyer need not invest in special equipment to use it. A product's trialability may be enhanced by coupons in newspapers, magazines, and the mail. New shampoos and laundry products are made available in small, inexpensive packages to encourage consumers to try them with little monetary risk. When companies give away free samples to possible buyers, bringing trialability to perhaps its highest level, the process is termed **trial sampling.** Sending computer discs and offering 10 or 50 hours of unlimited Internet and online service is America Online's major means of generating new customers.

Effective marketing management demands careful consideration of steps that may encourage buyer sampling of a new product. For example, marketers arranged for Kellogg's Nutri-Grain cereal bars to be given to passengers flying on Southwest Airlines. This is a situation where a high probability of trial exists. Items intended to be sold in cases or six-packs, like juices, sodas, and other drinks, might first be offered in single-drink packages or be given away by the cupful in shopping malls. Customers who are reluctant to buy 12 of a given product may be willing to try just one. Trialability is more appropriately referred to as **divisibility** when it refers to the opportunity to try a small amount.

OBSERVABILITY—THE CHANCE TO SEE THE NEWNESS

Some new products enter the marketplace with attributes or characteristics that are visible to the customer. The Kodak Photo CD, which stores photographs on

The FBI and other high-security facilities have had devices for scanning fingerprints or the iris of the eye, but American Biometric's BioMouse is a new product for PC users. A BioMouse user scans in a set of master fingerprints that are stored by the computer. After that, secure files can be opened only with a scan of a matching print. For consumers this is a product with relative advantage, one of the key features of new product success. (Courtesy of American Biometric Company, www.abio.com)

Trialability
The ability of a product to be tested by possible future users with little risk or effort.

Trial sampling
The distribution of newly marketed products to enhance trialability and familiarity; giving away free samples.

Divisibility
The ability of a product to be sampled in small amounts by consumers.

compact discs, displays them on ordinary televisions, and allows any portion of a photograph to be enlarged, has a relative advantage over regular film prints. Best of all for Kodak, the advantage is easy to see. The Kodak Photo CD is a product with **observability.**

Other products possess definite relative advantages that are not observable or so easily grasped. A new brand of allergy tablets with an advanced formula that relieves allergy symptoms without causing drowsiness has an advantage that is not observable by most buyers. Advertisements for products with hidden qualities frequently feature experts or credible users who attest to the products' worth, making hidden qualities observable.

SIMPLICITY OF USAGE

A complex product—or one that requires complex procedures for storage or use—starts out with a disadvantage. Polaroid Land cameras, at their introduction, were viewed by consumers as minor miracles. Therefore, the cameras themselves were designed for easy operation. The **simplicity of usage** offset the complexity of the product itself. Compact disc digital recordings were similarly surprising to consumers, who found it difficult to grasp the system by which these recordings were played. Makers of early CD players carefully trained salespeople to explain the new system and arranged for newspaper and magazine columnists to try it so that they could explain it to their readers.

New Product Development

What is the source of product innovations? How are new product ideas generated? There is no one answer to these questions. Some innovations are discovered by accident or luck, such as the vulcanization of rubber (discovered when a rubbery mixture was spilled on a hot stove) and Ivory's floating soap (first made when a mechanical mixer was left on overnight and whipped raw soap materials into a lightweight cleanser). Necessity, it seems, was the mother of invention for the ice cream seller in St. Louis who ran out of paper cups and rolled pancakes into serving cones—the first ice cream cones.

On occasion, the amateur inventor working in a basement comes up with an innovation that goes on to achieve great success. However, these days, when innovations require sizable financial investments and other resources for support and commercialization, most innovations come from serious research and development efforts undertaken with the support of formal organizations. For example, the Piccolo Point-of-Care Whole Blood Analyzer mentioned at the beginning of this chapter was developed only after years of research and development at NASA and later at Abaxis Corporation.

The new product development process can be quick, the result of a sudden flash of insight. But in many cases, such as in the development of space satellites, telecommunication systems, and other highly technical products, the process can take years. The development process may be lengthy not so much because of technical problems but because it takes time to research and understand potential market resistance to a new product. Even when a new product has a technological advantage, customers may not accept it.

Exhibit 10-2 shows the five general stages in the new product development process: idea generation, screening, business analysis, development, and commercialization. Products pass through these stages at varying rates. A product may stall for a time in one, for example, and pass through another so quickly that it appears to have skipped it entirely.

IDEA GENERATION

In marketing-oriented organizations operating in dynamic environments, **idea generation**—the exploration stage of new product development—is less a period

---

Observability
The ability of a product to display to consumers its advantages over existing products.

Simplicity of usage
Ease of operation. This product benefit can offset any complexity in the product itself.

Idea generation stage
The stage in new product development in which a marketer engages in a continuing search for product ideas consistent with target market needs and the organization's objectives.

The General Stages in the Development of New Products

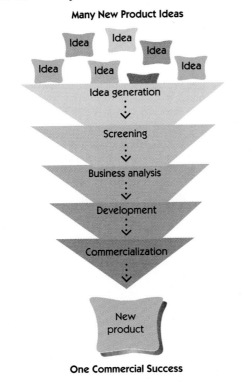

Many New Product Ideas

Idea generation

Screening

Business analysis

Development

Commercialization

New product

One Commercial Success

Source: Adapted from Roger A. Bengston, "Nine New Product Strategies: Each Requires Different Resources, Talent, Research Methods," *Marketing News,* March 19, 1982, p. 7. Reprinted with permission of the American Marketing Association.

of time than an ongoing process. Thus, the idea generation stage involves a continuing search for product ideas that are consistent with target market needs and with the organization's objectives.

In many organizations, particularly those in industries with complex technology, generating ideas and searching for technological breakthroughs are likely to be the tasks of the research and development (R&D) department. R&D personnel may focus creative thinking on transferring a technology from an existing product category to a new product, on miniaturization, or on basic research to create new-to-the-world products. For example, the idea for Eastman Kodak's digital camera was technology-driven. This filmless camera allows a customer to store digital images, display them on a television or a computer monitor, exchange photographs on the Internet, and print as many copies as desired. R&D engineers creatively applied consumer electronics technology from the personal computer industry to generate the idea for this product.

Although a large proportion of new product ideas flow from technology-driven research departments, other sources should not be ignored. New product suggestions may come from customers. Sales representatives may uncover or be told about new product opportunities. Marketing research can yield new product suggestions. An employee, a supplier, or a distributor may come up with a good—or even brilliant—idea.

Companies can stimulate the generation of ideas by encouraging employees to think about new products that could address consumer complaints, make a task easier, add benefits to existing products, or provide new uses for existing products.

Yamaha Insights into possibilities for new products that are fundamentally different—that is, new-to-the-world products—may be garnered in ways that go beyond traditional modes of marketing research.

Toshiba has a Lifestyle Research Institute; Sony explores "human science" with the same passion with which it pursues the leading edge of audiovisual technology. The insights gained allow these firms to answer two crucial questions: What range of benefits will customers value in tomorrow's products, and how might we, through innovation, preempt competitors in delivering those benefits to the marketplace? Yamaha gained insights into the unarticulated needs of musicians when it established a "listening post" in London, chock full of the latest gee-whiz music technology. The facility offered some of Europe's most talented musicians a chance to experiment with the future of music making. The feedback helped Yamaha expand the competitive space it had staked out in the music business. Yamaha's experience illustrates an important point: To push out the boundaries of current product concepts, it is necessary to put the most advanced technology possible directly into the hands of the world's most sophisticated and demanding customers. Thus arose Yamaha's London market laboratory. Japan is still not the center of the world's pop music industry.[5]

Many organizations have instituted reward systems to encourage employee suggestions. The focus at this stage is on encouraging creativity rather than on evaluating suggestions. The organization wishes to generate ideas, not kill them.

SCREENING

Screening stage
The stage in new product development in which a marketer analyzes ideas to determine their appropriateness and reasonableness in relation to the organization's goals and objectives.

The **screening stage** of the product development process involves analyzing new ideas to determine which are reasonable, compatible with the organization's goals, and appropriate to the organization's target markets. This step is extremely important, because the underlying assumption of the entire product development process is that risky alternatives—possibilities that do not offer as much promise for success as others—should be eliminated from consideration. Resources can then be concentrated on the best prospects so that market failures can be avoided.

The screening stage is also important because it is the first stage at which alternative ideas are sorted. New ideas may now be rejected. From time to time, of course, any management team is likely to reject some ideas that they later wish they had accepted. Because mistakes will be made, managers must screen ideas with caution. In fact, because an idea rejected at this stage is eliminated from further consideration, some companies prefer to allow a marginal idea to progress further rather **BALANCING THE COSTS OF ADDITIONAL INVESTIGATION AGAINST THE LOSS OF A VIABLE PRODUCT IDEA IS ONE OF MANAGEMENT'S MOST DELICATE TASKS.** than risk rejecting it too early in the process. However, at later stages, the costs of analysis and evaluation are substantially increased. Balancing the costs of additional investigation against the loss of a viable product idea is one of management's most delicate tasks.

At Procter & Gamble, three basic questions are carefully answered before new product projects are approved. These questions are general enough to be used by almost any organization in its own product screenings. These deceptively simple questions demand hard answers on which more than a few managers' careers may depend:

1. Is there a real customer need for the product?
2. Does the organization have the scientific and technological ability to develop the product?
3. Is the potential for such a product large enough to offer some promise of making a profit?

Extensive marketing research is associated with later stages in the development process, but some marketing research and discussions with salespeople, executives, and knowledgeable consumers could be used to answer these questions and thus help screen new product ideas. The discussion on exploratory research in Chapter 5 suggested forms of research appropriate to this stage.

BUSINESS ANALYSIS

A product idea that survives the screening process enters the **business analysis stage,** at which point it is expanded into a concrete business recommendation. This recommendation includes both qualitative and quantitative means of evaluation. The qualitative evaluation seeks such specifics as a listing of product features, information on resources needed to produce the product, and a basic marketing plan. Creativity and analysis come together at this stage.

Although qualitative evaluations of the product and its likely success are still important, business analysis requires quantitative facts and figures. The new product idea is evaluated with increasingly detailed quantitative data on market demand, cost projections, investment requirements, and competitive activity. Formal buyer research studies, sales and market forecasts, break-even analyses, and similar research efforts are undertaken. In short, the business analysis is a review of the new product from all significant organizational perspectives. It emphasizes performance criteria and chances for success in the marketplace.

Business analysis stage
The stage in new product development in which the new product is reviewed from all organizational perspectives to determine performance criteria and likely profitability.

DEVELOPMENT

A new product idea that survives the preliminary evaluative stages is ready for the fourth stage, development. In the **development stage,** the proposed new product idea is transformed from a product concept to a product prototype. The basic marketing strategy is developed, and decisions are made about the product's physical characteristics, package design, and brand name, as well as about market segmentation strategy. Specific tactics within the product strategy are also researched during this stage.

In the development stage, paper-and-pencil concepts become demonstrable products. Research and development or production engineers give marketers a product that can be tested in customer usage studies, sold in test markets, or investigated in other limited ways. This is not to say that the product is in its final form. For example, if soft drink marketers convene a panel of consumers to taste-test a new formulation and the product is not well accepted, it might be reformulated or its package might be changed. The product can be retested until the proper set of characteristics has been discovered. We discuss three popular forms of testing here.

Development stage
The stage in new product development in which a new product concept is transformed into a prototype. The basic marketing strategy also develops at this time.

Concept Testing Concept testing is a general term for many different research procedures used to learn consumers' reactions to a new product idea. Typically, consumers are presented with the idea—illustrated in graphic form or described in writing—and asked if they would use it, if they like it, if they would buy it, and so on.

Concept testing helps to ensure that product concepts are developed with the needs of the consumer or user in mind. For example, General Electric's design engineers are sent out to talk with dealers and customers about new product concepts to ensure that market feedback goes where it can do the most good—to the engineers who design the products. GE wants design engineers to get their directions from customers. GE's objective is to bring the technology and the consumer demand together.

Concept testing
Research procedures used to learn consumers' reactions to new product ideas. Consumers presented with an idea are asked if they like it, would use it, would buy it, and so on.

Test marketing investigates how consumers react in actual marketplace settings.

Test marketing
A controlled experimental procedure in which a new product is tested under realistic market conditions in a limited geographical area.

Test Marketing Test marketing is an experimental procedure in which marketers test a new product under realistic market conditions in order to obtain a measure of its potential sales in national distribution. Test markets are cities or other small geographical areas in which the new product is distributed and sold in typical marketplace settings to actual consumers. No other form of research can beat the real world when it comes to testing actual purchasing behavior and consumer acceptance of a product.

Note that test marketing involves scientific testing and controlled experimentation, not just trying something out in the marketplace. Simply introducing a product in a small geographical area before introducing it nationally is not test marketing.

Test marketing serves two important functions for management. First, it provides an opportunity to estimate the outcomes of alternative courses of action. Managers can estimate the sales effect of a specific marketing variable—such as package design, price, or couponing—and then select the best alternative action with regard to that variable. Second, test market experimentation allows management to identify and correct any weaknesses in either the product or its marketing plan before making the commitment to a national sales launch, by which time it is normally too late to make changes.

In selecting test markets, the marketer must choose cities that are representative of the population of all cities and towns throughout the United States.[6] Test market cities should be representative in terms of competitive situation, media usage patterns, product usage, and other relevant factors. Of course, no single test market is a perfect miniature of the entire United States. Nevertheless, it is important to avoid selecting areas with atypical climates, unusual ethnic composition, or uncommon lifestyles, any of which may have a dramatic impact on the acceptance of a new product. Some of the most popular test markets are midsized cities where costs won't be prohibitive, such as Tulsa, Oklahoma; Charlotte, North Carolina; Green Bay, Wisconsin; Odessa, Texas; Nashville, Tennessee; Omaha, Nebraska; and Portland, Maine.

Test marketing is expensive. Developing local distribution, arranging media coverage, and monitoring sales results take considerable effort. The cost of test marketing a consumer product can be several million dollars. However, if a firm must commit a substantial amount of money to investments in plant and equipment to manufacture a new product, the cost of test marketing may be minimal compared with the cost of a possible product failure. The marketer, then, must balance the cost of test marketing against the risk of not test marketing.

Beta Testing Marketers of new software or Internet products wish to avoid selling poor-quality programs that have "bugs." *Beta testing* is the second and final phase of bug-catching in the development of software. Customers who are representative users receive free copies of the initial software. They run the new application on their computer systems to check for any bugs and incompatibilities with hardware or other software and report back to the software organization. In exchange for their efforts, they are the first to receive the final version of the software, thereby getting a head start in using the new product.[7]

COMMERCIALIZATION

After passing through the filtering stages in the development process, the new product is ready for the final stage of **commercialization.** The decision to launch full-scale production and distribution entails risking a great deal of money, because commercialization involves a serious commitment of resources and managerial effort. This stage is the last chance to stop the project if managers think the risks are too high. Many successful marketing firms, such as Procter & Gamble, remain willing to stop a project right up to the last moment. Although a lot of money may have been spent in reaching the commercialization stage, any amount is small compared with the sums that full commercialization will demand.

Even when marketers use great caution, product failures still occur. It is not difficult to find products that should have been killed before commercialization. For example, the Dow Chemical Company developed a compound of resins and methanol to be sprayed on car tires to increase their ability to maintain traction on ice. The product, Liquid Tire Chain, truly did work, as proved by in-use testing. Not surprisingly, however, buyers stored the pressurized cans of the product in their cars' trunks. When the aerosol containers froze in winter weather, the material within them solidified, making the product useless. The in-use tests Dow had undertaken somehow missed this factor. Unfortunately for Dow, the product failed after commercialization. Had testing been more complete, this failure could have been avoided.

Commercialization
The stage in new product development in which the decision is made to launch full-scale production and distribution of a new product.

Why Do New Products Fail?

New product failures and near-failures occur with some regularity. As was pointed out earlier, it is estimated that there is a one-in-three failure rate among new product introductions. Consider that Pillsbury's Oven Lovin', a cookie dough loaded with Hershey's chocolate chips, Reese's Pieces, and Brach's candies in a resealable tub, failed after millions of dollars had been spent in the new product development process. After researching the Oven Lovin' concept by surveying consumers, the company in a cost-saving effort skipped test marketing and launched the product nationally. Unfortunately for Pillsbury, consumers, based on limited experience during the survey, said they liked the Oven Lovin' resealable tubs. At home, however, many shoppers found they ended up baking the entire package at once—or gobbling up leftover dough raw instead of saving it— eliminating the need for the pricier packaging. The product failed within two years of its introduction.[8]

Cajun Cola tried to compete regionally against Pepsi and Coke at a time when the two cola giants were engaged in an intensive cola war involving reduced prices and increased advertising. Cajun Cola didn't have the resources to compete. In introducing Benefit, a high-soluble-fiber cereal made with psyllium, General Mills stressed the cereal's ability to reduce cholesterol levels. When sales did not meet expectations, the company learned that although consumers understood the role of oat bran in reducing cholesterol levels, they were confused about the term *soluble fiber*. The death knell for the product rang when a barrage of publicity questioned whether Benefit with psyllium was a drug or a cereal.

What are the most common reasons for product failures? Following are several:

- *Insufficient product superiority or uniqueness.* If a "me, too" product is merely an imitation of products that are already on the market and does not offer the consumer a relative advantage, the product may be doomed from the start. Although the Everlast brand has been around boxing for years, Everlast sports drink was not much different from Gatorade. It took only a short time for the product to fail.
- *Inadequate or inferior planning.* Many product failures stem from failure to conduct proper marketing research about consumers' needs and failure to develop

realistic forecasts of market demand and accurate estimates of the acceptance of new products. Overly optimistic managers may underestimate the strength of existing competition and fail to anticipate future competitive reactions and the need for sizable promotional budgets. Too often, the enthusiastic developer of the product is surprised to find that it takes more time and effort than expected to launch the product successfully or that the market for the product is not as substantial as forecasts suggested. When Colgate-Palmolive, anxious to beat its rivals to market, commercialized Fab 1 Shot without test marketing, it quickly learned that the single-packet detergent and fabric softener was not cost-effective for large families. Colgate-Palmolive learned its lesson in the marketplace, while Procter & Gamble and Clorox learned the same thing in test markets.

- *Poor execution.* No matter how good the plans are for commercializing a product, adequate resources must be allocated so that strategies can be properly executed. Many new products fail because managers who think the product is so good it will sell itself do not provide adequate resources for tactical execution. For example, Pillsbury failed with Appleeasy because, in response to increasing apple prices, the company reduced the amount of apples in its recipe rather than increase the production budget. Sometimes a new product fails because the organization lacks the expertise to carry out required production or marketing activities.

- *Technical problems.* Problems may stem from the product itself—failures in production or design. For example, Hot Scoops, a microwavable hot fudge sundae, left the consumer with a mess rather than a sundae if the microwave timer wasn't set exactly right.

- *Poor timing.* The market may change before the new product is introduced, or the company may enter the market too early or too late in the product life cycle. For instance, if a new luxury product is introduced just as a downturn in the economy occurs, the product's chances for success are substantially reduced.

All managers planning new product introductions have one thing in common: They must attempt to predict the future. The product designed in 1998 but commercialized in 2000 is likely to meet an environment somewhat different from the one that existed when the product was being designed. Hence, marketing plans may not work as well as expected. New product marketing deals with forecasting. As the wry adage goes, "Forecasts are dangerous, particularly those about the future."

The Product Life Cycle

Product life cycle
A marketing management concept, often depicted graphically, that traces a product's sales history. The cycle is depicted as having four stages: introduction, growth, maturity, and decline.

The **product life cycle** is a depiction of a product's sales history from its "birth," or marketing beginning, to its "death," or withdrawal from the market. Generally, a product begins its life with its first sale, rises to some peak level of sales, and then declines until its sales volume and contribution to profits are insufficient to justify its presence in the market. This general pattern does vary from product to product, however. Products such as salt and mustard have been used for thousands of years. Arm & Hammer baking soda has been used for over 150 years. Cellular phones and fax machines are mere youngsters by comparison. Some products, such as Topp's Talking Baseball Cards, fail at the very start of their lives. But whether a product has a very short, short, long, or very long life, the pattern of that life may be portrayed by charting sales volume.

Traditionally, the product life cycle has been thought of as reflecting the life of a product class or product category as a whole—for example, the life of hand-held video games as a group, without regard to model or brand. However, marketing managers also use the product life cycle idea in evaluating specific brands of products, because most brands, as well as most products, have limited market lives.

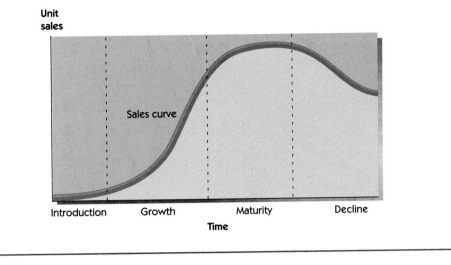

General Pattern of the Product Life Cycle

The product life cycle is illustrated in Exhibit 10-3. A product's life, as suggested earlier, typically flows through several distinct stages as sales volume is plotted over time. These stages are introduction, growth, maturity, and decline. As illustrated in Exhibit 10-4, both sales volume and industry profit change over the course of the life cycle. Exhibit 10-4 also shows the period of product development, which precedes the introductory stage. During this period, no sales are made, but investments are made in the belief that subsequent profitable sales will justify them.

The product life cycle, which is helpful for visualizing the stages of market acceptance, has its greatest practical use as a planning tool. Many successful marketing companies build their strategies around the concept, graph financial and market data against product life cycles, and develop long- and short-range plans for each stage.

THE INTRODUCTION STAGE

During the **introduction stage,** the new product is attempting to gain a foothold in the market. Sales are likely to be slow at the start of the period because the product is, by definition, new and untried. It takes time to gain market acceptance. Sales volume and sales revenues are still low relative to the high expenses associated with developing the product and the marketing mix necessary to introduce the product to the market. In most cases, profits are negative.

The marketing effort in the introductory stage is focused not only on finding first-time buyers and using promotion to make them aware of the product but also on creating channels of distribution—attracting retailers and other intermediaries to handle the product. It is also a time for attempting to recoup most of the research and development costs associated with the product. However, during this period, product alterations or changes in manufacturing may be required to "get the bugs out" of the new market offering. Thus, the introduction stage is typically a high-cost/low-profit period. Although it is an exciting time, it is also a time of uncertainty and anxiety about the new product's ability to survive.

Selecting strategies appropriate to the introductory stage is an important matter, yet organizations differ widely in their choices. Some companies believe that being a pioneer and risk taker is the best approach—the greater the risk, the

Introduction stage
The stage in the product life cycle during which the new product is attempting to gain a foothold in the market.

Industry Profit and the Product Life Cycle

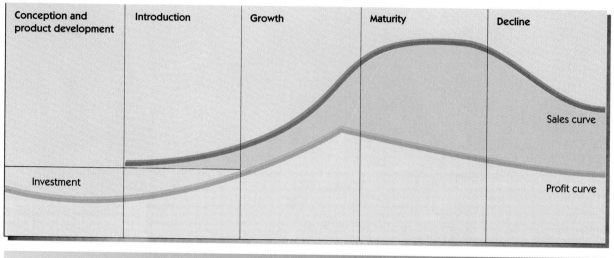

Unit sales/investment
profit (dollars)

Conception and product development	Introduction	Growth	Maturity	Decline

Sales curve

Investment

Profit curve

Time

	Introduction	Growth	Maturity	Decline
Sales	Low	Rapid growth	Slow growth, peak sales	Declining
Profits	Nonexistent or negligible because of high production and marketing costs	Reach peak levels as a result of high prices and rising demand	Increasing competition reduces profit margins and ultimately cuts into total profits	Declining volume pushes costs up to levels that lower profits
Competition	None of importance	Growing	Many rivals competing for a small piece of the pie	Few competitors, with a rapid shakeout of weak members
Customers	Innovative	Mass market	Mass market, differentiated	Laggards

greater the reward. Thus, in many industries, such as tires and aircraft, the same companies are the leaders in new product development over and over again. Other companies quickly follow the pioneer's lead, jumping into the market during the introductory stage. Still others hold back, waiting to see whether the new product will actually take off into a growth period. Each approach has obvious advantages and risks that management must weigh.

The length of the introductory stage varies dramatically. Personal computers and home video games gained market acceptance rapidly. Laser discs, on the other hand, took years to reach a modest level of popularity and experienced rapid decline as soon as the CD-ROM entered its growth stage. Another product category, concentrated laundry detergent, presents a further example of slow market acceptance. The first serious effort to introduce a product that cleans a full load of wash with only a quarter-cup of powder was made in 1976, when Colgate-Palmolive introduced Fresh Start, a powder in a plastic bottle. But rapid sales growth for the category did not occur until 1990, when two other brands, Ultra Tide and Fab Ultra, were successfully introduced. Their marketers succeeded, in part, by stressing the environmental advantage of small packages.

THE GROWTH STAGE

If a product earns market acceptance, it should, at some point, enter a period of comparatively rapid growth. The classic product life cycle portrays this **growth stage** as a period when sales increase at an increasing rate. In other words, sales grow slowly at first but increase at a faster rate later on.

When the product enters its growth stage, profits can be expected to be small. As sales continue to increase during this stage, profits increase, partly

Business people who travel need some way to maintain addresses and phone numbers, keep appointment schedules, perform basic computations, and, more recently, communicate electronically. AT&T's Personal Communicator 440 was the first personal digital assistant on the market; it was followed by Apple's Newton and Casio's Zoomer. These products were plagued by technical problems. Consumers also resisted the high price, which ranged from $1,599 to $2,999. As a result, unit sales volume was too low for the companies to hold out until the market matured. The lessons U.S. Robotics and other later market entrants learned from the first movers' mistakes kept the product from disappearing from the market.

www.usr.com/palm

because sales increase but also because the start-up expenses encountered earlier diminish. As a rule, profits peak late in the growth period.

A product that has entered the growth stage has shown that it may have a future in the marketplace. As a result, the number of competitors and the level of marketing activity can be expected to increase. Pioneering firms are often required to alter their products because competitors, having had the opportunity to learn from the pioneer's mistakes and the time to study the market, may have improved on the original. Competition also increases because of the industry's recognition of an untapped potential market. Competing firms seem to feel that there is enough profit to go around and that they may be able to grab a sizable market share without taking away from each other (as they must do during the maturity stage).

Products still in their growth stages include digital phones, zip drives, digital cameras, and computerized information and interactive shopping services. During their growth stages, the profits associated with these products will rise (although not for every company), peaking at the end of the period. Distribution costs will be brought under control as channels become more organized and able to perform their tasks routinely. Product quality will be stressed and improved. Persuasive efforts to create brand preference will become the emphasis of promotion. Promotion expenses will be adjusted as rising sales and profits indicate the product's potential.

THE MATURITY STAGE

As the product approaches the end of its growth period, sales begin to level off. A change in the growth rate—a decrease in the rate at which sales are increasing—heralds the end of the growth period and the beginning of the **maturity stage.** As

Growth stage
The stage in the product life cycle during which sales increase at an accelerating rate.

Maturity stage
The stage in the product life cycle during which sales increase at a decreasing rate.

Crayola Crayons are in the mature stage of the product life cycle. The company markets Magic Scent crayons, Glow-in-the-Dark crayons, Glitter crayons, and new crayon colors in specially marked boxes. Minor product modifications are typical efforts for products in the mature stage of the product life cycle.

Exhibit 10-4 showed, profits level off and then fall in the maturity stage. This is to be expected as competing firms try to operate within a static or slow-growth market. When the growth rate slows down, the product requires marketing strategies and tactics appropriate for the maturity stage. Later in this stage, for reasons such as diminished popularity, product obsolescence, or market saturation (which occurs when most target customers own the product), the product begins to lose market acceptance.

Most products on the market are in the maturity phase. During this stage, competition is likely to be intense. After all, one of the goals of effective marketing is to achieve brand maturity and to maintain it for as long as the market supports the product. Further, because a product in the maturity stage has achieved wide market acceptance, the primary means for any one company to increase its market share is to take market share away from competitors. For example, in the mature automotive business, strategies to maintain market share and defend against inroads from foreign competition are common.

adapting to change

The Recording Industry   The humble black phonograph record, a mainstay of the music industry for nearly a century, is a virtually extinct species. Because of consumer preferences for audiocassettes and runaway enthusiasm for the compact disc, conventional record albums now account for just a tiny portion of U.S. sales of recorded music (down from 30 percent of the market in 1985). Faced with this drastic decline, music marketers now are thinking about what was once the unthinkable—the prospect of a recording industry that doesn't sell records. Vinyl records are at the end of their life cycle.

In contrast, since the introduction of the compact disc player in 1983, CD sales have grown rapidly and now exceed sales of audiocassettes. In the 1980s, compact disc players were in the growth stage of their product life cycle. Today compact disc players are in the mature stage of their product life cycle. Digital versatile discs (DVD), an alternative to the CD, are brand new. If DVDs receive the support of recording studios, compact discs will go into the decline stage of the product life cycle.

It is interesting to note that, although new recording formats are far more popular than vinyl records, expensive, high-quality turntables for playing old vinyl records have seen a resurgence among musical purists. This small market segment believes that vinyl recordings, played on the right equipment, have a more realistic sound than digital recordings. And this has kept some vinyl records on the market.[9]

One strategy to increase market share is to produce private brands for distributors. Thus, private labels emerge in the maturity stage. An organization selling a mature product may pick up new business in the price-conscious segment of the market as other, less competitive companies withdraw. Persuading existing users to use more of the product may also be a major objective for marketers of mature brands. Many food companies advertise recipes that require their product as an ingredient in order to foster increased usage of that product.

Organizations in mature markets have solved most of the technological problems encountered early in the product life cycle. The products require little technological improvement, and changes become largely a matter of style. CD players, for example, are now offered in tiny sizes and in big sizes, with tape decks and without, with belt clips for joggers and with handles for toting them down the street. They run on house current, batteries, and solar power. Fashionable designs and model variations become important during a product's maturity.

Although Exhibit 10-4 showed that industry profits generally peak near the end of the growth stage, many individual firms in mature market situations are very profitable. A major reason for this continuing profitability is the experience gained during the earlier stages. Economies of scale also play a part. Organizations in mature markets whose brands are profitable typically use the funds these brands generate to support other items in the product mix. The laundry detergent industry is certainly in its mature stage, but industry leader Procter & Gamble uses the sizable profits generated by Tide and Cheer to pay for the development and introduction of new product items and lines.

Successful marketing managers, recognizing the onset of maturity, investigate the causes of that maturity. If a product is in the mature stage because it has become—and remains—widely used (like roofing supplies or tires), sales volume is likely to remain stable. In contrast, if an alternative product or brand has become popular owing to some environmental change, sales may have peaked. The effective marketer needs to know why a product is in its maturity stage, not just that it is there.

THE DECLINE STAGE

The **decline stage** in the product life cycle is marked by falling sales and falling profits. There is likely to be a shakeout in the industry, decreasing the number of firms, as managers become aware that the product has entered the decline stage. Survivor firms compete within an ever-smaller market, driving profit margins lower still. Ironically, the last surviving firm or firms may, as individual organizations, enjoy high profits at this point when the industry's profits are declining. This is because most competitors have withdrawn from the market, leaving what is left to one or two suppliers. Makers of parts for Edsel and DeLorean automobiles are neither large nor numerous, yet they can survive by catering to car collectors. Brylcreem, Ovaltine, Good & Plenty, and blacksmiths are not as common as they once were, but they still survive. Nevertheless, profits for the industry will be low, because only one or two producers are left. Eventually, the decline stage ends with the disappearance of the product from the market.

Exhibit 10-5 summarizes the typical marketing strategies over the course of the product life cycle.

DO ALL PRODUCTS FOLLOW THE SAME LIFE CYCLE?

All products follow a product life cycle. All products are introduced, and most eventually disappear. But the shapes of the product life cycles, the rates of change in sales and profits, and the lengths and heights of the cycles vary greatly. As Exhibit 10-6 shows, some products, like peanut butter, seem to be firmly preserved in the maturity stage forever, whereas others, such as novelty items like talking baseball cards, have very short life cycles.

Decline stage
The stage in the product life cycle during which the product loses market acceptance because of such factors as diminished popularity, obsolescence, or market saturation.

STAGE OF LIFE CYCLE	OVERALL STRATEGY	PRODUCT	PRICES	DISTRIBUTION	PROMOTION
Introduction	Market acceptance; foster product awareness and trial purchase	Basic design with competitive advantage	High, to recover some of the excessive costs of launching	Selective, as distribution is slowly built up	Informative, to generate brand awareness
Growth	Market penetration; persuade mass market to prefer the brand; expand users and use	Product improvements; expanding product line	High, to take advantage of heavy demand	Intensive, using few trade discounts, since dealers are eager to stock the product	Persuasive, to create brand loyalty and product differentiation
Maturity	Defense of brand position; prevent competition from making inroads	Product differentiation; full product lines	What market will bear; important to avoid price wars	Intensive, using heavy trade allowances to retain shelf space	Extensive, to retain existing customers and to stimulate brand switching
Decline	Reduction of expenses; prepare for removal of product from market; squeeze all possible benefits from the product	Minimal changes to product; product line reduced to best sellers	Low enough to permit quick liquidation of inventory	Selective, as unprofitable outlets are slowly phased out	Minimal to none

Indeed, marketers may expect specific brands to have short lives. Cereals, snack foods, and toys, for example, may gain considerable profits as fad items. Teenage Mutant Ninja Turtles cereal and Jurassic Park Raptor Bites candy were expected to be only short-term successes. Similarly, General Foods used carbonated confection technology to produce several fad bubble gum and candy items,

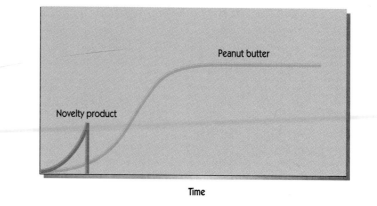

Long and Short Product Life Cycles

Suddenly the world's glass is half full again.

Drivers wanted. (VW)

The Volkswagen Beetle's life cycle differs from that of most automobiles. Introduced in the United States in 1949, the Beetle saw sales grow slowly for years. The Bug became highly successful during the 60s and 70s. In 1979, Volkswagen stopped selling the Beetle. However, after a lengthy absence from the U.S. market, the unpretentious, cute car reemerged in 1998.

www.vw.com

including Increda Bubble, Pop Rocks, and Space Dust. These fad candies, as well as some more familiar products, are marketed on a cyclical basis, reflecting a belief that their faddish nature does not justify year-round marketing expenditures. Other products are brought back in essentially unchanged form once a new generation of buyers has replaced the old. Many stories in Walt Disney comic books and movies

THE SHAPES OF THE PRODUCT LIFE CYCLES, THE RATES OF CHANGE IN SALES AND PROFITS, AND THE LENGTHS AND HEIGHTS OF THE CYCLES VARY GREATLY.

on videotape are reissued once an age cohort of readers has been replaced by a new group. These sorts of products have short lives. Marketers aware of this can develop strategies appropriate for short product life cycles.

IS THERE LIFE AFTER DECLINE?

Occasionally, a product life cycle changes slope, reversing the downward trend associated with the late maturity and decline stages. Some products and brands approach extinction, only to suddenly achieve a new-found popularity. Such a turn of events may be due to nostalgia or to the sudden realization that an old, familiar brand or product was really pretty good after all. A change in the marketing environment may bring this about.

In the last decade, for example, considerable medical attention has been given to proper nutrition and exercise as means of maintaining good health. Fiber in the diet has been an important issue. Some new products appeared in response to nutrition-related concerns, and certain old products—granola, soups, and natural sweeteners such as honey, among others—were suddenly more in demand and were marketed accordingly. Similarly, the concern with physical fitness helped the sales of jogging shoes, jump ropes, bicycles, and exercise machines.

Another social change has helped Erector sets, popular in the 1950s, to experience a revival in the 1990s. After a 10-year absence, Erector sets returned to the U.S. market for Christmas 1991. Santa Claus now finds Erector sets on the wish lists of both boys and girls. In fact, in December 1993, five 11-year-old girls won

Star Wars Few product introductions in 1997 had as much of an impact on pop culture as the *Star Wars* film franchise.

George Lucas created and Twentieth Century Fox Film Corp. distributed a film called *Star Wars* in 1977, and another called *The Empire Strikes Back* in 1981, and yet another called *The Return of the Jedi* in 1983.

But the new films Lucasfilms and Fox issued early in 1997 weren't mere re-releases. The movies included newly inserted scenes, technically impossible to create 20 years ago. The revised *Star Wars* trilogy reminded the world of the enduring power of the tales. The three movies generated a combined total of nearly $200 million at the U.S. box office, helping *Star Wars* become the highest-grossing film of all time until *Titanic's* blockbuster success in 1997–98. The film franchise also was the biggest movie property in entertainment licensing in 1997. Hasbro and Galoob put up about $1 billion to retain their toy licenses over the next 10 years.

The multigenerational appeal of the property underscored the powerful, and perhaps permanent, place *Star Wars* occupies in the global pop culture. Unquestionably, *Star Wars* sales history does not fit the traditional product life cycle for a movie.[10]

Erector building contests. Erector sets are part of a "crossover" trend; marketers now realize that toys once thought appropriate only for boys are popular with girls, too.

Products that appear to have stable or declining sales may also increase in popularity because of their close tie-ins with other products. For example, the popularity of products such as VCRs has increased consumer interest in high-quality color television sets.

The Adoption and Diffusion Processes

At all stages of the product life cycle, but especially during the introduction stage, organizations are concerned with who will actually buy, use, or in some other way adopt the product. Marketers who understand why and when customers accept new products are able to manage product strategy effectively over the course of a product's life cycle. This understanding requires familiarity with the related processes of adoption and diffusion.

A person who purchases a product he or she has never tried before, may ultimately become an adopter. The mental and behavioral stages through which an individual adopter passes before actually making a purchase or placing an order constitute the **adoption process.** These stages are awareness, interest, evaluation, trial, and—finally—adoption.

Not all potential buyers go through the stages of the adoption process at the same rate of speed. Some pass through them very quickly and are the first to adopt the new product. Others take longer to become aware of the product and to make up their minds to purchase it. Still others take a very long time to accept and adopt the product. This spread of the new product through society is called the **diffusion process.** The stages in the diffusion process can be charted, as shown in

Adoption process
The mental and behavioral stages through which a consumer passes before making a purchase or placing an order. The stages are awareness, interest, evaluation, trial, and adoption.

Diffusion process
The spread of a new product through society.

NOT **ALL POTENTIAL BUYERS GO THROUGH THE STAGES OF THE ADOPTION PROCESS AT THE SAME RATE. SOME PASS THROUGH THEM VERY QUICKLY AND ARE THE FIRST TO ADOPT THE NEW PRODUCT. OTHERS TAKE LONGER.**

Exhibit 10-7. As the exhibit shows, the cumulative pattern of adopters closely follows the shape of the product life cycle.

The Diffusion Process

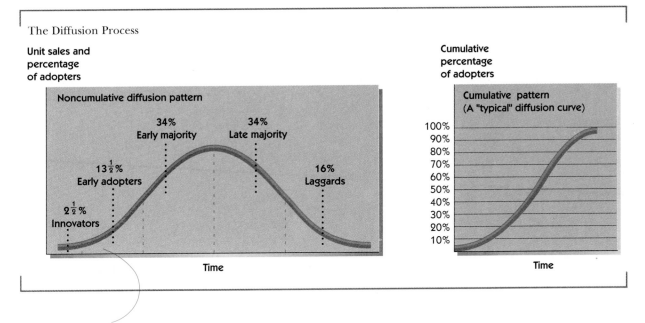

**Unit sales and
percentage
of adopters**

Noncumulative diffusion pattern

34%
Early majority

34%
Late majority

$13\frac{1}{2}$%
Early adopters

16%
Laggards

$2\frac{1}{2}$%
Innovators

Time

**Cumulative
percentage
of adopters**

Cumulative pattern
(A "typical" diffusion curve)

100%
90%
80%
70%
60%
50%
40%
30%
20%
10%

Time

To remember the difference between the adoption process and the diffusion process, keep in mind that it is individuals who go through the various psychological stages involved in adoption, while it is the new product that is diffused through the social system as it is purchased by the various groups of adopters.[11]

INNOVATORS—BEING VENTURESOME

Innovators—the consumers most likely to try something new—are the first to buy a new product. These people are venturesome, willing to be daring and different. They are the customers most confident about thinking for themselves and most likely to deviate from their local community's established way of doing things. Innovators, because they are eager to try new ideas, are extremely important in getting a new product accepted in the market. As Exhibit 10-7 shows, this venturesome group is small in number. As might be expected, members of this group are likely to be younger and better educated than the average consumer. They are generally higher-income buyers or financially stable individuals, who can afford to take a chance on something new.

EARLY ADOPTERS—FOLLOWING THE LEAD

A larger group than the innovators, but a somewhat less adventurous one, is the early adopter group. Many characteristics of the innovator group are also found among the early adopters, since to be an **early adopter** often requires the income, self-confidence, and education to use a product that has still not gained wide acceptance. A major difference, however, is that unlike innovators, who adopt the product during the introduction stage of the product life cycle, most early adopters buy the product during the growth stage.

Early adopters read more magazines than the average person and have high usage rates in the product category in which the innovation falls. Although members of this group follow the lead of the innovators, they are more integrated into their local communities. Early adopters are conceived of as opinion leaders, who help to determine which new products later adopters will find acceptable. Early adopters can be expected to influence their friends and coworkers and thus to

Innovator
A member of the first group of consumers to buy a new product.

Early adopter
A member of the group of consumers who purchase a product soon after it has been introduced, but after the innovators have purchased it.

contribute greatly to a new product's progress. Developers of new products therefore spend considerable time and resources in identifying and reaching this group. They are a significant target for advertisements and other promotions aimed at creating a market where none existed before.

EARLY AND LATE MAJORITIES—RIDING THE BANDWAGON

The early and late majorities, taken together, constitute approximately 68 percent of the overall group that adopts a new product (see Exhibit 10-7). They make up the mass market on which many products depend. The two halves of this market are seen as having similar characteristics in differing degrees.

The **early majority** is usually made up of solid, middle-class consumers, who are more deliberate and cautious in making purchasing decisions than are early adopters. Once this group adopts a new product, late in the growth stage, the product's acceptance and its diffusion throughout the social system are well established. In general, members of the early majority are of average socioeconomic status. Slightly less educated and financially stable than members of the early majority are those in the late majority. They also are older, more conservative, and more traditional. As time goes by and more and more consumers adopt an innovation, it is perceived to be less risky. At this time, the product has reached maturity, and the late majority adopts the innovation. Members of the **late majority** are skeptical about new product ideas and reluctantly adopt innovations only when the products no longer carry the risk associated with newness. Social pressure also may force late adopters to purchase a product.

LAGGARDS—BRINGING UP THE REAR

Laggards, or final adopters, make up the last group to adopt a product. These people see a need for the product but for economic, social, or educational reasons have been slow to accept it. Innovations are not welcome to this older group, which is lowest in socioeconomic status. Laggards resist challenges to past fashion and traditions. The laggard group is especially easily identified when the product in question is clothing. Frequently, a new clothing design is adopted by innovators, early adopters, and members of the majority groups, who then drop it as the laggard group begins to wear the style.

NONADOPTERS—HOLDING OUT

No matter what the innovation, there are always some individuals who never buy the new product or adopt the new style. These people are known as **nonadopters.**

USE OF THE ADOPTER CATEGORIES

Planners about to introduce a new product should give close consideration to the diffusion process and the various adopter categories. Characteristics of the various adopter groups may provide the basis for market segmentation efforts. As you have seen, youth, economic resources, adventurousness, and other possible segmenting variables are usually not spread evenly among the adopter groups. Thought and research intended to discover the characteristics of adopters can help the new product on its way and will surely pay off for marketing managers. As the target marketing and positioning focus shifts from early adopters to the early majority and late majority, promotional and other marketing plans, including pricing and distribution strategies, should be altered. Indeed, even the product strategy should be modified.

Strategies for Modifying Existing Products

New products should be carefully designed to appeal to well-researched target markets. However, most products and brands enjoy limited lives because of the dynamic nature of competition within target markets. Effective product strategy does not fulfill its obligation merely by contributing to the design of the product;

Early majority
A group of consumers, usually solid, middle-class people, who purchase more deliberately and cautiously than early adopters.

Late majority
A group of consumers who purchase a product after the early majority, when the product is no longer perceived as risky.

Laggard
A member of the group of final adopters in the diffusion process.

Nonadopter
A member of the group of consumers who never buy a particular new product or adopt a particular new style.

its role is ongoing. Dynamic markets must be monitored and researched so that appropriate strategies can be devised to keep old customers, to attract new ones, and to extend the product life cycle. Developing strategies for modifying existing products and managing the product mix is an important aspect of product management.

As we have stressed time and time again, no single facet of the marketing mix stands alone. Each facet must be viewed in light of what it contributes to the total mix, and each must be consistent with— and supportive of—the other variables. Despite these strong interrelationships, many marketing strategies have been developed that are specifically aimed at the product variable in the marketing mix. It is to these that we now turn our attention.

The marketer's decision about **product modification**—that is, the altering or adjusting of the product mix—is typically influenced by the competitive nature of the market (such as design changes made by competitors) and by changes in the external environment (such as the discovery of a new technology). For example, when Braun noticed a trend toward greater consumption of gourmet coffees in coffee shops like Starbucks and at home, the company conducted a scientific study of what makes coffee flavors different from one another. It then introduced a new coffee maker that allows a user to select where the water will flow through the coffee grounds and how long it will have contact with them, thus controlling the bitterness or robustness of the coffee flavor.[12] AT&T's Pocketnet is a mobile telephone that was improved by the addition of built-in e-mail, paging, and faxing capabilities. Most product modification decisions attempt to create a competitive

Product modification
The altering or adjusting of the product mix, typically influenced by the competitive nature of the market and by changes in the external environment.

focus on relationships

Silicon Graphics Inc. Cultivates Its Most Demanding Customers   If you're running a highly successful company, the vast majority of your customers are apt to be rather satisfied with your products. Great. Fine. Terrific. Maybe too terrific. How do you push your company to maintain the pace of innovation that will ensure its continuing prosperity? You seek out the customers most difficult to satisfy. Ed McCracken, chairman of Silicon Graphics Inc., has established a practice of actively cultivating customers who want to do things that just can't be done with Silicon Graphics Inc.'s products—or anyone else's, for that matter. Silicon Graphics Inc. then works closely with these cutting-edge customers to design the next generation of its computers. The customers' dreams and unmet demands drive the design of the new system, pushing Silicon Graphics Inc.'s engineers.

In the early Eighties the military was Silicon Graphics Inc.'s most demanding customer, the one that was willing and able to spend whatever it took to achieve the impossible. That stopped with the defense cutbacks following the end of the Cold War. Now that leadership role has been taken on by Hollywood's entertainment industry, which is entranced by high tech. Silicon Graphics Inc. has been developing the latest version of its most powerful and expensive product, its Onyx graphics supercomputer (price: $200,000 to $1 million), specifically to meet the demands of Walt Disney's Imagineering group, which creates attractions for the famous theme parks.

Disney's vision is a virtual-reality "ride" based on its movie *Aladdin*. Tourists strap on special headgear with visual displays that give them the illusion of flying on a magic carpet through Aladdin's home base, the desert town of Agrabah. Disney engineers had backed away from attempting a virtual-reality attraction because with earlier systems, the new medium's quality was still discouragingly spotty. Not only did the graphics lack truly realistic detail, but the motion sometimes seemed jerky or subtly out of sync—enough to make the viewer nauseated. The Disney people insisted on a computer graphics system that would closely re-create the look of the movie without compromises. Driven by this criterion, Silicon Graphics Inc. has been redesigning the Onyx, which it will sell to other corporate customers as well.[13]

advantage, through such means as product differentiation or reducing costs. We will discuss three general strategies for modifying existing products: cost reduction, repositioning, and total quality management strategies.

COST REDUCTION STRATEGIES

As new competitors, perhaps global competitors with factories in newly industrialized countries, enter the market, profits may be squeezed. The company with a product in the maturity or decline stage may choose to introduce a **cost reduction strategy.** This product strategy requires redesigning the product and working in harmony with production experts to lower factory costs or operating costs. For example, Chrysler is working on perfecting a plastic car body that would consist of only 6 big pieces instead of the typical 80 parts. The plastic parts need no paint and could halve the price of a car.

Implementing a cost reduction strategy may require moving production to another country. Stanley Works, a company that 30 years ago produced all its tools in New England, now operates a factory in Puebla, Mexico, to make its sledgehammers and wrecking bars. Low-cost labor was essential to compete with inexpensive imports from China.

Often, a company elects to produce a stripped-down version of the initial product with less expensive materials, aimed at price-conscious market segments. Shuttle by United, which United Airlines initiated to compete with low-fare airlines like Southwest, is an example. The cost reduction strategy need not mean a reduction in quality.

REPOSITIONING STRATEGIES

A **repositioning strategy** changes the product design, formulation, brand image, or brand name so as to alter the product's competitive position. Reformulating a soft drink to use NutraSweet instead of sugar, for example, may be intended to change the product's major benefit (from a sweet treat to weight control). Repositioning strategies usually include a corresponding change in promotion strategy.

A change in the market environment or an initial mistake in brand name selection may mean that a name or symbol has to be changed to reposition the brand. The original brand name may have been a bad choice that grew worse over time. This was the case with Heartwise cereal, whose name was changed to Fiberwise after the Food and Drug Administration argued there was no evidence that the cereal was good for the heart. In other instances, a brand name or trademark symbol may serve long and well but become inappropriate as the brand ages and times change. For example, Betty Crocker's looks have changed over the years to reflect current clothing and hairstyles.

Around the world, organizations are repositioning themselves to adapt to changes resulting from merger, diversification, or international interests. Southwestern Bell, which became SBC corporation, changed its name because it is no longer just a regional marketer in the Southwestern United States—it is a global marketer. As international trade becomes ever more important, companies are adding words like *International* and *Worldwide* to their official names. However, each name change, especially when the original name is well established, involves many risks. Goodwill may be lost if customers fail to realize that the new company is the same as the old one.

TOTAL QUALITY MANAGEMENT STRATEGIES

Total quality management strategies emphasize market-driven quality as a top priority. Chapter 2 indicated that for many years some U.S. corporations did not keep pace with the product quality offered by a number of overseas competitors. Today, with intense levels of global competition, most companies must adopt a total quality management philosophy. Total quality management involves properly implementing and adjusting the product mix (and procedures within the entire

Cost reduction strategy
A product strategy that involves redesigning a product to lower production costs.

Repositioning strategy
A product strategy that involves changing the product design, formulation, brand image, or brand name so as to alter the product's competitive position.

Total quality management strategy
A product strategy that emphasizes market-driven quality; also called a quality assurance strategy.

organization) to ensure customers' satisfaction with product quality. It is a strategy based on the conviction that if an organization wishes to prosper, every employee must work for continuous quality improvement.

What is quality? Organizations once defined quality by engineering standards. Most marketers today don't see quality that way. Some marketers say that quality means that their good or service conforms to consumers' requirements—that the product is acceptable. Effective marketers subscribing to a total quality management philosophy, however, believe that the product's quality must go beyond acceptability for a given price range. Rather than having consumers pleased that nothing went wrong, effective marketers want consumers to experience some delightful surprises or reap some unexpected benefits. In other words, quality assurance is

Jeep Chrysler Corporation, Jeep's parent company, asked the approximately 380 paint line workers who wash, wipe, and prepare Jeep Cherokees and Comanches for painting to stop using antiperspirants. Total quality management is the reason why. Chrysler's investigation showed that antiperspirants worn by workers flaked and fell onto the new paint. Antiperspirants contain chemicals, such as zinc zirconium, that can damage paint. The paint flows away from the fallen flake, causing a depression about the size of a baby's fingertip. "Who would've known that spraying that . . . under your arms would hurt the finish?" asked Freddie Robinson, a plant worker for eight years.

Chrysler looked into the matter after its quality control system reported that every vehicle coming off the line had up to 50 imperfections on the roof and hood. Such damage can be enough for an inspector to send a car back for thousands of dollars in repairs.

Jeep workers are not banned from wearing antiperspirants, but they are being educated about the problem. An awareness program that employees helped develop includes a training session that shows some of the common causes of paint flaws. "You do what you got to do," said one paint line worker. "We want to turn out the best Jeeps. If antiperspirants are causing problems, you got to give them up."[14]

more than just meeting minimum standards. Total quality management requires continuous improvement of product quality, enhancement of products with additional features as the products age, or both.

Managers continuously improve product quality to keep their brands competitive. Obviously, a Bentley from Rolls-Royce does not compete with a Geo Storm from General Motors. Buyers of these automobiles are in different market segments, and their expectations of quality differ widely. Nevertheless, marketers at both Rolls-Royce and General Motors try to determine what quality level their target market expects and then attempt to market goods and services that continually surpass expectations.

Marketers expect **product enhancement**—the introduction of a new and improved version of an existing brand—to extend a product's life cycle by keeping it in the growth stage. The Gillette Company is a master at this strategy. Exhibit 10-8 depicts the product life cycle for Gillette razors.

Notice how the company has managed to keep its basic product alive by steadily improving blades and razors. In 1990, Gillette introduced Sensor, a razor with a new suspension system. It provides a cleaner, smoother, and safer shave and has proved very successful. In 1994, Gillette upgraded the Sensor with SensorExcel, a razor that features rubber "microfins" (designed to stretch the skin for a closer shave) and a larger lubricating strip. It has not replaced Sensor but is sold alongside the original brand at a price about 15 percent higher. Gillette introduced the Mach3, a new, more advanced shaving system with the three blades, in 1998.

Gillette's strategy heavily emphasizes improving product performance—how well the razors remove whiskers. Product performance, however, is only one aspect of quality. Consumers perceive other dimensions of product quality, as defined in Exhibit 10-9. (The special aspects of service quality will be described in Chapter 11.)

Many of the dimensions of quality listed in Exhibit 10-9 are influenced by the quality of raw materials, production technology, and quality control at the factory.

Product enhancement
The introduction of a new and improved version of an existing product, intended to extend the product's life cycle by keeping it in the growth stage.

Gillette
www.gillette.com

Gillette Razor Blades' Product Life Cycles

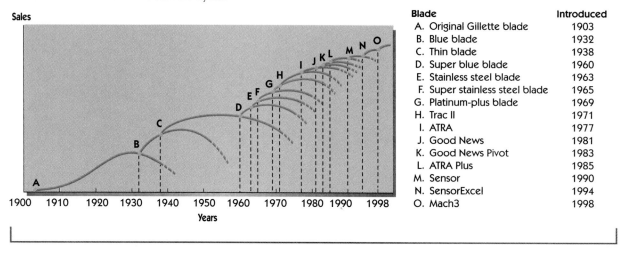

Blade	Introduced
A. Original Gillette blade	1903
B. Blue blade	1932
C. Thin blade	1938
D. Super blue blade	1960
E. Stainless steel blade	1963
F. Super stainless steel blade	1965
G. Platinum-plus blade	1969
H. Trac II	1971
I. ATRA	1977
J. Good News	1981
K. Good News Pivot	1983
L. ATRA Plus	1985
M. Sensor	1990
N. SensorExcel	1994
O. Mach3	1998

Although middle-level marketing managers have some influence in these areas, they do not have the primary decision-making responsibility for these activities. To ensure production quality, therefore, top management must communicate the consumers' needs to those who have production authority.

Top managers often have people from different functional areas of the company, such as finance, production, and marketing, work as a team to establish the appropriate processes for total quality management. Individuals in these cross-functional teams are empowered to organize their work and make decisions. They share a common goal and jointly design and develop processes so that the organization runs smoothly, efficiently, and effectively, without "bureaucratic red tape" and barriers that give functional managers exclusive control over certain operations. Cross-functional teams operate under the assumption that employees

Quality Dimensions for Goods

Performance	How well does the product perform its core function? (How well does a razor remove whiskers?)
Features	Does the product have adequate auxiliary dimensions that provide secondary benefits? (Does a motor oil come in a convenient package?)
Conformity to specifications	What is the incidence of defects? (Does a vineyard sell spoiled wine?)
Reliability	Does the product ever fail to work? Does the product perform with consistency? (Will the lawn mower work properly each time it is used?)
Durability	What is the economic life of the product? (How long will a motorcycle last?)
Aesthetic design	Does the product's design look and feel like that of a high-quality product? (Is a snowmobile aerodynamic?)
Serviceability	Is the service system efficient, competent, and convenient? (Does a computer software manufacturer have a toll-free telephone number and a technical staff to answer questions quickly?)

Source: Based on David A. Aaker, *Managing Brand Equity* (New York: Macmillan, 1991), pp. 90–95; David Garvin, "Product Quality: An Important Strategic Weapon," *Business Horizons,* May–June 1984, pp. 40–43; and David A. Garvin, "Competing on the Eight Dimensions of Quality," *Harvard Business Review,* November–December 1987, pp. 101–108.

actively involved in the quality process have valuable insight about ways to improve customer-driven quality.

Product Design   Product design—that is, a product's configuration, composition, and style—influences most quality dimensions. Marketers must work with engineers on product design to achieve quality goals. Assuring that a product design is aesthetically pleasing and fashionable often requires considerable consumer research, artistic creativity, and product planning.

Often, consumers' perceptions of quality are influenced by a noticeable aspect of product design or formulation. For example, the sound quality of stereo speakers can be difficult to assess, so many consumers believe that the larger the speaker, the better the sound. Consumers of tomato juice equate thickness with quality. With automobiles, a solid sound when the door closes symbolizes good construction and a solid, safe body.

Color contributes to the way people perceive products. When a Windex competitor tested a colorless window cleaner against the market leader, consumers did not perceive the new (and improved) cleaner to be better. However, when the product was tinted blue, consumer evaluation of product quality improved dramatically. When Igloo Products Corporation wanted to boost sales of its coolers, the company brought in a color consultant. She turned up her nose at Igloo's prosaic red and

blue coolers and advised the company to add turquoise- and raspberry-colored products to the line. After the new shades hit the shelves, sales jumped 15 percent. Igloo currently offers its coolers in purple, tangerine, and lime green, as well as in traditional red and blue.

The design of a building, an evening gown, a piece of furniture, or any other product may be influenced by what is currently in fashion. The terms *style, fashion,* and *fad* refer to specific concepts. **Style** refers to a distinctive execution, construction, or design. For

Design and style are important ways to differentiate a product from its competition. This Red Devil Ergo 2000 spackling knife is ergonomically designed with soft, oversized handles contoured to fit palm, thumb, and fingers. The design was based on research findings showing that people found conventional putty knives and scrapers too short, hard, and squared-off—a design that caused them to slam their thumbs against the side of the blade while using it. Simplicity of the functional design is reinforced by the aesthetic design, which evokes comfort.

Product design
A product's configuration, composition, and style. This characteristic influences most consumers' perceptions of product quality.

Talking Nano Baby says things like "I'm hungry" and "It's time to play." Talking Nano is a typical fad product, purchased for its novelty.

www.playmatestoys.com

Style
A distinctive execution, construction, or design in a product class.

Fashion
A style that is current or in vogue.

Fad
A passing fashion or craze that interests many people for only a short time.

example, paintings might be in the classic, impressionist, or modern style. A **fashion** is a style that is current or in vogue. A **fad** is a passing fashion or craze in which many people are interested for a short time. A fad item is purchased because of its novelty. For example, Tiger's Giga Pets, Tamagotchi's Virtual Pets, and Playmates' Talking Nano—digital "animals" on key chains—were hot items in 1997. The perceived quality of many products—especially clothing, such as a T-shirt from Chumbawamba's latest concert tour—is intertwined with consumers' feelings about fashion and fads. Marketers spend considerable effort trying to understand how styles, fashions, and fads influence perceived product quality.

Implementing a Total Quality Management Strategy As we have pointed out, the assumption underlying total quality management is that the voice of the consumer has to be brought into the quality improvement process. Thus, marketing research—specifically, customer satisfaction surveys—is an integral part of a total quality management strategy. Managers of quality assurance programs have found that companies that do not measure quality are less likely to improve product quality than companies that regularly measure quality against established standards.

Exhibit 10-10 illustrates the stages in the implementation of a total quality management strategy. The process begins with making a commitment to total quality assurance through a program that measures performance against consumers' standards, not standards determined by quality engineers within the company. All changes in the organization are oriented toward improvement of consumers' perceptions of product quality. Exhibit 10-10 indicates that establishing consumer requirements, quantifying benchmark measures, setting objectives, conducting marketing research studies, and making adjustments in the organization to improve quality go hand in hand. Total quality management is an ongoing process for continuous improvement.

The steps described in Exhibit 10-10 work for both goods and services. However, service products and customer services offered along with goods have some distinc-

e x h i b **10-10**   Implementing a Total Quality Management Strategy

STAGE	IMPLEMENTATION STEPS
Commitment Stage	Establish that it is the customers, not the organization, who define quality.
Exploration Stage	Discover what product features are important to customers: • What problems are customers having with the product? • What aspects of product operation or customer service have disappointed customers? • What is the company doing right?
Benchmarking Stage	Establish quantitative measures that can serve as benchmarks or points of comparison for evaluating future efforts: • Initial measures of overall satisfaction • Measures of the frequency of customer problems • Quality ratings for specific attributes Identify the brand's position relative to competitors' quality positions.
Initial Quality Improvement Stage	Establish the quality improvement process within the organization. Translate quality issues into the internal vocabulary of the organization. Establish performance standards and expectations for improvement.
Measurement Stage —Wave 1	Conduct Wave 1 to measure trends in satisfaction and quality ratings. Determine if the organization is meeting customer needs as specified by quantitative standards.
Continuous Quality Improvement Stage	Through quality improvement management, allow employees to initiate problem-solving behavior without a lot of red tape. Initiate proactive communications with consumers.
Measurement Stage —Wave 2	Conduct Wave 2 to track quality and compare results with earlier stages.
Continuous Quality Improvement Stage	Continue quality improvement management.

tive aspects. Chapter 11 discusses the influence of consumers' perceptions on the service encounter and how those perceptions determine service quality.

Matching Products to Markets—Product Line Strategy

The ultimate goal of the marketing manager is to develop a total product offering that satisfies the desires of target customers. Because most markets have heterogeneous needs, an organization ideally would develop a series of products so that each target market's needs and desires would be mirrored by a product offering. However, as discussed in the chapter on market segmentation, in reality a firm must select meaningful market segments that will be profitable. The **product line strategy** involves matching product items within a product line to markets.

The options an organization faces may be described in the following terms:

- The **full-line,** or **deep-line, strategy** means offering a large number of variations of a product.
- The **limited-line strategy** entails offering a smaller number of variations.
- The **single-product strategy** involves offering one product item or one product version with very few model options.

The product line strategy is influenced by the diversity of the market and the resources available to the company. In general, the deeper the product line, the higher the cost. Customers have more selection with a deep line, and this gives the marketer more opportunities to make a sale. However, offering too many product items may involve an economic penalty to the organization. Conversely, a sparse line may not match the market's demands, and the company may lose sales. However, high volume of one or a few items usually results in production and distribution economies of scale that increase profit margins.

A major product strategy question to consider is this: How many variations on a product can be presented to the market before the extra customer satisfaction achieved is no longer worth the expense to the company? The product line strategy alternatives must be evaluated in terms of the market addressed.

STRATEGIES FOR EXPANDING THE PRODUCT LINE OR THE PRODUCT MIX

Interpreting the market's needs often leads organizations to develop new product items that are very similar to existing products. These may be product line extensions or product category extensions.

A **product line extension** (or line extension) is an item added to an existing product line to provide depth. For example, when Uncle Ben's Inc. added Uncle Ben's Calcium Plus rice, it created a product line extension. A **product category extension** is a new item or new line of items in a product category that is new to the company. For example, Ultra Slim-Fast, which began as a diet drink (a meal replacement shake), expanded into microwavable meals and frozen desserts.

A product category extension may be called a brand extension if products in the new category use a brand name already used on one of the company's existing products. That is what Ultra Slim-Fast did. The term **brand extension,** however, may also refer to a product line extension. This can be a bit confusing. However, if you remember that the term *brand extension* involves the use of a brand name and may be used for either a new item in an existing product line or an item in a new product category, you will find the terminology easier to understand.

The concept of brand equity, introduced in Chapter 9, helps explain the reasons for brand extensions.[15] When a brand name like Weight Watcher's, Harley-Davidson, or Disney adds value to a product, the name is said to have brand equity. Market share or profit margins are greater because of the goodwill associated with the brand. Brand equity gives a brand higher financial value if the company is sold and also if the brand is used on other products. Brand equity is especially useful for brand extensions in similar product categories.

Product line strategy
The strategy of matching items within a product line to markets.

Full-line strategy
A product line strategy that involves offering a large number of variations of a product; also called a deep-line strategy.

Limited-line strategy
A product-line strategy that involves offering a smaller number of product variations than a full-line strategy offers.

Single-product strategy
A product line strategy that involves offering one product item or one product version with very few options.

Product line extension
An item added to an existing product line to create depth; also called a line extension.

Product category extension
A new item or new line of items in a product category that is new to the company.

Brand extension
A product category extension or product line extension that employs a brand name already used on one of the company's existing products.

Cannibalize
To eat into the sales revenues of another product item in the same line.

Flanker brand
A product that extends a product line as a means of denying shelf space to competitors.

Enhanced model
A model that extends a product line by virtue of its distinctive features, which consumers perceive as better than those of the original model.

Sometimes a product line extension will **cannibalize** sales from other items in the product line—that is, eat into the sales revenues from those items.[16] For example, Gillette's Sensor shaving system, the result of a 10-year development project, was intended to lure customers away from inexpensive disposable razors, which had achieved a 60 percent share of the market. Sensor did indeed take sales away from competitors' brands. However, it also cannibalized sales from Gillette's other razor brands. Gillette has a tradition of creating incremental technological advancements that lead to product line extensions. When SensorExcel was introduced in 1994, Gillette knew it would take sales away from Sensor, but the company also knew it would improve overall company profits.

Several strategies for product line extensions are shown in Exhibit 10-11. An item in a different-sized container, with a new flavor, with a style variation, or with some minor modification, is a brand extension within a product line if it uses the same family brand name. Among retailers, especially in the grocery industry, the term **flanker brand** is sometimes used to refer to an item introduced to extend the product line in order to deny shelf space to competitors. (Grocers place brand extensions next to the original items—that is, on their flanks.) Adding very similar items appealing to slightly different tastes or customer requirements is just one of many line extension strategies that may be implemented to extend a product line.

The initial product item may also be offered in an **enhanced model.** Product enhancement may take the form of introducing a fancier model with distinctive features for more discriminating consumers. For example, an enhanced model of a personal computer may have a built-in Zip drive, Dolby digital audio, DVD ROM, and greater memory capacity. It has all the bells and whistles. The difference between an enhanced model and a brand extension (flanker brand) is a matter of degree. Consumers perceive enhanced models as better rather than as just variations of the original item.

A company may choose to offer cost reduction, especially during the maturity or decline stage of a product's life cycle. This strategy requires working in harmony with production to lower factory costs. Often a stripped-down version of the initial product is produced with less expensive materials and then is marketed to the price-conscious market segment. The cost reduction strategy works for services, as well as goods. For example, Federal Express, well known for absolutely, positively delivering before 10:30 a.m. the next day, introduced an afternoon delivery service and a two-day economy service as cost reduction line extensions of its main service.

e x h i b i 10-11

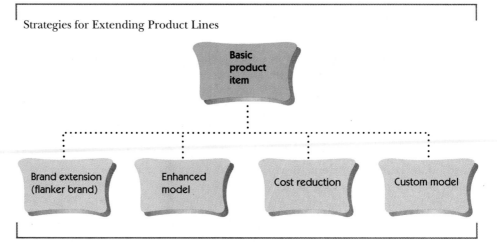

Strategies for Extending Product Lines

A custom model strategy requires producing a version of the product in relatively small lots for a specific channel of distribution or a specific customer. For instance, DuPont produces customized herbicides that attack specific problem weeds unique to Brazil and another that prevents damage to Japanese rice crops.

The most common custom models are private brands. This strategy does not always require a contract for a private brand. For example, many manufacturers of consumer electronics equipment use their own brand names on a unique model sold only to large retailers. The custom Panasonic model is very similar to another model in the Panasonic line, but it is available only at Wal-Mart, Sears, or some other large retailer. The Panasonic name remains a benefit to consumers, yet the retailer has an exclusive offering.

PRODUCT MODIFICATIONS FOR INTERNATIONAL MARKETS

The home-based international marketer must decide how much to adjust a product and its domestic marketing strategy for each foreign market. Similarly, the globally oriented multinational marketer must determine the extent to which market variations necessitate marketing adjustments.

A marketer adopting a **globalization strategy,** or standardization strategy, standardizes its product mix and promotion mix around the world. This strategy assumes that, in our modern era of global communication, the behavior of many consumers throughout the world has become very similar. For example, this strategy assumes that around the globe, members of market segments that can afford Panasonic videotape recorders desire the same features and buy for the same reasons. It also assumes that cost savings from production and marketing economies of scale will more than offset any sales lost because the organization's product and promotional strategies have not been adapted to local conditions. Using this strategy, a company will sell the same product, with no adjustments, in all markets. This works well for some products but not for others. Products vary in sensitivity to environmental conditions such as economic, cultural, and social factors. Industrial products, for example, may be used in much the same way in all markets in the world. Therefore, their use (and thus their marketing) is not sensitive to the peculiarities of separate cultures and economies.

At the opposite extreme are certain food items, whose use and acceptance vary among countries. Products that are highly sensitive to local conditions are not likely candidates for extension to foreign markets. Post-It Notes provides a good example. Post-It Notes are big sellers in the United States and Japan. In Japan, however, the shape of the paper is long and narrow to accommodate the vertical orientation of Japanese writing. Many situations call for a customization strategy.

A **customization strategy** adapts the product strategy to each country where the good or service is marketed. There are two basic approaches to a customization strategy. The company may sell the same product, adapted to a specific market, or it may sell a new product invention in a market.

Many products are best marketed with some sort of adaptation to local conditions. For example, Stanley Tools found that—despite the fact that the European Community offers the potential for a unified market for many of its products—the English and the French disagree on whether a handsaw should have a

Globalization strategy
A plan by which a marketer standardizes its marketing strategy around the world; also called a standardization strategy.

Customization strategy
A product line extension strategy that involves making a product in relatively small lots for specific channels of distribution or specific customers.

Bausch & Lomb uses a customization strategy for its Ray-Ban sunglasses. Sunglasses in Asian markets are designed to better fit the flatter bridge of the nose and higher cheekbones of the Asian face. The sunglasses sold in Europe are similar in shape to the Ray-Bans in the United States, but the styles tend to be more flamboyant and *avant-garde* than those of the U.S. counterparts.

wooden or a plastic handle. Sometimes adjustments are required because of government regulations. For instance, when Mentor O&O, a small manufacturer of surgical equipment used in eye care, decided to market one of its testing devices in Germany, the company had to modify its equipment to meet design specifications established by the German government. The Mentor testing device sold in the United States, which meets the rigorous standards of the U.S. government, has an alarm bell with an on-off switch. The German specifications required that the on-off switch be removed and dictated just how loud the alarm bell must sound.

Product invention requires the development of a new product for the international market. A company may opt to use *backward invention* (re-creating or reintroducing a product that is obsolete in the domestic market in another market) or *forward invention* (creating a new product for the new market conditions). Forward invention is the costliest and riskiest product strategy, but the potential for rewards is also the greatest.

The general approach taken by many marketers is to maintain a global corporate strategy with tactical adjustments where local conditions warrant them. If there were no strategic continuity of approach, the company would not gain a solid and cohesive global identity. Instead, its identity would consist of a patchwork of the fragmented efforts in its various markets. There is value in coordinating and standardizing strategic planning worldwide.

ELIMINATING OLD PRODUCTS

Many products that were once winners eventually become losers. However, managers, while stressing new product development efforts, often neglect product elimination efforts. Profits can be enhanced by eliminating certain costs associated with products in the later stages of the product life cycle, as well as by increasing the productivity of the resources released when older products are phased out. Hence, elimination of products is a strategic move that product managers should consider. The products may either be dropped entirely or be replaced by other products that better satisfy changing market requirements. Marketing managers should devote systematic attention to the elimination of products that are no longer profitable, although this is sometimes a painful process necessitating the realignment of company personnel and other assets. Every organization works with a limited pool of talent and resources. Expending these on products that are in the final periods of the decline stage detracts from efforts to pursue new opportunities.

focus on
global competition

Honda   Sometimes we are too close to our own culture. Sometimes it takes a person from another culture to see how to improve product quality.

Do you know what car manufacturer was the first to install coin trays in its cars? It was Honda. The founder of Honda, on his first visit to the United States, found it difficult to find change quickly for the automatic machines on parkway toll booths. Most Americans do not give a second's thought to this minor annoyance. However, as a newcomer to the country, the Honda executive had a different viewpoint. He saw it as a problem that an automobile maker could help solve.[17]

Ethical Considerations Associated with Product Strategy

When product strategy is viewed from a macromarketing perspective, it becomes apparent that marketers have certain responsibilities. For example, many laws require that marketers be accountable to customers, competitors, and the general public. This section discusses consumers' right to safety, their right to be informed, and their concerns about quality of life and ecology. It also addresses the issue of product obsolescence.

THE RIGHT TO SAFETY

Consumers have many expectations when they buy a product. They want it to work properly, to last a certain amount of time, and so on. But probably the most basic consumer expectation is that a product will be safe. Although most of us are willing to take certain reasonable risks, we do not want our use of a product to place us unnecessarily in danger.

The makers of Sudafed 12-hour capsules faced a safety problem when some of that product was found to contain deadly cyanide. The manufacturer did not place the cyanide in the capsules. However, was the company negligent in failing to package Sudafed in tamper-proof bottles so that no one else could put poison in the capsules? Should ketchup, mayonnaise, and milk all be in tamper-proof containers to guard against any similar attempts?

Clearly some reasonable risks must be taken. Most would agree, however, that consumers should be protected against products that are hazardous to life or health. The modern emphasis on the **right to safety** is a move away from *caveat emptor* ("let the buyer beware") to a philosophy that holds sellers responsible for their actions.

Right to safety
The right to expect the products one purchases to be free from unnecessary dangers. This is a right to which consumers assume they are entitled.

THE RIGHT TO BE INFORMED

In 1994, the Food and Drug Administration said that Calegene Incorporated's genetically engineered "Flavr Savr" tomato gene is considered a safe food additive. Critics, who contend the new genes that go into these tomatoes may be medically and environmentally unsafe, want genetically engineered tomatoes to be labeled. They want the **right to be informed.**

Most would concur that the consumer should not be exposed to grossly misleading information, deceptive advertising, fraudulent labeling, or other deceitful practices. The consumer has the right to be given the facts needed to make an informed choice. The right to be informed is reflected in laws and practices involving the inclusion on labels of such things as nutritional content, product content, country of origin, and quality. Requirements relating to truth in lending and package design also point out the importance of this right.

Right to be informed
The consumer's right to have access to the information required to make an intelligent choice from among the available products.

QUALITY OF LIFE AND ECOLOGY

As the United States, Canada, and certain other nations have become more affluent, the values of their citizens have changed. People are increasingly concerned with **quality of life.** This term, although difficult to define precisely, reflects a lessening concern with being economically well-off and an increasing concern with well-being.

This shift translates into a feeling on the part of consumers that organizations should be expected to be more than economically efficient. Customers call on business organizations also to preserve the environment and to conserve natural resources.

Issues of quality of life spring from the idea that citizens have certain rights that no organization can be permitted to violate. Meeting quality-of-life expectations while fulfilling other missions has caused organizations many problems. Yet if the demands of consumers—most of whom are interested in both quality-of-life

Quality of life
The degree to which people in a society feel a sense of well-being.

issues and the demands of the law—are to be met, organizations must address these expectations.

A major quality-of-life issue involves ecology and the protection of the environment. Many people believe that organizations, as important members of society, have a responsibility not to tamper with or damage the environment. However, this issue is complex, because people want other things as well. Environmental issues are loaded with trade-offs:

- People want low-priced electricity. Yet marketers of electric power are told that nuclear plants are disruptive to ecosystems and very dangerous. And many people do not want electric companies to burn coal in order to generate electricity, because burning causes air pollution. Coal mining too can create pollution and can leave a land area permanently scarred.
- Nonreturnable cans and bottles create litter problems and damage the environment in other ways. But people do not like the bother and expense associated with returnables and often just throw them away.
- People want clean air, but they do not want to car-pool or take buses to work.

That marketing has a social responsibility to preserve the environment is obvious. What is not obvious is how that responsibility will be met. Who will pay—in dollars and inconvenience—for a cleaner environment? Are consumers willing to pay higher prices for products that reduce pollution? Does society place a higher value on lower-priced automobiles or on clean air?

A cleaner environment can be achieved in part through producers' efforts to recycle waste products to make new products. Recycling efforts by both businesses and individual consumers can reduce trash and litter and conserve natural resources.

PRODUCT OBSOLESCENCE

The issue of **product obsolescence**—which occurs when an existing product becomes out of date because of the introduction of a new product—is another ethical concern. Some critics have said it is inappropriate for marketers to strive to make existing products obsolete, or out of date—especially when the obsolescence is related to a change in fashion rather than technology.

To be sure, no product lasts forever. When a product breaks down because of wear and tear, as when a lawn mower stops working after six years, the problem is **physical obsolescence. Planned obsolescence** is more controversial. Because new products yield the greatest profits, marketers plan product obsolescence to help maintain an adequate profit level and ensure corporate survival. Many products, then, are designed not to last a long time.

Although it may sound paradoxical, this planned obsolescence is generally an attempt to satisfy consumer needs. For most consumers, purchasing a $450 lawn mower that lasts for six summers is preferable to spending $1,900 for one that lasts 30 years. Furthermore, individuals in our culture find new styles of apparel, extra gadgets on appliances, and the latest automobile models more attractive. Although these style changes may not improve the performance of a product, they satisfy a number of psychological and social needs.

Product obsolescence
The process by which an existing product goes out of date because of the introduction of a new product.

Physical obsolescence
The breakdown of a product due to wear and tear.

Planned obsolescence
The practice of purposely causing existing products to go out of date by introducing new products at frequent intervals.

Marketers of haute couture are sometimes criticized for planning fashion obsolescence.

Product obsolescence is part of a broader issue that has been called the consumer's **right to choose** within a free enterprise system. Some argue that planned obsolescence violates consumers' right to have alternatives from which to choose; they suggest that consumers are being manipulated. Others argue that although the macromarketing system has occasionally failed to observe consumers' right to choose, if a poor product is offered or if a product becomes obsolete unnecessarily, competitors usually take advantage of the situation by offering those products demanded by consumers.

The free enterprise system, with rare exception, does serve the consumer's right to choose, and serves it well. The consumer's right to choose is interrelated with the need for competition in a free market. The Interstate Commerce Commission Act, the Sherman Act, the Clayton Act, the Federal Trade Commission Act, the Robinson-Patman Act, the Wheeler-Lea Act, and the Celler amendment to the Clayton Act all protect consumer choice. Each of these acts has been discussed elsewhere in this book.

Right to choose
The consumer's right to have viable alternatives from which to choose.

summary

Products differ in their degree of newness and in their chance of succeeding in the marketplace. Marketers must understand what is involved in developing and introducing new products. They must also understand the product life cycle and plan strategies to enable their products to succeed throughout the life cycle.

1   *Define product newness, and explain the chances of success and failure for new products.*
Managers and consumers view newness differently. Managers classify new products on the basis of newness to the company and newness to the market. Consumers distinguish products on a newness continuum that includes discontinuous innovations, dynamically continuous innovations, and continuous innovations. A new product's chances for commercial success are generally low. The failure rate is ordinarily greater for consumer products than for organizational goods, because the consumer market is more dynamic and organizational buyers are better able than consumers to express their needs to marketers.

2   *Identify general characteristics of successful new products.*
Five characteristics influence a new product's chances for success in the marketplace: (1) relative advantage, in the form of a clear-cut improvement over existing products; (2) compatibility with existing consumption and usage patterns; (3) trialability, which allows buyers to test the new product with little effort or risk; (4) observability, which allows buyers to see and understand the product's advantages over existing products; and (5) product simplicity, which allows the consumer to understand and operate the product.

3   *Characterize the stages of new product development.*
New product development involves five processes: (1) idea generation, the search for a new idea; (2) screening, the evaluation of an idea's suitability to the organization and target markets; (3) business analysis, the detailed study and testing of the new idea; (4) development, the construction and testing of the actual product; and (5) commercialization, the full-scale production and marketing of the new product.

4   *Identify some of the most common reasons for new product failures.*
Some of the most common reasons for new product failures are insufficient product superiority, inferior or inadequate planning, poor execution, technical problems, and poor timing.

5   *Describe the product life cycle, and characterize its stages.*
The product life cycle charts the sales history of a product from introduction to withdrawal. The life-cycle stages are introduction, growth, maturity, and decline. The introduction stage is characterized by large expenditures, an intensive marketing effort, and low profits. In this stage, the marketer must generate product awareness and create channels of distribution. The growth stage involves large expenditures and increasing competition, as well as rapid

sales growth. The marketer must create brand preferences and promote differential features. During the maturity stage, sales growth decreases, reflecting intense competition. The goal is to maintain or expand market share. Decreasing profits and decreasing expenditures mark the decline stage. Introducing a new and improved product may reverse declines in sales, but termination is typically the final phase.

6 *Describe the new product diffusion process, and list the groups of adopters to which marketers must direct their appeals.*

Not all buyers adopt a new product at the same time. The path is blazed by innovators, followed by early adopters, members of the early and late majorities, and finally laggards. Members of the first groups tend to be younger, more adventurous, better educated, and wealthier than members of later groups. Each group has characteristics and concerns that the marketer must address.

7 *Identify strategies for modifying existing products.*

Developing strategies for modifying existing products is an important aspect of product management. These strategies include cost reduction, repositioning, and total quality management. Decisions to modify products are typically influenced by the degree of competition in the marketplace and by changes in the external environment.

8 *Explain the total quality management process for goods and services.*

Total quality management programs measure quality from the customer's perspective and adjust product strategies accordingly. Implementing a total quality management strategy involves discovering what customers want, establishing quantitative measures to serve as benchmarks, establishing the quality improvement process within the organization, measuring customer satisfaction with the improvements, and so on, in a continuous process of quality improvement.

9 *Understand how marketers manage product lines.*

The product line strategy, which attempts to match product items to markets, is influenced by the diversity of the market and the resources available to the company. Marketers must ask themselves how many variations of a product can be offered before the extra customer satisfaction achieved is no longer worth the expense to the company.

10 *Identify some ethical questions associated with product strategy.*

Ethical issues associated with product strategy include those involving consumers' right to safety, consumers' right to be informed, and quality of life. The issue of whether product obsolescence, and especially planned obsolescence, is ethical is part of the broader issue of consumers' right to choose.

key terms

new product (p. 293)
discontinuous innovation (p. 294)
dynamically continuous innovation (p. 295)
continuous innovation (p. 295)
relative advantage (p. 296)
trialability (p. 297)
trial sampling (p. 297)
divisibility (p. 297)
observability (p. 298)
simplicity of usage (p. 298)
idea generation stage (p. 298)
screening stage (p. 300)
business analysis stage (p. 301)
development stage (p. 301)
concept testing (p. 301)
test marketing (p. 302)
commercialization (p. 303)
product life cycle (p. 304)
introduction stage (p. 305)

growth stage (p. 307)
maturity stage (p. 307)
decline stage (p. 309)
adoption process (p. 312)
diffusion process (p. 312)
innovator (p. 313)
early adopter (p. 313)
early majority (p. 314)
late majority (p. 314)
laggard (p. 314)
nonadopter (p. 314)
product modification (p. 315)
cost reduction strategy (p. 316)
repositioning strategy (p. 316)
total quality management strategy (p. 316)
product enhancement (p. 317)
product design (p. 319)
style (p. 320)
fashion (p. 320)

fad (p. 320)
product line strategy (p. 321)
full-line, or deep-line, strategy (p. 321)
limited-line strategy (p. 321)
single-product strategy (p. 321)
product line extension (p. 321)
product category extension (p. 321)
brand extension (p. 321)
cannibalize (p. 322)
flanker brand (p. 322)
enhanced model (p. 322)
globalization strategy (p. 323)
customization strategy (p. 323)
right to safety (p. 325)
right to be informed (p. 325)
quality of life (p. 325)
product obsolescence (p. 326)
physical obsolescence (p. 326)
planned obsolescence (p. 326)
right to choose (p. 327)

questions for review & critical thinking

1. What is your definition of a new product?
2. Classify the type of innovation represented by each of the following products.
   a. A personal communication device that combines a cellular phone, a pager, and storage spaces for keys and credit cards
   b. An identity checker for use by banks and organizations that need to control who enters the premises. The product verifies a person's identity in seconds, using magnetically coded cards and electronic sensors to check people's fingerprints.
   c. A new, aerodynamically designed car that has a wedge-shaped body with low wind resistance
3. For the products in question 2, identify salient product features that might speed acceptance.
4. Identify the steps in the new product development process. What takes place in each?
5. What are the main reasons new products fail?
6. What are the benefits and limitations of test marketing?
7. At what stage of the product life cycle would you place each of the following products?
   a. Cigars
   b. Coffee
   c. Digital personal assistants (stylus-activated personal computers)
   d. Theme amusement parks
   e. Tennis balls
   f. Slide rules
8. Trace the product life cycle for a particular brand, such as the Sony compact disc player.
9. Identify some typical marketing mix strategies used during each stage of the product life cycle.
10. Does marketing grow in importance as a product matures and moves from the introductory stage through the growth stage and into the maturity stage? Explain.
11. What are the most prominent characteristics of each adopter group in the diffusion process?
12. What guidelines would you suggest for rejuvenating old brands in the mature stage of the product life cycle?
13. How important is product quality to being competitive around the world?
14. Name some companies that have recently implemented cost reduction strategies. Are such strategies always incompatible with product quality strategies?
15. How important is brand equity to a line extension strategy?
16. What are the pitfalls of a brand extension strategy that, for example, extends a name from a hair spray product to a facial cream?
17. Some home builders are marketing houses with cable setups so that new owners can install computer terminals. What product strategy does this reflect?
18. SNOT (Super Nauseating Obnoxious Treat), Wurmz 'n Dirt, and Bubble Tongue are names of some recently introduced novelty candy items. Now it's your turn to come up with some new ones. Form groups as directed by your instructor.

    Step 1: Take 10 minutes to do some brainstorming to generate new product ideas for novelty candies. Do not evaluate the ideas; just generate as many as you can.

    Step 2: In the next 10-minute period, evaluate the ideas and decide which products should be considered for business analysis.

    Step 3: Discuss as a class how the groups' ideas emerged and whether each group was able to come to a consensus about which products were best.

marketing plan—right or wrong?

1. Windex NoDrip is a new product that is formulated not to drip when sprayed on a glass surface. The liquid stays where the user sprays.
2. In Japan, Sharp Corporation introduced a high-speed but low-capacity (6.6-pound-load) washer that can go though the wash cycle in 10 minutes.
3. Bioré Pore Pack is a box of lotion-covered sheets that users press on the nose to remove dirt and other deposits.

internet insights

exercises

1. Go to www.nabisco.ca and learn what new products are being offered by Nabisco Canada. Then go to www.nabisco.com to see what's new in the United States. Write a short statement comparing and contrasting the new products.
2. Go to www.mmm.com/quiz and take the 3M Innovation Quiz for long-term business strategy. How well did you score?

address book (useful urls)

New Product News	www.newproductnews.com
Inc. Magazine's Guide to Business Technology	www.inc.com/technology

ethically right or wrong?

Coffee is a product in the mature stage of its life cycle. It has been served for hundreds of years.

McDonald's franchisees are required to prepare coffee at very high temperatures because McDonald's coffee consultants say hot temperatures are necessary to fully extract the flavor during brewing. McDonald's operations and training manual says coffee must be brewed at 195 to 205 degrees and held at 180 to 190 degrees for optimal taste. Coffee made at home is normally 135 to 140 degrees.

An Albuquerque woman bought a 49-cent cup of coffee at the drive-thru window of a McDonald's and, while removing the lid from the top of the foam cup to add cream and sugar, spilled it, causing third-degree burns of the groin, inner thighs, and buttocks. She was in the hospital for over a week. Her lawsuit claimed the coffee was "defective" because it was so hot.

A jury awarded $2.9 million to the woman, who claimed McDonald's Corporation served dangerously hot coffee.[18]

QUESTIONS

1. If you had been on the jury for this case, what stand would you have taken?
2. If you owned a fast-food franchise other than McDonald's, at what temperature would you serve your coffee?

TAKE A STAND

1. What arguments are given by critics who say that it is inappropriate for marketers to strive to make perfectly good products obsolete?
2. Pet owners complain that a new flea and tick spray is making their dogs sick. Should the marketer take the product off the market?
3. A pajama manufacturer has developed a new fire-resistant chemical that will not wash out of children's pajamas until they have been washed more than 100 times. Should the pajamas be marketed as fire resistant?
4. A tampon manufacturer, after developing and marketing a superabsorbent product, learned that use of the tampon was related to a serious disease. The company immediately withdrew the product from the market. Should the

company be liable for damages suffered by consumers who used the product before it was taken off the market?

5. In the United States, packaged goods meant to be ingested by consumers must be approved by the Food and Drug Administration before they can be marketed. A multinational company, which has conducted its own laboratory test on a new over-the-counter drug, has not received approval from the FDA to market the drug in the United States. It plans to market the drug in several Asian countries where there are no such requirements for government approval. Is this approach socially responsible?

6. Marketers introduce more than ten new consumer package goods products every year. One year, 31 baby foods, 123 breakfast cereals, and 1,143 beverages were introduced. Does society need all these new products?

7. Is it ethical to initiate a cost-reduction strategy that requires closing a U.S. factory and opening a factory in an underdeveloped nation?

8. Do consumers really need flanker brands and line extensions?

10-1 video case

Etec

Etec was founded by an inventor and a former police officer. The company markets AutoCite, which is short for Automatic Citation Issuance System. Using this handheld computer and printing device, a police officer can write and record traffic violations much more efficiently. Today, AutoCite is used by police departments in more than 350 cities, municipalities, and college campuses. However, Etec sold only three units in its first 2 years of operation.

AutoCite is durable and works in all types of weather. A police officer who gives multiple tickets in a given location does not have to reprogram location information into the AutoCite. This allows the officer to produce more tickets in a given time period.

QUESTIONS
1. What are AutoCite's primary product characteristics and auxiliary dimensions?
2. How important are customer service and customer training for a product such as AutoCite?
3. In what stage of the product life cycle is AutoCite.
4. Products in the electronic industry often become obsolete because of new technology. How should AutoCite's marketing strategy deal with the issue of obsolescence?

vid**case**

Spanier & Bourne Sailmaker   *Focus on Small Business*

video case 10-2

A pleasure sail from New Zealand to the New Hebrides Islands in 1978 came to an abrupt end for Geoff Bourne and Barry Spanier. Their boat, a 38-foot one-master that Spanier had built, was destroyed in a violent storm, and they were shipwrecked on a small island. It took 22 days to get transport off the island. In a way, the misfortune made the fortunes of two men who, after getting out of college in California, had wandered from job to job—most connected with sailing—while taking lots of time off. The shipwreck left Spanier broke and Bourne with no plans. It seemed a time to reenter the world of employment.

From a visit to Maui, Spanier knew there were many charter sailboats there, but no sailmakers. With $10,000 of starting capital, the friends rented a loft and went into business. They had sailmaking experience and talent, and they soon had numerous customers in Maui's charter fleet.

In 1980 a monster storm hit Maui, wrecking many boats. Spanier & Bourne's customer base was wiped out. For some time to come, the charter skippers wouldn't be sailing or buying sails, just salvaging what they could.

Luckily, some California windsurfers, sailing in Maui's Hookipa area, brought in sails for repairs. "We suggested that we could improve on the design and construction of their rigs," Spanier says. The firm became so popular with windsurfers that international sailboard brands asked for its services. Later the company became the exclusive research and development facility for a major manufacturer of sailboards and other windsurfing equipment. Spanier & Bourne, which had two employees, hired more and invested in tools and material.

Things went swimmingly until, in 1986, the sailboard manufacturer lost its largest customer and in turn cut Spanier & Bourne's royalties. Unsure of the future, the firm concentrated on increasing its custom sail output—and on something new.

Spanier & Bourne applied the computer to sailmaking. With the aid of a skilled programmer, they developed a computerized system for designing windsurfing sails. The system cut costs and spurred sales by speeding design changes.

In the past few years, defense spending cutbacks have allowed competitors to hire many talented people. There has been a technological explosion as light but strong aerospace materials have been used in sailing.

But storm survivors Spanier and Bourne, who began using aerospace materials in 1983, will be taking the next steps first, they say. Their competitors will have to run just to keep up.[19]

QUESTIONS

1. Discuss the product life cycle for sails.
2. Spanier & Bourne is a small business. How does its new product development process differ from that of a large corporation?
3. How important are technology and the production process in the development of Spanier & Bourne's products?
4. What steps would Spanier & Bourne need to take to implement a total quality management program?

Water Joe—Johnny Beverages Inc.

First there was water. Then there was coffee.

Now, two of the hottest products in the beverage industry have been merged. The result is called caffeinated water.

Water Joe, bottled in Crivitz, Wisconsin, by Nicolet Forest Bottling Co., went on the market in Milwaukee, Madison, and Chicago.

The product, which tastes like water, sells for 89 to 99 cents per half-liter bottle. The amount of caffeine in the water equals that in one cup of coffee.

"It's really meeting all of our expectations," says Rick Nap, a representative for Nicolet in Wisconsin. "The key thing we want consumers to realize is it's a caffeine alternative in a healthier format."

David Marcheschi, now a 29-year-old real estate broker in Chicago, came up with the idea of putting caffeine in water when he was trying to stay awake while studying at Arizona State University. He found a chemist who created the proper formula, and Marcheschi then created a company, Johnny Beverages Inc., to market the concept.

Chris Connor, a 34-year-old furniture company owner, joined Marcheschi to help sell the idea. They spent a year promoting the concept before Nicolet Forest joined the project. The 8-year-old company helps finance Water Joe's production and distribution, but neither side will disclose the investment.

Water Joe's target market is working people and students, both of whom need a shot of caffeine at times.

The drink doesn't have the bitter taste and staining attributed to coffee, Marcheschi says.

His challenge is to distinguish Water Joe from the 50 or so bottled water labels that already crowd supermarket shelves. His solution: Put the drink closer to coffee items on store shelves.

That kind of talk gives pause to people in the coffee industry. "What?" asked Robert Nelson, president of the National Coffee Association of America, when told about the product. He couldn't recall a drink quite like it, then added that it seemed "twisted." "People don't just drink coffee for the caffeine," he said. "They drink it for the overall experience of coffee, which includes aroma and taste."[20]

QUESTIONS

1. In your opinion, what type of new product is Water Joe—if it is really a new product at all?
2. What should the marketing objectives for Water Joe be at this point in the product life cycle?
3. Evaluate the brand name Water Joe.
4. Summarize the product strategy for Water Joe, as it is described in this case. Can the strategy be enhanced?

chapter
11

Strategies for Services and Relationship Marketing

LEARNING OBJECTIVES

After you have studied this chapter, you will be able to:

Define service in its technical, specific sense.

1

Explain the four basic characteristics of services.

2

Understand demand management strategies.

3

Describe the strategies of standardization and customization.

4

Name some of the variables used to classify services.

5

(continued on next page)

the crash scene at the intersection of 40th Street and 26th Avenue in Tampa is chaotic and tense. The two cars are bent and battered. Their drivers and passengers are not bleeding, but they are shaken up and scared. Just minutes after the collision, a young man dressed in a polo shirt, khakis, and wingtips arrives on the scene to assume command. Bearing a clipboard, a camera, a cassette recorder, and an air of competence, Lance Edgy, 26, calms the victims and advises them on medical care, repair shops, police reports, and legal procedures. Edgy is not a cop or a lawyer or a good Samaritan. He is a senior claims representative for Progressive Corporation, an insurance company that specializes in high-risk drivers, high-octane profits—and exceptional service.

Edgy invites William McAllister, Progressive's policyholder, into an air-conditioned van equipped with comfortable chairs, a desk, and two cellular phones. Even before the tow trucks have cleared away the wreckage, Edgy is offering this client a set-tlement for the market value of his totaled 1988 Mercury Topaz. McAllister, who does not appear to have been at fault in this accident, is amazed by Progressive's alacrity: "This is great—someone coming right out here and taking charge. I didn't expect it at all."

Welcome to the front line of the new American economy, where service—bold, fast, unexpected, innovative, and customized—is the ultimate strategic imperative, a business challenge that has profound implications for the way business people manage companies, hire employees, develop careers, and craft policies.

WELCOME TO THE FRONT LINE OF THE NEW AMERICAN ECONOMY, WHERE SERVICE— BOLD, FAST, UNEXPECTED, INNOVATIVE, AND CUSTOMIZED—IS THE ULTIMATE STRATEGIC IMPERATIVE.

It matters not whether a company creates something you can touch, such as a computer, a toaster, or a machine tool, or something you can only experience, such as insurance coverage, an airplane ride, or a telephone call. What counts most is the service built into that something—the way the product is designed and delivered, billed and bundled, explained and installed, repaired and renewed.[1]

One of the Progressive Corporation's strategies for marketing its insurance service is to enhance its relationship with individual customers. This chapter discusses strategies for marketing services and building beneficial relationships. It first defines service and describes the characteristics of services. After discussing other issues related to services and service quality, it goes on to cover the marketing of goods with a high service component. Finally, it discusses how to develop and maintain long-term relationships with customers, suppliers, intermediaries, and employees.

Progressive Corporation
www.auto-insurance.com

What Is a Service?

Chapter 9 defined a product as a bundle of satisfactions. This definition holds as well for services as for tangible goods. However, to be more specific, a **service** is an instrumental activity performed for a consumer or a consummatory activity involving consumer participation in, but not ownership of, an organization's products or facilities.

This definition points out that the reason for purchasing one service may be very different from the reason for purchasing another service. Consumers purchase *instrumental services*—typically, work performed by others—to achieve a goal without being directly involved in the task. For example, a lawn care company provides an instrumental service. In contrast, a store that rents videotapes of movies provides a *consummatory service;* the consumer is directly involved and immediately gratified by use of the service. A skiing lesson may be both an instrumental and a consummatory service. The ski instructor performs an instructional task for the student, and the student receives gratification as the service is consumed.

Service
A task or activity performed for a buyer or an intangible that cannot be handled or examined before purchase.

The Characteristics of Services

Both instrumental and consummatory services have the following characteristics: (1) intangibility, (2) perishability, (3) inseparability, and (4) variability. The many marketing strategies associated with each of these service characteristics are discussed in this section.

INTANGIBILITY

Most services are intangible, even though their production may be linked to a tangible product (the transportation service an airline provides is tied to its fleet of airplanes, renting a videotaped movie is tied to the temporary usage of the videocassette, and so on). The element of intangibility makes the marketing of services different from the marketing of tangible goods. **Intangibility** means that buyers cannot see, feel, smell, hear, or taste before they conclude an exchange agreement with a seller. Because of this intangibility, consumers may misunderstand the exact nature of a service. For most of us, something that is intangible is more difficult to grasp than something that is tangible. Evaluating the quality of something intangible is difficult. To help consumers understand and evaluate the nature of their services, marketers often employ a marketing strategy to make the intangible tangible.

It can be argued that because customers cannot taste, feel, smell, or watch a product in operation in advance, they purchase promises of

Intangibility
The characteristic of services referring to the customer's inability to see, hear, smell, feel, or taste the service product.

Customers—who cannot taste, feel, or smell an intangible service in advance—purchase promises of satisfaction. The Chicago Cubs organization makes its service tangible by stressing symbolic clues, such as the familiar entrance to the "friendly confines" of Wrigley Field, and by providing supplemental tangible evidence, such as free baseball caps on special promotional days.

www.cubs.com

Demand management, then, involves managing the supply of a service so that it is in line with demand for the service. For example, restaurants often hire extra part-time employees to work during peak times or offer price reductions during slow times to even out demand.[5] Restaurant Daniel is among New York's most popular restaurants. Dinner reservations are in great demand because of its excellent service as well as its innovative cuisine. The restaurant has discreetly placed video cameras in the dining areas so that waiters and kitchen personnel can check monitors to determine exactly when guests are ready for their next course. Guests are delighted with the excellent service, and the restaurant efficiently manages demand.

Because service marketers can't store their products for sale at some other time, they must pay special attention to price adjustments. When prices fall, a dentist cannot warehouse her services until prices rise again. A hotel owner in Florida cannot suspend operations—at least not without considerable cost—while waiting for customers to return during the winter season. The service marketer must keep busy and, unlike the marketer of goods, cannot keep busy by building inventory. Pricing strategy provides an important tool for leveling the service marketer's demand.

To adjust for losses due to perishability, service marketers often implement **two-part pricing.** The user of the service pays two prices: the fixed fee (for example, a membership initiation fee) plus a variable usage fee (for example, a fee for tennis court time). Another strategy, used by many hotels, restaurants, and airlines, is to sell services in advance or require reservations to avoid problems associated with perishability. Airlines are known for overbooking flights because not all travelers are on time for their flights. When everyone does show up, the airlines offer free tickets or a monetary incentive to individuals willing to take an alternative flight. Selling services in advance and requiring reservations can be important aspects of a demand management strategy. Additional aspects of demand management are discussed later in this section in relation to intangibility.

INSEPARABILITY

In marketing exchanges of tangible goods, the producers (for example, industrial engineers or assembly line workers) need not come in direct contact with those who buy the goods. Because it is possible to separate production from consumption in exchanges of tangible products, distinct selling and marketing departments evolved naturally to handle the activities aimed at consummating these exchanges.

This type of separation is often impossible in marketing intangible services. In many cases, services are inseparable from their producers. **Inseparability** means that producer and consumer must be present in the same place at the same time for the

Two-part pricing
A pricing strategy in which the marketer charges a fixed fee plus a variable usage fee, in order to adjust for losses resulting from a service's perishability.

Inseparability
A characteristic of services referring to the fact that production often is not distinct from consumption of a service—that is, the producer and the consumer of a service must be together in order for a transaction to occur.

Leo Burnett, the founder of a major advertising agency, said, "All our assets go down the elevator every evening." He was referring to the fact that the service of creating promotional ideas and producing advertising is inseparable from those who work in an advertising agency.

www.leoburnett.com

service transaction to occur. Inseparability changes the sequence of events usually associated with the exchange of a product. In goods marketing, the product is first produced, then sold, and then consumed. Although some goods are not produced until a firm order has been received (specialty robots or custom-tailored dresses, for instance), in most cases producers of tangibles can produce, show, or display their

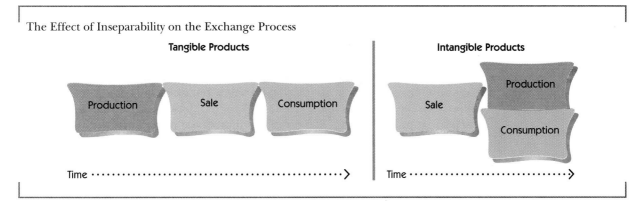

The Effect of Inseparability on the Exchange Process

Tangible Products — Production → Sale → Consumption — Time ·····>

Intangible Products — Sale → Production/Consumption — Time ·····>

offerings. Suppose, however, a patient is to be operated on by a surgeon. Delivering the promised service requires the simultaneous presence of both surgeon and patient. Should some problem prevent either from being present, the other is likely to suffer. If the surgeon does not appear, the patient will have to continue to suffer with his or her problem for an additional time or allow an unfamiliar surgeon to perform the operation. Conversely, if the patient fails to show up for the operation, the surgeon is left with unproductive time and therefore may lose some income. Exhibit 11-1 shows how the order of events in a typical service exchange differs from that in a typical exchange of goods.

Essentially, inseparability constrains the flexibility that service suppliers have in designing their offerings, because the amount of service they can produce depends largely on the amount of time they have available. Neither a surgeon nor a hairdresser nor a rock singer can squeeze more than a certain number of operations, haircuts, or live concerts into a given day or month.

For many services, the consumer actively participates in the production process. At a travel agency, for example, the agent interacts with the customer to make a reservation that suits the customer's desires. Because inseparability often demands such personal contact between buyer and seller, it can cause many distribution problems. Thus, most channels of distribution for services are direct channels in which the service provider markets the product directly to the consumer or organizational user. An accountant, for example, deals directly with a client. (However, it is possible to have intermediaries in the distribution of a service. We discuss such intermediaries in Chapter 12.)

Because of the element of inseparability, service organizations have been extremely production-oriented in their approach to

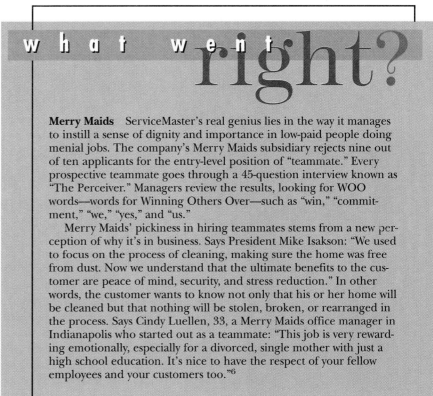

what went right?

Merry Maids ServiceMaster's real genius lies in the way it manages to instill a sense of dignity and importance in low-paid people doing menial jobs. The company's Merry Maids subsidiary rejects nine out of ten applicants for the entry-level position of "teammate." Every prospective teammate goes through a 45-question interview known as "The Perceiver." Managers review the results, looking for WOO words—words for Winning Others Over—such as "win," "commitment," "we," "yes," and "us."

Merry Maids' pickiness in hiring teammates stems from a new perception of why it's in business. Says President Mike Isakson: "We used to focus on the process of cleaning, making sure the home was free from dust. Now we understand that the ultimate benefits to the customer are peace of mind, security, and stress reduction." In other words, the customer wants to know not only that his or her home will be cleaned but that nothing will be stolen, broken, or rearranged in the process. Says Cindy Luellen, 33, a Merry Maids office manager in Indianapolis who started out as a teammate: "This job is very rewarding emotionally, especially for a divorced, single mother with just a high school education. It's nice to have the respect of your fellow employees and your customers too."[6]

distribution. For instance, traditionally hospitals had a single location and their clients were expected to visit the "factory." Today, under more competitive conditions, hospital administrators realize the need for convenient, multiple locations, emergency care centers, and ambulatory care centers that supplement the main hospital. Similarly, state universities traditionally were located in small rural towns, and students would come to the service facility to purchase the service. Today, however, universities offer extension programs, distance learning in remote classrooms, telecommunications via satellite, and classes in urban business centers. Banks no longer have a single place of business but offer many locations as well as automatic teller services.

Having a production orientation means that service providers tend to see themselves more as creators or producers of an offering than as its marketers. They tend to accent the pride, technical difficulties, and other elements involved in production instead of understanding the need to satisfy consumers. In other words, many service providers are production-oriented rather than customer-oriented. The What Went Right? feature describes one service provider that understands consumers' concerns and uses team building to satisfy the demand in the marketplace.

Overcoming this orientation problem leads to a strategy in which the production process is considered a marketing activity. Thus, managing personnel becomes a marketing activity, because the standards for personnel effectiveness and efficiency must be based on consumers' perceptions, not on assembly-line standards.

Most services are delivered by people. The quality of the contact between the customers and frontline staff provides the competitive edge, so employees are the key to success. The service marketer must therefore consider employees as part of the service offering. The doctor's bedside manner and the personality of a lawyer's receptionist are part of the product offered to consumers. Competent employees must be hired and trained so that they perform the service properly. Service employees need to know the organization's marketing goals and be trained to serve well and respond to any complaints. In short, they must be trained to assure consumer satisfaction.

VARIABILITY

Variability
The characteristic of services referring to the fact that services are heterogeneous—that is, the quality of delivered services can vary widely.

Because many intangible offerings are closely tied to the supplier's personal performance, there can be great **variability,** or heterogeneity, among the services provided. Standardizing services—that is, reducing service heterogeneity—is difficult. It is not possible to prescribe and deliver equal amounts of smiling by all employees at a service outlet, medical care of equal quality by several doctors at the same time, or even medical care of equal quality by the same doctor all the time. When a customer buys a service—say, in the form of an airline ticket—the customer can know only in a very general way what to expect from the pilot and flight attendants; knowing precisely what to expect ahead of time is impossible. Variability leads service marketers to choose one of two alternative strategies: standardization or customization.

The Strategy of Standardization Because of the heterogeneous nature of services, mass marketers may choose a strategy to standardize the service offered. For example, although a hotel room at the Hyatt Regency in San Francisco may be slightly different from a hotel room in the San Antonio Hyatt Regency, the company has made a great attempt to standardize its services. At McDonald's restaurants, all customers receive nearly the same courteous treatment.

The strategy of standardization emphasizes careful selection of personnel and extensive personnel training. In certain situations, it is possible to standardize services by using machines. Thus, automated car washes and electronic funds transfer systems ensure that service quality does not vary.

Standardization also emphasizes marketing research to discover if services fall below established standards. We will discuss the monitoring of service quality and customer satisfaction later in this chapter.

CHARACTERISTIC	PROBLEM(S)	POSSIBLE RESPONSE(S)
Intangibility	Customer cannot see or otherwise physically sense the product.	Associate service with a tangible product; use marketer's reputation or other clues to communicate the service's worth.
Perishability	Product cannot be stored; opportunity to sell or buy services is quickly lost.	Use demand forecasting and management of demand (for example, seasonal pricing).
Inseparability	Buyer and seller must both be present for exchange to occur; service producer is also a marketer.	Because direct distribution is nearly inevitable, locate near purchasers; train service providers to deal with customers.
Variability	Quality of delivered service can vary widely.	Standardize the service and its delivery to minimize variances; customize the service to best fit individual buyers.

The Strategy of Customization   In contrast to standardization, a customization strategy requires modifying or customizing a service for each individual customer. Such services are not mass produced but individualized. A chartered yacht may visit any destination chosen by the customer. A health club's fitness program may be customized to suit the customer's desires and individual physical condition.

We have discussed some major service-related problems and possible strategic responses for each of the four general characteristics of services. Exhibit 11-2 summarizes this information.

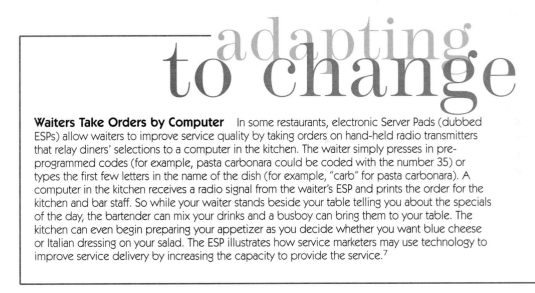

adapting to change

Waiters Take Orders by Computer   In some restaurants, electronic Server Pads (dubbed ESPs) allow waiters to improve service quality by taking orders on hand-held radio transmitters that relay diners' selections to a computer in the kitchen. The waiter simply presses in pre-programmed codes (for example, pasta carbonara could be coded with the number 35) or types the first few letters in the name of the dish (for example, "carb" for pasta carbonara). A computer in the kitchen receives a radio signal from the waiter's ESP and prints the order for the kitchen and bar staff. So while your waiter stands beside your table telling you about the specials of the day, the bartender can mix your drinks and a busboy can bring them to your table. The kitchen can even begin preparing your appetizer as you decide whether you want blue cheese or Italian dressing on your salad. The ESP illustrates how service marketers may use technology to improve service delivery by increasing the capacity to provide the service.[7]

The Total Service Product

Chapter 9 explained that a product should be thought of as consisting of a core product and several auxiliary dimensions that create an augmented product. For example, a package can be an important auxiliary dimension of the total product marketed by a manufacturer of consumer goods.

The total product concept applies to goods and services equally well.[8] However, service marketers often face product decisions somewhat different from those facing marketers of goods. Service marketers consider participants, physical evidence, and the process of service delivery to be the key auxiliary dimensions associated with the marketing of their core services.[9]

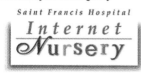

Meet the newest
Member of the Family

Nathaniel Joel S.
Born January 16, 1997
at 11:52 am
Weight 5 lbs. 13 ounces
Parents Melinda and Joel
Delivered by Dr. L. Montgomery

Saint Francis Hospital
Internet
*N*ursery

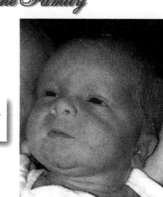

Message

Two presents from God. Mom is holding Nathaniel and Dad is holding Joshua.

Home Page • Special Deliveries • Saint Francis Internet Nursery • Contact Us

Shortly after Nathaniel S. was born, family and friends could see his picture on St. Francis Hospital's Internet Web site. Providing relatives and friends immediate access to new babies' photographs and vital statistics adds extra customer value to St. Francis' maternity service.

www.saintfrancis.com

Hertz, a rental car company, markets the temporary use of a car as its core service product. Transportation is the core benefit of a rental car. But Hertz knows its augmented product is what differentiates it from its competitors, so it carefully manages the auxiliary dimensions just mentioned. The attractiveness, dress, and demeanor of *participants,* such as the rental car counter personnel with whom the customer interacts, are an important part of the marketing mix. *Physical evidence,* which provides tangible symbols of the product concept, is equally important. Such evidence includes a modern counter near the baggage claim area, yellow counter signs displaying the Hertz brand name, covered parking lots, and Hertz Number One membership club cards. The *process of service delivery,* or process, also shapes consumers' perception of the total product. *Process* refers to how a service is delivered, as opposed to the technical activities required for performance of the core service. If the rental car starts and drives without incident, the basic transportation benefit is provided. However, customers also care about the process of renting a car. Do they have to wait in long lines or take a crowded shuttle bus before they are given the car keys? Making product strategy decisions about the process of service delivery involves understanding what happens during the service encounter.

focus on
global competition

British Airways   By looking beyond its core service, air transportation, British Airways redefined its view of what an airline does. British Airways recast its first-class transatlantic service to emphasize what happens on the ground as much as the service in the air. Most airlines want to turn New York–to–London flights into overnight fantasies; passengers simply want to sleep. Responding to this desire in an insightful way, British Airways gives premium fliers the option of dinner on the ground in the first-class lounge. Once they get on board, they can slip into BA pajamas (!) if they wish, put their heads on real pillows, curl up under a duvet, and then enjoy an interruption-free flight. On arrival, this presumably rested bunch can have breakfast, use comfortable dressing rooms and shower stalls, and even have their clothes pressed before they set off for business.[10]

The Service Encounter

A **service encounter** is a period of time during which a consumer interacts with a service provider. Production of a service often requires a great deal of time beyond the service encounter. For example, accountants may spend ten times as many hours

Service encounter
A period during which a consumer interacts with a service provider.

working on a tax return as they do interacting with the client. However, a consumer's evaluation of a service offering often depends on the physical surroundings and the behavior of the frontline employees during the service encounter. An accountant at an income tax preparation service who computed a client's taxes accurately but who smoked a cigarette during the service encounter with the nonsmoking client might find that the client didn't return the next year. The tax work was acceptable, but the smoking was not.

Study after study has shown a large difference between what customers expect during the service encounter and how frontline personnel actually deliver the service. Marketers who stress service quality strive to manage the service encounter because the evaluation of service quality depends so strongly on what takes place during this event.

Managing Service Quality

Evaluating **service quality** involves a comparison of expectations with performance. Consumers who perceive a service to be of high quality believe the service provider matched their expectations. Thus, marketers who wish to deliver high service quality must conform to consumers' service expectations consistently. Customers who receive high-quality service come back again.

In organizations that wish to improve levels of service quality, managers identify customer service needs and plan the level of service quality. These steps lead to specifications for the level of service to be delivered. Frontline personnel are then trained and given the responsibility for delivering high-quality service. These personnel need to be motivated to deliver the service according to the specifications planned by managers. Finally, the results are regularly measured against the standards.

Service quality
The degree to which the performance of a service matches customer expectations; the essential characteristic of a service that indicates its degree of excellence.

Gap Analysis

We have indicated that the effective marketing of services requires that managers learn what customers want and expect during the service encounter. If consumers' expectations do not match the perceived level of service received, a gap is said to exist. This gap is known as the **expected service–perceived service gap.**

Sometimes the difference between expected service quality and perceived service quality results in a negative gap—a fundamental determinant of consumer dissatisfaction. In other situations, consumers get better service than they expected. Avis's rent-a-car business, for example, trains its frontline employees to provide first-rate service. Employees enjoy the freedom to adjust their services to exceed customer expectations. Consider the experience of Ernesto Martinez, a U.S. government employee from El Paso, Texas.

Martinez, accompanied by his boss and a coworker, was standing at an Avis car rental counter in Monterey, California. He couldn't understand why the Avis sales agents were fussing over his license.

Expected service—perceived service gap
The gap between a service consumer's expectations and the person's perception of the level of service received. The gap can be negative or positive.

"Uh-oh," the agent, Suzy Caston, exclaimed after Martinez passed his license across the counter.

"Something is going to have to be done about that," said another.

"Do something," a third agent told Caston.

That day was Martinez's 57th birthday, and Caston did something about it. First, she gave Martinez a free upgrade to the biggest, whitest Cadillac on the Avis lot. Then she tipped off his hotel—a Hyatt Regency—which assigned him to a deluxe room with a king-size bed and a window facing the golf course.

"It's nice to be able to spoil people," says Caston, an Avis employee for eight years. "He was coming out of his skin, he was so excited."

Martinez still hasn't gotten over it. "I've been working for the government for 30 years and I've traveled on my birthday before. But nobody has ever treated me like that," he said. "Thanks to Suzy, it turned out to be a great day. Her gracious act impressed the heck out of a lot of seasoned travelers who thought they'd experienced about everything."[11]

Marketers use **gap analysis** to identify the sources of the consumer's expected service–perceived service gap. Exhibit 11-3 identifies four additional gaps that marketing and management activity influence.

Gap analysis
The type of analysis marketers use to identify the sources of the expected service–perceived service gap.

e   x   h   i   b   11-3

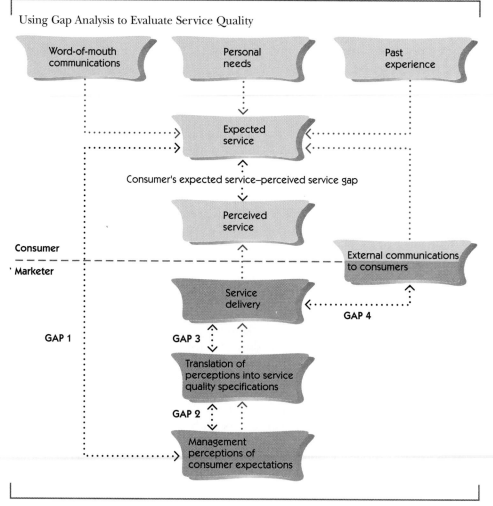

Source: Adapted from A. Parasuraman, Valarie A. Zeithaml, and Leonard L. Berry, "A Conceptual Model of Service Quality and Its Implications for Future Research," *Journal of Marketing,* Fall 1985, pp. 41–50. Reprinted by permission of the American Marketing Association.

Gap 1: A management perception–consumer expectation gap can exist if managers cannot identify or do not understand what aspects of the service encounter are important to consumers. Filling the gap between what customers perceive to be good service and what the company perceives to be good service is an essential aspect of service quality management.

Gap 2: When an unfavorable management perception–service quality specification gap exists, managers know what consumers expect, but the specifications they plan are less than what consumers expect. In other words, managers who should know better plan unacceptable standards for service delivery. This may occur in production-oriented organizations or in organizations that have not been allocated adequate resources.

Gap 3: Service quality specification–service delivery gaps occur when frontline personnel do not perform their tasks according to guidelines. Service managers may improve these situations with training and closer supervision of frontline personnel.

Gap 4: A service delivery–external communications gap can exist if advertising or other external communications promise more than the frontline personnel can deliver. A service marketing strategy, like other marketing strategies, must coordinate all aspects of the marketing mix. To achieve consumer satisfaction, service marketers must deliver what they promise. Marketers also must know what dimensions of the service are most important.

Consumers tend to use the same general criteria to determine the quality of many types of services. Exhibit 11-4 outlines some basic determinants of service quality. Marketing managers may use a list like this as a starting point for identifying service quality gaps. The use of gap analysis helps managers to think of service as a process instead of a series of isolated activities.

Marketing Tangible Goods with a High Service Component

The manager who said "Service is everybody's business" expressed a marketing truism. Even tangible products have intangible elements that enhance consumer satisfaction after the sale. For example, automobile retailers sell highly tangible products that have an extensive service component. How many customers have purchased an automobile only to be unhappy with the service department at the dealership? How many department store customers have been pleased with the

Determinants of Service Quality   e   x   h   i   b   **11-4**

Access	Contact with service personnel is easy. For example, a visit to the dentist does not require a long wait in the waiting room.
Communication	The customer is informed about and understands the service and how much it will cost. For example, the computer technician explains what repairs are needed without using overly technical terms.
Competence	The service provider has mastered the required skill and is proficient in managing support personnel. For example, the tax accountant has C.P.A. certification.
Courtesy	Personnel are polite and friendly. For example, the bank teller smiles and says "Have a nice day" after the transaction is completed.
Reliability	The service is consistently performed to meet standards, and the personnel are dependable. For example, the barber always cuts your hair the same length.
Credibility	The service provider has integrity. For example, the doctor who is performing a heart operation is trustworthy and believable.

Source: Adapted from A. Parasuraman, Valarie A. Zeithaml, and Leonard L. Berry, "A Conceptual Model of Service Quality and Its Implications for Future Research," *Journal of Marketing,* Fall 1985, pp. 41–50.

product they purchased but annoyed by the sales clerk or angry at having to wait a long time to get their gifts wrapped?

Servicing a product after the sale, then, may be as important as the tangible product itself. Imagine how important delivery service is to the organization that incorporates a just-in-time inventory system in its production operations, and how important quick repair is to a business with only one photocopying machine. Because service is so important, marketers of goods with a high service component should manage the service component with the same strategies that work for marketers offering pure services.

SERVICING A PRODUCT AFTER THE SALE MAY BE AS IMPORTANT AS THE TANGIBLE PRODUCT ITSELF.

Warranty programs, a no-questions-asked return policy, and other after-sale service programs can help create satisfied customers who will be repeat purchasers of tangible products. Unfortunately, implementing such programs can be difficult. As products become more complex, more skill is required of the technicians who work on them. There may be shortages of adequately trained personnel, and providing services may be expensive.

Sears knows that its after-sale service generates repeat purchases of tangible products. Its HomeCentral operation stresses "one-stop shopping" for repair services. So, no matter who made it, no matter who sold it, Sears can service it.

No matter who made them.
No matter who sold them.

The GE that came with the house.

The KitchenAid that's way past warranty.

The Frigidaire from who-knows-where.

The cooktop by Whirlpool. The installation by your brother-in-law.

One phone call fixes them all.

SEARS
HomeCentral
1-800-4-REPAIR

One phone call to Sears HomeCentral fixes your Kenmore, GE, Whirlpool, Frigidaire, KitchenAid or other major appliance brands.
No matter who sold it, our team of appliance repair specialists can service it. And guarantee it. So call someone you know. Anytime, day or night.
Call Sears HomeCentral. The Service Side of Sears.

Classifying Services

How are services classified? Like tangible products, services can be classified by type of market: whether they are purchased by the ultimate consumer or by organizational buyers. Organizational services generally include maintenance and repair, consulting and advisory, and transportation and storage services. Services also can be classified by the marketer's mission into not-for-profit service organizations and profit-seeking service organizations.

Indeed, if you think about services, you will realize that they can be classified using an almost infinite number of variables, just as markets can be segmented on the basis of almost any variable. Researchers have developed various classifications to suit their research purposes. Exhibit 11-5 shows how services can be classified according to selected variables related to market segment, type of organization, and service characteristics.

How Large Is the Service Economy?

During the past 50 years, the contribution of services to our economy has been steadily expanding. Today, the vast majority of U.S. jobs—about 80 percent—are service-related. Services generate three-quarters of the U.S. gross domestic product.

CLASSIFICATION BY A CHARACTERISTIC OF THE MARKET SEGMENT	CLASSIFICATION BY A CHARACTERISTIC OF THE ORGANIZATION OFFERING THE SERVICE	CLASSIFICATION BY A CHARACTERISTIC OF THE SERVICE
• Who is the buyer—the ultimate consumer or an organization? • If the buyer is an organization, what type is it (for example, health care, financial, educational)? • If the buyer is an organization, where is it in the channel of distribution—manufacturer, wholesaler, retailer?	• What is the mission of the service provider—is it a profit-making organization, a non-profit, or a government entity? • What experience or certification do the service providers have (for example, are they professionals, skilled labor, or unskilled labor)?	• What type of benefit does the service provide for the consumer—instrumental or consummatory? • How is the service delivered (for example, is it equipment-based, automated, or people-based)? • What function does the service provider fulfill for the consumer (for example, repair, storage, consulting)?

Service workers are often depicted as an army of hamburger flippers and car-rental clerks, but in fact they constitute a huge, diverse group. Service jobs come in every imaginable description: powerful (president of the United States), mechanical (maintenance engineer), nurturing (preschool teacher), outdoorsy (mountain-climbing guide), and indoorsy (computer programmer or accountant).

The Bureau of Labor Statistics expects service jobs to account for all net job growth through the year 2005.[12] Thus, the service economy offers a far brighter employment picture than does manufacturing. It is true that many service jobs, such as that of cashier, are relatively low paying. But the service sector also includes such highly paid groups as lawyers, psychiatrists, and professional athletes. Among the largest job classifications are professionals, executives and managers, sales workers, and secretaries.

Relationship Marketing

Service organizations have always been relationship-oriented.[13] They have learned that customers of services—buyers who purchase promises of satisfaction—prefer to do business repeatedly with people and organizations they trust.[14] The marketers of goods have also learned that establishing relationships with customers can increase long-run sales and reduce marketing costs. As we have already mentioned, the term **relationship marketing,** or relationship management, is used to communicate the idea that a major goal of marketing, whether the product is a good or service, is to build long-term relationships with the parties who contribute to the company's success. The marketer builds customer loyalty by fulfilling promises and satisfying customer wants and needs.[15]

SERVICE ORGANIZATIONS HAVE LEARNED THAT CUSTOMERS OF SERVICES—CUSTOMERS WHO PURCHASE PROMISES OF SATISFACTION—PREFER TO DO BUSINESS REPEATEDLY WITH PEOPLE AND ORGANIZATIONS THEY TRUST.

Relationship marketing
Marketing activities aimed at building long-term relationships with the parties, especially customers, that contribute to a company's success; also called *relationship management.*

Interior decorators realize that it costs much more to find new customers than to keep existing customers. Building relationships with customers is a major means to gain repeat business.

Once an exchange is made, effective marketing stresses managing the after-the-sale service process to create and maintain a relationship that will bring about additional exchanges. Effective marketers view making a sale not as the end of a process but as the start of an organization's relationship with a customer. When they need to repurchase the same product in the future, customers will return to the company that treated them best. If they need a related item, satisfied customers know the first place to look.

The major goals of relationship marketing are to solidify relationships, transform indifferent customers into loyal ones, retain customers, and serve customers as clients.[16] Theodore Levitt put it somewhat differently:

The relationship between a buyer and seller seldom ends when a sale is made. In a greatly increasing proportion of transactions, the relationship actually intensifies subsequent to the sale. This becomes the buyer's critical factor in the buyer's choice of a seller the next time around. . . . The sale merely consummates the courtship. Then the marriage begins. How good the marriage is depends on how well the relationship is managed by the seller.[17]

It is the marketer's job to create, interpret, and maintain the relationship between the company and the customer.[18] Companies that have adopted a relationship marketing perspective think about marketing as an activity aimed at *getting and keeping customers*. Marketing to existing customers to gain repeat business provides benefits to the marketing organization and to the customer.

BENEFITS TO THE ORGANIZATION

An old business adage says "It costs six times as much to get a new customer as it does to keep an old customer." Although the figures vary industry by industry, the point is valid. Working to retain customers by managing relationships with them will generally increase revenues and, in most cases, reduce costs. Thus, profits rise when companies retain customers.[19]

CONSUMER BENEFITS

Customers also profit from relationship marketing. First, the continuity derived from a relationship with the same seller simplifies the buying process. A Honda advertisement says: "Life is full of complicated decisions. Simplify." This advertisement reflects an understanding that consumers want many buying decisions to be easier. Many buyers do not to want to evaluate too many factors when choosing among alternatives. Feeling comfortable in a buyer-seller relationship is a major customer benefit.

Because services are intangible, they are difficult to evaluate prior to purchase. Buyers become loyal customers because they want to do business with organizations that will provide consistent service quality. For example, most consumers are very loyal to their hairdressers or barbers. They do not want to risk service quality that is below their expectations.

Another benefit customers gain from relationship marketing is increased customization of goods or services. The theme song for the television show *Cheers* said that Cheers is a place "where everybody knows your name." An ongoing relationship allows marketers to know their customers' names and the nature of their needs. People want to be dealt with on a one-to-one basis. Relationship marketing has been called "one-to-one marketing" because it allows marketers to tailor their offerings to individual consumers. Companies that wish to delight customers personalize the relationship and customize products.

Effective marketers who customize products and cater to individual lifestyles must learn a lot about their customers. Sales personnel at specialty clothing stores ask regular customers about their jobs, families, and lifestyles. They keep an eye out for clothes to suit their customers' tastes and put aside possible selections. They know that personalized service and their customers' trust in their ability to select items for them greatly enhance their relationship with customers. In the past, sales personnel noted such information in notebooks. Unfortunately, if they left, so did the client information.

In an age when personalization is rare, information technology is bringing it back. With today's information technology, personalized service can be greatly expanded through data-based marketing. Neiman-Marcus stores now track customers' buying habits, preferences, and special dates through their computerized cash registers. Sales associates can notify a client when new merchandise comes in or send a reminder about buying a gift for a personal event, like an anniversary.[20] Elsewhere in this book we will discuss some of the details of using data-based marketing in direct marketing and other promotional activities to build relationships.

Three Levels of Relationship Marketing Programs

It is possible to categorize three levels of relationship marketing: financial, social, and structural. The categories are based on the primary reason for the bond between the marketer and the customer.[21]

FINANCIAL RELATIONSHIPS: FREQUENCY MARKETING PROGRAMS

Most *frequency marketing programs* are based on financial incentives. Season tickets for professional basketball games or the opera provide discounts to fans who establish a relationship with the organization. Banks often offer higher interest rates for deposits that will be kept in an account for a longer duration. Frequent flyer programs offer a free trip after a customer flies a certain number of segments or miles. In effect, these programs provide a discount pricing incentive to reward consumers for high levels of spending or multiple purchases.

America West's FlightFund is a typical frequency marketing program. It offers travelers a chance to enjoy awards once they have accumulated a minimum of 20,000 FlightFund miles. Certificates are redeemable for award travel on America West, America West Express, and select domestic and international carriers. Awards can also be redeemed with participating FlightFund hotel and car rental partners, which include nine different hotel chains and five rental car agencies. In addition to being able to earn miles by patronizing car, hotel, and airline partners, FlightFund members can earn miles by using Sprint long distance service, America West Vacations, and the America West FlightFund Visa card. Thus, a financial benefit—in the form of travel, a hotel room, a rental car, or some other benefit—is the reward for increased patronage of America West and its partners.

SOCIAL RELATIONSHIPS

One form of relationship marketing involves the formation of a social bond between the company and its customers. Many people know about the thousands of Saturn owners who converge annually on the car company's headquarters in Spring Hill, Tennessee for a barbecue, a plant tour, and a chance to talk with other Saturn owners about how much they love their cars. However, this type of

Columbia House doesn't see itself as a marketer of CDs, but as a marketer of a long-term relationship. Columbia House learns its members' favorite kind of music—jazz, rap, country, rock, alternative—and enters this information into its database. Then, each month, it uses relationship marketing software to make a music selection that not only reflects an individual's tastes, but predicts them.

relationship marketing pales somewhat when compared to what Chrysler does to bond with its Jeep owners.

Jeep
www.jeep.com

One weekend each year, dozens of owners driving their Jeeps meet in the tiny mountain town of Blanding, Utah for Chrysler Corporation's "Jeep Jamboree."[22] The Jeep owners gas up and form a convoy to Arches Canyon National Park, a 20-minute drive away. There, for the next two days and nights, they get to test their vehicles on narrow roads in nature's roughest terrain. For the Jeep owners who participate, the Jeep Jamboree adventure offers a rare chance to experience the promise of Jeep commercials. (Only 10 percent of those who own sport-utility vehicles ever get a chance to drive off-road, studies show.) For Chrysler, this relationship marketing event provides an opportunity to bond with customers and establish brand loyalty. Chrysler expects participants in the jamborees to become ambassadors for the brand.

STRUCTURAL RELATIONSHIPS

Charles Schwab
www.schwab.com

When a stock broker, such as Charles Schwab, provides computer software so that a client can check stock quotes, evaluate portfolio histories, get information about companies, and trade stocks over the Internet, it has created a structural solution to an important customer problem. Relationships based on structural bonds do not depend on the relationship-building skills of a particular service provider, as in the traditional customer-stockbroker relationship, but on the service delivery system that is part of the company structure.

Share of Customer

Relationship marketing leads to a different kind of thinking about the nature of a business. Historically, marketers have thought in terms of a single product, and their goal has been achieving a high share of the market—more customers than their competitors have. In relationship marketing, the company objective often is to achieve a high *share of customer*. The company tries to sell an individual customer as many goods and services as it can over the lifetime of that customer's patronage.[23] An effective marketer determines the lifetime value of each of its customers and adjusts its marketing strategy accordingly. It treats its best customers differently than its other customers. It sends the right message to its best customers at the right time.

Increasing share of customer has become more popular as a marketing objective because customer databases and new information technologies allow marketers to track customers individually and then customize their marketing efforts. For example, American Express' CustomExtras program uses relationship marketing to attempt to get customers to charge more on their credit cards. Point-of-sale transactions feed into the American Express database; the company's relational database software tracks purchases, rewards, and promotions, and manages the printing of billing statements with customized offers and messages. American Express personalizes the customer relationship by targeting specific promotional offers, such as a discount on airline travel, to specific customers based on their spending patterns.

Customer Retention

Customer retention is a major objective of relationship marketing. An insurance agent may send a postcard to a client on his birthday. This is a friendly reminder that she thinks of him as an individual and wants the relationship to continue. Information technology and customer databases are making it possible for large organizations to focus on customer retention by treating their customers like individuals again. The rewards of focusing on customer retention can be enormous. Suppose a telephone company has 6 million customers using a call-waiting feature that costs $5 a month.[24] During the course of a year, a certain percentage of these customers cancel their service. If the organization could, through databased marketing and personalized promotional messages, stop 1 percent of these customers—or 60,000 accounts—from canceling, it would retain $3.6 million in annual revenue.

What Makes a Successful Relationship?

Relationship commitment and trust are the two essential factors required for successful relationship marketing.

Relationship commitment is defined as an enduring desire to maintain a valued relationship.[25] A strong commitment to a relationship develops if the relationship is mutually beneficial to the parties. A committed partner believes the relationship has value and is willing to work at preserving it. This is especially true of relationships among suppliers and intermediaries (see Chapter 12).

If a customer is committed to a relationship, he or she will resist attractive short-term alternatives in favor of the expected long-term benefits of staying with existing partners.[26] For example, a committed member of Delta Air Lines' Sky Miles program might forgo an opportunity to buy a low-fare, sale-priced ticket on Southwest Airlines and instead buy a regular-priced Delta ticket to reap the rewards of Delta's frequent flying program.

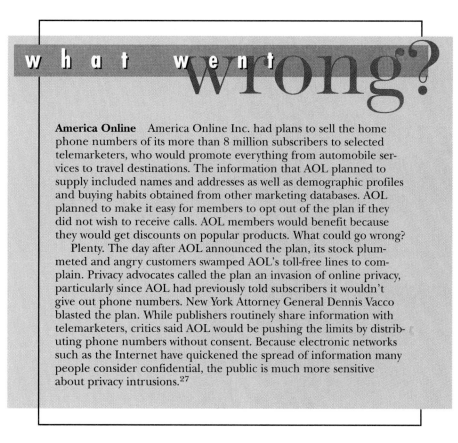

what went wrong?

America Online America Online Inc. had plans to sell the home phone numbers of its more than 8 million subscribers to selected telemarketers, who would promote everything from automobile services to travel destinations. The information that AOL planned to supply included names and addresses as well as demographic profiles and buying habits obtained from other marketing databases. AOL planned to make it easy for members to opt out of the plan if they did not wish to receive calls. AOL members would benefit because they would get discounts on popular products. What could go wrong?

Plenty. The day after AOL announced the plan, its stock plummeted and angry customers swamped AOL's toll-free lines to complain. Privacy advocates called the plan an invasion of online privacy, particularly since AOL had previously told subscribers it wouldn't give out phone numbers. New York Attorney General Dennis Vacco blasted the plan. While publishers routinely share information with telemarketers, critics said AOL would be pushing the limits by distributing phone numbers without consent. Because electronic networks such as the Internet have quickened the spread of information many people consider confidential, the public is much more sensitive about privacy intrusions.[27]

Trust exists when one party has confidence that he or she can rely on the other exchange partner. In many situations, trust means a customer believes that the marketer is reliable and has integrity.[28] In many personal selling situations, trust means that a customer has confidence that the sales representative is honest, fair, and responsible and that his or her word can be relied on. When there is trust in a relationship, all partners believe that none will act opportunistically. Marketers, especially the marketers of services, establish trust by maintaining open and honest communication and by keeping the promises they make.

MARKETERS, ESPECIALLY THE MARKETERS OF SERVICES, ESTABLISH TRUST BY MAINTAINING OPEN AND HONEST COMMUNICATION AND BY KEEPING THE PROMISES THEY MAKE.

We will mention more specific ways to establish relationship commitment and trust as we discuss other elements of the marketing mix. One of these ways, internal marketing, is addressed in the next section.

Internal Marketing Enhances Relationship Building

Marketers who stress service quality and relationship marketing strive to manage the service encounter. This is because the customer's evaluation of service quality and the building of a positive relationship between the customer and the organization are highly dependent on what takes place during the service encounter. Internal marketing is important in improving the service employees provide, which in turn improves relationships with customers.

The term **internal marketing** is often used by marketers, especially those in service businesses, when referring to public relations efforts aimed at their own employees who have contact with the ultimate consumer or who have a direct effect on the ultimate consumer's satisfaction with the product.[29] The objective of internal marketing may be to have employees recognize their role in the organization's effort to create customer satisfaction; these employees may better understand that their providing a high level of service is essential to the firm's existence.[30]

When Delta Airlines created its "We love to fly and it shows!" advertising campaign, the company realized that it would have to ensure that employee performance matched Delta's advertising claim. The company was following the trend toward increased internal marketing effort. Consider one ad

Internal marketing
Marketing efforts aimed at a company's own employees.

w h a t   w e n t   right?

Ritz-Carlton's Employee Empowerment Building customer loyalty requires empowerment with an entrepreneurial twist. It's easy to tell employees to do whatever it takes to satisfy a customer, as long as there is no cost. The Ritz-Carlton Hotel Co. brings an entrepreneurial dimension to it. Employees can spend up to $2,000 to redress a guest grievance. They have permission to break from their routine for as long as needed to make a guest happy. Expensive, perhaps, but customers who have problems resolved are more loyal than those who didn't have a problem at all, reports Jay Marwaha, a senior vice president with Technical Assistance Research Programs, a customer-service consultancy.

Recently, a member of the Ritz-Carlton cleaning staff at the Dearborn, Michigan, hotel noticed a guest waiting for the gift shop to open. The staffer, failing to find a key, kept watch until the shop opened, picked up what the guest had wanted, and camped outside a hotel conference hall to personally deliver the goods.

There is cold calculation behind such warm and fuzzy hospitality: Guests remember this level of service and tell their friends and colleagues. Says Patrick Mene, vice president of quality: "People don't have a rational understanding of quality. Personalized service is our method of driving retention." More than 90 percent of Ritz-Carlton's customers return, and the rate is even higher for customers who hold meetings there."[31]

in this campaign: a television commercial for Delta Airlines that portrays the soldiers of the U.S. Army's "Company B." The ad opens as a troop of soldiers in the pouring rain is being dismissed by a stern sergeant. Whooping with joy, the men stampede to the nearest telephone booth. "Even when Company B heads for the telephone," says an announcer, "it's no problem for Gail Godfrey." Godfrey, a real Delta reservationist, keeps her cool as the phone is passed from one soldier to another. Hailing from all over the country, they're all anxious to fly home.

As the last soldier hangs up, a fellow reservationist asks Godfrey if she's answered many calls that afternoon. "One," Godfrey replies, looking a little sheepish.[32]

This advertisement was designed to communicate what Delta believes is its unique competitive advantage: the service provided by its frontline personnel. The ad was designed to communicate how Delta employees go beyond the call of duty.

The advertising agency had developed a wonderful campaign. Delta realized, however, that before it went out to tell the world, internal marketing was necessary to ensure that its employees would deliver on the promise. Delta produced an employee video for the campaign, and every employee got a cassette explaining how important he or she was to the success of this campaign.[33]

summary

This chapter discussed the marketing problems faced by marketers of services and all marketers who need to engage in relationship marketing. Each type of marketing presents unique problems, which can be overcome by the judicious use of traditional marketing strategies.

1 *Define* service *in its technical, specific sense.*

A service is an instrumental activity performed for a buyer or a consummatory activity involving consumer participation in, but not ownership of, an organization's products or facilities.

2 *Explain the four basic characteristics of services.*

The four basic characteristics of services are (1) intangibility—buyers cannot normally see, feel, smell, hear or taste a service before agreeing to buy it; (2) perishability—unused productive capacity disappears in the sense that the provider's time cannot be used again if a customer does not make use of the service; (3) inseparability—the producer and consumer generally must be present at the same time and place, and the provider of the service cannot be separated from the service provided; and (4) variability—providers of services vary widely in their skills, and even a single provider cannot perform in the same way on every occasion. Marketers of services strive to control service variability to improve service quality.

3 *Understand demand management strategies.*

Service providers cannot store their products for future use, so forecasting and managing demand are of key importance. Altering prices to attract customers during off-season or off-hour times and two-part pricing (using fixed and variable usage fees) exemplify demand management strategies.

4 *Describe the strategies of standardization and customization.*

Standardization means attempting to control the inherent variability of services by such means as automation and strict controls on service-providing personnel. Customization involves modifying the service to fit the individual buyer's needs.

5 *Name some of the variables used to classify services.*

Services may be classified according to such characteristics as (1) market segment (for example, consumer versus organizational); (2) the organization offering the service (for example, profit-making versus not-for-profit); and (3) the service itself (for example, equipment-based versus people-based).

6 *Explain how to build and enhance relationships.*

Marketers have learned that establishing relationships with customers can increase long-run sales and reduce marketing costs. The term *relationship marketing* is used to communicate the idea that a major goal of marketing, whether the product is a good or a service, is to build long-term relationships with the parties who contribute to the company's success.

Once an exchange is made, effective marketing requires managing the after-the-sale service process to create and maintain a relationship that will bring about additional exchanges. There are three levels of relationship marketing: financial, social, and structural.

key terms

service (p. 337)
intangibility (p. 337)
perishability (p. 339)
demand management
    strategy (p. 339)

two-part pricing (p. 340)
inseparability (p. 340)
variability (p. 342)
service encounter (p. 345)
service quality (p. 345)

expected service–perceived service
    gap (p. 345)
gap analysis (p. 346)
relationship marketing (p. 349)
internal marketing (p. 354)

questions for review & critical thinking

1. What is the service element in each of the following, and how might each service be classified?
   a. A city zoo
   b. Avis car rental
   c. A shoeshine
   d. A taxicab ride
   e. New false teeth from a dentist
   f. Bungie jumping
2. Describe situations in which consumers might prefer consumption without ownership to actual ownership of products.
3. Describe a situation in which you paid in advance for a promise of satisfaction.
4. Give three examples of organizations that use slogans or images to impart believability or reliability to the services they offer for sale.
5. In what ways do inseparability and intangibility affect marketing planning for the following service providers?
   a. A church
   b. Your local public school board
   c. A ski resort
   d. A plastic surgeon
6. How does a service's perishability influence pricing?
7. How can the following service providers combat intangibility in their product and advertising strategies?
   a. A health spa
   b. A movie theater
   c. A hairdresser
   d. The bar near your university or college

8. Do sports figures and celebrities engage in service marketing? In what ways?
9. Give examples of the use of standardization and customization in the marketing of services.
10. Is it easier to market a service product with a high tangible component than to market one with a low tangible component? Why or why not?
11. What goals might a hotel have for its relationship marketing program?
12. Identify the three levels of relationship marketing programs.
13. Define the term *share of customer*. Why might this be an important concept for a Harley-Davidson retailer? A financial services company? A package delivery company?
14. You are a marketing consultant, and your city or town government has hired you to develop a marketing plan aimed at improving the public image of the local police department. What steps would you take to ensure a smooth introduction of the marketing approach to this organization?
15. a. Service workers often work in teams. The following questions will help you gain a better understanding of your orientation to work in a group. Respond either Y (yes) or N (no) to each of the following statements:
    1. I usually feel uncomfortable with a group of people that I don't know.
    2. I enjoy parties.
    3. I do not have much confidence in social situations.

4. I am basically a shy person.
5. I like going on job interviews.
6. I usually feel anxious when I speak in front of a group.
7. Large groups make me nervous.
8. I would rather work on a group project than an individual project.
9. I am basically a loner.
10. I find that groups bring out the best in me.

Scoring: Give yourself 1 point for each of your responses that matches the following answer pattern: 1 = Y, 2 = N, 3 = Y, 4 = Y, 5 = N, 6 = Y, 7 = Y, 8 = N, 9 = Y, 10 = N. Total your score.

Interpretation of score: If your score is 8 or higher, you probably prefer to avoid most group situations. This means you are a group avoider. If you have a score of 2 or lower, you probably seek out group situations and activities and are thus a group seeker. Unfortunately, it is not always possible to choose your preferred situation. When people get into situations that conflict with their orientation, they may not function as well as they would otherwise. Try to match your activities with your group preference style.[34]

b. Now form a small group, as directed by your instructor, and discuss how the scores of the group members differ.

c. How can you best match your work activities with your group preference style? Generate a list of ideas and share them with either your small group or the class, as directed by your instructor.

marketing plan—right or wrong?

1. Sears sells Florsheim Shoes but does not carry all styles and sizes. The plan is to install a computerized ordering system so that shoppers can look at pictures of Florsheim shoes at a kiosk and place orders for later delivery.
2. United Airlines contemplated sending flight attendants to classes at Ritz-Carlton hotels and other quality service organizations to learn how to serve food in United's first-class cabins.
3. A new Internet service lets customers buy theater and airline tickets, stock certificates, and savings bonds on-line. The marketer beta tested its service with ten consumers chosen for their technology expertise and found they had little concern about privacy or security.

internet i n s i g h t s

z i k m u n d . s w c o l l e g e . c o m

e x e r c i s e

Visit the Web sites of a hotel (www.hyatt.com), an airline (www.delta-air.com), a bank (www.citibank.com), and another service marketer of your choice. How do they use their Web sites to make the intangible tangible (if at all)?

a d d r e s s   b o o k   (u s e f u l   u r l s)

Journal of Service Marketing	www.mcb.co.uk/cgi-bin/journal1/jsm
The Cyber-Journal of Sport Marketing	www.cad.gu.edu.au/cjsm/home.htm
National Park Service	www.nps.gov

ethically right or wrong?

Political candidates spend a lot of money on their election and reelection campaigns. The laws covering political advertising differ from those for the advertising of consumer and organizational products. In general, political advertisers do not have to substantiate claims with evidence. Many negative advertising themes belittle opponents. Is this proper? Should any laws be passed or anything else be done to change the way political advertising is conducted?

TAKE A STAND

1. A doctor's bedside manner is part of the service offered to patients. From an ethical perspective, discuss the product strategy of emphasizing this service.

2. A restaurant customer asks the waiter if the fish on the menu is fresh. Although the fish was frozen, the waiter answers yes, because he knows it tastes great and the customer will love the chef's sauce. Take a stand.

3. Some people believe that not-for-profit service organizations that expect to bring about social change, like the National Rifle Association, have no business trying to change everyone's opinion to their point of view. Take a stand.

4. A small percentage of people suffer from allergies, asthma, or sensitivity to perfumes or other chemicals. Even a whiff of certain chemicals can cause respiratory problems, memory loss, or dizziness. Should restaurants and other service establishments offer customers seating in perfume-free sections?

Milton Seifert and Associates   *Focus on Small Business*

When Dr. Milton Seifert started his own practice in 1972, his goal was to satisfy patients with cost-effective, high-quality health care. He believed that he would have a good business if he practiced good medicine. When managing his business turned out to be a little more difficult than he had originally perceived, he realized his medical school training had not prepared him to be a businessman.

Seifert asked some of his patients for their advice. Thus, the business committee of the Patient Advisory Council (PAC) was formed. The business committee provided financial insight that dramatically improved Seifert's financial status. At the same time, the PAC as a whole acted as a support group for other patients by offering day care and transportation for the sick and the elderly.

Seifert's PAC has preserved goodwill in the face of complaints and was the primary reason for a 10 percent discount in Seifert's malpractice insurance. The PAC has also helped promote Milton Seifert and Associates by joining with the practice to put on a community health education forum.

Years later, however, many of Seifert's more affluent patients began joining health maintenance organizations (HMOs) and leaving his practice. To make a bad situation even worse, overhead rose to 77 percent and then to 86 percent. Seifert needed to expand and grow somehow in order to survive.[35]

QUESTIONS

1. Identify and evaluate the marketing mix of physicians like Milton Seifert and Associates.
2. How should Milton Seifert and Associates position itself in the health care marketplace?
3. How can service quality be evaluated at Milton Seifert and Associates?

Partnership for a Drug-Free America

The Partnership for a Drug-Free America used national TV advertising to try to change inner-city kids' perceptions about drugs. The campaign—including two ads, "Long Way Home" and "Who Wants"—was designed to change the way inner-city children thought about themselves in relation to drugs. First, in 1992, the Partnership surveyed 7,288 elementary school children in New York City to determine their attitudes about drugs. It also wanted to know what issues were most important and how best to reach the target group of second- through sixth-graders. In May 1993, after the advertisements had been televised, the organization surveyed 8,319 children and found marked attitude changes. "A lot of people think inner-city kids are unreachable and that they all use drugs," said Ginna Marston, director and executive vice president for research and strategic development. "That's just not true."

When questioned following the first series of ads, kids gave responses that showed their attitudes and feelings about drugs had changed perceptibly. Fourth-, fifth-, and sixth-graders questioned about their feelings toward drug dealers showed a significant change. In the first phase, 24 percent said they thought drug dealers had many friends; in phase 2, only 22 percent believed that statement. On a self-esteem question, second- and third-graders were less worried about wanting to try drugs, and more fourth- through sixth-graders felt they would walk away from drugs if they were offered. The ads themselves took a low-key approach. For example, "Long Way Home" illustrated the loneliness many inner-city children feel because of drugs in their neighborhoods. The ad, created *pro bono* by Goodby, Berlin & Silverstein, chronicles one child's efforts to get home without running into drug dealers. Instead of trying to force the idea of not taking drugs, the Partnership wanted to show support— ". . . we see you, we hear you."[36]

Marketing research in 1997 indicated that the Partnership should target younger children. To reach young preteen children, the Partnership's latest public service announcements are "Brain Damaged" and "Big Ol' Bug" from Saatchi & Saatchi Kid Connection in New York.

"Brain Damaged" shows a funny, likable brain talking about drugs in the first person, observing that drugs can "mess up your mind . . . they make me slow, confused . . . it's like I can barely think." The brain then goes on to swing at and miss a baseball to underscore that drugs throw off hand-eye coordination. It is later shown sunning itself to reflect how drugs make it "totally burned out." Then the gray matter jumps back into a young boy's head with a parting shot: "Get it into your heads—drugs are bad for your brain. So use your brain, and stay away from drugs."

Saatchi's "Big Ol' Bug" is set to rock music, with a kid shown ready to eat an insect. The lyrics relate: "I'd rather eat a big ol' bug than ever take a stupid drug." The song points out that drugs "make you sad and your parents mad." Again humor is employed, as the boy is shown putting a big, disgusting, talking bug on a slice of bread.

QUESTIONS

1. How is marketing by an organization like the Partnership for a Drug-Free America different from efforts by marketers of other services? How is it similar?
2. How can the Partnership for a Drug-Free America measure the success of its efforts?
3. Using your knowledge of consumer behavior, explain whether you think this promotional effort will accomplish the goals of the Partnership for a Drug-Free America.

You will find each exercise on the CD-ROM developed for use with this textbook. Each exercise has a name and is located within a module. For example, the first exercise can be found in the Micromarketing Module by clicking on Stages in the Product Life Cycle.

MICROMARKETING MODULE
Stages in the Product Life Cycle

1. Name some products in each stage of the product life cycle.

BUYER BEHAVIOR MODULE
PLC and the Diffusion Process

2. What is the relationship between the product life cycle and the diffusion process?

cross-functional
insights

Many theories and principles from other business disciplines can provide insights about the role marketing plays in an organization. The questions in this section are designed to help you think about integrating what you have learned in other business courses with the marketing principles explained in this book.

Trademarks   A trademark is a legally protected brand name or brand mark. The owners of trademarks have exclusive rights to their use.

What is the legal process required to obtain a trademark?

What can a marketer do if someone uses a trademark or patent without permission?

Warranty   A product warranty communicates a written guarantee of a product's integrity and outlines the manufacturer's responsibility for repairing or replacing defective parts.

According to U.S. law, what is an express warranty? What is an implied warranty?

New Product Development   New product development is the lifeblood of an organization. The process for developing new products starts with screening ideas and ends with commercialization of the new products.

How do the need to make a large investment in research and development for a new product and a financial manager's knowledge of net present value influence the decision to go ahead with the project?

How important is capital budgeting in new product development?

Should marketers expect higher rates of return on new-to-the-world products or on line extensions?

Can PERT (Program Evaluation and Review Technique) charts be used for new product development?

Product Life Cycle   The product life cycle is a depiction of a product's sales history from its "birth," or marketing beginning, to its "death," or withdrawal from the market. Products go through the stages of introduction, growth, maturity, and decline.

How does the return on investment (ROI) of a new product influence decision making? What is the relationship between ROI and net present value over the course of a product life cycle?

It is said that product life cycles are one of the justifications for the economic theory of comparative advantage. How is this so?

What role does ISO 9000 play in modifying products for the European market?

Which is more important to product managers during the growth stage of the product life cycle: financial accounting or managerial accounting?

Does the Occupational Safety and Health Act (OSHA) have any influence on product strategy?

Product Portfolio Analysis   Evaluation of a company's or a strategic business unit's product mix is called *product portfolio analysis*. Product portfolio analysis involves a matrix. The horizontal dimension of the matrix depicts relative market share on a scale from high to low. On the vertical scale, the same words refer to market growth rate. The combinations of these variables yield four quadrants: high-market-share product in a high-growth market; high-market-share product in a low-growth market; low-market-share product in a high-growth market; and low-market-share product in a low-growth market.

How are cash flow and product portfolio analysis related?

361

you seldom accomplish much by yourself; you must get the assistance of others

–WHO SAID THIS?

part 4

you seldom
accomplish much
by yourself; you
must get   THAT'S WHO SAID IT!
the assistance
of others

–HENRY J. KAISER

During World War II, West Coast industrialist Henry J. Kaiser was
able to construct roads, buildings, and ships for the government at
unprecedented speed by avoiding traditional methods and using
imaginative mass-production techniques. After the war, Kaiser
formed an association with Joseph W. Frazer to build innovative
small, economical front-wheel-drive cars (Kaisers) and upscale,
"modern" sedans (Frazers) and get them into the hands of car-
hungry Americans before the rest of the industry got into gear.
Kaiser's plan was to use his charisma and supplier contacts to cut
through the red tape of the war era, which still entangled the supply and distribution of raw materials necessary for the production
of auto-making machinery. Kaiser-Frazer dealers began selling
Kaisers and Frazers late in 1946.

chapter
12

The Nature of Distribution

After you have studied this chapter, you will be able to:

Explain the general purpose of distribution in the marketing system.

1

Show how distribution contributes to an effective marketing mix.

2

Understand why all marketers—even not-for-profit and service organizations—engage in distribution.

3

Characterize the functions of channel intermediaries.

4

Identify the major channels of distribution used by marketers of consumer and organizational products.

5

(continued on next page)

greens and fairways at the nation's

14,000 golf courses take a daily beating from golf carts and divot diggers. Keeping the grounds up to par can be tough for maintenance crews, so for help many rely on Lesco's "store on wheels." The company's fleet of 59 tractor-trailers delivers a full stock of Lesco fertilizers, pesticides, and equipment—just about any landscaping product a greenskeeper might need. Lesco brings the store to the clubhouse door at nearly half the courses in the United States, including such gems as Grand Cypress and Augusta National.

The manufacturing company, in Rocky River, Ohio, has three plants, where it makes more than 17,000 lawn care products for the professional landscaping market. It sells such tools of the trade as mowers and seed spreaders and their replacement parts. Lesco's other main products are fertilizers

MUCH OF LESCO'S SUCCESS CAN BE TRACED TO ITS EFFECTIVE PERFORMANCE OF THE DISTRIBUTION FUNCTION.

and turf-protection mixes, many of which it makes specifically for different regions of the country. In Florida, for example, it markets a special fertilizer to replenish the nutrients in sandy soil.

Although the stores on wheels have traveled to golf courses since 1976, the majority of Lesco's sales today occur at its 121 service centers, scattered mainly through the South, Northeast, and Midwest. The company plans to open more service centers, where most of the sales staff are trained as agronomists and are able to consult with customers on the latest products.

In 1993, Lesco entered the consumer market, and now it distributes its products through 103 Home Depot stores. Lesco executives see an opportunity for growth in the consumer products category, but the company is cautious because it doesn't want to risk losing focus on its efforts in the professional market.[1]

Lesco
www.lesco.com

Of course, Lesco products set the company apart from most others, but Lesco relies on a distribution strategy that utilizes a number of channels of distribution. Much of Lesco's success can be traced to its effective performance of the distribution function.

This chapter provides an overview of the purpose of the distribution element of the marketing mix. It defines channels of distribution and explores the functions intermediaries perform. It then explains the advantages and disadvantages of the many alternative channels of distribution. Next, it addresses the major decisions managers make in planning a distribution strategy. It discusses how the implementation of a distribution strategy may create channel conflict and, finally, describes some legal and ethical issues related to channels of distribution.

Distribution Delivers a Standard of Living to Society

The major purpose of marketing is to satisfy human needs by delivering products of various types to buyers when and where they want them and at a reasonable cost. A key element in this statement of marketing's mission is delivery. All marketing effort comes to nothing unless products are placed in the hands of those who need them. Thus, distribution is of overwhelming importance in any discussion of marketing functions. Distribution is estimated to account for about one-quarter of the price of the consumer goods people buy. Most would agree that this is a cost well worth bearing. Distribution creates time utility and place utility.

Distribution of products among the members of a society becomes necessary once people realize that, even in a primitive economy, efficiency can be gained if one person specializes in a certain activity, such as hunting, and another person specializes in a different activity, such as fishing or farming. In a primitive economy, distribution is straightforward; but in today's global economy, it is far more complex. For example, products shipped into Denver may ultimately be sold in Oregon, and Washington state apples may be consumed in Florida. One way or another, the distance between the grower or producer of a product and the final user of that product must be bridged. The distance to be covered can be quite long, as when Mexican oil ends up in Australia. It can also be quite short, as when a farmer at a roadside stand sells the watermelon that grew just a few yards away. Whatever the distance required to move a good from a producer to a buyer or consumer, society relies on the marketing function of distribution to do the job—to provide products in the right place at the right time.

Distribution in the Marketing Mix—A Key to Success

Increasing levels of competition, cost-consciousness brought on by world and national economic developments, and consumer concerns with efficiency in marketing are among the main reasons distribution has become increasingly important to organizations in recent years.

Some organizations compete successfully against much larger competitors by basing their market appeal almost entirely on distribution. Mary Kay Cosmetics, which has grown to be a large firm in its own right, competes against such giants as Procter & Gamble by employing a distribution system much different from Procter & Gamble's. Mary Kay's products go right to the consumer's door. Even activities not usually thought of as involving much in the way of distribution may rely heavily on this aspect of the marketing mix. Not-for-profit and social-service organizations such as the American Heart Association have used distribution effectively to perform their functions better. The American Heart Association makes blood pressure checks available in many locations, including schools, libraries, and fire stations, for example.

What Is a Channel of Distribution?

Channels of distribution were briefly discussed in Chapter 1. A channel of distribution may be referred to by other names, and terms vary from industry to industry. But whether *channel, trade channel,* or some other variant of the term is used, the functions performed remain the same. The term *channel of distribution* has its origins in the French word for canal, suggesting a path that goods take as they

The main business of the Hollywood movie studios once was simply making films—that is, production. Today, the crucial factor determining a studio's profitability is film distribution. Major U.S. film studios produce only about half the movies they distribute. They purchase many films from independent studios. The large studios concentrate on distribution and other marketing functions and are compensated for these efforts through a fee system, usually 25 to 30 percent of a film's rentals. Film distribution itself has also changed in recent years. Supplying films to theaters is no longer enough. Home Box Office, Showtime, and other cable systems, as well as TV networks, independent stations, and videocassette marketers, are now critical in the film marketing process. Distribution is the name of the game in Hollywood.

Channel of distribution
The complete sequence of marketing organizations involved in bringing a product from the producer to the ultimate consumer or organizational user.

Merchant intermediary
A channel intermediary, such as a wholesaler or a retailer, that takes title to the product.

Agent intermediary
A channel intermediary that does not take title to the product. Agent intermediaries bring buyers and sellers together or otherwise help complete a transaction.

flow from producers to consumers. In this sense, a channel of distribution is defined by the organizations or individuals along the route from producer to consumer. Because the beginning and ending points of the route must be included, both producer and consumer are always members of the channel of distribution. However, there may be intermediate stops along the way. Several marketing institutions have developed to facilitate the flow of the physical product or the title to the product from the producer to the consumer. Organizations that serve as marketing intermediaries (middlemen) specializing in distribution rather than production are external to the producing organization. When these intermediaries join with a manufacturer in a loose coalition aimed at exploiting joint opportunities, a channel of distribution is formed.[2] A **channel of distribution,** then, consists of producer, consumer, and any intermediary organizations that are aligned to provide a means of transferring title or possession of the product from producer to consumer. The channel of distribution can also be seen as a system of interdependent relationships among a set of organizations—a system that facilitates the exchange process.

All discussions of distribution channels assume that the product in question has taken on its final form. The channel of distribution for an automobile begins with a finished automobile. It does not include the paths of raw materials (such as steel) or component parts (such as tires) to the automobile manufacturer, which is an industrial user in these other channels. It should be emphasized that the channel's purpose in moving products to people is more than a simple matter of transportation. The channel of distribution must accomplish the task of transferring the title to the product as well as facilitating the physical movement of the goods to their ultimate destination. Although title transfer and the exchange of physical possession (transportation) generally follow the same channel of distribution, they do not necessarily need to follow the same path.

All but the shortest of channels include one or more intermediaries—individuals or organizations specializing in distribution rather than production. (In the past, intermediaries were called *middlemen.*) A distinction may be made between **merchant intermediaries,** which take title to the product, and **agent intermediaries,** which do not take title to the product. Although agent intermediaries never own the goods, they perform a number of marketing functions, such as selling, that facilitate further transactions in the exchange process.

Most intermediaries are independent organizations tied to the producers they deal with only by mutual agreement; they are not owned by the producers. Some intermediaries are owned by producers, such as the company-owned sales branches and sales offices that sell NCR office equipment. However, these company-owned sales branches and offices are clearly separate from the production facilities operated by the company.

In service marketing, it sometimes appears that there is no channel of distribution. When a beautician delivers a product, such as a haircut or make-up advice, he or she deals directly with the customer. But even in these shortest of distribution channels, involving no intermediaries, marketing functions are being performed. The required activities are simply performed by the provider of the service (or, in a self-service environment, by the ultimate consumer).[3]

When identifiable intermediaries are present, the channel members form a coalition intended to act on joint opportunities in the marketplace. Each channel member, from producer to retailer, must be rewarded or see some opportunity for continued participation in the channel. Ultimately, for the channel to work properly, the consumer, who is not an institutional member of the channel but is the final link in the process, must also perceive a likely reward. Thus, the large merchandise selection and low retail prices offered by a Venture or Target store must be seen as compensation for driving an extra mile or two to the store. The coalition between channel members may be a loose one resulting from negotiation or a formal set of contractual arrangements identifying each party's role in the distribution process. The conventional channel of distribution is characterized by loosely aligned, relatively autonomous marketing organizations that have developed a system to carry out a trade relationship. In contrast, formal vertical marketing systems are more tightly organized systems in which the channel members are either owned by a manufacturer or a distributor, linked by contracts or other legal agreements such as franchises, or informally managed and coordinated as an integrated system through strategic alliances. Vertical marketing systems are discussed in greater detail later in this chapter.

Not included in the channel of distribution are transportation companies, financial institutions, and other functional specialists selling services that assist the flow of products. They are *collaborators,* playing a specialized role by providing a limited facilitating service useful to channel members.

Marketing Functions Performed by Intermediaries

Perhaps the most neglected, most misunderstood, and most maligned segment of the economy is the distribution segment. Retailers are seen by some as the principal cause of high consumer prices simply because retailers are the marketers with whom consumers most frequently come into contact. Retailers collect money from consumers, so even though much of that money is passed to other distributors or manufacturers, retailers often bear the brunt of customers' complaints. Wholesalers are also seen as causing high prices, perhaps because much of what they do is done outside the view of consumers.

In either case, many suggest "cutting out the middleman" as a means of lowering the prices of consumer goods. For thousands of years, the activities of those who perform the distribution function have been misunderstood, and this viewpoint persists today.

Students of marketing should understand that an efficient distribution system must somehow be financed. Most of the time, "eliminating the middleman" will not reduce prices, because the dollars that go to intermediaries compensate them for the performance of tasks that must be accomplished regardless of the economic system in effect. In other words, a company can eliminate intermediaries, but it cannot eliminate the functions they perform.

> A **COMPANY CAN ELIMINATE INTERMEDIARIES, BUT IT CANNOT ELIMINATE THE FUNCTIONS THEY PERFORM.**

HOW INTERMEDIARIES FIT INTO DISTRIBUTION CHANNELS

Chapter 1 outlined a conventional channel of distribution consisting of a manufacturer, a wholesaler, a retailer, and the ultimate consumer. Not all channels include all of these marketing institutions. In some cases, a unit of product may pass directly from manufacturer to consumer. In others, it may be handled by not just one but two or more wholesalers. To show why these many variations exist, we will examine the role of intermediaries in marketing channels.

Consider this conventional channel of distribution:

Manufacturer → Retailer → Ultimate consumer

It is possible, as shown here, to have a channel of distribution that does not include a separate wholesaler. A manufacturer can choose to sell directly to retailers, in effect eliminating the wholesaler. However, the marketing functions performed by the wholesaler must then be shifted to one of the other parties in the channel—the retailer or the manufacturer. For instance, with the wholesaler out of the picture, the manufacturer may have to create a sales force to call on the numerous retailers. If the manufacturer assumes some or all of the marketing functions, they are said to have been shifted backward in the channel. If the retailer assumes them, they are said to have been shifted forward in the channel. For example, the manufacturer may decide to perform the function of breaking bulk by sending comparatively small orders to individual retail customers. On the other hand, the retailer may be willing to accept truckload lots of the product, store large quantities of it, and perform the activity of breaking down these larger quantities into smaller quantities.

In any case, the functions performed by the eliminated wholesaler do not disappear; they are simply shifted to another channel member. The channel member that assumes these functions expects to be compensated in some way. The retailer may expect lower prices and higher margins for the extra work performed. The manufacturer may expect larger purchase orders, more aggressive retail promotion, or more control over the distribution process.

The key to setting the structure of a channel of distribution is to determine how the necessary marketing functions can be carried out most efficiently and effectively. Certain variables, such as price, the complexity of the product, and the number of customers to be served, can serve as guides to the appropriate channel structures. However, the functions to be performed should be the primary consideration in the marketing manager's distribution plans. Let us consider some of the major functions performed by intermediaries: physical distribution, communication, and facilitating functions.

PHYSICAL DISTRIBUTION FUNCTIONS

Physical distribution functions include breaking bulk, accumulating bulk, creating assortments, reducing transactions, and transporting and storing.

Breaking Bulk   With few exceptions, intermediaries perform a bulk-breaking function. The **bulk-breaking function** consists of buying in relatively large quantities, such as truckloads, and then selling in smaller quantities, passing the lesser amounts of merchandise on to retailers, organizational buyers, wholesalers, or other customers. By accumulating large quantities of goods and then breaking them into smaller amounts suitable for many buyers, intermediaries can reduce the cost of distribution for both manufacturers and consumers. Consumers need not buy and store great amounts of merchandise, which would increase their own storage costs and the risks of spoilage, fire, and theft. Manufacturers are spared the necessity of dividing their outputs into the small order sizes retailers or consumers might prefer. Bulk breaking is sometimes termed "resolution of economic discrepancies," because manufacturers, as a rule, turn out amounts of merchandise that are vast compared with the quantity that an individual buyer might care to purchase. Breaking bulk resolves this discrepancy.

Accumulating Bulk   In the majority of cases, it is the task of the intermediary to break bulk. However, an intermediary may also create bulk, buying units of the same product from many small producers and offering the larger amount to buy-

Bulk-breaking function
An activity, performed by marketing intermediaries, consisting of buying products in relatively large quantities and selling in smaller quantities.

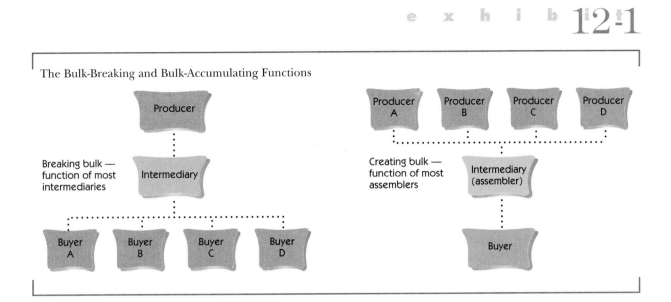

The Bulk-Breaking and Bulk-Accumulating Functions

Breaking bulk — function of most intermediaries: Producer → Intermediary → Buyer A, Buyer B, Buyer C, Buyer D

Creating bulk — function of most assemblers: Producer A, Producer B, Producer C, Producer D → Intermediary (assembler) → Buyer

ers who prefer to purchase in large quantities. These intermediaries are performing a **bulk-accumulating function.** An intermediary performing this function is called, not surprisingly, an **assembler.** The classic examples of assemblers are in agricultural and fishing businesses. A maker of applesauce, such as Mott's, or a fish canner, such as Bumble Bee, would probably not want to have to deal with many small farmers or independent owners of fishing boats. Assemblers gather large quantities of apples or tuna or other products attractive to large buyers. Exhibit 12-1 contrasts the operation of assemblers with that of bulk-breaking intermediaries.

After accumulating bulk, marketers of agricultural products and raw materials typically perform a **sorting function,** which involves identifying differences in quality and breaking down the product into grade or size categories. For example, eggs are sorted into jumbo grade AA, large grade AA, and so on.

Creating Assortments   Another function that intermediaries perform is the creation of assortments of merchandise that would otherwise not be available. This **assorting function** resolves the economic discrepancy resulting from the factory operator's natural inclination to produce a large quantity of a single product or a line of similar products and the consumer's desire to select from a wide variety of choices. Wholesalers that purchase many different products from different manufacturers can offer retailers a greater assortment of items than an individual manufacturer is able to provide. Consider how magazine publishers and retailers use intermediaries to solve a very big assorting problem. There are at least 30,000 different magazine titles available from U.S. publishers. No newsstand operator or other retailer carries anything like that number; a series of intermediaries is used to sort these many titles into appropriate groupings for individual stores.

National wholesalers, such as Hearst, ICD, and Select Magazines, move the thousands of titles to hundreds of local wholesalers. Their reward for fulfilling this gargantuan task is about 6 percent of the magazines' retail prices, out of which they must pay all expenses involved. The local distributors continue the task of breaking bulk, moving the magazines to countless supermarkets, newsstands, drugstores, and other retail spots. But there is more to the local wholesaler's task than simply breaking bulk and making delivery. The local wholesaler must select, from among the 30,000 available titles, the ones that are appropriate for the individual retailers' operations. Then, this assortment of titles must be

Bulk-accumulating function
An activity, performed by marketing intermediaries, consisting of buying small quantities of a particular product from many small producers and then selling the assembled larger quantities.

Assembler
A marketing intermediary that performs a bulk-accumulating function.

Sorting function
An activity, performed by marketing intermediaries, consisting of classifying accumulated products as to grade and size, and then grouping them accordingly.

Assorting function
An activity, performed by marketing intermediaries, consisting of combining products purchased from several manufacturers to create assortments.

Periodical Wholesalers of North America
www.periodical.org

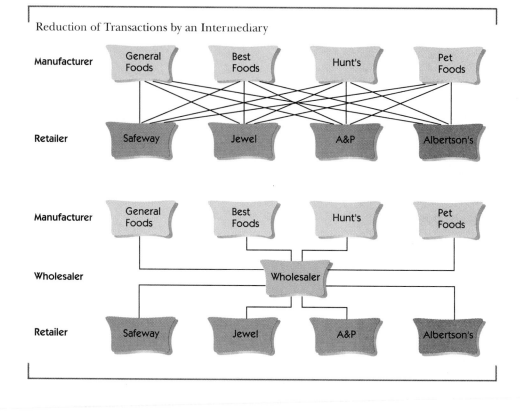

Reduction of Transactions by an Intermediary

assembled in the proper numbers for each retailer. The local wholesaler is paid about 20 percent of the cover prices.

Complicated as this sounds, the system is so efficient that less than 36 hours after a new *TV Guide* is printed, it has arrived at more than 150,000 retail establishments. Although the influence of wholesalers has declined in certain industries, it is obvious why wholesalers remain very important in the magazine distribution business.

Reducing Transactions   There is one underlying reason why intermediaries can economically accumulate bulk, break bulk, and create assortments. The presence of intermediaries in the distribution system actually reduces the number of transactions necessary to accomplish the exchanges that keep the economy moving and consumers satisfied.

As Exhibit 12-2 indicates, even if only four suppliers of grocery items attempt to transact business with just four supermarket buying headquarters, the number of interrelationships necessary is far greater than the number needed once an intermediary, such as a food wholesaler, is added to the system. Channel intermediaries, in their dual roles as buying agents for their customers and selling agents for the manufacturers with which they deal, simplify the necessary transaction process considerably. (Of course, channels of distribution can become too long. Such channels are common in Japan, as you will see later in this chapter.) Intermediaries not only reduce the number of transactions but also reduce the geographic distances that buyers and sellers must travel to complete exchanges and spare manufacturers the trouble of locating and contacting individual potential customers. These are some of the ways wholesalers and retailers can reduce costs. If manufacturers and consumers had to perform all these activities themselves, they would have to bear the costs involved.

Transporting and Storing Intermediaries, in most cases, perform or manage two other marketing functions: transporting and storing. Merchandise must be physically moved from points of production to points of con-

Storage, breaking bulk, and transportation are important distribution functions.

sumption. This process often involves storing, or holding, the product at various spots along the way. Intermediaries of all types, including retailers, frequently store goods until they are demanded by customers further along in the channel of distribution. Consider Busch beer—the most popular beer in the Cleveland, Ohio, market. If each person who wanted to buy Busch had to travel from Cleveland to the Busch brewery in St. Louis to make a purchase, those hundreds of thousands of customers—or Busch's employees, if the company chose to make home deliveries—would travel an incredible total distance. Wholesalers and retailers provide storage in the Cleveland market and enable Busch to send relatively few truckloads of beer to that city, greatly reducing the total distance otherwise traveled. It is clear that transportation and storage functions are necessary to satisfy the Cleveland area's demand for Busch beer. Although this example may seem far-fetched, it illustrates that one of the most important functions of intermediaries is to provide regional and local storage. The local Anheuser-Busch wholesaler, the neighborhood tavern, and the corner 7-Eleven all carry an inventory, and thus each performs the storage function.

We should mention that some types of intermediaries do not take possession of the goods whose distribution they facilitate. In such cases, the intermediary does not actually transport or store the merchandise. Instead, the intermediary coordinates transportation and storage or contributes in some other way to the creation of time and place utility. Thus, you should think of transportation and storage in a broad sense that includes the contribution of wholesalers that, for example, arrange for shipment of goods from a producer-owned place of storage to an organizational buyer's place of business.

COMMUNICATION AND TRANSACTION FUNCTIONS

Intermediaries perform a communication function, which includes buying, selling, and other activities involving gathering or disseminating information. The ultimate purpose of the communication link between the manufacturer and the retailer or between the wholesaler and the retailer is to transfer ownership—that is, to complete a transaction that results in an exchange of title.

Wholesalers and retailers may perform an important promotional function for manufacturers when they provide product information and price quotes. Most frequently, this communication is carried out by a sales force. However, intermediaries also use advertising and such sales promotion tools as retail displays. In other words, intermediaries perform a **selling function** for the manufacturer, often providing a sales force or other promotional efforts that they can supply more efficiently than the manufacturer can. The wholesaler provides a **buying function** for retailers, organizational users, and other customers. A wholesaler's contact with numerous manufacturers allows it to evaluate the quality of a wide assortment of goods from competing manufacturers. Thus, retailers and other customers are freed of the burden of evaluating every manufacturer's product assortments. This allows them more time to specialize in the retailing and merchandising of products.

Intermediaries further serve as channels of communication by informing buyers how products are to be sold, used, repaired, or guaranteed. They can even

Selling function
Activities, performed by intermediaries, that are associated with communicating ideas and making a sale, and thus effecting the transfer of ownership of a product.

Buying function
Activities, performed by intermediaries, that are associated with making a purchase and thus effecting the transfer of ownership of a product.

explain new product developments. (In fact, retailers should pass along more of this information to their customers; unfortunately many retail salespeople are not trained to provide information of this sort.) Because intermediaries typically deal with a number of manufacturers or other suppliers of goods, they are in a unique position to serve as conduits of information.

Intermediaries, being "in the middle," are well placed not only to pass information from producers to other channel members but also to collect information from channel members or retail shoppers and return it to producers. For example, suppose a retailer receives serious consumer complaints about a product or some product-related matter such as repair service. The retailer should pass this information backward in the channel to the wholesaler, who can bring the matter to the attention of the producer. *Should* is the key word here. Too often, whether because of apathy or the fear of somehow being blamed for a problem, intermediaries fail to perform this potentially valuable service. Marketers at all levels should encourage communication throughout channels of distribution because the satisfaction of all channel members and consumers is at stake.

FACILITATING FUNCTIONS

The transportation and storage functions of channel intermediaries are their most obvious contributions to the operation of the marketing system. However, intermediaries perform additional, so-called facilitating functions, which are not quite so apparent to observers of a channel in operation. Because the tasks of a channel intermediary can be so varied, it is nearly impossible to list all the facilitating functions a channel member might perform. However, three major categories of facilitating functions should be mentioned specifically: providing extra services, offering credit, and taking risks.

Service function
Activities, performed by intermediaries, that increase the efficiency and effectiveness of the exchange process. Repair services and management services provided by intermediaries are examples.

Extra Services   Channel members, particularly intermediaries, can and do provide a range of extra services that increase the efficiency and effectiveness of the channel; intermediaries thus perform a **service function.** For many products, the availability of a post-sale repair service is an absolute necessity. Office photocopiers always seem to need either routine maintenance or minor or major overhauls. Wholesalers and retailers of such machines usually offer repair services on either a contract or an emergency basis. They also carry necessary supplies like

paper. Other products—such as personal computers and cellular telephones—are not so prone to breakdowns, yet buyers like to know that repair service is available should it ever be needed. Honoring manufacturers' guarantees can be another responsibility of intermediaries.

Channel intermediaries can also provide a variety of management services. In the food industry, for example, wholesalers offer such services as computerized accounting systems, inventory planning, store site selection, store layout planning, and management training programs. The extra services offered are good business for the wholesalers in that (1) they attract customers and (2) they help their food retailer customers to stay in business and to remain successful. The services, if not offered by every competing wholesaler, can also provide a competitive advantage to the food wholesaler willing to invest in them.

Wholesalers may offer other services, too. They may help in preparing advertisements. Wholesalers sometimes offer a line of private brand goods or a wholesaler-owned label that smaller retailers can use to create an image similar to those of larger chains. Some "behind-the-scenes" wholesalers offering extensive services are McKesson, Supervalu, and Fleming Foods. Have you heard of them?

McKesson
www.mckesson.com

Credit Services   Most intermediaries perform a **credit function** by offering credit service of one kind or another. Although some wholesalers and retailers operate exclusively on a cash-and-carry basis, promising to pass related savings on to their customers, they make up a relatively small proportion of the millions of intermediaries operating in the United States.

Credit function
Provision of credit to another member of a distribution channel.

Some credit services provided by channel members may not be immediately obvious. A retailer that accepts MasterCard or Visa provides a credit service that in fact costs the retailer a percent of the sales fee, which it must pay to the credit card company. Sears, Montgomery Ward, and many other retailers offer their own credit plans, which involve a more clear-cut provision of service than accepting an "outside" card.

Wholesalers and other nonretailer channel members may provide credit in a number of ways. Although a supplier may have a credit system so unique that buyers pay particular notice, supplier credit systems are generally so widespread throughout a trade that buyers scarcely see the credit system as a true service. Intermediaries in many fields routinely offer 30, 60, or more days to pay for merchandise ordered. Often, the days do not start "counting" until the goods are delivered to the buyer's place of business. In effect, such a service permits the buyer to make some money on a product before having to pay for it.

Risk Taking   In almost everything they do, channel intermediaries perform a **risk-taking function.** When purchasing a product from a manufacturer or supplier of any type, intermediaries run the risk of getting stuck with an item that has fallen

Risk-taking function
Assumption of the responsibility for losses when the future is uncertain.

e   x   h   i   b   i   t   **12-3**   What a Channel Intermediary Does for Its Suppliers and Its Customers

MARKETING FUNCTION	PERFORMED FOR SUPPLIERS	PERFORMED FOR CUSTOMERS
Physical distribution functions	Breaking bulk Accumulating bulk Creating assortments Transportation Storage	Sorting into desired quantities Assorting items into desired variety Delivery (transportation) Storage
Communication functions	Promotion, especially selling and communication of product information Gathering customer information	Buying based on interpretations of customer needs Dissemination of information
Facilitating functions	Financing customer purchases Providing management services Taking risk	Credit financing Regular service Management assistance

out of favor with the buying public because of a shift in fashion or the death of a fad. It is also possible for the product to spoil while it is in storage or be lost through fire or some other disaster. Intermediaries bear these risks in addition to market risk.

Intermediaries run obvious risks in offering credit to the individuals and organizations to which they sell. They take legal risks in that intermediaries, not just manufacturers, can be held responsible for problems caused by faulty products or misleading claims.

When intermediaries, for whatever reason, seek to avoid the service of risk taking, the distribution system becomes less effective. In hard economic times, for example, retailers and wholesalers are tempted to engage in "hand-to-mouth" buying, ordering small quantities of products and attempting to sell them before placing yet another small order. Such behavior defeats the whole purpose of the marketing channel by eliminating the "buy in large quantities—sell in smaller quantities" premise on which most channels are based. Exhibit 12-3 summarizes the basic functions that channel intermediaries perform.

Typical Channels of Distribution

We have already suggested that not all channels of distribution are alike. In fact, the variety of distribution channels is extensive indeed. That is because marketers are constantly seeking new ways to perform the distribution function. Both manufacturers and intermediaries have developed all sorts of variations on the basic theme of distribution. Each variation was developed in an effort to perform the distribution function better and thereby attract business.

Channels may be distinguished by the number of intermediaries they include; the more intermediaries, the longer the channel. Some organizations choose to sell their products directly to the consumer or organizational user; others use long channels that include numbers of wholesalers, agents, and retailers to reach buyers.[5] This discussion focuses on the most common of the numerous channels of distribution available. Exhibit 12-4 shows the primary channels for consumer and organizational products.

CHANNELS OF DISTRIBUTION FOR CONSUMER GOODS AND SERVICES

Exhibit 12-4 gives examples of typical channels for the distribution of consumer goods and services.

In the United States, Gevalia Kaffe, fine coffees of Europe, are available only by express home delivery. The company's distribution strategy is to use a direct channel of distribution.

www.gevalia.com

Typical Channels of Distribution

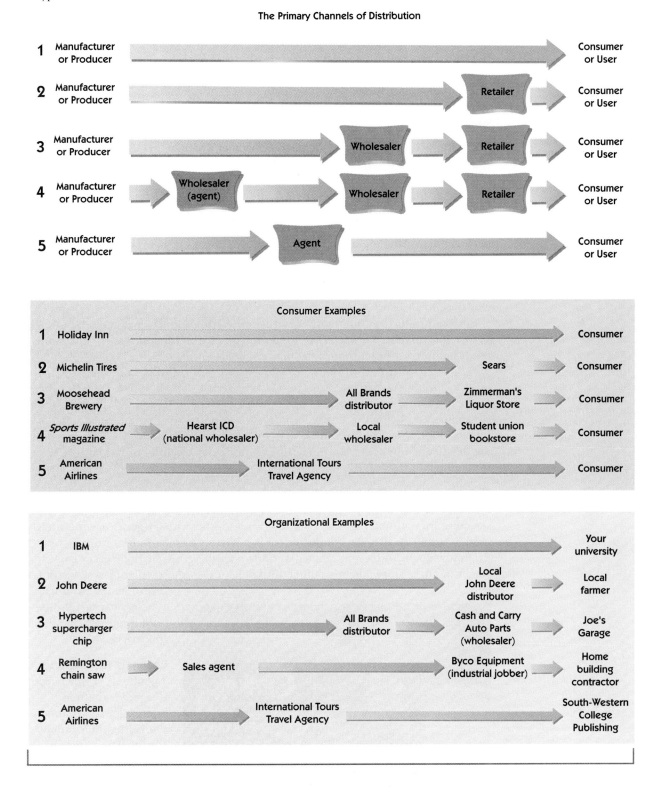

The Primary Channels of Distribution

1 Manufacturer or Producer → Consumer or User

2 Manufacturer or Producer → Retailer → Consumer or User

3 Manufacturer or Producer → Wholesaler → Retailer → Consumer or User

4 Manufacturer or Producer → Wholesaler (agent) → Wholesaler → Retailer → Consumer or User

5 Manufacturer or Producer → Agent → Consumer or User

Consumer Examples

1 Holiday Inn → Consumer

2 Michelin Tires → Sears → Consumer

3 Moosehead Brewery → All Brands distributor → Zimmerman's Liquor Store → Consumer

4 *Sports Illustrated* magazine → Hearst ICD (national wholesaler) → Local wholesaler → Student union bookstore → Consumer

5 American Airlines → International Tours Travel Agency → Consumer

Organizational Examples

1 IBM → Your university

2 John Deere → Local John Deere distributor → Local farmer

3 Hypertech supercharger chip → All Brands distributor → Cash and Carry Auto Parts (wholesaler) → Joe's Garage

4 Remington chain saw → Sales agent → Byco Equipment (industrial jobber) → Home building contractor

5 American Airlines → International Tours Travel Agency → South-Western College Publishing

The Direct Channel for Consumer Goods and Services   A good example of the direct channel is supplied by the neighborhood bakery, which converts flour, water, and other raw materials into baked goods and then retails these products, providing any other functions that might be necessary to complete the transaction. The direct channel is also familiar as the distribution method used by many marketers of services and not-for-profit groups that solicit donations.

Marketers of consumer goods and services that promote their products through mail-order catalogs, telemarketing (telephone sales), and toll-free numbers listed in advertisements and that distribute directly to consumers through the mail or a delivery service are also using direct channels. The strategies of these direct marketers, which do not use retail outlets or contact customers in person, rely largely on data-based management and certain direct-response promotional strategies. We will discuss direct marketing further in Chapters 14 and 15.

The Manufacturer (Producer)–Retailer–Consumer Channel   The *manufacturer–retailer–consumer channel* is commonly employed when the retailer involved is a sizable organization, such as a discount chain like Wal-Mart. This type of retail marketing organization may prefer to deal directly with manufacturers to be able to order specially made merchandise or obtain discounts or other benefits. Generally, the benefits must be important enough to make the retailer willing to perform many wholesaling functions. However, in an effort to please large retail customers, the manufacturer may agree to perform wholesaler functions. Efficiencies that accrue to a manufacturer because of the large orders placed by Sears or Wal-Mart can more than offset the wholesaling costs the manufacturer may have to absorb.

Service producers also use this channel of distribution. For example, HBO's Visitor Information Network (VIN) is a tourism channel that provides continuous programming for hotel rooms, highlighting local attractions, dining, and shopping. The channel of distribution for this service is VIN–hotel–consumer, or producer–retailer–consumer.

Many other service marketers use a producer–retailer–consumer channel when consumers can benefit from the location, product information, or other services a retailer offers. For example, many dry cleaners have their customers' suede clothing dry-cleaned by companies specializing in the dry cleaning process rather than in retailing.

The Manufacturer–Wholesaler–Retailer–Consumer Channel   The *manufacturer–wholesaler–retailer–consumer channel* of distribution is the most commonly used structure for consumer goods. This is because most consumer goods are so widely used. It would be virtually impossible for the Wrigley Company, for example, to deal individually with every retailer stocking chewing gum, let alone every consumer of gum. Thus, a long channel, with at least two intermediaries, is needed to distribute the product. Wholesalers can also be used in the distribution of services.

Channels That Include Agents   A familiar type of agent is the real estate agent. Consumers marketing their homes (or other used goods) often lack time and marketing skills, so they hire agents. Manufacturers, especially those lacking expertise in marketing a particular product line, may choose to permit manufacturers' agents or selling agents to handle the marketing of their products. Such agents do not take title to the goods they sell and usually earn commissions rather than a salary.

In marketing channels for consumer goods, agents may, depending on the circumstances and the product they offer, sell to retailers or wholesalers. The *manufacturer–agent–wholesaler–retailer–consumer channel* is widely used in the marketing of consumer products, especially convenience goods.

It might seem that travel agents used by airlines function as retailers. Technically, however, this is a channel involving an agent. The *service producer–agent channel* is common in marketing of consumer services. Ticketmaster provides such services for sports teams like the Chicago Bulls and the Chicago Cubs.

Ticketmaster
www.ticketmaster.com

ELECTRONIC INFORMATION BROKERS—AN EMERGING NEW INTERMEDIARY

The communication function of intermediaries has always been important because buyers need information to make decisions. In some situations, buyers also need to search to learn what organizations or individuals are marketing the product they desire. In the past, a consumer might buy a copy of *Consumer Reports* to reduce the time spent searching for information and to learn experts' evaluations of products. The consumer would then go to the store to purchase the desired item.

In today's digital world, a new form of intermediary, the electronic information broker, has emerged.[6] *Electronic information brokers* provide shopping or information buying assistance services that help buyers and sellers find each other. These services can offer sophisticated and highly specific information searches at a very low cost. Auto-By-Tel, for example, supplies its customers with the names of local

ELECTRONIC **INFORMATION BROKERS OFFER SOPHISTICATED AND HIGHLY SPECIFIC INFORMATION SEARCHES AT A VERY LOW COST.**

automobile dealers that will provide the exact car the buyer wants at a rock-bottom, no-negotiation price. Auto-By-Tel's role as an intermediary is to provide information. The physical transaction takes place elsewhere.

Auto-By-Tel
www.autobytel.com

CHANNELS OF DISTRIBUTION FOR BUSINESS-TO-BUSINESS MARKETING

Business-to-business marketers use channels that are similar to those used by the marketers of consumer products. The primary channels are illustrated in Exhibit 12-4.

The Direct Channel in Business-to-Business Marketing The name "business-to-business" suggests the importance of the direct channel in the marketing of organizational products. Indeed, the direct channel is the one most commonly used in the marketing of organizational goods. Direct organizational sales of industrial machinery such as escalators, power-generating machinery such as turbine engines, metals such as titanium, and many other products require well-informed salespersons, and perhaps engineers, who can help the buyer fit the product into its organizational facility or manufacturing process. Otis Elevator, for example, is a business-to-business marketer that uses a direct channel.

Many business-to-business marketers now use the Internet for electronic commerce. This constitutes a direct channel.

The Manufacturer–Wholesaler–Organizational User Channel Because, by definition, retailers deal with consumers, there is no distribution channel for organizational goods that directly parallels the manufacturer–retailer channel. However, there is a trade channel for organizational goods that relies on just one wholesale intermediary, which performs a function much like that of a retailer. This is

Auto-By-Tel If buying a new car gives you about as much pleasure as scheduling a root canal, take heart. Computer technology, modern merchandising, and old-fashioned entrepreneurial spirit are about to put traditional car dealers—among the most hated business people in America—on the endangered species list. Already about one in ten buyers has discovered how to bypass the dealer. . . . The information superhighway, it turns out, goes right past a car dealership. . . .

More and more car buyers are doing their shopping electronically. The experience of George Chin, 43, a technical services manager in upstate New York, is typical. Using the Internet, he compared the specifications of various models and learned their retail and wholesale prices. Then he placed an electronic order for a Ford Explorer XLT with Auto-By-Tel, a computerized broker service. A few days later, he got a call from a nearby dealer, Bill Colb Ford, which filled the order for a fixed amount over the wholesale price and delivered the vehicle. Says Chin: "The whole experience was painless. There was no price haggling. No psychological pressure. No surprises."

Auto-By-Tel is the creation of a former California Ford and Chrysler dealer named Peter Ellis. When his idea for selling cars on QVC television didn't work out two years ago, he decided to retail them in cyberspace. Ellis took sites on established online services like CompuServe, as well as on the World Wide Web, to solicit orders from customers. He relays an order to one of 1,200 dealers, each of which pays Ellis between $200 and $1,500 a month for referrals. The margins on each sale are low (about $600), but so are the costs. By snagging their customers electronically, the dealers can cut their marketing expense from $400 a car to $30.[7]

the *manufacturer–distributor–organizational user channel.* The names for this type of wholesaler vary from industry to industry; among the most common terms used are *jobber* and *distributor.*

Snap-On Tools, maker of socket wrenches and other hand tools, uses distributors who, working out of well-stocked vans, call directly on Snap-On's customers, professional mechanics. Distributors selling to organizational users may also operate store-like facilities that buyers such as electricians or plumbers may patronize. In either format, organizational distributors perform storage and communication functions. They may, as in the Snap-On example, provide delivery, and they may also supply credit or perform other functions. The organizational distributor is classified as a merchant intermediary, because this distributor takes title to the goods. Channels of distribution for organizational goods sometimes include more than one merchant wholesaler. This arrangement is most common in international marketing.

Business-to-Business Marketers Also Use Agents The *manufacturer– agent–organizational user channel* is commonly used in business-to-business marketing by small manufacturers that market only one product to many users. The wide range of customers to which agents sell suggests the main attraction of agents for manufacturers: flexibility. One type of agent intermediary, the broker, can be used on an occasional basis, as needed. No continuing relationship—and therefore no continuing financial remuneration or other obligation—is necessary. Similarly, manufacturers' agents operate on a commission basis within fixed geographic territories. Therefore, they appeal to small organizations whose limited financial resources make it difficult for them to fund their own sales forces. Manufacturers' agents are also attractive because they can be employed in "thin" market areas or in foreign countries where potential sales do not seem to justify a manufacturer's forming its own sales force.

Vertical Marketing Systems

In many industries, such as the fast-food restaurant industry, the dominant distribution structure is the vertical marketing system. The concept of a vertical marketing system emerged along with the need to manage or administer the functions performed by intermediaries at two or more levels of the channel of distribution.

Vertical marketing systems, or vertically integrated marketing systems, consist of networks of vertically aligned establishments that are professionally managed as centrally administered distribution systems. Central administration is intended to provide technological, managerial, and promotional economies of scale through the integration, coordination, and synchronization of transactions and marketing activities necessary to the distribution function. There are three types of vertical marketing systems: corporate systems, contractual systems, and administered strategic alliances.

CORPORATE SYSTEMS—TOTAL OWNERSHIP

The **corporate vertical marketing system** connects two or more channel members through ownership. It is exemplified by a retailer, such as Sears, that integrates backward into manufacturing to assure quality control over production and corporate control over the distribution system. A manufacturer may obtain complete control of the successive stages of distribution by vertically integrating through ownership. Sherwin-Williams administers a corporate vertical marketing system by owning more than 2,000 retail paint outlets.

CONTRACTUAL SYSTEMS—LEGAL RELATIONSHIPS

In a **contractual vertical marketing system,** channel leadership is assigned not by ownership but by agreement in contractual form. In such a channel, relationships are spelled out so that there is no question about distribution coordination. The relationship between McDonald's franchise holders and McDonald's headquarters is a contractual one wherein the rights and responsibilities of both parties are clearly identified. The idea behind such an approach to distribution is that if all parties live up to the agreement, the system will work smoothly and well. In the main, this has certainly been the case for McDonald's, although the secret of McDonald's success is not merely the employment of a contractual vertical marketing system but also the hard work required to make it succeed.

There are three subtypes of contractual systems: retailer cooperative organizations, wholesaler-sponsored voluntary chains, and franchises. A **retailer cooperative organization** is a group of independent retailers, such as Certified Grocers, that maintains a centralized buying center to perform a wholesaling function. These retailers have combined their financial resources and their expertise to more effectively control their wholesaling needs. By capitalizing on economies of scale, they lower wholesaling costs with their cooperative effort. At the same time, they retain independence.

The **wholesaler-sponsored voluntary chain** is similar to the cooperative organization except that the wholesaler initiates and manages the collaborative effort so that it has a strong network of loyal retailers. The independent retailers served agree to use only this one wholesaler, while the wholesaler agrees to service all the organized retailers. Ace Hardware is a voluntary chain. Each of their stores uses the common name and receives marketing support that helps the independent retailer compete with chain stores.

A **franchise** is a contractual agreement between a franchisor, typically a manufacturer or a wholesaler, and a number of independent retailers, or franchisees. The franchise agreement often gives the franchisor much discretion in controlling the operations of the small retailers. In exchange for fees, royalties, and a share of the profits, the franchisor offers assistance and, often, supplies. Franchise assistance may take the form of marketing research information or strategic marketing planning aids (for example, new product planning) from franchisor experts. The franchisee is usually responsible for paying for insurance, property taxes, labor, and supplies.

Corporate vertical marketing system
A vertical marketing system in which two or more channel members are connected through ownership.

Contractual vertical marketing system
A vertical marketing system in which channel coordination and leadership are specified in a contractual agreement.

Retailer cooperative organization
A group of independent retailers that combine resources and expertise to control their wholesaling needs, as through a centralized wholesale buying center.

Wholesaler-sponsored voluntary chain
A vertical marketing system, initiated by a wholesaler, that links a group of independent retailers in a relationship with the wholesale supplier.

Franchise
A contractual agreement between a franchisor and a franchisee by which the franchisee distributes the franchisor's product.

Obtaining a McDonald's franchise isn't easy. Potential franchisees go through a 2-year screening process. They must work at a store and undergo thorough training before gaining final approval, all for the right to plunk down tens of thousands of dollars and sign a 20-year contract that guarantees McDonald's a royalty of 4 percent of sales, plus another 8.5 percent or more of sales for rent, plus 4 percent of sales for advertising—over 16 cents of every dollar taken right off the top. But shed no tears, for McDonald's operators wind up taking home about $200,000 a year per store. High-volume stores can net three times as much.

The franchise has been popular and successful in the fast-food industry. Subway, Wendy's, Boston Market, and many other familiar fast-food restaurants are franchises. Subway is one of the fastest-growing fast-food franchise operations. Franchising is prominent in the service industry as well. Consider such familiar names as Brakeman, Midas, Mail Boxes Etc, and Century 21.

One of the main advantages of the franchise system, as well as some other contractual marketing systems, is that it offers brand identity and a nationally recognizable storefront for a retail outlet. Ethan Allen Carriage Houses, Holiday Inns, Burger Kings, and other franchise operations have strong identities. The person driving down the highway has a very clear conception of what products or services will be found at the franchise outlet.

Administered strategic alliance

A vertical marketing system in which a strong channel leader coordinates marketing activities at all levels in the channel through planning and management of a mutually beneficial program.

ADMINISTERED STRATEGIC ALLIANCES—STRONG LEADERSHIP

The third major type of vertical system is the **administered strategic alliance.** Here, a strong position of leadership, rather than outright ownership, may be the source of influence over channel activities. The "administrator" may be any channel member large enough or with enough market clout to dominate the others. Alternatively, a strategic alliance may be built on a commitment to establish a long-term relationship based on collaborative efforts. The services Caterpillar, Inc. offers its dealers are the subject of the Focus on Relationships feature.

focus on relationships

Caterpillar Caterpillar, Inc. wants to move mountains for its dealers. The dealerships are all independently owned, but Caterpillar considers its dealers as partners, not agents or intermediaries. Caterpillar is as concerned about dealers' performance as the dealers are, because the machinery and engine maker's enormous and loyal dealer network is one of its major competitive advantages.

Caterpillar maintains its position as a leader in the global machinery and engines market because of its strong focus on collaborating with dealers. It offers a range of support and consulting services aimed at helping dealers boost their profitability. "When you buy the iron, you get the company," Caterpillar literature says.

One Caterpillar service ensures that dealers' inventories are at the right level. An electronic data interchange linking all dealers to the computer at Caterpillar's Indianapolis distribution center enables dealers to order any part they need for delivery the next day. The company will buy back parts the dealers do not sell. And it tries to pace its introduction of new products according to dealers' capabilities. Caterpillar even has a subsidiary, Caterpillar Logistic Services, that distributes Caterpillar parts directly to its dealers' customers.

Caterpillar's dealerships have become diversified companies in their own right. With the strong encouragement of Caterpillar, many have established related businesses, such as refurbishing tractor parts and rebuilding diesel engines. Caterpillar loses some new-parts business this way, but it gains in the long run because its equipment becomes more economical for the customer.

Caterpillar has "customer sensitivity training" programs for its U.S. dealers' 2,400 salespeople. Caterpillar wants "the entire distribution network to focus on the customer first. [The company] trains its sales force to understand why customers buy [Caterpillar] products, what their needs are, the importance of follow-up, the need to let a customer vent his anger, and how to help a customer resolve problems without passing the responsibility on to someone else."

Caterpillar's focus on dealer relationships is not limited to the United States. The company has dealers around the world. In 1993, it positioned itself to take advantage of business opportunities as Russia and many other Eastern European countries strove to establish capitalist economies. In 1994, it entered into a joint venture with AMO-Zil, Russia's leading truck manufacturer, to produce parts for Caterpillar equipment. It is developing a network of dealers and support organizations in these countries to provide support for products powered by Caterpillar engines.

Perhaps the most significant indicator that Caterpillar believes in long-term relationships with its dealers is the fact that the company conducts a course at its headquarters to encourage dealers' children to remain in the business.[8]

Administered systems generally are constructed around a line of merchandise rather than the complete manufacturing, wholesaling, or retailing operation. For example, a manufacturer wishing to ensure that wholesalers and retailers follow its comprehensive program of marketing activities might use an administered strategic alliance to coordinate marketing activities and make them attractive to all parties (for example, by offering discounts or financial assistance). Administered strategic alliances may include arrangements to share or pool inventory information or exchange other databases so that purchase orders are executed automatically by computers. Examples of strong channel leadership through administered strategic alliances may be found in companies such as O. M. Scott and Sons Company (a producer of lawn products) and Baxter Healthcare. The position of leadership can be held by a wholesaler or a retailer as well as by a manufacturer.

Planning the Channel of Distribution

Distribution strategy requires two major decisions. The first involves the structure of the channel of distribution. The second concerns the number of intermediaries that will be used, or the extent of distribution.

DETERMINING THE STRUCTURE OF THE CHANNEL

What determines whether a channel of distribution should be short or long? The selection criteria are influenced by the other elements of the marketing mix strategy, by organizational resources, and by a number of external environmental factors.

The Marketing Mix Strategy In selecting the channel of distribution, the organization must consider other elements of the marketing mix. For example, an organization's long-term strategic pricing plan may determine whether it will distribute a product through high-margin outlets or through high-volume outlets appealing to price-conscious consumers. The product's characteristics, especially its tangible characteristics, may also play an important role in channel selection. For instance, if live Maine lobsters are to be sold in Tokyo, the channel of distribution will be largely dictated by the perishability of the product. Many products require after-sale service; hence, an intermediary's technical repair service often is an important consideration in selecting a channel of distribution. The size, bulk, and weight of a product will determine whether short channels are necessary to reduce transportation and handling costs. Other product considerations, such as the product's technical complexity, the replacement rate, the gross margin, and the image of the product, also influence the type of channel selected.

Organizational Resources Arm & Hammer Heavy Duty Detergent is marketed by Church & Dwight, a small company in comparison to Procter & Gamble and Colgate, its competitors. Church & Dwight works with 80 food brokers to market its product in supermarkets, whereas Procter & Gamble has the luxury of its own sales organization.

Utilizing one or more marketing intermediaries, as Church & Dwight does, disperses the responsibility for the performance of the distribution function. Thus, an organization that is unable to devote or uninterested in devoting financial resources to supporting its own sales force, storing a large inventory, or providing other distribution functions may use wholesalers or retailers to provide the resources or managerial expertise to handle these activities.

A company's existing channels of distribution for its other products are a tremendous resource—they may be the main determinant in the selection of a channel of distribution. Wow Lays, a new Frito-Lay snack food, was marketed through the same channel as Doritos and other Frito-Lay snacks. Relationships within this channel had already been established. Allowing one distribution channel to carry several items may lead to certain economies of scale.

External Environmental Factors Many elements of the external environment can affect channel selection. We will discuss market characteristics, consumer preferences and behavior, the nature and availability of intermediaries, and several other factors.

Market Characteristics The number of customers and the amount of the average purchase influence the length of the channel of distribution selected. If the market consists of a few large purchasers, channels are likely to be short. Conversely, if there are many small customers, channels are likely to be long.

Consumer Preferences and Behavior Customers' past behavior and preferences as to purchase location are major criteria that influence the selection of a distribution channel. Perhaps ultimate consumers prefer to buy a certain product in a wholesale club, such as Sam's. If Sam's prefers to purchase directly from manufacturers rather than through wholesalers, this preference has a dramatic impact on channel selection. At each market level, customer preferences must be considered. Furthermore, if a manufacturer finds that some of its buyers prefer to purchase its product in drugstores and others prefer to buy the product in discount stores, multiple channels of distribution may be necessary.

The Nature and Availability of Intermediaries In many cases, capable intermediaries are either unavailable or unwilling to handle a product. When the Levi Strauss Company tried to market its Tailored Classic men's suits, a high-quality, medium-priced product, the company found retailers resistant to handling the wool and wool-blend line because of the traditional Levi association with more casual clothing. Retailers insisted on displaying the Levi's suit and sport-coat line next to low-priced clothing and demanded price reductions. Furthermore, many retailers would not carry the line because their store images contrasted with the image of the traditional Levi product line. When the preferred intermediary is unavailable, a manufacturer may have to alter its channel of distribution, possibly by eliminating the wholesaler and going directly to the ultimate consumer in a certain territory.

Other Environmental Factors Any of the environmental forces discussed in Chapter 3 or Chapter 4 may have an impact on the channel of distribution. For example, the wholesaling and retailing structure in Japan is strongly influenced by political and legal factors. An organization must carefully consider all possible environmental forces before making a decision about a channel of distribution.

THE EXTENT OF DISTRIBUTION: HOW MANY OUTLETS?

Once the structure of the distribution channel has been determined, the manufacturer is faced with the problem of deciding on the intensity of distribution at each level

what went right?

American Greetings The big three card companies, led by Hallmark, with American Greetings right behind, and $546 million Gibson Greetings a distant third, favor different channels of distribution to reach card buyers. Hallmark is No. 1 in specialty stores, American Greetings is the leader in mass retail chains, and Gibson heads up deep-discount stores. This works out well for American Greetings, since there's no doubt that mass retail chains are now the place to be. For years, most women, 90 percent of card purchasers, bought their cards from specialty card shops. These days, however, 64 percent of cards are bought in mass retail outlets, while card purchases in specialty stores like Hallmark's have declined 36 percent since 1980.

American Greetings will be in good shape if it continues to grow with mass retail outlets like Wal-Mart and Target, whose sales are increasing 20 percent a year. If American Greetings continues to build its market share in these chains, it will likely take the leadership slot away from Hallmark within the next 5 to 10 years, even though both companies' annual sales growth has been about 8 percent over the past few years.[9]

within the channel. Determining the number of wholesalers and the number of retail outlets is an important decision that will determine the number of outlets where potential customers can expect to find the product. The various strategies, based on the degree of distribution intensity are (1) intensive distribution, (2) selective distribution, and (3) exclusive distribution.

Intensive Distribution   The strategy of **intensive distribution** seeks to obtain maximum product exposure at the retail level. When consumers will not go out of their way to purchase a product or will readily accept substitutes when the brand is not available, the appropriate strategy is to saturate every suitable retail outlet with the brand. Gasoline, chewing gum, and other convenience goods normally receive intensive distribution. Intensive distribution at the wholesale level allows almost all appropriate wholesalers to carry the product.

Products that are distributed intensively may be presold through mass media advertising or other means. Coca-Cola, for example, needs little personal selling and may be distributed in vending machines, supermarkets, drugstores, restaurants, and many other outlets. Pennzoil intensively distributes its motor oil in service stations, as well as in Kmart and Target stores and other mass merchandising outlets, where more than half of U.S. car motor oil is sold. To increase the intensity of its distribution, Pennzoil purchased a large share of Jiffy-Lube International, the leading oil-change-while-you-wait franchise.

Selective Distribution   At the retail level, a strategy of **selective distribution** restricts the sale of a product to a limited number of outlets. The manufacturers of Tommy Hilfiger shirts focus their marketing efforts on certain selected outlets with the desired store image. Each store must meet the company's performance standards while appealing to a specific target market. As distribution becomes more selective, the manufacturer may expect a greater effort on the part of the retailer (for example, a willingness to hold a larger inventory). Because retailers benefit from limits on the number of competitors, they are expected to be more willing to accept the manufacturer's suggestions and controls on the marketing strategy— for example, by supporting the list price.

Selective distribution is much more

Intensive distribution
A distribution strategy aimed at obtaining maximum exposure for a product at the retail level or wholesale level.

Selective distribution
A distribution strategy in which a product is sold in a limited number of outlets.

High-quality, prestigious brands such as Chanel No. 5 often use selective distribution strategies. Each store Chanel selects must meet certain standards and appeal to Chanel's target market.

commonly used for specialty and shopping goods than for convenience goods. However, Noxell Corporation, marketer of the Noxzema and Cover Girl brands of make-up and skin cream, selectively distributes its products in chain stores such as Kmart and Woolco. It lets its competitors vie for distribution in the more prestigious department and specialty stores. Its selective distribution strategy reaches its target market.

Exclusive Distribution   When a product requires aggressive personal selling, a complete inventory of the product line, repair service, or other special efforts, an intermediary may be granted an exclusive area. Generally, a manufacturer or wholesaler that grants a retailer **exclusive distribution** expects a maximum sales effort or expects to gain something from the prestige or efficiency of the retail outlet. Exclusive distribution agreements often involve contractual arrangements. Suppliers typically have written agreements with exclusive distributors stipulating

Exclusive distribution
A distribution strategy in which only one outlet in a given area is allowed to sell a product.

certain responsibilities that are too important to be left to a mutual understanding. Contracts outline tenure of appointment, trading area, sale conditions, warranty considerations, and extent of product line coverage. However, exclusive dealing may not be legal if it tends to lessen competition in a particular geographical area.

Caterpillar Inc. relies on a strong network of exclusive dealers. According to Caterpillar's president and chairman, "We have a tremendous regard for our dealers. We do not bypass or undercut them. Some of our competitors do and their dealers quit. Caterpillar dealers don't quit, they die rich."[10] This statement illustrates the cooperation and the degree of loyalty that can exist in an exclusive distribution system.

Note that the extent of distribution must be determined at each level in the channel. For example, a manufacturer like Coca-Cola may execute an intensive distribution strategy at the retail level and an exclusive distribution strategy at the wholesale level.

Channels of Distribution Around the World

There are many country-specific differences in distribution systems. For example, Japan has one of the most cumbersome distribution systems in the world. Most people think of Japan as the land of efficiency. They are surprised to learn that in Japan, most products en route from factory to consumer pass through countless wholesale distributors to tiny retail stores. In fact, the system is so expensive and inefficient by American standards that a Japanese camera costs more in Tokyo than in New York City. Many American companies find that distribution channels are the key barrier to marketing their products in Japan.[11] Japanese executives give four reasons why distribution is a problem in Japan:

1. Limited space and crowded conditions, necessitating low inventories and many small deliveries
2. Slow transportation because of congestion on an inadequate roadway system
3. Government regulations that protect small distributors and small retailers
4. Tradition-bound commitments and long-standing trading relationships among distributors, some of which have existed for generations

Although country-specific differences should not be ignored, sophisticated distribution systems exist in many parts of the world. As a general rule, international marketers experience few problems in planning distribution strategy as long as they stay within established routes. However, the task becomes more difficult when distribution deviates from these routes.[12]

Issues Surrounding Channel Relationships

Because the actions of one channel member may greatly influence the performance of another channel member, the relations among channel members are of considerable interest. The retailer relies on the manufacturer to create an adequate sales potential through advertising, product development, and other marketing strategies. An exclusive dealer's welfare is in jeopardy if a manufacturer's marketing strategy is not successful. A manufacturer may depend on the successful performance of a small number of wholesalers, which cannot be left to sink or swim on their own merits. In the following sections, we examine several issues related to relationships among interdependent channel members.

CHANNEL COOPERATION

The objectives and marketing strategies of two channel members—for example, a manufacturer and a retailer—may be in total harmony. Both parties may recognize that their tasks are linked and that by working together they can jointly exploit a marketing opportunity. The manufacturer promptly delivers a high-quality product with a good reputation; the retailer prices the product as expected and carries an inventory of the full product line. **Channel cooperation** exists when the marketing objectives and strategies of two channel members are harmonious.

Channel cooperation
Coordinated efforts by distribution channel members whose marketing objectives and strategies are harmonious.

CHANNEL CONFLICT

Channel conflict exists when channel members have disagreements and their relationship is antagonistic. Channel conflict often results from the absence of a clearly identified locus of formal channel power.[13] Channel members may disagree about the channel's common purpose or the responsibility for certain activities. The behavior of one channel member may be seen as inhibiting the attainment of another channel member's goals. (Channel conflict describes vertical conflicts among members of the same channel of distribution.[14] It should not be confused with economic competition between two like intermediaries at the same level in a channel, such as Macy's and Bloomingdale's, which is sometimes referred to as *horizontal conflict*.)

Channel conflict
Antagonism between distribution channel members.

CHANNEL **CONFLICT OFTEN RESULTS FROM THE ABSENCE OF A CLEARLY IDENTIFIED LOCUS OF FORMAL CHANNEL POWER.**

Consider the following instance of channel conflict. In 1992, Goodyear began selling its products to Sears—something it had not done before. In fact, for more than 60 years, Goodyear tires could be purchased only on new cars or from the company's exclusive network of independent dealers. Then in 1993, Goodyear started selling replacement tires to Discount Tire Company, a big independent tire retailer. These alignments with Sears and Discount caused considerable channel conflict. Goodyear's independent dealers expressed anger and feelings of betrayal. They protested that Goodyear's actions had eroded their competitive positions. Many dealers retaliated by taking on competing brands, especially private brands.

Vertical conflict can also arise when a wholesaler is frustrated because the manufacturer bypasses it and sells directly to larger accounts. Another typical source of conflict is a situation in which a dealer wishes to minimize its investment in inventory but cannot do so because the distributor does not maintain the proper inventory level and thus cannot be relied on to guarantee speedy delivery. Vertical conflict may occur when sales are down and, consequently, manufacturers accuse dealers or distributors of failing to promote aggressively. Conflict can also arise if manufacturers, wholesalers, or retailers believe that they are not making enough money on the product line.

In some cases, the causes of conflict are overt and readily identifiable; they arise from differences in channel members' opinions, goals, or attitudes. For example, when Levi's started marketing its five-pocket jeans through Sears and the JCPenney Company, there was no question about why managers of stores that had carried Levi's for years were upset. Department store chains interpreted the new Levi channel strategy as damaging to the brand's fashion credibility and a threat to their mark-ups. So they made the conflict more identifiable and more intense by ordering replacement brands such as Lee. In other instances, however, the cause of conflict may be latent frustration or slowly smoldering antagonism between parties. Disagreements may arise and cooperation break down when each party's objectives, strategies, and procedures are not adequately communicated or fully appreciated by other channel members.

Early theorists on channel conflict suggested that a channel system's goal should be to minimize conflict and maximize cooperation. Excessive conflict is likely to be detrimental to efficient performance in the channel of distribution; however, at times a certain level of conflict may be desirable. Conflict may be regarded as potentially beneficial to the system when it brings about a more equitable allocation of decision-making authority and economic resources and greater balance and stability within the system. Conflict is destructive when a lack of recognition of mutual objectives results.

Although there is some question about the most efficient level of conflict, it is generally agreed that conflict should not go unmanaged. Unfortunately, Mark Twain's comment about the weather ("Everybody talks about the weather, but nobody does anything about it") to some extent applies to discussions of conflict within channels of distribution. Once they recognize conflicts, channel members should discuss or negotiate the issues to try to resolve the problems before they lead to major confrontations.

CHANNEL POWER

Channel power
The extent to which a channel member is able to influence the behavior of another channel member.

Channel leader
A distribution channel member that is able to exert power and influence over other channel members; also known as a *channel captain*.

An organization that is able to exert its **channel power** and influence over other channel members is referred to as the channel leader or channel captain. A **channel leader** has mutually agreed-on authority to reward, punish, plan, coordinate, or otherwise dictate the activities of channel members. For instance, Home Box Office is the channel leader for the distribution of movies on pay TV. HBO virtually dictates how much it will pay for a film. Furthermore, HBO finances film production; in recent years, it has become a major source of financing for independent movie producers.

There are several sources of channel power. Because of the size of its purchases, a large retailer such as Wal-Mart may be able to dictate marketing strategy to less powerful channel members. In placing an order for a private-label brand, Wal-Mart may insist on certain product specifications, prices, or delivery dates. A small manufacturer may be so dependent on the Wal-Mart order that it changes the specifications on its own brand so that it can economically produce a product that meets Wal-Mart's specifications. Wal-Mart thus has channel power. More specifically, it has *coercive power*, the ability to force compliance from other channel members by threatening to take its business elsewhere, and *reward power*, the ability to offer an economic reward, such as a large, profitable order.

An organization such as a manufacturer of technical instruments may be able to wield channel power because of its expertise and ability to introduce technological innovations. It has *expert power* based on knowledge. Anheuser-Busch is a channel leader because of its marketing expertise. To support its wholesalers, Anheuser-Busch offers extensive training seminars on topics such as financial management and warehousing. It has developed a computerized shelf-space management program for retailers that audits sales, margins, and turnover by brand and package.

In addition to benefiting from Anheuser-Busch's expertise, channel members respect the brewery because they believe it is trustworthy and has other admirable characteristics. Anheuser-Busch thus has *referent power*, which stems from other channel members' respect, admiration, and identification with the channel leader.

When a Taco Bell franchise contractually agrees to perform specific activities, such as placing a common logo on all promotional materials, it grants legitimate power to Taco Bell's franchisor. *Legitimate power* results from formal agreements.

Reverse Distribution

In recent decades, the recycling of waste has become an important ecological goal. The major problem in recycling is determining who is responsible for the "reverse distribution" process it involves. The macromarketing task is to establish a **backward channel** of distribution, one in which the ultimate consumer who seeks to recycle waste materials must undergo a role change.

Backward channel
A channel of distribution for recycling, in which the customary flow from producer to ultimate user is reversed.

By recycling your old newspapers or metal cans, you become a "producer" of a usable product that has some economic utility. Thus, in this backward channel, the consumer is the first link in a process rather than the last. The backward channel in this case is likely to be run by traditional manufacturers of paper or cans. Yet the flow of goods is the reverse of what most descriptions of marketing operations suggest.

Backward channels of distribution have historically been very primitive, although some recycling has always existed. For example, ecologically concerned civic groups have sponsored paper drives and community clean-up days. Such groups are, in essence, performing channel intermediary functions.[15] In some cases, traditional intermediaries have long practiced as a sideline what have come to be recognized as recycling activities. Soda bottlers have accepted returnable bottles for years, but this practice was not seen as either a major part of their business or a contribution to the economy.

In recent years, however, a growing sophistication has been brought to the operation of reverse channels of distribution. For example, brokers are often employed to negotiate the sale of used packaging cardboard to paper mills that can reprocess the product. Larger supermarkets ship the "waste" directly to the mills, with the broker taking neither title nor possession but simply arranging the transfer. Such an operation reflects considerable thought in its development and requires a sizable management effort to succeed. Some soda vending machines have been modified or designed from scratch to accept empty aluminum cans for recycling and to reimburse the recycling patron with a small reward. This is clearly a step or two beyond having Boy Scouts scour roadsides for old containers.

Ethical, Political, and Legal Forces in Distribution Management

You might think of recycling as involving certain ethical issues as well as issues of distribution. Indeed, several ethical issues arise in connection with distribution and its macromarketing role. One such issue, already touched on earlier, is the supposed cost of distribution. Other issues have been dealt with institutionally and are now regulated by laws.

DOES DISTRIBUTION COST TOO MUCH?

As mentioned earlier, a commonly heard cry is "eliminate the middleman!" Previous discussions explored the reasons for specialization in the distribution channel. An intermediary may provide storage, selling, or other marketing functions more efficiently than either a manufacturer or a retailer. Eliminating the intermediary does not eliminate the functions intermediaries perform. Thus, a manufacturer that eliminates wholesalers will have to perform the wholesaling function itself. This may cost more than using independent wholesalers if the wholesalers were better at their job than the manufacturer can be. Or, performing intermediary functions itself may radically alter a company's marketing strategy. For example, a company that sells on the Internet has no intermediary to communicate persuasive information, so it must do this via other means.

A critic might note that some individual aspects of the distribution system are nonessential. Yet it has been shown repeatedly that "nonessentials" such as convenience are important to consumers. The success of 7-Eleven, Quick-Trip, and similar stores proves that consumers want—and will pay for—convenient location and quick service. The customers decide the trade-offs in this case, paying a little more money to avoid paying with their time. People can quickly and profoundly influence the distribution system simply by where they shop. It is arguable that distribution is the aspect of marketing that is most responsive to consumer demands. The high rate of business failure, especially among retailers, is strong proof that intermediaries must perform valuable functions if they are to survive.

LEGAL REGULATION OF DISTRIBUTION IN THE UNITED STATES

**Law Journal Extra—
Antitrust Law**
www.ljextra.com/practice/
antitrust

In the United States, in many other countries, and in international trade agreements, dealings in the area of distribution may be subject to numerous restrictions. For example, a manufacturer's ability to exercise power over channels is often regulated in an attempt to preserve the independence of intermediaries and to assure that unfair competition does not result.

The Sherman Antitrust Act, the Clayton Act, the Federal Trade Commission Act, and other laws dealing with antitrust policy are the bases for much U.S. legislation influencing distribution. In the United States, the three main legal issues surrounding distribution are exclusive dealing, exclusive territories, and tying agreements.

Exclusive dealing
A situation in which a distributor carries the products of one manufacturer and not those of competing manufacturers.

Exclusive Dealing   **Exclusive dealing** refers to a restrictive arrangement by which a supplier prohibits intermediaries that handle its product from selling the products of competing suppliers. A manufacturer may wish to deal only with those distributors that will agree to market its brand exclusively. Is such an arrangement legal? The answer to this question depends on whether the arrangement abuses the intermediary's right to act independently or the rights of other business competitors to succeed.

It is illegal for a manufacturer to prevent an intermediary from selling products that compete with that manufacturer's products if the activity tends to restrict competition. A new brand of refrigerator would never reach the marketplace if all makers of refrigerators already in the market enforced exclusive dealing agreements with their wholesalers and retailers. Such arrangements, in blocking entry of a new product, would appear to be restricting competition.

An exclusive dealing arrangement is likely to lessen competition if (1) it encompasses a substantial share of the market; (2) the dollar amount involved is substantial; or (3) it involves a large supplier and a smaller distributor, in which case the supplier's disparate economic power can be inherently coercive.

Exclusive dealing arrangements are generally legal if the parties to the arrangement can show that the exclusivity is necessary for strategic reasons, such as a franchisor's need to protect a product's image. Exclusive dealing may also be legal if the supplier's own sales are restricted because of limited production capacity.

Exclusive territory
An area defined by geographical boundaries or population and assigned to a retailer, wholesaler, or other dealer with the understanding that no other distributors will be assigned to operate in that area.

Exclusive Territories   A manufacturer that grants a wholesaler or retailer an **exclusive territory** may be acting illegally. The key point, as in so many legal matters relating to business, is restriction of competition. If the granting of exclusive territories does not violate the statutes relating to restriction of competition, then limiting the number of outlets within an area or assigning exclusive territories may be considered proper. Again, in many cases, this evaluation must be made by the legal system.

What about Cadillac? This organization attracts dealers in part by promising that no other dealers will be set up within the same areas. A number of defenses might be offered by organizations engaged in this sort of practice. They might argue that the investment expected from new dealers is so great that dealers could not be recruited unless they were offered some sort of exclusive territory. In this case, the defense is that the nature of the business demands such exclusivity. They might also argue that the image of the product offered demands some exclusivity. Cadillac, for example, is portrayed as a luxury product. Thus, excellent sales and service people are necessary; Cadillac dealers and mechanics are carefully selected and trained. If Cadillac dealerships were allowed to open on every other street corner, this might destroy the elite image Cadillac Motor Division is trying to create.

Tying Contracts   **Tying contracts** require a channel intermediary or a buyer to purchase lines of merchandise that the seller sees as supplementary to the merchandise the purchaser actually wants to buy. The seller tells the buyer, in effect, "If you want to have this product [say, a printing press], you must also buy my other product [paper]." Thus, two or more products are tied together. The Clayton Act makes tying contracts illegal, but whether a particular agreement is, in fact, a tying contract can be open to debate. Certain tying agreements can be legal—for example, in the case of a printing press, the seller could require a certain kind of paper if using other brands of paper would cause the press to break down.

Tying contract
An agreement tying the purchase of one product to the purchase of another. The buyer who wishes to purchase a certain product is required by the seller to purchase additional products, whether the buyer wants to purchase those products or not.

LEGALITIES OF INTERNATIONAL DISTRIBUTION
The many restraints on and problems associated with domestic distribution are compounded in the international marketplace. Domestic laws, the laws of the country to which goods are being shipped, the laws of the nations through which goods are being shipped, and the general conventions associated with international trade must all be obeyed. A full discussion of the many aspects of international constraints on distribution is beyond the scope of this chapter, but the immense problems that flow from them should be recognized by all students of marketing.

summary

Distribution is a necessary but often misunderstood marketing function. The common desire to "eliminate the middleman" shows that the general public has little appreciation for the role played by a channel of distribution.

1   *Explain the general purpose of distribution in the marketing system.*
A channel of distribution makes it possible for title or possession of a product to pass from producer to consumer. By common agreement, channel members share the responsibility for performing the basic functions of marketing. Distribution provides time and place utility to buyers by delivering the right products at the right time in the right place. It

bridges the gap between manufacturers and final users. In effect, distribution delivers a standard of living.

2   *Show how distribution contributes to an effective marketing mix.*
Effective distribution complements the other marketing mix variables and helps achieve the goal of effective marketing. Perishable products must be distributed quickly, expensive products must be offered for sale in stores or other locations consistent with the value of the products, delicate products must be handled with care, and widely promoted and demanded products must be distributed to large and geographically diverse markets.

12-2 video case

StockPot Soups

StockPot Soups is a manufacturer of homemade-style soup concentrates. The Fortun brothers founded StockPot Soups after 20 years in the food business. The company has 100 employees. The company's product line includes soups such as lobster bisque, chicken-flavored vegetable gumbo, cream of broccoli, and clam chowder. Production of the fresh soup product is labor-intensive, which drives up the cost of production.

Grocery wholesalers and retailers often stock five or six competing brands. Most competitors offer national brands. Like many small start-up companies in their early years, StockPot faces the daunting challenge of convincing distributors to carry its products. Wholesalers that supply grocers simply do not want to carry another soup. This is also true of wholesalers that supply food services and institutional customers.[17]

QUESTIONS

1. Describe StockPot's channel or channels of distribution.
2. What strategy can StockPot use to gain distribution?
3. Are there any innovative channels of distribution that StockPot can tap?

chapter
13

Retailing, Direct Marketing, and Wholesaling

After you have studied this chapter, you will be able to:

Describe the function of retailing and wholesaling in the distribution system.

1

Categorize the various types of retailers by ownership and prominent strategy.

2

Analyze the historical patterns in U.S. retailing and evaluate the theories proposed to explain them.

3

Understand the nature of retailers' marketing mixes.

4

Distinguish between merchant wholesalers and agents and describe their functions in the distribution system.

5

(continued on next page)

"i dress this way to bother you."

You can buy a T-shirt with that in-your-face motto emblazoned across the chest at Hot Topic, an upstart retail chain based in Pomona, California.

Well, you always knew that teenagers wanted to outrage their elders. Hot Topic has figured out how to make a business from it.

It peddles nipple rings, tongue barbells, purple hair dye, ghoulish white makeup and T-shirts lauding the Bible-trashing band called Marilyn Manson. Hot Topic took in $44 million last year selling kids the means to express themselves.

The stores have a gothic industrial look popularized by teen movies like *Batman:* wrought iron gates decorated with creepy bugs and guarded by gargoyles. A high-tech sound system blasts the likes of Nine Inch Nails and Rage Against the Machine. There are T-shirts with pictures of more than 150 bands, funky clothes, incense and candles, among other things. Morbid Metals, the company's line of body jewelry, is one of its more successful offerings.

Orval Madden, the man behind Hot Topic, is a teenager going on 49. He drives a Dodge Viper sports car, rides a Harley-Davidson and sports a couple of tattoos on his legs. Corporate headquarters is

TEENAGERS ARE EXPECTED TO NUMBER SOME 30 MILLION BY THE YEAR 2005. THEY HANG OUT AT MALLS AND SPEND, ON AVERAGE, $3,000 A YEAR EACH.

a warehouse-like space where 20 suspended television monitors pound out Viacom's MTV and M2 television channels. Even the workers sport brightly dyed hair, tattoos and rock fashions.

A typical client is 17-year-old Jacqui Badeau from Mesa, Arizona. She has two earrings in each earlobe and a clip attached to the top of her right ear. If her mother would let her, she would have a lot more Hot Topic paraphernalia. Says she: "I want to get my belly button pierced and my tongue done and a third hole in each ear and another in the top of my left ear. But my mom won't let me until I move out."

By then Jacqui will probably have lost interest in such things, but Orv Madden knows that she will not lack for successors. Teenagers are growing nearly twice as fast as the general population and are expected to number some 30 million by the year 2005. They hang out at malls and spend, on average, $3,000 a year each.

A native of Middle American Alton, Iowa, with an M.B.A. from the University of Chicago, Madden worked 20 years at mainstream retailers, including Federated. Funky his wares may be, but there's nothing funky about the business. Adjoining his Pomona office is a 45,000-square-foot, state-of-the-art distribution center linked to the stores by computers; inventory is monitored and shipped daily.

Madden opened his first store in the fall of 1989 in a Los Angeles suburb. After a slow start sales exploded, and Madden raised $11 million from venture capitalists and private individuals over the next 5 years to open additional stores. By the end of this year he expects to have 110. And, just what our economy needs, he expects to have 500 stores by 2007.[1]

Retailers like Hot Topic are vital components in the channel of distribution. This chapter begins by addressing the importance of retailing and classifying retailers according to several criteria. It then describes a theory proposed to explain the historical patterns of change in retail institutions. Next, it discusses retail management strategies, focusing on merchandise assortment, location, atmospherics, customer services, and data-based management. It then turns to wholesaling, examining types of wholesalers, their importance to the U.S. economy, and the strategies they use to market goods and services.

Hot Topic
www.hottopic.com

Retailing and Its Importance

Retailing consists of all business activities associated with the sale of goods and services to ultimate consumers. Retailing involves a retailer, traditionally a store or a service establishment, dealing with consumers who are acquiring goods or services for their own use rather than for resale. Of course, Wal-Mart, The Gap, Best Buy, and other familiar organizations offering products for sale to consumers are retailers. However, the definition of retailing includes some less-than-obvious service marketers, such as hotels, movie theaters, restaurants, and ice-cream truck operators. And even if an intermediary calls itself a "factory outlet," a "wholesale club," or a "shopping channel," it is a retailer if its purpose is to sell to the ultimate consumer.[2]

Viewed in the context of the channel of distribution, retailers are the important final link in the process that brings goods from manufacturers to consumers. Poor marketing on the part of retailers can negate all the planning and preparation that have gone into other marketing activities.

In the United States, there are more than 1.5 million retailing institutions accounting for well over $1.8 trillion in sales.[3] About 15 percent of U.S. workers are employed in retailing.

Retailing
All business activities concerned with the sale of products to the ultimate users of those products.

Retailing Institutions—Toward a System of Classifications

Retailers are a diverse group of businesses. In the distribution of food there are supermarkets, convenience stores, restaurants, and various specialty outlets. Merchandise retailers may be department stores, apparel stores, consumer electronics stores, home improvement stores, pet shops, or various types of retailing systems for home shopping. Service retailers, such as movie theaters and banks, are as diverse as the types of services offered for sale.

Retailing is dynamic, and retail institutions evolve constantly. For example, institutions such as "mom and pop" grocery stores are at the end of their life cycle. Individual companies like Sears, which began in the late 1880s as a mail-order retailer of watches and

RETAILING IS DYNAMIC, AND RETAIL INSTITUTIONS EVOLVE CONSTANTLY.

jewelry, are continually transforming themselves into new types of retailers. Warehouse clubs and interactive shopping at home via personal computers are but two retailing innovations that have developed in recent decades. In the next 20 years, retailers will inevitably adjust to their changing environments by making further transformations.

In light of this constant change, and of the very large number of retailers in the United States, how can retail institutions be sorted into more easily analyzed groups? Two commonly used methods classify retailers on the basis of ownership and prominent strategy.

CLASSIFYING RETAILERS BY OWNERSHIP

One popular method of categorizing retailers is by ownership. Most retailers are **independent retailers,** operating as single-unit entities. Independent operations may be proprietorships, partnerships, or corporations, but they are usually owned by one operator, a family, or a small number of individuals. They are not generally integrated into a larger corporation. These retailers are often thought of as small, but some are quite sizable. Taken together, they are an important part of the U.S. retailing scene.

An independent retailer that owns the merchandise stocked but leases floor space from another retailer is a **leased department retailer.** A leased department—for example, a jewelry, cosmetics, or pharmaceutical department—operates independently from the lessor retailer, although it often operates under the lessor's name. The lessor grants leased department retailers this degree of independence because they have special expertise in handling the particular product line, will increase total store traffic, or are necessary to the lessor because consumers expect to find the departments' merchandise in the store.

If a retail establishment is not independent, it is classified as either a chain or an ownership group. The more familiar of these classifications is the **chain store**—one of a group of shops bearing the same name and having roughly the same store image. Chain-store systems consist of two or more stores of a similar type that are centrally owned and operated.

Chains have been successful for a number of reasons, but one of the most important is the opportunity they have to take advantage of economies of scale in buying and selling goods. Conducting centralized buying for several stores permits chains to obtain the lower prices associated with large purchases. They can then maintain their prices, thus increasing their margins, or they can cut prices, attracting greater sales volume. Unlike small independents with lesser financial means, chains can also take advantage of promotional tools, such as television advertising, by spreading the expense among many member stores, thus stretching their promotional budget. Other expenses, such as costs for computerized inventory control systems, may also be shared by all stores.

Chains vary in size. Dean & DeLuca, with its 2 gourmet food stores, Hansen Galleries, with its 6 art gallery outlets, and Kmart, with its more than 2,500 stores, are all chain stores. The number of stores in a chain can make a big difference in the way the business operates.

According to the U.S. Department of Commerce, the term **corporate chain** is used for chains with 11 or more stores. Typically, as the number of units in a chain increases, management becomes more centralized, and each store manager has less autonomy in determining the overall marketing strategy. Although corporate chains possess many advantages over independents, some analysts say independents and smaller chains are more flexible. They may be better able to apply such marketing techniques as segmentation than are bigger operations, whose appeal must be more general.

Retail franchise operations are a special type of chain. Although the broad marketing strategy in such chains is centrally planned, the retail outlets are independently owned and operated. Franchises provide an excellent example of the evo-

Independent retailer
A retail establishment that is not owned or controlled by any other organization.

Leased department retailer
An independent retailer that owns the merchandise stocked but leases floor space from another retailer, usually operating under that retailer's name.

Chain store
One of a group of two or more stores of a similar type, centrally owned and operated.

Corporate chain
A chain consisting of 11 or more stores.

lution of retail institutions to fit the American culture. Midas Muffler Shops, Arby's, and other nationwide franchise chains are now found in nearly every population center. Thus, as the country's mobile citizenry moves from place to place, a familiar Midas shop or Arby's is "waiting" for them when they arrive. Each new franchise benefits from the company's experience, reputation, and shared resources.

The other type of retailing organization is the **ownership group**—an organization made up of various stores or small chains, each having a separate name, identity, and image but all operating under the ultimate control of a central owner. Typically, the members of such groups are former corporate chains bought out by much larger ownership groups. Dayton-Hudson, Federated Department Stores, and B.A.T. Industries are ownership groups that operate stores with different names. For example, Dayton-Hudson operates Target stores, Scribner's, Mervyn's, and others. Bloomingdale's, Lazarus, Burdines, Rich's, Jordan Marsh, The Bon Marché, Abraham & Straus, and Stern's are owned by the Federated ownership group.

Ownership group
An organization made up of stores or small chains, each with a separate name, identity, and image but all operating under the control of a central owner.

CLASSIFYING RETAILERS BY PROMINENT STRATEGY

Retailers can also be classified based on their most prominent retail strategies. The decision as to whether to market products and services with an in-store retailing strategy or a direct marketing (nonstore) retailing strategy is such an important discriminating factor that these two major groupings will be discussed separately. Exhibit 13-1 on page 403 shows these groupings and their subcategories.

In-Store Retailing Many fundamental strategies differentiate in-store retailers. The variety of products they sell, store size, price level relative to competitors, degree of self-service, location, and other variables can be used to categorize retailers. Each strategy has its particular advantages and disadvantages, and each fits particular markets and situations. Try to envision the following store classes as what they represent: responses to particular marketing opportunities.

Specialty Stores **Specialty stores,** also called *single-line retailers* or *limited-line retailers,* are differentiated from other retailers by their degree of specialization— that is, the narrowness of their product mixes and the depth of their product lines. These traditional retailers specialize within a particular product category, selling only items targeted to narrow market segments or items requiring a particular selling expertise, such as children's shoes, automobile mufflers, or clocks. Service establishments, such as restaurants and banks, are often classified as specialty retailers. These retailers do not try to be all things to all people.

General stores dominated U.S. retailing until after the Civil War because, except in large cities, too few people could be found to justify specialty retailers. The remarkable success enjoyed by specialty stores in recent years, however, illustrates the importance of effective market segmentation and target marketing. The major reason for their success is the development of considerable expertise in their particular product lines. Wallpapers to Go, for example, offers free wallpapering lessons to instruct consumers on what wallpapering techniques to use and what to buy.

Specialty store
A retail establishment that sells a single product or a few related lines.

A specialty store markets a single product or a few related lines. The Limited markets high-fashion specialty apparel for young women. Its merchandise assortment has a narrow selection of styles but a great depth of colors to give the impression of variety. The Limited can keep merchandise current because it has mastered the process necessary for quick turnover of inventory. The Limited regularly conducts marketing research on fashion trends and continually updates its merchandise needs. Once a trend has been spotted, the store quickly designs the new apparel. It then faxes designs to clothing manufacturers in the Far East. Within 6 weeks, the new fashion apparel is for sale in The Limited's stores.

Shop Our Most Loved...

Home Page

Spring 1998
Fashion Report

Ready-to-wear
Report

Shop our Most
Loved Items

Men's
Report

Early Spring
Items

Spring Shoes
and Accessories

Newest Spring
Items

© 1998 Bloomingdale's.
Electronic Commerce developed by Knowledge Strategies, Inc.

It's sometimes difficult to classify a retailer. Bloomingdale's is a progressive retailer that has adapted its marketing strategy to a changing retail environment. Bloomingdale's has stores, a mail-order catalog, and an Internet Web site for on-line shopping.

www.bloomingdales.com

Department store
A departmentalized retail outlet, often large, offering a wide variety of products and generally providing a full range of customer services.

Supermarket
Any large, self-service, departmentalized retail establishment, but especially one that sells primarily food items.

Scrambled merchandising
The offering of products for sale in a retail establishment not traditionally associated with those products.

Department Stores   **Department stores** are typically large compared with specialty stores. They carry a wide selection of products, including furniture, clothing, home appliances, housewares, and, depending on the size of the operation, a good many other products as well. These stores are "departmentalized" both physically and organizationally. Each department is operated largely as a separate entity headed by a buyer, who has considerable independence and authority in buying and selling products and who is responsible for the department's profits. Independent department stores do exist, but most department stores are members of chains or ownership groups.

Most department stores are characterized by a full range of services, including credit plans, delivery, generous return policies, restaurants and coffee shops, and a host of other extras such as fashion clinics, closed-door sales for established customers only, and even etiquette classes for customers' children. Such services, as well as the need to carry a wide variety of merchandise and maintain a large building, increase store operating costs and necessitate higher prices than those at discount stores. Some consumers seek the service and atmosphere of the department store but then make actual purchases at a discount store. In short, discounters and other types of store operators are formidable competitors for traditional department stores.

Supermarkets and Convenience Stores   The supermarket of today differs greatly from the "grocery store" from which it evolved. The grocery operator of the early part of this century knew most customers, personally filled customers' orders, and was likely to offer both delivery service and credit. With the advent of the telephone, the grocer accepted phone orders and dispatched a delivery boy to the customer's home. When the Great Atlantic and Pacific Tea Company discontinued its delivery service in 1912, A&P began the transformation from grocery to supermarket. In 1933, King Kullen Stores (Jamaica, New York) placed its cans, packages, and produce on crates and pine boards and introduced self-service. The evolution of the supermarket continues today.

Today's **supermarket** is a large departmentalized retail establishment selling a variety of products, mostly food items but also health and beauty aids, housewares, magazines, and much more. The dominant features of a supermarket marketing strategy are large in-store inventories on self-service aisles and centralized checkout lines. Often, supermarkets stress the low prices resulting from self-service.

The inclusion of nonfood items on supermarket shelves was once novel in that it represented the stocking of items that did not traditionally belong in the supermarket's group of offerings. The name given to this practice is **scrambled merchandising.** Scrambled merchandising permits the supermarket (as well as

MAJOR GROUP	RETAILER CLASSIFICATION	BRIEF DESCRIPTION
IN-STORE RETAILING	Specialty store	Narrow variety, deep selection within a product class, personalized service; makes up large bulk of all retailing operations
	Department store	Generally chain operations, wide variety, full range of services
	Supermarket	Wide variety of food and nonfood products, large departmentalized operation featuring self-service aisles and centralized checkouts
	Convenience store	Little variety, shallow selection, fast service
	General mass merchandiser	Wide variety, shallow selection of high-turnover products, low prices, few customer services
	Catalog showroom	General mass merchandiser that uses a catalog to promote items
	Warehouse club	General mass merchandiser that requires membership if customers wish to shop; goods stored warehouse-style
	Specialty mass merchandiser	Less variety but greater depth than general mass merchandiser, low prices, few customer services
	Off-price retailer	Specialty mass merchandiser that sells a limited line of nationally known brand names
	Category discounter	Specialty mass merchandiser that offers deep discounts and extensive assortment and depth in a specific product category
DIRECT MARKETING	Mail-order/direct response	Generally low operating costs; emphasis on convenience; often uses computerized databases; includes mail order, television home shopping, and telephone sales
	Door-to-door selling	High labor cost, image problems; decreasing in the United States, increasing in less-developed countries
	Computer-interactive retailing	Consumer initiates contact with retailer via computer and the Internet
	Vending machines	High-turnover products, low prices

other types of retailing institutions) to sell items that carry a higher margin than most food items; thus, it provides a means to increase profitability. Across the board, however, supermarket profit margins are slim—only 1 to 2 percent of total sales. Supermarkets rely on high levels of inventory turnover to attain their return on investment goals.

Supermarkets were among the first retailers to stress *discount strategies.* Using such strategies, large self-service retail establishments sell a variety of high-turnover products at low prices. A good part of a retailer's ability to hold prices down stems from the practice of offering few services. Other than the costs of the goods they sell, most retailers find that personnel costs are their largest financial outlay. Thus, by eliminating most of the sales help, having no delivery staff, and hiring stock clerks and cash-register operators rather than true salespeople, discounters are able to take a big step toward reducing their prices. Buying in large volume also reduces the cost of goods sold.

Convenience stores are, in essence, small supermarkets. They have rapidly developed as a major threat to their larger cousins. 7-Elevens, Quick-Trips, and other imitative convenience stores have sprung up and multiplied across the United States. These stores carry a carefully selected variety of high-turnover consumer products. As their names generally imply, the major benefit to consumers is convenience—convenience of location and convenience of time. By choosing handy locations and staying open 15, 18, or 24 hours a day, 7 days a week, convenience stores offer extra time and place utility. Consumers must pay for these conveniences and seem quite willing to do so.[4] Managers of these stores price most of their "convenience goods" at levels higher than supermarkets, to provide high

Convenience store
A small grocery store stressing convenient location and quick service and typically charging higher prices than other retailers selling similar products.

adapting to change

Supermarkets at the Turn of the Century   David McFarland makes daily jaunts to a grocery store two miles from his home, but not for bread or milk.

He goes to the Kroger supermarket in Alpharetta, a suburb north of Atlanta, to use the treadmills and stair-climbing machines in the store's fitness center. There is even a trainer with a degree in exercise physiology to guide him through his workouts.

Carmella Edelman has little use for the treadmills, but she has become a regular at the store for its cooking school, across from the aisle where Maybelline mascara and Stephen King paperbacks are sold. For about $30—food included—students learn to whip up duck ravioli with brown butter sauce, chocolate-chip biscotti and other such delights.

Is your driver's license about to expire? You can renew it at the store's customer service counter. Other chains are offering sushi bars and shoe repair, or providing baby-sitting while harried parents shop.

All this, of course, is intended to lure people into supermarkets, and not just to tighten abs or teach customers to stir-fry. Once they're inside, the grocery store of the '90s is designed to get shoppers not only to buy toothpaste and cereal but also to fill their carts with high-margin convenience items like boneless, skinless, marinated chicken breasts.

Behind the scenes, meanwhile, store operators are working to shave pennies off the cost of stocking chicken-noodle soup and other staples that add little to their bottom lines.

The goal is to push razor-thin profits closer to 2 percent than 1 percent, which is about all that even the best operators have been able to achieve in the supermarket industry. That challenge is attracting some of the smartest money in the United States and Europe to a business rarely regarded as innovative.

It is forcing supermarket operators to spend billions of dollars remodeling outdated stores and investing in technology. And it is driving already big chains into the arms of larger, more powerful merger partners.[5]

profit margins. Convenience stores are unusual among retailers because they have both a high margin and a high inventory turnover.

Mass merchandise retailer

A retailer that sells products at discount prices to achieve high sales volume; also called a *mass merchandise discount store*. There are two basic types of mass merchandise retailers: general mass merchandisers and specialty mass merchandisers.

Mass Merchandisers   **Mass merchandise retailers,** sometimes called *mass merchandise discount stores* or *superstores,* sell at discount prices to achieve high sales volume. Mass merchandisers cut back on their stores' interior design and on customer service in their efforts to reduce costs and maintain low prices.

Supermarkets were the forerunners of mass merchandisers. In fact, the term *supermarket retailing* has been used to describe Target, Venture, and many other stores that have adopted the supermarket strategy, incorporating large inventories, self-service, centralized checkouts, and discount prices. Using supermarket-style discount strategies helps mass merchandisers to offer prices lower than those at traditional stores.

Mass merchandisers can be classified as general or specialty. *General mass merchandisers,* such as Wal-Mart, carry a wide variety of merchandise that cuts across product categories. They may sell everything from drug and cosmetic items to electrical appliances to clothing, toys, and novelty items. The wide variety of goods general mass merchandisers offer at low prices means that they usually cannot afford to carry a deep selection of goods in any product line. Retailers usually carry either a wide variety or a deep selection, but not both. The expense associated with having many kinds of goods and many choices of each kind make the two possibilities largely mutually exclusive. (Indeed, small retailers can often compete with giant mass merchandisers on the basis of selection.)

In contrast with general mass merchandisers, *specialty mass merchandisers* carry a product selection that is limited to one or a few product categories. For example, some specialty mass merchandisers sell only clothing.

We will discuss two types of general mass merchandisers, catalog showrooms and warehouse clubs, and two types of specialty mass merchandisers, category discounters and off-price retailers.

Catalog showrooms, like Service Merchandise, publish large catalogs identifying products for sale in the store. Typically, these are high-margin items. The catalog—or an accompanying price list—shows the "normal" retail price of the items and the catalog discounter's much lower price. Often, the discounter's price is printed without a dollar sign in the form of an easily decipherable "code" to let the buyer know that a special deal—not available to just anyone—is being offered. Catalog discounters, like other discounters, do not offer customer conveniences or salesperson assistance. Service is slowed by the need to wait for purchased products to be delivered from a storage place. However, this successful formula permits lower prices. Some discounters operate a special sort of store called a **warehouse club** or *closed-door house.* At Sam's Wholesale Club and Price Club, cus-

Catalog showroom
A general mass merchandise outlet where customers select goods from a catalog and store employees retrieve the selected items from storage.

Warehouse club
A general mass merchandise outlet at which only "members" are allowed to shop; also called a *closed-door house.*

tomers are asked to become "members" and are issued cards that permit entry to the store. Some closed-door houses require that customers already be members of some specific group, such as a labor union or the civil service. While these operations run the risk of being seen as discriminating against persons not in the target customer group, the mem-

bership idea has been found by some retailers to be effective in building store loyalty. Moreover, if in building its membership base the club develops an actual list of customers, direct-mail advertisements can be sent to these people, eliminating, to a large extent, other forms of advertising with their large proportions of waste circulation. Warehouse clubs combine wholesaling and retailing functions. For these marketers, the showroom facility doubles as a storage place, or warehouse, allowing the retailer to hold far greater amounts of stock than traditional retailers retain. Furthermore, when they sell to service organizations or business members, such as schools, restaurants, and day-care centers, the clubs are actually wholesalers. However, many members who purchase as small-business customers also use these stores for personal shopping, and these are retail sales.

Warehouse clubs focus on sales volume and often sell in bulk. This requires that manufacturers change their packaging strategy. For example, Kellogg's, which initially refused to package in bulk, now provides dual packages of its cereals and Pop-Tarts for warehouse clubs.

Off-price retailers are specialty mass merchandisers that aggressively promote nationally known brand names of clothing at low prices. Dress Barn and T.J. Maxx stores are typical examples. Off-price retailers can purchase brand name goods such as apparel or footwear at below-wholesale prices (even below prices paid by traditional mass merchandisers) because they typically do not ask for promotional allowances, return privileges, extended payment terms, or the highest-quality merchandise. They also keep their costs low by offering few services. Off-price stores have evolved because many name-brand manufacturers that once sold exclusively to retailers such as Saks Fifth Avenue, Neiman-Marcus, and Bloomingdale's are now more willing to sell seconds, overruns, discontinued items, or out-of-season merchandise to large-volume retailers, even when retail prices are below sug-

Off-price retailer
A specialty mass merchandise outlet offering a limited line of nationally known brand names.

gested levels. When a manufacturer owns and operates an off-price store, the store is called a factory outlet.

Toys "Я" Us, Petsmart, and Sportsmart are specialty mass merchandisers that apply the supermarket format to the marketing of toys, pet food and supplies, and sporting goods. A mass merchandise discounter specializing in a certain product category is called a **category discounter,** or *category killer.* Sportsmart, which sells 100,000 different items, provides an example. It is radically different from the typical independent sports store because it stocks virtually all competing brands of soccer balls, baseball gloves, sports team jackets, and the like, rather than carrying a single brand, as most sports stores do. Category discounters apply a deep discount strategy, setting prices even lower than those of general mass merchandisers, and offer the most extensive assortment and greatest depth in the product lines they carry. This retailing strategy is expected to attain most of the local business for the product category and to eliminate ("kill") the competition.

Category discounter
A specialty mass merchandise outlet offering extensive assortment and depth in a specific product category; also called a *category killer.*

adapting
to change

Ford Retail Network With the advent of chain superstores like CarMax and AutoNation, the nature of automobile retailing has been changing over the last few years. However, for a glimpse at the future, look to Tulsa, Oklahoma. Ford Motor Company has reached an agreement with all of Tulsa's Ford and Lincoln-Mercury dealers to establish a joint-ownership Ford Retail Network (FRN). The new partnership approach to retailing cars and trucks creates a new entity encompassing all of the Ford and Lincoln-Mercury dealerships in the Tulsa market area. The Ford Retail Network concept involves fewer, larger full-service superstores supplemented by neighborhood service centers providing convenient, competitively priced service to customers. The new superstores will sell Ford, Lincoln, Mercury, Mazda, and Jaguar vehicles and offer no-negotiation, fixed pricing.[6]

Direct marketing
Marketing in which advertising, telephone sales, or other communications are used to elicit a direct response, such as an order by mail or phone; in a retailing context, also called *direct-response retailing.*

Direct Marketing **Direct marketing** involves the use of advertising, telephone sales, the Internet, or other communications to elicit a direct response from consumers. Direct marketing in a retailing context has also been called *nonstore retailing* and *direct-response retailing.* The many means of direct marketing include mail-order sales, door-to-door selling, computer interactive retailing, and vending machine sales.

Whether direct marketing uses telephone, catalogs, letters, other print media, television, or the Internet to reach consumers, it always calls for a direct response, generally an order by mail, telephone, or the Internet.

Mail-order retailing through catalogs is one of the oldest forms of direct marketing. Sears, Roebuck and Company began in the mail-order business and moved on to other types of marketing. Today, the famous Sears "wish book" catalog no longer exists. However, companies such as Banana Republic and Sharper Image still combine catalog advertising with both mail-order and in-store retailing. Others, like Sundance, are exclusively committed to direct marketing operations.[7] Consumers perceive mail-order buying as more risky than in-store shopping. In fact, catalog buying is among the shopping methods perceived as riskiest by consumers. Those who have had a favorable experience with this nonstore shopping method are more favorably inclined toward it.

Catalog retailers and some other mail-order marketers make extensive use of data-based marketing, discussed in Chapter 4. They buy computer-generated mailing lists from companies that specialize in developing them or they compile the lists themselves. As already discussed in previous sections on data-based marketing and relationship marketing, the lists can be narrowly focused on selected interest groups, age groups, homeowners, newlyweds, and so on.

Advertising in magazines and other print media may call for a direct response and thus may constitute direct marketing. Certain target customers may be reached effectively by such marketing efforts. Purveyors of vitamins and other health aids for senior citizens, for example, conduct a brisk business through advertisements placed in such magazines as *Modern Maturity*.

HEAR WHY THE BOSE® WAVE® RADIO WAS NAMED A "BEST NEW PRODUCT OF 1994" BY *BUSINESS WEEK*.

Tabletop radios are popular for their convenience and small size. But their sound quality leaves much to be desired. No one really expects high-fidelity sound from a radio. Until now.

Just as a flute strengthens a breath of air to fill an entire concert hall, the waveguide produces room-filling sound from a small enclosure. This technology and performance is available in no other radio.

You'll touch a button and hear your favorite music come alive in rich stereo sound. You'll hear

HEAR THE RADIO THAT WOKE UP AN ENTIRE INDUSTRY.

Bose presents the Wave radio. It's the one radio acclaimed by leading audio critics. Because it's the one radio that delivers big, rich, lifelike stereo sound *plus* a small, convenient size.

THE BEST-SOUNDING RADIO YOU CAN BUY.

We think the Wave radio is the best-sounding radio you can buy. And audio critics agree. *Radio World* called the sound "simply amazing... a genuine breakthrough in improved sound quality." *Business Week* named the Wave radio a "Best New Product of 1994." *Popular Science* called it "a sonic marvel" and gave it a prestigious "Best of What's New" award. The key is our patented acoustic waveguide speaker technology.

every note the way it's *meant* to be heard. The Wave radio measures just 4¼"H × 14"W × 8¼"D and fits almost anywhere. So you can listen in your bedroom, living room, kitchen, or any room. And with your choice of imperial white or graphite gray, the Wave radio not only fits in any room, it fits any decor.

REMOTE-CONTROLLED CONVENIENCE.
Operate the radio from across the room with the credit card-sized remote control. Set six AM and six FM stations, and switch between them at the touch of a button. You can even bring great Bose sound to recorded music, TV programs, or movies by connecting the Wave radio to your CD or cassette player, TV, or VCR.

CALL NOW AND MAKE SIX INTEREST-FREE PAYMENTS.

The Wave radio is available for $349 directly from Bose, the most respected name in sound. So call 1-800-681-BOSE, ext. R6899, to learn more about our in-home trial and satisfaction guarantee. When you call, ask about our six-month installment payment plan.

Or, if you prefer, return the coupon below.

Wired magazine said it has a "clean, sweet sound that will have your friends wondering where you've hidden your fancy speakers." But you have to hear the Wave radio for yourself to believe it. Call today.

ORDER BY MARCH 20, 1998, FOR FREE SHIPPING.

CALL 1-800-681-BOSE, EXT. R6899.
When you call, ask about our six-month installment payment plan. (Available on telephone orders only.) Also ask about FedEx® delivery service.
Please specify your color choice when ordering the Wave® radio:
☐ Imperial White ☐ Graphite Gray

Mr/Mrs/Ms. _____
Name (Please Print)
Address _____
City _____ State ___ Zip ___
Daytime Telephone _____
Evening Telephone _____

Mail to: Bose® Corporation, Dept. CDD-R6899, The Mountain, Framingham, MA 01701-9168, or fax to 1-800-862-BOSE (1-800-862-2673).

BOSE
Better sound through research.

©1998 Bose Corporation. Covered by patent rights issued and/or pending. Installment payment plan and free shipping offer not to be combined with any other offer. Installment payment plan available on credit card orders only. Price does not include applicable sales tax. Price and/or payment plan subject to change without notice. FedEx service marks used by permission. Wired, June 1994.

What started out as a product with no market has turned into a sound success via a direct marketing campaign.

In late 1993, Bose Corporation unveiled its Wave radio, not fully sure of its target audience. Bose elected to sell the device directly, to avoid possible problems on store shelves. The radio is much more expensive than a clock radio, which it resembles, and looks too different from traditional high-quality stereo components.

The solution: Bose used simple, black-and-white direct-response print ads in numerous publications to offer not just additional product information but also a 30-day home trial. The effort became more targeted as Bose honed in on its audience, mainly males who enjoy music but want simplicity in their electronic products.[8]

Direct marketers that advertise on television and fill orders via the mail or express delivery services have proliferated and now hawk everything from cutlery to Elvis Presley memorabilia. The familiar television campaigns that urge viewers to write or call a toll-free number are good illustrations of this approach to retailing.

Television home shopping is a direct marketing innovation developed with the advent of cable TV. Viewers tuning in to the cable shopping channel see a "show" where products are demonstrated by a "host." Consumers can call the host while the show is on the air to ask questions about the product or to purchase it.

Telemarketing, the selling of retail merchandise by telephone, is a growing aspect of direct marketing. It involves both database management and personal selling. This topic is discussed in Chapter 16, on personal selling.

What most attracts consumers to the various forms of direct marketing is convenience. Shopping at home, especially at such harried times of the year as the Christmas holidays, provides an undeniable attraction. So does the fact that many direct marketers will ship gift-wrapped orders directly to the person for whom the merchandise was bought, thus freeing the customer from wrapping and delivery chores.

Direct marketing may attract retailers because it offers many opportunities to reduce operating costs. No in-store salespeople need be hired, trained, or paid. Often businesses may be headquartered in low-rent areas that ordinary retailers would eschew. Indeed, the retailer that conducts business out of the consumer's view can cut many corners.

On the other hand, direct marketing retailers face certain special expenses. The catalog retailer incurs considerable expense in the preparation and mailing

focus on
global competition

European Direct Marketing   Figures from the European Direct Marketing Association show that the average Belgian gets 78 pieces of direct mail advertising a year. To most Americans, that would be a relief, because they get that many pieces of direct mail every month. But the average Belgian gets more mail than other Europeans. The typical German gets 61 pieces of direct mail a year; the typical French person, 55; and the typical English person, 42. In Spain, the average person gets only 24 pieces; and in Ireland, the average is 11, less than one catalog or letter every month.

The direct mail industry has developed much more slowly in Europe than in the United States because the various countries have vastly different privacy laws, postal rates, and postal delivery systems. For example, an automotive dealer in the United States can buy automobile registration information from state motor vehicle bureaus. However, the United Kingdom's Driving and Vehicle Licensing Center does not sell its data for commercial purposes.[9]

of catalogs, for example. Direct marketing retailers must also expedite shipments of goods so that customers receive their orders quickly and in good condition. In part to overcome the sense of unease some feel about buying merchandise they cannot examine, many direct retailers offer liberal return policies.

Door-to-Door Selling   Bibles, vacuum cleaners, magazines, and cosmetics are among the many products successfully sold door-to-door. This kind of retailing is an expensive method of distribution. Labor costs, mostly in the form of commissions, are quite high. Yet many consumers enjoy the personal in-home service provided by established companies like Cutco, Fuller Brush, and Avon. In general, products sold door-to-door are of the type that particularly benefit from demonstration and a personal sales approach. Vacuums and carving knives are among the many products that lend themselves to such demonstrations.

In-home retailing is often performed by organizations with outstanding reputations, including the Girl Scouts, Mary Kay, and the several Tupperware-style "party" merchants. Unfortunately for the many legitimate companies practicing this form of retailing, the image of the door-to-door approach has been tarnished by some unethical salespeople. A number of laws make door-to-door selling difficult. For example, *Green River ordinances*, in effect in many local areas, put constraints on the activities of door-to-door salespeople by limiting the hours or neighborhoods in which they may call or by requiring stringently controlled licenses.

It is interesting to observe that while door-to-door retailing is decreasing in importance in the United States, it is growing in some less-developed countries. Avon, for example, has a major door-to-door organization in China, and Tupperware parties are popular in many countries.

Computer-Interactive Retailing and Push Technology   Among the newer developments in nonstore retailing is **computer-interactive retailing,** through which consumers can shop at home by interacting with retailers via their personal computers. For example, America OnLine, Compuserve, and Prodigy are on-line interactive services that allow owners of personal computers to book airline flights and hotel reservations, buy and sell stocks, check weather forecasts, and shop for thousands of items ranging from encyclopedias to video games. The number of Internet Web sites, such as amazon.com and barnesandnoble.com, where products can be ordered has been growing very rapidly. The Internet, with its worldwide "audience," has the potential to dramatically change the nature of retailing.

Computer-interactive retailing
A retailing method whereby consumers shop at home using personal computers and interactive computer services.

Amazon.com Books
www.amazon.com

Interactive retailing represents a new generation of direct marketing, because the shopper goes to the seller electronically rather than waiting to receive a promotional message by mail, phone, or television. Viewers using the interactive system call up directories, as if they were using a computer menu. These directories list categories such as "what's on sale," "market-fresh grocery," and "apparel," from which the viewer can choose. In other circumstances the retailer can initiate the visit to the "store" or to a "shopping mall."

Excite Shopping uses personalized shopping technology to perform simultaneous searches for products on line.

www.excite.com/channel/shopping

Chapter 2 defined *push technology* as a means of delivering personalized content to the viewer's desktop. In a retailing context, computer software programs known as *smart agents* or *intelligent agents* learn a user's preferences and search for products available for sale on line. Excite Shopping (www.excite.com) uses personalized shopping technology, and its service can perform simultaneous searches for products available for sale on line based on various criteria like price and stock levels at different on-line stores. Technological improvements in the Internet and interactive television promise to make interactive retailing even more popular in the 21st century.

Vending Machines   The coin-operated vending machine is an old retailing tool that has become increasingly sophisticated in recent years. For the most part, items dispensed through vending machines are relatively low-priced convenience goods.

There is a vending machine for about every 40 people in the United States. They can be found almost everywhere—and this is a big part of their appeal to the marketers that use them. Cigarettes, gum, and other items can be sold in hotels, college dormitories, and church basements without an investment in a store or in personnel. Items sold through vending machines are generally small, easily preserved, high-turnover goods such as candy and soft drinks. Technological improvements in vending machines have allowed machines to dispense airline tickets, traveler's insurance, customized greeting cards, and breathalyzer tests.

Patterns of Retail Development

Many types of retailing institutions have been developed by marketers. Many more will be developed as retail marketing continues to respond to changes in its environment. If some pattern of retail institutional development could be identified, retailers would have a powerful management tool—a means of predicting

**what went wrong?**

American Greetings In 1992, American Greetings began introducing CreataCard kiosks in retail settings. These high-tech vending machines allow consumers to customize messages and print their own unique greeting cards. The company's marketing research showed that most card purchases are made on impulse. Recognizing that shoppers' attention needed to be drawn to the kiosks, American Greetings decorated the kiosks for Valentine's Day, Halloween, Christmas, and other holidays.

After 3 years of operation, the kiosks did not prove to be very popular. In 1995, American Greetings reduced the number of its kiosks from 10,000 to 7,500. What went wrong?

The company's marketing research found that women 40 and older—the most frequent purchasers of greeting cards—tended to buy them off the rack. Young adults, who tend to be more at ease with computers, were more likely to try CreataCard but became disenchanted with how slow the process was: about 8 to 10 minutes from start to finish. Today's kiosks produce cards at roughly the same speed as the first units introduced in 1992, but people's perception of speed and their willingness to wait for a slow computer have changed over the last few years. American Greetings also learned that many of its kiosks would be better located in retail areas where young adults gather.[10]

what new forms of retailing will emerge. Unfortunately, no hard and fast predictive method has yet been developed; but several theories have been formulated. Three such theories are discussed here.

THE WHEEL OF RETAILING

The best-known hypothesis relating to retail institutional development is called the **wheel of retailing.** This theory states that new retailing institutions enter the marketplace as low-status, low-margin, low-price operations and then move toward higher status, margin, and price positions. The formulator of the theory viewed this process as the spinning of a wheel, as shown in Exhibit 13-2. The emergence of discount stockbrokers like Charles Schwab illustrates the entry process. These brokers made an impact on the marketplace by charging low commission fees; however, they did not provide investment advice as traditional "full-price" brokers do.

Wheel of retailing
A theory positing that new forms of retail institutions enter the marketplace as low-status, low-margin, low-price operations and then gradually trade up, opening a market position for a new low-end retailer.

Retailing scholars have observed that a pattern of "trading up" does exist. As time goes by, retailers that started out small with inexpensive facilities begin to operate businesses far larger and fancier than those with which they began. One cause of this trading up is the American tradition of competing, at the retail level, more on the basis of nonprice variables than on the basis of price variables. Americans do not have a tradition of haggling over prices. Instead, retailers tend to compete with one another by such nonprice means as offering free services, frequent-purchaser programs, and more attractive stores. These things tend to drive up margins and prices. Whatever the causes of trading up, the end result, with respect to the wheel of retailing theory, is the same: A low spot on the wheel, once occupied by a

WITH **RESPECT TO THE WHEEL OF RETAILING THEORY, A LOW SPOT ON THE WHEEL, ONCE OCCUPIED BY A LOW-MARGIN RETAILER THAT HAS TRADED UP, IS LEFT OPEN FOR AN INNOVATIVE RETAILER THAT CAN OPERATE AT A MARGIN LOWER THAN THOSE EARNED BY EXISTING RETAILERS.**

low-margin retailer that has traded up, is left open for an innovative retailer that can operate at a margin lower than those earned by existing retailers. The lower margin should attract customers. The innovator is thus tempted to snatch that lower spot, and the evolutionary process continues. Many of the discounters of the 1930s and 1940s followed this pattern and eventually ended up much like the department stores from which they sought to differentiate themselves. The discounters then became vulnerable to the newer, low-margin, low-price retailers such as warehouse clubs and category discounters.

Some Positions on the "Wheel of Retailing" in Order of Decreasing Markups

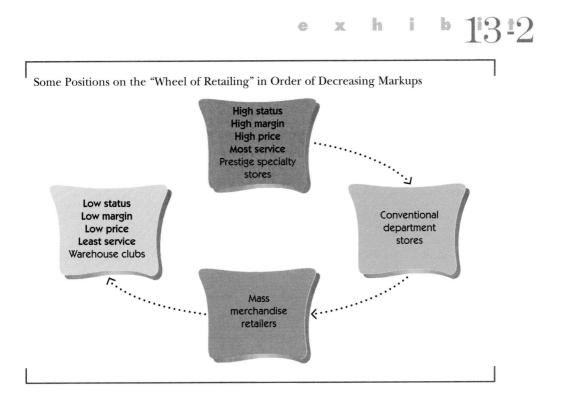

The wheel hypothesis has much intuitive appeal and has been borne out in general by many studies of retail development, but it only reflects a pattern. It is not a sure predictor of every change, nor was it ever intended to describe the development of every individual retailer. There are many nonconforming examples of retail managers who, for whatever reasons, have not traded their stores up from the positions they originally occupied. Some observers suggest that modern marketing methods, including research and positioning, will stop or slow the wheel of retailing as retail marketers resist abandoning market positions they have carefully selected.

THE DIALECTIC VIEW OF RETAIL DEVELOPMENT

In the early nineteenth century, the German philosopher G. W. Hegel proposed a logical view of change, a pattern that fits nearly every situation. Briefly stated, the **dialectic theory** is this: If a given institution exists, it will be challenged eventually by another. In Hegel's terminology, the original *thesis* will be opposed by an *antithesis*. Except in rare cases, both sides will have something to recommend them. As they interact, a new idea—some combination of the two—will develop. Hegel called this hybrid the *synthesis*. The synthesis will be challenged by another antithesis, and so on.

Patterns like this can be discerned in retailing. As Exhibit 13-3 shows, one type of retailing institution is challenged by another. What evolves from this confrontation is a new kind of institution combining elements of both. For example, out of the historical confrontation between the department store (the thesis) and the 1940s discount store located in spartan facilities in a low-rent district (the antithesis) emerged the discount department store like Kmart (the synthesis).

The challenge-and-response concept inherent in the dialectic process appeals to many observers of retailing because it suggests the competitive

Dialectic theory
A theory describing the interaction of an existing retail institution (the thesis) with a challenging institution (the antithesis), to yield a new retail institution (the synthesis) that has some characteristics of both.

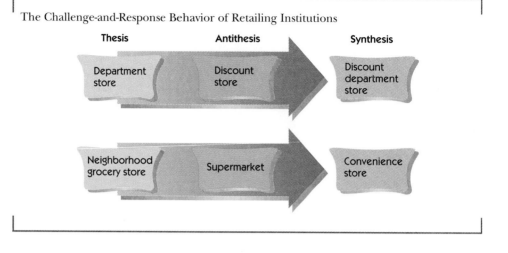

The Challenge-and-Response Behavior of Retailing Institutions

battles that retailers wage. And the wheel of retailing hypothesis alone is insufficient to explain institutional change because it lacks the elements of competition and response to competition that are inherent in retailing. Some combination of the wheel and the dialectic may therefore best explain retailing's changing patterns.

A GENERAL-SPECIFIC-GENERAL EXPLANATION

General stores once dominated the U.S. retailing scene. Then, as populations grew and became concentrated in cities, more and more stores specializing in just a few products began to appear. Recent years have seen the successful development of general mass merchandisers that sell enormous numbers of products under one roof. It is not too great a leap of the imagination to view these general mass merchandisers as giant general stores. Indeed, like the general stores of old, they are popular and successful in part because they offer one-stop shopping and something for everyone.

General-specific-general theory
A theory describing the development of retailing as a cyclic process in which general merchandisers are replaced by specialty merchandisers, which in turn are replaced by general merchandisers, and so on.

The **general-specific-general theory** suggests that retail change goes in cycles—from retailers offering general merchandise (that is, wide merchandise assortments) to retailers offering specific merchandise (that is, narrow assortments) and back to stores offering general merchandise. This theory is also called the *accordion theory*, because merchandise offerings, like an accordion, expand and contract over time.

USING THE THEORIES

The preceding explanations of retail institutional development do not and cannot explain how each and every change in the U.S. retailing system came about. Their predictive abilities are also imperfect, if only because marketing is so dynamic. The value of the theories lies not in the answers they give to planners but in their ability to raise questions. Their purpose is to generate thought. Why do these patterns appear to exist? What factors at play in the marketplace contribute to change? Is there an opportunity for a new positioning strategy? Coming to grips with questions like these is far more important to planners than simply being familiar with theories and historical patterns. The Adapting to Change feature illustrates a retailing change that is taking place in the grocery industry.

adapting to change

Natural Food Stores Supermarket-sized health foods stores are springing up in selected markets around the country. Produce is one of the keys to their growth because of a long-running trend: consumers' increased attention to, and knowledge of, nutrition.

Natural foods chains, such as Whole Foods Market, Wild Oats, and Fresh Fields, are setting the pace in a trend toward big stores. With selling floors that range from 20,000 square feet to 30,000 square feet, these operators can offer the variety that consumers normally associate with traditional supermarkets. Since natural foods stores traditionally have been small, ranging from 2,000 square feet to 5,000 square feet, the big stores represent just what supermarket operators might be expected to dread: yet another alternative type of food retailer.

The big health foods stores can knock smaller health foods operations in the same market for a loop. And while they pose less of a challenge to the supermarket industry, they tend to put upscale operators on red alert.[11]

Retail Management Strategies

Retailers, like all marketers, create marketing strategies. They analyze market segments, select target markets, and determine the competitive position they wish to occupy.

Like all marketers, retailers must develop a marketing mix. The concept of the marketing mix is essentially the same in all applications of marketing. Exhibit 13-4 shows some of the decision elements retail marketers face in developing a retail marketing mix.

No single chapter can discuss all aspects of the retail marketing environment. Here we will address six problem areas of special importance. These are merchandise assortment, location, atmospherics, customer service, store image, and database management.

MERCHANDISE ASSORTMENT

One image that comes immediately to mind when the word "store" is mentioned is a physical place where merchandise for sale has been assembled. This is because one of a retailer's prime functions is to provide a product assortment for customers. Stated in different terms, retailers perform an assorting function—they build desired assortments of varied goods so that

what went right?

Wal-Mart Despite its lofty status as the country's largest retailer, $104 billion Wal-Mart Stores Inc. works hard to cultivate the high-touch image of a country store in each of its 2,450 retail outlets. Company policy calls for "people greeters" at every front door. Fundraising bake sales for local charities are encouraged. All that's missing is a cat by the cash register and a checkerboard on the porch.

Behind the scenes, however, in the mission-critical logistical systems for replenishing the goods on store shelves, things are becoming less high-touch and more high-tech. In fact, Wal-Mart is now piloting an extension to its mainframe-based replenishment system, which uses a sophisticated decision support system to quickly recognize market trends and give human merchandising experts highly structured advice on what the merchandise assortment should be. In addition, the system automatically initiates actions in the replenishment system.

"In the future, our [merchandising] associates will be managing exceptions rather than making every replenishment decision that comes up," says Rob Fusillo, Wal-Mart's director of replenishment information systems. "In the end, we think we'll get better decisions."

Wal-Mart is just one of a growing number of companies attempting to get a jump on the competition by creating "closed-loop" decision support systems to improve their decisions about merchandise assortment.[12]

Elements of the Retail Marketing Mix

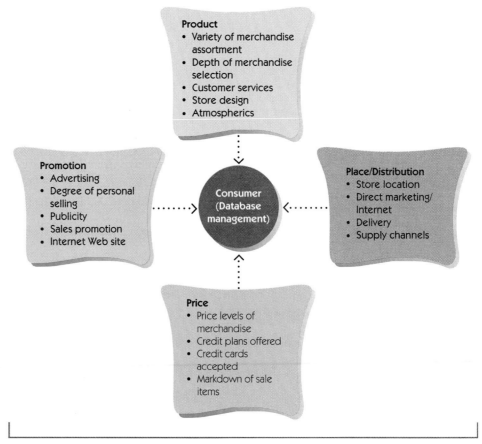

Product
- Variety of merchandise assortment
- Depth of merchandise selection
- Customer services
- Store design
- Atmospherics

Promotion
- Advertising
- Degree of personal selling
- Publicity
- Sales promotion
- Internet Web site

Consumer (Database management)

Place/Distribution
- Store location
- Direct marketing/ Internet
- Delivery
- Supply channels

Price
- Price levels of merchandise
- Credit plans offered
- Credit cards accepted
- Markdown of sale items

manufacturers and customers don't need to. It is clearly in the interests of both consumers and producers to allow retailers to perform this service and to reward them for it.

From the individual customer's perspective, a major advantage of one retailer over a competitor is merchandise assortment. Other things are important, of course, but no shopper will patronize a store unless he or she feels that there is some chance that the merchandise sought will be found there.

How does a retail marketer decide what merchandise assortment to carry? Information and suggestions are available from manufacturers and from intermediaries. Trade magazines and newspapers may offer useful insights. But most importantly, the retailer must carefully consider the target market's needs and wants and match the merchandise selection with those desires. This truth is elemental in effective retail marketing. Yet retailers frequently make buying mistakes, the costs of which must be absorbed through markdowns or other means. Buying errors cannot be totally avoided, but marketing research and careful planning can minimize their occurrence. The means of aligning merchandise offerings with customer desires cannot be detailed here, but it is important to note that marketing—not guesswork—must be the basis of all decisions in this area.

LOCATION, LOCATION, AND LOCATION
There is an old saying that the three most important factors in successful retailing are location, location, and location. This is not absolutely true—an out-of-the-way

location can be compensated for by other means, especially huge selections and low prices. Nonetheless, the adage makes a point. Retailers are justifiably concerned about locating in the right part of the right town. They must monitor changes that may affect the suitability of an existing location or make another site more attractive.

The right location depends on the type of business and the target customer, not on any formula or rule of thumb. As with merchandise assortment questions, the answer lies in careful marketing planning. Experience dictates certain guidelines, however. Toys "Я" Us, for example, has several specific guidelines for store location. In the United States, it requires that its outlets be placed in metropolitan areas with populations of at least 100,000 people, of which an established percentage must be children. Ideally, the selected location is a free-standing building near a major mall. Toys "Я" Us, which operates as a global retailer, has other criteria for other countries around the world. Locations in foreign countries are the topic of the What Went Right? feature.

Retail site selection experts note that an important attribute of any intended site is the other types of outlets around it.[14] Obviously, Toys "Я" Us expects major shopping malls to generate traffic near its toy store locations. More specifically, many retailers seek what are called *complementary businesses*. Placing a diner near a gas station makes more sense than locating a dress shop there. The nature of the retailer's business operations may affect whether the number or the nature of nearby businesses is important, however. Catalog discounters, for example, can rely on their customers to do some preshopping using the catalogs. This, plus lower prices and the immediate gratification of being able to take items home from the store, reduces the need for store locations in expensive, high-traffic areas. In contrast, the traffic generated by a shopping center is far more important to a Docktor Pet Center, a Sharper Image electronics store, or an Orange Julius shop.

Shopping centers are important locations for many retailers. As you are well aware, there are several kinds of shopping centers. Older versions are often long strings of stores set in a parking area. This design is called a *strip*. A design that

McDonald's International   McDonald's top managers in the United States learned much about efficiency from their colleagues abroad. Whereas the company built its American business in the suburbs, outside the United States it moves first to city centers, where space tends to be expensive and tight. "We had to become very flexible," says James Cantalupo, who oversees McDonald's International in 66 countries.

McDonald's has crammed restaurants into some tight spots—among them, a 13th-century building in Shrewsbury, England, and an 870-square-foot space in Tokyo's Ginza. (The traditional McDonald's occupies 4,500 square feet.)

Menus have also become flexible abroad. In Tokyo, McDonald's offers Teriyaki Burgers (sausage patties with teriyaki sauce) and Chicken Tatsuta (chicken breast in a tempura batter on a bed of sprouts with soy sauce and ginger).

Some overseas McDonald's restaurants, the Euro-195 models, are assembled on-site from five factory-built modules. They have inspired a U.S. counterpart, the Series 2000, named for its square footage. These models have enabled the company to drop its golden arches in towns once deemed too small, such as Holdredge, Nebraska (population 5,670).

McDonald's is eyeing more unusual locations. In the past, PepsiCo, which owns Pizza Hut and Kentucky Fried Chicken in addition to Taco Bell, has led the way in offbeat sites, such as mobile carts in airports. But now McDonald's runs restaurants inside 30 Wal-Marts and two Sears stores, and it is negotiating to open more such eateries in Home Depots. McDonald's is adding two new restaurants per day worldwide, giving it a count surpassing 14,000.[13]

It is a well-known fact that many shoppers view shopping as a source of enjoyment. A restaurant's or store's layout and appearance create an atmosphere. Retailers expend considerable effort to create an atmosphere conducive to shopping. And, in many instances, the longer shoppers stay in a store, the more they buy.

features stores built around a central area, in which shoppers can stroll, is called a *mall.* Technically, the heated and air-conditioned malls found in larger cities and towns are called *enclosed malls,* although most people simply call them malls.

You undoubtedly have also noticed that shopping centers come in different sizes, essentially small, medium, and large. The official size designations, however, are *neighborhood, community,* and *regional.* The neighborhood shopping center is likely to be a small strip containing such shops as a drugstore, a dry cleaner, and a supermarket. The community center is larger, with perhaps a variety store, clothing store, or small furniture dealer. The regional center is the largest, with 100 or even 200 stores, serving a large population and drawing customers from a wide geographic area. Although today people seldom think of it as such, the downtown area is, or at least used to be, a shopping center. For any number of reasons, including parking, crime, and a lack of public transportation, downtowns, or central business districts, have declined greatly in retailing importance since the post–World War II exodus of population to the suburbs.

The flight to the suburbs and the movement of retailers to suburban malls are difficult to overcome. Nevertheless, some city governments have successfully revitalized downtown areas. In some cities, "downtown malls" have been built to rekindle interest in downtown-based activities. Inner-city shopping malls such as the ones located in the rejuvenated Jax brewery in New Orleans, Boston's Faneuil Hall marketplace, and Chicago's Watertower Plaza are thriving. These urban malls often incorporate expensive restaurants, live theater, and other attractions that are better able to draw patrons in downtown locations than in the suburbs.

ATMOSPHERICS

Retail strategy includes managing every aspect of the store property and its physical characteristics to create an atmosphere conducive to buying. **Atmospherics** are physical characteristics of the environment, such as the store's exterior and interior appearance, layout, and displays, that contribute to a shopper's mental impression of

Atmospherics
Physical characteristics of a store's environment, such as appearance, layout, and displays.

RETAIL **STRATEGY INCLUDES MANAGING EVERY ASPECT OF THE STORE PROPERTY AND ITS PHYSICAL CHARACTERISTICS TO CREATE AN ATMOSPHERE CONDUCIVE TO BUYING.**

what the store is. Store atmosphere may influence store image, increase store traffic, influence the amount of time shoppers spend in the store, or encourage shoppers to make impulse purchases.[15]

Exterior atmospherics can exert a strong influence on new customers' willingness to enter a store. The building's architecture, parking facilities, storefront, and other outside features may either encourage or discourage patronage by communicating a certain message. The architectural motif of a Taco Bell, for example, makes an impression on the consumer and communicates a message about the restaurant's product line.

Planning the interior design and layout to influence the movement and mood of the customer is a primary concern of retailers. Atmospherics, such as lighting, music, colors, and the perception of uncrowded space, are used to foster favorable customer attitudes. Disney stores' layouts are designed to communicate the fun and excitement of Disney theme parks and characters. They are also designed to get customers to walk to the back wall; a large video

Retail marketers create and maintain a store atmosphere as part of their marketing strategies. In the Warner Studio Store shown here, a life-sized Bugs Bunny entertains the store's smallest customers. The store is filled with icons of Daffy Duck, Tweety Pie, the Roadrunner, Elmer Fudd, and, of course, that wascally wabbit Bugs. Walk into a Warner Brothers store and you are reminded of the characters you grew up with. The atmosphere shouts "fun!"

screen at the back of every store shows animated features, accompanied by familiar songs. The chances are good that customers will return to the front by a different route and see additional merchandise.

Retailers may plan atmospheres that appeal to any of the shopper's five senses: sight, hearing, smell, touch, and taste. The Hard Rock Cafe is loud, crowded, and bustling. The Ralph Lauren store on Fifth Avenue in New York City has colors, lighting, decorations, and mahogany furniture designed to communicate that the environment is quiet, plush, "upper class and quite British."

CUSTOMER SERVICE

The customer services a retailer offers may be as important as—or even more important than—the merchandise offered for sale. The courteous personal service and information provided by a salesperson may make the difference between success and failure in a retail setting. Maintaining convenient store hours, providing parking facilities, and offering product information are essential to the operation of many retail operations. Other services, such as delivery, alterations, repair, credit, return privileges, and gift wrapping, supplement the retailer's merchandise offerings. In some cases, the service offering (such as Domino's Pizza's in-home delivery) is the primary reason for selecting one retailer over another.

Development of the retailer's marketing mix thus requires decisions about the **service level**, or the extent of extra services that will be provided to consumers. Service-level strategies are often interrelated with pricing strategies. An organization that wants to be competitive in price will typically match competitors' service levels. Retailers that emphasize nonprice competition may be full-service organizations that provide extra services to create a competitive advantage. The level of service consumers expect is also a major determinant of service level. Many retailers regularly survey consumers to determine the amount and quality of services they expect.

Service level
Extent of extra services provided to customers. Service level is often related to price.

STORE IMAGE

Creating a store image is a primary aspect of a retail positioning strategy. Store image, like brand image, reflects consumers' mental impressions. Do consumers see the store as friendly or reserved, traditional or contemporary, prestigious or economical? How do they

Retailers talk about the importance of customer service, but many do a terrible job of delivering it. A MasterCard survey showed that 62 percent of customers left a store without buying an item because a sales clerk wasn't available. About 60 percent of those surveyed said they asked a question that sales clerks couldn't answer.[16]

feel about the store? Is it a place for them or a place where they would hate to be seen? The store's personnel, its merchandise, its immediate surroundings, its external and internal appearance, its prices, its customer services, and other aspects of the retailer's marketing mix all contribute to store image. In a sense, **store image** encompasses everything consumers see in a store that determines how they feel about the store.

DATABASE MANAGEMENT

Retailers, as the final link in the distribution channel, have always had direct contact with their customers and in many cases one-on-one relationships with individual customers. The local butcher knew when a customer walked in the shop how she wanted her steaks and chops trimmed. The jewelry store salesperson would often send a note to a male customer just before his wife's birthday. So it should come as no surprise that retailers, especially direct marketers, have recognized that customer databases can be used to better serve customers and to develop customer loyalty.

Retailers are in the ideal situation to build proprietary databases. When a consumer makes a purchase, information about it can be automatically entered into and stored on the store's or direct marketer's computer. When that purchase can be linked to the customer's name, phone number, or other information (such as demographic information) and to other purchases, the retailer has extremely useful information. For example, Helzberg Diamonds, which has 191 stores in 28 states, uses its database to identity customers who responded to special sales promotions in the past. The company then mails letters and brochures encouraging these customers to visit the store when similar promotions are occurring.

Supermarkets have learned from their databases that married men who purchase diapers between 6 p.m. and 8 p.m. are also likely to purchase beer. Data like these about past purchases and frequency of purchase have immense consequences for retailers. Data-based marketing is an important part of contemporary retailers' marketing efforts.

Global Retailing

Retailers, like manufacturers and service providers, have come to realize that their business future lies in international marketing. Some retailers, such as Southland's 7-Eleven stores, entered international markets because they faced a saturated market at home.[17] Others, such as McDonald's, see tremendous growth opportunities for their existing products as other countries become more affluent. Often, however, retailers entering foreign markets must develop merchandise assortments that appeal to the unique needs of those markets.

Developments in Mexico, which has become an increasingly important market for global retailers, illustrate how retailers, like other businesses, adapt to different retail buying behavior.[18] For example, warehouse clubs, which reject credit cards in the United States, have found that they can't maintain that policy in Mexico because so many Mexicans use credit cards to manage their cash flow on basic purchases.

In a large store's food section, Mexicans still prefer to see produce and meat displayed as they are in the local market. Both Wal-Mart and Kmart offer extensive fresh food sections. Kmart goes even further, displaying whole chickens stacked at the butcher's counter. Kmart does this because many Mexican consumers who see pre-packaged food don't think that it's fresh.

Many Mexicans, including members of the upper classes, still buy fresh meat, fresh produce, and tortillas at little stores in their neighborhoods. American-owned mass merchandisers carrying both food and nonfood items—and their Mexican competitors—have now incorporated small tortillerias to offer corner-store freshness.

Helzberg Diamonds
www.helzberg.com

7-Eleven Stores
www.7eleven.com

Mexicans tend to shop as families as part of a weekend's entertainment, so wide aisles are a necessity. Retailers have to place their stores close to residential areas to allow for low rates of car ownership. If prices are good, Mexicans will borrow cars or take public transportation to a faraway store, but they won't bother unless enticed, perhaps by a circular listing sale items. Consumers from the lower and working classes tend to be intimidated by "nice" stores and believe that prices at American-owned stores are higher. Capturing that lower-income market will become increasingly important as the retail chains expand and new entrants become established. Sales in retail chains have grown more slowly than the population since 1992. Retailers will have to look to grow by attracting the estimated 50 to 75 percent of consumer purchases made outside formal retail chains. That means they will have to woo lower-income shoppers from street vendors, local markets, and neighborhood stores.

Wholesaling

A wholesaler neither produces nor consumes the finished product. A **wholesaler** is a marketing intermediary that buys products and resells those products to retailers, other wholesalers, or organizations that use the products in the production of other goods or services. A wholesaler's primary function is facilitating either the transportation of products or the transfer of title to them.

Wholesalers have much in common with retailers; both of these types of marketers act as selling agents for their suppliers and as buying agents for their customers. Both are creators of time and place utility. Both must carefully evaluate the needs of their customers and deliver an appropriate total product of goods and services if they are to succeed in business. And both have developed ways of performing marketing functions that specially suit market conditions.

Wholesaler
An organization or individual that serves as a marketing intermediary by facilitating transfer of products and title to them. Wholesalers do not produce the product, consume it, or sell it to ultimate consumers.

Classifying Wholesalers

The functions of all intermediaries, including wholesalers, were discussed in Chapter 12. This section describes the different types of wholesaling establishments and institutions in the United States.

Intermediaries performing wholesaling functions are traditionally divided into two groups—merchants and agents. The only distinction between these categories lies in whether the intermediaries take title to the goods they sell. Merchant intermediaries take title; agent intermediaries do not. This has nothing at all to do with possession of goods. Some merchants take possession of merchandise and others do not. Some agents take possession of the goods they sell, but most do not. Taking title to goods does mean that the merchant intermediary owns that merchandise and must be prepared to handle any risks associated with ownership—including getting stuck with merchandise that, for whatever reason, turns out to be unsellable.

A recent Census of Wholesale Trade reported that there were 495,457 wholesale trade establishments in the United States.[19] Of these, 414,836 were merchant wholesalers, and they accounted for almost 60 percent of wholesale sales volume. There were 35,953 manufacturer's sales branches, and they accounted for slightly less than a third of the wholesale sales volume. The 44,668 agents and brokers accounted for approximately 11 percent of wholesale sales volume.

MERCHANT WHOLESALERS

Merchant wholesalers are independently owned concerns that take title to the goods they distribute. Merchant wholesalers represent about 80 percent of all wholesaling concerns in the United States.[20] Many of these operations are fairly small, and most of the small wholesalers restrict their business to a limited geographical area. Many merchant wholesalers cover single cities or areas stretching

Merchant wholesaler
An independently owned wholesaling concern that takes title to the goods it distributes.

only 100 or 200 miles from the main office. This allows them to replace retailers' inventory quickly. It also reduces or eliminates the need for overnight trips by trucks or sales personnel and so holds down expenses.

Merchant wholesalers may be classified in terms of the number and types of services they provide to their customers. In this regard, they provide perfect examples of how marketing firms adjust their total product offerings of goods and services to reflect the demands of particular situations and market segments.

Full-Service Merchant Wholesalers   As their name suggests, **full-service merchant wholesalers** provide their customers with a complete array of services in addition to the merchandise they offer. Such services include delivery, credit, marketing information and advice, and possibly even such managerial assistance as accounting aid or other nonmarketing aid. Full-service wholesalers are also called *full-function wholesalers.*

Within this category, three subsets of wholesalers are identifiable by lines of goods offered: **general merchandise wholesalers,** which sell a large number of different product types; **general line wholesalers,** which limit their offerings to a full array of products within one product line; and **specialty wholesalers,** which reduce their lines still further. A coffee and tea wholesaler or a spice wholesaler exemplifies this last class.

Wholesalers determine how wide or narrow a line to carry by carefully considering the customers they serve and the industry in which they operate. When the target customers are operators of general stores, the decision to be a general merchandise wholesaler is logical. In some industries, however, traditional marketing practices may require some degree of specialization. Occasionally, the specialization is required by law, as in the case of beer wholesalers, which in many states are not permitted to deal in any other alcoholic beverage.

Limited-Service Merchant Wholesalers   Regardless of the product line carried, full-service merchant wholesalers provide an essentially complete line of extra services. However, some customers may not want—or may not want to pay for—some of those services. They may prefer to sacrifice services to get lower prices. Thus, a group of **limited-service merchant wholesalers,** or *limited-function wholesalers,* has developed.

Cash-and-Carry Wholesalers   Buyers who are not willing to pay for and who do not need certain wholesaler services, such as delivery and credit, may choose to patronize **cash-and-carry wholesalers.** Such intermediaries eliminate the delivery and credit functions associated with a full-service wholesaler and permit buyers to come to the warehouse or other point of distribution to pick up their merchandise and to pay cash. Resultant savings are passed on to buyers, who are, after all, performing several functions normally associated with wholesalers.

Truck Wholesalers   **Truck wholesalers,** also called *truck jobbers,* typically sell a limited line of items to comparatively small buyers. Most of these merchant wholesalers sell perishable items. Their mode of operation, selling from a truck full of merchandise, can be justified by the increased freshness immediate delivery offers. Some truck wholesalers sell items that are not particularly perishable but that face keen competition. They might, for example, sell snack items to tavern owners. Although truck jobbing is an expensive means of distributing relatively small amounts of merchandise, it is an aggressive form of sales and provides instant delivery to buyers.

Direct Marketing Wholesalers   **Direct-marketing wholesalers** operate in much the same way as mail-order catalog retailers and other direct marketers. They use catalogs and direct mail, take phone and fax orders, and then forward merchandise to buyers via mail or a parcel delivery service. Traditionally, these wholesalers have been most important in reaching remote rural locations where market

---

Full-service merchant wholesaler

A merchant wholesaler that provides a complete array of services, such as delivery, credit, marketing information and advice, and managerial assistance; also called a *full-function wholesaler.*

General merchandise wholesaler

A full-service merchant wholesaler that sells a large number of different product lines.

General line wholesaler

A full-service merchant wholesaler that sells a full selection of products in one product line.

Specialty wholesaler

A full-service merchant wholesaler that sells a very narrow selection of products.

Limited-service merchant wholesaler

A merchant wholesaler that offers less than full service and charges lower prices than a full-service merchant wholesaler; also called a *limited-function wholesaler.*

Cash-and-carry wholesaler

A limited-service wholesaler that does not offer delivery or credit.

Truck wholesaler

A limited-service wholesaler that sells a limited line of items (often perishable goods) from a truck, thus providing immediate delivery; also called a *truck jobber.*

Direct-marketing wholesaler

A limited-service wholesaler that uses catalogs or the Internet; mail or telephone ordering; and parcel delivery.

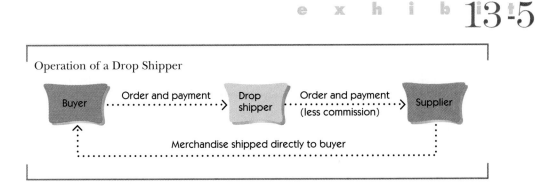

Operation of a Drop Shipper

potential is low. However, in recent years, many types of wholesalers, such as office supply wholesalers, have made strategic decisions to focus on direct marketing.

Drop Shippers   **Drop shippers** are merchant wholesalers that take title to goods but do not take possession of the goods or handle them in any way. Drop shippers accept a buyer's order and pass it on to a producer or supplier of the desired commodity, which then ships the product directly to the buyer. (See Exhibit 13-5.)

The big advantage of this system is that the product escapes double handling—that is, it need not be loaded and unloaded several times. Also, it goes directly to where it is needed, which lowers transportation costs. These advantages are especially important when the product is bulky, unwieldy, and comparatively inexpensive. Thus, drop shipping is most commonly used for products such as coal, cement, building blocks, and logs.

Because the drop shipper does not physically handle any products, no investment in warehousing facilities or equipment is required. In fact, so little equipment of any sort is required that these wholesalers can often get by with little more than a small office, a desk, and a telephone. For this reason, they are also called *desk jobbers*.

Rack Jobbers   **Rack jobbers** are a type of merchant wholesaler that came to prominence in the 1930s when supermarket operators began to practice scrambled merchandising and started selling cosmetics and other items they had not previously carried. To do this easily, they contracted with wholesalers willing to come to the store, set up a display rack, stock and replenish it, and give the supermarket operator a percentage of the sales. Now rack jobbers sell many different product lines, such as work gloves, paperback books, magazines, toys, cosmetics, and panty hose.

The attraction of this system for the store operator is the chance to stock and sell certain items at little risk. The great attraction for the rack jobber is the chance to place merchandise in a high-traffic supermarket location. Like most relationships between members of a channel of distribution, theirs is a mutually beneficial one.

AGENTS

Agents, the second general category of wholesalers, may take possession of goods they deal in but do not take title to them. Agents, as a rule, do not carry an inventory or extend credit, but they may provide physical facilities for conducting business. They may help to arrange for delivery or credit as part of their services, which can be generally described as bringing buyer and seller together. Agents typically receive commissions based on the selling prices of the products they help to sell. The commission percentage varies tremendously depending on the industry. Agents are expected to be familiar with their products and with who wants to

Drop shipper
A limited-service wholesaler, often dealing in bulky products, that takes customer orders and arranges for shipment of merchandise from the producer directly to the customer; also called a *desk jobber*.

Rack jobber
A limited-service wholesaler that contracts with a retailer to place display racks in a store and to stock those racks with merchandise.

Agent
A wholesaler that does not take title to goods. Agents sometimes take possession of goods but function primarily to bring buyers and sellers together or otherwise help consummate a marketing transaction.

sell and who wants to buy them. In short, they are expected to have an expert knowledge of the market in which they operate.

Broker
An agent intermediary whose major role is placing buyers and sellers in touch with one another and assisting in contractual arrangements.

Brokers   **Brokers** are agent intermediaries that receive a commission for putting sellers in touch with buyers and assisting with contractual negotiations. Brokers generally portray themselves as "neutral" in the selling process, working for both buyers and sellers. Brokers are found in many fields. Such commodities as coffee, tea, crude petroleum, and scrap metal are frequently brokered; so are the financial instruments handled by the familiar stock broker. Effective brokers are experts in the market for the products in which they deal. In effect, they sell their expertise. They have relatively low expenses. Their commissions are also likely to be small, generally 6 percent or less of the selling price.

Use of brokers holds particular appeal for sellers because brokers work strictly on commission and do not enter into long-term relationships with the companies that use them. A broker can be used only when needed and does not tie sellers to continuous expenses the way a full-time sales force does.

Because they are commonly used sporadically, brokers as a group do not constitute a major selling force in the day-to-day marketing activities of most organizations. A notable exception is the food broker, which represents a number of manufacturers of food products on a continual basis and actively attempts to sell their products to wholesalers or supermarkets. Such an operation really violates the standard description of a broker because food brokers may be seen as working more for the seller than for the buyer. In many ways, food brokers better fit other categories of agents. By tradition as much as anything else, however, they continue to be referred to as brokers.

Commission merchant
An agent intermediary similar to a broker but having certain additional decision-making powers, such as the power to make price adjustments.

Auction company
An agent intermediary that brings together buyers and sellers. Auction companies often assemble merchandise for sale in a central location and sell it by means of a bidding process.

Commission Merchants   The **commission merchant** is an agent intermediary similar to a broker. Unlike brokers, however, commission merchants are usually given certain powers by sellers. They might be empowered, for example, to attempt to bid up the selling price or to accept a selling price as long as it is above a previously agreed-on floor. Commission merchants thus perform a pricing function and more clearly work in league with the seller than do most brokers. They are most commonly found representing producers of agricultural products. Commission merchants, despite the name, are like other types of agents in that they do not take title to the goods they sell. However, they often take possession of those goods for inspection by potential buyers. Once a sales agreement has been reached, the commission merchant deducts a commission from the selling price and returns the balance to the producer.

Auction Companies   **Auction companies** are agent intermediaries that perform valuable services in the buying and selling of livestock, tobacco, and other commodities, as well as artwork and used mechanical equipment. In a sense, many of these companies take possession of the goods they deal in, because frequently they provide some special place in which the auction can be held. The auction company receives a commission based on the final, highest bid offered for an item or product, provided that this bid is above a minimum agreed-on figure.

The products sold through auction could be sold in some other manner, but auction companies offer a certain convenience in that they bring buyers together in one spot and expedite a bidding process that might otherwise take a long time. Some industries, such as the tobacco industry, have traditionally used auction companies and continue to do so for that reason.

The operation of the auction system provides some less-than-obvious advantages: (1) products can generally be examined by potential buyers; (2) sellers and buyers may, if they choose, remain anonymous; (3) buyers may enjoy the thrill of the auction and savor their victory over other bidders. This last factor may not be important to a tobacco buyer, but it is to a patron of art auctions.

Auction companies are beginning to appear on the Internet. For example, FastParts is an on-line auction for overstocked electronic parts. An auction on the Internet has the advantage of appealing to a greatly expanded geographical market.

Manufacturers' Agents and Selling Agents   **Manufacturers' agents,** also called *manufacturers' representatives,* are independent intermediaries that specialize in selling and are available to producers that do not want to perform sales activities themselves. These agents operate in geographically limited areas, such as a few states or a portion of a state, representing two or more noncompeting producers and spreading selling costs over all of them. Suppose a maker of photocopying equipment wants to employ a sales force only in major markets, not in smaller cities or rural areas. It might decide to hire a series of manufacturers' agents to cover areas with low market potential and to let the company's own sales force take the more important markets. The existence of markets with low market potential is not the only good reason to use manufacturers' agents. Their familiarity with local markets is often an advantage. Another reason is that the producer may lack the interest or expertise to perform sales and marketing functions. Still another is finances: A company that has relatively few financial resources is more likely to use an agent because the agent need not be paid until a sale is made.

Selling agents are also paid a commission and are expected to be familiar with the products they handle and the markets they serve. However, they differ from manufacturers' agents in one major respect. They sell the products manufactured by the producers they represent not in a single geographical area but in all the areas in which the products are sold. Because, in effect, they function as sales and marketing departments, they are often given more responsibility than manufacturers' agents. They may be permitted to handle the advertising and pricing of the products sold and determine any conditions of sale to be negotiated. The manufacturer that uses a selling agent obtains what might be called an external marketing department.

Exhibit 13-6 gives an overview of the various wholesalers in the two basic classifications.

MANUFACTURERS THAT DO THEIR OWN WHOLESALING

Throughout this section, we have been considering wholesaling as if it were performed entirely by independent organizations other than manufacturers. Actually, although the various agent and merchant intermediaries are extremely important, especially in particular lines of trade, many manufacturers perform the wholesaling functions themselves. Some manufacturers have become disenchanted with wholesalers for a number of reasons. They believe that wholesalers handling the products of many manufacturers cannot promote any one manufacturer's product as that producer feels it should be promoted.

When manufacturers do their own wholesaling, whether to retailers or to industrial users, they may use sales offices, sales branches, or both. (The U.S.

Manufacturers' agent
An independent agent intermediary that represents a limited number of noncompeting suppliers in a limited geographical area; also called a *manufacturers' representative.*

Selling agent
An independent agent intermediary similar to a manufacturers' agent but representing a given product in every area in which it is sold, rather than in a limited geographical area.

MERCHANT WHOLESALERS		AGENT WHOLESALERS	
Merchant wholesalers take title to goods and earn profits.		Agents do not take title but some may take possession of products; they receive a commission based on the product selling price; they usually do not extend credit.	
Full-service merchant wholesalers	Take title; take possession; deliver goods; extend credit; provide marketing information; provide managerial assistance	Brokers	Assist in contractual negotiations; bring buyers and sellers together
Limited-service merchant wholesalers		Commission merchants	Perform pricing function for sellers
• Cash-and-carry wholesalers	Do not provide delivery or credit		
• Truck wholesalers	Have a limited product line; deliver goods	Auction companies	Offer convenience in bringing buyers and sellers together
• Mail-order wholesalers	Are important in rural locations	Manufacturers' agents	Help manufacturers, often in "thin markets," to sell products
• Drop shippers	Don't handle products; generally deal in bulky products	Selling agents	Like manufacturers' agents, specialize in selling but also act as an external marketing department
• Rack jobbers	Handle wide variety of small products; responsible for stocking products		

Department of Commerce classifies sales branches and sales offices as wholesalers even though, according to our definition, they are not independent intermediaries.) **Sales offices** and **sales branches** are wholesaling establishments maintained by producers of the products sold, and both may serve as headquarters for "outside" salespeople or as offices for "inside" salespeople. The central difference between the two is that the sales branch carries an inventory of products while the sales office does not. The bulk of the product, the need for fast delivery, the technical aspects of the product, and the opportunity to sell a standardized product rather than a custom-made one all contribute to the decision as to whether to use offices or branches.

The reason manufacturers choose to do their own wholesaling can be expressed in one word: control. The maintenance of sales offices and branches permits manufacturers to control more effectively the flow of goods to their customers, the training and selling activities of their salespeople, and the flow of information returned to headquarters by a staff that is actually out in the field.

Sales office
A wholesaling establishment that is maintained by a manufacturer for its own product and does not carry an inventory of the product.

Sales branch
A wholesaling establishment that is maintained by a manufacturer for its own product and carries an inventory of the product.

WHOLESALERS THAT DISTRIBUTE SERVICES

Some wholesalers specialize in the distribution of services. For example, your college library may use the services of BRS (Bibliographical Retrieval Service), Lexis/Nexis, or the Dow-Jones News Retrieval Service. These organizations are wholesalers that market information services.

Chapter 5 discussed worldwide information systems, but not in the context of wholesaling and retailing. However, as you can now see, information and other services flow through channels of distribution. In the 21st century, when interactive media are even more prominent, the distribution channels for information and entertainment services will become even more significant.

Wholesale Management Strategies

Wholesalers, like all marketers, create marketing strategies. They analyze market segments, select target markets, and determine the competitive position they wish to occupy. To a great extent, the wholesaler's strategy is dominated by physical distribution concerns, the subject of the next chapter. However, two other aspects of strategy have dimensions that deserve special attention. They are (1) selecting target markets and creating assortments and (2) developing strategic alliances.

SELECTING TARGET MARKETS AND CREATING ASSORTMENTS

You have seen that wholesalers sell to three basic classes of customers: retailers that resell the product, other wholesalers that resell the product, and organizations in the business market that use the product. Each of these customers has different needs. The wholesaler must determine which target markets to serve and what product mixes to offer. Further, the depth of the product lines offered must be matched to the needs of the target market.

Consider this wholesaling strategy. Frieda's Finest is a produce grocery wholesaler that specializes in marketing uncommon fruits and exotic foods, such as tamarinds, bàbaco, and purple potatoes, to retailers. Its success with kiwi fruit, which is now stocked in most grocery stores, is typical. Once the pioneering company succeeds in gaining market acceptance for the product, larger produce companies like Chiquita enter the market with their brands and become such formidable competitors that Frieda's Finest must exit the market. Then it once again attempts to pioneer the wholesaling of another rare food.

Frieda's Finest
www.friedas.com

ORGANIZATIONAL COLLABORATIONS FOR LONG-TERM RELATIONSHIPS

A wholesaler and its customer determine the extent to which the wholesaler will be involved in the operation of the customer's business. In general, the customer expects, at the least, that the wholesaler will have an inventory of products in a quantity sufficient to make rapid delivery possible. But in many situations, the wholesaler goes on to form a strategic business alliance with its customer.

A *strategic business alliance* is a commitment between a wholesaler and its customer to establish a long-term relationship. Such alliances may include arrangements to share or pool inventory information or exchange other databases so that purchase orders are executed automatically by computers. Vertical marketing systems are, of course, the strongest type of strategic alliance. However, wholesalers that are not part of such systems may still concentrate on building long-term relationships with their customers. For example, Fleming Foods offers many managerial services to grocery retailers because it considers them partners. This wholesaler provides computer programs and other assistance to determine supermarket locations, design store layouts, and maintain the proper levels of on-shelf inventory.

summary

Retailing and wholesaling are the major distribution institutions that make the marketing system work.

1 *Describe the function of retailing and wholesaling in the distribution system.*
Retailers deal with ultimate consumers, people who buy products for their own use. Wholesalers deal with institutions that acquire products for organizational use or for resale. Both types of intermediaries buy, sell, and help to physically distribute products through the economy.

2 *Categorize the various types of retailers by ownership and prominent strategy.*
Retail establishments in the United States may be classified by ownership as independents, leased departments, chains, franchises, or ownership groups. They may also be classified by retail strategy as in-store retailers or retailers engaged in direct

marketing. In-store retailers may be further classified as specialty stores, department stores, supermarkets, convenience stores, general mass merchandisers, or specialized mass merchandisers. Discount department stores were the first general mass merchandisers. Catalog showrooms and warehouse clubs are among the more recent forms. Specialty mass merchandisers include off-price retailers and category discounters. Direct marketing by retailers includes mail-order selling, direct marketing via television, telemarketing, in-home retailing with computers, door-to-door selling, and selling from vending machines.

3 *Analyze the historical patterns in U.S. retailing and evaluate the theories proposed to explain them.*
American retailing has evolved to suit an ever-changing environment. Three theories are used to explain this evolution. (1) The wheel of retailing theory notes that low-price, low-status stores tend to trade up, leaving space for new low-status stores. (2) The dialectic view holds that the challenge of one type of institution by another leads to the development of a third that combines characteristics of the original two. The general-specific-general theory postulates that U.S. retailing began with the general store, progressed to the specialty store, and returned to the general store concept with the development of general mass merchandisers.

4 *Understand the nature of retailers' marketing mixes.*
Retail marketers of all types must develop effective marketing mixes aimed at attracting and satisfying target markets. Merchandise assortment, location, atmospherics, customer service, store image, and database management are of special importance to retailers.

5 *Distinguish between merchant wholesalers and agents and describe their functions in the distribution system.*
Independent wholesalers are either merchants or agents. Merchants take title to the goods they sell; agents do not. The wholesaler's primary function is facilitating transfer of products or title to them.

6 *Show how full-service and limited-service merchant wholesalers contribute to the marketing system.*
Full-service merchant wholesalers can perform credit and delivery functions and provide managerial assistance and market information. Limited-service wholesalers perform some, but not all, intermediary functions, eliminating those that particular buyers do not require. These intermediaries can therefore lower their costs of doing business and the prices they must charge their customers.

7 *Identify the marketing contributions of agent intermediaries such as brokers, auction companies, and selling agents.*
Agent intermediaries such as brokers, auction companies, and selling agents may offer expert knowledge of the marketplace, provide physical facilities for doing business, give advice to buyers and sellers, and help bring buyers and sellers together. They therefore play important roles in exchanges without actually taking title to the products.

8 *Understand the key elements of wholesalers' strategies.*
To a large extent, the wholesaler's strategy is dominated by physical distribution strategies. However, selecting target markets, creating assortments for customers, and developing strategic alliances are also important aspects of wholesale strategy.

key terms

retailing (p. 399)
independent retailer (p. 400)
leased department retailer (p. 400)
chain store (p. 400)
corporate chain (p. 400)
ownership group (p. 401)
specialty store (p. 401)
department store (p. 402)
supermarket (p. 402)
scrambled merchandising (p. 402)
convenience store (p. 403)
mass merchandise retailer (p. 404)
catalog showroom (p. 405)
warehouse club (p. 405)
off-price retailer (p. 405)
category discounter (p. 406)
direct marketing (p. 406)

computer-interactive retailing (p. 408)
wheel of retailing (p. 410)
dialectic theory (p. 411)
general-specific-general theory (p. 412)
atmospherics (p. 416)
service level (p. 417)
store image (p. 418)
wholesaler (p. 419)
merchant wholesaler (p. 419)
full-service merchant wholesaler (p. 420)
general merchandise wholesaler (p. 420)
general line wholesaler (p. 420)
specialty wholesaler (p. 420)

limited-service merchant wholesaler (p. 420)
cash-and-carry wholesaler (p. 420)
truck wholesaler (p. 420)
direct-marketing wholesaler (p. 420)
drop shipper (p. 421)
rack jobber (p. 421)
agent (p. 421)
broker (p. 422)
commission merchant (p. 422)
auction company (p. 422)
manufacturers' agent (p. 423)
selling agent (p. 423)
sales office (p. 424)
sales branch (p. 424)

questions for review & critical thinking

1. Give some examples of retailers in your area that fit the following categories:
   a. Warehouse club
   b. Specialty store
   c. Chain store
   d. Catalog showroom
2. Which of the following retailers would tend to use free-standing locations? Why? Why would the others not use such locations?
   a. Kmart
   b. McDonald's
   c. A local department store
   d. A popcorn shop
3. What are the advantages of direct marketing?
4. What are some of the disadvantages of using vending machines as retail outlets?
5. How can a small retailer use the Internet to market its products?
6. What trends do you predict in direct marketing by retailers?
7. Find out about furniture marketing in the United States, and discuss the evolution and development of retailing in this industry.
8. What are the key elements of a retailer's marketing mix? Provide examples.
9. Do you think executives in small independent retail organizations have the same growth orientation and business philosophy as executives in large corporations? Why or why not?
10. Find local examples of the following.
    a. Cash-and-carry wholesaler
    b. Rack jobber
    c. Manufacturer's sales office
    d. Auction company
11. What is the major difference between agents and merchant wholesalers?
12. What are the advantages and disadvantages for each of the following businesses of using manufacturers' agents?
    a. New company marketing voice synthesizers for computers
    b. Large established company marketing truck axles
    c. West Virginia coal company selling coal in Pennsylvania
13. What are the most important aspects of a wholesaler's marketing strategies?
14. A wholesaler states, "Retailers are our customers. Our allegiance lies with them, not with the manufacturers that supply products to us." Do you agree with this point of view?
15. Form small groups as directed by your instructor. Each group is to function as a department store buying center for women's casual fashion for either the upcoming winter season or the upcoming spring season. The group should come to a consensus and make a buying recommendation.

marketing plan—right or wrong?

1. A retailer believes that the longer shoppers spend in the store, the more they will buy. The plan is to play slow music through the store's speaker system so that shoppers slow down while shopping.
2. Disney began it. Then Warner Brothers opened its stores. Now Viacom plans to operate retail stores to market Nickelodeon, Mighty Mouse, and StarTrek products.
3. A small winery plans to set up an Internet site so that wine aficionados can purchase its limited supply of wines on line. It will then ship anywhere in the United States via FedEx.

exercises

1. Go to www.faoschwarz.com for the F. A. O. Schwarz toy store on the Internet. Then go to www.toysrus.com. Evaluate the toy stores' Web sites. Which is a better marketing tool? Why?
2. To learn what's hot in international retailing, go to the Imagine If . . . home page at www. imagine-if.com/retail/. Spend some time looking at the various options. What did you learn about international retailing? Do you think it would be difficult to understand international retail markets? Why?
3. Go to www.mallofamerica.com for the Mall of America and take a virtual tour. Is the shopping center's layout typical of most malls?

address book (useful urls)

Corporate Intelligence on Retailing	www.cior.com
International Council of Shopping Centers	www.icsc.org
Space Mall Internet Shopping Center	www.spacemall.com
iMALL	www.imall.com

ethically right or wrong?

A Utah ice-cream maker planned to market a new frozen novelty item in a 30-store California chain, until the chain demanded $20,000 to put the product in its freezers. This *slotting allowance* (also known in the grocery industry as a stocking allowance, an introductory allowance, or street money) is an admission fee that many packaged-goods marketers—large and small—must pay to squeeze their brands onto crowded supermarket shelves.

Retailers say they need the slotting allowance to compensate them for entering new product information into the computer, finding space in the warehouse, redesigning store shelves, and notifying individual stores about the latest entries. They also want to turn their buying efforts into new sources of profit. Is it ethical to charge a slotting allowance?

TAKE A STAND

1. A Wal-Mart moves into a small town, and many small retail establishments go out of business within a year. Is this right?
2. A major chain store has six supermarkets in a certain city but none on the poor side of town, where many minority consumers live. Should the store open a new branch on the poor side of town?
3. A wholesaler refuses to carry a lawn-mower manufacturer's product line because the wholesaler already represents a competitor's line. Is this legal? Ethical?
4. A manufacturer of office equipment used a manufacturer's agent on the west coast to sell to wholesalers for 6 years. The agent did a good job, and sales volume reached $1 million in the territory. When this happened, a sales representative was hired to replace the agent, and the long-standing relationship between manufacturer and agent was terminated. What obligation does the manufacturer have to the agent?

Muebleria La Unica

People often ask for Pichirilo, a general manager who offers deals so good they can't be for real, at the Muebleria La Unica furniture and appliance stores in western Puerto Rico.

Actually, Pichirilo himself isn't for real. This retailer with a soft spot for customers was created by MLU President Leandro Rodriguez for radio spot commercials, and he is so well known that many people think he exists. The spots have been a key weapon in a fight with chain stores for market share.

Rodriguez opened the first MLU store in Mayaguez in 1959, and his business grew as that city did. He opened two branch stores in smaller towns. Then two mainland U.S. chains moved into the area, followed by two more. Four Puerto Rican appliance/furniture chains also arrived. MLU's sales began to fall.

Volume-buying discounts allowed the newcomers to cut prices below locally owned stores' profit levels. MLU customers had been buying at good prices from salespeople they knew and trusted, but Rodriguez realized he couldn't count on customer loyalty alone to keep him in business. To get across the idea that MLU was as capable of offering low prices as the chains, he coined a slogan: "Ventas por millones, beneficios por centavos" ("sales by the millions, profits in pennies"). The slogan was incorporated in a catch jingle for radio spots—which were enhanced by the introduction of Pichirilo.

Showrooms at MLU's stores were spruced up. Storage space at the main store was remodeled as an extra showroom, after a storeroom was rented in a separate building. A fourth MLU outlet was opened in a Mayaguez location convenient to areas where many MLU customers live. Thanks to an excellent record at banks, Rodriguez was able to get funds for expanding and remodeling—and for purchase volumes large enough to win better discounts.[21]

QUESTIONS

1. What prominent element is the basis for Muebleria La Unica's retailing strategy?
2. Using the classification scheme in the chapter, determine what type of retailer Muebleria La Unica is.
3. Would Muebleria La Unica's strategy work in the continental United States?

EatZi's

At Brinker International Inc.'s latest restaurant innovation, you can hardly get a table—because there are only four of them indoors. Actually, EatZi's Market & Bakery, located in Dallas, Texas, is a New York–style gourmet grocery aimed at the takeout crowd. It features the sort of sushi and pasta dishes favored by young professionals on the go, along with fresh produce, flowers and pastries.

It may not be going too far to say that EatZi's—a Dallas deli/grocery/restaurant referred to by the management as EatZi's concept—has generated a revolution in food service that will have far-reaching repercussions. To give you an idea of the impact this rambunctious, 8,000-square-foot establishment has had on Dallas, just listen to what one customer said: "I've been here at least once a day for a month!" Most people don't even go to their jobs that often.

Here's what separates EatZi's from other grocery stores—it's really a restaurant. And don't let the fact that there are only four tables and two narrow counters on which to dine fool you either. EatZi's was created by restaurant genius Phil Romano, and it is definitely in the business of serving food to its customers.

In fact, "Food for the Taking" is their slogan. Although it's not that big, EatZi's has everything you could ever want for dinner, and management goes to great lengths to suggest that the possibilities are endless. And—there's opera music (no German or English operas, they insist) merrily blaring away on the sound system.

Chefs in their tall white hats welcome customers outside; inside they hand out free samples of cheese, seafood salad, smoked salmon, and more in the executional areas where bread is baked and food to go is prepared. There are 140 produce items, EatZi's ripens its own apples, and a third of EatZi's own produce goes to making the prepared food. The food bins are even custom-made, and everything but everything is for sale, even the baskets and totes. There are 700 specialty foods—oils, dressings, soy sauce, infused mayonnaise, roasted garlic, and even onion jam. In this world of plenty, the aisles have been made purposely narrow to create an intense atmosphere that's made even more intense because the chefs are constantly coming out from behind their counters to talk to the customers about the food.

In truth, much of the food EatZi's offers can be had at your local supermarket. But you won't feel as good shopping for it and you won't have nearly as much fun. And, you'll have to cook.

Take-home offerings at EatZi's can be amazingly good, particularly because you know that most of the preparation has already been done for you. The focaccia topped with tomatoes and caramelized onions redolent with garlic has gotten raves as the best in town; pizza also gets top honors. Thuringer salami is spectacular. A basic like roasted chicken shows thoughtfulness in the preparation—even with crisply browned skin, the meat is still tender and succulent. If you live in Dallas you have likely been to EatZi's or are planning to go; out-of-towners can easily add it to their list of compelling tourist attractions. But if you don't want to join the masses just yet, wait a while—the EatZi's concept management team has plans to roll out EatZi's all over the country. Probably even in your own home town.[22]

QUESTIONS

1. What prominent element is the basis for EatZi's retailing strategy?
2. Explain EatZi's in terms of the wheel of retailing theory.

chapter
14

Logistics and Physical Distribution Management

LEARNING OBJECTIVES

After you have studied this chapter, you will be able to:

Evaluate the role of logistics and physical distribution in the marketing mix. **1**

Show how distribution managers can make physical distribution provide maximum satisfaction to buyers while reducing costs. **2**

Explain the total cost approach to physical distribution. **3**

Compare the advantages and disadvantages of the modes of transportation available to shippers. **4**

Identify the purposes of warehousing, order processing, materials handling, and inventory control. **5**

(continued on next page)

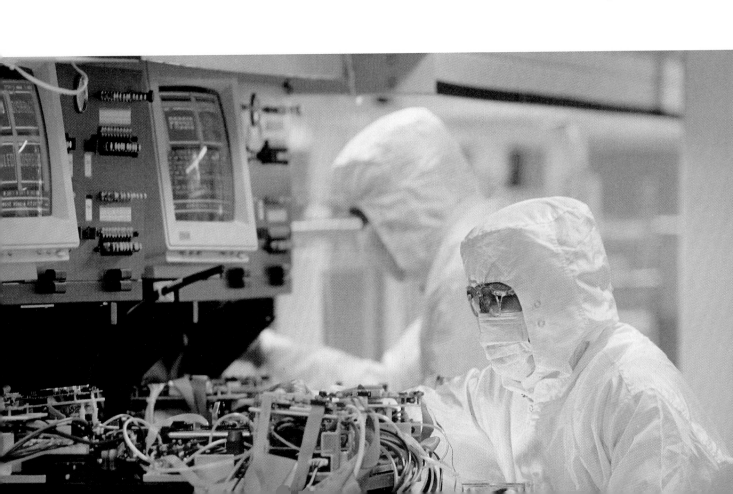

there is tumult in the personal com-
puter industry, and it is due largely to one man: Michael Dell. By sticking with a direct-order model—in which people buy goods directly from a manufacturer by phone, fax, or, increasingly, the Internet—Dell Computer has become the *cause célèbre* of the computer world.

The surging Texas company has given its competitors 10-gallon fits, igniting a tornado of reengineering of manufacturing and logistics strategies as they try to blunt Dell's momentum. All would love to match its ability to quickly accept orders, build the PCs, then move them to buyers.

But for now, Dell is setting the standard. In 1997 Dell surpassed Apple Computer and Packard Bell NEC to become the third-largest PC company in the United States.

Dell is shifting the nature of the PC business in a significant way: It's made the Internet a profitable and efficient way to sell products to home users and small businesses. It now sells nearly $2 million of products daily via its Web site. How much revenue does it want to flow over the Web? "We'd like to see it all on line," says Dell, 32, who famously founded the company in his college dorm room. "Why not?

DELL HAS MADE THE INTERNET A PROFITABLE AND EFFICIENT WAY TO SELL PRODUCTS TO HOME USERS AND SMALL BUSINESSES.

It is the most effective transaction medium we can think of except mental telepathy."

Dell began to explore Web opportunities in early 1995. In July 1996, with no promotional effort, the company offered a way to actually purchase products. Executives were astonished by the traffic. Soon, the site was selling 30 to 50 PCs a day. It never slowed down. Now, the company is on track to sell more than $500 million worth of goods this fiscal year on its Web site.

Dell's Web site (www.dell.com) lets you pick a model and see how the price changes when you add or take out various parts. You can buy directly on line by submitting a credit card number or print out a form and fax it to Dell. You get loads of product information and create your own Dell home page. Registered site users can track their orders on line, to see if they are in the mail or stuck in production. You can even access detailed PC diagrams for troubleshooting.

In the fast-moving PC market, Dell's chief advantage is price. By selling directly to buyers, it can offer prices about 10 percent below those of Compaq Computer, IBM, and Hewlett Packard. Those companies sell through distributors and other resellers, which, to turn a profit, mark up prices for the end user.

Dell also benefits from a well-honed manufacturing and logistics system. It doesn't build a PC until one is ordered. Then, workers in its plants retrieve the necessary parts, which suppliers have stored nearby. They assemble the PC according to buyer's specifications, and the PC is delivered to the customer, often within a week, assuming parts are available. That build-to-order process—and Dell's ability to steer callers to in-stock supplies—has given it big advantages over competitors that must forecast demand for various models, and build accordingly.

At times, Compaq, IBM, and others have built too few PCs and ended up losing sales. More often, they build too many PCs, which sit in their distributors' warehouses. If the price of a model drops while it is in inventory, the PC maker typically pays the distributor the difference between the new and old prices—boosting costs.

In the worst-case scenario, the inventory isn't sold, resulting in a write-down for the PC maker or the distributor. Dell's system allows it to turn over its PC parts inventory in 12 days. Meanwhile, finished PCs from IBM, Compaq, and H-P sit in warehouses an average of 4 to 6 weeks. To reduce their inventory risk, rivals are planning build-to-order manufacturing systems that give buyers a choice of purchasing directly or through a reseller. All share a key component: letting resellers assemble the PCs so that they can more efficiently customize the add-on hardware and the software ordered by end users.

For years, big companies bought mainly from value-added resellers—like Vanstar, Entex, and MicroAge franchises—because they also provided services such as installing software, setting up networks, and giving technical support. But Dell has matched some of the resellers' basic services, like software and hardware installation. And technology-savvy companies are now powering Dell's growth. Ford Motor, Oracle, and many others ". . . are saying instead of buying from 20 resellers, we'll just buy from Dell. . . . They're saying, 'Why should I pay a premium price when we don't get anything?'" Dell says.

Competitors say that's a gross simplification. The market "is much more complex than Michael Dell is trying to portray," Compaq CEO Eckhard Pfeiffer says. "He says everybody wants to buy direct. That is absolutely not the case." Most companies still demand services from resellers, he says, because they don't have the expertise or desire to completely set up, install, and service increasingly complex networks of PCs themselves. "Resellers aren't going to vanish," says Leslie Geezy, senior director of purchasing for Oracle. "But what I can tell you is that it is so simple to [buy] on a global basis with a direct company."

For Dell's competitors, however, electronic commerce is a dangerous game. By selling direct aggressively, PC makers would inevitably compete with and anger retail stores such as Computer City and CompUSA that distribute their products.

Dell is free of such constraints and is upgrading its on-line sales capabilities. The next step: moving big corporate purchases to the Web. It is setting up about 100 customized Web sites that will make it even easier for top customers to buy and track products and access various services. "For us, it's a natural thing to do," Dell says. "We are already in direct contact with our customers." A fact the industry knows all too well.[1]

Logistics and physical distribution have long been unsung, operations-intensive aspects of business that took a back seat to other areas of marketing strategy. However, at progressive companies, such as Dell, all that is changing as cross-functional activities, such as manufacturing and logistics, strongly influence the overall marketing strategy.

Some aspects of logistics and physical distribution can be found in every exchange situation. The chapter's opening story about Dell makes clear how important these activities are. In other instances, such as the marketing of services, physical distribution is not as obvious. But services, like goods, must be physically distributed. A rural university may decide that its target markets can be better served if off-campus branches are installed in major cities around the state. The school may also decide to have the same professors teach on all campuses. These are physical distribution decisions. The roles of logistics and physical distribution in an organization's value chain are the topics of this chapter.

The chapter begins by making a distinction between logistics and physical distribution and then discusses the objectives of physical distribution. It emphasizes the

Logistics deals with the "big picture" of an organization's distribution process.

importance of a systems approach and a total cost perspective in managing physical distribution activities. Next it identifies each individual physical distribution activity and discusses the management of these activities. The chapter ends with a brief discussion of future trends in physical distribution and logistics management.

Logistics and Physical Distribution Defined

Logistics
The activities involved in moving raw materials and parts into the firm, moving in-process inventory through the firm, and moving finished goods out of the firm.

Materials management
The activities involved in bringing raw materials and supplies to the point of production and moving in-process inventory through the firm.

Physical distribution
The activities involved in the efficient movement of finished products from the end of the production line to the consumer.

Logistics describes the entire process of moving raw materials and component parts into a firm, moving in-process inventory through the firm, and moving finished goods out of the firm. Logistics management thus involves planning, implementing, and controlling the efficient flow of both inbound materials and outbound finished products.

Clearly, the term *logistics* is broad in scope, because it encompasses planning and coordinating the physical distribution of finished goods and managing the movement and storage of raw materials and supply parts needed during the procurement and production processes. **Materials management** is concerned with only part of this process: bringing raw materials and supplies to the point of production and moving in-process inventory through the firm. General Motors Corporation wants to get to the point where every time a dealer sells a Cadillac, Firestone or Goodyear automatically sends another set of tires to one of GM's plants. This illustrates the importance of materials management and how a flexible company can coordinate logistical activities to react to the market faster.

Physical distribution is a term employed in manufacturing and commerce to describe the broad range of activities concerned with efficient movement of finished products from the end of the production line to the consumer.[2] In short, physical distribution refers to the flow of products from producers to consumers. Its major focus is the physical aspects of that flow rather than the institutional activities within channels of distribution dealing with changing title, facilitating exchanges, and negotiating with intermediaries. (The physical aspect of distributing ice cream is the subject of the What Went Wrong? feature.) As part of the "place" portion of the overall marketing mix, physical distribution activities contribute time and place utility.

Exhibit 14-1 shows the interrelationship of physical distribution, materials management, and logistics. It is common, as the exhibit indicates, to think of materials management as consisting of the activities performed up to the point of production and to think of physical distribution (narrowly

what went wrong?

A Triple Treat? The physical distribution system for McDonald's Triple Ripple, a three-flavored ice-cream product, was the major reason the product was dropped. Experiments indicated that the product would freeze, defrost, and refreeze in the course of distribution. Solving the problem would have required each McDonald's city to have an ice-cream plant with special equipment to roll the three flavors into one. As this example shows, physical distribution has a dramatic influence on a product's success.

Logistics Management and the Organization's Flow of Materials

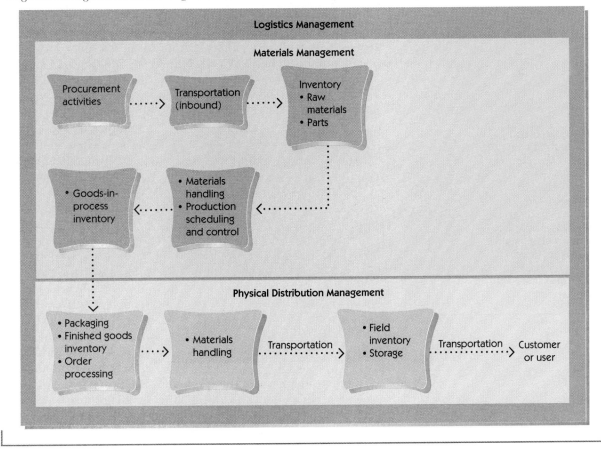

defined) as including the activities that occur after production. Logistics management encompasses these two functions, assuring coordination of their activities.

Logistics, dealing as it does with the "big picture" of an organization's distribution process, relies heavily on demand estimation (sales forecasting) to achieve its goal of smoothly controlling the physical flow of goods through the organization and its channels of distribution. Forecasting enables managers concerned with logistics to synchronize the activities that make up the distribution effort. With a properly constructed sales forecast at hand, indicating what sales totals are expected and when they are expected, the marketing manager can plan for the following events and needs (and many others):

LOGISTICAL **PLANNING IS MARKET-ORIENTED. IT STARTS WITH THE NEEDS OF THE CUSTOMERS AND WORKS BACK TO THE PLANT.**

• Handling and holding incoming inventories of raw materials, parts, and the like
• Monitoring stocks, materials, and finished goods inventories
• Handling finished goods and shipping them to points of storage or intermediaries
• Disposing of waste, by-products, and imperfectly manufactured output
• Monitoring and coordinating the members of channels of distribution

Note that logistical planning is market-oriented. It does not start at the production-related plant operations and work toward the customers. It starts with the needs of the customers and works back to the plant.

The Objectives of Physical Distribution

Physical distribution has many objectives. All of them can be condensed into one overall statement of purpose: to minimize cost while maximizing customer service. This goal is the statement of an ideal. Unfortunately, means of realizing the lowest total cost and the highest level of service almost always work at cross-purposes. For example, to achieve high-level customer service, an appliance marketer should operate many warehouses, each carrying a large inventory so that local customers' orders can be filled rapidly. In lieu of that, the marketer should

have a fleet of jet transports ready at all times to fly merchandise to customers within a few hours of receiving their orders. Both of these approaches to maximizing customer service are likely to prove inconsistent with the other half of the physical distribution objective, which calls for minimizing cost. Minimizing cost generally requires few warehouses, low inventories, and slow, inexpensive means of transportation. The twin goals of maximum service and lowest cost, while not necessarily totally contradictory, can rarely be fully met. It is usually necessary to compromise on one or both of them. Thus, physical distribution managers, while striving for the ideal, must work toward realistic objectives, performing a sort of balancing act in the process.

ESTABLISHING REALISTIC OBJECTIVES

How does marketing management develop reasonable objectives for physical distribution? A good place to start is with the marketing concept. The marketing concept dictates that marketing managers should strive for consumer satisfaction in all that they do, including physical distribution. Therefore, the distribution system should be designed to fit the wants and needs of the customer.

Just as in any other element of the distribution system, cost should be evaluated in terms of customer wants. Suppose an analysis of the market shows that customers are most concerned with rapid and on-time deliveries. If the marketing company determines that such service can be provided and guaranteed only at an increase in the product's price, does that mean customers cannot be served? No, but it does mean that a further step—determining whether customers are willing to pay a premium price for that service—is in order. For example, Federal Express's customers seem to be willing to pay for quick service, as are the customers who use the U.S. Postal System's Express Mail. In many cases, however, customers may have some priority other than rapid delivery. Buyers of furniture and appliances, though perhaps eager to possess their new purchases, often prefer to have the retailer from whom the purchase was made deliver, set up, or install the product, even if this means waiting a week or two to take delivery. These buyers are willing to pay a premium of time, sacrificing quick delivery for the feeling that installation was done properly by skilled workers. Other kinds of buyers, such as purchasers of repair parts for machinery, fall somewhere in the middle; they may seek both a steady flow of parts to maintain an in-shop inventory and access to parts on an emergency basis. Therefore, marketing managers must research and calculate how the customer sees the problem of balancing maximum service and minimum cost. An important consideration here is the competition's physical distribution policies. UPS, Emery Worldwide, Airborne, and other Federal Express competitors clearly have developed their distribution methods with Federal Express's market offering in mind. Each competitor is seeking a competitive advantage over the other.

ESTABLISHING A COMPETITIVE ADVANTAGE

In many cases, organizations can establish competitive advantages over rivals through more effective physical distribution. This is especially true where the products of one organization are essentially the same as those of competitors, as in the coal and the

Laura Ashley, the upscale clothing and home furnishings manufacturer and retailer, recently revitalized its information systems and consolidated warehouses as part of its physical distribution strategy. The British company now turns inventory roughly ten times a year, five times faster than before.

www.laura-ashley.com

steel industries. Marketers experience difficulty in establishing competitive advantages through price differentials or product superiority in such industries, but physical distribution offers an avenue to develop an advantage. Providing more reliable or faster delivery, avoiding errors in order processing, and delivering undamaged goods are all potential sources of competitive advantage. Should competitors be weak in any of these areas, opportunities for competitive advantage are especially attractive.

Many salespeople emphasize rapid delivery as a selling appeal. They may say, "We can provide you with the goods within 24 hours of the order, whereas competitors cannot guarantee delivery in under 3 days." Rapid delivery is especially important in certain industries. Pharmacists, for instance, may insist on 1- or 2-hour service from suppliers. If it is not available, the pharmacist may lose a sale and possibly even a regular customer. Auto repair parts are likely to be available with 24-hour notice even in smaller towns. Produce marketers and baked goods marketers, whose products are perishable, may seek a competitive advantage by marketing products fresher than those of their rivals.

Innovative organizations may employ the most advanced technology to establish rapid delivery, which becomes the basis for a competitive advantage. In no other area of marketing can computerization, automation, and modern quantitative techniques be so extensively and profitably employed as in physical distribution. Many of the marketing applications of computerization and automation are in the areas of handling inventory, recording orders, billing, and other aspects of order processing.

3M sells office items to Boise Cascade, which, in addition to selling lumber, distributes office products. 3M Corporation established a competitive advantage by reducing inventory by some 5 percent, or $500,000, for Boise Cascade and increasing inventory turns from 6 to 16 at a Los Angeles location. Among other initiatives, 3M speeded delivery by affixing logistics labels that mapped out slot locations in Boise Cascade's warehouse. 3M credits cross-functional teams that included people from logistics, management information systems, and sales. The basic idea: Understand and solve a customer's physical distribution problem and you've deepened the relationship.[3]

A Cross-Section of the Physical Distribution System

Physical distribution consists of several identifiable activities:

1. *Inventory management.* For example, a retailer determines how many Colorado Rockies hats is an adequate number to stock and when to order them.
2. *Order processing.* Sales office personnel receive customers' orders and then arrange for the requested merchandise to be shipped and for the customer to be billed.

Air-Vet   This story about a start-up veterinary supply wholesaler, Air-Vet, and FedEx is a lot like the old fable of the tortoise and the hare. Only in this true tale, the creatures put their heads together. The wisdom of the persistent turtle combines with the speed of the agile rabbit and they both win the race.

When Air-Vet entered the wholesale veterinary supply industry, it knew that with aggressive competitors already working out of regional and district offices across the country, Air-Vet could not enter the arena at a snail's pace. It was wise enough to know that it would have to have a competitive advantage. So the Memphis-based business developed an ambitious storage, inventory control, and delivery system that is unique in the animal pharmaceutical trade.

Air-Vet's parent company already had a strong reputation and years of experience as a successful sporting goods distributor. But animal pharmaceuticals and supplies were a different story. Start-up costs alone were prohibitive, and the company wanted to be unique. Research revealed what would distinguish Air-Vet from its competition: A survey of more than 400 veterinarians across the country indicated a strong preference for next-day delivery of orders.

"In our business," the company's vice president and general manager points out, "some wholesalers rely on 25 to 30 different shipping locations scattered around the country. We saw that as an inventory nightmare." The VP went on to say, "Air-Vet is not in the shipping business. In the beginning, we couldn't answer our own questions. If we'd relied on our parent company's distribution system, we would have been limited to regional distribution, with a national reach that took 2 days or more via UPS. And that didn't address our more immediate logistics needs."

A neighbor in Memphis, Business Logistics Services (BLS), a division of FedEx, offered the company a solution. Working as partners would allow Air-Vet to defer start-up costs without compromising a range of value-added services. Air-Vet believed that initial sales volumes would be low and the company needed to control costs. So it worked out with Federal Express a system that offers a unique way to control the operation's costs by keeping everything Air-Vet sells in the BLS warehouse system. The arrangement allows Air-Vet to cut labor expenses and physical expenditures for storage. And the company passes that savings on to its customers in fast service. Using BLS allows Air-Vet to ship orders to its veterinary customers overnight for any type of need: small or large animal products, topicals, fluids, dermatological applications, biological products, drugs, and basic supplies like bandages.[4]

3. *Warehousing and storage.* Producers of seasonal goods, such as air conditioners, bathing suits, and mittens, hold products in storage for distribution as needed through the seasons.

4. *Materials handling.* Forklifts, conveyor belts, and other means are used to move merchandise into and within warehouses, retail stores, and wholesalers' facilities.

5. *Protective packaging and containerization.* For example, paper for photocopiers is bound into packs of 200 sheets, the packs are put into cardboard boxes containing 10 packs, and the cardboard boxes are placed on pallets.

6. *Transportation.* For example, automobiles are shipped by rail from Detroit and other assembly points to dealers around the United States.

Regular physical distribution activities (excluding selection of a warehouse location) are shown in Exhibit 14-2.

Breaking physical distribution down into components permits us to concentrate on individual aspects of a complex subject. However, this approach is somewhat misleading, because it suggests that each component is carried out separately, without interacting with the others. It is important to understand that the components operate as a system.

The **systems concept**—the idea that elements may be strongly interrelated and may interact to achieve one goal—is of special value in considerations of distribution. Even the casual observer can see that a warehouse is of no meaningful use unless it fills and empties as part of a system intended to achieve some distribution goal. No shipment of merchandise via railroad or plane is of any real value unless it is taken from the carrier and moved to where it is actually needed. In seeking to satisfy customer service demands at reasonable cost, marketing managers can use each part of a distribution system to help attain that goal, but only within the context of the system. Each part affects the others. That is the very meaning of the word *system.*

Systems concept
The idea that elements of a distribution system (or another system) are strongly interrelated and interact to achieve a goal.

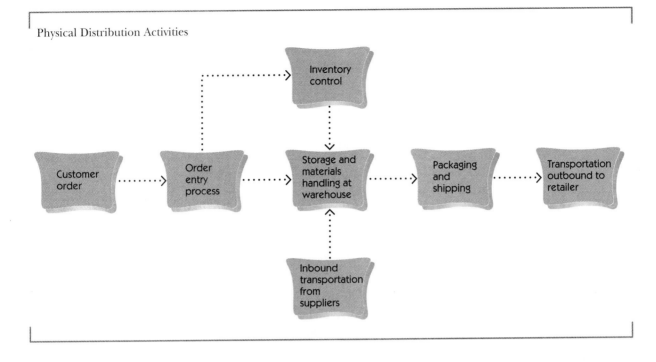

Physical Distribution Activities

Total Cost: A Systems Approach

The key ideas inherent in the systems approach to physical distribution have contributed to the development of the **total cost concept.** When marketing managers adopt this way of thinking, they see the answer to the distribution problem as a system—a system aimed at reducing total physical distribution cost.

What factors need to be contemplated by the distribution manager seeking to realize the physical distribution objective of holding down total cost? The number of variables can become quite large, but consider this partial list:

- Handling costs at the point of production
- Cost of transportation to a wholesaler, if necessary
- Handling costs at the wholesaler level
- Cost of transportation to a retailer or industrial user
- Handling costs at the retailer level
- Cost of transportation to a buyer, if necessary

Let's consider the case of an organizational good—a file cabinet, produced in California and intended for sale in New Hampshire. A partial list of physical distribution costs might include the following:

- Handling costs involved in moving the file cabinet from the factory to a warehouse on the west coast
- Storage costs at the warehouse
- Handling and shipping costs to a point of storage convenient to the New Hampshire buyer
- Storage costs on the east coast
- Local transportation costs to move the file cabinet from the east coast warehouse or another point of storage to the purchaser

Total cost concept
In relation to physical distribution, a focus on the entire range of costs associated with a particular distribution method.

- Expenditures for paperwork, local inventory taxes, and any additional handling or moving of the item, plus the further cost of customer concerns, worries, and dissatisfaction

A glance at this list of costs quickly reveals the basic lesson of the systems approach to distribution. A relatively slow means of transportation from west coast to east coast, such as ship or train, would reduce the cost of the transcontinental shipment. But if the purchaser of the file cabinet could not wait for a slow shipment, the distributor would have a problem. Should the manufacturer warehouse a large inventory on the east coast, thus incurring high expenditures for paperwork, inventory handling, and local taxes? The cost in terms of lost sales could be even greater if the inventory were not available. Or could the problem be solved simply by using a more expensive means of transportation directly from the west coast, eliminating the need for an east coast warehouse? Using air freight would likely reduce problems of storage and handling at both ends of the transaction and would probably lessen the total cost. Cheap transportation could prove more costly in the long run.

Clearly, minimizing the cost associated with only one or two steps of a multistep process can result in increasing the cost of the whole process. Systems-thinking managers make trade-offs, increasing the cost of some parts of the system to produce even greater cost reductions in other parts of the system—thus reducing the total cost.

SYSTEMS-THINKING MANAGERS MAKE TRADE-OFFS, INCREASING THE COST OF SOME PARTS OF THE SYSTEM TO PRODUCE EVEN GREATER COST REDUCTIONS IN OTHER PARTS OF THE SYSTEM—THUS REDUCING THE TOTAL COST.

Total cost is an important measure that was not always appreciated. At one time, shippers selected their transportation modes in a one-dimensional way. If management thought a product required quick delivery, the fastest mode of transportation was chosen. If quick delivery was thought not to be a major concern, the cheapest means of transportation, within reason, was selected. Looking back, you may wonder why transportation experts frequently did not bother to determine whether it was possible to lower the total cost of distribution, even if that meant using a more expensive means of transportation; but this approach was uncommon until relatively recently in marketing history. Sometimes the customer's satisfaction may be more important than a dollars-and-cents cost reduction. One possible payoff of increasing some system costs may come in the form of greater buyer satisfaction. Unfortunately, it is easy for distribution managers to become so wrapped up in dealing with dollars that they neglect customer costs and payoffs.

Many opportunities to cut distribution costs present themselves to the effective marketing manager because so much of the distribution system operates beyond the observation of target buyers. Customers are concerned with the results of distribution, not how it is accomplished. Often, management finds that costs can be reduced through improvements in existing physical distribution systems. Here are some examples of such improvements:

- Using robotics and automating warehouses, thereby reducing payroll expenses
- Replacing numerous small warehouses located near markets with a few large national warehouses that serve multiple markets, thereby reducing inventory carrying costs
- Correcting inefficient procedures in order processing, thus eliminating needless red tape and paper handling

- Using low-cost transportation carriers, such as barges
- Moving offices, plants, warehouses, and retail outlets to low-cost locations, perhaps in a foreign country where labor costs are low
- Requiring customers to perform some logistics functions (as when the marketer stipulates that retailers or wholesalers must carry certain minimum inventories), thus allowing the marketer to shift part of the warehousing and storage costs to customers

Cost-cutting measures can lower prices to buyers, increase the seller's margin, or achieve some combination of these goals. The extent of the possible savings from cost cutting is illustrated by the experience of one company that reported a potential savings of one-fifth of its total physical distribution costs of $40 million as the result of "a hardnosed physical distribution audit." Some of the problems that the audit uncovered were "small shipments moving separately to common destinations, fragmented inventories, different warehousing costs at different locations, and high costs per order."

Baxter International Baxter International, marketer of hospital products including instrumentation, custom procedure kits, diagnostic trays, and respiratory and anesthesia products, has responded innovatively to the pressure on hospital revenues brought by health maintenance organizations, insurance carriers, and the government. In the company's most recent variation on relationship marketing, Baxter has negotiated risk-sharing partnerships with a couple of hospitals: Baxter works with customers to set a cost target for supplies and shares the savings—or the additional costs if expenses overshoot targets.

With these and other hospitals, Baxter brings in consultants to streamline distribution. The company also works with hospitals to standardize instruments and bandages used for given procedures, and delivers the products to the site of the operation. Says Lester Knight, Baxter's executive vice president: "This goes beyond loyalty; you are sharing a common P&L [profit and loss]. You both make money by bringing costs down."

Participants in the company's ValueLink inventory management program relinquish ownership and management of inventory to Baxter, which will deliver supplies to hospital floors, often several times a day. Baxter has even taken over the task of cleaning and sterilizing equipment, freeing hospital staff to care for patients. At some hospitals, Baxter employees are on site 24 hours.

At Seton Medical Center, a 319-bed hospital in Daly City, California, George Ryan, the director of materials management, estimates that cost of supplies decreased some $300,000. True, the sales pie is smaller, but Baxter will keep a larger cut of it. Now Ryan wants to discuss changing the payment schedule from the standard 30 days to something more like the 87-day average float the government and insurance companies take to pay him. Says he: "I feel free to put out an idea like that and not have it laughed at."[5]

Managing the Components of Physical Distribution

As mentioned earlier, six major areas of concern may be isolated in the physical movement of products. They are transportation, warehousing, inventory control, materials handling, order processing, and packaging. As we look at each of these separately, keep in mind their interrelationships as well as their individual contributions to the overall physical distribution system.

LOW COST	SPEED	RELIABILITY OF DELIVERY	ABILITY TO DELIVER TO MANY GEOGRAPHICAL AREAS	REPUTATION FOR DELIVERING UNDAMAGED GOODS
(1) Pipeline	(1) Air	(1) Pipeline	(1) Motor	(1) Pipeline
(2) Water	(2) Motor	(2) Air	(2) Rail	(2) Water
(3) Rail	(3) Rail	(3) Motor	(3) Air	(3) Air
(4) Motor	(4) Pipeline	(4) Rail	(4) Water	(4) Motor
(5) Air	(5) Water	(5) Water	(5) Pipeline	(5) Rail

Note: These comparisons are of a very general nature intended only to show the trade-offs involved when cost of use is compared with other attributes of modes of transportation.

TRANSPORTATION

Transportation
The physical movement or shipment of products to locations in the distribution channel.

Transportation decisions involve selecting the specific mode that will be used to physically move products from a manufacturer, grower, wholesaler, or other seller to the receiving facilities of the buyer. The major alternative modes of transportation are motor carrier, air freight, water transportation, railroad, and pipeline. Their comparative rankings on various attributes are shown in Exhibit 14-3. Other means of transporting merchandise that may come to mind, such as parcel post or overnight delivery services, themselves use one or more of these major transportation methods.

The physical distribution manager, or transportation manager, must consider the cost trade-offs mentioned earlier in selecting one of the modes of transportation. The first consideration is always the needs of the buyer. If these needs are extraordinarily difficult or expensive to meet, the manager must investigate the buyer's willingness to bear extra costs to satisfy those needs. Other considerations include the nature of the product (bulk, perishability, weight, fragility), how fast and dependable the delivery must be, and the cost and availability of transportation methods and storage space. Alternatives may be evaluated in terms of these variables.

Motor carrier
A member of the trucking industry or another carrier, such as Greyhound's package service, that transports products over roads.

Damage in transit
Breakage, spoilage, or other injury to products that occurs while the products are being transported.

A load of margarine travels from Denmark to Tacoma, Washington, where a ramp worker notices a leak in the shipping container. The cargo is placed in a truck bound for a warehouse, but en route the driver looks in his rearview mirror and notices yellow globs flying out of the back of the truck. About 2,000 cartons of margarine have done a complete meltdown; the shipping documents from Denmark never specified a temperature setting for the cargo.[6]

Motor Carrier   At one time, the trucking industry was tightly regulated by the federal government. Implementation of the Motor Carrier Act of 1980 dramatically transformed this situation, essentially deregulating the trucking industry. Motor carriers are now able to set rates for individual customers based on costs rather than having to comply with a uniform set of rates. Although not all trucking industry members favor deregulation, it seems to have resulted in heightened competition, greater efficiency, enhanced services, and innovative pricing.

Trucks, and even the far less important **motor carrier** operations like Greyhound's package service, which uses buses as carriers, are preferred over rail

shipment—especially by marketers of consumer products in boxed cartons—despite the fact that trains can move great quantities of products at lower prices. One reason is that **damages in transit** are less likely with trucks than with trains. Furthermore, trucks are more accessible and more flexible than railroads, and they are generally more reliable in terms of delivery deadlines. Although they are most efficient moving comparatively small shipments over short distances, they are also effective for long distances. While trucking companies may not fully believe it, times of economic recession make motor carriers even more attractive to shippers. Manufacturers, forced by high cost or lower margins to reduce inventories, become increasingly vulnerable to delivery delays. With little or no cushion of spare parts or supplies, they depend on reliable trucking service.

Air Freight   The primary advantages of **air freight** are its speed and distance capabilities. For many shippers, these advantages compensate for the high costs associated with air transportation. There are other advantages as well. Fast transportation permits inventory reductions and savings in warehousing costs. Air freight has a superb reputation for seldom damaging goods in transit. In remote areas that are inaccessible by truck or railroad, air freight may be the only transportation choice available. Traditionally, air transportation has been used primarily to move goods of high unit value, perishable goods, and emergency orders. The growth of international trade has contributed to a dramatic increase in the use of air transport during the past two decades. As with trucking, recession and high interest rates have a significant impact on the use of air freight.

Air freight
The shipment of products by air carrier.

Manufacturers, especially producers of high-technology products, often choose to ship goods on demand via air freight rather than incur the costs of carrying inventory. Physical distribution has moved away from the old ways of using regional warehouses and trucks to an instant supply cycle.

A popular strategy among air carriers is the *hub-and-spoke* approach. For example, Federal Express's hub is in Memphis, Tennessee. All packages arrive in Memphis and then depart on jet airplanes to spoke locations throughout the United States and around the world. Hub routing of commercial airline flights through major airports such as Dallas–Fort Worth, Atlanta, and Chicago has also helped commercial airlines to establish new time and cost standards. The hub-and-spoke idea is not totally new. It was common in the early days of U.S. rail transportation marketing, when almost all livestock and grain were shipped into Chicago for sale, then resorted and redirected to new owners or food-processing facilities elsewhere. However, computerized resorting, reloading, and rerouting facilities have made major improvements in hub-and-spoke efficiency, allowing shippers to provide customers with major savings in both time and dollars.

At a sporting event so preoccupied with time, the choice of package delivery company was obvious.

There's a reason the Olympic Games depend on UPS. We guarantee two-day delivery to virtually every major business center worldwide. And to many places overnight, if you need an all-out sprint.

MOVING at the SPEED of BUSINESS. UPS

In the global economy, worldwide transportation service is an important aspect of the marketing mix. Companies like UPS deliver overseas overnight to hundreds of destinations, providing the kind of speed on which both businesses and organizers of events such as the Olympic Games have come to depend.

Both *warehouse* and *distribution center* are used commonly today because the newer terminology has not fully replaced the old. But whatever the storage place is called, the emphasis is on moving, not keeping, the product. After all, keeping products in a warehouse is not the goal of physical distribution managers. Their goal is to get products into the hands of buyers. As we have already noted, many large and small tasks are included in the warehousing function. Taken together, they comprise two primary activities: storage and breaking bulk.

> WHATEVER THE STORAGE PLACE IS CALLED, THE EMPHASIS IS ON MOVING, NOT KEEPING, THE PRODUCT.

Storage
The holding and housing of goods in inventory for a certain period of time.

Storage   Storage consists of holding and housing goods in inventory for a certain time period. It is necessary because of the almost inevitable discrepancies between production and consumption cycles. Consider this extreme example: The materials needed to operate midwestern steel mills are shipped across the northern Great Lakes via ship or barge. But shipment is impossible in the winter because the lakes freeze. Therefore, the materials must be stored at accessible locations. Such storage diminishes the effects that an uneven production cycle caused by a cyclical supply of raw materials would have on the steel business. In other cases, marketers store products because they have purchased large quantities and thus have more goods than they can sell at one time—another situation in which supply and demand are discrepant. Marketers may also store products in expectation that market prices for those products will be higher in the future. In any number of cases, cyclical demand brings about a discontinuity that has to be overcome by storing products. Products of a seasonal nature, such as air conditioners, class rings, skis, and wedding gowns, can be manufactured throughout the year. Regular schedules stabilize production and tend to minimize production costs. Storage permits the makers of these items to operate a steady production stream and hold the products until they are needed.

Storage does not always involve warehouses. The Magic Chef Corporation became a leader in the marketing of soft-drink vending machines when it designed a machine that stores three cans in a row instead of two, boosting the capacity of the machines by one-third and cutting the frequency of restocking. The company realized the importance of storage considerations to its customers.

Breaking Bulk   The second key function of warehousing is the physical task of breaking bulk. Shipments of any warehoused product are likely to arrive at the point of storage in large quantities and to leave in smaller quantities that are appropriate to the individual retailers or other buyers seeking them. A shipment of Toyotas arriving in California will be loaded on trucks and trains departing for various cities throughout the United States as the bulk-breaking function is performed.

Warehousing Strategy   A fundamental warehousing decision for marketing managers involves determining the optimal number, location, and types of warehouses needed. The warehousing choices open to marketing managers may be demonstrated in terms of two strategy extremes, between which lie many combinations of strategies. At one extreme, the manufacturer makes large shipments over short distances to high-capacity storage warehouses located near manufacturing points. Smaller shipments are then made to retailers or other purchasers. At the other extreme lies the strategy alternative of making relatively large shipments over long distances to various distribution warehouses located near the buyers rather than near the manufacturer. The function of the warehouses then becomes serving local buyers.

If one or the other of these strikes you as "obviously" the better plan, remember that each alternative has certain cost and customer-service advantages over the other. Locating warehouse facilities near buyers has a great deal of appeal but involves operating a larger number of storage points and dealing in smaller shipments, because local warehouses service only local markets. On the other hand, using a few large warehouses located near manufacturing points can yield economies of scale and other advantages but may contribute to a reduction of service to buyers in far-off locales.

In warehouse location decisions, the consumers' need for timely delivery is a major consideration. A company may try to win customers by emphasizing how quickly orders can be filled. For example, management may indicate that it can fill 20 percent of orders within 24 hours and the remaining 80 percent within 72 hours, given a particular warehouse-location network. For organizations that strive to provide quick and dependable delivery, speed and reliability are important factors in the warehouse location decision.

The best warehouse location is the one that maximizes customer service, gives the firm a competitive advantage over rivals, and minimizes cost. Finding the optimal location is difficult. Management, therefore, should turn to the marketing strategy for guidance as to the best site. If, for instance, the strategy calls for maximizing customer service, then cost considerations may be relatively unimportant. Where the strategy is to minimize cost and pass the resulting economies on to consumers in the form of low prices, however, cost may be the most important of the three variables.

In many instances, finished goods are warehoused at the factory. When this is the case, selecting the location of the factory becomes interrelated with physical distribution objectives. Management of production facilities clearly is not a marketing function. However, the location of a plant can be extremely important to the marketing strategy, and marketing personnel often provide information about market needs to top executives responsible for determining plant sites. The marketing strategy for Campbell's Fresh, a line of chilled fresh foods without preservatives, requires that processing plants be located within a 1-day drive of stores, to guarantee product freshness. Hewlett Packard moved its personal-computer headquarters to France because the company believed that Europe, not the United States or Japan, would be the growth market of the 1990s.

global focus on competition

National Semiconductor Streamlining processes that traverse companies and continents is about as easy as reforming the health care system. But the payback can be enormous. Companies that revamp their physical distribution operations often wind up adopting unconventional solutions. Why? In an age of delegation and empowerment, physical distribution can greatly benefit from centralized control. And sometimes the best way to get closer to your customer is actually to fold your tent—or your warehouse—and move that process to a more efficient location farther away. In a 2-year time period, National Semiconductor cut its standard delivery time 47 percent, reduced distribution costs 2.5 percent, and increased sales 34 percent. How? By shutting six warehouses around the globe and air-freighting its microchips to customers worldwide from a new, 125,000-square-foot distribution center in Singapore.[8]

INVENTORY CONTROL

Another fundamental concern of physical distribution management is control of inventory levels. **Inventory control** involves decisions concerning how large or small inventories should be and how overstocking of inventory can be weighed against the dangers of costly *stock-outs* (which mean that the product the customer desires is not on hand). The ideal level of inventory is one that provides adequate service to

Inventory control
Decision-making related to inventory size, placement, and delivery.

customers while keeping suppliers' costs as low as possible. The presence of these twin goals, set at cross-purposes, complicates inventory decisions.

Valuable guidance on questions of inventory control can be found in sales forecasts. Also useful is information about how much inventory was needed in past planning periods, how much was left over at the ends of past periods, the inventory turnover rates of the individual warehouses being used, the value of the inventories held, and the carrying costs. A great deal has been written on the matter of inventory control. The general approach involves reliance on data gathered in the past and on careful projections of future demand. Any number of simple and sophisticated quantitative tools have been developed to help marketing managers deal with this problem area.

Risk cannot be entirely removed from inventory control, but great strides have been made in the use of computerized inventory control systems. In fact, even figures seemingly impossible to gauge can be closely estimated. For example, the value of a lost sale can be defined either as the selling price of the product or as the price plus expected income from service work. The ill will of a customer who was not served cannot be accurately quantified, however.

The following three major costs associated with holding inventory are more amenable to quantitative treatment than are many other areas of marketing management:

- *Acquisition costs* are the expenses incurred in obtaining inventory. For a manufacturer, acquisition costs are the costs of production; for an intermediary, they are the cost of the goods bought plus any transportation or handling assessments.
- *Holding costs* are those incurred in housing inventory. Interest paid, taxes on inventory, and any costs associated with warehousing, spoilage, and obsolescence are included.
- *Out-of-stock losses* are those that occur when customers demand goods the marketer cannot provide. In addition to the loss of a sale, stock-outs may lead to the loss of customer goodwill or contribute to a bad reputation over the long term. Not all of these losses can be accurately calculated.

Management can, with care, minimize total inventory costs by setting inventories at levels that take into account the behaviors of all three sets of costs. Computerized inventory control systems have greatly facilitated this task. For example, Savin Corporation has a computer terminal in each of its warehouses to keep track of every item in its inventory. The computerized inventory control system identifies the quantity on hand, the location and movement of stock, and the status of all orders. The system helps in planning shipments, locating single items in inventory, and locating customer records.

Economic Order Quantity (E.O.Q.)   For intermediaries, inventory control includes ordering goods to replenish inventory levels. An organization considers several factors in determining the order size at which total costs can be minimized. Among these are the prices of materials, parts, and merchandise (especially the possible quantity discounts); order-processing costs; the cost of holding inventory in stock; predicted demand for the product; and the rate of turnover associated with the product.

The factors mentioned here can be weighed mathematically to determine the purchase order size yielding the lowest total cost of order processing and inventory holding. This is the **economic order quantity,** or **E.O.Q.** Visit zikmund. swcollege.com to find an Internet appendix that illustrates how E.O.Q. can be calculated with a simple formula.

International Sourcing   Multinational marketers face the same inventory control decisions as domestic marketers. "The buyer today, when looking for a source of supply, looks at the whole world to find where it's most economical to source it."

Economic order quantity (E.O.Q.)
A mathematically determined purchase order size that yields the lowest total order-processing and inventory-holding costs.

This statement, by an executive of Ford Motor Company, indicates one of the most pronounced trends in logistics: looking beyond the United States to solve physical distribution and materials management problems. Today's marketing managers make choices from a worldwide selection of supply sources and sites for manufacturing and physical distribution.

MATERIALS HANDLING

We have referred in this chapter to "moving" goods from manufacturer to warehouse and to the "movement" of products from one spot to another. This movement does not occur on its own. Personnel, machinery, and equipment are used to identify, check, load, and unload goods. These activities are fundamental to the task of **materials handling,** which can be defined as the physical handling and moving about of inventory. Throughout the 20th century, the materials-handling process has become increasingly mechanized. Workers with hand trucks and carts have been largely replaced by operators of forklifts and other mechanical tools such as conveyor belts, elevators, and cranes. Most recently, robots have been used to perform materials-handling tasks. In many warehouses, orders can be assembled and packed with almost no human involvement. Such systems have proved faster, more accurate, and, in the main, cheaper than systems using human workers to fill orders.

Materials handling
The use of muscle power, machinery, and other methods to identify, check, load, and unload goods in inventory.

ORDER PROCESSING

Like materials handling, **order processing** has become increasingly automated. Computerized order processing is common, because speed and accuracy are vital to this activity. For many buyers, high-quality order-filling procedures are a primary purchasing criterion. Because order processing is an early step in the process of getting merchandise to customers, mistakes made in this activity can carry through the whole process. Such mistakes result in lost time and money, as well as disgruntled customers and costly emergency shipments. Expedient and reliable order processing not only allows an organization to avoid these problems but also enables the organization to realize economies in related physical distribution areas; for example, it may allow the organization to carry reduced inventories or to use lower-cost transportation modes, such as trucks rather than air.

Order processing
A systematic procedure for filling customer orders. The process begins when orders are received and ends when goods have been shipped and bills sent to customers.

The computerized order-processing system at American Hospital Supply, a wholesaler, gives hospitals a direct computer-to-computer link. Direct ordering lowers order-processing costs, reduces the possibility of incorrect orders, and reduces the time between placing an order and receiving the goods.

Many retailers have order-processing and inventory management systems that are linked to bar-coding systems. Scanners or computerized wands at the checkout counters read the bar codes on all merchandise being purchased and then send the information via computer to vendors or other suppliers.

PACKAGING

Packaging has an important place in the field of physical distribution, because products must be properly packaged for protection during the distribution process. Damage, which is costly to marketers, can occur either during transportation or in storage. Protection means guarding against breakage, spoilage, mildew, insects, dirt, and any other significant threat. When designing packaging, marketing managers must evaluate the container's quality, appearance, and cost. Less obvious, but just as important, are the costs associated with repackaging products into larger or smaller quantities, such as cartons of grosses or dozens. Packages must also be designed to minimize difficulties in physical handling, such as stacking in piles. For some products, like machine parts, packages are color coded or in some other way marked for ease of use and to facilitate the process of filling orders. The requirements of the Interstate Commerce Commission and other considerations specific to particular customers or products present still other challenges in package design.

Materials Management

We have discussed many aspects of physical distribution, the first area of managerial responsibility associated with logistics. The second area is materials management. The function of materials management within this overall system is to evaluate alternative sources of supplies and acquire the raw materials necessary to ensure uninterrupted production at acceptable cost. Materials managers must procure materials of an acceptable quality that meet the organization's specifications and obtain an assurance that the materials will arrive at the manufacturing facility at the right time. As this goal suggests, materials management is concerned with materials that are inbound to the point of production, whereas *physical distribution management* is focused on outbound products. Materials management is of major importance to marketing because shortages of any needed materials interrupt both production and distribution processes, making it impossible to supply customers with the products they want. To ensure effective materials management, organizations perform **vendor analysis,** which is the comparative rating of alternative suppliers on attributes such as product quality, reliability of service assistance, speed of delivery, and competitive prices. Selection of suppliers may be an important determinant of the business strategy. For example, selecting a parts producer in Korea or Singapore because of its low cost of production may determine the marketer's pricing strategy. Exhibit 14-4 lists several logistical criteria for evaluating suppliers.

Materials managers strive to reduce inventory costs for parts and other items used in production by scheduling them to arrive just in time for use. A **just-in-time (JIT) inventory system** is a producer's (or reseller's) inventory control system, coordinated with a sophisticated ordering system, designed to minimize the amount of inventory kept on hand.[9] For example, Japanese and American automobile manufacturers have just-in-time inventory systems that closely coordinate shipments from suppliers with the demand for these items so that the desired part arrives just before it is needed at the factory.

The central idea behind a just-in-time system is to reduce the need to stockpile inventory by receiving smaller shipments more frequently. If the just-in-time system is to be efficient, the materials manager must understand the flow of products in the manufacturing (or distribution) process and carefully plan the organization's requirements for timely and reliable delivery. Furthermore, the supplier must be flexible, shipping inventory where and when it is needed. When demand for the final product, such as an automobile, rises dramatically, all suppliers' parts production must be sufficiently flexible to keep up with the demand. If, for example, a transmission maker cannot increase production, the entire just-in-time system suffers.

General Motors has a JIT system in place. Firestone, a major supplier of original equipment tires to the auto industry, has had to alter its own policies to meet GM's JIT requirements. Information about the automaker's tire requirements is

Vendor analysis
The rating of alternative suppliers on attributes such as product quality, reliability of service, delivery speed, and price.

Just-in-time (JIT) inventory system
A materials management system in which inventory arrives just in time for use.

exhib **14-4** Logistical Criteria for Evaluating a Vendor

Delivery time
Delivery reliability
Order accuracy
Access to interactive databases (order status, product availability, etc.)
Damage history
Ease of doing business
Facilitating services

continually transmitted via an on-line system to Firestone's Transportation Operations Department and the tire manufacturing plants. Each delivery to General Motors contains the number and types of tires required by the GM assembly line for a specified 6-hour period. Firestone switched from rail to truck transport so that smaller shipments could be delivered daily to particular loading docks at specified times. Firestone, in turn, has initiated a JIT system at its own plants, requiring its suppliers to deliver raw materials in small-lot sizes via trucks that arrive at Firestone plants at specific times.

Although we have discussed just-in-time systems from a materials management perspective, it is important to note that the JIT principles are equally applicable to inventory management by wholesalers and retailers.

Organizational Collaboration

Organizations heavily involved in distribution activities have deliberately sought ways to cooperate with one another and to share services. It makes little sense, for example, for every air freight company to support an entire complement of facilities and staff at every airport in the country. Realizing this, many companies sell ground support services to other cooperating organizations in an effort to eliminate duplicate investments.

Federal Express's BLS system provides an excellent example of organizational collaboration among a supplier, the supplier's customers, and a logistic service. This practice, whereby a marketing organization arranges for another organization, such as FedEx, to manage its logistic operation and to ship to its customers, is sometimes called *third-party logistics*.

New Information Technology

Distribution and materials managers have welcomed the use of computers, barcoding systems, laser scanners, and automation of materials handling because they make the jobs of distribution and supply easier and more efficient, thus contributing significantly to the overall health of the organization. Computers provide managers with detailed information that can be used to plan and control all types of decisions—from choosing sources of raw materials to determining the cheapest way to ship merchandise to retail dealers. Computer programs can simulate logistical problems, thus helping decision makers to weigh the many alternatives that confront them. Programs can also analyze the complicated cost variables so common to distribution decisions and calculate lowest-cost inventory levels and the most profitable warehouse location patterns. Procter & Gamble, for example, has a system called Direct Product Profitability, which provides computer-generated output measuring the cost of an item from the time it moves from the warehouse to the time it is sold at the retail level. Use of the system has resulted in the redesign of many product items based on information about size, shelf life, and purchase frequency.

Logistics management in general has become increasingly sophisticated because of the Internet and intranets. These media allow suppliers and customers to share data and make JIT systems and other logistical tasks involving two or more organizations easier to manage.

New technologies, such as *global positioning systems,* are changing the face of logistics. Schneider National, Inc., a coast-to-coast trucking organization, uses an innovative two-way satellite data communications link between a computer at the company's Green Bay, Wisconsin, headquarters and each of its 5,500 tractors. This allows Schneider to improve customer service and automate routing.

summary

The term *logistics* is broad in scope because it includes both planning and coordinating the physical distribution of finished goods and managing the movement and storage of raw materials and supply parts during the procurement and production processes. Physical distribution can be made more cost effective by the use of computerized technology and robotics, allowing an organization to obtain a competitive advantage not easily duplicated by competition.

1 *Evaluate the role of logistics and physical distribution in the marketing mix.*

Logistics describes the entire process whereby materials, in-process inventory, and finished goods move into, through, and out of a firm. Logistics management involves planning, implementing, and controlling the efficient flow of both inbound materials and outbound finished products. Materials management is concerned with bringing raw materials and supplies to the point of production. Physical distribution provides time and place utility by moving products from producer to consumer or organizational user in a timely and efficient manner. Transportation, warehousing, inventory control, materials handling, order processing, and packaging are the major areas of concern in physical distribution management.

2 *Show how distribution managers can make physical distribution provide maximum satisfaction to buyers while reducing costs.*

The central objective of physical distribution is to keep costs down while keeping the level of service up. Yet improving service raises costs, and reducing costs lowers levels of service. Distribution managers must balance these two elements. The marketing concept suggests that managers determine what level of service will fit the buyers' needs and what prices are acceptable to them.

3 *Explain the total cost approach to physical distribution.*

The total cost concept takes a systems approach to physical distribution. Placing the emphasis on controlling total cost forces the manager to focus on how the parts of the distribution system can be used to keep total costs down. Raising expenditures in one part of the system may reduce total costs; lowering expenditures in one part of the system might raise total costs.

4 *Compare the advantages and disadvantages of the modes of transportation available to shippers.*

The five major modes of transportation are motor carrier, air freight, water transportation, rail transport, and pipeline transport. These vary in flexibility, speed, reliability, tendency to damage goods, cost, and other variables. Water transportation is inexpensive but slow; air shipment is fast but often expensive. Trucks are flexible, relatively swift, and have a good reputation in terms of breakage of goods; however, they cannot move the volumes of freight railroads can. Pipelines are efficient movers of certain products but can deliver them only to specific terminals. Intermodal transportation, such as piggyback service, combines the advantages of two or more separate transportation modes.

5 *Identify the purposes of warehousing, order processing, materials handling, and inventory control.*

The purposes of warehousing are to hold merchandise until it is demanded by the market and to break bulk. The goal of order processing is to expedite orders quickly and economically. Materials handling focuses on moving inventories of products as needed. Inventory control is expected to manage inventory so that ideal inventory levels are maintained most of the time.

6 *Understand materials management activities and their influence on many marketing decisions.*

Materials management is the procurement of raw materials and parts and their movement to the point of production. Vendor analysis and just-in-time inventory systems are aspects of materials management that influence marketing mix decisions. International sourcing is a current trend in materials management.

key terms

logistics (p. 434)
materials management (p. 434)
physical distribution (p. 434)
systems concept (p. 438)
total cost concept (p. 439)

transportation (p. 442)
motor carrier (p. 442)
damage in transit (p. 442)
air freight (p. 443)
water transportation (p. 444)

rail transport (p. 444)
diversion in transit (p. 445)
pipelines (p. 445)
piggyback service (p. 445)
fishyback service (p. 445)

birdyback service (p. 445)
warehousing (p. 445)
storage (p. 446)
inventory control (p. 447)

economic order quantity (E.O.Q.)
(p. 448)
materials handling (p. 449)
order processing (p. 449)

vendor analysis (p. 450)
just-in-time (JIT) inventory system
(p. 450)

questions for review & critical thinking

1. Define *logistics*. What are its components?
2. What is meant by the systems concept in physical distribution? In what ways does the use of this concept benefit marketers?
3. What are the major ways in which an organization can use physical distribution as a means of establishing a competitive advantage?
4. What is the difference between warehousing and storage? How do they differ from breaking bulk?
5. Discuss the total cost approach to distribution. What are its advantages and disadvantages?
6. An overnight package service and a petroleum pipeline are both common carriers. How do they differ? How are they similar?
7. What type of physical distribution system would you use for each of the following products?
   a. Bird of paradise plants from Hawaii
   b. Kiwi fruit and avocados from California
   c. Barbie dolls
8. Why do organizations store goods? Provide an example of a storage problem faced by a marketing organization.
9. What factors should management consider in determining desired levels of inventory? What specific costs should management take into account for each of the following products?
   a. Candy bars
   b. Farm tractors

c. Sweaters
d. Personal computers

10. Define *order processing*. How can management use this function to attain a competitive advantage?
11. What are the advantages and disadvantages of using each of the following?
   a. Railroads
   b. Trucks
   c. Airlines
   d. Water carriers
12. Is it possible for a retailer to use a just-in-time system?
13. What is third-party logistics? What types of companies are most likely to use third-party logistics?
14. Form small groups as directed by your instructor. Select half of the group to represent an industrial supplier's logistical staff and half of the group to represent a customer's production and marketing employees. Identify the key aspects of the supplier's marketing strategy and the customer's buying behavior that will have to change when the customer adopts a just-in-time inventory system. Discuss as a class the decisions your group made.

marketing plan—right or wrong?

The DIAD (Delivery Information Acquisition Device) is a hand-held computer used by all UPS drivers to capture delivery information and customer signatures or pickup information. The parcel data from each driver's DIAD are routinely downloaded and transmitted via the UPSnet global telecommunications network for immediate access by customers. If a driver's DIAD malfunctions and transmission from the truck is not possible, the driver must call in the information, often from a customer phone, every half-hour or so.

exercise

Using a search engine such as Hotbot (www.hotbot.com), search the Web for information about logistics. What fields are represented in the search results? Select one document in the business field, and read it for information about logistics. Take notes and bring them to class for discussion.

address book (useful urls)

U.S. Department of Transportation, National Transportation Library	www.dot.gov/NTL.htm
Journal of Transportation and Statistics	www.bts.gov/programs/jts
Just-in-Time Solutions	www.justintime.com

ethically right or wrong?

A garment manufacturer located in the United States has been under increasing pressure to lower the prices of its products. The organization has explored the idea of moving much of its production operation to Asia, where labor costs are low. The move will cause a 50-percent reduction in domestic jobs because of changes in manufacturing and the physical distribution system. What are the ethical implications of such a move?

TAKE A STAND

1. A company's normal period from order entry to delivery is 9 days. A salesperson who very desperately wanted to make a sale told a retail customer that delivery could be made in 5 days. Was this right? What should the physical distribution manager do?
2. Suppose your petroleum company distributed its crude oil in tankers from Alaska. Knowing what happened to the environment after the *Exxon Valdez* spilled oil off the Alaska coast, would you continue to ship oil by tanker from Alaska? Would you recommend that more pipelines be built across Alaska?

The Limited

The Limited's marketing strategy is to ship products to its stores months before its competitors. It counts on its logistics system to allow it to reorder only the most popular colors and styles, based on sales performance of the item, while the competition is still stocking its first orders. The following steps outline The Limited's logistics operations:

1. Prior to the season, buyers analyze data from the company's database and search the world for new fabrics and styles that might be popular with consumers in The Limited's various stores.

2. These fashion ideas and trends are immediately sent to The Limited's stable of top designers at corporate headquarters, who come up with the season's designs. Mast Industries, a manufacturing company owned by The Limited, Inc., is brought into the loop for its input on design development.

3. At "warp" speed, the designers dispatch these designs via satellite (or fax) to manufacturing facilities wherever producers can turn out quality goods while coordinating fabric purchases and other logistical issues with vendors. Most of these independent producers are specialists in "manufacturing to design." Since they've formed such close relationships with The Limited, they function with the speed and quality of the firm's own manufacturing plant while still retaining the efficiency and flexibility of independent suppliers.

4. These producers rapidly supply the company with bids, usually within 3 days; buyers at The Limited or Mast Industries select the right facility within hours or even minutes and award a contract.

5. Within 3 weeks of receiving the design, the manufacturer ships much of the merchandise on Boeing 747s to The Limited's distribution center in Columbus, Ohio. (Competitors traditionally ship by water.)

6. The Limited's massive distribution center unpacks, reassembles, and ships the products with such blazing speed that most merchandise is in and out of the distribution center within 18 to 24 hours. Some of the merchandise is "cross-docked" at the rate of nearly 25,000 units an hour, meaning that the computers coordinate delivery so tightly that merchandise is unloaded from the airplane to the delivery trucks without ever entering a warehouse.

7. A merchandising team member at The Limited receives continuous consumer feedback about fashions, styles, and wants from the Information Technology, or IT, team. The IT team monitors high-volume stores every 2 hours to discover changes in consumer preferences for styles, color, and sizes and projects what stock needs to be replenished.

8. Visual displays for The Limited's stores are centrally planned, frequently changed, and dramatically executed so that what consumers see on the walls matches what's on the racks. The firm's IT and logistics systems function with state-of-the-art technologies, so that rapidly moving merchandise is replenished to meet the needs and desires of consumers instantly.

9. The Limited's highly trained associates work to meet customers' expectations for friendliness and helpfulness. To this end, associates are often hired because they match the customer profile. To cap a sale, associates emphasize that "no sale is ever final."

While the goal at The Limited is to speed consumer ideas to market within 1,000 hours of their conceptualization, the actual average for the process is 760 hours—making the company a leader in the logistics field among firms of all sizes and from all industries. The Limited has become so efficient at the entire process that management is considering raising the bar and setting even more aggressive goals.[10]

QUESTIONS

1. How important is time-based competition in the apparel business?
2. Identify the key factors in The Limited's logistical operation that help it achieve its strategic goals.

You will find each exercise on the CD-ROM developed for use with this textbook. Each exercise has a name and is located within a module. For example, this exercise can be found in the Micromarketing Module by clicking on Business Logistics.

MICROMARKETING MODULE
Business Logistics

As global trade between Asia and North America increases, water transportation has become increasingly important. What role does containerization play in the logistics of transportation by ship?

cross-functional
insights

Many theories and principles from other business disciplines can provide insights about the role of marketing in an organization. The questions in this section are designed to help you think about integrating what you have learned in other business courses with the marketing principles explained in this book.

Distribution Delivers a Standard of Living to Society
The major purpose of marketing is to satisfy human needs by delivering products of various types to buyers when and where they want them and at a reasonable cost.

How does the economic concept of scarcity relate to the distribution of a standard of living?

Channel Conflict   Channel conflict refers to a situation in which channel members disagree and their relationship is antagonistic. Disagreements may relate to the channel's common purpose or the responsibility for certain activities. The behavior of one channel member may be seen as inhibiting the attainment of another channel member's goals.

How are conflicts between channel members similar to conflicts that an organization's cross-functional teams experience? Can similar techniques be used to reduce these conflicts?

Retailers   Retailing consists of all business activities involving the sale of goods and services to ultimate consumers.

Are most retailers entrepreneurs? What characteristics of entrepreneurs would help them become successful retailers?

What stages of company growth would be typical for a successful retail business started by an entrepreneur?

If an entrepreneur were starting a retail business, what form of ownership would be best: a sole proprietorship, a partnership, or a corporation?

What would the typical small retailer's balance sheet look like?

What should a retailer know about teamwork? What types of teams might a retailer utilize?

What type of inventory cost system should a retailer have?

Merchant Wholesalers and Agent Wholesalers
Channel members may be merchant wholesalers, which take title to the goods, or agent wholesalers, which do not take title to goods.

Who may be a legal agent?

How is agency authority in a channel of distribution created?

How is an agency relationship in a channel of distribution ended?

How does the Uniform Commercial Code apply to the relationship between manufacturers and merchant wholesalers?

Logistics Logistics describes the entire process of moving raw materials and component parts into the firm, moving in-process inventory through the firm, and moving finished goods out of the firm. Logistics management thus involves planning, implementing, and controlling the efficient flow of both inbound materials and outbound finished products.

What factors should a company consider when determining locations for factories and company-owned warehouses? How important are logistics and physical distribution in this decision?

How do labor unions influence logistics management and physical distribution functions?

everyone lives by selling something

–WHO SAID THIS?

part 5

everyone

ives by

selling

something   THAT'S WHO SAID IT!

something

–ROBERT LOUIS STEVENSON

Robert Louis Stevenson (1850–1894), author and poet, was born November 13, 1850, in Edinburgh, Scotland. He traveled extensively despite being sickly as a child and having problems with tuberculosis as an adult. He wrote *The Strange Case of Dr. Jekyll and Mr. Hyde, A Child's Garden of Verses,* and many other commercially successful books. Stevenson's most famous book, *Treasure Island,* immortalized his tale about a young boy, a treasure map, and Long John Silver and his pirate crew.

chapter
15

Integrated Marketing Communications

LEARNING OBJECTIVES

After you have studied this chapter, you will be able to:

Discuss the three basic purposes of promotion.

1

Define the four major elements of promotion.

2

Describe the basic model for all communication processes, including promotion.

3

Explain the hierarchy of communication effects.

4

Explain how the elements of promotion can be used to support one another in a promotional campaign.

5

(continued on next page)

6 Describe the general promotional strategies known as push and pull strategies.

7 Classify the major approaches used by marketing managers to set promotional budgets.

8 Discuss promotional campaigns and provide examples.

9 Take a stand about the ethics of persuasion.

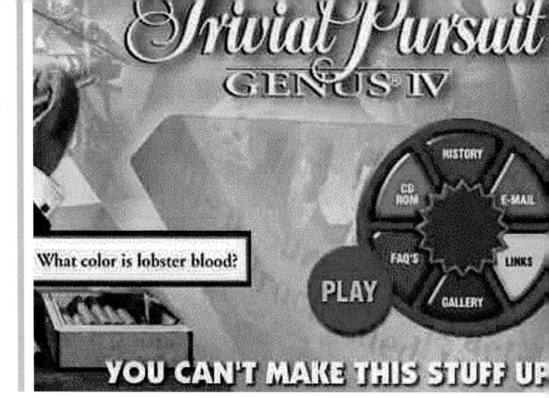

the Parker Brothers company had the best-selling trivia game of all time in Trivial Pursuit. But time had taken its toll, and the company was wondering if it could build top-of-mind awareness and purchase interest by prompting prospective customers to sample an Internet version of the board game.

"The board game business is a mature business now," says Joseph Serino, new media director at Parker's advertising agency. "You don't hear anything about a craze anymore. Trivial Pursuit was a fantastic success 15 years ago, but there's so much more competition now for leisure time. . . . But in the back of our minds we figured there were lots of people who were teens at the time who somehow missed the craze and who now would take to the game if given the opportunity."

So Trivial Pursuit went on the Web for a 2-month trial just before Christmas to see if it could recapture some of its past glory. Trivial Pursuit not only designed its own Web site, but also bought advertising banners on ten Web sites, including search engine keywords and categories and game and women's sites. "We wanted people to sample the game on line to see if they would be inclined to buy it," says Serino. And the results?

The campaign was a complete success. The site received more than 100,000 visitors. Over 50 percent played a complete version of the game, and 9 percent of all visitors completed the questionnaire that appears on the site. In addition, e-mail was overwhelmingly positive, and 98 percent of survey respondents say they would recommend Trivial Pursuit to a friend.

Activity on the Web grew steadily in September and October but really kicked in when the "You Can't Make This Stuff Up" cross-media campaign began in earnest. The number of visitors to the home page tripled.

Another factor that raised marketers' eyebrows was the amount of time visitors—particularly women—were willing to give the game. The real reason to come to the site was to sample the game, but this abbreviated form of the game takes at least 5 minutes to play, a substantial amount of time for anyone to spend.

Calculating a return on investment is always a tricky business, but on three levels, the Trivial Pursuit campaign scored high marks: (1) share of mind, which is basically the amount of time people will spend on the site; (2) gaining the 10,000 surveys (if the company had to pay outright for these surveys, taking into account all the work necessary to achieve this number, it probably would have cost well in excess of $100,000); and (3) good public relations generated for the product: it was mentioned at a Magazine Publishers Association conference, featured on the Web TV Network, and written about in several magazines.[1]

THE CAMPAIGN WAS A COMPLETE SUCCESS. THE SITE RECEIVED MORE THAN 100,000 VISITORS.

Parker Brothers' creation of a Web site to inform and amuse those who visit is but one example of how the Internet can be used to communicate an organization's message. Although the Internet as a promotional medium is in its infancy, success stories like Trivial Pursuit's demonstrate its remarkable potential.

Advertising, public relations/publicity, personal selling, and sales promotion are elements of the fascinating world of promotion, the subject of this chapter. The chapter begins by describing the three purposes of promotion and how the four basic promotional elements help accomplish promotion's purposes. It explains the new media that have emerged because of the revolution in digital technology and how these new media are dramatically influencing the promotional mix. It next examines the theory of communication and the hierarchy of communication effects. Then it discusses selecting a promotional mix and setting a promotional budget. After describing some strategies for promotional campaigns, the chapter ends by discussing the ethics of persuasion in our society.

Promotion: Communication with a Purpose

Effective marketers know that the old adage "Build a better mousetrap and the world will beat a path to your door" contains a basic flaw. If the "world" doesn't find out that there is a better mousetrap, the manufacturer will be a very lonely person, indeed. Having a great product is not enough. **HAVING A GREAT PRODUCT IS NOT ENOUGH. PEOPLE MUST BE MADE AWARE OF THE EXISTENCE OF A PRODUCT.** People must be made familiar with the product's benefits. Some form of promotion is necessary to make consumers, and other publics with which an organization interacts, aware of the existence of a product.

Recall that promotion is communication used by marketers to inform, remind, or persuade potential buyers. Personal selling, advertising, publicity and public relations, and sales promotion are promotional methods that may be used to communicate a message. Although promotion, and advertising in particular, is often singled out as a part of the marketing mix that society could well do without, a moment's reflection shows that this criticism is unwarranted. The job of marketing is to identify consumer needs and to try to satisfy those needs by developing appropriate products—priced right, packaged for convenience, and properly distributed. The role of promotion in the marketing function is to convey news—to tell consumers about the benefits of the product. This communication, often termed "selling the product," is an indispensable part of the marketing function.

PROMOTION INFORMS

Even critics of advertising might feel more comfortable with the job promotion performs in society once they realize that the essence of promotion is communication. If the management of Bloomingdale's is planning a sale, communicating price savings to potential customers must be part of the plan. Lowering prices will not benefit anyone unless promotion communicates to con-

This photo of Anakin Skywalker appears on Lucasfilm's Star Wars Web site. The studio's promotional purpose is to give fans information about the eagerly awaited *Star Wars* prequel, *Star Wars: Episode I,* due to be released in the spring of 1999.

www.starwars.com

sumers the fact that a sale is under way. The store's promotions also provide other information, such as store hours, whether returns will be allowed on sale merchandise, and whether customers can use credit cards. Thus, the broad goal of promotion is to inform potential buyers.

PROMOTION PERSUADES

Marketers rarely face a situation in which simple and plain communication of information is enough to make promotion effective. In the era of the production concept, when many organizations faced a seller's market, this may have been the case. But today's world is full of messages and distractions of all sorts. Consumers are often faced with many competing options. People find themselves increasingly rushed and harried. With less time for comparative shopping, consumers turn to advertising for product information. However, "pure information" is not all there is to be found in marketing communications. Marketing managers exist in a competitive environment, and as competitors they want consumers to buy their brands. Thus, persuasion that encourages purchases or attitude change is a primary goal of promotion. It is Bloomingdale's management's hope that the information that the store is having a big sale will persuade consumers to visit Bloomingdale's and see for themselves. In fact, a traditional definition of promotion is "persuasive communication."

PROMOTION REMINDS

Consider the customer who shops at Bloomingdale's regularly or the consumer who always buys Tide detergent. Do the marketers of Bloomingdale's or Tide advertise to this consumer? Yes. Is that a waste of money? The answer is no, for the very practical reason that even the most loyal customers must be reminded that a store or product has served them well over time and that it has features that make it attractive. This is especially true when competitors are free to tempt loyal customers with their own informative and persuasive messages. Thus, reminding customers, in addition to informing and persuading them, may be a promotional objective.

Reminding customers may be a promotional objective for marketers with loyal customers. In this advertisement, computer graphics remind consumers of the familiar shape of the Coca-Cola bottle.

Morton salt, Bayer aspirin, and Coca-Cola are all number one in their fields. They have achieved their goals to inform and persuade. The major goal of their promotion is to sustain their customers' preference for their products. Attracting new customers is a secondary promotional goal for these companies with loyal customers. Similarly, even people who buy Johnson & Johnson dental floss and believe that it is the best floss may forget to use it as much as they should (and so may not buy as often). They may be influenced by the message "a reminder to remember to floss."

adapting to change

The Coca-Cola Bottle   In an effort to distinguish the product further from a slew of brand-name and private-label competitors, advertisements from Coca-Cola emphasize the famous contours of Coke's bottle as much as the beverage it holds. Coca-Cola is attempting to capitalize on the symbolic nature of its proprietary package, a resource that none of its competitors has. Over the decades, the bottle has become a bona fide cultural icon, an obvious symbol of differentiation. Coca-Cola created a batch of television commercials whose messages simply remind consumers about the shape of its bottle.

One advertisement shows Coke being poured into a bottle while a female announcer goes on about the special shape of the bottle. The Coke logo is shown in various languages. The commercial is a celebration of the bottle.

In another commercial, a storm has caused a blackout. A man gingerly makes his way to the refrigerator in his apartment, where he is easily able to feel for a contoured Coke bottle. He also reaches for a box of animal crackers and shakes the contents into his open mouth. But the results are less than satisfying: "Bummer," says the poor soul, "baking soda."

In another commercial, a tourist wanders into a dusty store in a faraway country. Behind the counter are a beautiful Asian woman and her stern, watchful father. The tourist, trying to describe a Coke bottle, creates the shape of an hourglass with his hands. The father isn't amused and glares. When the point is made clear, the tourist smiles and says, "I'll have a Coca-Cola." The shop's owner—who the tourist believes cannot speak English—responds, "Sorry, this is a hardware store."[2]

New Communication Media Are Shaping Promotion

Advertising, personal selling, and publicity are among the traditional forms of promotion. Technical definitions of each will be provided in the following section. However, new media have emerged because of the revolution in digital technology. The availability of these new media dramatically influences the elements of promotion and how they are defined in our information age.

The traditional 20th-century view broke media into two categories: *mass media*, in which there was no interaction between the marketer and the audience, and *personal media*, such as personal selling, which involved a dialogue between buyer and seller. Today, advances in digital technology make this distinction outdated because of computers' capacity to interact with consumers.

For our purposes, we will use a simple threefold classification of media: mass media, human interactive media, and electronic interactive media. Exhibit 15-1 shows the individual advertising media in each of these classifications.

MASS MEDIA

Mass media are means of communication that reach large audiences without personal contact or instantaneous interaction between the marketer and the receiver of the message. Messages in print media, such as newspapers and magazines, and broadcast media, such as radio and television, are targeted at a general group of people rather than at any particular individual. When people think of advertising, they traditionally envision messages in mass media, but, as you will see, this is changing.

Mass media
Advertising media, such as television, radio, newspapers, and magazines, that reach a broad audience from many market segments and involve no personal contact or instantaneous interaction between the marketer and the target of the message.

the target audience through a medium such as national television. This expense tends to restrict all but the larger, better-financed organizations from using national advertising. Mass media advertising, unlike personal selling, does not allow the message to be personalized and tailored to the prospect. Immediate, direct feedback from a prospect is rare when mass media are utilized. In contrast, when marketers advertise on electronic interactive media, the audience has the opportunity to "customize" the nature of the information they receive and to interact with the marketer through the medium. Advertising via mass media and interactive media is the subject of Chapter 16.

PUBLICITY/PUBLIC RELATIONS

Advertising is a form of message delivery in which the sender pays to send the message. Publicity is similar to advertising in that it may use the same mass media. The difference between the two is that **publicity** involves a message that is not paid for and whose content is determined by the communication medium. When information about a company, a product, or an event is considered newsworthy, mass media may communicate that information "for free." Thus, the organization being publicized neither pays for the message directly nor is identified as the message sponsor.

An important distinguishing characteristic of publicity is that it always involves a third party, such as a newspaper reporter or editor, who has the ultimate power to determine the nature of the message. Because the third party usually has some credibility and because the information is generally factual rather than persuasive, publicity scores high in believability.

Publicity can be either positive or negative. In fact, because the message is in the hands of the media and not in the hands of the organization promoting the product, publicity can be terrible. Sunbeam Corporation and the American Medical Association planned an alliance in which the AMA would endorse and allow its seal of approval to be placed on a line of Sunbeam's health-care products, such as thermometers and heating pads. There were many news reports about this agreement. The AMA had little influence over what unidentified news writers, editors, and producers wrote or said about the plan. The negative publicity was intense. The media suggested that the AMA was selling its soul by taking money for its seal of approval. The product-royalty deal was renounced within ten days.

Similarly, negative publicity occurs whenever a recall of a popular product for repair or replacement makes the evening news. The makers of Firestone tires, Saturn automobiles, and Perrier bottled water have spent millions of dollars to develop fine products. Bad publicity about defects, however minor, can easily offset their efforts.

The Internet is a new medium for publicity that has, in many cases, increased the speed of message diffusion.

Although publicity is "free" in the sense that mass media are not paid to communicate the message, this does not mean that publicity should go unmanaged. For instance, you can be certain that every year the Neiman-Marcus Christmas catalog will generate a

Publicity

A message about a product, organization, or event carried by a nonpersonal medium but not paid for by a sponsor. Publicity involves a third party who determines whether the message is newsworthy enough to transmit and what the nature of the transmitted message will be.

Public relations

The activities involved in actively seeking to manage the nature of the publicity an organization receives.

When information about a business-sponsored sporting event is considered newsworthy, mass media will communicate that information for free. The fact that publicity is free does not mean that it goes unmanaged. Nike and Chevrolet are experts at carefully orchestrating publicity.

great deal of publicity. The organization manages to do this by its time-honored tradition of featuring spectacular "his and her" Christmas gifts. One year, Neiman-Marcus offered a set of wooden mosaic desks in the form of seven-foot-long ranch animals. For "him" the desk was a steer with authentic 42-inch horns. For "her" the desk was a custom-made likeness of a horse. The Christmas catalog is a carefully orchestrated annual publicity event.

Marketers may expend considerable time and effort in getting news releases and interviews with company spokespersons placed in newspapers and on broadcasts to promote a favorable organizational image. When an organization systematically plans and distributes information in an attempt to manage the nature of the publicity it receives, it is engaged in public relations. The purpose of **public relations** is to actively manage publicity (and sometimes other promotional elements) to establish and maintain a positive organizational image or to ensure that the public understands an organization's policies. Public relations is discussed in greater detail in Chapter 18.

what went right?

House of Blues   House of Blues night clubs in Los Angeles, Chicago, New Orleans, and Myrtle Beach, South Carolina, compete with chains such as Hard Rock Cafe and Planet Hollywood, but House of Blues positions itself as more than a theme restaurant. It also has its own record label, publishing division, production company, and news-media unit.

House of Blues doesn't do any mass media advertising. Public relations is the only promotional element that House of Blues uses. The publicity-driven company generates enormous media coverage every time it opens a club, releases a record, or revs up its Web site (www.hob.com).

House of Blues generated a great deal of publicity during the Olympic Games in Atlanta when it converted a Baptist church across from Centennial Park into a temporary House of Blues site. According to Burrelle's Newsclip Analysis Service, House of Blues' Olympics publicity achieved 1.34 billion total gross impressions in electronic and print media, for an advertising value of $19.3 million. For the opening of Chicago's House of Blues, the company's marketers devised a plan to surprise opening act hosts (and House of Blues investors) Dan Aykroyd and James Belushi with fellow alumni from Second City and *Saturday Night Live* and various movie co-stars. Chevy Chase, John Landis, Linda Hamilton, and others surprised the two on stage, and reporters had a heyday. A tour and talent division's 40-city "Smokin' Grooves" festival tour of urban hip-hop bands achieved enormous publicity after the company positioned the Lollapalooza-like event as "bringing House of Blues to you." The marketing effort goal is to keep inventing new ways to remind the world—via extensive media coverage—that House of Blues is an entertainment venue and more.[3]

focus on relationships

WordPerfect   "Please hold." Such are the words that every caller dreads. But many companies with toll-free numbers are using public relations efforts to make holding time more pleasant and thus reduce the "abandonment rate," or the number of callers who hang up. Perhaps nobody has gone to more elaborate lengths to enhance relationships with callers than WordPerfect in Orem, Utah.

Callers to the software maker get to listen to a live "hold jockey." One is Barbara Lee, a former radio newscaster. She entertains them with pop music interspersed with rush hour–style traffic reports, announcing "a three-call backup for Windows installation support," say, or "a two-minute delay for laser printers." Lee gets the information from a bank of 16 computer monitors that tell her how many calls are waiting on each of the more than 50 customer-service numbers that WordPerfect uses.

While automated phone-answering programs can perform a similar function, even computer nerds, it seems, respond to the warmth of a live human voice. WordPerfect is striving for the perfect relationship with its customers.[4]

Campbell Soup Company sponsored an "Art of Soup" contest in conjunction with the Andy Warhol Museum. Shown here are two entries in the contest. This sales promotion had the added benefit of generating considerable publicity.

Sales promotion
Promotional activities other than personal selling, advertising, and public relations that are intended to stimulate buyer purchases or dealer effectiveness over a specific time period.

SALES PROMOTION

Marketers use the term **sales promotion** to categorize a variety of promotional activities that are something other than personal selling, advertising, or public relations. Sales promotions are usually intended to induce buyers to make purchases or to stimulate dealer effectiveness in a specific time period. Sales promotions add value to the product offering or provide an incentive for certain behavior. Thus, special offers of free goods, coupon deals, display items for store use, training programs, in-store demonstrations, and vacation trips for top salespeople are sales promotions. With a few exceptions, these are not routine events but special, out-of-the-ordinary occurrences. Although they typically involve programs paid for by an identified sponsor, they are distinguished from advertising because they are temporary offers of a material reward to customers, salespeople, or sales prospects.

Sales promotion programs amplify or bolster the advertising and personal selling messages offered by an organization. More often than not, these effects occur at the point of purchase. For instance, advertising may create an awareness of a new product like Ivy Block, but the cents-off coupon is the enticement that gets the consumer to try the poison ivy lotion for the first time. Sales promotion is not a "poor cousin" of the other elements of promotion, however. American marketers spend billions of dollars on sales promotion, just as they do on advertising and personal selling. In fact, many consumer package goods companies spend more on sales promotion efforts than they do on advertising.

The main purpose of sales promotion is to achieve short-term objectives. Free samples or coupons encourage a first-time trial of a product. A premium offer or sweepstakes may stimulate interest in a product and encourage off-season sales. A contest may require that individuals visit a store or showroom to see if they have won. Whether the sales promotion takes the form of a trade show, a consumer rebate, a point-of-purchase display for retailers, or pens and calendars for wholesalers to give away, the best sales promotions support and are coordinated with other promotional activities. Sales promotion is discussed further in Chapter 18. The characteristics of the four elements of promotion are summarized in Exhibit 15-2.

e x h i b **15-2** Characteristics of the Four Elements of Promotion

	PERSONAL SELLING	ADVERTISING*	PUBLICITY	SALES PROMOTION
Mode of communication	Direct and personal	Indirect and nonpersonal	Indirect and nonpersonal	Indirect and nonpersonal
Regular and recurrent activity?	Yes	Yes	No—only for newsworthy activity	No—short-term stimulation
Message flexibility	Personalized and tailored to prospect	Typically uniform and unvarying	Beyond marketer's direct control	Uniform and unvarying
Direct feedback	Yes	No—if placed in mass media	No	No
Marketer control over message content?	Yes	Yes	No	Yes
Sponsor identified?	Yes	Yes	No	Yes
Cost per contact	High	Low to moderate	No direct costs	Varies

*Internet advertising is somewhat different from mass media advertising.

Integrated Marketing Communications— The Promotional Mix

The effective marketer recognizes that each of the four elements of promotion has certain strengths. The combination of elements a marketer chooses is the marketer's **promotional mix.** Some organizations, like the San Diego Zoo, emphasize advertising and public relations efforts in their promotional mixes. Others, especially those engaged in business-to-business marketing, make personal selling the main ingredient. No matter what the promotional mix, marketers should strive to blend the elements effectively, integrating and uniting the appropriate elements to accomplish their promotional objectives. The term **integrated marketing communications** is used to remind managers that all elements of the promotional mix should be coordinated and systematically planned to be in harmony with each other. Later in this chapter, we discuss what specific factors marketers consider when choosing a promotional mix. Before we do, however, we will consider how communication occurs.

Special K   Special K, the fat-free toasted rice cereal, having made its debut in 1955, is the grandmother of diet foods.

One television commercial showed a thin and beautiful woman expressing her happiness with Special K. She is shown in front of her bedroom mirror taking pride in the fact that she looks great in a skin-tight dress. What could go wrong with television commercials showing attractive models squeezing their drop-dead perfect bodies into clingy dresses and attributing it to Special K as part of their diets?

Plenty, as it turned out. Especially among baby boomers viewing the ad. The commercial communicated the wrong message. One woman's comment about the Special K commercial said it all: "When she was in that little dress saying, 'I'm hot, I'm great,' it really bothered me. Because I could never be like that."

In letters and in focus groups, women indicated they were alienated by the ads. They told Kellogg they really couldn't relate to advertising techniques that used unrealistic body images. So Kellogg dropped the ad campaign and started a new one that suggests that healthy—even chunky—can be beautiful.

In place of thin women tugging at their clothes, one commercial has men at a bar. It pokes fun at women's complaints about their bodies. "I have my mother's thighs. I have to accept that," one man says. "Do these make my butt look big?" another asks. The message: "Men don't obsess about these things. Why do we?"[5]

The Communication Process

Communication is the process of exchanging information with and conveying meaning to others. The goal of communication is a common understanding. That is, the goal is to have the **receiver** of the information understand as closely as possible the meaning intended by the sender, or **source,** of the message.

One communication theorist described communication as "who says what to whom through which channels with what effect."[6] In slightly different terms, he was saying that to achieve the desired effect, the marketer must consider the source, the message, the channel, and the receiver.

> TO **ACHIEVE THE DESIRED EFFECT, THE MARKETER MUST CONSIDER THE SOURCE, THE MESSAGE, THE CHANNEL, AND THE RECEIVER.**

Exhibit 15-3 summarizes the communication process graphically. In considering the exhibit, remember that it describes all types of communication—words, gestures, pictures, and so on. The model may be used to describe an advertisement, a telephone sales call, a point-of-purchase display, or any promotional communication.

ENCODING THE MESSAGE
Evaluate the Blazer advertisement shown in Exhibit 15-4 on page 473 in terms of the model in Exhibit 15-3. Who says what to whom? The communication source

Promotional mix
An organization's combination of personal selling, advertising, publicity and public relations, and sales promotion; its total promotional effort.

Integrated marketing communications
Marketing communications in which all elements of the promotional mix are coordinated and systematically planned so as to be harmonious.

Communication
The process of exchanging information with and conveying meaning to others.

Receiver
In communication theory, the one to whom a message is aimed.

Source
In communication theory, the one who sends a message.

exhibit 15-3

A Basic Model of the Communication Process

(the advertiser) wishes to communicate the notion that the Blazer is a durable, high-quality product that helps drivers enjoy driving in rugged terrain. This idea—not an easy one to get across—is the message of the advertisement. The message is communicated primarily in a visual and symbolic way, through the intriguing image of a Blazer easily negotiating a gravel road in the mountains. The sender's idea has been encoded by means of this picture. **Encoding** is the process of translating the idea to be communicated into a symbolic message consisting of words, pictures, numbers, gestures, or the like. Encoding is a necessary step—there is no way to send an idea from one person to another without encoding it.

As in the Blazer advertisement, nonverbal messages and nonrational symbolism are essential to the encoding process, because words can be hopelessly inadequate to express emotions. "There are just no words to express the various nuances of sensation and feeling, to express such things as mood and aesthetic impression. Try to describe to a child how a strawberry tastes compared to a raspberry, how a carnation smells, why it is pleasurable to dance, what a pretty girl looks like."[7] The emotional definition of a situation or the precise meaning of human feelings may be determined almost entirely from facial expressions; from movements of the body, such as the gestures of a traffic officer; from expressions of excitement, such as weeping, blushing, or laughter; or from involuntary exclamations and sounds, such as whistling or singing.

In Exhibit 15-4, the word *Chevrolet* appears only in the Internet address shown in very small print. However, the company's nameplate symbol communicates that the Blazer is part of the Chevrolet family of cars.

TRANSMITTING THE MESSAGE THROUGH A CHANNEL

Once the sender has created the message by encoding an idea into a transmittable form, it must be somehow conveyed to the receiver: It must be sent through a *channel of communication,* such as a magazine or other medium. Even people's casual conversations are sent through a channel, though the medium is the less obvious one of vibrating vocal cords, which send sound through air.

The message arrives at the receiver via the channel of communication. But some receivers will be more receptive than others. For example, some receivers of the communication about the Blazer will be consumers who for one reason or another (their age, their dislike of the outdoors) have little interest in a rugged vehicle that facilitates driving in mountains and rough terrain. It is the sender's job to pick the medium that will reach a maximum number of target receivers and a minimum number of nontarget receivers.

Encoding

In communication theory, the process by which a sender translates an idea to be communicated into a symbolic message, consisting of words, pictures, numbers, gestures, or the like, so that it can be transmitted to a receiver.

What Is Communicated in This Advertisement?

DECODING THE MESSAGE

The message arrives and is viewed, heard, or otherwise sensed by the receiver. But in order for communication to occur, the receiver must decode it. **Decoding** is the mental process by which the receiver interprets the meaning of the message. A difficulty encountered at this stage of the communication process is that receivers may interpret the message in different ways, given their particular biases, backgrounds, and other characteristics. That is, selective perception operates as the message is decoded. People interpret messages and give them meaning based on their personal experiences and backgrounds (see Chapter 5). An advertisement for cigarettes may be viewed differently by different people, for example. Nonsmokers may pass over the message entirely; antismokers may be angered by it; smokers satisfied with another brand may note the advertisement only casually. Some who see the advertisement may not "get it" at all; for whatever reason, the intended imagery may escape them completely.

In the Blazer advertisement, if the receiver interprets the message "like a rock" to mean that Blazers are tough, sturdy, and long lasting, the communication has worked.

Decoding
In communication theory, the process by which the receiver of a message interprets the message's meaning.

FEEDBACK

Often, the communication process includes **feedback,** communication of the receiver's reaction that goes back to the source of the message. In a personal selling situation, the feedback may be direct and immediate, as when the customer raises

Feedback
Communication of the receiver's reaction to a message back to the source.

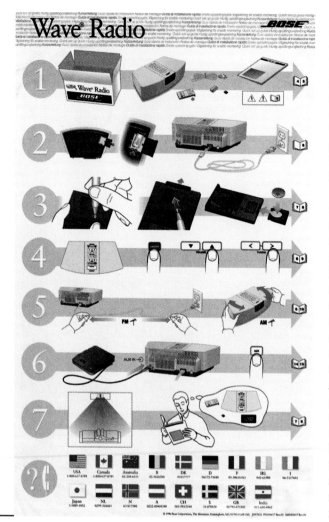

Noise
In communication theory, any interference or distraction that disrupts the communication process.

questions about the product or states why he or she will not purchase it. Indeed, as mentioned, the great attraction of personal selling is that there can be a two-way conversation, which ensures greater understanding between the people involved.

Feedback about advertising, sales promotions, or publicity and public relations is in most cases slower and less direct. For instance, advertisers may conduct surveys, count coupon redemptions, or evaluate letters and telephone calls from consumers to learn the audience's reactions. Although advertisers can get delayed feedback about an advertisement's effectiveness, the feedback rarely provides all the desired information about the receivers' responses to the message.

PERFECT COMMUNICATION

Ideally, in perfect communication, the message that was decoded and entered the mind of the receiver would be exactly the same as the one the sender had in mind, encoded, and transmitted. If the sender and the receiver share a common social background and have similar needs, they are more likely to similarly interpret the meaning of the words and symbols in the message. Perfect transmission, though, is never possible. In many cases, however, the sender can develop messages that will be decoded by the target audience to communicate approximately the message the sender had in mind.

It is likely—perhaps even inevitable—that any communication process will be interrupted or distorted by factors that communication experts term "noise." **Noise** is interference or distraction, and it may disrupt any stage of the communication process. Noise may come in the form of conflicting messages, misunderstood terminology, inadequacies in the channel of communication, and so on. A listener might not hear a radio advertisement because of loud traffic noises outside the car. In a cigarette advertisement, the Surgeon General's warning (a conflicting message) is noise. The sources of noise may be external to the individual, such as traffic noises, or internal, such as daydreaming that prevents a listener from concentrating on a sales presentation. Many advertising messages cause people to think of a competing product. Brand loyalties and past learning are internal distractions that may interfere with the decoding process.

The Hierarchy of Communication Effects

Ford has extolled the virtues of its "built to last" theme thousands of times. McDonald's has made hundreds of different advertisements for its burgers. Why are there so many commercials for the same products? Creativity aside, the main reason is that a single communication, no matter how cleverly designed and implemented, may not be enough to persuade a customer to change an attitude or make a purchase. Promotion, as a rule, becomes more effective with repetition. Promotion usually seeks to change people, and people tend to change very slowly. Habits and beliefs developed over long periods of time will not be altered quickly by just a few messages. The presentation of a message may be varied, as in the McDonald's example, because the effectiveness of a promotion wears out as the repetitive presentation becomes boring.

> A SINGLE COMMUNICATION, NO MATTER HOW CLEVERLY DESIGNED AND IMPLEMENTED, MAY NOT BE ENOUGH TO PERSUADE A CUSTOMER TO CHANGE AN ATTITUDE OR MAKE A PURCHASE. PROMOTION, AS A RULE, BECOMES MORE EFFECTIVE WITH REPETITION.

Marketers have come to expect various responses to their communications. To understand the different effects that promotion may bring about, it is useful to think of the promotion process as a staircase, or series of steps in a hierarchy.

THE PROMOTION STAIRCASE

Promotion can be thought of as a force that moves people up a series of steps called the hierarchy of communication effects.[8] This promotion staircase is shown in Exhibit 15-5.

exhibit 15-5

Promotion Moves Customers Up the Seven Steps in the Hierarchy of Communication Effects

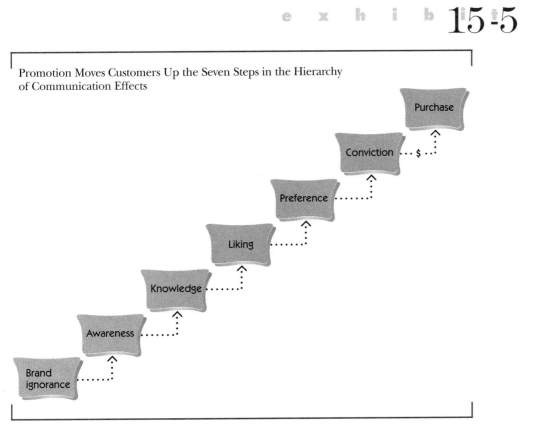

1. On the bottom step stand potential purchasers who are completely unaware of the existence of the product in question.
2. Closer to purchasing, but still a long way from the cash register, are those who are merely aware of the product's existence.
3. Up one step are prospects who know what the product has to offer.
4. Still closer to purchasing are those who have favorable attitudes toward the product—those who like the product.
5. Those whose favorable attitudes have developed to the point that they prefer the product in question over all other possibilities are up still another step.
6. Even closer to purchasing are consumers who couple preference with a desire to buy and the conviction that the purchase would be wise.
7. Finally, of course, is the top step, where consumers translate this intention into an actual purchase.

According to this somewhat idealized portrayal, consumers may move through the seven-step hierarchy, from total ignorance of a brand's existence to purchase of that brand. When the purchase decision leads to a reward, the result is a satisfied, or reinforced, customer.

The hierarchy model shown in Exhibit 15-5 suggests that communication may not be a one-step process. Marketers use promotion to induce buyers to change—that is, to move up the staircase. Communication may be aimed at any step, depending on the objective of the communication. The question is "What step should the marketer aim at?"

Part of the answer comes from the nature of the product. Marketers of a totally new product such as the Flashback electronic recorder—a miniature device that uses no tape, has no moving parts, and records sound digitally onto a flash-memory chip—face a different set of communication problems than marketers of fluoride toothpaste. The toothpaste communication need not include an extensive discussion of the fact that fluoride helps prevent cavities. Most consumers are already aware of fluoride's benefits. In contrast, the seller of a near-revolutionary product may need to devote considerable effort to explaining what the product is, how it works, and even that it works.

Whatever the product, the nature of the market is the most important consideration in deciding what step to aim at. The organization seeking to create an

An American visitor to Chinese cities like Shanghai and Beijing will see fleets of bicycles crowding the streets. So when Intel wanted to build awareness of its brand of computer chip in China, the company decided to use an inexpensive sales promotion. Intel distributed almost one million bike reflectors with the glow-in-the-dark message "Intel Inside. Pentium Processor."

www.intel.com

effective promotional message must begin with one of marketing's most basic rules: identify the target market or, in this case, the target audience.

As discussed earlier, the whole communication process must be built around the intended receiver of the message. A key question, then, is "What is the target audience's psychological state?" If the marketing organization is attempting to influence those who are currently on the Awareness and Knowledge steps, a primary promotional objective will be to provide factual information. For example, according to many petroleum companies,

WHAT PLAYS

RED, WHITE AND BUGLE BOY

www.bugleboy.com

The target audience in this case already knows about Bugle Boy classics and probably knows that the company is a respected manufacturer of fashionable clothing. Thus, the advertisement stresses emotional feelings toward the product. Similarly, advertisements for many soft drinks, beers, and wines accent the fun or sophistication associated with the drinks.

www.bugleboy.com

most citizens are totally unaware of how oil company revenues are allocated. Thus, some of these companies spend a good portion of their advertising budgets in an effort to inform people of the true nature of the oil business. They demonstrate that a large portion of revenues are spent on additional exploration, on the development of products that enhance the lives of consumers, and on protecting the environment.

Appealing to consumers who are on the Liking and Preference steps calls for promotional messages aimed at encouraging existing favorable feelings toward the good or service offered. For example, advertisements for many cosmetics, fashion items, soft drinks, and airlines emphasize the fun or sophistication associated with the products. The target audiences in these cases already know about the brands and probably know that the company is a respected manufacturer or service provider. Thus, the advertisements stress emotional feelings toward the product offered.

Prospective customers who are on the Conviction step of the model are very close to action, but they may need a little shove to get them to act. A bit of encouragement may be all that is required. Being reminded that now is the time to buy, warned that prices may go up, or notified that a two-for-one coupon is available may motivate these consumers to move up the staircase to the final step, the purchase.

As you saw in Chapter 6, the sale is not the end of the line. The marketer may continue to use promotional messages to reinforce the buyer's belief that he or she made a good buy or, later on, to remind the customer of the product and its value or effectiveness. For example, the advertisers of frequently purchased products like tomato sauce often remind buyers how satisfied they have been with the product. A promotion for an infrequently purchased durable good might advise the buyer to tell a friend about the purchase or to remember that the company sells other fine products. Such efforts often reduce consumers' post-purchase dissonance.

Sophisticated consumer behavior research suggests that some consumer purchasing decisions, especially those made when consumers have low involvement with the product, do not follow the steps in the hierarchy of communication effects. Nevertheless, this approach is useful in understanding how many promotions work.

THE HIERARCHY OF EFFECTS AND THE PROMOTIONAL MIX

As you have just seen, not all consumers are on the same step of the promotion staircase. Consumers on different steps will respond to different sorts of appeals. This suggests that different elements of the promotional mix may be more effective with different consumers.

To some extent, they are. Exhibit 15-6 illustrates, in general terms, the relative importance of advertising and personal selling at different steps in the hierarchy of effects, classified as pre-transaction, transaction, and post-transaction stages of the buying process. (The transaction may be roughly defined as the period in which the exchange agreement or the negotiation of the terms of sale becomes final.)

In the pre-transaction stage, the consumer becomes aware of a brand, acquires knowledge, and formulates likes, dislikes, and preferences. The purpose of promotion at this stage is to inform, and advertising generally plays a larger role than personal selling. In the transaction stage, personal selling is important because the consumer must be persuaded to make a positive evaluation, develop a conviction, and actually make the purchase. In the post-transaction stage, advertising reminds and reassures consumers about their satisfaction.

e x h i b 15-6

The Relative Importance of Advertising and Personal Selling Related to the Job to Be Done

	Steps in hierarchy of effects	Stage in consumer decision-making process	General purpose of promotion	Relative importance of advertising and personal selling
Pre-transaction	• Awareness • Knowledge • Liking • Preference	• Problem recognition • Search	Information to aid in recognition and understanding Information to create a positive feeling or affect	Personal selling Advertising
Transaction	• Conviction • Purchase	• Evaluation • Choice	Persuasion	Advertising Personal selling
Post-transaction		Post-purchase satisfaction	Reminder and reassurance	Personal selling Advertising

These relationships are strongly influenced by the many forces that contribute to the purchase decision. The characteristics of the marketplace, the state of the economy, the nature of the product, and the seller's overall marketing strategy vary from case to case, but these general statements illustrate the roles advertising and personal selling play at each stage.

Ideally, a promotional mix is planned to meet the information requirements of all target customers. That is, the mix is not designed to satisfy only the new buyer or only the regular buyer. Some elements of the mix may be aimed at target customers at a lower stage of the hierarchy of communication effects, others at potential customers near the top of the staircase. Even marketers of new and innovative products, such as portable, battery-powered global positioning systems, must keep this in mind. Although most customers are inexperienced, first-time buyers of this product, some people are computer and multimedia enthusiasts with a great deal of knowledge and experience with television, personal computers, and laser storage technologies. Potential buyers are to be found at all steps of the hierarchy staircase.

Let's consider how the promotional mix can work to move a consumer through several steps of the hierarchy. Suppose you want to purchase a laptop computer. You have probably advanced beyond total brand ignorance and are becoming increasingly aware of the different brands and their advertised benefits. Your interest in the product has led you to pay more attention to computer advertising and to magazine stories about laptops. Newspaper columnists may be writing about their own personal experiences, thus providing publicity for these brands. Your friend the computer expert may regularly read these columns and may talk to you about recent improvements in laptops. Sales promotions, such as the offer of a free software package or lessons in computer use, may ultimately bring you into a computer store, where personal selling communicates to you the benefits associated with a particular brand of computer. You may then decide to buy a particular brand, be it Macintosh, IBM, or Gateway.

Which aspect of the promotional mix brought you to the decision to buy the brand of computer you chose? Perhaps one factor, such as the expertise of the salesperson, was a major influence, but the fact is that all elements of the mix did their parts in bringing about the sale. Each had a role to play and a function to perform. In this case, advertising proved effective in generating awareness and, perhaps, positive attitudes toward the brand. The sales promotion offer of software led to the decision to visit the store. Personal selling proved, as it usually does, most effective in consummating the sale.

Commonly, there is an important interaction among the variables within the promotional mix. Consumers may be strongly influenced by the advertising for cold remedies, for example, but in-store displays, packaging, sales promotions aimed at retailers, and the activities of a personal sales force may all play some role in the ultimate purchase of a given medicine. The interaction of promotional mix variables is even more obvious in the business market. Here, advertising alone is unlikely to sell many products, yet it performs an important function in supplementing and supporting the personal sales force. The salesperson will get nowhere at all with a tough organizational buyer unless the buyer is at least familiar with the salesperson's company or line of goods. In other words, companies dealing with organizational buyers had better advertise and use personal selling because these promotional elements support each other.

While each promotional element has its relative strengths, any promotional element may be called on to accomplish a communication objective. Marketers select and combine the various promotional mix elements available to them as best they can. Some organizations have considerable flexibility in developing a promotional mix. Others, usually small companies without many resources, are primarily limited to personal selling by employees whose chief responsibility is running the business.

Push and Pull Strategies

The prime target of a promotional strategy may be either the ultimate consumer or a member of the distribution channel. Using the target as a basis for classification, we can identify the basic strategies of push and pull. No single strategy is purely one type or the other—but, in general, the strategies can be described as follows and illustrated as shown in Exhibit 15-7.

Push strategy
A promotional strategy whereby a supplier promotes a product to marketing intermediaries, with the aim of pushing the product through the channel of distribution.

A **push strategy** emphasizes personal selling, advertising, and other promotional efforts aimed at members of the channel of distribution. Thus, the manufacturer of a product heavily promotes that product to wholesalers and other dealers. The wholesalers then promote the product heavily to retailers, which in turn direct their selling efforts to consumers. Not infrequently, the wholesalers and retailers are offered strong price incentives or discounts as part of this process. The term *push* comes from the fact that the manufacturer, with the help of other channel members, pushes the product through each level in the channel of distribution. The push strategy may be thought of as a step-by-step approach to promotion, with each channel member organizing the promotional efforts necessary to reach the channel member next in line.

Pull strategy
A promotional strategy whereby a supplier promotes a product to the ultimate consumer, with the aim of stimulating demand and thus pulling the product through the channel of distribution.

In contrast, the manufacturer implementing a **pull strategy** attempts to stimulate demand for the product through promotional efforts aimed at the ultimate consumer or organizational buyer. The goal is to generate demand at the retail level in the belief that such demand will encourage retailers and wholesalers to stock the product. If the customer is pulled into the store, each channel member will "pass the demand back" through the channel. In other words, the demand at the buyer end of the channel pulls the product through the channels of distribution.

In sum, the push strategy suggests a step-by-step promotional effort, while the pull strategy attempts to develop ultimate buyer demand and a smooth flow of products from the manufacturer to the buyer via cooperative intermediaries. Consumers are most familiar with the pull strategy because they often encounter promotional messages that say, in effect, "go to the store and ask for this." However, a moment's thought will suggest products sold by the push approach. A consumer might purchase an imported watch or an expensive perfume even though the brand name is totally unfamiliar because the salesperson mentions that this product is "the best."

e x h i b i t 15-7

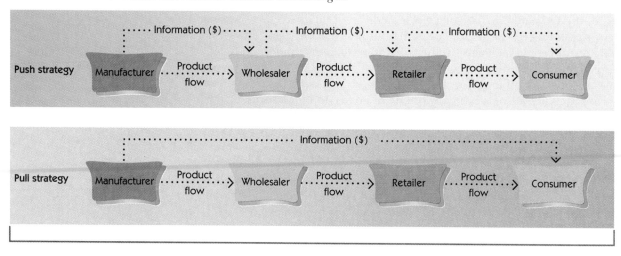

Flow of Promotional Dollars and Effort in Push and Pull Strategies

Marketing organizations do not limit themselves to using only a push or only a pull strategy. Effective marketing plans generally make use of both push and pull. Consider these remarks by Dr Pepper executives:[9]

> "We are a sales company."
> "The Dr Pepper bottler is the key to our success."
> "No matter how good a job we do, [consumers] can't get Dr Pepper unless [bottlers] have made the sale to the retailers."

These comments indicate that a push strategy is being used to motivate local salespeople. Yet consumers can see Dr Pepper commercials on television and in magazines and newspapers and hear them on radio. These commercials are obviously aimed at pulling the product through the channels of distribution. Here, the combination strategy employed acknowledges that the makers of Dr Pepper have more than one type of customer. Thus, a portion of the promotional campaign is geared toward channel members and has the objective of encouraging aggressive promotion by local bottlers. Another portion is intended to generate consumer purchases by developing favorable consumer attitudes toward the product.

focus on global competition

Coca-Cola Most people envision a pull strategy when they think about the promotion of Coca-Cola. However, when Coke decided to expand into international markets, access was by no means certain from the beginning; consumer preference was not inevitable. The company had to build up fairly complete local distribution systems and use a push strategy to establish local demand. In Japan, for example, the long-established preference was for carbonated lemon beverages know as *saida*. Consumer demand did not pull Coke into this market; the company had to persuade the bottlers to push it. Today, because the company properly executed its expansion, Coke is a highly desired brand in many countries. But it got there by recognizing the need for both push and pull strategies.

Determining the Promotional Budget

After managers have planned the promotional mix, they must determine if the organization can afford it. This is a matter of budgeting. Marketers attempting to determine the size of their promotional budgets are often reminded of the adage "If you can't make a splash, don't make a ripple." This piece of marketing wisdom suggests that marketers using a very small amount of promotion may not transmit their messages to buyers effectively. Giant organizations that can place promotional messages in many media and use other promotional tools as well are thus in an enviable position indeed. However, even smaller organizations can mount successful promotional campaigns by setting advertising budgets carefully and selecting those themes, media, and schedules that most effectively transmit the desired messages. These matters are dealt with more fully in later chapters because they concern advertising and personal selling specifically rather than promotion in general. Regardless of the promotional tools employed, however, the marketer must determine how much money will be available in the promotional fund before focusing on these other matters. Let's consider some methods used to determine the size of a promotional budget.

THE OBJECTIVE-AND-TASK METHOD

The **objective-and-task method** of setting a promotional budget, also called the *task approach,* is probably the most logical of the budget-setting techniques. It calls for first identifying the objective to be accomplished and then determining the costs and tasks necessary to attain the objective. An appropriate objective for a retail furniture marketer budgeting for 2001 might be to double 1999 sales, for example. Assuming that this objective was reasonable, the retailer would then budget the promotional resources necessary to achieve it. Such an approach has more logical appeal than does entrusting these important decisions to some mathematical formula based solely on quantitative data. Here, the job to be done, rather than sales figures or industry tradition, determines the size of the budget. Despite the clear logic underlying the objective-and-task approach, it is not the most commonly used method of setting a promotional budget. Using this approach is seldom easy, and it may require a great deal of time, mainly because it is difficult for a planner to develop obtainable objectives and then calculate what it would take to achieve these goals.

THE PERCENT-OF-SALES METHOD

The **percent-of-sales method** is probably the most commonly applied means of setting advertising budgets. The planner using the percent-of-sales method need only obtain a sales figure, take a percentage of that amount, and use that percentage as the promotional budget. For example, in the men's clothing business, 7 percent is considered a "reasonable" percentage of sales to spend on promotion. If sales for a period of time are $100,000, then the promotional budget "should" be $7,000. The percentage used varies from industry to industry; for example, the food marketing industry typically uses 1 percent of sales for promotion, and movie theaters generally spend about 14 percent for promotion.

A clear advantage of this method is that the marketer need only know sales totals to calculate the budget. Moreover, the appropriate percentage for a given industry—that is, the industry average or standard—can be obtained from trade associations or other sources. The user of this method is thus spared having to determine what percent-of-sales figure to use. He or she may also feel comfortable knowing that the budget developed is reasonable and is similar to that of other companies.

Although the percent-of-sales method is simple to use, it has many disadvantages. First, there is the logical problem of deriving a promotional budget from a sales figure. Supposedly, sales result from promotion. This method makes promotion a result of sales. In fact, the percent-of-sales method implies that the sales would have occurred with or without promotional expenditures. There is also the problem that such a method cannot cover all circumstances. For example, if sales are declining, it might be better to increase promotional expenditures rather than reduce them, as the formula would have the marketer do.

Two defenses of the percent-of-sales method have been offered. First, given that promotion is tied to sales, it is reasonable to assume that the sales have generated sufficient money to pay for the promotion. The logical flaws of the method, however, make this defense quite unsatisfying. Second, it is possible to defend use of the method in certain circumstances. Some industries—for example, electric power companies—are mature and face predictable market changes. A mathematical formula is more appropriate here than in more dynamic marketing environments.

THE COMPARATIVE-PARITY METHOD

The **comparative-parity method** for determining a promotional budget boils down to doing what the competitors do. Brewers compare their dollars-per-barrel promotional expenditures with those of competitors in an effort to assure that they are not falling behind. Supermarkets operating in a given city commonly spend almost precisely what their competitors in that city spend. In a two-department-store town, it is common to see both stores represented in the Sunday newspaper in ads that are nearly identical in size, placement, and cost.

The comparative-parity method for determining promotional budgets is based on the notion that marketers must somehow match the moves made by competitors or industry leaders. Like the percent-of-sales method, this technique takes little note of changes in the marketplace or of opportunities that may suddenly arise. In fact, the method makes one firm's promotion a near mirror image of another's. Each firm is thus allowing its competitors to determine its promotional budget. As suggested, this method has problems similar to those of the percent-of-sales method.

THE MARGINAL APPROACH

Theoretically, the **marginal approach** to almost anything in business is "the best." Applied to the setting of promotional budgets, such a method would have the organization spend promotional dollars until the payoff from the last dollar spent indicates that it is no longer worthwhile to continue to raise the budget. Unfortunately, the dynamic nature of markets, the actions of competitors, and the difficulty of determining exactly how much benefit was purchased with the "last promotional dollar spent" make this method difficult to implement.

Marginal approach
A method of setting a promotional budget in which the marketer attempts to spend resources until additional expenditures would not be justified by the additional sales and profits they would generate.

THE ALL-YOU-CAN-AFFORD METHOD

The name of the all-you-can-afford method is self-explanatory. Using this method, the marketer spends whatever is available for promotion. Organizations using this method typically do not have enough cash flow to justify using other methods. The owner of a new business, just starting out and facing the frightening statistics on new business failures, for example, would be well advised to spend, in effect, as much as is available for promotion. This method further implies that the promotional dollars are not borrowed but represent available cash on hand.

THE COMBINATION APPROACH

Solutions to real-world problems are seldom left to one formula or one method of analysis. Even a planner who can use the objective-and-task approach effectively might employ a percent-of-sales formulation to generate some ball-park figures to be considered as the planning process progresses. A planner relying on the comparative-parity method may be brought back to reality by the all-you-can-afford method when calculations yield a budget figure that is unreasonable, given the organization's assets.

COOPERATIVE PROMOTIONAL PROGRAMS

Many marketers at all levels in the distribution process employ a cooperative approach to advertising and other promotion. For example, a manufacturer of expensive wristwatches such as Rolex may offer to pay for a portion of a retailer's advertising with the understanding that the advertisements will feature that manufacturer's brand of wristwatch.

The attractiveness of these programs is clear. Every channel member gets some of the benefits of the others' promotional efforts, and no individual channel member must bear the full cost. All concerned parties realize savings. In some situations, the rates may even be reduced, because many newspapers and broadcasting stations charge lower rates to local businesses than to national advertisers. If a manufacturer paying part of the cost of the advertisement has a local retailer actually place the advertisement, the retailer will pay this lower rate. Cooperative advertising as a sales promotion incentive is discussed further in Chapter 18.

Promotional Campaigns

Throughout this chapter, we have considered the individual aspects of promotion while emphasizing that the parts of the promotional effort must fit together and complement each other. For example, a trade magazine mailed to owners of automobile muffler shops may do more than simply promote itself to potential buyers of advertising space as the place to advertise to reach target customers. The magazine's management may sponsor race cars or make awards to outstanding people in the muffler business, thereby building the magazine's image as a major force in the trade. All of these activities fit together into a unity of presentation that could be called the magazine publisher's total promotional effort or promotional mix.

Chapter 1 noted that military terminology is commonly used in football and in business. This tendency is evident in the term **promotional campaign.** A promotional campaign is a part of a firm's promotional mix, just as a military campaign is a portion of a total war effort. Thus, a promotional campaign is a series of promotional activities with a particular objective or set of objectives.

The phrase "particular objective" is important here, because it is this objective that indicates the goal to be reached. The campaign must be constructed to achieve that goal. The task of introducing a new product requires a promotional campaign considerably different from one intended to increase the sales of an established or widely recognized product.

Because most products are in the mature stage of the product life cycle, this section focuses primarily on promotional campaigns for these products. However, aspects of these strategies can also be applied to product introductions or to products in the growth stage. There are four major approaches to developing a promotional campaign for a mature product: image building, product differentiation, positioning, and direct response.

IMAGE BUILDING

The product or brand image is an individual's net impression of what the product or brand "is all about." It is the symbolic value associated with the brand. Buyers frequently prefer one product or brand over another because of its image. Thus, they often purchase or avoid brands or products not because of what they cost or how they work but because of what they say about the buyer-user—how they symbolize that person's personality or lifestyle. Marketers are properly concerned with this symbolic value or image. Thus, many promotional campaigns are aimed at **image building.**

Holiday Inn is one of the most recognized brands in the hotel/motel industry. However, over the years, many of the chain's hotels and motels had been neglected. Holiday Inn properties were often perceived as old, rundown, roadside motels with coffee shops. Today, the company is trying to polish its tarnished image and establish a more colorful, contemporary one, which communicates that it is a reinvigorated company.[10] The message communicated in its advertising is "On the way. Every Holiday Inn as good as the best Holiday Inn."

Not-for-profit organizations are also concerned with image building. Consider the image of a Girl Scout, which has traditionally been one of dependability, trustworthiness, and honesty. However, in the MTV era, many young girls had come to see this positive image as being too squeaky-clean.

Promotional campaign
A series of promotional activities aimed at achieving a specific objective or set of objectives.

Image building
A promotional approach intended to communicate an image and generate consumer preference for a brand or product on the basis of symbolic value.

For years, the Plymouth automobile appealed only to older consumers. The car had acquired a stodgy image. Marketers at Plymouth used a series of new product introductions and an advertising campaign with the tagline "One Creative Idea After Another" to overcome its image problems. Plymouth hopes to project an image of a car that is youthful, fun, and affordable.

Girl Scout membership had been dropping, especially in the 8–11 age group. Focus group research showed that these preteens perceived Girl Scouts as childish. So the organization's marketers decided that the Girl Scouts had to move away from the uniformed, goody-goody image and show that Girl Scout meetings were a fun, mature, cool place to be.

Girl Scouts of America
www.girlscouts.org

To overcome its image as an organization that was "locked in time," the Girl Scouts used a promotional campaign aimed at making the organization more relevant to the older age group while emphasizing the activities available to all girls who join. The new image portrayed Girl Scouts as more action-oriented. For example, cookie packages showed Girl Scouts engaged in outdoor games such as volleyball.

The not-for-profit organization developed an image-building advertising campaign that portrayed a hipper, more active organization. Using MTV-style graphics, TV advertising incorporated rap music and fantasy images, such as windsurfing, skiing, and parachuting, to suggest that the Scouts could offer girls a lot of fulfilling activities. One television ad closed with the line "The Girl Scouts. As great as you want to make it."[11]

In general, image-building promotional campaigns do not focus on product features but emphasize creating impressions. These may be impressions of status, sexuality, masculinity, femininity, reliability, or some other aspect of the brand's character thought to be alluring to target customers. Most advertisements for perfumes (such as Chanel No. 5 and Obsession) and clothing (Calvin Klein and Guess?) concentrate almost entirely on creating impressions.

PRODUCT DIFFERENTIATION

A promotional campaign aimed at developing **product differentiation** focuses on some dimension of the product that competing brands or competing products do not offer or accents some way in which using the product provides the solution to a consumer problem. For example, in its Piggyback suitcase advertising, Samsonite tries to persuade frequent flyers that they should think of this suitcase with wheels and a telescoping handle as a luggage cart that doubles as a suitcase.

Product differentiation
A promotional approach in which the marketer calls buyers' attention to those aspects of a product or brand that set it apart from its competitors.

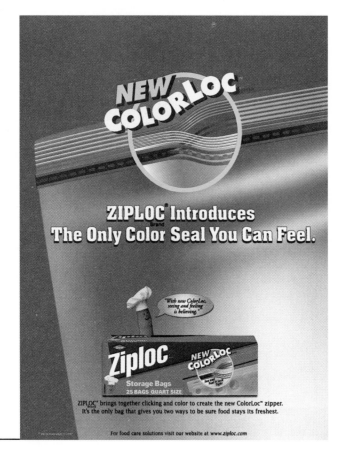

Ziploc's new Colorloc storage bags provide a unique selling proposition. This advertisement informs consumers that Ziploc's Colorloc, by bringing together clicking and color, gives consumers two ways to be sure food stays its freshest.

www.ziploc.com

Unique selling proposition (USP)
A unique characteristic of a product or brand identified by the marketer as the one on which to base a promotional campaign. It is often used in a product-differentiation approach to promotion.

The advertising shows how sturdy construction and tie-down straps, which allow customers to pile on several other carry-on bags, make the Samsonite Piggyback suitcase different from regular bags. The promotional campaign focuses on attributes of the product, not its image or price.

Product differentiation and related promotional efforts often take the form of the **unique selling proposition (USP).** As the name suggests, the basic idea of the USP is to identify and promote an aspect of the product that the competition does not offer or, because of patents or other reasons, cannot offer easily. Energizer batteries were the first to have an "on-battery tester." Initially, Eveready and the Coppertop had no such feature and no such benefit. The on-battery testing feature provided Energizer with a unique selling proposition around which a promotional campaign has been built. The USP tells buyers that if they buy the product, they will receive a specific, exclusive benefit.

Generally, mature products are not truly unique, especially from the point of view of performance. Yet *parity products*—those with ingredients nearly identical to those of competitors' brands, such as Tylenol's brand of acetaminophen—are often promoted as if they were special. This can be done because aspects of a product other than the strictly functional ones can be promoted as effectively as functional features. Elmer Wheeler illustrated this fact in the classic statement "Don't sell the steak, sell the sizzle."[12] Keep in mind, though, that the point stressed in the unique selling proposition, whatever it is, must be meaningful to the potential buyer. It is possible to "sell the sizzle" only if the sizzle means something to the buyer—that is, if it satisfies a need. If buyers do not care about the USP, it does not influence the purchasing decision.

POSITIONING

You may recall that a brand's *competitive position* is the way consumers perceive it relative to its competition. The positioning approach, which promotes a brand's competitive position, is often the focal point of promotional campaigns. The campaign objective is to get consumers to view the brand from a particular perspective.

In launching such a campaign, the marketer assumes that consumers have so much information about other brands and similar products that it must create a distinct position for the brand in the prospect's mind. The Avis campaign advertising "We're only number two" is a classic example of this strategy. By positioning itself as the second-largest automobile rental company, Avis dramatically increased market share. Avis took business away from the smaller rent-a-car companies,

Some people think the Pentium II is the fastest processor in the world. Not quite.   The chip inside every new Power Macintosh® G3 is up to twice as fast. 🍎 Think different.

In positioning campaigns, brands are often compared to competitors. This Macintosh advertisement positions the speed of its processor chip above that of its competitor Intel.

rather than Hertz (at the time the largest rental car company), because consumers remembered both the Avis and the Hertz positions—that Hertz was number one and Avis was in the number-two slot, where a company has to "try harder." Similarly, Xerox, long thought of as "the copier company," today positions itself as "the documents company," involved in faxing, scanning, copying, and printing. It wants to hold a position unoccupied by other competitors.

How do marketers go about positioning their brands? Exhibit 15-8 shows that there are many positioning strategies. It also suggests that brand image campaigns and product differentiation campaigns can be thought of as ways to position the product. Positioning strategies often communicate what the product does. Such strategies may promote a single product attribute—"the car dealer with the lowest prices in town"—or multiple attributes—"the high-performance luxury car." Sometimes the promotional campaign positions a brand in terms of its users—"for the working woman." In general, the important point about positioning is not what "selling point" is used as the basis of positioning but the idea that promotion can be used to position a brand relative to the competition. Note, too, that promotional campaigns that stress positioning are highly interrelated with the market segmentation strategy and the overall positioning strategy.

Positioning Strategies   e x h i b **15-8**

FOCUS OF POSITIONING STRATEGY	EXAMPLE
Image of user	Volkswagen Passat: Drivers wanted
Image of quality	Hallmark: When you care enough to send the very best
Value/price	Suave: Beautiful hair doesn't have to cost a fortune
Product attribute	Kellogg's Pop-Tarts: Frosted strawberry with Smuckers real fruit
Product benefit	Campbell's Soup: "Good for the Body. Good for the Soul"
Use or application	Arm & Hammer Baking Soda: Try adding Arm & Hammer along with your laundry detergent for a cleaner, fresher wash
Product class	Raid Baits: There's no better way to kill bugs dead
Competitor	Visa: The Olympics don't take American Express

NFL   When the National Football League launched the World League of American Football in Europe, the game was positioned somewhat differently than it is in North America. American football in Europe is marketed more as a fun outing for the family, not as the gladiatorial spectacle that it is in the United States. The focus of the promotions is to bring the family out to have an enjoyable afternoon. Emphasizing pregame festivities and postgame parties is part of the marketing effort.[13]

DIRECT-RESPONSE CAMPAIGNS

Recall our discussions in earlier chapters about direct channels of distribution, in which the manufacturer of a good or the producer of a service deals directly with the customer. The purpose of this "direct marketing" is to obtain a direct response, such as a sale.

Direct-response campaign

A promotional approach intended to elicit a direct, measurable response, such as an order.

A **direct-response campaign** is conducted specifically to elicit a direct, measurable response, such as an order, a donation, an inquiry, or a visit to a store or showroom.[14] For example, a mail-order company, such as L. L. Bean, engages in a direct-response campaign by sending out its catalog. Of course, most personal selling (discussed in Chapter 17) fits in this category. However, the growing availability of highly targeted computerized databases and the rapid expansion of Internet shopping have brought increased prominence to direct-response promotions conducted via mail, telephone, and other media.

A direct-response campaign, like the other major promotional campaigns, may be used in conjunction with other strategies. The advertising and personal selling tactics associated with direct-response campaigns will be addressed in the next two chapters.

The Ethics of Persuasion

Of all the macromarketing issues involving promotion, the use of persuasion has attracted the most attention. The most common target of critics of promotion is persuasion in advertising, but every element of promotion has been criticized at one time or another.

An important aspect of this issue is the difference between informative and persuasive promotion. Most people would grant that some advertising or other promotion is needed; otherwise, consumers wouldn't know where to buy a product they wanted, whether a gas station would accept a credit card, or what freeway exit leads to a motel. Thus, critics often maintain that informative advertisements are fine. They argue, however, that it is not right to use marketing skills, psychology, and expensive commercials to persuade consumers to buy a product, vote for a particular candidate, or give to a certain charity. For example, many would argue that all cigarette advertising should be banned because it promotes an unhealthful product. In summary, the basic argument is that persuasive advertisements are wasteful and manipulative.

A common defense against such criticism is that advertisements for an inferior product are almost certain to sell the product only once. Even the richest companies with the best sales records sometimes lose millions of dollars introducing products that fail in the marketplace. In fact, the quickest way to kill a poor product is to promote it aggressively. People will find out about its inferior nature just that much more quickly.

Your own answer to questions about the proper use of persuasion will be influenced by your view of whether people are—or should be—able to exercise freedom of choice. Are consumers able to control their own destinies? Do you ever not buy products you see advertised? Have you ever said "No" to a salesperson? Why? Rethinking the earlier discussions of the hierarchy of needs, selective perception, and other aspects of consumer behavior should help you to make a decision on this issue. Chapters 16, 17, and 18 address several specific issues involved in the ethics of advertising, personal selling, sales promotion, and public relations.

summary

Promotion consists of four elements: personal selling, advertising, publicity (as part of a public relations effort), and sales promotion. All must be integrated into the promotional mix.

1 *Discuss the three basic purposes of promotion.*

Promotion is communication designed to inform, to persuade, and to remind buyers about the existence and benefits of a good, service, or idea. Without promotion, buyers would have less information on which to base their buying decisions.

2 *Define the four major elements of promotion.*

Personal selling occurs when a seller communicates a persuasive message directly to a buyer. Advertising includes any persuasive message carried by a nonpersonal medium and paid for by an identified sponsor. Publicity involves a message that is not paid for and has no identified sponsor, delivered through a mass medium. Sales promotion consists of nonroutine, temporary promotional efforts designed to stimulate buyer purchases or dealer effectiveness in a specified time period.

3 *Describe the basic model for all communication processes, including promotion.*

The communication process occurs when a source encodes a message and sends it through a channel to a receiver, who must decode it and may respond with feedback. Noise may interfere. Each element in the process plays an essential role in the transference of a message from the source to the receiver.

4 *Explain the hierarchy of communication effects.*

Consumers often move through a seven-step hierarchy in relation to a product: ignorance, awareness, knowledge, liking, preference, conviction, and purchase. Consumers at different steps have different communication needs.

5 *Explain how the elements of promotion can be used to support one another in a promotional campaign.*

The effective marketer integrates all the elements of promotion—advertising, personal selling, public-

ity/public relations, and sales promotion—into a promotional mix. Such a mix is planned to meet the information requirements of all target customers. Each element of the mix performs a task. Some elements may be aimed at the target customer at a lower stage of the hierarchy of communication effects; others may be aimed at potential customers near the top of the staircase. Advertising's strength is in creating awareness and spreading information to a wide audience. Personal selling is best at moving buyers from liking to conviction to purchase.

6 *Describe the general promotional strategies known as push and pull strategies.*

A push strategy is directed toward members of a channel of distribution. A pull strategy is directed toward consumers in order to stimulate demand for the product.

7 *Classify the major approaches used by marketing managers to set promotional budgets.*

In setting promotional budgets, marketing managers can use the objective-and-task method, the percent-of-sales method, the comparative-parity method, the marginal approach, the all-you-can-afford method, cooperative promotional programs, or combinations of these. With the objective-and-task method, the budget is based on an estimate of the amount needed to accomplish established objectives. The percent-of-sales method bases appropriations on a standard percentage of sales. With the comparative-parity method, the appropriation is based on what competitors spend. The marginal approach considers the payoff from the last promotional dollar spent, and the all-you-can-afford approach uses whatever dollars are available. Cooperative programs involve a sharing of promotional expenses among members of a distribution channel.

8 *Discuss promotional campaigns and provide examples.*

A promotional campaign consists of promotional activities designed to achieve specific objectives. An image-building approach stresses the symbolic value associated with the product. A product-differentiation approach emphasizes unique product features. A positioning approach promotes a brand in relation to competing brands. A direct-response campaign seeks a direct measurable response.

9 *Take a stand about the ethics of persuasion.*

Every element of promotion has been criticized at one time or another. Critics argue that it is not right to use promotional efforts to persuade consumers. However, most people would grant that some advertising or other promotion is necessary to provide consumers with information. Thus, a central issue is whether promotions are informative or persuasive. Your own stand will depend in part on whether you think people are—or should be—able to exercise freedom of choice.

key terms

mass media (p. 465)
human interactive media (p. 466)
electronic interactive media (p. 466)
personal selling (p. 467)
advertising (p. 467)
publicity (p. 468)
public relations (p. 469)
sales promotion (p. 470)
promotional mix (p. 471)
integrated marketing
  communications (p. 471)

communication (p. 471)
receiver (p. 471)
source (p. 471)
encoding (p. 472)
decoding (p. 473)
feedback (p. 473)
noise (p. 474)
push strategy (p. 480)
pull strategy (p. 480)
objective-and-task method (p. 482)

percent-of-sales method (p. 482)
comparative-parity method (p. 482)
marginal approach (p. 483)
promotional campaign (p. 484)
image building (p. 484)
product differentiation (p. 485)
unique selling proposition (USP)
  (p. 486)
direct-response campaign (p. 488)

questions for review & critical thinking

1. Identify the type of promotion being used in each of the following cases, and comment on its effectiveness.
    a. A Chicago Cubs announcer wears a Budweiser jacket during a televised game.
    b. A TV ad says, "CNN Headline News: If you don't have it, [tell] your cable operator to get it."
    c. A Special Olympics representative telephones at 8:15 p.m. while you are watching your favorite TV show and asks you to make a donation.
    d. As a forward receives the basketball, the announcer says, "Here comes the Windex man."
    e. At the supermarket, a banner announces a scratch-and-win bingo game.
    f. During a corporate takeover attempt, a corporate raider invites television reporters from major cities to question him during a live satellite news conference. Reporters are allowed to splice in film of themselves for the evening news so that it appears that each local reporter has spoken to the corporate executive in an exclusive interview rather than via a satellite hookup.
2. What is sales promotion? Give some creative examples of sales promotion.
3. Using the communication model shown in Exhibit 15-3, give examples of the encoding and decoding that might take place during the personal selling process.
4. The "accommodation" symbol, a green and red, yin-yangish logo, has been used in Benson & Hedges ads to promote tolerance of smokers. Discuss the communication process, using the accommodation symbol as an example.
5. What is noise in the communication process?
6. How does selective perception enter into the communication process?
7. How does a push strategy differ from a pull strategy?
8. Comment on the following: "Promotion mirrors the values and lifestyles of the target consumers."
9. For each of the following brands, indicate whether the primary promotional strategy is likely to be image building, positioning, or a unique selling proposition.
    a. Mountain Dew soft drink
    b. MTV
    c. SnackWell cookies
    d. BMW convertibles
10. Form small groups as directed by your instructor. Outline a promotional campaign for your college or university in general or for the business department or school in particular. Be sure to keep your promotional budget in mind.

marketing plan—right or wrong?

1. An automobile manufacturer sets up a Web page to highlight the unique features of its cars. It plans to include an interactive e-mail feature so that visitors to the Web site can easily communicate with the company.
2. Dorf Industries, an Australian plumbing fixtures marketer, launched an ad campaign showing water faucets running. One commercial portrays a jilted girlfriend getting even with her ex-boyfriend by turning on all the taps and leaving his house to fill up with water. A follow-up commercial shows the man returning home to find water spouting through the keyhole. As he inserts the key, there is a "whoosh" of water, and the screen shows the tagline "Dorf, wherever water falls."

internet insights

zikmund.swcollege.com

exercises

1. The promotional mix and promotional strategy should be an integrated marketing communication. Take a look at Mama's Cucina, an Internet site at either www.eat.com or www.ragu.com, "brought to you by your fellow 'netheads at Ragú."
   This Web site is constantly changing. However, you should find selections such as Mama's New Sauces, Mama's Italian Cookbook, Goodies from Mama, Learn to Speak Italian, and What's New at Mama's. Select several options from the menu, and evaluate Ragú's promotional efforts. Answer the following questions, and bring your answers to class:
   a. Why does a spaghetti sauce company need a site on the Internet?
   b. Why does Ragú have recipes on this Web site?
   c. Why did Ragú use the personality of Mama rather than the authority of the company?
   d. Explain the messages communicated on the Ragú Web page in terms of the communication model presented in Exhibit 15-3.
2. Go to www.adage.com to learn the advertising news of the day. Write a short summary of an article you read.
3. Go to the PR Newswire Web site at www.prnewswire.com, and select two news releases. What do they have in common?

address book (useful urls)

KPMG Canada	www.kpmg.ca
Integrated Marketing Communications, Inc.	www.intmark.com
Communications Arts Magazine	www.commarts.com

ethically right or wrong?

Critics are outraged over a Benson & Hedges ad depicting the Statue of Liberty's crown as a swell place for tourists to smoke cigarettes. "Ever wonder why she's holding a light?" the print ad reads. "For a great smoke, take a few liberties."

The National Park Service isn't laughing. Neither are antismoking groups and the foundation that restored the statue. But Philip Morris says it won't kill the ad

International Management Group

The seeds for the International Management Group (IMG) sprouted when a college golfer named Mark McCormack realized he wasn't as good as one of his teammates. After concluding that he had no future as a professional golfer, McCormack decided to embark on another career. The college teammate, Arnold Palmer, became his first client, and McCormack became a manager—a sports agent.

When McCormack began, most athletes were amateurs, and television carried mostly black-and-white programming. However, as the business developed, McCormack anticipated the connection between sports, television, and global marketing. He thought of sports as a product; and ultimately, he created a multimillion-dollar operation based on sports marketing.

Today, McCormack's IMG represents hundreds of top athletes, including Joe Montana, Jim Courier, and Greg Norman, as well as sports announcers John Madden and Bob Costas. The company manages golfers, tennis players, NFL football players, and other athletes and entertainers. It negotiates contracts with many sporting organizations, including auto racing teams. And it works for clients like Martina Navratilova and Andre Agassi to obtain endorsement agreements with the marketers of consumer goods and services.

IMG even sponsors and manages its own tournaments and sporting events. It has created television shows such as *The Battle of the Network Stars* and *The Skins Game*. Many times, IMG athletes participate in these events.

QUESTIONS

1. Mark McCormack is a sports agent and a manager in charge of sports marketing. How important is personal selling in a job like this? What personal characteristics do you think would be important for a person in a job like McCormack's?
2. What promotional opportunities are available for athletes who wish to lend their names to goods or services? How might a marketer like Fila, Wilson, or Nike use McCormack's services?
3. What might IMG look for in an athlete it agrees to manage?
4. How global is the sports marketing business?

chapter
16

Advertising

After you have studied this chapter, you will be able to:

Understand the purpose of product advertising, direct-action advertising, and institutional advertising.

1

Differentiate between primary demand and selective demand advertising.

2

Discuss the stages in the development of an advertisement.

3

Analyze the role of communication objectives in the advertising process.

4

Show how advertisements for a product are likely to change over the course of the product's life cycle.

5

(continued on next page)

oh, no. Maybe Andre Agassi was right.

You may recall seeing him, beginning way back when he had enough hair to tie up in a do-rag, whacking tennis balls and snapping pictures with a Canon.

"Image is everything," he declared, and presumably he knew whereof he spoke, having become a Famously Iconoclastic Personality long before he actually began to win big tournaments.

But Agassi's pronouncement was dispiriting on the face of it. We like to think, after all, that image is superficial, that substance ultimately trumps artifice, that the sizzle is subordinated by the steak.

Alas, just when we let ourselves believe it's what's inside that counts, along comes someone or something to disillusion us. Such as Dennis Rodman. Or the matron formerly known as Madonna.

Or Sprite.

Yes, Sprite, the lemon-lime soft drink that declares, no less emphatically, that "Image is nothing. Thirst is everything. Obey your thirst." For the past three years, commercials from Lowe & Partners/SMS, New York, have systematically lampooned the phony quality of other soft-drink advertising. Now a new pool of spots is taking on other ad categories, as well. One spoofs VISA's overheated retail travelogues, another Cheer's quirky product demos. One makes fun of the entire genre of athlete endorsements and another trashes the trend of using animals in commercials.

And, excepting the animal one, which shows revolting things being eaten in revolting ways, they're all pretty amusing. The funniest, which purports to promote the fictitious "Jooky" cola, is one of those beach-party deals, where entirely-too-beautiful young people are having entirely too much fun. Finally it pulls back, where two dull-witted teens are watching the spot on the tube. But when they crack open their Jookys, no party breaks out.

"Oh, man," one moans. "Mine's busted."

Then the voice-over: "Trust your taste buds, not commercials."

Because, duh, commercials lie.

Such is the undergirding principle of so much anti-advertising. Marketers as varied as Nike, Energizer, and Miller Lite use ads to satirize ads, betting that media-wise young target audiences will credit the advertiser for being hip enough to understand that the audience understands that advertising is just a lot of smoke and mirrors obscuring the self-serving nature of the enterprise. So, the thinking goes, let's expose everybody else and stand alone in straightforward communication.

> JUST WHEN WE LET OURSELVES BELIEVE IT'S WHAT'S INSIDE THAT COUNTS, ALONG COMES SOMEONE OR SOMETHING TO DISILLUSION US.

But if image is nothing and thirst is everything, why is not one of the ads here about thirst? Why are none of the ads about taste? Why are none of the ads about anything intrinsic to Sprite? Why does the famous-athlete sendup use Grant Hill, a famous athlete? Answer: As far as this advertising is concerned, image is not nothing. Image is everything.[1]

The story behind Sprite advertising illustrates the fascinating world of advertising. The power of advertising can be amazing. It is a creative marketing tool whose influence may go far beyond the marketer's intended purpose. This chapter explores the captivating world of advertising. The chapter begins with a general discussion of the purpose of advertising. Next, it outlines the stages in an advertising campaign and describes each stage. It examines communication goals and advertising objectives, creative strategy, media strategy, and the use of research to evaluate these strategies. Finally, the chapter closes with a consideration of ethics.

The Nature of Advertising

Chapter 15 defined advertising as a persuasive message carried by a nonpersonal medium and paid for by an identified sponsor. This definition indicates two basic parts of advertising: the message and the medium. The two work together to communicate the right ideas to the right audience.

Advertising promotes goods, services, and ideas in mass media, such as television, radio, newspapers, and magazines, to reach a large number of people at once. It serves as a substitute for a salesperson talking to an individual prospect. Advertising is one-way communication and, unlike a salesperson, cannot receive direct feedback and immediately handle objections.

Advertisers, who must pay the mass media to present their advertisements, or commercials, control the exact nature of the one-way message that will be communicated to the target audience. The impersonal nature of advertising also allows marketers to control the timing and degree of repetition that are necessary. These features often provide benefits that far outweigh disadvantages associated with lack of feedback.

Marketers of soft drinks, cosmetics, soaps, and many other products that do not require direct and immediate feedback often rely heavily on advertising. For these marketers, the challenge is to present messages effectively to an audience that may not be interested in seeing or hearing them. They must contend with readers who quickly turn the magazine page or viewers who tape-record television programs and then fast-forward through commercials. They must cope with competitors that use advertising to compare brands. Because of these demands, advertising is often highly creative and innovative.

We all recognize and appreciate creative advertising. You probably remember a humorous Diet Pepsi commercial or dramatic Nike commercial that grabbed your attention. You may even have talked to your friends about some advertising you liked. Creative advertising can stimulate people to talk about products, services, and ideas. This word-of-mouth communication may be one of the most effective means of communicating a message to prospective customers. Advertising's power to influence word-of-mouth communication can be a great asset to a marketer.

Advertising supports other promotional efforts. It may communicate information about a sales promotion or announce a public relations event. Advertising helps the salesperson "get a foot in the door" by preselling prospects. A salesperson's job can be made much easier if advertising informs the prospect about unique product benefits or encourages prospects to contact a salesperson. Without advertising, the salesperson's efforts may be hindered by the prospect's lack of knowledge about the company or its products.

Advertising can be subdivided into many different categories. A very basic scheme classifies advertising as product advertising or institutional advertising.

PRODUCT ADVERTISING

Advertisements for Pert Plus shampoo/conditioner, Garth Brooks concerts, Hilton hotels, Lego building blocks, and many other brands are clearly intended to persuade consumers to purchase a particular product—indeed, a particular brand. These are **product advertisements.** An advertisement for Ford trucks that declares "Ford trucks—the best never rest" and suggests that viewers go down to the local Ford dealership is a product advertisement because it features a specific product.

If the Ford advertisement goes on to recommend that viewers go to the showroom for a test drive during an inventory reduction sale—that is, suggests an immediate purchase—it is also a **direct-action advertisement,** or *direct-response advertisement.* Many television advertisements and many direct-mail efforts are of this type. An increasing number of these involve direct marketing, which includes both direct-action advertising and a direct channel of distribution. For example, record companies frequently urge consumers to order special albums by calling a toll-free number and using a credit card. The Book-of-the-Month Club mails announcements of its latest offering to club members' homes and includes a return envelope so that the customer can order the latest selections. Direct-action advertisements, in general, utilize coupons, toll-free telephone numbers, or invitations to call collect in order to facilitate action and encourage people to "buy now." Much retail and Internet advertising emphasizes direct action.

BECAUSE WE'LL RECYCLE OVER 200 MILLION PLASTIC BOTTLES THIS YEAR, LANDFILLS CAN BE FILLED WITH OTHER THINGS. LIKE LAND, FOR INSTANCE.

We can't make more land. But we can do more to protect what we have. In fact, this year Phillips Petroleum's plastics recycling plant will process over 200 million containers. This effort will help reduce landfill waste and conserve natural resources. And that will leave another little corner of the world all alone. At Phillips, that's what it means to be The Performance Company.

PHILLIPS PETROLEUM COMPANY

For an annual report on Phillips' health, environmental and safety performance, write to HES Report, 16 AT-PB, Bartlesville, OK 74004, or visit us at www.phillips66.com.

Less assertive forms of product advertising are designed to build brand image or position a brand for an eventual sale rather than to sell merchandise right this minute. For example, consider an advertisement portraying the romance and adventure of Jamaica. The advertiser knows that the consumer is not going to run directly to a travel agency after seeing such an advertisement. The objective is to provide information so that the next time the family is considering a vacation, Jamaica will be among the spots considered. Such so-called **indirect-action advertisements** use a soft-sell approach calculated to stimulate sales in the long run.

INSTITUTIONAL ADVERTISING

Institutional advertisements aim to promote an organizational image, to stimulate generic demand for a product category, or to build goodwill for an industry. "Baseball fever . . . catch it" is an institutional advertising slogan. So is DuPont's "Better things for better living" and United Artists' "Escape . . . to the movies." These institutional advertising slogans do not stress a particular ball team, brand, or movie. Instead, they accent the sponsoring institutions. The baseball advertise-

---

Product advertisement
An advertisement promoting a specific product.

Direct-action advertisement
An advertisement designed to stimulate immediate purchase or encourage another direct response; also called a *direct-response advertisement.*

Indirect-action advertisement
An advertisement designed to stimulate sales over the long run.

For some years, Phillips Petroleum has been running institutional advertising to call attention to its involvement in worthwhile community projects and to tell consumers about its lesser-known activities beyond oil exploration and refining. The company's intent is to demonstrate that it is socially responsible and productive. It hopes to promote goodwill and increase investment in the company. The ad shown here and similar advertisements are aimed at people's roles as citizens, investors, and voters, rather than their roles as buyers.

www.phillips66.com

Institutional advertisement
An advertisement designed to promote an organizational image, stimulate generic demand for a product, or build goodwill for an industry.

ment, for example, attempts to build demand for the sport as a whole. The advertisements paid for by DuPont and United Artists stress how wonderful, responsible, or efficient those companies are. Contrasting the "baseball fever" slogan with such team slogans as "Royals baseball. You've got a hit on your hands" or "Wrigley Field—there's no place like it" makes the difference between institutional advertising and product advertising quite clear. Institutional advertising is often part of a larger public relations effort. (See Chapter 18.)

Planning and Developing Advertising Campaigns

Developing an effective advertising campaign requires a stream of interconnected decisions on such matters as budgeting and media, as well as a strong creative strategy. The process followed in planning and developing an advertising program is shown in Exhibit 16-1. The activities involved in the process are discussed in the following sections.

As you've seen throughout this book, goals and objectives must be established before work on specific plans and actions is begun. This relationship between objectives and plans holds true for advertising. Before developing a single advertisement, management must ask what the advertising is expected to do.

Of course, advertising is supposed to sell the product. That statement, however, is too broad to be truly useful to marketing planners. Advertising is, after all, only one element of the marketing mix. It affects and is affected by the product, the price, the packaging, the distribution, and the other elements of promotion. All these elements combine to sell the product; advertising does not do the job alone. Regardless of the appeal and longevity of advertising campaigns, such as those of De Beers diamonds, BMW, or United Airlines, successful advertisements do not stand by them-

e x h i b 16-1

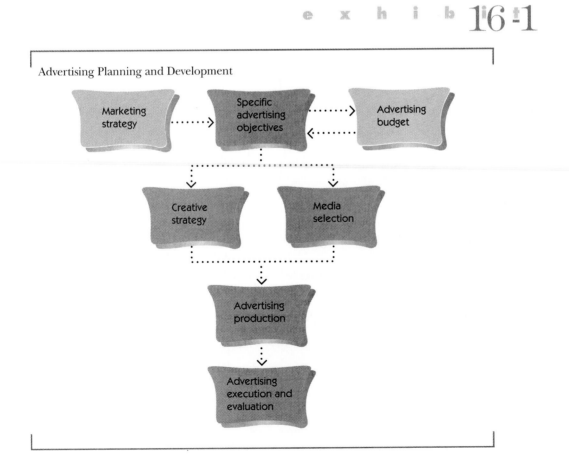

Advertising Planning and Development

selves. Effective advertising campaigns are developed as part of an overall marketing strategy and are tightly coordinated with the other facets of the promotional mix.

COMMUNICATION GOALS FOR ADVERTISING

What are appropriate goals for advertising? Because advertising is a method of communication, objectives directly related to advertising should be **communication goals.** In general, advertisers want to accomplish four broad communication goals: Advertisements are expected to generate attention, to be understood, to be believed, and to be remembered.

Communication goals
In the context of marketing, what the marketer wants a promotional message to accomplish: to gain attention, to be understood, to be believed, and to be remembered.

ADVERTISEMENTS ARE EXPECTED TO GENERATE ATTENTION, TO BE UNDERSTOOD, TO BE BELIEVED, AND TO BE REMEMBERED.

These goals relate to selling the product, but they are primarily matters of communication.

If these broad communication objectives are not considered and met, more specific objectives will not be met either. For example, if no one pays attention to an advertisement, the advertisement cannot achieve its more specific objective of, say, enhancing a romantic brand image. Likewise, an advertisement must be understood and believed if it is to reinforce or change perceptions and attitudes about a brand's characteristics. And if it is not remembered, an advertisement will have little effect on buyer behavior. With these broad objectives in mind, marketers developing advertising campaigns can set more specific objectives.

SPECIFIC ADVERTISING OBJECTIVES

Encouraging increased consumption of a product by current users, generating more sales leads, increasing brand awareness, increasing repeat purchases, and supporting the personal selling effort are typical specific objectives for advertisements. As Exhibit 16-1 illustrates, these objectives are developed from the marketing strategy and provide the framework for creative strategy and media selection.

Many advertisements have disappeared from the media, even

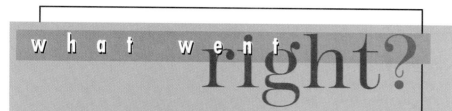

Snickers A Snickers television commercial is set in a football locker room, where a gruff, crew-cut head coach announces, "Listen up. This year we gotta be a little more 'politically correct' with the team prayer. [He turns to a priest, standing behind him.] Hit it, Padre."

"Let us take this moment to look inside and reflect on our good fortune," the priest says, but before he can go on, the coach butts in to introduce a second clergyman. "All right, Rabbi. Let's go."

"And may victory be with you," the rabbi says, before he too is cut off.

"Come on Shaman, let's move. [This time it's a Native American spiritualist, who utters one word, 'Minika.'] That was very touching. Come on, Bagwan."

Then, as the Indian mystic steps to the fore, the voice-over says, "Not going anywhere for a while? Grab a Snickers." Which one of the kneeling players does, as the Eastern Orthodox priest, black preacher, Hare Krishna, et al. wait for their turns. "Stay in line, no pushing" the coach tells them.

As the title card fills the frame, we hear the team chanting its mantra: "Ommmmmmmmmmm. . . ."

As funny as this gentle satire of diversity fever is, it pales next to the one about the end-zone painter, an elderly Chiefs employee whom we see painstakingly reproducing the team logo beneath the goalposts. As he steps back finally to admire his work, a player walks up behind him.

"Hey, that's great," says the lineman, "but who are the Chefs?"

Yeah, he left out the "i," which is amusing, but his reaction is hilarious.

"Great googily moogily!" he says. Then, he consoles himself with a Snickers bar as he contemplates starting from scratch. The player tries to help.

"You spell it . . ." But the old guy just snarls "Yahhhh!" and takes another bite. Yahhhh. It's not even a word, and you have to hear it to appreciate it.[2]

These two commercials are part of the Snickers "Not going anywhere for a while? Grab a Snickers" advertising campaign. The ads may be taken simply as comedy for comedy's sake, but beneath the jokes is a very serious selling proposition: what to eat when there's no access to real food. Therein is the big promotional idea.

though "everybody liked them," because they did not contribute to accomplishment of specific objectives. For example, almost everyone who saw it enjoyed a unique television advertising campaign featuring a fictitious (off-screen) giant armadillo that rambled across the Lone Star State, terrorizing Texans in its quest to satisfy its unquenchable thirst for Lone Star beer. Texans loved to talk to friends about the exploits of the state's favorite animal. However, the advertisements, while humorous and attention-getting, did not sell the product. Because the ultimate objective is to sell the product, the advertisements were changed. A "great" advertisement that does not contribute to success in increasing market share, introducing a new product, or the like is only great in the creative sense. In the business sense, it is far from great.

Opportunities in the marketplace, competitive advertising campaigns, and prior marketing strategy decisions, such as selection of a target market segment, all influence the development of specific advertising objectives. An important influence is the product's stage in the life cycle.

ADVERTISING OBJECTIVES AND THE PRODUCT LIFE CYCLE

Advertising objectives change with environmental conditions, as do all other aspects of marketing. Marketing is dynamic; advertising, as one of its most visible components, must be especially reflective of change.

Once again, the concept of the product life cycle can be used to illustrate the changes. Exhibit 16-2 shows how advertising objectives change over the course of

exhib 16-2

Objectives Change over the Product Life Cycle

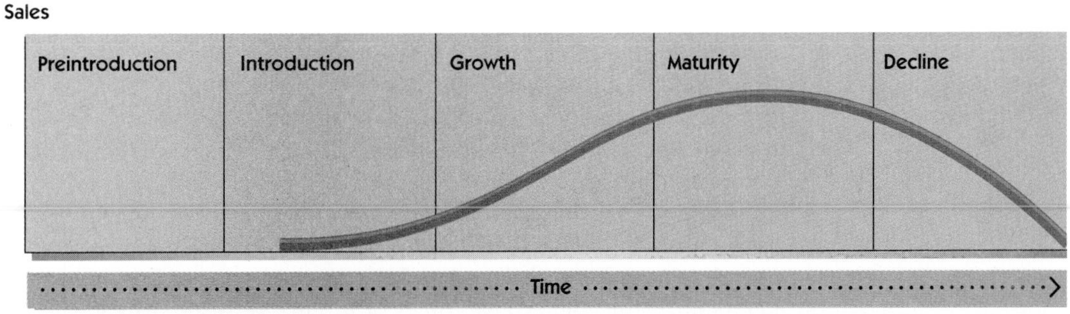

Sales

	Preintroduction	Introduction	Growth	Maturity	Decline
General promotional objective	Define objectives and plan promotional campaign	Develop product awareness, stimulate generic demand, and attract distributors	Create product acceptance and brand preference if there are competing products	Maintain and enhance brand loyalty; convert buyers and distributors of competing brands	Phase out product
Advertising strategy	Screen concepts, create advertisements, and plan media selection	Primary demand advertising to get potential purchasers to try product; trade advertising to introduce product	Extensive advertising expenditures emphasizing advantages of product and brand	Reminder and emotional advertising and promotions to promote repeat purchases and differentiate brands	Minimal advertising expenditures emphasizing low price to reduce inventory
Primary objective of message		Inform	Persuade	Remind	

Time

This AquafinA advertisement is a good example of an advertising campaign for a mature product. The advertisement does not explain anything about the product's characteristics. Rather, it reflects the psychological and emotional dimensions of the brand and consumers' enthusiasm for the product.

Take me to the water.™

Primary demand
Demand for a product class as a whole, without regard to brand; also known as *generic demand*.

Primary demand advertising
Advertising aimed at stimulating primary demand; also known as *pioneering advertising*.

a product's life. During the introductory stage of the cycle, developing consumer brand awareness and getting customers to try the product are normal advertising objectives. Trade advertising, which is aimed at attracting distributors and interesting them in carrying the product, is equally important, although less obvious, during this stage. Additional trade advertising may be developed later, with the objective of increasing the numbers of distributors and retail outlets.

At the start of the product life cycle, it may be necessary to develop **primary demand,** or *generic demand*, for the product—that is, demand for the product class as a whole. This kind of advertising, which often must be so basic as to explain what a product is and how it works, is called **primary demand advertising.** It seeks to introduce the product rather than to make brand comparisons. Advertising of this sort is also called *pioneering advertising*.

Advertising for a mature brand, such as French's mustard, may be aimed at regular, brand-loyal users. Its purpose is substantially different from that of advertising used to introduce a new product. Promotion to loyal customers requires a campaign designed to remind them of the product's image and of their satisfaction with the product; regular buyers do not need detailed information about the product. In the case of mature products, then, advertisers give relatively little emphasis to explaining product features. Messages become increasingly symbolic as the product "ages." Partly, this reflects the fact that mature products have found their niche in the marketplace. They have been positioned, either by marketers or by the competitive forces of the market itself, to appeal to smaller and more specialized market segments than when they were new and lacked intense competition.

An advertising campaign for a product in the maturity stage of the product life cycle may not explain anything about the characteristics of the product. Often the advertisements reflect the psychological or emotional dimensions of the brand or the situations in which it is consumed. For example, the essence of Campbell Soup's advertising is the emotional aspects of nurture and nourishment. One of its television commercials portrays a young girl's arrival at her new foster home. Overwhelmed, the child withdraws within herself—unable to speak until her foster mother brings her a steaming bowl of Campbell's soup. "My mommy used to fix me this soup," the child says quietly. The foster mother, fighting back tears, responds, "My mother used to make it for me too." The commercial closes with the woman and the child sharing memories.[3] Because most products on the market are in their maturity stages, much advertising emphasizes psychological benefits to differentiate brands. Such advertisements stress the reasons a brand is better than its competitors, instead of emphasizing the newness or uniqueness of the generic product, as is done at the start of the product life cycle. Advertising of this kind is called **selective demand advertising.**

The most commonly encountered advertising objectives for mature products may be summarized as follows:

1. Increase the number of buyers
   - Convert buyers of competing brands
   - Appeal to new market segments
   - Reposition the brand
2. Increase the rate of usage among current users
   - Remind customers to use the brand
   - Inform regular consumers of new uses
   - Enhance brand loyalty and reduce brand switching among current customers

After determining the advertising campaign's objective, marketing managers begin to develop a creative strategy and to select advertising media. These activities are interrelated. In fact, the interrelationship between advertisement and medium is so strong that it is often impossible to tell whether the selection of the medium or the development of the advertisement comes first. For the purposes of our discussion, we will first examine how marketers create and produce advertisements and commercials.

Creative Strategy

In advertising, the generation of ideas and the development of the advertising message or concept make up the **creative process.** Actually, creativity is necessary to all aspects of the marketing mix, but the term has come to be particularly associated with the people who actually develop and construct advertisements. Whether creative activity is based on information gathered by marketing research or on analysis by management, the basic thrust of an advertising message is developed primarily by the creative departments of advertising agencies.

Discussing creativity is a difficult task. It is possible to outline schematically the steps involved in the creative process, as illustrated in Exhibit 16-3. The role played by that elusive something called "creativity," however, can only be shown as a "creative spark." Advertising objectives provide a framework for creative efforts, but the creative spark is probably what makes an advertisement persuasive.

Selective demand advertising
Advertising aimed at stimulating demand for a particular brand.

Creative process
In the context of advertising, the generation of ideas and the development of the advertising message or concept.

exhib **16-3**

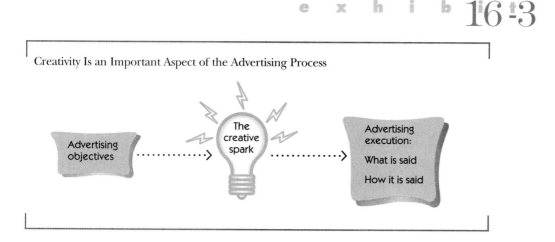

Creativity Is an Important Aspect of the Advertising Process

Advertising copy writers, art directors, and other creative people are responsible for the task of answering two questions: "What to say?" and "How to say it?" These questions reflect the two basic parts of the creative strategy.

"WHAT TO SAY?" AND "HOW TO SAY IT?" THESE QUESTIONS REFLECT THE TWO BASIC PARTS OF THE CREATIVE STRATEGY.

WHAT TO SAY—THE APPEAL

Advertising appeal
The central theme or idea of an advertising message.

The central idea of an advertising message is referred to as the **advertising appeal.** The purpose of the appeal, and of the advertisement, is to tell potential buyers what the product offers and why the product is or should be appealing to them. Thinking about advertisements you have seen will bring to mind the many kinds of appeals advertisers employ. It may be that the product offered has sex appeal, is compatible with the target customer's lifestyle (or desired lifestyle), or solves some particular problem such as "morning mouth," "medicine breath," or the need for healthy gums. Commercial messages that make firm promises, like "Never again will you have to weed your lawn, thanks to Jiffy Kill," are not uncommon. Many advertisers believe that specifically describing the answer to a problem in this manner is the most effective approach. Other advertisements are built around less straightforward appeals, such as cosmetic, beer, and hotel advertisements, that stress brand image.

When the same advertising appeal is used in several different advertisements to provide continuity in an advertising campaign, it is referred to as an **advertising theme.** The U.S. Army, for example, uses the theme "Be all that you can be" in its advertising to both high school dropouts and college graduates.

Advertising theme
An advertising appeal used in several different advertisements to give continuity to an advertising campaign.

To get a feel for how creative advertising appeals vary across an industry, it is useful to consider several brands of the same product and the advertisements developed for each.

The VISA credit card is positioned and advertised as the most widely accepted card. Advertising communicates the message that because VISA is accepted at more places, it is "Everywhere you want to be."

MasterCard takes a different approach, advertising itself as a smart payment service. For instance, one advertisement explains that if a MasterCard is stolen, the cardholder has to pay for only what he or she has bought—not what the thief has charged. Other advertisements appeal to consumers' emotions by discussing things the credit card cannot be used for. One MasterCard commercial shows a father and a son at a baseball game. It explains that tickets cost $28 and hot dogs, popcorn and soda cost $18, but "real conversation with an 11-year old is priceless." It then goes on to say "There are some things money can't buy. For everything else there's MasterCard."

The Discover card's appeal is different in that it stresses the fact that there is no annual fee for using Discover and that cardholders receive cash-back bonuses on purchases. Discover advertises, "People who really know money use the Discover Card. It pays to Discover."

Diners Club International's card uses the appeal "Rich in Rewards" as its theme. Its advertising points out that customers earn extra frequent flyer miles or other rewards each time they use the Diners Club International card to make a purchase.

American Express's advertising reminds viewers to "do more" with its card, which does not have spending limits. One advertisement has Jerry Seinfeld and Superman using the American Express card to help a shopper who has forgotten her wallet. Another shows a holder of the American Express card, who—unlike the users of its competitors—will never be embarrassed by a waiter saying that the card's credit limit has been reached.

The important thing to note here is that the advertisements for these products, as well as those for many others, feature different appeals. If every credit card company simply said, "Our credit card is more convenient than paying with cash," no brand's advertising would be unique or memorable. Creativity is responsible for this uniqueness.

But there's more to creativity than that. Many advertising appeals, such as the appeals for credit cards just described, are part of positioning promotional campaigns. Advertisers create these appeals so that consumers will perceive their brands as holding distinctive competitive positions. This strategy may be so successful that perfectly true claims made by the producer of one brand are not believable because of the competitive positions other brands hold in consumers' minds. Creativity, then, is more than an advertising tool. It is a competitive tool.

adapting to change

Sex Appeal   Be young. Have fun. Be sexy. Politically incorrect? Unabashedly. But, after several years of drab dress and neutered ads, consumers are craving a little levity. Bare asceticism in fashion is giving way to glamour: vibrant colors, coquettish skirts, corsets and bustiers that are bold enough to make Victoria's Secret blush.

Advertising, too, is loosening up. After a period when even fragrance marketers sublimated a sexy sell for one of self-affirmation, sex is creeping back into the lexicon. A model lip-synchs to the music of "I'm Too Sexy" in ads for the Head Over Heels fragrance; Brut Actif models are miming sex in a pool; and the Gianni Versace brand depicts woman as both dominatrix and mistress of her domain.

"We are dealing with a post-feminist moment in fashion, fragrance and a lot of areas," said Richard Martin, curator of the Metropolitan Museum of Art's Costume Institution. Observes psychologist and advertising consultant Carol Moog: "We've gone through this terribly serious period of time talking about sexuality, protesting it to the point where you have to deal with the existence of all levels of sexuality and all the pain that comes with it. To deal with the trauma you need to go through stages of healing. One helpful stage is playfulness."

A recent University of Chicago study on sexuality presents a culture more monogamous and less experimental than previously thought. "The majority of Americans approve of sex outside of marriage but in a relational context with love," said Edward Laumann, the University of Chicago sociologist who headed the research team. "That's why sex sells. It's appealing to everybody. But it's a turnoff if an ad emphasizes the casualness of sex and the promiscuity implied in it."

From an advertiser's perspective, the trick is to keep the mood of the advertisements playful. For example, a TV commercial for Diet Coke shows female office workers making sure they get a good look at a shirtless window washer.

"The wave of the future is if you have to use sex in advertising, it will be the men who are the sex objects," predicts Jordache Director of Advertising Kaaryn Denig, who created the commercial. "Woman are comfortable with and allowed to show appreciation for a man's body without being stereotyped in a negative sense. But there's a sense of humor."[4]

HOW TO SAY IT—EXECUTION OF THE APPEAL

Even when a copy writer or artist has an important and meaningful message to relate, its effect can be lost if it is not presented in the right way and in the right context. Marketing research can help in this regard. For example, an advertising agency's research indicated that many women who buy frozen dinners lead hectic lives and, because of time constraints, have trouble coping with everyday problems. So far so good. On this basis, advertising was developed for Swanson frozen dinners showing a rundown woman flopping into a chair just before her family is to arrive home demanding dinner. Suddenly realizing that she has a problem, the woman gets the bright idea of cooking a frozen dinner.

The problem was real enough, but the appeal was wrong. The last thing harried women want is to be reminded of how tired they are. Television viewers are fond of pointing out that married women in commercials are almost always peppy and well groomed even when they are doing the laundry or washing the floor. Advertisers use such images to focus the target customer's attention on the solution to a problem without making her feel like cursing the laundry or the dirty floor. Realizing this, Swanson changed its advertising appeal.

How to say something is as important as—and sometimes more important than—what to say. This is perhaps doubly true in advertising. The person delivering the message, the emotional tone, and the situation in which the action takes place all influence the effectiveness of the advertisement.

Although some advertisements are simple, straightforward statements about the characteristics of a product, creating advertisements that grab the intended audience's attention often requires some embellishment. Advertisements must say things to people both with and without words, and the creative spark clearly is vital to accomplishing this goal. The Suzuki motorcycle slogan "Suzuki—The ride you've been waiting for" tells the target customer something about the excitement of Suzuki motorcycles. "I'm stuck on Band-Aid, and Band-Aid's stuck on me" is a catchy phrase. The Hathaway man's eye patch is a symbol rich in meaning; so are the Marlboro man's cowboy hat and horse. One mark of the talent and success of creative individuals is that much of their work is so powerful that it can be used effectively in advertisements for decades. Many slogans, pictures, and other components of advertisements can be immediately identified with particular products by generations of consumers. Success depends on the creative person's ability to capture a feeling or fact with just the right phrase and the right symbols. Compare, for example, these common advertising phrases with the way they might have been written:

"Are you a saltaholic?"
"Is it possible that you ingest undesirable levels of salt?"

"Michelin—because so much is riding on your tires."
"Michelin tires are safe."

Creative platform
The style in which the advertising message is delivered; also known as *execution format*.

How an advertisement says something is its **creative platform,** or *execution format*. The creative platform is influenced by the medium that is used to convey the message. Obviously, a newspaper advertisement cannot duplicate the sound of a railroad train, but that sound might be used effectively in a radio advertisement. Determining how to communicate the message, then, is interrelated with selecting advertising media. Nevertheless, advertisers can present or creatively implement a basic appeal in a number of ways.

A Pizza Hut commercial spotlights a digitally reincarnated Elvis Presley singing to present the sales message. A Prudential Insurance company com-

The creative platform will be shaped by the medium in which the advertisement appears.

www.paramount.com

mercial tells a short story about a fellow who actually dies and goes to heaven. These two creative platforms are quite different. Decision making by the people assembling the advertisements about what creative platforms to select and how to use those creative platforms are part of the creative process.

Looking at some of the major creative platforms used in advertisements, especially TV commercials, helps put the creative strategies behind advertisements into perspective. The major creative platforms include storyline, product use and problem solution, slice of life, demonstration, testimonial and spokesperson, lifestyle, still life, association, montage, and jingle.

Storyline   The **storyline creative platform** gives a history or tells a story about the product. For example, initial advertising for the Saturn automobile told the story of how a town, a company, and its employees were changed when General Motors made the decision to build a new kind of automobile. Similarly, certain European vacation spots are shown in all their historical glory from the Middle Ages to the present.

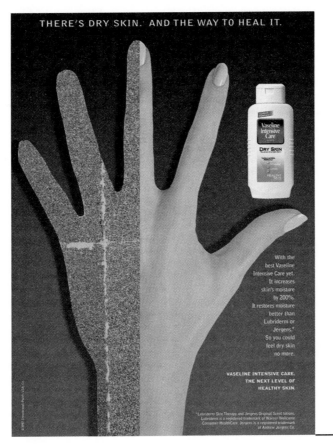

THERE'S DRY SKIN. AND THE WAY TO HEAL IT.

Problem-solution advertisements like this one straightforwardly describe how to solve a problem. The Vaseline Intensive Care advertisement shown here tells how the lotion, brimming with moisturizers, heals and restores dry, thirsty skin. The product's benefit is clearly presented as the solution to the problem.

www.unilever.com

In television commercials that use the storyline creative platform, unseen announcers (in a technique called *voice-over*) often narrate stories with recognizable beginnings, middles, and ends. Some copy writers attempt to make the product the "hero" of the story.

Product Use and Problem Solution   Straightforward discussion of a product's uses, attributes, benefits, or availability is a creative platform frequently utilized in advertising. A unique selling proposition, discussed in Chapter 15, is the central focus of such an advertisement. Comparatively simple advertisements for products ranging from Crest toothpaste to Texaco gasoline explain uses of the product and how the product can solve a problem. Crest toothpaste fights tooth decay. Texaco gas stops your car from "pinging." A maker of exercise equipment may point out that being fat and out of shape is a problem ("Your chest doesn't belong on your stomach") and may show that its product is a solution to the problem.

Slice of Life   The **slice-of-life creative platform** dramatizes a "typical" setting wherein people use the product being advertised. Most of these commercials center on some personal, household, or business situation. A seventh-grade romance that isn't a secret thanks to AT&T communications, an attractive neighbor going next door to borrow some Taster's Choice coffee, and two homemakers talking about a laundry problem are examples of slice-of-life advertisements.

The slice-of-life commercial often begins just before a character discovers an answer to a problem. Whether the trouble is dandruff, bad breath, or not being home for a holiday, emotions are running high. The protagonist may know of the problem or may be told about it by another character. The product is then introduced and recommended, and the needy person gives it a try. Just before

Storyline creative platform
An advertising creative platform that gives a history or tells a story about a product.

Slice-of-life creative platform
An advertising creative platform that dramatizes a "typical" setting wherein people use a product.

the end of the commercial, we are told—and, indeed, we can see for ourselves—that the new user of the product is now satisfied, a happier person. This creative platform is most common in TV commercials, but similar real-life stories can be developed in print media through the use of a series of pictures and in radio advertisements through the use of character voices. The slice-of-life creative platform is essentially a dramatized variation on the problem-solution creative platform.

Demonstration creative platform
An advertising creative platform in which a clear-cut example of product superiority or consumer benefits is presented.

Infomercial
A television commercial, usually 30 minutes long, that has the appearance of a program.

Comparative advertising
A type of demonstration advertising in which the brand being advertised is directly compared with a competing brand.

Demonstration   Certain products lend themselves to a **demonstration creative platform.** For example, a Master Lock advertisement in which bullets are repeatedly fired into a lock that does not open is suspenseful and self-explanatory. The demonstration creative platform makes its sales pitch by showing a clear-cut example of how the product can be used to benefit the consumer. It does this by either dramatically illustrating product features or proving some advertised claim. The Master Lock advertisement certainly seems to prove that product's claim to toughness.

Unusual situations, occasionally bordering on the fantastic, can draw attention to product benefits. A mosquito sucks a Tabasco eater's blood and explodes in a television commercial for E. McIlhenney's Tabasco Sauce. The novel situation draws viewers' attention and illustrates that Tabasco sauce is hot stuff.

Many demonstrations occur in **infomercials.** Infomercials are television commercials, usually 30 minutes long, that have the appearance of regular programs, such as cooking shows or talk shows. The product is repeatedly demonstrated on the infomercial. Often, telephone numbers are flashed on the screen so that the viewer can order the item.

Comparative advertising, which directly contrasts one brand of a product with another, is a form of demonstration advertising. In a comparative advertisement, the sponsor's product is shown to be superior to other brands or to Brand X in a taste test, laundry whiteness test, toughness test, or other appropriate contest. This creative platform is somewhat controversial on two counts.

First, some advertisers believe that calling attention to another company's brand helps that competing product by giving it free exposure. Certainly, the competing brand receives some attention, but this fact itself can be advantageous. Brands that do not have a high market share are intentionally compared with the best-known products to suggest that the two brands are equal. Pepsi, the challenger, thus urges comparisons with market leader Coke. For example, in one television commercial, delivery-truck drivers for both Coca-Cola and Pepsi-Cola order a meal at a diner. The Coca-Cola driver offers his competitor a sip from his Coke can. The Pepsi driver takes a sip, returns the Coke can, and then offers the Coke driver

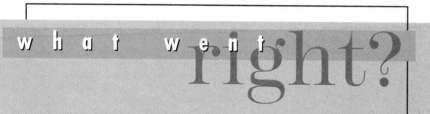
w h a t   w e n t   right?

Scotch-Brite Never Rust Soap Pads   Comparative advertising doesn't have to be scientific and dull. Scotch-Brite Never Rust soap pads from 3M associates its competitor Brillo with a dinosaur to illustrate its brand's quality.

"Steel wool," intones a voice-over in a television commercial, "a creature from a prehistoric age. . . ." On the screen, the viewer sees a steel wool pad metamorphose into a Tyrannosaurus Rex. ". . . Terrorizing us with splinters [the Tyrannosaurus Rex shakes itself, and thousands of steel fragments fly off like shrapnel], dripping with rust [the stalking dinosaur leaves a disgusting trail of rusty, sooty water]."

"Enter a superior species," the voice-over continues, "the new Scotch-Brite Never Rust soap pad. [Here the viewer sees the product in action, scouring grimy pots and pans.] It's made from an innovative fiber that never rusts or splinters, and no steel wool pad cleans better. The old dinosaur is history." [Now the Tyrannosaurus Rex melts like the Wicked Witch of the West in a ruddy puddle and is wiped away with a Scotch-Brite pad.][5]

a sip of his Pepsi. After the Coke driver takes a single sip of Pepsi, he wants more. He refuses to return the Pepsi, causing a commotion at the diner.

This commercial suggests a second point of controversy: Some people do not feel that such comparisons are fair or sporting. On the whole, however, advertisements using the direct-comparison creative platform have been increasing in number in recent years. The Federal Trade Commission, believing that honest comparisons will help the consumer to make choices, has supported this trend.

Testimonial   **Testimonials** and endorsements show a person, usually a prominent show business or sports figure, making a statement establishing that he or she owns, uses, or supports the brand advertised. The idea is that people who identify with the celebrity will want to be like that person and use the same product. Alternatively, the advertiser hopes that consumers will see the endorser as an honest person who would not lend his or her name to a product that is not good. Testimonials may also use speakers who, by virtue of their training or abilities, are seen as "experts" on the products being advertised.

A variation on the testimonial appeal is the use of a **spokesperson.** The spokesperson represents the company and addresses the audience directly, urging them to buy the company's product. Shaquille O'Neal is a spokesperson for Reebok. Reebok hopes that people who admire and trust "the Shaq" will associate his personable, warm, and humorous manner with its products. The spokesperson, often the commercial's central character, need not be a real person. The Poppin' Fresh Dough Boy for Pillsbury and the Keebler elves are well-known animated spokespersons.

Lifestyle   The **lifestyle creative platform** combines scenes or sequences intended to reflect a particular target market's lifestyle. Soft-drink and fast-food advertisements, as well as those for many other consumer goods, frequently show product users in a sequence of daily activities. Young people might be shown enjoying some weekend

Mountain Dew advertisements often show young people engaging in extreme sports such as skateboarding. The lifestyle creative platform combines scenes or sequences intended to reflect a particular target market's lifestyle.

www.pepsiworld.com

Testimonial
A type of advertising in which a person, usually a well-known or public figure, states that he or she owns, uses, or supports the product being advertised.

Spokesperson
A person who represents an advertiser and directly addresses the audience to urge them to buy the advertiser's product. Using a spokesperson is a variation on the testimonial.

Lifestyle creative platform
An advertising creative platform that reflects a target market's lifestyle or hoped-for lifestyle.

Honey & Bacon French

The still-life creative platform portrays the product in a visually attractive setting. This advertisement for Hidden Valley Honey & Bacon French salad dressing cleverly portrays the product's ingredients inside a bottle.

www.hiddenvalley.com

Chevy Trucks   There are good ideas. And then there are the kind of ideas that can lift a multibillion-dollar-a-year international corporation out of its doldrums. Ideas that can rebuild not just an image and a product but the morale of the army of employees who produce it as well.

This is the story of one of those ideas, and how it transformed the image of Chevy trucks with three notes and three words from a minor hit record by Bob Seger. The words are now legendary in the world of advertising and in the hallways of General Motors.

There, "Like a Rock" is not only the song that propelled one of the most successful and longest-lasting campaigns in automobile advertising, it's a three-word mission statement for the entire truck division.

When the ads began in 1991, you probably didn't think of Chevy trucks as being at all like a rock. Chances are pretty good you do now.

In that first ad, there were just 60 seconds of Chevy trucks being abused by heavy loads, muddy roads, bad weather, construction crews, ranchers, and a 1,500-pound prize bull. And, of course, Seger with his throaty, quarter-million-miles of wear-and-tear vocals proclaiming, "I was strong as I could be, nothin' ever got to me. . . . Like a rock."

The spot contained no performance stats, no product sell, and barely a mention of the vehicle it was pitching. But things have been looking up for Chevy trucks ever since. "Stood there boldly . . ."

Yet had it not been for an old record collection, a mysterious autoworker in a Detroit restaurant and a California carpenter known only as "Fred," it might never have happened.

[In 1990], Chevrolet was "in a battle for our very survival," says the company's Jeff Hurlburt. Sales were down, factories were shutting. Don Gould of Campbell-Ewald Advertising had to find a way to bolster the Chevy truck line, which accounts for well over half of all Chevrolet sales. The research said that Chevy trucks performed well and were viewed as good-looking, but wimpy. "We were perceived as the least dependable, least durable," says

R. M. "Mac" Whisner, manager of Chevy truck advertising. "We sought to reverse that."

Gould and his colleagues had two advertising campaigns ready to test, but he didn't like either. Desperate, he spent a weekend hunting through his music collection looking for inspiration.

"I was lying on my family room floor," he says. "I had this old tape of Seger's. . . . Right on the cover, it said, Like a Rock, and I thought, 'That is exactly what we need.'"

Gould patched together a mock-up commercial using old videotape with the song and rushed it to California for a focus group test, which is where Fred comes in. In the taped interviews before the presentation, Fred is the most vocal critic of American trucks. He considers them shoddy. After viewing the commercial, though, Fred is a changed man. "You got me!" he shouts.

He and the rest of the group say there is no way they could ever buy another truck without at least looking at a Chevy. "Good old Fred sold this," says Gould. "When he talked about goosebumps, we knew we had a hit."

They got the same response from every test they did. They didn't just have a great commercial, they had one that was making audiences stand up and cheer. The only problem was they didn't have the right to air it. In the rush to put the test commercial together, there had been no time to acquire the rights from Seger, and when they asked he turned them down. Flat. "That was a crazy time," says Gould. "We tried to get an audience with him . . . and nothing was working."

Seger, a work-a-day rocker with blue-collar Michigan roots, had not lasted to age 50 in the music business by bending easily nor doing anything that smacked of "selling out." "For the first six months, we just said, 'No!'" Seger says now. "We just didn't want to do any commercials."

Finally, Gould convinced Seger's manager, Punch Andrews, to watch the ad. After 15 seconds Andrews was convinced. "Punch came to me and said, 'I know I've been bringing you these commercials for years and you have always said no,'" recalls Seger. "But he said he

Still-life creative platform
An advertising creative platform that makes the product or package its focal point, emphasizing a visually attractive presentation and the product's brand name.

activity and topping off a perfect day with a Mountain Dew or a visit to Burger King. Thus, the enjoyable aspects of teenage life are shown in association with product usage. Important to such advertisements are the sorts of people actors portray.

Still Life   The **still-life creative platform** portrays the product in a visually attractive setting. The product or package is the focal point of the advertisement. Reminder advertising often uses still-life creative platforms because the most important purpose of the message is to reinforce the brand name. Absolut vodka has used this creative platform with great success.

thought this one made sense. 'This is trucks,' he said. 'You drive them. It's very American.'"

But Seger was not swayed until one night when he was dining with his wife at a place called the Venue on Detroit's Woodward Avenue—once famous for drag races, burger joints and rock clubs. An autoworker came up to the table and politely asked Seger to do something to help the auto industry.

"I had just read about how GM had lost over $1 billion in a single quarter, and I thought if I could do something to help I would. My dad worked at Ford for 19 years. I worked a little while in the plants making transmissions," says Seger. The next day he called Andrews and told him to accept. But not before first checking to make sure the autoworker was legitimate, and not working for the advertising agency. No one will discuss the terms of the deal, though experts say a total of $500,000 to $1 million would not be unusual. "Felt like number one . . ."[6]

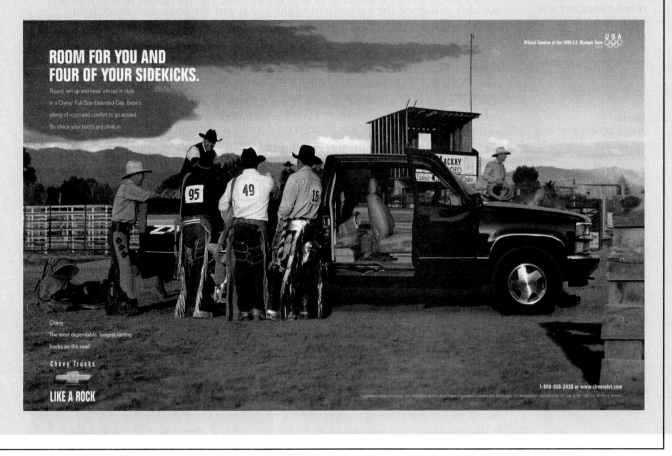

Association The **association creative platform** concentrates on an analogy or other relationship to convey its message. This creative strategy often "borrows interest" from another, more exciting product or situation. Thrilling activities, such as skydiving or windsurfing, and scenes of beautiful places, such as the coast of Maine or a mountain wilderness, are associated with a product in some way. The purpose of such analogies, which are often accompanied by music, is to create an emotional mood. Burger King, for example, has used popular tunes of the 60s and 70s as the primary element in commercials about its menu items. They link the good feelings associated with the music and Burger King. The psychological benefits of the product are communicated through the associations drawn by

Association creative platform
An advertising creative platform that uses an analogy or other relationship to stimulate interest and convey information.

COPY AND ART WORKING TOGETHER—THE AIDA FORMULA

Most advertisements, with the exception of radio advertisements, feature both copy and art. The two elements must work together to accomplish the communication objectives set by management. To ensure that copy and art complement each other, most advertisers follow a hierarchy of effects model known as the **AIDA** formula. AIDA stands for attention, interest, desire, and action.

AIDA

An acronym for *attention, interest, desire,* and *action.* The AIDA formula is a hierarchy of communication effects model used as a guideline in creating advertisements.

Attention An effective advertisement must draw the viewer's or listener's attention from the very first glance or hearing. Whatever follows will prove of little use if the member of the target audience has not first been influenced to pay attention to the message. Copy can be used to accomplish this, as when radio advertisements start out sounding like soap operas or mystery stories to draw attention. The copy can be enhanced by illustrations. Often a person representing the target customer is shown in situations that make the viewer think, "What's going on here?" or "What happened to these people?" For example, to attract the attention of luggage users, Samsonite luggage company has for years run advertisements showing suitcases falling out of airplanes or suitcases supporting automobiles that have flipped over on top of them. Humor is another attention-getting device, as the Focus on Global Competition feature illustrates.

focus on global competition

Translating British Humor for Americans While most Americans say they dislike advertising, polls show that the British seem to enjoy it. One reason, advertising people say, is the higher portion of humor and the softer sell in British ads.

Among the most popular figures in British advertising is a comic actor well-known to Americans: John Cleese, who is the spokesman for Schweppes soft drinks in the United States and Britain. Neither campaign bears any resemblance to the ads featuring the dignified, bushy-bearded Commander Whitehead; they were developed by David Ogilvy in the United States in the 50s and ran for 18 years.

The new, self-deprecating campaigns accept the notion that advertising is inherently silly. The British ads, which Mr. Cleese co-wrote . . . , begin with a voice-over in which he talks about the haggling that went on over his contract. He then appears on a beach flexing his biceps, in a parody of typically exuberant soft-drink commercials.

One of Schweppes's American ads . . . mocks British and American stereotypes. Mr. Cleese plays a stuffy British aristocrat who sips Schweppes by his fireplace and pontificates indecipherably. Then, dressed in shorts and a Hawaiian shirt, he takes on the Americans. He bursts through a Schweppes poster at a beach and lip-syncs to an ebullient voice-over that exhorts the viewer to "Buy a truckload today!"

This final version is more hyperactive than the original, Mr. Cleese says; in testing, American audiences did not recognize the parody.

"In England," Mr. Cleese said, "having someone scream out to buy something would be considered rude, and a bit vulgar." Advertising, he said, has its limits: "You can't sell in an advertisement. You can interest someone in a product by giving them a favorable association."[7]

Interest After the target consumer's attention has been attracted, the arousal of interest is next. If the attention-getter is powerful enough, interest should follow fairly automatically. However, it may be necessary to focus the viewers' or listeners' attention on how the product or service being advertised actually pertains to them.

Desire Immediately following the arousal of interest is the attempt to create a desire for the product. In a TV commercial for ChemLawn, the viewer first sees a homeowner carrying tools and bags of lawn chemicals. One of the bags breaks, and the exhausted do-it-yourselfer looks on helplessly. The viewer at home sees, however, that the unfortunate fellow's neighbor has a very nice-looking lawn but does not look harried or sweaty. Certainly he has no piles of spilled lawn-care products around his property. The viewer is interested in this story: Why is one fellow miserable while his neighbor smilingly pities him? The contented home-owner is a subscriber to the ChemLawn service, of course. The viewer is treated to some scenes of the ChemLawn man applying liquid lawn chemicals in one easy step. The ChemLawn people know what and when to spray—another load off the homeowner's mind. Thus, interest in and desire for the product are established in nearly simultaneous steps.

Action   Action is the last part of the AIDA formula. In the ChemLawn example, the commercial ends with a call to action. In effect, the advertisement urges viewers to phone the local ChemLawn dealer for an estimate of what it will take to make them as happy as the man who has a nice lawn with no effort. Thus, the means to act is provided. Usually, the advertiser makes the action seem as effortless as possible by giving a phone number or closing with a note that credit cards are accepted.

How the AIDA Formula Works   The AIDA formula is based on a consumer behavior theory that closely parallels the hierarchy of communication effects model discussed in Chapter 15. The formula describes consumers' behavior and serves as a guideline for creating advertising. AIDA makes good sense as an advertising tool and is widely known and followed.

Understand that it may not be possible for every advertisement to move the reader or viewer through the four stages to action with a single exposure. Repetition is usually necessary so that the advertisement's message can "sink in." Repetition also increases the chance that the target customer will see or hear the message at a time when there are no distractions. Finally, repetition recognizes the buyer's changing environment. The target buyer who has just been paid or has received a tax refund may perceive an advertisement that he or she has already seen in a different light. Eventually, if the advertisement is an effective one aimed at the proper people, buyers are likely to move psychologically through the AIDA stages and then act.

As we have already seen, developing a creative strategy and developing a media selection strategy are interrelated processes, and the planning of these activities occurs simultaneously. We now turn our attention to the selection of media.

Media Selection

Suppose you are about to open a retail store. You have already decided to have a Yellow Pages advertisement but are undecided about whether to use radio, television, or newspaper advertising as well. This choice is a matter of selecting a communication channel for your message. In making the choice, you are determining a **media selection strategy,** which must take into account the message you wish to transmit, the audience you want to reach, the effect you want to have, and the budget you have to support this effort.

Developing a media strategy requires answering two questions: "Which media will get the message to the desired audience efficiently?" and "What scheduling of these media will neither bore people with too-frequent repetition of the message nor let too many people forget the message?" Before we address these questions, let's look briefly at what the term *media* includes.

Media selection strategy
Plan for determining which media are most appropriate for an advertising campaign.

WHICH MEDIA?

Certain media lend themselves to certain tasks. If we assume, for the moment, that budget considerations can be set aside, certain factors become dominant in choosing the medium to carry a sales message. If demonstration or visual comparison of one brand with another is the goal, television becomes the most logical contender. If a lengthy explanation of sales points is required, print advertisements (magazines and newspapers) and the Internet come to mind. If consumers require a message to remind them of package identification or a short sales idea, outdoor advertising (billboards) makes sense. Thus, before a marketing planner starts thinking about what medium to use, he or she must know what is to be said. Once the marketer has decided what is to be said, attention can turn to which medium can best say it. Ultimately, several different media may be selected to carry the multiple messages the marketer wants to communicate.

Several media may appear to be able to do a particular job. When this is so, the marketing planner can narrow the choice by considering which media will hit the all-important target market. At this point, the media expert becomes a market expert. Knowing the target market—who the heaviest buyers are, what their demographic and psychographic characteristics are—leads to a determination of which media will deliver the message to these prospects. For example, a media planner in the insurance industry may be trying to target young males between the ages of 18 and 34; a European airline may be targeting well-educated, high-income men and women between the ages of 25 and 49; the primary customers for a sun-block cream may be youthful, fashion-conscious women. What media will reach each of these targets most effectively?

Mass Media   Most products can be related to a demographic profile. Data pertaining to mass media are geared to that same profile information. Thus, if the target audience includes men and women and it has been decided that television will do the best job and that the media budget permits such an expensive choice, the media planner may go for prime-time television—from 8 p.m. to 11 p.m. or 7 p.m. to 10 p.m., depending on the time zone. The next question becomes which television shows have audiences whose profiles most clearly match those of the target customers.

Careful analysis of any organization's marketing communication efforts might show that what appears to be the most appropriate advertising medium is, in fact, inappropriate. Where should one advertise a product like children's crayons? Saturday morning television shows, with their ability to show happy children drawing and coloring and with their excellent demographics, would seem to be an obvious choice. But when Crayola's marketing managers discovered that mothers were the prime factors in the purchase of crayons, they shifted a large portion of their advertising budget out of children's TV and into women's magazines, the Disney Channel, and family-oriented programming. The copy theme they developed to appeal to parents' nostalgia, "There is only one childhood. And only one Crayola," reflected the shift in audience and the new media strategy. The *Crayola Kids Adventures,* a family-oriented television program, was also used to reach children and parents at the same time.

The X-Files appeals to certain distinct demographic and psychographic market segments. An objective of a media selection strategy is to choose media that reach the desired segment.

www.thex-files.com

Each Medium Has Advantages and Disadvantages   Newspapers have the advantages of mass appeal within selected geographical markets, a general respect in the community, and a short lead time (that is, newspaper advertisements can be inserted, withdrawn, or altered quickly). Magazines have relatively long lead times but offer the advantages of selectivity of audience and far better reproduction of print and pictures than can be found in newspapers. Radio provides geographic and demographic selectivity because the programming of different stations attracts different sorts of listeners. Its lead time is short, and its usefulness in exposing listeners to frequent messages is obvious.

Television reaches a mass audience. However, specialization by type of show is possible. For example, *Moesha* appeals to preteens and teenagers; *Seinfeld* appeals to a range of young to middle-aged adults. Television allows advertisers to show and tell, because it can involve sight, sound, movement, cartoons, actors, and announcers. The strengths of television may be outweighed by its expensiveness. Cable television, with advertising rates lower than network television's, can be a good alternative for many products because it offers the advantage of greater psychographic selectivity. Even when the advertising rates for a particular program or station are relatively low, however, the costs to develop and produce a commercial keep many potential users away from TV.

adapting to change

Television in the 21st Century   Lately, there has been a lot of talk about phone companies merging with cable television companies to create interactive television systems. Fiber optics and telecommunications technologies will soon allow viewers to select from 500 channels. And consumers will not just receive programming; they will control it. Effective marketers are planning for a change from broadcasting to "narrowcasting" by which they will be able to direct fine-tuned messages to very specific groups of consumers. For example, an average commercial on the 24-hour golf channel may reach as few as 30,000 people, but it's highly likely that these viewers will be good prospects for golf shoes, clubs, and balls. And the viewers will be able to interact with their TV sets to place orders.

Furthermore, it is predicted that in the future television will not involve much real-time broadcasting but will consist of programs that are viewable on demand. The process by which this is expected to occur is called "broadcatching" and is possible because digital information does not need to be received in the same order in which—or at the same rate at which—it is consumed. Broadcatching will consist of asynchronous transmission of vast amounts of digital information to computerized television sets. A set will be programmed to examine the transmissions and save the few programs it concludes the household might choose to view at a later time.

Narrowcasting and broadcatching represent trends away from mass marketing. Such trends will have a tremendous impact on media selection strategies in the 21st century.[8]

WHAT SCHEDULING?

The **media schedule** is a time schedule identifying the exact media to be used and the dates on which advertisements are to appear. Media planners select not only the general media category (such as magazines and cable television) but also the specific media vehicles (such as *Sports Illustrated* and *Star Trek: Voyager*). Selecting the specific media vehicles requires advertisers to consider reach, frequency, and timing.

Reach—that is, the percentage of people exposed to an advertisement in a given medium—is an important factor in determining which media to use. Obviously, the advertiser wishing to reach the largest number of people in the target audience must take costs into consideration. A major aspect of the media selection job is making cost comparisons—evaluating whether, for example, *Sports*

Media schedule
A document identifying the exact media to be used and the dates on which advertisements are to appear; also known as the *media plan.*

Reach
The number of people exposed to an advertisement carried by a given medium.

You could read this whole magazine, or just call the new Jenny Craig.

NEW!

ABC

Program™

Jenny Craig®

1-800-448-6109

The media schedule is crucial for companies such as Jenny Craig. It is estimated that half of the weight-loss-industry diet-program business occurs between January and April.

www.jennycraig.com

Frequency
The number of times an advertisement is repeated in a given medium within a given time period, usually 4 weeks.

Illustrated has a lower cost per thousand readers than *Inside Sports*.

Another factor with cost implications is the repetition, or frequency, of the advertising message in a given medium within a given time period, typically 4 weeks. **Frequency** reflects the average number of times an average individual is expected to be exposed to an advertiser's message. An advertiser may decide to trade off reach for frequency. Placing two advertisements in *Forbes,* for example, may be more cost-effective than placing a single advertisement in *Fortune.*

Although cost is an important issue, strategy considerations may be equally important in choosing between reach and frequency. For example, frequency may be more important than reach when repetition will help the audience learn something new. If the advertising objective for a new brand is to establish awareness or to communicate a new product feature, the benefits of high frequency may outweigh the benefits of wide reach. Because the trade-off between reach and frequency is a complex issue, marketing managers often use marketing research to help them choose the best media schedule.

The timing of advertisements is another complex issue. Should advertising be spaced steadily throughout the year, concentrated in a particular season, or "pulsed" at regular or irregular intervals so that the company spends heavily during one period and then withdraws for a time? These are important questions, and they require a great deal of research and analysis by media planners.

In summary, the characteristics of advertising media vary greatly, and these variations play an important role in the marketing manager's choice of media. Most important of all, however, are the advertising objectives the marketer determined at the start of the advertising planning process. These objectives dictate which media will have the optimal impact. Then the choices regarding reach, frequency, and timing

MOST IMPORTANT OF ALL, HOWEVER, ARE THE ADVERTISING OBJECTIVES THE MARKETER DETERMINED AT THE START OF THE ADVERTISING PLANNING PROCESS. THESE OBJECTIVES DICTATE WHICH MEDIA WILL HAVE THE OPTIMAL IMPACT.

must be evaluated in terms of the realities of the budget. Cost is always a consideration in any organizational decision. However, careful and effective marketing planning can yield a communications effort that is both creative and successful.

Exhibit 16-4 highlights the general characteristics of several media. Today, U.S. advertisers spend more than $175 billion per year to place advertisements in various media.[9]

ELECTRONIC INTERACTIVE MEDIA

It has been said that "Computing is not about computers anymore. It is about living."[10] This observation certainly holds true with respect to the media people use to gather information and entertain themselves. This discussion of electronic interactive media will focus on advertising on the Internet, but the same principles apply to other media.

Interactive media allow an individual to seek information, ask questions, and get answers without the direct assistance of a human being. A company Web site is one of the most common forms of Internet advertising. For instance, The World of Clinique Web site offers on-line skin-type consultation. Consumers can find answers

Clinique
www.clinique.com

Advantages and Disadvantages of Selected Advertising Media

e x h i b 16-4

MEDIUM	ADVANTAGES	DISADVANTAGES
Newspapers	Geographic market selectivity Flexibility — easy to insert and change ads Editorial support (newspapers may write stories about paying advertisers)	Lack of permanence of advertising message Poor print/production quality Limited demographic orientation
Magazines	Demographic market selectivity Possibility of long life for ad Good print/production quality Editorial support	Lack of flexibility — difficult to make last-minute changes Limited availability Expensive, especially for color ads
Radio	Geographic and demographic market selectivity Flexibility Relatively inexpensive	Lack of permanence of advertising message "Clutter"—message may become lost in a group of several ads Lack of visual support Limited impact — radio is a background medium
Television	Advertiser can "show and tell"—demonstration is possible Geographic market selectivity Good market penetration because of large viewing audience	Lack of permanence of advertising message Expensive for national audience on major network Clutter Consumers videotape and skip ads
Direct mail	Highly selective Easy to measure results Lengthy copy possible Reader governs exposure	Expensive, especially on a cost-per-person basis Little or no editorial support Limited reader interest
Internet/interactive media	Easy to measure audience Lengthy copy possible Readers read and interact with what interests them Readers can request additional information Inexpensive, especially on a cost-per-person basis	Cannot reach consumers who have no access to Internet Difficult to gain advance knowledge of audience Not everyone has Internet access
Point-of-purchase materials	Promotes impulse buying "Sells" in nonpersonal selling environment Ties together product and ads	Difficult to obtain desired placements Clutter Limited creative possibilities
Directory (the Yellow Pages)	Permanence of ad High reach and frequency potential	Limited customer usage Market coverage limited to phone customers
Outdoor (billboards)	High reach and frequency potential Market selectivity High impact because of size Inexpensive	Message must be brief Image of billboards is poor in some markets Location choices may be limited

The initial idea for this table is based on William H. Bolen, *Advertising*, 2nd ed. (New York: John Wiley & Sons, 1984), pp. 601–602.

When a content provider, such as *Slate* magazine, publishes on the Web, it faces three challenges: how to get viewers to the Web site, how to get viewers to stay long enough to view the content, and how to get viewers to return.[11]

www.slate.com

to frequently asked questions about color and makeup and learn tips on topics such as sun protection. As the consumer interactively learns about skin care, she, of course, learns that Clinique cosmetic products are appropriate for her situation. Advertising on the Internet is ideal for consumers who want details about specific products. Interactive media can provide large amounts of information.

Of course, just because a company creates a Web site does not mean people will visit the site. When a content provider, such as *Slate* magazine, publishes on the Web, it faces three challenges: how to get viewers to the Web site, how to get viewers to stay long enough to view the content, and how to get viewers to return.[12] One way to get people to visit a Web site is advertising on another Web site. Advertising banners, another form of Internet advertising, are much like mass media advertising in the sense that a "space" is purchased on a search engine or on the commercial Web site of an information provider. However, banners are different because they are hypertext links to the advertiser's Web site. For example, a marketer of garden tools might work out an arrangement with the Yahoo search engine company to display its banner—which consists of a small flag-like rectangle—at the top of the results page whenever a user enters the key word "garden" as a search term. The advantage of this type of Internet advertising is that the audience has self-selected the topic so the marketer's message reaches an involved, highly targeted market.

Like many advertising banners, this one has a hyperlink.

Chapter 2 defined *push technology* as a means to deliver personalized content to a viewer's desktop. Computer software programs known as *smart agents* or *intelligent agents* find information without the user's having to do the searching and store that information—sometimes entire Web sites, complete with images and links—on the user's computer for later viewing.[13] Smart agent software that learns a user's preferences and searches out information is making advertising on the Internet and other interactive media more targeted and effective. Firefly makes recommendations about music, movies, and books by comparing one user's interests to the interests of his or her "nearest neighbors," other Firefly users who have similar demographics and interests.[14] Firefly also utilizes smart agents to make its selling of advertising "space" more attractive to its clients. Advertisers can have certain banners delivered to some target audiences, while other banner messages are served up to other users. An ad will appear only when someone with the appropriate demographics and entertainment preferences uses the service.

Firefly
www.firefly.com

TRUSTe   TRUSTe (www.etrust.org) is out to woo marketers and media companies to use the Internet equivalent of the Good Housekeeping Seal of Approval. Sites that pay to participate can display TRUSTe labels that describe how they treat personal data collected via registration forms. However, some concerns remain among privacy pundits and advertisers about the extent to which consumer information is really protected.

TRUSTe, which formed CommerceNet (www.commerce.net) and the Electronic Frontier Foundation (www.eff.org), has a mandate to promote electronic commerce by addressing privacy concerns among the online public.

"Privacy is one of the biggest impediments to electronic commerce, right behind security on most surveys," said Ira Machefsky, Vice President of Giga Information Group. "I think the TRUSTe initiative is an important one because the issue of what happens to information [on line] is of growing concern to individuals."

In fact, a recent study by Boston Consulting Group shows consumers hold businesses on the Net to a higher standard of privacy than real-world businesses. "I think this has to do with the fact that the Internet is mostly a visual, one-way medium," said Susan Scott, executive director of TRUSTe. "When you go into a store, you are subconsciously using all of your senses to determine whether you trust the place. . . . On the Net, basically a small, one-person business and a big, well-known company look exactly the same to the consumer."

TRUSTe evaluates sites' privacy policies based on data the owners of the sites volunteer as well as through personal interviews with Web site owners. The sites are then assigned to one of three categories: "no exchange"—no personal user data are collected; "1-to-1 exchange"—the sites collect user data for their own purposes but do not share them with third parties; and "3rd party exchange"—sites share the information with others. "1-to-1 exchange" sites are permitted to share user data—such as credit card numbers, names, and addresses—with business partners in order to complete transactions as long as the business partners agree not to collect the user data themselves, Ms. Scott said.

Participating sites will also be subjected to random audits. At launch, about 50 companies were participating in the program, including Excite, Four11, and America Online. Nine had signed on as "premier partner" sponsors, contributing $100,000 each, including AT&T and Netscape Communications. Some, however, question the organization's category definitions.

John Nardone, managing director of Modern Media, New York, said he understood the "no exchange" label to mean sites could not employ cookies to collect data from users' clickstream behavior, such as observing what pages in the site they visit, even if no personal data about the visitor are known. Ms. Scott said such anonymous cookies would indeed be acceptable under the "no exchange" label, "as long as no personal information, such as the user's name, was collected." She added that TRUSTe was currently updating its definitions.[15]

DIRECT MARKETING WITH DATABASES

Direct-marketing media, such as direct mail, can be very selective and can reach a clearly defined market, such as all families within a certain zip code area or all holders of American Express cards. But direct mail can also end up in the wastepaper basket.

Direct mail has been in existence for more than a century, but advances in digital technology have changed the nature of direct marketing in recent years. In particular, modern computer technology has improved the selectivity of this medium. Now computers can access databases to customize materials sent to different market segments and to personalize the message any individual consumer or household receives. For example, a personalized greeting may appear on a letter that, in addition to conveying an advertising message, indicates the name of a local retailer that sells the brand being advertised. If

the database records the ages of the children in households, an advertiser using direct marketing can send coupons only to those households with, say, children in diapers. Furthermore, if the database also indicates the brand of diapers a consumer regularly purchases, then an advertiser like Huggies can limit the mailing list to consumers who are loyal to Pampers or other competing brands.

Measuring the Effectiveness of Advertising

An advertiser about to commit more than $1,200,000 for a 30-second television commercial to be aired during the Super Bowl or for the development of a series of advertisements created especially for the Christmas season will want some way to measure the effectiveness of those advertisements. Measuring the effectiveness of advertisements in terms of the sales dollars generated is difficult. Despite that fact, several approaches to measuring effectiveness have been developed. These research techniques do not provide exact measures of effectiveness, but they do provide a systematic way of developing and testing advertisements to determine whether they are accomplishing the intended objectives. Advertising research may be divided into two phases: (1) the pretesting stage of developing and refining advertising and (2) the posttesting stage of evaluating its effectiveness.

DEVELOPING MESSAGES AND PRETESTING ADVERTISEMENTS

Effective marketers are reluctant to spend large sums of money running advertisements that have not been carefully pretested. Before advertisements are put on TV or in magazines, they may have gone through several stages of testing. The purpose of **pretesting** is to limit—or, even better, to eliminate—mistakes.

Pretesting may be conducted in the earliest stages of the development of an advertisement, and it may continue virtually until the advertisement is printed or broadcast. First, the basic appeal of an advertisement or of the concept around which it will be built may be tested. Then a headline, picture, or slogan may be tested. A "rough" version of the advertisement, featuring still photos in the case of a television commercial or a story acted out by nonprofessional actors in the case of a radio advertisement, can be assembled rather inexpensively and shown to a sample audience to measure appeal and believability. It does no good to create a funny, clever, or dramatic advertisement unless the impact of the advertisement comes through to the people it is supposed to affect.

Videotaping possible spokespersons for products and showing these tapes to panels of consumers to determine the appropriateness of the spokesperson is a worthwhile pretest. Consider, for example, the manufacturer of a hair-coloring kit that developed an advertisement featuring Raquel Welch endorsing the product. Tests of rough commercials showed that, although Welch was easily recognized and was perceived as an outstanding personality, she was not seen as an authority on the product or as a user of a home hair-coloring kit. The pretesting indicated

Pretesting
In the context of advertising, research carried out beforehand on the effectiveness of an advertisement. It begins at the earliest stages of development and continues until the advertisement is ready for use.

that, to enhance believability, advertisements for home-use products should feature "real people" rather than movie stars. Later research showed that, having reached middle age, Welch was perceived to be a very credible spokesperson for Bally Fitness Centers, because the target audience associated the need for fitness with movie stars of a "certain age" who must keep in shape.

Many of the marketing research tools discussed in Chapter 5 are used to pretest advertisements. Focus groups, discussions with consumers in malls, experiments, and other techniques can all be helpful. Rough or finished versions of television commercials may be shown in consumers' homes (in-home projector tests) or in specially equipped buses or trailers parked in shopping malls (trailer tests). After showing a commercial, advertisers use survey questionnaires or personal interviews to obtain viewers' reactions. No matter which method is used, pretesting attempts to evaluate the effectiveness of an advertisement before that advertisement is placed in the mass media.

POSTTESTING ADVERTISEMENTS

Once an advertisement has been developed and has run in the chosen media, **posttesting** should be used to determine if it has met the objectives set by management. There are many different objectives for posttesting and hence many kinds of posttests. To determine whether objectives have been met, posttests usually measure brand awareness, changes in attitudes toward the brand, or the number of inquiries generated about the product. Our discussion will focus on a few standard posttesting techniques.

Measuring Recognition and Recall   Because advertisers must gain the attention of buyers and have them remember the names of brands or the stores in which they can be found, many posttests are designed to evaluate recognition or recall. This is important even to advertisers of well-known brands, because advertisements for such products are intended to reinforce previously established good images. At the very least, a test showing that consumers remember particular advertisements gives advertisers a feeling that the money devoted to the campaign had some impact in the marketplace.

Recall tests can take many forms. For example, a telephone survey may be conducted during the 24-hour period following the airing of a television commercial to measure day-after recall. In such studies, the telephone interviewer first poses a question:

"Did you watch *60 Minutes* last night?"

what went wrong?

Reader's Digest   Begun in 1922, *Reader's Digest,* the world's most widely read magazine, sells nearly 27 million copies a month. Sold primarily by subscription, it is best known for its articles condensed from other publications.

For most of its history, *Reader's Digest* was a prosperous company, but operating earnings began falling in 1994 and kept falling for four straight years. Recently, the company indicated it was experiencing lower customer response to many of its promotional mailings in most markets. What went wrong?

Although the magazine accounted for only about 25 percent of the parent company's revenues, the world-famous brand was used as a "front door" to the company's books-and-entertainment unit, which used direct-mail promotions aimed at subscribers to Reader's Digest. The direct-mail promotions targeted magazine readers with premium-priced offers for glossy books on topics like home repair and gardening; specialty magazines such as *Family Handyman, New Choices, Walking,* and *American Health for Women;* audiocassettes; and videos. The typical promotion used a sweepstakes as a lure, and the strategy worked for many years. But customers started to complain about being bombarded with junk mail and grew tired of not winning the sweepstakes.

Many disgruntled customers cancel subscriptions to the flagship magazine. Hence, *Reader's Digest* must add 5 million new readers annually just to maintain its circulation of 27.5 million.

The view of the author Thornton Wilder appears to have gained currency. He described *Reader's Digest,* with its unremittingly positive tone, as "a magazine for bores, by bores about bores." Another view is that *Reader's Digest* is read mainly by "old folks and holy rollers." *Reader's Digest* products appeal primarily to a shrinking base of older readers. Adding to the company's problems is the fact that it has found it difficult to lure younger readers with the direct marketing methods and standard technologies it has used for years.[16]

Posttesting
In the context of advertising, testing that takes place after an advertisement has been run, to determine whether it has met the objectives set for it by management.

Recall test
In the context of advertising, a research tool used to determine how much people remember about an advertisement.

If the answer is positive, the next question might be

> "Do you recall whether there was a commercial on that program for an automobile?"

If the answer is again positive, the interviewer might ask

> "What brand of automobile was it?"

To this point, what has been measured is **unaided recall.** The interviewer gives no clue as to the brand of car advertised.

In an **aided recall** test, the questions might be phrased differently, as in these examples:

> "Do you recall the brand of automobile advertised? Was it an American compact car?"

> "I'm going to read you a list of automobile brand names. Can you pick out the name of the car that was advertised on the program?"

Aided recall is not as strong a test of attention and memory as unaided recall, but it still provides valuable information. After all, remembering the brand when you see it on the supermarket shelf may be all that is necessary.

Advertisers are also interested in **related recall**—the ability of a person who has seen an advertisement to repeat, or "play back," specific sales messages or images. Some advertisers set up booths in shopping malls and ask target customers to view one or more advertisements and then comment on or describe the advertisements. Researchers are thus able to determine which advertisements or portions thereof were most memorable to these subjects. This type of posttest allows researchers to determine if the advertisements accomplished their goals.

Another way to measure recognition involves showing an advertisement to a respondent and simply asking whether the respondent remembers having seen it before. If the answer is yes, the respondent is asked questions about particular portions of the advertisement. The Starch Advertisement Readership Service is a syndicated supplier of this type of information. It classifies readers into three types:

- "Noted" reader: A person who remembers having seen the advertisement in the magazine issue being studied
- "Associated" reader: A person who not only noted the advertisement but also saw or read some part of it that clearly indicated the brand or advertiser
- "Read most" reader: A person who read at least one-half of the written material in the advertisement.

Certainly, tests such as these are not perfect measures of recall and recognition. However, when they are conducted carefully, they provide marketing managers with helpful information.

Measuring Changes in Attitude about a Product   Effective advertisements can contribute to changing consumers' attitudes toward a brand. To measure and evaluate attitude change, researchers must record buyers' attitudes before and after they are exposed to the relevant advertisement. Thus, a two-part, before-and-after study must be undertaken.

For example, suppose a new Neutrogena advertisement states that Neutrogena hand cream has great powers to heal badly irritated skin on hands and feet. The effectiveness of Neutrogena's new advertisement can be measured by before-and-after surveys among target buyers. Suppose the results of the first survey show that few consumers know the product heals hands and feet. The new advertisement is now shown to a sample of these target buyers. A second survey is conducted after the advertisement has run. If the results of this survey show increased recognition of the product's healing properties, some measure of success in affecting attitude change is credited to the advertisement.

Measuring Inquiries about the Product   In certain situations, such as evaluation of one direct-mail piece versus another or evaluation of alternative Web pages, the generation of inquiries is a good measure of an advertisement's effectiveness. Advertisers of organizational products frequently count the number of inquiries generated by one magazine advertisement versus another to measure advertising effectiveness. Suppliers of such products often advertise in trade magazines that reach precisely those people and organizations most likely to be interested in their products. Many such advertisements include a phone number readers can call or a coupon they can return for additional information. Certainly, the number of calls or coupons the advertiser receives suggests how effective the advertisement was.

Inquiries usually come primarily from persons who are actually interested in the products being offered. Therefore, they are of particular use to marketing organizations whose promotional mixes include personal selling. Such organizations can use these inquiries to focus their sales forces' efforts on the customers most likely to buy. Thus, the number of inquiries provides a measure of an advertisement's pulling power, and the inquiries themselves are leads for the sales force.

SALES AS A MEASURE OF ADVERTISEMENT EFFECTIVENESS

After seeing some of the ways in which marketers try to measure the effectiveness of their advertising, you might ask, "Why not just use sales figures?" Unfortunately, this is easier said than done. Advertisers other than direct marketers have difficulty using sales as a direct measure of advertising effectiveness because many factors other than advertising influence sales. It is nearly impossible to separate the effects of the economy, the price, wholesaler and dealer activity, and so on from the effects of advertisements. Nevertheless, most marketers ultimately do use this measure, even if sales changes are not scientifically "proven" to result from advertising. Many popular and memorable advertising campaigns were removed from circulation when they did not positively affect sales.

Test marketing research and laboratory experiments designed to simulate sales behavior are the most sophisticated research tools available to evaluate advertising effectiveness when sales volume is the primary criterion. However, because advertising's effect on sales may not be immediate, even the most elaborate research may not establish a relationship between advertising and sales. Advertising researchers are constantly trying to improve techniques in this area because sales remain the bottom line for all advertisements. However, only in special cases, as when sales result from coupon or toll-free-number offers, will sales be a reasonably accurate measure of advertising effectiveness. Marketers must recall that research techniques intended to measure advertising's effects should be used carefully and with the understanding that they are usually very far from perfect.

Ethical Issues in Advertising

Social commentators frequently debate ethical issues concerning advertising.[17] We will discuss three of these issues: deceptive practices, public standards, and promotions aimed at children.

DECEPTIVE AND MISLEADING PRACTICES

Our society grants consumers the right to be informed and prohibits deceptive practices and promotions that intentionally mislead consumers. For example, consumers have the right to know how likely it is that they will win a contest or sweepstakes. State and federal regulations now require that the odds of winning such sales promotions be conveniently available to potential participants.

Misleading Advertising   Because of its direct effect on buyers, one area of particular concern is **misleading or deceptive advertising.** People feel strongly about this issue, largely because in almost all societies the truth is revered and lying is

Misleading or deceptive advertising
Advertising that leads consumers to inaccurate conclusions. Intentionally making false statements is an extreme case of deceptive advertising.

considered wrong. In the United States, the Federal Trade Commission Act of 1914 makes it illegal to run dishonest advertisements. Thus, laws and court cases aimed at ending the worst abuses have long been part of the American business scene.

Identifying what comprises misleading or deceptive advertising is not always easy. Although people disapprove of blatant deception and the legal system forbids it, hard-and-fast rules are difficult to develop and enforce. Consider the use of the terms "ozone-friendly," "biodegradable," "photodegradable," "recycled," and "recyclable" in advertising messages. When can a marketer honestly say that a product is conveniently recyclable? What constitutes proof of a claim that no chemical will migrate to the stratosphere and cause unnatural and accelerated deterioration of the ozone layer? Many contend that these terms, if used in advertisements, should conform to legal requirements.

Bait and switch
An advertising technique, usually associated with retailers, in which a product is offered at an extremely low price to attract customers, who are then told the product is unavailable and "switched" to a more expensive, higher-margin product.

Bait and Switch   Advertising that attempts to employ the tactic known as **bait and switch** offers another example of the difficulty in determining what is deceptive. The bait-and-switch technique involves advertising a product at an amazingly low price. Consumers, drawn to the store by the advertising, are "switched" to another, higher-priced item by salespeople who claim that the advertised item is, for some reason, no longer available.

Although this tactic is clearly deceptive, proving intentional deception is difficult. Would anyone claim that a salesperson should not try to sell an item that was not mentioned in the store's advertisement? What about the common sales tactic of trading up, whereby the salesperson tries to interest the customer in an item priced higher than the one the customer first mentioned? Because the marketing concept stresses honest attempts to create customer satisfaction, a salesperson might in good conscience point out a better, more expensive item. The question of the ethics of switching revolves around intentions and the actual availability of the product. Bait and switch occurs when a consumer cannot purchase the product because the marketer had no intention of selling it.

Puffery
The practice of exaggerating a product's good points in advertising or selling.

Puffery   Another gray area involves puffing. **Puffery** is the practice of stating opinions or making slight exaggerations, a practice that society in general considers harmless. Movie producers often publicize their films and publishers sometimes advertise their books by using puffery—who hasn't heard "the most exciting movie ever!" and "the funniest book you'll ever read"? Even though these are not provable statements, most would not favor banning them. But where does puffing stop and lying begin? Often, the Federal Trade Commission or a judge is required to make the final decision.

PUBLIC STANDARDS

Matters of law and ethics are frequently decided on the basis of public standards, or beliefs as to what is right and proper. Even more often, they are decided on the basis of what somebody thinks are public standards. Certain advertisements, such as the Calvin Klein perfume advertisements showing nude men and women in provocative poses, cause a stir because they challenge public standards or someone's ideas about public standards. But public standards are not always obvious. Try to decide what public standards dictate in regard to these marketing questions, for example:

- Should liquor advertising be allowed on television?
- Should minorities be portrayed in menial roles in television commercials?
- Should lawyers be allowed to send direct-mail materials to accident victims or their families in personal-injury and wrongful-death cases a week after the accident?

The public's sense of decency, then, is a tricky thing to deal with. Television networks are often accused of offering too much sex and violence. Groups condemn shows ranging from *The X-Files* to *South Park*. Other groups condemn the self-proclaimed TV watchdogs, saying no one should tell the American people what to do and "if you don't like it, you don't have to look at it."

Questions of public standards raise philosophical issues marketers must consider. Although the issues can be difficult, marketers can and do make choices. In many cases, marketers may decide to offend one market segment in order to satisfy the needs of another. Consider, as a case in point, the marketing of products such as Preparation-H. Clearly, many people find mass media advertising of this type of product offensive. Other segments of the population find the advertising perfectly acceptable. If the advertising for some product offends you, ask yourself if it would be acceptable to adults in another market segment who need the product.

PROMOTIONS AIMED AT CHILDREN

Marketing to children has always been an area of controversy.[18] Critics argue that advertising aimed at children fosters materialism, amplifies status inequalities, encourages the consumption of foods high in sugar and low in nutritional value, and induces conflict within families. They also maintain that children are especially susceptible to persuasion and that special protection should therefore be provided for them.[19] Others argue that children understand the purpose of commercials and must learn to be consumers. Marketing helps socialize them into the consumer role. Furthermore, parents—the ultimate arbitrators—have considerable influence on children, which they can choose to use to counteract marketers' influences.

Because of their importance to growth and health, food products sold to children are the focus of special concern. When, in a test market, General Mills advertised Mr. Wonderful's Surprise as "the only cereal with a creamy filling," consumer groups complained that the product, like other sweetened cereals, was not high in nutritional value. The cereal contained 30 percent sugar and 14 percent fat. General Mills argued, however, that the product should be considered as part of the child's total diet, not as an item "out of context."

We began this chapter by saying that advertising is a captivating topic. Now that you have read the chapter, you should recognize that marketers employ many different strategies and hold diverse opinions about how to manage advertising activities. This diversity exists in large part because advertising relies heavily on creativity. Careers in the advertising field can be fascinating indeed.

Ad Council
www.adcouncil.org

summary

Advertising is the promotional activity in which the art of marketing is most visible.

 Understand the purpose of product advertising, direct-action advertising, and institutional advertising.
Product advertising promotes the attributes, benefits, uses, and images of specific products. Direct-action advertising encourages immediate action. Institutional advertising promotes an organization or industry as a whole, stressing goodwill, image, and contributions to society, or stimulates generic demand for a product category.

 Differentiate between primary demand and selective demand advertising.
Primary demand, or generic demand, advertising promotes a product category without stressing par-

ticular brands. Selective demand advertising accents a particular brand.

3 *Discuss the stages in the development of an advertisement.*
Advertisements are developed in five basics steps: (1) setting objectives consistent with the marketing strategy and the advertising budget, (2) determining a creative strategy, (3) developing the advertising message, (4) formulating a media selection strategy, and (5) running the advertisements and measuring their effectiveness. Creativity is important throughout the process.

4 *Analyze the role of communication objectives in the advertising process.*
Because advertising must communicate with target markets, its communication goals must be clearly

defined. Effective advertisements must gain attention, be understood, be believed, and be remembered.

5 *Show how advertisements for a product are likely to change over the course of the product's life cycle.*
In the introductory stage, advertisements must help to develop primary demand for the product category by explaining what the product is and how it works, with little stress on brand name. In the growth stage, they seek to develop selective demand for particular brands and models. In the maturity stage, they stress product images or features that set the product apart from its competitors in order to maintain market share and enhance brand loyalty. During the decline stage, advertising efforts help phase out the product.

6 *Define advertising appeal and describe several commonly used creative platforms.*
The advertising appeal conveys information about product benefits to the target audience. After deciding what to say, the marketer must decide how to say it. Creative platforms include storyline, which features a story about the product or tells its history; product use and problem solution, which shows how a product can be employed to solve a problem; slice of life, which dramatizes how the product solved a particular problem; demonstration, which shows how the product is used; testimonial and endorsement, in which spokespersons attest to the product's worth; lifestyle, which links the product to the target customer's own lifestyle (or one the customer aspires to); still life, which focuses on visual aspects of the product; association, which draws an analogy to convey a message; montage, which blends a number of visual effects; and jingle, which is especially effective as a memory aid.

7 *Compare the advantages and disadvantages of various advertising media.*
Each medium has advantages and disadvantages. Magazines and newspapers, which permit the consumer to reread a message, are suitable for longer, more complicated messages. Magazines can reproduce pictures more clearly than newspapers. Radio seems best suited for reminders or other short messages for specific target groups. Television permits the use of music, motion, and color. Outdoor advertising is appropriate for short messages but may be limited in its reach. The appropriate mix of advertising media depends on the advertising budget and the advertiser's objectives.

8 *Explain how advertising effectiveness is measured.*
Pretesting evaluates effectiveness before an advertisement is placed in the mass media; posttesting determines if the finished version of the advertisement achieved its objectives. Sales are the ultimate measure of effectiveness, but the relationship of advertising to sales is difficult to measure.

9 *Discuss several ethical issues involving advertising.*
Our society grants consumers the right to be informed and prohibits deceptive practices and promotions that intentionally mislead consumers. Hence, deceptive advertising is illegal; but it may be difficult to identify. Questions about what public standards should be used in advertising may also present ethical dilemmas for marketers. Another issue involves advertising to children. Children are a special public, and there is disagreement about whether advertising aimed at this public is ethical.

key terms

questions for review & critical thinking

1. Indicate the advertising objective in each of the following instances:
   a. Macy's holds its Fourth of July sale.
   b. Sega advertises that its home unit would make a nice Christmas gift.
   c. "There is Hertz and not exactly."
   d. The California raisin growers promote raisins as a snack food.
2. When does advertising stimulate primary demand? When should it?
3. Watch several TV commercials, and determine the advertising objective of each one.
4. Identify three institutional advertisements and explain their purpose.
5. Identify some credit card advertisements other than those mentioned in the book, and compare them with the ones discussed in the book.
6. Does the AIDA formula have more relevance for the writing of advertising copy or the graphic aspect of advertising?
7. Describe the steps in developing a creative strategy.
8. What type of spokesperson would you hire to do a testimonial advertisement for each of the following?
   a. Campaign against alcohol abuse
   b. Campaign to encourage cigar smoking
   c. Campaign for high-quality luggage
9. Suppose you are the creative director for an advertising agency that has just landed the Cleopatra Soap account. You will be introducing the new brand to the market. Suggest a creative advertising strategy.
10. What advertising media would you select for each of the following? Why?
    a. Local zoo
    b. Local amusement park
    c. Local clothing store
    d. National soft drink
11. What products are most suited for advertising in mass media? Direct-marketing media? Interactive media?
12. What are some reasons for pretesting and posttesting specific advertisements? What are the best ways to do the testing?
13. Form small groups as directed by your instructor. Suppose an urban university is planning to advertise its educational programs in local newspapers and perhaps on radio. What creative strategy would you utilize? Be specific. Discuss as a class what decisions each group made.

marketing plan—right or wrong?

1. In magazine ads and commercials designed for Qantas Airways to promote the beaches and other pleasures of Australia, there was a picture of a man in an airplane seat placed at the water's edge. The headline read "You'll feel like you're in Australia as soon as you're on Qantas." In an attempt to be frugal, the D'Arcy Masius Benton & Bowles advertising agency sent the film crew to Hawaii instead of Australia. The shot they used was of a beach in Hawaii.
2. A goal of advertising for Haggar's slacks is to illustrate how loyal its customers are. The plan for a television commercial was to show a man going into a burning building to rescue the "Ultimate Pant."

internet insights

zikmund.swcollege.com

exercises

1. Go to www.usatoday.com and visit *USA TODAY's* Ad Track Index. Select the most current date and see if you agree with their ratings of commercials.

2. Enter the term "advertising agency" into a search engine such as Yahoo. Select an advertising agency and go to its home page. What is the agency's mission, and what business activities does it perform for its clients?
3. Many companies have created their own Web pages to offer interactive advertising. In addition, companies are advertising on other companies' Web pages, often using hyperlinks to their own pages. Go to the Time Warner Pathfinder page at www.pathfinder.com. Select the *TIME* Magazine link. Who is advertising on the *TIME* Magazine home page this week? Go back to the Time Warner Pathfinder page and select another magazine. The magazine selections vary from week to week, but you can expect to see magazines like *Fortune, Life, People,* and *Sports Illustrated.*
   a. Who is advertising on the home page of the magazine you selected?
   b. Go further into the magazine's home page to see what other ads you can find. In what ways is advertising on the Internet the same as advertising through any other medium?
   c. How is advertising on the Internet different from advertising in other media?
   d. What do you think is the future of advertising on the Internet?

address book (useful urls)

Clio Awards	www.clioawards.com
J. Walter Thompson Advertising Agency	www.jwtworld.com
Fallon McElligott	www.fallon.com
Advertising Research Foundation	www.arfsite.org
American Association of Advertising Agencies	www.commercepark.com/aaaa

ethically right or wrong?

After Swedish copywriter Michael Malmborg wrote his very first commercial, he didn't suffer the creative's chronic anxiety about whether or not his work was going to get noticed. The first night Malmborg's commercial ran on Sweden's TV3, it created what the Swedish called a "folkstorm." The TV station was flooded with calls from viewers, most of them outraged, some in tears. By the time the news media picked up the story, Malmborg more than once had heard himself called a "murderer."

The source of the stir indeed appeared to be the piscine equivalent of a snuff film, the victim being a goldfish (actually a carp) that suffers a dramatic death by detergent right before our eyes. The spot, opening with a stark white-on-black written question—"Are you taking overdoses?"—starts out innocently enough as a man prepares to do his laundry.

As a voice-over explains how 10,000 tons of excess washing powder pollutes Swedish waters, the man takes a heaping cup of detergent, pushes the excess on top into the goldfish bowl and pours the rest into his washing machine. The big, beautiful fish thrashes, and it seems to stare into the camera in horror as it gasps for air. Its demise dramatized by sound effects, the fish gives a final shudder and sinks to the bottom of the cloudy bowl with a thud. Then, ending with a flourish to show the potential polluter how his habits come back to haunt him, the man in the commercial picks the fish out of the tainted bowl and throws it into a sizzling frying pan. "It's all going to end up on your own plate," concludes the announcer.

Of course there was no way for the TV viewers to know that the fish in question (four altogether) were killed relatively humanely during this shoot. (Since detergent truly would have caused a slow, tortured death, marine biologists recommended shots of phenobarbital.) Outraged reactions from mothers such as "How can you do this?" caused TV3 to move the spot from its original prime-time airing to a later time slot.

On a more professional front, Morkman Film Co. and director Ola Mork in Stockholm, who had donated their services to get the spot produced, got an unpleasant surprise when they sent out an updated reel that included the "Goldfish" spot. One Danish agency reportedly objected so strongly that it said it would never hire the production house.

Yet the commercial's most rewarding ramifications were manifested when Michael Malmborg's neighbors came up to him outside his house in a Stockholm suburb and told him that they thought of that goldfish every time they stood over their washing machines measuring out powder and resisted the urge to overdo it.

This was just the type of reaction that Malmborg had dreamed of when this project began.[20]

QUESTIONS

1. Do you find this commercial objectionable? Why?
2. If a similar ad were produced in the United States, should it be allowed to run during the prime-time viewing hours?
3. When the purpose of an advertisement is to create a better society for everyone, does the end justify the means?

TAKE A STAND

1. Madonna wrapped herself in an American flag, but was otherwise scantily clad, during a public service announcement urging young Americans to vote. Was this approach appropriate?
2. A consumer advocate wishes to create a center for the study of commercialism because the public needs to be aware of the insidious nature of advertising. "The whole emphasis of our society has become 'buy, buy, buy,'" she claims. Do you agree?
3. While visiting in Kentucky, an outdoor advertising executive saw a billboard for a car dealer that claimed "We'll beat the pants off any deal in town." The billboard featured a mannequin with undershorts down around its ankles. The executive decided to use a mannequin with its pants down and the same lowest-price-in-town theme for an automobile dealer located in another state. Is this ethical?
4. Is it ethical to advertise beer on a televised college football game?
5. Superstar athletes are used to advertise a basketball shoe priced at over $150. Poor inner-city teenagers are frustrated because they cannot afford the shoes their heroes wear. Is this situation good for society?
6. A retailer of roller skates uses the attention-getting headline "Kick some asphalt" and an action shot of a helmeted skater. Is this advertisement decent?
7. Is American-style advertising good for third-world countries, where most of the citizens are poor and cannot purchase the goods that are attractively advertised?

W. B. Doner Advertising Agency

In 1973, Red Roof Inn started building economy lodging motels along interstate highways in the midwest. Its basic strategy was to give travelers a clean, comfortable room at a great price. Red Roof's promotional effort emphasized the slogan "Sleep Cheap." Its media plan used highway billboards to communicate the "sleep cheap" concept.

During the 1970s and early 1980s, Red Roof Inn's business grew rapidly. There was little competition in the economy segment of the lodging market. Gradually, however, this lucrative segment began to draw increased competition from Hampton Inn, Budget Inn, and others. Occupancy at Red Roof Inns began to decline as sophisticated new competition using aggressive advertising began to take some of the company's business away.

Red Roof began searching for a new advertising agency. W. B. Doner, an advertising agency with headquarters in Southfield, Michigan and Baltimore, Maryland, won the account for Red Roof's business. W. B. Doner clients at the time included Chiquita International and British Petroleum.

The advertising agency analyzed customer research and concluded that although the "sleep cheap" slogan communicated the idea that Red Roof Inns were economical, many people not familiar with the motels had a negative perception. For them, the slogan brought to mind an image of a run-down motel. The agency's analysis also suggested that the typical Red Roof Inn customer was a business traveler, often a sales representative, on a per diem expense account.

QUESTIONS

1. What factors are critical if an advertising agency is to win a client's business?
2. What type of creative strategy for Red Roof Inn should the advertising agency recommend?
3. What type of media and integrated marketing communications strategy would you suggest?

chapter 17

Personal Selling and Sales Management

LEARNING OBJECTIVES

After you have studied this chapter, you will be able to:

Describe the role of personal selling and relationship management in the marketing process. **1**

Identify marketing situations in which personal selling would be the most effective means of reaching and influencing target buyers. **2**

Show how the professional salesperson contributes to a modern marketing firm. **3**

Outline the steps involved in making a sale. **4**

Explain why the marketing process does not stop when the sale is made. **5**

(continued on next page)

"i see them everywhere, and I have come to understand that they are among the bravest of us. They face on a daily basis what we all dread the most: flat, cold rejection. Even the best of them hears 'No' more than he hears 'Yes'. . . . Yet all of them get up each morning and go out to do it again." So says Bob Greene, describing salespeople in his book *American Beat*. Probably many of us share Greene's image of what salespeople's lives are like.

But salespeople don't just make sales. For many, if not most, salespeople, servicing accounts—working with existing customers—is a big part of the job. That means they hear questions like "Can you help me solve this?" as often as simple "Yes" and "No" answers. To prosper, most salespeople need to know more than the customer about some aspects of the customer's own business. Today's salesperson is often a cross between a consultant and a vendor.

Also, many of today's salespeople are women— 28 percent of sales jobs are held by women, according to a recent survey of sales forces. More than 80 percent of salespeople have at least some college education. On average, salespeople (including sales managers) work 49 hours a week and earn almost $50,000 a year.

> FOR **MANY, IF NOT MOST, SALESPEOPLE, SERVICING ACCOUNTS—WORKING WITH EXISTING CUSTOMERS—IS A BIG PART OF THE JOB.**

Christine Sanders, a top sales representative for Eastman Kodak copiers, typifies today's successful salesperson. Selling and leasing machines that cost from $18,000 to $105,000, Sanders may spend up to 6 months closing a sale. Her commission ranges from a few hundred to a few thousand dollars. The sales she feels best about are the ones "you earn because you really understood a customer's applications or because you worked hard or were persistent in the face of a lot of competition," she says.

At Northwestern University, Sanders earned a bachelor's degree in a special program that combined economics and communications. She didn't plan on a sales career, but she effectively trained for one through extracurricular activities that often involved fund-raising.

After recruiting her in a campus interview, Kodak sent Sanders through a 10-week training program that included classroom work, real and simulated sales calls, and many sessions probing the innards of the copiers she would eventually sell. The training was "intense," she recalls, "good preparation for the real world."

Sanders shone in the suburban Chicago territory she was given and quickly advanced, eventually to a territory that includes a handful of major accounts in downtown Chicago. Forty-hour work weeks are uncommon for Sanders; the job typically demands 50 to 60. "Whatever it takes to satisfy the customer," she says.

Companies that buy or lease Kodak copiers get a package of services along with their hardware. Training is one of these services, and if a customer with 24-hour administrative operations needs to conduct late-night training sessions, a Kodak sales representative may oblige. For one such session, Sanders got up at 4 a.m. and drove to the customer's office. No trainees appeared that morning. "But I was there," she says, "and the customer will never forget that."

Her advice to newcomers in the sales profession is to know their product, their competitors' products, and their customers. That way, they can sell the benefits of their product without slamming a rival firm. A salesperson may need to understand what bothers a prospective customer about a competing product, Sanders says, "but you don't need to harp on that. I'd rather sell the benefits of my company and myself than ever bad-mouth the competition, because I think it's unprofessional and it doesn't really buy you anything—and it could come back to haunt you."[1]

This chapter begins by explaining the nature of personal selling in organizations and its importance in the economy. It discusses the various types of personal selling jobs and then describes the creative selling process and the tactics that order-getting salespeople use in each stage of this process. Next, it explains how sales careers can provide entry into managerial positions and why many managerial and executive jobs require personal selling skills. After describing the basic principles of sales management, the chapter ends with a discussion of some ethical issues facing both salespeople and sales managers.

Personal Selling Defined

Personal selling, as noted in Chapter 15, is a person-to-person dialogue between the prospective buyer and the seller. Thus, it consists of human contact and direct communication rather than impersonal mass communication. Personal selling involves developing customer relationships, discovering and communicating customer needs, matching the appropriate products with these needs, and communicating benefits.[2]

The salesperson's job may be to remind, to inform, or to persuade. In general, the salesperson's responsibility is to keep existing customers abreast of information about the company's products and services and to convey a persuasive sales message to potential customers. Salespeople are also expected to be aware of changes in the markets they serve and to report important information to their home offices. Professional sales personnel are vitally important as a direct link to a company's customers. Salespeople communicate a company's offer and show prospective buyers how their problems can be solved by the product. They finalize the sale by writing orders.

Many different businesses—farms, factories, retailers, banks, transportation companies, hotels, and other enterprises—use personal selling. Each business faces personal selling tasks that are unique. Various methods of personal selling may be used to accomplish these tasks.

We are all familiar with **retail selling**—selling to ultimate consumers. In business-to-business transactions, field selling, telemarketing, and inside selling are the three basic methods of personal selling. **Field selling** is performed by an "outside" salesperson, who usually travels to the prospective account's place of business. **Telemarketing** involves using the telephone as the primary means of communicating with prospective customers. **Inside selling** is similar to retail selling by store clerks; a salesperson using this approach sells in the company's place of business and deals with customers on a face-to-face basis. For example, the

Retail selling
Selling to ultimate consumers.

Field selling
Business-to-business selling that takes place outside the employer's place of business, usually in the prospective customer's place of business.

Telemarketing
Using the telephone as the primary means of communicating with prospective customers. Telemarketers often use computers for order taking.

Inside selling
Business-to-business selling in the salesperson's place of business.

typical plumbing wholesaler employs inside sales personnel to assist customers—plumbers—who travel to the wholesaler's place of business to obtain fixtures, tools, or parts.

The Importance of Personal Selling

Personal selling is the means most widely used by organizations to communicate with their customers. In other words, it is the most commonly used promotional tool.

It is possible to find for-profit and nonprofit organizations that make no use whatsoever of advertising. For example, for decades the Hershey Company did not advertise. Certainly, there are companies so obscure that they get no publicity at all. It is, however, difficult to imagine any organization making no personal contact with its clients. Even the one-person machine shop deals with clients through some kind of personal contact and sales effort. And although you may not have thought of them in this way, accountants, stockbrokers, dentists, lawyers, and other professionals are personal salespeople in that they deal with clients and sell a service. For example, when hard-working accountants (who generally were not marketing majors) get promoted to partnerships in accounting firms, many find that they spend more time trying to generate new business than working out accounting problems. Robert Louis Stevenson was not far from the mark when he said, "Everyone lives by selling something."

In terms of dollars spent, personal selling is again the foremost promotional tool. Money spent on personal selling far exceeds money spent on advertising, despite advertising's costs and visibility. This becomes clear if you consider the number of people engaged in selling and the cost of training, compensation, and deployment of sales forces.

Personal selling is also the most significant promotional tool in terms of the number of people employed. It is estimated that at least 12 million people, or 10 percent of the U.S. work force, are engaged in sales. In contrast, fewer than 200,000 people work in advertising. As impressive as these statistics are, they underestimate the importance of personal selling in the economy and in other aspects of social life. Professional selling is an activity of many individuals whose job titles may obscure this fact. For example, company presidents, advertising executives, and marketing researchers are frequently engaged in personal selling.

Why is personal selling so important in the economy? The answer is that the salesperson is the catalyst that makes the economy function. The adage "nothing happens until a sale is made" reflects the importance of personal selling in all aspects of business. Few of us have ever purchased a car from a plant engineer or a financial manager; we buy cars from salespeople. Salespeople build and maintain relationships that stimulate economic activity and produce revenue for the organization. They keep the economy going.

> WHY IS PERSONAL SELLING SO IMPORTANT IN THE ECONOMY? THE ANSWER IS THAT THE SALESPERSON IS THE CATALYST THAT MAKES THE ECONOMY FUNCTION.

The Characteristics of Personal Selling

Two basic characteristics that contribute to the importance of personal selling are its *flexibility* in adapting to the prospect's needs and its value in *building relationships*. We will look more closely at these characteristics before discussing the disadvantages of personal selling.

PERSONAL SELLING IS FLEXIBLE

The key to personal selling's advantage over other means of promotion is its flexibility. Personal selling is flexible because it allows the carrier of an organization's message to discover new sales prospects and concentrate on the best ones. In contrast, a television advertisement might be seen by just about anyone, including many people who will never be interested in the product offered for sale. This "waste circulation," as marketers call it, can be reduced or even eliminated by effective personal sellers. Salespeople can visit or call on large-volume buyers frequently. Personal selling allows efforts to be concentrated on the profitable accounts because it is a selective medium.

Another aspect of its flexibility is the salesperson's ability to adapt a sales presentation to a specific situation. When a sales prospect has a particular problem or unique series of problems to solve, the professional salesperson can adjust the presentation to show how the good

An old business adage says "It costs six times as much to get a new customer as it does to keep an old customer." Although the figures vary industry by industry, the point is valid. Cost-effective marketers work to retain customers by managing relationships with them.

or service offered can solve these problems and satisfy the individual needs of the potential customer. Similarly, the salesperson can answer questions and overcome objections that may arise. The salesperson can even "read" the customer. Sensing that the client agrees with a certain aspect of the presentation or is not interested in a given point, for example, the salesperson can shift gears and move to another benefit or adjust the sales talk in some other way.

All this is possible because personal selling entails a two-way flow of communication. Listening is important. Direct and immediate feedback is elicited. Consider the following examples of how feedback allows the salesperson to gather information as well as to impart it.

- The salesperson discovers in casual conversation that potential buyers have problems that no products on the market can solve.
- A customer suggests how existing products can be modified to better suit customer needs.
- A customer provides the salesperson with new sales leads by mentioning other firms that could use the salesperson's merchandise.
- The salesperson elicits a customer's view of the competition's sales message and uses it to good advantage.

PERSONAL SELLING BUILDS RELATIONSHIPS

Throughout this book, we have emphasized that the relationship between marketer and buyer does not end when the sale is made. Long-term success often depends on the sales force's ability to build a lasting relationship with the buyer. This is especially true in business-to-business marketing. For many business-to-business marketers, the relationship intensifies after the sale is made. How well the marketer manages the relationship becomes the critical factor in the buying decision the customer makes the next time around.[3]

In the context of personal selling, relationship management is often called *relationship selling.* We prefer the term *relationship management* because it has a broader application. **Relationship management** refers to managing the account relationship and ensuring that buyers receive the appropriate services. The goal of relationship management is for the marketer to help customers expand their own organizational resources and capacities through the relationship. The salesperson is the key in relationship management, for it is the salesperson who

Relationship management
The sales function of managing the account relationship and ensuring that buyers receive appropriate services.

Building and managing relationships with customers is a major selling objective. A good track record and a loyal relationship are often critical factors in buying decisions.

makes sure the product solves the customer's problems and contributes to the success of the customer's organization. When a salesperson understands and solves a customer's business problems, the relationship will deepen.

SOME LIMITATIONS OF PERSONAL SELLING

Our emphasis on the advantages of personal selling as an effective communication tool should not overshadow its major limitations. Personal selling cannot reach a mass audience economically and therefore cannot be used efficiently in all marketing situations. For example, face soaps, such as Ivory and Dove, may be used by tens of millions of people; millions more are potential users. Reaching these target customers by personal selling would be too expensive. Advertising via mass media is the appropriate tool in cases like this because it can reach a mass audience economically. (Personal selling does, however, play a role in marketing such products when sales representatives call on the major retailers and wholesalers that distribute them.)

Personal selling is expensive because it involves one-on-one communication. The cost per thousand viewers and cost per sale for a high-priced TV advertisement are quite small because the ad is seen by a vast audience. In contrast, the average cost per call for personal selling exceeds $300 for many organizational products. The high cost results from the fact that recruiting, training, and paying salespeople costs the marketer a great deal. Each salesperson, because of the nature of the job, talks to only one or a few people at a time. Furthermore, a great deal of time may be spent just driving to and from appointments and waiting in reception rooms. Because numerous sales calls may be needed to generate a single sale, you can see that the cost per sale can be tremendously large. The many advantages of personal selling, however, often offset the high cost per sale. In some cases, as in selling machinery that must be custom-made for the buyer, personal selling is the only way a sale can be made. Fortunately, fax machines, e-mail, company Web pages, and other advances in information technology are helping to counter the cost of in-person sales calls.

The Types of Personal Selling Tasks

The importance of personal selling varies considerably across organizations. Some organizations rely almost entirely on their sales forces to generate sales; others use them to support a pulling strategy based on advertising. Some organizations employ salespeople who do little professional selling, such as store clerks at Target and Kmart; others employ engineers and scientists as technical sales representatives. Clearly, these two types of sales representatives are not comparable.

Because of this diversity, it is useful to differentiate among selling tasks. The marketing manager must do this, for example, in deciding which selling skills and job descriptions are appropriate to the sales objectives to be accomplished. To assign a highly skilled salesperson to a task that could be accomplished as efficiently by a less skilled individual or an interactive data-based marketing system is a waste of an important resource. Here, we discuss three kinds of personal selling tasks: order taking, order getting, and sales support.

ORDER TAKING

Millions of people are employed in routine sales jobs. These people, who do very little creative selling, are called **order takers.** They write up orders, check invoices for accuracy, and assure timely order processing. The term *order taking* is appropriate here, because the customer decides on the appropriate products and then tells the salesperson what the order is to be. The order taker's job is to be pleasant and helpful and to ensure that the order truly satisfies the customer's needs. Further, the order taker should spend adequate time with the customer and otherwise go out of his or her way to solidify the long-term relationships between the company and the customer.

The order taker may engage in **suggestive selling** by suggesting that the customer purchase an additional item ("Would you like French fries with your hamburger?"). Suggestive selling is important. However, the typical order taker's primary task is to keep selling existing products to well-established accounts.

In general, order-taking salespeople are divided into the "inside" sales group and the "outside," or field, sales group. Inside order takers are exemplified by auto parts salespeople. The customer for auto parts comes to the shop seeking the part; the salesperson does not seek out the customer. The inside salesperson may provide some advice on product quality or installation and may even suggest that additional parts or tools would make the job easier or that the customer might as well change the oil filter while handling the other repairs. However, the order taker typically does not extensively modify the basic order presented by the customer.

Telemarketing is becoming a major activity of many inside order-taking sales representatives. Telemarketing involves the use of telephone selling in conjunction with computers for taking orders. Of course, all salespeople telephone prospects and customers, and telephone selling is an important part of many order-getting sales jobs. However, here the term *telemarketing* means using the telephone as the primary means of communication.

Outside, or field, salespeople may also be order takers. Manufacturer or wholesaler representatives selling such well-known products as Campbell's soups find themselves in this position. The question they ask their customers is essentially "How much do you want?" Because nearly every grocery store stocks Campbell's soups, there is little need for aggressive selling. Some sales representatives in sales positions of this sort do a better job than others in enlarging order size, tying the product to special promotional opportunities, and so on. Such efforts are likely to be rewarded with a promotion or a bonus. Overall, however, taking orders requires less persuasive skill than selling expensive computer systems to corporate executives or new airplanes to the transportation industry. Thus, order takers in general make less money than order getters.

In recent years a number of order-taking tasks have been automated. Interactive Web sites on the Internet often have order-taking software that performs this task more quickly than a salesperson and at a reduced cost to the organization.

ORDER GETTING

In **order getting**—also called *creative selling*—the sales job is not routine. Order getters must seek out customers, analyze their problems, discover how the products for sale might solve those problems, and then bring these solutions to the customers' attention. Creative selling calls for the ability to explain the product and its auxiliary dimensions in terms of benefits and advantages to the prospective buyer and to persuade and motivate the prospect to purchase products of the appropriate quality and in the appropriate volume. Whereas the order taker's job is to keep the sale, the order getter's job is to make the sale. Put another way, the primary function of the creative salesperson is to generate a sale that might not occur without his or her efforts.

Order taker
A salesperson who is primarily responsible for writing up orders, checking invoices, and assuring prompt processing of orders.

Suggestive selling
Suggesting to a customer who is making a purchase that an additional item or service be purchased.

Order getting
An adaptive selling process that tailors sales efforts and product offerings to specific customer needs; also known as *creative selling*. An order getter is primarily responsible for developing business for the firm. Order getters seek out customers and creatively make sales.

Creative salespeople generally invest far more time and effort in making a sale than do order takers. And although it is possible to engage in creative selling in either an inside or a field environment, it is far more common for creative salespeople to go to the customer's place of business to evaluate the needs to be addressed. This process can take a very long time. A salesperson for Boeing/McDonnell Douglas, attempting to demonstrate that a particular airplane is the best available to meet the needs of an airline, can literally spend years preparing to make a sale.

Order getters may specialize in certain types of selling. For example, some organizations have sales personnel, often called **pioneers,** who concentrate their efforts on selling to new prospects or selling new products. Selling an established product or service for the first time to a new customer or selling an innovative product new to the market to an existing customer generates new business for the organization. In contrast, **account managers** concentrate on maintaining ongoing relationships with existing customers and actively seek additional business for reorders or orders for other items in the product line. Although pioneering and account management activities may be carried out by separate salespeople in some organizations, in many instances the creative salesperson is involved in both. Organizations that segment their markets based on account size often make a distinction between major accounts and smaller accounts. For major accounts, a field salesperson may spend a considerable amount of time at the client's headquarters. For small accounts, telemarketing is often the primary means of selling. For example, most local telephone companies use telemarketing to manage any accounts with fewer than ten lines. The sales representatives for these accounts never see customers. To monitor customers' use of the company's service, they use a database that shows sales and telephone activity levels. Based on this information, they telephone clients with suggestions: "Here's a better way to do it; here's a less expensive way to do it. We've noticed you're making a lot more long-distance calls; how about a toll-free number?"[4]

An order-getting salesperson's primary responsibility is, of course, selling. However, order getters, especially account managers, may spend a great deal of time engaged in other activities. Exhibit 17-1 classifies the job activities of order getters.

Pioneer

A salesperson who concentrates on selling to new prospects or on selling new products.

Account manager

A salesperson who concentrates on maintaining an ongoing relationship with existing customers.

e x h i b i t 17-1   Activities of Order-Getting Salespeople

GENERAL ACTIVITY	SPECIFIC ACTIVITIES
Selling	Prospect for and qualify leads; prepare sales presentations; make sales calls; overcome objections
Working with orders	Enter orders; expedite orders; handle shipping problems
Servicing the product	Test equipment; teach safety instructions; supervise installations, minor maintenance
Information management	Receive feedback from clients; provide feedback to superiors
Servicing the account	Perform inventory control; set up point-of-purchase displays; stock shelves
Conferences/meetings	Attend sales conferences; set up exhibitions, trade shows
Recruiting/training	Recruit new sales representatives; train new sales representatives
Entertaining	Take clients to lunch, sporting events, golfing, tennis, etc.
Traveling	Visit prospects in other cities, regions
Working with distributors	Establish relations with distributors; extend credit; collect past-due accounts

Source: Adapted from William C. Moncrief, "Selling Activity and Sales Position Taxonomies for Industrial Salesforces," *Journal of Marketing Research,* August 1986, pp. 261–270. Reprinted by permission of the American Marketing Association.

relationships

Hallmark Cards and James River Corporation Building durable customer relationships is one thing when you're hawking mainframes, cars, or organs; it's a rather different story when you're pushing a product as short-lived as a greeting card. That's why the sales force at Hallmark Cards, the world's largest greeting card company, concentrates on pleasing retailers. Says Al Summy, a vice president of sales and service for cards sold through large merchandisers like Target, Kmart, and A&P: "We're not selling to the retailer, we're selling through the retailer. We look at the retailer as a pipeline to the hands of consumers."

Anything his salespeople can do to make Hallmark products more profitable for retailers, he figures, will ultimately benefit Hallmark.

As a result, Hallmark is reorganizing its entire sales and marketing operation into specialized teams designed to work effectively with product managers at major retailers. In the old days Hallmark sold pretty much the same mix of cards to every store. Now, using data derived from bar codes at the checkout counter and laptops that supply merchandising information from Hallmark headquarters, salespeople can tailor displays and promotions to a retailer's demographics.

James River Corporation, which sells toilet tissue, napkins, Dixie cups, and the like, also understands that when it puts its head together with its retailers' both sides benefit. Specifically, James River shares proprietary marketing information with its customers that enables them to sell more paper products. For instance, it told its West Coast client, Lucky Stores, how often shoppers generally buy paper goods and which items they tend to buy together. Lucky has since reshelved all its paper products and managed to win market share in the category from competing stores.

James River has reorganized the way it calls on customers. Previously, three or more salespeople would approach a company like Lucky Stores: one with plates, one with cups, and one with toilet paper. If all three secured orders, Lucky was obliged to buy three full truckloads, one for each product, to get the lowest price from James River. Today, a unified team from James River will sell Lucky Stores one truckload with a mix of paper products at the lowest price.[5]

SALES SUPPORT AND CROSS-FUNCTIONAL TEAMS

Many salespeople hold jobs whose titles suggest that they are involved in special selling situations. One salesperson of this sort is the so-called **missionary.** Pharmaceutical manufacturers, for example, employ missionaries, called *detailers,* to call on doctors and provide them with information on the latest prescription and nonprescription products. Detailers do not take orders; sales occur only when the doctor prescribes medication for patients. Missionary sales personnel in fact rarely take or actively seek orders; their primary responsibility is to build goodwill by distributing information to customers and prospective customers and by "checking in" to be sure that buyers are receiving satisfactory service from company representatives and other relevant channel members such as wholesalers.

Even missionary salespeople working for consumer goods companies and calling on retailers do not sell anything directly. If a retailer insisted on placing an order, the missionary would not refuse to accept it but would simply pass it on to the salesperson who

Missionary
A salesperson who visits prospective customers, distributes information to them, and handles questions and complaints but does not routinely take orders. Missionaries really serve as customer relations representatives.

Forget the mythic lone-wolf star salesman; today's salespeople tend to work in teams. The traditional sample case? It's more likely to hold spreadsheets than widgets, and the team member hauling it around probably regards herself as a problem solver, not a vendor.

Cross-functional sales team
The sales representative and those who support his or her efforts in making sales and servicing accounts. Support personnel may include technical specialists and missionary salespeople.

Account service representative
A sales employee at company headquarters or at a branch office who corresponds with clients and provides customer service to established accounts; sometimes called a *sales correspondent*.

regularly handles the retailer's account. Missionaries are, in effect, employed by the manufacturer to perform a public relations function. In some industries, scientists and engineers serve as specialized sales support people; these technical specialists support the regular field sales force. The credentials and expertise of these sales engineers, applications programmers, and other technical support personnel are often helpful in concluding sales of complicated products such as nuclear reactors, computer installations, and advanced jet engines.

Some firms, especially those whose customers may require a little extra push at some point in the selling process, have master salespeople or sales experts on their selling staffs. These salespeople are held in reserve until less senior or less capable salespeople need help. Real estate sellers frequently find a sales expert helpful when, for example, a customer on the verge of buying a new house gets cold feet because of financing worries. At that point, the salesperson may call on the owner of the agency to "clinch" the sale by working through contacts at the bank or simply lending a hand in moving the customer to the purchase point. Car dealers and retailers of major appliances also use this approach at the consumer level. Suppliers of organizational goods adapt the technique to their selling situations.

In many organizations, the salesperson in contact with the customer is supported by a **cross-functional sales team.** A creative salesperson who is trying to close a deal may call on a technical specialist in engineering or logistics or a master salesperson for aid. Or, the path to a successful sale may have been made easier by a missionary salesperson. After the sale, the missionary may play a further role in keeping the buyer content and certain that he or she made the best choice. Order takers, whether in the field or at the home office, may see to it that orders are handled promptly and without error. The customer may be provided with the name and phone number of an **account service representative,** someone at company headquarters who can answer questions about delivery, post-sale service, installation, and repair parts when the salesperson is away from the home office. The company may also have a toll-free number for customers to use.

The effective cross-functional sales team is a good illustration of the marketing concept in action. It reflects an effort to satisfy customers, not just sell products. Many people in the organization, from accountants to engineers, engage in a unified effort to build relationships. The What Went Right? feature describes effective sales teams at IBM.

what went right?

Client Teams at IBM For IBM a sales force remake was simply a matter of survival. The company cut its cost of selling by close to $1.5 billion in a two-year period. Its worldwide sales and marketing team, 70,000 strong, is close to half the size it was in 1990.

Those who survived are part of a new operation that is a cross between a consulting business and a conventional sales operation. Big Blue now encourages buyers to shop for a salesperson before they shop for products. [John] Gorney, [head of information systems at Cleveland's] National City Corporation, a superregional bank (assets: $30 billion), handpicked Don Parker as the bank's sales representative after interviewing a half dozen IBM candidates. Says Gorney: "I wanted this person to be a member of my team." An engineer by training, Parker maintains an office at National City, and Gorney has sought his help to drive down the bank's costs of delivering services within the bank and to retail customers in the branches.

Consultants need a more sophisticated set of skills than metal pushers, and IBM has not stinted on their training. For the 300 people like Parker who head client teams, the company has developed a voluntary, year-long certification program. The classroom component consists of a 3-week stint at Harvard: one week devoted to general business knowledge, one to consulting, and one to the industry the consultant specializes in serving. For the rest of the year, enrollees work on case studies and then write a thesis on their particular customer. Harvard professors grade the papers. "Graduates" receive the certification, along with a raise. Those who fail can keep trying.

In their new role as purveyors of solutions rather than products, IBM's sales teams don't always recommend Big Blue's merchandise. About a third of the equipment IBM installs is made by DEC and other competitors. Says senior vice president Robert LaBant: "In the Eighties we never would have recommended another company's product because all we were paid to do was install Blue boxes."[6]

The Creative Selling Process

As you have seen, some salespeople do little true selling. Perhaps the least creative selling situation involves the "canned presentation." The salesperson memorizes a descriptive or persuasive speech and is directed to give that speech without variation to any and all potential customers. Such an approach is common in many door-to-door and telemarketing selling situations. Although such a strategy may have little appeal for most customers, telemarketers and door-to-door sales organizations frequently devote much time and effort to developing what is thought to be the "best" sales talk. These organizations obviously believe that the method's likelihood of success justifies the lack of individual selling creativity.

Except perhaps for the person whose job is to deliver a canned sales talk, all salespeople can benefit from knowledge of the **creative selling process.** This series of steps provides guidelines to help the salesperson satisfy the prospect's needs. It suggests that professional selling is an adaptive process that begins with the identification of specific potential customers and tailors the sales dialogue and product offering to each

Creative selling process
The six-step process by which creative selling is carried out: (1) locating and qualifying prospects, (2) approaching the prospect, (3) making the sales presentation, (4) handling objections, (5) closing the sale, and (6) following up.

PROFESSIONAL SELLING IS AN ADAPTIVE PROCESS THAT BEGINS WITH THE IDENTIFICATION OF SPECIFIC POTENTIAL CUSTOMERS AND TAILORS THE SALES DIALOGUE AND PRODUCT OFFERING TO EACH PROSPECT'S NEEDS. THE SALESPERSON SELLS A SOLUTION TO THE CUSTOMER'S PROBLEM.

prospect's needs. The salesperson sells a solution to the customer's problem. The ultimate goal is customer satisfaction.

The creative selling process includes the following steps: (1) identifying and qualifying prospects, (2) approaching the prospect, (3) making the sales presentation, (4) handling objections, (5) closing the sale, and (6) following up. These steps are portrayed in Exhibit 17-2. Again, the steps represent guidelines to help

e x h i b i 17-2

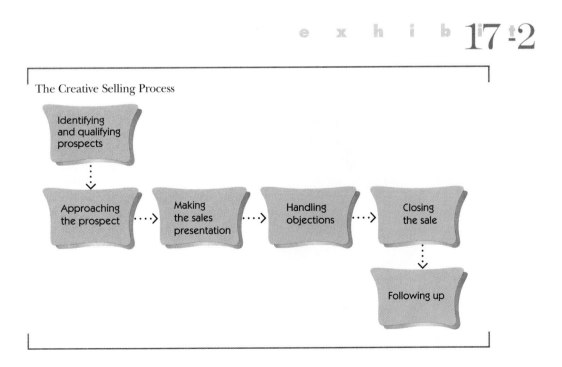

The Creative Selling Process

- Identifying and qualifying prospects
- Approaching the prospect
- Making the sales presentation
- Handling objections
- Closing the sale
- Following up

salespeople think about the tasks that face them. Unlike the canned sales presentation, they are not to be followed slavishly.

STEP ONE: IDENTIFYING AND QUALIFYING PROSPECTS

Established sales representatives may rely on regular customers for most of their business, but a successful salesperson is not content to service only existing accounts. Sales calls to regular customers are only part of the sales job. New customers or new accounts must be sought. However, making a sales presentation to someone who has no need for the product, who cannot pay for it, or who is not empowered to purchase it is not an efficient use of time unless the person being addressed may become a customer at some time in the future. The salesperson must thus identify likely customers, or prospects.

Prospecting
Identifying likely customers. In prospecting, the salesperson may search lists of previous customers, trade association lists, government publications, and many other sources.

Identifying Prospects Identifying prospects is called **prospecting.** Lists of previous customers, referrals, trade association lists, advertising inquiries from postcards or coupons, records of visitors to company Internet Web sites, and other sources may provide the names of prospects. While each industry or line of business has its traditional means of generating "leads," such as membership lists published by trade associations, good salespeople are prepared to dig harder for prospects. Government publications providing breakdowns of business patterns in particular states and counties can be used, and perhaps even cross-referenced with other sources, to develop lists of likely buyers. Some salespeople spend considerable time on the telephone screening possible clients. Others talk with organizations that supply or buy from firms that seem like possible customers. The number of prospecting tools is nearly unlimited.

Qualifying
Evaluating a prospect's potential. Key questions are whether the prospect needs the product, can pay for it, and has the authority to make—or at least contribute to—a decision to buy.

Qualifying Prospects Identifying prospects is only the beginning. Prospects must need the product, must be able to pay for it, and must be in a position to make—or at least contribute to—the buying decision. Determining that a prospect meets these conditions is called **qualifying** the prospect. Another part of the qualifying process is determining whether the prospective buyer's order will be of sufficient size—that is, whether the account has an adequate sales potential. On the basis of the qualification process, a potential customer may be assigned to a qualified group, a nonqualified group, or a group falling somewhere in between. Thus, careful consideration of

The communication revolution has freed sales representatives from the office. Computers enormously increase the amount of information a salesperson can gather about his or her customers. With cell phones, fax machines, portable computers, and information systems, a sales representative can tap into company databases and transmit information from any remote location.

a prospect may lead a salesperson to conclude either that the prospect has insufficient potential and should receive no further attention, that the prospect is worthy of close attention and a series of sales calls and presentations, or that the prospect is worth a phone call or two but not a full presentation. Care must be taken to assure that a highly qualified prospect is not relegated to the wrong category because of inadequate investigation.

Another important fact to be learned through qualifying is what member of an organization should be contacted. Who has the authority to make the purchase decision? Who else strongly influences the purchase decision? A plant superintendent may be a "boss," but calling on only the superintendent is the wrong tactic if the vice president makes all the buying decisions.

The process of qualifying is difficult and may require considerable tact and effort. Qualifying is sometimes called the *preapproach*, because the information gained in this step, especially information about the prospect's requirements, lays the foundation for planning the other steps in the selling process, including the next step, the approach itself.

Salespeople engaged in international sales must understand the cultural differences that will affect the way they do business. For example, customs concerning the exchange of business cards vary around the world. Although exchanging business cards may seem of trivial importance, observing a country's customs for card giving is a key part of business protocol. In Japan, the Western practice of accepting a business card and pocketing it at once is considered rude. The proper approach is to look at the card carefully after accepting it, observe the person's title and organization, acknowledge with a nod that the information has been understood, and perhaps make a relevant comment or ask a polite question.

STEP TWO: APPROACHING THE PROSPECT

The **approach** involves making an initial contact and establishing rapport with the prospect. If the prospect is already familiar with the salesperson and the company, the approach may be as simple as making a telephone call to request an appointment or knocking on the prospect's door with a friendly greeting. In other situations, the salesperson may have to be more creative to obtain an appointment with the prospect or get past the prospect's secretary.

The salesperson may approach the prospect by mentioning an offer that can benefit the prospect. What better way to persuade a prospect to grant time for a sales presentation than to offer a benefit that will save the prospect money, make the company's products more attractive, or add prestige to the customer's good name?

The approach is intended to make a good impression and to solidify the prospect's willingness to listen to the sales presentation. Effective sales personnel recognize the importance of making a good impression during the first few seconds of the approach. Experience is a great asset in this matter, but research and caution can serve the seller well, too. For example, smoking a cigar or cigarette in a non-smoker's office may doom a sale before the presentation has even begun. Not wearing a hard hat in a location where protective gear is required may undermine the salesperson's credibility: If the salesperson is so unfamiliar with the situation, how is he or she going to solve the client's problem? The importance of making a good impression should not be underestimated. The best way for a salesperson to build a creative sales approach is to do some homework on the prospect, gathering specific information about the prospect's needs for the products being offered. Once these needs have been identified, they can provide the basis for effective personal communication by phone, letter, or direct personal contact.

Approach
The step in the creative selling process wherein the salesperson makes initial contact and establishes rapport with a prospect.

STEP THREE: MAKING THE SALES PRESENTATION

The **sales presentation** is the salesperson's attempt to persuasively communicate the product's benefits and to explain appropriate courses of action to the potential buyer. Typically, effective presentations tell the product's story.

The presentation begins by focusing the prospect's attention on the story. Some salespeople do this by producing a physical object—the product itself (if it is both portable and eye-catching), a model of the product, or something that relates to the product in an interesting or even humorous way. It is more common, however, to use an opening statement designed to attract attention. Thus, salespeople often begin with opening lines such as "I'm here to show you how we can save $5,000 a week in your factory" or "I've got a computer networking system that everyone in your organization will consider user-friendly."

After focusing the prospect's attention, the salesperson must generate interest in the product being offered. An opening comment that the salesperson can save

Sales presentation
The step in the creative selling process wherein the salesperson attempts to persuasively communicate the product's benefits and to explain appropriate courses of action.

Salespeople should be aware of nonverbal communication. This is especially true in international sales, where nonverbal communication can take on unfamiliar meanings because of cultural differences. For example, a salesperson should never touch or pass an object over the head of a Thai; the head is considered sacred in Thailand.

the client a great deal of money in income taxes may gain attention, but it must be followed by development of interest in the product that is designed to save the money. Describing the product's benefits in an interesting way, explaining how it works, or demonstrating its use can all be part of an effective presentation.

Arousing interest in the product itself is still not enough to make a sale. A desire to purchase the product must also be generated. A scale model of an executive jet plane may be interesting, but it is of little use if it does not help bring about a desire to own the plane itself.

In formulating an effective sales presentation, the salesperson may find visual aids such as PowerPoint presentation graphics and video recordings helpful in illustrating a product's benefits. In recent years, many salespeople have come to rely on computers in their presentations. They may use laptop units to illustrate some aspect of the product or offer computer-generated data to answer the customer's "what if" questions. For example, a representative of an industrial robotics firm may bring a laptop computer into the prospect's office; ask for information such as production schedules, delivery requirements, and so on; and enter that information into the computer. Within minutes, the computer can yield output that shows exactly how the salesperson's product will affect the prospect's business operations.

Note that some of the communication in the sales presentation may not be verbal. Many successful salespeople use body language, seating arrangements, and clothing colors to communicate important nonverbal messages to their clients.

STEP FOUR: HANDLING OBJECTIONS

Most sales presentations do *not* involve the salesperson's making a one-way presentation while the customer passively listens. The customer, no matter how friendly or interested in the product, may have reservations about committing money or other resources in a purchase agreement. Questions or strong objections are likely to arise. Because objections explain reasons for resisting or postponing a purchase, the salesperson should listen and learn from them.

Indeed, the sales call should be a dialogue or conversation in which objections are expected to arise. It is undesirable to have the prospect sit quietly until the end of the talk and then say no without any explanation. Effective salespeople encourage prospects to voice reasons why they are resisting the purchase. Even though the well-prepared sales presentation covers such topics as the quality of the product, the reputation of the seller, post-sale services, and the like, objections or questions tell the salesperson which points are most important to the customer.

Occasionally, an objection comes as a surprise to the salesperson. For example, a representative of a pest-control company may launch into a lengthy discourse on his company's reputation and demonstrate the product by poisoning a bug right before the prospect's eyes. It may take an objection for him to discover that the prospect is quite willing to buy the exterminator's service but is concerned that neighbors will see the pest-killer's truck parked in front of the house or place of business. In such a case, the salesperson might promise to have a nonuniformed exterminator drive to the client's location in an unmarked truck. Such a response is a means of **handling objections.**

There are many ways to handle objections. When an objection indicates that the prospect has failed to fully understand some point that was made, the sales-

Handling objections
The step in the creative selling process wherein the salesperson responds to questions or reservations expressed by the prospect.

person can explain the area of uncertainty. A question about a product characteristic may mean that the prospect has not grasped how the product works or seen the benefits it can provide. A salesperson who encounters an objection of this type can provide additional persuasive information, clarify the sales presentation, or offer the basic argument for the product in a different manner.

Objections can also be turned into counterarguments by experienced sales representatives. A stockbroker might say, "You're right, Dr. Johnson. The price of this stock has dropped one-third in the last six months. That is exactly why I am recommending it to you. At this low price, it is now underpriced and is an excellent investment opportunity, in the opinion of our analysts."

One tactic for handling objections, then, is to agree with the prospect, accepting the objection but with reservation. This is consistent with the marketing concept's prescription to sell the product from the customer's point of view. The salesperson's counterargument is intended to refute the objection: "Yes, that is true, but this is also the case." The purpose of this method of dealing with objections is to avoid getting into an argument with the prospect. If the customer says the price is high and the salesperson says it is low, the discussion goes nowhere fast. But if the salesperson responds, "Yes, it is priced higher than many, but our product's quality is higher than our competitor's, so you get more for your money," the salesperson has agreed and counterargued at the same time. More importantly, the seller has given a reason for the higher price. Another approach to a price objection is described in the What Went Right? feature.

The prospect's questions, objections, and other comments may reveal how close the prospect is to making a purchase decision. Good salespeople use such clues to determine whether they should attempt to enter the closing stage of the sales presentation.

STEP FIVE: CLOSING THE SALE

Ultimately, a salesperson must make the sale. In selling, the term **closing** indicates that the sale is being brought to a finish. The main advantage of personal selling over other forms of promotion is that the salesperson is in a position to conclude negotiations by actually asking for an order. Unfortunately, many salespeople are knowledgeable and convincing when making sales presentations, but they never get around to asking for the order. Sometimes this failure is due to the presenter's genuine belief in the product being offered—a belief so strong that he or she can barely stop talking about it. In other cases, worry about receiving a negative answer or misreading the client's willingness to deal may be the cause. (Experienced salespeople know that they will hear the word no most of the time—or at least more than they hear yes. Rejection is never a source of enjoyment, but there are many times when the sales representative is better off

what went right?

SOQ NOP The senior regional sales manager from John Deere was wearing an odd tie tack. It was in the shape of a cross. The vertical letters spelled out DEERE, the horizontal SOQ NOP. When asked what the letters stood for, his reply was "Sell on quality, not on price." He added, "It's my toughest job, in down markets, to make my own people realize that the objective is to sell the benefits, not just resort to price. I tell them a story. I was going after a sale some years ago. It came down to two final contenders. The fellow making the buy called me in to give me one last chance. His message in a nutshell: 'You're just too high on the price side. No hard feelings, and we hope we can do business with you again in the future.' I was about to walk out the door, unhappy to say the least. Then I had an inspiration. I turned and said, 'Those are nice-looking boots you've got on.' He was a bit surprised, but said, 'Thanks,' and he went on to talk for a minute or so about those fine boots, what was unique about the leather, why they were practical as well as fine. I said to him, at the end of this description, 'How come you buy those boots and not just a pair off the shelf in an Army-Navy store?' It must have taken 20 seconds for the grin to spread all the way across his face. 'The sale is yours,' he said, and he got up and came around his desk and gave me a hearty handshake."[7]

Closing
The step in the creative selling process wherein the salesperson attempts to obtain a prospect's commitment to buy.

accepting a negative response gracefully and moving on to prospects who may be more likely to buy.) In any case, there comes a point when the salesperson must draw the presentation to its logical conclusion. Because closing the sale is so vital, experienced sales personnel constantly try to read prospects' reactions to the presentation for signs that a conclusion is in order. Signs revealing that prospects are ready to buy are called **closing signals.** For example, a comment such as "These new machines should reduce the number of breakdowns we've been having" may indicate a readiness to purchase. Should the prospect offer a signal like this, the sales representative should quickly respond and ask for the prospect's signature on the order. When the prospect's willingness to close is not clearly revealed, the salesperson may utilize what is called the trial close. A **trial close** is a tactic intended to draw from the prospect information that will signal whether a sale is imminent. For example, the salesperson may attempt to focus the conversation on closing the sale by asking which model the customer prefers. If the customer indicates a preference in a positive way, the sale may almost be made. If the customer is unable to decide or if he or she asks for another comparison of the two models, more information is necessary. Closing techniques include the following:

1. Narrowing the alternatives to a choice. The salesperson asks, "Do you want the deluxe model or the standard model?"
2. The direct, straightforward approach. The salesperson requests the order.
3. The assumptive closing technique. The salesperson takes out the order forms or in some other way implies that an agreement has been reached, saying something like "Let's see here, you'll need 20 units by the first of the month."
4. The "standing room only" closing technique. The sales representative indicates that time is an important factor and perhaps that supply is limited. Typical phrases used are "We've been selling a lot of these lately, and I want to make sure that you get what you need" and "This offer will be withdrawn soon, and then it's back to the old higher prices."
5. The summative approach. The salesperson summarizes, usually on paper, the benefits of buying the product, perhaps mentioning some disadvantages that are outweighed by the advantages. When the product's benefits have been summarized, the salesperson asks for the order.

focus on global competition

Selling in Japan—A Lengthy Process International sales negotiations can break down through failures in cross-cultural communications, even when both parties have much to gain from an agreement. Cultural understanding begins with a sensitivity to cultural differences and a willingness to learn more about the precise meaning of agreement in the host culture.

In Japan, prospective clients allow plenty of time to gain trust in the salesperson. Thus, negotiating a sale with Japanese executives is a lengthy exercise, not only because of cultural gaps but also because the Japanese will not take a position until they have achieved an internal consensus among a great many organizational members. However, once an internal consensus is achieved, the Japanese organization can move very quickly.

Patience, a virtue in Japan, can also be used as a valuable asset in obtaining the best sales terms, especially with impatient Americans. Misreading the situation, U.S. sales executives often make ill-considered concessions just to keep negotiations moving forward.

Ultimately, the Japanese prefer broad agreement rather than a detailed contract. Like the Greeks, the Japanese do not view the signing of a contract as the end of negotiations. Japanese firms want long-term, exclusive business relations based on *Kan,* a word that can be translated as "emotional attunement."[8]

STEP SIX: FOLLOWING UP

Organizations that have truly adopted the marketing concept do not view getting an order as the end of the selling process. It can, in fact, be seen as a beginning. Satisfied customers will return to the sales organization if they need to repurchase the same product at some time in the future or need a related item. A happy customer may even recommend the sales representative to new sales prospects. The professional salesperson, knowing these things, does not neglect the follow-up.

During the **follow-up,** salespeople make sure that everything was handled as promised and that the order was shipped promptly and received on schedule. Few things are worse than promising a delivery date and having the goods arrive weeks or months late. Sales personnel should also check with the customer to determine whether there were any problems such as missing parts or damage to the merchandise during shipping. The customer, once in possession of the product, may need additional help in integrating it into company operations. Post-sale services such as repairs or returns may also be necessary.

In a sense, how well the follow-up is performed differentiates between a simple selling job and marketing. After all, if customer satisfaction is not achieved or if the organization appears not to even try to achieve it, the company is unlikely to enjoy anything more than a one-shot sale. When the possibility of repeat purchase or expanded business seems strong, a single follow-up call after the transaction may not be enough. In many situations, the salesperson, with the help of others in the organization, must initiate a relationship emphasizing ongoing follow-up. Buyers—especially buyers of technically complex products—may expect salespeople and their companies to offer continuous, long-term help in solving problems and contributing to organizational success. If a marketer does not meet a buyer's expectations with excellent service, the buyer may terminate its relationship with the seller. And in many situations, if an account is lost, it is lost for good.

There are many ways a salesperson can foster an ongoing relationship; showing appreciation for an order, expediting delivery, and resolving complaints are but a few. Often, as noted, the salesperson engaging in relationship management obtains help from others in the organization. For example, WordPerfect Corporation has an extensive sales support service that offers customers technical assistance with its software via a series of toll-free numbers.

Sales Force Automation and Integrated Marketing Communications

The application of digital and cellular technologies to personal selling is known as *sales force automation.* Cell phones, fax machines, e-mail, and voice messaging systems have changed the way sales representatives communicate with prospects and clients. Laptop computers, database marketing systems, mass customization systems, and the Internet have also dramatically changed the personal selling process.

Many aspects of relationship marketing have already been discussed. However, from the perspective of the sales force, the establishment and maintenance of mutually beneficial long-term relationships with customers is *relationship selling.* The goal of relationship selling is to earn the position of preferred supplier by fostering trust among key accounts.[9]

Follow-up
The final step in the creative selling process, wherein the salesperson, after the sale has been made, contacts the buyer to make sure everything connected with the sale was handled properly.

Today, many companies employ call report–generating software that is easy to use and easy to read. Using standardized software, such as ACT! and Lotus Notes, requires a minimum of time, so the salesperson can spend more time with customers. For example, ACT! allows sales representatives to track their customers daily, using a calendaring program to improve time management, remember important phone calls and meetings, and report what is occurring at a customer's site of operations. In addition to making paperwork easier for sales representatives, the software allows a company to build a sophisticated customer database with long-run benefits for business.

www.symantec.com/act

Sales representatives used to keep facts such as a client's birthday, whether she plays golf, and her favorite restaurants in their own notebooks; if the representative left the company, so did the client information. Today, this type of information, along with past purchasing history and responsiveness to promotions, is kept in the company's database. Data-based marketing software can help the salesperson personalize the sale call. In fact, data-based marketing systems can analyze customer and prospect data to provide the salesperson with a list of who should be visited in person, who should receive a phone call, and who should receive a customized letter. Sales automation can also help with follow-up. The computer can be used to send e-mail to the sales representative to indicate that a shipment has been sent on time or that a delay can be expected and a computer-generated letter has already been sent explaining the problem.

This discussion of sales automation has just scratched the surface of information about new technologies, but these examples should give you some insight into how much different the sales process in the 21st century will be from selling in the 20th century.

adapting to change

IBM's Virtual Sales Office   Out in the heartland of America, IBM has eviscerated that most sacred of corporate perks: the corner office. Today, all the company's salespeople and sales managers in the midwestern region, as well as in other locations, are no longer assigned specific offices. They work from home, where extra phone lines, computers, fax equipment, desks and chairs have been provided at IBM expense. And they work from their cars, with cellular phones and laptops. None of the sales teams, a total of 15,000 employees and growing, have fixed work locations provided by IBM.

If they need an office for the day, they go to one of a series of "office hotels." These are scattered throughout the region of eight (plus portions of three more) midwestern states. Each has been designed to be nearly interchangeable "to minimize disruption on the road." Mail rooms are in the same place (near the entry); physical components such as paint, color schemes, and cubicle layouts are similar; check-in procedures are identical. Check in for the day, get an assigned cubicle or team or conference room, have all your telephone calls routed automatically to your new desk and get to work.[10]

Salespeople as Future Managers

Sales experience, including management of customer accounts, is often a requirement for upper-level management positions. Entry-level sales positions train future management prospects to emphasize customer orientation and to allocate resources efficiently. Sales experience provides the opportunity to learn many skills. For example, Bill Kelly, manager of systems development for Amoco Corporation, one of the world's largest energy corporations, began his career with IBM in marketing, initially as a systems engineer and eventually as a salesperson. He feels that his start in sales was helpful in many ways:

> The primary benefit of a start in sales is a firm and practical grounding in interpersonal skills. If you can't work with and communicate with a

wide variety of people with diverse backgrounds, you don't sell anything, and that gets very lonely. These skills are absolutely essential to the effective manager and business person. The sales training supplied by an organization like IBM speeds development of those skills. Of course, many individuals have good skills to start with, but I have seen them passed by salesmen who have worked at their craft.

The second benefit of a sales career is the ability to understand and appreciate business decision processes from an executive viewpoint. The nature of the products I sold brought me into contact with customer management much earlier than I would have had I worked for those organizations. Marketing training on the products as well as personal development courses prepared me for that role more thoroughly than some organizations train their staffs. The marketing objective was to allow me to sell products to customer executives. In the process I became comfortable in the company of decision makers and find I work easily with them. Without the sales training, I am convinced this would have taken much longer, if it even happened at all.

A third benefit, which may be most important, is the acceptance of individual responsibility for performance. The sales job by its nature is quantified and measured—you make your quota or you don't. This fact is impressed on the individual very early in his career in sales and leads to better personal organization. The salesperson's role as the company representative to the customer requires him to coordinate the activities of many others, often without direct authority, to meet his commitments to his customer. The focus on measured results forces the salesperson to concentrate his time and effort and the efforts of others on specific objectives. The salesperson understands that he has to make things happen if the objectives are to be met. He expects he will be rewarded for achievement and is prepared to accept that responsibility and challenge.

The critical role of selling for most organizations should not be overlooked as a good place to start a career. The selling experience and the lessons permeate my day-to-day life. As Manager, Systems Development, I am still dealing with computers, but that is incidental to the task of planning and managing. I am responsible for Corporate Systems Development through a group of 700 professionals [with a] budget [of] $65 million. . . . Without the selling skills, I don't think I could handle the job. In fact, I don't think I would have the job.[11]

Executive Selling

In some businesses, such as in an advertising agency, the organization's president may be the most important salesperson. But even in other industries, an organization's top executives may engage in personal selling when an individual transaction is more substantial and meaningful than the typical sale. The trend to enter into long-term relationships with suppliers, perhaps involving just-in-time production systems, has increased the need for top-level executives to make sales calls on major accounts. This is especially true if decision makers in the client organization are top-level executives, as they may want to deal with executives on the same organizational level. Members of the regular sales force may lay the groundwork and take the process to the closing stage, but finalizing the sales transaction with a major account may require an executive's involvement. The What Went Wrong? feature illustrates one of the subtle aspects of executive selling and relationship building.

Sales and Marketing Executives International
www.smei.org
www.sell.org

Sales Management

Sales management is the marketing management activity dealing with planning, organizing, directing, and controlling the personal selling effort. Sales managers are responsible for a number of administrative tasks. These include planning and organizing the efforts of the sales force, as well as recruiting, training, supervising, motivating, evaluating, and controlling sales personnel. The major activities involved in managing a sales force are shown in Exhibit 17-3.

Sales personnel, like most employees, require some degree of supervision and management. However, the typical salesman or saleswoman, especially one operating in a business-to-business setting, is responsible for setting priorities and managing his or her own time. Although they maintain contact with sales management and may ask for advice or other support, most of the time such salespeople are not in daily contact with their direct supervisors. For this reason, the job of the sales manager differs significantly from that of other managers.

The sales manager's responsibilities may also include selling activities. After all, virtually every sales manager earned the job by performing well in the field. A sales manager may accompany a less experienced salesperson during the training period or work with a veteran salesperson when a particularly significant account needs to be sold. Thus, while sales managers are primarily responsible for planning, organizing, directing, and controlling the sales force, they have ample opportunity to engage in the personal selling process.

what went wrong?

Global Myopia? Not long ago, the chief executive officer of a major Japanese capital goods producer canceled several important meetings to attend the funeral of one of his company's local dealers. When asked if he would have done the same for a dealer in Belgium, one who did a larger volume of business each year than his late counterpart in Japan, the unequivocal answer was no. Perhaps headquarters would have had the relevant European manager responsible for Belgium send a letter of condolence. No more than that. In Japan, however, tradition dictated the chief executive officer's presence.

But Japanese tradition isn't everything, Kenichi Ohmae, managing director of an international management consulting firm, reminded the CEO. After all, he was the head of a global, not just a Japanese, organization. By violating the principle of equidistance— viewing all key customer accounts as equidistant from the corporate center—his attendance underscored distinctions among customers. He was sending the wrong signals and reinforcing the wrong values. It may be unfamiliar and awkward, but the primary rule of equidistance is to see—and to think—globally first.[12]

Sales management
The marketing management activity that deals with planning, organizing, directing, and controlling the personal selling effort.

e x h i b i t 17-3 The Managerial Activities of Sales Managers

MANAGEMENT FUNCTION	SALES MANAGEMENT ACTIVITY	EXAMPLE
Planning	Setting sales objectives	Determine specific sales objectives that reflect the organization's overall strategy
Organizing	Organizing sales activity	Determine if sales territories should be based on geography, customer type, product line, or selling tasks
Directing	Recruiting and selecting personnel	Determine the best individuals to hire
	Training and development	Determine how much knowledge sales personnel need to have about customers' businesses
	Managing compensation	Determine if a straight commission, a salary, or some combination is the best compensation plan
	Motivating	Determine how much praise and reinforcement each salesperson needs
Controlling	Evaluating and controlling	Determine if sales quotas have been met

PLANNING SALES OBJECTIVES

All good managers, before setting out to accomplish a task, first give considerable thought to what that task should or must be. In other words, they plan and set objectives. The reason a statement of sales objectives is so important is that much of sales management involves the assignment of resources. How can the manager know, for example, how many salespeople to hire unless the manager first understands the tasks to be accomplished?

Sales objectives should meet the criteria by which objectives are generally evaluated in the marketing world. They should be precise, be quantifiable, include a time frame, and be reasonable given the organization's resources, its overall promotional strategy, and the competitive environment in which it operates. If the objectives are not precise, managers won't know what they are trying to accomplish. If they are not quantifiable, managers cannot know when an objective has been reached. If no time frame is included, the manager has "forever" to reach the goals. If the sales objectives are not reasonable, the manager can waste time and effort in a pursuit that was doomed to failure from the start.

Sales objectives can be expressed in many ways—as sales totals in dollars, as sales totals in units of products, as percentage increases over previous sales totals, as market share, as number of sales calls completed, as number of sales calls on new customers, and as dollar or unit sales per sales call made. An example of a sales objective stated in terms of sales volume is "expand annual sales in the Virginia/West Virginia sales territory by 10 percent over last year's dollar volume." A market share objective might be to "increase market share by 1 percent every year for the next 5 years." The sales forecast—which may or may not be the responsibility of the sales manager, depending on the organization—strongly influences decisions about sales objectives.

ORGANIZING THE SALES FORCE

Because nonretail sales forces typically must contact their customers either in person or by telephone, sales departments are generally organized so that sales personnel are responsible for certain accounts. Calling regularly on the same organizations and individuals leads to a better understanding of their problems and needs and provides sales representatives with an opportunity to develop personal relationships with clients. Further, some form of organization is required to prevent several company representatives from calling on the same customers where this is unnecessary. Duplication of calls wastes resources and may annoy clients.

The specific accounts and prospects assigned to a salesperson comprise the **sales territory.** A sales territory is commonly thought of as a geographical area. Territories are not always so defined, however. Sales territories may also be determined according to customer type, product line, or selling task. Every method of creating territories has advantages and disadvantages. Whatever the method employed, the characteristics and needs of the customers to be served should always take precedence over the convenience of the sales force.

Geographically Based Sales Territories Sales personnel are frequently assigned to particular geographical sales territories. Exhibit 17-4 shows an organization chart for a company using this approach. Notice that as an individual manager moves higher in the organizational scheme, he or she becomes responsible for increasingly larger territories, with the vice president for marketing ultimately responsible for the entire country or even the world.

District sales managers and regional sales managers, who are held accountable for the activity of sales personnel operating within specific areas, are referred to as **field sales managers** because of their direct concern with salespeople out in the field. Their primary concern is management of the field sales personnel who report to them. Much attention has been given to the design of geographic sales territories. A number of variables must be considered as the market is being "cut

Sales objectives
The specific objectives that an organization's sales effort will attempt to meet. Sales objectives should be precise and quantifiable, should include a time frame, and should be reasonable given the organization's resources.

Sales territory
The specific and prospective accounts assigned to a salesperson. They may be based on geographical divisions, customer types, or product lines.

Field sales manager
A district or regional sales manager, so called because his or her main concern is the salespeople in the field.

Example of a Geographic Sales Organization

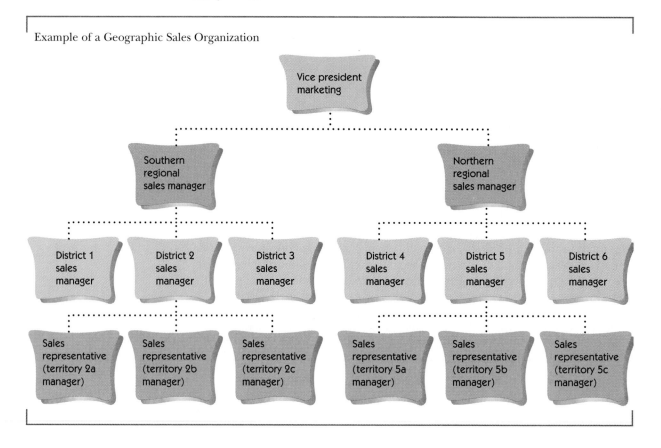

up" into sections for assignment to individual sales representatives. Clearly, even though each company's situation is different, all companies must weigh similar factors when determining geographic sales territories. A major concern is creating territories that are roughly equal in terms of physical size, available transportation within the territory, number of current and potential customers, general economic state, sales volume, and sales potential.

Personnel problems result when one salesperson gets a "bad" territory and another gets the "best" territory. Thus, equality and fairness are important goals in establishing territories. A related goal is the development of geographic territories that allow the sales manager to maintain as close a working relationship with the sales representatives as necessary. In some cases, the relationship may primarily involve telephone conversations and the filing of reports rather than actual face-to-face meetings. For example, in the sparsely populated western United States, consumer goods companies such as Clairol typically have very large territories, which may include Montana, Idaho, Wyoming, the Dakotas, Nebraska, and parts of other states. When a sales territory is that large, the opportunity for close personal contact between supervisor and salesperson is small. Personal encounters may be limited to occasional meetings at the home office. To encourage closer contact between sales manager and sales representatives, some firms require that the manager periodically travel with individual salespeople. This travel provides opportunities for sales managers to serve as role models.[13]

Sales Territories Organized by Customer Type When a sales organization specializes by customer type, two or more salespeople may cover the same geographical area. For example, a chemical manufacturer may have one sales representative call on users of petrochemicals in the Southwest and another representative call on users of other chemicals in this region. Similarly, a textbook publishing company may cover Georgia with one sales representative who calls on business and engineering professors and another who deals with professors in colleges of arts and sciences. In both cases, more than one representative of the same company may call on a single organization, and the representatives may call on different individuals within this organization. Obviously, decision makers at both the chemical company and the publisher believe that their customers are better served by dealing with a salesperson who is a specialist rather than a generalist. Yet even when salespeople are assigned by customer type, the matter of geography still enters the picture. The bookseller specializes by buyer type within a specific area, as do the chemical company's representatives. Thus, the sales force is organized through a combination of geography and customer type. In fact, the inescapability of the geographic factor makes a combination approach the most commonly employed method of assigning sales territories.

Sales Territories Organized by Product Line   Within large, multi-product companies, it is not uncommon for each division or product line to have its own sales force. As with organization by customer type, the emphasis is on specialization. Multi-line organizations often find that their salespeople must know a great many technical details about their products and customers. The need to remember too many details about too many products will almost certainly reduce the salesperson's ability to sell a product effectively.

The net result of specialization may be a situation in which several sales representatives from a single company call on the same client organization. However, as with organization by customer type, the specialized nature of the products may be reflected in specialization by the buyers. Thus, a single purchaser may not have to deal with several representatives of the same firm.

Sales Territories Organized by Selling Task   Sales forces can also be organized according to selling task. Some salespeople are judged to be best at sales development—that is, they are pioneers who specialize in bringing in new accounts. Others seem best at sales maintenance and account management—that is, calling on existing accounts and making sure that these customers continue to purchase the products being offered. Individual attitudes, aptitudes, and personalities play a part in determining who fills each of these roles.

RECRUITING AND SELECTING THE SALES FORCE

Sales tasks and activities are unlikely to be completed effectively unless a manager directs them. Directing involves first recruiting and then training, compensating, and motivating sales personnel to accomplish the organization's objectives.

According to the president of a shoe company, two shoe salespeople were sent to a poverty-stricken country. The first e-mailed, "Returning home immediately. No one wears shoes here." The second, more optimistic salesperson e-mailed, "Unlimited possibilities. Millions still without shoes."[14] This apocryphal story illustrates that one of the most important jobs sales managers perform is the personnel function. The personnel function starts with finding and hiring individuals for sales slots in the organization—people who are both interested in sales jobs and qualified to fill them. An important point here is that no salesperson, whatever his or her qualifications, is universally acceptable in all selling situations. Thus, the sales manager must decide what characteristics a given sales position requires. Selling people-mover systems to airports may call for engineers attired in three-piece suits; selling manure spreaders to Iowa farmers probably requires another form of dress. The job requirements for an order taker may be quite different from those for an order getter. These requirements must be carefully thought out and matched with job candidates, not only for the sake of the sales organization but also for the sake of the individuals hired. Clearly, the task is to get the right person for the job. Because selling situations vary tremendously, the analysis of a

One of a sales manager's more important activities is recruiting. Finding the right person for an open sales position can make other sales management tasks easier.

sales position should include a list of traits that an applicant should have. Some traits and accomplishments commonly considered in recruiting sales personnel are educational background, intelligence, self-confidence, problem-solving ability, speaking ability, appearance, achievement orientation, friendliness, empathy, and involvement in school or community organizations. Having many positive accomplishments does not guarantee that an applicant will be a successful sales representative, but the accomplishments may be indicators of attributes that are difficult to determine. For example, a friendly and helpful personality may be considered a meaningful trait, and membership in clubs and service organizations may suggest that a person has that trait. If the applicant's resume indicates that he or she is a loner, a recruiter may consider that possibility worthy of further investigation.

Related to this point is the matter of testing. Certainly no personality test or other test proves that a person will or will not be a good salesperson, and this fact concerns job applicants who feel that they have been denied a position on the basis of a pencil-and-paper quiz. Sales managers are willing to admit that no test is right in every case. However, many sales organizations continue to use tests because the test results have shown some validity over a long period of time. Thus, although tests are not right all the time, they may serve to improve the odds of making a correct choice.

TRAINING THE SALES FORCE

After sales personnel have been recruited and selected, they must be trained. Training programs vary from company to company. Some companies use an apprentice-type system, sending the newcomer into the field with an experienced salesperson to "learn the ropes." Others put the recruit through an intensive training program at headquarters or at a regional office before sending him or her into the field. A few organizations believe in a "sink or swim" method, whereby new people are sent out on their own to succeed or fail.

A sales training program for a recent college graduate hired by a company that markets office photocopiers and document systems might cover the following areas: (1) company policies and practices, (2) background on the industry and competitors, and (3) product knowledge and selling techniques. The graduate might receive several weeks of instruction at a center run by staff that specialize in training recruits. The instruction would probably feature guest lectures by both field salespeople and company executives. Next, the graduate might be required to work as an account service representative for several months, becoming familiar with customer needs and complaints and handling them by telephone or letter. The next phase might be on-the-job training that involves making sales presentations under the supervision and guidance of the sales manager or a senior salesperson. Programs like this are usually varied to suit the needs of the incoming employee. If the new person is experienced in sales, for example, less emphasis will be placed on selling skills than on company policies and product information.

In many successful sales organizations, training to develop the skills of sales personnel is an ongoing process. Most sales representatives can benefit from a refresher course, a few days spent learning about new products, or just a break from their regular schedules. Thus, continuing training is often carried out at the home office, at sales conventions, or even at a local hotel or conference center.

COMPENSATING THE SALES FORCE

Sales work—unlike certain other business professions, such as accounting and personnel management—is generally highly visible. It involves the attempt to achieve clearly measurable results: Did sales go up or did they fall? How many new accounts were opened? How many calls were made? For this reason, most sales managers believe that salespeople who achieve the highest performance in terms of some specific measure should receive the highest compensation. Financial incentives are not the only way to motivate salespeople, but they are important and deserve the sales manager's close attention.

What is the ideal compensation plan for salespeople? It should be simple so as to avoid disagreements over the size of paychecks and bonuses. It should be as fair as possible to avoid petty jealousies among the sales team members. It should be regular so that salespeople will be able to count on a reasonable reward coming to them steadily. It should provide security to the salesperson and yet provide an incentive to work harder. It should give management some control over sales representatives' activities. Last, it should encourage optimal purchase orders by the customer. (For example, a heavily incentive-based plan might encourage salespeople to engage in extra-hard-sell activities, including selling customers items that they really do not need. This is not optimal ordering; ordering should promote the development of a profitable long-term relationship with clients.)

Unfortunately, no compensation plan completely satisfies all these criteria. Based on the desires of the sales manager and his or her salespeople and also on the nature of the selling job, management must select from among the available compensation plans described below. The range of compensation plans used in selling situations represents a continuum, as shown in Exhibit 17-5. At one end is

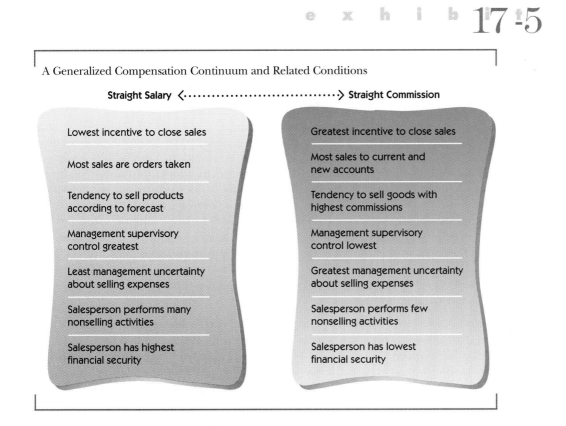

e x h i b 17-5

A Generalized Compensation Continuum and Related Conditions

Straight Salary <......................> Straight Commission

Lowest incentive to close sales	Greatest incentive to close sales
Most sales are orders taken	Most sales to current and new accounts
Tendency to sell products according to forecast	Tendency to sell goods with highest commissions
Management supervisory control greatest	Management supervisory control lowest
Least management uncertainty about selling expenses	Greatest management uncertainty about selling expenses
Salesperson performs many nonselling activities	Salesperson performs few nonselling activities
Salesperson has highest financial security	Salesperson has lowest financial security

the straight salary approach. At the other end is the straight commission plan. All other possible compensation plans are trade-offs between these two extremes; they attempt to borrow the good points from both salary and commission approaches.

Straight salary
Compensation at a regular rate, not immediately tied to sales performance.

Straight Salary or Wage The **straight salary** method or an hourly wage plan offers the salesperson compensation that is not directly tied to sales performance. With this plan, management has the greatest control over sales personnel and the least uncertainty about selling expenses, because earnings are not tied to sales. Many creative salespeople dislike this plan, preferring to accept the risks of a commission plan in the hope of achieving high earnings. However, there are some selling situations that require use of the straight wage or salary plan. The common denominator among these situations is management's desire to control a salesperson's time and activity. Straight salary is most likely when the job requires the salesperson to engage in nonselling activities. For example, retail sales personnel may be expected to arrange stock, clean up spills, feed the fish in the display tank, and fill in whenever an extra worker is needed. Paying these people on anything other than a straight wage or salary plan would reduce management's control.

Straight commission
Compensation based strictly on sales performance.

Straight Commission Unlike the salary plan, the **straight commission** plan rewards only one thing: sales performance. A clear-cut financial incentive is its prime advantage. On the surface, this plan would seem to have considerable appeal to most managers. However, the plan has a number of disadvantages. As suggested, salespeople paid this way cannot be expected to perform additional activities that do not lead directly to a sale. In other words, their activities are difficult to control. Furthermore, they may be reluctant to try to sell to new accounts that may develop slowly or to sell merchandise that is difficult to move, preferring instead to raise their short-term compensation by concentrating on products they know they can sell quickly. Management may decide to discourage this understandable behavior by lowering the commissions on easy-to-sell goods and raising them on hard-to-sell goods. This, however, destroys one of the straight commission plan's key advantages—simplicity. In addition, salespeople will resent changes that are likely to reduce their incomes. Straight commission has other shortcomings, too. The salesperson has little security. If the economy slows down or if sales fall off for some other reason beyond the salesperson's control, the incentive in the plan may be lost if the sales representative fails to achieve a satisfactory income over a period of a few weeks or more. Finally, when managers do not know exactly what commission expenses will be, they cannot predict selling expenses with complete accuracy.

Commission with Draw Management, seeking to keep the incentive of the commission plan while softening the blow that a run of bad luck might deal a salesperson, can move toward the middle of the compensation continuum. One possibility is the plan known as **commission with draw.** Under this plan, the salesperson is still on straight commission but can dip into a "drawing account" to increase his or her pay during slack seasons. This pay plan is especially common when demand for the product being sold is seasonal, as it is for certain construction materials. The important thing to remember about commission with draw is that it is, at base, a true commission plan because the amount taken as a "draw" must be paid back into the drawing account once the sales representative's commission returns to higher levels.

Commission with draw
Compensation based strictly on sales performance, but with the provision that the salesperson can borrow from a drawing account if necessary.

Quota-bonus plan
Compensation plan whereby a salesperson is paid a base salary related to achievement of a quota and a bonus for sales exceeding the quota.

Quota-Bonus Plan Under a **quota-bonus plan,** each salesperson is assigned a sales quota—a specific level of sales to be achieved over a specified period. However, an incentive is built in because salespeople who exceed their quotas receive bonuses. The base salary is related to the quota total, while the bonus provides a commission-like incentive. This plan, like others in the compensation continuum, provides aspects of both straight salary and straight commission.

While the quota-bonus plan has a good deal of appeal, inherent in it are possibilities for friction between salespeople and management. For example, expert sales representatives may find that they can make their quota very quickly. If some flat bonus amount is offered for any number of sales over quota, the salesperson may be tempted to take it easy for a time, then make just enough sales to earn the bonus. This behavior will make managers unhappy. As a result they may raise the quota, making the salespeople unhappy. In contrast, if more and more bonus money can be earned for more and more sales over quota, the salespeople may be motivated to maximize their bonuses.

Salary Plus Commission   As the name suggests, the **salary plus commission** compensation plan combines the two pay methods by granting the salesperson both a straight salary or wage and a commission on sales. Typically, because a salary is provided, the commission is smaller than would be expected in a straight commission pay package. The intent of this plan is to allow management to ask salespeople to engage in nonselling work (since they are on salary) but also reward them for successful sales efforts (with a commission). For example, increasingly sales representatives are being asked to enter customer data into their laptop computers. When a salesperson must give up selling time to help the company build its database, the compensation system is often salary plus commission.

Salary plus commission
Compensation consisting of a regular salary plus a commission based on sales performance.

MOTIVATING THE SALES FORCE

As mentioned, many salespeople work alone in the field, often at great distances from their home offices and far from direct supervision. This unique situation—this feeling of working for oneself—draws many talented individuals into selling. But it can also create problems and thereby strongly influence the role of supervision.

Many salespeople are high achievers and seldom require supervision from sales managers. For these people, selling itself is highly motivating. There is a challenge intrinsic in the selling process and a related challenge in trying to understand and solve customers' problems. Despite all this, most salespeople need at least occasional support from management. Sales personnel are often subject to broad fluctuations in morale and motivation, from the lows that accompany a string of customer rejections or a sense of being alone on the road to the highs of obtaining major orders,

THERE IS A CHALLENGE INTRINSIC IN THE SELLING PROCESS AND A RELATED CHALLENGE IN TRYING TO UNDERSTAND AND SOLVE CUSTOMERS' PROBLEMS.

enjoying peaks of success, and earning substantial commissions and bonuses. Sales personnel, especially young trainees, may become discouraged if they do not receive proper help, supervision, and attention to morale. Because sales personnel do need a "listening ear" as well as direction and advice, telephone contact can help the sales manager supervise the sales force.

While experienced sales managers may know how, by words and actions, to properly reward and encourage salespeople to keep them fresh and interested in the job, many corporations use another element of the promotional mix to help in this matter: the sales promotion. Sales contests, bonus plans, prizes and trips, and sales conventions in exciting cities can all help a sales manager keep motivation high among the sales force. Periodic sales meetings are also useful, both for creating a feeling of group support and mutual interest and for providing training and transmitting information.

Sales organizations, such as Tupperware, rely on sales meetings as the primary means of motivating the sales force. Every Monday night, Tupperware distributors hold a rally to announce sales successes with considerable hoopla and celebration.

engage in special activities such as providing service and technical expertise.

4 *Outline the steps involved in making a sale.*

The steps involved in making a sale are (1) identifying and qualifying prospects, (2) making the approach, (3) making the sales presentation, (4) handling objections, (5) closing the sale, and (6) following up.

5 *Explain why the marketing process does not stop when the sale is made.*

Obtaining an order is the beginning of an organization's relationship with a customer. Satisfied customers provide repeat sales and positive word-of-mouth recommendations. To ensure an enduring buyer-seller relationship, sales personnel should follow up on orders to guarantee that products are delivered in proper condition on schedule and that post-sale services are provided.

6 *Characterize the major aspects of the sales manager's job.*

Members of the sales force must be managed so that their efforts are directed toward organizational goals. A sales manager is responsible for (1) setting sales objectives, (2) organizing the sales force, (3) recruiting and selecting sales personnel, (4) training the sales force, (5) developing an effective compensation plan, (6) motivating the sales force, and (7) evaluating and controlling the sales force.

7 *Classify the various forms of sales compensation.*

Sales personnel may be compensated with a straight salary, a commission based on sales, or a combination of these plans, such as a commission with draw, a quota-bonus plan, or a salary plus commission.

8 *Identify some of the ethical issues facing sales personnel.*

The ethical issues facing sales personnel are as numerous as those involved in any human interaction. In general, companies expect their salespeople to comply with the law and be honest and straightforward in all their dealings.

key terms

retail selling (p. 535)
field selling (p. 535)
telemarketing (p. 535)
inside selling (p. 535)
relationship management (p. 537)
order taker (p. 539)
suggestive selling (p. 539)
order getting (p. 539)
pioneer (p. 540)
account manager (p. 540)
missionary (p. 541)

cross-functional sales team (p. 542)
account service representative (p. 542)
creative selling process (p. 543)
prospecting (p. 544)
qualifying (p. 544)
approach (p. 545)
sales presentation (p. 545)
handling objections (p. 546)
closing (p. 547)
closing signals (p. 548)

trial close (p. 548)
follow-up (p. 549)
sales management (p. 551)
sales objectives (p. 553)
sales territory (p. 553)
field sales manager (p. 553)
straight salary (p. 558)
straight commission (p. 558)
commission with draw (p. 558)
quota-bonus plan (p. 558)
salary plus commission (p. 559)

questions for review & critical thinking

1. For each of the following, tell whether you would expect the salesperson to be an order taker or an order getter.
   a. Selling satellite TV subscriptions to homeowners
   b. Selling industrial power tools to purchasing agents in the aircraft industry
   c. Selling blocks of Oakland A's season tickets to businesses that entertain customers at the games
   d. Selling paper products to office supply stores

2. How would you prospect for and qualify customer accounts if you were selling each of the following?
   a. Chain saws to hardware wholesalers
   b. Installation of cables for office computer networks
   c. Life insurance
   d. Executive jet aircraft

3. "Salesmen are born, not made." Do you agree? Why or why not?

4. What are the steps in the personal selling

process? Which is the most important step?

5. As a salesperson, how would you handle the following objections?
   a. "The price is too high."
   b. "I don't have enough money. I'll have to wait a month or two."
   c. "I'm just not certain if I need one or not."

6. The sales volume of a person with 25 years of selling experience begins to slip. How would you motivate this person to work harder?

7. How have changes in technology changed the way salespeople do their jobs?

8. How could a sales manager determine the number of salespeople to hire? Be creative.

9. Over a 5-year period, a company keeps the same sales personnel in the same geographical territories. What problems might this policy create?

10. Why do most college students avoid careers in personal selling?

11. What do you think is the average cost per contact of having sales representatives personally visit customers?

12. How important are personal appearance and proper dress in personal selling?

13. Many salespeople take clients to restaurants for lunch. What should a young salesperson be told about entertaining at lunch?

14. Field sales representatives often work in teams. Describe some situations in which team selling is most likely.

marketing plan—right or wrong?

1. Xerox thinks its sales training program is so good that it will train other companies' sales personnel if the other companies are willing to pay its price.

2. A director of business marketing estimates how much an individual customer will buy over a given time period, then subtracts the cost of goods or services sold to calculate a gross margin. Next, the cost of acquiring a new customer and the cost of customer retention are deducted to come up with the lifetime value of a customer.

3. A marketing vice president tells the sales force they should encourage their customer accounts to buy directly from the company Web site. If customers use the Web site, the sales representative will be required to make fewer sales calls.

internet insights

zikmund.swcollege.com

exercises

1. Visit the Web site of Jacques Chevron's consulting company at www.cl.ais.net/jchevron. List at least three suggestions for sales representatives selling in Europe.

2. The Executive Woman's Travel Network offers tips on travel safety, health and fitness when traveling, and other travel information. It can be found at www.delta-air.com/womenexecs. What information do you think women sales representatives would find most useful?

3. Sales managers need to understand their markets thoroughly before they can set sales objectives. Sales managers may find the market information they need by speaking with others in their own organizations. In addition, they may find it necessary to seek information from sources outside the firm. Companies like FIND/SVP conduct research and compile market reports for many different industries. Go to the FIND/SVP home page at www.findsvp.com. Select the links that describe the services provided by FIND/SVP. Then go back to the FIND/SVP home page and select the link called Search Our Catalog (which leads to thousands of Market and Industry Reports). On the next page, select Market & Industry Reports. Suppose you were the sales manager for a large paper products distributor. Select a category that might be of use to you, such as the Office Supplies category. Next, select a category that looks relevant, like Business Forms.

a. Would the report you selected be of use to you in forecasting the demand for envelopes and file folders?
b. How could you use this information to help you set your sales objectives?
c. How much would the report cost you?
d. Would you be willing to pay this price?

address book (useful urls)

SalesLeads USA   www.lookupusa.com

Time Service Department, U.S. Naval Observatory   http://tycho.usno.navy.mil

Canadian Professional Sales Association   www.cpsa.com

ethically right or wrong?

A sales manager tells the sales force that he is under a lot of pressure to increase sales for the quarter, which ends in a week. Afterward, a salesperson calls a prospect who has recently mentioned that she is almost ready to place an order for a competitor's product and arranges to take her to dinner at an expensive restaurant. At dinner, after ordering the best of everything, the salesperson says a number of negative things about the way the competitor does business. Some of these statements are not completely accurate. The salesperson normally would not be misleading but really wants to make a quick sale to help the sales manager out. Did the salesperson do the right thing?

TAKE A STAND

Are the following sales activities ethical?

1. A salesperson skips lunch but adds the typical $10 charge to her expense account.
2. In a hotel bar, a salesperson recognizes a sales representative from a competing company, and they discuss each company's prices, discounts, and terms of sale.
3. A salesperson gives a Christmas gift worth $50 to a purchasing agent responsible for buying for a major account.
4. A salesperson offers a customer who is "difficult to deal with" a higher discount than the typical prospect.

Closing Techniques: Five Top Salespeople

Elaine Bailey sells a sophisticated computer network product called Connect. By adapting her sales presentations to fit different prospects, she has built a million-dollar career selling computer products.

Rick Brown is National Sales Manager for Ben & Jerry's Ice Cream. He sells established flavors like Cherry Garcia and new products such as Peace Pops. Ben & Jerry's sells to wholesale distributors, which in turn sell to supermarkets and other retailers. The company stresses long-term relationships with its customers.

LeRoy Leale sells financial services for a full-service financial firm. Estate planning, insurance, and stocks are among the products he sells. He has been the company's national sales leader twice. He truly believes in his product. He seeks referrals and spends quite a bit of time developing qualified leads. He closes more than fifty percent of the sales presentations he makes.

Bob Hopkins sells a cash register that has a built-in vault. The notion of a theft-proof cash register is the primary benefit he sells. Many of his prospects are large organizations with many cashiers, like 7-Eleven, or banks with extensive teller operations. They are often concerned with the cost of the machines. Many of these prospects have video camera surveillance and/or hire an armored-car service to pick up money each evening.

Jim Kilcoyne sells heart-lung machines. In most situations he sells to more than one person at a medical facility.

Think about what these salespeople have in common.

QUESTIONS

1. In each of the selling situations mentioned above, what types of signals might indicate that a prospect was ready to buy?
2. What is a trial close? What type of trial close would be best for each of the salespersons mentioned above?
3. What should the above salespersons do when the prospect shows no interest?

chapter
18

Sales Promotion, Publicity, and Public Relations

LEARNING OBJECTIVES

After you have studied this chapter, you will be able to:

Explain the purposes of sales promotion.

1

Identify each of the major sales promotion tools at the wholesale and retail level.

2

Identify each of the major sales promotion tools aimed at the ultimate consumer.

3

Explain why tie-ins are popular as sales promotions.

4

Define public relations and explain how publicity should be managed.

5

(continued on next page)

6   Define publicity and discuss how it is different from public relations.

7   Understand the basics of crisis management.

cakebread cellars of

Rutherford, California, ranks as a small winery, producing 45,000 cases a year. But the brand, distributed by Kobrand Corporation of New York, has a steadfast following of 10,000 who receive its chatty food and wine newsletters. The quarterly routinely sings the praises of such offbeat pairings as peanut butter sandwiches and Cakebread Zinfandel. Through the mailing list, vp-sales/marketing Dennis Cakebread, son of winery founder Jack Cakebread, had no trouble rounding up 20 fans to go salmon fishing with him.

Cakebread and crew set off from San Francisco at 6 a.m., returning in the late afternoon. The outing wrapped with a dinner of the day's catch at

IT'S A LOT OF EFFORT FOR SMALL GROUPS OF PEOPLE, CAKEBREAD ADMITTED. "BUT I THINK WE EARN CUSTOMERS FOR LIFE."

Aqua, a local seafood restaurant. "We were all exhausted," recalled Cakebread. "But we forgot that as we all sat down and clinked our first glass."

Cakebread, which also has attracted Californians with fly-fishing seminars, is planning an out-of-state event in Chicago, where the winery is sponsoring a mushroom-foraging trip, complete with an appropriately wined dinner of the finds. It's a lot of effort for small groups of people, Cakebread admitted. "But I think we earn customers for life," he said. "The people on our fishing trip should go back to where they work and spend all day Monday talking about the trip. Every time they order salmon they should recount the trip. Every time they see a fishing boat, they should talk about the trip."[1]

Cakebread Cellars
www.cakebread.com

Cakebread's salmon-fishing event and its fly-fishing seminars are sales promotions. Often these events receive considerable publicity. Small businesses like Cakebread often concentrate their promotional efforts on sales promotions and public relations. When properly planned and executed, they can produce amazing results. The purpose of this chapter is to explain how sales promotions and public relations can be important parts of an integrated communications plan.

Sales Promotion

Chapter 15 indicated that the typical purpose of a sales promotion effort is to bolster or complement other elements of the promotional mix during a specific time period. Thus, a sales promotion program—say, a contest—may be used as an incentive to motivate the sales force, may play a part in company advertising, or may serve as the basis for a publicity campaign. Here are some examples of sales promotions that illustrate a variety of objectives at various levels of the marketing channel:

- Sales promotions may be used to encourage a wholesaler's sales force to sell more aggressively to retailers. For instance, the salesperson with the highest sales volume for a particular period might win a trip to Hawaii.
- A sales promotion may be conducted to obtain retailers' cooperation with a consumer-targeted promotion. A marketer of videotaped movies wishing to reach consumers at the retail level could provide a special promotional allowance to retailers who agree to place displays in key locations in their stores.
- A sales promotion's objective may be to add an attention-getting quality to consumer advertising and to stimulate consumers to make an immediate purchase. Offering McDino toys with a purchase at McDonald's gets the attention of members of a certain target market and stimulates them to act.

As with all promotional mix decisions, the marketer planning a sales promotion should carefully determine the organization's objectives and create a budget that can realistically be expected to achieve these objectives. The cost of some promotions can be rather small. For this reason, sales promotions may be especially important to small businesses. The expense of a promotion such as giving away a free calendar or ball-point pen may be affordable, while network television advertising may be out of reach.

SALES PROMOTION IS GROWING IN THE UNITED STATES

In the United States, sales promotion spending exceeds $250 billion per year. The exact expenditures are difficult to pinpoint because private companies' sales promotion expenditures are not as available to the public as their spending on mass advertising media.

Nevertheless, one thing is clear. The proportion of the promotional dollar spent on sales promotion is rapidly growing, especially in consumer goods and consumer services companies.[2] The average consumer goods company spends more on its consumer sales promotion budget than it does on mass media advertising.

There are several reasons for this increase in spending. One of the most important is that the growth in the number of retail stores operating electronic scanners has allowed marketing managers to more carefully monitor the results of many types of sales promotions. Managers can evaluate the impact of a sales promotion almost immediately. This ability has led to increased confidence that sales promotions can be very effective in the short run. And, because many managers face immense pressure to improve sales in the short run, they have gravitated to sales promotions. When this occurs, competitors often respond with equivalent sales promotion efforts.

The growth of sales promotions is especially dramatic when products are in the mature stage of their life cycles and there is little differentiation among competing brands. If there is little difference between two flashlight batteries, a contest that offers the chance to win a trip to Australia may be enough to make one brand more attractive than another. Marketers of mature products striving to break down brand loyalties and to encourage brand switching often use sales promotions as an alternative to permanent price cuts. If one brand uses sales promotions extensively, the competitive reaction is much the same as with a price cut: Most competitors will follow suit.

SALES PROMOTIONS AIMED AT WHOLESALERS AND RETAILERS

In this chapter, we examine sales promotions in two general categories: promotions aimed at wholesalers and retailers and promotions aimed at ultimate consumers.

The main purpose of a trade show is to serve as a central marketplace where members of the trade can find many vendors.

Sales promotions targeted at wholesalers and retailers—trade promotions—are generally intended either to motivate these channel members to make special efforts to market a product (for example, by devoting more shelf space to display the product) or to increase the number of distributors and dealers handling the product. The major forms of sales promotion at the wholesale and retail level are trade shows, contests, point-of-purchase displays, cooperative advertising and promotional programs, and allowances.

Trade show
A meeting or convention of members of a particular industry where business-to-business contacts are routinely made.

Trade Shows **Trade shows** are extremely important in business-to-business marketing. Industry-wide conventions and trade association meetings are scheduled throughout the year at hotels and convention centers across the country. The typical trade show features many booths where producers, suppliers, and other marketers display and provide information about their products, in effect using the booths as temporary bases of sales operations. You may be familiar with boat and auto shows, where hundreds and even thousands of products and services are shown and demonstrated. Most trade shows are organized along the same lines, though of course the shows vary widely in size, ranging from a few hundred people to tens of thousands. Most trade shows are not open to the general public, because marketers use these shows to distribute literature, obtain sales leads, and sell products to wholesalers, retailers, organizational buyers, and others in the trade. The main purpose of a trade show is to serve as a central marketplace where trade members, by making a single trip to the city in which the trade show is held, can view many products and discuss industry trends with other professionals.

Contest
In the context of a wholesaler's or retailer's sales promotion, a means of motivating a sales force by offering bonuses or prizes for sales performance.

Contests **Contests** to motivate a manufacturer's, wholesaler's, or retailer's sales force are very common sales promotion activities. The purpose of these contests is to increase sales levels by stimulating individual competition among salespeople. Competition is, of course, stimulated by the chance to win bonuses or prizes. In short, the salespeople are rewarded for extra effort.

Sales contests add some excitement to regular activities and provide the opportunity for a salesperson to gain personal recognition as well as extra compensation and prizes. The major problem with sales contests is that the sales increases that result are often temporary. Furthermore, salespeople who wish to improve performance in the contest often shift sales that would have occurred in another time period to the contest period.[3]

Point-of-purchase materials
Promotional items intended to attract attention to specific products in the places where those products are purchased. Signs and displays in supermarkets are examples.

Display Equipment and Point-of-Purchase Materials Display equipment and other **point-of-purchase materials** are often provided to retailers or other members of distribution channels so that they can conveniently display or highlight the product to be sold. Display equipment and point-of-purchase items come in many forms. Convenience stores and bars almost always display clocks supplied by soft-drink or beer marketers. Bookstore operators often receive new books in shipping packs that can be converted into book display racks.

Cooperative advertising
Advertising paid for jointly by a supplier and a customer—for example, by the manufacturer of a product and a retailer.

Cooperative Advertising and Promotions Manufacturers frequently use **cooperative advertising** and other cooperative promotions to increase promotional activity at local wholesale and retail levels. Programs vary, but the essence of all of them is that suppliers share promotional expenses with their customers. For example, a 50/50 co-op program offered by the manufacturer of La-Z-Boy chairs or their wholesalers would induce retailers to advertise the product in their local markets. In a 50/50 program, half of the retailer's advertising expense is borne by the supplier, so the retailer pays just half of what the ad would ordinarily cost. The retailer gets to promote its own name as well as the La-Z-Boy brand name. The reward for the supplier that offers such a program is the active local support of dealers and the increased likelihood of immediate consumer purchases.

Cooperative advertising approaches are of two general types: vertical and horizontal. *Vertical cooperative promotion* involves channel members at different levels, as when La-Z-Boy offers to pay for a portion of a retailer's advertising with the understanding that the advertisements will feature La-Z-Boy recliners. *Horizontal cooperative promotion* involves channel members at the same level, as when retailers in a town get together to promote shopping in general or to conduct a "sidewalk" promotion.

Allowances   An **allowance** is a reduction in price, a rebate, merchandise, or something else given to an intermediary for performance of a specific activity or in consideration for a large order. For example, a manufacturer may offer free merchandise to retailers that feature its product in point-of-purchase displays.

Allowance
A reduction in price, a rebate, or the like given to a marketing intermediary in return for a large order or the performance of a specific activity.

SALES PROMOTIONS AIMED AT ULTIMATE CONSUMERS

Like other forms of promotion, sales promotion at the consumer level can inform, remind, and persuade. Specific objectives of sales promotions may be to attract more attention to a product once it is in the store, to serve as a reminder at the point of purchase, to help break down loyalty to competing brands, to add value to the product in the consumer's eyes, to make short-term price adjustments, to provide consumers with an incentive to try the product for the first time, to offer an incentive for repeat purchases, or to induce large-volume purchases. The objectives of sales promotions are almost limitless, and the possibilities for their nature are bounded only by the marketer's imagination. For convenience, however, sales promotions can be grouped into these categories: product sampling, coupons, rebates, contests and sweepstakes, premiums, multiple-purchase offers, and point-of-purchase materials.

> THE **OBJECTIVES OF SALES PROMOTIONS ARE ALMOST LIMITLESS, AND THE POSSIBILITIES FOR THEIR NATURE ARE BOUNDED ONLY BY THE MARKETER'S IMAGINATION.**

Product Sampling   The purpose of **product sampling** is to reach new customers by inducing trial use. A free trial or trial sample of the brand is given to consumers to stimulate product awareness, to provide first-hand knowledge about the product's characteristics, and to encourage a first purchase of a previously untried brand. Typically, miniature packages of the product are distributed to homes, in retail settings, on airplanes, or at public events. Product sampling is an expensive method of promotion, but good for new brands in mature markets where strong brand loyalties may exist.

Product sampling
A sales promotion in which samples of a product are given to consumers to induce them to try the product.

Coupons   Coupons, which generally offer price reductions of some kind, are one of the most widely used sales promotions. Like other kinds of price reductions, coupons have an established record of increasing short-term sales. They attract new users to a brand, encourage brand switching, and stimulate increased purchases by existing users. It should be noted that occasionally cutting prices with coupons does not damage a product's long-term quality or value image—many price-conscious consumers always clip coupons.

Coolsavings
www.coolsavings.com

Coupons designed to grab the consumer's attention are often included in print advertisements or in free-standing inserts in newspapers. They may be printed on packages or placed inside packages. Coupons are increasingly being distributed in stores and by direct mail. With the growth of data-based marketing, the nature of coupon distribution strategies has changed. Coupons may be distributed to specific consumers who are known to use particular competing brands or who are identified in the database as having certain purchasing behaviors of interest to the marketer. This strategy helps minimize a major disadvantage of coupons: the fact that most coupons are redeemed by consumers who already buy the brand.

Rebate
A sales promotion wherein some portion of the price paid for a product is returned to the purchaser

Rebates A **rebate,** like a coupon, is a price reduction designed to induce immediate purchase. However, with a rebate the consumer gets money back from the manufacturer rather than a price break at the retail level. Rebate offers often require that the consumer purchase multiple units (for example, three boxes of cereal) to qualify for the refund. Typically, the consumer must then send in some proof of purchase, after which the company sends a check to the consumer. For many consumers, this time lag makes rebates less attractive than an immediate price reduction at the retail level. Less price-sensitive shoppers often do not bother to follow the steps necessary to get the rebate payment. Marketers, however, know that rebates are most attractive to price-sensitive shoppers, who will generally spend the time and effort to obtain the rebate. Thus, unlike a price cut, which everyone gets, a rebate goes to only the most price-sensitive shoppers. Because rebate offers are typically printed on the packages or placed inside them, costs for rebate distribution are lower than those for circulating coupons through means other than the packages themselves. Also, retailers recognize that in a rebate promotion the manufacturer, not the retailer, pays for the discount in price.

Contests and Sweepstakes Contests and sweepstakes stimulate purchases by giving consumers a chance to be big winners. Certain types of consumers enjoy these exciting promotions. Contest participants have to complete some task, such as submitting

Odor-Eaters International sponsors an annual Rotten Sneaker Contest. The contestant with the smelliest old sneakers wins a $500 savings bond and a trophy. As you can imagine, the contest is newsworthy, and it generates a lot of publicity.

www.odor-eaters.com/ halloffumes.html

a recipe to the Pillsbury Bake-Off, and are awarded prizes when their entries are judged to be among the best. Sweepstakes participants become winners based on chance. Sweepstakes are easily tied to repeat purchases of a brand when the chances of winning increase with each purchase. If sweepstakes promotions require the purchase of a unit of the product, however, state or local lottery laws may prohibit them.

Premium
A product offered free or at reduced charge with the purchase of another product.

Premiums and Self-Liquidating Premiums A **premium** is a product offered free or at a reduced charge with the purchase of another product, the *key brand*. A premium, such as a Beanie Baby given to children attending an L.A. Dodgers' game, is a giveaway. Consumers see themselves as getting something for nothing. *Self-liquidating premiums* are special types of premiums that consumers obtain by using proofs of purchase, trading stamps, cash, or a combination of these.

Premium offers are quite diverse. Usually the more imaginative premiums are the most effective. Fast-food franchises often offer sets of cups, Christmas tree ornaments, or other premiums tied to the promotion of a movie. Advertisements feature action scenes from the movie, along with a message about the premium offer, to generate widespread interest in collecting every item in the set.

Hotels, airlines, and many service organizations offer their own products as premiums for frequent users. Unlike most sales promotions, promotions to encourage brand loyalty and increased usage, such as the Delta Frequent Flyer program, have evolved into long-term programs. The term *frequency marketing* is sometimes used to describe these brand loyalty programs that are highly interrelated with capacity management strategies and pricing strategies.

Multiple-Purchase Offers   Two-for-one deals, or multiple-purchase offers, are tied to price or to some other promotion. Offering four bars of Dial soap for the price of three is a typical example of a multiple-purchase offer; it encourages a bigger-than-normal purchase and helps maintain customer loyalty.

Point-of-Purchase Materials   Banners, pamphlets, coasters, and similar materials may be used to provide information at the point of purchase. Point-of-purchase materials serve as reminders. Reminding a shopper of an appeal used in advertising may trigger a sale. In-store videos, shopping-cart videos that are started electronically when the cart moves toward the aisle where the product is stocked, and other technological innovations are changing the nature of these sales promotions.

Exhibit 18-1 summarizes the major forms of consumer sales promotions. As a final note, we should mention that sales promotions can be overused. A number

A Summary of Consumer Sales Promotions   e   x   h   i   b   18-1

ACTIVITY	DESCRIPTION	FEATURES	EXAMPLE
Product sampling	A sample of the brand is given to consumers	Expensive but good for new brands in mature markets where brand loyalties may exist	Free sample of Doritos WOW Chips
Coupons	Most often, a temporary price reduction coupon is found in an advertisement, but it may be located in the store or the package	Cutting the price does not damage long-term quality or value image; many price-conscious consumers always clip coupons	Save 50¢ on Kellogg's Smart Start
Rebates	Consumer is offered the opportunity to get money back from the manufacturer rather than receive a price break at the retail level	Lower cost than circulating coupons because rebate coupon is inside package and fewer consumers participate	Mail-in rebate for $5 on Black and Decker drill
Contests and sweepstakes	Consumer is given a chance to be a big winner	Some consumers like contests; they may be tied to repeat purchase of a brand	Safeway Bingo Game Sweepstakes
Premiums and self-liquidating premiums	Another product is offered free or at a reduced charge if the key brand is purchased	Consumers see themselves as getting something for nothing	Oscar Mayer wiener whistle given away with each pack of hot dogs
Multiple-purchase offers	Multiple purchases are tied to price or another promotion	Induces heavier-than-normal purchases and maintains customer loyalty	Four bars of Dial soap for the price of three
Point-of-purchase materials	Banners, pamphlets, coasters, and similar materials are used to provide information at the point of purchase	Reminders at the point of purchase may trigger a sale	Cardboard display for Stephen King's latest book
Product placements	Products appear in movies	Communicates a positive message in a noncommercial setting	Movie scene filmed inside Taco Bell

In one scene in the James Bond movie *Tomorrow Never Dies,* Bond drives a BMW motorcycle. In another, he crashes a car into a Heineken truck. This was not just good luck for BMW and Heineken. These are product placements, and arranging for the products to be seen by moviegoers is part of these companies' promotional budgets.

www.tomorrowneverdies. com

of sales promotions, such as coupons, rebates, and premiums, lower the price of the product or similarly enhance the product offering. If these special incentives are used regularly or if consumers can predict their timing, then consumers may buy only during sales promotions. Marketers who continually use this type of sales promotion risk the loss of sales at traditional prices to price-conscious consumers. Obviously, a strategy of continually using sales promotions can lead to spiraling costs.

Product Placements   A product or company that appears in a movie scene will be exposed to millions of movie viewers. If an actor consumes a particular brand of soft drink or wears a certain brand of clothing, a very positive message can be communicated in what most consider a noncommercial setting. In recent years, movie studios have come to recognize that selling *product placements* in their movies can be a profitable side business. Marketers of widely used consumer goods and services are often willing to pay large fees for product placements. In some cases, the product placements are tied in to other promotional efforts.

Sales Promotions Often Use Tie-Ins   A *tie-in* involves a collaborative effort between two or more organizations or brands that work as partners in a promotional effort. Tie-ins generally borrow interest value from movies, sporting events, or other marketing efforts. When Burger King sells soft drinks in Anastasia cups, its sales promotion effort is based on a tie-in to the popularity of the cartoon movie about a snowbound Russian orphan. Burger King expects its soft drink sales to increase because of the popularity of the movie.

   The benefits of tie-ins with premiums are easily appreciated, but contests,

Burger King offered Rugrats merchandise as a tie-in with the popular Nickelodeon cartoon TV show. The bags for meals were printed with games and puzzles and drawings of Tommie, Chuckie, Phil and Lil, and Angelica.

sweepstakes, coupons, and other sales promotion elements can also benefit from a tie-in approach. For example, the National Basketball Association and Sprite's tie-in collaboration ranged from having NBA promotional information appear on special Sprite cans to sending a portable playground to state fairs. Tie-ins such as this one can be rather elaborate, with integrated marketing communications ranging from mass media advertising to Web site promotions.

Public Relations

Chapter 15 stated that publicity always involves a third party, such as a newspaper reporter or editor, who has the ultimate power to determine the nature of the message. Since the marketer does not pay for space in a newspaper or time on a

McDonald's and Disney   McDonald's has a 10-year multinational promotional alliance with Disney. McDonald's is Disney's primary promotional partner in the restaurant industry, with exclusive rights linked to Disney theatrical releases, theme parks, and home video releases in more than 93 countries.

television program, publicity is "free." However, because favorable publicity can have the same impact as advertising, effective marketers plan publicity with as much care as they give to the rest of the promotion mix. This effort is often the responsibility of the organization's public relations department. The concepts of publicity and public relations are not the same, and they should not be confused.

Public relations is the managerial activity that involves identifying, establishing, and maintaining beneficial relationships between an organization and the publics on whom its success or failure depends.[4] Although the purpose of public relations is to actively manage publicity, maintaining the goodwill an organization has established or providing the public with information about an organization's plans, policies, or personnel may also be accomplished by managing promotional elements other than publicity. In this sense, public relations is more clearly defined by its goal of building acceptance for a company as a whole rather than by its strong association with publicity as a means to accomplish this goal.

Effective marketers are proactive in shaping how each of their publics perceives the organization. Public relations efforts often target stockholders, government agencies, local community organizations, citizen action groups, the news media, and the organization's own employees, as well as the general public that includes its customers. Planning an organization's public relations requires establishing public relations objectives that focus on the exact message the organization wishes to communicate. Generally, the reputation or image to

BECAUSE FAVORABLE PUBLICITY CAN HAVE THE SAME IMPACT AS ADVERTISING, EFFECTIVE MARKETERS PLAN PUBLICITY WITH AS MUCH CARE AS THEY GIVE TO THE REST OF THE PROMOTION MIX.

be communicated is closely linked to the organization's mission statement. Most public relations efforts are ongoing. However, under certain circumstances, such as during a product recall, the objective of the public relations effort will be quite specific and will be designed to be accomplished in a limited period of time.

PUBLICITY

Publicity, when properly managed by a public relations department, can serve many purposes. Marketers often hope to attract the public's attention or maintain public visibility. Many organizations wish to provide consumers or public interest groups with useful information. Others use public relations to change attitudes or to combat negative publicity from another source. Here are some examples:

- Nissan Motor Company, a company that recently developed a fuel-efficient engine system combining an electric motor with a gasoline engine, may use

adapting to change

3M's Identity   At 3M, D. Drew Davis, staff vice president, corporate marketing and public relations, says the corporate reputation was created by people who have since retired. Public relations' role is to continue to build on the previous reputation. "Our public relations people can't create a spin."

3M manufactures products for industrial, commercial and consumer markets. The mission of public relations at 3M "is to support the growth of the company and promote understanding of it," Davis continued. Of particular importance is "making sure that the value and the history of the company are alive with 3M stakeholders. We're an innovative company that started with sandpaper and today has 66,000 products."

One way that 3M's public relations people promote understanding of the company is with a recently initiated identity strategy. Those who identify the company with Scotch tape and computer diskettes may not know that it is involved in many other industries. That lack of knowledge can be a liability for 3M. "We want to hire the best and the brightest, and they don't want to work for an unknown company," Davis explained.

Hence the identity strategy is "to help people understand who we are and what we're about," Davis explained. An integrated approach to communications ties in advertising, internal communications, packaging, and literature, grouping discrete divisions under rubrics such as 3M Health Care. "It communicates that we're in that business," Davis said.

"The identity strategy was co-developed by all layers of management," Davis said, describing the contribution of public relations to the program. "Once the philosophy was in place, the professionals took over and began to implement. We're proactive once we establish the philosophy."[5]

publicity to attract attention to its hybrid electric engine system, which cuts exhaust emissions dramatically.

- Political candidates routinely use "photo opportunities" to maintain visibility among apathetic voters.
- The Surgeon General of the United States uses publicity to inform the public about the dangers of teenagers' smoking.
- The owner of an NFL football team calls a press conference to announce that the rumor that the team's coach will be fired is false.

In general, no matter what the marketer's purpose, the information offered must be timely and interesting—that is, newsworthy—if it is to result in publicity for the marketer. Usually, the more engrossing and captivating the material, the more likely it is to be publicized. Celebrities are often asked to work with charity organizations because their fame and personalities help get the much-needed "free" publicity. Information offered by public relations departments often takes the form of news releases and press conferences.

Public relations efforts are aimed at customers, stockholders, and many different publics. Public relations efforts targeted at legislators (or environmental groups) are common. Often they are called lobbying, but they are public relations activities nonetheless.

www.sierraclub.org

News Releases
Marketers may spend considerable time and effort in getting news releases and interviews with company spokes-

persons placed in newspapers and on television news broadcasts, to promote a favorable corporate organizational image.

Suppose, for example, that you are in charge of public relations for Campbell Soup Company and the company has just introduced a new 32-ounce resealable carton for Swanson Chicken Broth. Your publicity objective is to provide information about the product's characteristics and potential benefits to make the public aware of its existence. You might issue a **news release**—a relatively brief typewritten statement—describing a newsworthy aspect of the product. The news release would announce that Campbell Soup Company has begun offering Swanson Chicken Broth in a 32-ounce resealable carton.[6] It might go on to say that according to Swanson research, more than 88 percent of the published recipes that use chicken broth call for either less than or more than the traditional-size can. It might explain the reason for the product and its benefits. It might say that the new, 99 percent fat-free product was created specifically to be easy to use in cooking, providing a more convenient way for chefs at home to use broth as a replacement for butter, margarine, or oil in recipes. The news release could conclude by pointing out that broth is no longer an occasional ingredient, but an essential tool in modern cooking. The resealable carton provides easy accessibility in the refrigerator so that cooks can instantly add flavor to their recipes.

Well-executed news releases are written in a form that a newspaper, magazine, or broadcast editor can easily incorporate into a news story. Photographs, films, and videotapes are often distributed to the media to accompany news releases. For example, videotapes of company operations and interviews with company spokespersons are often distributed to television broadcasters. Organizations with Web sites often post their press releases on their Web sites after the releases have been distributed to the media.

Press Conferences The **press conference** is another form of publicity that can create goodwill and positive relations between an organization and the public. When an organization wishes to make a specific announcement, it may schedule a press conference so that company officials can make a statement and reporters can ask questions. For example, the professional football

Mattel Inc. used publicity to announce the introduction of a less busty Barbie. The makeover was designed to give a more realistic profile to the curvaceous, best-selling doll. Barbie's new look also includes a thicker waist and slimmer hips. Changes above the neck include a new nose and softer, straighter hair. This story was so newsworthy that it was published in almost every major newspaper in the United States.

www.barbie.com

News release
A brief written statement sent to the press or others, describing a new product, a product improvement, a price change, or some other development of interest. The release is intended to be newsworthy.

Press conference
A meeting called by an organization to announce a newsworthy event to the press.

Enhancing corporate visibility is one objective of public relations. This photograph shows the Gothic-style headquarters of the *Chicago Tribune* ablaze in colored light. The lighting was part of a publicity campaign to celebrate the *Tribune's* 150th anniversary.

www.chicago.tribune.com

team with the worst record in football will inevitably call a press conference to announce the signing of its recently drafted Heismann Trophy candidate. The organization's public relations department thus seeks to promote next year's team via publicity.

Appearances   Talk shows are known for inviting guests who promote their books, CDs, and concerts. The entertainment business is one of the most extensive users of public relations. Performers' appearances are often part of well-planned marketing strategies. For example, sales of Tony Bennett's recordings of pop songs that made him famous in the 1950s and 1960s have been revitalized because of a savvy public relations effort by his son and manager. Tony Bennett's appeal to young audiences—fans of alternative rock—was enhanced by carefully exposing the entertainer with guest appearances on programs such as *The Simpsons* and *The Late Show with David Letterman*. Bennett also appeared with one of the Red Hot Chili Peppers on an MTV award show, shared concert bills with groups such as Smashing Pumpkins, and recorded an MTV *Unplugged* show.[7]

Sports figures, politicians, environmentalists, and activists for social causes use their guest appearances on television programs to promote their agendas. *Person marketing* is a term sometimes used to describe marketing when the product is a person. If baseball and football star Deion Sanders wishes to promote his image, appearances are a very cost-effective medium. Further, viewers do not perceive his appearance on a television show as an advertisement.

PUBLIC RELATIONS GOES BEYOND PUBLICITY: AN INTEGRATED MARKETING COMMUNICATIONS APPROACH

Although management of an organization's public image through publicity is the cornerstone of public relations, all forms of promotion may influence an organization's relationship with the general public. Thus, managers must not overlook the coordination of public relations efforts with other promotional efforts. Many of the objectives of publicity are the same as those of other promotional efforts—and all of these activities may be carried out by a public relations department. For example, the Macy's Thanksgiving Day parade is a sales promotion event that enhances Macy's public image. And the lobbying effort by the Friends of Kuwait is a form of personal selling, even though the public relations workers involved have titles other than sales representative. (The term *public relations* may be used in preference to the term *sales* by government officials, who would rather go to lunch with a lobbyist than a salesperson, or by a charity, which wishes to talk about its fund-raising as something other than a sales promotion.)

> PUBLIC **RELATIONS EFFORTS HAVE VARIOUS TARGET AUDIENCES—NOT JUST CONSUMERS BUT ALSO STOCKHOLDERS, GOVERNMENT ENTITIES, ENVIRONMENTAL GROUPS, AND THE LIKE.**

Exhibit 18-2 illustrates the fact that public relations to enhance organizational image and to communicate product information includes more than just public-

The Late Show
www.cbs.com/lateshow

The Scope of Public Relations

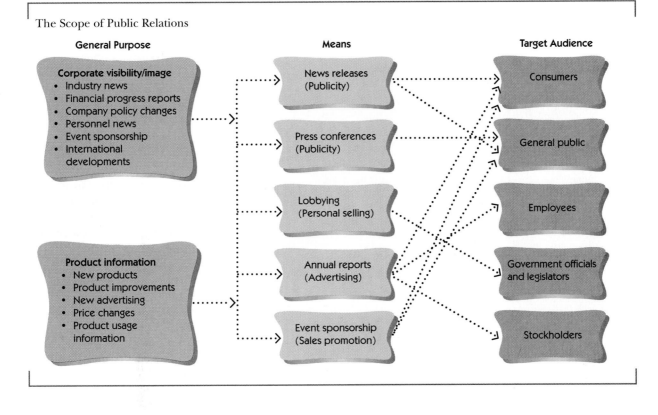

General Purpose	Means	Target Audience

Corporate visibility/image
• Industry news
• Financial progress reports
• Company policy changes
• Personnel news
• Event sponsorship
• International developments

Product information
• New products
• Product improvements
• New advertising
• Price changes
• Product usage information

News releases (Publicity)

Press conferences (Publicity)

Lobbying (Personal selling)

Annual reports (Advertising)

Event sponsorship (Sales promotion)

Consumers

General public

Employees

Government officials and legislators

Stockholders

ity. It also illustrates that public relations efforts have various target audiences—not just consumers but also stockholders, government entities, environmental groups, and the like—which can be reached in various ways.

EVENT SPONSORSHIP

Sponsorship of sporting events and charity causes can be very effective for marketers who wish to generate publicity or reinforce a certain image with a tie-in to a special event. A sponsor collaborating on an event or helping out with a charitable cause provides financial resources, personal services, equipment, and/or facilities to create an alliance with the event or organization. In return, the company obtains direct exposure to the public targeted by the event and the ability to transfer the sporting or charitable organization's image to its products. MasterCard was a major sponsor of the first World Cup soccer games held in the United States. The

The growing global presence of the National Basketball Association will serve as the vehicle for a major international push for Miller Genuine Draft beer. Miller's sponsorship of the NBA will be a key promotional element in the international expansion of Miller Genuine Draft, which has garnered some degree of distribution in more than 70 countries, but has yet to put forth a concerted marketing promotional effort. The company hopes to evolve from being export-sales driven to being more closely associated with the local markets.[8]

www.nba.com

what went right?

Chemical Bank Corporate Challenge Begun in 1977, the Chemical Bank Corporate Challenge Series attracted 200 runners from 50 companies to its inaugural event in New York. Since then the bank (now known as Chase Bank as a result of a merger) has expanded to 19 markets across the nation, plus London and Frankfurt, with 150,000 participants. The 3.5-mile road races are open to full-time employees of corporations, businesses and financial institutions—prime targets for the marketers at New York–based Chemical Bank.

The company considers this event a cost-effective means to enhance its image in its targeted markets, according to Barbara Paddock, vice president/director of event marketing at Chemical Bank.

Races take place on weeknights, after work, and runners compete as a company team. The local events are staged throughout the summer. The promotion culminates with a championship race when the winning teams from all sites compete on Park Avenue in New York City.

Prime sponsor objectives are to generate publicity for the institution and to provide bank officers a platform for inviting companies from a client and prospect base to participate.

There is scant advertising for the event, primarily in the *New York Times* and *Business Week*. Chemical Bank counts on attendant coverage and publicity in respective markets to spread the word. Direct-mail entry application kits are also sent to corporations and business institutions.

Sponsor tie-ins are generated by the bank, which extends marketing opportunities to others. Major affiliated sponsors include the two aforementioned publications, plus PowerBar, Tiffany & Company, Hyde Athletic Industries, Saucony, and American Airlines. Races have VIP tents.

The bank retains local public relations firms to generate publicity and solicits regional running groups to help conduct the races and generate participants.

"In many ways this is a unique event," said Paddock. "It's something we created and no one else does."[11]

MasterCard logo was prominently displayed behind the goal—visible to an estimated two billion fans who watched as Brazil won the championship, beating Italy in a penalty-kick shootout.[9] However, sponsors of televised sporting events such as the World Cup must rely on the TV camera to show their banners and signs. The lack of complete control over promotional efforts is a disadvantage of event sponsorship. Nevertheless, the Wimbledon Tennis Championships, the PGA Championships, and the World Series are global events that receive media coverage, and sponsoring these events generates considerable publicity around the world. NationsBank Corporation spent approximately $120 million on its sponsorship of the 1996 Olympic games in Atlanta. Besides choice seats and hospitality tents, what did the Charlotte-based banking giant get for its $40 million sponsorship fee?[10] The bank gained national name recognition beyond anything any advertising campaign could buy, because the Olympics reach people of a wide spectrum of ages and cut across all socioeconomic lines. But the heart of NationsBank's strategy was to associate the bank as often as possible with world-class athletes and teamwork.

When a marketer such as Yukon Jack creates a special event to sponsor, such as the Yukon Jack Wrestling Championships, the company is the *title sponsor* and the activity is called *event marketing*. Thus, event sponsorship can be an integrated marketing communication that is both a public relations effort and a sales promotion effort. The What Went Right? feature explains how the Chemical Bank/Chase Corporate Challenge has grown into a major event.

CRISIS MANAGEMENT

Sometimes unfortunate executives find that a tragic event, such as an airplane crash or criticism from an activist group like Greenpeace, creates a public relations crisis. **Crisis management** is a public relations effort aimed at disseminating information during an emergency.

Public relations specialists believe that managers should make themselves available to journalists as quickly as possible after a crisis strikes. In the case of a plane crash or a health care scare, the public has an urgent need for information. Thus, the company should not delay; it should respond immediately.

Another guideline for public relations efforts is to ask top executives to get involved when a crisis occurs. Top executives can be very effective as company spokespersons. During a crisis, executives should take time to communicate

Crisis management
A public relations effort that involves disseminating information during an emergency.

important information about company policy regarding the emergency. Experience shows that it is vital that these executives tell the truth, rather than using subterfuge to buy time. It is also wise to apply the K.I.S.S. formula—Keep It Short and Simple (or Keep It Simple, Stupid)—in their remarks. A message that is too complicated for the public to understand can defeat the purpose of crisis management.

Sometimes rumors about a company's operations or products reach near-crisis proportions. When a company wants to cope with rumors, it should develop a plan of action. The following steps are recommended for *rumor control:*[12]

1. Create a rumor center and appoint a person to be responsible for its operation on a constant basis. Have the rumor center trace the rumor's origins.
2. Send out the correct facts—don't just deny the rumor. Demonstrate the truth to dispel the rumor.
3. Hold press conferences when appropriate.
4. Ask a respected third party, such as an outside expert, to comment on the rumor.
5. Treat the rumor locally when appropriate.

INTERNAL MARKETING AND EMPLOYEE RELATIONS

One of an organization's most important publics is its managers and employees. Employees who feel that they are important parts of a worthwhile activity, who identify themselves with the creation of good products for others, who take pride in the delivery of outstanding service, and who understand the workings of the organization are likely to be satisfied employees.[14] Giving them a sense of identification and satisfaction with the company should be a priority for every organization.

Internal marketing was discussed in Chapter 11.

INTEGRATED MARKETING COMMUNICATIONS AND PUBLIC RELATIONS

In a small company, the primary promotional tool of public relations is often publicity. However, major corporations use all forms of promotion for public relations. For example, product recall efforts often combine advertising with press conferences and news releases. Public relations campaigns, like all promotional campaigns, should use an integrated marketing communications approach. Each

---

what went wrong?

Intel Intel Corporation, the leading maker of computer chips, had sold more than 3 million Pentium chips to computer manufacturers when revelations that the Pentium chips were flawed became public late in 1994. The original Pentium chips made mistakes in some mathematical calculations when converting complex decimal numbers into binary numbers. Intel discovered the error in the summer of 1994 and changed the chip's design. The company, however, remained silent about the flaw until a mathematics professor documented the bug. After the company pleaded ignorance about the flaw, the professor posted the results of his research on the Internet.

Intel then responded by saying that a Pentium user was likely to encounter an error only once in 27,000 years and that off-the-shelf software was not affected. The company said that the flaw was a serious problem only for people who use computers in specialized math and scientific calculations. The company would, however, replace the chip for customers who could demonstrate that they used their Pentium-based PCs for such complex calculations.

However, soon after the news broke, jokes like the following appeared on the Internet.

Question: What do you get when you cross a Pentium PC with a research grant?
Answer: A mad scientist.

When IBM's research lab found that certain calculations on common spreadsheet programs could turn up an error as often as once every 24 days, the incident became a full-blown public relations disaster for Intel. On December 12, 1994, IBM stopped shipping its personal computers with the Pentium chip. Then the Food & Drug Administration announced that it was investigating whether the Pentium chip may have caused inaccurate data to be supplied by pharmaceutical manufacturers seeking approval for drugs. Attorneys General in two states called on Intel to be honest with consumers. More than 10,000 messages about Intel were posted on the Internet. By December 21, Intel had been humbled. The company's new policy was to replace any customer's chip. The president of the company said, "To some users, the [old] policy seemed arrogant and uncaring. . . . We were motivated by a feeling that this [replacement of the chip] was not necessary for many people. We still believe that, but want to stand behind our product."[13]

promotional element should be employed so that its unique characteristics can help the company communicate a unified message. Because integrated marketing communication is so important, large public relations companies such as Hill & Knowlton and Ketchum PR are as familiar with the use of advertising as they are with publicity to tell a company's story.

INTERNATIONAL PUBLIC RELATIONS

Throughout this book, the importance of understanding local cultures has been stressed. As you can imagine, understanding language, norms, values, religious traditions, government regulations, and other dimensions of the culture is absolutely vital in international public relations. This topic is complex and cannot be dealt with here in any depth. Suffice it to say that employing public relations consultants with experience in local areas should always be considered by any multinational organization.

EVALUATING AND MONITORING PUBLIC RELATIONS

Public relations managers should not just rely on their own intuition about what the public thinks of their company. If managers really want to know what people think about the company's reputation, they need to systematically gather information from the public. Marketing research should be used to ask customers and noncustomers how they feel about the company. Focus groups and surveys are common ways of gathering information about the public's attitudes toward the company image. In most image research, attitudes toward competitors are also measured and used as a benchmark. That way, a company will know, for example, whether it is seen as more socially responsible or as less socially responsible than the competition.

Monitoring newspaper, television, and radio news coverage is another means to learn the public's thinking. Press clippings and videotapes of television news stories are often systematically analyzed to quantify the content of these communications.

summary

1 *Explain the purposes of sales promotion.*

Sales promotion programs support other promotional elements, which in turn support the sales promotion. The purpose of a typical sales promotion effort is to bolster or complement other elements of the promotional mix during a specific time period. Sales promotions occur at both the wholesale and retail level and the consumer level.

2 *Identify each of the major sales promotion tools at the wholesale and retail level.*

Sales promotions at the wholesale and retail level include trade shows, contests, point-of-purchase displays, cooperative advertising, and allowances.

3 *Identify each of the major sales promotion tools aimed at the ultimate consumer.*

Popular sales promotion tools at the consumer level are product sampling, coupons, rebates, contests and sweepstakes, premiums and self-liquidating pre-miums, multiple-purchase offers, and point-of-purchase materials.

4 *Explain why tie-ins are popular as sales promotions.*

A tie-in involves a collaborative effort between two or more organizations or brands that decide to be partners in a promotional effort. Tie-ins borrow interest from movies, events, or other marketing efforts. Tie-ins with premiums are popular, but contests, sweepstakes, coupons, and other sales promotion elements can also use a tie-in approach.

5 *Define public relations and explain how publicity should be managed.*

Public relations is the managerial activity that involves identifying, establishing, and maintaining beneficial relationships between an organization and its publics. Its specific purposes are to enhance the organizational image and to convey product information. Favorable publicity can have the same impact as advertising. Hence, effective marketers plan publicity with as much care and consideration as they give to the rest of the promotional mix.

6 *Define publicity and discuss how it is different from public relations.*

Publicity involves the communication of information about a company or its products by a third party. In general, the information must be newsworthy if it is to result in publicity for the marketer. Publicity can be positive or negative. Usually, the more engrossing and captivating the material, the more likely it is to be publicized. Publicity and public relations are not the same, and they should not be confused. *Public relations* is a broader term that refers to all means of enhancing organizational image and communicating product information; it includes more than just publicity. Public relations efforts have various target audiences—not only consumers but also stockholders, government bodies, environmental groups, and the like.

7 *Understand the basics of crisis management.*

Crisis management is a public relations effort aimed at disseminating information during an emergency. Company officials should make themselves available to journalists as quickly as possible after a crisis strikes. Executives should get involved when a crisis occurs because they can be very effective as company spokespersons.

key terms

trade show (p. 570)
contest (p. 570)
point-of-purchase materials (p. 570)
cooperative advertising (p. 570)

allowance (p. 571)
product sampling (p. 571)
rebate (p. 572)
premium (p. 572)

news release (p. 577)
press conference (p. 577)
crisis management (p. 580)

questions for review & critical thinking

1. Define sales promotion, and explain why it might be used instead of advertising or personal selling.
2. Some sales promotions are geared toward stimulating activity among wholesalers and retailers; others are geared toward influencing ultimate consumers. How do the objectives of these types of promotion differ?
3. Give your opinion on the likely effectiveness of each of the following sales promotion tactics.
   a. A rebate offer on a car battery
   b. Selling four pairs of panty hose for the price usually charged for a three-unit package
   c. A sweepstakes contest conducted by a regional airline
   d. A free screwdriver with a can of WD-40
4. What type of marketers emphasize public relations in their promotional mixes? Why?

5. Discuss how a political candidate for a national office might develop an integrated communications strategy for both advertising and public relations.
6. Identify two separate marketing organizations that might jointly benefit from a tie-in collaboration. Explain how.
7. Provide some examples of unethical sales promotion and public relations efforts. Why are they unethical?
8. Form small groups as determined by your instructor. Each group should brainstorm ideas about how a local restaurant or bar could use sales promotion creatively. After 10 minutes of brainstorming, the group should evaluate these ideas and select three for presentation to the class.

marketing plan—right or wrong?

1. In the 1994 remake of the classic *Miracle on 34th Street,* the Santa who claims to be the authentic Kris Kringle works for the C. F. Cole department store—not Macy's as in the 1947 original. Macy's declined to have its name used in the film and passed up the potential publicity.

2. *Baywatch* is planning a promotion on 100 college campuses to discover college men and women who have what it takes to be on *Baywatch*. The program will involve product sampling, premium giveaways, and coupons. A new microbrewery is considering getting involved in the sales promotion.
3. A major oil company wants to understand why the business media seem to be out to get them. The plan is to hire a public relations company that tracks and analyzes articles. The PR firm says it can tell its clients how many relevant articles were published over time; rate them as positive, negative, or neutral toward the company; identify the authors who wrote the articles; and determine whether these individuals are objective.

zikmund.swcollege.com

exercise

Go to www.mypoints.com to see a system for earning redeemable points while using the Internet. How does this differ from the typical frequency marketing program, such as an airline frequent flyer program?

address book (useful urls)

Sweepstakes Online	www.sweepstakesonline.com
Publicity Club of Chicago	www.publicity.org
Public Relations Society of America	www.prsa.org

ethically right or wrong?

A large computer company was downsizing its operation by offering employees early retirement and telling some people that they would be laid off if they did not accept the retirement package. At the same time, the company spent almost a quarter of a million dollars to construct a Rose Bowl float that was used for only a few hours during the New Year's Day parade. Was this public relations effort proper, in light of the company's financial problems?

TAKE A STAND

1. Marketers of tobacco are restricted from using television advertising. Self-regulation among liquor marketers keeps most companies from advertising on television. Should such companies be allowed to sponsor sporting events that children might attend?
2. A business-to-business marketer holds a sweepstakes that requires visitors to its booth at an industry trade show to fill out a form. The marketer does not use a random drawing, but picks as the winning company a company that is a good prospect for future business.
3. A prankster writes a phony Microsoft press release that says the computer software giant is planning to buy the Catholic Church. Microsoft says the story has no truth to it. The person starting the rumor just wanted to have some fun. Was this wrong?

Stone Hill Winery

Changing tastes in wines during the late '70s and early '80s were hard for vintners Jim and Betty Held to swallow.

Baby-boomer professionals were replacing older, blue-collar types as the predominant U.S. wine drinkers, and dry wines were replacing the sweet in consumer preferences. The Helds' Stone Hill Winery, of Hermann, Missouri, wasn't suited to the shift. Its products were sweet and semisweet; Missouri's harsh winters were unfriendly to now-favored European grape varieties such as cabernet, chardonnay, and zinfandel.

With an onslaught of competition from new California wineries and waves of advertising that put Stone Hill's low-budget advertising in the shade, Stone Hill wines went from top to bottom shelves in the stores.

Other Missouri wineries also suffered, and some went under. Not Stone Hill. The Helds charted a new course, aided by the expertise of three of their children, who had won grape-growing and wine-making degrees from the University of California, Fresno.

Investment in new vineyards and equipment would enable Stone Hill to compete with California wines—in price as well as quality, if the investment was large enough to provide economies of scale. To raise the money, Stone Hill had to grow significantly.[15]

QUESTIONS

1. Suppose Stone Hill decided that sales promotion was the only way it could afford to promote its product. What sales promotion strategy would you recommend?
2. How would you implement your strategy?

Gourmet Our Way

Cascia Hall Preparatory School, in Tulsa, Oklahoma, was Oklahoma's first Augustinian prep school. From its initial enrollment of 25 boys, Cascia Hall has successfully educated and graduated over 2,400 young men and women.[16] In 1995, Cascia Hall facilities included a high school, library, chapel, middle school, tennis complex, two gymnasiums, numerous playing fields, and a running track. The clinker brick, slate-roofed buildings of Neo-French-Norman architecture make Cascia Hall's 40-acre campus very attractive. "Truth, Unity, and Charity" are the essence of the school's tradition.

In an effort to help parents and alumni all feel part of the Cascia Hall "family," the school undertook an effort to produce a cookbook. All proceeds from the non-profit cookbook were slated to go to the charitable trust at Cascia Hall.

A cookbook committee, chaired by three strong-willed women, was formed in 1993. They arranged for a contract to publish the cookbook with Wimmer Press of Memphis. Two and one-half years later, their effort resulted in Gourmet Our Way.

Hundreds of Tulsans—Cascia Hall families, friends, and professional chefs—contributed recipes that focus on fresh flavors and seasonal sensations. The result is a collection of unique recipes that reflect lifestyles in the gracious, cosmopolitan city of Tulsa. *Gourmet Our Way* is filled with simple-to-prepare recipes for garden fresh soups and salads, flavorful entrees, and luscious desserts. Spinach Crepes Stuffed with Tomato-Pesto Cheese, Tomato Angel Hair Pasta with Basil and Crab, Pork Roast with Peppercorn Mustard Crust and Cider Gravy, and Asparagus Lasagna are among the dishes evaluated and tested by Cascia Hall's cookbook committee. In addition to recipes designed to tantalize any family's palate, there are menus for casual entertaining and memorable dinner parties. Stories on the early beginnings of Tulsa, its history, architecture, community events, family gathering places, and volunteerism in Tulsa and at Cascia Hall add spice to the book, making it a pleasure to read and give to friends. The watercolor that graces *Gourmet Our Way*'s unique cover was painted by P. S. Gordon, renowned Tulsa artist.

Although Wimmer would advertise *Gourmet Our Way* at trade shows and in its catalog, the primary job of promoting the cookbook rested with the volunteers from Cascia Hall. The cookbook committee wanted to make sure the cookbook-buying public understood that this was an upscale book—more like a Junior League book than a "family favorites" collection of the kind published by many local organizations. However, they had not prepared for a formal public relations program.

QUESTIONS

1. What public relations objectives should be set for *Gourmet Our Way?*
2. What specific public relations efforts would you recommend for the volunteers on the cookbook committee?
3. Write a press release for the cookbook.

enhance your marketing skills

You will find each exercise on the CD-ROM developed for use with this textbook. Each exercise has a name and is located within a module. For example, the first exercise can be found in the Micromarketing Module by clicking on Marketing Communications.

MICROMARKETING MODULE
Marketing Communications

1. What factors influence effective communication in advertising, public relations, and personal selling?

MICROMARKETING MODULE
Advertising

2. If the California Fluid Milk Processors Association wanted your recommendation for an advertising agency, what would you tell them?

cross-functional insights

Many theories and principles from other business disciplines can provide insights about the role marketing plays in an organization. The questions in this section are designed to help you think about integrating what you have learned in other business courses with the marketing principles explained in this textbook.

Promotional Budget   After managers have planned a promotional mix, they must determine if the organization can afford it. Determining how much money to allocate to each promotional element is a matter of budgeting.

Should advertising be treated as an expense or a capital expenditure?

Advertising   Advertising includes an informative or persuasive message carried by a nonpersonal medium and paid for by a sponsor whose product is in some way identified in the message.

When is deceptive advertising considered to be fraud?
How does the organizational mission affect advertising?
What is the nature of the collaborative relationship between the advertiser and the advertising agency?
What is the Federal Trade Commission's primary function? What types of penalties can the FTC impose on marketers who have used deceptive or unfair advertising?

Personal Selling/Creative Selling   Personal selling is a person-to-person dialogue between buyer and seller.

What should a sales representative know about listening skills?
Is on-the-job training or classroom training more important for a sales representative?
How is information technology changing field selling?

Is diversity training necessary for sales personnel?
As a company becomes more involved in using sales teamwork, will the entire department come to be composed of self-managed work teams? Will the teams assume many of the tasks normally believed to be managerial functions, such as making decisions about job assignments, budgeting, scheduling, and hiring?

Sales Management   Sales management is the marketing management activity dealing with planning, organizing, directing, and controlling the personal selling effort.

What planning activities are required of sales managers?
What human relations skills are important to sales managers?
How much authority should a national sales manager delegate to regional sales managers?
What should a sales manager know about the reinforcement theory of motivation?
Write a job description, and give job specifications for the following: sales representative; regional sales manager; national sales manager.
What should a sales manager know about the Uniform Commercial Code for sales contracts?
What should an international sales manager know about the Foreign Corrupt Practices Act?

Integrated Marketing Communications   The term *integrated marketing communications* is used to remind managers that all elements of the promotional mix should be coordinated and systematically planned so that they are in harmony.

What management skills are helpful in developing integrated marketing communications?
How important to effective integrated marketing communications efforts is a company's management information system?

everything is worth what its purchasers will pay for it

Pricing Strategy

–WHO SAID THIS?

part

6

Everything is worth what
its purchasers will pay
for it

THAT'S WHO SAID IT!

—SYRUS

Publius Syrus was born in Rome during the first century B.C.
A former slave who achieved the status of full citizen, Publius
Syrus became the creator of mimes, Roman farces peopled by
slapstick characters. His life experiences gave him a great sense
of value.

chapter
19

Introduction to Pricing Concepts

LEARNING OBJECTIVES

After you have studied this chapter, you will be able to:

Define price and discuss it.

1

Tell how price interacts with the rest of the marketing mix.

2

Analyze price's place in the economy.

3

Outline the fundamentals of pricing strategy.

4

Characterize the relationship between price and organizational objectives.

5

(continued on next page)

6 Relate the demand in a target market to the prices charged.

7 Understand that demand and cost considerations influence pricing.

8 Differentiate among price elasticity, price inelasticity, and price cross-elasticity.

in telephone lingo, Ruth Holder is a "spinner." She can't say no when long-distance carriers dangle lower phone rates in front of her.

Holder—who often spends more than $100 a month on calls to Florida, Ohio, and the Virgin Islands—used AT&T when she moved to Washington "because that was the carrier I knew." She later switched to MCI to join a Friends and Family calling circle.

"At that time, MCI was giving frequent-flier miles and AT&T was not," says Holder, an editor with the non-profit Alliance for Public Technology, a telecommunications group. "That played a part in my decision."

She returned to AT&T when it mailed a $75 check to win back her business, but went back to MCI when it came courting with an offer of 50 percent off all her calls for 6 months.

Her savings so far: more than $445. She also makes the new company pay the transfer fee—usually $5—to the local carrier. And her switching days might not be over.

"Recently I got a call from AT&T offering to pay me $75 plus give me 50 percent off my bill for 6 months," says Holder. "I haven't yet. But I'm thinking about it."

Spinners are among the most fickle of the estimated 16.1 million households (about 16.6 per-

cent) that changed long-distance carriers at least once in a 12-month period, according to a survey by the Yankee Group in Boston. About 97,000 households changed four or more times.

AT&T says there are about 27 million residential switchers each year. Spinners were created by the mud-slinging competition for customers by the long-distance industry.

That competition is fierce because big bucks are involved. The long-distance consumer market had revenue of about $35 billion in 1994.

MCI promotes New Friends and Family calling circles, AT&T its True Savings and True USA plans, and Sprint its 10-cents-a-minute offer. Special incentives to get customers to switch can range from cash, free calls, and Walt Disney merchandise to travel discounts and plane tickets.

Some consumers ditch carriers because they are unhappy with service. But spinners switch repeatedly because of marketing incentives. As the stakes soar, more spinners are entering the fray. Michelle Margolis had been with AT&T, then switched to an MCI calling circle, but returned to AT&T when it sent her a $100 check earlier this year.

"Over time I've gotten $25 or $50 checks," Margolis says. "I just threw them out. But for $100 I figured it was worth it."[1]

> SPINNERS **WERE CREATED BY THE MUD-SLINGING COMPETITION FOR CUSTOMERS BY THE LONG-DISTANCE INDUSTRY. THAT COMPETITION IS FIERCE BECAUSE BIG BUCKS ARE INVOLVED.**

The influence of spinners on the long-distance telephone market presents a dramatic example of the importance of pricing in marketing strategy and brand-switching behavior. Price, as the story about spinners illustrates, plays a major role in the marketing mix. A lower price can be a means to enter a market or to gain a competitive advantage. A proper price can make the difference between success and failure.

This chapter focuses on the nature of price as a marketing mix variable and the role of price in the economy. The chapter provides a framework by examining the fundamental concepts underlying pricing strategy. It shows the interrelationship between overall organizational and marketing objectives and an organization's pricing objectives. In doing this, it addresses target market considerations, supply and demand, price elasticity, and the nature of costs.

What Is Price?

As you have seen, marketing involves exchanging things of value. **Value** is a quantitative measure of the power one good or service has to attract another good or service in an exchange. An auto mechanic could exchange four tuneups for two months of coffee and doughnuts from a nearby diner. Such a trade is possible because the tuneups, the coffee, and the doughnuts all have value. When products are exchanged for one another, the trade is called **barter.**

While it would be possible to value every product in the world in terms of every other product, such a system would be complicated and unwieldy. It is far easier to express these many values in terms of the single variable of money. Price is thus a statement of value, because it is the amount of money or other consideration given in exchange for a product.

Price has many names. These names vary according to tradition or the interests of the seller. *Rent, fee,* and *donation* are terms used in specific exchange situations to describe price. Some sellers avoid using the word *price* in order to make what is offered for sale appear to be of a quality that price cannot fully describe. Thus, a student pays tuition, not a price, for education. A commuter pays a toll. A professor who gives an off-campus speech "accepts an honorarium." A physician charges a fee for professional services. Universities, governments, professors, and doctors all sell their services for a price, no matter what that price is called.

In brief, marketing involves exchanges of things that have value. The name most commonly used to describe this value is price. In the United States, price is most commonly expressed in dollars and cents.

Price As a Marketing Mix Variable

Price has a special significance in that it ultimately "pays" for all of a firm's activities. Because sales revenue equals price times unit sales volume, the price of a product is one of the prime determinants of sales revenues. If the price can be increased while unit volume and costs remain the same, revenues and profits will be increased. For this reason alone, pricing decisions are important. But price is important for another reason. Like other marketing mix variables, price influences unit sales volume. Thus, proper pricing of a product is expected to increase the quantity demanded. Price is perhaps the most flexible element of the marketing mix because it can be changed rapidly in response to changes in the environment.[2]

In setting prices, many marketers start with a basic price quote, called a **list price.** Price adjustments may be made when the season changes, when a buyer purchases a large quantity of a good, or for other reasons. Many marketers adjust list price with discounts or rebates. For example, retailers often mark down, or reduce, the list price when merchandise is out of season or moving slowly.

A list price functions as a communication tool by adding symbolic value to a good or service and by helping to position the brand in relation to competitors.

Value
The power of one product to attract another product in an exchange.

Barter
The exchange of products without the use of money.

List price
The basic price quote, before adjustment.

A high price may suggest a high-status good, a low price may suggest a bargain, and a discount coupon or rebate may encourage purchases by people who would otherwise not buy the product. Entire positioning strategies may revolve around price. For example, Tiffany & Company, a chain of exclusive jewelry stores, maintains an image as a seller of products of the

A LIST PRICE FUNCTIONS AS A COMMUNICATION TOOL BY ADDING SYMBOLIC VALUE TO A GOOD OR SERVICE AND BY HELPING TO POSITION THE BRAND IN RELATION TO COMPETITORS.

highest quality by stocking reliable products and providing special services and also by charging comparatively high prices. Wal-Mart and Price Club stress bargains and must therefore keep prices at the lowest levels.

Price is closely related to other marketing variables and cannot be discussed without simultaneous consideration of product, place, and promotion. Pricing strategies must be consistent with the firm's other marketing mix decisions and must support the firm's other marketing strategies. For example, the Maytag product strategy—ensuring that customers will have "ten years of trouble-free operation"—stresses the quality and reliability that is highlighted in its advertising strategy, which is compatible with its premium pricing strategy. Although mechanical problems with its product are infrequent, Maytag's strategy requires the proper distribution system, for both its product and its service technicians. The premium pricing strategy, which allows an adequate profit margin for intermediaries, helps support the distribution strategy.

Price bears a special relationship to promotion. One job of promotion is to show potential buyers that an item is worth the price demanded. We can all think of products we bought or services we used because we believed that we were getting a good deal, a bargain, or high-quality workmanship. But after a bit of thought, we might admit that our favorable perception of the price or the quality originated in a familiar advertisement or a television salesperson's convincing presentation. In such instances, the consumer more willingly pays the asked-for price because promotion has convinced him or her that the price is justified.

Price competition
Competition based solely on price. It is especially important in the marketing of products that are not distinctive, such as raw materials.

what went *wrong?*

USA TODAY   An entirely new publishing and advertising economy is taking shape because of the Internet and the World Wide Web. It is changing the way information is priced.

In April 1995, *USA TODAY* announced it would begin providing software for people to access its Web site, charging $12.95 per month for 3 hours of access to its online newspaper, $2.50 for every hour beyond that. But after 4 months, it managed to attract only about 1,000 subscribers, a disastrous showing for a newspaper with a daily print circulation topping 2 million. A postmortem analysis indicated the paper's first mistake was the "unnecessary" move into the Internet access business, a commodity market well served by dozens of other companies. The second mistake was charging a subscription fee. In August 1995, *USA TODAY* began phasing out its software business and made its Web site free.

Consumers will rarely pay a subscription fee for access to a Web site. There are vast amounts of free information and users "treat information charges as damage, and route around them." In this sense, the Web is like cable TV: People will pay for delivery of the medium itself, but will pay extra for only one or two premium channels, if any.[3]

PRICE COMPETITION

The degree of **price competition** influences the nature of the marketing mix. Intensive price competition exists in many industries, especially those dealing with raw materials such as crude petroleum. Because competing products are not distinctive, price becomes the key marketing variable. In other product categories, price may be less important to the consumer than a distinctive product feature or a differentiated brand image. For products in these categories, the firm that emphasizes low price exclusively may find that competitors will meet this low price. Shortly after Tylenol was introduced, its maker, Johnson & Johnson, built strong brand-name recognition by emphasizing that acetaminophen is less irritating to the stomach than aspirin. Datril was introduced as a "me too" brand. The gist of its advertising campaign

Price is a primary consideration in the selection of brands of shopping goods. During periods of recession, consumers look for value. Everyday low prices work best during periods when consumers are price conscious.

was that Datril was lower in price than the leading brand, Tylenol. Unfortunately for Datril, when Tylenol marketers saw that Datril was becoming serious competition, Tylenol met Datril's price—thereby forcing Bristol-Myers to change all of the Datril advertising. The primary Datril strength, low price, was no longer an issue. Today, Datril itself is no longer an issue.

If price is the sole basis of competition, then competitors can easily take away a product's competitive advantage. Of course, if the low price is the result of technology and production efficiency that competitors cannot easily match in the short term, then a low-cost, lowest-price strategy may be effective.

PRICE AND MARKETING EFFECTIVENESS

As mentioned, in some competitive situations price may be less important than some other feature. Effective **nonprice competition** allows a marketer to charge premium prices. Indeed, price is often indicative of overall marketing effectiveness. Lego gets a price substantially above that of many of its competitors but nevertheless sells far more building-block toys than any of them. This is fairly substantial proof that Lego's overall marketing strategy produces a product, promotion, and distribution mix consistent with and supportive of its pricing strategy. Lego is thus better off than its competitors. The ability to maintain prices and sales volume in the face of relatively stiff competition certainly indicates an excellent marketing strategy and effective execution of that strategy.

Nonprice competition
Competition emphasizing marketing variables other than price—for example, product differentiation.

Price in the Economy

The main function of price in our relatively free-market economy is to help allocate goods and services. Most items of value are distributed to those who demand them and have the means to pay for them. When products are scarce or in short supply, prices are high, and wealthier citizens are better able than poorer citizens to afford them. Thus, from a macromarketing perspective, price allocates available goods and services within the economy by determining who will get them.

THUS, **FROM A MACROMARKETING PERSPECTIVE, PRICE ALLOCATES AVAILABLE GOODS AND SERVICES WITHIN THE ECONOMY BY DETERMINING WHO WILL GET THEM.**

Price also determines the quantity of goods and services that will be produced and marketed. An economist's explanation of demand and supply helps clarify the role of pricing in the economy.

The salary of a professional baseball player is a price—the price a team is willing to pay for the player's services. The ballplayer's position—whether he is a pitcher, outfielder, or infielder—partially establishes the demand for the player. However, a pitcher with a low E.R.A. or an outfielder with a batting average above .300 is in greater demand. Outstanding pitchers like Toronto's Roger Clemens, with a 2.07 E.R.A. and 21 wins in the 1997 season, are in great demand because the supply of such players is limited. His salary: $8,400,000 per year.

Demand curve
A graphic representation of the relationship between various prices and the amount of product that will be demanded at those prices; also called a *demand schedule.*

Supply curve
A graphic representation of the relationship between various prices and the amount of product that will be supplied at those prices; also called a *supply schedule.*

DEMAND CURVE

Demand is the quantity of a product consumers are willing and able to buy at a given price. Usually, the quantity demanded changes as price changes. Thus, you might be willing to pay someone $10 to clean your untidy bedroom each week. But you might have the room cleaned only every two weeks if the price rose to $25, and not at all at a price of $100. At $100, you would either clean the room yourself or leave it dirty! This relationship can be shown either as a table or as a curve, as in Exhibit 19-1.

The **demand curve,** or *schedule of demand,* is a graphic representation of the relationship between the various prices sellers might charge for a product and the amount of that product that buyers will demand at each price. Clearly, it would be a great help to marketers to have access to a specific demand curve for their industry. While marketers seldom have an exact demand schedule showing how much they can sell at price 1, price 2, and price 3, they may have some demand information from marketing research. At the very least, when precise demand curves cannot be drawn, marketers make assumptions about demand. A demand curve is represented by the line labeled *D* in Exhibit 19-2. Note that as price declines, an increasing quantity of the product is demanded.

SUPPLY CURVE

Supply is the quantity of a product that marketers are willing and able to sell at a given price in a given time period. A **supply curve,** or *supply schedule* (labeled *S* in Exhibit 19-2), graphically represents the amount of goods or services marketers will supply at various prices.

e x h i b i t **19-1**

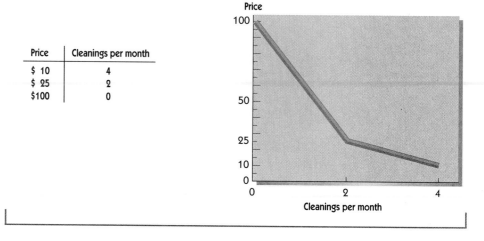

Changes in Cleanings Demanded As Price Increases

Price	Cleanings per month
$ 10	4
$ 25	2
$100	0

The Intersection of Supply and Demand

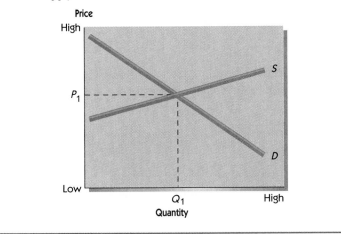

A supply curve shows that as prices become more attractive to suppliers (marketers), those suppliers will try to provide more of the product. Thus, in most cases, as prices rise, suppliers are encouraged to supply more product; and as prices fall, they will prefer to supply less.

The intersection of the industry demand and supply curves establishes the market price (P_1) and the quantity produced (Q_1), or size of the market. Thus, economic theory shows how price determines how much will be produced and distributed to members of society.

We have focused here on price for an industry, not for an individual firm marketing a product. We now turn our attention to pricing strategy for a firm.

focus on relationships

Hyatt Hotels   In the old days, large companies were famous for ruthlessly driving down supplier prices. Pitting one against another, for example. Or not paying bills until the supplier buckled under pressure. But Hyatt Hotels Corporation's president, Darryl Hartley-Leonard, has a better idea. "The best way to drive down supplier prices is to find additional customers for the supplier," he says. Rather than beat up suppliers in negotiations where both sides usually end up losing, Hartley-Leonard offers public testimonials and letters of support designed to create new business for Hyatt's suppliers. "The more money you help someone make, the more responsive they are going to be," he says.[4]

The Fundamentals of Pricing Strategy

Many mathematical tools can be used to determine the specific price that should be assigned to a particular product. Most marketing managers, however, would be reluctant to trust such an important matter as price setting exclusively to any mechanical technique. Company objectives, costs, and demand need to be considered. Further, managerial judgment, supported by marketing research, knowledge of competitors' actions, and an understanding of the target market's reaction to prices, plays an important role in pricing decisions. In setting prices, the following activities are essential:

1. Determine your pricing objectives.
2. Know the importance of price to your target market.
3. Know the demand for your product.
4. Understand your costs.
5. Determine your pricing strategy.

Of course, like other marketing mix decisions, pricing decisions are also influenced by environmental forces. Competitive forces and legal influences are extremely important factors. This chapter discusses the first four items listed above. Chapter 20 focuses on pricing strategies and tactics, as well as the legal aspects of pricing.

Pricing Objectives

Pricing objective
The desired result associated with a particular pricing strategy. The pricing objective must be consistent with other marketing objectives.

Although we are concerned here with pricing, we should mention again that **pricing objectives** must be coordinated with the firm's other marketing objectives. These must, in turn, flow from the company's overall objectives. Thus, if Toshiba seeks to become the leader in developing and marketing high-technology electronics products, all of its marketing objectives, including its pricing objectives, must be consistent with that broad company mission. For example, the objectives associated with a high level of product differentiation at the overall marketing level would not generally be compatible with an objective of always setting prices below competitors' prices.[5] The relationship of pricing decisions to organizational objectives is diagrammed in Exhibit 19-3.

With organizational objectives firmly in mind, marketers pricing a good or service must determine what specific objectives are to be accomplished with the pric-

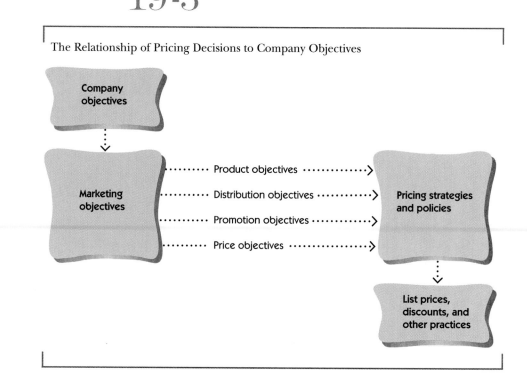

The Relationship of Pricing Decisions to Company Objectives

ing strategy. Managers should know why certain prices are being charged, as well as why these prices might differ from buyer to buyer and from time to time. A firm may face any number of problems and opportunities, and these may give rise to many pricing objectives. Some possible objectives are shown in Exhibit 19-4, along with possible pricing steps to be undertaken for each objective. We discuss some of these objectives in the remainder of this section.

The important thing to note is that each pricing strategy—each type and level of price—has logic and reason behind it. Prices are set to help bring about a result. The hoped-for result is the pricing objective. Clearly, objectives narrow the

Some Organizational Objectives and the Role Pricing Can Play in Attaining Them

e x h i b 19-4

MAIN FOCUS OF OBJECTIVES	PRICING STEPS TAKEN*	WHY TAKE SUCH STEPS?
Income		
Achieve a target return on investment (ROI)	Identify price levels that will yield the required return on investment.	Firm may have a required return on investment and may drop product lines that cannot reach that return.
Maximize profits	Control costs and adjust prices to achieve profit maximization.	All companies would like to achieve profit maximization. Some come close to this goal, particularly for certain items in their product mixes.
Increase cash flow	Adjust prices and discounts to encourage purchases and rapid payment.	The company may face a serious cash-flow problem and be unable to meet its obligations.
Survive/Keep a concern going	Adapt prices to permit the organization to "hold on" in periods of business downturns or until a buyer can be found.	The organization may be seeking to weather an economic storm or simply hold on for a few years. The organization may be for sale, and it is easier to sell a going concern than one that is out of business.
Sales		
Maintain market share	Assure that prices contribute to keeping sales in roughly the same position relative to those of competitors.	Many companies (such as Procter & Gamble in detergents) are long-time leaders and want to keep leadership positions.
Encourage sales growth	Adjust prices and discounts to encourage more purchases by existing buyers and to attract new buyers.	The firm may need a larger group of customers to ensure growth.
Competition		
Meet competition	Set prices about equal to those of competitors. Do the same with discounts offered.	Many firms avoid price competition and compete by means of nonprice competitive moves.
Avoid competition	Set prices at a level that will discourage competition in the firm's markets.	A firm with a local monopoly might choose to keep prices low so that no new competitors will be attracted to its market.
Undercut competition	Set prices lower than the competition's.	The organization might undercut competition to project a bargain image or to draw customers away from competitors.
Social Concerns		
Behave ethically	Because of special considerations, set prices at levels lower than they would have been set based on income, competition, or similar market factors.	A manufacturer of prescription medicines could charge almost any price for effective drugs but "does what's right," though this is partly to avoid government regulation.
Maintain employment	Set prices at levels that will maintain production and employment of workers.	An organization with strong community ties may seek to keep townspeople employed at least until a buyer for the company can be found.

*Notice that no consideration is given here to possible responses by competitors or shifts in demand.

range of pricing possibilities considerably and thus greatly facilitate the determining of price.

INCOME-ORIENTED OBJECTIVES

Organizations may focus on income-oriented pricing objectives because they find these goals compatible with the profitability dimension of the marketing concept. Although income-oriented objectives may be stated as short-term or long-term objectives, management should concentrate on the long run. In the short run, changes in the external environment, such as changes in a competitor's strategy, may hinder the achievement of an income target. Establishing a price that will ultimately achieve the desired profit level should remain the objective. Here, we discuss income-oriented objectives that involve achieving a target return on investment and maximizing profit.

Return on investment (ROI)
The ratio of profits to assets (or net worth) for an organization, a unit of an organization, a product line, or a brand; also called the *profit target*.

Target Return on Investment **Return on investment (ROI)** is the ratio of profits to assets (or net worth) for an organization, an organizational unit (such as a division), a product line, or a brand. (See our Internet Appendix on Financial and Economic Analysis for Marketers for a discussion of how to calculate return on investment and other financial measures.) The ROI is also called the *profit target*. If management has determined that a certain ROI is needed from each product or product line, the prices for these must be set with the return objective in mind. Such a price is referred to as an *ROI price*.

Return on investment considerations are important to many pricing decisions because they provide a means to evaluate alternative marketing opportunities (or other investment options). Suppose two proposed products are expected to generate approximately the same sales volume, but one product can be priced to yield an ROI of 10 percent and the other an ROI of 30 percent. The latter product will be selected, unless a factor such as greater risk renders it less attractive. The choice between the two marketing opportunities is made easier because the ROI pricing method suggests a standard that the marketing manager can use for reference as the decision-making process continues.

Turnover
Sales divided by average inventory. Turnover measures the speed with which merchandise is sold.

Turnover (sales divided by average inventory) is an important factor in influencing the ROI of many organizations, especially retailers and wholesalers. Grocery store pricing strategies, for example, recognize that a higher return on investment may be generated if there is a rapid turnover of inventory. Thus, a grocery store might have a profit margin of less than 5 percent but a higher return on investment.

Profit Maximization A form of pricing is suggested by the expression "all that the traffic will bear." Perhaps this is a distasteful idea, but in certain circumstances it works. Faced with a shortage of apartments in California's Silicon Valley, newcomers are willing to pay more rent than they had planned to pay rather than have no place to stay. Victims of cancer or other serious diseases frequently demonstrate that they will pay any price for a cure. In these and similar situations, sellers might try to raise their prices to the highest levels. This course of action is exemplified by the classic, but rare, monopolist that prices a good or service at the highest possible level. However, few, if any, businesses are free to behave in this manner, since legislation has restricted the extreme forms of profit maximization sometimes practiced by monopolies.

Aside from questions of ethics, an "all the traffic will bear" approach violates a major premise of the marketing concept: the idea that a consumer orientation and relationship building will lead to long-term profitability. Maximizing prices, even if it is tempting in the short run, can be disastrous if it results in threats, boycotts, bad public relations, or government action. Furthermore, a business charging a very high price over a short period runs the risk of being driven out of business by competitors willing to provide the same service or a substitute good at a more reasonable price. Given the realities of our market economy, then, effective marketers focus on maximizing profits over the long term and, accordingly, charge prices that will keep customers and the government comparatively content.

SALES-ORIENTED OBJECTIVES

Prices may be set to encourage sales growth or to maintain or increase market share. Sales-oriented pricing objectives are often intertwined with competitive objectives and with the company's commitment to the marketing concept, which emphasizes profitable sales volume. We limit our discussion here to objectives concerning market share.

Market share refers to the percentage of total industry sales accounted for by a particular firm. Caterpillar accounts for a large portion of the total sales in the excavator and road-building-tractor industry and thus has a large share of the market. In the soft-drink industry, the same is true of Coca-Cola. These companies, for financial reasons or for reasons of pride, seek to protect their impressive shares of the market. They keep their prices at reasonable levels even when it might appear that the popularity of certain items would permit them to raise prices without losing sales. The objective of this type of pricing is to maintain market share.

Price might also be used aggressively by firms seeking to enlarge market share. Such firms may cut prices drastically in an attempt to attract customers away from competitors. However, such a move can backfire. Competitors may begin to lower their own prices, setting off a price war. Or customers may come to believe that the price reduction signals a cutback in the product's quality. Thus, price cuts are generally used to attract customers on a temporary basis. Coupons that expire on a certain date, rebates available for a short time, and January white sales are examples of temporary price cuts.

Market share
The percentage of total industry sales accounted for by a particular firm or the percentage of sales of a given product accounted for by a particular brand.

COMPETITION-ORIENTED OBJECTIVES

The effective marketer invariably tempers pricing judgments with considerations related to competition. Several situations in which competition is an issue in pricing decisions are discussed here.

Avoiding Competition One pricing objective is to underprice goods and services to avoid attracting competitors. Businesses using this approach reason that it is better to own the only store in the neighborhood and make a reasonable profit than to make a large profit that attracts other marketers to the service area.

Meeting Competition Businesses may find it necessary to price goods or services at approximately the levels charged by competitors. Indeed, unless the marketer is in the rare situation of holding an unbreakable patent on a product that is unique, difficult to copy, and in great demand, it is impossible to set prices without at least considering this strategy. Many goods are so similar that buyers can and do consider them to be virtually the same, forcing the individual firm to set its prices at the level established by competitors. New brands of coffee, for example, are generally priced at the going rate because one coffee is highly substitutable for another. Most consumers will not buy a brand of regular coffee that costs $3 more per pound than the others.

Where a brand is considerably more expensive than others, the higher pricing must be supported by other marketing strategies. These might include producing a genuinely better coffee blend, promoting the brand with an extensive advertising campaign, positioning it as a gourmet coffee, or packaging the coffee in attractive reusable containers.

Stabilizing Prices A marketer may aim to match competitors' prices or maintain existing price differentials in order to avoid injurious price wars and help stabilize the general price level. This is a **price stabilization** strategy. It is fairly common, particularly in the retailing of gasoline and groceries. Though price wars in these

Price stabilization
A pricing objective aimed at avoiding widely fluctuating prices. The marketer with this objective sets prices to match competitors' prices or to maintain existing price differentials.

fields are not unheard of, normally all gas stations in town charge roughly equal prices for fuel, and all grocery stores charge approximately the same price for milk. Thus, prices remain stable and predictable.

OBJECTIVES RELATED TO SOCIAL CONCERNS

Many organizations, especially not-for-profit organizations, set pricing objectives on the basis of social concerns. For example, zoos might be able to raise prices but refuse to do so because the organizational mission stresses public education above profit maximization. Pricing objectives for other organizations, especially sole proprietorships, might simply be to make enough to meet the payroll. Pricing objectives based on social concerns are highly interrelated with the ethical and legal aspects of pricing. We discuss this topic further in Chapter 20.

Target Market Considerations

Pricing decisions are affected by many factors. The most significant of these is demand from the organization's target market. Even when a competitor making the same product changes its price, target market considerations are important because the competitor's move may affect only the competitor's target market. In essence, the question the marketing manager faces is this: "Who are our customers and what do they want the price to be?" Many market segments are price-conscious. Recall that

> IN ESSENCE, THE QUESTION THE MARKETING MANAGER FACES IS THIS: "WHO ARE OUR CUSTOMERS AND WHAT DO THEY WANT THE PRICE TO BE?"

Pillsbury's Oven Lovin' cookie dough, loaded with Hershey's chocolate chips, Reese's Pieces, and Brach's candies and packaged in a resealable tub, was a failure. One reason for the failure was that price-conscious shoppers didn't think the product was worth 20 cents more than the company's conventional tube of dough, especially since the new package was 10 percent smaller.

Nevertheless, the notion that the customer wants the lowest price is not always correct. Diamonds and Rolls Royce automobiles are expensive partly because people expect them to be expensive. A $100 bottle of perfume may contain only $10 to $20 worth of scent; the rest of the price goes to advertising, packaging, distribution, and profit. When consumers buy such perfume, they are buying atmosphere, hope, the feeling of being someone special, and pride in having "the best."

Even frequently purchased products can benefit from the customer's willingness to pay a higher price rather than a lower one. Parents do not usually brag about buying bargain-priced baby food for their infants, nor do most hosts discuss what an inexpensive brand of whiskey they've been able to buy while offering their guests a drink.

When targeting certain markets, then, marketers can expect to sell more at a higher price than at a lower one. However, most successful marketers do not employ high prices to appeal to buyers. Instead, they offer reasonably priced products that prove popular to target markets.

Know Your Demand

Marketers need to know how many people will buy their products. How many people are willing to buy and how much they will buy are primarily functions of price. Marketers use the concept of price elasticity to describe how sensitive demand is to price.

PRICE ELASTICITY OF DEMAND

Price elasticity measures the effect of a change in price on the quantity of a product demanded. Price elasticity refers to price sensitivity. Specifically, price elasticity measures what percentage change in quantity demanded is induced by a percentage change in price. Exhibit 19-5 illustrates the concept of *price elasticity of demand.*

Logic would lead us to predict that (1) a decline in the price of a product might lead to an increase in the quantity of it demanded and (2) the rate of increase might differ from case to case and from product to product. For example, we would expect that bread sales might increase as prices went down. However, the rise would be slight and would happen slowly, because bread is a common, unexciting product that most people can afford and are already buying. Demand increases are also limited by the fact that there is a limit to how much bread people can eat.

This situation is demonstrated in Exhibit 19-5(a). A decrease in price from P_1 to P_2 increases demand from Q_1 to Q_2. The gap between the two Qs is far less than the gap between the two Ps, illustrating *relative price inelasticity* of demand.

Price elasticity
A measure of the effect of a change in price on the quantity of product demanded.

e x h i b 19-5

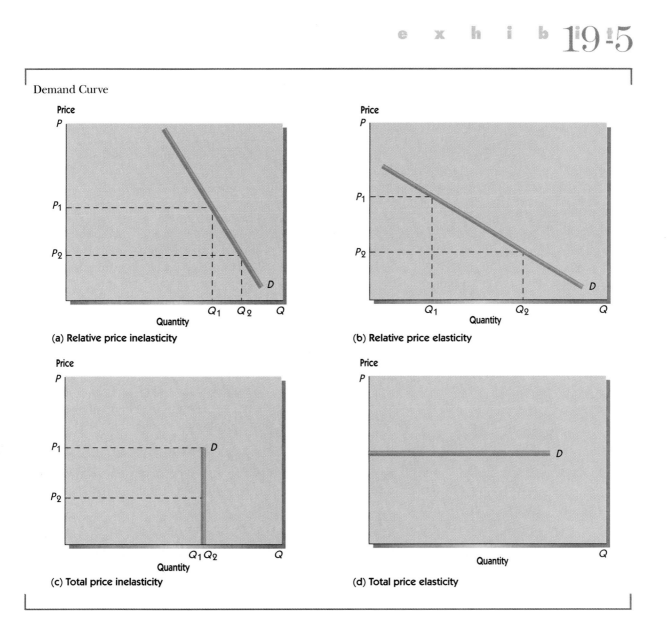

Demand Curve

(a) Relative price inelasticity

(b) Relative price elasticity

(c) Total price inelasticity

(d) Total price elasticity

That is, demand is not very flexible when price is changed. Thus, when price is raised from P_2 back to P_1, demand does not decrease rapidly; it is price inelastic.

The opposite situation is shown in Exhibit 19-5(b), in which a downward change in price does increase demand significantly. More than that, the increase in demand appears to be greater than the decrease in price might warrant. This curve might apply to, say, filet mignon. This product is very much in demand even though most families buy it in limited amounts because of its high price. The shopper who finds that the price of the steak has been reduced is likely to stock up. Thus, the demand for the product is highly flexible, or *elastic,* in terms of price.

If the slope of the demand (*D*) line in Exhibit 19-5(a) increases so that it becomes straight up and down as in Exhibit 19-5(c), the line shows absolute and complete inelasticity of demand. Regardless of the price charged, be it high or low, the same quantity is demanded. No change in price will affect demand. The classic example of this phenomenon is medicine sales. Suppose a patient needs one dose per day of a certain drug—say, insulin—to stay alive. If the price fell, the patient would not buy more than the prescribed amount. If the price became extremely high, the same single treatment would be demanded, even if the patient had to resort to drastic measures to meet the bill.

Another special case is shown in Exhibit 19-5(d). Here, the demand curve is perpendicular to the price axis. In this situation, there is a single price, and customers demand various quantities at that one price. Sometimes they demand no goods; sometimes they demand many units of goods. Whereas the vertical curve shows absolute price inelasticity, the horizontal line demonstrates *total price elasticity*—no change in price is needed to increase or decrease quantities demanded. The classic example of this situation involves the wheat farmer who grows a product that is nearly identical to that of all competitors and who is unable to influence market price. Such a farmer can only earn the going price and sell as much wheat as he chooses at that price.

The demand schedules for most products lie somewhere between the extremes of total price inelasticity and total price elasticity. It is the often-difficult task of the marketer to determine the nature of the demand curve for each product offered to the market. Information published by trade associations and information from other sources should assist in this chore. Experimenting with different price levels may also provide insights. Marketers experiment in this way every day. When items don't sell at one price, they charge a different price or offer a discount. They move, either consciously or unconsciously, to a new point on the demand schedule.

CROSS-ELASTICITY OF DEMAND

Cross-elasticity
Elasticity in the demand for one product in relation to the prices of substitutable or complementary products.

One other aspect of elasticity of demand should be mentioned here. Many products depend partially on cross-elasticity for their sales. **Cross-elasticity** describes how demand for one product responds to changes in the price of another product. The demand for laser printers, for example, is closely related to the demand for personal computers; they are complementary—they go together. Conversely, if the price of beef rises sharply, thereby reducing the demand for beef, the demand for lower-priced meat or for fish might increase. Effective marketers thus study not only their own product's demand schedule but also the demand schedules of substitute and complementary products.

Know Your Costs

Pricing methods based only on the seller's costs fail to include the all-important buyer in the pricing effort. Nevertheless, the seller's costs are a major area of concern. Although some products may occasionally be sold at a loss, cost must be recouped sooner or later. Cost thus provides the "floor" on which to build a pricing strategy.

Marketers often use **marginal analysis** in examining costs. This measure allows them to determine the costs and revenues connected with the production and sale of each *additional* unit of a product. The concept of marginal analysis can be demonstrated by example: If only one unit of a product or service is produced, all the costs of production and marketing must be

Airlines use special off-season fares to fill empty seats that would otherwise go unsold. They know that the costs and revenues associated with the production of "one more unit" of a product can be marginal when demand is low. Low off-season fares encourage more purchases by existing buyers and attract new buyers.

assigned to that single unit. Thus, the cost associated with the very first brake repair job performed by a Brakeman franchise would be immense. All the fixed costs (that is, the expenses associated with entering the business) would have to be covered by that first repair job. However, each *additional* brake repair would take over some portion of these costs. When there were many brake repair jobs, only a small portion of the fixed cost would have to be allocated to each one.

The costs and revenues associated with the production of one more unit of a product are the marginal costs and marginal revenues. **Marginal cost** is the net addition to total costs created by the production of one more unit of a product. **Marginal revenue** is the net addition to the total revenue of the firm from the sale of one more unit of a product. The basis of marginal analysis is the idea that these combine to create a point of maximum profitability for a firm. As shown in Exhibit 19-6, that point is where marginal cost equals marginal revenue.

Move a pencil point along the horizontal, or quantity, axis of Exhibit 19-6 and note the behavior of the variables shown. Begin by looking at **average cost,** which represents the total costs divided by the number of units produced. Moving from the extreme left, where the quantity produced and sold is zero, the average cost at first declines as quantity increases, because the cost of the first unit produced is

Marginal analysis
A method for determining the costs and revenues associated with the production and sale of each additional unit of a product.

Marginal cost
The net addition to a firm's total costs that results from the production of one additional unit of product.

Marginal revenue
The net addition to a firm's total revenue that results from the sale of one additional unit of product.

Average cost
The total costs divided by the number of units produced.

e x h i b i t 19·6

Behaviors of Costs and Revenues As Demand and Quantity Produced Increase

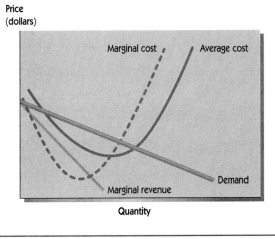

Intersection of Marginal Cost and Marginal Revenue Curves

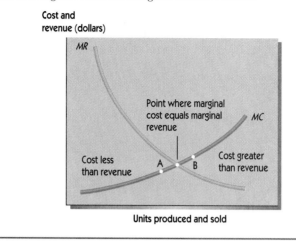

Cost and
revenue (dollars)

MR

Point where marginal
cost equals marginal
revenue

MC

Cost less
than revenue

A   B

Cost greater
than revenue

Units produced and sold

far greater than the cost of the thousandth. The marginal cost also declines at first as we move along the quantity axis. In the case of the Brakeman franchise, this is because the same garage, using the same equipment and instruments, is handling an increasing number of cars. The marginal revenue declines because the revenue generated from each additional sale is an increasingly smaller portion of Brakeman's total income. The two cost curves eventually move upward because, after a certain level of output has been reached, production inefficiencies, such as overcrowding in the workplace, cause cost per unit to rise.

The important point is that *profit is maximized where marginal cost equals marginal revenue (MC = MR)*. Consider Exhibit 19-7, which shows only these two variables. Suppose a seller of a good or service discovered that the cost of producing one more unit was less than the revenue to be realized by producing that unit (in other words, suppose the firm was at point *A*). Management would logically decide to produce and sell that additional unit. That is, there would still be some profit to be made, because the cost would be less than the revenue to be gained. However, if management discovered its operation to be at point *B*, where cost per unit is *greater* than revenue, it would realize that the one more unit would cost *more* than it would bring in—that the

what went wrong?

AT&T and MCI   AT&T and MCI, leaders in the long-distance calling business, are constantly at loggerheads about who has the lowest long-distance prices. Third-place Sprint Corporation, rather than enter the "our rates are the lowest" fray directly, chose to have a Fridays Free program. The company promised to give small-business customers free long-distance calling every Friday for a year. Many small businesses found the offer attractive and switched to Sprint. What could go wrong?

Plenty, as it turned out. Sprint found that its Fridays Free promotion ran out of control. Its costs were too high. Many residential customers signed up for the service, even though the program was originally targeted at businesses. And many small businesses, as it turns out, do a lot of international marketing. Calling volumes to nine countries—China, India, Pakistan, Israel, Ecuador, Bolivia, Thailand, Iran and Myanmar—increased 800 percent.

Startled by the high volume of free calls placed by its business customers in the promotion, Sprint beat a hasty retreat. It barred any free calls to overseas destinations for new customers who sign up for the service. Moreover, for current customers, Sprint effectively banned freebie Friday traffic to those nine countries that became especially popular targets.

The move angered many customers, who accused the company of luring them to convert to Sprint with terms that have now been withdrawn. Some complained Sprint's actions were not professional.[6]

company would take a loss on that unit. The sensible thing to do would be to cut back—not to point *A*, where the cost is still less than the revenue to be made, but to the point where cost and revenue levels come together; that is, production should be at the level where *MC = MR*.

summary

Marketing involves the exchange of something of value. Value is generally represented by price. Price plays an important role in the marketing mix and in the attainment of marketing objectives.

1 *Define price and discuss it.*

Price represents value, which is the power of one product to attract another in an exchange. Price enables buyers and sellers to express the value of the products they have to offer.

2 *Tell how price interacts with the rest of the marketing mix.*

In an effective marketing mix, product, distribution, promotion, and price decisions must be consistent with and must support one another. For example, high price is consistent with high product quality, an image-oriented promotion, and exclusive distribution in prestigious stores.

3 *Analyze price's place in the economy.*

Price plays a major role in the allocation of goods and services in market economies. In addition, price encourages or discourages demand; it often gives products a symbolic value that can easily be perceived by buyers; it helps achieve financial or market-share objectives; and it can be used in a rapid-response adjustment to environmental changes.

4 *Outline the fundamentals of pricing strategy.*

In setting prices, it is important to (1) determine your pricing objectives, (2) know the importance of price to your target market, (3) know your demand, (4) understand your costs, and (5) determine your pricing strategy.

5 *Characterize the relationship between price and organizational objectives.*

Organizational objectives are the basis for pricing strategies and are achieved partially as a result of those strategies. Price affects income generation, sales, competitive moves, and attainment of social objectives.

6 *Relate the demand in a target market to the prices charged.*

The price of a product must suit the target market. For example, the decision to target potential buyers of extremely expensive jewelry means that the prices charged can be high if they are supported by the appropriate product quality, promotion, and distribution choices.

7 *Understand that demand and cost considerations influence pricing.*

Marketers need to know how many people will buy their product and how much it will cost to meet this demand. Cost provides the "floor" on which to build a pricing strategy. Marginal analysis is a technique that helps marketers determine the cost and revenue associated with production and sale of each additional unit of a product.

8 *Differentiate among price elasticity, price inelasticity, and price cross-elasticity.*

Price elasticity exists when the change in quantity demanded exceeds the change in price that brought it about. Price inelasticity exists when the change in quantity demanded is smaller than the change in price. Cross-elasticity exists when price changes for one product affect demand for another, as when a rise in the price of beef contributes to an increase in the demand for fish.

key terms

value (p. 593)
barter (p. 593)
list price (p. 593)
price competition (p. 594)
nonprice competition (p. 595)
demand curve (p. 596)

supply curve (p. 596)
pricing objective (p. 598)
return on investment (ROI) (p. 600)
turnover (p. 600)
market share (p. 601)
price stabilization (p. 601)

price elasticity (p. 603)
cross-elasticity (p. 604)
marginal analysis (p. 605)
marginal cost (p. 605)
marginal revenue (p. 605)
average cost (p. 605)

questions for review & critical thinking

1. What are some other names given to price? Why are these names used instead of price?
2. What is the main macromarketing function of price in the economy? Differentiate between that function and the role of price as a micromarketing tool.
3. "A high price policy needs supporting policies." Explain.
4. Give examples of situations in which a low price might not suit other aspects of a firm's marketing plan.
5. Why does the consumer often view price as the most important part of a transaction?
6. Consumers can rent everything from houses, yachts, and luxury cars to televisions and other home appliances. What price-related advantages might renting bring to consumers? What aspects of buyer behavior are brought into play when a consumer compares renting a TV or refrigerator with buying the item?
7. Days Inn of America, a chain of 325 motels, adopted a slogan for use in its advertisements: "Inexpensive. But not cheap." What does this slogan say about Days Inn motels, their prices, and the target market Days Inn is trying to attract?
8. The price a firm charges for its goods or services often depends primarily on how the customer is expected to react to the price charged. In what situations have you, as a customer or seller, encountered this approach to pricing?
9. Differentiate among organizational objectives, marketing objectives, and pricing objectives.
10. Why must managerial judgment play a role in determining prices even though many mathematical techniques have been developed for that purpose?
11. How can target market considerations affect a firm's pricing policies?

marketing plan—right or wrong?

1. A Ford dealership in a city of 500,000 people plans to switch to a "no haggle," one-price policy similar to that used at Saturn dealerships. Each Saturn dealership typically is the exclusive dealership in an area. The Ford dealer is one of three competing Ford dealerships in the metropolitan area.
2. When McDonald's opened in Moscow, lines were extremely long. There were as many as 50,000 customers daily, some of whom waited 2 hours for a Big Mac. The restaurant manager's plan was to raise its prices by 85 percent.

internet insights

exercise

Much pricing theory is related to economics. Amos World is A Guide to All Things Economic and the Home of Mr. Economy. Go to http://amos.bus.okstate.edu and you will find, among other things, the *AmosWorld Encyclopedic Glossary*. It is a searchable, cross-referenced database of economic terms. You should find it quite useful.

address book (useful urls)

The Economist newspaper	www.economist.com
The Conference Board	www.conference-board.com
The Professional Pricing Society	www.pricing-advisor.com

ethically right or wrong?

1. Some roses-only stores import roses from South America. They sell imported roses at much lower prices than domestic roses. Some domestic rose growers believe that these low prices will increase the demand for roses and make roses widely available. They fear the market will become saturated and roses will lose their image as special flowers. Some suggest that the government should pass laws to restrict the importation of roses into the United States. How would you feel about this if you were an American rose grower? A retailer who imports roses from South America? A consumer who wants to buy roses for her mother's birthday?

2. Supply-and-demand theory suggests that prices should find their own level—that is, they should represent "all the traffic will bear." Is such pricing ethical? Is it good for society?

3. "Consumers want lower prices. If the marketing concept means being oriented toward the consumer, prices should be lowered." Comment.

World's Gym

World's Gym–Showcase Square in San Francisco began operations in 1989. The company's objective was to meet the fitness needs of a diverse clientele, from the professional body builder to the overweight person.

World's Gym's pricing plan was to have a fitness facility that targeted the common person—a fitness facility that was not on the high end or the low end, but in the middle price range. In the beginning it planned to challenge the price of the top-of-the-line facilities. It offered its services in a big cavernous space in a high-traffic area, a part of town that was becoming gentrified. There was little competition in the area. The establishment's "warehouse" space, with natural light coming in, set it apart from competitors.

The company expected its members to come from other clubs and facilities not only in the immediate neighborhood, but all around San Francisco. It saw its trade area as the neighborhoods within an 8- to 10-minute drive.

The company decided to begin by marketing its product to people who were already working out but wanted something unique. When the company opened its fitness facility, consumers readily accepted it. World's Gym membership far exceeded expectations. It now has 8,000 members. As many as 2,000 people come through the door on a given day.

For years World's Gym has had few serious competitors. In San Francisco, permits are required to open a gym and thus are an obstacle to potential competitors. And the cost of opening a 35,000-square-foot facility is an additional barrier to entry.

QUESTIONS

1. Was World's Gym pricing plan appropriate in a market where there was a relatively low supply of services?
2. Over time World's Gym membership exceeded expectations. Demand was strong and constant. What impact might this situation have on the company's pricing strategy? On product strategy?
3. Suppose the company learns that two new competitors plan to open fitness facilities within a mile of World's Gym. How might the increased supply of services affect World Gym's pricing policy?

Scalper

It is 8 a.m., and a Target store [in Ypsilanti, Michigan] has just opened for business. Dennis Barger, who has been waiting in the parking lot since 7:30, races in to buy a toy.

A few minutes later, he is down the road at a Wal-Mart, then on to a Kmart and two Toys "Я" Us stores. At 10:30, a weary Mr. Barger finds a coffee shop, sits down to an iced tea, and surveys his haul: one Captain Kirk, three Guinans, two Cygors, one Hamburger Head, one Worf, one Violator—13 action figures in all, from the world of *Star Trek* or *Spawn* comic books. Total price: $55.

Mr. Barger didn't get everything he was looking for, but not to worry. "I'll sell two figures and get my money back," he says. The entire purchase, he reckons, should fetch him more than $200. Mr. Barger, 24 years old, is a toy scalper. By staying alert to the latest fads, moving fast and using special purchasing channels, he makes his living buying toys that are in short supply and then selling them at huge markups to collectors, other resellers, or parents and children who are desperate to have them.

In the toy business, where shortages are increasing, the role of scalpers is growing. For reasons that are hotly debated, temporary unavailability of certain toys has plagued consumers ever since the big run on Mighty Morphin Power Rangers began [in 1993]. Parents agonized when Mattel Inc.'s Happy Holiday Barbie sold out weeks before last Christmas morning. Not long before that, stores were cleaned out of Earring Magic Ken. More recently, Mattel's Treasure Hunt cars, Toy Biz Inc.'s Xena the Warrior, and the Cal Ripken Jr. replica from Hasbro Inc.'s Starting LineUp have been scarce.

Some buyers speculate that shortages are designed by manufacturers seeking to create cachet for toys and stir consumer interest. Others say supply problems are the result of a highly unpredictable market in which toy makers aren't really sure what products will become hot. "The penalty for overproducing product in the toy industry is so huge, many toy companies have gone out of business. And because of that, manufacturers would rather deal with a shortage than overproduction," says Sean McGowan, an analyst for Gerard Klauer Mattison & Amp Co., a New York investment bank.

Toy makers say their calculations have been upset by collectors, such as the Barbie devotees who gobbled up so many Happy Holidays last Christmas. Estimates on the number of collectors vary widely, from 200,000 to three million. Judging from ads in toy-collector magazines, there is a thriving business for scalpers as well.

A Toys "Я" Us store in New Hampshire banned a collector—for the first time—from buying any more toys there. The company says the collector had become too frequent a customer, purchasing thousands of dollars of hot figures.

While some stores set limits on the number of certain items each customer can purchase, "It's very hard to police" scalping, says Michael Goldstein, chairman of Toys "Я" Us Inc., the nation's largest toy retailer. "Scalpers can easily sidestep the customer limit by having relatives or friends come in to buy for them."

Toys "Я" Us has investigated a number of deals made between its employees and scalpers, Mr. Goldstein says, leading to the dismissal of some workers.

One of the biggest current squeezes is on Hasbro's new line of Star Wars figures linked to a coming re-release of the space-movie trilogy. At Toys "Я" Us stores, characters such as Obi Wan Kenobi and Princess Leia retail for $4 to $5—if you can find them. Eleven-year-old Kilian Ellison couldn't. After what he calls "an endless search for the Princess," he ran into Mr. Barger at a comic-book store, and paid $55 for one. "I get $15 for mowing people's lawns," shrugs Kilian, who lives with his mom in Ann Arbor, Michigan. "So I'll mow a few more lawns." Mr. Barger has a wide reputation—and an eclectic clientele. During the Power Ranger drought, he sold scarce versions of the drop-kicking avengers for about $120 apiece to film stars Tim Robbins and Susan Sarandon, who gave them to their children for Christmas. Specialty shops paid plenty for his Earring Magic Kens, which had become a novelty item among gays. "He's like Indiana Jones," says Rex Schroeder, owner of Total Entertainment, a comic-book and video store in Ypsilanti. "If there's a Holy Grail in toys, he'll find it." But collectors are outraged at scalpers' prices. Mr. Barger's inventory includes a hard-to-get World War II G.I. Joe for $150, a replica of Los Angeles Dodgers pitcher Hideo Nomo for $35, and a Commander Riker Star Trek doll at $225. Each has, or had, a retail price of about $5. "When will the escalation end?" asks Sean MacIntyre, a Dallas collector. "His type of price inflation we see in Argentina, not America." There is nothing illegal about what Mr. Barger does, but that doesn't make kids any happier when they can't find their favorites. "The adults beat us to the store every time," says Jon Iwata, 10, combing shelves for Star Wars and Hercules figures at a Caldor store in Braintree, Massachusetts. "It's like little kids racing against these big adults in a 100-yard dash or something."

Mr. Barger says he doesn't feel guilty, reasoning that he deals mostly with adult collectors and owners of small toy stores. He blames toy makers for shortages, saying they don't make enough toys to go around. He adds that he makes donations to Toys for Tots and other children's charities as a way of saying to kids: "I'm sorry for buying up all your toys."

A stocky figure with a penchant for black T-shirts and baseball caps worn backward, Mr. Barger graduated from Eastern Michigan University earlier this month with a major in marketing. He declines to discuss his income, but says he paid for college with scalping profits. "I almost never sell my stuff for less than a 100 percent markup," he says. "What stock on any of the exchanges offers that kind of return in just a few weeks?" Industry estimates are that a good scalper can make upward of $50,000 a year. Mr. Barger's biggest concern at the moment is moving his bulging inventory—which he values at $200,000 in street prices—to a larger home.[7]

QUESTIONS

1. How important is price in a person's decision to buy a toy? A collector's item?
2. How do the forces of supply and demand operate in the toy industry?
3. In your opinion, are toy scalpers' activities ethical? Should toy scalping be legal?

chapter
20

Pricing Strategies and Tactics

After you have studied this chapter, you will be able to:

Identify the various pricing strategies.

1

Discuss the nature of differential pricing strategies.

2

Describe skimming and penetration pricing.

3

Show how competition affects pricing activity.

4

Discuss the effects of inflation on pricing.

5

(continued on next page)

circuit city, the electronics retailer with almost 500 stores, has launched a five-city experiment. In these cities, it requires customers returning nondefective items to pay 15 percent of the purchase price as a restocking fee if the box or packaging was opened. Circuit City also adopted a policy nationwide requiring the 15 percent fee for opened boxes on nondefective personal computers or peripherals.

It's the latest example of how retailers are getting tougher on returns.

In the past few years, some retailers have put limits on "lifetime" guarantees.

Some stores have added tags to the fronts of women's dresses warning that the garment can't be returned if the tag is removed.

The goal is to prevent a dress from being worn for an event, then returned for a refund.

Circuit City rival Best Buy has charged 15 percent restocking fees on certain unboxed electronics

IN THE PAST FEW YEARS, SOME RETAILERS HAVE PUT LIMITS ON "LIFETIME" GUARANTEES.

products for nearly 2 years to try to stop abuse of its liberal return policies.

Best Buy says students were buying laptop computers to write term papers and then returning them. A camcorder was returned as defective; the videotape left inside showed the camera had been dunked in a swimming pool.

"There are abuses that unfortunately caused us to revise our policies," says Laurie Bauer, spokeswoman for 285-store Best Buy, based in Eden Prairie, Minnesota. The fee applies to opened boxes for nondefective notebook computers, radar detectors, camcorders, and digital cameras.

In Circuit City's case, "Some consumers were, in effect, borrowing the product," spokesman Morgan Stewart says. "Once you have an opened box, it's a markdown."[1]

Circuit City
www.circuitcity.com

This chapter begins with a discussion of common pricing strategies. It then focuses on techniques and methods of analysis for establishing a product's price and explains how marketers adjust list prices. The remainder of the chapter focuses on legal and ethical issues associated with pricing.

An Overview of Pricing Strategies

A wide range of pricing strategies are available to marketing managers, as shown in Exhibit 20-1. Managers may use several of these strategies to arrive at a price that reflects market realities, costs, consumer perceptions, and other considerations. Pricing strategies may be broadly categorized under five headings:[2]

1. Differential pricing strategies
2. Competitive pricing strategies
3. Product-line pricing strategies
4. Psychological and image pricing strategies
5. Distribution-based pricing strategies

Differential Pricing Strategies

Organizations that sell the same product to different buyers at different prices use a **differential pricing strategy.** The type of industry strongly influences whether an organization uses differential pricing.

ONE-PRICE POLICY VERSUS VARIABLE PRICING

Determining whether to maintain a fixed price for all customers or to vary the price from buyer to buyer is a basic pricing decision. Organizations that vary the price from buyer to buyer are said to have a **variable pricing strategy.** Holding the price the same for all buyers is termed a **one-price strategy** (or a one-price policy, if it is routinely used for all pricing decisions).

In the United States, most retailers follow a one-price policy. Whether a billionaire or a child with only 50 cents enters the candy store, the price of the candy bar is the same. Some marketers defend this strategy on the grounds that it is fair and democratic not to charge prices that might favor one customer over another.

A one-price policy provides the advantage of simplicity of administration, which leads, in turn, to lower personnel expenses. This is the main reason most retailers use it. Salespeople and clerks need not debate the price of a loaf of bread or a yard of cloth with each customer.

However, many marketers allow customers to haggle in an attempt to secure a favorable price.[3] In many foreign markets, variable pricing is the rule. In the United States, automobile and real estate purchases often present such an opportunity. Variable pricing developed in the automobile industry as a response to

Differential pricing strategy
A strategy whereby different prices are charged to different buyers of the same product.

Variable pricing strategy
A strategy whereby an organization varies the price from buyer to buyer.

One-price strategy
A strategy whereby a single price is charged for a product regardless of the circumstances surrounding the sale, the quantity bought, or any other unique aspect of the exchange.

The Basic Pricing Strategies

e x h i b 20-1

Differential pricing strategies	Product-line pricing strategies
Variable pricing	Total-profit pricing
Second-market discounting	Captive pricing
Skimming	Leader pricing
Periodic discounting	Bait pricing
Random discounting	Price lining
	Price bundling
	Multiple-unit pricing
Competitive pricing strategies	**Psychological and image pricing strategies**
Meeting competition	Reference pricing
Undercutting competition	Odd and even pricing
Price leadership	Prestige pricing
Following the leader	**Distribution-based pricing strategies**
Penetration pricing	F.O.B.
Predatory pricing	Delivered pricing
Traditional pricing	Zone pricing
Inflationary pricing	Uniform delivered pricing
	Basing-point pricing

Although one-price policies are common in the United States, markets in many other countries are based on variable pricing. Negotiating and bargaining are common in markets like the one shown here in Peru.

customers' desire to trade in their older models. When variable prices are used, each salesperson must be able to handle customers' questions, complaints, and attempts to have the price reduced. While the supermarket's one-price policy allows it to employ less experienced, lower-paid clerks, the automobile dealer must hire active salespeople—and pay them comparatively high commissions—to administer its variable price policy.

Where haggling is allowed, large companies usually find themselves in a better position than weaker firms to drive a hard bargain with suppliers. Federal legislation prohibits the use of variable pricing policies when they might give large or powerful organizational buyers competitive advantages over small organizational buyers. (This legislation, the Robinson-Patman Act, is discussed later in the chapter.) However, there are many situations in which seller and buyer engage in a bit of give and take. The variable pricing policy allows for this.

SECOND-MARKET DISCOUNTING

Second-market discounting
A differential pricing strategy whereby a product is sold at one price in the core target market and at a reduced price in a secondary market.

Second-market discounting is a differential pricing strategy designed to sell a brand at one price in the core target market and at a reduced price in a secondary market segment. For example, art museum memberships are often discounted to students and senior citizens. Theaters, airlines, and utilities may vary their prices among buyers. A theater's matinee price is ordinarily less than the evening price; a plane ticket is less expensive if one flies on a weekend; the industrial user generally pays less for electricity than the homeowner. The price differences are usually treated as "discounts" rather than price variants. They are not illegal under the Robinson-Patman Act because the groups of buyers are not considered to be in competition with one another.

Excess capacity is a requirement for a second-market discounting strategy. An organization exporting products to foreign markets may choose this strategy to make use of its excess capacity and to reduce its average production costs.

SKIMMING

Skimming price
A relatively high price, often charged at the beginning of a product's life. The price is systematically lowered as time goes by.

A **skimming price** is a high price intended to "skim the cream off the market." It is best employed at the start of a product's life, when the product is novel and consumers are uncertain about its value. For example, compact disc players first sold at prices of about $800. Now they can be purchased for as little as $60. Similarly, in 1991, adding a first-generation sound card, a CD-ROM drive, and some speakers to a personal computer cost more than $1,000; today, this combination of devices costs less than $250.

This pattern—pricing high and systematically reducing price over time—allows companies to establish a flow of revenue that covers research and development expenses, as well as the high initial costs of bringing the product to market. A skimming strategy assumes the existence of a relatively strong inelastic demand for the product, often because the product has status value or because it represents a true breakthrough. Price is used as a means to segment the market on the basis of discretionary income or degree of need for the product. As the product life cycle progresses, prices are reduced in response to competitive pressures, and new market segments become the key targets. Marketing managers are most likely to embrace a skimming strategy when production capacity limits output or when competitors face some barrier to market entry. For instance, during early stages of NutraSweet's product life cycle, when G. D. Searle and Company had a patent

On Valentine's Day, roses are no bargain. Florists charge a premium for Valentine's Day roses because prices tend to climb with demand, and Valentine's Day is the biggest rose day of the year. Lower prices for roses during the summer are quite predictable.

www.america.net/
seasonal/valentine/
history.html

on the product, Searle charged the highest possible prices to soft-drink companies, the customers with the greatest need for the artificial sweetener. As it increased production capacity and as other food manufacturers began to demand NutraSweet for diet versions of their products, Searle progressively lowered prices. In 1992, when its patent expired, it lowered its prices again and began heavily promoting the NutraSweet brand name to solidify brand loyalty.

OTHER PRICE-REDUCTION STRATEGIES

Periodic discounting, like skimming, uses price reductions that are predictable over time. The basic strategy is to price high and to discount systematically as time elapses. Summer fashion items are reduced in price in midsummer. Long-distance telephone calls are cheaper on weekends. The price changes associated with periodic discounting take place over shorter time periods than those associated with skimming. Further, prices may be expected to rise in subsequent periods.

The **random discounting** pricing strategy involves lowering the price of a product randomly to entice new customers, perhaps by means of coupons or featured prices. It is designed so that customers do not anticipate the reduced prices and therefore do not postpone purchases at the regular price. In its simplest form, the strategy is designed so that regular and high-income customers routinely buy at the normal (high) price and price-conscious shoppers purchase at the sale price. The key to implementing this strategy is to ensure that consumers can't predict the timing of the discounts.

Periodic discounting
A pricing strategy whereby discounts are offered systematically and predictably.

Random discounting
A pricing strategy whereby discounts are offered occasionally and unpredictably.

Competitive Pricing Strategies

Competitive pricing strategies are used by organizations that have competitive pricing objectives. Dominant firms may use pricing to exploit their positions. Weak firms may opt for the role of follower.

MEETING THE COMPETITION

Organizations concerned with meeting competition quite naturally set prices at levels equal to those of competitors—the going rate. Many U.S. firms choose a **meeting-the-competition strategy** to avoid price competition and price-cutting wars. This approach tends to shift competition to areas other than price. Setting prices for organizational products may be considerably different from setting prices for consumer products. An organizational buyer may solicit competitive bids, asking various suppliers to submit independent price quotations for a specific order. This permits the buyer to obtain the lowest possible price for products that meet certain predetermined specifications. When they must submit price quotes, many marketers adopt competitive pricing strategies.

Meeting-the-competition strategy
A pricing strategy whereby an organization sets prices at levels equal to those of competitors.

Sony MiniDisc Sony's MiniDisc was one of the biggest product failures ever in consumer electronics. Sony made an ambitious effort to persuade consumers to swap their compact discs for a premium-priced new format: a cute little disc that records as well as plays.

To introduce its new product, Sony launched what is widely regarded as one of the biggest music promotion giveaways ever: 1.1 million MiniDiscs to subscribers to *Rolling Stone,* plus a huge magazine campaign. It didn't work. Today, the MiniDisc has all but disappeared in this country, the victim of poor marketing and overpricing. What went wrong?

When Sony first introduced its MiniDisc player in December 1992, it anticipated a huge market for a portable machine that could play prerecorded MiniDiscs ($549) and for one that also could record ($750). Sony, basking in the glow of its famed Walkman product, as well as the compact disc that it co-created with Philips Electronics N.V., was convinced that consumers would welcome a new, easy-to-carry digital format.

However, Sony mistakenly targeted its advertising and marketing efforts at the MTV generation, which couldn't afford MiniDisc players or recorders. And an effort to re-launch the product in 1994 was widely regarded as unsuccessful. Overall, fewer than one million MiniDisc players/recorders have been sold in the United States.

Despite its past failures, Sony decided to test-market its palm-sized recorder/players with a new marketing strategy. This time around Sony believes it will prevail, in part because it has completely revamped its advertising strategy with a new advertising campaign that asks "Why Make a Copy of Your CD When You Can Make a Clone?" Instead of promoting the MiniDisc as a portable country cousin of the Walkman, Sony is offering a home-deck unit, together with a portable player and two blank discs, that it has priced at $599.

Sony also has slashed the prices of blank 74-minute MiniDiscs from $16.99 in 1992 to $9.99. In addition, Sony is offering a bundle of three blank MiniDiscs for $21.99, or only $7.33 a disc. That's about half of what a recorded compact disc costs. Sony research shows its target customers are 18 to 34 years old, buy 12 or more compact discs a year, have a higher-than-national-average income, and prefer to do their recording at home. Only time will tell if Sony's persistence pays off.[4]

For many custom-made products, the supplier may request a proposal from the buyer indicating the exact nature of the product or service that will be sold. Often, the buyer and the seller will then negotiate a price.

UNDERCUTTING THE COMPETITION

An **undercutting-the-competition strategy** emphasizes offering the lowest price among available choices. Marketers implementing this approach often use price as the focal point of the entire marketing strategy. For instance, most discount stores highlight undercutting the competition (traditional retailers). Their lower markup helps generate a higher volume of merchandise sales.

Many large organizations, especially those that compete in the global marketplace, also favor this strategy. Multinational organizations and others that price to undercut the competition often have certain advantages because of production costs. For example, many Asian electronics manufacturers pay relatively low wages, and their low labor costs allow them to undercut prices in many of their export markets. Organizations experienced in producing a product often find that their know-how and technical expertise provide economies of scale, which allow them to undercut competition with a discount strategy.

Undercutting-the-competition strategy
A pricing strategy whereby an organization sets prices at levels lower than those of competitors.

Price leadership strategy
A strategy whereby organizations with large market shares and production capacities determine a price level that other, weaker organizations in the same industry will follow.

PRICE LEADERS AND FOLLOWERS

Price leadership strategies are generally implemented by organizations that have large shares of the market and of the production capacity in their industries. Such organizations have enough market information and enough control over their distribution systems to determine a price level that others will follow. Price leaders typically are able to make price adjustments without starting price wars and can make their announced prices stick. Price leaders are often sensitive to the price and profit needs of the rest of the industry. Some organizations, especially those in weak competitive positions, adopt a **follow-the-leader strategy** by simply pricing as the market leader does.

PENETRATION PRICING

A **penetration price** is a low introductory price. In the short run, it may even result in a loss. A penetration pricing strategy is implemented when a competitive situation is well established (or soon will be) and a low price in the introductory stage of the product life cycle will be necessary to break into the market. Penetration pricing is an alternative to skimming. Its objective is to enable a new product to become established and survive in the long run. A company achieves this objective by pricing so low that a profit is possible only if the company sells a relatively high volume and obtains a large market share. Penetration pricing is likely to be the most effective and desirable approach under one or more of the following conditions:

1. When demand for the product is very sensitive to price (elastic demand)
2. When it is possible to achieve substantial economies in the unit cost of manufacturing and/or distributing the product by operating at high volume (economies of scale)
3. When a brand faces threats of strong competitive imitation soon after introduction because there is no patent protection, no high capital requirement for production, and no other factors to keep competition out of the market (strong competitive threat)
4. When market segments do not appear to be meaningful and there is mass market acceptance of the product (mass market acceptance)

When Motorola, Apple, and IBM jointly introduced the Power PC microprocessor, they used a penetration pricing strategy. They priced the microprocessor very low relative to Intel's Pentium, assuming that the production cost per chip would be dramatically lowered if they produced at high volume and obtained a high market share in the long run. This would have been a successful pricing strategy if it had eliminated competitors. Unfortunately for Motorola, Apple, and IBM, Intel was too well established in the computer chip market to be dislodged strictly on the basis of price.

The logic of penetration pricing is that the strategy will reduce the threat of competitive imitation because the small profit margin will discourage low-cost imitators from entering the market. Furthermore, by increasing the size of the total market or of its market share, the marketer establishes strong brand loyalty and increases the brand's dominance in consumers' minds.

An organization trying to establish a monopoly might set prices low to restrict or eliminate competition and then raise prices high, after all competition had been eliminated. This **predatory pricing strategy** is illegal under the Sherman Antitrust Act and the Robinson-Patman Act.

TRADITIONAL PRICING

Certain prices are set largely by tradition rather than by individual marketers. These customary prices may remain unchanged for long periods. The 10-cent phone call, although now a thing of the distant past, was priced at the same level for decades. Candy bars tended to be priced so that they could be paid for with coins. As chocolate and sugar prices rose or fell, the bars got smaller or larger, but the price (a nickel, dime, quarter, etc.) remained the same. It was only when candy bars had diminished to near invisibility that manufacturers broke with tradition and raised the price. Until that time, only a few bars were priced higher than the traditional price, and these were backed by appropriate supporting policies. The 10-cent bar in the 5-cent era was bigger than the others and of better quality, and it was heavily promoted. Today, candy bars that break with the going rate have similar attributes.

Exhibit 20-2 portrays the demand situation faced by firms in industries where prices have become established at particular levels. Should a company attempt to raise prices above the traditional level, the result will be considerably decreased sales. On the other hand, notice that a reduction in price will not produce sales increases that justify the price cut. Demand is thus elastic above the traditional price (P_t) but inelastic below it. The resulting curve is "kinked." This condition arises because consumers' beliefs and habits are so ingrained that price reductions are attributed to some negative change, such as a perceived lowering of quality, rather than to competitive market pressures.

Follow-the-leader strategy
A pricing strategy whereby an organization sets prices at the level the market leader has established. It is used especially by organizations in weak competitive positions.

Penetration price
A low introductory price meant to quickly establish a product in the market.

Predatory pricing strategy
An illegal pricing strategy whereby the price of a product is set low to eliminate competition and then raised to a high level after competition has been eliminated.

Kinked Demand Curve Facing Marketers of Products Sold at a Traditional Price

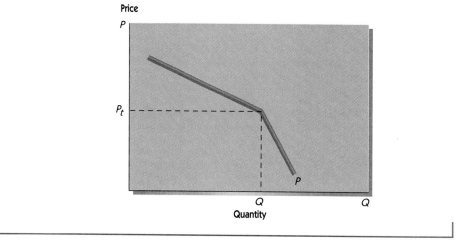

The kinked demand curve also characterizes oligopolistic markets, in which a small number of marketers must price at traditional market levels to maximize profits. Oligopolists, which are highly sensitive to competitive price shifts, generally respond in kind to price reductions. Thus, there is no advantage in price reductions; they will only lead to a lower market price adhered to by all of the oligopolists.

INFLATIONARY PRICING

Executives focus increased attention on pricing strategies when inflation rates are high. During periods of inflation, buying power declines for consumers as well as for many organizational buyers, and most buyers become more price conscious and sensitive to price changes. Increased price awareness heightens price competition. Products may be altered to permit the offering of lower-priced alternatives. For example, during an inflationary period, an airline may continue to offer dependable air service while cutting some of the "free" frills and extra services rather than increasing price.

Organizations may react to inflation by changing the size or amount of the product sold. When the candy bar manufacturers raised prices and enlarged bar size, perceived value was enhanced even though price per ounce increased. Alternatively, distribution systems may be tightened in an effort to hold costs down. Advertising and personal selling messages can stress lower prices and better values when customers are known to be especially sensitive to price.

Gillette   To make sure its brands offer value, Gillette bases its pricing on a market-basket approach. Marketing managers keep daily track of a collection of lowly items, including a newspaper, a candy bar, a can of Coke, that are all priced under a dollar. Then Gillette never raises its prices faster than the rate of increase in the price of the market basket. The company does not believe in a what-the-market-will-bear pricing strategy. Gillette believes that consumers have a relative-value consciousness. If the price of some things gets out of whack, consumers feel as if they are getting ripped off.[5]

Product-Line Pricing Strategies

Many pricing strategists consider the product line, rather than individual product items, to be the appropriate unit of analysis. The objective of product-line pricing is to maximize profits for the total product line rather than to obtain the greatest profits for any individual item in the line. Marketers who do this are said to focus on *total-profit pricing* rather than on *item-profit pricing*.

CAPTIVE PRICING

A camera manufacturer may set low prices on cameras in the hope of making significant profits on film. Firms such as Schick and Gillette sell their razors at low prices to encourage long-term purchase of blades that fit the razors. In a **captive pricing strategy,** the basic product is priced low, often below cost, but the high markup on supplies required to operate the basic product makes up for that low price.

LEADER PRICING AND BAIT PRICING

A common pricing strategy that sacrifices item profit for total profit is *leader pricing*. Most consumers are familiar with the concept of the **loss leader,** the product that the seller prices at a loss so as to attract customers, who may then buy other goods or services. Consumers are perhaps less aware of similar strategies involving *cost leaders* and *low-profit leaders*. Here again, products are priced to attract bargain-hunting customers, who may make additional purchases. The leader items, however, are sold not at a loss but at the seller's cost (the cost leader) or at a very small profit (the low-profit leader). Such pricing strategies can be quite effective. For example, when Target discount stores priced selected popular video games at two-thirds of the regular price, they tripled store traffic. Goods so priced are usually familiar, frequently purchased items that customers will be able to recognize as bargains. Reduced prices on caviar and goat meat would not accomplish the same objective.

Bait pricing involves attracting customers by advertising low-priced models of, for example, televisions. Although the bait item is available for sale in sufficient quantity, the marketer's expectation is to trade the customer up to a higher-margin model that is also available for sale. This strategy may be an effective means to sell higher-margin items.

The term *bait and switch*, however, is used when the merchant has no intention of selling the bait merchandise but only intends to convince the customer to buy more expensive goods. In fact, the item used in the bait-and-switch scheme is sometimes referred to as the "nailed-down model," so unlikely is it that it will be sold. Bait and switch has an unsavory reputation and is often the target of attention from the Federal Trade Commission.

Captive pricing strategy
A strategy whereby a basic product, such as a razor, is priced low but the profits from associated products needed for operating the basic product, such as razor blades, make up for the lack of profit on the basic product.

Loss leader
A product priced below cost to attract consumers, who may then make additional purchases.

Bait pricing
A method of attracting customers by offering low-priced items for sale with the intention of selling more expensive goods.

Selling video games is much like the razor and blade business. Sony sells five pieces of PlayStation software for every one piece of hardware.[6] Only PlayStation games will fit Sony's compact disc–based PlayStation console. Marketers of products requiring consumers to repurchase operating supplies are using captive pricing strategies.

www.sony.com

PRICING LINING

A marketer using a **price-lining strategy** prices the products in a product line according to a number of "price points." Price points are simply specific prices. A marketer selling a full product line establishes certain price points to differentiate the items in the line.

Many retailers, especially clothing retailers, practice price lining. A dress store ordinarily does not stock dresses priced at $299.99, $299.87, $299.76, and so on, down to $55. Instead, the prices offered are $299, $249, $199, and the like. These prices are believed by the store owner to be "strong price points," or prices that are greatly attractive to buyers. The assumption is that a good number of dresses will be sold at $249 but that not many more will be sold at prices lower than $249 until the price reaches the next strong price point, $199. Similarly, if the price is raised from $249, there will be a rapid drop in sales until the next strong price point is reached.

Price lining simplifies consumers' buying decisions. Shoppers can first select a price point and then choose from the assortment in the price line based on color, style, or other product characteristics. It also simplifies the retailer's decisions about what specific prices should be selected.

what went right?

Parker Pen   It would be tough to outflank Parker Pen in the arena of high-low marketing. On the low end, the Gillette Stationery Products subsidiary markets the refillable Jotter Ball Pen for $4.99. On the high end, Parker offers the Limited Edition Gold Snake Fountain Pen, yours for a mere $12,000. The Parker brand, by price, can quite obviously mean greatly different things to different scribblers.

But if Parker has the high and the low down pat, other price points in between have proven more problematic. It needed more of a compelling draw into the crucial $10–$40 range—a necessary next step in keeping the discerning pen-user in the brand franchise. Parker didn't just revise its existing product in the tier, the slim-barreled Classic, it launched a whole new subbrand, the Frontier Collection, a line of eight basic wide-barreled pens ranging in price from the $12.50 translucent ball pen to the $32.50 two-tone fountain pen with gift box. Initially, Parker expected to sell 250,000 units in 1996, but the brand more than doubled that projection, selling 580,000 pens throughout the gift-giving season. In 1997, the company will sell more than 1 million Frontier units, according to company estimates.

"The Frontier has helped bridge the gap between [Parker's] commodity pens and the high-priced models," said Robert George, a merchandise buyer at office superstore Staples. "It's been a great seller for us."

Parker, in conjunction with British design firm Hollington Associates, constructed the new line to satisfy a variety of tastes and budgets while capitalizing on the "corporate casual theme" that's becoming increasingly popular in U.S. workplaces. The unifying brand strategy is to encourage consumers to trade up to higher price points, a classic Gillette strategy. The less expensive translucent models are generally sold on a counter display rack, while the more expensive two-tones are merchandised under glass. The line and in fact its breadth has become the bridge by which Parker hopes to usher consumers eventually to the next level of the brand, the Insignia Custom pen, a line that runs $40–$70, a point at which a writing instrument becomes, truly, an accoutrement of lifestyle, and the brand becomes a badge. Parker Pen's product line strategy is designed to keep customers for life.[7]

PRICE BUNDLING AND MULTIPLE-UNIT PRICING

With a **price-bundling strategy,** a group of products is sold as a bundle at a price lower than the total of the individual prices. The bargain price for the "extras" provides an incentive for the consumer. Selling a car with an "options package" is an example of a price-bundling strategy.

Microsoft Corporation combines a price-bundling strategy with a product strategy in its Microsoft Office97, a so-called suite of software. Suites are bundles of applications—for example, spreadsheets, word-processing programs, and graphics programs—sold together for a fraction of what they would cost if purchased separately. Microsoft Office97 combines Microsoft Word, Microsoft Excel, Microsoft Powerpoint, Microsoft Access, and Microsoft Explorer.

The marketer using a price-bundling strategy benefits by increasing total revenues and, in many instances, reducing manufacturing costs. Inventory costs may also be reduced when marketers bundle slow-selling items with popular items to deplete inventory.

Price bundling differs from **multiple-unit pricing** (as in a two-for-one sale) and quantity discounts because "enhanced" products or multiple products are sold rather than increased quantities of a particular product.

Multiple-unit pricing, in addition to attracting new customers through lower prices, may increase overall consumption of the product. Consumers who bring home two six-packs rather than a single six-pack may increase consumption, for example. The major disadvantage of multiple-unit pricing is that regular customers may store the product in their pantries, postponing future purchases until other "specials" appear.

Psychological and Image Pricing Strategies

Like any other stimulus, a price may be selectively perceived by consumers. Consumers may infer something about a brand's value or image from its price. When customers choose brands because their prices send

CONSUMERS MAY INFER SOMETHING ABOUT A BRAND'S VALUE OR IMAGE FROM ITS PRICE.

a message, they are responding to a psychological or image pricing strategy.

REFERENCE PRICING

Retailers often use a **reference pricing strategy,** in which they choose a moderate price for a version of a product that will be displayed next to a higher-priced model of the same brand or a competitive brand. This strategy is based on the **isolation effect,** which suggests that a choice looks more attractive next to a high-priced alternative than it does in isolation. Reference pricing is also used by catalog retailers such as Service Merchandise to convey the idea that they offer bargain prices. The catalog may show "reference price," "store price," and sometimes "sale price."

ODD VERSUS EVEN PRICING

One seldom sees consumer packaged goods priced at $2.00, $5.00, or $10.00. Instead, they are normally priced at odd amounts such as $1.87, $4.98, and $9.99. Odd prices have, in fact, become traditional.

The use of odd prices is based on the belief that, for example, a price of $1.95 is seen by consumers as only a dollar plus some small change. Advocates of odd pricing assume that more sales will be made at certain prices than at prices just one or two cents higher. However, the published research findings in this area are inconclusive about the benefits of odd pricing. There are those who suggest that a price of $1.98 is seen as $2.00 and that deeper cuts—say, to $1.75—are necessary to achieve the intended psychological effect. The practice of odd pricing does have a practical purpose. It forces clerks to use the cash register to make change, thus creating a record of the sale and discouraging employee dishonesty.

Even prices are often used to good effect by the marketers of services and high-quality merchandise. A physician charges $175 for your annual check-up. A

Varsity Spirit trains more than 100,000 cheerleaders at more than 500 camps held on college campuses across the country. Varsity charges a small tuition fee for a 4-day session, where students learn numerous cheerleading routines and stunts. The tuition barely covers the company's costs, but Varsity gets to showcase its products. In addition to its cheerleading school, Varsity markets cheerleading uniforms, shoes, pom-poms, ribbons, jewelry, megaphones, and other sundry items. Most schools let the cheerleadering squad select which supplier to use, and Varsity does quite well. This pricing strategy, which takes the total product line into account, is a strategy that wins.[8]

www.uca.com/varsity/index.html

Multiple-unit pricing
Selling more than one unit of a product at a price lower than the sum of the individual unit prices, as in a four-for-the-price-of-three sale.

Reference pricing strategy
A strategy whereby a moderate price is set for a version of a product that will be displayed next to a higher-priced model of the same brand or next to a competing brand.

Isolation effect
An effect by which a product appears more attractive next to a higher-priced alternative than in isolation.

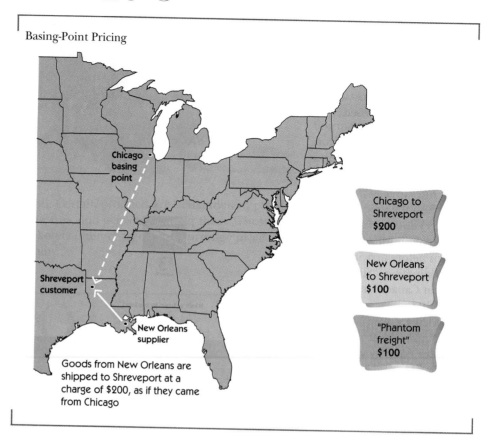

Basing-Point Pricing

Chicago
basing
point

Shreveport
customer

New Orleans
supplier

Chicago to
Shreveport
$200

New Orleans
to Shreveport
$100

"Phantom
freight"
$100

Goods from New Orleans are
shipped to Shreveport at a
charge of $200, as if they came
from Chicago

The services of many professionals, such as doctors and lawyers, are often priced at a figure that suggests that the physician or attorney has been involved totally in the client's case and therefore will present a bill that is free of itemized, penny-counting entries. Thus, the professional charges $2,000 for a gall bladder operation or $700 for a quick divorce. Such prices are called *professional prices* or *gentleman's prices.*

Another sort of price is the so-called *ethical price.* Supposedly, ethical prices are lower than what could have been charged; the marketer chooses the lower price for ethical or humanitarian reasons. Drug companies claim that they set the price of insulin at a reasonable level, even though they could charge more, because it is the right thing to do.

Establishing the Exact Price

Marketers use many methods to assign specific prices to the products they sell. Here, we discuss the logic of several types of calculations: the markup on selling price or cost, the cost-plus and average-cost methods, target return pricing, and break-even analysis. See our Internet Appendix, Financial and Economic Analysis for Marketers, for additional details.

MARKUP ON SELLING PRICE AND MARKUP ON COST

Markup on selling price

A markup expressed as a percentage of the selling price of an item.

Many marketers, especially retailers and wholesalers, rely on a comparatively uncomplicated method for determining their resale prices: A simple percentage markup is added to the cost of the product to reach the selling price. When a markup is expressed as a percentage of the selling price, it is called a **markup on selling price.** For example, a cost of $1.00 and a selling price of $1.50 means a markup on selling price of 33.3 percent. The 50-cent markup is 33.3 percent, or one-third, of the selling price of $1.50. When only the term *markup* is used, it refers to markup on selling price. However, in many industries, pricing focuses on costs.

Consider an example comparing a focus on selling price with a focus on cost. Suppose an item costs a retailer $50, and the retailer sells it for $100. The markup on selling price is calculated by dividing the amount added to the cost of the product by the selling price of the product:

$$\frac{\$50 \text{ added on}}{\$100 \text{ selling price}} = 50 \text{ percent}$$

In contrast, the **markup on cost** is calculated by dividing the amount added to the cost of the product by the cost:

$$\frac{\$50 \text{ added on}}{\$50 \text{ cost}} = 100 \text{ percent}$$

Markup on cost
A markup expressed as a percentage of the cost of an item.

As you can see, using a markup based on cost makes the retailer's markup appear higher (100 percent versus 50 percent here), even though the dollar figures are exactly the same. Distinguishing between markup on selling price and markup on cost is important. Our Internet Appendix, Financial and Economic Analysis for Marketers, discusses formulas for calculating the relationship between these markups. Users of the markup method almost always use the selling price rather than the cost of the product in figuring the markup percentage. The reason is that many important figures in financial reports, such as gross sales, revenues, and so on, are sales figures, not cost figures.

Effective use of markup based on cost or selling price requires that the marketing manager calculate an adequate *margin*—the amount added to cost to determine price. The margin must ultimately provide adequate funds to cover selling expenses and profit. Once an appropriate margin has been determined, the markup technique has the major advantage of being easy to employ.

As Exhibit 20-4 shows, a series of markups is used as products move through channels of distribution. Certain industries have established traditional markups for the various channel members. The ultimate markup—that of the retailer—results in the price paid by the consumer.

THE COST-PLUS METHOD

Manufacturers often use a pricing method similar to markup in which they determine what costs were involved in producing an item and then add an amount to the cost total to arrive at a price. Like markup, this cost-plus method is easy to use once an appropriate amount to add to the cost has been determined. Much government contracting is done on this basis, with the supplier of a good or service

Markup Through a Channel of Distribution

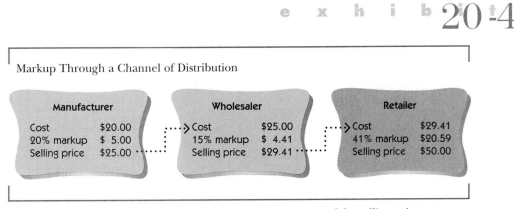

Note: At each step, markup is expressed as a percent of the selling price.

submitting the cost figures associated with a particular project and adding a reasonable profit margin to yield a total price for the project.

THE AVERAGE-COST METHOD

Identifying all the costs associated with the manufacturing and marketing of a good or the provision of a service should make it possible to determine what the average cost of a single unit of the good or service might be. Consider an example.

$$\frac{\text{All costs}}{\text{Number of units produced}} = \text{Average cost of a single unit}$$

$$\frac{\$80,000}{100} = \$800$$

(Note that to make this calculation, it is necessary to predict how much of the product will be demanded and produced.) Adding a margin for profit to the total cost figures allows calculation of a likely price for a unit of product.

$$\$80,000 \text{ all costs} + \$20,000 \text{ margin for profit} = \$100,000$$

$$\frac{\$100,000}{100 \text{ units}} = \text{Average cost of a single unit including the profit margin}$$

$$= \$1,000$$

While the average cost method can suggest a price, there is a serious risk that the quantity demanded by the market will not match the predictions of the marketing manager. If in the above example only 50 units were demanded at the price of $1,000, the firm's revenue would be only $50,000, but the costs of production and marketing would remain at

IT IS EXTREMELY RISKY TO BASE PRICING DECISIONS ON COSTS ALONE.

$80,000. This demonstrates that it is extremely risky to base pricing decisions on costs alone. The market—the demand generated by customers—must be carefully considered in any calculation of price. Changes in demand can turn profit into loss.

TARGET RETURN PRICING

If you've taken an accounting class, you probably remember that **total costs** are the sum of fixed and variable costs. **Fixed costs** are incurred with the passage of time, regardless of volume. **Variable costs** fluctuate with some measure of volume. These costs are used in calculating a target return price.

Hotel and motel chains operate computer systems similar to the one airlines use. The systems track reservations (demand) and available rooms (supply). Travelers who book early get lower rates, and those who reserve a room late pay the highest rates. The pricing strategy, which takes fixed costs into account, uses a traditional economic model to price high when supply is low and demand is high.

A marketing manager using **target return pricing** first calculates a total fixed cost figure. This figure includes such items as executive salaries, rents, and other expenses that must be paid even when no units of a product are being produced. A target return, usually represented as a percentage of investment, is added to total cost to yield a figure representing total fixed costs and target return. To illustrate, assume a fixed cost of $400,000 and a target return of $100,000, for a total of $500,000.

Now the marketer must estimate demand. For an estimated demand of 1,000 units, if the total of fixed costs and target return is $500,000, each unit produced would cost $500 in fixed costs and target return.

$$\frac{\text{Fixed costs} + \text{Target return}}{\text{Units to be sold}} = \frac{\$500,000}{1,000} = \$500 \text{ per unit}$$

But the production and sale of each unit involves variable costs as well. Suppose these costs are calculated to be $75 per unit. This figure is added to the already determined cost per unit of $500 to indicate that the price per unit should be $575.

$$\begin{array}{ccccc} \text{Fixed costs and} & & & & \\ \text{target return} & + & \text{Variable costs} & = & \text{Suggested price} \\ \text{per unit} & & \text{per unit} & & \text{per unit} \\ \\ \$500 & + & \$75 & = & \$575 \end{array}$$

As in the case of average-cost pricing, a miscalculation of the demand for the product can be disastrous. If the firm's customers demanded only 500 units of the product, not the expected 1,000, the carefully calculated price of $575 would lead to a loss.[9]

BREAK-EVEN ANALYSIS

As you have seen, all marketers, whether of consumer goods, organizational goods, or services, face costs that must somehow be recovered. These include fixed costs and variable costs. Variable costs would be zero if no products were produced and marketed, but fixed costs would remain at their established level even if production and sales were zero.

Exhibit 20-5 portrays fixed costs as the horizontal line *FC*. Variable costs added to fixed costs give the total cost figures shown by the line marked *TC*. This curve rises to the right because total costs should increase as production and sales increase.

The hope is that each additional unit of goods manufactured and sold or each additional service performed and paid for will raise the firm's total revenue (total revenue equals price per unit times units sold). This relationship is shown in

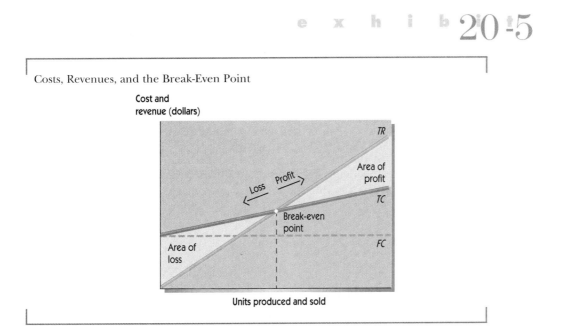

Costs, Revenues, and the Break-Even Point

Exhibit 20-5 by the total revenue curve labeled *TR*. Obviously, marketers hope that total revenue will exceed total costs, resulting in a profit. If total costs exceed total revenue, the result is a loss.

At the start of operations, zero units are being produced, and total revenue is zero because no sales are being made. However, fixed costs such as rent are already being incurred. Therefore, the company is suffering a loss at this point. If all goes well, however, and sales rise, revenue will also rise. If the firm is successful, revenue will continue to rise until it meets and exceeds the costs associated with production and marketing. Now, with revenue greater than costs, the company is making a profit. The point at which costs and revenue meet is called, logically, the **break-even point.** At this point, the money coming in is equal to the money going out. (Our Internet Appendix, Financial and Economic Analysis for Marketers, describes a formula for calculating the break-even point.)

Break-even point
The point at which an organization's revenues and costs are equal.

Price and Break-Even Analysis   Price clearly plays an important role in break-even analysis. For example, raising the price of the product may enhance revenue, allowing revenue to catch up to cost more quickly; lowering the price may have the opposite effect. It might also be demonstrated that a cost-control program would increase profit by lowering the total cost curve. In any case, every organization has a break-even point. If it achieves and surpasses that point, the organization makes a profit. Price has an impact on when the break-even point is met. The concept, though simple, is important.

Demand and Break-Even Analysis   Break-even analysis should deal with demand as well as cost. As price changes, the quantity demanded will change. It might be expected that an increase in price will lead to fewer sales and a drop in price will generate more sales. The marketing manager's problem in employing break-even analysis is to determine just what effect a change in price will actually have on demand.

Simple manipulation of cost and revenue figures is not enough, nor are graphs (such as the one in Exhibit 20-5) that seem to portray ever-increasing profits as more and more units are sold. There is no reason to assume that a product is going to sell at either a higher price or a lower price. An effective marketer, aware of the changes and uncertainties in the marketplace, knows that raising prices will not necessarily increase revenues and lower the break-even point.

In short, determining a break-even point is only the beginning. Break-even analysis may be of most use in conducting preliminary studies to eliminate certain extreme pricing situations. For example, a restaurant might be so poorly run that its costs necessitate menu prices that start at $10 for a hot dog—a price at which few are likely to be sold. Break-even points are also of use in

DETERMINING **A BREAK-EVEN POINT IS ONLY THE BEGINNING. BREAK-EVEN ANALYSIS MAY BE OF MOST USE IN CONDUCTING PRELIMINARY STUDIES TO ELIMINATE CERTAIN EXTREME PRICING SITUATIONS.**

evaluating alternative pricing strategies. But no matter how carefully costs and revenues are portrayed on a graph, the underlying problem of estimating demand remains. Thus, break-even analysis must be used with the customer in mind.

Price Adjustments

Recall that the list price is the basic, "official" price of a product. In many industries, it is common for list prices to be adjusted with rebates or discounts. Rebates reduce the list price by giving back to the consumer part of the amount paid. Rebates generally are reimbursements from the manufacturer rather than the retailer. By passing savings directly to the consumer, a rebate policy assures that the consumer, and not the retailer, will benefit from the price adjustment.

The most common price adjustments are **discounts,** reductions from the list price or reimbursements for performing a specific action, such as maintaining a sales force or carrying inventory. Common discount schemes are discussed briefly below. Notice that each discounting technique provides an incentive to potential buyers but also yields some advantage, such as speedier payment of bills, to sellers.

CASH DISCOUNTS

Cash discounts may take the form of the common "2/10 net 30" payment scheme, which indicates that payment made within 10 days of the date on the invoice will be discounted 2 percent and that full payment, with no discount, must be made within 30 days. The amount of discount, the time allowed, and when the counting of days begins vary from industry to industry. The discount offered is usually large enough that it is worthwhile for the buyer to borrow from a bank, if necessary, to pay what is owed to the supplier. An **anticipation discount,** an additional discount to encourage even faster payment, may also be offered. The purpose of each form of cash discount is to encourage prompt payment of bills. All forms of cash discounts are legal if offered equally to all similar buyers.

TRADE DISCOUNTS

Trade discounts are discounts given to members of the trade. Electricians receive discounts on wire and tape because they are in the electrical trade. Electrical distributors (wholesalers) get even larger discounts because they must make a profit on the products they sell to electricians. Because the recipient of the discount is performing a function, such as holding an inventory of electrical parts, these discounts are also called *functional discounts.*

The types and sizes of discounts for wholesalers, retailers, or other tradespeople vary considerably by industry. Generally, the discount rate, which reflects the intermediary's percentage margin on the goods sold, increases as the intermediary's role in marketing to the customer increases. Thus, discounts are higher in the furniture industry than in the grocery industry.

QUANTITY DISCOUNTS

There are two types of quantity discounts: noncumulative and cumulative. In the case of **noncumulative quantity discounts,** each order is treated separately. The buyer's discount is calculated on the basis of the size of a single purchase, without consideration of past purchases or planned purchases. Obviously, the purpose of this discount is to encourage large orders.[10]

Cumulative quantity discounts, on the other hand, allow the buyer an ever-increasing discount with each purchase made over some period of time—say, a year. The more the buyer orders, the larger the discount becomes. The intent of the cumulative quantity discount is to keep the customer coming back. Stated another way, the supplier's aim is to build a relationship and to tie the buyer to the seller.

SEASONAL DISCOUNTS

As you probably can guess, the **seasonal discount** is intended to help level out the marketing workload by encouraging buyers to make purchases and take delivery of out-of-season merchandise. Products such as bathing suits, winter clothing, paint, and lawn furniture are obvious candidates for seasonal discounting at various times during the year.

CHAIN DISCOUNTS

In many purchasing situations, a buyer qualifies for a series of discounts. A wholesale buyer quoted terms of 40/10/5 net 30 realizes that he or she will receive a

Discount
A reduction from list price or a reimbursement for performance of a specific task.

Cash discount
A price discount offered for early payment of bills.

Anticipation discount
A discount over and above the regular cash discount, meant to encourage even faster payment.

Trade discount
A discount given to wholesalers, retail dealers, or others in a particular trade as repayment for the performance of certain functions; also called a *functional discount.*

Noncumulative quantity discount
A price discount determined by the size of an individual purchase order. The larger the order, the larger the discount.

Cumulative quantity discount
A price discount determined by the amount purchased over some specified time period.

Seasonal discount
A price discount intended to encourage purchase of products during a time of year when sales are traditionally low.

series of discounts by using all the appropriate options. For example, for a machine with a list price of $995, the chain discount on the above terms is calculated as follows:

List price	$ 995.00
Less trade discount (40 percent of $995)	−398.00
Balance	$597.00
Less seasonal discount (10 percent of $597)	−59.70
Balance	$ 537.30
Less cash discount (5 percent of $537.30)	−26.86
Price wholesaler pays	$510.44

PROMOTIONAL ALLOWANCES

A manufacturer may partially reimburse wholesalers or retailers for promotional assistance at the local level. These reimbursements may be in the form of either cash or merchandise, with the value commonly restricted to a percentage of sales or a discount off the list price.

Exhibit 20-6 summarizes the various discounts and allowances.

Pricing and the Law

Fed Law
http://fedlaw.gsa.gov

Law Mall-Antitrust
www.lawmall.com

Robinson-Patman Act
Federal law passed in 1936 and intended to halt discriminatory pricing policies by specifying certain limited conditions under which a seller may charge different prices to different buyers.

Because pricing strategies can be used to harm the competition and because price so clearly affects the consumer as well as the business person, a number of national and local laws have been passed that influence pricing practices. The Sherman Antitrust Act (1890) and the Clayton Act (1914) were early attempts to curb price fixing, restraint of trade, and other unfair and monopolistic practices. Additional legislation amended these acts. Here we discuss the Robinson-Patman Act, the fair trade acts and their repeal, and various state laws. Such laws, and court cases based on them, are so numerous that a service industry has grown up to supply companies with the latest information on legislation and litigation that may affect their pricing and other marketing plans.

ROBINSON-PATMAN ACT

Price discrimination occurs when a manufacturer or supplier charges a lower price to one customer than to another, similar customer. The **Robinson-Patman Act** of 1936 is a federal law that makes it illegal to give, induce, or receive discriminatory prices except under certain conditions specified in the law. The act's sponsors believed it would wipe out chain stores. Under the law, a supplier of, say,

e x h i b 20-6 Discounts and Objectives

DISCOUNT	OBJECTIVE
Cash discount	To encourage customers to pay their bills within a given period of time, such as 10 days
Anticipation discount	To encourage even faster payment of bills by offering additional discounts if the customer pays within, for example, 5 rather than 10 days
Trade or functional discount	To "reward" a customer for functions performed, such as installing a particular brand of storm windows in new houses or stocking a particular brand of clothing in a store
Noncumulative quantity discount	To encourage buyers to place a larger order each time they buy merchandise
Cumulative quantity discount	To encourage buyers to return to a particular supplier for repeat business
Seasonal discount	To encourage buyers to make purchases during the "off season"—for example, to buy house paint and bathing suits in the fall and winter and to visit winter resort areas during the summer
Promotional allowance	To encourage intermediaries to promote the product to their local customers

meat products may not give a large discount to a supermarket chain just because that chain is an important customer. But the supplier may give the discount if a "proportional" discount is offered to the corner grocer. In the event of litigation, a judge must decide what is proportional and what is not.

The law also prohibits the granting of a wholesaler's discount, or broker's discount, to a business that does not meet criteria identifying it as a true wholesaler. The effect of this brokerage provision is that a large retailing organization cannot demand to be given a wholesaler's discount even though it may buy merchandise in larger quantities than do typical wholesalers. The law does allow for the offering of cooperative advertising and other promotional assistance if the promotional help is offered to all customers on proportionally equal terms.

The Robinson-Patman Act includes two provisions that can be used to defend prices that could appear to be discriminatory. One of these allows for the use of several prices if the competitive situation demands it. Thus, a marketer may charge one customer a lower price if this price is granted to meet the equally low price of a competitor. For example, a marketer may lower its price for a buyer in one city who is faced with a price war but charge a higher price to a buyer in another city who is not. The second provision is the so-called cost-justification provision. If the seller can prove that granting a lower price to one buyer simply represents passing on cost savings—for example, savings that result from producing and shipping in large quantities—the seller has successfully employed the cost-justification provision.

The Robinson-Patman Act, along with the Federal Trade Commission Act (discussed in Chapter 3), is one of the most important laws affecting the daily dealings of marketers. But mere observance of its major provisions is not enough to avert legal troubles. As with all legislation, its content is open to interpretation and reinterpretation by the courts and government agencies.[11]

THE REPEAL OF FAIR TRADE ACTS

Before 1975, the states were empowered under federal law to pass fair trade or resale price maintenance acts. Most states enacted laws that allowed manufacturers to fix the prices of their goods and prohibited wholesalers and retailers from offering reduced or discount prices. Although it was argued that these laws would protect small companies by forcing all businesses to charge the same prices for goods, their main purpose was to stabilize prices at comparatively high levels.

Enforcement of these laws was difficult, and growing consumer awareness that certain prices were being kept artificially high contributed to the passage of the Consumer Goods Pricing Act (1975), which repealed the right of individual states to allow price maintenance in interstate commerce.

adapting to change

Ceilings Are Legal Consumers can shop for that hot new car with less fear of having to pay a premium. The Supreme Court, in one of its most important antitrust decisions in years, ruled unanimously that a manufacturer or supplier does not necessarily violate Federal antitrust law by placing a ceiling on the retail price a dealer can charge for its products. The decision was widely welcomed by manufacturers, notably those in the auto and computer industries, who said it could lead to lower consumer prices. Justice Sandra Day O'Connor noted that it remained illegal for manufacturers to impose minimum prices on dealers.[12]

UNFAIR SALES PRACTICES ACTS

Unfair sales practices acts are state laws that limit or prohibit the use of certain sales and marketing techniques. They commonly require that certain items be sold at prescribed markups. The markups may range from zero (thus eliminating loss leaders) to a relatively high percentage. Generally, some provision is made to allow for the sale of old or out-of-style merchandise at a reduced price. Dealers covered by such laws may charge more, but not less, than the specified markups allow. Thus, the laws are also termed *minimum markup laws*. These acts are intended to protect the small business using a relatively high markup by assuring that even a discount store must mark up its merchandise by the minimum amount. The smaller dealer then has a cushion that brings its prices closer to those charged by the chain store.

OTHER STATE AND LOCAL LAWS

Many states and cities further restrict the pricing freedom of firms within their boundaries. For example, several states set limits on the number of times per year that wholesale beer prices may be changed. Many cities require that a "fire sale" actually follow a fire and that "going out of business" sales be followed by a cessation of business operations.

Pricing and Social Responsibility

Most people in this society believe that an organization has a right to make a profit. And as our discussion of the legal aspects regulating price shows, society cares a great deal about the consumer's right to fair pricing. Laws address many ethical issues involving price. However, even some legal pricing practices can create ethical dilemmas. For example, should zoos and museums be free to the public? If public institutions such as these do charge an admission fee, should it be waived for disadvantaged segments of society?

Elsewhere in this book, we have discussed the complaint that certain marketing efforts, such as advertising, increase prices. Many ethical issues involving price are not independent of other marketing mix decisions. Changing one marketing mix element may lead to higher prices. This fact leads us to one of the most fundamental questions concerning ethical pricing: Are corporate social responsibility and the corporate profit motive compatible?

It has been argued that "welfare and society are not the corporation's business. Its business is making money, not sweet music."[13] A number of managers believe that profit maximization is the only legitimate goal of business. Furthermore, they argue that business's pursuit of economic self-interest is what's best for the country.

Goodwrench Service Plus dealers focus on up-front pricing because GM wants to promote the idea that its prices are fair and socially responsible. There will be no pricing surprises at a GM Goodwrench Service Plus dealer. GM's lifetime guarantee on parts and labor supports its responsible pricing strategy.

www.gmgoodwrench.com

*"Up-front pricing? What do you think this is...
GM Goodwrench Service Plus!?"*

If it were, you'd get up-front pricing.
Plus a lifetime guarantee on parts and labor. Plus courtesy transportation.
For the select GM Goodwrench Service Plus dealer
near you, call 800 96 GM PLUS.

Goodwrench
Service
Plus

The *Plus* means better.

Pursuing goals related to social responsibility may place a company at a competitive disadvantage. Consider some examples. Ingersoll-Rand developed a quiet air compressor to silence noisy jack-hammers. Unfortunately, this product, which provided a clear social benefit in the form of noise abatement, had to be sold at a 25 percent premium because of its higher manufacturing cost. In effect, the question here is "Would a buyer rather buy a jack-hammer for $5,000 or for $6,250?" And suppose a manufacturer of coal-mining equipment believes a certain safety feature will save lives. If this marketer adds the feature as standard equipment and increases the price of the equipment but other competitors are not forced to do so, will the company be at a competitive disadvantage?

It is unlikely that one manufacturer will add an expensive safety feature to a product aimed at a price-conscious market segment unless all competitors are forced to do the same. Like it or not, this kind of problem is often settled by legislation requiring that socially desirable, but costly, features be added.

summary

Pricing is one of the most critical aspects of marketing. Prices must appeal to buyers and offer them satisfaction. Costs and profit considerations are important, but prices that do not appeal to customers are of no use, no matter how they are determined. Effective marketers employ a combination of pricing strategies to arrive at prices that appeal to buyers first and then meet other organizational goals.

1 *Identify the various pricing strategies.*

Broadly stated, there are five categories of pricing strategies: (1) differential pricing, (2) competitive pricing, (3) product-line pricing, (4) psychological and image pricing, and (5) distribution-based pricing.

2 *Discuss the nature of differential pricing strategies.*

Maintaining a single fixed price for all buyers is a one-price strategy. Organizations that sell the same product at different prices to different buyers use a differential pricing strategy. Second-market discounting, skimming, periodic discounting, and random discounting are differential pricing strategies.

3 *Describe skimming and penetration pricing.*

The skimming strategy involves charging a high price to "skim" the market. It is most appropriate when demand for a product is strong and there is little competitive pressure to lower price. A penetration strategy is employed by an organization seeking to enter a competitive market. By charging a low price, the organization hopes to establish market share quickly.

4 *Show how competition affects pricing activity.*

Several types of prices result directly from the competitive structure of the marketplace. Charging the going rate or pricing above or below that rate is clearly a response to competition. Similarly, charging a traditional price or following the lead of the industry's leading firms is a competition-influenced policy. Competition, though only one of many variables affecting prices, is among the most powerful influences on pricing activity.

5 *Discuss the effects of inflation on pricing.*

When inflation rates are high, buyers become increasingly price-conscious. Effective marketers can meet this challenge by attempting to maintain their prices or control their upward spiral. They can also alter their products, improve distribution, and use promotional methods to help allay buyer concern over rising prices. The total marketing mix, not just price, can be adjusted to respond to high inflation rates.

6 *Discuss product-line pricing strategies.*

Many pricing strategies consider the product line the appropriate unit of analysis. The objective of product-line pricing is to maximize profits for the total line rather than for an individual item in the line. Captive pricing, leader pricing, bait pricing, price lining, price bundling, and multiple-unit pricing are product-line pricing strategies.

internet insights

exercises

1. The Professional Pricing Society's home page is located at www.pricing-advisor.com. Each month, excerpts from the Pricing Advisor Newsletter appear with information about topics such as value-added pricing. What is the subject matter of the current newsletter?
2. You might be surprised to find out that even bands like Pearl Jam need to know a lot about pricing. Using your Web browser, search the Web for information about Pearl Jam. When you find information about the band, search the Pearl Jam pages for articles that mention Ticketmaster. (Hint: You may find the information under headings like "statement before Congress" or "article on Ticketmaster.") What problem did Pearl Jam run into? What did the group learn about pricing? Given what you have learned about pricing in this book, how would you respond to their complaints?

address book (useful urls)

World Currency Exchange Rates	www.rubicon.com/passport/currency/currency.htm
Bloomberg's Exchange Rate Service	www.bloomberg.com
Consumer Price Index	http://stats.bls.gov/datahome.htm
United States International Trade Commission	www.usitc.gov/taffairs.htm
Bureau of Export Administration	www.bxa.doc.gov

ethically right or wrong?

1. A retailer uses a 150-percent markup on cost for an item with a cost of $10. When the item is put on sale, the retailer advertises 50 percent off (markdown on selling price) and sells the item for $12.50. Is this deceptive?
2. A salesperson is allowed to vary the price quoted to a customer by 10 percent. The salesperson sells 100 units to one wholesaler for $3,500. The next day, another wholesaler says he will buy 100 units only if the price is $3,000. The salesperson writes up the order and says, "I hope this clears the order-processing department." Did the salesperson do the right thing?
3. A retailer's advertisement for fine china compares "our everyday price" with the "manufacturer's suggested retail price." A statement in small print at the bottom of the page says: "Manufacturer's suggested retail price is not a price at which our store offered or sold this merchandise and may not be a trade area price." Is the retailer's advertising ethical?
4. An airline arranges with a national association to offer a special discount fare to association members who are attending a convention. A travel agent uses these group fares for regular clients, who are not association members, so that they can get the lowest possible air fares. Is this good business?
5. For more than 30 years, StarKist Seafood packaged 6½ ounces of tuna in its regular-sized can. During a period of inflation, the can's weight was reduced by ⅜ ounce, but the price remained the same. Detecting this subtle change, which resulted in a 5.8 percent price increase, was a challenge for most consumers. The weight was clearly marked on the package, but the size of the can did not change. Was StarKist's action ethical?

Pacific Paper Tube   *Focus on Small Business*

The earthquake that struck the San Francisco area during the 1989 World Series gave Patrick Wallace's paper-tube manufacturing company quite a jolt—but it was nothing like the impact of strictly business events that followed.

Wallace and his father had founded the Pacific Paper Tube, Inc. that July in Oakland, California across the bay from San Francisco. On October 17 they were reveling in news that a competitor was closing when the Cypress Freeway collapsed a block from their plant.

Crawling up into the structure, Wallace located two children, trapped in a car containing dead adults. Emergency crews couldn't complete the rescue until late that night.

The event attracted media attention, and precious days went by before Wallace could focus on his embryonic company. Other business delays were considerably longer. Demolition of the freeway disrupted transportation in the area, and closing of the Bay Bridge separated the company from many customers, primarily small businesses.

There was much more turmoil for the company when one of its two production employees quit, started a rival enterprise, and cut prices below break-even. Many customers were lured away because of these lower prices.[14]

QUESTIONS

1. Pacific Paper Tube's new environment has increased price competition. What should its pricing objective be?
2. What role will cost play in Pacific Paper Tube's marketing strategy?

Outfitters USA—Pricing a New Product Line

Outfitters USA is a national store chain that specializes in outdoor casual footwear for men and women. The 300 retail outlets in the United States appeal primarily to young and middle-aged adult consumers. The success experienced by Outfitters USA is attributed to its ability to market fashionable and functional high-quality merchandise at competitive prices. The company carries a limited assortment of national manufacturers' brands (such as Timberland and Bass) to stimulate demand and to enhance its store image. However, the majority of each outlet's merchandise consists of private retailer brands owned by the firm.

In 1995, Outfitters USA purchased the Sports Club Shoe Company, a well-established national footwear manufacturer whose product line features high-quality casual footwear. SCSC produces men's and women's leather and non-leather casual shoes. The management of Outfitters USA feels that the takeover will ensure a reliable source of supply for its private labels.

Recently, marketers have observed an increased demand for casual footwear that is not so "athletic" looking. The all-white canvas shoe is popular with both male and female market segments. The favorable demand for this type of shoe prompted Cynthia Huffman, the national merchandise manager for Outfitters USA, to assess the feasibility of adding a new line to the current collection of footwear. After a preliminary investigation, Cynthia concluded that the canvas footwear line would appeal to the "casual wearers"—a consumer market segment seeking the comfort and leisure of an athletic shoe but the style and looks of a dressy casual shoe. This segment is concerned primarily with quality, although price is also an important factor in the selection of footwear. Given the relatively low cost of canvas, price may play a more important role than usual in the purchasing decision for this new footwear.

Cynthia believes the canvas shoe line will fit appropriately with the current store theme of casual footwear. Although she believes the addition makes good merchandising sense, the final decision will be made by the SCSC's production department. It must determine the feasibility of the new product line given the price, cost, and profit constraints under which it must produce the product.

In order to make an evaluation of the canvas shoe product line, Tony Pescatore, manager of new product development, must collect certain information. This information will be used to perform cost and break-even analysis, to project expected profits, and to recommend a suggested retail price as well as a manufacturer's price (the price that Sports Club would charge Outfitters USA).

The following is a review of the relevant data Tony collected for his evaluation of the proposed line of canvas shoes.

1. Similar lines of canvas shoes have recently been introduced by several competitors. Market research indicates that these lines have been selling well. The following prices have been observed in competitors' lines:

Retail Selling Price	Number of Times Observed
$18.00	5
$20.00	7
$22.00	3
$24.00	2

2. Outfitters USA will apply a 40-percent initial markup on the retail price of shoes.
3. Production costs for the new canvas shoes are estimated as follows:

Material	$1.75 per pair
Soles	$2.75 per pair
Thread	$.05 per pair
Direct labor	15 minutes per pair
Shipping weight	1 pound per packaged pair

4. Marketing costs associated with the introduction of the new line of canvas shoes are estimated to be $350,000 during the first year if a penetration pricing strategy is used or $475,000 if a skimming pricing policy is used.
5. Sports Club is a fairly large company with 14 production facilities strategically located throughout the United States. The average round-trip distance from these production facilities to Outfitters outlets is 200 miles. The new line of canvas shoes will be produced at all of the production facilities.
6. A review of Sports Club's annual report reveals the following information:

Managerial salaries	$ 1,600,000
Rent and utilities expense	$ 1,300,000
Transportation costs (1,500,000 miles)	$ 900,000
Depreciation on plant	$ 1,400,000
Other overhead	$ 2,225,000
Direct labor costs (1,000,000 hours)	$ 5,000,000
Total company sales	$50,000,000
Average order size	600 pounds

7. Outfitters USA hired the Central Market Research Company to develop a sales forecast for the new line of shoes. Its research findings estimate that if a skimming pricing policy were used, Outfitters could expect to sell approximately 120,000 to 150,000 pairs of shoes. With a penetration pricing policy, Central estimates a unit sales volume of approximately 150,000 to 170,000 pairs of shoes.

QUESTIONS

Assume that Tony Pescatore was suddenly required to go out of town and he asked you to prepare the analysis and written report on the feasibility of the new product line. You will also be responsible for recommending a pricing strategy. At a minimum, include the following in your analysis:

1. Cost analysis (variable cost per pair of shoes, fixed allocation for the line, and total cost per pair of shoes)
2. Break-even analysis in units and dollars
3. Suggested manufacturer's price and suggested retail price
4. An estimate of the profit Outfitters USA can expect to derive from the new line

enhance your marketing skills

with CD-ROM

You will find each exercise on the CD-ROM developed for use with this textbook. Each exercise has a name and is located within a module. For example, the first exercise can be found in the Macromarketing Module by clicking on Marketing's Contemporary Environment—Global Markets.

MACROMARKETING MODULE
Marketing's Contemporary Environment—Global Markets

1. What impact do trade agreements like GATT and NAFTA have on prices in the United States?

The following CD-ROM skill-building exercises relate to materials in several parts of the book.

STRATEGY MODULE
Military Strategy As an Inspiration for Marketing Strategy

2. What analogies can be made between military strategy and marketing strategy?

STRATEGY MODULE
Writing the Marketing Plan

3. What elements should be included in a marketing plan?

cross-functional insights

Many theories and principles from other business disciplines can provide insights about the role of marketing in an organization. The questions in this section are designed to help you think about integrating what you have learned in other business courses with the marketing principles explained in this textbook.

Monopoly and Oligopoly   Markets with only one seller are called monopolies. Markets with only a few sellers are called oligopolies.

According to economic theory, what pricing strategies are utilized by marketers operating in monopolies and oligopolies? In what industries are these situations most likely?

Competitive Pricing Strategies   Competitive pricing strategies are used by organizations that set pricing objectives based on the actions of their competitors. Dominant firms may exploit their positions. Weak firms may opt for the role of follower.

Economists use the *ceteris paribus* ("other things being equal") assumption. Do marketers setting prices agree that they should assume that everything except price is held constant?

What is monetary policy? How does it influence a marketer's competitive pricing strategy?

What is the effect of a tariff on domestic equilibrium price?

Change in Supply   Supply is the quantity of a product that marketers are willing and able to sell at a given price in a given time period. A supply curve graphically represents the amount of goods or services marketers will supply at various prices.

What impact does a technological innovation in the production process have on the supply curve?

Change in Demand   Demand is the quantity of a product consumers are willing and able to buy at a given price. Usually, the quantity demanded changes as price changes, and a demand curve can be used to represent this change.

Many Americans' tastes have changed in recent years. More and more consumers enjoy Mexican and Southwestern cuisine. What impact does this have on the demand curve for salsa?

Price Elasticity   Price elasticity measures the effect of a change in price on the quantity of a product demanded. Price elasticity refers to price sensitivity.

What is the relationship between price elasticity and revenue? (Use perfectly elastic, downward-sloping, and perfectly inelastic demand to illustrate your answer.)

Consumer Price Index   The consumer price index is a measure of inflation compiled by the federal government.

How is the consumer price index calculated? How has it changed in the past five years?

Geographical Pricing   Pricing strategies are sometimes based on geographical considerations.

What roles do letters of credit and bills of lading play in a marketer's international pricing strategy?

642

epilogue

A Closing Note

In the preface to this book, we said that marketing is a fascinating subject. Now that you are about to finish your first course in marketing, we hope you agree. Before we end this book, however, we must add some final comments.

As a marketing plan is being executed, and afterward, it is referred to as the *marketing program,* a term that embraces all of the activities associated with marketing research as well as implementation and control of the individual elements of the marketing mix. All of the elements of the marketing program must come together as a synchronized, integrated whole. The parts of the program are so tightly interrelated that any change in one area almost certainly affects all others. The goal is a unified program made up of pieces solidly put together.

An effective marketing program requires the proper implementation of new strategies and the effective execution of continuing strategies. As we mentioned in Chapter 2, execution requires organizing and coordinating people, resources, and activities. Staffing, directing, developing, and leading subordinates are major activities used in implementing plans. Properly executing these activities—that is, doing things right—can make the difference between success and failure. A marketing program has the greatest chance for success if the appropriate strategy is chosen and then is effectively executed. But the marketer is in for trouble if the proper strategy is selected and then is not properly executed. Clearly, even the best of marketing plans, if not well implemented, is likely to result in disappointment, if not failure.

Now that you have read this entire book, it is important to remember that marketing success depends on the interaction of strategy and implementation. It is also important to think about what you have learned from this book. We would like you to think about the big picture and try to put the many aspects of marketing all together. Listed below are just some of the important marketing themes and trends that you should remember if you are to be an effective marketer:

The primary emphasis of marketing is on the exchange process.

Marketing in the global economy requires understanding consumers and knowing how to satisfy them.

Listening to consumers and buyers, whether through marketing research or other means, is the way to discover opportunities.

Not all groups of customers are alike. Selecting target markets and positioning brands remains central to marketing management.

Marketers focus on building relationships with customers, suppliers, and distributors.

It is possible to satisfy customers while being socially responsible.

Marketing organizations are increasingly focusing on core competencies to achieve competitive advantages.

A worldwide trend toward working with collaborators in strategic alliances has created many "virtual corporations."

Around the globe, new markets and new opportunities are constantly emerging. Marketers should use marketing research to keep abreast of these changes.

Rapid changes in information technology are transforming the nature of marketing.

Data-based marketing and mass customization illustrate the magnitude of this trend.

A market position represents the way consumers perceive a brand relative to its competition.

The total product includes a broad spectrum of tangible and intangible benefits. Brand image is important.

The product life cycle influences most aspects of the marketing mix. It is an important planning tool.

Product innovation, product differentiation, and continuous quality improvement are vital to marketing success.

Product quality and value are defined by the customer.

Distribution is a means for delivering a standard of living to society.

Channels of distribution, especially retail institutions, are constantly evolving.

Distribution, especially logistics, should not be overlooked as a means to gain competitive advantage in the global economy.

Marketing communications are in the eye of the beholder—when devising communications, be sure you know who the recipients will be so that you can tailor the communications to them.

Marketers should strive for integrated marketing communications within all media. New media are developing. The Internet is changing the way marketers communicate with customers.

Personal selling remains the most common form of promotion, but wireless communication of digital information has changed its face. Teamwork, especially cross-functional teamwork, is becoming increasingly important.

Prices have names like *fee*, *rent*, and *donation*, but they are always an expression of value.

Price and value are determined by many factors. Increasingly, the ability to produce around the globe has a dramatic impact on the nature of pricing.

We could go on and on. However, we hope we have communicated the notion that marketing involves a company and its ever-changing relationship with customers, collaborators, and competitors. Marketing is dynamic because it must change in response to events within society and the global economy.

We hope we have answered many of your questions about the nature of marketing. We know we have not answered them all. You now know that marketing is not a black-and-white area in which there is always one best strategy. There are many gray areas that require analysis, considerable experience and skill, and a touch of creativity. And because marketing is dynamic, yesterday's answers will not be suitable as the world changes.

If our book has instilled in you the desire to continue to ask questions about marketing, we have done our job. We sincerely hope you are a satisfied customer.

appendix
A

Internet Insights into Marketing Careers

Marketing is a fascinating field. Students interested in a challenging career will find that it offers many opportunities that are hard to equal elsewhere. College students who have studied marketing provide a fresh source of talent for major corporations as well as smaller organizations.

The Zikmund and d'Amico home page (zikmund.swcollege.com) discusses a variety of marketing careers and provides a great deal of information about job opportunities available to students who major in marketing. It also provides tips on resume writing, job interviewing, and sources of information on the availability of jobs.

The American Marketing Association is one of the most respected professional organizations for people working in the field of marketing. Its home page (www.ama.org) gives additional information about careers in marketing.

The remainder of this appendix provides some Internet exercises that will help you learn more about the jobs available to you.

zikmund.swcollege.com

exercises

1. Use your Web browser to go to the Career Mosaic home page at www.careermosaic.com. Read through the information on the home page to see what is going on at CareerMosaic this month. Then select College Connection to get information on internship opportunities, entry-level jobs, resumes, and the like. Select one of the companies on the Employers list, and find out what marketing-related employment opportunities are available. (If the company you selected doesn't have any marketing jobs listed, select another company.)
   a. What marketing jobs did you find available?
   b. What advice did the company offer potential employees?
   Go back to the CareerMosaic home page and select Jobs. Read the directions for entering a job search. Then enter a search on something like sales and marketing. Submit your search and let the computer do the work. Read through some of the many job postings to see if any look interesting to you.
2. Go to the Career Magazine home page at www.careermag.com. Select the Job Openings link and search for marketing-related jobs that have been posted on the Internet. Leave the Location field empty, enter Marketing in the Skills field, and enter Manager in the Title field. Then submit your search by clicking on the Submit Search button. Browse through the jobs

you find. Pick a job that looks interesting to you, write down the information, and bring it to class for discussion and to share with others.

3. Go to the following address: www.job-hunt.org. You will find a fantastic connection to career resources. In the General Job Listings, select College Grad Job Hunter. Take a look at Job Postings, Interviews and Negotiations, Resumes and Cover Letters, and any other topics that interest you.

4. The Internet's Online Career Center (OCC) is a wonderful resource for people seeking jobs, as well as companies seeking new employees. Check out the Online Career Center home page at www.occ.com/occ. From the Online Career Center home page you can choose Search Firms, which will lead to job listings for dozens of companies. Choose several companies and look for marketing-related positions. Why are there so many technology-related positions on the OCC? Is this good target marketing? Why? Check out the other options at the OCC. You will find information under Post Resumes, Career Forum, Salary Information, Career Fairs and Events, and other categories that may help you find a job or internship.

5. Go to the JobNet home page at www.westga.edu/~coop. Read through the information on the JobNet home page to learn about the services available at JobNet. Selecting Tips, Jobs, or Research will lead to more information about the current condition of the job market.

6. Go to the NPD Group, Inc., home page at www.npd.com. Choose the Career Opportunities option to find out what a career in marketing research might look like. Look at the link called Current Career Opportunities. In what areas does the company hire new recruits? What qualifications is it looking for? What tasks is a marketing service director expected to perform? What types of training does the company offer?

appendix
B
The Marketing Audit

A **marketing audit** is a comprehensive appraisal of an organization's marketing activities. It involves a systematic assessment of marketing plans, objectives, strategies, programs, activities, organizational structure, and personnel. Such a thorough study of a marketing operation requires an objective attitude. Thinking about bank auditors, whose cautious care makes them hard to fool, provides good insight into the marketing audit process. A good marketing audit, therefore, has the following characteristics:

Systematic. It follows a logical, predetermined framework—an orderly sequence of diagnostic steps.

Comprehensive. It considers all factors affecting marketing performance, not just obvious trouble spots. Marketers can be fooled into addressing symptoms rather than underlying problems. A comprehensive audit will identify the real problems.

Independent. To ensure objectivity, outside consultants may prepare the marketing audit. Using outsiders may not be necessary, but having an objective auditor is essential.

Periodic. Many organizations schedule regular marketing audits because marketers operate in a dynamic environment.

Managers often describe the audit process as costly, complex, and upsetting to organizations and individuals. This is because the audit emphasizes not only what is being done but why it is being done and it evaluates both current tactics and past strategies. Ideally, the audit should stress correcting procedures rather than assigning blame to individuals. Organizations that conduct regularly scheduled marketing audits can avoid problems by pointing out that the process is scheduled from time to time and is not aimed at criticizing an individual or a part of the organization.

Marketing audits typically begin with a meeting between the organization's officers and the outside people who are to conduct the audit. They decide on the audit's objectives, report format, timing, and other matters. A typical audit consists of numerous sections, as shown in Exhibit B-1.

FOCUS OF AUDIT	QUESTIONS TO CONSIDER
Environment	How are environmental trends monitored?
	What population trends are expected to affect existing and planned strategy?
	What social and psychological patterns (attitudes, lifestyle, etc.) are expected to affect buyer behavior patterns?
	How are present and pending legal developments affecting your operation?
	What are the effects of competitors (their products, services, technologies) on your operation?
Objectives	Are the marketing objectives of your department consistent with overall company objectives?
	Should these objectives be altered to fit changing environmental variables?
	Are objectives consistent with one another?
	How do objectives relate to marketing strengths and market opportunities?
Strategy	What is the relationship between objectives and strategies?
	Are resources sufficient to implement the strategies?
	What are the company's weaknesses?
	How do you compare your strategies with those of competitors?
Product Decisions	How are new products developed within your business unit?
	How are existing products evaluated?
	How are products phased out of the line?
Pricing Decisions	How are pricing decisions made?
	How do pricing decisions reflect the influences of competitors and the concerns of channel members?
Distribution Decisions	How are channel members selected, evaluated, and dropped if necessary?
	How are channel members motivated?
	How are decisions to modify channel structures reached?
Promotion Decisions	How are promotion mix decisions made?
	How are salespeople selected, monitored, and evaluated?
	How are payoffs associated with promotional efforts estimated?
Market Information	How is marketing research information transmitted to, and used by, the business unit?
	Is a global information system in place?
Activities and Tasks	How are tasks scheduled, described, and planned? How are the responsibilities of individuals determined?
	What spans of supervision, reporting relationships, and communication patterns exist? How are they evaluated?
Personnel	What level of competence has been attained by personnel in each position?
	Are remedies to problems, if necessary, being planned? What are they?
	What is the state of morale? Motivation? What are present plans in these areas?
	Describe career development paths. Are replacements for personnel in key positions being groomed?

NOTE: This list of items is intended to represent matters typically treated in a marketing audit. It is not intended to be a complete checklist.

appendix C

Organizing the Marketing Function

Organizing the marketing function consists of assigning tasks, grouping tasks into organizational units, and allocating resources to organizational units. This activity determines the structure of the marketing organization and assigns responsibilities for the implementation of marketing activities.

Organizational design emphasizes the efficient allocation of marketing personnel and other resources. Each organizational structure has advantages and difficulties, but all provide ways to assign authority and responsibility for marketing activities to individuals and divisions within the total organization.

The Marketing Era Organization

The marketing concept mandates two major features of the marketing organization. One is that there is one person in the organization (or in each strategic business unit, if SBUs are identified) who is clearly responsible for managing all marketing activities. This manager holds a title such as vice president of marketing. The second feature is the concentration of all marketing subfunctions under the direction of the primary marketing officer.

All firms can make use of the marketing concept's organizational prescription: assigning marketing responsibilities to a single executive and placing all marketing subfunctions under the control of that person. Yet each organization, especially if it is diversified, will be faced with the problem of refining its organizational structure to fit individual circumstances. Experience has shown that many types of organizational structures are well suited to marketing operations. We discuss some of them here.

THE FUNCTIONAL ORGANIZATION

Marketing is divisible into many specific functions, or areas of specialization. It makes sense to consider organizing marketing activities around such functions or activities as sales, advertising, marketing research, and so on. The type of organization that results is the functional organization.

A functional organization is considered appropriate for small companies with centralized operations, and for some larger firms if their marketing operations are not complex. However, for firms, especially large ones, that serve multiple market segments with many products and brands, this form of organization can lead to coordination problems.

ORGANIZATION BY PRODUCT TYPE

Organizations that produce a wide variety of products often find it best to organize marketing activities around those products. The major rubber producers, for example, typically focus one set of managers and efforts on the sale of standard automobile tires and another on the sale of off-the-road tires—the huge tires used for construction vehicles, tractors, and the like. Still another group of managers handles marketing of specialty tires for racing, motorcycles, and other specific uses. Belts, gaskets, and other products are handled by yet another part of the firm. The product-based organization allows product or brand managers to concern themselves with a relatively small number of products or brands. This is especially efficient when managers must have extensive knowledge of technical, industrial products.

ORGANIZATION BY MARKET

Another form of organization involves a market manager who is responsible for administering all marketing activities (forecasting, product planning, pricing, and so on) that relate to a particular market. In this context, *market* is typically defined as a customer group (industry) or product application. A manufacturer of forklift trucks might sell to grocery wholesalers, but also to steel mills, and perhaps even to firms engaged in pulpwood logging. Because these types of customers clearly differ in what they expect from the forklift manufacturer, an organizational structure built around varying customer needs may be appropriate. Differences in the marketing mix required for each customer group may be so great that it is most efficient to have separate market managers, each with considerable knowledge about customer needs in a specific industry. Organization by market, or customer type, is most efficient when the strategic business unit has a single or dominant product line and divergent customer types that are readily identifiable.

GEOGRAPHY-BASED AND COMBINATION ORGANIZATIONS

In more complex marketing operations—those active in numerous markets, those marketing numerous and varied products, or both—marketing activity may become decentralized and may be divided by geographic region. This is often the case with sales territories. In addition, entire strategic business units may be based on geographical decentralization. Geography-based organizations are used by companies that market to customer groups whose needs vary significantly from one geographic area to another. For example, Ford Motor Company has a North American division, a European division, a Latin American division, and so on.

Often there is a certain amount of overlap among functional, product-based, market-based, and geography-based organizations. Usually, all factors—product mixes, customer needs, geography, marketing functions—are considered. Thus, the organization model followed by many companies is that of the combination organization.

Organizing for New Product Development

New product development is a key to long-term success in the marketplace. Therefore, the organization must be structured to permit and encourage innovation. However, many organizations are constructed around the day-to-day chores needed to keep operations moving smoothly and successfully in existing marketing areas.

In many cases, product managers or market managers are responsible for new product development. Product managers are extremely knowledgeable individuals who theoretically are well placed to detect market opportunities, to identify or conceptualize appropriate additions to product lines, and to evaluate the chances of success or failure for new product offerings. It is easy to see the disadvantages in this arrangement, however. Product managers, as specialists, may be unlikely to develop product ideas outside their limited areas of specialization. They may be concerned that new products will undermine their established products. Product managers may be so busy safeguarding current success that they have no time for new product development. It can also be argued that the abilities needed to manage an existing product or brand are not necessarily those appropriate for developing new product ideas. Furthermore, although individual product managers are responsible for the product's or brand's success, they rarely have authority over many of the individuals with whom they must work. Managers of sales and other marketing functions do not report directly to the brand or product category manager. Thus, brand managers must rely on the cooperation of the sales manager and sales force, because they do not have direct authority over these individuals or their activities.

Managers in each functional area understandably concentrate on meeting immediate objectives and solving current problems. Despite the fact that everyone knows forecasting the future is important, current problems can easily blot the future from view. Individual managers may defend this situation with the observation that if they don't solve today's problems, there will not be any future. Although there is an element of truth in this statement, long-range survival of an organization requires that long-range problems be solved. The organizations that enjoy the most success in new product introductions are the ones that have given the greatest care to organizing for developing those products. Many organizational forms have been designed in an effort to encourage the smooth development and introduction of new products.

THE VENTURE TEAM

The venture team is a group of specialists in the various functional areas of the organization who operate in an entrepreneurial environment. Team members are freed from their daily organizational responsibilities. The team is supposed to develop a new business—a new venture—instead of operating as a closely controlled part of the whole organization. The team plays an independent role, therefore, in developing a new product, as well as in testing and commercialization. If the new product or new business is brought into full commercialization, the team members may be assigned to manage it. This assignment, as well as financial bonuses tied to the venture's success, may serve as a significant reward for team members.

THE NEW PRODUCTS DEPARTMENT

A new products department, unlike a venture team, is a permanent department within an organization, headed by a director or even a vice president. Under this system, a high-ranking organizational official has clear-cut responsibility for new products and, by virtue of the position, can deal with other important executives as an equal. Furthermore, because the new product manager or director is a high-level officer dealing directly with the chief executive officer, he or she can expedite matters related to product development.

The new product manager is most likely to be found in a consumer goods company confronting a market in which marketing issues (rather than production or technical problems) predominate. New product managers are expected to be creative people who understand the unique problems of introducing new products to the market. The new product manager is a specialist in activities such as concept testing and test marketing.

In general, new products departments work in one of two ways. The department may be fairly large and have its own research staff and other experts, or it may be small and call on people from other areas of the corporation as needed. Once a new product has reached the commercialization stage, in either type of organization, responsibility for the new product is turned over to the regular departments of the firm, perhaps with the new products department maintaining some coordinating role. This is in contrast to the venture team approach, in which the venture team often maintains full responsibility for the new product or business.

THE NEW PRODUCTS COMMITTEE

A new products committee is a group similar to any other committee. Usually, the heads of the organization's functional departments constitute the committee membership, and the chair is the chief executive officer. The committee also includes the new products director or other officer directly involved in such matters. New products committees create and review new product policies, assign priorities to various new product options, evaluate progress, and ultimately decide whether to commercialize new products. In fact, new products committees are frequently used in connection with other new product management formats, such as new products departments. The committee can help new products departments or new products managers with its input into the decision-making process. Most important, however, the new products committee puts the weight of its high-ranking, executive membership behind new product plans.

THE TASK FORCE

Task forces are used in new product development situations much as they are used in government. A group is created whose membership spans numerous groups within the organization, typically the functional department. This task force ensures that a specific new project gets the support and resources that the various departments are able to offer. Unlike the new products committee, which is a permanent group, the task force is disbanded at product completion. Task forces also differ from the venture group because they handle task force duties in addition to their usual assignments. However, a few members are sometimes given leaves of absence from their regular jobs to devote their full attention to the task until it is completed.

glossary

A

Account manager A salesperson who concentrates on maintaining an ongoing relationship with existing customers.

Account service representative A sales employee at company headquarters or at a branch office who corresponds with clients and provides customer service to established accounts; sometimes called a *sales correspondent*.

Administered strategic alliance A vertical marketing system in which a strong channel leader coordinates marketing activities at all levels in the channel through planning and management of a mutually beneficial program.

Adoption process The mental and behavioral stages through which a consumer passes before making a purchase or placing an order. The stages are awareness, interest, evaluation, trial, and adoption.

Advertising An informative or persuasive message carried by a nonpersonal medium and paid for by an identified sponsor whose organization or product is identified in some way.

Advertising appeal The central theme or idea of an advertising message.

Advertising theme An advertising appeal used in several different advertisements to give continuity to an advertising campaign.

Agent A wholesaler that does not take title to goods. Agents sometimes take possession of goods but function primarily to bring buyers and sellers together or otherwise help consummate a marketing transaction.

Agent intermediary A channel intermediary that does not take title to the product. Agent intermediaries bring buyers and sellers together or otherwise help complete a transaction.

AIDA An acronym for *attention, interest, desire,* and *action.* The AIDA formula is a hierarchy of communication effects model used as a guideline in creating advertisements.

Aided recall tests In the context of advertising, a test of consumers' memory of an advertisement in which clues are provided to the specific material to be remembered.

Air freight The shipment of products by air carrier.

Allowance A reduction in price, a rebate, or the like given to a marketing intermediary in return for a large order or the performance of a specific activity.

Anticipation discount A discount over and above the regular cash discount, meant to encourage even faster payment.

Antitrust legislation Federal laws meant to prohibit behavior that tends to lessen competition in U.S. markets. The major antitrust laws are the Sherman Antitrust Act (1890), the Clayton Act (1914), and the Federal Trade Commission Act (1914).

Approach The step in the creative selling process wherein the salesperson makes initial contact and establishes rapport with a prospect.

Art Any aspect of an advertisement other than copy, including pictures, layout, and white space.

Aspirational group A group to which an individual would like to belong.

Assembler A marketing intermediary that performs a bulk-accumulating function.

Association creative platform An advertising creative platform that uses an analogy or other relationship to stimulate interest and convey information.

Assorting function An activity, performed by marketing intermediaries, consisting of combining products purchased from several manufacturers to create assortments.

Atmospherics Physical characteristics of a store's environment, such as appearance, layout, and displays.

Attitude An individual's general affective, cognitive, and behavioral responses to a given object, issue, or person.

Auction company An agent intermediary that brings together buyers and sellers. Auction companies often assemble merchandise for sale in a central location and sell it by means of a bidding process.

Auxiliary dimension An aspect of a product that provides supplementary benefits, such as special features, aesthetics, package, warranty, repair service contract, reputation, brand name, or instructions.

Average cost The total costs divided by the number of units produced.

B

Backward channel A channel of distribution for recycling, in which the customary flow from producer to ultimate user is reversed.

Bait-and-switch advertising An advertising technique, usually associated with retailers, in which a product is offered at an extremely low price to attract customers, who are then told the product is unavailable and "switched" to a more expensive, higher-margin product.

Bait pricing   A method of attracting customers by offering low-priced items for sale with the intention of selling more expensive goods.

Barter   The exchange of products without the use of money.

Basing-point pricing   Charging for shipping from a specified basing point, or location, no matter where the shipment actually originates.

Belief   A conviction concerning the existence or the characteristics of physical and social phenomena.

Benefit segmentation   A type of market segmentation by which consumers are grouped according to the specific benefits they seek from a product.

Birdyback service   Transport of containers by air to destinations from which they are then moved by truck.

Boycott   The refusal of some group to buy certain products. A government may enforce a boycott of the products of some other country.

Brand   An identifying feature that distinguishes one product from another; more specifically, any name, term, symbol, sign, or design or a unifying combination of these.

Brand equity   The value associated with a brand. Where a brand has brand equity, market share or profit margins are greater because of the goodwill associated with the brand.

Brand extension   A product category extension or product line extension that employs a brand name already used on one of the company's existing products.

Brand image   The complex of symbols and meanings associated with a brand.

Brand mark   A unique symbol that is part of a brand.

Brand name   The verbal part of the brand—the part that can be spoken or written.

Break-down method   A sales forecasting method that starts with large-scale estimates (for example, an estimate of GDP) and works down to industrywide, company, and product estimates. See also *build-up method*.

Break-even point   The point at which an organization's revenues and costs are equal.

Broker   An agent intermediary whose major role is placing buyers and sellers in touch with one another and assisting in contractual arrangements.

Build-up method   A sales forecasting method that starts with small-scale estimates (for example, product estimates) and works up to larger-scale ones. See also *break-down method*.

Bulk-accumulating function   An activity, performed by marketing intermediaries, consisting of buying small quantities of a particular product from many small producers and then selling the assembled larger quantities.

Bulk-breaking function   An activity, performed by mar-keting intermediaries, consisting of buying products in relatively large quantities and selling in smaller quantities.

Business analysis stage   The stage in new product development in which the new product is reviewed from all organizational perspectives to determine performance criteria and likely profitability.

Business cycle   Recurrent fluctuations in general economic activity. The four phases of the business cycle are prosperity, recession, depression, and recovery.

Business-to-business marketing   Marketing aimed at bringing about an exchange in which a good or service is sold for any use other than personal consumption. The buyer may be a manufacturer, a reseller, a government body, a nonprofit institution, or any organization other than an ultimate consumer. The transaction occurs so that an organization may conduct its business.

Buy phase   One of the stages of the multistage process by which organizations make purchase decisions.

Buyer   The buying-center role played by the organizational member with the formal authority to purchase the product.

Buying center   An informal, cross-departmental decision unit, the primary objective of which is the acquisition, dissemination, and processing of relevant purchasing-related information.

Buying function   Activities, performed by intermediaries, that are associated with making a purchase and thus effecting the transfer of ownership of a product.

C

Cannibalize   To eat into the sales revenues of another product item in the same line.

Captive pricing strategy   A strategy whereby a basic product, such as a razor, is priced low but the profits from associated products needed for operating the basic product, such as razor blades, make up for the lack of profit on the basic product.

Cash-and-carry wholesaler   A limited-service wholesaler that does not offer delivery or credit.

Cash cow   A high-market-share product in a low-growth market.

Cash discount   A price discount offered for early payment of bills.

Catalog showroom   A general mass merchandise outlet where customers select goods from a catalog and store employees retrieve the selected items from storage.

Category discounter   A specialty mass merchandise outlet offering extensive assortment and depth in a specific product category; also called a *category killer*.

Census   A survey of all the members of a group (an entire population).

Chain store   One of a group of two or more stores of a similar type, centrally owned and operated.

Channel conflict Antagonism between distribution channel members.

Channel cooperation Coordinated efforts by distribution channel members whose marketing objectives and strategies are harmonious.

Channel leader A distribution channel member that is able to exert power and influence over other channel members; also known as a *channel captain*.

Channel of distribution The complete sequence of marketing organizations involved in bringing a product from the producer to the ultimate consumer or organizational user.

Channel power The extent to which a channel member is able to influence the behavior of another channel member.

Choice criteria The critical attributes a consumer uses to evaluate product alternatives.

Closing The step in the creative selling process wherein the salesperson attempts to obtain a prospect's commitment to buy.

Closing signals Signs from the prospect revealing that he or she is ready to buy.

Closure An element of perception whereby an observer mentally completes an incomplete stimulus.

Co-branding The use of two individual brands on a single product.

Code of conduct A statement establishing a company's or a professional organization's guidelines with regard to ethical principles and acceptable behavior.

Coding Establishing meaningful categories for responses collected by means of surveys or other data collection forms so that the responses can be grouped into usable classifications.

Cognitive dissonance The tension that results from holding two conflicting ideas or beliefs at the same time; in terms of consumer behavior, the negative feelings that a consumer may experience after making a commitment to purchase.

Collaborator A person or company that works with a marketing company. Collaborators help the company run its business but are not actually part of the company.

Commercialization The stage in new product development in which the decision is made to launch full-scale production and distribution of a new product.

Commission merchant An agent intermediary similar to a broker but having certain additional decision-making powers, such as the power to make price adjustments.

Commission with draw Compensation based strictly on sales performance, but with the provision that the salesperson can borrow from a drawing account if necessary.

Communication The process of exchanging information with and conveying meaning to others.

Communication goals In the context of marketing, what the marketer wants a promotional message to accomplish: to gain attention, to be understood, to be believed, and to be remembered.

Company A business or organization that offers products and services to consumers.

Comparative advertising A type of demonstration advertising in which the brand being advertised is directly compared with a competing brand.

Comparative-parity method A method of setting a promotional budget in which the marketer tries to match competitors' prices.

Competitive advantage Superiority to or favorable difference from competitors along some dimension important to the market.

Competitor One of two or more rival companies engaged in the same business.

Computer-interactive retailing A retailing method whereby consumers shop at home using personal computers and interactive computer services.

Concentrated marketing Development of a marketing mix and direction of marketing efforts and resources to appeal to a single market segment.

Concept testing Research procedures used to learn consumers' reactions to new product ideas. Consumers presented with an idea are asked if they like it, would use it, would buy it, and so on.

Conspicuous consumption Consumption for the sake of enhancing social prestige.

Consumer behavior The activities people engage in when selecting, purchasing, and using products so as to satisfy needs and desires.

Consumer involvement The extent to which an individual is interested in and attaches importance to a product and is willing to expend energy in making a decision about purchasing the product.

Consumer market The market consisting of buyers who use a product to satisfy personal or household needs.

Contest In the context of a wholesaler's or retailer's sales promotion, a means of motivating a sales force by offering bonuses or prizes for sales performance.

Continuous innovation A new product that is characterized by minor alterations or improvements to existing products and that produces little change in consumption patterns.

Contract manufacturing In international marketing, an agreement by which a company allows a foreign producer to manufacture its product according to its specifications. Typically, the company then handles foreign sale of the product.

Contractual vertical marketing system A vertical marketing system in which channel coordination and leadership are specified in a contractual agreement.

Control The process by which managers ensure that planned activities are completely and properly executed.

Convenience product A relatively inexpensive, regularly purchased consumer product bought without much thought and with a minimum of shopping effort.

Convenience store A small grocery store stressing convenient location and quick service and typically charging higher prices than other retailers selling similar products.

Cooperative advertising Advertising paid for jointly by a supplier and a customer—for example, by the manufacturer of a product and a retailer.

Copy Any words contained in an advertisement.

Core competency A proficiency in a critical functional area, such as technical know-how or a specialization in a particular aspect of a business, that helps provide a company's unique competitive advantage.

Corporate chain A chain consisting of 11 or more stores.

Corporate vertical marketing system A vertical marketing system in which two or more channel members are connected through ownership.

Cost reduction strategy A product strategy that involves redesigning a product to lower production costs.

Creative platform The style in which the advertising message is delivered; also known as *execution format*.

Creative process In the context of advertising, the generation of ideas and the development of the advertising message or concept.

Creative selling process The six-step process by which creative selling is carried out: (1) locating and qualifying prospects, (2) approaching the prospect, (3) making the sales presentation, (4) handling objections, (5) closing the sale, and (6) following up.

Credit function Provision of credit to another member of a distribution channel.

Crisis management A public relations effort that involves disseminating information during an emergency.

Cross-classification matrix A grid that helps isolate variables of interest in the market. For example, a geographic variable might be cross-classified with some other variable of interest, such as income.

Cross-elasticity Elasticity in the demand for one product in relation to the prices of substitutable or complementary products.

Cross-functional activity An activity carried out by individuals from various departments within an organization and from outside the organization, all of whom have a common purpose.

Cross-functional sales team The sales representative and those who support his or her efforts in making sales and servicing accounts. Support personnel may include technical specialists and missionary salespeople.

Cross-functional team A team made up of individuals from various organizational departments who share a common purpose.

Cross-selling Marketing activities used to sell new services to customers of an existing service.

Culture The institutions, values, beliefs, and behaviors of a society; everything people learn, as opposed to the basic drives with which people are born.

Cumulative quantity discount A price discount determined by the amount purchased over some specified time period.

Custom marketing A marketing effort in which a marketer seeks to satisfy each customer's unique set of needs. In effect, each customer is an individual market segment.

Customer One who buys a company's goods or services.

Customization strategy A product line extension strategy that involves making a product in relatively small lots for specific channels of distribution or specific customers.

D

Damage in transit Breakage, spoilage, or other injury to products that occurs while the products are being transported.

Data Facts and recorded measures of phenomena.

Data analysis Statistical and/or qualitative consideration of data gathered by research.

Data-based marketing The practice of using databases of customers' names, addresses, phone numbers, past purchases, responses to previous offers, and demographic characteristics in making marketing decisions.

Data mining The use of powerful computers to dig through large volumes of data to discover puchasing patterns among an organization's customers.

Database A collection of data, arranged in a logical manner and organized in a form that can be stored and processed by a computer.

Decider The buying-center role played by the organizational member who makes the actual purchasing decision.

Decision support system A computer system that stores data and transforms data into accessible information. It includes databases and software.

Decline stage The stage in the product life cycle during which the product loses market acceptance because of such factors as diminished popularity, obsolescence, or market saturation.

Decoding In communication theory, the process by which the receiver of a message interprets the message's meaning.

Delivered pricing Pricing that includes delivery within a specified area; also known as *freight-allowed pricing*.

Demand curve A graphic representation of the relationship between various prices and the amount of product that will be demanded at those prices; also called a *demand schedule*.

Demand management strategy A strategy used by

service marketers to accurately forecast the need for services so that supply is in line with demand.

Demarketing A strategy (or strategies) intentionally designed to discourage all or some consumers from buying a product.

Demography The study of the size, composition, and distribution of the human population in relation to social factors such as geographic boundaries.

Demonstration creative platform An advertising creative platform in which a clear-cut example of product superiority or consumer benefits is presented.

Department store A departmentalized retail outlet, often large, offering a wide variety of products and generally providing a full range of customer services.

Derived demand Demand for a product that depends on demand for another product.

Development stage The stage in new product development in which a new product concept is transformed into a prototype. The basic marketing strategy also develops at this time.

Dialectic theory A theory describing the interaction of an existing retail institution (the thesis) with a challenging institution (the antithesis), to yield a new retail institution (the synthesis) that has some characteristics of both.

Differential pricing strategy A strategy whereby different prices are charged to different buyers of the same product.

Differentiated marketing A marketing effort in which a marketer selects more than one target market and then develops a separate marketing mix for each; also called *multiple market segmentation*.

Differentiation strategy A strategy whereby a marketer offers a product that is unique in the industry, provides a distinct advantage, or is otherwise set apart from competitors' brands in some way other than price.

Diffusion process The spread of a new product through society.

Direct-action advertisement An advertisement designed to stimulate immediate purchase or encourage another direct response; also called a *direct-response advertisement*.

Direct foreign investment Investment of capital in production and marketing operations located in a host foreign country.

Direct marketing Marketing in which advertising, telephone sales, or other communications are used to elicit a direct response, such as an order by mail or phone; in a retailing context, also called *direct-response retailing*.

Direct-marketing wholesaler A limited-service wholesaler that uses catalogs or the Internet; mail or telephone ordering; and parcel delivery.

Direct-response campaign A promotional approach intended to elicit a direct, measurable response, such as an order.

Discontinuous innovation A product so new that no previous product performed an equivalent function. Such a product requires the development of new consumption or usage patterns.

Discount A reduction from list price or a reimbursement for performance of a specific task.

Distributor brand A brand owned by a retailer, wholesaler, or other distributor rather than by the manufacturer of the product; also called a *private brand*.

Diversification A strategy of marketing new products to a new market.

Diversion in transit Direction of a rail shipment to a destination not specified at the start of the trip.

Divisibility The ability of a product to be sampled in small amounts by consumers.

Dog A low-market-share product in a low-growth market.

Domestic environment The environment in an organization's home country.

Drop shipper A limited-service wholesaler, often dealing in bulky products, that takes customer orders and arranges for shipment of merchandise from the producer directly to the customer; also called a *desk jobber*.

Durable good A physical, tangible item that can be used over an extended period.

Dynamically continuous innovation A product that is different from previously available products but that does not strikingly change buying or usage patterns.

E

Early adopter A member of the group of consumers who purchase a product soon after it has been introduced, but after the innovators have purchased it.

Early majority A group of consumers, usually solid, middle-class people, who purchase more deliberately and cautiously than early adopters.

Economic order quantity (E.O.Q.) A mathematically determined purchase order size that yields the lowest total order-processing and inventory-holding costs.

Economic system The system whereby a society allocates its scarce resources.

Economic utility The ability of a good or service marketed by an organization to satisfy a consumer's wants or needs. Economic utility includes form utility, place utility, time utility, and possession utility.

Editing Checking questionnaires or other data collection forms for omissions, incomplete or otherwise unusable responses, illegibility, and obvious inconsistencies.

80/20 principle In marketing, a principle describing the fact that usually a relatively small percentage of customers accounts for a disproportionately large share of the sales of a product.

Electronic interactive media Media, such as the Internet, touch-tone telephone systems, and on-line information services, that allow marketers to reach large audiences with personalized individual messages and that provide an opportunity for immediate interaction.

Embargo A government prohibition against trade, especially trade in a particular product.

Emotion A state involving subjectively experienced feelings of attraction or repulsion.

Encoding In communication theory, the process by which a sender translates an idea to be communicated into a symbolic message, consisting of words, pictures, numbers, gestures, or the like, so that it can be transmitted to a receiver.

Enhanced model A model that extends a product line by virtue of its distinctive features, which consumers perceive as better than those of the original model.

Entrepreneur A risk-taking individual who sees an opportunity and is willing to undertake a venture to create a new product or service.

Environmental monitoring Tracking certain phenomena to detect the emergence of meaningful trends.

Environmental scanning Information gathering designed to detect changes that may be in their initial states of development.

Ethical dilemma A predicament in which a marketer must resolve whether an action that benefits the organization, the individual decision maker, or both may be considered unethical.

Ethnocentrism The tendency to consider one's own culture and way of life as the natural and normal ones.

Exchange process The interchange of something of value between two or more parties.

Exclusive dealing A situation in which a distributor carries the products of one manufacturer and not those of competing manufacturers.

Exclusive distribution A distribution strategy in which only one outlet in a given area is allowed to sell a product.

Exclusive territory An area defined by geographical boundaries or population and assigned to a retailer, wholesaler, or other dealer with the understanding that no other distributors will be assigned to operate in that area.

Execution The carrying out of plans; also called *implementation*.

Expected service–perceived service gap The gap between a service consumer's expectations and the person's perception of the level of service received. The gap can be negative or positive.

Experiment A research method in which the researcher changes one variable and observes the effects of that change on another variable.

Exploratory research Research to clarify the nature of a marketing problem.

Export A domestically produced product sold in a foreign market.

Export management company A company that specializes in buying from sellers in one country and mar-

keting the products in other countries. Such companies typically take title to the products.

Exporting Selling domestically produced products in foreign markets.

Extensive problem solving In-depth search for and evaluation of alternative solutions to a problem.

F

Fad A passing fashion or craze that interests many people for only a short time.

Family A group of two or more persons related by birth, marriage, or adoption and residing together.

Family branding The practice of using a single brand name to identify different items in a product line.

Family life cycle A series of stages through which most families pass.

Fantasy creative platform In the context of advertising, a type of association creative platform used to link a product with the target buyer's wildest dreams and hopes.

Fashion A style that is current or in vogue.

Federal Trade Commission (FTC) Federal agency established in 1914 by the Federal Trade Commission Act to investigate and put an end to unfair methods of competition.

Feedback Communication of the receiver's reaction to a message back to the source.

Field sales manager A district or regional sales manager, so called because his or her main concern is the salespeople in the field.

Field selling Business-to-business selling that takes place outside the employer's place of business, usually in the prospective customer's place of business.

Fishyback service Transport of containers by water to destinations from which they are then moved by truck.

Fixed cost A cost that is incurred with the passage of time and is not a function of volume of production or sales.

Flanker brand A product that extends a product line as a means of denying shelf space to competitors.

Flexible manufacturing system A group of machines integrated through a central computer and able to produce a variety of similar but not identical products.

F.O.B. "Freight on board" or "Free on board"; a term used to identify the point at which title passes from seller to buyer. For example, "F.O.B. factory" means that the buyer takes title at the factory and is responsible for all shipping charges.

Focus group interview A loosely structured interview in which a group of 6 to 10 people discuss a product or focus on some aspect of buying behavior.

Follow-the-leader strategy A pricing strategy whereby an organization sets prices at the level the market leader has established. It is used especially by organizations in weak competitive positions.

Follow-up   The final step in the creative selling process, wherein the salesperson, after the sale has been made, contacts the buyer to make sure everything connected with the sale was handled properly.

Foreign environment   The environment outside an organization's home country.

Form utility   Economic utility created by conversion of raw materials into finished goods that meet consumer needs.

Four Cs   A name for the microenvironmental participants that perform essential business activities: company, customers, competitors, and collaborators.

Four Ps of marketing   The basic elements of the marketing mix: product, place (distribution), price, and promotion; also called the *controllable variables of marketing,* because they can be controlled and manipulated by the marketer.

Franchise   A contractual agreement between a franchisor and a franchisee by which the franchisee distributes the franchisor's product.

Frequency   The number of times an advertisement is repeated in a given medium within a given time period, usually 4 weeks.

Full-line strategy   A product line strategy that involves offering a large number of variations of a product; also called a *deep-line strategy.*

Full-service merchant wholesaler   A merchant wholesaler that provides a complete array of services, such as delivery, credit, marketing information and advice, and managerial assistance; also called a *full-function wholesaler.*

G

Gap analysis   The type of analysis marketers use to identify the sources of the expected service–perceived service gap.

Gatekeeper   The buying-center role played by the organizational member who controls the flow of information related to the purchase.

General line wholesaler   A full-service merchant wholesaler that sells a full selection of products in one product line.

General merchandise wholesaler   A full-service merchant wholesaler that sells a large number of different product lines.

General-specific-general theory   A theory describing the development of retailing as a cyclic process in which general merchandisers are replaced by specialty merchandisers, which in turn are replaced by general merchandisers, and so on.

Generic name   A name so commonly used that it is part of everyday language and is used to describe a product class rather than a particular manufacturer's product.

Generic product   A product that carries neither a manufacturer nor a distributor brand; also known as a *generic brand.* The goods are plainly packaged with stark lettering that simply lists the contents.

Geodemographic segmentation   A type of market segmentation by which consumers are grouped according to demographic variables, such as income and age, as identified by a geographic variable, such as zip code.

Globalization strategy   A plan by which a marketer standardizes its marketing strategy around the world; also called a *standardization strategy.*

Green marketing   Marketing ecologically safe products and promoting activities beneficial to the physical environment.

Gross domestic product (GDP)   The total value of all the goods and services produced by capital and workers in a country.

Gross national product (GNP)   The total value of all the goods and services produced by a nation's residents or corporations, regardless of their location.

Growth stage   The stage in the product life cycle during which sales increase at an accelerating rate.

H

Handling objections   The step in the creative selling process wherein the salesperson responds to questions or reservations expressed by the prospect.

Head-to-head competition   Positioning a product to occupy the same market position as a competitor.

Human interactive media   Personal forms of communication involving face-to-face interaction and person-to-person interaction (as by telephone).

Hypothesis   An unproven proposition that can be supported or refuted by market research. Research objectives are often stated as hypotheses.

I

Idea generation stage   The stage in new product development in which a marketer engages in a continuing search for product ideas consistent with target market needs and the organization's objectives.

Image building   A promotional approach intended to communicate an image and generate consumer preference for a brand or product on the basis of symbolic value.

Import   A foreign product purchased domestically.

Import quota   A limit set by a government on how much of a certain type of product can be imported into a country.

Incentive   Something believed capable of satisfying a particular motive.

Independent retailer   A retail establishment that is not owned or controlled by any other organization.

Indirect-action advertisement An advertisement designed to stimulate sales over the long run.

Individual brand A brand that is assigned to a product within a product line and is not shared by other products in that line.

Individual factor With reference to perception, a characteristic of a person that affects how the person perceives a stimulus.

Influencer The buying-center role played by organizational members (or outsiders) who affect the purchase decision by supplying advice or information.

Infomercial A television commercial, usually 30 minutes long, that has the appearance of a program.

Information Data in a format useful to decision makers.

Information search An internal or external search for information carried out by a consumer to reduce uncertainty and provide a basis for evaluating alternatives.

Innovator A member of the first group of consumers to buy a new product.

Inseparability A characteristic of services referring to the fact that production often is not distinct from consumption of a service—that is, the producer and the consumer of a service must be together in order for a transaction to occur.

Inside selling Business-to-business selling in the salesperson's place of business.

Institutional advertisement An advertisement designed to promote an organizational image, stimulate generic demand for a product, or build goodwill for an industry.

Intangibility The characteristic of services referring to the customer's inability to see, hear, smell, feel, or taste the service product.

Integrated marketing communications Marketing communications in which all elements of the promotional mix are coordinated and systematically planned so as to be harmonious.

Intensive distribution A distribution strategy aimed at obtaining maximum exposure for a product at the retail level or wholesale level.

Internal marketing Marketing efforts aimed at a company's own employees.

International franchising A form of licensing in which a company establishes foreign franchises. Franchising involves a contractual agreement between a franchisor, often a manufacturer or wholesaler, and a franchisee, typically an independent retailer, by which the franchisee distributes the franchisor's product.

International marketing Marketing across international boundaries; also called *multinational marketing.*

Internet A worldwide network of private, corporate, and government computers that gives users access to information and documents from distant sources.

Intranet A company's private decision support system that uses Internet standards and technology.

Intrapreneurial organization An organization that encourages individuals to take risks and gives them the autonomy to develop new products as they see fit.

Introduction stage The stage in the product life cycle during which the new product is attempting to gain a foothold in the market.

Inventory control Decision-making related to inventory size, placement, and delivery.

Isolation effect An effect by which a product appears more attractive next to a higher-priced alternative than in isolation.

J

Jingle A song or other short verse used in an advertisement as a memory aid.

Joint decision making Decision making shared by all or some members of a group.

Joint ownership venture In international marketing, a joint venture in which domestic and foreign partners invest capital and share ownership and control.

Joint venturing In international marketing, an arrangement between a domestic company and a foreign host company to set up production and marketing facilities in a foreign market.

Just-in-time (JIT) inventory system A materials management system in which inventory arrives just in time for use.

L

Label The paper or plastic sticker attached to a container to carry product information. As packaging technology improves, labels become incorporated into the protective aspects of the package rather than simply being affixed to the package.

Laboratory experiment An experiment in a highly controlled environment.

Laggard A member of the group of final adopters in the diffusion process.

Late majority A group of consumers who purchase a product after the early majority, when the product is no longer perceived as risky.

Learning Any change in behavior or cognition that results from experience or an interpretation of experience.

Leased department retailer An independent retailer that owns the merchandise stocked but leases floor space from another retailer, usually operating under that retailer's name.

Legal environment Laws and regulations and their interpretation.

Licensing In international marketing, an agreement by

which a company (the licensor) permits a foreign company (the licensee) to set up a business in the foreign market using the licensor's manufacturing processes, patents, trademarks, trade secrets, and so on, in exchange for payment of a fee or royalty.

Licensing agreement   A legal agreement allowing an organization to use the trademark (or other proprietary rights) of another organization.

Lifestyle   An individual's activities, interests, opinions, and values as they affect his or her mode of living.

Lifestyle creative platform   An advertising creative platform that reflects a target market's lifestyle or hoped-for lifestyle.

Limited-line strategy   A product-line strategy that involves offering a smaller number of product variations than a full-line strategy offers.

Limited problem solving   An intermediate level of decision making between routinized response behavior and extensive problem solving, in which the consumer has some purchasing experience but is unfamiliar with stores, brands, or price options.

Limited-service merchant wholesaler   A merchant wholesaler that offers less than full service and charges lower prices than a full-service merchant wholesaler; also called a *limited-function wholesaler*.

List price   The basic price quote, before adjustment.

Location-based competition   Competition based on providing place utility by delivering a product where the consumer wants it.

Logistics   The activities involved in moving raw materials and parts into the firm, moving in-process inventory through the firm, and moving finished goods out of the firm.

Logo   A brand name or company name written in a distinctive way; short for logotype.

Loss leader   A product priced below cost to attract consumers, who may then make additional purchases.

M

Macroenvironment   Broad societal forces that shape the activities of every business and nonprofit marketer. The physical environment, sociocultural forces, demographic factors, economic factors, scientific and technical knowledge, and political and legal factors are components of the macroenvironment.

Macromarketing   The aggregate of marketing activities in an economy or the marketing system of a society, rather than the marketing activities in a single firm (micromarketing).

Magnuson-Moss Warranty Act   Federal law requiring that guarantees provided by sellers be made available to buyers before they purchase and that the guarantees specify who the warrantor is, what products or parts of products are covered, what the warrantor must do if the product is defective, how long the warranty applies, and the obligations of the buyer.

Majority fallacy   The blind pursuit of the largest, or most easily identified, or most accessible market segment. The error lies in ignoring the fact that other marketers will be pursuing this same segment.

Manufacturer   An organization that recognizes a consumer need and produces a product from raw materials, component parts, or labor to satisfy that need.

Manufacturer brand   A brand owned by the maker of the product; also known as a *national brand*.

Manufacturers' agent   An independent agent intermediary that represents a limited number of noncompeting suppliers in a limited geographical area; also called a *manufacturers' representative*.

Marginal analysis   A method for determining the costs and revenues associated with the production and sale of each additional unit of a product.

Marginal approach   A method of setting a promotional budget in which the marketer attempts to spend resources until additional expenditures would not be justified by the additional sales and profits they would generate.

Marginal cost   The net addition to a firm's total costs that results from the production of one additional unit of product.

Marginal revenue   The net addition to a firm's total revenue that results from the sale of one additional unit of product.

Market   A group of potential customers who may want the product offered and who have the resources, the willingness, and the ability to purchase it.

Market development   A strategy by which an organization attempts to draw new customers to an existing product, most commonly by introducing the product in a new geographical area.

Market factor   A variable, associated with sales, that is analyzed in forecasting sales.

Market factor index   An index derived by combining a number of variables that are associated with sales.

Market penetration   A strategy that seeks to increase sales of an established product by generating increased use of the product in existing markets.

Market position   The way consumers perceive a product relative to its competition; also known as *competitive position*.

Market potential   The upper limit of industry demand; that is, the expected sales volume for all brands of a particular product during a given period.

Market/product matrix   A matrix that includes the four possible combinations of old and new products and old and new markets. The purpose of the matrix is to broadly categorize alternative opportunities in terms of basic strategies for growth.

Market segment   A portion of a larger market, identified according to some shared characteristic or characteristics.

Market segmentation Dividing a heterogeneous market into segments that share certain characteristics.

Market share The percentage of total industry sales accounted for by a particular firm or the percentage of sales of a given product accounted for by a particular brand.

Marketing The process of planning and executing the conception, pricing, promotion, and distribution of ideas, goods, and services to create exchanges that will satisfy individual and organizational objectives.

Marketing audit A comprehensive review and appraisal of the total marketing operation, often performed by outside consultants or other unbiased personnel.

Marketing concept Organizational philosophy that stresses consumer orientation, long-range profitability, and the integration of marketing and other organizational functions. The marketing concept, which focuses on satisfying consumers' wants and needs, is the foundation of a marketing orientation.

Marketing ethics The principles that guide an organization's conduct and the values it expects to express in certain situations.

Marketing management The process of planning, executing, and controlling marketing activities to attain marketing goals and objectives effectively and efficiently.

Marketing mix The specific combination of interrelated and interdependent marketing activities in which an organization engages to meet its objectives.

Marketing myopia The failure of a company to define its organizational purpose from a broad consumer orientation.

Marketing objective A statement of the level of performance that an organization, SBU, or operating unit intends to achieve. Objectives define results in measurable terms.

Marketing orientation Organizational philosophy that emphasizes developing exceptional skill in understanding and satisfying customers so the organization can offer superior customer value.

Marketing plan A written statement of the marketing objectives and strategies to be followed and the specific courses of action to be taken when (or if) certain events occur.

Marketing research The systematic and objective process of generating information for use in marketing decision making.

Marketing strategy A plan identifying what marketing goals and objectives will be pursued and how they will be achieved in the time available.

Markup on cost A markup expressed as a percentage of the cost of an item.

Markup on selling price A markup expressed as a percentage of the selling price of an item.

Mass customization A strategy that combines mass production with computers to produce customized products for small market segments.

Mass media Advertising media, such as television, radio, newspapers, and magazines, that reach a broad audience from many market segments and involve no personal contact or instantaneous interaction between the marketer and the target of the message.

Mass merchandise retailer A retailer that sells products at discount prices to achieve high sales volume; also called a *mass merchandise discount store*. There are two basic types of mass merchandise retailers: general mass merchandisers and specialty mass merchandisers.

Materials handling The use of muscle power, machinery, and other methods to identify, check, load, and unload goods in inventory.

Materials management The activities involved in bringing raw materials and supplies to the point of production and moving in-process inventory through the firm.

Maturity stage The stage in the product life cycle during which sales increase at a decreasing rate.

Media schedule A document identifying the exact media to be used and the dates on which advertisements are to appear; also known as the *media plan*.

Media selection strategy Plan for determining which media are most appropriate for an advertising campaign.

Meeting-the-competition strategy A pricing strategy whereby an organization sets prices at levels equal to those of competitors.

Membership group A group to which an individual belongs. If the individual has chosen to belong to the group, it is a voluntary membership group.

Memory The information-processing function involving the storage and retrieval of information.

Merchant intermediary A channel intermediary, such as a wholesaler or a retailer, that takes title to the product.

Merchant wholesaler An independently owned wholesaling concern that takes title to the goods it distributes.

Microenvironment Environmental forces, such as customers, that directly and regularly influence a marketer's activity.

Misleading or deceptive advertising Advertising that leads consumers to inaccurate conclusions. Intentionally making false statements is an extreme case of deceptive advertising.

Missionary A salesperson who visits prospective customers, distributes information to them, and handles questions and complaints but does not routinely take orders. Missionaries really serve as customer relations representatives.

Modified rebuy An organizational buying situation in which a buyer is not completely satisfied with current suppliers or products and is shopping around rather than rebuying automatically.

Monopolistic competition A market structure characterized by a large number of sellers offering slightly differentiated products and exerting some control over their own prices.

Monopoly   A market structure characterized by a single seller in a market in which there are no suitable substitute products.

Montage creative platform   An advertising creative platform that blends a number of situations, demonstrations, and other visual effects into one commercial to emphasize the array of possibilities associated with product usage.

Moral behavior   Individual or organizational marketing activity that embodies the ethical values to which the individual or organization subscribes.

Motivation   An activated state that causes a person to initiate goal-directed behavior.

Motive   An aroused need that energizes behavior and directs it toward a goal.

Motor carrier   A member of the trucking industry or another carrier, such as Greyhound's package service, that transports products over roads.

Multinational economic community   A collaboration among countries to increase international trade by reducing trade restrictions. Typically, a group of countries forms a unified market within which there are minimal trade and tariff barriers; the European Union is an example.

Multinational marketing group   A group of countries aligned to form a unified market with minimal trade and tariff barriers among participating member countries.

Multiple-unit pricing   Selling more than one unit of a product at a price lower than the sum of the individual unit prices, as in a four-for-the-price-of-three sale.

N

Need   The gap between an actual and a desired state.

New product   A product new to a company. The meaning of this relative term is influenced by the perceptions of marketers and consumers; in general, it refers to any recently introduced product that offers some benefit that other products do not.

New task buying   An organizational buying situation in which a buyer is seeking to fill a need never before addressed. Uncertainty and lack of information about products and suppliers characterize this situation.

News release   A brief written statement sent to the press or others, describing a new product, a product improvement, a price change, or some other development of interest. The release is intended to be newsworthy.

Noise   In communication theory, any interference or distraction that disrupts the communication process.

Nonadopter   A member of the group of consumers who never buy a particular new product or adopt a particular new style.

Noncumulative quantity discount   A price discount determined by the size of an individual purchase order. The larger the order, the larger the discount.

Nondurable good   A physical, tangible item that is quickly consumed, worn out, or outdated.

Nonprice competition   Competition emphasizing marketing variables other than price—for example, product differentiation.

Nonprobability sample   A sample chosen on the basis of convenience or personal judgment.

Norm   A social principle identifying what action is right or wrong in a given situation.

North American Industry Classification System (NAICS)   A numerical coding scheme developed by the governments of the partners in the North American Free Trade Agreement and used to classify a broad range of organizations in terms of the type of economic activity in which they are engaged.

O

Objective-and-task method   A method of setting a promotional budget in which the marketer decides the objective to be accomplished, determines the tasks necessary to achieve the objective, and budgets amounts sufficient to accomplish the tasks.

Observability   The ability of a product to display to consumers its advantages over existing products.

Observation research   The systematic recording of behavior, objects, or events as they are witnessed.

Off-price retailer   A specialty mass merchandise outlet offering a limited line of nationally known brand names.

Oligopoly   A market structure characterized by a small number of sellers who control the market.

One-price strategy   A strategy whereby a single price is charged for a product regardless of the circumstances surrounding the sale, the quantity bought, or any other unique aspect of the exchange.

Operant conditioning   The process by which reinforcement of a behavior results in repetition of that behavior.

Operational planning   Planning that focuses on day-to-day functional activities, such as supervision of the sales force.

Opinion leader   A group member who, because of some quality or characteristic, is likely to lead other group members in particular matters.

Order getting   An adaptive selling process that tailors sales efforts and product offerings to specific customer needs; also known as *creative selling*. An order getter is primarily responsible for developing business for the firm. Order getters seek out customers and creatively make sales.

Order processing   A systematic procedure for filling customer orders. The process begins when orders are received and ends when goods have been shipped and bills sent to customers.

Order taker   A salesperson who is primarily responsible for writing up orders, checking invoices, and assuring prompt processing of orders.

Organizational buying behavior   The decision-making activities of organizational buyers that lead to purchases of products.

Organizational market   The market consisting of buyers who use a product to help operate a business or for resale; also known as *business market.*

Organizational mission statement   A statement of company purpose. It explains why the organization exists and what it hopes to accomplish.

Organizational opportunity   An environmental opportunity that fits a particular organization's capabilities and resources.

Organizational product   A product or service that is used to produce other products and/or to operate an organization.

Outsourcing   Buying or hiring from outside suppliers.

Ownership group   An organization made up of stores or small chains, each with a separate name, identity, and image but all operating under the control of a central owner.

P

Packaging   An auxiliary product dimension that includes labels, inserts, instructions, graphic design, shipping cartons, and sizes and types of containers.

Penetration price   A low introductory price meant to quickly establish a product in the market.

Perceived risk   Consumers' uncertainty about the consequences of their purchase decisions; the perception on the part of a consumer that a product may not do what it is expected to do.

Percent-of-sales method   A method of setting a promotional budget in which the amount budgeted is some set percentage of sales, often a standard percentage for a given industry.

Perception   The process of interpreting sensations and giving meaning to stimuli.

Periodic discounting   A pricing strategy whereby discounts are offered systematically and predictably.

Perishability   The characteristic of services referring to the fact that they cannot be stored and used later.

Personal selling   Person-to-person interaction between a buyer and a seller wherein the seller's purpose is to persuade the buyer to accept a point of view, to convince the buyer to take a course of action, or to develop a customer relationship.

Personality   The fundamental disposition of an individual; the distinctive patterns of thought, emotion, and behavior that characterize an individual's response to life situations.

Physical distribution   The activities involved in the efficient movement of finished products from the end of the production line to the consumer.

Physical environment   Natural resources and other aspects of the natural world that influence marketing activities.

Physical obsolescence   The breakdown of a product due to wear and tear.

Physiological need   A need based on biological functioning, like the needs for food, water, and air.

Piggyback service   Transport of loaded truck trailers or other sealed containers by rail to destinations from which they are then moved by truck.

Pioneer   A salesperson who concentrates on selling to new prospects or on selling new products.

Pipelines   Systems of pipes through which products, such as oil and natural gas, are transported.

Place (distribution)   The element of the marketing mix that encompasses all aspects of getting products to the consumer in the right location at the right time.

Place utility   Economic utility created by making goods available where consumers want them.

Planned obsolescence   The practice of purposely causing existing products to go out of date by introducing new products at frequent intervals.

Planning   The process of envisioning the future, establishing goals and objectives, and designing organizational and marketing strategies and tactics to be implemented in the future in order to achieve the goals.

Point-of-purchase materials   Promotional items intended to attract attention to specific products in the places where those products are purchased. Signs and displays in supermarkets are examples.

Political environment   The practices and policies of governments.

Population   In marketing research, any complete group of entities sharing some common set of characteristics; the group from which a sample is taken.

Positioning   Planning the market position the company wishes to occupy. Positioning strategy is the basis for marketing mix decisions.

Possession utility   Economic utility created by transfer of physical possession and ownership of the product to the consumer.

Posttesting   In the context of advertising, testing that takes place after an advertisement has been run, to determine whether it has met the objectives set for it by management.

Predatory pricing strategy   An illegal pricing strategy whereby the price of a product is set low to eliminate competition and then raised to a high level after competition has been eliminated.

Premium   A product offered free or at reduced charge with the purchase of another product.

Press conference   A meeting called by an organization to announce a newsworthy event to the press.

Prestige price   A high price meant to convey an impression of high quality.

Pretesting Conducting limited trials of a questionnaire or some other aspect of a study to determine its suitability for the planned research project. In the context of advertising, research carried out beforehand on the effectiveness of an advertisement. It begins at the earliest stages of development and continues until the advertisement is ready for use.

Price The amount of money or other consideration—that is, something of value—given in exchange for a product.

Price-bundling strategy A strategy whereby the price of a group of products is lower than the total of the individual prices of the components. An example is selling a new car with an "options package."

Price competition Competition based solely on price. It is especially important in the marketing of products that are not distinctive, such as raw materials.

Price elasticity A measure of the effect of a change in price on the quantity of product demanded.

Price leadership strategy A strategy whereby organizations with large market shares and production capacities determine a price level that other, weaker organizations in the same industry will follow.

Price-lining strategy A strategy whereby a seller prices products in a product line in accordance with certain "price points" believed to be attractive to buyers.

Price stabilization A pricing objective aimed at avoiding widely fluctuating prices. The marketer with this objective sets prices to match competitors' prices or to maintain existing price differentials.

Pricing objective The desired result associated with a particular pricing strategy. The pricing objective must be consistent with other marketing objectives.

Primary characteristic A basic feature or essential aspect of a product.

Primary data Data gathered and assembled specifically for the project at hand.

Primary demand Demand for a product class as a whole, without regard to brand; also known as *generic demand*.

Primary demand advertising Advertising aimed at stimulating primary demand; also known as *pioneering advertising*.

Probability sample A sample selected by statistical means in such a way that all members of the sampled population had a known, nonzero chance of being selected.

Problem child A low-market-share product in a high-growth market.

Problem definition The crucial first stage in the marketing research process—determining the problem to be solved and the objectives of the research.

Problem recognition The awareness that there is a discrepancy between an actual and a desired condition.

Product A good, service, or idea that offers a bundle of tangible and intangible attributes to satisfy consumers.

Product advertisement An advertisement promoting a specific product.

Product category A subset of a product class containing products of a certain type.

Product category extension A new item or new line of items in a product category that is new to the company.

Product class A broad group of products that differ somewhat but perform similar functions or provide similar benefits—for example, all automobiles made for personal use.

Product concept The end result of the marketing strategist's selection and blending of a product's primary and auxiliary dimensions into a basic idea emphasizing a particular set of consumer benefits; also called the *product positioning concept*.

Product design A product's configuration, composition, and style. This characteristic influences most consumers' perceptions of product quality.

Product development A strategy of marketing innovative or "new and improved" products to existing markets.

Product differentiation A promotional approach in which the marketer calls buyers' attention to those aspects of a product or brand that set it apart from its competitors.

Product enhancement The introduction of a new and improved version of an existing product, intended to extend the product's life cycle by keeping it in the growth stage.

Product item A specific version of a particular good or service.

Product life cycle A marketing management concept, often depicted graphically, that traces a product's sales history. The cycle is depicted as having four stages: introduction, growth, maturity, and decline.

Product line A group of products that are fairly closely related. The number of different items in a product line determines the depth of the product line.

Product line extension An item added to an existing product line to create depth; also called a *line extension*.

Product line strategy The strategy of matching items within a product line to markets.

Product mix All the product offerings of an organization, no matter how unrelated. The number of product lines within a product mix determines the width of the product mix. A wide mix has a high diversity of product types; a narrow mix has little diversity.

Product modification The altering or adjusting of the product mix, typically influenced by the competitive nature of the market and by changes in the external environment.

Product obsolescence The process by which an existing product goes out of date because of the introduction of a new product.

Product portfolio   A collection of products to be balanced as a group. Product portfolio analysis focuses on the interrelationships of products within a product mix. The performance of the mix is emphasized rather than the performance of individual products.

Product sampling   A sales promotion in which samples of a product are given to consumers to induce them to try the product.

Product strategy   The planning and development of a mix of the primary and auxiliary dimensions of a product.

Product warranty   A written guarantee of a product's integrity and the manufacturer's responsibility for repairing or replacing defective parts.

Production orientation   Organizational philosophy that emphasizes physical production and technology rather than sales or marketing.

Promotion   The element of the marketing mix that includes all forms of marketing communication.

Promotional campaign   A series of promotional activities aimed at achieving a specific objective or set of objectives.

Promotional mix   An organization's combination of personal selling, advertising, publicity and public relations, and sales promotion; its total promotional effort.

Prospecting   Identifying likely customers. In prospecting, the salesperson may search lists of previous customers, trade association lists, government publications, and many other sources.

Psychographics   Quantitative measures of lifestyle.

Public relations   The activities involved in actively seeking to manage the nature of the publicity an organization receives.

Publicity   A message about a product, organization, or event carried by a nonpersonal medium but not paid for by a sponsor. Publicity involves a third party who determines whether the message is newsworthy enough to transmit and what the nature of the transmitted message will be.

Puffery   The practice of exaggerating a product's good points in advertising or selling.

Pull strategy   A promotional strategy whereby a supplier promotes a product to the ultimate consumer, with the aim of stimulating demand and thus pulling the product through the channel of distribution.

Purchase satisfaction   The feeling on the part of the consumer that the decision to buy was appropriate because the product met expectations.

Pure competition   A market structure characterized by free entry, a homogeneous product, and many sellers and buyers, none of whom can control price.

Push strategy   A promotional strategy whereby a supplier promotes a product to marketing intermediaries, with the aim of pushing the product through the channel of distribution.

Q

Qualifying   Evaluating a prospect's potential. Key questions are whether the prospect needs the product, can pay for it, and has the authority to make—or at least contribute to—a decision to buy.

Quality-based competition   Competition based on quality. Quality-based competition is associated with form utility.

Quality of life   The degree to which people in a society feel a sense of well-being.

Quota-bonus plan   Compensation plan whereby a salesperson is paid a base salary related to achievement of a quota and a bonus for sales exceeding the quota.

R

Rack jobber   A limited-service wholesaler that contracts with a retailer to place display racks in a store and to stock those racks with merchandise.

Rail transport   The shipment of products by train over railways.

Random discounting   A pricing strategy whereby discounts are offered occasionally and unpredictably.

Reach   The number of people exposed to an advertisement carried by a given medium.

Rebate   A sales promotion wherein some portion of the price paid for a product is returned to the purchaser.

Recall test   In the context of advertising, a research tool used to determine how much people remember about an advertisement.

Receiver   In communication theory, the one to whom a message is aimed.

Reference group   A group that influences an individual because that individual is a member of the group or aspires to be a member.

Reference pricing strategy   A strategy whereby a moderate price is set for a version of a product that will be displayed next to a higher-priced model of the same brand or next to a competing brand.

Reinforcement   Reward. Reinforcement strengthens a stimulus-response relationship.

Related recall test   In the context of advertising, a test of consumers' memory of an advertisement in which recall of specific messages or images is required.

Relationship management   The building and maintaining of long-term relationships with the parties that contribute to an organization's success; the sales function of managing the accounting relationship and ensuring that buyers receive appropriate services.

Relationship marketing   Marketing activities aimed at building long-term relationships with the parties, especially customers, that contribute to a company's success; also called *relationship management*.

Relative advantage   The ability of a product to offer clear-cut advantages over competing offerings.

Repositioning Changing the market position of a product.

Repositioning strategy A product strategy that involves changing the product design, formulation, brand image, or brand name so as to alter the product's competitive position.

Research design A master plan that specifically identifies what techniques and procedures will be used to collect and analyze data relevant to the research problem.

Retail selling Selling to ultimate consumers.

Retailer An organization that sells products it has obtained from a manufacturer or wholesaler to the ultimate consumer. Retailers neither produce nor consume the product.

Retailer cooperative organization A group of independent retailers that combine resources and expertise to control their wholesaling needs, as through a centralized wholesale buying center.

Retailing All business activities concerned with the sale of products to the ultimate users of those products.

Return on investment (ROI) The ratio of profits to assets (or net worth) for an organization, a unit of an organization, a product line, or a brand; also called the *profit target.*

Right to be informed The consumer's right to have access to the information required to make an intelligent choice from among the available products.

Right to choose The consumer's right to have viable alternatives from which to choose.

Right to safety The right to expect the products one purchases to be free from unnecessary dangers. This is a right to which consumers assume they are entitled.

Risk-taking function Assumption of the responsibility for losses when the future is uncertain.

Robinson-Patman Act Federal law passed in 1936 and intended to halt discriminatory pricing policies by specifying certain limited conditions under which a seller may charge different prices to different buyers.

Role A cluster of behavior patterns considered appropriate for a particular person in a particular social setting, situation, or position.

Routinized response behavior The least complex type of decision making, in which the consumer bases choices on his or her own past behavior and needs no other information.

S

Salary plus commission Compensation consisting of a regular salary plus a commission based on sales performance.

Sales branch A wholesaling establishment that is maintained by a manufacturer for its own product and carries an inventory of the product.

Sales forecast The actual sales volume an organization expects during a given period.

Sales forecasting The process of estimating sales volume for a product, an organizational unit, or an entire organization over a specific future time period.

Sales management The marketing management activity that deals with planning, organizing, directing, and controlling the personal selling effort.

Sales objectives The specific objectives that an organization's sales effort will attempt to meet. Sales objectives should be precise and quantifiable, should include a time frame, and should be reasonable given the organization's resources.

Sales office A wholesaling establishment that is maintained by a manufacturer for its own product and does not carry an inventory of the product.

Sales orientation Organizational philosophy that emphasizes selling existing products, whether or not they meet consumer needs, often through aggressive sales techniques and advertising.

Sales potential The maximum share of the market an individual organization can expect during a given period.

Sales presentation The step in the creative selling process wherein the salesperson attempts to persuasively communicate the product's benefits and to explain appropriate courses of action.

Sales promotion Promotional activities other than personal selling, advertising, and public relations that are intended to stimulate buyer purchases or dealer effectiveness over a specific time period.

Sales territory The specific and prospective accounts assigned to a salesperson. They may be based on geographical divisions, customer types, or product lines.

Sample A portion or subset of a larger population.

Sampling Any procedure in which a small part of the whole is used as the basis for conclusions regarding the whole.

Science The accumulation of knowledge about humans and the environment.

Scrambled merchandising The offering of products for sale in a retail establishment not traditionally associated with those products.

Screening stage The stage in new product development in which a marketer analyzes ideas to determine their appropriateness and reasonableness in relation to the organization's goals and objectives.

Seasonal discount A price discount intended to encourage purchase of products during a time of year when sales are traditionally low.

Second-market discounting A differential pricing strategy whereby a product is sold at one price in the core target market and at a reduced price in a secondary market.

Secondary data Data previously collected and assembled for some purpose other than the one at hand.

Selective attention A perceptual screening device whereby a person does not attend to a particular stimulus.

Selective demand advertising Advertising aimed at stimulating demand for a particular brand.

Selective distribution A distribution strategy in which a product is sold in a limited number of outlets.

Selective exposure The principle describing the fact that individuals selectively determine whether they will be exposed to certain stimuli.

Selective interpretation A perceptual screening device whereby a person forms a distorted interpretation of a stimulus whose message is incompatible with his or her values or attitudes.

Selective perception The screening out of certain stimuli and the interpretation of selected other stimuli according to personal experience, attitudes, or the like.

Self-concept An individual's perception and appraisal of himself or herself.

Selling agent An independent agent intermediary similar to a manufacturers' agent but representing a given product in every area in which it is sold, rather than in a limited geographical area.

Selling function Activities, performed by intermediaries, that are associated with communicating ideas and making a sale, and thus effecting the transfer of ownership of a product.

Service A task or activity performed for a buyer or an intangible that cannot be handled or examined before purchase.

Service encounter A period during which a consumer interacts with a service provider.

Service function Activities, performed by intermediaries, that increase the efficiency and effectiveness of the exchange process. Repair services and management services provided by intermediaries are examples.

Service level Extent of extra services provided to customers. Service level is often related to price.

Service mark A symbol that identifies a service. It distinguishes a service in the way a trademark identifies a good.

Service quality The degree to which the performance of a service matches customer expectations; the essential characteristic of a service that indicates its degree of excellence.

Shopping product A product for which consumers feel the need to make comparisons, seek out more information, examine merchandise, or otherwise reassure themselves about quality, style, or value before making a purchase.

Simplicity of usage Ease of operation. This product benefit can offset any complexity in the product itself.

Single-product strategy A product line strategy that involves offering one product item or one product version with very few options.

Single-sourcing Purchasing a product on a regular basis from a single vendor.

Situation analysis The interpretation of environmental attributes and changes in light of an organization's ability to capitalize on potential opportunities.

Skimming price A relatively high price, often charged at the beginning of a product's life. The price is systematically lowered as time goes by.

Slice-of-life creative platform An advertising creative platform that dramatizes a "typical" setting wherein people use a product.

Social and psychological need A need stemming from a person's interactions with the social environment.

Social class A group of people with similar levels of prestige, power, and wealth whose thinking and behavior reflect a set of related beliefs, attitudes, and values.

Social responsibility The ethical principle that a person or an organization must become accountable for how its acts might affect the interests of others.

Social value A value that embodies the goals a society views as important and expresses a culture's shared ideas of preferred ways of acting.

Socialization process The process by which a society transmits its values, norms, and roles to its members.

Societal marketing concept Organizational philosophy that stresses the importance of considering the collective needs of society as well as individual consumers' desires and organizational profits.

Software Various types of programs that tell computers, printers, and other hardware what to do.

Sorting function An activity, performed by marketing intermediaries, consisting of classifying accumulated products as to grade and size, and then grouping them accordingly.

Source In communication theory, the one who sends a message.

Specialty product A consumer product that is not bought frequently, is likely to be expensive, and is generally purchased with great care.

Specialty store A retail establishment that sells a single product or a few related lines.

Specialty wholesaler A full-service merchant wholesaler that sells a very narrow selection of products.

Spokesperson A person who represents an advertiser and directly addresses the audience to urge them to buy the advertiser's product. Using a spokesperson is a variation on the testimonial.

Standard Industrial Classification (SIC) System A numerical coding system developed by the U.S. government and (until the advent of NAICS) widely employed by organizational marketers to classify organizations in terms of the economic activities in which they are engaged.

Star A high-market-share product in a high-growth market.

Still-life creative platform An advertising creative platform that makes the product or package its focal point, emphasizing a visually attractive presentation and the product's brand name.

Stimulus factor A characteristic of a stimulus—for example, the size, colors, or novelty of a print advertisement—that affects perception.

Storage The holding and housing of goods in inventory for a certain period of time.

Store image Everything consumers see in a store that affects how they feel about the store. Store image is determined by such factors as personnel, merchandise, external and internal appearance, prices, and services.

Storyline creative platform An advertising creative platform that gives a history or tells a story about a product.

Straight commission Compensation based strictly on sales performance.

Straight rebuy A type of organizational buying characterized by automatic and regular purchases of familiar products from regular suppliers.

Straight salary Compensation at a regular rate, not immediately tied to sales performance.

Strategic alliance An informal partnership or collaboration between a marketer and an organizational buyer.

Strategic business unit (SBU) A distinct unit—such as a company, division, department, or product line—of an overall parent organization, with a specific marketing focus and a manager who has the authority and responsibility for managing all unit functions.

Strategic corporate goals Broad organizational goals related to the long-term future. An organization's primary strategic corporate goal is identified in its organizational mission statement.

Strategic gap The difference between where an organization wants to be and where it is.

Strategic marketing process The entire sequence of managerial and operational activities required to create and sustain effective and efficient marketing strategies.

Strategic planning Long-term planning dealing with an organization's primary goals and objectives, carried out primarily by top management; also called *corporate strategic planning.*

Strategic window of opportunity The limited time during which an organization has an advantage over its competition because of its capabilities and resources.

Style A distinctive execution, construction, or design in a product class.

Subculture A group within a dominant culture that is distinct from the culture. Members of a subculture typically display some values or norms that differ from those of the overall culture.

Suggestive selling Suggesting to a customer who is making a purchase that an additional item or service be purchased.

Superior customer value The consumer's attribution of greater worth or better ability to fulfill a need to a certain product compared to its competitors.

Supermarket Any large, self-service, departmentalized retail establishment, but especially one that sells primarily food items.

Supplier An organization that provides raw materials, component parts, equipment, services, or other resources to a marketing organization; also called a *vendor.*

Supply curve A graphic representation of the relationship between various prices and the amount of product that will be supplied at those prices; also called a *supply schedule.*

Survey Any research effort in which data are gathered systematically from a sample of people by means of a questionnaire. Surveys are conducted through face-to-face interviews, telephone interviews, and mailed questionnaires.

SWOT Acronym for internal strengths and weaknesses and external opportunities and threats. In analyzing marketing opportunities, the decision maker evaluates all these factors.

Systematic bias A research shortcoming caused by flaws in the design or execution of a research study.

Systems concept The idea that elements of a distribution system (or another system) are strongly interrelated and interact to achieve a goal.

T

Tactics Specific actions intended to implement strategies.

Target market A specific market segment toward which an organization aims its marketing plan.

Target population The population of interest in a marketing research study; the population from which samples are to be drawn.

Target return pricing Setting prices to yield a particular target level of profit for the organization.

Tariff A tax imposed by a government on an imported product. A tariff is often intended to raise the price of imported goods and thereby give a price advantage to domestic goods.

Technology The application of science for practical purposes.

Telemarketing Using the telephone as the primary means of communicating with prospective customers. Telemarketers often use computers for order taking.

Test marketing A controlled experimental procedure in which a new product is tested under realistic market conditions in a limited geographical area.

Testimonial A type of advertising in which a person, usually a well-known or public figure, states that he or she owns, uses, or supports the product being advertised.

Time utility Economic utility created by making goods available when consumers want them.

Time-based competition Competition based on providing time utility by delivering a product when the consumer wants it.

Total cost   Fixed costs plus variable costs.

Total cost concept   In relation to physical distribution, a focus on the entire range of costs associated with a particular distribution method.

Total product   The wide range of tangible and intangible benefits that a buyer might gain from a product after purchasing it.

Total quality management (TQM)   A management principle calling for managers to seek to instill the idea of customer-driven quality throughout an organization and to manage all employees so that there will be continuous improvement in the quality of products and/or services.

Total quality management strategy   A product strategy that emphasizes market-driven quality; also called a *quality assurance strategy.*

Trade discount   A discount given to wholesalers, retail dealers, or others in a particular trade as repayment for the performance of certain functions; also called a *functional discount.*

Trade show   A meeting or convention of members of a particular industry where business-to-business contacts are routinely made.

Trademark   A legally protected brand name or brand mark. Its owner has exclusive rights to its use. Trademarks are registered with the U.S. Patent and Trademark Office.

Transaction   A single exchange agreement; the completion of a one-time sale.

Transportation   The physical movement or shipment of products to locations in the distribution channel.

Trial close   A personal selling tactic intended to elicit from a prospect a signal indicating whether he or she is ready to buy.

Trial sampling   The distribution of newly marketed products to enhance trialability and familiarity; giving away free samples.

Trialability   The ability of a product to be tested by possible future users with little risk or effort.

Truck wholesaler   A limited-service wholesaler that sells a limited line of items (often perishable goods) from a truck, thus providing immediate delivery; also called a *truck jobber.*

Turnover   Sales divided by average inventory. Turnover measures the speed with which merchandise is sold.

Two-part pricing   A pricing strategy in which the marketer charges a fixed fee plus a variable usage fee, in order to adjust for losses resulting from a service's perishability.

Tying contract   An agreement tying the purchase of one product to the purchase of another. The buyer who wishes to purchase a certain product is required by the seller to purchase additional products, whether the buyer wants to purchase those products or not.

U

Ultimate consumer   An individual who buys or uses a product for personal consumption.

Unaided recall tests   In the context of advertising, a test of consumers' memory of an advertisement in which no clues are provided as to the specific material to be remembered.

Uncontrollable variable   A force or influence external to the organization and beyond its control.

Undercutting-the-competition strategy   A pricing strategy whereby an organization sets prices at levels lower than those of competitors.

Undifferentiated marketing   A marketing effort not targeted at a specific market segment but designed to appeal to a broad range of customers. The approach is appropriate in a market that lacks diversity of interest.

Unfair sales practices acts   State laws that limit or prohibit the use of certain sales and marketing techniques; most commonly, laws requiring that certain types of merchandise be sold at prescribed markups.

Uniform delivered pricing   A type of delivered pricing in which an organization charges the same price for a given product in all locations.

Unique selling proposition (USP)   A unique characteristic of a product or brand identified by the marketer as the one on which to base a promotional campaign. It is often used in a product-differentiation approach to promotion.

Universal product code (UPC)   The array of black bars, readable by optical scanners, found on many products. The UPC permits computerization of tasks such as checkout and compilation of sales volume information.

User   The buying-center role played by the organizational member who will actually use the product.

V

Value   The power of one product to attract another product in an exchange.

Value chain   Chain of activities by which a company brings in materials, creates a good or service, markets it, and provides service after a sale is made. Each step creates more value for the consumer.

Variability   The characteristic of services referring to the fact that services are heterogeneous—that is, the quality of delivered services can vary widely.

Variable cost   A cost that varies directly with an organization's production or sales. Variable costs are a function of volume.

Variable pricing strategy   A strategy whereby an organization varies the price from buyer to buyer.

Vendor analysis   The rating of alternative suppliers on attributes such as product quality, reliability of service, delivery speed, and price.

W

Warehouse club A general mass merchandise outlet at which only "members" are allowed to shop; also called a *closed-door house.*

Warehousing All the activities necessary to hold and house goods between the time they are produced and the time an order is shipped to the buyer.

Water transportation The shipment of products by ship, boat, or barge.

Wheel of retailing A theory positing that new forms of retail institutions enter the marketplace as low-status, low-margin, low-price operations and then gradually trade up, opening a market position for a new low-end retailer.

Wholesaler An organization or individual that serves as a marketing intermediary by facilitating transfer of products and title to them. Wholesalers do not produce the product, consume it, or sell it to ultimate consumers.

Wholesaler-sponsored voluntary chain A vertical marketing system, initiated by a wholesaler, that links a group of independent retailers in a relationship with the wholesale supplier.

World brand A product that is widely distributed around the world with a single brand name that is common to all countries and is recognized in all its markets.

World Wide Web A portion of the Internet; a system of Internet servers that support specially formatted documents.

Worldwide information system An organized collection—of telecommunications equipment, computer hardware and software, data, and personnel—designed to capture, store, update, manipulate, analyze, and immediately display information about worldwide business activity.

Z

Zone pricing A type of delivered pricing in which prices vary according to the number of geographic zones through which a product passes in moving from seller to buyer.

endnotes

chapter 1

1. Adapted with permission from Jill Lieber, "Braves Bank on Future: Converted Olympic Stadium Incorporates Latest Technology," *USA TODAY*, April 3, 1997, p. 3C. Copyright 1997, USA TODAY. Reprinted with permission.

2. Elizabeth Sanger, "Morphin Rangers Overpower Rivals," *New York Newsday*, June 27, 1994; and Carol Wolf, "Zapped by High Demand: Shortage of Power Ranger Toys Tests Parents, Stores," *Crain's Cleveland Business*, June 6, 1994.

3. Jennifer Cody, "Power Rangers Take On the Whole World," *Wall Street Journal*, March 23, 1994.

4. For a full treatment of the exchange process, see Franklin S. Houston and Julie B. Gassenheimer, "Marketing and Exchange," *Journal of Marketing*, October 1987, pp. 3–18.

5. For an excellent discussion of not-for-profit marketing issues, see P. Rajan Vardarajan and Anil Menon, "Cause-Related Marketing: A Coalignment of Marketing Strategy and Corporate Philosophy," *Journal of Marketing*, July 1988, pp. 58–74. See also C. Scott Greene and Paul Miesing, "Public Policy, Technology, and Ethics: Marketing Decisions for NASA's Space Shuttle," *Journal of Marketing*, Summer 1984, pp. 56–67.

6. This is the American Marketing Association's definition of marketing, as published in *Marketing News*, March 1, 1985, p. 1.

7. See Regis McKenna, "Marketing Is Everything," *Harvard Business Review*, January-February 1991, pp. 65–79.

8. The word *marketing* comes from the Latin *mercatus* ("marketplace"), which in turn comes from the word *mercari*, "to trade."

9. Neil H. Borden, "The Concept of the Marketing Mix," *Journal of Advertising Research*, June 1964, pp. 2–7.

10. E. Jerome McCarthy, *Basic Marketing: A Managerial Approach* (Homewood, IL: Richard D. Irwin, 1960).

11. Gay Jervey, "New Products Painting Rosy Future for Crayola," *Advertising Age*, January 11, 1982, p. 4.

12. Reprinted with permission from "McDonald's Tartan Choice Upsets Scottish Clan," in the May 12, 1997 issue of *Advertising Age*. Copyright, Crain Communications Inc., 1997.

13. The fact that marketing has implications that extend beyond the traditional marketer–marketing intermediary relationship is discussed in P. R. Vardarajan and Daniel Rajaratnam, "Symbiotic Marketing Revisited," *Journal of Marketing*, January 1986, pp. 7–17.

14. When one or more elements of the marketing mix are altered or controlled, as by a law or other environmental influence, the other elements of the mix, as well as consumer behaviors, are affected. See, for example, Susan L. Holak and Srinivas K. Reddy, "Effects of a Television and Radio Advertising Ban: A Study of the Cigarette Industry," *Journal of Marketing*, October 1986, pp. 219–227.

15. Matt Murray, "What Kids Eat: Snacks, Meals, Snacks, Snacks," *Wall Street Journal*, October 20, 1994.

16. For a seminal work on historical marketing philosophies, see Ronald A. Fullerton, "How Modern Is Modern Marketing? Marketing's Evolution and the Myth of the 'Production Era,'" *Journal of Marketing*, January 1988, pp. 108–125. Also see D. G. Brian Jones and David D. Monieson, "Early Development of Marketing Thought," *Journal of Marketing*, January 1990, pp. 103–113; and Terence Nevett, "Historical Investigation and the Practice of Marketing," *Journal of Marketing*, July 1991, pp. 13–23.

17. For discussions on this contemporary issue, see George Day, "The Capabilities of Market-Driven Organizations," *Journal of Marketing*, October 1994, pp. 37–52; John C. Narver and Stanley F. Slater, "The Effect of Marketing Orientation on Business Profitability," *Journal of Marketing*, October 1990, pp. 20–35; A. K. Kohli and B. J. Jaworski, "Market Orientation: The Construct, Research Propositions, and Managerial Implications," *Journal of Marketing*, April 1990, pp. 1–18; Bernard J. Jaworski and Ajay K. Kohli, "Market Orientation: Antecedents and Consequences," *Journal of Marketing*, July 1993, pp. 53–70; Stanley F. Slater and John C. Narver, "Does Competitive Environment Moderate the Market Orientation–Performance Relationship?" *Journal of Marketing*, January 1994, pp. 46–55; Gary L. Frankwick, James C. Ward, Michael D. Hutt, and Peter H. Reingen, "Evolving Patterns of Organizational Beliefs in the Formation of Strategy," *Journal of Marketing*, April 1994, pp. 96–110; and James M. Sinkula, William E. Baker, and Thomas Noordewier, "A Framework for Market-Based Organizational Learning: Linking Values, Knowledge, and Behavior," *Journal of the Academy of Marketing Science*, Fall 1997, pp. 305–318.

18. Theodore Levitt, "Marketing Myopia," *Harvard Business Review*, July-August 1960, pp. 45–56. For an excellent discussion of customer value, see Robert B. Woodruff, "Customer Value: The Next Source for Competitive Advantage," *Journal of the Academy of Marketing Science*, Spring 1997, pp. 138–153; A. Parasuraman, "Reflections on Gaining Competitive Advantage through Customer Value," *Journal of the Academy of Marketing Science*, Spring 1997, pp. 154–161; and Stanley F. Slater, "Developing a Customer Value–Based Theory of the Firm," *Journal of the Academy of Marketing Science*, Spring 1997, pp. 162–167.

19. Although the marketing concept has clear applications to many situations, the point has been made that it need not be applied to every possible situation. Franklin S. Houston, "The Marketing Concept: What It Is and What It Is Not," *Journal of Marketing*, April 1986, pp. 81–87.

20. Fred J. Burch, "The Marketing Philosophy as a Way of Business Life," in *The Marketing Concept, Its Meaning to Management*, Marketing Series no. 99. See also Theodore Levitt, "Marketing Myopia," *Harvard Business Review*, July-August 1960, pp. 45–56.

21. Excerpted with permission from Jaclyn Fierman, "The Death and Rebirth of the Salesman," *Fortune*, July 25, 1994, p. 86.

22. Reprinted with permission from "William Spain—Sauder (Marketing 100)," in the June 30, 1997 issue of *Advertising Age*,. Copyright, Crain Communications Inc., 1997.

23. Mary Kuhn and Kitty Kevin, "The 1995 New Product Hit Parade," *Food Processing*, November 1, 1995.

24. Theodore Levitt, "Marketing Myopia," *Harvard Business Review*, July-August 1960, pp. 45–56.

25. For an interesting study, see Anusorn Singhapakdi, Kenneth L. Kraft, Scott J. Vitell, and Kumar C. Rallapalli, "The Perceived Importance of Ethics and Social Responsibility on Organizational Effectiveness," *Journal of the Academy of Marketing Science*, Winter 1995, pp. 49–56.

26. Excerpted with permission from *Insights and Inspiration: How Businesses Succeed*, pp. 3-4, Copyright 1995, by Connecticut Mutual Life Insurance Company, now known as Massachusetts Mutual Life Insurance Company.

chapter 2

1. Adapted with permission from Brian O'Reilly, "The Rent-a-Car Jocks Who Made Enterprise #1," *Fortune*, October 28, 1996, pp. 125–128.

2. Pamela S. Lewis, Stephen H. Goodman, and Patricia M. Fandt, *Management* (St. Paul, MN: West Educational Publishing, 1995), pp. 5, 15.

3. See, for example, Richard L. Daft, *Management* (Hinsdale, IL: Dryden Press, 1994), p. 5; and William G. Zikmund, R. Dennis Middlemist, and Melanie R. Middlemist, *Business: The American Challenge for Global Competitiveness* (Burr Ridge, IL: Austin Press, 1995), pp. 11–15.

4. Alfred D. Chandler, *Strategy and Structure* (Cambridge, MA: MIT Press, 1962), p. 13.

5. Mission statement of The Limited Corporation reprinted by permission.

6. Theodore Levitt, "Marketing Myopia," *Harvard Business Review,* July/August 1960, p. 45.

7. Michael E. Porter, *Competitive Strategy* (New York: Free Press, 1980). See also William L. James, John M. Planchon, and Alan Joyce, "Porter's Generic Marketing Strategies in the Computer Industry: An Empirical Investigation," *Journal of the Midwest Marketing Association,* vol. 4, no. 1 (1989), pp. 57–61; and Shannon H. Shipp, William C. Moncrief, III, and David W. Cravens, "Marketing and Sales Strategy Requirements for Competing in Turbulent Markets," *Journal of Marketing Management,* Spring/Summer, 1992, pp. 55–62.

8. Janice Castro, "Making It Better," *Time,* November 13, 1989, pp. 78–81; and David A. Gavin, "Competing on the Eight Dimensions of Quality," *Harvard Business Review,* November/December 1987, pp. 101–108.

9. "Burger King Opens Customer Hot Line," *Marketing News,* May 28, 1990, p. 7.

10. Adapted with permission from T. L. Stanley, Karen Benezra, Betsy Spethmann, Gerry Khermouch, and Elaine Underwood, "Brand Builders (Promotion Marketing Association of America's Reggie Awards)," *Brandweek,* March 11, 1996. © 1996 ASM Communications, Inc. Used with permission from *Brandweek* magazine.

11. Marshall Loeb, "How to Grow a New Product Every Day," *Fortune,* November 14, 1994, p. 269.

12. Adapted with permission from Faye Rice, "The New Rules of Superlative Service," *Fortune,* Autumn–Winter 1993, pp. 50–53.

13. Gene Bylinsky, "Manufacture for Reuse," *Fortune,* February 6, 1995, pp. 110, 112.

14. Sarah Schafer, "Gimmie a Break," *Inc. Technology,* No. 1, 1997, p. 19.

15. Michael A. Hitt, R. Duane Ireland, and Robert E. Hoskisson, *Strategic Management: Competitiveness and Globalization* (St. Paul, MN: West Educational Publishing, 1995), p. 46.

16. Adapted with permission from Thomas A. Stewart, "Welcome to the Revolution," *Fortune,* December 13, 1993, pp. 66–67.

17. Hallie Forcinio, "Form Follows Function," *Prepared Foods,* April 15, 1994; "In a Pickle," *Prepared Foods,* May 5, 1994.

18. Doug Levy, "Ads of Dubious Distinction," *USA TODAY,* December 15, 1997, p. 6b.

19. Reprinted with permission from "Computer Firm Lists Wrong No.," *AP Online,* June 21, 1996.

20. Peter D. Bennett, *Marketing Terms* (Chicago: American Marketing Association, 1988), p. 189.

21. Ray Billington, *Living Philosophy: An Introduction to Moral Thought* (London: Routledge, 1988), p. 17.

22. See Geoffrey P. Lantos, "An Ethical Base for Marketing Decision Making," *Journal of Business and Industrial Marketing,* Spring 1987, pp. 11–16; and R. Eric Reidenbach, Donald P. Robin, and Lyndon Dawson, "An Application and Extension of a Multidimensional Ethics Scale to Selected Marketing Practices and Marketing Groups," *Journal of the Academy of Marketing Science,* Spring 1991, pp. 90–91. For formal theories of marketing decision making and ethical dilemmas, see Shelby D. Hunt and Scott Vitell, "A General Theory of Marketing," *Journal of Marketing,* Spring 1986, pp. 5–16; and O. C. Ferrell, Larry G. Gresham, and John Fraedrich, "A Synthesis of Ethical Decision Models for Marketing," *Journal of Macromarketing,* Fall 1989, pp. 87–96.

23. For a general discussion of ethical dilemmas in business, see Anusorn Singhapakdi and Scott J. Vitell, "Marketing Ethics: Factors Influencing Perceptions of Ethical Problems and Alternatives," *Journal of Macromarketing,* Spring 1990, pp. 4–18; P. J. Forrest, Daniel S. Cochran, Dennis F. Ray, and Donald P. Robin, "An Empirical Examination of Four Factors Thought to Be Influential in Ethical Business Judgements," *Proceedings of the Midwest Marketing Association,* 1991, pp. 133–138; M. Alan Miller, "A Holistic Approach to Marketing," *Proceedings of the Midwest Marketing Association,* 1983, pp. 26–31; Steven Pharr, "A Research Agenda for Marketing/Business Ethics," *Journal of the Midwest Marketing Association,* Vol. 4, no. 1 (1989), pp. 133–138; and Scott J. Vitell and Anusorn Singhapakdi, "Ethical Ideology and Its Influence on the Norms and

Judgements of Marketing Practitioners," *Journal of Marketing Management,* Spring/Summer 1993, pp. 1–11. Code of Ethics of the American Marketing Association on p. 53 reprinted by permission of the American Marketing Association.

24. For an interesting study of this issue, see Michael J. Dorsch and Scott W. Kelley, "An Investigation into the Intentions of Purchasing Executives to Reciprocate Vendor Gifts," *Journal of the Academy of Marketing Science,* Fall 1994, pp. 315–327.

25. For a general discussion of ethical dilemmas in business, see John R. Schermerhorn, Jr., James G. Hunt, and Richard N. Osborn, *Managing Organizational Behavior* (New York: John Wiley & Sons, 1991), p. 27. See also Anusorn Singhapakdi and Scott J. Vitell, "Marketing Ethics: Factors Influencing Perceptions of Ethical Problems and Alternatives," *Journal of Macromarketing,* Spring 1990, pp. 4–18.

26. George Izzo, "A Theoretical Perspective of the Effects of Moral Intensity on Consumers' Ethical Judgments of Marketers' Non-Normative Behavior," in Joyce A. Young, Dale L. Varble, and Faye W. Gilbert, eds., *Proceedings of the Southwestern Marketing Association* (Terre Haute: Indiana State University and Southwestern Marketing Association, 1997), pp. 53–59.

27. For investigation of ethical awareness and values among marketing executives and marketing students, see Anusorn Singhapakdi, Kenneth L. Kraft, Scott J. Vitell, and Kumar C. Rallapalli, "The Perceived Importance of Ethics and Social Responsibility on Organizational Effectiveness," *Journal of the Academy of Marketing Science,* Winter 1995, pp. 46–56; David J. Fritzche, "An Examination of Marketing Ethics: Role of the Decision Maker, Consequences of the Decision," *Journal of Macromarketing,* Fall 1988, pp. 29–39; M. M. Pressley, D. J. Lincon, and T. Little, "Ethical Belief and Personal Values of Top Level Executives," *Journal of Business Research,* December 1982; Shelby D. Hunt, Van R. Wood, and Lawrence B. Chonko, "Corporate Ethical Values and Organizational Commitment in Marketing," *Journal of Marketing,* July 1989, pp. 79–90; R. Eric Reidenbach, Donald P. Robin, and Lyndon Dawson, "An Application and Extension of a Multidimensional Ethics Scale to Selected Marketing Practices and Marketing Groups," *Journal of the Academy of Marketing Science,* Spring 1991, pp. 83–92; Jerry R. Goolsby and Shelby D. Hunt, "Cognitive Moral Development and Marketing," *Journal of Marketing,* January 1992, pp. 55–68; David J. Burns, John M. Lansasa, and Jeffrey K. Fawcett, "Ethical Perceptions of Undergraduate Business Students: Does the Nature of the Institution Matter?" *Journal of the Midwest Marketing Association,* Spring 1990, pp. 84–156; James B. Deconinck and Paul C. Thistlethwaite, "Gender Differences in Ethical Evaluations," *Proceedings of the Midwest Marketing Association,* 1991, pp. 139–143; and Margery S. Steinberg, Robert F. Dyer, and Hiram C. Barksdale, Jr., "Marketing Ethics: An Examination of the Values and Attitudes of Today's Students/Tomorrow's Professionals," *Journal of the Midwest Marketing Association,* Fall 1989, pp. 65–67.

28. Adapted from "Lanier: Customer Vision Gives Clear Market Focus," Copyright © by Quality Publishing, 10200 Grogan's Mill Rd., Suite 150, The Woodlands, TX 77380. Reprinted from *Managing Office Technology* with permission July 1993.

29. Excerpt from Roy Furchgott, "You Say You Didn't Buy It. But Did You Read the Tiny Type?" *New York Times,* December 7, 1997, p. bu–9. Copyright © 1997 by The New York Times Company. Reprinted by permission.

chapter 3

1. Excerpt reprinted with permission from Karl Schoenberger and Melanie Warner, "Motorola Bets Big on China," *Fortune,* May 27, 1996.

2. See, for example, Terry Clark, "International Marketing and National Character: A Review and Proposal for an Integrative Theory," *Journal of Marketing,* October 1990, pp. 66–79; Duane Davis, Michael Morris, and Jeff Allen, "Perceived Environmental Turbulence and Its Effect on Selected Entrepreneurship, Marketing and Organizational Characteristics in Industrial Firms," *Journal of the Academy of Marketing Science,* Winter 1991, pp. 43–52; Leopoldo G. Arias Bolzmann, "Retailing in a Developing Economy: A Case Study in the Peruvian Retailing Economy," in Joseph F. Hair, Jr., Daryl O. McKee, and Daniel L. Sherrell, eds., *Advances in Marketing* (Baton Rouge, LA: Southwestern Marketing Association, 1992),

pp. 250–258; Eshghi Abdolreza, Joby John, and Charlie Van Nederpelt, "Marketing Strategy in an Integrated Europe: Some Research Propositions," in Victoria L. Crittenden, ed., *Developments in Marketing Science, Volume XV* (San Diego: Academy of Marketing Science, 1992), pp. 131–135; and Ravi S. Achrol, "Evolution of the Marketing Organization: New Forms of Turbulent Environments," *Journal of Marketing,* October 1991, pp. 77–92.

3. Joe Schwarts, "Climate-Controlled Customers," *American Demographics,* March 1992, pp. 24–32.

4. www.patagonia.com, February 19, 1998.

5. Adapted with permission of the Associated Press from "Japanese Like Seafood Really Fresh," *Tulsa World,* April 27, 1991, p. C2.

6. Ian Robertson, *Sociology* (New York: Worth Publishing, 1987), pp. 64–65.

7. For some recent studies on this issue, see Lalita A. Manrai and Ajay K. Manrai, "Effects of Cultural Context, Gender, and Acculturation on Perceptions of Work versus Social/Leisure Time Usage," *Journal of Business Research,* February 1995, pp. 114–128; James W. Gentry, Sunkyu Jun, and Partiya Tansuhaj, "Consumer Acculturation Process and Cultural Conflict," *Journal of Business Research,* February 1995, pp. 129–139; and Ruby Roy Dholakia and Luis V. Domingues, "Special Section on Marketing Strategies and the Development Process," *Journal of Business Research,* February 1995, pp. 113–114.

8. Humberto Valencia, "Snafus Persist in Marketing to Hispanics," *Marketing News,* June 24, 1983, p. 3.

9. From DO'S AND TABOOS AROUND THE WORLD 3rd Edition, by Roger E. Axtel. Copyright © 1993 by Parker Pen Company. A Benjamin Book distributed by John Wiley & Sons, Inc. Adapted by permission of John Wiley & Sons, Inc.

10. "Don't Drip on Me," *Time,* March 7, 1988, p. 45.

11. For an interesting study in this area, see Terence Shrimp and Subhash Sharma, "Consumer Ethnocentrism: Construction and Validation of CETSCALE," *Journal of Marketing Research,* August 1987, pp. 280–289.

12. Martha Farnsworth Riche, "We're All Minorities Now," *American Demographics,* October 1991, pp. 26–34.

13. Unless otherwise noted, the statistics in this section are from the U.S. Bureau of the Census.

14. For additional information see "Geographical Mobility: March 1993 to March 1994," www.census.gov/population/www/socdemo/mig-94.html.

15. Peter Francese, "America at Mid-Decade," *American Demographics,* February 1995, p. 28.

16. Peter Francese, "America at Mid-Decade," *American Demographics,* February 1995, p. 28.

17. Larry S. Lowe and Kevin McCrohan, "Gray Marketing in the United States," *Journal of Consumer Marketing,* Winter 1988, pp. 45–51; and Haya El Nasser and Andrea Stone, "Study: 2020 Begins Age of the Elderly," *USA TODAY,* May 21, 1996, p. 4A.

18. Cheryl Russell, "The Aging of Two Generations," *Marketing Power,* November 1995, p. 6; and Melinda Beck, "Next Population Bulge Shows Its Might," *Wall Street Journal,* February 3, 1997, p. B1.

19. Peter Francese, "America at Mid-Decade," *American Demographics,* February 1995, p. 26.

20. Adapted with permission from Antonia Barber, "Take-Out Has Bigger Place on Home Tables," *USA TODAY,* January 27, 1997, p. D1. Copyright 1997, USA TODAY. Reprinted with permission.

21. Except where indicated, information in this section comes from U.S. Department of Labor, Bureau of Labor Statistics, "Outlook 2000," Bulletin 2352, April 1990 (Washington DC: Government Printing Office, 1990) and from the following publications of the U.S. Bureau of the Census (all published by the Government Printing Office): "Household and Family Characteristics, March 1990 and 1989," *Current Population Reports,* Series P-20, no. 447; "How We're Changing: Current Population Special Studies," Series P-23, no. 170, December 1990, and Series P-23, January 1990; *Statistical Abstract of the United States: 1990,* pp. 444, 445, and 451–453; and "Consumer Income," *Current Population Reports,* Series P-60, no. 157, July 1987, p. 15.

22. Paul Overberg, "Rich Earn More than All of the Middle Class," *USA TODAY,* June 20, 1996, p. A-1.

23. U.S. Bureau of the Census, "U.S. Population Estimates, by Age, Sex, Race, and Hispanic Origin: 1989," *Current Population Reports,* Series P-25, no. 1057 (Washington, DC: Government Printing Office, 1990), pp. 2–7; and Peter T. Kilborn, "The Middle Class Feels Betrayed, but Maybe Not Enough to Rebel," *New York Times,* January 12, 1992, p. 1e.

24. John Huey, "Waking Up to the New Economy," *Fortune,* June 27, 1994, p. 36.

25. Adapted with permission from Vivian Pospisil, "Global Paradox: Small Is Powerful," *Industry Week,* July 8, 1994. Copyright Penton Publishing, Inc., Cleveland, OH.

26. GNP and other measures of the economy are not always accurate. Unmeasured, or "underground," activities take place throughout the economy. See Kevin F. McCrohan and James D. Smith, "A Consumer Expenditure Approach to Estimating the Size of the Underground Economy," *Journal of Marketing,* April 1986, p. 48.

27. Integration of technology and marketing strategy is discussed fully in Noel Capon and Rashi Glazer, "Marketing and Technology: A Strategic Coalignment," *Journal of Marketing,* July 1987, pp. 1–14.

28. Julie Liesse, "Oat Bran Popularity Hitting the Skids," *Advertising Age,* May 21, 1990, p. 3.

29. Neil Postman, *Technopoly: The Surrender of Culture to Technology* (New York: Vintage Books, 1993), pp. 6–15.

30. James P. Ronda, "Thomas Moran and the Eastern Railroads," *The Gilcrease Journal,* Spring/Summer 1997, p. 38.

31. Neil Postman, *Technopoly: The Surrender of Culture to Technology* (New York: Vintage Books, 1993), pp. 6–15.

32. Kevin Goldman, "Video Explosions Sell Technology to Teens," *Wall Street Journal,* October 5, 1993.

33. Nicholas Negroponte, *Being Digital* (New York: Knopf, 1995), p. 6.

34. Christine Dugas, "Banks See Deep Pockets in Cash-free Customers," *USA TODAY,* July 1, 1996.

35. Four excellent articles about the Internet and its impact on marketing in the 21st century are Paul Pallab, "Marketing on the Internet," *Journal of Consumer Marketing,* Vol. 13, No. 4, 1996, pp. 27-39; Robert A. Peterson, Sridhar Balasubramanian, and Bart J. Bronnenberg, "Exploring the Implications of the Internet for Consumer Marketing," *Journal of the Academy of Marketing Science,* Fall 1997, pp. 329–346; John Deighton, "Commentary on 'Exploring the Implications of the Internet for Consumer Marketing'," *Journal of the Academy of Marketing Science,* Fall 1997, pp. 347–351; and Raymond R. Burk, "Do You See What I See? The Future of Virtual Shopping," *Journal of the Academy of Marketing Science,* Fall 1997, pp. 352–360.

36. Nathaniel Sheppard, Jr., "Information Service Links Professors," *Tulsa World,* February 5, 1995, p. 12.

37. www.pcwebopedia.com, October 15, 1997.

38. Bruce J. McLaren, *Understanding and Using the Internet* (St. Paul, MN: West, 1996), p. 99.

39. Adapted from Internet information published by the Netscape Communications Company (www.netscape.com).

40. Lee Fleming, "Digital Delivery: Pushing Content to the Desktop," downloaded from the *Digital Information Group,* 1997

41. Lee Fleming, "Digital Delivery: Pushing Content to the Desktop," downloaded from the *Digital Information Group,* 1997.

42. Joshua Quittner, "Invasion of Privacy," *Time,* August 25, 1997.

43. Kenneth G. Hallgren, "Marketing in an Electronic Age: Profession in Transition," *Proceedings of the Midwest Marketing Association,* 1993, pp. 43–47.

44. Kevin Goldman, "Video Explosions Sell Technology to Teens," *Wall Street Journal,* October 25, 1993.

45. Michael D. Hutt and Thomas Speh, *Industrial Marketing Management* (Hinsdale, IL: Dryden Press, 1988), p. 39.

46. Michael D. Eisner, "Critics of Disney on the Wrong Track," *USA Today,* July 12, 1994, p. 10A.

47. Adapted from Patti Cignarella, "A New Pepsi Challenge in India," *Adweek's Marketing Week,* April 30, 1990, p. 17. © ASM Communications, Inc. Used with permission from *Adweek.*

48. Tim Friend, "Cosmetic Ads Must Tone Down Claims," *USA Today,* April 5, 1988, p. 1D.

49. For a survey of this topic, see Bruce D. Fisher and Michael J. Phillips, *The Legal, Ethical, and Regulatory Environment of Business* (St. Paul, MN: West Publishing Company, 1992), pp. 627–893.

50. M. Jeffrey Kallis, Kathleen A. Krentler, and Dino J. Vanier, "The Value of User Image in Quelling Aberrant Consumer Behavior," *Journal of the Academy of Marketing Science,* Spring 1988, p. 30.

51. Information and quote from Andrew Serwer, "McDonald's Conquers the World," *Fortune,* October 17, 1994, pp. 103–117.

52. Excerpted with permission from *Real-World Lessons for America's Small Business,* pp. 181–182, copyright 1992 by Connecticut Mutual Life Insurance Company, now known as Massachusetts Mutual Life Insurance Company.

53. Reprinted with permission from Margot Hornblower, "Learning to Earn," *Time,* February 24, 1997, p. 34. © 1997 Time Inc. Reprinted by permission.

chapter 4

1. Excerpts reprinted from "Whirlpool: U.S. Leader Pursues Global Blueprint," *Appliance Manufacturer,* February 1997, p. 21.

2. The concept of the four Cs of business is copyrighted by William G. Zikmund, 1991. Use of this conceptual scheme elsewhere is not permitted without written permission from William G. Zikmund. For an alternative conceptualization, see Kenichi Ohmae, *The Mind of the Strategist* (New York: Penguin Books, 1982), p. 91.

3. See Michael H. Morris and Joan M. Jarvi, "Making Marketing Curriculum Entrepreneurial," *Marketing Educator,* Fall 1990, pp. 1, 8.

4. Patricia Sellers, "John Bryan's Sara Lee," *Fortune,* February 6, 1995, p. 24.

5. Excerpt reprinted with permission of Harvard Business School Press from *Real Time: Preparing for the Age of the Never Satisfied Customer* by Regis McKenna. Boston, MA 1997, pp. 3–4. Copyright © 1997 by the President and Fellows of Harvard College, all rights reserved.

6. Thomas A. Stewart, "Welcome to the Revolution," *Fortune,* December 13, 1993, p. 76.

7. Adapted with permission of the Associated Press from "IBM on the Ball under Gerstner," *Tulsa World,* May 1, 1995, Business Sec., p. 14.

8. John A. Byrne, "The Futurists Who Fathered the Ideas," *Business Week,* February 8, 1993, p. 103.

9. For an alternative view of this concept, see Michael E. Porter, *Competitive Advantage* (New York Free Press, 1985), pp. 36–43.

10. Rosabeth Moss Kanter, "Collaborative Advantage: The Art of Alliances," *Harvard Business Review,* July-August 1994, p. 97; and Joel Bleeke and David Ernst, "Is Your Strategic Alliance Really a Sale?" *Harvard Business Review,* January-February 1995, p. 104.

11. "Will Kodak Get Lucky in China?" *Business Week,* July 28, 1997, p. 48.

12. James Brian Quinn and Frederick G. Hilmer, "Strategic Outsourcing," *Sloan Management Review,* Summer 1994, p. 43.

13. Peter F. Drucker, "The Information Executives Really Need," *Harvard Business Review,* January–February 1995, p. 59.

14. Shawn Tully, "You'll Never Guess Who Really Makes," *Fortune,* October 3, 1994, p. 127.

15. Harry Berkowitz, "Here Comes a Whopper for One Agency," *New York Newsday,* March 21, 1994.

16. Kenichi Ohmae, "The Equidistant Manager," *Express Magazine,* Fall 1990, pp. 10–12.

17. Adapted with permission from Myron Magnet, "The New Golden Rule of Business," *Fortune,* February 21, 1994, pp. 60–61.

18. Philip R. Cateora, *International Marketing* (Homewood, IL: Richard D. Irwin, 1990), p. 2.

19. "No Beef in India McDonald's," Associated Press, October 11, 1996.

20. Laurel Wentz, "Multinationals Tread Softly While Advertising in Iran," *Advertising Age International,* November 8, 1993, p. I-21.

21. See, for example, Nancy D. Albers-Miller, "Appealing to Values in Advertising Across Cultures . . ." in Joyce A. Young, Dale L. Varble, and Faye W. Gilbert, eds., *Proceedings of the Southwestern Marketing Association* (Terre Haute: Indiana State University and Southwestern Marketing Association, 1997), pp. 105–114.

22. Adapted from Ron Tempest, "Europeans Use American Images to Hawk Wares," *Tulsa World,* December 30, 1990, p. D1. Copyright 1990, *Los Angeles Times.* Reprinted by permission.

23. Bill Montague, "Worst Fears of Free Trade Have Cooled," *USA Today,* November 25, 1994, p. B-1.

24. "Boone Set for Showdown with Japanese Business Culture," *Tulsa World,* June 27, 1990, p. 2B.

25. Geoffrey Lee Martin, "P&G Puts Nappies to Rest in Australia," *Advertising Age,* September 19, 1994, p. I-31.

26. Information from "Buy American Sentiment Backfires," *Tulsa World,* January 25, 1992, p. 6B; and Robert Reich, "Who Is Us?" *Harvard Business Review,* January-February 1990, pp. 53–54.

27. Reprinted from "Pepsi Egypt Crippled after 48 Years," in the September 18, 1994 issue of *Advertising Age.* Copyright, Crain Communications Inc., 1994.

28. Reprinted by permission from *Real-World Lessons for America's Small Business: Insight from the Blue Chip Enterprise Initiative 1994,* pp. 120–121. Copyright 1994 by Connecticut Mutual Life Insurance Company, now known as Massachusetts Mutual Life Insurance Company.

29. Excerpted with permission from *Insights and Inspiration: How Businesses Succeed,* pp. 106–107. Copyright 1995 by Connecticut Mutual Life Insurance Company, now known as Massachusetts Mutual Life Insurance Company.

chapter 5

1. Karen Benezra, "Fritos Around the World," *Brandweek,* March 27, 1995, p. 32; "Chinese Chee-tos," *New York Times,* November 27, 1994, p. 31; and "Chee-tos Make Debut in China but Lose Cheese in Translation," *USA TODAY,* September 2, 1994, p. B-1.

2. See Thomas G. Exter, "The Next Step Is Called GIS," *American Demographics Desk Reference,* May 1992, p. 2.

3. Ralph H. Sprague, Jr., and Hugh J. Watson, *Decision Support Systems: Putting Theory into Practice* (Englewood Cliffs, NJ: Prentice Hall, 1986), p. 1. See also Jim Bessen, "Riding the Marketing Information Wave," *Harvard Business Review,* September-October 1994, pp. 150–160.

4. "Three Visions of an Electronic Future," *New York Times,* March 24, 1996, p. 22F.

5. Paul Schneider, "Behind Company Walls: It's the Intranet," *Arizona Business Gazette,* March 7, 1996.

6. "Technology: Sun Microsystems Planning to Unveil 'Intranet' Products," *Wall Street Journal,* March 26, 1996.

7. Andrew J. Kessler, "The Database Economy," *Forbes,* April 21, 1997, p. 168.

8. This section is based on William G. Zikmund, *Essentials of Marketing Research* (Fort Worth, TX: Dryden Press, 1998).

9. Based on material from DataMind's home page, which can be found at www.datamindcorp.com. For an interesting article see Peter R. Peacock, "Data Mining in Marketing: Part 1," *Marketing Management,* Winter 1998, pp. 9–18.

10. IBM Business Intelligence-Data Mining, www.software.ibm.com, December 8, 1997.

11. Ira Sager, "Big Blue Wants to Mine Your Data," *Business Week,* June 3, 1996.

12. Adapted from the definition of research in the report of the American Marketing Association Committee on Definitions of Marketing Research, 1987. The official AMA definition is as follows: "Marketing research is the function that links the consumer, customer, and public to the marketer through information—information used to identify and define marketing opportunities and problems; generate, refine, and evaluate marketing actions; monitor marketing performance; and improve understanding of marketing as a process. Marketing research specifies the information required to address these issues; designs the method for collecting the information; manages and implements the data collection

process; analyzes the results; and communicates the findings and their implications." See also Morris B. Holbrook, "What Is Marketing Research?" and Shelby D. Hunt, "Marketing Research: Proximate Purpose in Ultimate Value," both in Russell W. Belk and Gerald Zaltman, eds., *Proceedings, 1987 Winter Educators' Conference* (Chicago: American Marketing Association, 1987).

13. P. J. Runkel and J. E. McGrath, *Research on Human Behavior: A Systematic Guide to Method* (New York: Holt, Rinehart and Winston, 1972), p. 2.

14. A. Einstein and L. Infeld, *The Evolution of Physics* (New York: Simon and Schuster, 1942), p. 95.

15. "Rubbermaid Tries Its Hand at Bristles and Wood," *Adweek's Marketing Week*, March 5, 1990, pp. 20–21.

16. Adapted with permission of the author from Doug Stewart, "In the Cutthroat World of Toy Sales, Child's Play Is Serious Business," *Smithsonian*, December 1989, pp. 76–78.

17. Peter Francese, "Grill of My Dreams," *Marketing Tools*, July 1997.

18. For further insight into problems associated with surveys, see Philip E. Down and John R. Kerr, "Recent Evidence on the Relationship between Anonymity and Response Variables for Mail Surveys," *Journal of the Academy of Marketing Science*, Spring 1986, pp. 72–82; Jon M. Hawes, Vicky L. Crittenden, and William F. Crittenden, "The Effects of Personalization, Source, and Offer on Mail Survey Response Rate and Speed," *Akron Business and Economic Review*, Summer 1987, pp. 54–63; and three articles in Joseph F. Hair, Jr., Daryl O. McKee, and Daniel L. Sherrell, eds., *Advances in Marketing* (Baton Rouge, LA: Southwest Marketing Association, 1992): Robert E. Stevens, David London, and C. William McConkey, "Does Questionnaire Color Affect Response Rates?" pp. 80–85; Ronald D. Taylor and Michael Richard, "Mail Survey Response Rates, Item Omission Rates, and Response Speed Resulting from the Use of Advanced Notification," pp. 67–72; and David Strutton and Lou Pelton, "Surveying the Elderly," pp. 264–268.

19. Gloria E. Wheeler, "Yes, No, All of the Above: Before You Conduct a Survey," *Exchange* (a publication of Brigham Young University School of Management), Spring/Summer 1979, p. 21.

20. Reprinted with permission from "ResearchWeb Mines the Net for Effective Survey Results," in the July 21, 1997 issue of *Advertising Age*. Copyright, Crain Communications Inc., 1997.

21. "You Say Tomato, I Say Tomahto," *Express Magazine*, Spring 1992, p. 19.

22. Thomas J. Meyer, "Slicing the Japanese Pie," *American Way*, November 1989, pp. 40–43. Thomas J. Meyer, 1989. Reprinted by permission of the author.

chapter 6

1. Adapted with permission from Beth Burkstrand, "Scrapbook Mania: Pricey Labor of Love," *Wall Street Journal*, July 16, 1997. Reprinted by permission of *Wall Street Journal*, © 1997 Dow Jones & Company, Inc. All Rights Reserved Worldwide.

2. Adapted with permission from Barbara Carton, "Hold On to Your Tupperware—The Home Sales Party Is Back," *Wall Street Journal*, March 26, 1997. Reprinted by permission of *Wall Street Journal*, © 1997 Dow Jones & Company, Inc. All Rights Reserved Worldwide.

3. William L. Wilkie, *Consumer Behavior*, 2nd ed. (New York: John Wiley & Sons, 1990), p. 12.

4. Kurt Lewin, *A Dynamic Theory of Personality* (New York: McGraw-Hill, 1935).

5. This model is a variation of the one discussed by John C. Mowen in *Consumer Behavior*, 4th ed. (New York: Macmillan, 1997).

6. William L. Wilkie, *Consumer Behavior*, 2nd ed. (New York: John Wiley & Sons, 1990), pp. 220–225. See also Mark E. Slama and Armen Tashchian, "Validation of the S-C-R Paradigm for Consumer Involvement with a Consumer Good," *Journal of the Academy of Marketing Science*, Spring 1987, pp. 36–45; Joseph J. Belonax, Jr. and Rajshekhar G. Javalgi, "The Influence of Involvement and Product Class Quality on Consumer Choice Sets," *Journal of the Academy of Marketing Science*, Summer 1989, pp. 209–216.

7. For an interesting article, see Jeffrey B. Schmidt and Richard A. Spreng, "A Proposed Model of External Consumer Information Search,"

Journal of the Academy of Marketing Science, Summer 1996, pp. 232–245.

8. Information from Wilton Woods, "A PC Learns How to Kiss," *Fortune*, September 5, 1994, p. 107.

9. Marketers are interested in dissatisfaction as well as satisfaction; but since complaints are only one measure of dissatisfaction, this result is difficult to measure. See Marsha Richins, "A Multivariate Analysis of Responses to Dissatisfaction," *Journal of the Academy of Marketing Science*, Fall 1987, p. 24.

10. A. Maslow, *Motivation and Personality* (New York: Harper & Row, 1954), p. 92.

11. Excerpted from Lisa Gubernick and Marla Matzer, "Babies as Dolls," *Forbes*, February 27, 1995, p. 79. Reprinted by permission of FORBES Magazine. © Forbes Inc., 1995.

12. Matthew Grimm, "Coors Serves Taste-Test Results in Ads," *Adweek*, July 1, 1991, p. 9. For interesting studies on perception in marketing, see R. I. Allison and K. P. Uhl, "Impact of Beer Brand on Taste Perception," *Journal of Marketing Research*, August 1964, pp. 36–39; Gordon L. Patzer, *The Physical Attraction Phenomena* (New York: Plenum Publishing, 1985); William L. Rhey, Hemant Rustogi, and Mary Anne Watson, "Buyers' Perceptions of Automobile Saleswomen: A Field Study," in Joseph F. Hair, Jr., Daryl O. McKee, and Daniel Sherrell, eds., *Advances in Marketing* (Baton Rouge, LA: Southwest Marketing Association, 1992), pp. 41–46; and Donald R. Lichtenstein, Nancy M. Ridgway, and Richard Netermeyer, "Price Perceptions and Consumer Shopping Behavior," *Journal of Marketing Research*, May 1993, pp. 234–245.

13. Adapted from Damon Darlin, "Where Trademarks Are Up for Grabs: U.S. Products Widely Copied in South Korea," *Wall Street Journal*, December 5, 1989. Reprinted by permission of *Wall Street Journal*, © 1997 Dow Jones & Company, Inc. All Rights Reserved Worldwide.

14. A review of the 25-year history of subliminal cues is found in Sid C. Dudley, "Subliminal Advertising: What Is the Controversy About?" *Akron Business and Economic Review*, Summer 1987, pp. 6–18. See also Robert E. Widing II, Ronald Hoverstad, Ronald Coulter, and Gene Brown, "The VASE Scales: Measures of Viewpoints about Sexual Embeds in Advertising," *Journal of Business Research*, January 1991, pp. 3–10.

15. Debra L. Nelson and James Campbell Quick, *Organizational Behavior: Foundations, Realities, and Challenges* (St. Paul, MN: West Educational Publishing, 1994), pp. 112–113.

16. William L. Wilkie, *Consumer Behavior*, 2nd ed. (New York: John Wiley & Sons, 1990), p. 311.

17. Excerpted from Marcia Berss, "Whirlpool's Bloody Nose," *Forbes*, March 11, 1996, pp. 90–92. Reprinted by permission of FORBES Magazine. © Forbes, Inc., 1996.

18. Kenneth R. Evans, Tim Christiansen, and James D. Gill, "The Impact of Social Influence and Role Expectations on Shopping Center Patronage Intentions," *Journal of the Academy of Marketing Science*, Summer 1996, pp. 208–218.

19. See, for example, Van R. Wood and Roy Howell, "A Note on Hispanic Values and Subcultural Research," *Journal of the Academy of Marketing Science*, Winter 1991, pp. 61–67.

20. See Lawrence F. Feick and Linda L. Price, "The Marketing Maven: A Diffuser of Marketplace Information," *Journal of Marketing*, January 1987, pp. 83–97.

21. Levitt material excerpted from Theodore Levitt, "The Morality(?) of Advertising," *Harvard Business Review*, July-August 1970, p. 91. Hayden material from Sterling Hayden, *The Wanderer* (New York: Knopf, 1963).

22. Reprinted with permission from "Ore-Best Goes for Rabbit Punch," in the February 13, 1984 issue of *Advertising Age*. Copyright, Crain Communications Inc., 1984.

23. This case was prepared by Professor Barton A. Weitz, JCPenney Eminent Scholar in Retail Management, College of Business Administration, University of Florida. It is adapted with permission of the author and publisher from Michael Levy and Barton A. Weitz, *Retailing Management*, 2nd ed. (Homewood, IL: Richard D. Irwin, 1995), pp. 578–580.

chapter 7

1. Reprinted with permission from Roberta Maynard, "Striking the Right Match," *Nation's Business*, May 1, 1996, pp. 18–20. Reprinted by permis-

sion, Nation's Business, May 1996. Copyright 1996, U.S. Chamber of Commerce.

2. This paragraph is based on F. E. Webster, Jr. and Y. Wind, *Organizational Buying Behavior* (Englewood Cliffs, NJ: Prentice Hall, 1972), p. 1.

3. Claudia H. Deutsch, "A Matter of Supplier-Customer Trust," *New York Times*, February 17, 1991, p. F25.

4. Though these three situations are common and widely recognized, some research offers alternative viewpoints. See Erin Anderson, Wujin Chu, and Barton Weitz, "Industrial Purchasing: An Empirical Exploration of the Buyclass Framework," *Journal of Marketing*, July 1987, pp. 71–86; and Morry Ghingold, "Testing the Buygrid Buying Process Model," *Journal of Purchasing and Materials Management*, Winter 1986, pp. 30–36.

5. It appears that organizational buyers and sellers develop mental "scripts," which they tend to follow in dealing with each other. Salespeople should devote some effort to understanding these "cognitive scripts." See Thomas W. Leigh and Arno J. Rethans, "A Script-Theoretic Analysis of Industrial Purchasing Behavior," *Journal of Marketing*, Fall 1984, pp. 22–32.

6. For an interesting article on business-to-business marketing on the Internet, see Doug Bartholomew, "Trawling for $1 Billion," *Industry Week*, April 21, 1997, p. 68(4).

7. Reprinted with permission from *Industry Week*, April 21, 1997, p. 68. Copyright, Penton Publishing, Inc., Cleveland, Ohio.

8. "A Survey of Electronic Commerce—Business-to-Business e-Commerce Is a Revolution in a Ball Valve," *The Economist*, downloaded from www.economist.com, June 1997.

9. It has been suggested that there is a "marketing strategy center," the seller's equivalent of the "buying center." See Michael D. Hutt and Thomas W. Speh, "The Marketing Strategy Center: Diagnosing the Industrial Marketer's Interdisciplinary Role," *Journal of Marketing*, Fall 1984, pp. 53–61.

10. Excerpt reprinted from Brad Ketchum, "Faux Pas Go with the Territory," *Inc. Magazine*, May 1, 1994.

11. R. D. Buzzell, R. E. M. Nourse, J. B. Matthews, Jr., and T. Levitt, *Marketing: A Contemporary Analysis* (New York: McGraw-Hill, 1972), pp. 205–206.

12. Adapted with permission from Calmetta Y. Coleman, "Fliers Call Electronic Ticketing a Drag," *Wall Street Journal*, January 17, 1997, p. B1. Reprinted by permission of *Wall Street Journal*, © 1997 Dow Jones & Company, Inc. All Rights Reserved Worldwide.

13. Adapted with permission from Ronald Henkoff, "The Hot New Seal of Quality: ISO 9000 Standard of Quality Management," *Fortune*, June 28, 1993, pp. 116–117.

14. Sue Davis, "New Product Pioneers Garner Grand Awards," *Prepared Foods*, April 15, 1993.

15. Excerpt reprinted from "At DEC, Someone Is Breathing on the Phone Line," *Time*, February 17, 1997, p. 70. © 1997 Time Inc. Reprinted by permission.

16. From a press release issued by the Executive Office of the President, Office of Management and Budget, Washington, DC.

17. Excerpted with permission from *Insights and Inspiration: How Businesses Succeed*, pp. 135–136, copyright 1995 by Connecticut Mutual Life Insurance Company, now known as Massachusetts Mutual Life Insurance Company.

chapter 8

1. Adapted with permission from "Trend: Women Buy Themselves Jewelry," Associated Press, May 6, 1997.

2. Adapted with permission of the *Orlando Sentinel* from Rene Stutzman, "Sports Marketers Focusing on Women," *Tulsa World*, October 9, 1994, Business Section, p. 7.

3. Segmentation strategies can be very specific. See, for example, Morris B. Holbrook and Douglas V. Holloway, "Marketing Strategy and the Structure of Aggregate, Segment-Specific, and Differential Preferences," *Journal of Marketing*, Winter 1986, pp. 62–67; Jo Ann Stilley Hopper, "An Investigation of the Roles of Husbands and Wives in Family Financial

Decision Making Processes: Preliminary Results," in Michael Levy and Dhuruv Grewal, eds., *Developments in Marketing Science*, vol. XVI (Miami Beach: Academy of Marketing Science, 1993), pp. 75–81; Don R. Rahtz, M. Joseph Sirgy, and Rustan Kosenko, "Using Demographics and Psychographic Dimensions to Discriminate between Mature Heavy and Light Television Users: An Exploratory Analysis," in Kenneth D. Bahn, ed., *Developments in Marketing Science*, vol. XI (Montreal: Academy of Marketing Science, 1988), pp. 2–7; Glen Riecken and Ugur Yavas, "Who Uses Prepared Food? Psychographic and Demographic Correlates," in Michael Levy and Dhuruv Grewal, eds., *Developments in Marketing Science*, vol. XVI (Miami Beach: Academy of Marketing Science, 1993), pp. 542–546; and Cynthia Webster, "Spanish- and English-Speaking Hispanic Subcultural Consumption Differences," in Kenneth D. Bahn, ed., *Developments in Marketing Science*, vol. XI (Montreal: Academy of Marketing Science, 1988), pp. 18–22.

4. David Field, "Business-Flier Plan Paying Off for United," *USA TODAY*, August 5, 1997, p. 8b.

5. Reprinted with permission from "Barbie Fashion Designer—Marketing 100," in the June 30, 1997 issue of *Advertising Age*. Copyright, Crain Communications Inc., 1997.

6. Joshua Levine, "Relationship Marketing," *Forbes*, December 20, 1993.

7. Steven L. Goldman, Roger N. Nagel, and Kenneth Preiss, "Why Seiko Has 3,000 Watch Styles," *New York Times*, October 9, 1994, p. F9.

8. Reprinted with permission from "A Car or a Club?" in the November 8, 1993 issue of *Advertising Age*. Copyright, Crain Communications Inc., 1993.

9. Adapted from Sarah Jay, "Getting Beyond Beep-Beep, Pow and Zap," *Wall Street Journal*, September 23, 1994, p. B1. Reprinted by permission of *Wall Street Journal*, © 1994 Dow Jones & Company, Inc. All Rights Reserved Worldwide.

10. "The Country Club Set," *Brandweek*, September 2, 1996, p. 18.

11. Alex Taylor III, "Porsche Slices Up Its Buyers," *Fortune*, January 16, 1995, p. 24.

12. Judann Pollack, "Sampling, Ads May Be Key for Products Using Olestra," *Advertising Age*, April 1, 1996, p. 16.

13. Adapted with permission from Alex Taylor III, "Porsche Slices Up Its Buyers," *Fortune*, January 16, 1995, p. 24. Pricing information from Wilton Woods, "Not Priced for the Nineties," *Fortune*, September 22, 1993, p. 87.

14. Adapted from Sally Goll, "Emerging Markets Report: New Market Caters to China's Little Emperors," *Wall Street Journal*, February 8, 1995. Reprinted by permission of *Wall Street Journal*, © 1995 Dow Jones & Company, Inc. All Rights Reserved Worldwide.

15. Information from Patricia Sellers, "Keeping the Buyers You Already Have," *Fortune*, Autumn-Winter 1993, p. 57; and Bob Dorf, "Phone-to-Phone Marketing," *Brandweek*, September 1997, p. 27.

16. Michael J. McCarthy, "Marketers Zero In on Their Customers," *Wall Street Journal*, March 18, 1991, p. 1B.

17. "Hot Spot: Ethan Allen," *Advertising Age*, January 13, 1997, p. 38.

18. Adapted with permission of SRI Consulting from "The VALS™ 2 Typology," © 1994, SRI Consulting.

19. From Diane Toroian, "Making the Point: A Collection of Savvy and Irrepressible Staffers Have Turned KPNT into One of the Top Alternative Radio Stations in the Nation," *Everyday Magazine*, St. Louis Post-Dispatch, November 9, 1996. Reprinted with permission of the St. Louis Post Dispatch copyright 1998.

chapter 9

1. Adapted with permission from Stephanie Thompson, "Making Lunch Cool," *Brandweek*, October 6, 1997, pp. 18–19. © 1997 ASM Communications, Inc. Used with permission from *Brandweek* magazine.

2. Theodore Levitt, *The Marketing Imagination* (New York: Free Press, 1986), p. 79.

3. Reprinted with permission from Earle Eldridge, "Hood Ornaments Become Endangered Species," *USA TODAY*, June 18, 1997.

4. Estimates of the importance of services vary because of definitional problems. For example, U.S. government statistics omit transportation from the definition of services and thus estimate services to account for

approximately 30 percent of the gross national product.

5. All but the first paragraph excerpted with permission from Daniel Imhoff, "Tree-Free 2: Moving beyond Wood-Based Paper," *Communication Arts*, January–February 1995, pp. 104–105.

6. Excerpted from Rita Koselka, "Hope and Fear as Marketing Tools," *Forbes*, August 29, 1994, p. 78. Reprinted by permission of FORBES Magazine. © Forbes, Inc., 1994.

7. Suzanne Oliver, "New Personality: Black and Decker's DeWalt Line of Industrial Power Tools," *Forbes*, August 15, 1994, p. 114.

8. Information from Bruce I. Knoviser, "A Czech Entrepreneur Makes Names for Himself," *New York Times*, February 19, 1995, p. 4F.

9. Information from John Gilbert, "Fans Love That Moose," *Minneapolis Star Tribune*, April 22, 1995, pp. 1D–2D.

10. For an interesting article see Kevin Lane Keller, Susan E. Heckler, and Michael J. Houston, "The Effects of Brand Name on Suggestiveness in Advertising Recall," *Journal of Marketing*, January 1998, pp. 48–57.

11. Adapted from "Sony," *Express Magazine*, a publication of Federal Express Corporation, Winter 1992, p. 14.

12. All but the first paragraph excerpted from "Technology to Watch," *Fortune*, September 5, 1994, p. 109.

13. Information from Stephanie Strom, "High Noon for Big Maker of Toy Guns," *New York Times*, October 22, 1994; and Joseph Pereira and Barbara Carton, "U.S. Toy Retailer to Ban 'Realistic' Toy Gun Sales," *Wall Street Journal*, October 14, 1994.

14. Adapted by permission from *Insights and Inspiration: How Businesses Succeed*, pp. 116–117, copyright 1995 by Connecticut Mutual Life Insurance Company, now known as Massachusetts Mutual Life Insurance Company.

15. Wording of Dirty Potato Chips label reprinted courtesy of Chickasaw Foods.

chapter 10

1. Adapted with permission from Allison Sprout, "Blood Test While You Wait," *Fortune*, June 27, 1994, p. 125.

2. Kevin J. Clancy and Robert S. Shulman, *The Marketing Revolution* (New York: Harper Business, 1991), p. 6.

3. Excerpt reprinted with permission from Bob McMath, "Beverage Blips: Even Good Beverages Aren't Immune from Failure," *Beverage Industry*, October 1996, p. 18.

4. E. M. Rogers and F. F. Shoemaker, *Communication of Innovation* (New York: Free Press, 1971). See also Vijay Mahajan, Eitan Muller, and Frank M. Bass, "New Product Diffusion Models in Marketing: A Review and Directions for Research," *Journal of Marketing*, January 1990, pp. 1–26; and Fareena Sultan, John V. Farley, and Donald R. Lehmann, "A Meta-analysis of Diffusion Models," *Journal of Marketing Research*, February 1990, pp. 70–77.

5. From Gary Hamel and C. K. Prahalad, *Competing for the Future*. Boston: Harvard Business School Press, 1992, pp. 101–102.

6. For some products, psychographic variables may be more important than demographic variables. See Judith Waldrop, "Markets with Attitude," *American Demographics*, July 1994, pp. 22–33.

7. Chris Bucholtz, "Ironing Out the Bugs Through the Internet," *Telephony*, January 1, 1996, p. 16.

8. Kathleen Deveny, "Failure of Its Oven Lovin' Cookie Dough Shows Pillsbury Pitfalls of New Products," *Wall Street Journal*, June 17, 1993.

9. Adapted from Michael Ceiply, "Popularity of Compact Disks and Cassettes May Take Record Out of Record Industry," *Wall Street Journal*, October 16, 1986, p. 3. Reprinted by permission of *Wall Street Journal*, © 1986 Dow Jones & Company, Inc. All Rights Reserved Worldwide.

10. Reprinted with permission from "Year in Review: Star Wars," in the December 22, 1997 issue of *Advertising Age*, December 22, 1997, p. 16. Copyright, Crain Communications Inc., 1997.

11. E. M. Rogers and F. F. Shoemaker, *Communication of Innovation* (New York: Free Press, 1971); see also Vijay Mahajan, Eitan Muller, and Frank

M. Bass, "New Product Diffusion Models in Marketing: A Review and Directions for Research," *Journal of Marketing*, January 1990, pp. 1–26; and Fareena Sultan, John V. Farley, and Donald R. Lehmann, "A Meta-analysis of Diffusion Models," *Journal of Marketing Research*, February 1990, pp. 70–77.

12. Rita Koselka, "It's My Favorite Statistic," *Forbes*, September 12, 1994.

13. Reprinted from Alan Deutschman, "The Managing Wisdom of High-Tech Superstars," *Fortune*, October 17, 1994, p. 200.

14. Adapted with permission of the Associated Press from "No Deodorant? No Sweat!" *Tulsa World*, December 18, 1991, p. A1.

15. For an interesting study, see Vicki Lane and Robert Jacobson, "Stock Market Reactions to Brand Extension Announcements: The Effect of Brand Attitude and Familiarity," *Journal of Marketing*, January 1995, pp. 63–77.

16. For an interesting article, see Deborah Roedder, John Barbara Loken, and Christopher Joiner, "The Negative Impact of Extensions: Can Flagship Products be Diluted?" *Journal of Marketing*, January 1998, pp. 19–33.

17. Based on Calvin L. Hadock, "The Decline and Fall of Marketing Research in Corporate America," *Marketing Research*, June 1991, pp. 12–22.

18. Andrea Gerlin, "A Matter of Degree: How a Jury Decided That One Coffee Spill Is Worth $2.9 Million," *Wall Street Journal*, September 1, 1994, p. A1; and "Jury Says Coffee Too Hot," *USA TODAY*, August 19, 1994, p. B-1.

19. Adapted with permission from *Real-World Lessons for America's Small Business: Insights from the Blue Chip Enterprise Initiative 1994*, pp. 91–92. Copyright 1994 by Mass Mutual—The Blue Chip Company.

20. From "New Twist on an Old Cup of Joe; Caffeinated Water Joins Beverage Fray," *Dallas Morning News*, April 16, 1996, Copyright 1996. Reprinted with permission of the Dallas Morning News.

chapter 11

1. Adapted from Ronald Henkoff, "Service Is Everybody's Business," *Fortune*, June 27, 1994, p. 48.

2. Theodore Levitt, *The Marketing Imagination* (New York: Free Press, 1986), p. 96.

3. Adapted from Alan Salomon, "Doubletree—Marketing 100," *Advertising Age*, June 30, 1997, p. S36.

4. Adapted with permission from Roger D. Blackwell, *From Mind to Market* (New York: Harper Business, 1997), pp. 105–107.

5. Leonard L. Berry, Valerie Zeithaml, and A. Parasuraman, "Responding to Demand Fluctuations: Key Challenges for Service Businesses," in R. Belk et al., eds., *A.M.A. Educators' Proceedings* (Chicago: American Marketing Association, 1985), pp. 231–234.

6. Adapted from Ronald Henkoff, "Service Is Everybody's Business," *Fortune*, June 27, 1994, p. 48.

7. Jack Bishop, "Waiters Take Orders by Computer," *Cook's*, July-August 1990, p. 11.

8. For some interesting research on this topic, see John Ozment and Edward A. Morash, "The Augmented Service Offering for Perceived and Actual Service Quality," *Journal of the Academy of Marketing Science*, Fall 1994, pp. 352–363.

9. Mary Jo Bitner, "Evaluating Service Encounters: The Effects of Physical Surroundings and Employee Responses," *Journal of Marketing*, April 1990, pp. 68–82. See also Ruth N. Dolton and James H. Drew, "A Longitudinal Analysis of the Impact of Service Changes on Customer Attitudes," *Journal of Marketing*, January 1991, pp. 1–9; Keith B. Murray, "A Test of Service Marketing Theory," *Journal of Marketing*, January 1991, pp. 10–25; Raymond P. Fisk, Stephen J. Grove, and Mary Jo Bitner, "Dramatizing the Service Experience: A Managerial Approach," in Teresa A. Swartz, Stephen W. Brown, and David E. Bowen, eds., *Advances in Services Marketing and Management: Research and Practice* (Greenwich, CT: JAI Press, 1992).

10. Adapted from Rahul Jacob, "Why Some Customers Are More Equal Than Others," *Fortune*, September 14, 1994, p. 215.

11. Adapted from Doug Carroll, "Avis Has a License to Celebrate," *USA*

TODAY, October 30, 1991, p. 10E. Copyright 1991, USA TODAY. Reprinted with permission.

12. Ronald Henkoff, "Service Is Everybody's Business," *Fortune*, June 27, 1994, p. 49.

13. Christian Gronroos, "Relationship Marketing: The Strategy Continuum," *Journal of the Academy of Marketing Science*, Fall 1955, p. 252.

14. Patricia M. Doney and Joseph P. Cannon, "An Examination of the Nature of Trust in Buyer-Seller Relationships," *Journal of Marketing*, April 1997, pp. 35–51.

15. Mary Jo Bitner, "Building Service Relationships: It's All About Promises," *Journal of the Academy of Marketing Science*, Fall 1995, p. 246.

16. Leonard L. Berry, "Relationship Marketing of Services," *Journal of the Academy of Marketing Science*, Fall 1995, pp. 236–245.

17. Theodore Levitt, "Marketing Intangible Products and Product Intangibles," *Harvard Business Review*, May-June 1981, pp. 94–102.

18. Regis McKenna, "Marketing Is Everything," *Harvard Business Review*, January-February 1991, pp. 65–79.

19. Frederick F. Reichheld and W. Earl Sasser, Jr., "Zero Defections: Quality Comes from Services," *Harvard Business Review*, September-October 1990, pp. 105–111.

20. Eleena de Lisser, "Retailing: Retailers Are Trying Harder to Please Regular Customers," *Wall Street Journal*, May 5, 1994.

21. Leonard L. Berry, "Relationship Marketing of Services," *Journal of the Academy of Marketing Science*, Fall 1995, pp. 236–245.

22. Nichole M. Christian, "Autos: One Weekend, 52 Jeeps, a Chance to Bond," *Wall Street Journal*, May 23, 1997.

23. Don Peppers, "How Technology Has Changed Marketing," *Forbes ASAP: A Technology Supplement*, April 10, 1995.

24. John Foley, "Market of One: Ready, Aim, Sell!" *Informationweek*, February 17, 1997.

25. Christine Moorman, Rohit Deshpande, and Gerald Zaltman, "Factors Affecting Trust in Market Research Relationships," *Journal of Marketing*, January 1993, pp. 81–101.

26. Robert Morgan and Shelby Hunt, "The Commitment-Trust Theory of Relationship Marketing," *Journal of Marketing*, July 1994, pp. 20–38.

27. Adapted with permission from "AOL to Give Out Home Phone Numbers," Associated Press, July 24, 1997, and "AOL Won't Give Out Numbers," Associated Press, July 25, 1997.

28. Christine Moorman, Rohit Deshpande, and Gerald Zaltman, "Factors Affecting Trust in Market Research Relationships," *Journal of Marketing*, January 1993, pp. 81–101.

29. Greg W. Marshall and Stephen J. Miller, "Does the Domain of Marketing Include Internal Customers within the Total Quality Management Movement?" *Proceedings of the 1991 American Marketing Association's Summer Educator's Conference* (Chicago: American Marketing Association, 1991).

30. For an interesting article see Mary C. Gilly and Mary Wolfinbarger, "Advertising's Internal Audience," *Journal of Marketing*, January 1998, pp. 69–88.

31. Excerpted with permission from Rahul Jacob, "Why Some Customers Are More Equal Than Others," *Fortune*, September 19, 1994, p. 224.

32. Adapted by permission from Debbie Seaman, "In Company B, Delta Snaps to Attention," *Adweek's Marketing Week*, April 11, 1988, p. 26.

33. "What's Ahead for Travel Industry," *Advertising Age*, January 22, 1990, p. 22.

34. Adapted from R. A. Baron and P. B. Paulus, "Group Seekers and Avoiders: How Well-Suited Are You for Working in Groups?" in *Understanding Human Relations*, 2d ed., pp. 286–287. Copyright © 1991 by Allyn & Bacon. Reprinted by permission.

35. Adapted by permission from *Strengthening America's Competitiveness*, pp. 78–79, copyright 1991 by Connecticut Mutual Life Insurance Company, now known as Massachusetts Mutual Life Insurance Company.

36. Adapted from "A Winning Partnership," *Brandweek*, June 13, 1994, and Millie Takaki, "Proposal for Big Bucks Against Drugs May Mean More PSAs," *SHOOT*, March 28, 1997, p. 7. © 1994/97 BPI Communications, Inc. Used with permission from *Brandweek* and *Shoot* magazines.

chapter 12

1. Adapted with permission from John Labate, "Companies to Watch," *Fortune*, May 2, 1994, p. 79. © 1994 Time Inc. All rights reserved.

2. Wroe Alderson, *Marketing Behavior and Executive Action* (Homewood, IL: Richard D. Irwin, 1957).

3. For an interesting study, see Charles R. Duke and Margaret A. Persia, "Purchasing Issue Importance in Service Channels of Distribution: Tour Operators and Travel Agents," in Michael Levy and Dhuruv Grewal, eds., *Developments in Marketing Science*, Vol. XVI (1993), pp. 405–408.

4. Excerpted from Peter T. White, "The Power of Money," *National Geographic*, January 1993, p. 82; as it appears in John Naisbitt, *Global Paradox* (New York: Morrow, 1994), pp. 10–11.

5. For an excellent discussion of the environmental forces that affect channel length, see Arun Sharma and Luis Dominguez, "Channel Evolution: A Framework for Analysis," *Journal of the Academy of Marketing Science*, Winter 1992, pp. 1–16.

6. Paul Resnick and Richard Zeckhauser, "Roles for Electronic Brokers," based on a paper presented at the Twenty-Second Annual Telecommunications Policy Research Conference, October 1994. Downloaded from the Internet June 1, 1997.

7. Excerpt reprinted with permission from Alex Taylor III, "How to Buy a Car on the Internet . . . and Other New Ways to Make the Second-Biggest Purchase of a Lifetime," *Fortune*, March 4, 1996, pp. 163 and 167.

8. Information from "Caterpillar's Backbone: A Long Dealer Network," *Business Week*, May 4, 1981, p. 77; Geoffrey Brewer, "Industrial and Farm Equipment: Caterpillar Inc.," *Sales and Marketing Management*, September 1, 1993; Hillary Durgin, "The Caterpillar's Meow," *Crain's Chicago Business*, March 21, 1994; Bob Bouyea, "This Competitive Edge No Longer Seems Jagged," *Peoria Journal Star*, October 19, 1993; "Cat Signs New Joint Venture, Puts Down More Roots in CIS," *Peoria Journal Star*, February 8, 1994; and "Cat Joins with Russian Truck Maker," *Peoria Journal Star*, December 4, 1993.

9. Excerpt adapted and reprinted with permission from Debra Sparks, "The Card Game," *Financial World*, July 5, 1994, pp. 28–29.

10. "Caterpillar's Backbone: A Long Dealer Network," *Business Week*, May 4, 1981, p. 77.

11. Marshall Fisher, "Japanese Distribution," *The Wharton Report*, Financial News Network, December 4, 1989.

12. Michael R. Czinkota, Ilkka A. Ronkainen, and Michael H. Moffett, *International Business* (Ft. Worth, TX: Dryden Press, 1994), p. 656.

13. Kenneth A. Hunt, Susan P. Keaveney, and Jeffrey E. Danes, "Power and Compliance: An Investigation in a Channel Behavior Setting," in Michael Levy and Dhuruv Grewal, eds., *Developments in Marketing Science*, Vol. XVI (1993), pp. 589–593; Jeffrey C. Dilts and George E. Prough, "Perceived Environmental Uncertainty and Perceptions of the Channel Relationship," in Robert L. King, ed., *Developments in Marketing Science*, Volume XIV (1991), pp. 96–100; David H. Strutton, Lou E. Pelton, and R. Keith Tudor, "The Relationship of Channel Structure, Climate, and Power to Exchange: Pennington Revisited," in Victoria L. Crittenden, ed., *Developments in Marketing Science*, Vol. XV (1992), pp. 11–15; William H. Redmond and Nancy Merritt, "Multifunctional Relations in Channel Partnerships," in Michael Levy and Dhuruv Grewal, eds., *Developments in Marketing Science*, Vol. XVI (1993), pp. 119–123; and Kaushik Mitra, Samantha J. Rice, and Stephen A. LeMay, "Postponement and Speculation in Exchange Relationships: A Transaction Cost Approach," in Joyce A. Young, Dale L. Varble, and Faye W. Gilbert, eds., *Proceedings of the Southwestern Marketing Association* (Terre Haute: Indiana State University and Southwestern Marketing Association, 1997), pp. 18–25.

14. A detailed discussion of conflict within the channel of distribution can be found in John F. Gaski, "The Theory of Power and Conflict in Channels of Distribution," *Journal of Marketing*, Summer 1984, pp. 9–29. For more recent research in this area, see Gary L. Frazier and Raymond C. Rody, "The Use of Influence Strategies in Interfirm Relationships in Industrial Product Channels," *Journal of Marketing*, January 1991, pp. 52–69; Jakki Mohr and John R. Nevin, "Communication Strategies in Marketing Channels: A Theoretical Perspective," *Journal of Marketing*, October 1990, pp. 36–51; and James C. Anderson and James A. Narus, "A Model of Distributor Firm and Manufacturer Firm Working Partnerships," *Journal of Marketing*, January 1990, pp. 42–59.

15. Madeline Johnson and Charles R. Strain, "Retailers' Perceptions of Their Recycling Programs," in Joyce A. Young, Dale L. Varble, and Faye W. Gilbert, eds., *Proceedings of the Southwestern Marketing Association* (Terre Haute: Indiana State University and Southwestern Marketing Association, 1997), pp. 128–134.

16. Excerpted by permission from *Real World Lessons for America's Small Business*, pp. 52–53, copyright 1992 by the Connecticut Mutual Life Insurance Company, now known as Massachusetts Mutual Life Insurance Company.

17. Adapted by permission from *Strengthening America's Competitiveness*, p. 56, copyright 1991 by the Connecticut Mutual Life Insurance Company, now known as Massachusetts Mutual Life Insurance Company.

chapter 13

1. Excerpted from Mary Beth Grover, "Teenage Wasteland," *Forbes*, July 28, 1997, pp. 44–45. Reprinted by permission of FORBES Magazine. © Forbes Inc., 1997.

2. It is common to use sales figures to differentiate between retailers and other intermediaries. If an intermediary makes more than 50 percent of its sales to consumers, that intermediary is counted as a retailer in the U.S. government's Census of Retail Trade.

3. U.S. Bureau of the Census, *1992 Census of Retail Trade*, found at www.census.gov/econ/www/retmenu.html.

4. The convenience shopping style, the price trade-off, and the convenience shopper are examined in Joseph A. Bellizzi and Robert E. Hite, "Convenience Consumption and Role Overload," *Journal of the Academy of Marketing Science*, Winter 1986, pp. 1–9.

5. Excerpt reprinted with permission from Dana Canedy, "Supermarkets Get a Brand New Bag," *New York Times*, August 31, 1997, p. 3–1. Copyright © 1997 by The New York Times Co. Reprinted by permission.

6. Becky Tiernan, "Area Ford Dealers to Unite," *Tulsa World*, November 25, 1997, p. A-1; "Ford Announces New Retail Distribution Initiatives in Tulsa and San Diego," *PRNewswire*, November 24, 1997; and Earle Eldridge, "Ford Dealers in Tulsa Plan Joint Venture," *USA TODAY*, November 24, 1997, p. 23b.

7. Troy A. Festervand, Don R. Snyder, and John D. Tsalikis, "Influence of Catalog vs. Store Shopping and Prior Satisfaction on Perceived Risk," *Journal of the Academy of Marketing Science*, Winter 1986, p. 37; and Jon M. Hawes and James R. Lumpkin, "Perceived Risk and the Selection of a Retail Patronage Mode," *Journal of the Academy of Marketing Science*, Winter 1986, p. 37.

8. Adapted from Junu Bryan Kim, "Bose Wave—Marketing 100," *Advertising Age*, June 30, 1997, p. S29.

9. Information from Beverly Martin, "Machine Dreams," *Brandweek*, April 26, 1993, pp. 17–22. © 1993 ASM Communications, Inc. Used with permission from *Brandweek* magazine.

10. Information from Erin Flynn, "American Greetings Cards Creates a New Card Pitch," *Brandweek*, November 14, 1994, p. 24. Adapted with permission from M. R. Kropko, "Card Makers Struggling with Computer Kiosks," *Marketing News*, June 3, 1996, p. 6.

11. Adapted with permission of *Progressive Grocer* from Stephen Bennett, "Natural Foods: A Fad No More," *Progressive Grocer*, May 1, 1994.

12. Reprinted from Jeff Moad, "Taking Stock: New Closed-Loop Decision-Support Systems Are Helping Companies Such as Wal-Mart Automate Fast Responses to Market Changes," *PC Week*, May 26, 1997. Copyright © 1997 Ziff-Davis.

13. Adapted with permission from Patricia Sellers, "Look Who Learned about Value," *Fortune*, October 18, 1993, pp. 75, 78; with updates from Andrew Serwer, "McDonald's Conquers the World," *Fortune*, October 1994, pp. 103–117.

14. Ronald D. Taylor and Blaise J. Bergiel, "Chain Store Executives' Ratings of Critical Site Selection Factors," *Journal of Midwest Marketing*, Fall 1988, pp. 37–49.

15. For interesting discussions of this issue, see Mary Jo Bitner, "Servicescapes: The Impact of Physical Surroundings on Customers and Employees," *Journal of Marketing*, April 1992, pp. 57–71; and Joseph A. Bellizzi, Ayn E. Crowley, and Ronald W. Hasty, "The Effects of Color on Store Design," *Journal of Retailing*, Spring 1983, pp. 21–57.

16. Eleena de Lisser, "Retailing: Retailers Are Trying Harder To Please Regular Customers," *Wall Street Journal*, May 5, 1994.

17. Michael Levy and Barton A. Weitz, *Retailing Management* (Burr Ridge, IL: Irwin, 1992), p. 101.

18. This section is adapted with permission from Elizabeth Malkin, "Mexican Retail Can Be a Game of Chicken," *Advertising Age International*, November 21, 1994, p. I21. Copyright Crain Communications Inc. All rights reserved.

19. U.S. Bureau of the Census, *1992 Census of Wholesale Trade*, found at www.census.gov/epcd/www/wc92html.html.

20. U.S. Bureau of the Census, *1992 Census of Wholesale Trade*, found at www.census.gov/epcd/www/wc92html.html.

21. Adapted by permission from *Insights and Inspiration: How Businesses Succeed*, pp. 100–101. Copyright 1995 by the Connecticut Mutual Life Insurance Company, now known as Massachusetts Mutual Life Insurance Company.

22. Reprinted with permission from *Texas Monthly's* Internet Web site located at www.texasmonthly.com/food/resto/lakes.html. Additional information from *Wall Street Journal* Interactive Edition, "Marketplace Front, Latest Restaurant Innovation Looks a Lot Like a Grocery," www.interactive.wsj.com.

chapter 14

1. Adapted with permission from James Kim, "Dell: Built-to-Order Success," *USA TODAY*, June 30, 1997. Copyright 1997, USA TODAY. Reprinted with permission.

2. James C. Johnson and Donald F. Wood, *Contemporary Physical Distribution* (New York: Macmillan, 1986), p. 415.

3. Rahul Jacob, "Why Some Customers Are More Equal Than Others," *Fortune*, September 19, 1994, pp. 218–220.

4. Adapted from Martin Keller, "A Pet Project," *Express Magazine*, a publication of Federal Express Corporation, Winter 1990, pp. 6–7.

5. Adapted with permission from Rahul Jacob, "Why Some Customers Are More Equal Than Others," *Fortune*, September 19, 1994, p. 220.

6. Adapted with permission from Steve Bates, "The Dog Ate My Shipment!" *Nation's Business*, December 1997, p. 37.

7. Adapted from Jon Tevlin, "Mexico Calling," *Express Magazine*, a publication of Federal Express Corporation, Winter 1992, p. 19.

8. Adapted with permission from Ronald Henkoff, "Delivering the Goods: Logistics Has Become a Hot Competitive Advantage as Companies Struggle to Get the Right Stuff to the Right Place at the Right Time," *Fortune*, November 11, 1994, pp. 64, 75, 76.

9. For an interesting discussion of JIT, see Joyce A. Young and Faye W. Gilbert, "Just-in-Time Purchasing: A New Commitment between Manufacturers and Suppliers," in Joseph F. Hair, Jr., Daryl O. McKee, and Daniel L. Sherrell, eds., *Advances in Marketing* (Baton Rouge: Southwest Marketing Association, 1992), pp. 157–163.

10. Adapted with permission from Roger D. Blackwell, *From Mind to Market* (New York: Harper Business, 1997), pp. 152–153.

chapter 15

1. Adapted with permission from "Return of the Best-Seller: Trivial Pursuit Attracts New Converts on the Web," *MediaWeek*, May 5, 1997, p. S60. © 1997 ASM Communications Inc. Used with permission from *MediaWeek* magazine.

2. Adapted from Kevin Goldman, "Coke Contours New Ads to Fit Cultural Icon of Shapely Bottle," *Wall Street Journal*, February 14, 1995, p. B6. Reprinted by permission of *Wall Street Journal*, © 1995 Dow Jones & Company, Inc. All Rights Reserved Worldwide.

3. Reprinted with permission from "House of Blues—Marketing 100," in the June 30, 1997 issue of *Advertising Age*. Copyright, Crain Communications Inc., 1997.

4. Adapted from Mark D. Fefer, "Taking the Pain Out of Holding Patterns," *Fortune*, January 10, 1994, p. 20.

5. Adapted from "Special K Drops Thin Models," Associated Press, February 6, 1998.

6. H. D. Lasswell, *Power and Personality* (New York: W. W. Norton, 1948).

7. Pierre Martineau, *Motivation in Advertising* (New York: McGraw-Hill, 1957), p. 154.

8. The hierarchy of communication effects model has been portrayed in several other forms. A common one includes awareness, interest, evaluation, trial, and adoption. Another model includes attention, interest, desire, and action (AIDA). The nature of the model depends on consumer involvement.

9. Based in part on Thomas E. Barry, "The Dr Pepper Company," in W. G. Zikmund, W. Lundstrom, and D. Sciglimpaglia, eds., *Cases in Marketing Research* (Hinsdale, IL: Dryden Press, 1982), p. 151.

10. Mark Gleason and Alan Salomon, "Fallon's Challenge: Make Holiday Inn More 'In'," *Advertising Age*, September 2, 1996, p. 14.

11. Adapted from Jane Weaver, "Girl Scout Campaign: Shedding Old Image for MTV Cool," *Adweek*, September 11, 1989, p. 68. © ADWEEK, L.P. Used with permission from Adweek.

12. Elmer Wheeler, *Tested Sentences That Sell* (Englewood Cliffs, NJ: Prentice Hall, 1937).

13. Adapted from "Border Crossings: Brands Unify Image to Counter Cult of Culture," *Brandweek*, October 31, 1994. © 1994 ASM Communications Inc. Used with permission from *Brandweek* magazine.

14. Herbert Katzenstein and William Sacks, *Direct Marketing*, 2nd ed. (New York: Macmillan, 1992), p. 5.

15. Copyright 1994 Bill Communications. All but the questions at the end excerpted from Bruce Horovitz, "Statue of Liberty Tobacco Ad Ignites Firestorm," *USA TODAY*, April 27, 1995, p. B1.2. Copyright 1995, USA TODAY. Reprinted with permission.

16. Adapted by permission from *Strengthening America's Competitiveness*, p. 93. Copyright 1991 by Connecticut Mutual Life Insurance Company, now known as Massachusetts Mutual Life Insurance Company.

chapter 16

1. Reprinted from "Sprite Raps 'Image,' While Embracing It," in the April 21, 1997 issue of *Advertising Age*. Copyright, Crain Communications Inc., 1997.

2. Reprinted from "Snickers Ads Grab the Elusive 'Big Idea'," in the September 2, 1996 issue of *Advertising Age*. Copyright, Crain Communications Inc., 1996.

3. "Campbell Launches New Soup Campaign: M'm! M'm! Good for the Body, Good for the Soul," *PR Newswire*, February 9, 1998.

4. Reprinted from "Fashion Gives Sex Another Try," in the October 31, 1994 issue of *Advertising Age*. Copyright, Crain Communications Inc., 1994.

5. Reprinted from "A Powerful Message," in the September 16, 1996 issue of *Advertising Age*. Copyright, Crain Communications Inc., 1996.

6. Excerpts reprinted from Joe Urschel, "The Song That Chevy Rocks to: Three Words That Evolved into a Corporate Hymn," *USA TODAY*, January 5, 1996. Copyright 1996, USA TODAY. Reprinted with permission.
Lyrics to "Like a Rock":
Stood there boldly sweatin' in the sun
Felt like a million, felt like number one
The height of summer, I'd never felt that strong
Like a rock
My hands were steady, my eyes were clear and bright
My walk had purpose, my steps were quick and light
And I held firmly to what I thought was right
Like a rock
Like a rock, I was strong as I could be
Like a rock, nothing ever got to me
Like a rock, I was something to see
Twenty years now, where'd they go
Twenty years I don't know
I sit and I wonder sometimes
Where they've gone
And sometimes late at night when I'm bathed in the firelight
The moon comes callin' a ghostly white
And I recall . . . I recall
Like a rock . . .

7. Excerpted from Craig Bloom, "Translating Quintessential British Humor for Americans," *New York Times*, August 19, 1990, p. F5. © 1990 by The New York Times Company. Reprinted by permission.

8. First paragraph adapted from Patricia Sellers, "The Best Way to Reach Your Buyers," *Fortune*, Autumn-Winter 1993, pp. 14, 16. Second paragraph adapted from Nicholas Negroponte, *Being Digital* (New York: Knopf, 1995), pp. 168–169.

9. Robert J. Coen, "Ad Spending Tops 175 Billion during Robust '96," *Advertising Age*, May 12, 1997, p. 20.

10. Nicholas Negroponte, *Being Digital* (New York: Knopf, 1995), p. 6.

11. Lee Fleming, "Digital Delivery: Pushing Content to the Desktop," downloaded from the Digital Information Group, 1997.

12. Lee Fleming, "Digital Delivery: Pushing Content to the Desktop," downloaded from the Digital Information Group, 1997.

13. Lee Fleming, "Digital Delivery: Pushing Content to the Desktop," downloaded from the Digital Information Group, 1997.

14. Debra Aho Williamson, "The Agents of Change Are Sweeping into Internet Advertising: Smart Agents Build Brains into Net Ads," *Advertising Age*, April 8, 1996.

15. Reprinted from "TRUSTe Pitches Its Seal of Approval," in the June 9, 1997 issue of *Advertising Age*. Copyright, Crain Communications Inc., 1997.

16. Based on information from I. Jeanne Dugan, "Pain in Pleasantville: Reader's Digest's Scary Story: Lower Profits, Fewer Readers," *Business Week*, July 14, 1997, p. 62; "Reader's Digest CEO Schadt Quits Abruptly," *Los Angeles Times*, August 12, 1997, p. D-3; Tracy Corrigan, "Investors Impatient with Reader's Digest," *Financial Times—London Edition*, August 13, 1997; G. Bruce Knecht, "Reader's Digest Replaces Its CEO with George Grune," *Wall Street Journal*, August 12, 1997.

17. Steve J. Grove and William E. Kilbourne, "A Mertonian Approach to the Analysis of Advertising's Role in Society: From Polemics to Discourse," in Robert P. Leone, V. Kumar, Peter J. Gordon, and Bert J. Kellerman, eds., *1992 AMA Educator's Proceedings: Enhancing Knowledge Development in Marketing* (Chicago: American Marketing Association, 1992), p. 441; and Joe F. Alexander, Ernest F. Cooke, and Michael A. Turk, "An Examination of that Form of Deception Called Puffery," in Kenneth D. Bahn, ed., *Developments in Marketing Science*, vol. XI (Montreal: Academy of Marketing Science, 1988), pp. 247–250.

18. See, for example, Lois J. Smith, "Children's Advertising: Difference in Advertisers' Approaches for Girls and Boys," in *Proceedings of the Midwest Marketing Association* (1994), pp. 79–84; Lois J. Smith, "Children and Television Violence: Public Policy and Advertisers' Perspectives," in *Proceedings of the Midwest Marketing Association* (1991), pp. 88–91; Michael L. Klassen, Lisa Barkema, and Fred Meisenheimer, "Nutrition Claims in Children's Food Commercials," in *Proceedings of the Midwest Marketing Association* (1993), pp. 79–82; Srivatsa Seshadri and C. P. Rao, "Considerations in Advertising Directed toward Children," and Les Carlson, Russell N. Lacznik, and Darrel D. Muehling, "Antecedents of Mother's Perceptions of Toy-Based Programming—An Empirical Investigation," in Robert P. Leone, V. Kumar, Peter Gordon, and Bert J. Kellerman, eds. *1992 AMA Educator's Proceedings: Enhancing Knowledge Development in Marketing* (Chicago: American Marketing Association, 1992).

19. V. Kanti Prasad and Lois J. Smith, "Television Commercials in Violent Programming: An Experimental Evaluation of Their Effects on Children," *Journal of the Academy of Marketing Science*, Fall 1994, pp. 340–351.

20. Reprinted from "Carpe Dyin'," in the February 1991 issue of *Advertising Age, Special Creativity Insert*. Copyright, Crain Communications Inc., 1991.

chapter 17

1. Adapted from Kevin McManus, "Selling," *Changing Times*, October 1990, pp. 48–56. Copyright © 1990 The Kiplinger Washington Editors, Inc.

2. Gerald L. Manning and Barry L. Reece, *Selling Today: A Personal Approach* (Boston: Allyn and Bacon, 1990), p. 6.

3. Theodore Levitt, *The Marketing Imagination* (New York: Macmillan, 1986), p. 111.

4. Nancy Arnott, "Selling Is Dying," *Sales & Marketing Management*, June 1, 1994.

5. Excerpted with permission from Jaclyn Fierman, "The Death and Rebirth of the Salesman," *Fortune*, July 25, 1994, pp. 86, 88. © 1994 Time Inc. All rights reserved.

6. Adapted with permission from Jaclyn Fierman, "The Death and Rebirth of the Salesman," *Fortune*, July 25, 1994, p. 86. © 1994 Time Inc. All rights reserved.

7. From A PASSION FOR EXCELLENCE by Thomas J. Peters and Nancy K. Austin. Copyright © 1985 by Thomas J. Peters and Nancy K. Austin. Reprinted by permission of Random House, Inc.

8. Reprinted with permission from Franklin R. Root, *Entry Strategies for International Markets.* Copyright © 1987 Jossey-Bass Inc., Publishers. First published by Lexington Books. All rights reserved. See also John L. Graham, "The Influence of Culture on the Process of Business Negotiations: An Exploratory Study," *Journal of International Business Studies*, Spring 1985, pp. 81–96.

9. Stephen X. Doyle and George T. Roth, "Selling and Sales Management in Action: The Use of Insight Coaching to Improve Relationship Selling," *Journal of Personal Selling and Sales Management*, Winter 1992, pp. 59–64.

10. Excerpted from Jeffery Young, "Hit the Road, Jack: IBM's Wandering Tribe," *Forbes ASAP*, August 28, 1995, p. 93. Reprinted by permission of FORBES ASAP Magazine. © Forbes Inc., 1995.

11. Personal correspondence to William G. Zikmund from Bill Kelly, January 29, 1988.

12. Adapted from Kenichi Ohmae, *The Borderless World* (New York: McKinsey & Company, Inc., 1990), pp. 17–18. Copyright © 1990 by McKinsey & Company, Inc. Reprinted by permission of HarperCollins Publishers Inc.

13. Gregory A. Rich, "The Sales Manager as a Role Model," *Journal of the Academy of Marketing Science*, Fall 1997, pp. 319–328.

14. Eric Sevareid, *Enterprise: The Marketing of Business in America* (New York: McGraw-Hill, 1983), p. 13.

15. For an excellent discussion of some of the issues faced by salespeople, see Karl A. Boedecker, Fred W. Morgan, and Jeffrey J. Stoltman, "Legal Dimensions of Salespersons' Statements: A Review and Managerial Suggestions," *Journal of Marketing*, January 1991, pp. 70–80.

chapter 18

1. Reprinted with permission from Elaine Underwood, "U.S. Vintners Are Bearing Fruit with a Cultural, Culinary Approach," *Brandweek*, September 5, 1994, pp. 28–29.

2. Donnelley Marketing, *Annual Survey of Promotional Practices*, 1993.

3. William H. Murphy, "Even Roses Have Thorns: Functional and Dysfunctional Effects of Sales Contests on Sales Personnel," in Robert P. Leone, V. Kumar, Peter J. Gordon, and Bert J. Kellerman, eds., 1992 *AMA Educator's Proceedings: Enhancing Knowledge Development in Marketing* (Chicago: American Marketing Association, 1992), p. 402.

4. Scott M. Cultip, Allen H. Center, and Glen M. Broom, *Effective Public Relations* (Englewood Cliffs, NJ: Prentice Hall, 1985), p. 4.

5. Reprinted with permission from Rayna Skolnik, "Portraits of the 'Most Admired' Companies: How Public Relations Helps Build Corporate Reputations," *Public Relations Journal*, May 1, 1994. Copyright Public Relations Society of America 1994.

6. Adapted from "Campbell Soup Company Introduces Convenient, 32-Ounce Resealable Carton for Swanson Chicken Broth," *PRNewswire*, October 31, 1996.

7. "Tony Bennett," *Advertising Age*, July 4, 1994, p. S-25.

8. Gerry Khermouch, "It's Miller Time Around the World: NBA's International Expansion Should Boost Genuine Draft Beer," *Adweek* Eastern Edition, July 11, 1994.

9. Terry Lefton, "MasterCard World Cup Promotion," *Brandweek*, September 19, 1994, p. 34.

10. Robert Morris, "Banking on the Olympic Games," *Business Journal–Charlotte*, August 15, 1994.

11. Adapted with permission from Chuck Stogel, "Chemical Bank Corporate Challenge," *BrandWeek*, September 19, 1994, p. 43. © 1994 ASM

Communications, Inc. Used with permission from *Brandweek* magazine.

12. Philip Lesly, ed., *Lesly's Handbook of Public Relations and Communications*, 4th ed. (New York: AMACOM, 1991), p. 340.

13. Michael Himowitz, "Pentium Flaw May Be More Important Than Intel Says," *Tulsa World*, December 11, 1994, p. B-10; Kevin Maney, "IBM Won't Sell PCs with Flawed Intel Chip," *USA Today*, December 13, 1994, p. 1A; "IBM Stops Pentium PC Shipments," PRODIGY® interactive personal service, December 12, 1994; James G. Kimball, "Can Intel Repair Pentium PR?" *Advertising Age*, December 19, 1994, p. 36; and James Kim, "Intel Puts Chips on the Table," *USA TODAY*, December 21, 1994, pp. B1–B2.

14. Philip Lesly, ed., *Lesly's Handbook of Public Relations and Communications*, 4th ed. (New York: AMACOM, 1991), p. 15.

15. Adapted by permission from *Insights and Inspiration: How Businesses Succeed*, pp. 27–28. Copyright 1995 by Connecticut Mutual Life Insurance Company, now known as Massachusetts Mutual Life Insurance Company.

16. *Gourmet Our Way* (Memphis: Wimmer, 1996), p. 11.

chapter 19

1. From Barbara Woller, "Long-Distance Callers Cash In on Incentives," *USA TODAY*, July 27, 1995, pp. 1C–2C. Copyright 1995, USA TODAY. Reprinted with permission.

2. During periods of inflation, price's importance in the marketing mix is rated higher by managers. See Saeed Samiee, "Pricing in Marketing Strategies of U.S.- and Foreign-Based Companies," *Journal of Business Research*, February 1987, pp. 17–30.

3. © 1996 Wired Magazine Group, Inc. All rights reserved. Adapted with permission from "Advertising Webonomics 101" by Evan Schwartz. *Wired* 4.02.

4. Adapted from "Business 2000: The New World Order" (Special Advertising Section), *Inc.*, December 1993, p. 51. Copyright © 1993 by Goldhirsh Group, Inc.

5. See Hugh M. Cannon and Fred W. Morgan, "A Strategic Pricing Framework," *Journal of Consumer Marketing*, Summer 1990, p. 62. The relationship of price and product quality over time is discussed in David J. Curry and Peter C. Riesz, "Prices and Price/Quality Relationships: A Longitudinal Analysis," *Journal of Marketing*, January 1988, pp. 36–51. See also Jerry B. Gotlieb and Dan Sarel, "The Influence of Type of Advertisement, Price, and Source Credibility on Perceived Quality," *Journal of the Academy of Marketing Science*, Summer 1992, pp. 253–260.

6. Adapted with permission from Gautam Naik, "Sprint Scales Back Fridays Free Plan," *Wall Street Journal*, April 11, 1996. Reprinted by permission of *Wall Street Journal*, © 1996 Dow Jones & Company, Inc. All Rights Reserved Worldwide.

7. Excerpt reprinted from "Toy Scalpers Buy Scarce Items, Then Resell Them at a Profit," *Wall Street Journal Interactive Edition*, June 24, 1996. Reprinted by permission of *Wall Street Journal*, © 1996 Dow Jones & Company, Inc. All Rights Reserved Worldwide.

chapter 20

1. Adapted from Chris Woodyard, "Circuit City Tacks 15% Fee on Some Returns," *USA TODAY*, December 26, 1997, p. 1b. Copyright 1997, USA TODAY. Reprinted with permission.

2. This chapter has been greatly influenced by the work of Gerald J. Tellis. The authors strongly suggest that readers review his important paper on pricing strategy; see Gerald J. Tellis, "Beyond the Many Faces of Price: An Integration of Pricing Strategy," *Journal of Marketing*, October 1986, pp. 146–160. Because our purpose differs from his, terminology employed here differs somewhat from Tellis's.

3. Some prices are actually "consumer negotiated." See Kenneth R. Evans and Richard F. Beltramini, "A Theoretical Model of Consumer Negotiated Pricing: An Orientation Perspective," *Journal of Marketing*, April 1987, pp. 58–73.

4. Adapted from Jeffrey A. Trachtenberg, "Sony, Unfazed by Flops, Rolls Out MiniDisc for Third Time in U.S.," *Wall Street Journal*, July 24, 1996, p. B5. Reprinted by permission of *Wall Street Journal*, © 1996 Dow Jones & Company, Inc. All Rights Reserved Worldwide.

5. Erin M. Davies, "The Brand's the Thing," *Fortune*, March 4, 1996.

6. Robert LaForbes Franco, "Take That, Nintendo," *Forbes,* June 3, 1996.

7. From Becky Ebenkamp, "Drawing a New Frontier," *Brandweek,* May 5, 1997, p. 17. © 1997 ASM Communications Inc. Used with permission from *Brandweek* magazine.

8. R. Lee Sullivan, "School for Cheerleaders," *Forbes,* October 25, 1993, p. 118.

9. The per-unit loss is $300. The fixed cost per unit is $400,000/500 = $800. The variable cost per unit remains at $75. However, because there is a loss, there is no target return per unit. The total per-unit cost (fixed cost + variable cost) is thus $875. Subtracting the selling price of $575 yields a $300 per-unit loss. Calculating the target return at 500 units would have yielded a selling price of $1,075: Fixed cost and target return per unit ($1,000) + variable cost per unit ($75) = suggested price per unit ($1,075).

10. Marketers must be careful not to structure discount schedules in ways that encourage buyers to purchase more product than they need and sell the excess on the "black market." See James B. Wilcox, Roy D. Howell, Paul Kuzdrall, and Robert Britney, "Price Quantity Discounts: Some Implications for Buyers and Sellers," *Journal of Marketing,* July 1987, pp. 60–70.

11. For an excellent discussion of the Robinson-Patman Act, see James C. Johnson and Kenneth C. Schneider, "Those Who Can, Do . . . and Those Who Can't . . . : Marketing Professors and the Robinson-Patman Act," *Journal of the Academy of Marketing Science,* Summer 1984, pp. 123–138.

12. Reprinted from "Ceilings Are Legal," *New York Times,* November 9, 1997, p. BU2. © 1997 by the New York Times Co. Reprinted by permission.

13. Theodore Levitt, "The Dangers of Social Responsibility," *Harvard Business Review,* September-October 1958, p. 47.

14. Adapted by permission from *Insights and Inspiration: How Businesses Succeed,* pp. 37–38. Copyright 1995 by Connecticut Mutual Life Insurance Company, now known as Massachusetts Mutual Life Insurance Company.

photo credits

name index

Farley, John V., 296n, 313n
Fawcett, Jeffrey K., 55n
Fefer, Mark D., 469n
Feick, Lawrence F., 185n
Ferrell, O. C., 51n
Festervand, Troy A., 406n
Field, David, 231n
Fierman, Jaclyn, 19n, 541n
Fisher, Bruce D., 88n
Fisher, Marshall, 386n
Fisk, Raymond P., 343n
Fleming, Lee, 84n, 520n
Flynn, Erin, 410n
Foley, John, 353n
Forcinio, Hallie, 45n
Ford, Henry, 18, 35, 229
Forrest, P. J., 52n
Fraedrich, John, 51n
Francese, Peter, 72n, 73, 74n, 76, 140n
Franco, Robert LaForbes, 621n
Frankel, Steven, 272
Frankwick, Gary L., 18n
Frazer, Joseph W., 364
Frazier, Gary L., 387n
Friend, Tim, 88n
Fritzche, David J., 55n
Fujii, Toshio, 67
Fullerton, Ronald A., 17n
Fusillo, Rob, 413

G

Gandhi, Rajiv, 87
Gardner, John, 96
Garvey, Dick, 240
Garvin, David, 318
Gaski, John F., 387n
Gassenheimer, Julie B., 8n
Gassner, Rudy, 106
Gaston, Jim, 120
Geezy, Leslie, 433
Gentry, James W., 69n
George, Robert, 622
Gerlin, Andrea, 330n
Gerstner, Louis, Jr., 102
Ghingold, Morry, 200n
Gilbert, Dennis, 184
Gilbert, Faye W., 54n, 108n, 387n, 398n, 450n
Gilbert, John, 274
Gill, James D., 182n
Gilly, Mary C., 354n
Glazer, Rashi, 81n
Gleason, Mark, 484n
Godfrey, Gail, 355
Goldman, Kevin, 81n, 85n, 465n
Goldstein, Michael, 611
Goll, Sally, 243n
Goodman, Stephen H., 32n
Goolsby, Jerry R., 55n
Gordon, P. S., 586
Gordon, Peter J., 525n, 527n, 570n

Gorney, John, 542
Gotlieb, Jerry B., 598n
Gould, Don, 510
Graham, John L., 548n
Greene, Bob, 534
Greener, C. Scott, 9n
Gresham, Larry G., 51n
Grewal, Dhuruv, 227n, 369n, 387n
Grimm, Matthew, 175n
Gronroos, Christian, 349n
Grove, Stephen J., 343n, 525n
Grover, Mary Beth, 399n
Gubernick, Lisa, 171n

H

Hadock, Calvin L., 324n
Hair, Joseph F., Jr., 65n, 143n, 175n, 450n
Hakmi, Claire, 109
Hallgren, Kenneth G., 85n
Hamel, Gary, 300n
Hamilton, Linda, 469
Hartley-Leonard, Darryl, 597
Hasty, Ronald W., 416n
Hawes, Jon M., 143n, 406n
Hayden, Sterling, 190–191
Heckler, Susan E., 277n
Hegel, G. W., 411
Held, Betty, 585
Held, Jim, 585
Henkoff, Ronald, 208n, 336n, 341n, 349n, 447n
Hill, Barrington, 109
Hill, Grant, 497
Hilmer, Frederick, 105n
Himowitz, Michael, 581n
Hint, James G., 54n
Hint, Shelby, 353n
Hite, Robert E., 403n
Hitt, Michael A., 44n
Holak, Susan L., 16n
Holbrook, Morris B., 134n, 227n
Holder, Ruth, 591
Holloway, Douglas V., 227n
Hopkins, Bob, 565
Hopper, Jo Ann Stilley, 227n
Hornblower, Margot, 96n
Horovitz, Bruce, 492n
Hoskisson, Robert E., 44n
Houston, Franklin S., 8n, 18n
Houston, Michael J., 277n
Hoverstad, Ronald, 176n
Howell, Roy D., 183n, 631n
Huey, John, 79n
Huffman, Cynthia, 640
Hugo, Victor, 126
Hunt, Kenneth A., 387n
Hunt, Shelby D., 51n, 55n, 134n
Hurlburt, Jeff, 510
Hutt, Michael D., 18n, 86n, 201, 205n

I

Imhoff, Daniel, 271n
Infeld, L., 135n
Ireland, R. Duane, 44n
Irwin, Richard D., 107n
Isakson, Mike, 341
Iwata, Jon, 612
Izzo, George, 54n

J

Jacob, Rahul, 344n, 354n, 437n, 441n
Jacobson, Robert, 321n
James, William L., 37n
Jarvi, Joan M., 99n
Javalgi, Rajshekhar G., 163n
Jaworski, Bernard J., 18n
Jervey, Gay, 11n
John, Joby, 65n
Johnson, James C., 434n, 633n
Johnson, Madeline, 389n
Joiner, Christopher, 322n
Jones, D. G. Brian, 17n
Jordan, Michael, 115, 177
Joyce, Alan, 37n
Jun, Sunkyu, 69n

K

Kahl, Joseph, 184
Kaiser, Henry J., 364
Kallis, M. Jeffrey, 90n
Kanter, Rosabeth Moss, 103n
Kantor, Mickey, 94
Kasten, Stan, 4
Katzenstein, Herbert, 488n
Keaveney, Susan P., 387n
Keller, Kevin Lane, 277n
Keller, Martin, 438n
Kellerman, Bert J., 525n, 527n, 570n
Kelley, Scott W., 54n
Kelly, Bill, 550, 551n
Kelly, Mary A., 114n
Kennedy, John F., 54
Kerr, John R., 143n
Kessler, Andrew J., 132n
Ketchum, Brad, 205n
Kevin, Kitty, 20n
Khermouch, Gerry, 39n, 579n
Kijowski, John, 254
Kilborn, Peter T., 76n
Kilbourne, William E., 525n
Kilcoyne, Jim, 565
Kim, James, 433n, 581n
Kim, Junu Bryan, 407n
Kimball, James C., 581n
King, Robert L., 387n
Klassen, Michael L., 527n
Knecht, Bruce G., 523n
Knight, Lester, 441
Knoviser, Bruce I., 275n

Kohli, Ajay K., 18n
Koselka, Rita, 272n, 315n
Kosenko, Rustan, 227n
Kraft, Kenneth L., 23n, 55n
Krentler, Kathleen A., 90n
Kropko, M. R., 410n
Kuhn, Mary, 20n
Kumar, V., 525n, 527n, 570n
Kurth, Terry, 28
Kuzdrall, Paul, 631n

L

LaBant, Robert, 542
Labate, John, 366n
Lacznink, Russell N., 527n
Landis, John, 469
Landon, Alf, 146
Lane, Vicki, 321n
Lansasa, John M., 55n
Lantos, Geoffrey P., 51n
Lasswell, H. D., 471n
Laumann, Edward, 505
Lavalle, Nye, 226
Leale, LeRoy, 565
Lee, Barbara, 469
Lefton, Terry, 580n
Lehmann, Donald R., 296n, 313n
Leigh, Thomas W., 202n
LeMay, Stephen A., 387n
Leone, Robert P., 525n, 527n, 570n
Lesly, Philip, 581n
Levine, Joshua, 234n
Levitt, Theodore, 18n, 19n, 20n, 36n, 190–191, 206n, 267n, 338n, 350, 537n, 635n
Levy, Doug, 49n
Levy, Michael, 194n, 227n, 369n, 387n, 418n
Lewin, Kurt, 161n
Lewis, Pamela S., 32n
Lichtenstein, Donald R., 175n
Lieber, Jill, 5n
Liesse, Julie, 81n
Lincon, D. J., 55n
Lipshultz, Alfred, 395
Lipshultz, Mitchell, 295
Little, T., 55n
Loeb, Marshall, 41n
Loken, John Barbara, 322n
London, David, 143n
Lowe, Larry S., 73n
Lucas, George, 312
Luellen, Cindy, 341
Luke, Alex, 254–255
Lumpkin, James R., 406n
Lundstrom, W., 481n
Lynn, C. Stephen, 121

M

Macdonald, Godfrey Lord, 11
Machefsky, Ira, 521

company index

subject index

Retail selling, 535
Retailer, 13
   sales promotions aimed at, 570–571
Retailer cooperative organization, 381
Retailing, 399
   global, 418–419
   in-store, 401–406
   management strategies for, 413–418
Retailing institutions
   classifying, 399–409
   theories of development of, 409–412
Return on investment (ROI), 600
Reward power, of channel member, 388
Right to be informed (of consumers),
   325
Right to choose (of consumers), 327
Right to safety (of consumers), 325
Risk
   to consumers, 165
   to intermediaries, 375–376
Robinson-Patman Act, 89, 327, 616, 619,
   632–633
Roles, 181–182
   in buying decisions, 187
Routinized response behavior, 162
Rumor control, 581
Russia, 86
Rwanda, 86

S

Salary plus commission, 559
Sales, as measure of advertising
   effectiveness, 525. *See also*
   Personal selling; Sales management
Sales & Marketing Management, 152
Sales branch, 423, 424
Sales force
   automation of, 549–550
   compensation of, 557–559
   evaluation and control of, 560
   motivation of, 559–560
   recruitment of, 555–556
   training of, 556–557
Sales forecast, 150, 553
Sales forecasting, 149–153, 435
   conditional, 150
   levels of, 150
   methods of, 151–153
   by time periods, 150–151
Sales management, 552–561
   ethical issues in, 561
Sales objectives, 553
Sales office, 423, 424
Sales orientation, 17, 18
Sales potential, 150
Sales presentation, 545–546
Sales promotion, 470, 559, 568–574
Sales territory, 553–555
Sales volume, 21
Salespeople, as managers, 550–551
Sample, 145, 146
Sampling, 145–146
Science. *See* Technology
Scrambled merchandising, 402–403
Screening stage, of new product

development, 300–301
Search engines, 83, 84, 141
Seasonal discount, 631, 632
Second-market discounting, 615, 616
Secondary data, 130, 138, 139–140
Segmentation. *See* Market segmentation
Selective attention, 173, 174
Selective demand advertising, 503
Selective distribution, 385–386
Selective exposure, 173, 174
Selective interpretation, 173, 174
Selective perception, 172–173, 176, 473
Self-concept, 180
Selling agent, 423
Selling function, of intermediaries, 373
Service(s), 266
   characteristics of, 337–343
   classifying, 348, 349
   customization of, 343
   definition of, 337
   distribution of, 368–369
   as portion of U.S. economy, 348–349
   production orientation of providers
     of, 341–342
   standardization of, 342–343
   wholesaling of, 424
Service encounter, 345
Service function, of intermediaries,
   374–375
Service level, of retailer, 417
Service mark, 276
Service quality, 345, 346
Share of customer, 352–353
Shelf impact, 282
Sherman Antitrust Act, 87, 89, 327, 390,
   619, 632
Shopping centers, 415–416
Shopping product, 268–269, 595
Simple random sample, 146
Simplicity of usage, 298
Singapore, 447
Single-line retailers, 401
Single-product strategy, 321. *See also*
   Market segmentation
Single-sourcing, 210
Situation analysis, 43–44
Skimming price, 615, 616–617, 619
Slice-of-life creative platform, 507–508
Slovakia, 40
Small Business Administration, 141
Smart agents, 84, 409, 520
Social class, 183–184
Social needs, 169
Social responsibility, 51, 634–635
Social situations, and buying
   behavior, 186
Social values, 67
   and consumer decision-making, 181
Socialization process, 186
Societal marketing concept, 23
Sociocultural forces, 67–70, 181–186.
   See also names of specific
   countries
Socioeconomic variables, 240
Software, 132
Sorting function, of intermediaries, 371
Source, of communication, 471

South America, 98, 149, 278
South Korea, 175
Spain, 108, 115, 408
Specialty product, 269
Specialty stores, 401, 403
Specialty wholesaler, 420
Spokesperson, 509, 522–523
Sponsorship, 579–580
Standard Industrial Classification (SIC)
   system, 213–215
Standardization strategy. *See*
   Globalization strategy
Star (product), 273
Still-life creative platform, 509, 510
Stimulus factors, 174
Stock-outs, 447
Storage, 373, 438, 446
Store image, 417–418
Storyline creative platform, 507
Straight commission, 558
Straight rebuy, 200, 201, 202
Straight salary, 558
Strategic alliances, 199, 210, 425
Strategic business unit (SBU), 36–37
   growth strategies for, 39–42
Strategic corporate goals, 35
Strategic gap, 44
Strategic marketing process, stages of,
   42–50
Strategic planning, 33, 34. *See also*
   Planning
Strategic window of opportunity, 46
Strips, 415
Style, 319–320
Subliminal perception, 175–176
Success, of new products, 296–298
Suggestive selling, 539
Sunbelt, growth in, 71–72
Superior customer value, 18
Supermarket, 402–403, 404
Superstores, 404
Suppliers, 103
Supply curve, 596–597
Survey, 142–144
   of customer expectations, 152
   of executive opinion, 151–152
Sweden, 108
Sweepstakes, 572
Switzerland, 109, 183
SWOT, 44
Systematic bias, 142
Systems concept, 438

T

Tactics, 33
Tangibility, 266, 337–338
Target market, 224. *See also* Positioning
   and pricing decisions, 602
   selecting, 46–47, 225, 477, 516
   for wholesalers, 425
Target population, 145
Target return pricing, 628–629
Targeting, 224
   strategies for, 228–236
Tariffs, 109, 110, 111